MW00358661

Appreciation of *The IT/Digital Legal Companion*

As an entrepreneur founder and CEO of several tech companies, I appreciate the insight into IP, strategy and deals that this book provides. I wish there were a book like this when I started my first company. The book is easy-to-read, comprehensive and up-to-the moment. It covers everything from basic IP and deal negotiations to mobile media, software IP and the Internet. There is lots of detail, sample forms, and practical tips. This book is the first comprehensive and intelligent resource for creating real value through IP. More entrepreneurs and engineers need to pay attention to what the real world of IP is about.

> **– Beth A. Marcus, Ph.D., CEO and Director, Zeemote, Inc.** *(www.zeemote.com)*

The title says that the book is a legal companion, and that is precisely what it is. Gene has put together years of a lawyer's wisdom into this companion, but without burdening it with any legal language at all. Keep this companion next to you if you are a practicing manager involved with IT or digital content transactions.

> **– Dr. G. Venkatesh, Chief Technology and Strategy Officer and Executive Director of Sasken Communication Technologies Ltd., Bangalore, India** *(www.sasken.com)*

Gene Landy's book allows insight into the critical decisions that individuals and companies need to make in deciding how to build and protect digital and online products, services, and businesses.

> **– Charles Nesson, Professor, Harvard Law School and Founder and Co-Director of the Berkman Center for Internet & Society** *(www.cyber.law.harvard.edu)*

The IT/Digital Legal Companion is like a Department Store where you easily find the part of the store where you want to go shopping but may also stop in other areas to browse. With this book, the organization makes it easy to find the area of greatest interest relating to a particular business issue.

The book covers a wide range of topics—from contract and intellectual property law to more specialized issues including Software as a Service, Open Source and digital content. The book covers legal issues facing both technology suppliers (e.g., software vendors) and consumers (e.g., companies contracting for services). Service providers working with these organizations will also find the book useful.

> **– Jim Geisman, President, MarketShare, Inc.** *(www.marketshare.com)*, **software marketing consultant and advisor and mentor to technology companies**

I found Gene Landy's latest publication *The IT/Digital Legal Companion* to be a clear and comprehensive book from an attorney who specializes in helping technology companies build and preserve the value of their companies and intellectual property. I appreciate how this publication clarifies IT agreements and complex IP arrangements. I was also amazed at the breadth and level of detail in this book.

> **– Peter Duflo, President and CEO, Strategic Ventures, LLC** *(www.strategicventures.com)*, **consulting for mergers, acquisitions and executive search for information technology companies**

The IT/Digital Legal Companion

A Comprehensive Business Guide to Software, Internet, and IP Law
Includes Contract and Web Forms

Best Wishes

The IT/Digital Legal Companion

A COMPREHENSIVE BUSINESS GUIDE to
SOFTWARE, INTERNET, AND IP LAW
INCLUDES CONTRACT
AND WEB FORMS

Gene K. Landy

Editing and Additional Content by
Amy J. Mastrobattista

SYNGRESS®

AMSTERDAM • BOSTON • HEIDELBERG • LONDON
NEW YORK • OXFORD • PARIS • SAN DIEGO
SAN FRANCISCO • SINGAPORE • SYDNEY • TOKYO

ELSEVIER

Morgan Kaufmann Publishers is an Imprint of Elsevier

Elsevier, Inc., the author(s), and any person or firm involved in the writing, editing, or production (collectively "Makers") of this book ("the Work") do not guarantee or warrant the results to be obtained from the Work.

There is no guarantee of any kind, expressed or implied, regarding the Work or its contents. The Work is sold AS IS and WITHOUT WARRANTY. You may have other legal rights, which vary from state to state.

In no event will Makers be liable to you for damages, including any loss of profits, lost savings, or other incidental or consequential damages arising out from the Work or its contents. Because some states do not allow the exclusion or limitation of liability for consequential or incidental damages, the above limitation may not apply to you.

You should always use reasonable care, including backup and other appropriate precautions, when working with computers, networks, data, and files.

Syngress Media®, Syngress®, "Career Advancement Through Skill Enhancement®,""Ask the Author UPDATE®," and "Hack Proofing®," are registered trademarks of Elsevier, Inc. "Syngress: The Definition of a Serious Security Library"™, "Mission Critical™," and "The Only Way to Stop a Hacker is to Think Like One™" are trademarks of Elsevier, Inc. Brands and product names mentioned in this book are trademarks or service marks of their respective companies.

KEY	SERIAL NUMBER
001	HJIRTCV764
002	PO9873D5FG
003	829KM8NJH2
004	BAL923457U
005	CVPLQ6WQ23
006	VBP965T5T5
007	HJJJ863WD3E
008	2987GVTWMK
009	629MP5SDJT
010	IMWQ295T6T

PUBLISHED BY
Syngress Publishing, Inc.
Elsevier, Inc.
30 Corporate Drive
Burlington, MA 01803

The IT / Digital Legal Companion: A Comprehensive Business Guide to Software, Internet and IP Law

Copyright © 2008 by Elsevier, Inc. All rights reserved. Printed in the United States of America. Except as permitted under the Copyright Act of 1976, no part of this publication may be reproduced or distributed in any form or by any means, or stored in a database or retrieval system, without the prior written permission of the publisher, with the exception that the program listings may be entered, stored, and executed in a computer system, but they may not be reproduced for publication.

Printed in the United States of America
1 2 3 4 5 6 7 8 9 0
ISBN 13: 978-1-59749-256-0

For information on rights, translations, and bulk sales, contact Matt Pedersen, Commercial Sales Director and Rights, at Syngress Publishing; email m.pedersen@elsevier.com.

The IT/Digital Legal Companion and its content, including these forms, are for educational purposes only and is provided with the understanding that the authors and the publisher are not engaged in rendering legal, accounting, investment, or any other professional services.

THE AUTHORS AND PUBLISHER MAKE NO EXPRESS OR IMPLIED WARRANTY OF ANY KIND and assume no responsibility for errors or omissions. No liability is assumed for incidental or consequential damages in connection with or arising out of the use of the information or digital files contained or supplied with or for use with this book. Changes occur in legal matters and in the interpretation of law. Some legal matters are subject to opinion and judgment rather than definite rules. If you require legal, accounting, or other expert assistance, you should consult a professional advisor.

Knowledge is power.

—Sir Francis Bacon, philosopher

Knowledge shared is power multiplied.

—Robert Noyce, co-inventor of the semiconductor, co-founder of Intel

Contents

CHAPTER 7   **Confidentiality, Rights Transfer, and
Non-Competition Agreements for Employees 165**

Acknowledgment by Gene Landy

This work is founded on the insights and experience of many.

Most important is the contribution of Amy Mastrobattista, who edited the text, contributed forms, and provided many suggestions for improvements. You can find Amy's touch throughout the book.

I also gratefully acknowledge the help of persons who contributed ideas and insight or kindly reviewed the text, including:

Mike Dornbrook, Executive Vice President, Harmonix Music Systems, Inc.

Peter Duflo, President and CEO, Strategic Ventures, LLC

Andrew Feinberg, General Counsel, Brightcove, Inc.

Jim Geisman, CEO, Marketshare, Inc.

George Grey, CEO & Founder, Mobicious Inc.

Beth A. Marcus, Ph.D., CEO and Director, Zeemote, Inc.

David Marglin, San Francisco attorney; formerly General Counsel, Gracenote, Inc.

Charles Nesson, Professor, Harvard Law School and Founder and Co-Director of the Berkman Center for Internet & Society

Jeffrey Steefel, Franchise Executive Producer, The Lord of the Rings Online, Turbine, Inc.

G. Venkatesh, Chief Technology Officer, Sasken Communication Technologies Ltd.

Aaron von Staats, Senior Vice President and General Counsel, Parametric Technology Corporation

Anyone who wants to reaffirm their belief in the essential goodness of human nature should write a book. Of course, any inadequacy in this work is solely my own responsibility.

I am indebted to Chris Williams and Amy Pedersen and all the other good people at Elsevier who helped with this book.

I am also grateful to my assistant Cindy Scolamiero and the others at my law firm that suffered through proofing of the text.

In addition to these individuals, I thank the countless innovators and risk takers in digital technology companies around the world. Their creativity and effort advances and continually renews the world that this book describes.

Finally, I owe the greatest debt to my wife Sylvia who put up with me while I worked on this book.

A Note from the Authors

We would like to hear from you about the ways in which this book has helped you and about ways that it could be improved.

We are always interested in new technologies, innovative legal techniques, new legal issues, and new problems to solve. If you have a need for business law services that require a sophisticated understanding of digital technology business and legal issues, please let us know.

Feel free to write us at our firm:

Gene K. Landy
Chair, Technology Business Group
e-mail: gkl@riw.com

or

Amy J. Mastrobattista
e-mail: ajm@riw.com

Ruberto, Israel & Weiner, P.C.
100 North Washington Street
Boston
Massachusetts 02114
USA
www.riw.com

About the Authors

Gene K. Landy is a shareholder of Ruberto, Israel & Weiner, P.C., Boston, Massachusetts, USA and Chair of the firm's Technology Business Group. His practice has a concentration on technology companies and digital technology transactions. He is a graduate of the Massachusetts Institute of Technology (SB 1969) and Harvard Law School (JD 1975 cum laude).

Mr. Landy handles domestic and international transactions for high technology businesses, from start-ups to publicly traded companies. He represents companies in software, integrated circuits, telecommunications technology, IT hardware, Internet applications, e-commerce, computer games, and other technology fields.

His work includes licensing, intellectual property, technology transfer, business sales and acquisitions, and investments. He has served non-US technology firms that operate in the United States, including companies in India, Australia, Ireland, England, Switzerland, and Scotland. Mr. Landy also works with investors in technology opportunities.

In addition to this book, Mr. Landy is the author of an earlier lay person's guide to software law entitled *The Software Developer's and Marketer's Legal Companion*, published by Addison-Wesley in 1993, as well as a number of articles in the field of information technology law published in law journals and other publications.

Mr. Landy frequently lectures on legal topics and has spoken at e-Commerce Expo, Lotusphere, the Computer Games Developer Conference, and other industry trade shows, as well as the Massachusetts Technology Leadership Council, Massachusetts Continuing Legal Education, and the International Federation of Computer Law Associations. He has spoken at the invitation of the Comsware Communications Technology Conference in Bangalore, India and the Irish Software Association in Dublin, Ireland. He has been named a Massachusetts Super Lawyer in 2004 to 2007.

Amy J. Mastrobattista is a shareholder at Ruberto, Israel & Weiner, P.C. and a member of the Corporate Department and Technology Business Group. She is a graduate of Smith College (A.B. 1988 magna cum laude and Phi Beta Kappa) and New York University School of Law (JD 1991).

Ms. Mastrobattista has extensive experience structuring financings, including "seed rounds," angel investments, and venture capital transactions. She has represented both emerging companies and investors. She is also very active in technology licensing for companies small and large.

Ms. Mastrobattista has successfully structured and negotiated the purchase and sale of numerous businesses. She was recognized as one of Boston's Top 10 Lawyers in Women's Business Boston reader's poll, January 2006.

About the Authors' Law Firm

RUBERTO, ISRAEL & WEINER, P.C.

SERVICES OF THE TECHNOLOGY BUSINESS GROUP

Focus on Technology and Business

Ruberto, Israel & Weiner is a Boston-based business law firm. Our Technology Business Group is focused on information technology, digital products and services, and high technology manufacturing.

- We understand the interaction of intellectual property and technology in a global marketplace

- We have sector-specific knowledge. We understand technologies, business practices, intellectual property assets, and transactions

- We can execute sophisticated and complex technology sector deals

Technology Sectors that We Serve

Our firm has clients in many technology product and service fields. They include both US-based and non-US businesses. RIW represents emerging technology companies as well as established players expanding into new technologies. Specific industry segments served include:

- Software including business products, infrastructure, financial software, Internet, open source and communications products

- Consumer products, social applications, Web sites, and content, including Web and mobile media and games

- IT services and consulting

- Web businesses and software-as-a-service (SaaS)

- Communications technology

- Silicon products, including semiconductors, ASICs and MEMS

- High tech materials and manufacturing companies

Business Services for Technology Companies

Our services for technology companies include:

Company Formation

- Incorporation, tax strategy, capital structure, shareholder agreements
- Formation and operation of US-based subsidiaries of non-US companies

Financing Transactions

- Seed capital, angel and venture financing, commercial loans, private placements, and securities offerings

Employment

- Employment law generally, employee agreements, option plans and other equity compensation plans

Trademarks and Copyrights

- US and worldwide trademark registration
- Management of global trademark portfolios
- Copyright registration

Technology M&A and Strategic Licensing Transactions

RIW handles technology merger and acquisition transactions. We also can carry out strategic licensing deals, including acquiring or granting key licenses for product line expansion, patent portfolios, or enabling technologies.

Strategic Guidance

We provide advice and guidance on legal aspects of:

- Technology and intellectual property strategies
- Distribution strategies
- Branding strategies

Information Technology Transactions

We handle domestic and international transactions for technology businesses ranging from start-ups to publicly-traded companies that are essential for technology companies, such as:

- Licensing and technology transfer
- Customer, reseller, VAR and OEM agreements
- Development agreements
- Technology acquisitions and transfers
- Outsourcing agreements
- Internet and mobile distribution deals
- Web agreements and online documentation
- Patent, copyright and trademark licensing
- Open source licensing
- International distribution arrangements
- Strategic alliances and joint ventures
- Multimedia, entertainment and game deals
- Content acquisition and licensing

Litigation

We provide civil litigation services, including trade secret matters, copyright and trademark infringement, contract disputes, and non-competition and confidentiality agreements

Global Affiliations

Through our network of affiliations across the globe, we partner with other law firms as needed for global distribution agreements, trademarks, partnerships and other international matters.

Contact

Contact us to discuss your technology business needs and strategies. Please feel free to contact Gene Landy, Technology Business Group Chair, gkl@riw.com.

Ruberto, Israel & Weiner, P.C. 100 North Washington Street, Boston, MA 02114 USA
(617) 742-4200 Phone / (617) 742-2355 Fax
www.riw.com

Form Downloading Instructions

About the Forms in **The IT/Digital Legal Companion**

There are 38 contract and web forms in the Appendix at the end of this book. The purchaser of this book can download the forms from a special web page at no additional charge. The forms are available in PDF and Microsoft Word format. You can also download a zip file on the web side that includes all of the forms in both formats.

To get the forms, you need to register and then downloading just requires a few clicks.

The site is optimized for Internet Explorer v6+ or Firefox v2.0+.

How to Register

You must register to download the forms.

1. Find the 8-digit passcode listed at the back of this book inside the cover.

2. To access the website, go to this URL: http://booksite.syngress.com/ Landy

3. Beneath the "Log In" button, you will see a "Register" link. Click this link to open the registration form.

4. Enter your 8-digit passcode. Choose a username and password. Enter your first and last name as well as a current email address. This information can be used to retrieve your password if you lose it. If you would like to receive additional information on product updates, you may opt-in by checking the Opt-In box.

5. Be sure to write down or save your username and password. It is your key to downloading forms. Once you have obtained a username and password, your 8-digit passcode will be invalid.

Downloading Forms

Once you have registered, you are redirected to the Logon Page. Use your username and password to logon to the site.

You may open the forms through the browser and then save them or you may right-click on the form links and save them directly to your drive.

You may logon to and use the download site as often as you wish.

If You Have a Problem or Lose Your Password

If you have problems in registration or downloading forms or if you lose your password, please contact Technical Support at technical.support@elsevier.com.

Use of Forms

Please note that the forms are subject to copyright and are provided for your own personal or business use. You should not use them for distribution or sale.

Introduction: Using this Book to Build Value

YOUR NEED TO KNOW DIGITAL BUSINESS LAW

To compete effectively in any digital business in a changing world, you need to understand how to use the law to advantage.

This book will empower you to:

- Understand the interaction of law, business, and technology.

- Exploit emerging technologies and intellectual property (IP) assets.

- Negotiate better deals.

- Build and reinforce positive relationships with other companies.

- Leverage digital media.

- Perceive and manage risk.

- Benefit from Internet and mobile networks.

- Act more decisively and confidently in legal matters.

WHO IS THIS BOOK FOR?

This book is written for anyone in the world of digital technology business, including:

- Business owners, executives, and decision-makers

- Entrepreneurs

1

- Business development executives
- Sales and product line managers
- Technology developers, consultants, and advisors
- Chief information officers who make important software and IT decisions
- In-house lawyers, contracting officers, and paralegals
- Anyone managing and protecting software or digital technology IP

ORGANIZATION OF THIS BOOK

This book consists of 25 chapters. The subject matter includes:

- **Chapters 2-7: Intellectual Property in Digital Business**—Copyrights, trademarks, domain names, patents, trade secrets, and nondisclosure agreements, explained with a focus on digital business, digital media, the Internet, and mobile networks.

- **Chapter 8: Digital Contract Fundamentals**—The key principles and strategies in digital licensing and contracting.

- **Chapter 9: Open Source**—A practical guide to open source licensing, including open source business models.

- **Chapter 10: Development and Consulting**—A how-to guide for the deal-making process (including RFPs and agreements) for digital technology services, consulting, Web development, and outsourced development.

- **Chapters 11-15: Business IT and Software, including Licensing and Distribution**—Beta test agreements, commercial end-user license agreements, distribution and reseller deals, partnering agreements, component distribution, OEM deals, and software-as-a-service agreements.

- **Chapters 16-17: Web and Internet Agreements**—The law and practice of business and consumer clickwrap and browsewrap agreements, Web site terms of use, Weblog terms, and Web site rules of conduct.

- **Chapter 18: Privacy**—The rules on privacy and acceptable use of personal data in the digital world, including privacy law, privacy policies, child protection issues, and trans-national issues.

- **Chapter 19: Standards**—Legal strategies, opportunities, and risks in the system for setting new technical standards for software, digital products, and communications. How you can use this process to get ahead of the curve.

- **Chapter 20: Clearance of Content**—An overview of getting licenses and clearance for use of media assets for Web and mobile consumer applications and games, including text, graphics, music, and video. Also the legal rules about user-contributed content, mashups, and spidering the Web.

- **Chapter 21: Web and Mobile Deals**—Guidance for deals in technology licensing, providing services, and media distribution for the Internet and mobile networks.

- **Chapter 22: Video Game Deals**—Doing deals in the video game sector, including IP, clearance issues, and publishing agreements. The chapter includes discussion of console, PC, mobile, and online games, including multi-player games.

- **Chapters 23 and 24: International Distribution**—IP and deal issues for digital business in going global, distributing in world markets, international partnering and joint venturing, localization, setting up operations abroad, and protecting your rights in other nations, together with an overview of the US export controls.

- **Chapter 25: Legal Affairs Management**—Practical measures to manage your legal affairs in order to execute legal strategies effectively and build value in your business.

- **Forms Appendix**—38 sample forms agreements for deals and transactions addressed in this book.

APPROACH OF THIS BOOK

The book is based on three concepts:

- First is that all legal issues are business issues—they have meaning only in their business context.

- Second is that essential legal principles can be made comprehensible when explained in straightforward English.

- Third is that once you understand basic concepts of IP and contracts, you will be ready to put to good use the more advanced deals and strategies discussed in this book.

UNDERSTANDING AND USING INTELLECTUAL PROPERTY

Digital technology companies gain power from their "intellectual property space"—the zone where their IP helps them be dominant, overcoming competition, gaining customers, and pricing at a premium.

This book introduces you to the IP rights that underlie all digital technology. This book will help your business to secure and expand its IP assets. It will help you fully understand what rights you have, can acquire, and can license, assign, or enforce.

The discussion in this book about IP includes digital technology and digital content issues of a networked world. For example, the discussion of copyrights includes anti-circumvention and peer-to-peer file sharing; the explanation of trademarks includes the trademarks on the Internet and domain names; and the discussion of patents includes a review of software and business method patents. There is also a discussion of IP in digital media. You can factor this information into your company's IP strategy.

DOING DEALS

This book can help your company make better deals. Software and digital technology contracts span a huge range. They include consumer online or mobile transactions that are over in an instant and multiyear global relationships involving hundreds of millions of dollars of commerce. Agreements allocate valuable intellectual property. Contracts allow sharing of opportunities and transfer of risk. They are the means to getting paid.

Nothing combines, replicates, interfaces, embeds, or distributes like software and digital data. Technology deals can provide leverage and extend the distribution reach of small and large companies. Most digital technology companies license technology *in* from suppliers as well as licensing it *out* to customers and distributors, so every company needs to know how to function on both sides of the license equation. This book covers a variety of up-to-date contract types that are the tools of the trade for digital business.

There is no such thing as a perfect contract, but there are good deals and bad ones. This book explains the goals and key provisions of digital technology and content deals, as well as common traps and critical issues.

UNDERSTANDING AND DEALING WITH LEGAL RISK FACTORS

The information here can help you manage risk. Digital businesses have been sued by competitors, employees, contractors, licensors, licensees, and IP owners. Legal mistakes can result in bad relationships, wasted opportunities, lost IP, unprofitable deals, litigation, and lost business value.

No one can guarantee your business a risk-free existence, but the discussion here will help you recognize legal contingencies, make intelligent risk management decisions, and conduct smarter negotiations to reduce risk. We also discuss legal "safe harbors" that can protect against liabilities.

GLOBAL PERSPECTIVE

Digital technology is global. You may need to provide technology products or services locally or in Russia. Your technology may come from Silicon Valley or from India and China. While the majority of the content in this book is about US law, there is substantial discussion on dealings in non-US markets and on international aspects of IP, privacy, contracting, export controls, and other topics.

FOCUSING ON YOUR END GAME FROM THE BEGINNING

Understanding your legal environment can help you build value in your business.

From the founding of each digital technology company and during every working day, you should be thinking about securing the assets and building the relationships that will be of value at the end—that sale of business exit deal where you will reap the many millions of dollars of value that you have created. When the buyer's lawyers begin to review your company's files in the investigative process known as "due diligence," good legal planning will pay off.

During the Internet boom of late 90s, my law firm saw a $400 million proposed sale of start-up Internet software company stopped dead because of a very bad distribution deal the start-up had signed. The company had granted a small distributor in a key market a very broad, very long lasting exclusive license to its technology. The would-be acquirer saw this flawed distribution deal as a fundamental obstacle to its own use of the technology.

Each legal move that your company makes—each distribution deal, each strategic partnership, each investment in a technology, each trademark or patent filing, each license granted—can make your company more or less valuable. This book will help you use the law to maximize the value of your business.

HOW TO USE THIS BOOK

Readers will make different decisions on which content in this book they need to read.

This book is written to be used in two ways. First, it is a plain-language primer on digital technology law, designed to give you a basic understanding of law that affects your business. Second, the book is designed as a reference book for practical guidance—a resource to pick up when you face legal problems or important negotiations.

Each chapter begins with basic concepts and proceeds to discussions in more detail. You can decide which content in each chapter suits your needs. In addition the early chapters on IP and contract basics serve as a foundation for the deal discussions that follow.

There are many connections between these chapters. You will find frequent cross-references in the text. Some will bring you back to basics and some will bring you forward to new topics.

USING THE LEGAL FORMS

This book includes an Appendix of legal form agreements. As you will see, each of the forms in the Appendix has an introduction that provides information about the contents and use of the form. Many of the forms also have annotations with further explanatory material.

These forms are largely based on deals that we have seen or forms that we have used at our law firm. They should be used as checklists of issues and examples for what may work. They are forms, but not templates. We do not believe it is meaningful to consider contracting (except for the simplest forms) as "fill in the blank."

The reality is that most types of agreements have endless variations, and forms used in most deals require adjustments. Changes in one part of a deal inevitably affect provisions and force changes elsewhere, so that adjusting forms requires legal insight, drafting skill, and the ability to spot issues that comes with experience. You can use these forms to guide your thinking and to understand issues, learn typical contract wording, and for a contractual starting place. However, they are not magic and not a substitute for legal help in significant deals.

The forms are also available online at a special web site. You can download them in both Word and PDF format. You can find instructions on downloading the forms at the beginning of this book and also in the introduction to the Appendix.

LIMITS TO THE CONTENTS OF THIS BOOK

While this book is intended to be your need-to-know legal companion, there are some limits to its contents.

While there is a lot of substance and detail in this book, it does not deal with legal issues at the most technical level. This is a layperson's guide, not a lawyer's treatise. Inevitably there are going to be questions on which you will have to consult legal counsel.

This book focuses on the legal aspects of digital business that are distinctly associated with digital business and are central to its technology, business, and IP strategies and tactics. While we believe these are the core issues, there are more general legal aspects of doing business that we left outside the scope of this book. The business subjects that this book does not cover are company formation, taxation, equity investment deals (by "angel" investors, venture capital firms, or others), employment law matters (except for employee agreements and IP aspects which are covered), and the buying and selling of digital technology companies. For these matters, you should consult your attorney and your accountant. We also have not included (except in passing) discussion of the criminal law aspects of the regulation of technology.

While this book mentions statutes and some key decisions by the courts, it does not contain legal citations of the sort that lawyers use. There are two reasons for this. First, they are meaningless for most readers. Second, anyone who wants to find the original materials can easily do so using the information in this book and a Web search engine.

LEGAL COUNSEL

This book is not a substitute for hiring legal counsel. Each digital technology business needs to use legal services. Good legal counsel can add value to your business. Even companies that have in-house counsel need the services of outside law firms from time to time.

How should you select counsel to best serve your business? In the final analysis, you are looking for more than just a person to carry out tasks. Your lawyer, like your accounts, should be a trusted partner and should be someone that you can rely upon.

The important criteria are apparent: knowledge, skills, and experience. You want counsel that has experienced the challenges your business will face, that follows digital technology law issues, and understands your business and your technologies. Digital business exists at the intersection of technology, law, and markets. Your counsel should have knowledge of IP law as well as the other legal, business, and financial issues that affect your technology businesses. Your lawyer should speak your language and provide practical guidance and solutions.

Digital Copyright Basics

2

It's not manufacturers trying to rip anybody off or anything like that. There's nobody getting rich writing software that I know of. There are people who would like to stay in business and earn a salary writing packages for these low-cost computers.

—Microsoft CEO, Bill Gates, then 25 years old, in a 1980 interview with
80 Microcomputing, a computer hobbyist magazine

SOME HISTORY

Back in 1980, Bill Gates was upset. Microsoft was a tiny company serving an infant personal computer market and selling copies of BASIC, a programming language. Most personal computer users were hobbyists who felt free to make copies of Microsoft's commercial software programs and give them to friends for free. Gates told anyone that would listen that it was important that PC software companies get paid for copies!

In those days, it was unclear whether copyright law, the body of law that governs making and selling copies of books, movies, and music, could be used to protect software too. Gates (as well as everyone else that wanted to make money from software for PCs) was hoping that Congress would pass a proposed change in US federal law to make it clear that copyright law covers software.

Gates was facing a fundamental fact: digital products are incredibly cheap to copy. Copying is the key to turning digital products into wealth—but only if you can *control* copying. The law that provides legal control of digital copying is copyright law.

9

In 1980, not long after Gates gave that interview, Congress amended the Copyright Act to give express copyright protection to software. It is hard to overestimate the importance of this legal protection for digital industries.

COPYRIGHT COUNTS!

Why does copyright law matter to you? Copyright law grants the copyright holder exclusive rights that are at the heart of licensing and distribution deals. Copyright law is also an important legal weapon against unauthorized copying of software and digital content. When copyright law is violated, most often copyright holders use civil law—a lawsuit—to protect their copyrights; sometimes the authorities enforce criminal copyright provisions.

While copyright is your friend, there are copyright doctrines that surprise, and in some cases, bedevil digital product and content companies. To function effectively in any digital business, you need a grasp of the basics of copyright law.

IN THIS CHAPTER

This chapter is about the fundamentals of copyright law, including:

- How you get copyright protection.
- Legal rights a copyright gives you.
- Legal provisions that restrict "cracking" copy protections and access control.
- An overview of copyright registration.

In the next chapter, we will examine some advanced copyright topics regarding the application of copyright law to the Internet and to software products, as well as international aspects of software law.

THE NATURE OF A COPYRIGHT

Fundamentally, a copyright is just what it sounds like: the legal right to control copying. Copyright law also governs distributing and selling copies, preparing works based on earlier works (known as "derivatives"), and public display and public performance of works. Copyright protection in the United States is governed by the Copyright Act, a statute passed by Congress. (There is no state copyright law.) The purpose of copyright law is to encourage creation and expression. Copyright law does this by granting a legal monopoly on copying, distributing and performing works to the copyright holder. Nations around the world also have copyright statutes, and there are international copyright treaties.

What Is Covered by US Copyright Law?

Something that is protected by copyright is referred to as a "work." Modern copyright law began in 18th century England with books and expanded to other media of expression. Today, US copyright law covers the following works:

- Literary works: novel, stories, articles, advertisement text, manuals, and so forth
- Computer programs
- Musical works and sound recordings
- Choreography
- Visual arts
- Motion picture and audiovisual works
- Architectural works

Works in the form of digital goods are covered by copyright law. A motion picture, photograph, song, or novel can all be distributed and copied in digital form. Even choreography can be in the form of a digital file. There is therefore an extensive overlap between digital technology and all media under copyright law. The Internet, wireless networks, CDs, and DVDs have accelerated the trend for copyrighted goods to become digital.

Copyright law affects any business that communicates (which means all of them). Industries that are the most reliant on copyright law to protect their core products and services include the software industry, video game developers and publishers, Web-based businesses, the recording industry, the motion picture business, publishers, and broadcasters.

Any contract that deals with the creation or modification of software or any digital content must consider issues of rights under copyright law.

What Is a Computer Program under Copyright Law?

As noted above, computer "programs" are protected under copyright law. What is meant by a "program" under copyright law? In the Copyright Act, we find the following definition:

> *A computer program is a set of statements or instructions to be used directly or indirectly in a computer in order to bring about a certain result.*

Under copyright law, a program can be written in any computer language: C++, Java, SQL, COBOL, or anything else. A Web page written in HTML meets the definition. A program could be an operating system, Web server, video game, a word processor, a software component meant to be incorporated in a device, or anything else that runs on a computer or processor. It could be a few lines of code or millions of lines. A program under the Copyright Act may also be a combination of programs that work together.

The (Very Modest) Requirement of Originality

Under copyright law, you can only get a copyright on a work, including a computer program, that is *original*. However, the required level of originality required is very low, and meeting this requirement is easy. The legal test contains two elements: (1) a level of originality described by judges as "very slight" or "minimal" and (2) independent creation. This means that if you wrote a software program or created any other original work, even if quite pedestrian and ordinary, it will be original enough under this test. What falls outside of copyright is pure data or facts.

Copyright and Musical Works

Music recordings (including those in digital form) are subject to two different copyrights:

- **The Composition Copyright**, which covers the words and musical notes.

- **The Sound Recording Copyright**, which covers the recorded sounds—also known as the master recording copyright.

You will find much more about music copyrights and the application of copyright law to digital music (including special webcasting rules) in Chapter 20, which is about clearing digital content.

Exclusive Rights under Copyright Law

What rights does a copyright include? Here is a list of exclusive rights held by a copyright holder under US law:

- **Reproduction**—The right to make copies.

- **Distribution**—The right to sell or rent copies.

- **Public Performance**—The right to perform, display, or play the copyrighted work in public. (There are some limitations on this exclusive right with regard to recorded music that we will review in Chapter 20.)

- **Derivatives**—The right to create works based on a work.

Expressions vs. Ideas and Methods

A fundamental concept of copyright law is that it grants exclusive rights to the particular *expression* that constitutes the work—but not the *ideas* in the work.

The Copyright Act expressly provides that copyright protection does *not* extend to any idea, procedure, system, method of operation, concept, principle, or discovery underlying the program. A news story reported on CNN.com is protected by copyright, but the facts reported are not. An article describing a new theory in biophysics would be protected by copyright, but the theory itself would have no copyright protection.

How to Get a Copyright

To get a copyright is amazingly easy. All you have to do is get your work into some fixed form. Copyright applies, for example, to a sketch that you draw on a paper napkin and to every email you compose and send. For software or digital content, fixed form could mean a printout, storage on a hard drive, network storage, diskette, or ROM chip. The rule is that a copyright is secured *automatically* when the work is recorded in some reasonably persistent form for the first time.

Although the question is not completely settled, it is probable that works that exist only in RAM memory are sufficiently "fixed" to be copyrighted, but in any case, as soon as they are saved, they are undoubtedly within the scope of the Copyright Act.

Copyright vs. Other Kinds of Intellectual Property (IP)

As you can see above, copyright law is for works in which there is some kind of original content. Copyright protection is very different from other types of IP protection. Here are some key differences.

Copyright vs. Patents

Let us say that you make an invention implemented by software—for example, a new way of encrypting data. Copyright will not stop other persons from making other programs that use the same invention. Inventions are covered, not by copyright law, but by patent law. A copyright on a software program that has patentable elements would only cover the code itself, not the inventions or any concepts or methods used in the invention. Software and patents, a topic of growing importance in the digital technology industry, are discussed in Chapter 5.

Copyright vs. Trade Secrets

Software may use secret methods of data storage, graphics display techniques, character recognition methods, encryption and compression techniques, speed optimization methods, and so forth. The law that may protect these secrets from unauthorized appropriation is state trade secret law, discussed in Chapter 6, not copyright law. However, copyright law may be relevant to reverse engineering, a topic discussed in Chapter 3.

Copyright vs. Trademark

The brands of your digital products (used on packaging, CD-ROM discs, Web sites, screen displays, and so forth) are covered by trademark law. If someone is using your brand (or a confusing similar brand) without your consent and causing market confusion, you can use trademark law in a court of law to stop that use or obtain money damages from the infringer.

Copyright does cover graphic art, so that someone else's unauthorized use of your unique logo might be both copyright and trademark infringement. Trademarks are discussed in Chapter 4.

Duration of Copyright Protection

Copyrights last a *very long* time. In the United States and many other countries, for copyrights now being created:

- For works created by individual authors, under US law, the copyright lasts for the *life of the author plus 70 years*. In the case of a joint work, that is a work prepared collectively by two or more authors, the term lasts for 70 years after the last surviving author's death.

- For works by employees of a company and other works made for hire (see discussion below of the "work made for hire" concept), the duration of copyright will be *95 years from first publication* or *120 years from creation*, whichever is shorter.

Stanford law professor Lawrence Lessig once remarked: "By the time Apple's Macintosh operating system finally falls into the public domain, there will be no machine that could possibly run it." For *technology*, the life of copyrights might as well be forever. As is discussed below, the duration of copyright often matters for *content*.

PUBLIC DOMAIN

Works that are not subject to copyright at all are in "the public domain." Anyone can copy, distribute, and make derivatives of works that are in the public domain freely and without permission. The public domain includes works on which the copyright has expired, US government works, and works dedicated by the copyright owner to the public domain.

The rules on copyright have changed several times and so there are some technicalities to the rules. Subject to some exceptions, the copyright on a *published* work will have expired if:

- The work was created and first published before January 1, 1923, or, if published later, then

- Seventy years after the death of the author, or if work made for hire for a company, 95 years from publication

There are other technical rules under which works published before 1989 may have lost copyright protection (such as the pre-1989 rule regarding omitted copyright notices discussed below or a pre-1964 rule that required copyrights to be renewed). There are also rules on the duration of copyrights on unpublished works. Other nations may have different rules. If you want to rely on the public domain status of a work, you may want to consult your attorney to be sure you are correct.

Whether a work is the public domain can have more than one answer, because there may be more than one applicable copyright. For example, a 19th century tune will be out of copyright, but not its 1975 sound recording. A 19th century novel will be out of copyright, but not a translation of the novel made in 1985.

Notice

You have seen *copyright notices* (also called copyright *legends*) on books and on digital products many times. A typical notice looks like this:

> *Copyright © 2008 Jack Smith, Inc.*
>
> *All rights reserved*

Is a notice legally required to secure copyright protection? Under the Copyright Act, the answer is "No," if the work was first published *on or after March 1, 1989*. (A work is "published" when it is first put into general distribution or made available for public sale. Private showings to friends, investors, or publishers are not publication.) If the publication took place after that date, there is no legal requirement that you mark your product in any special way in order to preserve your copyright. You won't loose the protection of copyright law by failing to use a notice. This is the rule not only in the United States, but also around the world.

Nevertheless, it is a good idea to always use a copyright notice on software, documentation, and digital content—even before publication. This is because the notice serves to put others on notice of your ownership claim. The copyright notice might deter unauthorized copying. It also helps you if you ever have to bring litigation against infringers because it makes it clear that unauthorized copying was done in the face of your claim of ownership. The date that you should put in the copyright notice is the first publication date of the work, and you should use the name of the copyright owner. You can find more details about proper copyright notice formats on the Web site of the US Copyright Office at www.copyright.gov.

For works published *before* March 1, 1989, putting that copyright notice on all versions of the work was essential. If you fear that you might have inadvertently lost a copyright for a work published before March 1, 1989 because of a failure to include a proper notice, you should consult legal counsel.

Copyright Registration

A frequently asked question is: Do I have to register my work with the US Copyright Office in order to get a US copyright? The answer, which surprises many, is "No." Copyright law protects works without registration. Your works are subject to copyright even if not registered.

Even though you won't lose your copyright if you do not register, registration with the US Copyright Office is required in order to bring a lawsuit to enforce your copyright. You can also get better remedies in a copyright lawsuit (as explained below) if you register your copyright *before the infringement began*. As we will discuss later in this chapter, registration is easy and inexpensive, and many companies routinely register their US copyrights in software and other digital content.

INFRINGEMENT

Violation of the rights of a copyright holder is called "infringement." Copyright law gives the copyright owner a remedy in court when someone else infringes the copyright. However, there are some important defenses discussed below and in the following chapter. In some cases, which we will also discuss below, violation of copyright law is *criminal*.

There are several different kinds of infringement under US law:

- **Direct Infringement**—consists of exercising one of the exclusive rights of copyright without consent of the party that owns or controls the copyright. Copying copyrighted software or digital files without permission (unless a defense applies) is direct infringement.

- **Contributory Infringement**—applies when a party knowingly materially contributes to the directly infringing conduct of another. For example, helping another person make or sell infringing copies would be contributory infringement.

- **Vicarious Infringement**—apples when a party (1) has the right and ability to supervise or control infringing activity; and (2) receives a direct financial benefit from that activity. The classic example of vicarious infringement is a flea market where infringing goods are sold by a person that rents a booth; the owner of the flea market may be liable for vicarious infringement.

- **Inducing Infringement**—occurs when a party knowingly encourages or induces another party to engage in direct infringement. The US Supreme Court added this final category in its 2005 decision of *MGM Studios, Inc. v. Grokster, Ltd.* in the context of peer-to-peer file sharing. Grokster was liable because it made and distributed software that facilitated peer-to-peer filing sharing, and Grokster *knew* that illegal file sharing would be the software's main use. The application and limits of this "inducement" doctrine are still not clear. What *is* clear is that this is a very important extension of copyright law.

DERIVATIVE WORKS

Suppose that you write a brilliant software game program based on the latest Stephen King's novel and begin selling it. What will happen? Unless you have a *license* from the holder of the rights to create computer games from the novel, you will surely be sued. This is because your software is a *derivative work*.

In copyright law, a *derivative work* is a fundamental concept. It means a work based on another work. The legal rule on derivative works is quite clear and is just what you would expect: If you want to create, make copies of or sell a derivative work, you need the permission of the holder of the rights that your work is based on.

If you create a derivative work without permission, you infringe the copyright in the underlying work. Moreover, while you will have the copyright in your derivative work, your rights will cover only your own contribution and creation—and any acts to distribute the derivative work without permission from the owner of the underlying work will be acts of infringement.

Examples of derivative works are a translation, a sequel or an adaptation of a work for another medium—for example, a movie based on a novel. A derivative software program could be:

- An update, new release, or new version of any existing computer program

- A "localized" version of a program with foreign language content

- A "port" of a program into a different software-operating system

- A program substantially derived from another computer program (or portions of the program)

- A program based on another medium such as a novel, a movie, or a game that is copyrighted

A novel, television show, or movie based on a digital product, such as a video game, would also be a derivative work. Processing works electronically also creates derivatives. For example, if you take a digital music file from a music CD and process it to create an MP3 file, you have created a derivative of the original file.

The concept of what is derivative is logically related to the concept of copyright infringement. In contracts we often define a derivative work as: "A work sufficiently based on a copyrighted work such that copying it without permission would infringe the copyright of the prior work."

WORKS MADE FOR HIRE

A basic concept of the Copyright Act, and one that is much misunderstood, is "work made for hire," often shortened to "work for hire." The concept of "work made for hire" is important for two purposes:

- It may control who is the author of a copyrighted work.

- It may govern the duration of a copyright license or transfer (as discussed below).

If an *employee* of a company creates a work while on the job, the program is automatically "work made for hire." This means that the *employer company* is legally the *author* of the program and owns the copyright. The concept follows federal employment law. If the person gets W-2 compensation, has FICA withholding, gets unemployment insurance and the like, he or she will be an employee. If the person gets a Form 1099 and is paid on a per-job basis, the person will be a contractor and not an "employee" under this doctrine.

This very important rule of US copyright law has the following effect:

- If an *employee* develops a work, it will belong to the *employer* because the employer is considered the author.

- If an *independent contractor* develops a work under contract with a *customer*, unless a contract says otherwise, the *independent contractor* will own the copyright. The customer will likely receive a *nonexclusive license* for the intended use of the software. This is a result that often comes as a shock and surprise to companies that have paid contractors to develop software without using a proper contract.

More on Work Made for Hire

There is another rather technical circumstance in which a program is work made for hire under the Copyright Act: A work also classifies as work made for hire if (1) there is a written contract, (2) the contract *states* that the work will be work made for hire, *and* (3) the work is part of a larger work, is a translation, is supplemental to another work, is part of a fact compilation, or is an instructional text. This concept is relevant when a company hires a person to provide copyrighted work product, including software code or other digital products.

Work Made for Hire Clauses in Contracts

In contracts for development of software or other digital products, you will often see "work made for hire," clauses, which say, in essence: "This work is to be a work made for hire of Customer, but if not work for hire, the work is hereby assigned to Customer."

The reason that these clauses have the "but if not" language is that work made for hire status is technical, as noted above. So lawyers want the "assignment" language as a back-up, in case the attempt to classify the work as "work made for hire" is ineffective.

These clauses are necessary to capture for the customer the copyright that otherwise would go to the independent contractor. This is one reason why a carefully written contract with every independent contractor is so important.

Note on the Right to Revoke Copyright Grants and Transfer after 35 Years

There is another legal impact of the work for hire classification; it affects a special rule under which authors may revoke copyright transfers or licenses. This rule in the Copyright Act applies if an author has licensed or transferred any rights to a copyright: The author (or his or her heirs) has the right to revoke the transfer or license 35 years after publication or 40 years after the transfer or license grant, whichever comes first, by serving written notice on the licensee or transferee within specified time limits.

The purpose of this rule is to protect the creators of works of literature and art that show their true value only many years after creation. It gives creators a "second bite at the apple" in transfer or licensing. However, if the work was work made for hire, *this rule does not apply*, and as a result the assignee or licensee of the work (often the publisher) keeps control of the work for the full life of the copyright.

If you sign an agreement with a developer in which the developer *assigns* your company the copyright to the resulting product, but it is *not* work made for hire, then the author (or his or her heirs) will have this right to revoke. On the other hand, if your written contract with the developer had a proper "work made for hire" clause (and the other qualifications for work made for hire apply), your company is deemed the author of the program, the copyright belongs to your company, and there is no right to revoke.

Because this rule requires the passage of such a long time, it might appear to have no practical relevance to digital products and digital technology. However, it might affect you if you have licensed content (say music, a film, or a short story) that was created years ago for new use in software or in a multimedia product.

California Law Issue Involving Work Made for Hire Clauses

There is a California state law aspect of the work made for hire that might affect you—and will probably be a surprise if you are not expecting it. Under the California Labor Code, if your company engages any individual as an independent contractor under a written contract to create any "work made for hire," that individual is treated as your employee for the purposes of worker's compensation insurance (which covers on the job injuries). This means that you will need to obtain in advance and pay for worker's compensation insurance covering the contractor during the period of the assignment as if he or she were your employee.

What does this mean for you if your company retains independent contractors that reside in California but does not want to incur the cost of worker's compensation insurance? You have two basic options:

- Retain only *corporations* as independent contractors—rather than individuals. (As your lawyer will tell you, there are other legal benefits from this practice.)

- Have your individual contractor *assign* the copyright (and all other rights) to your company and *not* have a work made for hire clause in the written contract.

If you have questions about the effect of this California law, you should consult a lawyer that practices in California.

Problems When Parties Fail to Specify Who Is to Own the Copyright

When a contractor or consultant provides software or other digital products under a contract, the parties all too often forget to specify who will *own* the copyright. The following example illustrates the problem.

Example: A large manufacturer, United Inc., wants a program to calculate and optimize its capital expenditures. United asks Smith, a programmer, to write the required program, and the contract says nothing about who will own what.

Smith writes computer code at home. After six months, Smith has done everything required, including the creation of a brilliant software program that saves United millions of dollars each year.

After the program is written, Smith sees that he has created a winning program that United's competitors will all want. He puts his copyright notice on the program, and advertises it for licensing. Meanwhile, believing it has all rights to the program, United has registered the copyright in its own name. Seeing Smith's advertisement, United sues Smith to stop him from selling the program.

Who really owns the copyright, and who will win the struggle for ownership? The answer is that in all likelihood it is Smith, as the independent contractor, who owns the copyright to the software, and United will likely have only a non-exclusive license. This will leave Smith free to license the program to others.

Would United have the right to distribute the program? It's not clear. If Smith is the copyright owner, United would have only whatever license the parties agreed upon. Whether Smith and United agreed that United would have distribution rights requires interpreting the facts and circumstances regarding the business understanding of the parties. If Smith and United are unable to come to some agreement, the matter could only be resolved by trial in court.

The important point to remember is that every development contract should make it explicitly clear who will own the rights to the product. In addition, if a contractor is permitted to use subcontractors, it is advisable to require the contractor to have written work made for hire agreements with each subcontractor.

FAIR USE

Does all copying of other person's copyrighted materials without permission constitute infringement? The answer is no. One important exception and defense to liability for infringement is "fair use," which is a very important US copyright law concept.

To introduce the subject of fair use, here are some fact patterns to consider:

Example One: *Jack the Poet wrote a poem that he published on lovetalk.com. Joe the Literary Blogger writes an article about Jack's poem which he posts on Joe's poetry blog. Without the author or publisher's permission, Joe downloads and reproduces the entire text of Jack's poem in his blog article.*

Example Two: *Jill is an art lover. Without obtaining any permission, Jill assembles and puts on her advertising-supported Web site, artfavorites.com, her 500 favorite works of modern visual art, all of which are subject to copyright.*

Example Three: *Jeff Gamer, a computer game developer, creates a commercial shareware PC video game that is a parody of the Lara Croft Tomb Raider computer game. Without getting permission from Aspyr Media, the Tomb Raider game publisher, Jeff includes many of the characters and themes of Tomb Raider in his own game.*

All of these persons are either making copies of copyrighted works or making derivative works. Are all these persons infringers? Are *any* of them? If any of them were sued for copyright infringement, each would claim that their copying was permissible "fair use."

Legally, fair use is a *defense* to a suit for copyright infringement. The rationale of the fair use defense is that there is *some* copying where the social benefits of copying outweigh the benefits of copyright protection. Fair use law is a kissing cousin of First Amendment law. Fair use law is based on part of the idea that copyright law needs to be balanced against free speech.

You may have heard that fair use law is complex. Conceptually it's not complicated at all. The problem with fair use is rather that its *application* is often uncertain. What constitutes fair use is based on an analysis of all the facts—and on the same facts different judges may disagree on what constitutes fair use.

Factor-Based Analysis

Under the Copyright Act, there are four factors that a US federal court is supposed to consider when deciding whether copying is subject to the fair use defense. None of the factors, by itself, is determinative. Some have more weight than others.

Factor One: What Is the Character of the Use?
This factor relates to *how* the copied material is used.

Commercial vs. Commercial

If the use is noncommercial, the copying is more likely to be deemed fair use. Commercial use is less likely to be found to be fair use.

Commentary and Criticism

The court is more likely to find fair use if the copying is commentary or criticism. This is a very strong factor in favor of a finding of fair use, even if the use is commercial. This is because these types of speech are given broad protection under the First Amendment. A parody (which is a form of commentary and criticism) will nearly always be deemed a fair use.

Factor Two: What Is the Nature of the Work that Is Copied?

This factor relates to *what kind* of work the alleged infringer is copying.

Generally speaking, works that are creative (songs, poems, and stories) will get more protection than items that are factual (reports and news stories). This means that a court is less likely to find fair use where the original work is a novel as opposed to a news story.

Factor Three: How Much of the Work Was Copied?

Copying a small portion of a work is more likely to be deemed fair use. Copying a lot means that it is less likely that the doctrine will apply. For the same reason, a low-resolution reproduction of a digitized picture, such as a Web page "thumbnail," is more likely to be a fair use than a reproduction of the picture in its original resolution.

Factor Four: What Is the Effect on the Market for the Copied Work?

This factor is based on the commercial impact on the copied work. If actual or potential sales are not going to be hurt, then the challenged copying is more likely to be fair use. If sales of the copied work are adversely impacted, then a finding of fair use is less likely. Under this factor, if the use is "transformative" —it uses the work in a wholly new and noncompetitive way—it is more likely to be seen as fair use.

Applying the Factors

If we apply these factors to our examples above, we see:

> **Example One**: *Jack the Poet is in a gray area. His use is noncommercial and for the sake of criticism, but he has taken the entire poetry work and by doing so may have diminished the market for its sale. It would be unclear if this is fair use.*

Example Two*: Jill, the art lover's use is likely not fair use. Her site is commercial. She is exploiting entire art works. Arguably her distribution for free diminishes the for-pay market for the image of the artworks. Jill's use is unlikely to be fair use.*

Example Three: *Jeff Gamer's parody is probably fair use. Even though his use is commercial, under court rulings, a true parody is deemed to be fair use.*

Getting Permissions

Sometimes it is really quite clear whether use is or is not fair use. Sometimes the conclusion is very much in doubt. Getting permissions from rights holders, in proper legal form, avoids the need to rely on the fair use doctrine. You will find that publishers (including publishers of digital content) often prefer permissions and hesitate to rely on the uncertain doctrine of fair use. (Chapter 20 of this book is about getting clearance under copyright and other IP law.) Note also that there are special fair use issues in software reverse engineering that we cover in our next chapter.

Fair Use and Personal Copying

In 2001, Apple used this cool slogan to sell Macintosh computers: "Rip, mix, burn. After all, it's your music." The fact, of course, is that the music on your Mac's hard drive is not "your music" at all because the copyrights are controlled by the record label and the music publisher. However, a user does nonetheless have the right to "rip" tracks from music CDs, "mix" the sound together, and "burn" music on CD-ROMs—as long as it is done for his or her own personal use.

Uses have this freedom to rip, mix, and burn because the US courts have decided that, generally speaking, copying of content lawfully in a person's possession for his or her own personal noncommercial use is "fair use." That conclusion is important, because it allows companies to make hardware and software for such copying without being liable for contributory infringement.

The case that established this aspect of fair use law was the important 1984 US Supreme Court case of *Sony v. Universal Studios* (known as "the Betamax case"). The case involved video cassette recorder (VCRs) that allowed people to record movies from television. Universal Studios argued that makers of VCRs like Sony should pay money damages to Universal Studios because the machines contributed to massive copyright infringement.

The US Supreme Court held that individual use of VCRs for "time-shifting"— viewing of broadcast performances at other times—was a fair use. The court held that selling VCRs was not contributory infringement of copyright despite the fact that VCRs could also be used for infringing uses, such as making pirated videocassette copies. The general rule is that if a software or hardware personal copying product has "substantial noninfringing use," contributory infringement will not apply.

This is the reason that it is legal for you to copy TV shows on a VCR or digital video recorder. This is also the reason that it is legal for you to make and distribute software to allow persons to make personal copies of music CDs or (as noted above) to "rip" MP3s. (Note, however, that the makers of such devices cannot include provisions for defeating digital rights management also known as DRM protections because of the anticircumvention provisions of US law discussed below.)

By contrast, making copies of copyrighted works for *others* without permission is illegal. This is why peer-to-peer file sharing is illegal. In addition, as noted above, the Supreme Court has made it illegal to *induce* copyright infringement. On this theory, companies such as Grokster that made software to enable peer-to-peer file sharing have been held liable for inducing infringement.

THE FIRST SALE RULE

Another important principle under the Copyright Act is known as *the first sale rule*. The basic concept is that once I *sell* a copy of a copyrighted work, I cannot forbid or control the resale of *that copy*. For example, if I sell you a copy of a copyrighted novel by Stephen King, you can resell *that copy* of the novel whenever you want, to whomever you please, for any price that you can get. You do not need permission of the copyright holder to sell your copy whenever and however you want. (Of course, it would be illegal to reproduce the novel without the permission of the holder of the copyright.)

The first sale principle is not a good fit for the world of digital goods and content. That is because suppliers of software or other digital products often want to restrict how the product can be used or transferred after it is delivered to the user.

We avoid the first sale rule by *licensing rather than selling* software and digital goods. If you license a digital product to Smith, then you and Smith can validly agree that the license cannot be transferred to a third party without your permission. You and Smith can also agree on how Smith may and may not use the software.

The licensor's control of the transfer and usage of the digital product by means of a license agreement is a feature of most digital product industries. There are some exceptions, however. For example, when music publishers *sell* music CDs, which are digital goods, the first sale rule applies.

In common language, everyone talks about "selling" software. It is very cumbersome to speak of everyone who deals in software products for a living as a *licensor* rather than a *salesperson*. It is odd to refer to a company's "sales" for the month as its "revenue from licensing activities." In this book, we will often use ordinary language and refer to "sales" of software products. Nonetheless, you should note that it is primarily *licensing* that we are usually discussing—and you should remember that the use of licensing terminology in your business is important. You should be more formal in choice of words in contracting. In your business correspondence, use the terminology of licensing. Avoid the words "sell" and "sale" in writings when referring to digital product transactions unless you really *mean* a sale.

Legal doctrine can be complicated if not paradoxical. In many cases, a software transaction can be a *licensing* transaction under copyright law and nonetheless may be considered a *sale* under the contractual law relating to sale of goods and warranties. (There is an introduction to the contract aspects of software transactions in Chapter 8.) It is a sign of the complexity of our legal system that inconsistent concepts of the nature of a bargain can coexist in a single software transaction.

THIN COPYRIGHT PROTECTION FOR COMPUTER DATABASES

Copyright law may apply to databases, that is, digital data compilations. However, there is an important limit to that protection under US law. If the data itself is not copyrighted, then your copyright extends only to the arrangement of the database, and if there is little or no originality to the arrangement, you may have no copyright protection at all. Lawyers say that the protection afforded to databases is "thin."

There are some databases that may totally fail the originality test of US copyright law. These are databases where there is no creative work in selecting and displaying the data.

> **Example***: You distribute a computer database consisting of the names and addresses of all restaurants in southern Florida. Your database supplies the data in alphabetical order.*

In this example, you certainly have no ownership interest in the names and addresses, which are public information. The alphabetical arrangement is not even slightly original. There would therefore be no valid copyright. Even if you arranged the names and data in some original way, your copyright would only extend to the arrangement itself. Others would be able to copy the names and addresses for their own database without violating copyright law. The fact that it costs you hundreds of thousands of dollars to assemble the data would be irrelevant.

It is possible to have a database in which each entry in the database, and therefore the contents of the database as a whole, is protected by copyright law. For example, the entries in a database might be brief custom-written reviews of southern Florida restaurants.

Even if your database is not copyright protected, you may be able to get protection for your database (if it is distributed online or on disk) in another way under US law—by means of contract. Using clickwrap or browsewrap agreements, containing limitations on the use and copying of your database as well as prohibitions on reverse engineering of encryption protection measures, can protect your database even if the US copyright laws do not. This is because US courts have shown a willingness to enforce these types of contracts and contractual provisions. (For a discussion of clickwrap agreements, see Chapter 16.)

The 27-member countries of the European Union (EU), under the EU Database Directive, extend legal protection to databases created within the EU, even for data not protected by copyright. Under the Database Directive, as implemented by the law of the various EU nations, database rights last for 15 years from the end of the year that the database was made available to the public, or from the end of the year of completion for private databases. Protection is very similar to copyright law. For many years, database companies have been asking Congress to create similar protection for databases in the United States. So far these efforts have come to nothing, but it is likely the database owners will keep lobbying Congress for this protection.

COPY PROTECTION TECHNOLOGY AND ANTICIRCUMVENTION LAW

In 1998, Congress passed the Digital Millennium Copyright Act (or DMCA). This was an important collection of amendments to the Copyright Act. (We will encounter provisions of the DMCA in various parts of this book.) One of the significant DMCA provisions was a section that made it illegal to circumvent copyright-protection technology or to distribute or sell programs or devices for defeating such protections. Copyright holders may sue violators of these "anticircumvention" provisions. In addition, violation of these provisions may be a crime. This was an important extension of the protection of copyright law.

Digital Rights Management Technology and Anticircumvention

The anticircumvention provisions of the DMCA reinforce technological anticopying measures. If you want to control the copying or use of your digital product, you do not have to rely solely on the law; you can also use technology; there are many well-known schemes for controlling access and copying. These so-called "DRM" technologies include:

- Software solutions (including online authentication) that limit use or copying of programs or digital content

- Hardware devices (such as so-called "dongles") that are required for use of a software product

- "Watermarking" technology that allows distinctive but invisible marking of content so that illegal copying can be detected

- Encryption schemes that require "keys" for accessing digital content

- Web-based software that permits viewing of content, but not printing or saving

- On-line passwords that open access to otherwise unavailable content

While there are many such solutions, they are often defeated by "crackers." An ideal technical solution is one that is cheap to implement, easy to use, but very hard to defeat. This perfect technical solution has been hard to find. Piracy of copyrighted goods has been slowed but not stopped by technology. For that reason, a number of countries, including the United States, have acted to provide legal reinforcement of access control and copy protection devices. The EU countries have similar laws.

Anticircumvention Law Concepts

Here are some basis concepts of anticircumvention law under the DMCA:

- "Access control measures" are technologies that permit or forbid access to a copyrighted work. An example is a password, a "dongle," or encryption of content.

- "Copy control measures" control copying. Examples are software-based copy protection schemes, such as the DVD copy protection scheme known as CSS or Apple's AAC protection system that limit users' copying of down-loaded music files.

- "Access control circumvention devices" are hardware methods, software or services that defeat access control measures and have only "limited com-mercially significant purpose or use" other than to circumvention. Examples are password "cracking" programs.

- "Copy control circumvention devices" are methods, hardware software or services that defeat copy control measures and have only "limited commer-cially significant purpose or use" other than to circumvention. An example is the software program developed in 1999 by three young Norwegian pro-grammers called DeCSS, which defeats CSS protection and permits copying of DVDs on ordinary Windows PCs.

What Is Illegal under Anticircumvention Law?

Under the relevant sections of the DMCA, it is illegal:

- To circumvent an access control measure

- To build, import, or distribute any access control circumvention device or copy control circumvention device (This is sometimes called the "Trafficking Ban" because it is designed to stop sales and distribution of such devices.)

It is also illegal under the DMCA to remove intentionally from a copyrighted work any "copyright management information" which means the title of a work, the name of the author, the copyright notice, and other identifying information.

Violation of these DMCA provisions can have unpleasant consequences. The criminal penalties include fines of up to $500,000 and up to five years in prison. Parties whose anticircumvention rights are violated may sue for actual damages or up to $2,500 per violation in statutory damages. The impact even of the civil remedies can be severe. If a user cracked the copy protection of 100 music record-ings, he or she could be liable to the record labels for $250,000.

Absence of Defenses

Anticircumvention under the DMCA is rather controversial because the penalties are high and the law has virtually no exceptions. *In particular, there is no "fair use" defense.* Say that you circumvent an access control to extract content that fair use law permits you to copy. In that case, you will have a fair use defense to infringement, but no defense to anticircumvention liability.

There are only a few exceptional cases in which you are legally entitled under the DMCA to "crack" access controls. These include:

- For reverse engineering of software for the purpose of achieving interoperability with another program. (However, as discussed in the next chapter, such reverse engineering may nonetheless be illegal under the "clickwrap" agreement that accompanies software.)

- For encryption research.

- When malfunctioning or damaged access control mechanisms prevent you from accessing literary works that you are otherwise entitled to use.

- When you want to determine whether a Web site is blocked by filtering software (such as NetNanny, CyberPatrol or SurfWatch) and the filtering software has an encrypted list of blocked sites.

REGISTERING YOUR COPYRIGHT

Copyright registration in the United States is optional—but it is often a very good practice.

To best protect your software and digital products in the United States, you should register their copyright *before* you start sending them out into the world—at the time of first commercial sale or even earlier. The reasons that you should register early in the life of your computer program are:

- Registering your work is *very* easy.

- Registering is a bargain. At the time that this book is being written, the fee for most registrations is $45. (Under an electronic filing system in beta test at the Copyright Office as we write this book, the fee is $35.00.) This is a fraction of what it costs the government to examine and process your application and store your deposit of computer code.

- Timely registration, as discussed shortly, gives you important litigation advantages, including access to "statutory damages" in civil litigation and a good shot at an award of attorneys' fees. These advantages are quite valuable if you need to threaten or sue an infringer. If you have waited too long to register your copyright, these advantages are lost.

For business products, early registration is recommended. For consumer products, it is essential because publishers need the enhanced remedies that registration provides to battle software "piracy."

How Copyright Registration Works

The US Copyright Office is a branch of the Library of Congress set up by Congress, and it runs the copyright registration system. Its staff members examine applications, issue certificates of registration, classify and maintain materials sent to the office, and aid the public in the registration process.

The copyright registration system is based on the proposition that any work that meets the easy standard for copyright protection is acceptable for registration. As long as the (rather simple) formalities are done correctly, you will find that nearly every software and digital work is accepted.

To register a copyright you send an application, a deposit of copyrighted material and the applicable fee to the Copyright Office. Most digital technology companies do their own copyright registrations without using their attorney. For text and graphic works, the deposit is usually a copy of the work; for software, the deposit is usually a printed listing of part of the source code. For most software, you should use Form TX, the form used for written works. Registration times can vary, but it normally takes about four months from the submission of a correctly filled out application until you get a certificate of registration back from the Copyright Office.

Details of the process, additional important information and the applicable forms can be found on the Copyright Office Web site. Be sure to follow the instructions stated on the application forms.

If you mail computer media to the Copyright Office, be sure to follow the instructions on the Web site about how to package your materials for mailing. In response to the anthrax mail attacks in Washington D.C. in 2001, mail addressed to the Copyright Office is currently irradiated before it is delivered. Unless you follow the rules, your deposit of copyright materials may be ruined by the irradiation process.

ADVANTAGES OF COPYRIGHT REGISTRATION

Many digital technology companies never bother to file a copyright registration until they are faced with infringement. However, waiting until the time of suit to file the application may cost your company advantages in litigation. Our advice is that for every new version of any significant digital technology product, including every significant revision (beyond minor repairs and bug fixes), you should file another copyright registration. Here's why:

Statutory Damages under the Copyright Act

In most lawsuits, you need to prove actual damages in order to recover money. Actual damages usually will mean the amount of profits that you lost due to the wrongdoing or the wrongful profits that the infringer gained.

Under copyright law, however, you can get monetary damages *even if you do not or cannot prove actual damages*. These damages without proof are called *statutory damages*. The amount you get under this provision is set by the judge in his or her discretion; the award can be as high as $30,000 per work, and, if the infringement was intentional, as high as $150,000 for each work infringed.

The right to claim statutory damages gives you the option of a simpler and less costly lawsuit. However, the judge has discretion to grant you these statutory damages *only* if you have made a timely registration as discussed below.

Getting a Good Shot at Attorneys' Fees

Also important is the opportunity to seek an award of attorneys' fees after trial. An award of attorneys' fees under this provision again is discretionary; that is, the judge can freely decide whether or not to award fees. In practice, attorneys' fees are granted quite often to prevailing plaintiffs. The clearer and more blatant the infringement is, the more likely you are to get an award of attorneys' fees, the amount of which can be *very* substantial. Even the availability of the remedy gives you important settlement leverage. But if you don't register your copyright in a timely way, the judge has no power to award you *any* attorneys' fees at all.

Filing for Timely Copyright Registration

Statutory damages and attorneys' fees are available only if:

- For Infringement of Unpublished Programs: If you registered your program before the infringement began.

- For Infringement of Published Programs: If you registered before the infringement began or within three months of publication.

In calculating whether you filed in time, the key date is the *effective date* of registration, which is the date on which the Copyright Office *receives* your properly prepared application, together with the appropriate fee and your deposit of program code. The date the Copyright Office finally issues the Copyright Certificate, which may be months later, is irrelevant.

Presumption of Validity of Your Copyright

If you have registered your copyright either *before* publication or *within five years* of publication, the law also gives you another procedural benefit. In a copyright lawsuit, until proven otherwise, your copyright is presumed valid; and until proven otherwise, all the statements in your copyright registration are taken as true.

These presumptions can simplify proof somewhat at trial and are meant to be another incentive to prompt registration. However, the matters of proof that are the subject of this rule are really not very difficult to prove in litigation. This is a less important advantage than statutory damages and attorneys' fees.

Making Copyright Registration a Regular Practice

Registering early gives you the legal advantages outlined above and thereby strengthens your hand against an infringer. As a practical matter, you should register your product, and any new release or substantial revision, before circulating it widely. At the latest, registration should take place during the three-month window allowed by the Copyright Act discussed earlier in this chapter. Registration is particularly important for widely used products that are commonly the target of piracy or illegal use and copying.

Recording Assignments and Exclusive Licenses

If you have received an assignment of a copyright or obtained an exclusive license to software, you can and should get the assignment or license on record at the Copyright Office. You should promptly *register* the copyright if it is unregistered, as discussed above. If the copyright has been previously registered, you can *record* at the Copyright Office the contract or other instrument that granted you your exclusive license interest. (You can register nonexclusive licenses to registered copyrights as well, but that is not commonly done.)

Why would you want to record a transfer or exclusive license? The reason is that recordation establishes priorities between conflicting transfers. The priority date is the date of transfer as long as the transferee or licensee records the transaction document at the Copyright Office within 30 days after the transfer or license grant (60 days if the transfer took place outside the United States).

When there are priority conflicts in copyright transfers or exclusive license grants, it is most often a matter of accident rather than deliberate fraud. But whatever the cause, it is best to get the law on your side by making the proper recordings. Details of the process and the applicable forms can be found on the Copyright Office Web site. Your attorney can also help you with these matters.

CRIMINAL COPYRIGHT VIOLATIONS

Intentional copyright infringement can be a criminal offense. Infringement is a crime if done for financial gain; or if not for financial gain, if it involves the copying of works with total retail value of over $1,000. Infringement is a felony if the infringer distributes ten or more copies of copyrighted works valued at more than $2,500 during a 180-day period. For felony violations, federal law allows punishment of up to three years in prison and a fine.

Does this mean that if anyone is pirating your software or digital goods, you call the FBI and have the government begin an investigation? Unfortunately, it is not that simple. Governmental agencies have limited resources and priorities driven by policy and politics. Federal authorities will be most interested in cases involving large amounts of copied products or organized crime. For matters that are not enforcement priorities, the government will leave you to file your private lawsuit.

If you do want to try to get a criminal case under way, you should be prepared to assist the government by providing ample documentation of large scale unauthorized copying.

MORE ON COPYRIGHT LAW

If you want to know more about copyright law issues, please read on to the next chapter. The subject matter is the application of copyright law to the Internet and digital products. There is also a deeper discussion on what it means to "copy" a computer software program. For example, there is a legal distinction between "literal" and "nonliteral" copying of software. The next chapter also explores the copyright issues in reverse engineering and includes information on international copyright law.

We will revisit copyright issues throughout this book, because copyright is essential in digital transactions. Copyright is at the heart of open source contracting (discussed in Chapter 9) and is very important in clearance of content (discussed in Chapter 20).

More information on copyright law and procedures is also available online from the Copyright Office at the URL mentioned above.

CONCLUSION

The protection of software and digital goods under the US Copyright Act and its counterparts around the globe is far from perfect or complete. Nonetheless, it is vitally important because it rewards originality and deters unauthorized copying. Your commercial digital product creation, distribution, and sales depend on it. Your business needs to be constantly aware of how copyright can protect your works and what copyright law allows and forbids you to do.

Copyrights on the Internet, for Software Protection and Around the World

3

When I took office, only high energy physicists had ever heard of what is called the Worldwide Web…. Now even my cat has its own page.

—Bill Clinton, US President, 1996, referring to the Web page for Socks, then the nation's First Cat

When we were developing the Macintosh we kept in mind a famous quote of Picasso: "Good artists copy, great artists steal." What do I think of the suit? I personally don't understand it…. Can I copyright gravity? No.

—Steve Jobs, commenting on Apple's unsuccessful copyright suit against Microsoft for allegedly illegally copying of the Macintosh interface in Microsoft Windows 2.0

IN THIS CHAPTER

In Chapter 2, we looked at copyright basics. This chapter extends our discussion of copyrights deeper into the digital world. You can consider this chapter as "advanced topics" in digital copyrights. There are three distinct topics covered.

- First is copyrights applied to the Internet and the Web, which as President Clinton observed has penetrated our society. (Of course, in 1996, we had only an inkling of what was yet to come.) This includes a discussion of copyright issues involved in linking, framing, peer-to-peer file sharing, and user-provided Web content. Included is a discussion of the important "notice-and-takedown rules" under the Digital Millennium Copyright Act (DMCA).

37

- Next you will find a discussion of the subject that Steve Jobs touched upon in his quote, the different ways one might "copy" a software program or digital product. Topics covered included protection (or lack thereof) of interfaces and look and feel. There is also a discussion of reverse engineering.

- Finally, you will find a discussion of international copyright protection.

TOPIC ONE: COPYRIGHT AND THE INTERNET

The Internet, you might say, is built on copying. It is also built on links. Both of these topics and their relation to copyright are explored in this section.

Example

Let us say that you have a Web site about automobiles and you want to add a picture of a car. The photo is a copyrighted work. If you "touch up" the photo (say with Photoshop), you create a derivative work which you will copy to your hard drive. Processing to compress the file (for example to make a jpeg file) is creating a further derivative work. Composing a Web page that includes the graphic file requires accessing and copying the file again. When you put the graphic file and the rest of the Web page into your Web server (or back-end database) you make another copy. When a user of the Internet browses to your Web site and accesses the page that contains the photo, more copying happens. The compressed file is copied from the disk and sent into the Internet. In its traveling through the Internet, the file (and the rest of the page content) may be cached by one or more internet service providers, which constitute more copies. Then the compressed graphic file is transmitted to the user's PC, which copies the file in both memory and on disk and then accesses it, decompressing in memory to create a screen display.

As you can see from this example, if the original copy of the photo is used without permission, you have a long series of copying (and creation of derivatives) with no consent—and therefore potentially dozens of infringements of the copyright.

There is a section of the DMCA, a statute that we met in the last chapter, that provides a "safe harbor" for some Internet copying. (There is a discussion of these DMCA provisions below.) If anyone is sued for infringement when copying or distributing copyrighted works, unless there is consent, fair use or another defense such as under the DMCA, the copying will be infringing.

Analysis of Web Functions

The foregoing example illustrates the way to analyze question of copyright and possible infringement in the Internet context. The first step is to get a good understanding of the technology and the flow of content. Then one applies copyright principles to each copy and each derivative to see if it is infringing or not. Technologies change and Congress gives us new laws from time to time; but this approach to the analysis is constant.

Links

Generally speaking, there is no copyright issue under US law in providing a link. If I put a link on my Web page to www.cnet.com, it does not matter whether CNET Networks, Inc., the site owner, consented or not. That's because I am not providing a *copy* of the CNET content—a link is just the *address* where that content can be found.

Deep Linking

Some commercial companies on the Web have complained about (and even sued over) "deep linking," which is linking to content on pages of a Web site other than the home page. The famous case was the 1997 litigation between Ticketmaster and Microsoft. Microsoft had a service called Sidewalk that included concert listings with links to specific pages on the Ticketmaster site where the tickets could be bought. Ticketmaster prefers that customers come to its home page where it displays advertising and where it tries to interest the Web viewer in other offers as well.

The Microsoft case was settled (and ironically Sidewalk was later sold to Ticketmaster), but in a later and similar case, a US federal court in California ruled in 2000 that deep linking is permissible so long as it is clear to the user who is the owner of the linked-to site. (Avoiding source confusion is a trademark rather than a copyright concern. Trademarks are discussed in the next chapter.)

Framing

Framing occurs when a Web page is designed to link to another Web site, but includes its own page display over or around the framed page. An example of framing is Google Image Search. When you click on a thumbnail Google image search result, Google displays an images.google.com Web page with another provider's embedded page, together with a message such as "Below is the image in its original context." Google also provides the embedded page's URL which is also a link. Clicking on the link takes the user to the page in an unframed form.

Framing is generally permissible under US copyright law as long as the source of the famed page is made clear. That is because the framing mechanism is just a link. The framing Web page does not copy the framed page; it just sends the user a Web page that includes a link to the framed page.

Companies that do framing can get into trouble if they do more than just framing. For example:

- Changing the appearance of the framed content (or juxtaposing it with other content) so that the result is arguably the creation of an unauthorized derivative work

- Creating confusion about the source of the framed page

- Giving a false impression that the owner of the framed page has consented to its use

If you are using framing in your Web site or Web service, it is always good practice to include a link to the framed page and its URL, just as Google does.

Linking and Peer-to-Peer Copying

Napster, as you recall, was the first of the peer-to-peer music-sharing services. It launched in 1999 and soon had tens of millions of users. Napster functioned by indexing users' collections of music mostly mp3 songs "ripped" from CDs. Napster's servers created, and made available to users, a searchable central directory of links to all user music collections. Using the Napster application, users could search the central directory, click on song titles, and obtain peer-to-peer transmission of recorded music from other users.

The music industry sued Napster. By March 2001, a federal appeals court had ruled that Napster's service was illegal and shut it down. Napster soon went bankrupt. (While you can buy music from Napster.com today, this is a legal download service that bought the "Napster" trademark; it is not the same company that caused such a popular and illegal sensation.)

From a technical perspective, Napster's service did not copy copyrighted music—Napster simply provided links—but those links were a centralized mechanism, run from Napster's servers, to permit users to engage in copyright infringement. The Napster case indicates that while linking is permissible in general, providing links knowingly to contribute to or induce copyright infringement, is not permitted.

As noted in the last chapter, the courts have extended this analysis to decentralized peer-to-peer file-sharing programs such as Grokster. With Grokster's application, the directory of links was not in company servers, but rather was spread about in thousands of users' computers. The US Supreme Court found this to be inducing infringement nonetheless because it found that Grokster *intended* that the technology be used for infringement and *induced* copying of infringing content.

The bottom line is that enabling peer-to-peer content sharing of copyrighted content is likely to be infringing in the United States.

The DMCA Notice-and-Take-Down Rules

The DMCA, mentioned above, has provisions that can act as a shield against copyright liability, informally known as the "safe harbor" provisions. The most important of these is the "Notice-and-Take-Down" rules of the DMCA (also known as DMCA Section 512(c)). This is a vital protection for online businesses. *If you have a Web site or service and allow users (including any content suppliers) to provide content that users download or access, then you unquestionably should take advantage of this protection.* The basic idea is that if you have the right policy and follow a specific process for removing infringing content after notice, your company is not liable for inadvertent copyright infringement.

Why Were These Rules Enacted?
Generally speaking, ignorance and good faith is not a defense to direct copyright infringement. If you include infringing content in a publication, you will be liable even if you believed in good faith that the content was noninfringing. This principle has the potential to create real problems in Internet (and other network) applications where users contribute or include content freely—for example in email attachments, blogs or chat rooms.

During the late 1990s, Internet companies went to Congress to lobby for protection from copyright liability. The 1998 DMCA with its Notice-and-Take-Down Rules were the results of intense negotiations between the lobbyists for content owners and Web companies. Like many compromises made in a hurry and under pressure, they are an inelegant solution. On the whole, the Internet companies seem to have come out ahead.

Who Do the Rules Protect?

The protection of the Notice-and-Take-Down Rules applies to any "service provider," which defined as "a provider of online services or network access." This is a very broad definition. The beneficiary of these rules could be any company that allows posting of content or messaging. This could be any blog site, any instant messaging service, a user-contributed video service, a Web portal, an online video game that allows communication, a chat room, or any Web content-sharing site.

The Big Change in the Legal Environment for User-Supplied Content

The importance of these Notice-and-Take-Down Rules has been magnified by the explosion of Web video and audio content, and it has had unexpected consequences.

When this law was passed in 1998, the category of content of most concern was email and its attachments and chat rooms. Internet access was mostly dial-up and user-posted content was mostly prose and some graphics. There was then no blogosphere, YouTube, or MySpace, and none of the hundreds of other sites that feature and audio content.

We now live in a broadband world of user-posted content. Enormous amounts of user-posted content consist of or contain movie and television content or popular recorded music. As you will see in Chapter 20 (which is about clearing digital content) getting permissions for video and music can be complex. But individual users of the Internet don't bother getting permission; they just use, alter, combine, or copy copyrighted content at will and then post it online. Needless to say, individual-user-posted content is filled with copyright infringement. This fact, and the fact that infringing content attracts millions of viewers every day to Web sites that do not pay content owners for the content, has raised the stakes on these rules enormously.

Content owners (like the record labels and the movie studios) would like to compel sites like YouTube and MySpace to pay for this content use but find themselves thwarted by Section 512(c) of the DMCA.

What Activities Are Protected?

These rules provide protection to the service provider against claims of infringement of copyright by reason of the "storage at the direction of a user" of material on the service provider's systems. This in essence means any user-initiated storage and permitted downloading of uploaded content. A "user" in this sense could be anyone—a corporation or other business entity or an individual.

Limitations to the Rule

There are some limitations to this protection:

- Protection will not apply if the service provider has "actual knowledge" that the material is infringing.

- Protection will not apply if the service provider is aware of *"facts or circumstances from which the infringing activity is apparent.* This phase about "facts or circumstances" makes the scope of protection somewhat unclear, because it is not clear what facts or circumstances would make infringement "apparent."

- Protection will not apply if *"the service provider does not expeditiously remove or disable access to the material upon obtaining such knowledge or awareness of the infringing material."* The courts have interpreted the DMCA to require online services that want the protection of the DMCA safe harbor to adopt, give notice of, and implement a policy to terminate the accounts and access of repeat infringers. This means that online services must track infringement incidents and have its staff assigned whose job is to terminate accounts of offending users. (We discuss the policy and notice requirement below.)

No Direct Financial Benefit from Infringement

Under the terms of the DMCA, the Notice-and-Take-Down Rules only apply if the service provider *"does not receive a financial benefit directly attributable to the infringing activity, in a case in which the service provider has the right and ability to control such activity."*

What does this mean? We can illustrate it with an example: Say that you have a Web business that allows indie bands to post their music on your Web site. Let's say that someone posts a downloadable copyrighted song without permission, and the copyright holder sues your company for copyright infringement. Your company unquestionably controls downloading, so the DMCA will only protect your company if there is no "financial benefit" to your company that is "directly-attributable" to the infringing song.

Your company clearly *would* get a "directly-attributable" financial benefit if your company charges the Web site users for each download of the song or if your company plays (and gets paid for) a video or audio advertisement when a user plays the song.

There is also a 2007 federal appellate court decision that declared that a firm gets a "directly-attributable" financial benefit if the infringing activity constitutes a draw for users. So it is possible that the DMCA will not protect your company for its featured content.

Let's take the same fact pattern, but assume that your indie music site uses a monthly subscription-based revenue model, does not charge per song, and does not specifically feature the infringing song. Your company would now have a reasonable argument that the DMCA safe harbor *should* apply, because the revenue is now likely not "directly attributable" to the infringement.

This means that the way that a Web site gets paid for and uses content may affect its copyright infringement exposure and its protection under the DMCA. Web site owners should not have their revenue "directly attributable" to content that has high infringement risk. There is still uncertainty in the law as to what does or does not qualify as a "financial benefit directly attributable" to infringement. You should consult your lawyer before you make any important decision that turns on this distinction.

Appointing an Agent and Posting a Policy

To be eligible for protection of these DMCA rules, a Web site owner must designate an agent for notification about claimed infringements. The Web site must register the agent with the US Copyright Office. It is very easy to do this. There is a form on the Copyright Office Web site, www.copyright.gov. All you need to do is download it, fill it out and send it to the address indicated.

Once the Web site owner has completed this registration process, its Web site needs to clearly identify that person as the agent for notice under the DMCA and inform users of the DMCA procedure. That notice should be made part of a "Copyright Policy" on the site that also includes language like this:

> We respect the intellectual property rights of others and we prohibit users from uploading, posting or otherwise transmitting on this Web site or service any materials that violate another party's intellectual property rights. When we receive proper Notification of Alleged Copyright Infringement as described below, we promptly remove or disable access to the allegedly infringing material and terminate the accounts of repeat infringers in accordance with the Digital Millennium Copyright Act.

Many thousands of Web sites have a "Copyright Policy" provision, so examples are easy to find on the Web. (YouTube has one, for example, as does Yahoo! and FaceBook.) For your convenience, we have included an example (Form 3-1) in the form appendix to this book. To take advantage of the safe harbor, put a notice like this into your Web site. Usually, there is a link at the bottom of the site home page to this legal notice.

Once the Web site owner has its registered agent and the right form of copyright policy up on its Web site, then the Web site owner can avoid most or all US copyright infringement due to user-contributed content—as long as it complies with some formal procedural rules as follows.

Notice

The Notice-and-Take-Down rules spring into action when the Web site receives a notice of claimed infringement from a copyright owner (or its agent or licensee). To be effective, the notice from the copyright owner must include:

- Identification of the copyrighted work that the owner claims is infringed.

- Particular content from the work that was copied.

- Page or location on the Web site where the infringing content can be found.

- A statement that, to the good faith belief of the copyright owner, there was no permission for use.

- A statement that the information in the notification is accurate, and under penalty of perjury, and that the complaining party is authorized to act on behalf of the copyright owner, agent or licensee.

After notice, the Web site owner must "expeditiously remove, or disable access to" the material that is the subject of the notice. Having done so, the Web site owner is protected under the DMCA provisions.

Put-Back Provisions

Under the rules, the Web site is supposed to notify the user whose material was removed. The user may then provide a "counter-notice" asserting that the material does not infringe.

The counter-notice must include:

- The user's name, address, phone number and physical or electronic signature

- Identification of the material and its location before take-down

- A statement under penalty of perjury that the material was removed by mistake or misidentification

- The user's consent to local federal court jurisdiction (or if the user is in another nation, to the local court system)

If the user provides a counter-notice, the Web site must notify the copyright owner. Fourteen days later, the Web site owner is required to put the content back up on its site unless within that 14-day period, the copyright owner has sued the user for copyright infringement.

Some Notes and Take-Aways

Here are some comments on the "safe harbor" of the DMCA:

- The shield against copyright liability provided by the rules under the DMCA "safe harbor" is broad. It covers any form of "monetary relief" which would include damages or attorneys fees, and prevents most injunctions as well.

- This shield only works for copyright claims. While copyright is clearly the main concern, it is possible that clever content owners might come up with some other type of legal claim.

- This shield works in the United States, but has no effect in other nations.

- An unknown is how far the rules go to protect against a claim of inducing on contributing to infringement. This question is posed by the litigation (going on as this is written) between media provider Viacom and YouTube Web (owned by Google). Viacom has demanded a billion dollars in money damages. YouTube has had lots of Viacom content (for example from Viacom's Comedy Channel) uploaded by users. YouTube's claim is that the Notice-and-Take-Down rules provide a defense. Viacom says that the rules do not apply to infringement because allegedly YouTube knew of the infringing activity. This is certainly a case to watch.

- There is more information and details about these important rules at the US Copyright Office Web site, www.copyright.gov.

- This is absolutely essential protection for Web sites, but the law is quite technical—you may want to check with your legal counsel to be sure you are in compliance with the rules, particularly if you expect to have lots of user-contributed content on your site.

- There are some other, more technical, "safe harbors" in the DMCA that apply to transitory network communications and system caching (under DMCA secs. 512(a) and (b)). Generally speaking, these provide protection to routine content copying by Internet service providers and Internet carriers. These sections have no takedown provisions. If you want more information about these protections, you should contact your legal counsel.

Protection from Libel Claims

Federal law provides another important shield. There is a 1996 federal statute called the Communications Decency Act (or CDA). While the "decency" provisions of that act (which attempted to restrict indecent content) were held unconstitutional, there remains in effect a provision that most often provides site owners with immunity from defamation (libel) suits for user-supplied content in posting such as blogs and chat.

More on Copyright and the Internet

There is more about copyright issues and digital applications in this book:

- Chapter 20 is about clearance issues for digital media such as music, video, text, and graphics and also covers copyright issues for Internet applications such as search engines and mashups.
- Chapter 21 discusses content deals in the Web and mobile value chains.

TOPIC TWO: COPYRIGHT AND SOFTWARE PROTECTION

We now change the topic and look at another important aspect of copyright law and digital goods. This is the issue raised by Steve Jobs (in the quote at the beginning of this Chapter) regarding what aspects of software are protected by copyright law.

Copyright law needs to take account of the fact that software programs are fundamentally different from other copyrighted media:

- In a novel every element of a work relevant to copyright is in black and white: the words, phrases, plot, and characters—everything can be found on the printed page. With software, the images and words that the user sees on the screen are only one small element of the program. Indeed many programs have no visible aspect and operate only in the background or in a device. Any visible (or audible) elements of a program are merely an output of the binary code of the program, which consists of the on–off signals that the machine perceives and executes.

- Binary code that runs in a computer is quite different from the source code that the author wrote and used to generate the object code.

- All these elements are conceptually different from the internal organization and structure of the program.

What is it then about software that the Copyright Act protects from copying? What copying is deemed infringing? We know that infringement is making or selling unauthorized copies. But what is included in copying software? Is it copying pictures and words on the screen, object code, source code, internal structure, overall appearance, or something else? Are the programming concepts protected? Is reverse engineering also infringement?

In the course of decisions rendered over the last two decades, the courts have had to sort out which of the many elements and aspects of software are protected by the Copyright Act. We now have many answers. In the next several sections, you will learn some of the limits of copyright protection for software.

Unauthorized Copying of Copyrighted Computer Code

One aspect of the law is crystal clear. It is almost always an infringement to copy binary code or source code without permission for the purposes of commercial use or sale. Similar protection against copying applies to the text of the user documentation that comes in the program, in printed form, on CD-ROM or is available online.

> Note: There is a narrow exception to this rule against literal copying. Under the Copyright Act, the software licensee has the right to make one copy of the program for archival purposes only.

Piracy

A great deal of the PC software in use in the world consists of illegal copies. No one really knows how many billions of dollars worth of infringing copying takes place each year. Every year major software companies catch business users committing wholesale infringement of the Copyright Act. Because piracy involves literal copying of the binary code, it is clearly copyright infringement. (Piracy is almost always trademark infringement as well.)

How do copyright holders take action against illegal copying of software? The copyright holders must threaten suit or actually sue to terminate these violations and to collect the money that should have been paid for the software. Enforcement of this kind is an imperfect remedy, because only a small percentage of violators get caught. In most third world countries, unauthorized copies are the rule rather than the exception.

Private Illegal Copying

Private unauthorized copying of software happens commonly as users pass software to their friends or take software home from work to put on their own machines. There is of course, also illegal Internet distribution. An individual user of mass-market software can make an illegal copy without much fear of repercussions, because it is usually not cost effective for a publisher to pursue an individual in court. For this reason, PC software publishers rely on the customer's desire for the benefits that come only from purchasing the program, such as the user manual, technical support, access to upgrades, and bug fixes. Some publishers use copy protection software.

More at risk are businesses that make illegal copies. It is not uncommon for a business to buy a single copy of a program and then install it illegally on a large number of computers within the office. When this sort of illegal copying comes to light, the copyright holder's usual remedy is to request compliance. If that does not work, the next step is to threaten and, if necessary, bring litigation against the infringer. In my experience, it is employees who have been laid off or fired that are most likely to "drop a dime" on their former employers and report illegal copying.

Pieces of Software Programs

Under copyright law, it is also generally illegal for someone without authorization to copy *part* of the code of a copyrighted program. Illegal copying of this sort is more common than you might think. Programmers sometimes leave a job with pieces of source code or object code that they or others have developed, and use the code in their next job. Sometimes developers reuse code without paying required license fees. Sometimes developers sell ownership of the same software code to several customers.

As a general rule, if someone else's software code gets into your software without permission, it is copyright infringement. The fact that it was inserted without your knowledge or consent is not a defense. On the other hand, infringement that is hidden in the internals of your software program may be very difficult to discover.

No Protection for Functional Elements Inherent in the Idea of the Application

Software copyright protection does not cover *functional elements* that are inherent in the *idea* of a particular application.

> **Example:** *You write and market a copyrighted medical office program that manages a doctor's appointments, bills, and patient records. Your program allows the physician to input the time of her appointments and to display each patient's medical history, and it allows the staff to print out an invoice before the patient leaves. Your competitor sees your program and brings out a program that also provides for patient names, appointments, medical records, and invoices. Is your copyright infringed?*

It is clear that the features of the competitive program—managing appointments, bills, and medical records and the like—are part of the *concept* of a medical office system, and the competitor may use them all. Copyright does not cover ideas and methods.

No Protection for Commonly Used Software Elements

Copyright protection does not extend to software elements that are in common use. Suppose that you write a program that uses the following message when a user exits without saving a file: "Do you want to save your file?" and prompts the user to click 'yes' or 'no.' A competitor can use exactly the same message without raising any infringement concerns, because hundreds of programs use essentially the same message. The same applies for common icons concepts, such as a trash case for file deletion.

No Protection for Use of Interfaces and File Formats Needed for Compatibility

It is generally accepted that copyright protection does not prevent use of interfaces or file formats needed to achieve compatibility or allow interaction with another program. If you want to make a program that generates files in

Microsoft Word format, nothing in copyright law prevents it. Similarly, if you create a file format, copyright law does not prevent other from using it. (Unauthorized use of a *patented* technology affecting the way that programs interact with files could be patent infringement. See Chapter 4 for a discussion of how patents work. In addition, "cracking" encryption or other file protection measures would likely violate the DMCA anticircumvention rules discussed in Chapter 2.)

External Characteristics of Computer Programs

A computer program is *active*. It may display a list of commands for you to choose from, retrieve data, display Web pages, receive your mail, solve equations, encrypt data, enable video chat, or play MP3s, and so forth, all in response to instructions delivered by keystrokes and mouse clicks. One term for these visible and audible aspects of a software program is *external characteristics*. Another is *user interface* or just *UI*. Sometimes the external characteristics of the program, together with its internal structure, sequence, and organization are called the *nonliteral elements* of a program, because the *literal elements* are the source and object code.

For some of the external characteristics of computer programs, copyright protection applies. For example, copyright law will protect the original pictures and designs that appear on the computer screen, including animation, as well as music and sound—as long as they are part of the program itself. A copyrighted picture that is part of a screen design cannot be copied and sold without permission—any more than a picture from a copyrighted magazine or a scene from a movie can be. If your computer program displays an original poem, that text would be protected by the Copyright Act just as much as any poem that appears in *The New Yorker*.

Copyright Law and the User Interface

The courts in the United States have limited the degree to which external characteristics are protected by the Copyright Act.

The PC "desktop" graphical user interface ("Desktop GUI") is so familiar that it seems intuitive: a screen divided into tiled or overlapping "windows," icons that represent programs or documents, on-screen documents that look rather like paper versions, the use of mouse to "click" icons, and so forth. We forget that all of this was invented. Xerox came up with the all the basic concepts back in the 1970s at its laboratory in Palo Alto. Apple Computer improved upon the Xerox design and first commercialized the Desktop GUI successfully in 1984 with its introduction of the Macintosh.

Apple vs. Microsoft

In 1985, Apple and Microsoft signed a secret agreement under which Apple licensed to Microsoft certain elements of the Macintosh desktop environment. Microsoft used the licensed elements in what now seems a rather crude first version of the Microsoft Desktop GUI, Windows 1.0. In 1987, Microsoft brought out Windows 2.0, which went beyond the scope of the license, and Apple saw clearly that Microsoft would be a competitive threat in this technology. Apple was correct in this assessment, as Windows 3.1 became the dominant PC interface.

In 1988, Apple sued Microsoft, claiming that its copyright in the Macintosh operating system precluded Microsoft from implementing a Mac-like "look-and-feel" for representing and controlling a PC operating system environment. The course of justice is not quick and it was not until six years later, in 1994, that a federal court of appeals issued a definitive ruling.

Apple lost the case on all points. The reason is that, as the court found, it was the *idea* of the Desktop GUI that Apple was trying to protect, and copyrights do not protect ideas. Using an icon to represent a document is an idea. The idea of windows on the screen gives a programmer very limited choices: the windows must either tile or overlap. The *idea* of windowing determined the look and feel.

Lotus vs. Borland

In 1990, Lotus Development Corp. (now part of IBM) sued Borland International, Inc. for "cloning" the menu structure of the Lotus spreadsheet program known as 1-2-3.

In the late 1980s, Lotus was the largest PC software company, with revenues and profits bigger than Microsoft. Its "cash cow" money-earner was Lotus 1-2-3, a spreadsheet program that was the *de facto* standard for DOS computers. When the case began, Lotus saw "clone" spreadsheets as its main competitive threat and sued Borland, which made a similar program. Ironically, Lotus lost the spreadsheet market to Microsoft Excel while *Lotus vs. Borland* was in litigation.

In its suit against Borland, Lotus argued that its menu structure for 1-2-3 was unique "expression." It noted that there were millions of possible menu structures for a spreadsheet. Borland, it said, could compete by choosing another menu structure.

However, in a 1995 decision, a federal court of appeals rejected these arguments. The court said that it made no sense to require users to learn a new spreadsheet interface in order to switch products. The court likened the pattern of user interface command in 1-2-3 to the shift-pattern in a manual shift automobile. The 1-2-3 interface, it said, was a "method" that is unprotectable under copyright law. Lotus brought the case to the US Supreme Court, but the justices on the court split four-to-four (one abstained), and the result was left intact.

The Bottom Line

Since the *Apple* and *Lotus* cases, it has become well accepted that GUIs, menu and command structure and the overall interface structure of a program do *not* have copyright protection. Rather copyright protection for on-screen elements is limited to creative, decorative, and design elements.

The bottom line is that you cannot depend on copyright law to protect a means of presenting information or a new GUI. If you invent one, patent law might help you, but copyright law will not.

Analysis of Similarity of External Characteristics

You may have heard that one can copyright the "look and feel" of a computer program, but that is not accurate. In the days before the *Apple* and *Lotus* cases, there were some courts that used the term as a shorthand expression, but the term is now out of vogue and reasoning of the old decisions has been rejected.

There are software products where there is nonetheless some substantial protection to the external characteristics of software: games and multimedia. In that case, the analysis of external characteristics is done by comparing the visual and audible and other "creative" elements of the two programs in question. Let us take an example from the software game world, where programs have many artistic and expressive elements.

> **Example:** *You get an inspiration for a computer combat game based on the legend of a macho superhero, and then you program a highly original game called Hercules. You register the game copyright with the US Copyright Office and publish it. Then your competitor brings out a strikingly similar game—so similar in every feature, element, and design that clearly is a copy—called Thor. What are your rights? Can you and your lawyer get Thor off the market?*

To begin with, you cannot copyright the *concept* of a game based on a mythological hero. You cannot protect the idea of a game based on the life of Hercules. As we have discussed, the Copyright Act forbids extending copyright protection to any idea or concept. On the other hand, your competitor cannot evade copyright law just by giving his game a different name and making a few minor changes.

A lawsuit would usually turn on an analysis of the functional, thematic, sound, and graphic elements of the two games. The more the author of Thor borrows the external characteristics of your game, the more likely it is that he will be found liable for infringing your copyright. Elements that are common to similar combat games, however, will receive no protection. The test is one of substantial similarity of the copyright-protected elements.

Clean Rooms: Duplicating Without Copying

Perhaps it is an obvious point: There can be no copyright infringement unless there is *copying*, and a key element of proving infringement is proving that the alleged infringers had *access* to the allegedly copied material. If one person *independently* creates a program, it does not matter if it is very much like another program. This principle has been used in so-called "clean room" software operations to duplicate the functions of a competitor's program without copying. Sometimes this process is called the "Chinese wall" method.

A clean room operation works as follows: Say that you wish to duplicate the functions of a competitor's computer program. You are not permitted under copyright law to decompile it and copy it in detail. (See the discussion of reverse engineering later in this chapter.) So instead: (1) you have your engineers study it, and produce a detailed list of its functions and interface specifications, but nothing about its programming; (2) you hire a second set of engineers who know nothing about the workings of the competitor's program (because of their lack of knowledge of the competitor's code, these engineers are sometimes known as "virgins"); (3) you have your virgin engineers in an environment where they learn nothing about the competitor's code; and (4) you have the virgins write a new program that duplicates these functions and interfaces. All of these procedures to isolate the engineers from the other product are scrupulously documented.

The end result of this clean room operation should be a program that acts the same as the competitor's program—but nothing was copied. It is generally believed that this clean room process avoids copyright infringement claims.

This sort of operation requires careful planning and documentation, and must be carried out with the assistance of counsel. It is also very expensive—and there is no assurance that the virgins will produce the required program on time.

Is There Any Protection for the Internal Structure of a Program?

Does any copyright protection extend to the "internal structure, sequence, and organization" of a program? Even if you do not copy the code of a program or its appearance, you might copy its overall internal structure. For example, one might copy the way that the program modules are organized, internal data structures are arranged, errors are monitored, or techniques are used for managing memory, and so forth. (One might learn these things, say, by means of reverse engineering or simply by observing a program and figuring out how it must work. Alternatively you may learn such information from a former employee of the other company, a situation that may raise serious issues under trade secrets law, the subject of Chapter 6 in this book.)

The courts now tend to conclude (correctly in my opinion) that these internal structural elements are in fact ideas and methods of operation that cannot be covered by copyright protection. However, I cannot promise you that every federal judge will conclude that copying the structure of another program is noninfringing under copyright law.

Reverse Engineering

Reverse engineering means decompiling or disassembling the object code of a program to figure out how it works.

Reverse Engineering and Copyright Infringement

It seems quite clear that reverse engineering—for whatever purposes—is unauthorized *copying*. In reverse engineering of commercial software, the first step is to decompile the program in question and then get a listing of the resulting form of source code (sometimes called pseudo-code) for detailed study. The listing itself is an unauthorized copy. The question is whether it is *infringing* copying.

First Question: Is Some Reverse Engineering Fair Use?

Court decisions under copyright law have said that reverse engineering will be considered fair use if discovery of information for interoperability, rather than reproduction of the program, is the goal, and as long as other means of discovering information about the program are unfeasible. As we will see, a related question is whether the "clickwrap" agreement that came with the software nonetheless forbids the reverse engineering.

In a 1993 case, Accolade, a California software game company, reverse engineered part of the operating system software used by Sega Enterprises of Japan in its Genesis game console. Accolade did not seek to use Sega's code or to market copies of the Sega Genesis software. Rather, Accolade used reverse engineering only to learn the interface between the Sega game console and the game cartridge. Accolade wanted this information to make its own game cartridges work with the Genesis unit (and Accolade did not want to pay royalties to Sega).

The reverse engineering was necessary (at least a federal appeals court thought so) because no other means of access to the interface information was available. The court found that under these circumstances the fair use doctrine of copyright law protected Accolade from an infringement claim.

However, the Accolade decision was not the last word on this topic.

Second Question: Is Reverse Engineering Forbidden by the EULA?

Every time you install software, you click to accept the end user license agreement (or "EULA"). EULAs for commercial programs routinely have a provision that says that the licensee "may not reverse engineer" the licensed software. What is the effect of that contractual provision? Does it overrule your "fair use" right to reverse engineer for interoperability? (EULAs and other "clickwrap" type agreements are the topic of Chapter 16 of this book.)

Since the Accolade cases, other courts have held that the anti-reverse engineering provision in a EULA is *enforceable*. Although it is not 100 percent free from doubt, it appears that your limited "fair use" right to reverse engineer under copyright law is lost when you click to accept the EULA on installation. Most reverse engineering will likely be illegal under contract law in the United States for any software that requires EULA acceptance.

Reverse Engineering and Anticircumvention Law

The anticircumvention provisions of the DMCA that we discussed in the last chapter also address reverse engineering in a limited way. The DMCA provides that anticircumvention prohibition does not apply if you need to reverse engineer for the purpose of "identifying and analyzing those elements of the program that are necessary to achieve interoperability of an independently created computer program with other programs."

However, this is a narrow exception. The wording of the exception does not, for example, permit reverse engineering for interoperating with protected content such as an electronic book, game, or a video. Moreover, there is nothing in this part of the DMCA that appears to override the "no-reverse engineering" clause of a EULA.

Reverse Engineering in the EU

If you want to reverse engineer for interoperability, you need not necessarily despair. There is a provision in the European Union's Software Directive that allows reverse engineering of computer programs for interoperability purposes. Most lawyers consider that this provision of European law will *override* a EULA in the EU and permit reverse engineering there for this limited purpose. However, before you begin the reverse engineering in a European nation, I strongly suggest that you contact legal counsel both in the European nation and in the United States to get some comfort that this will really work.

Reverse engineering in general is a tricky subject. If you are thinking of reverse engineering another company's software product, you need to get the advice of counsel first.

TOPIC THREE: INTERNATIONAL COPYRIGHT PROTECTION

Copyrights are the most international of intellectual property. If you have a US copyright (which are created automatically when a software work is made), then you can also get copyright protection in most other countries in the world. In addition, most nations follow the United States in including computer software within the scope of copyright protection, classifying them as literary works. That means that if there is illegal copying of your computer program or digital content, the law of most nations will provide you with a legal claim against the infringer of your copyright. (How effectively you can enforce those rights will vary of course.)

Copyright Treaties

As are mentioned in Chapter 8, there are two very important international treaties that govern copyrights, the Berne Convention and the WIPO Copyright Treaty.

Berne Convention

The Berne Convention (formally the Berne Convention for the Protection of Literary and Artistic Works) sets the world's minimum standards for copyright. One hundred and sixty-two countries (including the United States and all major European and Asian nations) have signed under the Berne Convention:

- Copyright protection of works is automatic—registration cannot be required as a condition of protection. (Note, however, that under US law, a copyright holder can get statutory damages if he or she registers before infringement begins.) Also no special marking on works is required for them to be protected.

- Each signatory nation must protect the copyright of other signatory states with the same rules that it applies to copyrights of its own citizens. If you take your copyrighted work to Brazil, you get the same protection for copyright as a Brazilian. This is known as "national treatment." Of course, if you want to fully understand your legal protections in Brazil, you still need to review the copyright laws there.

WIPO Copyright Treaty

"WIPO" stands for the World Intellectual Property Organization, which is a United Nations agency that promotes the protection of intellectual property throughout the world. The WIPO Copyright Treaty was adopted in 1996 as an attempt to bring international copyright protections up-to-date and make them stronger.

- The treaty requires countries to protect computer software as literary works under copyright.

- The treaty provides that the holder of the copyright control renting of works.

- Most importantly, the treaty prohibits "circumvention" of technological measures for the protection of copyrighted works or any unauthorized modification of rights management information in the works. This provision was implemented in the United States by the "anticircumvention" provisions of the DMCA. The European Copyright Directive requires all EU nations to prohibit such circumvention.

Thus far there are about 60 signatories to the WIPO Copyright Treaty. That there are not more signers is due in part to the fact that the anticircumvention provisions are controversial. At the time of writing this book, neither China nor India are signatories. Over time, it is likely that more companies will sign, which should increase international protection of digital goods.

EU Software Directive

The European Union's Software Directive requires that all EU countries adopt software protection for software under their own legal systems, and they have all done so. Under the Software Directive, software in the EU has legal protection roughly comparable to that provided in US law. As noted above, reverse engineering of copyrighted software is allowed under the Software Directive's terms to achieve interoperability.

About "Moral Rights" and Copyright

You often see a reference in agreements to waivers of "moral rights." These are rights granted to the creators of copyrighted works in some countries, particularly in Europe. The country that takes moral rights most seriously is France.

In countries that recognize them, moral rights include the right to have a copyrighted work accurately attributed to the author (called the right of paternity), the right to have a work published anonymously or pseudonymously, and the right to the integrity of the work. These rights, which are personal to the creator, are deemed "moral" because they apply even if the author of a work has transferred away all economic interest in a work. Moral rights are not transferable—only the author and his or her heirs can assert them.

Moral rights are recognized in the Berne Convention, which states: "Even after transfer of rights, the author shall have the right to claim authorship of the work and to object to any distortion, mutilation or other derogatory action in relation to the work which would be prejudicial to his honor." In 1995, a French court relied on moral rights law to ban a colorized version of the black-and-white firm "Asphalt Jungle." Director John Huston's heirs successfully sued MGM to stop any showing in France of the colored version because they regarded it as a mutilation of the original work.

Although the United States is a signatory to the Berne Convention, there is limited application of moral rights here. Moral rights in the United States are limited to visual arts under the Visual Artists Rights Act of 1990 (or "VARA"). Visual arts are narrowly defined in VARA and do not include electronic media.

Moral arts are not often relevant to digital technologies and products, but might apply with regard to electronic derivatives of works of copyrighted art that is modified in ways that authors disapprove of. To minimize these rights, we attorneys include moral rights waivers in many contracts for development or transfer of digital works. VARA allows moral rights waivers for visual art, but only by a signed, written agreement specifying the work and the uses to which a waiver applies. In many European countries moral rights waivers are likely to be ineffective.

Caution about Law in Other Nations

Copyright law in its basic concepts is the same in many different countries, but there are differences in detail of the law and in procedures. To understand your legal rights under copyright law in other nations, you will need to consult local counsel.

Trademarks and Domain Names

4

No one was ever fired for buying IBM.

—Anonymous

This chapter is about brands, the words and symbols that identify the source of products and services. A strong brand can help bring customers to your products and services. Brands provide credibility. Building and implementing legal protection for your brand are essential ingredients in the success of a digital technology business. The legal name for a brand is a trademark.

IN THIS CHAPTER

This chapter covers the following topics, all from a software, Internet and digital technology perspective:

- Introduction to trademark law
- Strong and weak trademarks
- Trademark priority
- Trademark searches
- US trademark registration
- Trademarks around the world
- Trademark licensing
- Trademarks on the Internet

- Domain names
- Trademark disputes

WHAT IS A TRADEMARK?

You have an everyday sense of trademarks that identify companies as the source of goods and services—such as Microsoft, Apple, IBM, and Intel. You know that trademarks also apply to particular products—for example, an Excel spreadsheet, an iMac computer, an Electronic Arts video game, or a Core2 Duo processor. Trademarks for products and services appear on screen displays, on packaging, in advertising, on Web sites, and in computer manuals.

A trademark can consist of:

A name like Microsoft.

A slogan like EA Sports' "It's in the Game!"

Letters and/or numbers like AS/400, an IBM computer hardware brand.

A design or logo like Apple Inc.'s various apple-shaped logos.

A sound like the familiar Yahoo! yodel sound.

Trademarks are source identifiers that carry an emotional charge. They can be conservative and safe, for example, IBM's brand WebSphere. They are sometimes quirky like Google or hip like Java. They can come in families, like iTunes, iPod, iLife, iPhoto, iPhone and iMac. Selecting good brands is an art.

Many digital technology products have more than one trademark; for example, Symantec, the Symantec logo and pcAnywhere are all trademarks of Symantec Corporation and all are used on pcAnywhere products. A trademark can also be used to show one company's component in another product. An example is the famous "Intel Inside" logo and sound.

Service marks are trademarks that apply to services. Companies that provide online services such as software-as-a-service vendors use service marks. So do service Web sites such as online travel services, auction sites, or dating services. Other digital technology businesses that use service marks include developers, contract programmers, data recovery services, data and media conversion services, and system integrators. (For convenience, we will refer only to trademarks or just use the term "marks"; aside from some details of the procedure for registration, the rules for service marks are the same as trademarks.)

Countries around the world protect trademarks under their national law. (In the European Union (EU), one "Community Trade Mark" or "CTM" registration can cover all 27 member countries.) While this chapter is primarily about US federal trademark law, some important international aspects of trademarks are discussed later in this chapter.

In the United States, trademark rights may arise under both federal and state law. The federal trademark statute is called the Lanham Act. Generally speaking, the Lanham Act will apply with regard to trademarks used in US interstate or international commerce. We will discuss state trademark law only in passing in this chapter. Because most digital technology and software companies have inter-state (and international) operations, they rarely bother with state trademark filings.

Domain names are different from trademarks of course, but they overlap with trademark law because they also can serve as important identifiers of products and services. (There are some cases where domain names are also trademarks; for example, Salesforce.com is a trademark of Salesforce.com, Inc.) You will find a discussion of the legal rules that apply to domain names later in this chapter.

Trademark Goals

Brands are built through smart selection, advertising, public relations, and promotion (including Web promotion) and labeling of products. When a brand helps close a sale or allows a company to charge a premium price, the investment in branding pays off.

From a legal perspective, your goal should be to create a "trademark space" that defines your products, services, and company now and for the future. That means companies should:

- Get a strong and defensible trademark or family of trademarks.

- Have protection for the trademarks in every market in the world where the brand is used.

- Be proactive in trademark protection, so that legal protection is secured not only for existing product brands and product types, but for product extensions and not only for current geographic markets, but for future sales territories as well.

- Actively exclude others from using confusing similar trademarks in each relevant product market.

We recommend that every technology company think long and hard about its brands and review its branding strategy periodically. Product development and branding should be coordinated. Companies need to allow for the time required to select a protectable brand and, if needed, secure the corresponding domain names. Trademark registration should be secured in all relevant markets in time for launch of each new branded product and service. If you want to have a family of marks (like the iTunes, iLife, iPhone series), apply for them in advance.

If your company properly establishes and protects its trademarks, the law can be a powerful tool to stop competitors from using or blurring the name and reputation that it has established. When you sell your company, its value will be much greater if it has a well-known and legally protected brand.

Trademark Risks

Bad things can happen if you neglect trademark law. For example, if you do not take proper steps under trademark law:

- You could introduce a new product and be forced to withdraw it until you change its branding.

- A competitor could start eroding your business and confusing customers by using your trademark or one that looks confusingly similar to your trademark. You might not be able to stop it from doing so.

This chapter will help you avoid these disruptive results.

Company Names vs. Trademarks

Company names (also known as "trade names") may often be very similar to trademarks, but they are not the same. For example, "Sun Microsystems, Inc." is a company name. The United States Trademark and Patent Office site has a trademark search function that shows that Sun has more than 150 trademarks registered in the United States. These trademarks include: Solaris, Sparc, Java, Sun, and Sun Microsystems. However, "Sun Microsystems, Inc." is not claimed as a trademark. When a company has a main trademark that is used across a line of products or services, such as "Sun," "Nokia," or "Motorola," it is commonly called a "house mark."

Scope of Legal Protection

Here, in one sentence, are the two concepts at the heart of American trademark law: the law generally protects the owner of a *distinctive* trademark that has *priority*.

- A *distinctive* trademark is one that is capable of distinguishing one company's goods from other similar goods made by someone else.

- *Priority*, generally speaking, goes to the first user of the trademark in the relevant market or the owner of a trademark registered with the US federal government.

The law gives such an owner a remedy in court when someone else, without permission, uses the same or a similar trademark if customers are likely to be confused about the source of the goods or services. Let's now take a closer look at these two concepts.

Distinctiveness of Trademarks

Trademark law protects only *distinctive* marks. Broadly speaking, the more distinctive the trademark, the better the legal protection. Why does the law emphasize distinctiveness? The answer is that the law seeks to balance trademark rights on one hand with the freedom to use ordinary language on the other. For example, only one software business needs to label its goods "Symantec," but many businesses legitimately need to label a program a "Utility." Symantec therefore is a strong trademark, and "Utility" is a generic term that has no trademark protection at all.

In order to understand how to choose a trademark, or how much protection an existing trademark can get, you have to understand what makes a trademark more or less distinctive—what separates trademarks into "strong" marks and "weak" marks. We are talking here about *legal* strength, recognized in a court of law. Generally speaking the stronger (that is, the more distinctive) your trademark is, the easier it is to get strong legal protection for the trademark in court and the easier it is to get federal registration.

Two Kinds of Distinctiveness

The law in fact recognizes two types of distinctiveness. The first is based on *inherent distinctiveness.* This means using brands consisting of words and symbols that *look and sound distinct* when applied to a particular kind of goods. "Apple," for example, sounds distinctive when applied to a computer, music player, or software although it would be generic when applied to pies or jam.

The second type of distinctiveness is based on *secondary meaning*—that is, the power that a trademark gets when many customers have come to recognize it. Secondary meaning is also called *acquired distinctiveness*. A rule of thumb often used in the law is that a trademark in continuous use for five years is presumed to have secondary meaning, but there are exceptions. In this mass-media age, recognition can possibly come in a few weeks through intensive advertising and public relations. "Windows" is a good example of a word that has acquired distinctiveness in the software world through use. At one time a software "window" was simply a screen or part of a screen in which content might be displayed; now of course it is distinctively associated with Microsoft operating system products.

Strong and Weak Marks

Strong marks are good. When you go about choosing a trademark or evaluating the inherent strength of an existing trademark, you need to know how the law classifies trademarks. There is a ranking based on how inherently distinctive types of marks are. As mentioned, the more distinctive, the stronger the trademark; the less distinctive, the weaker the trademark. Here are the categories:

Arbitrary Marks—An arbitrary trademark is one that bears no logical relation to the goods that it labels. Examples are *coined* marks, like Xerox, eBay, or Symantec, or marks with meaning wholly unrelated to the function of the product, like Apple, Adobe, or Amazon. Arbitrary marks have the strongest inherent distinctiveness.

Suggestive Marks—A suggestive trademark is one that suggests but does not describe a product's function. Examples are Autodesk (for design and drafting software), iTunes (for an online music store), Intuit (for financial software), and VeriSign (for encryption and security products). None of these marks states what the products do, but each product trademark suggests what the product line does. Suggestive marks are also strong, but not as strong as arbitrary marks. That is because similar products can justifiably have similar names. For example, another online music store could justifiably include the word "tunes" in its brand.

Descriptive Marks—A descriptive trademark primarily describes (as opposed to suggests) the characteristics of a product, such as its performance, function, features, quality, or capacity. An example is Virusafe anti-virus software. Some marks are more descriptive than others. For example, marks such as "Calendar Maker" or "Business Plan Maker" are deemed very descriptive and therefore legally very weak marks. In general, descriptive marks are weak. If marks are wholly descriptive, trademark law protects them only if they have acquired significant secondary meaning.

Surnames as Marks—Common family names as trademarks are weak, and like descriptive marks, will often be protected only if they have acquired secondary meaning. Norton (anti-virus software) would be an example of a surname that has this kind of acquired distinctiveness. Surnames can be more distinctive if unusual or used in association with other words or in a distinctive design.

Place Name Marks—Place names also make weak marks and normally will have protection only if they have secondary meaning. The trademark will be a bit stronger if the place name is less well known.

Generic Marks—Generic marks identify a category of goods recognized by an industry. For digital technology products, this would include the terms Works, Draw, Database, Graphics, OS (for operating system), Utilities, and so forth. These marks are the weakest. By themselves they have no protection at all. However, it is possible sometimes to protect the combination of words that is generic in part but has a nongeneric component, for example: Microsoft Works, Norton Utilities, or CorelDraw. Under US trademark law, if a generic term is given a novel spelling, it is nonetheless generic.

Rules of Proper Trademark Use

Sometimes trademarks that were originally distinctive become generic because they come to be identified not as a trademark for a product but with the product itself. Examples of common words that started out as trademarks are aspirin and dry ice. Because aspirin and dry ice are now generic, any company can call its acetylsalicylic acid "aspirin" or its frozen CO_2 "dry ice." So when a trademark becomes generic, it loses all protection and anyone can use it. Lawyers refer to this as *genericide*.

Genericide applies in the digital technology world. A federal court in California ruled in 1991 that "386," a variant of Intel's 80386 brand for a family of microprocessors, had become generic and could therefore be used by AMD, a competing maker of compatible microprocessors. This is one reason that Intel switched to arbitrary marks like Pentium and Centrino.

How do companies stop genericide? Here are some often quoted guidelines:

- Use the trademark together with the product description and make the trademark look different, such as "**AppleWorks** Word Processing Program" or "AppleWorks Word Processing Program."

- Do not use the trademark in the possessive. Avoid "AppleWorks's features."

- Don't use the trademark as a noun or a verb; always use it as an adjective. For example, refer to "**Microsoft Excel** Spreadsheet Program" rather than "Microsoft Excel."

- Always use a trademark notice (see discussion later in this chapter on these notices).

There is a problem with these rules as commonly prescribed. They are just too cumbersome to follow religiously. For example, think how the Microsoft Excel user guide would read if Microsoft had to add the words Spreadsheet Program every time it used the word Excel. What many companies do with these rules in real life is compromise. The first page of the Excel User Guide may have the words Spreadsheet with Business Graphics and Database, but the text just refers to the product as Excel, using the trademark as a noun. Most software companies reach the same type of compromises and have avoided genericide. Carelessly casual use of trademarks is still a risk.

The bottom line is that every advertisement, piece of packaging, and manual should make it clear to the reader that your trademark *is* a trademark.

Confusingly Similar Marks

Preventing customer confusion regarding the source of goods and services is the cornerstone of trademark law. Trademark law protects a distinctive trademark with priority against other companies that are using marks that are *confusingly similar*— that is, marks that cause customer confusion about the source of the goods.

This means that you may be sued if you adopt or are using a trademark confusingly similar to another distinctive trademark that has priority over your mark. (Principles of priority are discussed in detail below.) Similarly, you may have a litigation remedy if someone else adopts a trademark that is confusingly similar to yours, but only if you have priority. Use of a trademark that is confusingly similar to a trademark that has priority without permission constitutes *trademark infringement*.

Deciding When Two Marks Are Confusingly Similar

How do courts decide if marks are confusing similar in infringement lawsuits? There are a variety of relevant factors:

- Fame of the priority trademark (judged based on sales, advertising, length of use)

- Whether the priority trademark is strong or weak

- Similarity or dissimilarity of the marks in appearance, sound, connotation, and commercial impression

- Similarity or dissimilarity and nature of the goods or services

- Number and nature of other similar marks in use on similar goods

- Similarity or dissimilarity of trade channels

- Conditions under which, and buyers to whom sales are made, for example, "impulse" sales where risk of confusions is high vs. careful planned purchasing

- Nature and extent of any actual confusion—or the length of time during, and the conditions under which there has been concurrent use without evidence of actual confusion

- Variety of goods on which the priority trademark is used

Applying these factors to decide whether a trademark is confusingly similar to another is normally a matter of common sense, based on the facts of the situation. For example, if you choose as your software trademark "Orracle" or "Microsof," it is a good bet that you will be sued and will lose. Customers or potential customer could be confused. You can also run into problems if *part* of your trademark is the same or similar as prior trademark.

On the other hand, if the field of use of two marks is very different, the same or similar marks may not be confusingly similar. An example of this principle is the trademark Lexis, which is the name of a database service for law firms owned by Mead Data. In 1989, Mead Data sued Toyota Motor Co., trying to prevent Toyota from using the trademark Lexus for its luxury automobiles. Mead lost the case, because the judge decided that the field of use of the two marks was just too dissimilar. (Different rules apply, however, for "famous" trademarks. This topic is discussed below.)

Distinctiveness in Selecting a Trademark

You should apply the concepts discussed above to select a new trademark. A trademark will have the best legal protection if it is arbitrary or suggestive. Most of the marks that are powerful in the computer field have those characteristics. Strong marks such as Sun, Cisco, Intel, Oracle, and Apple are examples.

Often new companies are inclined to choose marks that tell the consumer what the product does, which means that they will select a weak trademark like Virusafe. Short-term marketing reasons support this type of choice. However, the price for picking a weak trademark is that competitors may be able to enter the market with products bearing quite similar names. In general, lawyers consider that it is best to choose a strong trademark—particularly for your company's principle brands.

Choosing good new marks for technology companies is not easy. That is because there are many tech companies with many brands already. In addition, many companies want the brand and a domain name to be the same, and that may be difficult or costly to accomplish. Nonetheless the power of brands is strong—and it is worth the effort and time to find a good brand name.

Even the most distinctive trademark will not be protected, however, if the same or a confusingly similar trademark of another company already has priority. Therefore, before adopting a new product trademark, you should understand how trademark priority works and learn how to investigate the other marks that are already out there.

Obtaining Priority Rights

As we have discussed, distinctive marks are protected against infringement if they have *priority*. Following are the three ways that distinctive marks get priority.

Priority from First and Continuous Use

To some extent under US state and federal law, the user of a trademark may obtain some priority rights to use a trademark just by using it first and continuously. However, we do not recommend relying on use to establish priority. Here is why:

- Use alone will provide priority in the United States only in the geographic markets and product markets in which the trademark is actually marketed and known. Use does not provide priority in any region where someone else is already using the same or a confusingly similar mark.

- Use does not provide priority if the same or a confusingly similar mark has already been registered by someone else in the federal Principal Register before your use began. (Registration is discussed below.)

- A party relying on use will normally lose to a prior state trademark registrant of the same or a confusingly similar mark.

Due to these many limitations, relying on use alone to establish priority is not recommended.

In most foreign nations, trademark registration is required, and there is no such thing as priority based on use. (There is more about foreign law priority rules below.)

Priority from Obtaining Federal Intent-to-Use Registration

Federal trademark law has a provision under which a trademark application can be filed *even before first use*—with the result that the registrant normally gets nationwide priority from the application date if the trademark meets the legal requirements for federal registration. Before making any heavy investment in a trademark, prudent companies take the precaution of filing an *intent-to-use application* for trademark registration on the federal Principal Register. (The registration process is explained below.) We strongly recommend intent-to-use filings before you introduce any significant trademark or family of trademarks. This is the smartest way to get priority. (You will need to check first to be sure that the mark is available. See the discussion of trademark searches below.)

Most foreign nations also permit pre-use registration, and, as noted, in most nations registration is the only way to obtain priority.

Priority from Federal Registration after Use

If you are the first user, and your trademark meets the legal qualifications regarding distinctiveness, you can normally extend priority for your trademark throughout the United States by registration on the federal Principal Register. If you have trademarks that are important to your business, you should get them registered.

Most states have their own copyright registration laws, but these are of very limited utility. Rights granted by state statutes are limited to the state's borders, and rights created by federal trademark registration generally override any state-created rights.

NECESSITY OF A TRADEMARK SEARCH BEFORE ADOPTING NEW MARKS

Before your company adopts a new trademark, or before you can conclude whether it has the right to use its existing trademark(s), you must find out whether anyone else is already using, or has already registered, a trademark that is the same or confusingly similar to the one(s) you want to use. Your company also needs to steer clear of famous marks. *It is your obligation to find out whether a trademark that you wish to use is available.* It is not a defense when you get sued for trademark infringement that you did not know that you were infringing another owner's trademark.

There are thousands of computer products and hundreds of thousands of trademarks used in other products. How do you find out if the trademark you want to use is available? The answer is that you must do a *trademark search.* A trademark search is also the normal first step toward filing for federal registration.

If, as a result of the search, you find that a trademark you want to use is confusingly similar to an existing trademark in your business or trade channels, you may be blocked. Sometimes, you can get permission to use the mark from the holder of the pre-existing trademark, but often you will be forced to choose another mark. Your attorney can help you decide the best strategy.

Scope of the Trademark Search

If you are going to sell your software or services nationwide, you need to conduct a trademark search that is nationwide in scope. You want to be sure that no one in the United States might stop you from using your chosen trademark. International searches are appropriate as well if international expansion is part of your plan.

Getting Searches Done

We recommend having the searching done through legal counsel because it will likely give you a more reliable conclusion.

Comprehensive searches using trademark search services can be expensive, so trademark lawyers normally start with what is known as a "knock-out" search. A knock-out search is meant to quickly identify marks that are obviously unavailable. Typically a knock-out search consists of preliminary searching with the online trademark databases.

If a proposed mark survives the knock-out test, we do more thorough searching based on a thorough written report from a search service. The cost of the search report (as of this writing) is about $200 to $500 per trademark depending on the scope of the search. To search a proposed symbol or design, as opposed to words, may be more expensive.

What will a search service do? It normally will search:

- Computerized database of federal trademark registrations and applications

- Computerized database of state trademark registrations and applications

- Various legal databases (to see whether trademarks have shown up in litigation)

- Domain names and Web searching

- Trade directories

The search service will use computerized tests for similarities in look, sound, impression, and use. A trademark lawyer will examine the search report and make a judgment as to whether or not the mark is likely to be available.

Limitations of a Trademark Search

Even the best trademark search does not produce perfect information. It is possible that the search may miss current users of the name of a similar trademark. Some businesses use unregistered trademarks that may not appear on any of the sources normally searched. It is also possible that someone will register a name or introduce a product with the same or a similar name after the date of your search.

These imperfections mean that you could do all these searches, come to the conclusion that you have no trademark problems, introduce your product, and *still* get sued by a prior user. Nonetheless, the search is your best means of finding out what trademarks are in use. Most of the time, those who use the process and trademark counsel get the information they need to make the right choices for their companies.

One more note about searches: If your search shows that a similar trademark has been registered, it does not necessarily mean the trademark is in use. It is possible that the user went bankrupt or gave up on the product line that used the trademark. However, sometimes trademarks that are not currently used can be revived by their original owners. Your trademark lawyer can help you determine what is available.

Once the results of the search are in, they have to be evaluated. This is where the advice of competent trademark counsel is crucial. Trademark counsel can help you to interpret the results of the search and decide if the trademark is worth pursuing. Counsel can also craft an application for trademark registration so that it avoids objections and covers the business areas that are most important to your business.

Prescreening Potential New Trademarks

Coming up with new trademarks for technology products and services is not easy. That is because there are now so many trademark and service marks already in use and registered. It is hard to find names that are original. When you are selecting a mark, you might want to do some trademark prescreening on your own before you submit a mark to your trademark lawyer. This is a way to avoid wasting time and money for reviews of marks that are already taken. It is not a substitute for having a thorough search and an analysis by a trademark attorney. (You may also need to secure corresponding domain names—this is a topic discussed below.)

If you do wish to do your own trademark screening, here is some guidance on how to proceed. A good starting point is the online trademark database provided by the United States Patent and Trademark Office (USPTO). The system is called the Trademark Electronic Search System or "TESS." You can find it at www.uspto .gov. TESS includes registered trademarks and applications. TESS is free, which certainly is a plus. However, TESS has a number of limitations. First, it includes only federal registered trademarks and applications and provides no access to other sources. Second, it provides only alphabetical searching; there is no provision for sound-alike searching.

Another tool that you can use is the Web. Putting your desired trademark into a search engine such as those offered by Google or Yahoo may lead to other users of trademarks. However, search engines also lack "sound alike" searching.

A more sophisticated tool for searching is Saegis, a trademark database search environment provided by Thomson & Thomson, which is a resource used by many law firms for searching. To use Saegis, you must sign up online to become a subscriber and pay for online use. The advantage of the Thomson & Thomson databases is that they include both state and federal registered trademarks, including pending applications and expired registrations. There are also additional resources to search for "common law" (unregistered) trademarks. The system includes a sound-alike searching function. In addition, Saegis also provides trademark databases for a number of foreign states, including Japan, Canada, and many European states.

There are two drawbacks to searching through Saegis. One is the cost; it is not cheap, especially for inexperienced users that may spend time learning the system. A thorough search done right may well cost several hundred dollars per mark. The second drawback is that lack of experience may lead you to do an incomplete or inaccurate search. You can find more information at www.thomson-thomson.com.

The Advantage of Federal Registration

Whenever a trademark is important to your business, you should register it with the federal Patent and Trademark Office (USPTO) on what is called the Principal Register.

Why register? Because, as noted, federal registration extends the geographic scope of your trademark, and registration makes your trademark easier to enforce in a variety of ways. Registration makes your trademark a more potent weapon.

Federal Trademark Registration System

Under the federal trademark system, the USPTO maintains two lists of trademarks and service trademarks: the Principal Register and the Supplemental Register. Greater rights are granted by registration on the Principal Register, which is designed to protect *distinctive* trademarks. The Supplemental Register, which allows registration of trademarks that are not distinctive, grants significant, but more limited benefits.

Principal Register

Generally speaking, the USPTO will put a trademark on the Principal Register if the trademark meets the following conditions:

- The trademark is distinctive: that is, it is arbitrary or suggestive, or if descriptive has demonstrable secondary meaning.

- The Trademark is not primarily geographic.

- The Trademark has not become generic.

- There is no significant likelihood of confusion with a trademark already registered.

If your trademark is enrolled on the Principal Register, you have the following very significant benefits:

- You can bring a federal infringement action in any federal court.

- Nationwide use of the trademark is presumed to have occurred from the application date. (You can prove earlier use as well.) If this date precedes all other users, this date will usually establish a right of priority to the trademark.

- Every user of the same or a similar trademark is presumed to have notice of the trademark (and therefore cannot claim to be an innocent infringer) from the registration date, that is, the date the trademark registration certificate is issued.

- In any lawsuit, during the five years after registration, there is a presumption that your use of the trademark is valid, that the trademark is your property, and that your right to use it is exclusive. During the five years after the registration, a prior user can still challenge your right to priority—but registration forces the other party to present affirmative proof that you do not have priority.

- After five years of continuous use after registration (and the filing of an affidavit at the USPTO affirming this use), the right to use the trademark becomes, with certain limited exceptions, incontestable. This means that even if a prior user then appears, in most cases it can do nothing to deprive your company of the right to use the trademark.

- You may use the ® symbol with your trademark.

Supplemental Register

The USPTO also maintains a list of trademarks and service marks known as the Supplemental Register. The Supplemental Register was originally begun to allow nondistinctive trademarks to gain federal registration, which in turn helped owners get protection in foreign countries. Even if the USPTO rejects your trademark for the Principal Register, the trademark may qualify for the Supplemental Register. The benefits from such registration, while significant, are much more limited.

Generally the trademarks registered on the Supplemental Register are weak trademarks: descriptive, surname, or geographic trademarks without proven secondary meaning. The USPTO will approve an application for registration on the Supplemental Register if the USPTO decides that the trademark meets these criteria:

- The Trademark is not a generic term.
- The Trademark is not already registered in the federal system for your field of use by someone else.

If your trademark is on the Supplemental Register, you have the following rights:

- You can bring a federal infringement action in any federal court.
- You can file a later application for registration on the Principal Register, if, for example, you can prove secondary meaning at that later time.
- You can use the ® symbol with your trademark.

Trademark Classes

To make trademarks searchable, the patent office has developed a trademark classification system. (There is also a similar international trademark classification system.) Trademarks are divided into classes based on business type. Each application to register a mark has to specify the applicable class. Marks can be (and often are) registered in more than one class, but there is only one class per application. US trademark classes that are likely to be relevant to digital technology businesses are:

- Class 9 (Electrical and Scientific Apparatus)—includes computer and computer software.
- Class 35 (Advertising and Business)—includes Web shopping services and Web-based advertising services.
- Class 38 (Telecommunications)—includes traditional telecom and Internet-based communications.
- Class 42 (Computer, Scientific & Legal)—includes technical services such as software and Web development and programming.

Word Trademarks and Logo Trademarks

It is good practice to register both the word and logo forms of trademarks by means of separate applications. Intel, for example, has registrations on both "Intel Inside" as a word trademark and the familiar "Intel Inside" logo. Logos cover just the particular logo itself. If you have used the same text in a new logo, the old registration would not cover it, and you would have to file a new application. The word trademark registration covers the words themselves, and therefore is broader. However, the word trademark registration would not cover a competitor's logo that looked very much like yours, but used different words.

If you have a descriptive trademark, it may not be possible to get the word trademark on the Principal Register; however, it may be easier to register the logo version on the Principal Register, because the logo design will supply distinctiveness.

Trademark Record Keeping in Support of Registration

Because the time and manner of your usage of a trademark may be a crucial factor in determining priority, and may sometimes become an issue in litigation (or important in registering a trademark), you should, as a matter of routine practice, keep complete sales and shipment documentation for any new product. Especially important is your documentation of the first use of the trademark for bona fide commercial transactions and, in addition, the first use of the trademark in interstate or US foreign commerce.

It is also important to keep records of the promotional use of each trademark, such as samples, advertisements, and direct mail materials, and copies of paid invoices for your promotion and advertising. These materials can help establish secondary meaning.

TRADEMARK REGISTRATION PROCESS

The registration process begins with an application filed by an attorney that concentrated in trademark matters. (You normally would have a trademark search done before you decide whether to file an application, although this is not a legal requirement.) An examiner at the USPTO reviews the application, examining the trademark's distinctiveness, searching for other similar trademarks, and scrutinizing evidence of secondary meaning if that is submitted.

You may recall that in our discussion of software copyrights, we said that virtually every program and digital work is copyrightable and that you can easily copyright your own software or other digital product yourself. The trademark system is different; the USPTO rejects or requires changes in a considerable proportion of the trademark applications that it receives. Many trademarks do not qualify for registration because they are not distinctive enough, and many are disallowed on the basis of other confusingly similar, previously registered trademarks or for other reasons. The registration process can slow down if the examiner at the

USPTO raises questions about the application, as they frequently do. Sometimes your attorney can overcome the USPTO's objections to registration, and sometimes not. In some cases the description of the trademark use is narrowed in the process.

If the examiner determines that the trademark passes muster, it is then published in the *Official Gazette*, a government publication. With luck, after publication, no one will file an opposition to the registration. Then the USPTO will issue you a Certificate of Registration. As of this writing, the time from the filing of the application to the issuance of a certificate, absent any opposition, is approximately 15 months.

If you are not so lucky, someone will file an objection to the registration. The USPTO will then conduct proceedings over a period of months to resolve the objection. Your trademark counsel will represent you in this process. If there is a conflict over the right to use the trademark between two companies that want to register it, the company that used the trademark first usually prevails. Appeals to the federal court system seeking review of USPTO decisions are also possible and will drive the legal costs higher still. If all objections are rejected, the USPTO will register the trademark.

Keeping Your Federal Registration In Effect

Once you have registered a trademark, if you want to keep your registration in effect, you must continue to use the trademark. Nonuse for two years often is presumed to be abandonment of a trademark.

In addition, to keep your trademark registered, you *must* submit an Affidavit of Use during the sixth year after registration to certify that the trademark is still in use. In addition, your trademark gets incontestable status only if you also submit an Affidavit of Continuous Use during the same sixth year to certify that use since registration has been continuous. Normally both these requirements are met by filing a single form known as a Sections 8 and 15 of Affidavit. In addition, you *must* renew the registration during the *tenth* year and *every tenth year* after that. These are all documents that your trademark lawyer can prepare for your company. Failure to file can constitute an abandonment of the mark.

Timely compliance with these requirements is essential. (Trademark lawyers have database systems in which they track required filing and renewal dates, but it is a good idea to keep track yourself of key renewal dates.) All of these forms are available online and can be filed through the Trademark Electronic Application

System (TEAS). If your company complies with these requirements, trademarks may be kept registered indefinitely—some US registrations have been in effect for more than 100 years.

DO-IT-YOURSELF REGISTRATION OF US TRADEMARKS

Some people simply cannot afford the cost of trademark counsel's advice. It is also true that the USPTO lets businesses register their own trademarks. Our advice, however, is that you use an attorney for trademark matters. As you can see in this chapter, federal trademark law is full of distinctions and rules. There are possible errors and traps that can prevent federal registration, limit the scope of protection, or even make the registration invalid later on.

We therefore suggest that you consult a capable trademark lawyer to submit your trademark application and to advise you on trademark issues. Having a lawyer bring the trademark through the federal registration process normally costs about $2,000 to $3,000, assuming that the process does not run into complications. (The registration process and its possible complications are discussed in the following section.)

However, for those that do want to do their own registration, here are some tips on going forward.

The place to start is the USPTO's Web site at www.uspto.gov, which has a wealth of information about trademarks. On the site, TEAS allows you to fill out a form and check it for completeness over the Internet. Using TEAS you can then submit the form directly to the USPTO via the Internet. There is useful information about the TEAS system at: www.uspto.gov/teas/index.html. There are also instructions on the online form.

Here are a few things to keep in mind:

- You may only register one trademark in one class per application.

- Application gives you an option of filing based on use or intent to use. You can only choose one of these two options.

- If you check the box for an application based on use, the application requires you to give a date for first use of the trademark in commerce that the US Congress may regulate, also referred to as the "use in commerce" date. Generally speaking, Congress regulates transactions between states of the United States, between the United States and foreign countries, or involving a territory of the United States. Therefore the form is asking for the date of first use that fits one of these categories. The form also asks for the date of first use anywhere. This date will differ from the in commerce date only if there were earlier transactions that were entirely within a single state or solely in a foreign state. For product trademarks, transactions count to establish the date of first use only if the trademark was in fact *on* the goods involved or, for services, if the use was in connection with your services. Transactions must be for genuine commercial dealings.

- In specifying dates of use, be as accurate as possible. Check whatever records you have. If you are not absolutely sure of the exact dates of first use and first use in commerce, use phrases such as "no later than." Misrepresentations about the dates of use, even if inadvertent, may render the registration invalid later on.

If you file an intent-to-use application, you will have to file a later Allegation of Use to show that you are actually using the trademark within stated time frames. The Allegation of Use is due within six months after the mailing date stamped on the Notice of Allowance, which is USPTO's notice that it has approved your trademark registration application. The date for filing the Allegation of Use can be extended, by filing the appropriate form, for up to 36 months.

ESSENTIAL ACTIONS TO PROTECT YOUR TRADEMARKS

Whether you have registered your trademark or not, there are certain essential steps that you should take to protect it.

Trademark Notices

Whenever you use your trademark (registered or not), you should use a trademark notice. The notice should appear together with the trademark on every product, package, user manual, label, advertisement, and brochure for the product. The notice serves two functions. First, it puts all would-be trademark infringers on notice that you claim trademark protection. Second, it helps fend off claims that your trademark has become generic. In some cases, failure to use a notice will impair your ability to sue for trademark infringement.

Notice for a Federally Registered Trademark

If your trademark is registered on either the Principal Register or the Supplemental Register, it is *very important* to give notice of federal registration. In some cases, you may not be able to get monetary damages in a lawsuit for infringement unless there is such a trademark notice on your goods and on advertisements and promotional materials. To give notice of federal registration, the "®" symbol is used, like this: Adobe ® or IBM®.

If you want, instead of the "®" symbol, you can use your trademark with the words: "Registered in U.S. Patent and Trademark Office" or "Reg. U.S. Pat & Tm. Off." (You must use *exactly* these words.) Most companies just use the symbol.

Notice for a Trademark That Is Not Federally Registered

If you have an unregistered trademark (including one for which there is a pending application for registration), it is still vitally important to give notice of your trademark. For an unregistered trademark, you should use the "TM" symbol. For an unregistered service mark, use either the "SM" or the "TM" symbol. These symbols are used like this: Works™. It is illegal to use the ® symbol in the United States if you do not have federal registration.

Vigilant Defense of Your Trademark to Prevent Dilution

To protect your trademarks, a certain degree of vigilance is required. The protection given to a trademark will be narrowed if you allow other companies to use the same or confusingly similar trademarks. It is good practice to send cease-and-desist letters to infringers and to bring suit where necessary to stop blatant infringement. Most companies learn of infringement by chance, but you can (and should) make arrangements (for a fee) to have a trademark search company monitor all federal and state trademark filings as well as domain name registrations and notify you when a similar name appears in an application. In addition, some companies do a periodic sweep of the Web for infringing trademarks. Your attorney can obtain these watch service subscriptions for you.

It is also a good idea to insist that when another company uses your trademark in an advertisement that refers to your products that the company acknowledges your ownership of the trademark. (This is the reason that advertisements often, in fine print, include a listing of the owners of each trademark referred to, or sometimes statements such as "Company, product, and service names are trademarks or service marks of other companies.")

If someone mentions your trademark in an advertisement without such an acknowledgment, and if it appears that there is a likelihood of confusion about the source of the goods or about whether your company has endorsed the advertised product, it would be a good idea to write to the advertiser and ask that it cease and desist from improper trading on your company's reputation.

Legal Protection of Famous Trademarks

There is another form of protection for trademarks, *beyond* the protection against infringement. This form of protection is called "anti-dilution" and it generally applies only to "famous" trademarks. The basic idea is that famous marks may be harmed or "diluted" by goods that are not confusingly similar, but that "tarnish" or "blur" the famous trademark. Federal law generally allows the holder of a famous trademark to enjoin use of the diluting trademark. There are also state laws that protect against dilution of famous marks.

Here is an example of tarnishing a famous trademark. Hasbro Inc. is a toy company that publishes the child's game Candyland. In 1996, a company known as Internet Entertainment Group, Ltd. (IEG) began to use the trademark Candyland and the domain name "candyland.com" for a sexually explicit Web site. When Hasbro sued IEG, Hasbro was not claiming that the consumers were confused about the source of the soft porn Web site. Rather, Hasbro's claim was that the use of the brand "Candyland" for selling sex was "tarnishing" Hasbro's own Candyland trademark. IEG lost the case, and the court ordered IEG to cease use of the "Candyland" trademark and to turn over the candyland.com domain to Hasbro.

"Blurring" is a similar dilution theory. Blurring typically refers to the "whittling away" of distinctiveness of a famous trademark. It would be blurring, for example, for you to use the brand Google as a brand name for a line of books, even if Google is not in the book publishing market.

How do the courts decide if a trademark is "famous?" To some extent it is common sense and common knowledge. Relevant factors include:

- Duration and extent of use of the trademark

- Duration and extent of advertising and publicity of the trademark

- Geographical extent of the trading area in which the trademark is used

- Degree of recognition of the trademark in the channels of trade used by the marks' owner and the person against whom the enforcement is sought

- Whether the trademark was registered and if so, for how long

TAKING TRADEMARKS GLOBAL

Your approach to obtaining international trademark registration should have the same goals as for US trademarks: you want to keep other companies from using your marks in your markets, and you want to avoid being sued for infringing others' marks. In the Internet age, brands "go global" faster than ever before. (See discussion of trademarks and the Internet below.) Law firms that do trademark work, as we do, have correspondent counsel in other countries around the world that assist in trademark matters.

First a few fundamental facts about trademarks around the world:

- If you have trademark registration in the United States only, those registrations provide no trademark protection in any other country.

- In most countries trademark rights are based on a "first-to-file" principle. This is different from the United States, where you can get some (albeit sometimes limited) trademark rights just from use. In most nations, if your trademark is not registered, you right to use your brand is at risk. Your company must register its trademarks abroad as part of an international expansion strategy. It is absolutely essential.

- Many foreign jurisdictions permit broader trademark descriptions in trademark filings for software products and services than would be permitted by the USPTO. A company might register its trademark in the EU for "software"—and thereby get a trademark that covers all kinds of software from games to operating systems. That would never fly in the United States. The USPTO allows trademarks to be registered only for a particular type of software. The broad trademark filings allowed in many foreign jurisdictions increase the risk that your trademark may be blocked abroad. It makes it even more important to get your trademark applications on file in foreign jurisdictions as early as possible.

- There is an international registration system that covers many countries under the Madrid Protocol (discussed below). And there is a EU-wide trademark system known as the Community Trademark (also discussed below).

- Some words and symbols that are acceptable in American English may sound odd, funny, improper, or offensive in other languages. A famous example is the Chevy Nova automobile, which became a joke in Spanish-speaking countries because "No va" means "It doesn't go." You need to check out trademarks with native speakers in each jurisdiction.

- In countries that use symbols other than roman letters, you may want to register both English and local language versions of word trademarks. For example, in China, the Microsoft house mark is both "Microsoft" and these two Chinese words: 微软, pronounced "Wei Ruan." The first character means "small and delicate" (suggesting "micro") and the second means "soft."

Paris Convention and Trademarks

As a general rule, the priority date for a trademark in most nations is the date of filing for of the trademark registration. However, you can often obtain the benefit of your earlier first filing date in another nation under the Paris Convention. (This is the short name for "The Paris Convention for the Protection of Industrial Property of 1883.") The rule is that you can use your first Paris Convention nation trademark priority date in other Paris Convention nations as long as you file in the other nations *within six months* of your original filing date. This means, for example, you can use your US filing date as your priority date in Japan as long as you file your Japanese application within six months of your US trademark application filing date.

Most counties in the world are members of the Paris Convention. (An important exception is Taiwan.) The European CTM system discussed below also recognizes Paris Convention priority.

Madrid Protocol

The Madrid Protocol is the name of a unified international process for registering trademarks. As of this writing, about 80 countries around the world, including the US and the EU, have accepted it.

Here is how it works:

- The Madrid Protocol system is administered by the World Intellectual Property Organization (WIPO), a UN agency headquartered in Geneva, Switzerland.

- The process starts with an existing trademark application or registration (known as the "basic application" or "basic registration"). For a US company, citizen, or resident, this would be the USPTO application or registration.

- Under the Madrid Protocol system, a US-based company, citizen, or resident can extend the base application or registration internationally by means of the USPTO. The Madrid Protocol system requires that the trademark owner "designate" on the Madrid Protocol application each nation that it wants the application to cover. Thus, the system allows use of a single application (which can be in English) to reach many other nations.

- The application is first accepted or rejected by WIPO. If it is accepted by WIPO, then any designated jurisdiction may still reject the application for any reason that it would reject a normal national registration, such as undue descriptiveness or because of conflict with a prior registered mark.

- Wherever the application is rejected in a particular nation, the trademark owner can appeal to the nation's trademark registration authorities. This will normally require getting local counsel or a local trademark agent.

- If the Madrid registration is not rejected by a nation's trademark registration authorities in the time allowed (usually within a year), it will become effective in that nation.

- The Madrid Protocol system also allows trademark holders to take advantage of Paris Convention priority date rules.

- The Madrid Protocol system can be used to apply for CTM registration in the EU (discussed below).

- An international registration under the Madrid system lasts for 10 years from the date of registration and may be renewed for additional 10-year periods by paying a renewal fee at WIPO.

Sometimes registration under the Madrid System is called an "international trademark," but it would be more accurate to call it a multinational trademark filing system. The holder of an effective Madrid Protocol registration gets the same rights as would apply for registration in the member jurisdiction. Say, for example, if you wanted trademark protection in Australia, you could apply at the USPTO under the Madrid Protocol and then designate Australia. If your application was accepted by WIPO and not rejected by Australia, you would have a registration that was equivalent in rights to any trademark that was registered in Australia.

The Madrid Protocol system is not for every trademark and every company. The Madrid Protocol system is quite technical, so it is important that the filings be done correctly. You should discuss with your trademark attorney whether the Madrid Protocol is right for your business and your trademarks.

CTM Registration in the EU

The EU has set up a unified system that allows one trademark registration to cover all 27 nations of the EU. A trademark registered under this system is a Community Trademark or CTM. An EU agency in Alicante, Spain known as the Office for Harmonization in the Internal Market (OHIM) administers the CTM system. This system functions in addition to the national systems of trademark filings.

The great advantage of the CTM system is its extraordinary reach on the European continent. A CTM registration is the best deal in the world in trademarks. A disadvantage is the fact that if OHIM finds your CTM application blocked in any EU country—say on the basis of a prior registration in England—OHIM will reject your CTM application as a whole. At that point, your only recourse is to apply in various nations individually.

A US applicant that wants to use the CTM system can apply in Europe—normally you would use a trademark agent or attorney in one of the EU countries. Or, as noted above, the US applicant could apply at the USPTO under the Madrid Convention process. There are advantages and disadvantages to each approach and they are quite technical. Your trademark attorney can advise you about the best strategy on applications for registration under the CTM system.

EXPLOITING TRADEMARKS IN DISTRIBUTION, LICENSING, AND OTHER DEALS

It goes without saying that technology companies use trademarks on their products and in advertising and promotional material for their services. But that is not the only use. There are many other ways in which you can build and promote your trademark.

In addition to the business discussion in this section, you will find discussion of trademark issues in Chapter 14 (on distribution deals), Chapter 20 (on licensing and clearing digital content), Chapter 21 (on Web and mobile deals), and Chapter 22 (on videogame deals).

Trademark Guidelines

There are many ways in which companies permit their trademarks to be used by other companies. The most common is in distribution. Companies often allow authorized distributors and dealers to use trademarks on Web sites, business cards, advertising, and so forth. In some cases, trademark use is mandatory.

Whenever your company permits another company to use your trademarks, you should do so pursuant to written "trademark guidelines" (also known as "branding guidelines") that the other company agrees in writing to follow. In distribution agreements there will normally be a clause on trademark matters that requires the distributor to comply with the supplier's current branding guidelines. (For more information on distribution deals, see the discussion in Chapters 14 and 15.) There are countless examples of trademark guidelines that you can find on the Web.

Guidelines need to be tailored to fit the particular use of your brand. For example, branding guidelines for packaging may be quite different than bran-ding guidelines for Web sites. Included in branding guidelines are typically such items as:

- Detailed instructions about trademark placement, size, and color

- Rules on correct trademark use (similar to those to prevent "genericide" mentioned above)

Prohibitions against uses that might taint or dilute the trademark. The more important your brands are, the tighter branding guidelines need to be.

Co-branding

Co-branding is the use of more than one trademark on a product or to promote a service. Because computer products and Internet services readily combine, co-branding is a common strategy used in the digital technology business. If you buy a Samsung mobile phone from Verizon, you will usually find that it has both Verizon and Samsung branding and that it has been programmed to display the Verizon logo on start-up.

The place that co-branding is most common is on the Web, where suppliers of content or functionality will often obtain secondary branding. For example (at least as of the time this is written) the "Automotive" page of nytimes.com recites that it is provided "in partnership with" Edmunds.com, which is an automobile information portal. The Edmunds.com brand is prominently displayed. This tells us that there is a deal between Edmunds and the *New York Times* under which Edmunds provides access to its portal content and functionality and the parties share resulting revenue.

Combined Trademarks

Co-branding can take the form of trademark combinations. An example is the "ATT Yahoo" DSL Internet service. The branding combines the ATT brand with that of Yahoo! the Internet portal. ATT is the company that actually provides the DSL service; Yahoo! markets online services under the "ATT Yahoo" brand to its customers. The combined brand is used by both parties. From a legal perspective combined trademarks are tricky because they involve creation of new trademarks in which each party may own only in part. Creation of these combined marks requires carefully drafted agreed rules on ownership, registration, and use.

Branded Components

Let's say that you make component software and that you license your software (for a license fee) for inclusion in another software vendor's product. If you have sufficient leverage in the deal, there are a number of different ways in which you could require under the license agreement to promote your trademark. For example:

- **Brand Display**—You could require that your branding be prominently displayed on the licensee's product interface—for example, on the main interface screen or splash screen. Often this is done with a phrase suggesting a technology–supply relationship, such as "Powered by XYZ."

- **Packaging**—You could require that your branding be included on the packaging of the licensee's product.

- **Public Display**—You could require that the licensee feature your branding at its trade show exhibit and mention your product in its trade show public presentations of its product.

- **Advertisements**—You could require that your brand be included in advertisements for the licensee's product and on its Web site.

Where an agreement has these kinds of mandatory branding provisions, the licensor imposes binding guidelines for trademark use of the type discussed above. The brand owner may also require an opportunity to review and approve materials and advertisements that use its brands.

Trademark Licensing

Sometimes companies simply license their trademark to another company for its use on the licensee's products. This type of licensing is quite common for use of famous marks on consumer products (think Duke Blue Devil t-shirts). This kind of licensing occurs with some digital technology consumer products. For example, you can purchase Polaroid brand electronic cameras, but they are not made by Polaroid. Rather the owner of the Polaroid brand (a company called Petters Group Worldwide) has licensed the brand to a distributor of cameras. Video game companies do a lot of trademark branding (along with licensing of content).

When licensing a trademark, the licensor must have trademark guidelines and the contractual right to monitor the *quality* of the licensed goods and to prevent licensing from continuing if quality is not maintained. Where licensing is done without control of the licensed goods (called "naked licensing") it is treated under US law as an abandonment of the trademark. Abandonment can lead to loss of all trademark rights and the cancellation of trademark registration. This means that a bad license agreement may kill the trademark. Generally, brand licensors keep control in two ways: they inspect the goods for quality, and they have strict trademark guidelines. Your lawyer can help put the right clauses in place.

To help you with trademark licensing, we have included two sample trademark license agreement forms in the Appendix to this book:

- Form 4-1 is for a royalty-free trademark licensing agreement. This form is designed for the situation in which a licensor has component software that is included in the licensee's software product, and the licensor wants to permit the licensee to use the licensor's branding on the resulting product. This form is for the kind of trademark licensing strategy under which Intel allowed PC makers to use its "Intel Inside" branding. This form agreement is written to be permissive (the Licensee may use the branding), but could be made mandatory (the Licensee must use the branding).

- Form 4-2 is for a royalty-bearing arrangement. The licensee pays the licensee for use of the brand. This is for a situation where the licensor's brand is valuable and the licensee expects to be able to increase sales and prices by use of a well-known trademark.

Trademark Transfers

When companies are sold, trademarks are usually important assets. The buyer will normally conduct "due diligence" into the seller's trademarks to confirm that they have been property protected. Properly protected marks make companies worth more.

Generally speaking, under US law, you can only transfer trademarks together with the product rights and the "customer goodwill" to which the trademarks relate. This is because the transfer of the trademark by itself would, like "naked licensing" discussed above, be treated as an abandonment of the trademark. (If you are starting a business and want to buy someone's trademark, be sure to remember this rule.)

The Web makes national and global publishing cheap. This means that the cost of introducing and promoting new branded products has gone down.

- The Web also makes it easy to offer products and services in remote locations. This makes national or international brands that, in an earlier time, would have been purely local.

- The Web is indexed by the major search engines, such as Google and Yahoo!, and since search engines are free, new brands are readily discoverable.

In the age of the Internet, there is more brand friction. There is also more reason than ever to consider an international branding strategy.

Meta-tags

Meta-tags are HTML text data in Web pages which are invisible when a user views a Web page with a browser but are visible to search engines that index it. Meta-tags typically describe the site's content and create key words. If you had a Web site that sold coffee, you might include "Coffee," "Java," and "Kona" in your site's meta-tags.

It is possible for a company to use another company's brand as a meta-tag for its site in order to fool search engines. In one litigated case, Natural Answers, an herbal medicine company, sold a "natural tranquilizer" called "Herbrozac," and included in its Web site the meta-tag "Prozac." As Natural Answers intended, search engine users who were looking for information about Prozac saw Natural Answers' site show up high in search results. When Prozac's maker Eli Lilly sued, the court held that Natural Answers had engaged in trademark infringement. Even though a consumer who got to the Natural Answers' site would surely realize that Herbrozac was not Prozac, this use of meta-tags to create "initial source confusion" has consistently been held to be wrongful under trademark law.

DOMAIN NAMES

A domain name functions as a unique Internet resource locater. Domain names are used to locate network resources for Internet applications such as email, FTP (fire transfer protocol), or, most significantly, the Web. Domain names are organized into top level domains such as .com, .org., .edu, and .net. There are also national domains such as .uk for United Kingdom, .jp for Japan, and .in for India.

A nonprofit corporation called the Internet Corporation of Assigned Names and Numbers (ICANN) administers the domain name system and appoints private companies as "registrars" that register domain names and keep them in effect in exchange for modest fees. You can find a list of registrars at www.icann .org. Each registrar provides a means of searching domain names—and will allow you to determine if a domain name is available. In many—but not all—cases, the online record will indicate the registered owner of the domain name. The registrars also provide procedures for transferring of domain names, which is something you might do, for example, when selling a business or a product line.

Domains and Brand Identity

Because the Web is so important as a communications medium, domain names are critical to brand identity. When selecting trademarks, you should, as a matter of course, try to obtain the corresponding domain name. For example, the house trademark of International Business Machines Corporation is "IBM" so it obtained the Web address, "ibm.com." When IBM acquired Lotus in 1995, it also obtained "lotus.com."

If you are starting a company in technology, you should try to secure both the ".com" and ".net" version of your company name if at all possible. Getting those domain names—even if you have to buy them from third parties—will likely be a key asset. It may also be prudent to secure confusingly similar or sound-alike domains.

Domain Names vs. Trademarks

In some ways, domain names have characteristics that are quite different from trademarks. For example:

> *Domain names are unique.* More than one company can have the same brand. An example is "Delta" used by Delta Airlines, Delta Dental, and Delta Faucets. There can be only one delta.com, currently owned by Delta Airlines.
>
> *Domain names may be generic.* Generally speaking, trademark law will not grant trademark status to generic words. Therefore, you could not use as a trademark the word "computer" and stop other persons from using that word to describe their computer products. But there is a "computer.com" domain (currently linked to the home page of CNET consumer electronic reviews). Many generic terms are in domain names.

During the Internet boom of the late 90s, it was believed that generic domain names such as "computers.com" and "pets.com" were the key to great riches. Such domain names do have value, but the market for them has certainly cooled. People have realized that it takes a lot more than a domain name to build a successful business.

Sometimes companies want to register a domain name as a trademark. The USPTO will permit this, but only if the applicant provides exemplars that show the domain name actually being used as a service mark. "Salesforce.com," for example, is clearly being used as the brand for an online sales force management service. So saleforce.com would qualify. Contrast General Motors use of "gm.com," which is not a service mark, but rather only as an address for the company's Web site.

This means that trademark registration is likely to be available to companies that engage in e-commerce or offer services through the Internet. Note, however, that the USPTO will likely reject trademark registration for domains name that are generic or highly descriptive, such as "homefinder.com" or "computers.com."

Cybersquatters and Remedies

It is less a common problem now, but in the 90s, there were a number of individuals and companies that registered domain names and held them for ransom—hoping that legitimate trademark owners would pay large sums for them. There were public disputes when individuals registered mcdonalds.com, mtv.com, and other domains that include famous trademarks. This kind of bad faith registration of domains is known as "cybersquatting."

Cybersquatting cases were, at first, dealt with under trademark law. Congress, under pressure from brand owners, then enacted the Anticybersquatting Consumer Protection Act in November 1999. This Act allowed courts to transfer a domain name that is confusingly similar to a trademark to the owner of the trademark. To obtain the domain name, the trademark owner is required to establish that the domain name holder acted in bad faith.

Because litigation is expensive and can be prolonged, a more efficient way of dealing with domain name disputes was needed. For this reason, ICANN created the Uniform Domain Name Dispute Resolution Policy (UDNDRP). This is a relatively simple arbitration process, based on submitted papers and without any testimony. Under the UDNDRP, a trademark owner can challenge the holder of a domain name. If the trademark owner wins, the domain name is transferred to the trademark holder. In order to win, the trademark owner has to persuade the arbitrator that: (1) it has a trademark that is the same or substantially similar to the domain name; (2) the domain holder does not have a legitimate interest in the domain name; and (3) the current domain holder registered in bad faith.

What counts as proof that a domain is held in bad faith? Signs of bad faith owner are:

- Registering numerous domains that correspond to others' brands

- Demanding a high price for the domain

- Threatening to sell the domain to a competitor

The domain owner can defend its position by showing that it had a legitimate reason to register the domain and has used it legitimately.

If you have a problem of this kind with a domain name that is similar to your company's brand, you should seek legal counsel without delay.

TRADEMARK INFRINGEMENT LITIGATION

For our final topic in this chapter, let us take a look at trademark infringement litigation in the United States. If you believe someone has infringed your trademark, or if you are accused of using someone else's trademark, you should see an attorney immediately. Delay may hurt your case.

The Litigation Process

What do you do if an infringer is using or harming your brand? The process normally begins with a cease-and-desist letter from legal counsel.

When the infringement is clear, the dispute will often be settled before litigation is filed. Quite commonly, the alleged infringer simply agrees to stop using a trademark immediately, or more commonly after a few months' transition period. However, if the alleged infringer of the trademark has some hope of defending its trademark, and if it has had considerable success (and has earned real money) with the trademark, litigation may be necessary.

Sending a cease-and-desist letter is not completely risk free. There is a risk that the alleged infringer will sue first, to get the advantage of having the lawsuit in the alleged infringer's home jurisdiction. (We call this kind of first strike by the accused a *declaratory judgment* action, because the alleged infringer asks the court to *declare* that it is not infringing.) For this reason, in some cases, the trademark holder will sue as the first move.

While most trademark law suits end quite quickly, it is possible for seriously contested cases to cost substantial amounts. Proof of secondary meaning or to establish the likelihood of confusion may be expensive, because it can require customer survey evidence, which is costly to produce. Proof of distinctiveness, customer confusion, and damages all may require expert testimony. A contested case between two substantial trademark users can cost hundreds of thousands of dollars.

Proof of Infringement

Generally, the owner of the trademark has to prove these elements to establish infringement:

- That the owner has a valid trademark
- That the trademark is distinctive
- That the trademark has priority
- That there is a likelihood of confusion about the source of the goods bearing the trademarks

Fair Use under Trademark Law

In our discussion of copyright law, we reviewed the doctrine of "fair use," a defense to a claim of copyright infringement. There is also a similar "fair use" defense in trademark law. The rationale of fair use in trademark is similar to that in copyright law; it is based on the principle that some uses of trademark are consistent with free speech and are not harmful to others' trademarks. As in copyright law, fair use is a defense to a claim of infringement.

Generally speaking fair use under trademark law permits good faith use of terms that are descriptive of goods or services. For example, you should be able to advertise that you provide the "best buy in consumer software" without infringing the trademark of "Best Buy" stores. In addition, it is generally held to be a fair use to refer to a competitor's product, as in "our word processor costs much less than Microsoft Word." This is called "nominative use" because you are using the trademark only to refer to the other product by name.

Infringement Remedies for Federally Registered Trademark

If you have a federally registered trademark and someone uses a confusingly similar trademark, what happens when you *win* a trademark infringement trial in federal court?

Remedies for infringement can include:

- Your lost profits due to the infringement or the profits wrongfully made by the infringer (whichever is greater)

- In case of willful infringement, up to three times the actual damages, as the court deems just

- In egregious cases, an award of attorneys' fees

In addition, the court may order the destruction of the improperly labeled goods and of all copies of the improper labels and packaging.

If the violation is counterfeiting, that is, if the defendant was using an exact copy of your trademark with the intent to deceive customers, the court may also order seizure of the counterfeit goods by the United States Marshall at the beginning of the case. Where there is counterfeiting, the court often will award three times the actual damages and attorneys' fees.

A holder of trademark on the Principal Register may also request the United States Customs Service to prevent the importing of goods labeled with its trademark.

The Customs Service, unfortunately, does not have the resources to police all US imports, and thus the amount of protection you can get from this system is uncertain.

Infringement Remedies for Unregistered Trademarks

Even if you do not have federal registration, state and federal law may give you protection if someone uses your trademark (or one confusingly similar) and harms your business. (But as noted above, federal registration can provide much better protection.)

There is a section of the Lanham Act that grants a remedy in federal court against anyone that damages another by using a name or trademark that is likely to cause confusion or is deceptive. This statute has often been used to protect unregistered trademarks. In addition, state law is likely to protect unregistered trademarks against infringement.

Remedies under these provisions may include monetary damages and court orders (including preliminary relief early in the case) to stop the infringer's use of the trademark.

CONCLUSION

Building and implementing legal protection for your brands is essential for the success of a digital technology business. You should be proactive in registering and managing your trademarks to secure and expand the "trademark space" that defines your company and its products and services.

Patents and Digital Technology Companies

5

Patents have "added the fuel of interest to the fire of genius in the discovery and production of new and useful things."

—Abraham Lincoln on the patent laws, 1859

They have been called the "heavy artillery" of intellectual property. They are expensive to get, but can have great value. Investors love them. They can multiply the value of your company when you sell it. Sometimes, they can pose a serious threat. If your digital business involves innovation, you *have* to be interested in patents.

IN THIS CHAPTER

The topics covered in this chapter are:

- The power of patent and patent law
- The nature of patents
- How to read a patent
- The patent application process
- Software and business method patents
- Deciding when to patent based on the value and strategic importance of an invention
- International aspects of patents

- Patent licensing
- Patent enforcement and patent risks
- Your company's patent strategy
- Possible "reforms" of the US patent system

THE POWER AND USE OF PATENTS

You have probably heard about patent lawsuits involving digital technology. These lawsuits highlight the power of patent rights.

- In 2005, Ariba Inc., a maker of e-commerce software, agreed, after losing at trial, to pay $37 million to settle a patent-infringement lawsuit filed by its smaller competitor, ePlus Inc. ePlus sued on patents for procurement systems that search for goods in online catalogs.

- In 2001, NPT, Inc., a company that specializes in holding and enforcing patents sued Research in Motion Ltd. (RIM), the maker of Blackberry devices. NPT has patents on the implementation of wireless e-mail. RIM lost at trial, and agreed in 2006 to pay NPT $612 million to resolve the suit.

But there is more to patents than getting home run results in litigation. Here are some key factors about patents and digital technologies:

- **Increased Importance in Digital Technology**—As a result of court decisions that transformed the law in the United States, many digital technology and software innovations are eligible for patent protection in this country. Thousands of software patents and so-called "business method patents" have been issued in the last decade. In addition, patents have long been important in telecommunications, computer hardware, and semiconductors.

- **Opportunities**—Patents are business tools. If you hold patents on technology of significance in your field, your company may be able to exclude competitors from your market or reduce their competition. Your company may be able to license patents for royalties. Patents can also be important bargaining chips against other patent holders.

- **Risk Factors**—Patents are a potential threat to any technology company. A single patent can cover many different products. Some patents are very hard or prohibitively expensive to design around. If your company infringes another company's patent, your company may be liable for damages or a court order that it stop infringing. Under US law, willful infringement can lead to payment of treble damages (that is, the infringer must pay the amount of actual patent damages determined by the court multiplied by three).

- **Standards and Patents**—Many commonly used standard-based technologies, such as MP3 encoding, DVDs, or RSA encryption, are subject to patents. Patent holders can function like tax collectors in the information economy. (For a discussion of standards and patents, see Chapter 19.)

- **Badge of Innovation**—Many companies use patents for marketing and public relations, because patents can make a company appear innovative and technically advanced.

- **Relationship to Business Value**—Investors put a premium value on patent portfolios. Patents on key innovations can make it easier to raise money for your company.

- **Cashing In**—Patents can have their biggest impact in a company's sale-of-business transaction. An acquirer will pay more to get control of key patents—and to keep the patents out of the hands of competitors.

Every company that makes technology innovations must consider the use of patents in its business strategy.

NATURE OF UNITED STATES PATENTS

Under US law, a patent is an exclusive right, a monopoly, granted by the federal government, to exclude others from exploiting an *invention*. Patents become effective only when granted. They generally expire *20 years* measured from the *application date*. There are no state law patents.

In the United States, patents cover any process, machine, manufacture, or composition of matter. If someone makes, sells, or imports products incorporating a patented invention or uses a patented method without the patent holder's permission, the law grants the patent holder the right to sue the that person. Violating the patent holder's rights is called *patent infringement* and the person who does it is called an *infringer*.

Patents may apply to devices and methods, and many patents refer to both. A patent grants the patent holder the right to prevent all others from using the rights to the invention defined by the patent.

The reach of a patent is national, which means that to obtain optimum protection of your inventions you may have to do filings in a number of nations. In some cases, in the Internet age, it may be possible to avoid using technology covered by US method patents by doing the same electronic processing outside the United States.

The patents that we discuss in this chapter are known as "utility patents." There are other types of patents: design patents and patents on plants (as in living green plants). Design patents, which protect novel nonfunctional designs for products, may be important for some digital technology companies. If you are interested in these other types of patents, you should consult patent counsel.

How Do You Get a Patent?

The process of applying for and seeking a patent is called "patent prosecution." You can get help in patent prosecution matters from a patent lawyer or a patent agent. Both are licensed by the US Patent and Trademark Office (USPTO).

There are some persons that manage to apply for and get patents without professional legal assistance, but they are rare, and this go-it-alone method is not recommended for anyone who is not *very* familiar with patent matters.

If you want a US patent, your patent attorney or patent agent will file an application with the USPTO. A patent examiner at the USPTO will review the patent and decide whether the patent should issue. The process of filing applications and dealing with the patent office is very specialized, and it is not cheap. A typical application can take two years or more and cost $20,000 or $30,000 in legal fees and patent office fees before the US patent issues. Sometimes, it will cost more. And sometimes, even after you have spent thousand and thousands of dollars, the USPTO may narrow or even reject your application. So there are no guarantees in patenting. There is more information about this process and the decision on whether to patent or not below.

Legal Standard for Patents

Not every new digital technology idea or development can be patented. Under US law, patents are granted for a claimed invention only when the USPTO finds that your device or process meets three tests:

1. **The claimed invention must be useful**—This means that unless you have an invention with some form of practical application, there is no patentable invention. Abstract ideas and theories without real world application, however astoundingly brilliant, are not patentable.

2. **The claimed invention must be novel**—This means that the claimed invention must be something that has not been invented before. If the same invention can be found in earlier work, which patent lawyers refer to as "prior art" (discussed further below), then the claimed invention should be rejected.

3. **The claimed invention must not be obvious to a reasonably skilled practitioner in the field at the time of invention**—This means that the claimed invention must be a genuine advance over what people already know how to make or do. The patent system is not supposed to reward trivial or self-evident advances.

Reading Patents

Patents have specialized and stylized language, and only someone trained in patent law understands all aspects of their interpretation. However, a software engineer that is skilled in the technology described can read a digital technology-related patent and get the gist.

If you take a look at a patent (try the patent search database at the United States Patent Office, uspto.gov), you will find that it is divided into three sections:

- The *cover page*, which provides some raw facts about the patent, such as the patent number, inventor, assignee (owner), application and patent grant date, and its classification codes (which reflect its general subject matter)

- The *specification*, which usually includes background to the invention, a short summary of the invention, a description of drawings (which in digital technology often includes process flow charts) and a more detailed description of the invention

- The *claims*, which define the scope of what the patent covers

The Importance of the Claims in the Patent
Before issuing you a patent, the USPTO must approve a definition in English works stating what constitutes the invention. This definition is referred to as the "claims" of the patent. The patent's claims are the heart of a patent because they

specify the legal scope of the patent. Patents typically have more than one claim. Claims may stand on their own, known as "independent claims," or may be subordinate to other claims, in which case they are "dependent claims."

Let's take a look at a simple (but real) example of claims. This example is from a patent application for an electronic remote key system to turn on a machine. The system operates by having a "remote" send a signal (here called a "challenge") to a receiver that decides whether the challenge should be accepted or not by checking a "key." Here is an independent claim followed by a dependent claim:

1. *A portable electronic equipment key system comprising*:

   a transponder for receiving a challenge and transmitting a response thereto; and

   an electronic apparatus, comprising;

   a memory circuit for storage of a key;

   a reader for transmitting said challenge and for receiving said response, and for enabling the electronic equipment in response to said response being a predetermined response.

2. *The portable electronic equipment key system according to claim 1, wherein said predetermined response comprises a function of said challenge and said key.*

This is the typical format of a claim. The first part of the claim is a "preamble," which states generally what the claim is about. Here it is a "portable electronic equipment key system." Then there is a "connector" word; here it is the word "comprising." Finally there are the "elements" of the claim, which are the parts or steps that make up the invention. As you can see, the dependent claim 2 adds an additional element to claim 1.

While the general idea of the claims will be clear to anyone that understands the technology, reading claims requires both legal knowledge as well as technical background. That's because claims are written in a specialized way that can be quite abstract, are often affected by other parts in the patent, and in some cases, can be narrowed by statements that the patent applicant made to the USPTO during the patent application and approval process.

The Relationship of Claims and Infringement

The elements of the claim are very important in determining if there is an infringement. As a general rule, in order to prove that another company is infringing your company's patent, you need to show that the other company's technology uses every one of the elements of your patent's claim. If your patent claim has five elements, generally speaking, a device that uses only four of them is not infringing. So writing claims is really a precise and calculating art, the aim of which is to cover as many different implementations as possible and thereby help exclude competitors from entering or besting you in the market.

Equivalents

In some cases, if another company's product or method has very minor variations on elements in your patent's claim, so that the company's technology does essentially the same thing in essentially the same way, it might still be infringing under a rule called the "Doctrine of Equivalents." However, patent holders do not like to rely on this doctrine because its application is uncertain and has a number of legal technicalities. There are a lot of judgment calls that go into deciding whether something is really an "equivalent."

Broad and Narrow Claims

Lawyers often talk about patents and patent applications with "broad" claims or "narrow" claims.

We call claims "broad" when they are written with relative few claim elements and they are worded to cover many different implementations. Narrow claims are the opposite; they cover less because they have more claims or more specific wording. Narrow claims are more specific. Broader claims are more abstract.

Patents that have broad claims can be very valuable if they cover a lot of commercially valuable implementations. (A patent can be broad but worthless if it covers many implementations that no one would pay for.) Broader patents can be harder to design around. They may also be easier to invalidate by means prior art (a subject discussed below).

Apparatus Claims, Method, and Article-of-Manufacturing Claims

There are three kinds of claims that may normally be included in a utility patent involving digital technology: "apparatus claims," "method claims" and "article-of-manufacture claims." The first, the apparatus claim, describes a mechanism, object, or system. The second, the method claim, describes a method of operation or getting something done. The third is a result of a manufacturing process.

Apparatus claims and method claims are often aspects of the same invention. For example, the telephone (as invented by Samuel Morse) was an *apparatus*. But in inventing the telephone, Morse also invented a *method* of turning sound into electrical signals and then turning those signals back into sound.

With software inventions:

- A *method* claim is usually defined as performing a set of programmed operations on stated computer hardware components. (The technology is thus described as carrying out various steps to get a particular result.)

- The corresponding *apparatus* claim would consist of the computer hardware components executing a set of programmed operations. (The same technology but described as a machine or system that performs such steps.)

- The *article-of-manufacture* claim would often be the computer medium (an optical or magnetic disk, for example) or digital file that will contain such programmed instructions and can be installed and used in such a computer system.

Patents and Software

We often hear people say that they want to patent their software, but in fact, you cannot patent a software program or digital technology system per se. Rather you would patent one or more inventions that might be used in many different software programs.

An example: Let's say that in the course of programming a digital music player, you invent a better way to analyze a digital music file to detect the mood of the music. Let's assume you get a patent on (a) that mood-detecting method and (b) on the corresponding apparatus (a program running software that uses that method).

If you do so, your patent would cover only what is in your mood-detecting patent. Your patent could be infringed by other person's products (not limited to digital music players) that include your invention. On the other hand, any other technologies in digital music players would not be covered by your patent.

Patents and Disclosure

A key concept behind patents is that they exchange public disclosure of your invention for legal protection. Patent law allows you to get a defined legal monopoly excluding others from exploiting an invention, but only if you disclose what your invention is.

Most patent applications are published 18 months after the application is filed. (There is a provision in the United States for keeping patent applications secret until the patent is granted if the applicant agrees not to seek foreign patents on the invention. In some cases, patents are not published for national security reasons.)

In order to get the application approved, the applicant must satisfy the USPTO that the patent application discloses the claimed invention's implementation with sufficient detail that a "reasonably skilled practitioner" can build the device or practice the method. This is known as an "enabling disclosure." There is also a legal requirement that the applicant must also disclose the "best mode" of implementation known to the inventor.

If the patent application fails to make the required disclosures, the patent may be subject to legal challenge. There is considerable art and skill in deciding how much to disclose in the application. This is an area where a good patent lawyer's skill matters a great deal.

Types of Infringement

Patent infringement under the Patent Act occurs when someone uses in the United States without permission the rights granted in a US patent. This is called "direct infringement."

You infringe an apparatus claim or an article of manufacture claim of a US patent if you *make, sell, or import* a patented item in the U.S. without the patent holder's consent. You infringe a method claim if you *use the method* without the patent holder's consent. This means that a *seller* of an electronic product might infringe an apparatus claim in *making* and *selling* it; and the *user* of the product might infringe the corresponding method claim.

There are two other kinds of infringement under US law:

- **Contributory Infringement**—A company becomes a contributory infringer by knowingly selling a product or a component *specially made* or *specifically designed* for infringing use. A company will *not* be a contributory infringer if it sells a general-purpose product that the buyer puts to an infringing use.

- **Inducement to Infringe**—A company will be liable for inducing infringement if it either knowingly aids and abets infringement by another or if it actively and knowingly induces another to infringe.

Contributory infringement and inducement to infringe are called "indirect infringement."

Limits to the Right to Exclude Others

The right to exclude others is not necessarily the same thing as the right to use an invention. In many cases, a patent covers an *improvement* to other patented technology; in that situation, the patent holder (or licensees of the patent holder) may need a license from *another* patent holder (or perhaps more than one patent holder) in order to have the right to use the invention.

In addition, systems may need many patented technologies to function. Complicated products, for example today's multifunction cell phones, can require technology under dozens of patents.

A US patent's legal power of exclusion extends to the products made and sold and methods used in the United States. This right to exclude others, however, is not self-enforcing. The mere fact that you have patent does not by it put a stop to infringement. In order to enforce a patent, you need to bring a civil lawsuit. (Unlike trademark and copyright law, there is no US criminal statute dealing with patent infringement, so the authorities cannot help you stop patent infringement through criminal enforcement.) In some cases, it is also possible to bring a civil administrative proceeding to stop importation of infringing products.

Although importation is infringing, a US patent's reach stops at the border. If you have a US patent, it will not stop use of your invention on a Web server in Mexico City—even if the Web service can be accessed by Web users inside the United States. This is an important limitation of patents in the Internet age.

About Prior Art

Broadly speaking, the term "prior art" refers to publicly available information before the date of invention of a patent or claimed invention. Most patent systems around the world use and apply this concept of "prior art." Under US patent law, the concept is bit different in some technical ways, but the general concept is the same. One significant difference is that under US law, an invention *used* in the United States can be prior art.

Prior art is important in the patent application process. If the patent examiner finds prior art that covers a claim sought in a patent application, the examiner will disallow the claim. In patent litigation, prior art can also be used to invalidate patent claims after the patent has issued.

Most often prior art is a prior written publication (including electronic publication) or a prior patent of the invention. You can hunt for prior art in patent records and in other publicly available materials, such as scientific journals, professional publications, academic theses, textbooks, product documentation, and so forth.

The availability of databases on the World Wide Web has made this task much easier, but there is still much information that is not available electronically. Many of the world's patent records are on the Web. Some of the unpatented prior art in digital technology is also online, but much is not. Finding unpatented prior art often calls for extensive research.

When applying for a patent, the applicant is required to disclose all known relevant prior art. Patent attorneys strive to write patent applications so that the claimed inventions are clearly distinguishable from the prior art.

Searching in Patent Databases

Patent files are organized in hierarchical subject matter classifications. There is a US classification system and an international classification system.

As noted, patent filings are computerized in patent systems around the world. There are easily accessible public databases, such as the free US patent database at www.uspto.gov and the commercial database operated by Thomson Corporation under the Delphion brand, www.delphion.com. The Delphion system permits a variety of international searches as well. There is also a valuable free international search service provided by the European Patent Office (EPO), ep.espacenet.com. With these various systems, you can search patents by classification number, inventor, assignee (current owner), date, and key words.

If your business is involved in technology innovation (or your competitors are), it is a good idea for your company to use online patent resources regularly. Here are some reasons why your company would do so:

- **Prior Art Searches and Patentability**—Searching prior art can help determine patentability of an invention.

- **Learning the "Lay of the Land"**—You can investigate a technical field that you are considering entering and discover prior patents that might be problems or barriers to your entry.

- **Monitoring Your Competitors**—You can monitor your competitors' patent filings. These filings can tell you what technologies competitors are working on and what patent positions they are staking out. If you are diligent, you may be able to discern your competitors' technical strategies and priorities.

- **Technology Discovery**—You may be able to use patent search to help solve technical problems by looking for patented solutions in technology areas that are similar to but not the same as your own.

It is also a good idea to keep abreast of patent lawsuits filed against other companies in your line of business. They will allow you to gage the risk of your company's using technologies claimed by patent holders that are aggressively enforcing patents in your field.

SOFTWARE PATENTS AND BUSINESS METHOD PATENTS

Software patents and business method patents are topics that are important to digital technology businesses.

Patents on Software Generally

There is no legal definition of a "software patent" in the Patent Act. As noted above, we refer to a software patent, we mean generally, a patent that involves the use of stored instructions and algorithms designed to operate in a system that includes a processor. There is, of course, no limit to the type of functions or the kinds of uses that such system could have.

Major digital technology companies, such as Cisco, IBM, Microsoft, Apple, and others have built substantial digital technology patent positions. In 2005, Microsoft was awarded 746 US patents, and IBM received 2972! Although statistics are hard to come by, it is clear that thousands of patents are obtained every year by small and mid-size technology companies.

For years, it was said that "you cannot patent software." It is an axiom of patent law that you cannot patent mathematical concepts and formulas. Because computer programs are intangible and algorithmic, they were long thought to be similarly unpatentable. The USPTO accepted this reasoning and for years rejected most software patent applications (although some did get through the system). However nothing in the Patent Act states any such restriction, and in the 1980s and 1990s, federal court decisions made it clear that patents on inventions involving software are no different than any other invention. These decisions opened the door in the United States to patents on software-based inventions. (In other nations, software patents are still harder to obtain, and many US software-based patents would not be granted abroad.)

The result has been a flood of US software-related patents in the past decade. This makes the United States a more complicated and dangerous place for software companies. It also means that every innovative entrepreneurial software company should try to maintain awareness of its competitors' patents and seriously consider adopting a patent strategy of its own.

Here are a few examples of digital technology and software-related patents. You will notice how varied they are, and you will also notice that they are related to the business purpose and objectives of their owners:

- IBM has a 2001 patent on a method for object replication in a content management system (US Patent Number 7,054,887).

- Google has a 2006 patent on a method for serving advertisements based on content (U.S. Patent No. 7,136,875).

- Merrill, Lynch (the stockbrokers) owns a 2001 patent for a stock option control system (U.S. Patent No. 6,269,346).

Business Method Patents

What is a business method patent? Again, this is not a definition in the Patent Act, but a practical one. Business method patents involve methodologies for running a business operation. They frequently overlap with the "software patent" category, because the majority of patented business methods involve systems that are implemented with computers and software.

Patents on business methods have a history similar to that of software patents. For many years, it was the conventional wisdom that a "mere business method" was unpatentable. The USPTO rejected many (but not all) applications that described methods of business operations. However, as in the case of software, nothing in the Patent Act prohibits granting business method patents.

The door to business method patents was open wide with the 1998 decision of a case entitled *State Street Bank & Trust Co. v. Signature Financial Group*. The case involved a patent on a method of managing a number of mutual funds with a "hub and spoke" computerized system architecture. In holding the patent valid, the court held that inventions involving business method were under the same standards of patentability as any other invention.

Many of the business method patents have been in the financial, business system, and e-commerce fields. Here are some much publicized examples of computer-implemented business method patents that have been granted for e-commerce inventions over the past few years:

- The Interactive Coupon Network (also known as "coolsavings.com") obtained a patent on a method of issuing and tracking use of coupons over the Internet.

- Priceline.com obtained a patent on a method for operating "reverse auctions" (also know as "Dutch auctions") under which would-be buyers place offers online which sellers may accept.

- Home Gambling Network obtained a patent on a method for remote "real-time" gambling.

There have been many thousands of business method patents granted and many more are pending. These patents are not limited to systems implemented by computers and networks; for example, the USPTO has granted patents for tax strategies.

Doubts about Some Business Method and Software Patents

There has been some concern that the USPTO has issued some "bad" business method and software patents. What makes a patent "bad?" In this case, we are talking about patents for inventions that aren't really new. The problem is that sometimes the examiners at the USPTO fail to find prior art and incorrectly conclude that the claimed invention is new, when it is not.

One problem is the fact, noted above, that much of the prior art in software and computer inventions is unpatented and not readily available to patent examiners. There are currently thousands of software and network products on the market (and many thousands more that were marketed in the past), but many are not extensively described in the published literature. Some of the prior art is found only in user manuals and other manufacturer documentation that is not collected anywhere.

As if to underline the potential issues with these patents, in 2001, Amazon.com ran into a roadblock when it tried to enforce its famous "one-click-check-out" patent against barnesandnobles.com. A federal Court of Appeals overturned an injunction that Amazon had obtaining against Barnes and Noble, ruling that prior art found by Barnes and Noble raised "serious questions" about the validity of the patent. (The case subsequently settled.)

The USPTO has implemented a program to increase the quality of its examination of applications for computer-implemented business method patents. This includes additional training of selected examiners, improvement of prior-art search strategies, and increased supervisor review of examiner's work. The goal is to make it harder to get "bad" computer-implemented business method patents.

THE PATENT APPLICATION PROCESS

The following is an overview of the patent application process for the United States.

Patent Lawyers and Patent Agents

Only lawyers that have passed a special federal examination can file a patent application for you, or represent you before the USPTO in patent-related proceedings. The fact that other American lawyers (who are allowed to practice in all the other areas discussed in this book) are excluded from the patent application process gives you some sense of the special complexity of patent applications and the application process. Most patent lawyers are engineers or have a considerable engineering or science background. (Patent-related transactions and patent litigation are often done by attorneys who are not patent lawyers.)

The USPTO also permits applications by *patent agents*, nonlawyers who are legally qualified to prepare and prosecute patent applications. You can probably get a broader view of the legal issues from a patent attorney, but patent agents can be less expensive than patent attorneys. Whether you get a patent attorney or a patent agent, be sure to get one with digital technology experience. The government publishes a directory of patent attorneys and agents that is available on the USPTO Web site. However, most people find patent lawyers and agents by asking for a referral from an attorney who represents them in other matters.

Although in theory you can represent yourself and prepare and file your own patent application, in reality most programmers and publishers (and indeed most nonpatent lawyers) could not competently draft a high-quality patent application. If you hire a competent patent lawyer or agent, you are more likely to get patent if one is obtainable—and to find out in advance whether applying would be a waste of time.

If you decide that you want to try your hand at a patent application, there is one very well written book on do-it-yourself patents, although it is not focused on digital technology or software. The book is *Patent It Yourself* (Nolo Press, 2005), written by California patent lawyer David Pressman. (This is also a good book to buy if you just want to know more about the details of the patent application process.) Even Attorney Pressman's fine book states that the *claims* section of a patent application should be drafted by a patent professional.

Provisional Applications

Since 1995, US patent law has allowed *provisional applications* for patents. A provisional application is a simplified version of a regular patent application and therefore the legal cost for the filing is less. The provisional application does have to describe the invention, but other formal requirements of a full patent application do not apply; in particular, the claims section is not required. The USPTO does not examine and process provisional applications to determine patentability. They proceed with the examination process only when a follow-on full patent application is filed.

If you do file a provisional application, you will have *12 months* to file a full patent application. *This deadline cannot be extended*. This means that if you do not file a full application within the 12-month period, your patent application will die.

Many start-up companies use provisional applications as a way to keep costs down while they hunt for more capital to fund their company. Provisional patent applications will also allow your company to file patent applications when you are not yet sure of the value of an invention—and allow your company to decide later whether or not to pursue the application.

Provisional patent applications typically cost anywhere from $5,000 to $10,000, far less than the costs of preparing and filing a full patent application. Not only do start-up companies save money by filing provisional applications, but it also gives them the right to legitimately claim "patent pending" status, which may impress potential investors or customers.

Patent Priority and Documenting Inventions

Under the American system, if two inventors file for the same invention, the patent rights go to the first person to invent something, even if the inventor is not the first to file a patent application. Under the laws of just about every other country, the patent goes to the first person to file a patent application, regardless of who invented the method or device first. We say that the United States has a "first-to-invent" priority system, and other nations have a "first-to-file" system.

Under US law, the invention occurs when there is "conception"—the formulation of the invention in mind of the inventor—*plus* "reduction to practice." Reduction to practice occurs either when the invention is actually made to work or the date of a filed patent application. When reduction to practice is based on a patent application, we call it a "constructive reduction to practice." ("Constructive" is a legal term that means "it may not have happened, but the law will consider that it did.")

The rule on "constructive reduction to practice" is an important reason to file patent applications as early as you reasonably can. Filing patent applications promptly is also important because (as is discussed below) the US filing date can often be used to obtain patent priority in other nations.

This "first-to-invent" rule in the United States means that any company that is serious about US patents must be diligent about creating and keeping records about when inventions are conceived and how they are put into operation. When the invention date depends on an actual reduction to practice, proof of the date and time when this occurred may be critical under the US system. This is best done with notebooks that record concepts and development work. Nothing beats contemporaneous and witnessed records of intentions. A patent lawyer can provide guidance about documenting inventions.

Don't Delay Filing that Patent Application!

If you want patents, do not delay in filing those patent applications. Another reason that you need to move quickly is because the Patent Act has what are called "statutory bars." Here the word "bar" means an absolute barrier that prevents you from getting a patent. There are two kinds of statutory bars that may apply:

- **Publication Bar**—You cannot get a patent unless you apply within one year from *the date the invention was disclosed in a printed publication anywhere in the world*.

- **On-Sale Bar**—You cannot get a patent unless you apply within one year from *the date that the invention was first sold or offered for sale within the United States*. The key point here is that this includes *offers* even if no sale results.

In many other countries, the rules are even stricter; disclosing an invention often bars patent protection altogether and immediately. Therefore it is always best to contact patent counsel as early as possible and plan a patent strategy that beats the clock.

CAPTURING EMPLOYEES AND CONTRACTORS' INVENTIONS

If your company's employee makes an invention, does the company own the patent rights, or does the employee own them? In the absence of a proper employment agreement, the general rule in the United States is that when an employee is "hired to invent" inventions of the type involved, the employer is entitled to the invention. But disputes are inevitable, and lawsuits are an expensive and uncertain process. Therefore it is vital that every employer has employment agreements in place with every employee that mandate employer ownership of inventions and require employees to cooperate in the patenting process. These agreements are discussed in Chapter 5 of this book, and there is a sample form agreement (From 5-1) in the Appendix.

There is another factor that employers should be aware of. Under US law, the patent is issued in the name of the inventor, and only the inventor can apply for one. (If there are co-inventors, all of them need apply.) Corporations that want to own patents arrange for employees to *assign* the inventions. For example, US Patent No. 6,317,826, entitled "Booting a computer system from a network" shows as "Inventors" Colin McCall and Jane Shaw, but lists IBM as the "Assignee." The inventors were IBM employees when they made the invention, and they assigned the invention to IBM. It is typical for companies to file patent assignments at the same time as they file the patent application. This is another reason that there should be a contract in place that requires employees to cooperate. (Clauses that do this are also discussed in Chapter 5.)

What if your company hires an independent contractor to do work and in the course of the work the contractor makes an invention, what then? Does the contractor own the patent or does your company? The answer is that, absent an agreement with the contractor that covers the point, the independent contractor will likely own the patent rights. If you want to capture IP created by a contractor that you hire, you need a written agreement that covers the point. This topic is covered in Chapter 10 of this book in its discussion of IP clauses in consulting and development agreements. The wording of the IP clauses in independent contractor contracts is critical (and errors are common). Be sure to consult with lawyer on these form agreements.

The Patent Issuance Process

Patent applications are highly technical. A full application itself includes:

- An Abstract summarizing the invention.

- Technical drawings that illustrate the invention, which in the case of inventions involving networks or software, would often be detailed process flow diagrams.

- A discussion of the prior art and the ways in which the invention is an advance.

- A detailed discussion of the structure, operation, features, and advantages of the invention. As noted above, the application must (1) describe the invention in sufficient detail that a person skilled in the field of the invention can make and use the invention, and (2) describe the "best mode" to create and use the invention known to the inventor at the time of filing.

- The claims, a logical and precise statement of exactly what aspects of the technology in the application constitute the invention.

After the application is filed, the USPTO does its own investigation to decide whether the purported invention is patentable. The USPTO often raises questions and objections on patent applications. All the examiner's objections must be answered and overcome by the applicant. It is frequently necessary to amend or narrow the scope of claims. Even in the simplest cases, the applicant normally has to respond to at least two office actions by the USPTO requiring further information, amendment of claims, and the like. Assuming that your application is successful and faces no more than normal red tape, you can expect to get a patent in about two or three years.

It often happens that the USPTO denies a patent application. Then, the applicant must decide to either appeal or abandon the attempt to get a patent. An appeal is an additional cost, with no guarantee as to outcome. More infrequently, the USPTO declares an "interference" between two persons who are both claiming the same invention, and may conduct hearings to determine who invented it first—at considerable expense to the parties.

Foreign Patent Applications and PCT Applications

Patents are national in scope. There are no international patents. The United States is a large market. For some technology fields, it may be sufficient to have only the US patent rights. However, if you have an invention that is likely to have significant international use, you will want to consider pursuing patenting your invention in other nations. A patent in another nation that is based on your US patent or patent application is known as a "foreign counterpart" of your US patent. Your patent lawyer will manage the international filing process for you. Most US patent lawyers have a network of "correspondent" legal counsel and patent agents that can help them in foreign patent matters.

You will usually target filings in nations that are either (a) important target markets for your invention or (b) are locations where a patented product is likely to be manufactured. You may decide to file only your more important patents in other nations. You may want to consider how effective each nation is in its enforcement of IP rights. You should discuss these matters with patent counsel.

The European Patent System

In Europe, there is a way to get your patent examined (and hopefully allowed for registration) in more than one country at once. This is because of the European Patent Office (EPO) with its main office in Munich, Germany. The EPO is created under a treaty that many European nations (including some non-EU members) have approved.[1]

This is how it works: The EPO permits filings of applications in English, French, or German. The EPO's process of examining patent works much like that used in the United States. An EPO examiner must judge if the patent meets the applicable criteria for patents. In general, these are similar to those in the United States, but the system does not readily grant patents in for software- or computer-operated business methods. In some cases, the patent may be narrowed in the process of examination. If the patent application (with any amendment) passes muster, the EPO will allow the application.

Once the EPO allows a patent application, the allowed application can be filed in any nation that accepts EPO decisions. You will still have to file your patent separately in each nation where you want a patent—and you will still have to pay national fees and get the patent translated into the relevant national language, but there is no further examination and review of your patent. So, in the end, even though you still get a French patent, an English patent, a Swiss patent, a German patent, and so forth, you only had to go through a single examination process. You save the expense of applying for the patent and dealing with the process of examination in each nation.

The EPO system is not exclusive of national systems. If you want, you can file your patent counterpart applications county-by-country under as many national

---

[1] As of the time this chapter is written, the following 31 nations belong to the EPO system: Austria, Belgium, Bulgaria, Cyprus, Czech Republic, Denmark, Estonia, Finland, France, Germany, Greece, Hungary, Iceland, Ireland, Italy, Latvia, Liechtenstein, Lithuania, Luxembourg, Monaco, The Netherlands, Poland, Portugal, Slovenia, Spain, Romania, Slovakia, Switzerland, Sweden, Turkey, and the United Kingdom. The following five additional nations are not members of the EPO, but will accept EPO-allowed patent applications: Albania, Bosnia and Herzegovina, Croatia, Macedonia, and Serbia.

systems in Europe as you like. However, most US companies prefer the EPO route, because it is cost-effective and because its processing and examination of patent applications, while not prefect, are considered to be good. EPO patent files become public 18 months after the applicable priority date and (as mentioned above) are available on the Internet.

Priority Date for Foreign Applications

It is important to get an early priority for foreign nations. As mentioned above, most countries in the world determine patent priority by a "first-to-file" rule. Also, in many nations, any publication of an invention before the priority date will preclude any patent grant. This means that the priority date for foreign applications is all important.

The Paris Convention

As a general rule, the date of filing for a patent is the priority date in each nation. However, you can often obtain the benefit of an earlier first filing date under an international treaty called the Paris Convention. (This is the short name for the "The Paris Convention for the Protection of Industrial Property of 1883.") You can get a patent application priority date in a Paris Convention nation based on your original filing in another Paris Convention nation as long as you file *within one year of your original filing date*.

Most counties in the world have accepted the Paris Convention, but a few have not. Your patent lawyer can help you understand how the Paris Convention affects your foreign patent filing deadlines. The Paris Convention also covers trademarks, but supplies only six month's grace for trademarks.

The Patent Cooperation Treaty

There is another way to extend that deadline for foreign patent filings and still get the benefit of your US filing date. This is done by filing (within one year of your US filing date) a PCT application. PCT stands for "Patent Cooperation Treaty," which is an international pact on patent procedures among more than 100 countries. The PCT filing can give you up to an extra 18 months for most nations. The PCT also has the benefit of a single form of filing that can be used for many nations. The PCT process also (optionally) can get you a pretty good international search of prior art.

PCT applications are rather expensive themselves (figure on about $5,000 or so in fees and costs) and the process does not suit all cases. Also note that, in addition to the PCT costs, obtaining and maintaining patents are still a costly proposition in many nations, requiring substantial fees. Your patent attorney can give you more details about PCT and foreign filings and the costs involved.

More about Priority

Foreign parties can use the same Paris Convention and PCT rules to file for patents in the United States. The same rules allow foreign parties to use their earlier foreign priority dates for their US patent applications.

You should note that there is one technically advanced country, Taiwan, that in not part of the Paris Convention or the PCT system. Taiwan is a leader in semiconductor manufacturing, consumer electronics design and manufacturing, and other technical fields. So early filing in Taiwan is required to get an early priority date there.

Differing Patent Systems

Each country's patent system is different, so your rights and remedies as a patent holder can vary from country to country. Some are better for patent holders than others. There are some unifying principles and practices, due in part to international treaties and pressure by advanced nations on developing states to do more to protect IP. As a broad generalization, advanced nations tend to have systems that are more protective of patent rights than developing nations. Here are just a few examples of differences that may be important to your company:

- In the United States (as we mentioned), a patent holder can get an award of triple damages for willful infringement. Other nations have a single damages system.

- In the United States, patent cases can be tried to a jury. Other countries have judge-run trial systems.

- Patent litigation in other nations, while certainly not cheap, generally costs less than US patent litigation.

- In some countries, the judicial determination of whether a patent is invalid is in a separate proceeding from litigation about alleged infringement. In the United States, both issues are in the same case.

- Patent systems in individual countries each have their own characteristics. For example, in China, the procedures of the legal system places make it difficult to get large patent damage awards. In India, patent infringement cases move very slowly in the courts.

- In many countries, there are restrictions on the grant of software and business method patents. The most tolerant nation for these types of patents is the United States.

You should consult with your patent lawyer about the advantages, disadvantages, and limitations of different patent systems.

INVENTING AND PATENT STRATEGICALLY

Let's now turn to the all-important topic of patent strategy for your business.

If your company is involved in innovation, it must consider getting patents. Building a patent portfolio requires planning and effort. It is not just a matter of making a "eureka" discovery and then filing for a patent. Inventing and patenting should be a *pro active* process.

Your business can *plan* to invent—by focusing the intention of the innovators in your company on the new technology areas where you want your company to go and the ways in which your existing products and technologies can be extended.

Here is an example of targeted innovation. At the time, we are writing this book (late in 2007), Google has recently disclosed to the world that it wants to make and market mobile phone technologies. Google mobile device technologies are, we are told, going to feature Web-like functionality providing a mobile device open platform. An online search of US patent filings shows that Google has been working on patent protection for this Google Phone project *for at least three years*. Google already has three patents in the mobile telephony space—the first application was filed in 2004—and has six publicly disclosed patent applications in the field. (Because patent applications are secret for 18 months, it is a good bet that there are more Google mobile patents to come.) The Google mobile telephony patent portfolio covers mobile payments systems, data retrieval, advertising delivery, and more. You can see that Google is targeting its patent filings on what it perceives as key business and consumer functions. Google is carving out a "patent space" for itself through innovation in *anticipation* of a Google product line and "open mobile phone" technology and service market that does not yet exist.

Your company can do the same thing—innovate and patent not only for the markets and products that exist now, but for those in your company's planned future as well.

Strategic Factors

Here are some key strategic factors that you should consider in deciding whether, how, and when to innovate and patent.

Relationship to Core Business

Patents can function as a circle of protection—a patent space that your competitors may fear to enter due to patent risk. Any invention that has the potential to establish or extend that patent circle of protection around your core business should be a high priority. Think not only about current products and markets, but also about future products and markets.

Extending Existing Patent Positions

If you have a key patent or patents (or pending applications), a common strategy is to extend out existing patent space by patenting improvements or inventions that work with, enhance, or improve the core functionality.

Watch for Unexpected Uses

If a customer turns up with a use for your product or technology in a new market, don't just take the order. Think about how the customer's needs can be met through innovations that are patentable. You may be able to obtain a patent position in a new business sector.

Fundamental Patents Are Not a Necessity

While broad patents that cover fundamental inventions can be the most valuable, there is also value in patents on key incremental improvements. A patent does not have to be a "blockbuster" to have value.

Listen to Customers and Partners

When developing technologies and products, listen to what your business partners and customers (actual and prospective) tell you about unsolved problems and needed functionality. These can be areas where innovation and patents will pay off.

Blocking Competitors

It may also be of value to patent inventions that improve or extend your competitor's product or services, because those patents can be used a leverage points if your competitor sues or threatens to sue your company for patent infringement.

Up-Market and Down-Market

One entrepreneur we spoke with advised patenting both the best versions of an invention and also the "cheesy" variations. The concept is that innovation spawns imitators that provide solutions that provide similar, but somewhat inferior and cheaper, functionality. To block competitors with low-end solutions, you should consider getting patent coverage on "low-end" variants to your innovation.

Other Factors

Other factors to consider in inventing and patenting are:

- **Trends**—Can you stake out a proprietary position covering technology that is likely to be important to the future of your business sector as a whole? Does your technology extend an existing industry standard?

- **Your Stakeholders**—Make sure that your investors understand and support your patent strategy. They may be willing to provide additional resources to support it.

- **Your Employees**—Make sure your employees understand your patent strategy, because they need to carry it out.

- **Geography**—Decide what nations and regions of the world will be the focus of your patent position.

- **Your Competitors**—Do they have patents? Do you need to carve out your own proprietary position in response?

- **Your Budget**—How much patent development can your company afford?

Once you have patents and filed applications, you should evaluate (and periodically re-evaluate) your patents and patent strategy.

Deciding to Patent a Particular Invention

Some innovations are worth patenting—and others are not worth the cost. To determine whether a patent on a particular invention would have value, consider the following factors:

- **Advancement Over Prior Solutions**—Does the invention materially extend or improve the solutions currently available? If your invention is only a marginal improvement, it may be less likely to result in a valuable patent.

- **Marketability**—Does your invention have a good chance to generate a marketable product or feature?

- **Will the Technology Stand the Test of Time?**—It takes two years or more to get a patent, and digital technology changes quickly. Will your technology be useful or obsolete when the patent is issued?

- **Are You Willing to Disclose the Technology?**—Much of digital technology is kept as a trade secret. When a patent issues, it must disclose the technology sufficiently to enable the invention to be practiced by anyone skilled in the art. You cannot get a patent without making some of your trade secrets public.

Your patent lawyer can help you with the legal aspects of this analysis. Usually for under $2,000 or $3,000, you should be able to get a preliminary opinion on whether it is worthwhile to proceed with a patent application from a legal point of view. A favorable opinion from an attorney, however, is by no means a guarantee that the USPTO will issue a patent for your digital technology invention or that you will be granted the patent claims that would be most advantageous to your company.

GETTING SERIOUS ABOUT PATENTS

If you decide that a patent strategy is important for your business, you need to get serious about developing a patent position. Here are some steps to take inside your business:

- Form a patent committee with senior technicians and managers. Have the committee meet regularly (monthly or quarterly) to review technical developments.

- Have the committee formulate a plan targeting technical areas that are important for patenting. Update the plan from time to time.

- Establish a process for employees to document and disclose inventions for the committee to review.

- Make identifying potentially patentable innovations part of technical managers' job responsibilities.

- Provide a budget for patent expenses.

- Monitor your competitors' patent positions.

- Reward employees that make inventions with recognition and bonuses.

- Work with a good patent lawyer.

YOUR STRATEGY FOR USE OF PATENTS

When you have patents, you can put them to use. One use, of course, is to use the patented technologies in your own products and services. Other actions and strategies to consider are:

- **Publicity**—Do you want to publicize your patents as a badge of innovation?

- **Enforcement**—Do you want to enforce your patents aggressively against competitors?

- **Defensive Assets**—Do you want to use patents defensively—to assert against competitors when they assert patents against you?

- **Licensing**—Do you want to license your patents to competitors in your own field? Can they be licensed for use in other market sectors?

- **Selling**—If your patents are no longer relevant to your core technology, but useful to others, do you want to sell them?

We discuss licensing and enforcement later in this chapter.

PATENTS IN BUSINESS DEALS

If your company has a patent position (or wants to have one), you should make obtaining patent rights a goal in your business deals. For example:

- If you engage in development funded by a customer, negotiate for an agreement under which your company ends up with the resulting patent rights. (Avoid jointly owned patents, as they provide no control of the technology under US law.)

- If you engage in a strategic partnership or joint venture with another company that includes research and development, try to obtain resulting patent rights that are relevant to your field.

- Watch for opportunities to purchase valuable patents or to obtain exclusive patent licenses as part of a business deal.

PATENT LICENSING AGREEMENTS

As you have seen, patent law is multifaceted. Methods of patent licensing (which we do in our law office frequently) often mirror that complexity. The following is a high-level overview of the subject of patent licensing. The form Appendix in this book includes a form of patent license agreement for your review. (While this form includes many common provisions, it does not include all variations and may not fit your particular licensing needs.)

Why Engage in Patent Licensing?

There are many reasons why you may be licensing patents. Here are some of the reasons that might apply:

- A third party may want to or need to license your patents for use in its own business.

- You may be licensing your patents to another company as part of the settlement of an infringement suit that you brought against it. Or a company may be taking a license because they fear your company will sue them for patent infringement if they do not.

- You may be cross-licensing your patents and those of another company. (Note that cross-licenses and patent consortiums can raise antitrust issues if they result in domination of a market. This issue should be reviewed with your lawyer if there is any antitrust law risk that might apply.)

- Your business may be licensing a patent from another company or a university as the key to entering a new line of business.

- Patents may be licensed together with other digital technology assets, such as a license to software that is primarily covered by copyright but uses the patented invention.

- You may be licensing patents that cover an industry standard technology. Common examples are MP3 encoding technology under patents held by

Thomson Multimedia and Alcatel-Lucent or DVD technology, which is under patents held by the DVD Licensor Consortium. (As noted above, Chapter 19 discusses patents in the context of digital technology and communications standards setting.)

Business Terms

Patent license agreements require negotiating some basic business terms. These vary according to technology type, industry, and the goals of the parties. Here are a few of the items that might go into a written patent license agreement:

- **Patents Included**—Does the license cover all of the licensor's patents or only listed patents? Does it cover improvements? Does the license cover future patents in the same technology field that are not technically classed as improvements? Does it cover foreign counterparts?

- **Field of Use**—What kinds of products or services of the licensee are permitted by the license?

- **Duration**—How long does the license last? Is it for the life of the patent or a shorter period? Will the license be lost if not used?

- **Royalty Structure**—What is the basis for charging a royalty? Is it based on licensee product sales? Is it flat fee? Are there different rates for different products or services? An overall license cap? Are there minimum royalties? There are endless variations.

- **Exclusivity**—Is the license exclusive at all? Exclusive only for a time? Exclusive only for certain uses?

- **Grant backs**—If the licensee invents an improvement to the patent, does the licensee grant back the patent rights (or a license to the improvement) to the licensor?

Covering Contingencies

Patent license agreements, particularly when they are expensive or involve large amounts of money, also cover many contingencies. Some are listed below.

- **Invalidation**—There may be a provision that patent royalties end when a patent has been found invalid in a final judicial decision.

- **Unenforced Patents**—A licensee will not want to pay license fees while its competitors freely infringe the licensor's technology. The licensee may want a clause that suspends or reduces fees if the licensor fails to aggressively enforce the licensed patents.

- **Weakened Patents**—Sometimes, patents are so weakened by discovery of prior art that they become effectively unenforceable. A licensee may want a clause stating, in essence, that if this happens, the licensee can terminate the patent agreement. The licensee may also want the licensor to warrant that it has no knowledge of any invalidating prior art.

- **Applications Delayed or Granted in Part**—Sometimes, we do license agreements based on patent applications, which grant no enforceable rights until the patent actually issues. The agreement might provide that there will be no license fees while the application is still pending and there is as yet no patent—or it may provide for payment to begin without any delay. The licensee may have a right to terminate if the USPTO rejects the patent—or if key claims are watered down in the course of proceeding in the USPTO.

- **Equal Pricing**—The licensee may want assurance that it is not paying more than others for the license. Sometimes, this is referred to as a "most favored nations" clause.

- **Freedom to Practice**—In some cases, the licensor may promise the licensee that it will be free to practice the licensed patent in a particular way, and may agree to indemnify the licensee for any third party lawsuit that results if it turns out other third party patents are infringed by a particular implementation. (See Chapter 8 for a discussion of indemnification provisions in digital contracting.)

- **Dealing with Infringers**—The parties may decide whether the licensor or the licensee controls decisions on dealing with infringers of the licensed patents as well as cooperation in such enforcement. The license agreement may also stipulate who gets the proceeds of such enforcement.

- **Disputes**—The parties will usually specify how disputes between them will be resolved. (See Chapter 8 for a discussion of dispute resolution provisions.)

Clauses on these various topics are often negotiated. Many provisions will need to be adapted to fit particular markets, technologies, and deal terms. You may want to have a lawyer skilled in licensing that understands your technology help you outline the key terms of your licensing deal and assist you in negotiating a patent license agreement that covers the key contingencies.

Assignments

In some cases, you may wish to buy or sell all rights to a patent. Patent assignment agreements raise many of the same issues as license agreements. These should be done with the assistance of counsel as well. Assignments should be registered with the USPTO (and foreign patent offices if applicable).

HOW PATENTS CAN BE USED AGAINST YOUR BUSINESS

For better or worse, patents are potentially a risk factor for every digital technology company. Here are some facts that you should know about how patents held by others may affect you.

- **The Breadth of Patented Digital Technology**—Patents now cover discrete pieces of technology in a wide variety of digital technology fields, including: operating environments, relational databases, financial data analysis, computer games, banking transactions, e-commerce, computer graphics, CAD/CAM, screen displays, networks, telecommunication, memory management, electronic mail, semiconductor technologies, and many others. Whatever digital technology or software field you are in, there are probably patents that cover some technology in that field.

- **Independent Creation Is Not a Defense**—In patent law (unlike copyright law), independent creation is not a defense. In patent law, you might be liable for infringement even if you did not know of the relevant patent when you adopted the technology.

- **The Difficulty of Patent Infringement Determinations**—It may be difficult to know if you are an infringer. Searching every function in a large and complex digital technology system to see if any of it infringes one or more patents would be prohibitively expensive.

- **Applications for Patents Are Kept Secret after Filing for 18 Months or More**—In the US (like most other countries) patent applications are normally published 18 months after the application date. There are some exceptions, however. Applicants who do not intend to apply in any foreign nations can keep applications secret until the patent issues. This means that you could be using an invention in your product that is subject to a pending application and not know it, even if a patent search was done. As soon as the patent is issued, you will infringe the patent.

■ **The Expense of Resisting Claims**—If you are sued for patent infringement, it will be very expensive to resist. The litigation costs in patent cases are among the highest. Damage awards can be substantial. If your company knowingly infringes, it can be liable for triple damages.

WHO IS AT RISK OF PATENT CLAIMS?

No one is immune. It is quite common for makers of software or hardware to receive a notice from an agent claiming infringement of one patent or another, seeking royalties and threatening an infringement lawsuit. Many digital technology businesses pay substantial patent royalties. Others make a lot of money from licensing patents. Texas Instruments, for example, gets a substantial percentage of its revenues from patent royalties.

Sometimes, smaller companies can fly "under the radar." Small firms and start-up IT companies are more likely to be less threatened by patent infringement claims, because they are often too poor for the patent holders to bother with and because they often do not have high-volume patent use. When a company has yearly sales of several tens of million dollars, it is much more likely to be targeted with a demand for patent royalties. The more successful you are in digital technology, the more you are at risk of a patent problem.

Companies that are on the cutting edge, using new methods and exploring new computer applications, are also at a higher risk. This is because there is a reasonable likelihood that other companies that are working in the same field are seeking patents.

It is also common for large companies to grant one another royalty-free cross-licenses of patents in a particular area of interest to both. The cross-license gives both large companies free rein to use the patented technology, but may force smaller companies to pay patent license fees to enter the area. The effect may be to exclude competition in a technological market. (As noted above, cross-licenses can raise antitrust issues.)

However, you are by no means helpless in dealing with this potential patent threats:

- You can keep aware of patents that are enforced in your technology field.

- You can monitor the patents and patent filings of your competitors.

- You can establish your own patent position as a counter-weight.

- With the help of patent counsel, you can make efforts to avoid or "design around" patents held by others.

IF YOU RECEIVE A CEASE-AND-DESIST LETTER FROM A PATENT HOLDER

If you get a cease-and-desist letter from a patent holder, you should not panic. You need to carefully assess your position and then respond.

First, you should get a good lawyer with expertise in digital technology disputes to advise you. After speaking with counsel, you may also need an engineer or computer scientist to work with the attorney to read the patents that are allegedly infringed and look for prior art. You should not attempt to formulate a strategy or respond to a cease-and-desist letter unless you have first consulted with counsel, who will be better able than you to analyze the breadth of the claims in the patent and the significance of the prior art. (If you find the right prior art, your attorney may be able to get the patent holder to settle cheaply—or just go away.) Your attorney can also advise you of the steps that should be taken to keep your own factual and legal investigations strictly confidential.

If your company is at risk because of an infringement claim and the problem looks like it is not going to go away, the company should discuss its options with its legal counsel. The available options might include designing around the problem or licensing alternative technology (to stop damages from accruing), paying for a license from the patent holder, or, as the last resort, leaving the field.

A further note on patent-related letters: The beginning of the game is sometimes not a cease-and-desist letter, but rather an almost innocent sounding letter from a patent holder that expresses a wish to draw your attention to a particular patent and suggests that your own product is infringing. If you receive such a letter that appears in any way relevant to your own technology, you should take it seriously and contact counsel. The lawyer will counsel you on the risks and options.

Patent Infringement Lawsuits

What happens if you are sued for patent infringement, or if you bring your own patent infringement suit?

Patent disputes normally start with a cease-and-desist letter, but sending such a letter is not completely risk free. There is a risk that the alleged infringer will sue first, in order to get the advantage of having the lawsuit in the alleged infringer's home jurisdiction. (We call this kind of first strike by the defense a declaratory judgment action, because the accuse infringer asks the court to declare that it is not infringing.) For this reason, in some cases, the patent holder will sue on the patent as the first move.

The alleged infringer might capitulate and agree to pay a royalty—or it might deny infringement or insist that the patent is invalid. Settlement before suit is always possible. Absent settlement, litigation often follows. Litigation is in federal court and runs in fits and starts over a period of months or years, leading, if not settled, to a trial and possibly to appeals. Patent litigation is legally complex and uncertain. Either party has the right to claim a jury trial, although it is the judge's job to interpret the patent's claims.

Patent litigation can be shockingly expensive. Patent litigation requires sophisticated expert testimony and skilled patent litigators. These cases can easily run tens of thousand of dollar *per month* or more for the two or three years or so that the pretrial and trial process typically takes. When parties take patent cases through trial, it is not uncommon for each party to spend more than $2,000,000 in legal and expert fees. This level of cost, and the risks of litigation, pushes the parties on both sides to resolve these cases. For this reason, most patent suits settle before trial.

When a patent holder (the plaintiff) sues an alleged infringer (the defendant), the dispute focuses on two issues. Is the plaintiff's patent valid? (Patents are presumed valid, and the burden is on the alleged infringer to prove them otherwise.) Does the patent cover the defendant's product? If the court finds that the answer to both of these questions is yes, it must find that the patent was infringed.

Every time that the patent holder sues, it runs the risk that the court may find the patent invalid and render it worthless forever. Prior art can emerge in the course of court proceedings that had not been found before. If the patent is weak—if there is a danger that the court will find that the patent should not have been issued—or if infringement is in doubt, the holder will be more likely to settle the case for a relatively small amount of money or a low royalty amount. If the patent is strong—if there is little risk that the court will invalidate the patent and if infringement is clear—then the defendant will be forced to settle at a higher price.

When the court finds patent infringement, it has the power to:

- Award damages to the patent holder equal to a reasonable royalty on the defendant's sales for the period of infringement, or in some cases, the profits made by the infringer by use of the patent holder's invention

- Issue a court order to prevent further infringement (including a preliminary injunction stopping infringement early in the case if the infringement is clear)

In cases of willful infringement, the court may also:

- Award treble damages

- Award attorneys' fees

What the patent holder normally wants, of course, is money, together with recognition that the patent is valid and covers the defendant's product. Where there is a settlement, the most common result is that the defendant pays some amount for past use of the patent and a royalty on future sales.

Criticism of the Current US Patent Critique and Proposed "Patent Reform"

As patents have become more powerful in digital technology and other technology fields, patent-related issues have become more political. As a result, there may be changes coming in the US patent system.

This is a topic that anyone interested in patents should be aware of because it adds an element of uncertainty to US patents. It is unclear whether there will be changes in US patent law. What *is* clear is that there is considerable pressure on Congress to make changes. Whether these changes will "reform" the patent system or make it worse depends on your point of view.

A number of major companies—particularly companies in computers, software, and electronics—are seeking changes in the US Patent Act and have lobbied the US Congress intensely to change the system. Other companies (notable biotech companies) and universities oppose most of the changes.

The proponents of change criticize, in particular, what they call "patent trolls"—a pejorative term. The more polite term would be "patent investor." Whichever term you prefer, the concept is about companies that purchase patents, not to use them, but to enforce them for royalties. These patent investors have had success suing major IT companies and obtaining infringement judgments and settlements in the tens or hundreds of millions of dollars. Whether this is good or bad depends on your point of view. Some would say that they are just obtaining the real value of the patents.

The proposed changes in patent law would generally favor big corporations over smaller company and individual inventors. They would also likely make patents more expensive. The advocates of change are trying to reduce the amounts of court patent damage awards and make challenging patents easier. Here are some of the proposals for change in the US patent system that Congress is considering at the time that we are writing this book:

- **Priority**—Changing the US patent law to a "first-to-file" system (like that used in the rest of the world) rather than a "first-to-invent" system. This change would likely benefit large corporations, because they are better positions to file many applications and to file quickly.

- **Prior Art Searching**—The Patent Office would have the power to require applicants to do extensive prior art searches and disclose the results. This would assertedly result in higher-quality applications, but also raise the cost of patent applications.

- **Open Prior Art Submission**—Allowing any person or company to submit prior art to challenge or narrow pending patent applications.

- **Postissuance Challenges**—Allowing any person and company to challenge issued patents by means of proceedings in the Patent Office. This could result in cancellation of wrongfully issued patents, but could also impose substantial additional costs on patent holders to defend proper patents.

- **Limiting the Damages**—Changing (and reducing) patent judgment amounts by permitting money damages only for the value added by the patented invention over the prior art—rather than the fair value of the patented technology. (How this value-added would be determined is unclear.) Also, placing limitations on circumstances under which treble damages could be awarded.

This is a topic that digital technology companies should follow closely.

More Information

Want to learn more about patents? You can find a lot on the topic by searching the Web. A good place to start is the site of the United State Patent and Trademark Office at www.uspto.gov.

For patent-related advice specific to your business and technologies, you need a good patent lawyer or patent agent. For patent-related transactions or licensing, you should consult an attorney with knowledge and experience in software, IP, and digital technology transactions.

Trade Secrets and Non-Disclosure Agreements

6

Secrecy is the practice of hiding information from others.

—Wikipedia

For technology businesses, hiding information can be good. Does your business have technology, strategies, and other knowledge that you do not want competitors or customers to know? Can your business maintain its secrets? Can you get a remedy in court if your secret information is stolen? The subject of these questions is trade secret law.

IN THIS CHAPTER

In this chapter, we will cover:

- The legal requirement of trade secret law
- A comparison of patents vs. trade secrets
- The practices and agreements used for trade secret protection
- The risks from mishandled trade secrets
- Remedies when trade secrets are wrongfully taken or used
- Non-Disclosure agreements
- Confidentiality provisions in contracts

137

WHAT IS A TRADE SECRET?

As the name suggests, trade secrets are valuable information kept secret. But trade secrets are more than information—they are also a form of intellectual property. Indeed, they are the only way that you can "own" unpatented concepts and ideas. Under American law, trade secrets have legal protection, but that protection is far from complete. The law protects only against *wrongful* appropriation, disclosure, or use of trade secrets.

The law will protect your trade secrets only if you do. Because trade secrets are information, they can easily slip away. Trade secrets can be stolen in an instant by electronic transfer or can be carried out the door by departing employees. Trade secrets that are made public are destroyed, for example, by publication on the Internet. So your company's measures to protect trade secrets are critical for practical as well as legal reasons.

Trade secrets are a source of competitive advantage—but other person's trade secrets in your possession are often a legal risk for you. If you use or disclose another's trade secret when you have a legal obligation not to, you can be sued and may be liable for large sums.

BASIS OF TRADE SECRET LAW

Trade secrets are governed mainly by state law. There is a great deal of uniformity in this body of law. In 40 states, the main source of trade secret law is the Uniform Trade Secrets Act (UTSA). Even in those states that have not adopted the UTSA, the same basic rules apply either under other statutes or legal principles adopted by judges in their case decisions.

The term "trade secret" may bring to mind an image of a scientist in a white coat crafting complex chemical formulas. In reality, the definition of a trade secret is much broader. A trade secret can be any kind of information, technical or non-technical, that fits the legal tests discussed below. There is no requirement that trade secrets be written.

To be a trade secret, your company's information must pass three tests:

- **Unavailability**—The information must not be generally known or available. Information that can be found from an available public source is not a trade secret.

- **Value**—The information must have actual or potential economic value. In order to prove that information is a trade secret, your company must show how the information—actually or potentially—confers an economic advantage in the marketplace over those that do not have it.

- **Protection**—A company claiming a trade secret must prove that the company uses (and has used) reasonable measures to maintain its secrecy. This means that to prove a trade secret, your company must make an affirmative showing that at all times it has used and is using reasonably confidentiality procedures and protections.

Whether any particular information is or is not a trade secret is always a factual inquiry. It is a matter of proof based on the factors listed above. This makes trade secrets very different from copyright (where the particular copyrighted work is the basis of protection), patent law (which is based on a patent issued by a government patent office), or trademark law (which is based on particular trademarks and trademark registrations). In trade secret litigation, it is very common for the parties to dispute whether a particular piece of information is a trade secret at all.

Trade Secret Law vs. Contractual Protection of Confidential Information

In digital contracting, it is very common that contracts contain provisions to protect Confidential Information. (These are discussed in Chapter 8.) Protecting Confidential Information contractually is very important for trade secret law, but it is not the same.

- Contracts bind only those that sign them. Trade secret law would bind a stranger to the contract. For example, a hacker that broke into your information system and took secret information would be liable under trade secret law.

- Breach of contract can cover (depending on how the clause is written) failures to protect Confidential Information that occur without fault or purely accidental. Trade secret law protects only against wrongful violation (discussed below).

- Contractual definitions of Confidential Information are often broader than what is legally protected under trade secret law.

- These two bodies of law may overlap. For example, an exemployee who uses Confidential Information without permission may breach both her employee agreement and also be liable under trade secret law.

- Contractual protection of Confidential Information is often a precondition to trade secret protection, because it is part of the "reasonable measures" that companies must use if they are to have legally protected trade secrets.

Technology as a Trade Secret

For digital technology companies, trade secret technologies can often be vital assets. Many different software technologies and techniques could classify as trade secrets if not generally known, for example, methods of data storage, data analysis methods, graphics display techniques, encryption and compression techniques, optimization methods, and so forth. The list is endless and always growing through creation of technology—but also always eroding as once-secret techniques become generally known.

A trade secret may exist in various forms and formats. Say, for example, that you have a new algorithm for efficient high-speed data transmission. Trade secret law would cover the algorithm itself, flow chart that describes it, and the computer code that implements it. Each of these might be deemed as a trade secret.

Some trade secrets are more valuable than others. If you make a quantum leap ahead of the competition, if you solve a problem that others have tried to solve in vain, yours will be a much more valuable trade secret. From a practical point of view, you would be well advised to provide extra protection to the most valuable secrets.

Source Code as a Trade Secret

Many software companies do business under a propriety business model in which their commercial products are provided only in binary form. These companies treat their source code as a valuable trade secret. Most resist disclosing their source code to any customer or outsider. Disclosure of source code to trusted contractors will be under a form of agreement with clauses designed to protect trade secrets.

Many software vendors use source code escrow agreements (discussed in some detail in Chapter 12) as a means to provide customers access to source code *only if* the software vendor fails to maintain the software or goes out of business. Controlling disclosure is vital to maintaining the trade secret status of the source code.

Product Ideas—Flying Under the Radar Screen

In the world of software, fundamental trade secrets may not last long. That is because clever programmers can often figure out how a rival company's software works. There is a saying in digital technology that "today's innovation is tomorrow's commodity." However, even short-lived trade secrets may be priceless.

A good example of a brief but extremely valuable start-up trade secret was webmail—the Web application that allows users to access e-mail online through a Web browser. Hotmail was the first webmail company, launched on July 4, 1996. Hotmail quickly obtained millions of users. As a result, Hotmail was sold to Microsoft in January 1998, just 18 months after launch, for $400 million—a smash hit deal even by the extravagant standards of the '90s Internet boom.

Hotmail's advantage was to get webmail first. After Hotmail was launched, its secret was out. Any sophisticated Web developer who saw the Hotmail service in operation could figure out how to build a competing service—but it was then too late. The key trade secret of Hotmail was having the *concept* of webmail before others knew it. As a result, Hotmail launched first, getting the jump on competitors that was the key to its success.

To protect product concepts and business plans, many start-up technology companies begin their business life in "stealth mode" or "under the radar screen." They swear all officers, employees, and investors to secrecy, and they try to keep even the basic outlines of their product secret as long as possible.

Confidential Business Information

Software companies also have nontechnical trade secrets that can be quite valuable. Examples are confidential customer databases, contact lists, prospect lists, mailing lists, lists of suppliers and contract programmers, product development and acquisition plans, cost and profit margin information, contract bids, and business strategy documents.

Confidential Information from Third Parties

Much of the most important Confidential Information used in your business may not be yours at all. You may have received a third party's Confidential Information under the terms of an agreement that requires you to keep the information secret. In that case, in accordance with your contractual obligations, you must take steps to protect that third party information, to use it only as permitted in the agreement, and otherwise to comply fully with the terms of the agreement under which you received the other party's secret information.

Limits to Trade Secrets

Trade secrets do not include information that is not really secret. For example, techniques or information generally known to skilled personnel in any technical field are not trade secrets—even if they were taught to an employee at great expense to the employer.

Sometimes in trade secret litigation, lawyers will try to make rather mundane techniques and informations look like well-guarded secrets—and opposing lawyers try to portray genuine secrets as common knowledge. Most often, the courts see through all this legal sleight-of-hand—but in a world where many judges have nontechnical backgrounds, sometimes the courts get it wrong. This makes trade secret law an area where rights are often uncertain and contingent.

How Long Trade Secrets Last

Trade secrets last as long as the information remains secret and valuable. For some trade secrets—for example, the formula for Coca-Cola—that can mean a very long time. The longest lasting secrets are those that are not apparent from the products or services they are used to create.

Patents vs. Trade Secrets

Sometimes companies have a choice as to whether to patent an invention or to keep it as a trade secret. Not all trade secrets are potentially patentable—only those that meet the legal tests for patentability (as discussed in the Chapter 4 of this book).

If an invention appears to be patentable—a company has to choose which route to protection it wants to take. Here are some of the factors to consider in making this choice:

- **Time to Obtain Protection**—Patents take a long time to obtain—usually two or three years—but they last a long time—20 years from the application date. Some digital technologies quickly become "old" and are "leapfrogged" by other technologies. Patenting best fits technologies that can be expected to have continuing value over time.

- **Disclosure**—Patents are public—they *disclose* technology. Most patent applications are published within 18 months of filing. There is a risk that after this disclosure, your competitors may figure out how to design around your patent but obtain the same general results. An invention might be used in foreign nations where no patent was obtained. There is also a risk that the Patent Office will disallow or narrow the patent application. Where disclosure is risky, trade secret protection may be preferable.

- **Patenting by Others**—In some cases if you chose trade secret protection, your innovation will be patented by some other company that independently invents it—in which case you could end up being the infringer. Your patent counsel can help you evaluate this risk.

- **Legal Protection**—Legal protection under patent law is broader. Independent invention is not a defense to a patent claim. As is discussed below, trade secret law protects against wrongful appropriation only.

- **Expense**—Patent filings are costly. The expenses of trade secret protection are those for the security measures that are used to protect secrets generally in your company; the marginal cost of protecting each additional trade secret is small.

The bottom line is that important technology advances need to be reviewed to determine which kind of protection is best. Consult with your technical staff and patent counsel and make the determination that best suits your market, technology field, and business strategy.

Can More Than One Company Have the Same Trade Secret?

More than one company *can* have the same trade secret technology. As long as the technique is not generally known in the industry, the trade secret can continue to exist in several companies. Unlike patents, trade secret protection does not provide the owner any ability to halt the use of technology by another company unless the other company obtained the trade secret from the owner by improper means or is using it in violation of a duty not to do so.

CARE AND PROTECTION OF TRADE SECRETS

Trade secrets are legally protected only if their owner uses "reasonable measures" to safeguard their secrecy. Unless you use reasonable measures to safeguard your new technologies, legal protection under trade secret law is lost. Your investors will expect that you will protect trade secrets. When you sell your company, you will be expected to warrant that you have used reasonable trade secret protections. Any innovative digital technology company should make trade secret protection part of its culture.

So what does the term "reasonable measures" really mean? In this context, "reasonable" means what a sensible person who was interested in keeping information would do under all the circumstances. So to some extent, the answer is context-driven; some business and some secrets demand more protection than others. Companies should be especially careful about core technologies that are the keys to their competitive advantage. A defense contractor is naturally expected to invest more on security of information than a software game development company. A company with three employees will need fewer formal confidentiality procedures than a business with 20,000 employees.

While there are these variations and degrees, there is a common set of security and confidentiality measures that are used in technology companies throughout the world. The following list of security measures are those commonly used. Not all of them are needed for every business, and this is not an exhaustive list of every measure that might apply.

One Person in Charge of Confidentiality Measures

A sensible basis for adequate trade secret protection is to put a single responsible person in charge of security and protection measures for the company—and in large companies, for each business unit. This will help you obtain implementation and follow up on a consistent basis.

Controls on Access to Confidential Data

The company must control access to Confidential Information within the company. The methods are straightforward:

- **Computer Access Protection**—Where Confidential Information is accessed by computer, whether in a single machine or on a network, use password protection. Passwords should be changed frequently, and passwords for departing employees should be deleted promptly. For very secret information, you may want to consider biometric protections, such as fingerprint or retinal scan systems.

- **Need-to-Know Access**—Access should be limited for directories where source code, product plans, customer lists, or other confidential data is stored. Access should be permitted on a need-to-know basis only. It is usually a mistake to let all employees have access to all data. There are many software tools that allow system administrators to control access to information.

- **System Protection**—Computer systems that interface with the Internet or other networks (as most do) need protection by means of firewalls and intrusion detection systems. It is a good idea to hire consultants that do periodic "white hacking" penetration testing—so that you can find and fix points of vulnerability. You can also have security audits for your information systems.

- **Encrypted Transmission and Storage**—Data is more secure if it is in encrypted form. This applies especially to transmission through open networks such as the Internet. When data is particularly valuable or sensitive, you may want to consider implementing encrypted internal storage as well. (Encrypted storage is an especially good idea for personal data including names, addresses, and social security numbers, because your company can face statutory liability for release of such data. See the discussion of data security breach notification laws in Chapter 18, which is about privacy laws.)

- **Permanent Copies**—Where confidential data is stored on tape, CD-ROM, or hard copy, access to the information should be controlled by lock and key, which sign out systems to record access. You may want to restrict use, storage, and access to particular locations.

- **Laptops and Storage Devices**—One way that Confidential Information can be lost or compromised is to allow it to get into portable form in a laptop or flash drive. In some companies, there are strict limitations on putting company data on these devices. Others have procedures to require storage in such devices to be in encrypted form. Some companies forbid visitors to bring storage devices on site (even iPods) or into secure areas.

Entry Control and Badges

Physical access control is important.

- **Entry and Exist Control**—It is standard procedure at many high-technology companies to monitor who comes in and out. Visitors sign in and out, and should be issued "visitor" badges that they surrender on leaving. Visitors should always be escorted.

- **Employee Badges**—As soon as the company is large enough that all employees are not known to one another, the employees should get numbered identification badges that include a photo. Systems to generate the badges are commercially available. In many companies, the identification badges also serve as keys to otherwise locked access doors.

- **Security Systems and Personnel**—After-hours access should be controlled by a security system, and there should be an intruder alarm. Larger companies will consider hiring guards and having security cameras.

Confidentiality Legends on Documents, Code, and Other Data

Materials that contain (or may contain) trade secrets must be marked. They should have a clearly visible legend or notice. The legend alerts anyone who sees the document—employees and nonemployees alike—that trade secret protection is claimed.

Your confidentiality legend should normally be typed in all capital letters (in order to be more conspicuous) and read like this:

NOTICE: THE CONTENTS CONSIST OF TRADE SECRETS THAT ARE THE PROPERTY OF [NAME OF COMPANY]. THE CONTENTS MAY NOT BE USED OR DISCLOSED WITHOUT EXPRESS WRITTEN PERMISSION OF [NAME OF COMPANY].

Confidentiality legends should be used regardless of the form in which Confidential Information is maintained. For example, the legend should be placed conspicuously in or on:

- Every source code file (written into the source code, including at the top and the end)

- Every propriety database

- All laboratory notebooks or other records of research

- Product plans, specifications, and so forth

- Customer lists, projections, market research results, and so forth

- Every printout or other hard copy of every type of Confidential Information

If in doubt, mark the information with the legend. Most often, you will do this electronically. It is also a good idea to get an old-fashioned rubber stamp reading: "CONFIDENTIAL TRADE SECRET: PROPERTY OF [NAME OF COMPANY]" and use it to mark documents, optical disks, and other media that contain trade secret matter.

While use of a confidentiality legend is very important for secret information used within a business, the notice is even more important for information provided in confidence to someone outside. We have seen a judge deny trade secret protection to a graphics video board design based on the disclosure of a single schematic with no confidentiality legend and no confidentiality agreement to a potential business partner.

We recommend that each technology company configures their e-mail program (such as Outlook) at the company level so that it automatically adds a confidentiality message for each outgoing e-mail. For example, the following:

> *This e-mail message and any attachments are confidential and proprietary information of [NAME OF COMPANY]. If you are not the intended recipient, please immediately reply to the sender or call [NUMBER] and delete the message from your e-mail system.*

A note of caution: A confidentiality notice is important, but is not a substitute for a non-disclosure agreement (NDA) with the other party. Your unilateral assertion of confidentiality will probably not bind the other party—you also need to get the other party to *agree* to hold your information confidential.

Agreements with Third Parties to Protect Confidentiality

It is essential to use the correct form of NDA to protect trade secrets to be disclosed to third parties. In the following section of this chapter, we will discuss the goals and terms of such agreements. In any negotiations where there may be any disclosure of any Confidential Information regarding your business, you should get an NDA in place before discussions take place.

In addition, as mentioned above, it is essential to have confidentiality clauses in a great variety of contracts between a technology company and third parties, including business partners, independent contractors, and consultants that the company uses. You can find many samples in the agreement forms in the Appendix to this book and discussions of these clauses throughout this book.

Confidential Undertakings by Employees and Contractors

Your company needs to obtain confidentiality undertakings from employees and contractors. These clauses are contained in the employee agreements of the type discussed in Chapter 7 of this book. It is a good policy to have every employee sign such agreements, not just technical and sales staff. These agreements should be signed by each officer and director and members of any advisory board.

Employee Guidelines
Every company should have an employee manual (a topic to discuss with your lawyer). Your company's employee manual must include the company's policies on confidentiality. That section will contain guidelines as to what sort of information the company considers confidential and how that information should be treated. It is a good idea to prepare and use similar guidelines for contractors.

Speeches, Paper, and Presentations
Many companies unwittingly lose trade secret protection when they allow scientists and engineers to publish and speak in public. Sometimes your technical staff will disclose information over cocktails in idle chat with their peers. It is important for companies to do their best to screen and preapprove any public discussion of their technology—and to impress upon all the need not to discuss secret technology with third parties. You may wish to assign an employee or employees the task of screening and approving public disclosures of technical information.

New Employee Orientation
When new employees or officers are hired, an explanation of the company's trade secret policies and protections should be part of their introduction to the company. On or before the first day of employment, they should sign the company's confidentiality agreement and receive a copy of the company's policy on protection of intellectual property.

New hires should be counseled not to bring with them or to use any information or materials belonging to another company, such as telephone directories, organizational charts, salary schedules, and the like, as well as technical and business information that were protected as confidential by that company.

They should not be permitted to bring computer files from their former employer. You may make an exception for materials that are publicly available or for materials that the employee is bringing pursuant to the signed consent of an authorized officer of the former employer. A similar process should apply for your company's onsite independent contractors.

If you are going to discuss technical or other nonpublic matters with a prospective employee, you should have them sign an NDA before such discussions.

Exit Process

When employees leave or the services of independent contractor are ended, there should be an exit process, where, among other matters, trade secret matters are covered. Here are some pointers for this process:

- Be sure each departing employee or contractor returns his or her access cards, ID badge, keys, laptops, PDA or Blackberry, company flash drives, and the like.

- Disable the employee's access to computers, voicemail, and e-mail. Be sure that the appropriate usernames and passwords are deleted from all company systems.

- Make the employee return any documents or company material in his or her possession, including things kept at home (such as company files on his or her home computer or storage device), in his or her car, as well as such items in his or her office or work area. The employee's supervisor can help verify that this has been done correctly.

- Some companies archive the contents of the departing employee's computer records, including those on the server and on his or her workstation or laptop. Then you may erase the computer files to free up the storage area.

- It is a good practice to wind up the affairs of departing employees or independent contractors very quickly. If they stay on the job, they will have more opportunity to remove confidential data for use in the next job. You may want to check his or her recent access to computer systems; heavy activity may indicate that he or she has been improperly downloading files.

- An exit interview that covers confidential matters (and any noncompetition agreement) is recommended. In many companies, departing employees are asked to sign a written statement that they have returned all materials belonging to the company, and that they will maintain trade secrets and

Confidential Information in confidence after leaving. During the exit interview, give the departing employee a copy of his or her employee agreement and should remind the employee of its obligations, including confidentiality and (if applicable) noncompetition.

NON-DISCLOSURE AGREEMENTS AND CONFIDENTIAL DISCLOSURE

Aside from clickwrap agreements, perhaps the most common intercompany agreements in the world of information technology are NDAs, the confidentiality agreements that companies routinely sign before they talk about non-public matters. NDAs are designed to cloak discussions in secrecy to allow parties to have freer discussions. You will find an example of a conventional reasonably balanced mutual NDA (Form 6-1) in the Appendix to this book.

It is a mistake to consider an NDA as "just a form." Most companies that deal with NDAs have their own favorite versions that fit their business—and are constantly adjusting and editing forms that come from other companies. Some of these adjustments can make a real difference. Many of the variations that you see in these forms are discussed below.

Some NDAs provide inadequate protection or may allow the receiving party to use the disclosing party's information. You should read these agreements from the other party very carefully. Many companies will not sign NDAs from other companies without legal review.

NDAs are not self-enforcing. You can enforce them only through litigation—and you can sue only after you discover the violation of confidentiality. Litigation is expensive and uncertain. So NDAs are imperfect protection. You should be careful about what you disclose to other companies even if an NDA is in place. Never "lift the kimono" more than you have to.

Of course, contractual provisions on confidential disclosure are not limited to NDAs. As noted above, many technology agreements have confidentiality provisions. These clauses also have variations. The considerations and analysis discussed in the following sections apply to the confidentiality clauses in contracts as well.

Mutual or Unilateral NDAs

There are some NDAs that are mutual; they cover both parties in their roles of "disclosing party" and "receiving party." Some NDAs are unilateral; they are a disclosing party's form of agreement that requires the other party to protect the disclosing party's Confidential Information—based on the assumption that no protection will apply to the other party's information.

We tend to be skeptical of unilateral NDAs. In most serious technical and business discussions, both sides have Confidential Information to disclose. Mutual NDA forms tend to be fairer, because they force the drafter to state rules the both sides must live with. Often, we will respond (with our client's permission) to a proposed unilateral NDA form by just sending our client's favorite mutual NDA form.

Defining "Confidential Information"

Definitions of "Confidential Information" in NDAs are often in this format:

> *"Confidential Information" means all nonpublic information provided by the Disclosing Party including, but not limited to, the following: [INSERT LIST OF EXAMPLES].*

When you are drafting or editing this kind of clause, be sure that this list of examples includes the type of materials and technology that you are actually likely to disclose. In addition, you should avoid narrowly drafted definitions of Confidential Information—because you might be waiving protection for anything that you leave out. (In this discussion, we use the term "Confidential Information"—with initial caps— to refer both to the defined term in an NDA and the information that it covers.)

What Written Information Is "Confidential Information"?

There are variations in the way that NDAs deal with confidential documents that are disclosed under the NDA:

- Some NDA forms are written so that documents are Confidential Information only if they are marked "Confidential" or "Proprietary." With this language, any contents of unmarked documents will be deemed nonconfidential and subject to unrestricted use by the receiving party.

- Some NDA forms are written so that any written information disclosed is deemed designated as "Confidential Information."

- Some NDA forms are written so that any written information disclosed that the recipient "reasonably understands to be confidential" is deemed "Confidential Information."

Many high-technology companies tend to prefer the forms that require written information to be specifically marked confidential—because this makes it less likely that they will accidentally use information that is subject to a confidentiality agreement. On the other hand, if only marked information is deemed "Confidential Information," there is a risk that the disclosing party will accidentally fail to mark their disclosed information properly and lose protection.

If your company ever enters into agreements in which you need to designate written information as confidential, be sure to remember that this requirement applies to e-mail, instant messaging, electronic white boards, and every other form of electronic information exchange.

What Oral or Visual Information Is "Confidential Information"?

NDAs vary in the way that they treat information that is disclosed orally or visually. (An example of visual disclosure would be showing a PowerPoint presentation that is not provided in written form.) The concern here is that there is no record of the fact of the disclosure. Unless there is a mechanism for creating a record, the only evidence would be by the testimony of participants in the disclosure.

- Some NDAs are written to protect all oral or visual information that otherwise meets the Confidential Information definition.

- Some NDAs require the disclosing party to provide a written summary of its oral or visual disclosures in confirmation of the disclosure—typically within 30 days of disclosure. With this language, failure to provide the summary will waive confidentiality protection.

- Some NDAs include a written list of proposed discussion topics, which are deemed designated as confidential, and require a written summary of anything else.

If your company enters into agreements that require a written summary of confidential disclosure, it is important that you make sure that this task actually gets done. Unfortunately, many forget to do this, and much Confidential Information is therefore put at risk. It is a good idea for each party to put one of its participants at the meeting in charge of such designations.

Carve-Outs from Confidential Information

NDAs virtually always have a provision (commonly called a "carve-out") stating what is *not* Confidential Information. Here is a typical provision:

"Confidential Information" will not include information that:

(a) was known by the Receiving Party prior to disclosure thereof by the Disclosing Party;

(b) was publicly available through no wrongful act of the Receiving Party;

(c) is disclosed to the Receiving Party by a third party legally entitled to make such disclosure without violation of any obligation of confidentiality to the Disclosing Party;

(d) is required to be disclosed by applicable laws, court order, or regulations (provided that the Receiving Party notifies the Disclosing Party and provides the Disclosing Party the opportunity to challenge or seek a protective order for the Confidential Information); or

(e) as the Receiving Party can demonstrate was independently developed by the Receiving Party without reference to any Confidential Information of the Disclosing Party.

This kind of provision is designed to remove Confidential Information status for information that the Receiving Party legitimately obtains by other means. These provisions vary, so you should always pay attention to them. Sometimes they include a requirement that each exception be "proved by documentary evidence"—and this may be unreasonable. Depending on the nature of the exception and the information, there may be situations where documentary proof of the exemption may not be feasible.

Prohibition of Disclosure

Virtually every NDA has provisions on nondisclosure of Confidential Information but they are often not absolute.

You should pay attention to provisions in the NDA that say how Confidential Information may be disclosed. Most forms allow no disclosure to third parties.

Some allow confidential disclosure to accountants, advisors, or other third parties. Some impose an unqualified nondisclosure obligation, and some require only that the receiving party use "reasonable measures" to protect the disclosed information. You need to judge which level of protection is sufficient.

NDAs normally have provisions for return of Confidential Information either upon demand or the end of negotiations between parties.

Use of Confidential Information

NDAs should have restrictions on how Confidential Information can be used. Sometimes you see NDA forms that have restrictions on disclosure but not on use—a circumstance that a disclosing party should find unacceptable.

It is common for NDAs to have clauses that permit only evaluation. Some NDAs allow use "for the purposes of the relationship of the parties"—which strikes me as too vague and broad. If you disclose valuable Confidential Information, you will usually want to narrow its permitted use carefully.

Many NDAs for disclosed hardware or software expressly prohibit reverse engineering and provide for return of samples upon demand.

When Does Protection Time-Out?

Some forms of NDA are designed to be in effect permanently and to protect Confidential Information forever. Others have time limits—there are two kinds that may apply.

First is a time limit on disclosure—for example,

This Agreement covers disclosures made during one year from the Effective Date of the Agreement.

Some NDAs have a limit on how long the obligation of confidentiality last. For example,

The receiving party agrees to hold in confidence the disclosing party's Confidential Information for five years from the date of disclosure.

When entering into an NDA, be sure that the period of protection lasts as long as your secrets are likely to be valuable. When our client has a secret that is likely to be long-lasting, we recommend against *any* "time-out" of Confidential Information.

Risks from Others' Confidential Information

Exchanging Confidential Information may be a benefit because it facilitates deals and cooperation—but confidentiality carries danger as well. If your company discloses or uses another company's Confidential Information improperly, the disclosing party may sue you—and seek money damages or seek injunctions to terminate the violation.

The problem is that in some cases, it may be unclear after the fact whether you did or did not misuse Confidential Information. Say, for example, that another company reveals to your company a technology in your field that your company did not then know—but which your company was very close to developing itself. Or say that the disclosed technology is new but it is an obvious extension of your company's current technology. In that circumstance, if your company releases a product that is similar to the disclosing party's product, you may be accused of improper use of the disclosing party's technology—and bitter litigation may follow.

Another risk is that you may inadvertently use another's technology. Sometimes a company's engineers and programmers discuss ideas and concepts informally among themselves without making it clear that they are subject to confidentiality restrictions—or they may simply not remember the context in which they learned about a particular technical approach. In this way, companies sometimes stray into use of the other's Confidential Information.

The bottom line is that obtaining disclosure under an NDA (or any other confidentiality clause) may create a legal vulnerability that you—and your technical staff—need to manage with great care.

Two-Stage Disclosure

To minimize the risk of receiving unwanted confidential disclosure, companies sometimes use an (admittedly rather awkward) two-stage disclosure. First, the would-be disclosing party has to supply an initial nonconfidential summary of the proposed disclosure—telling the other party the general nature of what it plans to disclose. Then if the other party agrees to accept the information, it would get the burdens of confidential disclosure. If the other party says "no," it will remain unburdened by confidential disclosure.

As you may imagine, this two-stage process for confidential disclosure is burdensome—and greatly slows communications. So this form of disclosure is relatively uncommon—we usually reserve it to critical high tech disclosures between competitors.

Watch Out for "Residuals" Clauses

Another way in which companies try to limit their exposure to the risks of receiving Confidential Information is by use of a "residuals" clause. The concept of "residuals" is information that is left in the unaided memory of the receiving party's head after the Confidential Information is returned. The residuals clause provides for the receiving party to keep the right to use residuals. Microsoft Corporation, for example, commonly includes a residuals clause in its form of NDA.

Here is a typical residuals clause:

Either party shall be free to use for any purpose the residuals resulting from access to or work with such Confidential Information, provided that such party shall maintain the confidentiality of the Confidential Information as provided herein. The term "residuals" means information in non-tangible form, which may be retained by persons who have had access to the Confidential Information, including ideas, concepts, know-how, or techniques contained therein. Neither party shall have any obligation to limit or restrict the assignment of such persons or to pay royalties for any work resulting from the use of residuals. However, the foregoing shall not be deemed to grant to either party a license under the other party's copyrights or patents.

If you are likely to be *getting* Confidential Information, a residuals clause can be very beneficial—if you are *providing* Confidential Information, a residuals clause can be very dangerous. Here are some key points to know about residuals clauses:

- These clauses are in fact technology licenses. They permit permanent use of the residuals and trump a trade secret claim.

- If a company duplicates your disclosed technology and relies on the residual clause in the NDA, you will be at a disadvantage in litigation. You will need to prove that the other company's employee did not remember your technology—and that is very difficult to do.

- *Unless carefully worded, residuals clauses are broad intellectual property licenses.* This is because of the doctrine that when you grant permission for use of a technology, your permission, unless otherwise stated, covers all rights you may have. So even if you had a patent or copyright that would otherwise block use of the residual, the recipient of the residual is free to use it nonetheless, because you have given permission. To prevent this result, if you do use a residuals clause, you must use language like that quoted above: *"However, the foregoing shall not be deemed to grant to either party a license under the other party's copyrights or patents."*

■ Residuals are especially dangerous when you have a secret innovative or unique technology or product. In that case, the concepts—rather than the code—may be the key to the value of your technology.

You need to consider carefully when use of the residuals clause is right for your company—and when it will be a threat. Note that the great majority of NDAs do not have this kind of provision.

Are There Oral Agreements for Non-Disclosure?

It is *possible* to have enforceable oral agreements for confidentiality, but it's never advisable to rely on such agreements. While the courts have enforced such agreements on occasion, it is never smart to rely on an oral agreement to keep information confidential. The other party may deny that the agreement exists. There is also a risk that court may consider that someone who relies on oral promise of confidentiality is not using "reasonable means" to protect its trade secrets. And, of course, it may be very hard to prove with specificity the terms of an oral confidentiality agreement. So our advice is always: Get it in writing.

Disclosure Agreements that Are the Opposite of NDAs

Some companies use form documents that you might consider a kind of "anti-confidentiality agreement." They are designed to protect against a claim of wrongful use. These agreements are commonly used in the video game business and have language such as this:

We may, from time to time, receive submissions of material similar to yours, or we may be developing similar products. You agree that we are not bound to treat as confidential your idea or any information that you may choose to disclose to us during the course of our evaluation whether or not marked as confidential or proprietary.

Our acceptance of your material for evaluation does not imply that we will market your material nor does it prevent us from marketing or developing other products that may be similar in idea or concept so long as we do not infringe your copyright or patent rights.

We have included an example of such a prorecipient disclosure agreement in the form appendix to this book (Form 6-2).

When You Negotiate a Deal, Should NDAs Be Superseded?

When the parties move from talking about a possible relationship to actually negotiating the business agreement between them, we think it is the better practice to include a confidentiality clause in the business agreement that will supersede the NDA. We don't generally recommend agreements that have language that merely continues the existing NDA in effect. This is because most NDAs are written to facilitate discussions—not for an ongoing relationship. There are often new and different issues regarding confidentiality to be dealt with in the resulting agreement—and you are likely to miss these by just continuing the NDA in effect.

Confidentiality Clauses Generally

Many agreements have confidentiality provisions. The same considerations that we discussed with regard to NDAs should be considered when you craft any agreement that includes Confidential Information. Remember that restraints on misuse of your Confidential Information may be a key strategic and competitive factor in any agreement.

You should also pay very close attention to how confidentiality clauses in your various agreements may interact with other clauses—particularly clauses regarding limitations on consequential damages and damage caps. If you are not careful, you may find out that your agreement limits or even eliminates any money damage remedy for breach of confidentiality by the other party. Claims for breach of confidentiality obligations are often important exceptions or "carve-outs" from liability limitation clauses. You can find more on this topic in Chapter 8.

VIOLATIONS OF TRADE SECRET LAW

Let's assume that you have protected your trade secrets by all the requisite reasonable measures. What protection then do you get under trade secret law? (Remember that this protection is in addition to whatever remedies might apply under contract law.)

Trade secret law provides protection only against wrongful appropriation, disclosure, or use of trade secrets. The key word in that sentence is "wrongful." There are improper ways of obtaining and exploiting the trade secrets of another person that are illegal—and there are proper ways that are perfectly lawful under trade secret law.

What Is Illegal under Trade Secret Law?

Violations of trade secrets involve wrongful acquisition, use, or disclosure of another's trade secret. Here are some examples of trade secret violations:

- Obtaining secrets by industrial espionage

- Breaking into another company's computer systems and taking files

- Inducing an employee or former employee of another company to reveal trade secrets

- Receiving trade secrets from someone that the recipient knew (or should have known) is not entitled to disclose them

- Using or disclosing trade secrets in violation of your duty of good faith as a director or employee of a business

- Using or disclosing trade secrets in violation of an NDA or the confidentially clause of an agreement

All of these violations involve activities that the recipient should know to be improper.

What Is not Illegal under Trade Secret Law?

Here are some examples of what's not illegal under trade secret law:

- It is not a violation to replicate a trade secret by independent invention.

- It is not a violation to reverse engineer another product—unless you have validly agreed not to do so.

Be careful about reverse engineering. Software and hardware contracts often contain broad prohibitions against reverse engineering, and these clauses are usually enforceable in the United States. (In the European Union, you may have a statutory right to reverse engineer for the limited purpose of making an interoperable product.) This means that reverse engineering of software in many cases will be illegal under contract law even if it is permitted under trade secret law. (There is a discussion of copyright and contractual issues in reverse engineering in Chapter 3 of this book.)

What if Trade Secrets Are Disclosed?

If trade secrets are wrongfully disclosed and if the disclosure is limited, trade secret protection will usually not be lost. On the other hand, permitted publication or public disclosure will destroy any trade secret. Even illegal disclosure, if broad enough, will destroy trade secret status. If your former employee publishes your trade secrets on the Internet or if they show up on the *New York Times*, you can consider them gone. Your employee may be liable for damages, but you will no longer be able to get legal protection for the information under trade secret law.

DEALING WITH VIOLATIONS OF TRADE SECRETS

The most egregious violations of trade secrets are theft and espionage—but more common by far is wrongful use and disclosure of trade secrets by former employees (and their new employers), contractors, or "business partners."

When you know or strongly suspect that someone has violated your valuable trade secret rights, you should consider taking immediate steps to stop the violation, including litigation if necessary. Delay can be dangerous. If you do nothing, you risk letting your secrets circulate—and once they circulate, they are not secret anymore. Moreover, judges will likely rule later that if you didn't care enough about your secrets to enforce your rights promptly, the secrets probably do not deserve protection. You should seek legal advice immediately.

Sometimes the holder of a trade secret gets an early warning that there has been a violation or probably violation—as, for example, when a key scientist or engineer quits and immediately goes to work for a competitor where he or she begins work on a competing product. Sometimes it is only long after the fact that the violation manifests itself—for example, when the competing product hits the market and an examination of the product shows that a trade secret was wrongfully taken or used.

To prevail in these cases, as the purported wronged party, you must identify the trade secret, prove it is valuable, prove that it is protected by reasonable measures, and show the wrongful removal, use, or disclosure.

In trade secrets cases, the wronged party will seek injunctive relief or damages or both.

- Injunctive relief means a temporary or permanent court order that the other party stops using the trade secrets. Where a former employee or contractor has taken trade secrets, the trade secret owner may also seek a court order mandating a separation between the employee or contractor and the new employee—or ordering the employee to work only in areas unrelated to a trade secret technology.

- The wronged party may also be entitled to money damages to recover its lost profits or the wrongdoer's ill-gotten profits.

Remedies Short of Litigation

Let's say that you find that your senior employee has left and gone to a competitor—and you fear that your trade secrets are going with him or her. What can you do, without the expense of litigation, to stop third parties from wrongfully delivering trade secrets to a new employer? There are steps that you can take (with the advice of an attorney); although none of them provide absolute assurance that the trade secrets will be safe:

Notice to Respect Trade Secrets. If the threat of a trade secret violation is moderate, a pointed reminder of the employee's obligations may suffice. The employer may give the employee a written reminder of his or her trade secret obligation as a routine part of the exit interview process. Then the employer can follow up with a letter to the former employee and his or her new employer stating the areas of technology involved and insisting that the confidentiality agreement be adhered to. In either case, it is best to supply both the employee and the new employer with a copy of the employment agreement signed by the employee so that the new employer will understand that a wrongful disclosure will violate a contractual duty of the employee.

Demand for Measures to Prevent Disclosure. If the disclosure risk is high, a more forceful letter is called for. This sort of letter is meant to be part of a strategy in which litigation is a possible outcome, but the preferred goal is a negotiated solution in which the former employer obtains reasonable assurance that trade secrets will not be disclosed. Such a letter might state:

- That procedures should be put in place immediately at the new employer's business to prevent use or disclosure of trade secrets.

- That employees at the new company must be instructed not to discuss the subject matter of the trade secrets technology with the employee.

- That the former employee should be assigned only to work areas and to projects that are technologically distinct from and physically separate from any work area that might want to use any relevant trade secret information.

- That the new employer should confirm in writing that these safeguards will be put in place immediately and will remain in place for an agreed-upon period.

- That the former employee and the new employer should confirm in writing that no trade secrets have been or will be revealed.

- That litigation may result if suitable assurances are not received. (Note, however, that you should never threaten litigation unless you are absolutely prepared to follow through on the threat.)

The employer needs to discuss an overall strategy with counsel before sending any letter concerning a suspected trade secret violation. When nonlitigation methods fail, you must seriously consider prompt litigation.

IS TAKING TRADE SECRETS A CRIME?

In a number of states, it is a crime to wrongfully appropriate the trade secret information of another. There is a similar federal law, known as the "The Economic Espionage Act." The federal act is best known for provisions on trade secret theft for the benefit of foreign governments, but it also makes intentional appropriation of trade secrets a crime if the trade secret is "related to or included in a product that is produced for or placed in interstate or foreign commerce." This would cover almost all commercial products sold in the United States.

Criminal prosecutions in trade secret cases are relatively uncommon. Most trade secret litigation is civil, not criminal. Criminal prosecutions in trade secret cases are most likely to occur when there is a truly egregious violation that causes major harm. Criminal prosecution is also much more likely if there is other criminal activity involved as well. For example, if there was an illegal wiretap or a break-in or bribe to steal trade secret materials, then a prosecutor might become sufficiently interested to take action.

CAN SOFTWARE TRADE SECRETS BE LICENSED OR SOLD?

Where a company is selling technology, rather than just a software application, it is not unusual that trade secret techniques (or confidential know-how) are licensed. And trade secrets can also be sold by agreement. Licensing deals involving trade secrets are often similar in legal issues and in pricing structures to other digital technology licenses of the type discussed in this book. Because trade secrets are vulnerable to destruction by disclosure, any such agreement must include carefully crafted confidentiality provisions.

USE OF COUNSEL IN MANAGING TRADE SECRETS

Trade secrets are often key assets in a digital technology business. You should be sure that they are protected by confidentiality measures and by careful contracting. Your attorney can help you assess and improve your confidentiality practices, can advise you on trade secret protection, can help you include trade secrets in your strategic plans, and can help craft agreements that protect and extend the value of confidential technologies. Where there are threats to your trade secrets by employees or others, you should contact counsel without delay.

Confidentiality, Rights Transfer, and Non-Competition Agreements for Employees

7

Knowledge worker, a term coined by Peter Drucker in 1959, is one who works primarily with information or one who develops and uses knowledge in the workplace....

A knowledge worker's benefit to a company could be in the form of developing business intelligence, increasing the value of intellectual capital, gaining insight into customer preferences, or a variety of other important gains in knowledge that aid the business.

—From Wikipedia on "Knowledge Worker"

IN THIS CHAPTER

The topic of this chapter is employee agreements for technology business. Your technology company needs clear, reasonable, and legally enforceable form agreements with your employees to secure intellectual property for the company, protect your confidential information, and secure protection against competition. Employee agreements help secure for your company the value that employees create.

These agreements are fundamental for every technology company and using them should be a routine part of the hiring process at your company. Venture capitalists and other investors will insist on their being in place—so will any potential purchaser of your business. We recommend that these terms and conditions be used, to the maximum extent possible, with *all* employees from the CEO to interns and that you get them signed before the first day of work for each employee.

The discussion of employee agreements in this chapter is focused on agreements that you would use in the United States for persons who are "W-2 employees," that is, persons who are classified as employees under federal and state tax reporting. For similar agreements in foreign nations, you will need local legal advice. For similar issues in consulting and contractor agreements, see Chapter 10.

You will find in the Appendix in this book a form of employee agreement (Form 7-1) for technology companies. The contents of these form agreements may require changes to adapt it to your company's situation. In addition, as is discussed in this chapter, there are state laws that may affect whether an employee non-competition restraint is enforceable or unenforceable wholly or in part. For this reason, you should have your attorney advise you as to the right form (or forms) of employee agreement and any applicable state law rules.

A Note on Terminology

We attorneys generally make a distinction between "employee agreements" and "employment agreements." They sound the same but are different.

- **Employee Agreement**—This is a *form* agreement of the type that is the subject of this chapter. It covers topics such as the employee's obligations regarding confidential information and the company's ownership of intellectual property. The document often has postemployment restriction against competition with the company and against hiring company employees. It is a document that is focused on employee obligations, not on employee rights.

- **Employment Agreement**—This is a *negotiated* agreement (typically with a senior executive or lead technical employee) that includes employee compensation, title, responsibilities, minimum duration of employment, and benefits. An employment agreement may also include the subject matter of an employee agreement. Often an executive will sign a negotiated employment agreement and the form employee agreement.

The role of your legal counsel in these agreements is quite different:

- For the *employee agreement*, you use a lawyer to make sure you have the right form or forms in place. Thereafter, unless you need to change or update the form or you negotiate a special deal with an employee, you will use the agreement without further involvement of legal counsel.

- For an *employment agreement*, you will use your lawyer to help negotiate and fine tune each agreement with each key employee. There are a lot of legal issues in these agreements, and you will likely need legal advice on each one. Negotiated employment agreements are beyond the scope of the discussion that follows.

Because these terms sound so similar, they are sometimes confused, and you may see inconsistent use of these terms.

About Employment Law Generally

There are many topics covered in this book, but the general field of employment law is not one of them. Employment is a fundamental relationship in our society and one that is much regulated. It is also a legal specialty at our law firm and at many others. Employment law covers compensation, taxation, social security, health insurance, retirement plans, discrimination, sexual harassment, layoffs, unemployment insurance, privacy rights, wage and hour law, and many other topics. There are also many documents relevant to employment that are not covered here, such as offer letters, employment manuals, ethical rules, employee e-mail policies, and so forth. In Wikipedia, the page on "Employment Law" has links to 75 subtopics.

It goes without saying that every employer needs to learn the applicable state and federal employment rules that apply to its business. Every technology company should discuss with legal counsel and its accountant the fundamental rules of employment. You should consult counsel as needed when employment law issues arise. There are many laypersons' books on employment law that may help. The employee agreements discussed here are just one aspect—albeit an important one—of employment in the technology economy.

THE CONTENTS OF EMPLOYEE AGREEMENTS

Let's now turn the heart of our discussion, the provisions that are in an employee agreement and the reasons that they are there. The main subject matter of employee agreements are: confidentiality, intellectual property rights transfers and—often—non-competition and non-solicitation provisions.

Confidentiality Provisions

Employee agreements always contain confidentiality agreements. Here is why:

- Confidentiality has obvious advantages in competition and negotiation with customers.

- As discussed in Chapter 6, trade secret law protects your valuable non-public information only if you use reasonable efforts to keep it secret, including reasonable employee agreements.

- When your company holds confidential information of other companies, you will breach your contract with the other party unless your employees protect it.

- Public disclosure of information can often eliminate your ability to patent inventions, particularly outside the United States.

- If you do deals with public companies (or if your company is a public company), you may possess nonpublic information that under the securities laws it is illegal to disclose.

Confidentiality needs to be part of the culture of each technology company—and the employee agreement is one important ingredient in accomplishing that.

Definition of "Confidential Information"

In employee agreements, confidential information is always defined broadly to include all non-public information regarding the company and its business affairs. Here's a sample provision:

> *Confidential Information means any information or data, whether in oral, graphic, written, electronic, machine-readable or hard copy form, possessed by, used by, or under the control of the company that is not generally available to the public. Confidential Information includes but is not limited to inventions, designs, data, source code, object code, programs, other works of authorship, know-how, trade secrets, techniques, ideas, discoveries, technical, marketing and business plans, customers, suppliers, pricing, profit margins, costs, products, and services.*

You may want to add to the long descriptive list in this clause those information items that are particularly important to your business. For example, if your company made voice recognition software, the list might include "speech interpretation and generation methods and algorithms." If your company made stock market analytical software, you might add "securities analysis methods and techniques." And so forth.

In many technology agreements, we put "carve outs" or exceptions into confidentiality clauses—a listing of things that are *not* within the definition of Confidential Information. No carve-outs of this kind belong in employee agreements. The goal here is to keep in place the broadest definition. In case of doubt, the employee agreement should err in classifying information as confidential and subject to employer control. Some agreements add this additional provision:

> *Where the employee has any doubt whether information in his or her possession is confidential information, the employee shall request a determination from his or her supervision.*

Regarding Use and Protection of Confidential Information

Employee agreements restrict the use of your company's confidential business information and forbid unauthorized disclosure. Here is a typical provision:

> *Employee agrees not to make any unauthorized disclosure of any Confidential Information. Employee agrees not to make any use of any Confidential Information except in carrying out of his or her employment responsibilities.*

This general language is broad enough to cover third party information held in confidence by the company. Nonetheless many employee agreements contain provisions that expressly require the employee to treat third party confidential information as Confidential Information under the employee agreement:

> *Employee also agrees to preserve and protect the confidentiality of third party Confidential Information.*

Employee agreements require that employees return confidential information either at the employers' request or upon the termination or expiration of employment.

Confidentiality and Pre-Employment Communications

Employee agreements apply after hiring—that means they do not normally cover any confidential information given to employees *before* they were hired. If you are going to be discussing your technology and other confidential matters with the person that you are interviewing or to whom you have offered employment, the best practice is to have them sign your form of non-disclosure agreement before any confidential communications.

Provisions in Aid of Enforcement

If an employer learns that a former employee has taken confidential information after termination of employment in violation of the Agreement, the employer may send its lawyers to court to get an emergency court injunction. The injunction sought would normally be a court order that the former employee and the new employee cease immediately use of disclosure of the information. In some cases, the former employee may seek an order that the former employer not be permitted to work for the new employer in any role that would be likely to include use of confidential information.

Court orders of this kind are classified as "extraordinary relief." To get that injunction, the employer must demonstrate to the court that the harm is immediate (so that the matter cannot wait), that the harm to be stopped is irreparable (it cannot be fixed) and that money damages (also known as an "at law" remedy) are an inadequate remedy (recovering money would not solve the problem). To get a leg up on this relief, employment agreements usually have a clause such as the following:

> *Employee acknowledges that that immediate and irreparable damage will result to the Company and its business and properties if an employee breaches these confidentiality obligations and that the remedy at law for such breach will be inadequate. Accordingly, in addition to any other remedies and damages available, the Company shall be entitled to injunctive relief (without the necessity of posting a bond), and the employee may be specifically compelled to comply with his confidentiality obligations under this Agreement.*

These clauses will help the employer make its case, but they do not have any magic effect. The employer will still have to convince the judge that it really needs that injunction. Judges are obligated to rule on the facts and the law.

Why does the clause say that the injunction should be issued "without the necessity of posting a bond"? Sometimes an injunction turns out (when all the facts come out) to be unjustified. Judges frequently require a party that obtains an injunction to post a bond (which is a form of financial guarantee issued by a bonding company) to protect the enjoined party. If the injunction turns out to be wrongful, the judge will have the legal power to award compensation from the bond to the enjoined party. This clause in the employee agreement is the employer's attempt to get the injunction without the cost of bond. In spite of these words, judges would still have the power to require a bond as a condition of the injunction.

Capturing Intellectual Property Rights

Intellectual property rights generally include copyrights, patents, trade secret rights, and trademarks. A key function of employee agreements is to capture all of these rights that the employee may create for the employer. The normal way to do this is to define the "Work Product" that the employee will create and then provide for all rights in the Work Product to belong to the employer.

Here is a typical Work Product definition:

"Work Product" shall mean all items created or made, discoveries, concepts, ideas and fixed expressions thereof, past, present and future, whether or not patentable or registrable under copyright or other statutes, including but not limited to software, source and object code, hardware, technology, products, machines, programs, process developments, formulae, methods, techniques, know-how, data and improvements, which Employee makes or conceives or reduces to practice or learns alone or jointly with others that (1) are made, conceived, reduced to practice or learned during employment by the Company; (2) occur or have occurred during the period of, as a consequence of, or in connection with employment by the Company; (3) result from tasks assigned to Employee by the Company; or (4) result or have resulted from use of property, premises or facilities owned, leased or contracted for by the Company.

This is another provision that you could tailor to your business by including in the list of items those technologies or categories of secret information that are most important in your business.

Next comes the provision that is designed to make the Work Product the property of the employer:

Employee agrees that any Work Product shall be the property of the Company and, if subject to copyright, shall be considered a "work made for hire" within the meaning of the Copyright Act of the United States (the "Act"). If and to the extent that any such Work Product is not to be a "work made for hire" within the meaning of the Act, Employee hereby expressly assigns to Company all right, title and interest in and to the Work Product, and all copies thereof, and the copyright, patent, trademark, trade secret and all other intellectual property or proprietary rights in the Work Product.

You notice that this text treats copyright differently from other intellectual property and specifically declares it to be "work made for hire." There is an explanation in Chapter 2 of the "work made for hire" provisions of the US Copyright Act. As noted in Chapter 2, any works generated by a W-2 employee is automatically "work made for hire" under the Copyright Act. So this language mandates a legal result that ought to occur by default. This language is thus a form of legal backup. It is designed to supply a "work made for hire" agreement if, for some unforeseen reason, the default rule does not apply. As you see, all other intellectual property rights are *assigned* to the employer.

172 CHAPTER 7 Confidentiality, Rights Transfer

Employee agreements commonly have provisions that make it clear that the agreement does not cover employee works and inventions that the employee makes on his or her own time and unconnected with work. This is a fairness provision. Here is common language:

> *For clarification, the term "Work Product" does not apply to any invention, work product, or development which meets all of the following three conditions: (1) Employee does the work entirely without use of Company's facilities, property or resources, (2) Employee does the work entirely on his or her own time, and (3) the development does not relate to the Company's business or research or to its planned business or research. However, employee agrees to disclose to the Company during the term of his or her employment in confidence each invention in order to permit the Company to make a determination as to compliance by Employee with this Agreement.*

Special Rule for California and Certain Other States

There is a provision of California law that mandates that an employee to include provisions in employee agreements rather similar to the last provision that we discussed. This is Section 2870 of the California Labor Code, and it applies to "inventions" that the employee makes unconnected with his or her employment. Here is a typical California employment agreement text that addresses Section 2870:

> *The provisions above regarding ownership of Work Product do not apply to Employee's inventions which qualify for protection under California Labor Code ("Section 2870"). As currently in effect, Section 2870 covers inventions for which no equipment, supplies, facility or trade secret information of Company was used and which was developed entirely in Employee's own time, and (i) which does not relate, at the time of conception or reduction to practice of the invention, to the business of Company, or to Company's actual or demonstrably anticipated research or development, or (ii) which does not result from any work performed by Employee for Company. Employee agrees to disclose to Company during the term of his or her employment in confidence each invention in order to permit the Company to make a determination as to compliance by Employee with this Agreement. Employee acknowledges that it is the Employee's burden to prove that Section 2870 applies.*

As you can see from this text, Section 2870 allows the employer to require confidential disclosure to the employee of his or her inventions during the term of employment so that the employer can verify that Section 2870 applies. The wording of the provision closely follows the text of the statute.

There are very similar laws and required notices for employees in Illinois, Kansas, Minnesota, and Washington (state). See your attorney for the right form of employee agreement you have for employees who work in any of those states.

Cooperation in Rights Transfer

Employment agreements have provisions that require employees to cooperate in transfer of intellectual property rights to their employer. These provisions also permit the employer to sign documents on the employee's behalf if the employer cannot locate the employee or if the employee is uncooperative. These provisions are needed because patent rights, under US law, vest in the inventor. Patent applications become the employer's property only when the employee assigns them. So these cooperation provisions come in handy in situations where the employee cannot or will not sign the necessary documents. Here is sample text for this rather technical provision:

> *Employee will, during his/her employment and at any time thereafter, at the request and cost of the Company, execute all such documents and perform all such acts and provide such cooperation as the Company may reasonably require (i) to apply for, transfer, obtain, and preserve in the name of the Company (or its designee) any patents, copyrights or other intellectual property or proprietary rights and (ii) to assist in any proceeding or litigation regarding such intellectual property or proprietary rights.*

> *In the event that the Company is unable for any reason to secure Employee's signature through reasonable effort on any assignment or application or other document or instrument that the Company requires regarding intellectual property or proprietary rights, Employee hereby irrevocably appoints the Company and its duly authorized officers and agents as his/her agent and attorney-in-fact, to act for and on his or her behalf to execute and file any such documents and to do all other lawfully permitted acts to further the assignment, prosecution and issuance of patents, copyrights and other intellectual property or proprietary rights with the same legal force and effect as if personally executed by Employee.*

Documents and Records

Employee agreements also have provisions to secure for the company the relevant documents and records that the employee prepares during the term of employment. Here is typical language:

> *All written materials, records, data, and other documents prepared or possessed by Employee during Employee's employment by the Company are the Company property.*

At the termination of Employee's employment with the Company for any reason, Employee shall return all of the Company's materials, records, data, and other documents, together with all other Company property.

NONCOMPETITION AND NONSOLICITATION PROVISIONS

Noncompetition provisions restrict ex-employees from working for your competitors. Nonsolicitation provisions restrict ex-employees from soliciting your customers for business or luring away your employees. We lawyers refer to noncompetition and nonsolicitation provisions together as "restrictive covenants."

Employees do not like restrictive covenants because they limit their freedom. However, these provisions are very commonly used by digital technology companies. Here are some ways that restrictive covenants can help your business:

- Restrictive covenants can lessen the impact of losing key technical and sales personnel.

- Investors in your business—and potential purchasers of your business—will expect you have restrictive covenants in place.

- Restrictive covenants work together with confidentiality provisions. If your company's ex-employee does not work for your competitor, your secrets will be safer.

State with Limitations on Restrictive Covenants

There is a widespread myth that the restrictive covenants are unenforceable—perhaps this is employees' wishful thinking. Under the laws of most states, restrictive covenants are enforceable—although the employee will need to prove they are needed and fair. (The general tests for enforceability are discussed below.)

However, in one state, California, restrictive covenants in employment agreements are generally unenforceable. This is because of California Civil Code Section 16600, first adopted in 1872, that says: "every contract by which anyone is restrained from engaging in a lawful profession, trade, or business of any kind is to that extent void." In spite of the "every contract" language, California may permit restrictive covenants in employee agreements to the limited extent that the court finds them necessary to protect the employer's trade secrets.

The California limit on restrictive covenants is important because of the large number of digital technology companies that operate in that state. Because of this law, restrictive covenants are much less common in California than in other high-tech economy states such as Virginia, Texas, North Carolina, or Massachusetts. Many companies with national operations that have major operations in California omit restrictive covenants from their employment agreements nationwide.

There are other states that permit restrictive covenants—but limit them under state statutes in various ways. The limitations may include duration (how long the restriction can last) and what they can protect (primarily limiting them to protecting secret information). States that have statutes limiting restrictive covenants (as of the time that this is written in 2007) are Colorado, Louisiana, Hawaii, Missouri, Montana, North Dakota, Oklahoma, Oregon, Nevada, and South Dakota.

About Consideration

When your company enters into a restrictive covenant with an employee, the agreement will be binding on the employee only if, under applicable state law, there is "consideration" for the agreement. "Consideration" is something of value given for a promise. The law of what constitutes sufficient consideration varies from state to state. Your attorney can tell you the rule that applies in states where your business has operations.

Here is an overview of the rules that apply in most states:

- When at-will employment is the only consideration for a restrictive covenant, the agreement must be executed when the employee is first hired as a condition of employment.

- If the restrictive covenant is executed later (after hiring), then in most states, in addition to continued employment, the employer must provide the employee with something extra. The something extra could be a cash bonus (this is the most common), extra training, stock options, or another benefit—but it will count as consideration only if the employee would not otherwise have been entitled to the benefit. It is important that the consideration be specifically identified in the employee agreement. There are some states, however, in which continued employment without more is sufficient.

Getting Employees to Sign

Some companies fail to get these agreements in place in early days of their operations—and then find that key employees resist signing any employee agreement with a restrictive covenant.

We have found that a good way to deal with this is to tie signing the restrictive covenant agreements to stock option grants. If the employee won't sign the employee agreement, he or she gets no options. In our experience, most employees will sign with this inducement. It is good practice to have employee signatures witnessed.

Enforceability of Provisions

Even where restrictive covenants are generally permitted, the courts will enforce them only when justified. Two factors generally determine whether a restriction is enforceable: (1) the nature of the employment and (2) the reasonableness of the restrictions. This means that enforcement will never be automatic in court.

The Nature of the Employment

The courts generally enforce restrictive covenants against only two types of employees:

- *Employees who have access to trade secrets or confidential information—usually technical and scientific employees.* The rationale is that the restraint preserves legitimate trade secrets. To enforce restrictions on this theory requires proof (1) that the employer actually has trade secrets, (2) that the employee knows the secrets, and (3) that the employer otherwise protects trade secrets with reasonable security measures.

- *Employees who have gained customer loyalty—usually sales staff.* The rationale is that the restraint allows the employer to protect its customer relationships. In this case, enforcement of the restriction requires proof (1) that customer contacts are important in the employer's business and (2) that the employee had significant customer contact on the job.

Both these factors are matters of proof. When the employer wants to enforce a restrictive covenant against an employee, it will be the employer's burden to show that these factors apply.

Reasonable Scope and Duration

There is another important limitation on restrictive covenants. The courts enforce agreements only if they are reasonable in duration and geographic scope. This rule is a balancing test—pitting the employer's need for protection against the employee's interest in employment freedom.

- **Duration of Restrictive Covenants**—Normally a one-year restraint is considered reasonable. In many states, when good reason is shown, two-year restraints are enforced. A three-year restraint is a stretch but will be allowed for good cause in some states. In general, the shorter the restraint, the more likely that it will be enforced.

- **Geographic Scope**—The court will expect the restraint to be limited to a relevant area. Technical employees and sales employees may have very different relevant geographic areas. For a company with global competition, it may make sense to have a global restraint on a technical staff member's employment with a competitor. If a sales person has only a local territory, you may want to have his or her non-competition restraint cover just the same territory. Some businesses have different forms for sales and technical staff members.

Here is the text of a typical non-competition provision:

Except with the prior written consent of Company, during his or her employment with Company and for a period of one year after that employment ends, Employee will not directly or indirectly run, operate, control, be employed by, hold an interest in or participate in the management, operation, ownership or control of any business if such business is in competition with Company [in the following geographic area: ___]. As used in this Agreement, "business" includes any corporation, company, association, partnership, limited partnership, or other entity. Notwithstanding the above, Employee will not violate this Agreement solely by owning less than one (1) percent of the publicly traded shares of a competing business.

Getting these limitations correct is primarily a matter of thoughtful and careful drafting. If you craft provisions that don't overreach, you are more likely to be able to enforce them in court.

The Non-Competition Clause

Here is typical language for non-solicitation provisions that covers customers:

> Nonsolicitation of Customers and Prospects. *Except with the prior written consent of Company, during his or her employment with Company and for a period of one (1) year after that employment ends, Employee will not directly or indirectly, either for himself or herself or for any other business or person, solicit, call upon, attempt to solicit or attempt to call upon any of the customers or prospective customers of Company with whom Employee has had contact while employed at Company, and Employee will not accept any business from such customers or prospective customers of Company for his or herself or for any employer during such period.*

When you hire a salesperson, don't be surprised if he or she says: "I own my contacts." You may need to compromise on your non-solicitation language when hiring sales personnel. A common way to do this is to edit the text to exclude customers resulting from the salesperson's pre-existing contacts.

Here is typical language for non-solicitation provisions that covers solicitation of other employees:

> Non-Solicitation of Employees. *Except with the prior written consent of Company, during his or her employment with Company and for a period of one (1) year after that employment ends, Employee will not solicit or have any discussion with any employee of Company concerning employment for any business other than Company, and Employee will not induce or attempt to influence any employee of Company to terminate his or her employment with Company.*

Automatic Extension of Restricted Period

Often the restrictive covenant will include a provision stating that if an employee violates her non-compete or non-solicitation obligation, the duration of the restrictions shall be extended by the length of the breach. This clause is designed to take away the benefit of any cheating.

The "Blue Pencil"

If a restrictive covenant is too broad, in some states it will be unenforceable. In other states the judge will have the power (but not the obligation) to adjust or "blue pencil" the restriction. What this means is that a court will narrow the restriction and enforce it as rewritten. To encourage the court to save restrictive covenants in this way, many employee agreements include text like this:

> *If any restriction set forth in this Section is found by any court of competent jurisdiction to be unenforceable because it extends for too long a period of time or over too*

great a range of activities or in too broad a geographic area, it shall be interpreted to extend only over the maximum period of time, range of activities or geographic area for which it may be enforceable.

If the judge does "blue pencil" the agreement, the judge will be deciding how much of a restriction is fair as applied to the particular employee under all the circumstances.

Enforcement of Noncompetition Agreements by Employers

What do you do if you think that your company's ex-employee is violating a restrictive covenant? This section will explore your options.

Don't Delay in Addressing a Breach

If you discover that an ex-employee is breaching a restrictive covenant, call an attorney who knows employment litigation without delay. Both the practical and legal remedies may evaporate if you wait too long. How long is too long? There is no fixed rule, but even a few weeks delay means that your trade secrets have been spilled everywhere and your legal case for an injunction could be impaired.

Remedies Short of Litigation

What can you do, before starting litigation, to stop a former employee from violating an employee agreement? Generally speaking, the best bet is to send to both the former employee and the new employer a demand letter insisting that the former employee and the new employer observe the restraint. Sometimes it will be sufficient if the new employer promises specified compliance, for example, that a salesperson will be given a territory different from that which is forbidden in the agreement. In other cases, there is no adequate remedy other than separation of the former employee from his or her new job at the new company.

Any demand letter should be written by your legal counsel or approved by your attorney before it is sent. Together with the letter, the former employer should send to both the former employee and the new employer a copy of the restrictive covenant. A demand letter will normally state that litigation will result if the adequate assurances of compliance are not forthcoming. Of course, a company should never threaten litigation unless it is prepared to follow through.

The Preliminary Injunction

Like trade secret and employee agreement confidentiality clause cases (with which they are often combined), litigation on the basis of a restrictive covenant normally turns on a preliminary injunction hearing. For this reason, these cases may be relatively inexpensive as litigation goes. In most cases, the decision on the preliminary injunction (or an expedited appeal of a preliminary injunction decision) is effectively the end of the case, one way or the other. The party that won the opening round usually has a strong advantage in settlement talks.

The "smell" of the case plays an important role. If the employee has walked away with papers, disks or other property of the former employer, downloaded files, or has otherwise failed to leave "clean," a preliminary injunction enforcing a restrictive covenant will be easier to get. Similarly if the employee was your company's top scientist and he went to a direct competitor, that will help get the injunction.

If the court issues a preliminary injunction, what will the injunction require? Normally the court will order, in quite specific terms, that the restrictive covenant must be complied with. The court has great discretion in fashioning relief, but it is common that the court will be guided by the terms of the covenant.

Obtaining Assurance of the Absence of Conflicting Prior Agreements

Prior to hiring an employee, you should do your best to ensure that he or she is not subject to any restrictive covenants with prior employers. Be sure to ask every prospective employee about this subject. Sometimes employees are not aware that they are subject to a restrictive covenant with a current or former employer either because they do not have copies of the written agreements that they have signed or, if they do, they do not understand the provisions. Ask about restrictive covenants when talking to a prospective employee's references if they are former employers.

Employee agreements often include clauses that provide the employee's assurance that he or she is not breaching a prior employee agreement. Here is what this type of provision looks like:

> *Employee represents that entering into employment with the Company under this Agreement does not constitute a breach of any contract, agreement or understanding and that Employee is free to enter into the employ of Company. Employee promises to (a) remain in full compliance with the terms of any agreement with any previous employer or other party and (b) to refrain from using or disclosing to the Company any trade secret or confidential information of such previous employer or other party.*

What do you do if you find out that a prospective employee is subject to a legally enforceable restrictive covenant? If you go ahead and hire the person, you may be sued for inducing the employee to breach her restrictive covenant.

If a job applicant is potentially valuable and if there is a problem with a contract that the applicant has signed with a past employer, you will need to consult with legal counsel. Counsel will do the requisite analysis—looking at the agreement itself, at the facts, and at the law—and determine the legal risk. Needless to say, this should be done *before* offering the applicant a job.

Introduction to Digital Product and Service Contracts

8

Con·tract (kŏn'trăkt) 1. An agreement between two or more parties, especially one that is written and enforceable by law .... 2. The writing or document containing such an agreement.

—American Heritage Dictionary

Digital companies live and grow through contracts.

A few contracts can change a company's destiny. Microsoft's first operating system was MS-DOS 1.0, a legendary world-changing success. Yet Microsoft did not originate MS-DOS. Bill Gates learned in 1980 that IBM was having trouble finding an operating system for its planned IBM-PC. There was a small development shop, Seattle Computer Products (SCP), that had written an operating system called QDOS (for "quick and dirty disk-operating system") in just six weeks. In September 1980, Microsoft made an agreement with SCP to license QDOS on a non-exclusive basis for $25,000. Microsoft then sublicensed the software to IBM. In July 1981, a month before the launch of the first IBM PC, Microsoft shrewdly acquired all rights to QDOS from SCP for an additional $50,000. Through two contracts for $75,000, Microsoft obtained exclusive control of the operating system for the IBM-PC. Renamed MS-DOS, it ended up in tens of millions of PCs and was the basis of a worldwide computing empire.

A successful software or digital technology company may enter into thousands of contracts. Mass market software companies make tens of millions of contracts. Contracts manage relationships with suppliers, business customers, distributors, partners, and consumers. This book surveys many, but certainly not all, of the categories of digital technology agreements.

Mass market contracts are accepted with a click. But many contracts are the subject of negotiation. Contract negotiations are an art, a combination of law, tactics, market savvy, risk analysis, and sales psychology. You want to "make hay" but not "give away the farm." You want to obtain opportunities but manage risk. This chapter is about how to accomplish these goals. This chapter is a "must read" for anyone that engages in negotiations or is involved in deals. This chapter is also a conceptual guide for chapters that follow and discuss deals of various types.

Forms contracts are essential tools. You are encouraged to find and use them. But they will do you little good, and indeed can hold many traps for you, unless you have an understanding of the contractual concepts and language that they contain.

IN THIS CHAPTER

In this chapter, you will find an introduction to the principles that underlie crafting and negotiating contracts that digital companies use to obtain, develop, distribute, and license software and digital products and services of all kinds. The chapters that follow will then cover specific types of commercial transactions and deals: end-user agreements, consulting and IT service agreements, distribution deals, shrinkwraps and "clickwraps," software-as-a-service agreements, game publishing agreements, and so forth. The basic principles in this chapter are relevant to those digital deal types—and many more.

In this chapter, you will find three distinct contract topics:

- First, some basic concepts of contract law as applied to software and other digital product and service deals

- Second, a survey of the key sections, clauses, and provisions that are found in most digital product and service contracts

- Third, a discussion of the bargaining process and techniques for contract negotiations

This chapter is not a substitute for a course in basic contract law or digital technology agreements. This chapter cannot replace the assistance of a skilled lawyer with experience in drafting and negotiating digital technology agreements. This chapter will, however, help make you better-informed and more effective deal negotiator and a smarter consumer of legal services. The result should be better deals at lower cost.

There are other bodies of law that might be relevant to agreements (and might affect particular deal terms) that will not be discussed in this chapter, such as antitrust law, securities law, bankruptcy law, consumer protections law, privacy law, corporate law, the law of taxation, and so forth. This chapter is a discussion of contracts under US law, with reference (only in passing) to the law of other nations and cross-border deals. (You will find more on this subject of foreign law in Chapter 23, which is about "going global.")

In the form Appendix to this book, you will find many sample agreements of various types. Reviewing these sample agreements will give you additional insight into the way contracts work.

The words "contract" and "agreement" have the same meaning. When writing and negotiating these deals, lawyers more commonly use the term "agreement" because it sounds friendlier. In court of law, lawyers are more likely to call them "contracts." You will find the terms used interchangeably in this book. In this chapter, for convenience, we call the company that is supplying software the "vendor" (meaning a seller) although in fact digital technology companies usually *license* their digital products and *sell* their services.

FIRST TOPIC: CONTRACT CONCEPTS

Contract law allows individuals and businesses to make legally binding promises. It is based on the concept of freedom of contract—the idea that making commercial promises enforceable is both fair and beneficial to society. Contracts are primarily governed by state law in the United States.

Contracts arise from a process of "offer and acceptance." This is the process by which the parties agree to a bargain. A contract can cover a commercial interaction that is completed in a few moments or govern a complex business relationship that lasts for years. A contract can cover one transaction or millions of transactions. A contract can govern rights for an instant or day or forever.

Practically speaking, contracts serve two functions. First, contracts act as guidebooks for the parties; the parties can consult the contract to find out their rights and determine what actions are required or optional, allowed or forbidden. Second, contracts act as binding legal rules for a judge, jury, or arbitrators in deciding a dispute between the parties and awarding legal remedies. In contract drafting and negotiations, you need to keep your eye on both functions at all times.

Limits to Freedom of Contract

There are contracts that are illegal (for example, contracts to gamble in most states) and restrictions on contracting (such as antidiscrimination laws or laws on unfair business practices), but within very broad limits, contracts are limited only by the will of the parties and their ability to reduce their bargain to writing.

Contracts Are Binding and Enforceable

There are reasons to abide by contractual obligations that have nothing to do with legal remedies. Keeping your word builds solid relationships. Satisfied customers will recommend your business to others.

On the other hand, it is important to understand that contracts have legal force. There is a saying: "The wheels of justice are slow, but they grind exceedingly fine." The mechanisms for resolution of contract disputes in the justice system are time-consuming and expensive, but in the end the law can often provide a strong remedy against a party found to have breached a contract in a serious way. The most common remedy for breach of contract is what the law calls a "judgment" for "money damages." This means an award of money—or more precisely the legal right to collect money from the party found liable.

Where there is a judgment for money damages, the power of the law is considerable. If the money is not paid, the holder of the judgment can use the judicial process to seize the losing party's assets and have them sold at a sheriff's sale or push the losing party's business into receivership. Losing parties that have exhausted all appeals can be forced to pay up if they have the resources to do so and may end up in bankruptcy if they do not.

In some situations, particularly those involving unauthorized use of intellectual property (IP), the courts will issue an "injunction," a court order requiring a party to cease and desist from a particular course of action. In some cases, but less commonly, the courts will issue "mandatory injunctions," which are court orders requiring a party to perform some or all of its obligations. A party that disobeys a court order may be cited by the judge for civil contempt, which can result in fines or in extreme cases, incarceration of the recalcitrant party until he or she obeys the court. Most parties understand that they have to obey court orders.

This is why it is important to write agreements carefully. It is also why risk limitation clauses in agreements are very important. Indeed, it is sometimes the case that a rather grievous breach of contract is not worth suing over because of tight risk limitation clauses. Your lawyer can help you evaluate the risk of contractual failures and understand what is the likely outcome and options if an agreement goes bad.

Oral and Written Agreements

Attributed to Film magnate Louis Mayer is the saying: "Oral contracts are not worth the paper they are written on." In fact, many oral contracts are enforceable, while many are not. (The rules on binding and non-binding oral contracts are technical and can depend on the subject matter of the agreement, the amount to be paid, or duration of the contract.)

If you are not careful, if you shake hands on a deal before the contract is drafted, if you declare that a deal has been made, you might make an oral contract. After you've made this type of statement—and after you have refused to sign the "confirming" contract draft that the other side sent—it is easy to spend a great deal of money litigating whether you have a contract or not.

Oral contracts and handshake deals have always been a fertile field for litigation. Where there are no records of a bargain, either side is free to invent or elaborate on the facts. Even well meaning people may have their recollection of a conversation colored by their self-interest. Oral contracts are also dangerous for what they leave out. For example, in most written contracts to license software or other digital products the vendor will disclaim warranties and limit liability. Informal oral contracts invariably leave such matters out.

You should avoid making bargains orally. Every contract you make—from a transfer of a single software copy, to distribution deals, to the sale of your business—should be made in writing and done carefully. This applies to contracts with long-time business partners as well as strangers. A deal is made when you sign.

Trust but Verify

All promises made by the parties should be in the written contract. You should be wary of undocumented side promises. Ronald Reagan's famous motto, in dealing with Gorbachev on nuclear arms reduction deals, was "Trust, but verify." That wise advice should always be in your mind when documenting deals. If a promise is made, verify it by adding the promise to the agreement. If someone wants to leave a promise undocumented, it is a sign of trouble to come.

Contracts Are More than the Words

Written contracts are best. But it is also important to understand that there is often more to contracts than what you read on the written page. In some cases, wording has specialized or customary meanings that laypersons might not expect. In some cases, the omission that you might not notice can give the agreement an unexpected meaning. There are default rules (some are discussed below) that may apply when your contract is silent to "fill in the gaps" or supply additional rules—so your contract might include rules that you never discussed or considered. Under some circumstances, provisions that you might write will be void because they are illegal, overreaching, or against public policy. In some cases, your contract may be affected by law external to your agreement, such as the Patent Act or the Copyright Act. Some provisions of the contract may interact with others in ways that you did not anticipate.

The principles and examples in this book will help you with these issues and reduce the risk of the unknown in your contracts—but not end this risk altogether.

LOI and MOUs

On the path to a contract, particularly for deals with some complexity, preliminary documents that outline the proposed deal are often used. These documents are called "term sheets," "letters of intent," or the like. No matter what these kinds of documents are called, they should include the word "non-binding" in the text as well as in the title (for example, "Non-Binding Letter of Intent"). We have seen clients who signed hastily drafted documents end up in wasteful disputes or litigation over whether preliminary documents are or are not binding contracts.

If you sign a quick-and-dirty document that is or might be binding, you will usually be rolling the dice with your business. That is because the terms of these documents are often ambiguous and incomplete. These documents often lack the risk-limiting clauses and disclaimers that we discuss below. They may have loose or incorrect allocations of IP. In short, they can pave the road to litigation.

Watch out in particular for a "Memorandum of Understanding" or "MOU." The term "memorandum" means a record and "understanding" means agreement; so an MOU is a record of an agreement—in other words, MOU means "contract." (Sometimes, we hear the redundant term "Binding MOU.") MOU documents are almost always binding agreements.

If you (or your sales staff) want to sign MOUs, you can do it, but be very careful. Often an MOU recites that it is binding and calls for negotiation of a more formal "definitive agreement" within 30 or 60 days. In our experience, the follow-on definitive agreements often do not get signed, and the parties are left with an ambiguous or incomplete contract.

When a client wants to sign an MOU, we normally suggest a "Non-Binding Letter of Intent" instead. There are some circumstances when the binding MOU is needed because there is no time to negotiate anything else. If our client wants a binding MOU, we will make sure that it is edited before signing—and we will add in protective disclaimers and risk-limiting clauses. In other words, we will try to make the MOU less risky for our client. This will provide some assurance that when the deal blows-up—as hasty deals often do—there will be limitations on our clients' contractual risk exposure.

Another legal tip: getting good legal counsel involved early in important deals can avoid legal problems later on. That is because knowledgeable counsel can help structure the deal to avoid traps.

The Myth of the Two-Page Contract

Albert Einstein said that "Things should be made as simple as possible, but no simpler." This certainly applies in contracting. Many times a client has brought us a complex multiyear distribution deal and wanted a "simple two-page agreement." Sometimes, they even ask for a one-page deal! The ostensible goal is to cut down negotiation time. But for most negotiated deals, it is a myth that adequate contracts can be super-short in this way. If the lawyer tries to comply (and we have tried), the result will almost always be to make the deal ambiguous.

The wish for a super-short agreement is a reaction to the unfortunate fact that the world is full of hopelessly bloated agreements produced (alas) by the legal profession. These documents are full of verbose legalese, convoluted paragraph-long sentences, unneeded Latinate words, and redundancies.

It is possible to cut away the bloat of legalese with careful, tighter drafting and use of plain English and make contracts better and shorter. But if the trimming goes too far and core language is cut, the text will be increasingly imprecise. Then there will be an increased risk that a judge or jury will get the meaning of the deal wrong in ligation or that important issues will not be addressed at all.

Managing complex deals full of contingencies with as imprecise a tool as the English language is tough enough; it is not prudent to try (or to force your lawyer to try) to make agreements more risky than they have to be.

Contracts, Company Sales, Investments, and Due Diligence

Poorly drafted contracts can hurt your business in two ways. First, the deal itself may go bad, with the failure caused by the mistakes that you made in the contract or its unclear or unfavorable language. Second, the deal can hurt you when you sell your company or seek to raise capital. This is because the prospective buyer or investor will have its lawyers scrutinize all your significant contracts—in the pretransaction examination process known as "due diligence." Therefore, in addition to the gaze of the judge and jury, your contracts need to be ready for the scrutiny of a buyer or investor's legal counsel.

No "Agreements to Agree"

In our law, there is no such thing as an "agreement to agree." Very often parties would like to sign what appear to be contracts with essential terms to be filled in later "by mutual agreement"—for example, features of a product to be developed. If the parties fail later to agree, they are likely to find that the document they signed is entirely unenforceable—a failed attempt at a contract. This is the result even if both parties really intended to enter into a binding contract.

The reason for this result is that the courts do not want to write contract terms for parties that fail to do so. The general rule is that every "essential" term of an agreement must be agreed to in the contract. In simple contracts, the law may allow the court to fill in the gaps by assuming market pricing for commodity products or "reasonable" delivery times. But parties cannot leave open the nature of the product to be delivered or the price of a custom product.

There is a work-around for the "agreement to agree" problem. Your attorney can draft contracts that operate in stages, with provisions for termination if the parties fail to reach agreement on the next stage.

Your attorney can help you avoid "agreements to agree" and reduce the risk that your agreements will be found unenforceable in this way.

Form Agreements for Your Business

If you are a vendor of software or digital products or services, you will need a set of forms for the transactions that are most common to your business. These might include end-user licenses, reseller agreements, online software-as-a-service agreements, non-disclosure agreements and other forms. You will find that you can cut negotiation time and expense if you make these forms easy to read, use more "plain English" and make them less one-sided. Also you can have a "play book" of preapproved attachments and variations that can be cut-and-pasted into your form agreements.

Sometimes, the other party will just sign your company's standard form. On the other hand, for significant deals between sophisticated companies, standard forms are rarely sufficient. Usually adjustments are needed to conform the pre-existing text to the current deal terms. The back-and-forth process of contract negotiation changes them much more.

CONCEPTUALIZING THE CONTRACT

While there is an endless variety of digital technology contracts, there are concepts and themes that repeat. Let us present a conceptual framework that will give you a way of thinking about the clauses we find in an agreement. We divide the parts of a contract into four elements:

- Core Economic Bargain

- Rules of Behavior

- Contingencies and Risk Allocation

- Mechanics and Boilerplate

These categories are discussed in detail below.

First: the Core Economic Bargain

You can think of the Core Economic Bargain as the provisions that express the basic commercial terms of a deal—who gets what and who pays what. This category could include:

- Deliveries of software, other digital goods, or services

- Development, installation, or customization of software

- Acceptance rules

- Price and payment

- Maintenance and support
- The license grant or access rules for online services and its limitations
- Transfer or ownership of IP
- The duration of the deal.
- Warranties of quality

There are basic business terms that most every business person will find easy to understand.

Second: the Rules of Behavior

The Rules of Behavior specify how the parties (sometimes, just the licensee) are supposed to behave or use technology. For example:

- No unauthorized copying
- No "service bureau use"
- No reverse engineering
- No disclosure of confidential information
- Required cooperation

You can think of these as rules and restrictions to prevent activities that may undermine the bargain.

Third: the Contingencies (Risk Allocation)

These are the provisions about events that are likely low probability, but will have a large impact if they occur. For example:

- IP warranties and indemnification
- Breach, express remedies, and early termination
- Disclaimer and remedy limitations
- Force majeure ("Act of God" clauses)

- Source code escrow

- Effect of termination

- Procedures for disputes

- Jurisdiction for disputes

- Assignments and changes of control

Fourth: the Mechanics and Boilerplate

These provisions provide for the administration of the Agreement. Here are some examples of this category.

- Audit rights

- Notice

- Nature of relationship ("independent contractor" clause)

- Waivers

- Entire agreement clause

Some Limits to this Conceptual Framework

This framework is an aid for analysis and understanding, but has its limits:

- This analysis follows in part the order that we use in the United States to write agreements, but it does not match up exactly. For example, the duration of a license is a key value term, but it is often stuck near the end of the Agreement. IP ownership provisions may be put in the middle. So the logical way to think about deals and the conventional order in which we write them is often not the same.

- We need to understand provisions conceptually, but it is also important to know that some provisions have technical and seemingly stylized language that is based on legal custom and culture. In a few cases, there are formulations of language that are akin to "magic words" that you have to use.

With this overview in mind, let's take a deeper look at these types of provisions—after two short digressions.

Note about the Uniform Commercial Code

Let me introduce you to an important statute. It is called the Uniform Commercial Code or "UCC." The relevant part of the UCC is Article 2, which is about sales of goods. UCC Article 2 has been adopted as the law in all states except Louisiana and is in force also in the District of Columbia, the Virgin Islands, and Puerto Rico—so it functions as America's law of sales.

If UCC Article 2 is about *sales*, why is it relevant to *licensing* of software and digital products? The UCC predates the digital world, but judges have used it for digital products anyway. Court decisions regularly interpret Article 2 to cover most software licensing, with the exception of custom-programmed software. Even when the UCC does not apply, for example in contracts that are predominantly for services, it may be used by court as a source of principles to apply by analogy.

UCC Article 2 covers many important aspects of licensing contracts including contract formation, interpretation, performance, warranties, and remedies. Much of the statute is quite technical and beyond the scope of this book. However, there are some key UCC provisions regarding warranties and damages that are discussed below. It is important to understand that the UCC applies by default, which means that your contracts may include UCC provisions, particularly as "gap fillers," even if you never thought about the UCC when you did your negotiation.

About UCITA

There is another so-called "uniform" statute that you may have heard about. It is called the Uniform Computer Information Transaction Act or "UCITA." UCITA is widely regarded as a botched experiment in legislation about digital technology agreements. We mention UCITA only because it may affect your contracting under the laws of Virginia and Maryland.

UCITA was proposed in 1999 and was specifically written to cover only contracts involving software and digital products. UCITA was widely criticized (rightly or wrongly) as a big software vendors' proposal that undermined consumer protections. UCITA was also criticized as unduly complex. The law was opposed by consumer groups and the attorneys general of many states.

As a proposed uniform law, UCITA was a flop. Only Virginia and Maryland adopted UCITA, and there is no movement in other states to pass it. A few states have expressly disapproved it. In our law firm, when we do contracts under

Virginia or Maryland law involving digital content or technology, we normally include a provision that:

The Uniform Computer Information Transaction Act (UCITA) will not apply to this Agreement.

(UCITA has a provision that allows parties to "opt-out" from its application.)

Because UCITA so rarely applies, we will not address its provisions here. If you have a contract under Virginia and Maryland law to which UCITA applies, you should consult legal counsel to understand its effect, if any, on your deal.

SECOND TOPIC: CONTRACT PROVISIONS

Now, let's take a look at the categories of clauses typically found in digital product and service contracting in the United States. We will go through them in the order that they are generally found in agreements, but we will also tie them into the four basic elements discussed above. Of course, not every contract has every one of these clauses—and some have provisions not discussed here.

In the following discussion, we look mainly at software products and service contracting. The same principles apply in deals involving digital content or online and mobile services. We will go into more detail on these variations in the chapters to come.

The following discussion includes some sample language. You can find examples of *all* provisions discussed below in the forms included in the Appendix to this book.

The Promised Performance

In most digital product and service contracting, you will find a promise of some kind of performance by each party. This is a key element of the economic bargain. For example, a vendor promises to deliver software, and the licensee promises to pay for it. Or, a software vendor agrees to supply packaged software to a reseller, and the reseller agrees to use commercially reasonable efforts to resell it.

In contract law, this undertaking to provide products or services is called the "promised performance." It is also sometimes called the "consideration." There is a general rule that commercial contracts (with some exceptions) cannot be unilateral—that each party to a contract must give or promise some consideration in order for the contract to be binding.

Most software contracts have one or more sections that discuss the promised performance. Usually the sections have titles that reflect the nature of the performance, such as "Delivery" or "Development Obligations." These clauses say: "Vendor will deliver…," "Vendor will develop and supply…," "Licensor agrees to ship to Licensee…," and so forth.

The promise can be an unqualified promise to provide—for example, "Vendor will develop and deliver the Software" or it can be just a promise to make an attempt—for example, "Vendor will make commercially reasonable efforts to develop and deliver." In the first case, failure to deliver is a breach; in the second, if the vendor has made a good faith attempt, it is not a breach.

The performance to be provided can vary enormously. It might include, for example:

- Development services (covered in Chapter 10)

- Delivery and customization of a business application (covered in Chapter 12)

- Software-as-a-service delivered through the Internet (covered in Chapter 13)

- A licensed content download (covered in Chapters 20 and 21).

Some Legal Tips on Promises

- Failure to perform the promise to any significant extent, unless cured as permitted in the contract, will usually be a breach of contract. The vendor's goal is to promise only performance that it is highly confident it can supply. Over-promising or loose language can be dangerous.

- The customer should make sure that the performance it expects from the vendor is accurately described in the contract.

- The promised performance may be controlled by milestones and specifications—matters that are discussed in Chapter 10 in the context of development and consulting agreements.

The Acceptance Clause

The acceptance clause provides for a process for the customer to determine whether or not it has received the promised digital product or service. Through the acceptance process, the customer validates the "value" received. Parties use acceptance procedures, which in some cases can be multistage and complex, when digital products are being developed, enhanced, customized, or installed.

The acceptance process normally includes "acceptance criteria" and may include "acceptance testing." There is usually a requirement that the customer lists any defects and gives the vendor a chance to cure them. Often the customer can terminate the contract and reject the product if the defects are not fixed.

This is what an acceptance clause looks like:

Customer will have fifteen (15) business days after receipt of any Deliverable to test and review such Deliverable ("Acceptance Period"). If Customer does not accept or reject a Deliverable within the Acceptance Period, such Deliverable will be deemed to be accepted by Customer. Acceptance by Customer shall not be unreasonably withheld. If a Deliverable does not materially comply with the specifications for such Deliverable ("Specifications") in material respects, Customer may reject such Deliverable by written notice of rejection to Supplier. Such notice will specify in detail the reasons the Deliverable fails to meet the relevant Specifications.

Supplier will use commercially reasonable efforts to correct any material deficiencies and provide Customer with a revised Deliverable fifteen (15) business days after receipt of such a notice of rejection.

Customer will have the right to accept or reject the corrected Deliverable in accordance with this Section. If Supplier does not correct a material deficiency after two cycles of this process, either party may elect to terminate this Agreement or the applicable Statement of Work in which event Customer's sole and exclusive remedy shall be to receive a refund of the fees paid to Supplier for the non-conforming Deliverable.

The License Grant

License means permission. The license grant is a fundamental element of the economic bargain in digital product contracting. A software license gives the licensee permission to do something with software, such as to use it, copy it, modify it, combine it with other products, or distribute it.

We sometimes analogize the IP rights that relate to a product or services as a "bundle of rights" and speak of a vendor as giving some (but not all) of those rights permanently or temporarily to the licensee. There are an endless variety of possible license grant clauses.

The Philosophy of License Grants

- From the vendor's point of view, licenses should be thoughtfully drawn and narrow. The vendor's goal, in crafting license grant clauses, is so-called "value licensing." The vendor wants to match the intensity of use of the software to the amount of money that the licensee pays. The more that licensee uses the software—the more copies installed, the more users, the more online access—the greater the license fee should be. Calculating the right measure of use and setting the pricing equation is an art.

- A corollary of the value-licensing concept is that the vendor wants to grant the licensee only the rights that the licensee really *needs* to use. From the vendor's viewpoint, all uses that are not expressly permitted should be forbidden, and the vendor will want the license agreement to make that clear.

- When the licensee demands increased freedom in using licensed software, the vendor's challenge is to permit some flexibility while making sure that the licensee pays for any additional use. It is in the vendor's interest to permit increased use of its digital product, as long as the use is monitored, controlled, and monetized.

Contingencies

Part of the craft of license grants is drafting to anticipate contingencies. For example:

- When you license to a corporation, what happens to the license if the customer merges with another corporation—does the enlarged company get the benefit of the license with no additional payment?

- Say that your game development company created a video game and licenses it to a publisher. If the publisher wants to market a sequel game, does your company get to program the sequel too? If not, does the publisher nonetheless have to pay your company royalties on the sequel?

It is impossible to cover all contingencies, but carefully drafted agreements cover those that are most important in the particular business context.

Maintenance and Support

Maintenance and support for software and other digital products are at the economic core of most software and digital product deals. Maintenance and support help insure that the customer actually obtains the benefit of its bargain.

Software and digital technology goods are among the most complex commercial products sold. Because of their complexity, software licensees need maintenance and support. *Maintenance* means fixing software to cure bugs and other errors. *Support* means advice on using the features and functions of a product. Most vendors offer some form of maintenance and support so most software licenses have provisions on this topic. (Sometimes, we use stand-alone maintenance and support agreements.)

What maintenance and support consist of varies greatly by product type and context. Here are some possible variations:

- Some freeware and open source come without any formal maintenance or support. (But new and better version may be released from time to time.)

- Many mass market products have Web-based maintenance and support systems that consist primarily of downloadable updates and online information. It is common for vendors to allow downloads of fixed versions even after the warranty has expired. This is particularly true when the newer version cures a significant product defect, such as a security hole that exposes the user's computer to hacker intrusions.

- Business products normally offer phone maintenance and support for a price.

- When products are mission-critical—for example, safety or security systems, trading systems or transaction processing systems, maintenance and support are extensive—usually offered 365 days per year, 24 hours a day—and quite expensive.

Here are some general points to keep in mind when designing or reviewing maintenance and support provisions for commercial software products:

- From a vendor's point of view, maintenance and support can be an important source of revenue that continues even during recessions and downturns. This means that it is important for the vendor to charge enough for these services to cover costs and generate a profit. It is not uncommon for companies with mature products to earn more from maintenance then from new product licensing.

- A provision of a typical digital product contract (often in a schedule) usually states what maintenance and support are available and at what price. There can be more than one "level" and the contract may offer the customer a choice of maintenance and support plans.

- Payment for maintenance and support is usually charged annually in advance, although, like most payment items, this may be negotiable.

- In many cases, maintenance and support are priced as a percentage of the software product license fee, but the agreement allows for pricing to increase after a few years. Sometimes, customers negotiate limits on how much the vendor can increase maintenance and support charges in any year.

- Many agreements include a form of service response requirement that classifies software errors as "Critical," "Serious," "Non-Serious," or the like and have different required responses to different error classifications. If the problem is more serious, the vendor is required to provide a faster response.

- Maintenance and support provisions usually give the licensee the right to get *updates* (which are versions of software with error fixes) and may also provide for *upgrades* (which are enhanced products with new functions).

- The maintenance and support provisions may require that the vendor have remote access to the licensee's system. This common provision can raise security issues, because access may provide a potential "back door" through the licensee's firewall.

- The vendor may want the right to discontinue maintenance and support at some point in the future especially when it phases out the product.

- Software products that are licensed on a subscription basis usually include service and support "bundled" with the product license.

Pricing and Payment

It goes without saying that the price is a core element of the bargain.

Pricing is often highly negotiated. Pricing is tied to the value of products, IP, and services received. There are many ways to adjust pricing in an agreement. For example:

- Payments can be fixed or depend on usage. There can be quantity and early payment discounts.

- There may be required minimums. There can be license fee caps.

- The timing of payment can vary. Payments can be in advance or in arrears. Upfront payments are a common way to get customer commitment.

- There can be refundable or nonrefundable advances.

- Payments can be tied to product or milestone deliveries.

- Payment can be subject to product or milestone acceptance.

- There can be guaranteed minimum payments.

- Late payments can trigger late fees and interest.

And so forth—with infinite numbers of combinations. You will find (as it will become clear in chapters to follow) that certain pay structures tend to fit particular deals.

Payment clauses should be precise. No matter how complicated, the goal should be to make it completely clear how amounts due are calculated and when amounts are billable and payable. If there is any complexity in the formula for payment, examples of calculations should be included in the contract.

"Equity Kickers"

In some deals (particularly major deals done by early stage companies with much larger ones), technology vendors sometimes include a grant to the customer of equity securities of the vendor. Usually these are *warrants*, a form of stock option, but (less commonly) they could be in the form of stock. Because these are "equity" (as opposed to debt) securities and because they are "thrown in" to make the deal, we call them "equity kickers." These equity kickers are most common during hot stock markets and in "hot" market segments.

Don't even think of tackling this kind of deal on your own without the aid of your lawyer. Equity kickers raise issues under state and federal securities laws. We have seen some early stage entrepreneurs give away warrants like they were candy—this is always a mistake and often illegal.

"Most Favored Pricing" Clauses

These are also sometimes called "most favored nation" (or "MFN") and "most favored customer clauses." The term "most favored *nation*" is used because very similar concepts are used in trade and tariff treaties between nations.

The idea of a most favored pricing clause is that the vendor charges a customer the lowest prices and terms then offered or provided to any other customer. The clauses may be limited to "comparable products" or "comparable terms of sale" or "comparable volumes," and so forth. Most clauses are prospective only, but some are retroactive in form—adjusting prices back in time.

We generally recommend that vendors not use these MFN clauses. Many companies simply refuse to do any most favored pricing deals. Vendors resist these clauses because they are dangerous and can have serious adverse unintended consequences. There is a risk that some special deal offered for some special reason by some salesperson will trigger an unexpected huge cut in price. In addition, "comparables" are hard to determine because of the variability of offerings, product combinations, and pricing structures. If you must offer a customer this protection, the clauses should be as narrow and specific as possible.

Here is the text of such a clause:

> *For so long as Vendor continues to make available the Product for license to any third party, Vendor agrees to license to Customer the Product on terms no less favorable than Vendor licenses the Product during the Term.*

Here is some added language that qualifies and limits that provision:

> *Such most favored terms, to be comparable, shall be similar in price, quantity of licenses purchased, functionality of the Product and payment terms and shall be granted to Customer upon the condition that Customer accept all material terms upon which such most favored customer licensed the Product. Price adjustments under this provision will be prospective only.*

Revenue Recognition

One important issue in digital technology licensing generally is revenue recognition. Revenue is a fundamental concept in accounting. In accrual basis accounting, revenues are recognized and can be recorded, not based on cash receipts, but when they are earned and realized. This is an *accounting* issue, but companies that get it wrong can get into severe *legal* trouble.

The General Rule

Naturally, a vendor wants to record as much revenue as possible for their income statement to please shareholders, lenders, and investors. Under US Generally Accepted Accounting Principles (or GAAP), a digital product license fee is earned when *all three* of the following have occurred:

1. Delivery of the digital product has occurred.
2. The vendor has no obligations or only insignificant obligations remaining to be done.
3. Collectibility of payment is probable.

Additional Considerations

Here are some points to keep in mind:

- **Customization and Acceptance**—If there is any professional services being provided to the customer before acceptance of a software solution (as, for example, any material customization or installation), there will be no revenue recognition until all significant work is done and customer acceptance has occurred.

- **Subscriptions**—If software is licensed on a subscription basis, then recognition of subscription revenue for accounting purposes normally occurs over the course of the subscription period.

- **Maintenance and Support**—Maintenance and support revenue is recognized not when paid, but when these services have been rendered. When the vendor "bundles" maintenance and support (say for a year) into the initial license fee, only the amount of the initial license fee attributable to the software will be recognized as revenue initially. The portion of the license fee attributable to the service obligation will be recognized over the course of the prepaid maintenance and support period.

- **Sales to Distribution**—You should discuss with your accountant how your sales to distributors should be treated for revenue recognition purposes. There are two methods that might apply. If the rate of likely product returns is uncertain (for example, for new or low volume products), the method normally used is known as "sell-through." Under the sell-through method, the vendor cannot recognize revenue from a shipment to a distributor until the distributor provides the vendor with evidence of a sale of the product through to the end customer. The alternative method, normally used for products with a well-established rate of return, is called "sell-in." With the sell-in method, revenue recognition occurs upon the vendor's sale to the distributor, but subject to a reserve (deduction) for the cost of likely returns. You should see your accountant for details on these methods and to determine which is most suitable for your business.

- **Other Factors**—Additional complications in revenue recognition arise from extended payment terms, discounts on future products, cancellation and refund rights, acceptance clauses, "equity kickers," and price protection.

Software and digital product revenue recognition can be *very* complicated. In some cases, the correct accounting for software revenue can be unclear. You should talk to your company's accountant to be sure you understand the rules applicable to your business. If "making the numbers" is important to your shareholders or investors, you want to make sure that you report numbers calculated in compliance with the accounting rules.

Abuses of Revenue Recognition

Some software companies, particularly in the 1990s, were overly aggressive in recognizing revenue under end-user agreements. Some of the executives involved ended up in prison for stock market fraud because of it.

Some of the more common abuses were:

- Recording revenue from products that are subject to acceptance but do not yet meet the acceptance criteria

- Keeping the quarter "open" for a few days after it ends in order to "squeeze" in more sales

- "Stuffing the channel" with sales on special terms to distributors that allow them to return software or postpone payment

- Back dating agreements

- Failing to deduct product returns

A cautionary tale is the case of Sanjay Kumar, the former CEO of business software giant Computer Associates (CA). Kumar was considered to be an outstanding software industry leader, but in 2006, he and other former CA executives pleaded guilty to fraud in federal court in connection with CA's revenue recognition misdeeds. The principle revenue recognition transgression was backdating deals to make them appear to be in an earlier quarter. Kumar was sentenced to 12 years in prison and fined $8 million. The lesson is that boldness and risk-taking in digital technology can be good, but not when it comes to revenue recognition.

Reports and Audit

Provisions of agreement regarding reporting and auditing are part of the deal mechanics. These clauses allow a vendor to verify that it is getting the benefit of its bargain. These provisions are necessary whenever the amount of payment is contingent upon intensity of use. For example, a reseller may owe license fees to a vendor based on the total number of vendor products that reseller licenses to its customers. A corporate customer of enterprise software may owe the vendor license fees based on the number of work stations on which the software is installed. And so forth.

Whenever payment is contingent in this way, the vendor must include a contract provision that requires the licensee to provide periodic reports of sales or results. In addition, the vendor will always require that the licensee keep detailed financial records. The contract will give the vendor a right to audit the records.

These provisions will state how long records much be maintained, how the audit is to be done (usually by independent accountants), when it can be done, and how often. It is common to have a provision that requires the licensee to pay for the cost of the audit if material underpayments are found. You will find examples of typical audit clauses in various agreements in the form Appendix to this book.

The vendors' right to audit can be backed up with technology that protects the vendor. For example, the vendor can use "software locks" or "license managers" in its software that are designed to stop or discourage unlicensed use.

Sometimes, it is the *customer* that wants the right to reports and audit. For example:

- If the vendor is providing development services to the customer on a time and materials basis, the customer may wish to audit the project records to be sure it was not overcharged.

- If the vendor is providing "software-as-a-service" (a topic covered in Chapter 13), the vendor will determine the quantity of the customer's use (and therefore the charges to the customer) from data recorded on the vendor's own servers. The customer may ask for an audit right to be sure the charges are correct.

Never be shy about using the audit rights if you think there is any risk that your company is not being paid correctly. Remember Ronald Reagan's motto as quoted above: "Trust, but verify."

Warranties

Under the law of every state, a warranty is a promise that products or services, as supplied, will have certain characteristics or that other relevant facts will be true. We often talk about "representations" and "warranties," but in reality a representation about a product or service is the same as a warranty.

Warranties are, to some extent an element of value, but in software they also serve other functions because they are intimately tied to warranty disclaimers (what's not covered in the warranty), remedies and remedy limitations (what happens if the warranty is breached), and risk limitation clauses (what are the limits of the vendor's liability).

Express Warranties

An *express warranty* is an affirmatively stated warranty. Under the UCC, the default rule (which may be changed in the written contract) is that any statement or presentation made in the sales process is a warranty. This would include assertions the vendor might make in selling—including those in the vendor's sales literature, proposals, and even those made in oral discussions. Needless to say, this is a dangerous rule for vendors, so vendors almost always include language to limit warranties.

As noted below, vendors normally include in contracts "entire agreement" clauses (also called "integration clauses") that expressly exclude any promises or assurance other than those expressly stated in the contract. We also normally include warranty disclaimers (discussed below). These important provisions are designed to limit warranties to those express warranties in the text of the agreement.

In digital product contracting, most warranties are about product quality. Sometimes, we see warranties of non-infringement (discussed below). In theory, one could make a warranty about anything.

Some Tips about Warranties

Here are some guidelines about the substance of warranty provisions:

- A common express warranty in contracts for software or other digital product is an affirmations that software "*substantially* conforms" or "conforms in all *material* respects" to its documentation. We use this kind of qualifying language because software is rarely perfectly conforming or fully defect-free.

- Warranties of software often "time out" (come to an end) after 30 or 90 days, based on the theory that any defects found thereafter should be "under maintenance and support."

- Software warranties often have built-in remedy limitations as well. Most commonly, the stated remedy is maintenance and support—which means the warranty period really amounts to a period of no-additional-charge maintenance and support.

You can see examples of common software warranties in the form Appendix to this book.

Some contracts include warranties of non-infringement. These causes need to be read together with the infringement indemnification provisions of the agreement. We address the topic of these IP risk clauses later in this chapter.

"No Open Source" Warranties

Some warranties are about what the software or digital product is *not*. For example, a customer may insist on a "no open source" warranty. If your company is committed to the use of only non-open source tools and platforms, it will be easy to give the customer these warranties. (Chapter 9 is about open source licensing and its opportunities and risks.)

Here is a typical customer clause that would be used to guard against inclusion of open-source-licensed software:

Developer represents and warrants that the Software will not contain any Open Source Software. As used in this Agreement, "Open Source Software" means any software that consists, contains, or is derived in any manner (in whole or in part) from, any software that is distributed as free software, open software, open source software, or similar licensing or distribution models.

Some customers are worried only about so-called "Copyleft" licenses (discussed in Chapter 9) so a warranty like the following might satisfy them:

Developer represents and warrants that the Software will not contain any Copyleft Software. As used in this Agreement, "Copyleft Software" means any software that (a) requires as a condition of distribution of such software or any derivative that such software or derivative be disclosed or distributed in source code form or (b) requires that such software or derivative can be licensed to others only under the same or a similar license as that under it was received. Examples of Copyleft licenses are the GNU General Public License (GPL) or Lesser General Public License (LGPL).

Other customers simply want all open source programs disclosed so that they can decide for themselves if the open source licenses are satisfactory. For them, a warranty like the following might work for them:

Developer represents and warrants that the Software will not contain any Open Source Software except for those programs listed on Schedule X or as expressly approved by Customer in writing.

Date-Related Processing

In the run up to the year 2000, digital technology business and its enterprise customers engaged in a round of "Y2K" frenzy—dealing with fixing thousands of software programs that could not handle four digit dates. This anxiety has largely faded away. However, there are still some application programs out there that do not process four digits and are operating in the 21st century only by means of a two-digit-based "work around." So four-digit date functionality is still the subject of warranties for some classes of hardware and software, primarily mainframe software.

Implied Warranties

The UCC includes implied warranties for digital product contracts. These are warranties that apply by default, although, as discussed below, if a vendor uses the right language, it can effectively disclaim (eliminate) the implied warranties. You should understand these warranties, because they can trap an incautious software vendor. For example, if your company licenses software with a simple letter agreement, without proper disclaimers, then your company will be bound by all the implied warranties.

Here are the implied warranties under the UCC:

- **Implied Warranty of "Merchantability"**—This means, in essence, that a reasonable buyer would find the products of acceptable quality and performance.

- **Implied Warranty of Fitness for a Particular Purpose**—This is a warranty that the product provided to the licensee will meet the needs of the licensee stated in the communications that led to the agreement—including the customer's oral or written statements. Most vendors do not want to give this warranty; rather they want the licensee to determine on its own if the product is suitable for its needs.

- **Implied Warranty of Title**—This is a warranty the vendor owns and has the rights that it provides to the customer (that is, a warranty that the product is not stolen or misappropriated).

- **Implied Warranty of Non-Infringement**—This is a warranty that the product can be used as intended without infringing third party IP rights.

Disclaiming Implied Warranties

The UCC does allow a vendor to disclaim implied warranties, but *only by use of* *"conspicuous" provisions*. This is why you often see warranty disclaimer provisions in all capital text or bold letters. Usually digital product and service contracts disclaim most or all of the implied warranties. Here is a typical provision:

EXCEPT AS EXPRESSLY PROVIDED IN THIS AGREEMENT, LICENSOR MAKES NO REPRESENTATIONS OR WARRANTIES WITH RESPECT TO PRODUCTS, SERVICES, OR OTHERWISE. LICENSOR DISCLAIMS ALL OTHER WARRANTIES, EXPRESS OR IMPLIED, INCLUDING BUT NOT LIMITED TO, THE IMPLIED WARRANTIES OF MERCHANTABILITY AND FITNESS FOR ANY PARTICULAR PURPOSE. NO WARRANTIES OF NON-INFRINGEMENT ARE MADE EXCEPT AS EXPRESSLY STATED HEREIN.

In many cases, state law may not allow or limit exclusion of implied warranties for consumer transactions, and consumer transactions require different wording for disclaimers. Consumer and mass market product warranties' issues are discussed in Chapter 16, which is about "clickwrap" and "browsewrap" agreements.

Prohibitions

Most software and digital product contracts include prohibitions. These rules of behavior are designed to stop customer exploitation of the product that is beyond the boundaries of the economic bargain made by the parties. The most common prohibitions include:

- **No Unauthorized Use**—This provision is designed to prohibit the customer from selling, leasing, transferring, assigning, licensing, sublicensing, or exploiting the product other than as expressly authorized in the agreement. These clauses, in essence, provide that anything not allowed is forbidden.

- **No Reverse Engineering**—These provisions are designed to prohibit the customer from any decompiling, disassembling, or otherwise processing the software to learn its inner workings. (Legal aspects of reverse engineering of software are discussed in Chapter 3.)

The particular prohibitions in an agreement need to be tailored to your company's products and technologies and the characteristics of the business deal.

Confidentiality Clauses

Confidentiality is a rule of behavior—and a reinforcer of trust. It is designed to set up rules under which the parties can communicate without fear that the information will become public or go to third parties. For some simple licensing transactions that do not require exchange of information, confidentiality clauses may be unnecessary.

In these clauses, "Confidential Information" is normally defined as non-public information provided by a party. Confidential clauses normally require each party not to disclose such information and to use it only for the purposes of the agreement.

Confidentiality clauses can serve different business purposes:

- **To Protect the Customer**—Sometimes, the customer needs to disclose secret information to a vendor in order to enable the vendor to supply development, customization, or installation services. The information disclosed could be the customer's internal systems, security procedures, proprietary technologies, financial data, business processes, and so forth. In this case, the confidentiality clause is designed primarily to give the customer comfort that it is safe to make the necessary disclosure.

- **To Protect the Vendor**—Sometimes, the vendor will try to keep the features, functions, and interfaces of its digital product secret—and prevent competitors from seeing and testing it. In this case, the vendor may use a confidentiality clause to impose an obligation on the customer not to disclose the software or information about it.

- **To Protect Both Parties**—In many cases, both parties to an agreement have confidential information to exchange.

A few more observations:

- Many, but not all, confidentiality clauses require that a party can claim confidential information status only for (i) written information that is marked or stamped "confidential" or "proprietary" or the like and (ii) for oral information that is summarized in a follow-up writing sent by the disclosing party. Because some will not bother to send such written summaries, these clauses risk "leakage" of confidential matters provided in oral form.

- Some confidential clauses are in essence guarantees that no confidential information will be misused or be disclosed. Some are "softer" and promise only "reasonable efforts" to keep information confidential.

Intellectual Property Clauses

It is common to have provisions in digital product contracts that address owner-ship of IP. Provisions on IP ownership are part of the core economic bargain.

In most license agreements, these clauses are generally very simple. There is really little that needs to be said other than the agreement grants a license only—and that no transfer of ownership is intended. Here is typical language:

> *This Agreement grants a non-exclusive license only. No ownership interest in the Software or Documentation is transferred by this Agreement. Licensor and its sup-pliers retain all ownership and intellectual property rights.*

The provisions on IP can be more complicated (and tougher to negotiate) when IP will be created during the performance of the agreement. In that case, it will be important that the agreement address with clarity which party will receive the ownership of which of the rights that will be created. This is a topic that is dis-cussed in considerable detail (with sample contract clauses) in the discussion of development deals in Chapter 10.

Risk Allocation: Remedies, Limitations, and Damage Caps

Some of the provisions of agreements are invoked only occasionally—the vendor in fact hopes they are never used. These provisions manage situations where expectations have broken down and bad things have happened. Although they are not the economic heart of the bargain, they are important. They involve situa-tions where the financial consequences of failure can be severe.

The risk allocation provisions, typically found near the end of the document, are quite technical. Negotiating them effectively requires knowing a fair amount about the law, including the law of contract damages and patent and copyright law. It also requires the knowledge to evaluate risks in both the business and legal context—to know whether a particular risk is high or low and whether the damages it is likely to cause are large or small.

Each word in these clauses can matter. The risk allocations provisions are such that altering a single word or phase can dramatically change the coverage of the provision—a layperson might not notice the difference. It is also an area where the provisions interact with one another. Changing a warranty might affect the indemnification clause. Changing the indemnification clause might undo a disclaimer of damages. We will discuss some of the fine points below, but we do suggest that you consult your lawyer with regard to these more technical provisions.

A couple of basic principles for risk allocation:

Watch out for "risk multipliers." There are some situations where the risk of harm is multiplied—which makes allocation more critical. Here are some examples:

- Assume a small software vendor supplies a critical $1.00 software component for a cell phone that sells at wholesale for $45.00. The cell phone vendor might lose tens of millions of dollars in sales and millions of dollars in profit if the component is late or does not function correctly. The small software vendor cannot afford to take all that risk.

- Assume that a video game developer supplies software for distribution by a publisher and it turns out that the game infringes a third party's patent. If the publisher has sold millions of copies of the game, and if a reasonable patent royalty, payable to the patent owner, is $1.00 per game, there will be millions of dollars of patent infringement damages. The publisher will want to recover (to the extent it can) from the video game developer.

In general, the vendor's goal will be to keep its worst case exposure within bounds that it can afford to pay—even if the payment amount is painful—without being driven into bankruptcy.

Categories of Contract Damages

In order to understand contract risk, you need to understand contract damages. As we noted above, the remedy in a court of law for breach of contract is an award of "money damages." (For lawyers and judges, "damages" are the money awarded by a court in litigation.) Let's now dig deeper into this topic and review the measure of damages and the ways that vendors routinely limit the damages that apply.

In theory, contract damages are intended to put the non-breaching party in the economic position reasonably expected to result of the successful completion of the contract. This is usually called the "benefit-of-the-bargain" measure of damages. (Contract damages do not include non-economic harm, such an emotional distress.) We break down "benefit of the bargain" damages into the following components.

Direct Damages

Direct damages are the difference in the value of the product or service as promised and as actually delivered. (In addition to the term "direct," we sometimes call this "cover damages." That is because if you were to go out into the market and purchase products or services reasonably required to make up for my breach, you would be expending money to "cover" the lost value.) Here is how this measure works:

- *Assume that I promise in a contract to deliver to you a software product at a price of $50,000.00 of a type that has a fair market value of $75,000, and assume that, in breach of the contract, I deliver nothing, and you pay nothing. In this case, the value of the performance is $75,000. If the agreement was performed, you would have paid $50,000. Therefore your direct damages are $25,000.*

Direct damages also apply to breach of a promise to provide services such as maintenance and even a failure to provide indemnification.

- *Assume that I promise to, but fail to, provide indemnification for a lawsuit that costs you $500,000 to defend. In that case, your direct damages would be $500,000.*

For the vendor, recovering direct damages normally means an award of the agreed (but unpaid) contract payments, such as the license fee.

Consequential Damages

Consequential damages are the additional costs and expenses (beyond direct damages) that the non-breaching party foreseeably incurs because of the breach (minus any savings due to the breach). These might include lost profits that a party would have obtained except for the other party's breach of contract.

- *Assume that I agree to deliver to you software for resale. Assume that in breach of the contract, I deliver nothing, and that, as a result, you lose the opportunity to sell it to your customer. If your reasonably expected resale profit were $250,000, your consequential damages are $250,000.*

- *Assume that I promise you software to run a factory. The software I supply is six months late, and you have to shut down a product line as a result. You lose $1,000,000 in production profits as a result. In this scenario, your consequential damages are the lost $1,000,000.*

Consequential damages are very dangerous from a vendor's point of view (and are therefore often disclaimed). This is because they are not in the vendor's control and might easily become very large. In a case litigated in Massachusetts some years ago, a software developer's failure to provide working inventory and order management software at a price of $250,000 led to a $5,000,000 damage award at trial. The customer proved that the developer's failure to deliver the promised software in accordance with the agreement led to *lost cost savings* equal to *20 times* the contract price. Lost savings are a type of consequential damages.

Incidental Damages

Incidental damages are incidental costs due to the breach, such as the cost of storage of any defective goods or the cost of shipment to return them. Incidental damages in software and digital technology contracts are usually very small.

Legal Defaults

As a legal default under US law (under UCC Article 2), the non-breaching licensee would normally be entitled to *all* the above: direct damages, consequential damages, and incidental damages. As you can see, these legal defaults tend to be pro-buyer and pro-licensee.

Option to Return

There is another possible remedy. Licensees often seek to include clauses that permit the return of software product for a full refund in case of an uncured breach of warranty.

Contractual Damage Limitations

Fortunately for vendors, it is possible to limit exposure in agreements in contracts. (As discussed in Chapter 16, when vendors deal with consumers, the law regulates and restricts the remedy limitations that are allowed.)

Most reasonable limits written into agreements in commercial deals will be accepted by the courts. Contract clauses on the measure of damages are important risk allocators and can be the subject of considerable negotiation, particularly in large deals. Most commonly, vendors limit damages in the following ways:

- **Damage Exclusions**—Most commercial contracts contain language that completely excludes consequential and incidental damages. The most important component of this is the consequential damages exclusion.

- **Damage Caps**—Most commercial contracts contain language that puts a limit on the total amount of damages that the licensee can recover. The most common cap is the contract price or the license fee. There are many other variations.

Here is some typical contract language designed to limit a vendor's exposure to large damages claims that might be asserted by its customers:

Damages Exclusion. Vendor will not be liable for any lost profits, lost savings, or exemplary or consequential damages of the other party, even if Vendor has been advised of the possibility of or could have foreseen such damages.

Damages Cap. Vendor's aggregate liability under this Agreement shall be limited to the total fees paid under this Agreement.

The reference to "exemplary" damages in this clause is a reference to what is also called "punitive damages." In some states, the judge or jury is permitted to impose extra money damages for a *willful* contract breach in order to punish the wrongdoer. Your lawyer can provide you guidance on this subject for the states where you do business. We cannot guarantee you that a contractual exclusion of exemplary damages will be effective in every state or in every circumstance, but it is good practice for vendors to include this language.

Also note that in most states, you cannot limit damages for fraud, which normally means sales made through deception.

Mutual Damage Limitations Provisions

In many digital technology agreements, the parties make the damages limitations mutual, because it is often easier to "sell" provisions that appear to treat both parties the same. However, sometimes sauce for the goose should not be sauce for the gander.

Although vendors may want to be free from all consequential claims, they usually need to preserve the right to collect certain consequential damages from their licensees. Attorneys that represent vendors do more than just making the consequential damages exclusion mutual; we also include "carve-outs" —a lawyer's name for exceptions.

Mutual Consequential Damages Exclusions and Carve-Outs

The most common carve-outs from the consequential damages exclusion are for the following:

- Misuse of confidential information

- Unlicensed use of software supplied

- Misuse of the vendor's IP

Here is a mutual consequential damages exclusion clause *without* carve-outs (which is *not* good for vendors):

Neither party shall be liable for any lost profits, lost savings, or exemplary or consequential damages of the other party, even if such party has been advised of the possibility of or could have foreseen such damages.

Here is a consequential damages exclusion clause *with* carve-outs (which is what vendors normally want). The underlined text is the carve-out:

<u>Except with regard to breach of the parties' obligations regarding Confidential Information, Intellectual Property, or unlicensed use of the Software</u>, neither party shall be liable for any lost profits, lost savings, or exemplary or consequential damages of the other party, even if such party has been advised of the possibility of or could have foreseen such damages.

The carve-outs are important. For the contract breaches included in the carve-out, *the only damages that* apply are consequential damages. There are *no* "direct damages." Unless a vendor reserves its right to claim consequential damages in these situations, the vendor would likely end up with *no remedy* at all. Note that the carve-out for "Confidential Information" is a two-edged sword, because either party might have a claim for the other's misuse of its confidential materials or data.

Mutual Damage Caps and Carve-Outs

Mutual damage caps need carve-outs too. That's because in some cases the mutual damage cap will leave the vendor or the customer with an inadequate remedy. Say, for example, the customer pays $10,000 for a software license and then makes $500,000 worth of illegal copies. In that case, it would not be good to make the amount paid, $10,000, to be the limit of the vendor's damages.

With regard to the damage cap, the vendor will often use the same carve-outs that we discussed above *plus* indemnification. Here is a typical provision:

<u>Except with regard to breach of the parties' obligations regarding indemnification, Confidential Information, Intellectual Property, or unlicensed use of the Software</u>, the aggregate liability of each party under this Agreement to the other party shall be limited to the total fees paid and fees required to be paid under this Agreement.

The rationale for the indemnification carve-out is different. Here the goal is not self-protection, but making the deal. This carve-out provision most often favors the licensee, who is the most likely beneficiary of indemnification. (See discussion of indemnification below.) Usually this carve-out is included because sophisticated licensees commonly insist on it. The vendor may seek to place a separate and higher dollar limit on this exception. For example:

> *Except with regard to breach of the parties' obligations regarding indemnification, Confidential Information, Intellectual Property, or unlicensed use of the Software, the aggregate liability of each party under this Agreement to the other party shall be limited to the total fees paid and fees required to be paid under this Agreement, <u>provided that each parties' aggregate liability with regard to indemnification will not exceed one million dollars ($1,000,000)</u>.*

Variations on Damages Limitations

There are many other variations on these damage cap provisions. You can have damage limits set at defined dollar amounts, different amounts for different types of claims, or have the damages limited to the licensee's payments over a set period, or combinations and permutations of these provisions. The larger the deal and the higher the technological, financial and/or IP risks, the more incentive for the parties to bargain over risk limiters.

The Risk of Overreaching

Caution is required with these provisions. This is a situation where you do not want *too* good a deal. If a party overreaches on drafting damage limitations and provides no meaningful remedy to the other party, the judge may "throw out" the damage limitation. If that happens, then the damage limitation will fail altogether and the amount of potential damages will be unlimited.

Indemnification Clauses

Indemnification clauses are key risk allocation provisions. They are often bargained over. The fact that there are so many software patents and business method patents in the United States (discussed in Chapter 5) has raised the patent risk profile of digital business. This has made indemnification more critical and more contentious.

Indemnification means a promise to protect a person or company against a contingent financial loss and normally also include the obligation to provide a legal defense. They say, in essence, if a defined adverse event happens to you, the indemnitor (the party providing indemnity) will see that you suffer no financial loss. Indemnification can be seen as a kind of insurance offered by a party to a contract. Or to put it another way—an indemnification clause re-allocates a specified risk from one party to another.

In digital product and service contracts, indemnification clauses most often provide protection from third party IP infringement claims, although they often cover many other contingencies. For contracts involving lots or money, the indemnification provisions are the subject of considerable negotiation. They can even be deal killers.

The Details of Indemnification

Indemnification clauses can provide vital protection—or they can provide very little protection. Unfortunately, these provisions are by their nature so technical and full of legalese that they are frequently written in ways that are traps for the unwary. Companies may use indemnification clauses that sound good to a lay reader but, on analysis, do not promise much. With indemnification, it is surely true that the "devil is in the details."

Here is a typical IP indemnification clause that provides a licensee with a broad promise of protection:

> *Vendor shall defend, indemnify and hold Licensee and any of its officers, directors, agents and employees harmless from and against any and all third-party claims, actions, proceedings, and suits and all related liabilities, damages, settlements, penalties, fines, costs or expenses (including reasonable attorneys' fees and other litigation expenses) incurred by Licensee, arising out of or relating to any alleged infringement of any patent, trademark, or copyright or other proprietary right of any other entity or person arising from the Licensed Product.*

There are many ways to edit and limit IP indemnifications clauses so that they provide materially less protection to a licensee. Sometimes, these limitations are quite justified and sometimes not. Here are some examples:

- **Limiting Coverage by Type of IP**—The clause is written to cover copyright only or copyright and trademark—but leaves out patents, which are normally the area of greatest risk.

- **Limiting Coverage by Geography**—The clause covers only IP claims under the IP laws of the United States. (In one license agreement that we saw, the grant was for worldwide distribution, but the indemnification covered only IP rights arising under the laws of Ireland.)

- **Limiting Coverage by Issue Date**—The clause covers only patents issued as of the contract's effective date. Needless to say, this leaves the licensee uncovered for all later issued patents.

- **Knowledge Qualifier**—This type of clause limits indemnification to "IP known to the vendor" or "infringements known to vendor." Sometimes, we write these clauses so that copyright and trademark claims are fully indemnified but patent indemnification is limited to known infringements. These clauses protect vendors that have a "pure heart and empty head."

Licensees, large or small, want to get unlimited IP indemnification from the vendor. Software suppliers will usually fight hard to put some limitations on patent indemnification. A knowledge qualifier can be valuable protection for a vendor—as can damage caps for indemnification claims.

Limitations on indemnification are particularly valuable for those companies that make software components that are incorporated in another software or hardware product. Here's why:

- Patent infringement is without fault. An infringer will be liable even if it had no knowledge of the patent involved. Software suppliers (particularly smaller companies) often are unaware of the patent risks and may not have the resources to find out if there are relevant patents.

- There is a risk that a component supplier will be swept up into a wider patent struggle between its licensee and the licensee's competitors. Patent litigation is often unleashed for competitive reasons that have little to do with the software supplier. There is an African saying: "When the elephants fight, the grass gets trampled."

- Patent damages may far exceed the license fee payment to the software supplier. Let's say that LittleCo supplies a relatively small software component that is incorporated into BigCo's software product. Assume that BigCo's product is priced at $500.00 per unit and that each time BigCo licenses a unit, it pays LittleCo a license fee of $1.00. Let's also assume that a patent holder that sues BigCo and bases its patent infringement damage claim on the price of BigCo's product. If the jury determines that a "reasonable royalty" is one percent, BigCo's exposure would be $5.00 in royalties for each product unit. If LittleCo completely indemnifies BigCo, then LittleCo is burdened with $5.00 of liability for each $1.00 of royalties it receives.

Added to the risk of infringement damages is the fact that typical, legal, and expert fees for a patent litigation defense—from start of the lawsuit to the end of trial—is two to three million dollars (not including appeals).

You can see that patent indemnification can be a "bet-your-company" risk for smaller companies. When you are providing IP indemnification, you should be looking to make sure that risk is commensurate with the benefit from the contract. It is a mistake to give unlimited indemnification for unknown patent claims when all your company is getting is a small royalty or a fixed fee.

Indemnification as Sole Remedy for Infringement

Sometimes, a vendor provides a *warranty* of non-infringement and in addition *indemnification* for infringement. They are not the same. Including both gives a licensee two potential recoveries against a vendor for infringing software:

- The licensee will be entitled to compensation for breach of the warranty. The measure of compensation would be the fair value of the non-infringing software that the vendor promised, but failed to provide.

- The licensee will also be entitled to indemnification against the third party's lawsuit.

When we represent vendors, we often seek to include a clause stating that:

"Indemnification under this Section is each Party's sole and exclusive remedy for actual or alleged infringement of third party rights."

This language is designed to be sure that vendor's exposure is limited to protecting licensee from losses due to third party lawsuits.

Indemnification for Personal Injury

Another subject on which vendors commonly provide indemnification is personal injury or property damage caused by the negligence of its personnel on-site at the customer's location. Here is a typical provision:

Vendor agrees to defend, indemnify, and hold Customer harmless from and against any claims, damages or liabilities asserted by any third party alleging personal injury or physical property damage arising from the negligent act or omission of Vendor's employees or agents at Customer's premises.

Indemnification by Licensees

Indemnification can be crafted to cover many different situations. In some cases, the *vendor* wants indemnification *from the licensee*. Here are some common examples:

- **Technology Combinations**—If the licensee is permitted to combine the vendor's technology with other technologies, the vendor may insist on indemnification by the licensee if the combination causes an infringement (where the vendor's software alone was non-infringing).

- **Hosted Information**—Online service vendors that host software and hold customer information (such as companies that provide enterprise solutions on a "software-as-a-service" or "SaaS" basis) want to be indemnified by customers for lawsuits arising from any "bad" data. For example, the customer (or its employees) might store information that is infringing, defamatory, or obscene. If customer-supplied bad data leads to liability or legal costs, the SaaS vendor will want the customer to take care of it. (For further discussion of this point, see Chapter 13, which deals with SaaS agreements.)

- **Misrepresentation by Reseller**—Resellers often must indemnify software vendors against any customer claims that arise from unauthorized promises or representations made by the reseller.

Avoiding Indemnification for "Any Breach"

Sometimes, in a negotiation, a party (usually the customer) will propose indemnification language like this:

> *Vendor shall fully indemnify Customer for any loss or damage suffered by Customer arising from any breach of this Agreement by Vendor.*

This might look innocuous, but actually it is a very dangerous provision for a vendor. It is a back door—the effect of which is to circumvent the consequential damages exclusion that we discussed above. This provision will likely result in the vendor having unlimited exposure for lost profits, lost cost savings, or any other kind of loss arising from any vendor breach of contract.

This kind of provision does have a place in the law. If you have sold your company for $100 million, you would normally give an indemnity like this—subject to a negotiated dollar limit. However, this open-ended provision does not belong in digital licensing agreements because neither party is likely to expect, or be receiving sufficient compensation for, such open-ended and unlimited financial exposure.

Procedure for Indemnification

Indemnification clauses (of all kinds) normally have procedures for handling indemnification claims. Here is a typical simple provision:

> *Licensee shall (a) promptly notify Vendor in writing of any claim subject to indemnification hereunder; (b) permit Vendor to assume control of the defense and settlement of any such claim; and (c) reasonably cooperate with Vendor, at Vendor's*

expense, in defending or settling such claims. Licensee shall have the right to participate, at its sole expense, in the defense or settlement of any such claim.

Indemnification provisions for infringement claims often have added procedural language which permits the vendor to cure the infringement problem:

At any time, should Vendor reasonably become concerned about a claim or potential claim regarding the Software, Vendor shall have the right, but not the obligation, at its sole option and expense, to either procure for Licensee the right to continue using the Software or replace or modify the Software so that it becomes non-infringing. Licensee is obligated to distribute only modified Software if it is supplied under this Section.

Sometimes, vendors also have the right to terminate licenses with regard to software that become the subject of a third party IP claim. This is another way that vendors can limit indemnification risk. Here is a typical provision:

At any time, should Vendor reasonably become concerned about a claim or potential claim regarding the Software, Vendor shall have the right, but not the obligation, at its sole option and expense, to either procure for Licensee the right to continue using the Software or replace or modify the Software so that it becomes non-infringing. Licensee is obligated to distribute only modified Software if it is supplied under this Section. If vendor determines that the foregoing remedies are not practicable, Vendor may terminate the license granted herein on 90 days written notice and refund to Licensee any prepaid license or maintenance fees.

Term, Termination, and Survival

The term of the agreement and the rights granted is a fundamental part of the economic bargain.

Some software licenses are permanent, and others are for a limited term. Software can be licensed by the year, by the month or even by transaction. Even when the license is permanent, maintenance and support are not. Distribution deals are almost always limited in time. Development deals often permit the customer to terminate for no reason on short notice. The duration of an agreement and allowed reasons for its termination are determined by the nature of the agreement and by the particular deal. These concepts, as applied to different agreement types, are discussed in the following chapters.

Most agreements provide for termination for uncured material breach; there is some variation on how this works. Cure periods can vary. Where licenses are for mission critical software, licensees may seek provisions that do not allow termination of the license even for breach, but only permit money damages unless the breach is willful.

Usually agreements provide that some provisions and obligations survive termination. These usually include provisions on confidential information, indemnification, IP ownership, accrued warranty claims, and accrued amount due. Sometimes, a licensee will be permitted to keep copies of licensed software post-termination for use in providing support or maintenance to its existing customers.

You will find examples of clause on contract term, termination, and survival in the various contract forms that are included in the form Appendix to this book.

Source Code Escrows

Source code escrow agreements are another component of risk management. They are designed to provide a safety net of sorts to customers.

Source code escrow agreements are side agreements that permit the licensee to obtain access to the software's source code under specified conditions—usually if the vendor discontinues a product line, goes out of business, becomes insolvent, or ceases providing maintenance. We discuss code escrow agreements in some detail in the section of this book below in Chapter 12, the chapter on commercial end-user licenses. There is a sample source code escrow agreement in the form Appendix (Form 12-3).

Dispute Resolution

Another contingency that contracts must provide for is resolution of disputes between the parties. This is a necessary subject that nobody (but the lawyers) likes to discuss.

We believe that every dispute should be settled. Litigation usually represents a failure of reason and good sense. When there is a contract dispute that cannot be settled, by default, it will end up in court for resolution—often by jury trial.

Because litigation is a public and expensive process, the parties sometimes include "alternative dispute resolution" or "ADR" provisions in agreements. There are various kinds of ADR and a great variety of ADR provisions, as is discussed below.

Dispute Escalation Clause

This type of provision provides a set "cooling off period." The parties agree to meet and talk, normally each will be required to "escalate" the matter to a senior executive on each side who has not previously been involved in the disputed matter. This is a low-cost ADR measure.

Mediation

Mediation is a process in which both parties are obligated to hire an outside facilitator who will meet with the parties and attempt, by convincing and cajoling both sides, to bring about a settlement. Mediation is a non-binding process.

Arbitration

Arbitration is, in essence, a private and confidential form of litigation. An arbitration clause requires that disputes be submitted to a binding decision-making process consisting of a hearing before one or more arbitrators, rather than tried before a judge and jury in a court of law.

The arbitrators can be chosen by any procedure agreed to by the parties. They are usually attorneys. Often parties use the procedures and rules of the American Arbitration Association or AAA (informally referred to as "triple-A arbitration"), which arranges commercial arbitrations and has a set of arbitration rules. International private disputes are often heard under the procedures of the International Chamber of Commerce or ICC. Most cases are heard by one arbitrator or a panel of three arbitrators. Compared to litigation in court, arbitration can be a streamlined process, although it often still may take many months or even years to resolve. Arbitration usually is less costly than litigation, but it is not cheap. In addition to legal fees, parties that arbitrate must pay arbitration fees, which may be quite substantial. Arbitration clauses normally specify the place of arbitration and (in international deals) the language of the proceedings.

Arbitration awards are almost always final. They are normally enforceable in court (including courts in many foreign nations), and quite difficult to appeal, reverse, or alter in the courts.

For international disputes, arbitration has another advantage over litigation—its awards are more likely to be enforceable in foreign courts. That's because there is a treaty known as the Convention on the Recognition and Enforcement of Foreign Arbitral Awards (known informally as the "New York Convention") that makes them enforceable in 141 countries around the world (as of the time this is written). Judicial rulings are often not enforceable in other nations. For example, the judgment of US court is not enforceable in China, but an arbitration award rendered in the US normally is enforceable there. Some of the more commonly chosen locations for international arbitrations are London, Paris, Geneva, Singapore, and Hong Kong.

There are other advantages and disadvantages to ADR procedures. There are many variations on how to write these clauses. ADR provisions may not fit small or simple contracts. Your legal counsel can help you determine which provisions are best for your digital deals.

The Injunctive Relief Clause

As we explained earlier in this chapter, one type of relief that courts can issue in litigation is a court order, known as an "injunction." These orders are classified as "extraordinary relief." To get a court to issue an injunction in a lawsuit, a party must show the court that money damages (also known for historical reasons as a remedy "at law") are an inadequate remedy so that recovering money would not solve the problem.

If a party wants an injunction early in a lawsuit (or any time before trial), the party seeking an injunction must show that it has a reasonable likelihood of winning the case, that the harm it will suffer will be immediate (so that the matter cannot wait) and irreparable (so it cannot be remedied later). Most commonly, digital technology companies seek such "preliminary injunctive relief" to protect confidential information from disclosure or to stop unauthorized use of technology or IP. These clauses are also used in conjunction with non-competition clauses.

To provide a party a better chance to obtain this injunctive relief when most needed, companies often include an "injunctive relief clause" in digital technology agreements. Sometimes, these are written to be unilateral, that is, protective of only one party; often they are mutual, that is, protective of both parties.

Here is an example of a *unilateral* injunctive relief clause that covers both proprietary rights and Confidential Information:

> *Injunctive Relief. Licensee acknowledges that any breach of its obligations under this Agreement with respect to the Licensor's proprietary rights or Confidential Information of Licensor will cause Licensor immediate and irreparable injury for which there are no adequate remedies at law, and therefore Licensor will be entitled to injunctive relief in addition to all other remedies provided by this Agreement or available at law.*

Here is an example of a *mutual* injunctive relief clause. This particular example was written to cover only confidentiality.

> *Injunctive Relief. The parties agree that any threatened or actual violations of any of a party's confidentiality obligations of this Agreement would cause immediate and irreparable harm to the non-breaching party and that a remedy at law would*

be inadequate. Therefore, in addition to any and all remedies available at law, the non-breaching party shall be entitled to seek an injunction without any require-ment of posting of a bond.

Note that the first example says the Licensor "will be entitled to injunctive relief" whereas the second example says that a party is entitled to "be entitled to *seek* an injunction." The second clause might be read as a more tentative assertion that injunctive relief is required.

These clauses will likely help the party seeking an injunction make its case, but they do not make getting an injunction automatic. The proponent of the injunction still must convince the judge that it really needs that injunction. If it cannot bear the burden of persuasion, the court will say "no" to the injunction, regardless of what the contract says.

Why does the second example clause say that the injunction should be issued "without any requirement of posting of a bond"? Sometimes, an injunction turns out (when all the facts come out) to be unjustified. Judges frequently require a party that obtains an injunction to post a bond (which is a form of financial guarantee issued by a bonding company) to protect the enjoined party. If the injunction turns out to be wrongful, the judge will have the legal power to award compensation from the bond to the wrongfully enjoined party up to the amount of the bond. This language is an attempt to get the injunction without the requirement of bond. In spite of these words, judges would still have the power to require a bond as a condition of an injunction.

Choice of Law

Agreements almost always have provisions for choice of law. Usually the agreement recites that it is governed by the law of a particular US state (because contract law is primarily state law in the United States) or that of a particular foreign nation.

There is some variation in the laws of the US states. But the reality is that the interpretation of well-written digital product and service contracts does not often turn on differences in state law. So choice of law is not usually a deal killer. Many lawyers will prefer their own state's law, just because they know it. All else being equal, it is probably better to enter into contracts that select state law that has a fair amount of written case law involving software and digital issues, such as the law of California, New York, Illinois, Massachusetts, Texas, or Virginia (subject to the comment above about UCITA in Virginia).

You should be careful in choosing foreign law—not that there is necessarily anything wrong with the law of other nations. Basic contract legal principles in most developed nations will be much the same there as under US law, but there are significant differences in detail and major differences in customary practices. Any significant contract under foreign law should be reviewed by foreign counsel before signing. (See also the discussion in Chapter 23 on "going global.")

Choice of Jurisdiction

Contracts often (but not always) have clauses that select the exclusive jurisdiction for the litigation of a dispute. You will normally be better off if the clause selects your home jurisdiction. This is because it is less expensive to litigate a case in your hometown. You have legal counsel there that already knows your business. You don't have to travel and live on the road to attend hearings or the trial. For these reasons, having an exclusive jurisdiction clause that picks your hometown can be an important leverage point in a dispute. The same advantage applies to arbitration clauses that select your own hometown as the place of arbitration.

Here are some pointers on jurisdiction clauses:

- If you cannot get your hometown as the site for jurisdiction, try to get a neutral location. Some contracts choose the courts of Delaware. Many choose the courts located in the borough of Manhattan, New York City.

- Some lawyers recommend clauses that put exclusive jurisdiction for disputes between the parties in the hometown of the party that did not start the litigation; so, if the vendor sues the licensee, jurisdiction will be in the licensee's hometown; and vice versa. The theory is that this kind of provision discourages litigation. However, another way to look at this is that it rewards the party that breaches the contract with home court advantage. For example, if the licensee refuses to pay its license fees, the vendor must sue the licensee in the licensee's hometown. Don't use this clause if it will lead to rewarding bad behavior.

- Jurisdiction selection clauses normally choose "exclusive" jurisdiction. If they leave out the word "exclusive" or its equivalent, they are "permissive" —that is they say the jurisdiction that either side *may* use for litigation, but is not obligated to use. You need to read these clauses carefully.

- If there is no exclusive jurisdiction clause, then there is often a "race to the court house" —with each side trying to get the case filed first in its own hometown. This is often followed by an expensive dispute over the highly technical subject of whether the defendant is subject to jurisdiction in the chosen court and whether the "venue" (place of litigation) is fair and convenient.

- If you get into litigation in a foreign court system, you will need foreign counsel to handle the dispute. That can add considerable expense—as can the cost of traveling to trial and the cost of translations.

Restriction on Assignment Clauses

Another contingency that contracts must manage is assignments and changes of control. Often contracts have clauses that forbid one party or both from assigning the agreement without consent. Here is a sample:

> *Neither party may assign, directly or indirectly, all or part of its rights or obligations under this Agreement without the prior written consent of the other party, which consent shall not be unreasonably withheld or delayed. The rights and obligations of this Agreement shall bind and benefit the permitted successors or assigns of the parties.*

The purpose of these clauses is to avoid substitution of the other party by a less creditworthy or trustworthy company.

The common objection to this kind of clause is that it can prevent or slow down an asset-sale "exit" transaction or a "spin-off" of a business operation. Many companies resist any clause that makes them less free to sell their operations. For this reason, parties often use clauses such as the following:

> *Neither party may assign this Agreement without the prior written consent of the other party, which consent shall not be unreasonably withheld or delayed. Notwithstanding the foregoing, either party may, without the consent of the other, assign the Agreement to (i) a subsidiary that it controls or (ii) a purchaser of all or substantially all of that party's assets related to this Agreement, provided that the assignee has unconditionally assumed in writing the obligations of the assignor under this Agreement. The rights and obligations of this Agreement shall bind and benefit permitted successors or assigns of the parties.*

Because these clauses can be technical—and because they potentially affect exit transactions—you should get your lawyer's advice on provisions that purport to restrict contract assignments.

Change of Control

There is a difference between an assignment and a "change of control." In an assignment, the party to a contract passes the contract rights on to another party. For example:

- *You signed an agreement with Company A. As permitted in the contact, Company A assigns the contract to Company B. Your licensee is now Company B as a result of the assignment.*

In a change of control, ownership of a party to a contract changes.

- *First example: You signed an agreement with Company A. The shareholders of Company A all sell their shares to Company B. Your agreement is still with Company A, but ownership and control of Company A have changed.*

- *Second example: You signed an agreement with Company A. Company A merges with Company B, leaving majority control of the resulting entity in the hands of the shareholders of Company B, which is the surviving corporation. Your agreement is now with Company B, but there was no contract assignment. The change happened as a matter of corporate law.*

Here is a common contract definition of change of control:

- *"Change of Control" means the occurrence of any of the following with regard to a party: (i) consolidation or merger with any other corporation or entity in which the shareholders of a party as constituted immediately before the transaction own less than fifty percent (50%) of the voting shares of the combined entity or (ii) a transaction or related series of transactions effecting a change in ownership of more than fifty percent (50%) of the voting shares of a party held by shareholders as of the effective date of the Agreement.*

Many run-of-the-mill software licenses have no change of control provision. Simple end-user licenses never have them. On the other hand, they need to be considered for every contract that has a strategic impact. For example:

- A party may not want its technology or trade secrets getting into the hands of a competitor.

- A party simply does not want to deal with a different customer or vendor.

- A party is concerned that a change of control will affect contract performance or quality or render the other party less creditworthy.

Most often the company looking for this kind of protection will want the right to terminate the contract in an unwanted change of control situation.

In some cases, a party will bargain for a right to have *its own* change of control trigger a termination right. This kind of clause is designed for easy exit transactions. They allow the party to shed its "partners" when it sells control.

Miscellaneous "Boilerplate" Clauses

At the end of the contract, we often find "miscellaneous" provisions—what law-yers call "boilerplate." Even in these common clauses, you will find variations and occasionally a trap or two. Here are some that you commonly will find:

Force Majeure. This is a provision excusing late performance if due to events beyond a party's control (often called an "Act of God"). These clauses are for contingen-cies such as earthquake, hurricane, fire, flood, war, and so forth. Sometimes, they also cover strikes and other labor actions. Some clauses permit agreement termi-nation if the force majeure stoppage in performance goes on too long.

Notice. These provisions provide procedures for giving notice. They are usu-ally not controversial. Some versions provide for notice by courier (such as DHL or FedEx) and some have provision for use of fax or e-mail. Notice provi-sions will often specify when a notice is "deemed" delivered—for example, on the second business day following its deposit in the US mail. Depending on how they are written, deemed delivery clauses can create that risk that a party will be deemed to have notice when it actually had none.

Waiver. This provision makes it clear that a waiver of a provision on one occa-sion will not mean that it is waived on another. Sometimes, the provision also requires that all waivers be in writing.

Severability. This provision states that if the court for legal reasons nullifies a clause, the remaining clauses will be unaffected. This is a very common provi-sion, but the nullification of a provision is actually quite rare.

Counterpart Originals; Fax Signature. This provision allows fast execution of an agreement by permitting the parties to sign the agreement in different places. Sometimes, we substitute PDFs for faxes.

Entire Agreement. This important provision says that the agreement supersedes earlier or concurrent discussions and agreements. If there are agreements that should not be superseded, the text should make that clear as well.

THIRD TOPIC: CONTRACT NEGOTIATIONS

The final section of this chapter is about the tactics and methods of negotiation. These methods are not new. Although software and digital technology agreements provide a particular business context, the basic tactics of contract negotiation are probably unchanged from the days of early written contracts in ancient Egypt and Babylon. If you are a veteran of many negotiations, the discussion in this section may be old hat. If you are new to the process, it will help you.

Some software and digital technology agreements are negotiated and some (such as shrinkwraps and clickwraps) are not. However, major deals come from negotiations. Companies that acquire products to resell, that have complex products, or work through distribution and "partners" have negotiations all the time.

The negotiation of a contract is a process that requires time and attention as well as business savvy. When an agreement is poorly conceived or important issues are missed, conflict and litigation wait in the wings.

Preparation for Negotiation: the Overall Strategy

As all veterans of negotiations know, a good agreement comes together as the result of a sound strategy and a lot of hard work. Contract negotiation must be seen as a process. First, there is a period of selling. Then there is serious negotiation on terms—the most important issues first, then all the others. Finally, a deal is documented. The process can take days, weeks, or months.

Before any negotiation, you need to formulate your bargaining position and strategy. As the negotiating process goes forward, of course, your plan for the negotiation should be constantly re-evaluated and adjusted. As noted above, your attorney may be able to help you structure deals as well as "papering" them when the deal structure is in place.

Get the Background Information You Need

It is always good to get as much information as you can about the company that you are negotiating with—and what its needs are. You should find out what the other side has done on similar deals. How much has it paid or charged? On what terms has it insisted, and on which issues has it been flexible?

It is also important to find out who are the key decision-makers for the other side. To make that key deal with another company, you will usually need an advocate on the inside of the other company. You should try to understand the players on the other side and their roles. In many cases, you will be dealing with a team on the other side, including representatives from the legal department, the finance department, production, information services, and so forth. You should understand the role and concerns of each player. It is important to find out who inside the other side's organization has to approve the deal and who has the clout to conclude a deal.

Be Sure That You Can Deliver Value to the Other Side

You need to analyze realistically how your product can help the other side. If you have an enterprise software product, you need to explain how it will solve a problem, cut costs, or increase profits. If you want to license software for distribution to a large reseller, you need to analyze how your software will help sell the reseller's other products. The better you can sell your product's benefits, the more likely it is that you will close a deal.

Assess Your Credibility

An important quality in software negotiations is credibility. Established companies often have it, and small early stage companies often don't.

The history of software is full of long delays and vaporware (promised software that never appears). Many software products have failed to perform adequately. Some custom software and new products are delivered with unacceptable amounts of bugs and errors. If you have a startup business, you will need to bolster your case with testimonials and case studies from existing customers and demonstrate that you have the wherewithal to deliver and support the product. Some customers may want you to prove your financial viability and profitability.

Look for a Deal that Works for Both Sides

Before negotiating, you should have a fairly good idea of the deal that ought to come out of the process—a deal that makes economic sense for both sides. This means having a sound grasp of your own costs and margins and an understanding of the economic value of your goods and services to the other side. If you cannot see how the dollars work for both sides, it may not make sense to negotiate in the first place.

Try to Start with Your Own Form

Negotiation is easier if your own form agreement or proposed contract is the starting point for the negotiations. Vendors of software and digital products and services usually put their own form contract on the table. Many submit it in PDF format in the hope (often the vain hope) of preventing negotiation. On the other hand, some large corporations have a policy of using their own forms for all acquisition negotiations.

Negotiating from the Other Side's "Standard Agreement"

Aside from simple consumer shrinkwraps, there is really no such thing as a "standard" commercial digital contract. There is no objective standard as to what should be in an agreement. There are only agreements and provisions that favor one side or another.

You should study carefully any form sent to you, then negotiate to modify the draft to make the bargain more balanced. It is not enough simply to react to what is *in* the other side's draft; you also have to pay attention to the important issues that have been *left out*. This chapter can help, but you may well need an attorney to understand the issues fully and frame an appropriate response.

When the other side has sent a proposed agreement, a common and effective response is to send back a marked-up copy of the draft with suggested changes. You can also raise the issues that you have with the other side's draft by sending a list of issues for discussion. In any case, it is usually best to meet (or have a conference call) and go through the issues one by one.

Sometimes, a party has a bargaining position so weak that it is forced to accept a one-sided agreement lock, stock, and barrel. But in the overwhelming majority of deals, there is room for bargaining and some pressure on both sides to compromise.

A word of warning about negotiating changes in other parties' form contracts when acquiring software or other digital licenses. Some form contracts have language prohibiting sales staff from changing terms absent a sign-off by headquarters. Those clauses can invalidate side letters or additions grafted on by salespersons acting without authority. If you negotiate to modify such a form, get the changes in writing in the text, or an addendum to the original agreement, and get the agreement, with its modifications, signed by the right person.

Develop Justifications for Your Positions

To negotiate effectively, you need to develop justifications for your positions. Be prepared to sell your positions just as you might sell a product. This applies to the technical legal terms just as much as the core business terms. When you are attempting to resolve open items, try to emphasize the ways in which your proposals benefit the other side—or advance the mutual aims of both parties.

Negotiating in the Right Setting

Negotiations are more likely to succeed in a setting—such as a conference room—where there will be no distractions. Try to block out enough time for conference calls to cover all outstanding issues.

It is important to get everyone to set aside enough time to explore the full set of issues. A meeting that is too short or constantly interrupted by telephone calls will not accomplish anything. Don't underestimate the value of face-to-face meetings for overcoming hard negotiation points.

Deal with the Most Important Terms First

It is best to focus on the key issues first. In negotiations involving software, the most important terms are usually features, time of availability, integration, maintenance, support, and price. If those terms come into place, the parties will have a substantial incentive to resolve all the other terms.

Where business points are at issue, sometimes the parties can be most effective in bargaining without counsel present. However, attorneys need to be involved soon thereafter to make sure that there actually is an agreement. Often parties think they have resolved a point, but have not addressed the key points where their interests differ.

Listen Hard

It may be the case that the other party has agendas you don't understand. It is important to listen carefully to what they say and what they leave unsaid. Sometimes, you can infer a lot from the way the other side discusses an issue. If you get a surprising position from the other side or any unexpectedly easy concession, you should try to figure out why; there may be a concealed message.

Contract drafts can likewise be used to discover information from the other party. When the other side refuses to accept a provision that seemed reasonable or proposes unexpected language, it may be the sign of an agenda or a problem that they have not yet disclosed.

Make Trades Rather than Concessions

Don't be quick to offer concessions. Negotiations are like a ratchet mechanism—once you've made a concession, you cannot take it back without putting the negotiating process at risk. It is much better to propose trade-offs, in which you give up something in exchange for some concession on the other side. This is why it is important not to bargain piecemeal, one issue at a time. Get all of the important issues out on the table and be prepared to systematically horse trade.

Smart bargainers map out positions that leave them bargaining room—so that they can trade concessions when it gets them an advantage in return.

Negotiate Price Terms with Firmness

Price negotiation is usually a process of give and take. It is best to position yourself for price negotiations by starting out with a figure or pricing formula that leaves room for bargaining to get to your real figure.

Don't be quick to drop your position on price. You want to avoid bidding against yourself.

Often disagreements on the price terms can be closed with an offer of something extra—an additional program or function—rather than a price concession. When opposing positions on price are very close, then it is often the right time to split the difference and arrive at the final price.

Knowing When to Say "No" and When to Say "Yes"

The word "no" is both the most powerful and the most dangerous word in negotiations. When you make it clear that a key point is "deal killer," you force the other side to compromise or walk away from the deal. This is something that you need to be prepared to do—or your position may be steamrollered.

Negotiating tough issues requires patience and it may take time to get the other side to come around to your position—or it may be impossible to get them to do it. Sometimes, negotiators simply become tired and begin to make concessions just to get the deal done. We call this "deal fatigue." Too often we have seen companies make unwise concessions to get a deal closed by quarter end in order to "make their numbers." Remember that very bad deals are most often worse than no deal at all.

It is also important for the negotiators to understand when offers from the other side, even if far from ideal, are good enough. That involves an analysis of all the factors discussed in this chapter.

THE ROLE OF LEGAL COUNSEL

Some agreements are simple variations on your own contract forms. In some cases, the only issues are features and price. Many companies have lists of approved contract language variations. For negotiations within set parameters, there may not be much for a lawyer to do—and you may be comfortable doing the deal without a lawyer's assistance. However if the stakes are high, the matter is very complicated or you if are working from the other side's form, a lawyer's assistance can be indispensible.

No agreement can completely eliminate business risk, and no contract can cover every possible contingency that might arise. It follows that even using a lawyer will not ensure a perfect agreement. So then why is counsel needed? Good attorneys in this field will understand how to draft agreements that fit your business context. They know what clauses and language are normally found in agreements for a particular type of transaction or relationship. They also know how the use of certain terms and provisions can shift the risks. Having a competent attorney on your deal team will help you know the issues, avoid errors, and close on your best deal.

Legal representation can also be used tactically in negotiations. Sometimes, lawyers play the "bad cop," taking hard line positions that coming from the business person might seem too tough. At other times, lawyers play the "good cop," making the peace when negotiations break down.

A Pragmatic Guide to Open Source

I'd like to say that I knew this would happen, that it's all part of the plan for world domination. But honestly this has all taken me a bit by surprise.

—Linus Torvalds, chief architect of Linux, speaking of its success, in *Open Sources: Voices from the Open Source Revolution* (1999)

INTRODUCTION

Open source licensing is an important software and IT licensing tool. You need to know its opportunities, advantages, challenges, tricks, and traps. This chapter is a practical guide to open source licensing.

IN THIS CHAPTER

This chapter covers the following:

- The nature of open source licensing and how open source licensing differs from proprietary licensing

- The advantages and disadvantages of open source

- The two major categories of open source licenses: "BSD-Type" licenses and the GNU General Public License (GPL) and other "Copyleft" licenses. This discussion covers both GPL Version 2 and GPL Version 3, which was issued in mid-2007

- Implied and express patent licenses in open source licensing

237

- Open source and trademarks

- Copyright and patent risks in open source

- Business models—how to make money with open source products and open source licenses

- How software under Copyleft licenses (like the GPL) can be made (almost) proprietary

- Combined open source and proprietary licensing strategies

THE POPULARITY OF OPEN SOURCE SOFTWARE

The open-source "movement" is a major factor in the computer industry and in information technology in general.

The best-known open source program is Linux, a collaborative effort begun and still guided by Finnish programmer Linus Torvalds, with the aid of many other contributors and collaborators. This operating system software is available as open source software under the GPL Version 2 license (discussed below).

The Linux operating system is widely used in the commercial world as well as in science and engineering. Linux runs on a great variety of computer and consumer electronics hardware—from PCs to mainframes, from video recorders to PDAs. IBMs endorsement of Linux and its adapting IBMs enterprise software programs to the Linux operating system gave Linux, and open source licensing in general, legitimacy in the enterprise. Oracle's database management software and many other mainstream programs now run on Linux. Red Hat, a profitable company that provides open source Linux under commercial subscription licenses, is listed on NASDAQ. Google's huge Internet search operation runs on Linux servers.

In addition to Linux, there are thousands of other programs available under open source licensing. Some of the best known are Apache (the most popular Web server in the world), MySQL (a popular database), Firefox (the Web browser), Open Office (a "productivity suite"), and Perl (a very widely used scripting language for Internet applications). A number of mainstream software companies have released their own open source products. These include IBM, Real Networks, Sun Microsystems, and Apple. Open source components are commonly embedded in commercial software products and devices, as well.

The best-known open source software is written for broad "horizontal" applications, where there are likely to be many users and many adapters across many economic sectors. Open source is part of a long-term trend in computing toward a commodity infrastructure where all the basic building blocks are inexpensive. These days, processing power is inexpensive, storage is cheap, and now the software infrastructure is becoming low cost due to open source.

What Is Open Source Software?

Open source is not a technology. There is nothing about any piece of software itself that makes it open source. Open source is rather an increasingly popular licensing and distribution method. When we refer to "open source software," we simply mean a computer program that can be obtained under an open source license.

Open source licensing, paradoxically, is not about licensing source code per se. Usually open source involves licensing binary computer programs where the source code is available. In some cases, users of open source programs do make use of the source code. But many—indeed most—users of open source-licensed products do not use the source code at all; they simply run and use the binary versions of the program.

However, the availability of the source code and distinctive features of open source licenses (discussed below) are important determiners of how the product can be distributed and exploited, and therefore they make open source software different in very important ways.

Source Code vs. Binary Code

Source code access is important. If one has only the binary code for a particular program (without the source code), it is extremely difficult and expensive to reverse engineer the program to recover and read its logic and underlying algorithms. It is also prohibitively difficult to enhance complex programs that are available only in binary form or fix errors that they may contain. Source code is thus the key to maintaining and improving any software program.

Proprietary Source Code in Software Business

Microsoft, Oracle, SAP, and thousands of other software vendors operate their businesses under what is called the "Proprietary Model." Under the Proprietary

Model, source code is kept as a closely guarded trade secret. By maintaining the secrecy of the source code, the software vendor has sole control of the contents of its software products, the development of new features, and maintenance.

It is a cliché in the software business that to create the first copy of a commercial software program may cost millions, but the next million copies cost pennies each. In fact, packaged goods can be created for a few dollars each, and as electronic downloads, the cost is a fraction of a cent per megabyte. So the goals for software vendors are to sell repeatedly high margin licenses for the same software, periodically create new and better versions of that software (licensing the new versions for additional fees), and sell support and maintenance services for that software. Having sole access to the source code is necessary for the Proprietary Model to work.

Commercial Source Code Licensing

There are commercial models for licensing source code as well. Some vendors are in the business of licensing of proprietary source code. This is particularly true for makers of programs that are used as components of other programs, where the ability to modify and customize the source code is important to the licensee.

Commercial licensing of proprietary source code is a variant of the Proprietary Model; vendors keep the source code a trade secret. They do this by imposing a contractual obligation on every licensee to keep the source code secret and to distribute only binary derivatives of the source code.

Origins of Open Source

Open source was born from a desire to step away from the Proprietary Model.

Open sharing of source code was routine in the early days of mainframe and minicomputer computing. In the 1960s and 1970s, commercial and academic programmers and computer researchers often made source code available freely. However, by the late 1970s and early 1980s, the wealth that software produced and the increased application of copyright law to computer programs changed the computer world. The Proprietary Model of software development came to dominate. Source code became closed.

As the Proprietary Model took hold, former MIT computer researcher Richard Stallman was frustrated by the privatization of UNIX and other programs. In 1985, Stallman founded the Free Software Foundation (www.fsf.org or www .gnu.org) as a nonprofit organization to serve as a platform for holding, creating, and promulgating software that would be open and free. The organization serves that function to this day. In 1989, Stallman created the GNU GPL, discussed below, which became a widely used open source contract form. GNU, which has become a brand name for his model of licensing, stands for "GNUs Not UNIX." (As is discussed below, the most common version of the GPL is Version 2, issued in 1991.)

Another nonprofit organization, the Open Source Initiative (OSI, www .opensource.org), was formed in 1998 to help popularize this new model of shared software creation. It is said that the OSIs founders coined and promoted the term "open source" in hopes of making the software sound more acceptable to the mainstream software community. The term caught on in the mass media almost immediately. The OSIs Web site remains one of the best sources on the Web for information about open source licenses and software.

The Generations of Open Source

Open source licensing began as an attempt to capture and formalize an early model of collaborative, open, and free software development. In the paradigm of such development, a cadre of unpaid but dedicated collaborators jointly creates noncommercial high-quality products that may be spread around the globe for free by means of open source licenses. Important open source products such as Linux and Apache did indeed arise from dedicated small groups of innovators who were assisted by many individuals and companies that contributed (and continue to contribute) code for free. This collaborative enterprise takes enormous amounts of time and has no profit motive. This is indeed about as far as one can get from the Proprietary Model.

However, the profit motive is irrepressible, and it has now invaded the open source world. It turns out that you can make a lot of money with open source. We will discuss below some of the business models that companies use to profit from open source.

The Open Source Model of Licensing

There are a great variety of open source licenses, and therefore the term "open source licensing" can vary somewhat in meaning. However, all open source licenses share a few common elements. Open source licenses all give the licensee:

- The grant of a license to the source code for a program along with the binary version. (Under some license forms, each licensee is required to make source code available to sublicensees. In some cases, the source code is simply widely available as a matter of custom and practice.)

■ The grant of a license to make derivative works of the program using the source code without paying a license fee.

■ The grant of a license to make and distribute unlimited copies of the program, including the source code, the binary product, and derivative works without paying a license fee.

Note that open source licensing is not the same as licensing for free. Although many open source programs often are widely available for free, there are open source programs commonly licensed for a fee. Moreover, open source licensing is not the same as granting a license to the public generally or dedicating a program to the public domain. The copyright(s) for open source software is licensed, but it is not given away.

Perceived Advantages

Some of the claimed advantages of open source software and the collaborative manner in which some (but by no means all) open source software is created are these:

■ Because the source code is available, open source proponents claim that logical errors and security "holes" are more likely to be found and fixed quickly. This means that open source programs are assertedly more reliable and secure than proprietary programs.

■ Because many open source programs are available for free or at low prices, proponents claim that they provide more value.

■ Open source licensing allows for fast spreading and adoption of new products and features.

■ Because open source has so many contributors and potential distributors, proponents contend that they are less vulnerable to competitive forces. If the supplier of a proprietary software program goes out of business, its product may die. It is much harder to kill an open source product, because any licensee can become a licensor.

While assertions of technical superiority or value are hard to prove, it is undeniable that the ability to obtain software at a low price or for free drives the adoption of open source programs. This is particularly true where there is a need to deploy low-cost commodity software over a large number of desktops, devices, or applications.

Perceived Disadvantages

Critics of open source software point out the following risks associated with open source programs:

- Many open source products come without warranty or support. Open source critics therefore contend that at least some errors in community-supported products will not be repaired.

- Where there are many contributors, it is possible that some code may be wrongfully inserted without copyright owners' permission.

- Most open source products come without intellectual property indemnification. Therefore, open source critics point out that there is a risk that the licensee will have no remedy in case of an infringement claim.

- Open source critics claim that "Copyleft" open source licenses, particularly the GNU Public License (discussed below), can cause inadvertent loss of proprietary rights.

Users will have to make their own assessment of the risk that errors will be unrepaired. We will discuss the other key matters on this risk list—intellectual property matters and "Copyleft" clauses—below.

OPEN SOURCE LICENSES

There are scores of open source license forms. You can, at the time this is being written, see 64 open source licenses on the Web site of the Open Source Initiative and more are invented from time to time. Anyone can write his or her own open source license. (Our law firm has created new open source licenses for its clients.) The license forms have proliferated because different licensors have sought to craft license provisions to serve their own goals. There is certainly no substitute for reading the licenses, and I recommend that any one involved with open source read at least a few.

If you review many open source forms, you will find that common open source licenses fall into two broad categories: One category, which as we will see has very few restrictions, is called "BSD-Type" or "Open." The other category, which is more restrictive, is called "Copyleft" or "Free." The "Free" categorization is somewhat ironic because a Copyleft license permits a developer considerably less freedom of action than a BSD-Type license. Also any person or company is completely free to charge money for software under a "Free" license. Copyleft licenses are "Free" in a rather special and somewhat ideological sense; they are designed to stop code from being transformed into proprietary products. Figuring out that a license could be made to have a perpetual anti-proprietary function and be "Copyleft" in this way was Richard Stallman's great and brilliant innovation.

Common open source licenses in the BSD-Type category, aside from the BSD License itself (first used for the BSD UNIX operating system from the University of California at Berkeley), are the MIT License and the W3C Software License (from the World Wide Web Consortium).

The best-known Copyleft licenses are the GNU GPL (Version 2 of the GPL is the most famous open source license because it is used for Linux) and its somewhat less restrictive cousin, the GNU Lesser General Public License or "LGPL." Also in this category, but somewhat less restrictive than the GPL, are the Apple Public Source License (used by Apple to license Darwin, a version of UNIX that is at the core of the Macintosh operating system OSX), the IBM Public License, and the Mozilla Public License (MPL) (used to license the Mozilla browser).

BSD License

To get an idea of how permissive a license can be, let's take a look at the current BSD License itself. (This is sometimes called the "New BSD License" because it superseded a pre-1999 version.) It is a simple half page agreement widely available on the Web. It has a copyright notice at the beginning and an "AS IS" disclaimer at the end, together with this text:

> *Redistribution and use in source and binary forms, with or without modification, are permitted provided that the following conditions are met:*
>
> 1. *Redistributions of source code must retain the above copyright notice, this list of conditions, and the following disclaimer.*
>
> 2. *Redistributions in binary form must reproduce the above copyright notice, this list of conditions, and the following disclaimer in the documentation and/or other materials provided with the distribution.*

3. *The name of the author may not be used to endorse or promote products derived from this software without specific prior written permission.*

That's it! Including the copyright notice and disclaimer, it is about half a page. The license has no restriction on what you can do with the licensed code or how you can use it. There is no obligation that sublicenses be under any open source license; nothing stops use of a typical proprietary license. There is no obligation for the licensee to redistribute binary derivatives with source code. The only limitation is a requirement for a notice in documentation and other materials, which most likely few users will bother to read.

Taking BSD-Licensed Code Private

If you are the licensee of a BSD-licensed program, you can modify the source code and keep the resulting modified source code completely private. You are allowed to add in any other code you want. You may, if you like, distribute only binary versions of the resulting versions. You are free to put BSD-licensed code into your existing proprietary application without disclosing the resulting source code. You can put the resulting combined binary code under a proprietary license as long you also supply to your licensees the notices required by the BSD form as cited above.

If you do modify the BSD-licensed code (or combine it with other code) and keep the resulting source code in your sole possession, you thus can become the only person in the world who can maintain the resulting product or create upgrades of it. You can also assert the legal monopoly granted by copyright law over whatever portion is your own contribution. This means that, by modifying the BSD-licensed program or combining it with your own source code into a new product, you can effectively bring BSD-licensed open source software across the line into the Proprietary Model.

This is what developers like about BSD licenses. These licenses allow great freedom of use. However, this ability to privatize and commercialize is a bit at odds with the ideological goal of some open source licensing to keep code "free" from commercial control, which is why other open source license forms are much more restrictive.

GPL Version 2

The GNU GPL of the Free Software Foundation is an early open source license that is widely used. It is also one of the most restrictive of common open source licenses. (The commonly used version of the GPL is "Version 2" issued in 1991, and that is the subject of the discussion in this section. There is a discussion of the 2007 GPL Version 3 below.)

In some ways, the GPL Version 2 grants a great deal of freedom. Like a BSD-Type license, the GPL grants the licensee unlimited rights to use the software, make and distribute copies, and make derivatives. However, the GPL, true to its anti-proprietary origins, also has added restrictions that are designed to keep the software from coming under any particular licensee's control. The GPL has provisions of a type that are never found in the BSD-Type license but are characteristic of Copyleft licenses generally.

Required Source Availability

When you, as a GPL licensee, license the GPL-licensed code (or any derivative) to someone else, you are required to make the source code available to each licensee of distributed binary copies. While you can charge as much as you want for each copy of the program, you must provide the source code (including source code changes that you distribute in binary form) either without charge or for a charge that covers only the cost of reproduction. You are not permitted to make binary-only distribution. We call this "Required Source Availability."

License Inheritance

The GPL provides that you can modify and distribute a program, but only on the condition that you distribute the resulting work (called a "work based on the Program") under the terms of the GPL.

The GPL also provides that:

Each time you redistribute the Program (or any work based on the Program), the recipient automatically receives a license from the original licensor to copy, distribute or modify the Program subject to these terms and conditions. You may not impose any further restrictions on the recipients' exercise of the rights granted herein.

This means that any GPL licensee can distribute the software code or derivatives under the GPL and only the GPL. You cannot add or subtract any license term or condition. We call this "License Inheritance."

Being Copyleft

These two features—Required Source Availability and License Inheritance—give the GPL its "Copyleft" aspect. Unlike code under a BSD-Type license, a GPL licensee cannot bring code into the Proprietary Model. Rather the GPL is designed to perpetually lock each licensee into the GPL model for any further distribution. As copyright is a right to *exclude* others, the "Copyleft" is a requirement that licensees be *included* in development, distribution, and source code access rights, but always under the Copyleft license.

Copyleft licenses exclude other inconsistent licenses—which renders them "incompatible" with commercial licenses and some, but not all, open source licenses. To determine whether two open source licenses are compatible, you need to read and compare both. When two licenses are incompatible, you cannot mix software under the two licenses and distribute the resulting code without violating one or both licenses. Version 2 of the GPL is incompatible, for example, with the Apache Public License, a Copyleft agreement that covers the popular Apache server. Incompatibility is not a problem, however, as long as you keep the two programs separate—even if they both operate in the same computer.

The GPL also has a feature that makes it particularly "sticky" when GPL code is mixed with other programs. The GPL says that it applies to "any work that you distribute or publish, that *in whole or in part contains or is derived from the Program or any part thereof …*" (Emphasis supplied.)

Because of this phase, many fear the GPL, and indeed some call this a "viral" license. For example, if you take a small GPL-licensed program and combine it with a million lines of your own proprietary code, the GPL requires that you distribute the entire program under the GPL—or refrain from any distribution at all.

- If you licensed the resulting combined program under the GPL, you would, of course, grant all subsequent licensees a license for unlimited royalty-free distribution of your proprietary source code.

- Let say that, ignoring the GPL terms, you distribute the resulting combined program under a proprietary license. Then the included GPL-licensed code would be unlicensed (because you distributed it under an incompatible license)—and your unlicensed distribution therefore would infringe the copyright on the GPL-licensed code. The copyright owner of the GPL-licensed code presumably could sue you for copyright infringement.

Some critics of open source have seized upon the Copyleft or "viral" nature of the GPL to charge that open source licensing is a kind of IP cancer. It is important to keep this in perspective:

- It is a misconception that mixing all or part of a GPL program with your proprietary code, without more, somehow converts the whole into GPL code. In fact, the GPL gives you a choice. You can distribute the combined work under the GPL or not at all. The GPL has no affect at all on an enterprise that obtains a GPL-licensed product and just uses it internally (including use in an online application that allows third parties to use it remotely).

- Copyleft clauses do not affect programs that are clearly separate. For example, IBMs Websphere, a Web portal manager program, runs on GPL-licensed Linux and may be shipped with Linux, but it remains fully an IBM proprietary program.

- Many open source programs use the much less restrictive BSD-Type licenses. There are also other Copyleft licenses that are less "sticky" than the GPL.

On the other hand, GPL-code should not be combined in the same work with any program that is intended for proprietary distribution for the reasons related above. This means that developers and their legal counsel must act with caution when planning for proprietary products that come with code licensed under the GPL or other Copyleft licenses. In some cases, the issues involved in deciding whether the GPL code is a different program or part of a combined program are quite technical. The *"Frequently Asked Questions about the GNU GPL"* document found online at the Free Software Foundation Web site may help with some of the subtleties of Copyleft under the GPL. We also recommend that you read the entire GPL Version 2 text.

There are other quirky aspects of GPL Version 2 that the reader will discover. One notable provision requires that when a licensee distributes the Program (or a work based on the Program), he or she must have all rights and permissions for unlimited royalty-free distribution, including all patent licenses. If you, as a would-be distributor, cannot get those permissions, then the GPL says you must "refrain entirely from distribution" of the Software. What happens if a GPL licensor distributes GPL-licensed software products in violation of this provision? The test of the GPL does not say. This is not a purely academic question. For example, there are a number of MP3 encoders available under the GPL that do not come with the required patent licenses for MP3 encoding. Presumably the GPL licenses granted are valid notwithstanding this language, but no one knows for sure.

The courts have provided very little guidance to date about this or other open source license interpretation issues. There is an April 2, 2004 German opinion involving the GPL issued by the Munich District Court. The court in that case ruled in a suit brought by a copyright holder of software called "netfilter/iptabes project" against a licensee Sitecom. Sitecom was shipping products that included the plaintiff's GPL-licensed software but failed to make source code available. The court found this to be a breach and enjoined Sitecom from distributing its product unless Sitecom complied with its GPL obligations.

The first ever US open source lawsuit was filed in September 2007 by the two developers and copyright owners of a UNIX toolkit who released it under the GPL. The suit was against a licensee that allegedly refuses to distribute the source code for its software program that incorporates the toolkit. As of the time we are writing this chapter in 2007, there has been no court ruling.

While there are precious few case decisions on open source licensing, most lawyers who practice in the area consider the GPL and many other open source licenses to be enforceable in the United States and in other countries only by the *owners of the copyright* to the program code that is being used in a manner inconsistent with the license.

GPL Version 3

On June 29, 2007, the Free Software Foundation issued a new version of the GPL, known as Version 3—16 years after Version 2. It is not clear yet how important or popular Version 3 will be. For the present, at least, Linux remains under Version 2 and it is unclear how many developers will ultimately opt to put new works under Version 3. The following is an overview of Version 3, but there is no substitute for reading the document itself, which you can find at www.fsf.org.

A Lot of Continuity
As a whole, Version 3 is more verbose, more complex, and more like a lawyer-drafted license than Version 2. Nonetheless, GPL Version 3 is very much like Version 2 in effect. It is still Copyleft in nature and just as "viral."

The new version introduces new terminology and definitions. For example, in Version 3 you "propagate" programs rather than "copy and distribute" them as in Version 2. Version 3 is more precise about exactly what source code you are required to make available under the GPL and how you can provide it to licensees.

Incompatible and Compatible
GPL Version 3 and GPL Version 2 are incompatible. If you combine code that you got under GPL Version 3 with code you received under GPL Version 2, neither

GPL license version can be used for the combination. That's because each license, in effect, excludes the other. This means that the resulting code is not legally distributable at all. There is no way to evade this incompatibility. (You could, of course, distribute separate programs under GPL Version 3 and GPL Version 2 on the same disk.)

On the other hand, GPL Version 3 was drafted to be compatible with the Apache public license—which, as noted, is incompatible with GPL Version 2.

Differences and New Sections

Here are some of the more important new features in GPL Version 3:

Waiving Anticircumvention

The Free Software Foundation (and particularly its founder Richard Stallman) does not like anticircumvention law under the DMCA (discussed in Chapter 2), which the Foundation considers contrary to the principle of fair and legitimate access to copyrighted information. Version 3 provides that any licensor under the GPL waives its applicable anticircumvention rights.

Anti-Tivoization

If you buy a Tivo-brand digital video recorder (DVR), you get a product that runs on Linux and other GPL Version 2 licensed software. Tivo is in compliance with GPL Version 2, because Tivo makes the source code available to anyone. However, anyone who edits the Tivo software will find that the modified version won't run on the Tivo device. That's because every Tivo DVR is programmed not to run if there is any change in its software. The Free Software Foundation considers this practice, which it calls "Tivoization," to be inconsistent with the freedom of software users. (Tivo considers it a security feature.)

To combat Tivoization, Version 3 provides that the license does not apply to software in a consumer product unless the product permits modification without interfering with its "continued functioning."

Anti-Microsoft-Novell

If you follow software news on the Web, you know that Microsoft has publicly claimed that Linux infringes 235 Microsoft-owned patents. Distributors of Linux disagree and say Linux is non-infringing. (As of the time this is written, Microsoft had not sued any Linux publisher or user for patent infringement.)

Novell (which distributes Suse Linux) was concerned that these Microsoft patent assertions cast a cloud of doubt over Linux that might chill Linux sales.

So Novell entered into an agreement with Microsoft in which each company agreed not to sue each other's customers for patent infringement and Novell agreed to pay Microsoft a royalty on Linux sales.

The Free Software Foundation believes that Novell's deal with Microsoft compromises the freedom of Linux under the GPL and of Linux users. To stop this kind of deal for any software under Version 3, the Free Software Foundation inserted a provision that makes the Version 3 license ineffective if the would-be GPL licensor is party into an arrangement like the Microsoft-Novell deal—in which the GPL licensor pays for a patent license that benefits some, but not all, users of the program. Version 3 calls such a patent license "discriminatory" based on the concept that a legitimate license would be for all.

Express Patent License

Version 3 has an express patent license grant. If your company creates or modifies and distributes a program under Version 3, you grant a patent license covering the entire program to your licensee. If your company merely distributes a program without changing it at all, your company would not grant such patent license. This provision of Version 3 provides a clear set of patent license rules, which is a GPL first.

Which Version Should You Use?

If you write a new software program and want to release it under the GPL, which version should you select—Version 2 or Version 3?

The main reason for selecting Version 3 would be that you agree with the goals of the new license—that you want to discourage Tivoization for example—or that you like some of the more detailed and precise provisions.

You may have reasons for selecting GPL Version 2. For example, if you want your software to be used as embedded code in a consumer device, you might want to allow "Tivoization." Also if your product is intended to be integrated into a Version 2 product (for example, added to the Linux "kernel"), you may want to use GPL Version 2 so that your license and code will be compatible.

The Lesser General Public License or LGPL

There is another Copyleft License from the Free Software Foundation known as the Lesser General Public License (LGPL), formerly the "Library General Public License." The LGPL is designed for publication of code libraries that are called by other programs.

Generally speaking the LGPL applies the rules of Required Source Availability and License Inheritance discussed above, but only as to the library itself—not to "the work that uses the library." This license allows you to use an open source library under the LGPL and still keep the bulk of your program outside the open source world. Therefore, the LGPL is less "viral" than the GPL. However, the LGPL has its own special rules that limit its flexibility. You should read the LGPL carefully if you wish to use code received under it.

The Mozilla Public License

In part because of perceived problems with the GPL, and also because open source licensors are becoming more legally sophisticated (and are allowing their attorneys to write open source licenses), there are Copyleft licenses that are less restrictive and clearer in their provisions. A good example is the MPL, written by Netscape, Inc., which applies to the well-known Mozilla Web browser.

The MPL is longer and more detailed than GPL Version 2, and it looks like a document created by lawyers rather than a programmer. Under the MPL:

- One can release code that is subject to a patent that the licensor does not control (although the licensor is required to provide notice of known patent issues).

- One can combine MPL code with a proprietary "Larger Work" without affecting or restricting the proprietary licensing of the larger work.

Quasi-Open Source License

In addition to "true" open source licenses, there are licenses that permit source code access, but do not grant the licensee freedom to make and distribute derivatives. These licenses are somewhere between open source and proprietary licenses. One example is Microsoft's "Shared Source" program, under which academics may experiment with certain Microsoft source code, but are forbidden to distribute the results.

Which Open Source License Form Should a Developer Use?

If a developer has created software that it wishes to release under an open source license, how does the developer choose the type of open source license to use? The choice will depend on the application type and on what the developer hopes to achieve.

If the program is a stand-alone application, the developer may want to release it under one of the Copyleft type licenses, because that will allow users to adopt the application, but will help prevent competitors from appropriating the benefits of the developer's work and "taking it private." If competitive exploitation is not a concern, the developer could distribute a product under the less restrictive BSD-Type license.

If the program is one that is normally embedded in another application, then the developer will need to make sure that the open source license chosen is not a barrier to adoption. The viral nature of the GPL, for example, may scare off would-be licensees who are afraid of losing control of their own proprietary code. In that case a less restrictive Copyleft license or a BSD license would more likely promote widespread adoption of the open source code.

If you are in doubt as to your choice of open source licenses, a lawyer familiar with these documents will be able to help you.

Risks in Using Collaboratively Developed Open Source Products

There is some risk in licensing any software—open source or proprietary. A licensee never really knows the provenance of any software it obtains. The licensor may say that the code is original or properly licensed, but there is no way to know for sure if that is true.

While this risk exists for all software, the risk is clearly higher for collaboratively developed open source software. (This risk would likely be much lower for open source programs created by a single company.) As discussed above, some very important open source products, such as Linux and Apache, are the result of a process in which hundreds of individuals have contributed code. For those products, there is no way to be sure that each contributor actually had the rights under copyright law to make the contribution. Therefore, collaboratively developed open source products carry an inherent risk that they might include code included without permission and in violation of some unknown copyright holder's rights.

SCO Litigation

This inherent risk in collaboratively developed open source software has been underscored by the various SCO cases. The litigation was initiated by SCO Group, Inc. (SCO).

In August 2000, SCO, formerly know as Caldera, bought the rights to the version of UNIX known as SCO Linux. In March 2003, SCO sued IBM. SCO alleges that in the mid-1980s IBM entered into a series of agreements to license UNIX from ATT, the originator of UNIX. SCO claims to have acquired ATTs rights under these agreements. SCO alleged that IBM used the UNIX source code and trade secrets that it contains in breach of the various ATT-IBM agreements to make contributions to Linux. Linux is very much like UNIX in logical structure, and this fact perhaps lends weight to SCOs claims. On the other hand, prior to suit, SCO itself licensed Linux to many users under the GPL license, a fact that surely weakens its case. SCOs ownership of the UNIX copyrights has been challenged by Novell.

SCO has also sued two corporate users of Linux, AutoZone and Daimler-Chrysler, alleging wrongful use of SCOs copyrighted content, and SCO has sent letters to many leading corporations claiming that use of Linux is infringing. Red Hat, in turn, has sued SCO; Red Hat is seeking a declaratory judgment that Red Hat Linux code is non-infringing.

While the outcome of the various SCO cases is still uncertain, here are some observations about the litigation:

- The case has gone badly for SCO so far. On August 10, 2007 a federal court ruled that the UNIX copyrights belong to Novell rather than SCO.

- SCO, as of the time this is written, has gone into Chapter 11 proceedings under the Bankruptcy Act.

- So far no major open source program other than Linux has been subjected to a public litigation based on alleged unauthorized contributions of code or trade secrets.

Ironically the SCO litigation has been a marketing opportunity for some Linux vendors. Novell, unlike most Linux providers, now offers indemnification to commercial licensees of its SuSE Linux. Hewlett-Packard (HP) offers indemnification that covers Linux bundled with HP computers, including Linux from Red Hat, SuSE, and Debian. Commercial customers nervous about such claims can now buy protection.

Patent Risks

Aside from the potential copyright risks illustrated in the SCO cases, there is also the matter of potential patent infringement risk from open source programs. However, to date, we have not seen publicized patent suits against open source vendors. (As noted, Microsoft claims that Linux infringes many Microsoft patents, but it has not brought infringement lawsuits so far.)

In some cases, open source programs may use technology widely known to be patented such as telecommunications, encryption, or data compression protocols. In other cases, a licensee of an open source program may have no low-cost way to find out if the product infringes a third party's patent rights—other than to wait to see if anyone asserts a claim. It is reasonable to assume that most open source products have never been subjected to a non-infringement review by patent counsel so their patent risk is unknown.

Dealing Pragmatically with IP Infringement Risk

How will customers deal with the potential intellectual property infringement risks that open source products pose? For most users and licensees, the answer is that reasonable comfort, rather than perfect safety, will be the goal. Licensees will never know for sure that popular open source products such as Linux or the Apache server are free from infringement claims. Rather, users will decide over time whether the risks are real and how serious they may be. If millions are using a program and few or none are sued over the course of years, adoption will continue. For the most risk averse, however, the answer may be to avoid open source software.

Open Source and Implied Patents License Grants

Some forms of open source licenses have express patent license grants and many (particularly the BSD-Type licenses) are silent on patent matters. The GPL Version 2, while containing the quirky patent clause mentioned above, lacks an express patent grant. (As noted, Version 3 includes an express patent license.)

It is likely—but not certain—that a grantor of an open source license which is silent on patent matters does, nonetheless, grants an implied license under US federal law for use of patent rights held by the licensor that are necessary to exercise the license.

As noted, open source licenses all permit licensees to make derivative works. Where the open source license contains no express patent license, does the implied patent license given by the open source licensor under US law extend to all the new functions and features that a licensee may add in creating a derivative product? The answer is unclear but, if so, this could mean that the licensee would potentially have a license to all of the licensor's patents.

On the other hand, the patent licensing issue is expressly managed in some other open source license forms. For example, under the MPL, a licensor grants a patent license that covers only the licensor's own version of the software product, not code that may be added later. The GPL Version 3 license is similar.

The lesson here is that open source licensors that have patents should choose their open source licenses with care.

Open Source License and Trademarks

Trademarks are an important differentiator in open source commercial distribution. For example, there are several suppliers that have created branded versions of Linux. These include Red Hat, SuSE, TurboLinux, and Debian, among others. While these suppliers all distribute Linux under the GPL that permits copying, nothing in the GPL Version 2 permits licensees to use a licensor's trademark. GPL Version 3 allows the licensor to exclude any trademark license.

The "Linux" trademark itself is owned by the Linux Mark Institute, which is controlled by Linus Torvalds, www.linuxmark.org. The Web site includes a license agreement for royalty-free use of the mark subject to the institute's guidelines and provides instructions on how to register for the license.

Open Source Use by Software Vendors

Companies should manage the acquisition of open source products and components. Unfortunately, open source products often enter companies "under the radar screen." Developers often take free software from the Web and include it in products. This often happens without management or the board of directors even knowing it has occurred.

It is good practice for IT companies to implement a process to screen and review open source products and licenses *before* open source software is incorporated into products. The technical staff should be educated about open source issues. Each open source acquisition should trigger a review. With notice, licensing managers and counsel can deal with license and potential infringement issues.

Open Source Software and Due Diligence in Company Sales or Investment Deals

Open source issues often arise when software companies are bought and sold or in investment transactions. Acquirers and investors commonly ask for warranties on open source issues. A typical warranty that an acquirer might ask for is:

Seller represents and warrants that Seller's software does not contain any portion of any open source software.

Due diligence on open source issues has become a regular part of the acquisition and finance landscape. Your company should be prepared to make disclosure of the open source components in its products and to make available to potential buyers and investors the applicable open source licenses.

Making Money with Open Source Programs Generally

Open source licensing began as a reaction against the Proprietary Model, but it is now of great interest to entrepreneurs, established IT vendors, and investors. There are a number of ways to make money with open source products. Here are some of them:

- **Proprietary Products on Open Source Platforms**—Some companies offer proprietary products built on an open source platform. For example, many of IBMs major product offerings, such as its Web Sphere Web application development environment or its DB2 enterprise database, are offered in Linux versions. The open source platform is used primarily because it is reliable, popular, and costs much less than the proprietary products that it replaces.

- **Open Source as Components of Proprietary Products**—Many proprietary software products now include open source components. At our law firm, we have seen products that include half a dozen or more open source components. For example, a number of Web products have embedded copies of the Apache Web server or the Tomcat applications server. Another example was mentioned above: the DVR from Tivo, Inc. which includes a version of Linux adapted for devices (known as "embedded Linux").

- **Proprietary Vendors That Release Open Source Products**—Some companies use open source products tactically to popularize and spread adoption of other products. For example, Apple has released the "Darwin core" underlying its current Macintosh OS-X operating system under an open source license. Apple's hope and expectation is that open source developers will use the code to build more products that run on Apple hardware and thereby add to the market for Apple Macintosh products. Sun Microsystems released its Star Office product, a multiplatform alternative to Microsoft Office, under the GPL in 2000 in hopes of creating desktop competition to Microsoft that would run on Sun hardware (as well as other platforms). The open source version is now known as OpenOffice (available at www.OpenOffice.org).

- **Providing Services and Maintenance for Open Source Software Products—** Some companies provide open source products without charge, but do charge for maintenance, consulting, support, and other services. A company that uses this strategy successfully is JBoss, which offers open source-licensed Web application products. When enterprise customers obtain JBoss software, they want a reliable source of maintenance and support and are willing to pay JBoss for a service agreement.

- **Using Open Source in Consulting—**There are also many integrators, programmers, and other providers of IT services that use open source programs to create and deliver applications to customers under a consulting (fee for service) model.

How Copyleft Programs Can Be Made Quasi-Private

Copyleft licensing was founded out of a desire to keep code free forever. But even GPL-licensed programs, in the right circumstances and with the right strategy, can be "tamed" and brought into a commercial model that gives the GPL licensor control that is quite close to the Proprietary Model.

Red Hat is a profitable public company that has been able to get many large companies to pay for its Linux products on a subscription model (that is, the customer pays every year) in spite of the fact that any licensee of Red Hat Linux is free under the GPL to make copies or even post the source and binary versions of the product on the Internet. So how does Red Hat charge for something that any customer can replicate and give away for free?

Red Hat's strategy (like that of JBoss described above) works primarily because Red Hat is targeting its products at the enterprise market. In this market, most customers do not really care much about source code access. They want reliable, up to date, standardized, and well-supported products that are comparatively inexpensive.

To serve this enterprise market, Red Hat provides standardized periodic releases of its Linux product. Although Red Hat Linux is an open source product, the enterprise version is not freely available from Red Hat. In fact, neither source code nor binary code of its enterprise versions is on its Web site for free downloading. If you want the official enterprise version of Red Hat Linux for free, you need to find someone else who is willing to make a copy available (remember this is permissible under the GPL Version 2 license). Most companies would rather pay to get the product from Red Hat or an authorized distributor. Red Hat also provides user support and maintenance only to subscribers. Red Hat has invested in building its brand, which provides comfort to buyers. Most importantly, perhaps, Red Hat provides subscribers with a suite of *proprietary* (not open source) software tools for installing and managing networks that run Linux. This combination of open source and complementary proprietary products gives Red Hat Linux an added value that cannot be obtained without becoming a subscriber. A subscription agreement with additional products and services therefore complements the GPL that covers Red Hat Linux itself.

This is a business model that will work best for large complex products in mission critical applications where users need and will pay for support, consistency, and complementary products.

Dual Licensing

Some open source vendors use a business model in which the same software is available under a "dual licensing" model, that is, the vendor makes available its product both under open source and commercial licenses. Under this model the developer can choose either to obtain a copy of the software under an open source license at no charge or can obtain a commercially licensed copy for a fee. Why would anyone pay for software that they can also get for free? The answer is that some companies (particularly large companies that want to redistribute the product or incorporate the product in their own software offerings) do not want an obligation to make source code available or to give the software supplier attribution. Some companies may also want support for the software product. To get these benefits, the licensee is often willing to pay for a commercial license for software that is also available for free in open source form.

Why does this strategy benefit the vendor? The answer is that as the open source-licensed copies spread throughout the user community, knowledge of the product and its effectiveness grow. The open source side of this "dual licensing" strategy has a marketing function.

To carry out a dual license strategy, the licensor needs to have these elements in place:

- The licensor needs the legal right to license the software in both a proprietary and open source manner. Companies that use this strategy are normally the copyright owners, a circumstance that gives them the greatest flexibility in licensing choices. However, the licensor could also have the right under a commercial license that is broad enough to permit it.

■ The licensor needs to give the licensee a choice between some kind of Copyleft license and a proprietary license. In order for the proprietary license to be a benefit, the open source license must impose some burdens.

So far the dual licensing strategy has worked best for products that are components of other products. The successes have been MySQL of Sweden and Sleepycat Software of California (which was bought by Oracle), both of which make database products that are intended for embedding in other applications.

In June 2003, MySQL announced that it was changing the license to certain MySQL database components known as libraries from the less restrictive LGPL to the more restrictive GPL license. This was an attempt to force many developers to purchase proprietary licenses rather than using open source software, because it was no longer "safe" for developers to mix their own code with library code from MySQL. Developers protested, particularly users of PHP, another popular open source product used with the MySQL code libraries to develop applications. In face of this resistance, by March 2004, MySQL had beaten a partial retreat and resumed licensing of MySQL libraries in PHP without the burden of the GPL. This example indicates how crucial it is that open source vendors carefully consider the licensing strategies that they use.

Sources of Information on Open Source Matters on the Web

For more information on open source, see

Free Software Foundation—www.fsf.org or www.gnu.org. This is the copyright holder for many GPL- and LGPL-licensed programs. The site contains useful information on the GPL and LGPL open source license forms.

Open Source Initiative—www.opensource.org. The site contains articles on open source concepts and issues and the text of many open source license forms.

CONCLUSION

Open source licensing presents important opportunities. Open source products are widely used in the digital infrastructure. Open source licensing is an ideal model for enabling fast, low-cost diffusion, and adoption of new software products. It can be very profitable with the right business model. However, you should be aware of the challenges and risks that may apply.

IT Services—Development, Outsourcing, and Consulting

10

> *One of my favorite interview questions is, "How would you characterize your approach to software development?".... My favorite answer came from a job candidate who said, "During software design, I'm an architect. While I'm designing the user interface, I'm an artist. During construction, I'm a craftsman. And during unit testing, I'm one mean son of a bitch!"*

> —Steve McConnell, Development Consultant, from *IEEE Software*, January/February 1998

There are many thousands of companies in the business of providing custom IT services, commonly known as "IT consulting." IT consulting is a technology service business; but, because its product is code, it is also an intellectual property business.

In this chapter, you will find a discussion of consulting in general, with particular emphasis on the methods and mechanics of development deals. This chapter looks at deals from both the developer's and the customer's point of view.

IN THIS CHAPTER

This chapter covers:

- The business of consulting and development

- The development process, including characteristic risks

- The request for proposals (RFPs) and project planning processes

- Development agreements, including typical provisions and common negotiation issues

- Issues in offshore IT development

- More consulting deals (other than development agreements)

- Some legal issues in the operation of a consulting business

THE IT CONSULTING BUSINESS MODEL

Consulting companies depend on a cadre of highly trained and well-compensated employees who deliver professional services. Consulting companies usually pay these professional employees generous salaries and benefits. Consulting companies make their profits by charging even more for these employees. This means that personnel costs are high and fixed costs are substantial. (This is the reason that the cost-saving opportunities for offshoring can be very significant.)

Sales are all-important because consulting companies need to keep the "pipeline" full. Consulting companies lose money if they have their highly paid personnel "on the bench." Service companies therefore try their best to find large clients that will provide long-term projects—or project that lend themselves to extensions and follow-up.

Business-oriented consulting is—and always will be—a field where demand fluctuates. Changes in technology stimulate the consulting market. Billions of dollars of consulting came from the introduction of enterprise information systems, client–server and Web architectures, and the deployment of networks, including the Internet. There have been IT booms driven by year 2000 compliance and more recently by the Sarbanes-Oxley Act. Recessions can reduce new business sharply. Consulting firms must meet the demands of the market and must be ready to grow or contract at any time.

Consulting is a fiercely competitive business. Consulting companies compete on price, service, reputation, and expertise. There is a premium on specialization.

DEVELOPMENT DEALS

Development has been a basic part of the IT industry since its infancy. As the quotation at the start of this chapter suggests, development is a tough business requiring many different skills. Without IT consulting, our knowledge-based economy could not exist.

This chapter discusses development deals in some depth. Development agreements are sophisticated contracts involving all the issues that affect IT consulting deals generally, such as the delivery of sophisticated IT-related services, payment matters, risk management, and intellectual property ownership.

Mention IT development and the first thing that comes to mind for most people are projects for big business. Enterprise software development is indeed a major part of the information industry. Major IT service firms, such as Accenture, EDS, Computer Sciences Corporation, or offshoring firms such as Wipro, Infosys, or Tata Consulting Services, have thousands of professionals that span the IT spectrum. There are also thousands of smaller firms in IT consulting. Many software or hardware product companies have development arms to provide customized business solutions based on their technology.

At our law firm, we work on development agreements for enterprise software but we also do development agreements for many other types of software, components, and applications. Whenever one business needs to have another business build some software or a system, there must be a development agreement. The same development agreement issues apply to developing e-commerce solutions, networking software, middleware, messaging applications, games, entertainment, and any other software or IT system. Contracting for IT services covers projects that range from simple one-day consulting jobs to complex multimillion dollar, multideveloper development projects.

Development can meld with other deal types. In some cases, we combine development projects with distribution or marketing arrangements of the type that we discuss in the chapters on distribution deals (Chapters 13 and 14) later in this book. Sometimes we merge development deals with strategic investments. If you are doing such a composite deal, you will need your attorney to create a hybrid of these various deal types.

The combination of a development project with mass-market distribution is a special case, which we call a "publication" arrangement. Chapter 22 discusses publication agreements for video games.

Why Outside Development?

Let's begin with the business background of development engagements. Why do the customer companies do these deals? They do, after all, have a choice—which is to hire staff and do the development jobs themselves. So why do customers go outside? Here are the typical reasons:

- Companies perceive that developers are "experts" who will provide solutions faster and with less risk.

- Development projects are based on the use of third party software products put together with hardware, networks, programming, and configuration to create a solution. Companies want vendors that have existing expertise in the underlying products.

- Companies may see advanced technology solutions from expert developers as conferring a competitive advantage.

- Vendors may have prebuilt software modules that can reduce development time and cost and development risk.

- Companies often want to concentrate on their core technologies and business processes rather than investing time and attention in software systems.

In the contracting process, the key customer goal is likely to be getting a solution quickly and efficiently with low technical risk. Control of the intellectual property may also be a customer goal. The developer's main goal is usually the money but it may also want marketing opportunities, experience, and control of newly created intellectual property.

Scale of Development Deals and the Development Forms

Development engagements come in all sizes. Large deals are distinguishable from small deals on a number of levels including:

- Pricing and pricing structures

- The number of technical managers and the size of the programming staff involved

- The process and procedures necessary to manage the project

- The life span and technical complexity of the project including its innovative aspects as well as the degree to which existing third party technology is used

- The role of the completed application in the customer's business.

What all of these factors translate into is a risk profile for the deal. Large deals with big price tags that involve a high degree of technical innovation and/or mission critical systems are much more risky to both the customer and the developer than smaller jobs.

At the conceptual level, the legal and business and contract issues for big and small development jobs are much the same. However, larger jobs have much more process and procedures (which we will discuss below) to manage complexity and risks.

In the form Appendix to this book, you will find a "long form" of development agreement (Form 10-1) that you may want to review. The long form is a starting point for a contract covering a major development project. Also included in the form appendix are more general forms of consulting agreement (Forms 10-2 and 10-3) that can be used in smaller development products. We also provide a form of web site development agreement (Form 10-4) and, for companies that provide hosting as well as development, a web hosting agreement (Form 10-5). You can also find many examples of development agreements at legal sites such as findlaw.com and onecle.com.

Development Can Be a Risky Business

There is no doubt that developers and customers strive for good results on budget and on time. Notwithstanding these worthy goals, study after study has shown that major IT development projects have a remarkably high rate of bad results. One 1997 study, for example, surveyed large enterprise IT managers and found that the managers consider over 60 percent of their IT development projects to be "unsuccessful." Moreover, three-quarters of projects reviewed in the same study were significantly late in completion, and more than half were significantly over budget.

Each large IT development project gone wrong has its own tale of woe, but there are some common factors. Here, as a word to the wise, are some of the factors commonly cited as the cause of failure and disputes. You will see that many (but not all) of these problems come from inadequate planning at the start and poor controls.

- **Unclear Specifications**—Creating thorough specifications requires time and money at the outset, so all too often projects are based on written specifications that are lacking in detail or vague. This leads to disagreements over the functionality and performance the developer was obligated to deliver.

- **Lack of Communication; Lack of User Involvement**—Sometimes the customer's management has an unclear idea of what it wants—or wants something that differs from what the intended users want. The result can be a product that does not serve the customer's real needs and disappoints all.

- **Technical Risk**—Large projects may have technical challenges where the level of effort required is simply unknown. New feature creation can be an iterative process of uncertain duration. If the project does not provide enough money and time, the project will run into trouble.

- **Aggressive Pricing and Scheduling**—To secure contracts, developer's sales staff may base bids on unrealistic assumptions about the time and labor needed to complete the project. If the fixed price or estimate turns out to be too low, the developer will start asking for more money. That's when conflict can begin.

- **Lack of Monitoring and Control**—Customers sometimes let projects go without close monitoring. Sometimes customers do not have the technical means to monitor progress. This can lead to unpleasant surprises when the problems finally emerge.

- **Poor Change Control**—When changes are required in the course of a project, they should be documented. There needs to be a formal process to assess the impact of each change on project cost and its schedule. This is best done by means of a formal change order process. Unfortunately, some project just "evolves," and changes are left undocumented. This leads to disagreements about specifications and schedules, as well as to developer demands to be paid for "out of scope" work.

- **Low Wages and High Turnover in Staff**—In some cases, the developer may be cutting corners in staff salaries or benefits to keep costs down; the resulting high turnover rate can slow progress and compromise quality.

Experience shows that the bigger and more complicated the project, the more risk there is that things will go wrong. However, smaller projects are certainly not immune to problems. The loose specifications in smaller jobs can often lead to conflicts about what was supposed to be done. In either case, it is not unusual for failed IT projects to end up as a dispute in the hands of the lawyers.

Need for Planning and Risk Management

Good planning, frequent communication, and sensible development contracts will not guarantee that there will be no disputes or failures, but these sensible measures can help reduce the number of problems and help manage them if they occur.

Before entering into any IT service agreement, each side should make an assessment of risk factors. Where there are special risks—whether it is a large quantum of technical risk, untried software components, an insufficient number of trained staff, a tight schedule, or other uncertainties, each side will need to devote more resources to risk management. In addition, both parties should monitor and discuss progress and problems throughout the project. The customer may need contingency plans so that it can take action if the project is very late or fails altogether. Contract provisions need to be adjusted to compensate for perceived risks.

Because development deals can go bad, customers should understand clearly what contractual remedies will apply if the project fails. For the same reason, smart developers should always put clear risk limitations in development deals, including damage exclusion and limitation of liability clauses. (These contractual provisions are discussed below.)

PROCESS OVERVIEW

Let's look at the stages of a typical significant software development project.

- **Needs Assessment**—Every development project begins with the customer and its needs. The customer begins by assessing, sometimes with the assistance of an outside consultant, what it needs in terms of new or different products or services. Often the customer assembles an internal system acquisition team, which may include representatives of management, users, information services, and the legal department.

- **Acquisition Team**—If the customer decides to go forward, the needs assessment team will likely become the acquisition team. The team may also consider whether to do the project in house rather than hiring an outside developer.

- **Setting Goals**—The customer needs to decide what the functionality and performance needs are and what its preliminary expectations are as to how long development will take and how much it will cost.

- **RFPs**—To get the best combination of high skill and reasonable price, there is nothing better than competitive bidding. To start that process, the customer will often assemble RFPs—sometimes called an "invitation to bid"—to use in soliciting bids. Sometimes the customer will start with a "call for expressions of interest"—a preliminary document about the project used to identify developers that are interested in the project and who will be provided with the fuller RFP. The customer may retain an outside consultant to help prepare the RFP and to help evaluate responses.

- **Response to RFP**—The developer becomes part of the process when it submits a written response to the RFP. Often the developer will assemble its own team of sales people, managers, and technicians who will put the response together.

- **Developer Selection**—The customer reviews the responses and selects a developer.

- **Contracting**—After the customer chooses a developer, the parties will negotiate a development agreement to govern the development process.

- **Development Services**—The developer will perform the development services under the development agreement—hopefully to the customer's satisfaction. Development normally ends with acceptance of the final deliverables.

- **Postdelivery Services**—The developer will normally provide postdelivery services, such as ongoing maintenance and training and follow-on development work.

Lawyers are primarily involved in the contracting process—and, of course, in resolving any disputes. However, all the other phases of the process have significance for contracting and legal matters—the initial phases—because they help define the deliverables and set the parties' expectations and the final phases because they determine success or failure.

Smaller projects will have similar stages—although needs assessment may be informal and the parties may not bother to use a formal RFP process to obtain bids.

WRITING AND RESPONDING TO RFPS

In the RFP process, the customer invites bidding on a project, states its requirements in a formal document, and seeks key information from the bidders. In some cases, particularly when a government entity is seeking bids, anyone who is qualified may submit a response to the RFP. More often, the customer chooses the developers that it wants to engage in the process.

Elements of an RFP—From the Customer's Point of View

Say that you want to retain a developer to supply development service for an IT project. Here are some pointers that you may want to consider in drafting your RFP.

Confidentiality is the first order of business. In order to explain your procurement requirements, you are likely to disclose confidential information about its business. Therefore, you will want to impose a requirement that respondent not disclose your confidential information or use it other than to prepare a response. This is best done by requiring the respondent to sign a non-disclosure agreement (NDA) before you deliver your RFP. For more information on this topic, please see Chapter 7.

The RFP is designed to elicit key information that will enable you to choose a respondent that will provide the best value. A well conceived and written RFP will cover the following:

- **Background**—State the reason for the project, including the current situation and the business problem that you seek to solve.

- **Your Goals**—State the business and practical results that you expect to achieve.

- **Required Functionality**—Explain what you want the resulting system to do. The more detail the better. Require the respondent to state that it will provide all expected functionality or explain any exceptions. If there are features that are not essential but "nice-to-have," consider adding those. Often this portion of the RFP goes on for many pages. You cannot be too inclusive or too careful about stating your needs in detail.

- **Importance**—If the project involves a core or critical business function, this should be made very clear.

- **Technology Requirements**—Explain the information system environment that the project needs to support and any decisions that you have made as to the technologies to be used in the project. Require the respondent to state that it can provide the required solution for the specified environment.

- **Developer Qualifications**—Explain the particular qualifications and skills that you expect the developer to demonstrate in its response. You should also inquire as to the developer's (and that of its key staff members) experience with similar projects. And be sure to seek references to other customers for whom the developer has done similar work.

- **Development Team Size and Composition**—Ask the developer to explain the project staffing and management, including the specific persons to be assigned. You may want to ask for recent employee turnover rates. Ask about any subcontracting that is contemplated.

- **Time Frame Expectations**—State how long the project is expected to take. Require the respondent to state whether it can do the project in the expected time frame. Where timing is critical, this should be stated.

- **Budgetary Expectations**—State the range of spending expected. Require the respondent to state its best price for performing the services.

- **Communications and Management**—Explain how you want communications and reporting of progress to be managed.

- **Acceptance**—Explain your expectations for implementation, testing, and acceptance of the project deliverables.

- **Maintenance and Support**—Explain your expectations regarding continuing hardware repair and repair of the system, bug fixing, and the like.

- **Training**—State what you expect the respondent to provide to train system users.

- **Risk and Risk Management**—Ask the developer to evaluate the risks and explain how they can be mitigated. If you want an off-site disaster recovery system, make sure to mention it.

- **Security Needs**—Explain your security requirements, both with regard to the development process and security features of the proposed project.

- **Legal Terms of Importance**—Include proposed legal terms. Require the respondent to state whether it will agree to them, and if not, to indicate those that require negotiation. You may want to include insurance requirements.

- **RFP Process**—State when responses are due, and when you will get back to the respondents. Explain the criteria for acceptance. Be sure to reserve expressly the right to reject all responses if you choose.

Responding to RFPs—From the Developer's Point of View

If your company provides IT services and wants to respond to an RFP, here are a few general observations on how to put together a winning response:

- **Be Aware of the Uses of Your Response**—It is common for customers to ask that the RFP and your response be included as part of the final development agreement. Even if you are going to resist this (as most IT service companies do), it is a virtual certainty that much of the content of your response will go into the final contract. Therefore, you should not promise anything in the response that you would not want to promise in a contract.

- **Be Very Responsive**—Be sure to address every point of the RFP in a way that demonstrates knowledge of both the business and technical issues and a capability to perform.

- **Provide a Detailed Response**—State clearly what you can or cannot do. With regard to proposed features or functions, your response should explain if it is "fully supported," "partially supported," "not available," or "available at extra cost." Avoid general responses that leave in doubt what you are willing to provide. If further work is required to define the scope of the project, you should say so. If requirements are unclear, you should say so. If there are ways to get clarification before responding, you should use them. The goal is to avoid unpleasant surprises later on.

- **Avoid Sales Talk**—Avoid sweeping and glib language in the response such as "instant response," "everything that you could want," "best performance in the market," and the like. There are problems with this kind of talk. First, it sounds slick and may be a turn-off. Second, it could cause legal risk if it is incorporated into your consulting agreement—and thus become a legally binding warranty. If the project ends up in a lawsuit, the judge and jury may weigh these over-the-top promises and representations against the actual results that you deliver.

- **Explain the Technologies That You Propose to Provide**—Explain the preferred technology solutions and how they will be implemented. Use graphics as necessary to explain the architecture and designs you recommend.

- **Explain How You Bring Extra Value**—Most projects are awarded based on value—which may or may not be the same as the lowest price. If your company provides additional value, explain why.

- **Subcontracting**—If you are planning to use subcontractors, explain why. Note that you, as the prime contractor, will normally be legally responsible for the performance of your subcontractors—or their lack of performance.

- **Communication**—Explained proposed communications and reporting methodologies. Explain how project setbacks or delays will be reported and treated.

- **Be Careful with Pricing**—Be as responsive as possible regarding the expected price of your company's services and any goods that may have to be purchased. However, if you do not have enough information to state the final cost, say so. If there are contingencies that affect pricing, explain them.

- **Post-Acceptance**—Explain post-acceptance support for the project.

- **Legal Terms**—If there are particular legal terms that are important to your company, be sure to say so. If you have standard terms that you want to use, you should include them.

- **Proof and Polish**—Some companies lose out in the bidding process because they submit responses that are sloppy and filled with errors. Take the time to make it right.

THE AGREEMENT

After selection of a vendor comes the negotiation of the development agreement. This is sometimes done under pressure—as both sides want to "get going." Sometimes the parties will start work while the contract is worked out under an informal MOU (Memorandum of Understanding)—often a risky course for both sides. (See discussion of MOUs in Chapter 8, our chapter on digital contracting basics.)

In this section, you will find a discussion of the typical issues and provisions in development agreements. There are innumerable variations on development deals of course—but from a lawyer's perspective these are usually variations on the same themes. This section is designed to help you see the issues and find solutions. The development agreement manages:

- What development work will be performed

- How the project will be managed

- What will happen if the project goes wrong or contingencies arise

Each side should bring its technical, business, and legal resources to bear on this negotiation process. Both parties should be trying to minimize its risks and maximize its gains.

Getting the First Draft on the Table

There is an old adage in diplomatic negotiations: "The first draft on the table wins." This is an overstatement to be sure—but it is usually a negotiating advantage to have your form of agreement as the starting point for negotiation.

Most often, the party that gets this first draft advantage is the developer—because it does many deals of this type. However, customers that do a great many software or IT acquisitions often have their own acquisition form agreement—or sometime key clauses that they want in agreements.

Smart developers begin with a "user friendly" form that is reasonably protective but fair. That is more likely to lead to a smooth negotiation and faster conclusion of the deal. Developers that look for perfect legal protection probably won't close many deals. On the other hand, developers that take unwise risks may end up in litigation. For the developer, the key often is knowing what is a reasonable compromise and knowing how to "sell" the other side on its "must have" positions.

STRUCTURE OF A DEVELOPMENT AGREEMENT

Development projects require contract provisions that provide for the management of many moving parts: complex tasks, complex specifications, third party tools, a team of professionals, and substantial sums of money over time to reach defined goals. For this reason, development projects usually require lots of documentation (discussed in more detail below) that specifies what is to be done and when and how it is to be accomplished. This task-oriented documentation normally becomes "schedules" to the agreement, placed at the end. The "body" of the agreement for the most part consists of the "legal terms" that interact with and govern the task-oriented content of the schedules.

One development job often leads to another. After systems are built, the customer often wants them enhanced, extended, updated, or integrated with other systems. For this reason, most development agreements are designed so that a single set of "legal terms" can be used with a variety of development projects. Such a form of agreement is sometimes called an "umbrella" agreement, because it "covers" a variety of tasks. In other cases, particularly for larger more complex projects, there will be a single highly customized agreement to cover a series of development tasks. Some large projects may have different contracts for different development phases or services.

DEVELOPMENT PLANNING

There is a saying: "One who fails to plan, plans to fail." A large development agreement needs task schedules that explain in reasonable detail what is to be done. Even after the RFP process, the customer usually will have only a general idea of the functionality it needs, and the developer may have only a general idea of what it is going to supply. This means that there must be a planning process in place.

Development agreements for complex projects most often include provisions for a planning phase, designed for the creation of a development plan. The planning process can take days, weeks, or months, depending on the scale and complexity of the undertaking.

Sometimes the parties will sign a separate consulting agreement just to cover the project planning process—to be followed by the negotiation of a full development agreement. Alternatively, planning can be the first phase of a multiphase process under a comprehensive development agreement. From the customer's point of view, there are advantages and disadvantages from either course.

- If the customer negotiates the full contract first, it will spend time and money on contract negotiations covering the entire project before it has a clear idea of the project price and duration.

- If the customer has planning done first, it will spend money on planning without a clear idea of the legal and business terms under which the project will be built.

In either case, the customer normally gets to see the development plan first—and then decide if it wants to proceed with the rest of the development project. If the customer does not go further, the customer will have to pay for the creation of the development plan only.

A good planning process will generate much of the key project documentation that will be used to define the scope of the work. This documentation will often become a part of a detailed "statement of work," or "work order."

Here are some of the elements that might be in a development plan—whether in the form of one document or many. For convenience, we have arranged common development plan elements by subject matter below:

Deliverables

- **Software Deliverables**—The software deliverables for the project may be alpha, beta, and final versions of each module. The agreement should state whether each deliverable includes source code and binary code or any software tools.

- **Documentation Deliverables**—There should be a listing of documentation to be created and supplied, including any user document and system operator or maintenance documentation.

- **Data Conversion**—If data is to be converted or processed from a pre-existing software application, the process for doing this needs to be stated.

Requirements for Providing the Deliverables

- **Specifications**—Written specifications should include functional specifications (what the software will do) and technical specifications (how the software will be built). There may also be performance specifications (for example, the rate of transaction processing on a designated platform). These sometimes are preliminary specifications—with detailed specifications to be created later as part of the development process.

- **Standards**—There should be a listing of applicable technical standards for performance, interoperability, or quality. There may be applicable code development standards, such as naming conventions, rules on structure and modularity of code, and required formats. (Note that there is a discussion of the creation of technical standards in Chapter 19 of this book.)

- **Milestone Schedule**—This is a schedule for the performance of tasks—generally in the form of a table listing dates and deliverables and the party responsible for each task. In many deals, selected milestones trigger payments to the developer.

- **Location**—There should be a statement of the place (or places) that the services will be performed. There may be a listing of customer location workspaces or development hardware to be made available to developer.

- **The Team**—There is normally a listing of the developer staff members to be assigned to the project.

Software and Data to Be Provided for Use in Development

- **Third-Party Products and Services**—There will need to be a statement of third party products to be supplied (and it needs to be stated who will supply them). There may be a need for third party services, such as telecommunications lines or services for hardware installation or configuration. In some cases, third party services might include subcontracting or off-shoring part of the work.

- **Pre-Existing Software**—If the developer or the customer is providing pre-existing software code or products, those programs should be listed.

- **Data**—In some cases, the customer must supply sample data and/or information about its data structures, equipment configuration, or business processes.

- **Access**—The developer may require remote access to the customer's computer systems.

Oversight and Management

- **Management and Communications Plan**—The parties will need a structure for meetings, progress and problem reporting, documenting decisions, and follow-up. There may be a process for escalation of problems and disputes.

- **Risk Management Plan**—For complex projects, there should be a process for reporting problems and managing project risks, which include delays, dependencies on third parties, quality issues, staffing changes, or other risk factors.

- **Quality Assurance**—Depending on the product, there may be a plan for regular quality checking, reviews of software for functional completeness, error logging, and follow up with error correction. There may be periodic reviews to check conformity of product to specifications.

Price and Costs

- **Payments to Developer**—The amounts and timing of payments to the developer (which may be subject to adjustment) should be clearly stated. Cost variables should also be clearly stated. Normally payments will be tied to the successful completion of designated milestones. Expense reimbursement and the reimbursement process should be explicit.

- **Third Party Payments**—Estimates of payments for third party hardware, software, and services should be provided. The party responsible for making those payments—the developer or the customer—should be stated.

Acceptance

- **Acceptance Process**—The acceptance standards and acceptance process, including any applicable testing, should be made clear.

Postacceptance

- **Training**—Planning should include adequate training for administrators and users.

- **Maintenance**—There should be planning for maintenance and support after acceptance. If the developer is going to provide maintenance and support, a fee schedule should be provided.

"Detailed Design"

Depending on the complexity of the project, the parties may agree on the creation of a "detailed design" document that refines and "fills in the blanks" of the original preliminary design documentation. In some cases, there may be more than one of these more detailed documents. Work may proceed in some areas while detailed design work proceeds in others.

Detailed design documents often lead to a change in the projected work. (It often means an increase in the amount of services.) This can trigger negotiations about repricing of the project.

In each case, the development agreement will need to contain a process for customer "sign-off" of the design documents as they are created, including any change in price. The customer will want the option not to proceed or pay for development under documents that are not yet approved.

Here is typical language regarding such a provision:

In accordance with the Milestone Schedule, prior to beginning the development services, Developer will prepare a detailed design document ("Detailed Design") for the System that will be submitted to Customer at least two weeks in advance of a detailed design review meeting including Developer and Customer ("Design Review"). The Detailed Design will incorporate and comply with the Specifications and Requirements.

In the event that Customer approves the Detailed Design, Customer may provide Developer with written notice ("Design Approval Notice"). In any case, Developer may not proceed with the development services until Customer provides a Design Approval Notice.

Dealing with Informal Specifications

For small projects, it is often the case that neither the customer nor the developer wants to invest the time and money required to develop a detailed specification. What they use instead is a more informal "high level" specification that outlines the functionality of the desired system in a general way.

Development tools that allow for rapid development of applications and prototypes have caused a shift toward more informal specifications. This is true, for example, in Web development. These tools allow for iterative styles of development: the developer creates an initial version, gets customer feedback, and makes changes—until the parties agree that the application is as desired.

What is good about this informal specification methodology is that it can be fast and efficient. What is not so good is that it can cause uncertainty. And that uncertainty increases with the size of the project. Uncertainty makes it harder to contract on a fixed price and milestone basis. Informal processes are a better fit for time-and-materials billing. Fixed price deals with soft specifications create more risk for developers and customers alike.

Project Management Provisions

Development agreements normally include provision for management. These can be simple or quite elaborate depending on the needs of the project. The types of provisions normally included are:

- **Representatives**—The parties appoint administrators who communicate on their behalf regarding the project. These administrators are authorized to make decisions and receive notices. Sometimes roles are divided. For example, the parties may each have a "Contract Representative" and a "Technical Representative."

- **Reporting**—There may be provisions for written reports on a weekly or monthly basis. Normally, the development agreement will specify the types of information to be reported, such as progress, delays, decisions made, and so forth. These may require specific testing procedures or quality reports.

- **Code Reviews**—In some agreements, there are requirements that the developer makes the current version of the source code or each interim version of the executable files available for FTP download by the customer for monitoring and review. The customer may want the right to have one or more third party consultants download and review the work product.

- **Inspections**—The customer may negotiate for the right to visit the developer's locations to verify processes for quality and security.

Personnel Assigned to Development

Because the people staffed on a project can be critical to its success, the customer often wants control over personnel assignments. This control can take many forms:

- The initial staff assignments to the project may be specified.

- There may be stipulations as to whether specified staff assignments are full time or part time.

- There may be prohibitions on reassigning key personnel to other projects for other customers.

- Additions to, or changes of staff, may be made subject to the customer's approval.

- There may be requirements that the developer promptly report staff turnover—and its impact on the project.

- There may be a requirement that persons who depart be replaced with personnel of "at least equal skill and experience."

Change Management Provisions

Most development contracts have provisions that manage requests for changes in the specifications and development tasks. This is required because any material change in the specifications or development tasks can impact the developer's workload and the scheduled completion of milestones. Of course, this means price adjustments. There are many ways to write these provisions, but the basic concept is always the same: any change order has to be reduced to writing, and it is effective only when signed by both parties.

If not managed properly in the development agreement, change requests frequently cause trouble. Often customers will ask for additional features without expecting to pay more. The developer will do extra work to respond to a request and expect extra pay. The result can be conflict. Litigation involving millions of dollars of disputes about liability for "out of scope" work (that is, work not covered by the specification) are not uncommon. Good contract language—combined with discipline in following the rules—can avoid this kind of problem.

Acceptance Procedures

Development agreements have provisions for the acceptance or rejection of deliverables. Here is how it normally works:

- The developer submits the deliverable.

- The customer is given a set amount of time to accept or reject the deliverable.

- If the customer takes no action in a specified amount of time, the deliverable is deemed accepted.

- If the customer rejects the deliverable, it must give a written statement specifying the reasons for the rejection. The developer is then given a set amount of time to cure the specified defects and resubmit the deliverable for acceptance under the same process.

There are some variations. For example:

- Some agreements provide for acceptance of deliverables only in writing.

- Some agreements require that specified key deliverables can be accepted only in writing.

- Some agreements provide that if the developer fails to cure the deliverable after two tries, the customer can terminate the agreement.

- Some agreements provide that if the developer fails to cure the deliverable after two tries, then *either* party can terminate the agreement. (This version—which we often recommend for developers—allows the developer to escape from the agreement if its staff is simply unable to meet the requirements.)

In some development agreements, the final deliverable (that is, the finished product) may have a different acceptance process than interim deliverables. For example, the final version may be subject to:

- A much more thorough testing process, including trial use by the intended users

- A longer time period for acceptance

- A provision that acceptance occurs only when the customer affirmatively accepts in writing (with a provision that such acceptance may not be "unreasonably withheld").

Payment Provisions

Probably there is nothing that is more bargained over in development agreements than price. And, of course, there are many different ways to write pricing provisions. Here are some common pricing mechanisms.

Milestone-Based

The most common payment structure for major development agreements is the "milestone-and-specification" structure. This is also known as "fixed price" although, of course, the parties can build in variables. Payment is based on "milestones" defined as acceptance of deliverables in accordance with the specifications.

We have seen development contracts where there are monthly payments that are not tied to a particular milestone—other than the final product. Obviously this kind of deal leaves the customer with much less leverage if the project is delayed or otherwise runs into trouble.

Structuring milestone payments is a mixture of skill, analysis, and negotiation. The customer will (if it is wise) have used competitive bidding to get a general idea of the market price of the project. (Some companies hire outside purchasing consultants to help in estimating likely costs.) The developer will have the advantage in understanding the approximate cost of meeting the milestones. The developer will want to be sure that pricing is high enough to leave a reasonable profit margin and to include a margin of error in case estimates are off.

Here are some of the goals that the parties may strive for in setting milestones:

- The developer would like significant "down money" (due on signing the agreement) as a "cushion."

- The developer may seek to include "easy" milestones in the early stages of the project.

- After its initial payment, the customer may want significant work done before major payments.

- The customer may bargain for a right to refund if milestones go wrong.

- The customer may want to "hold back" an amount that is due only after acceptance of the final deliverables.

Time and Materials

As the name indicates, this method of payment is based on the developer's level of effort—normally with different professional service rates for different classes of professional staff. From the customer's perspective, the time-and-material pricing method is risky because the price may get out of control. It is more typical to see this method for smaller jobs where costs are easier to track and control. In those rare cases where the unknowns predominate, the creation of milestones and a specification may be just too speculative, and time and materials may then be the logical pricing option for both parties.

There are many variations on time-and-materials arrangements. For example:

- The parties may work under an estimate, and may have arranged to suspend work if charges exceed a defined level.

- The parties may have negotiated a maximum price cap for completing the assignment, so that risk of exceeding the cap is significantly shifted to the developer.

- Many customers require expenses to be preapproved—and specify a procedure for expense reimbursement.

When the parties use a time-and-materials structure, the customer will want to be sure that it has the means to evaluate the developer's progress and verify the developer's time. Often the agreement will require the developer to deliver monthly or weekly reports to the customer and give the customer the right to audit the books and records of the developer.

A variation on the time-and-materials method—often used in state and federal contracting—is "cost-plus." This is a method under which the developer tracks and reports all its out-of-pocket costs (including labor) and adds an agreed markup to establish its billings.

Combinations and Variations

There are, of course, other ways to price development work. For example, one could have:

- Combinations of fixed and variable charges

- Provisions for relief from fixed pricing for "major unanticipated obstacles"

- Bonus payments for early completion

- Loss of retainage or reduced pricing for late delivery.

The Right Schedule

One issue that is a perennial problem in development deals is the time allowed to complete the project. Sometimes it is possible to estimate the amount of effort required with reasonable accuracy, because the task is routine. Sometimes estimating the effort is nearly impossible. For example, the team that wrote the first commercial spell checker could not have known in advance how many months of work would be required.

It is best that the schedule for delivery of new software be as realistic as possible. It is a common perception that software development is *always* late. Developers sometimes promise delivery when the customer wants it, fearing to tell the customer about probable delays. Lack of realism and candor in the beginning may lead to frustration and anger later on.

If there are delays, the timeframes can be extended by mutual agreement in writing. But if the customer is looking for an excuse to terminate the contract or force a price reduction, late delivery will often provide it.

Under contract law a modest delay in delivery is not always fatal. The courts generally hold that some minor tardiness in delivery is tolerable. However, where the fine print of the agreement states that "time is of the essence," any delay past the stated deadline will probably be ruled a material breach of the contract. Some software development agreements are written to provide the developer an express option to extend the time for delivery by a specified time if the development pace is slower than expected.

Developers who are late in their delivery run other risks. If completion of the software is behind schedule, the developer must incur payroll expenses for staff and contractors not provided for in the budget. In addition, delay in producing the software means delays in payment—and this too may cause financial strains on the developer. Customers hate it when developers come asking for more money—particularly when the product is late. Again the moral is that realism in time and cost estimates are important.

Intellectual Property—Ownership and/or License

Development agreements must provide for ownership and/or rights to use the intellectual property that is related to the deliverables or that is created in development work. There is no doubt that many companies negotiate intellectual property clauses without fully understanding what they have done. This is due to the subtleties of intellectual property law.

The Intellectual Property at Stake

To understand the variety of intellectual property provisions, we need first to survey what intellectual property interests are likely to be in play. We can then look at who is likely to want—or to get—the various intellectual property interests. You may want to refer back to the chapters of this book on copyrights (Chapters 2 and 3), trade secrets (Chapter 6), and patents (Chapter 5) as you read this discussion.

Copyright in the Software

In most development agreements, the intellectual property interest that we absolutely must manage carefully is the copyright in the code and documentation delivered by the developer. Copyright controls the right to make and sell copies of the program. Copyrights are created automatically.

By default the developer will own the copyright for code written by the developer's employees. Because the developer owns the copyright in the code by default, the customer will not get copyright ownership rights unless the development agreement provides for the customer's ownership.

As is discussed in the chapters on copyright, the developer that subcontracts work will need to be sure that it has arranged to get relevant intellectual property rights from its subcontractors; otherwise it cannot provide these rights to its customer.

Patentable Inventions

In building "run-of-the mill" business applications using standard tools, there is probably not much likelihood that the developer will be making inventions (although you never know for sure). On the other hand, in developments requiring creation of innovative or cutting edge products, there is a reasonable likelihood that the developer may well have to do some inventing—and if so will create potentially valuable patent rights.

Patents, unlike copyrights, do not come into existence automatically—they are the result of an expensive technology review and application process. Unlike software copyrights, any resulting patent most likely would not cover the whole of the code, but rather a discrete invention. And unlike software copyrights, the coverage of patents is not limited to particular code—patents potentially cover any code or systems within the borders of a nation that constitutes a product or uses a method covered by the patent.

However, patents are like copyrights in that the developer will usually own patent rights it creates by default. (A joint invention would be jointly owned by default.) Due to this legal rule, the customer will not get the rights to inventions created in the development process unless the development agreement provides for the customer's ownership.

Trade Secrets

In a trivial sense, confidential information is involved in every development deal. The customer's data and business processes are usually confidential. Certainly the source code to be delivered will be held in confidence by both the developer and the customer.

However, it is less common that the developer is providing a valuable trade secret of broader application—that is, a valuable processing method or software design that is not generally known. If that is the case, however, the developer's trade secret would need to be dealt with explicitly (and carefully) in the development agreement.

By default, the unrestricted delivery of trade secret information by the developer to the customer will permit the customer to use or disclose the developer's trade secret as it sees fit (of course, public disclosure means the loss of trade secret status). Moreover, most development deals require delivery of source code—which will disclose the program logic and therefore most likely fully reveal to the customer (if it takes the trouble to look) all the processing methods that constitute the trade secret.

Goals in Negotiating Intellectual Property Clauses

Ownership of intellectual property is largely a "zero-sum game"; any intellectual property ownership assigned to one party is lost to the other. So there is often bargaining about who will own what. Often each party begins with the assumption that intellectual property ownership is good, and that owning as much of it as possible is a worthy goal. Here are some other relevant considerations:

- If the developer's business model is to create and "resell" applications, it should try to retain ownership of the copyright to all or key portions of the code. If the developer's business model is to build intellectual property value in its business, it may want to retain patent rights in its area of expertise.

- A developer that sees its business as purely being a seller of programming services (with no ambition to be an intellectual property owner) may regularly give up intellectual property ownership just to keep the customers happy.

- The tenacity with which a customer will seek intellectual property ownership is frequently related to its core competency. If you develop accounting software for an auto company, the customer might not much care who owns the copyright. If you develop automobile engineering software for an auto company, the customer will likely insist on owning it. Companies in the IT and software businesses are often looking to acquire intellectual property rights to developed software.

- Developers find that many customers are not aware that patents are a potential outcome of development services. However, due to the publicity of "business method patents" and "software patents," it has now become more likely that customers will care about patent rights that the developer may invent. (See discussion of these patent categories in Chapter 5.)

- In some cases, the developer may be able to make a deal in which it retains the intellectual property in exchange for agreeing not to supply similar software to other customers for a specified period of time. Typical restraints are for periods from six months to two years. On the other hand, the customer might want to own the intellectual property *and* also impose a restraint against the developer providing similar solutions to others.

Common Means to Deal with Intellectual Property in Agreements

There is no end to the possible ways to deal with intellectual property rights in development agreements. Here are some of the most common methods:

Developer Owns/License Grant Clause

One common model—much loved by developers—is to make the developer owner of all intellectual property rights. Under this model, the developer simply licenses the deliverables to the customers. Here is a typical clause of this type:

> *Subject to payment in full of the Development Fee, the Developer grants to the Customer a perpetual nontransferable license to use the Software on computers and networks owned or controlled by Customer for its own internal business purposes, and make sufficient copies of the Software for such use. This Agreement grants license rights only.*

This clause is great from the developer's point of view, but may meet a number of customer objections:

- As noted, the customer may insist that ownership is needed for its business strategy.

- The license grant is very narrow, and a customer may well find it too constraining. For example, the license that is "nontransferable" might prevent the customer from transferring the license to a buyer of its business. The license "for its own internal business purposes" makes no provision for use of the software by the customer's subsidiary or "sister" corporations. The clause similarly makes no provision for sublicensing to a "spin-off" operation or for use by the customer's contractors, business "partners," or clients. There is no grant for the customer to modify the software. And so forth. The basic problem is lack of flexibility.

Some of these objections may be met by drafting a different kind of license grant. The developer can add license grants to address the customer's specific objections—or it can grant broad rights for copying, sublicensing, and modification. There are many possible variations.

Work-Made-For Hire Clause/Patent Clause

At the other end of the spectrum, one often sees "work made for hire" clauses that grant ownership rights to the customer. (See discussion of the "work made for hire" concept in Chapter 2.) Here is a typical clause of that kind:

> *The parties agree that all work product resulting from the Services performed by Developer hereunder (the "Work Product"), including, but not limited to, the Software, and documentation prepared by Developer, if any, shall be considered to be a "work made for hire" for the Customer, and to the extent not "work made for hire" are hereby assigned to Customer. In addition such work product and the intellectual property rights embodied therein are and shall be the sole exclusive property of Client.*

This clause sounds pretty comprehensive, but it's not quite what it seems. It covers copyright, but the clause may leave out patentable inventions. Although the phase "the intellectual property rights embodied therein" is very common, it may not be sufficient to grab inventions that the developer created during the development work. Here's why:

- One could argue that the rights to patentable inventions are not "embodied" in the work product at all. Patent lawyers will tell you that patents are rights to exclude others from a claimed invention and therefore are not really "embodied" in any technology. So this language is ambiguous at best with regard to covering patents.

- Moreover, the developer might have made inventions during the development work that are broader or different from the implementation in the "work product" or not used in the deliverables. These would not be covered by the clause.

- The language leaves unstated the duty, if any, of the developer to cooperate in patenting.

If the customer really wants these rights as well, it needs a clause that is broader. Here is the type of language that effectively grabs patent rights:

The parties agree that all Inventions developed by Developer in the course of the development services shall be the property of the Customer and not the Developer. "Inventions" shall mean and include any and all ideas, concepts, inventions, discoveries, designs, improvements, and creations, regardless of whether the same are patentable or protected under any Federal or State law, rule, or regulation or under the common law of any state. Subject to Customer paying Developer's reasonable out of pocket costs, Developer agrees to (i) execute an assignment or other document reasonably requested by the Customer in order to document, assign, and convey all Inventions arising from the development project to the Customer and for Customer to perfect its ownership rights and (ii) to cooperate in the registration, perfection, and enforcement of any resulting patent rights.

Foreground Intellectual Property and Background Intellectual Property Clause

From the developer's point of view, there is another potential problem with the sample "work made for hire" clause quoted above—it may give too much away. If a developer designates the entire delivered software application as "work made for hire," it loses the copyright to the whole application. That language can give away the developer's pre-existing ownership of software.

Many developers have some pre-existing custom-made software code that they use as a "common code base" for a variety of solutions. Some developers are content to convey to their customers any code written "on the customer's dime," but they don't want to surrender ownership of their own pre-existing code.

One common way to deal with this issue is to divide the rights to be delivered into "background technology" and "foreground technology" or "background IP" and "foreground IP." The developer then transfers the "foreground" and licenses the "background" to the customer.

Here is typical language:

1. *"Intellectual Property Rights" means any and all intellectual property rights including, without limitation, copyrights, trademarks, patents, and trade secrets.*

2. *"Developer's Background IP" means all Intellectual Property Rights which are owned by the Developer and are in existence prior to or independent of providing the Services.*

3. *"Foreground IP" means all Intellectual Property Rights arising as a result of providing the Services.*

4. *All right, title, and interest in and to any Developer's Background IP shall remain the property of Developer. Developer hereby assigns to Client its entire right, title, and interest in Foreground IP. Developer shall execute and aid in the preparation of any documents that Customer deems appropriate to document, secure, evidence, and perfect such rights.*

5. *The Developer hereby grants to Customer a perpetual, irrevocable, royalty-free, worldwide nonexclusive license (with the right to grant sublicenses) to use the Developer's Background IP for the purpose of exploiting the Foreground IP as Customer deems fit.*

A note about this text: You can see in paragraph "5" an example of an extremely broad license of the Developer's Background IP. The grant is essentially unlimited. This contrasts with the rather narrow grant we saw in the "Developer License" example above. There are, as discussed above, many variations as to how broad or narrow these licenses might be.

Another potential issue to take note of: In this type of deal, the customer may not be able to easily sort out what is "background" and what is "foreground." The application as delivered will often be an inextricable mixture of both. As a practical matter, this means that the customer's use of the application will be limited by the license grant to the background technology. Some customers may ask that "background technology" be designated and separable to avoid this limitation.

Other Variations

There are many more ways that a developer and a customer might divide intellectual property ownership. Sometimes we divide the software into "reusable code" which will belong to the developer and code and data "unique to the customer's implementation," which will belong to the customer.

We can also divide ownership by data type, function, or software module.

- For example for a multimedia application, the customer might own the media files, while the developer keeps ownership of the applications that manage and play them (including any changes made in the development project).

- In a product used for management of mutual funds, the customer might own the code that represents particular management rules created at the customer's request, while the developer keeps ownership of the "rules engine" that makes them operate (including any changes during the project).

The ways to divide intellectual property ownership is limited only by the imagination of the parties (and the lawyers) doing the deal.

Avoiding Jointly Owned intellectual Property

Sometimes parties think that the best way to deal with intellectual property is to jointly own it. However, this is rarely the best solution unless great care is taken in setting forth each party's rights and obligations.

This is because there are counterintuitive default rules about the exploitation of jointly owned intellectual property, which differ for different types of intellectual property. For example, in the United States, joint owners of a *copyright* can each use the copyright without the co-owner's permission, but each must account to the other party (that is pay) 50 percent of the profits that he or she obtains from the copyright. The rule in the United States on jointly owned *patents* is that either can use the patent without an obligation to account to the co-owner. These default rules vary from country to country.

The bottom line is: To handle joint intellectual property, you need to have clear rules in the development agreement as to who can do what with the jointly owned intellectual property. Although it is possible to write workable provisions handle jointly owned intellectual property, it is better and simpler just to allocate ownership to one party and have the other's use and exploitation regulated by a license grant.

When the Web Developer Is Also Providing Web Hosting

Agreements for building Web applications are, for the most part, the same as any other form of development. The underlying technology is distinct, but the contract issues are the same. However, an extra issue may apply when the vendor is going to act both as the party that develops the application and the party that provides hosting—mixing two different forms of services. The development deal and the hosting arrangements can be in two distinct agreements or combined. (We have included a form of simple hosting agreement [Form 10-5] in the form Appendix.)

If the developer is planning to provide hosting or other Web functionality by means of the developer's own proprietary background and infrastructure management software (Let's call this "background Web software.") there may be a difference of opinion between the developer and the customer as to how the background Web software can be used by the customer.

- From the developer's perspective, its background Web software may not be considered "deliverables" at all. The developer may think of them as part of its "hosting service" and not a portable component of the application.

- Smart customers on the other hand want the hosted application to be "portable" from one hosting vendor to another. So this customer will want all background Web software: (i) to be deliverables, (ii) to be licensed to the customer with broad rights to copy and use, and (iii) will usually want them in source code form. The customer will also normally want the right to transfer such a license together with the rest of the Web application.

This issue can often be compromised by means of a carefully written provision that allows the customer to transfer the license to the background Web technology in connection with the sale of its business subject to carefully written confidentiality protections. The developer will have to decide whether it will provide source code or, perhaps, offer a source code escrow, for any proprietary hosting software.

Subcontractors

If you are a developer, you need to be sure that you have contracts in place with your subcontractors under which they pass all intellectual property rights that they develop for or supply to your company. If you are not careful with documentation, the subcontractors will end up owning the intellectual property that they create— and you will have no way to deliver it to your customer. You should use a form of subcontractor agreement that has intellectual property ownership, confidentiality, and (if you want) non-competition provisions.

Noncompetition Clauses

Customers sometimes want to include in development agreements a form of non-competition clause. This kind of clause is designed to keep the developer from using expertise it developed "on the customer's dime" to benefit the customer's competition. A customer will typically ask for a non-competition clause when the developer has created a unique application—or at least one that is not generally available. Here is a sample:

Developer agrees that during the term of the Services and for one year thereafter, Developer will not develop or seek to develop any application or system with functionality similar to or competitive with the application developed for Customer under this Agreement.

This kind of clause is often coupled with an injunctive relief clause, which invites a court of law to stop any violation of this clause by means of an injunction, that is, a court order. (Injunctions as a remedy and the language typical of injunctive relief clauses are discussed in Chapter 8.)

Provisions on Confidential Information

Almost every development agreement has a conventional mutual confidentiality agreement provision. There is a discussion of clauses of this type in Chapter 8 as well. The gist is that each party agrees not to disclose the other party's confidential information and agrees to use the other party's confidential information only as reasonably needed for the purposes of the agreement.

In many cases, the customer will not consider this clause good enough. The customer may want an additional provision stating that ownership of certain confidential information, particularly information relating to the deliverables or created during a project, will pass from the developer to the customer. Here is typical language:

The parties agree that data and information comprising or regarding the source code that Developer creates under this Agreement will become the exclusive Confidential Information of the Customer upon creation. Developer shall not disclose, use, or exploit such Confidential Information except to carry out its obligations under this Agreement or as Customer may expressly authorize in writing.

This kind of clause, as well, is usually coupled with the agreement's injunction relief clause in language that asks the court to enjoin any breach by the Developer of this obligation.

Training and Support

In order for the customer to use a new sophisticated software or computer system, the customer's staff usually requires training. The developer's work may include preparation of training materials. Some agreements provide for "training the trainers"—that is the developer must train a group of customer employees who will train others employees.

Warranties

It is normal for development agreements to have warranty clauses of the sort discussed in Chapter 8 in which the developer warrants that the application (after acceptance) "substantially conforms to the specifications" and makes available "maintenance" to fix logical errors in the code.

Pricing of maintenance for custom-developed software and systems is tricky. It's not like supporting commercial-off-the-shelf software, because:

- Custom software is more likely to be buggy at first. There is often a sharp demand at first for maintenance services that trails off over time.

- The developer usually does not have staff dedicated solely or even primarily to maintenance tasks.

For these reasons, developers often charge for maintenance for custom-developed software on a "time and materials" basis. Sometimes the customer gets a "warranty period" during which errors may be reported and fixed without additional billing to the customer. (Of course, this is built into the price of the project.) All of this is frequently the subject of negotiation. Usually a warranty period of this kind kicks in after acceptance. A typical period would be 60 or 90 days.

Disclaimers and Limitations

Development deals will almost always have the risk limiter provisions discussed in Chapter 8. These include:

- Exclusions of implied warranties

- Limitations of remedies for "bugs" or "errors" to specified repair processes

- Exclusions of consequential damages

- A damage cap—often set at the amount paid to the developer

You can find examples of these clauses in the sample contracts for this chapter in the form appendix to this book.

Date Processing (Y2K) Warranties

There was a time not long ago when every development agreement had elaborate (and a bit paranoid) warranties that the application to be developed would handle four digit date data (such as the year 2000) correctly. You may occasionally see these "Y2K" clauses, but they are becoming rare. That is because common development tools include full date functionality. It is also because the dire predictions of "Y2K" meltdown failed to materialize.

Open Source Provisions

Customers frequently ask for assurance that the application contains no software under any open source license. "No open source" warranties are discussed in Chapter 8. Chapter 9 which is our discussion of open source licensing, reviews the advantages and risk of open source products, including the more restrictive so-called "Copyleft" form. If you are interested in open source issues, you may want to refer to these chapters.

These "no open source" restrictions will not fit all projects. In fact, more and more development project applications are being built with open source foundations and components and delivered to the customer wholly or in part under one or more open source licenses. If that is the case, the development agreement should make clear which open source licenses will apply and what software programs they will cover. Any company that receives such a program should be sure it fully understands the open source licenses involved.

Note that a customer that takes open source software commonly takes it with any infringement risks that may arise from using or distributing the program.

Intellectual Property Warranties and Indemnities

The general topic of intellectual property warranties and indemnities is discussed in Chapter 8. You may want to review that discussion as background—particularly with regard to the important difference between warranties and indemnities.

The negotiation of intellectual property warranties in development deals has become more complicated due to the explosion of software and business method patents and the growth of intellectual property litigation. A decade or so ago, the odds of a developer accidentally infringing a third party's intellectual property were quite low. There is no doubt that the risks are higher now.

Developers and customers come at this question from different viewpoints:

- The customer will say: I paid good money for this application; I want the developer to stand behind its work. If the developer delivers an infringing application, the developer should take care of the problem.

- The developer's attitude is: I am paid for developing software, not for underwriting an intellectual property risk. I am certainly not going to run an intellectual property risk that might be much higher than the contract price. Besides the customer selected the functionality, so it should be responsible.

In determining a fair allocation of the intellectual property risk, it is important to distinguish between types of intellectual property:

- **Copyright**—The developer cannot infringe a third party's copyright in a business application unless it copied someone else's code. So normally it is fair to hold the developer responsible for copyright infringement, unless the customer selected the offending code.

- **Trade Secret**—The situation with trade secrets is much the same. If the developer had access to a third party's trade secrets and took them for its development work, it should be responsible for this misdeed (unless it was the customer that wrongfully acquired the trade secret).

- **Patents**—It is patents that are the tough case. Most often, patent infringement in development is innocent—but it can lead to liability just the same. Moreover, depending on the nature of the patent claim, the potentially liability—not to mention the costs of defense—can be much higher than the developer's profit margin. The patent risk has grown in recent years due to thousands of new software patents. When both parties are innocent of fault, the parties will have very different viewpoints on which party should bear the loss.

Who bears the risk of patent infringement is frequently the subject of hard bargaining and compromise. Here are some of the provisions that developers can propose as alternatives to the unlimited indemnification requested by customers:

- The developer may propose that it bear responsibility only for "knowing" infringement. This "knowledge qualifier" will usually free the developer from indemnifying the customer, as long as it stays ignorant of the patents that might apply to its development task. We sometimes call this the "pure heart and empty head" standard—because, under this clause, the less you know about the patented technology in the field the better.

■ The developer may propose that its liability for patent infringement indemnification be "capped" at an agreed figure. This is a shared risk proposal.

■ The developer may propose a reverse indemnity—that is, indemnification by the customer if technology or functionality proposed by the customer leads to an infringement.

In the final analysis, this is a bargained-for risk allocation. You should be careful that your company puts limits on its exposure and does not "bet the company" on contracts.

Insurance

Insurance companies love software development firms, because they buy lots of insurance. It is not that they want to; their large customers *make* them buy it.

Most large companies that purchase development services will require that their developers obtain specified categories and amounts of insurance. The one that is most commonly required is "Errors and Omissions" insurance which covers losses due to the developer's negligent or erroneous services. If the developer's employees will be on-site at the customer's premises, customers may require that developers have additional coverage as well—consisting of:

■ **General Liability**—This insurance covers personal injury and injury to tangible property.

■ **Automotive**—This insurance covers injury and damage caused by vehicles.

■ **Worker's Compensation**—This insurance covers claims of the developer's employees for on-the-job injuries.

Insurance provisions often include some rather technical requirements:

■ A **"certificate of insurance"**—This is a written certification from the insurance company that the required coverage is in place.

■ A **requirement that the customer be a "named insured"**—This means that the customer becomes the direct beneficiary of the insurance coverage and, if need be, can sue the insurance company directly.

- **A requirement that the insurance be primary and not contributory—** This means the customer does not have to exhaust other insurance coverage first.

Developers should not be shy about faxing any requested insurance clauses to their insurance broker and making sure they have the required insurance coverage. Never guess.

Clause on Customer Non-Solicitation of Developer Employees

Developers fear that their employees will be hired away by the competition—this is one reason that developers want their employees to sign non-competition clauses in states where they are enforceable. However, sometimes the "raider" is not a competitor but, in fact, the developer's customer.

This kind of problem arises when the customer begins to rely on the services of a particular developer's employee, and the customer believes that it can save money and get more control by inducing the employee to move from the developer's payroll to its own.

In order to deter "raiding" by customers, some developers try to include a "non-solicitation" provision in their development agreements. Here is a sample:

During the term of this Agreement and for a period of one (1) year after termination, Customer shall not hire or solicit for employment (or for engagement as a contractor) any of Developer's current employees or persons who were employees during the preceding twelve (12) months.

There are many variations on this kind of customer non-solicitation clause. For example:

- The provision can be made mutual—applying to both parties.

- The restriction can be written so that it applies only to employees that actually worked on the project in question.

- The restriction can be written so that it only applies to intentional solicitation.

- The restriction can have a "carve-out" (so that it does not apply) for hiring an employee that answers a mass-market recruiting request, such as an employee that answers an advertisement on the Web or in the local newspaper.

- The provision may be written so that the customer pays "liquidated damages" (often fixed in relation to the employee's compensation) for violating the restriction. For example, the provision might state that, in case of violation, the customer will be obligated to pay to the developer one-half of the purloined employee's yearly salary.

From the developer's viewpoint, these customer non-solicitation clauses have an important drawback—no developer wants to sue its own customers. As a result, these clauses are not often enforced. They do serve to deter "employee raiding" by customers, but they are far from the perfect answer.

Termination

Development agreements normally contain termination provisions allowing either side to terminate the agreement for the other side's uncured default (this is known as a termination "for cause."). Where there are "umbrella" agreements covering more than one "work order," the customer may want the option of terminating only a particular work order or the entire agreement if the developer fails to perform.

Customers often want the right to terminate a development project or any work order for convenience (meaning with no stated reason). This is because there may be situations where the customer is unhappy with the developer, but does not have sufficient reason to terminate for cause. Developers working on a major project may resist such a provision—or it may want compensation for lost opportunity and shut down costs if the customer terminates for convenience. These provisions are often highly negotiated.

If the agreement is terminated before the development is finished, what happens to the partially completed computer code—and what are the customer's rights to it? Of course, the parties may make any provision they want for this situation—but the most common provision is that the developer delivers to the customer whatever software it has completed in exchange for partial payment of the contract price. Sometimes a customer will negotiate a provision under which it can get some or all of its money back if the developer fails to deliver early milestones in accordance with the agreement.

Where the agreement can be terminated early and provides that the customer will be entitled to keep possession of the code, the developer may want provisions that make clear that, in that scenario, the developer makes no warranty with regard to the quality or completeness of the code or has no maintenance obligations.

Dispute Resolution

Dispute resolution clauses are also discussed in Chapter 8. The principles discussed there apply to software development agreements. However, there are a few additional applicable considerations for development agreements that we wish to bring to your attention.

As we mentioned above, large development projects have a troubled history, and for this reason are comparatively dispute-prone. While no one likes to dwell on negative outcomes, it is a good idea to build dispute management into every major development project. Here are a few suggestions:

- It may be a good idea to have a "dispute escalation" process—whereby matters in dispute must be discussed by senior executives before litigation starts.

- If the developer and customer are based in different jurisdictions, it may discourage litigation and encourage settlement if adjudication of disputes (whether by litigation or arbitration) is in a neutral location.

- Beware of "attorneys' fees" clauses that provide for an attorneys' fee award to the "prevailing party" in a dispute. While there is a certain appeal to this kind of "winner take all" provision, the downside is that these clauses tend to make parties feel more comfortable about starting litigation and may make settlement harder.

- Disputes over development projects may be well suited for mediation and arbitration.

Boilerplate Provisions

The general topic of the "boilerplate" provisions found at the end of US contracts is discussed in Chapter 8. The principles discussed there apply to software development agreements.

One clause to pay attention to is the assignment clause. The customer may want the right to prevent the developer's assignment of a development contract—or any change of control of the developer if the customer believes that the change will impair the development project. On the other hand, customers often resist contract assignment provisions that would impair their own exit transactions.

ABOUT OFFSHORING

Enormous amounts of development are now done offshore. Many buyers of IT services get them directly from an offshore supplier. Many developers subcontract work offshore.

There is nothing different in principle between a contract with a US-based developer and one in a "lower-wage" country such as India, China, or Russia. The same planning, contracting, and development processes need to take place. There are some additional challenges and uncertainties associated with emerging countries, but thousands of companies have had favorable experiences when outsourcing development offshore. The price advantages in nations such as India are obvious (although price differentials are falling, due to wage inflation in foreign labor markets and the decline of the value of the US dollar). The worldwide telecommunications infrastructure makes foreign suppliers accessible. While Bangalore is nine and half hours ahead of New York, managers there understand full well that they have to be available to talk to the Americans in the early evening.

Let us assume that—as a customer or developer doing subcontracting—you are actively considering having development done half a world away. Here are some factors (in addition to those that apply to development deals generally) to consider. Note that this is by no means an exhaustive list:

- **Right Tasks**—Not all development tasks are suitable for offshore work. If the specifications are vague and completing the design requires frequent interaction with users, the offshoring effort may bog down or produce poor results unless the US party has staff onsite at the foreign location.

- **Knowing the Developer**—It is important to deal with companies that you trust. That means that you should check references and get to know your vendor. You should be sure the offshore developer has the right technical skills and experience in similar projects. It is also a good idea to find out what you can do about the rate of employee turnover. One or more onsite visits at the vendor location in advance of any agreement are recommended.

- **Communications**—Make sure that communications are good. This means that the developer should have good English language skills—unless you speak developer's language.

- **Deal Exits**—You should consider having "termination for convenience" provisions in any major agreement, so that you get out easily if things are not going well.

- **Confidentiality and Intellectual Property**—You should be sure that confidentiality and intellectual clauses are tight and take reasonable steps to make sure the offshore developer has contracts in place with its employees to obtain all required rights and impose all relevant confidentiality restrictions.

- **Security**—You should check both the physical security and the electronic and network security measures used by any offshore developer.

- **Your Management Resources**—You need to be sure that you have the skills and staff in place on your side to generate tight specifications, and review work product. The management requirements are generally higher for offshore work.

- **Frequent Reviews**—You should require frequent reporting and reviews of code, testing, bugs, integration, and so forth. For large projects, you will likely want to visit and speak with managers on site. If payment is on a "time" basis, you will need to do your own verification of whether projected savings are being realized.

- **Possession of the Code**—It is a good idea to obtain the most current build of the software frequently, say by daily or weekly FTP transfer. This will give you the ability to monitor the work—and to take it over if need be.

- **Discretion in Disclosure of Trade Secrets**—While there is no reason to consider foreign citizens more or less trustworthy than Americans, it is certainly true that tracking down stolen trade secrets is harder in Moscow or Shanghai than in Silicon Valley. So you may want to think twice about exposing your "crown jewel" source code. On the other hand, many companies conduct all of their product development offshore; in the final analysis, it is a business risk decision.

- **Regulatory Issues**—For some industries, there may be privacy law or export control law issues in offshore development. You should discuss these with your legal counsel.

- **Governing Law**—If possible negotiate deals governed by the laws of a US jurisdiction. Many deals with foreign developers are done under New York or California law.

- **Jurisdiction for Disputes**—It is often best to have disputes resolved by arbitration. This is because many nations do not recognize foreign court judgments but do recognize arbitration decisions. You may want to have the arbitration in a convenient US venue. Alternatively, you might consider a neutral site in a legally sophisticated city, such as London, Geneva, Singapore, or Hong Kong as the site for arbitration.

Other Types of Consulting Business and IT Services

There are, of course, other types of IT consulting and IT services work beyond the development engagements that we have discussed above. Consulting and IT services can include routine maintenance for computer systems and service and "help desk" support for enterprise IT networks and computers. Some companies simply provide "programmers for hire" on a daily or weekly basis. In some cases, an IT service provider will engage in a type of "outsourcing" transaction in which it buys a company's computers, storage systems, and information systems and operates them for their former owner—a deal that includes elements of finance, employment, and services. Some consultants provide advice on IT strategy and planning. There is really no end to the variations.

This chapter could not possibly deal with all consulting variants. However, we have included in the form Appendix to this book a general forms of consulting agreement that you can think of as containers in which many consulting engagements would fit. (These are Forms 10-2 and 10-3.) As you will see by reviewing the forms, the issues in consulting, in general, are the same as those that we discussed above in the context of the development agreements. In preparing consulting or IT services agreements regardless of the variant, you will typically give attention to the following:

- Assessment of customer needs.

- Identification of services and/or deliverables.

- A process for customer acceptance or sign-off.

- Apportionment of any intellectual property created—although some simple engagements may not generate any intellectual property of significance.

- Confidentiality.

- Provisions for the upkeep and maintenance of computer code, if any, are involved.

- Warranty disclaimers and remedy limitations.

- Indemnification in some cases.

- Dispute resolution procedures and other "boilerplate."

Because the issues recur, this chapter and the various sample agreements provided should be a good introduction to IT consulting agreements generally.

Note that automated IT services provided remotely are discussed in Chapter 13, our discussion of software as a service or "SaaS."

Legal Issues in Development and Consulting Businesses

In this chapter, we have emphasized the importance of good contracting to build value in a consulting business. Let's look at a couple of other legal issues that development, consulting, and IT services businesses need to keep in mind.

Employment Issues

It almost goes without saying that consulting companies need to pay careful attention to all the legal issues that relate to employment. Here are some issues that you should attend to if you own or operate a consulting company:

- Be sure that all employees sign employee agreements. (See the discussion of employee agreements in Chapter 7.) These should normally include non-competition provisions in each state or country where these agreements are enforceable.

- Be very careful in classifying staff as contractors as opposed to temporary employees. Consulting companies can face tax and other legal problems if they classify workers as "contractors" when the law considers them to be employees. See your accountant or your lawyer about this important distinction.

- Consult legal counsel in case of any employment dispute and in case of any major reduction in force.

It is also recommended that you review your employment policies with a lawyer familiar with employment law in each state where you conduct business.

Building a Brand

Some consulting companies begin with just a few individual consultants or developers. Getting bigger means being able to sell the services of hundreds or thousands of professionals rather than those of just a few founders. To sell the services of a company rather than a founder requires building a strong brand. Some world-famous brands in this field are Accenture (formerly Andersen Consulting) and BearingPoint (formerly KPMG Consulting). Any brand worth using should be properly protected under trademark law. See Chapter 4 for information on trademark and branding.

CONCLUSION

If your company is careful in its development contracting, it can obtain expected results, make smart choices about intellectual property, manage risk, and build sound relationships.

Beta Test Agreements

11

Six Software Testing Axioms

1. *It is impossible to test a program completely.*

2. *Software testing is a risk based exercise.*

3. *Testing cannot show that bugs don't exist.*

4. *The more bugs you find, the more bugs there are.*

5. *Not all the bugs you find will be fixed.*

6. *Product specifications are never final.*

—From Wikipedia on "Software Testing."

IN THIS CHAPTER

This chapter covers beta test agreements for software products and services.

Software vendors find that there comes a time in software product development when the product is close to done but not quite ready for prime time. Perhaps most bugs are fixed, but undiscovered glitches and gremlins are surely lurking in the code. Products are tested internally, but there is a need for testing and evaluation by actual users. The vendor may want its prerelease software to be taken on a "trial run" by potential customers—in the hope that they will soon become paying customer when the product is released.

In this setting, vendors often provide copies of the premarket software to customers and prospects without charge for a tryout. The trial user is often promised a free or discounted copy of the final released version when it comes out on the market. The trial users provide reports on bugs and problems in the software and suggest needed improvements or desired additional features. The trial users also may report on whether the software is easy to use.

The software released to testers in this way is often called a *beta* version. The trial users are commonly known as *beta testers*. Before the software is released for this kind of testing, it is customary (and important) that the beta licensee (which might be a company or an individual) signs or agrees to a *beta test agreement*. Beta test agreements are simple documents as software agreements go. This is because they are designed to be operative for a relatively short time, they do not involve any rights of distribution, and they normally do not require payment.

There are different kinds of beta tests. Complex products may require lengthy tests that last many months. For simpler products a few weeks may suffice. Wholly new products or major upgrades of products may require tests for multiple versions each with incremental improvements and corrections. Consumer and mass market products, such as games or personal computer applications, may require many individual beta testers. Corporate applications may have a handful of beta users, but require lots of communication and cooperation between the vendor and its beta licensees.

A NOTE ON TERMINOLOGY

The *alpha* version of a product includes major features but with some functionality yet to be completed. A *beta* version usually represents a status in development at which all planned features have been coded and are working, but the software is not ready for release because it has bugs and errors—and sometimes because minor improvements may still be added.

Further more refined prereleases are sometimes called *"gamma"* or *"delta."* Microsoft and others use the term "release candidate" for a version where (hopefully) nothing is left to be done but some bug fixing.

The version that is "beta tested" by third parties may, of course, be beta, gamma, or delta software. The version that is actually released for commercial use is typically called version 1.0.

GOALS AND CONTENTS OF A BETA TEST AGREEMENT

Beta test agreements have provisions designed to serve some important goals for the vendor.

- **Limiting Liability**—It is possible that due to errors and bugs, the software in beta testing may fail, crash, or corrupt data. The vendor wants the tester to help discover these flaws to be sure, but does not want the tester to be able to sue if something goes wrong. Accordingly, beta test agreements state that the licensed software is not market-ready and have broad warranty disclaimers and risk limitation clauses.

- **Reporting Errors**—The beta test agreement either requires or invites the beta licensee to report errors or problems in use.

- **Defining the Use of the Software**—The agreement will state that the tester is licensed to use the program only for a defined test period. In many cases, the license is for test use only, but some agreements permit the licensee to use the software internally as it deems fit.

- **Keeping the Software and Its Features Confidential**—Many beta test agreements have provisions that require the licensee to keep the software and its features confidential until the launch of the commercial release. This is hardly a perfect barrier, of course. Information from beta tests (and copies of beta software) are often leaked. Nonetheless, this provision may help keep the new product and information about it out of the hands of the competition.

- **Public Betas**—Not all beta tests are confidential. In some cases, there are widely distributed "public betas" under beta test agreements in which there are no confidentiality limitations. With some consumer applications, beta tests may cover millions of copies and many months of testing.

- **Establishing Proprietary Rights in the Program**—In most beta test agreements, the beta licensee acknowledges the vendor's ownership of the program, its copyright, and trademarks.

- **Consent for Automated Monitoring**—If the beta test software includes any mechanism for automated Internet reporting on usage or errors, the beta test agreement should provide for the licensee's express consent to this functionality.

- **Coping with Unsolicited Advice**—Sometimes, a beta tester will send the vendor ideas for improvements in the product or even provide a flow chart for additional functions and features that the beta tester thinks should be added to the vendor's software. If the vendor makes a change that looks like one of the tester's ideas, there is a risk that the tester might demand to be paid for his contribution. If he is not paid, he may sue. To head off this type of problem before it happens, beta test agreements have provisions that give the vendor unlimited rights to use any feedback.

VARIATION IN BETA TEST AGREEMENTS

Not all beta test agreements are the same. They vary greatly based on the product type and the user type. Beta test agreements need to be adapted for these variations:

- Consumer and mass market products will often be under "click-through" beta test agreements. (See the discussion of "click-through" agreements in Chapter 16.)

- Complex products, with major corporations as beta licensees, often must include provisions for installation and/or configuration services. For this reason, the beta test agreement may be a signed and negotiated document. There will often be a written beta test plan agreed between the vendor and the beta licensee and referred to in the beta test agreement. (These plans are discussed below.)

- Software-as-a-service (or "SaaS") applications that are provided remotely will normally be written as service beta tests—rather than as beta test product licenses.

MARKETING USES OF BETA TESTS

In addition to testing functions, beta test agreements can serve a marketing agenda especially for companies or product marketer with a new product entry. The marketing functions include the following:

- **Getting a Foot in the Door**—The beta test stage may provide an opportunity for the vendor to introduce its product to the potential customer. The beta test agreement thus can be a prelude to a commercial license.

- **Establishing a Pedigree**—If the test is successful, the vendor may be able to arrange for the customer's permission in using its name in promotion as a "representative customer" for the application.

The vendor should be sure that the software to be supplied is reasonably bug-free in order for this type of beta testing-as-marketing strategy to work. If the software vendor wishes to use the name of the tester and the results of the test in advertising and promotions, the beta test agreement should grant the vendor the right to do so.

FOLLOWING UP ON A BETA TEST

It is a good idea, from a business and a legal perspective, to follow up on the beta licensees to see if they had trouble with the software and whether there were problems. Often beta test software includes functionality for feedback for bug reporting and for feedback on feature use and on errors. Vendors also often follow up on beta software with phone or e-mail communication.

BETA TEST PLANS

For sophisticated business and industrial applications, beta testing may require coordination and cooperation between vendor and customer. To carry out such a beta test, the vendor needs first to create a separate document, often called the "beta test plan," after discussions with the beta licensee.

While the beta test plan may be attached to the beta test agreement, it is really a business document that spells out the intended working relationship of the two parties. The details of the plan will be largely dictated by the product and its business setting. Here is a list of some items that you may wish to cover in a beta test plan:

- **Equipment and Scale of the Test**—The number of computers or workstations to be involved and the hardware and software platforms to be used

- **Test Sites**—The business locations where the software will be installed and used

- **Installation Details**—The timing and sequencing of installation (including any integration) and the work needed from both sides to set up for and carry out installation

- **Training and Technical Support**—Provision for how and when the vendor will make available training and technical support for users, often including a hot line

- **Contact Persons**—The personnel at the beta licensee company who will be in charge of coordinating the beta test, and the contact persons for the supplier

- **Bug Reports**—The method and format of reporting on problems and bugs

- **Meetings**—The scheduling of regular meetings with the beta licensee's staff to access problems and progress

- **Final or Periodic Evaluation of the Software**—Evaluation procedures in which the software is compared to projected results or to the competition, and user satisfaction is rated

When a beta test agreement incorporates such a beta test plan, the parties normally agree to use reasonable efforts to carry out the agreed-upon plan. However, the beta test plan is a document that will never be enforced in a court of law—it is designed to give structure to a voluntary cooperative effort.

TWO FORMS OF BETA TEST AGREEMENT

Included in the form appendix are two sample forms of beta test agreement. The first (Form 11-1) is for a mass distribution single user product. The second (Form 11-2) is for a cooperative beta test, where the software will require installation, training, and support from the vendor, and where a beta test plan has been agreed upon.

As noted above, these forms may require variations depending on product type, technology, market or other factors. If you have questions about the right beta test agreement for your product, you should seek the advice of legal counsel.

Commercial End-User Agreements

12

The process of negotiating a contract can help the parties get to know each other better, clarify their objectives and expectations, and thereby strengthen their relationship.

—Constance Bagley, Harvard Business School Professor

At our law firm, we have helped vendors license an endless variety of applications to end users: stock portfolio management systems, "add-in" programs for Web servers, retail cash register systems, database management systems, stock trading systems, programs for managing machine shops, payroll management systems—even computer software for managing pizza parlors.

If licensing commercial software is your business, you regularly use form agreements as the basis (or at least the starting point) for negotiations. In doing deals, you have some simple goals: You want to close sales. You don't want to get bogged down in long legal negotiations. On the other hand, you don't want contracts that expose your company to large legal risks or that will look bad when your company is up for sale.

As the quotation above indicates, contracts are an important part of the relationship with commercial customers. They set expectations and impose boundaries. Done right, contracts will reinforce relationships.

IN THIS CHAPTER

This chapter covers the end-user agreements that vendors use to license software to commercial customers. This form of licensing is also used to license nonprofit corporations and national and state governments. This chapter also **313** covers some important related topics: software escrow agreements, accounting for software transactions, and the application of sales tax to software licensing deals.

The contracts discussed in this chapter are *signed* agreements on paper, and they are often negotiated. They are primarily for business and industrial software products. Commercial end-user agreements cover a great variety of transaction sizes. At the modest end of that range might be a simple application with a permanent license price of a few thousand dollars. At the high end are software packages that are a million dollars or more for a permanent license or costing hundreds of thousands of dollars annually on a subscription basis. These license agreement forms are used in "direct sales" (actually direct *licensing*) to customers and also are often provided to "channel partners" for use in their licensing.

We often refer to these commercial end-user agreements as "enterprise license agreements" to distinguish them from non-negotiated and automatically accepted "clickwrap" license agreements. (Clickwraps and related "browsewraps" are discussed in Chapter 16.)

Contracts for offerings where the software functionality is provided as a service accessed remotely, known as "software as a service" (or "SaaS"), are discussed in Chapter 13. In some cases, customers may have the option to convert an enterprise license agreement to a SaaS agreement or vice versa, in which case the agreement would be a hybrid of the type discussed here and those considered in Chapter 13.

In this chapter, we refer to the party supplying the software as the "vendor" and end user as the "customer."

BUSINESS SETTING FOR SOFTWARE END-USER AGREEMENTS

A commercial end-user agreement is often entitled "License Agreement," "Enterprise License Agreement" or the like. These agreements fit the following product setting:

- **A Finished Product**—The vendor provides an existing product or suite of products. Because pre-existing software is used, the technical risk of the solution is low.

- **Standard Environment**—The software runs on widely available hardware and software platforms that are standard products.

- **Limited Customization and Integration**—The vendor's customization and integration work typically consists of such straightforward tasks as setting up data files, creating forms and screens, creating report formats, adapting the product to the user's network and systems, creating inter-application interfaces, and the like.

- **Maintenance and Support**—The customer requires (and will pay for) continued maintenance and support services after the software is delivered and installed.

- **Training**—The customer often pays for training in use of the software.

Some Guidance on License Design

Here are a few guidelines for designing contract forms for this kind of licensing:

- **Keep it Simple**—Essential legal protections must be in the documents, but they can be written simply and directly without excess amounts of "legalese." (Note, however, that the "one-page agreement" for sophisticated business software is a myth, unless the type is "mouseprint" size.)

- **Know What You Need and Eliminate What You Don't**—This chapter outlines the many provisions that could be in your agreements, and some provisions that must be in them. The vendor's challenge is to keep the text as straightforward as possible. Try to eliminate what you don't need.

- **Build in Flexibility**—Keep contract forms "modular," so that deal terms like pricing or service terms are in schedules. This makes it easy to add, remove, or change products or services. Often these agreements are written so that multiple product deliveries can occur over a long period of time without the need to negotiate or sign another agreement.

- **Find the Middle Ground**—Try to make form agreements fair and balanced. Making form agreements one-sided will delay closing deals—often for marginal advantages.

- **Formatting**—You may wish to put contracts into double column form so that they look more like "standard" forms. This formatting can make contracts look less "negotiable."

The commercial end-user agreements are not the most complex contracts, but they do have some subtleties and raise legal issues that you might miss.

They need to be adapted to different software types and markets. The vendor should have an attorney's assistance in creating these forms or negotiating major modifications. Similarly, an end-user company that is investing a large sum in the procurement of a major software system should not sign or assent to an end-user agreement until legal counsel has reviewed the document.

Form of Software End-User Agreements

As an aid for designing and negotiating agreements discussed in this chapter, we have included a sample evaluation license agreement (Form 12-1) and a sample commercial end-user agreement (Form 12-2) in the Appendix. In addition, one can find countless examples of end-user license agreements (ranging from very good to very bad) on the Internet, including on such legal sites as findlaw.com and onecle.com. If you examine a few, you will see a great variety in provisions reflecting the variations in business settings and technologies.

Forms should be considered as examples, not as models. They may be perfectly good agreements but just not be right for your deal. There is no such thing as a universal form document for IT licensing.

Agreements for Software Plus Hardware

Often customers will buy or lease their own computer hardware and use the vendor only for the applications software. The computer hardware is commonly considered a commodity item and is usually obtained through mass-market channels. But sometimes the vendor will provide the customer with a complete system (sometimes called a "turnkey system") with both computer hardware and application software. Sometimes the computer "box" acts as a delivery container for the software inside. In some cases there is other hardware in the sale, such as network or storage devices.

When the transaction involves hardware, customers may want a single agreement to cover both the hardware and software, so that if the system is defective, the customer can return the entire system, or if there are problems with the system, one vendor is responsible for fixing it.

This is not a book about hardware sales, but I note in passing that hardware agreements have their own issues: delivery, installation, acceptance, warranties, remedies for defective equipment, replacements and returns, upgrades, normal wear and abuse, useful life of components, service, and support. This is all pretty simple to manage if the vendor simply "passes though" the hardware vendor's sales documentation and refers the customer to the hardware vendor's service offerings. It gets more complicated if the vendor is taking more responsibility for the hardware. If you need a contract to cover hardware issues, you should consult your attorney.

BARGAINING BETWEEN VENDOR AND CUSTOMER

The bargaining process for software end-user agreements usually depends to a large degree on these factors:

- The price of the software license and the follow-on fees for support and additional software licenses. Most companies are reluctant to spend time and effort in negotiating small-ticket software license purchases. As the price climbs, so does the extent of bargaining you should expect.

- The competition (or lack of competition) for the customer's business.

- The customer's sophistication about computers and contract negotiations.

The vendor will usually go into discussions with the customer with a form contract in hand. The more money that is at stake and the hotter the competition, however, the more likely it is that vendors—large and small—will have to negotiate changes and concessions in their standard terms.

Probably the most frustrating situation from the vendor's point of view is dealing with an inexperienced acquisition team or legal counsel. Inexperience coupled with customer leverage often results in excessive or unrealistic requests for changes that can slow negotiation down. There is no remedy for this other than patiently explaining contract terms. Educating the customer about normal software industry contracting practices can be an essential part of the sales process.

The customer should make sure that all promises made actually end up in the contract—rather than in side letters signed by sales persons who may lack authority to bind the vendor. Some large vendors have policies that prohibit the modification of their standard form agreements without approval from headquarters—and language to that effect included in their standard form agreement. Such contract language is usually upheld by the courts, so "side letters" may be unenforceable in many cases.

Large corporate customers often have their own standard forms for *purchasing* software licenses. Needless to say, from the vendor's point of view, these forms contain any number of unfavorable provisions. Sometimes the vendor is forced to choose between accepting some bad terms and losing the deal. In our experience, vendors often can negotiate fair bargains that start with the "customer's paper," but it takes longer and requires patience. It also can cost more, because the vendor will need to have its lawyer review the proposed agreement and propose edits.

Vendor and Customer Goals

The vendor normally has the following goals in the negotiation of an end-user agreement:

- A price with a reasonable profit margin and a reasonable amount of cash early in the transaction

- The customer's irrevocable acceptance of the software as soon as possible after the contract is signed

- Continuing revenue stream for software support and services

- Flexibility in pricing for follow-on orders and future services

- Limitations on potential liability

The vendor will normally require revenue sources in addition to the software license fee. When the customer licenses a major new software system, there may be professional service fees for software integration and configuration, training, data conversion, and ongoing maintenance and support. In some cases these additional costs over time equal or exceed the license fee for the software.

The sophisticated customer's goals will be:

- A software product that genuinely meets its needs

- Favorable pricing on software license fees and reasonable fees for software support

- A firm commitment on the delivery and installation date and a right to cancel if the software is not delivered or installed within a specified time

- The opportunity to test the software for a reasonable period with real data under real conditions before paying the major part of the price, and the right to return it if dissatisfied

- Flexibility for future needs, including options for increasing overall system size and capacity, adding functions, ordering more software, enhancing performance, downsizing, and so forth.

The Request for Proposal Process

Many customers initiate the process of a major software or computer system acquisition with a Request for Proposal (RFP). The RFP states what the customer's needs are, what tasks the software will be required to perform, what volume of data the software will need to process, and the like. RFPs are circulated to vendors to elicit bids. Some RFPs are very tightly drafted, but many are quite vague about what is really required of the software. Where the required system is complex and performs a crucial business function, smart customers will often hire a computer consultant to write a carefully considered RFP. (See the discussion of the RFP process for development deals in Chapter 10.)

Some customers place their form software procurement contract in the RFP with a condition that any bidder must agree in advance to accept it. Whether or not that tactic actually works to cut off negotiations varies with the leverage of the parties.

COMMON ISSUES IN NEGOTIATING END-USER AGREEMENTS

In the following sections we discuss some of the provisions included in an end-user agreement and the topics that are often the subject of negotiation. You may want to review the discussion in Chapter 8 on IT contracting basics before diving into this discussion. If you look at the form of commercial end-user license agreement included in the Appendix to this book, you will see contractual language on many of the points discussed here.

Delivery and Acceptance

The delivery, installation, and acceptance of the software are important topics in commercial end-user agreements.

Delivery
The end-user agreement should specify *what* has to be delivered, and *when*. If no delivery time is specified, the vendor must arrange for delivery in a

reasonable time. As a practical matter, vendors must deliver in a time frame that keeps its customer reasonably happy or the customer may seek to cancel the agreement.

In addition, shipment is often important for revenue recognition purposes, and under many contracts, the vendor bills for some or the entire license fee on shipment. Therefore the vendor shares an interest in setting a prompt shipment date.

Customization

Software may require heavy customization or none. Any customization required should be spelled out in the end-user agreement in reasonable detail. Pricing of customization is often negotiated.

Installation

Some software is easy to install, and the vendor simply sends it to the customer with installation instructions. When installation is more complex, installation services will be provided. Sometimes installation is included in the licensing fee and sometimes the vendor provides installation on a time and materials basis as specified in the end-user agreement. Data conversion (conversion of data stored in the format used by the customer's old software into a new format) may be needed as part of the installation process, and is often supplied for a negotiated additional fee.

Acceptance

Vendors prefer agreements in which there is no acceptance process. They want to just bill for the software upon shipment or delivery. Customers, however, often want acceptance clauses. The more expensive the software, the more likely that there will be an acceptance process.

In most agreements that include a software acceptance procedure, part of the license fee is due on signing of the agreement and the final portion of the license fee is due on acceptance of the software. There are several types of provisions for acceptance commonly found in end-user agreements:

- **Performance Criteria**—This type of provision says that the customer must accept the software if it substantially performs according to specified criteria: Sometimes, the specified criteria are that it runs the functions described in the user manual.

- **Specified Customization or Installation**—Where the agreement includes development or installation services, the agreement will need to be drafted to cover delivery and acceptance of any custom software code or services.

- **Customer-Specified Acceptance Criteria**—In many cases, the customer may negotiate custom acceptance criteria—which may include processing actual data from the customer's operations and running real reports.

- **Specified Corrections**—Under this common provision, the customer must list any bugs or other needed corrections in a specified number of days after delivery. If these are fixed, the customer must accept the software. Sometimes the agreement has a time frame in which the vendor must provide corrections—if the vendor fails to meet the time limits, the customer may have the right to terminate the agreement and receive a refund of all amounts paid.

- **Deemed Acceptance**—Normally vendors insist upon a "deemed acceptance" provision. If the customer fails to deliver a list of defects to the vendor in a defined number of days, the software will be automatically deemed accepted. It is also common to provide that any use of the software in the customer's business (often called "productive use") will be deemed acceptance.

- **Free Trial and Optional Acceptance**—Under this alternative, the customer makes the up-front payments and then obtains and tests the software. If it chooses, the customer may accept or reject it. If the software is not rejected in a specified number of days, the software is automatically accepted. This try-before-you-buy provision has marketing advantages, but it also gives the customer an easy way out of the agreement if there are problems with the software. Any vendor that uses such a right-to-return provision should be sure that the end-user agreement states that if the customer returns the software within the stated time period, the return of the software and return of any down payment is the customer's sole and exclusive remedy for any product defect.

The Permanent License Model: Initial License Fees and Support Fees

As noted earlier, under the terms of a commercial end-user agreement, the customer pays a license fee to obtain the software. The most common model is the "permanent" or "perpetual license." Under this model, the customer pays one license fee and obtains the right to use the software forever (as long as it does not materially breach the license in some way). The fee typically (but not always) also includes software maintenance and support for a limited period—often 90 days, six months, or one year. Installation, if required, may be included in the license fee or more commonly is an extra charge.

In addition to a license fee for the permanent license, the vendor hopes to get maintenance and support fees over time. Usually the vendor offers one or more "Maintenance and Support Plans." Maintenance means that the vendor resolves software malfunctions and fixes bugs. Support means technical advice to the customer on the use of the software. After the initial period of maintenance and support is over, the customer will need to pay a quarterly, yearly, or other periodic fee to obtain these services.

Vendors get their customers to pay for maintenance and support year after year by providing knowledgeable and prompt product advice, resolving bugs, and (where upgrades are included in maintenance) releasing new versions of their products with better or enhanced functionality and features. Because sophisticated software is rarely completely bug-free, software maintenance and support may be essential assurance that the program will keep performing its normal business functions. Indeed the process of improving software will itself often create new bugs that make support essential. For large customers with "mission critical" applications, obtaining software without maintenance and support is unthinkable. (There is more about maintenance and support later in this chapter.)

Software maintenance and support fees can be due yearly, or less commonly over shorter periods, and are normally due in advance. The maintenance and support fee may be a specified amount or may be stated as a function of the license fee charged for software, often 15 to 20 percent of total fees. A smart vendor will make sure that it does not get locked into a set price over a long period of time. Here are some ways that vendors get price increases:

- Tying yearly maintenance and support fees to the percentage of the license price set in vendor's *then current* price list. This ensures that as the vendor increases (or decreases) its license fees, the maintenance and support fees of its existing customers also increases (or decreases). Such provisions allow the vendor to increase (or lower) maintenance and support prices in response to market conditions.

- Fixing support and maintenance fees for a specified period with the vendor thereafter free to increase or decrease the fees at its discretion.

- Providing for automatic price adjustments based on inflation using some recognized measurement for inflation.

Customers will resist price increases, especially increases at the discretion of the vendor. Usually the vendor and the customer will agree to some form of price increase using one, or a combination of the methods referenced above. If the customer has leverage, it can usually successfully negotiate longer term price caps.

Software by the Month, Quarter, or Year

An increasingly common model for licensing software is the "subscription model" in which customers pay for use of the software month-to-month, quarter-to-quarter, or year-to-year. Under this model, the license fee, and maintenance and support are all "bundled" into a single fee. If the customer keeps paying, it keeps using the software. Fees are often due in advance. Most subscription model agreements require that the customer agrees to use, and pay for, the software for a defined minimum initial term of at least a year although longer minimum periods are not unusual.

Under this model, in the short run the customer pays less for the software, but in the long run, it pays more. That's because subscription pricing is commonly set so that in three or four years the vendor gets just as much money as it would have received by charging for a permanent license plus maintenance and support. Over time, subscription payments will far exceed the price of a permanent license. Another advantage for the vendor is that subscription license receipts continue year to year. Permanent license revenues for business products tend to slow down greatly during economic recessions. Many vendors have aggressively promoted subscription licensing.

Permitted Use and Pricing

The scope of use and the payment terms are key interrelated elements of end-user agreements. Vendors design the end-user license grant clause with several goals in mind:

- The grant is designed to delineate clearly the customer's permitted use of the software, so that the customer has a guide to what use is allowed and what is forbidden.

- The grant must be designed to fit the technology. For instance, the permitted use of desktop software is different from that of a Web server.

- The grant is closely coordinated with the pricing provisions. Vendors most often permit use that is measurable in units. The customer is then charged for the use of those units.

Here are some customary ways in which the customer's use is defined and measured in an end-user agreement:

- Specified number of workstations

- Specified number of named users

- Specified number of concurrent users

- Specified numbers of servers

- Site licenses

- Single corporation (and perhaps subsidiaries and affiliates)

- Variations on the above

In the following sections, we will examine the distinctions among these permitted uses and their corresponding price plans.

Servers and Workstations

There are many software programs that have a client–server architecture in which both the client and server software is supplied by the vendor. This type of system has one or more servers and also has client software that is installed in various workstations or PCs in a network (which often will include a local area network (LAN) as well as access by authorized users in remote locations). Most computer aided design (CAD) systems, for example, have this kind of architecture. With this system, the server provides administration, storage, and communication, and the client software provides the functionality that allows the user to create, manipulate, and move data.

Common end-user licensing for this system requires the customer to obtain a license for the software installed on the server and a workstation license for each network workstation or PC. If the customer wants to add more servers or use more workstations, it must buy more server or workstation licenses at a preset license fee. The vendor may include license management software that will prevent access to the server by more than the allowed number of client installations. The disadvantage of this system to the customer is that access is tied to the workstation and installed client software.

License for Use by a Specified Number of Users

Another very common scheme for licensing is based on the number of individual "named users" that may access a system. This way of metering use works on client–server systems, but also can readily be adapted to Web-based client–server architectures, which permit users to access the software from any Web browser.

With the "named user" method, user access is usually authorized by a system administrator at the customer's location. Each user typically has his or her own user name and password that is required for a user to "log on" to the software from a workstation or PC. Limiting the number of permitted user names and passwords means that the customer is required to purchase additional named user licenses to enlarge the capacity of the software system.

Often software licensed in this way also has built-in license manager software that blocks assignment of user names in excess of the limit set by the license agreement. If the customer pays for more users, the vendor will supply a software key that resets the number of permitted named users.

Using this model, the vendor can impose substantial controls over the access to the software through a license manager and the customer has the flexibility of access through any number of workstations, PCs, or (if the technology allows) Web browsers.

License for a Specified Number of Concurrent Users

Another common option is to grant a license that allows installation on one or more servers with a specified number of "concurrent users." In such systems, license manager software is often used. The metering system monitors the number of workstations that are using the software at any one time. When the maximum number is reached, the metering system shuts out any additional workstation that attempts to access and use the software. A customer that purchases a two-user concurrent license can make the software available on as many internal workstations as it wishes, but only two users can access the software at the same time; others are locked out unless the customer buys additional licenses.

Some companies, in this global economy, make a distinction between a "national" concurrent license (which can be used only within one nation) and a higher priced "global" concurrent license (which can be used anywhere in the world). That is because the license to use concurrently licensed software in different time zones can increase its utilization and value to the customer. If, for example, a software development company has locations in both Boston and Beijing, it might use a single concurrent "seat" for a software development tool for 12 hours a day in Boston and for another 12 hours a day in Beijing, thereby doubling the value that it obtains from the single "seat."

Specified Number of Servers

Some applications are commonly licensed on a per-server basis. To add a server, the customer pays an additional license fee. This kind of license is most common when a single server provides a specialized function that serves a network, rather than just one PC, for example, Web servers, file storage servers, or e-mail servers.

Under this option, the number of users is limited only by the capability of the software and hardware. There are likely to be other contractual limitations—for example, use may be limited to a particular department or grouping of employees.

Site License

The classic meaning of a "site license," a term first used in the mainframe computer era of the 1950s, is licensing for use at a single location. Site licenses of this kind are much less common today than they were 20 years ago, because it's now so easy to extend access outside a single location. We still see site licensing in some sectors, for example, software products that manage manufacturing or other location-based activities. When there is site licensing of this kind, users are often limited to those physically present at the site, although sometimes there are provisions for some limited remote access. There may be extra fees for "moving" the license to a new site. Site licenses can be for software with client–server or Web architectures—or even for single PC applications. Vendors may include audit clauses in site licenses allowing the vendor's representatives to come on site at the customer's location and verify that the license is being used only as permitted.

The term "site license" also can bear another, quite different meaning. The term refers to deals made by large institutions such as universities for discounted purchases of mass-market software by affiliated persons. For example, Microsoft has a so-called "site license" agreement with the University of Michigan that permits the faculty and students to obtain software at a discount off retail price.

Corporate and Operating Unit License

Sometimes a license simply grants a corporation (and often its subsidiaries) a license to use software in its operations, with the right to make as many server or client software copies as it pleases. This type of license is normally available only to a customer that is willing to pay a premium for this freedom of use.

Unless the vendor is careful, a corporation-wide license may yield unexpected results. What happens, for example, if the customer corporation carries out an acquisition and doubles in size overnight? Does the license now cover all the newly acquired operations? It might, or might not, depending on how the scope of use clause is drafted. Similar problems occur when software is licensed for use in a particular department or business unit and the unit merges with another.

The limit to use is an issue in any corporation-wise license because of the consolidation in corporate America. Banks, insurance, automobiles, telecommunications carriers, Web hosting firms, and many other industries continue to undergo massive consolidation.

This means that any vendor that grants licenses that are for use in a company or business unit must consider provisions that limit the expansion of the license if the customer merges or combines with another company. Another potential solution is to have provisions that increase the license and maintenance fees if there are abrupt transaction-driven changes in the size of the customer's operations. Your attorney can help you craft clauses that deal with these contingencies.

More Scope-of-Use Provisions

In commercial end-user licensing agreements, the grant clause may address other matters regarding scope of permitted use, including the following:

Subsidiaries and Affiliates

Often a corporate customer will ask that a license be granted to the corporation and its subsidiaries and affiliates. These terms can make the scope of the software license uncertain, because they are often vague.

- Subsidiaries are companies that are owned, wholly or in part, by another corporation; the term thus can include 100-percent ownership, 50-plus percent ownership, or less ownership. A "majority owned" subsidiary is one where one company has over 50 percent ownership of the other.

- Affiliates are companies that share some or all of the same owners—but the degree of common ownership required may be undefined. In some cases the customer corporation may have no legal control of the subsidiary or affiliate.

If you are a vendor and granting a broad license (or giving large discounts), you may want to consider limiting use by subsidiaries and affiliates to those that are majority owned and controlled by the primary customer. You may also want to be sure that when an entity cease to be a subsidiary, its rights of use lapse.

Supplemental Uses

Customers commonly want extra copies of software programs for uses that supplement its main commercial use of the software. Examples would be an extra "instance" of the software running in a disaster recovery location that would be put to work in case the main computing location was out of operation. Another example is the "test server" used to do development or testing with the software. Vendors commonly expand licenses to accommodate these supplemental uses of the licensed software.

Internal Use or Customer's Own Data Restrictions

End-user agreements often specify that software is for "customer's internal use only" or for "customer's own data only." The vendor does not want its software to be used by the customer to process data for a variety of *other* businesses or allow the customer to make the software available remotely to its clients or business partners. While this sounds simple enough, the question of what is "internal use" or a software customer's "own data" can be unclear.

Take, for example, a bank that licenses software from a vendor. Assume the commercial end-user agreement signed by the bank contains these "internal use only" and "own data" restrictions. And suppose the bank allows depositors to log on to the bank's computer, examine their own accounts, check market yields for certificates of deposit and other investments, and to transfer funds or pay bills.

- Is it the bank's "own" data that is being accessed by depositors or is it the data of the depositors?

- Is the bank breaching the "internal use only" contract with the software vendor by offering this service to its depositors?

There has been litigation between vendors and customers over questions like these. Thinking through the issues and being more specific in the licensing provisions can avoid disputes over the scope of use.

Home Use of Office Software

If a vendor has granted a site license for a PC software program, are employees of the customer allowed to install a copy of the program on their home PCs? Can employees access the functionality remotely though a remote access product such as Citrix? If the license has a specified license fee per workstation, must the company pay an additional fee for use on or access from a PC at home?

Some vendors' commercial end-user agreements permit their customers' employees to use the program at home without extra charge; however many do not. Some agreements require extra payment for additional access locations.

A similar issue is the use of PC software on portable computers. Some vendors permit a portable computer and a desktop computer to be counted as a single installation, so long as only one person has sole use of both machines. Other vendors will demand two license payments for such use.

Nonassignable Agreement

Software end-user agreements often state that the license is nonassignable and nontransferable. The vendor wants each new prospect to license software from the vendor, *not* from an existing customer. Most customers find that restriction reasonable.

But there is one situation where a strict no-assignment provision can cause a customer an unpleasant surprise: That is when the customer tries to assign an expensive software license, together with all the other assets of customer's business, as part of the sale of all of the assets of the customer's business operations. Smart customers will negotiate a right to assign to cover this situation.

Some vendors include a provision that allows the assignment of the license, subject to vendor approval "not to be unreasonably withheld."

Limitation to Specified Hardware and Software Platforms

It is common for an end-user agreement to specify the type of hardware and software platforms that the software will be running on. The most common reason for this provision is to limit use of the software to computers and operating systems that are known to work with the software. Many vendors have lists of supported platforms for their products.

Software platforms change over time. In many end-user agreements, the software vendor reserves the right to require that the customer upgrade its operating system or its hardware to a listed version as a condition for continued software maintenance and support. The reason is that the vendor does not want to incur the costs of maintaining many versions of the software.

License Managers or Monitoring Software

If you supply software that has a license manager—to limit the number of users or to limit the time that the software can be used—be sure to include language in the end-user agreement that mentions the manager—so that it is clear that the customer has consented to its use. The same is true of any software function that reports back to the vendor aspects of the customer's use—such as functionality that reports the number of users. Disclosure to the customer is essential. Software that has hidden functionality that is harmful to the customer's property or business may be deemed an unfair business practice.

Make it clear to the customer that defeating or working around the license manager is a breach of contract. (As we saw in Chapter 2, doing so would also likely be a violation of the "anti-circumvention" provisions of the Digital Millennium Copyright Act.) Here is typical language to do this:

> *Licensee may not utilize any equipment, device, instruction, program or other means designed to circumvent or remove any License Manager.*

Dealing with the Future Needs

Many end-user agreements manage the future needs of the customer for additional software.

- **Additional Users or Workstations**—When the license is limited to a certain number of workstations or concurrent users, the agreement will almost always include an opportunity for the customer to increase the scope of the license for a set price.

- **Additional Modules**—Often software is licensed in modules that allow the vendor to sell additional functions separately. An example would be an accounting program that licenses separate modules for general ledger, payroll, and tax returns. An end-user agreement can specify the terms for adding such modules.

Agreements normally provide that to obtain maintenance and support for any additional software licensed, the customer must pay additional software maintenance and support fees.

Regulatory or Industry Changes

Some software needs to change to meet new requirements issued by government or by business. For example, income tax return software needs to be updated for changes in federal and state tax rules. Reimbursement software for doctors, hospitals, and clinics may need updating to provide for new forms required by insurers or federal or state government. Accounting software needs to change with changes in accounting rules.

The end-user agreement can specify that the vendor will provide updates that meet changing requirements for a specified fee or sometimes on a time and materials basis. (Note, however, the vendors will normally expressly disclaim any guarantee of legal or accounting accuracy.)

Pricing Variations

Pricing of software is more an art than a science. In addition to the pricing metrics discussed above (pricing by user, workstation, concurrent user or server), there are an infinity of possible variations. For example, a pricing schedule may include minimum purchase commitments over time or it may include options for a fixed amount of additional software at a set price if licenses are purchased by a set date. Sometime client licenses are sold in blocks, often called "license packs," with lower prices for higher volumes. Often there are quantity discounts.

Pricing Increases

Software licenses may last for many years. Inflation is a fact of life. From 1995 to 2005, the US dollar lost about 20 percent of its value. In the past, inflation has been much higher. For that reason, smart vendors build into their end-user agreement the ability to raise prices for individual server or client licenses and for maintenance and support.

The parties may negotiate a freeze on pricing increases (for software or maintenance or both) for a fixed number of years. Or the parties may negotiate a limit on periodic pricing increases. For example, a price clause may say:

Prices may not increase more than eight percent per year.

Or the limits may be based on an inflation measure. For example:

Licensor may increase fees and pricing under this Agreement yearly by no more than two percent over the increase in the cost of living as measure by the Consumer Price Index—All Urban Consumers as maintained by the US Bureau of Labor Statistics.

You may want to use other measures of inflation that fit particular markets or circumstances.

Software licenses also often have clauses that impose interest on late payments. Sometimes they have clauses requiring the customer to pay attorney's fees of the vendor if the vendor sues them successfully for nonpayment or other material breach of the Agreement.

Technology Change

Clauses defining the scope of use and related pricing metrics must take into account changes in technology.

For example, processors often now have multiple processing cores. Does this extra computing power count as installation on one computer or many? There are different approaches possible. One approach (from a Sybase form) treats a multicore processor the same as a single core:

> *As used in this Agreement, either a single or multi-core processor is considered a single CPU.*

Another approach (from an IBM form) is this:

> *Unless otherwise announced, with multi-core technology, IBM considers each core to be a physical processor.*

Virtualization software allows a single server to run many "instances" of client software on "virtual servers." We now commonly see license grant clauses like this:

> *Instance Licensing*
>
> *An instance of the Software is in "use" when it is being executed on a computer, virtual computer, or virtual machine. The use of multiple instances of the Software on a Single Computer requires a multiple instance license. If you have purchased a multiple instance license, you are authorized to use the number of instances for which you have paid. The term "Single Computer" means a stand-alone workstation.*

In these and many other cases, the vendor must imaginatively adapt its license agreement to fit the new technology. When technology changes the concepts that you use in your licensing, you should discuss with your counsel the adjustments that will be required in your company's form end-user agreements.

Software Maintenance and Support Provisions

As a practical matter, most customers will feel that it is necessary to purchase maintenance and support for any sophisticated software.

When Support Provisions Become Effective

Maintenance and support usually "kick in" after the end of an initial period of maintenance and support provided under the commercial end-user agreement, typically called the "warranty period." This initial warranty period is most often 90 days, six months, or one year.

The typical commercial end-user agreement will provide that if the customer finds errors in the software, the vendor will fix the problems and deliver corrected software. In reality the warranty period in most software license agreements is just a period of support and maintenance at no extra charge. After acceptance, there is typically no provision for the customer to return the software or to get the license fee back if software has errors.

Diagnosis and Response Time

Under most commercial end-user license agreements, when the customer reports a software error, the vendor's first task is to reproduce and diagnose the error. Many commercial end-user agreements include language to classify customer-reported software errors as "Critical," "Serious," "Non-Serious," or the like and have different required responses to different error classifications.

- "Critical" errors are those that stop the software from running or cripple critical functions.

- "Serious" errors are those that cause significant inconvenience, but do not stop business from being done.

- "Non-Serious" errors are those that do not substantially interfere with use of the software.

Many agreements include a "response matrix" that specify the number of hours within which the vendor will assign staff to a reported error and respond and report to the customer.

Vendors often guarantee a prompt response to the customer but are very reluctant to guarantee that errors will be fixed in a set amount of time. That's because there is no way to know in advance how long finding and fixing a particular software bug will take. Some customers manage to negotiate a "right to return" remedy (and a full or partial refund) if the time to repair critical errors takes longer than a specified number of days.

If the software is used at a site far from the vendor's location, the customer may have to pay travel and other out-of-pocket costs for on-site service. Many vendors offer a service in which vendor's technicians access the customer's system remotely and run diagnostic programs in order to diagnose the problem.

Maintenance Releases

When significant software errors are reported by customers, the vendor will often issue to customers a new release that fixes them, known as a "maintenance release." Usually the maintenance release is provided only to customers that are paying for maintenance and support.

Some end-user agreements provide for termination if the vendor is unable to fix a serious problem with the software. Typically, the vendor is allowed to pull the plug, that is, to discontinue support, refund some or all of the license fee or support fee, terminate the license, and cease further obligation to the customer. These provisions are most common in situations where the software requires considerable development before delivery and there is a high degree of technical risk.

New Versions of the Software

It is normal for the vendor (or a company that supplies the vendor) to release improved versions of software from time to time—versions with faster operation, greater ease-of-use, more functionality, or that take advantage of new features of hardware and operating systems. Vendors often make a distinction between software "Updates" and "Upgrades." Here are typical definitions:

> "*Update*" *means any version or release of the Software that corrects or remedies an error or provides minor enhancements to the Software.*

> "*Upgrade*" *means any version or release of the Software that adds capabilities or functionality (other than minor enhancements) or otherwise materially enhances the Software.*

Maintenance and support plans almost always include Updates. Whether it also includes Upgrades is a matter of vendor choice or negotiation. The more the customer pays for a maintenance and support plan, the more likely it is that Upgrades are included.

Support Only for Current Versions

It is normal for the commercial end-user agreement to provide software support only if the customer is using the most recent release (or one of the two most recent releases). This policy is born of necessity. No vendor can afford to be fixing and supporting obsolete versions of software used by only a few customers. This policy is one reason why the vendor may want to include Upgrades in its maintenance and support plan offerings.

Continuing Technical Support

Under most maintenance and support plans, the vendor will provide technical advice on use of the program. Sometimes there is a limit as to the number of hours included, with additional hours available on a "time and materials" basis.

Many agreements require that the customer appoint employees trained in use of the software to make all requests for maintenance and support. Vendors do not want calls from untrained employees that have poor understanding of the software's functionality.

Training Employees to Use the Program

New software often requires training, therefore provisions regarding training are often included in the commercial end-user agreement. A certain number of person–days of training may be included in the license fee, or training may be separately priced. The agreement (or a schedule to the agreement) may specify the number of trainers and trainees, the days or hours of training to be provided, the qualification of trainers, the curriculum, the place where the training will occur, the hardware to be used, the sample data to be used, and so forth. Some customers want to obtain training materials in advance of training sessions. Some vendors offer online training "webinars," DVD training materials, or tutorial software. Many vendors also offer, on an ongoing basis (and at additional charge), training on the use of their programs or on features of new releases of its software products.

Restrictions

Most commercial end-user licensing is for binary code only. End-user agreements always have clauses forbidding decompiling, reverse engineering, and/or use of the code in other products. Commercial end-user agreements also contain provisions making it clear that the software is licensed and not sold and that the vendor retains all of its ownership rights in the software.

Confidentiality Clause

Many commercial end-user agreements have confidentiality clauses—but in some cases they are not necessary. Here are some situations to consider:

- If an application is widely circulated—so that its functionality is not secret—there may be no need to include any confidentiality clause.

- For applications that are not in broad circulation—for example, specialized products for niche markets, the vendor may want a confidentiality clause directed at protecting and keeping secret the functionality of the software.

The goal of such a provision is to make it harder for competitors to gain access to the vendor's software and learn in detail how it functions.

- Where there is likely to be significant communication between customer and vendor—for example, when customization or integration is required for a particular product, then the agreement should have a conventional mutual confidentiality agreement.

Intellectual Property Indemnification

In many commercial end-user agreements, the vendor agrees to indemnify and defend the customer if the software program infringes another party's rights under patent, trademark, copyright, or other intellectual property law. The customer is obliged to cooperate with the vendor in defending any such infringement claim. The vendor typically has the right to procure a license for any infringing technology or to supply noninfringing code and to require that the customer switch to the noninfringing version. It is also common that the vendor maintains, as a last resort, the right to "pull the plug" and terminate the customer's use of the program, if the vendor cannot find a suitable and cost-effective way to allow the customer to use the program without infringement. The key here is to provide fair coverage for the customer, but to provide the vendor with an escape hatch in case infringement is unavoidable.

For more on indemnification and on the following topics of warranty disclaimers and remedy limitations, see Chapter 8.

Warranty Disclaimers and Remedy Limitations

All software vendors should insist that their end-user agreements contain language limiting warranties and the amount of potential damages. (For a more thorough discussion of these clauses and what they are designed to do, see Chapter 8.)

Warranty Disclaimers

Commercial end-user license agreements limit warranties to those expressly stated in the agreement and will disclaim "implied warranties." Customer claims for money damages for product defects, late delivery, or other causes arise primarily under the Uniform Commercial Code (UCC), a statute that governs sales of goods (with some minor variations) in all states but Louisiana.

Under the UCC, language that disclaims warranties needs to be "conspicuous," therefore this disclaimer is usually printed in ALL CAPITAL LETTERS. It is common (although not required) that other boilerplate language, such as exclusions of consequential damages and damage caps to be in all caps. The form commercial end-user agreement (Form 12-2) in the Appendix to this book (and many other Appendix forms) contains this kind of provision on limitation of liability.

Remedy Limitations

Commercial end-user agreements normally contain the following provisions:

- During the warranty period, the vendor has the option to replace or repair any defective software, and if this is done, it is the exclusive remedy.

- License fees are nonrefundable.

- There is restriction on the type of injury to the customer that is compensable—usually the agreement permits only so-called direct damages, the cost of replacing the defective software or system. The agreement disclaims liability for incidental or consequential damages. Incidental damages are costs incidental to replacement of defective software, such as shipping and installation costs. Consequential damages, usually by far the larger item, are damages for interruption of business, lost data, loss of production, or lost profits. This clause is called a "consequential damages exclusion." There may be exceptions or "carve outs" from the consequential damages exclusion as is discussed below.

The Damage Cap

Commercial end-user agreements normally contain restrictions (or a "cap") on the total dollar amount of damages that the customer can recover from the vendor in a lawsuit. Typically the limit is the license fee that the customer has paid. There may be exceptions or "carve-outs" for indemnification claims or confidentiality breaches.

In most cases, it is a mistake for a vendor to try to eliminate *all* liability for software errors or to reduce damage much below the price paid by the customer. There is a significant risk that the courts will find such a limitation to be unreasonable and nullify it. The effect will be to expose the vendor to unlimited liability. However, the courts have generally upheld clauses that cap a vendor's liability to the amount paid in fees for the software in question.

Mutual Clauses

When there are substantial transactions with sophisticated customers, you can expect that the customer will insist that the consequential damages exclusion and damage cap clauses be *mutual*.

For that reason (and to streamline negotiations) many vendors start with a form contract in which these clauses apply to *both* vendor and customer. The vendor using mutual clauses of this type should make sure that there is an exception (or "carve-out") to the mutual damage cap and the mutual exclusion of consequential damages for:

- Unlicensed use or exploitation of the vendor's software or intellectual property
- Breach of the confidentiality provisions

The vendor *needs* these carve-outs. This is because:

- The customer's unlicensed use or exploitation or breach of confidentiality might cause only consequential damages to the vendor (such as lost sales);
- The amount of the harm to the vendor may be much greater than the amount of the fees paid to the vendor.

This means that, without the carve-outs, the vendor might have no remedy—or too limited a remedy—for the customer's unauthorized use and copying of the software.

Many variants on these clauses are possible. This is a highly technical legal area and the degree of risk your company can accept may vary. You should seek the advice of legal counsel on the best way to negotiate these risk allocation matters.

The Customer's Obligation to Back-Up Its Data

When something goes wrong with software, important data can be lost or garbled. The damage will be minimized, however, if the customer has backed up its data to disk, tape, or other storage media. Although vendors normally expressly disclaim any liability for lost data, as an additional line of defense against damage claims, many end-user agreements require that the customer regularly back up all data. If data is lost that was not backed up as specified in the end-user agreement, it will be because the customer did not comply with the requirements of the end-user agreement.

Term and Termination

In most commercial end-user agreements, the vendors grant the customer a license to the software that has no stated end of term, that is, a permanent (sometimes called "perpetual") license. This is the Permanent License Model that we discussed above. As a practical matter software life is often limited by technology. While some companies run 30-year-old mainframe software, current experience is that most commercial software gets replaced in less than a decade by newer and better programs running on richer platforms and communication environments. Vendors keep customers over the long term by upgrading them. Once the customer permanently discontinues using a program, the license remains in effect as a legal matter, but has little practical effect.

Perpetual end-user agreements do provide for termination of the agreement and all license grants under specified circumstances. For example, agreements will give the vendor the option to terminate the license if required payments are not made or if the customer otherwise materially breaches the agreement and fails to cure the breach after notice.

Subscription licenses, paid for year to year, will normally terminate if the subscriber ceases its year-to-year (or other periodic) payment for licenses.

Upon termination, the agreement usually provides that the customer must erase the software from hard drives or other storage media, destroy any archival CD-ROMs or other copies, and return the original media and documentation to the vendor and certify that it has done so in writing.

There are usually certain clauses, such as disclaimers, confidentiality, and indemnity that survive termination.

General Provisions

Most end-user agreements have at the end "boilerplate" provisions. These provisions are discussed in Chapter 8. The most important issues here are likely to be the jurisdiction for resolution of any dispute (each party will want to specify the court located in its own home town) and whether to provide for alternative dispute resolution (such as mediation or arbitration) instead of litigation.

SOURCE CODE ESCROW AGREEMENTS

Many commercial end-user license agreements have a provision requiring that the vendor and the customer enter into a separate source code escrow agreement.

This is an agreement under which a third party holds the application source code and will release it to the customer under specified circumstances.

Why source code escrows? Escrows are most often used for software that plays an essential role in a customer's business. For those applications, software maintenance is critical. This means that the customer's business will be threatened if the vendor goes bankrupt, stops supporting the product, or fails to fix a serious error. Binary software is compiled, and that means it cannot be fixed (or enhanced) without the source code.

One answer to the dilemma might be for the vendor simply to deliver to the customer a copy of the source code of each version of the software so that the customer can have it ready if needed. Most vendors will not do this. Here's why:

- The source code is the vendor's trade secret. Vendors do not want customers (and their contractors and advisors) examining the internal workings or their programs. (See the discussion of trade secrets in Chapter 6.)

- Vendors make money by selling maintenance and support. They do not want third parties (such as contractors) providing that service using the source code.

- Vendors want to maintain sole control of the evolution of their products over time, and that control could be threatened by providing source code to third parties.

The most common answer to this dilemma is to set up a source code escrow.

When to Offer Escrow

The first question for a vendor regarding a source code escrow is whether to offer it at all. Vendors with lots of leverage simply do not make it available at all. There is, for example, no software source code escrow available to licensees for Microsoft business applications. Some escrow agreements offer less protection than others. Key provisions of the escrow agreement (discussed below) are often a matter of negotiation.

The Problem with Escrow

While very common, a source code escrow is far from a perfect solution from the customer's viewpoint. The common weaknesses of this practice are:

- It may take a long time to learn how the source code works and how to fix it. (When the vendor is out of business, customers may try to hire the vendor's former employees to maintain the code.)

- It may be expensive to maintain and enhance the source code.

- The legal process required to get the code over the vendor's objection may take months. (The release process is discussed below.)

In spite of these drawbacks, the practice persists because customers see source code escrows as the last resort protection of business continuity.

Two-Party and Three-Party Agreements

In source code escrow agreements, the vendor that puts the source code and other material into escrow is called the "depositor" and the customer who has a conditional right to receive the source code is called the "beneficiary."

Source code escrow agreements come in two flavors: two-party and three-party.

- In a two-party source code escrow agreement, the agreement is between the vendor and the escrow company. While written to protect the customer, the customer is not a party to the agreement. This means that the customer's legal right to enforce the agreement may be unclear.

- In a three-party source code escrow agreement, the agreement is among the vendor, the escrow company and the customer. The customer is a legal party to the three-party agreement and has the clear right to enforce the agreement.

Sophisticated customers strongly prefer three-party source code escrow agreements.

Multi-Beneficiary Escrow

Some source code escrow agreements (both two-party and three-party variants) include a mechanism in which any number of customers can be added on to the same escrow agreement. This "multi-beneficiary" version allows a vendor to deposit the source code materials once to serve many.

It is possible to do multiparty agreements and yet customize the release conditions (discussed below) that apply to any individual customer. This is often the most cost-effective way to provide source code escrow protection for many customers. If you are interested in this option, you should discuss it with your attorney or with the escrow company.

Contents of an Escrow Agreement

Here are some key provisions of source code escrow agreements:

The Deposit

The "deposit" is the source code and other materials that the vendor sends to the escrow agent. Customers often want the deposit to include "all source code," "all tools required to compile the source code," "instructions for use of the source code" as well as "fully commented source code."

Vendors usually want to soften these requirements. For example, there may be third-party products (such as code libraries or the compiler) that the vendor uses to create the commercial product. Most often, the vendor will have no right to put these third party products into the escrow account. So the defined escrow deposit will be written to "carve out" third party products. (The vendor will normally agree to provide a list of such materials for the escrow.) The vendor also may not want any obligation to put comments (explanatory notes) into source code other than what is already there. Whatever deposit requirements are negotiated should be documented in the escrow agreement.

Frequency of the Deposit

An important question is how often the vendor is required to make a deposit of source code. Customers would ideally want each release of the software (including bug fixes and maintenance releases) to trigger a deposit.

However, assembling the source materials in a form suitable for deposit (normally on CD-ROM) takes time and effort. So vendors want to limit the deposit. Commonly a vendor will agree to make updating deposits twice a year or quarterly.

Another question is whether the source code to be kept in escrow will be only the most recent release (with each older version discarded as a new one arrives) or whether the escrow agent is required to retain in escrow all the "legacy" versions of the product. The escrow agreement should define precisely what the rules are on retaining old versions.

Release Conditions

The most important provision of the Agreement is the *release conditions*, that is, the triggering conditions under which the escrow agent is required to release the deposited source code materials to the customer. There are several classes of common release conditions:

- The vendor ceases operations.

- The vendor ceases providing maintenance for the licensed product.

- The vendor is in bankruptcy or another insolvency procedure.

- The vendor is unable to fix a software error within a specified amount of time or otherwise "fails to fulfill the vendor's maintenance obligations."

The most controversial of these conditions is the last. Many vendors will refuse to agree to escrow provisions that make a failure to provide a bug fix into a release condition.

The Source Code Release Process

Every source code escrow agreement includes a *release procedure*, that is, a process for releasing source code to the customer. Most agreements allow for the customer to make a demand to the escrow agent for the release of the deposited materials and allow the vendor to object. If the vendor does not object in a specified amount of time (often 10 days), the deposited materials will be released.

Most source code escrow agreements provide that if the customer and the vendor disagree on whether a release condition exists, the escrow agent will continue to hold the source code until a court of law or an arbitrator orders that the source code be released to the customer.

Sometimes customers will push for the opposite process—that the code will be *released* to the customer unless a court or arbitrator orders, within a specified number of days, that it *remain* in escrow. This provision is not common, but customers that have a lot of leverage may get it.

Permitted Use of Released Code

Normally the source code escrow agreement specifies what the customer is licensed to do with the source code materials after release. Again there are some common variations:

- The customer can maintain the software product by fixing bugs and errors.

- The customer may enhance the software product.

- The customer may use contractors do carry out the above.

Some vendors will insist upon limiting the customer's use to fixing bugs and errors.

Smart vendors put additional conditions on the use of the released escrow materials. For example:

- The materials are confidential information of the vendor and therefore their disclosure is restricted.

- Disclosure to contractors must be under a confidentiality agreement.

- Any limitations on the use of the software product as specified in the underlying license (such as limits on duration of use or number of users) apply equally to versions of the software product that are created by use of the released escrow materials.

Verification

Some source code escrow agreements provide for a *verification* process at the customer's request. Under this provision, the escrow agent will provide confirmation of the contents of the escrow on request, for a fee.

To perform this service, the escrow agent will compile the escrowed source code and compare the compiled program to the binary code regularly supplied by the vendor. To perform verification, the escrow agent will depend on the vendor to provide any third-party software needed to carry out this test.

Other Escrow Provisions

Other provisions of the source code escrow agreement relate to administrative matters. These include:

- The amount and payment of the escrow fees. (The agreement will normally state if it is the vendor's or the customer's obligation to pay escrow fees.)

- Provisions that the escrow agent will not be liable to either party (for wrongful release, wrongful failure to release or anything else).

- Provisions on termination of the agreement.

Caution in Using Form Source Code Escrow Agreements

Most escrow companies make available escrow agreement forms that you can download for free from their Web sites. So it is very easy to get sample forms.

However, these forms will not fit all transactions. At our law firm, when we represent vendors, we rarely use these off-the-Web forms without making some edits. (The escrow companies will not mind at all if the parties edit the escrow form—as long as they leave intact the provisions that protect the escrow company and fix responsibility for payment.)

These online escrow agreements forms tend to be "pro customer" rather than "pro vendor." The provisions we most often change are:

- Contents of the deposit

- Release conditions

- Conditions that apply after release

A more "pro vendor" form of escrow agreement is included in the form appendix to this book.

NOTE ON COMMERCIAL LICENSING SOFTWARE TO THE GOVERNMENT

One of the largest customers in the world for software is the United States government. The government obtains software under rules in the Federal Acquisition Regulations (FAR) and the Department of Defense FAR Supplement (DFARS). These rules are administered by the General Services Administration (GSA), by the Department of Defense (DOD), or by various federal agencies that need software.

Under these rules, if your software product was created without any government funds *and* is a commercially released product (which the government calls "commercial computer software"), federal regulations mandate that the government gets whatever commercial license agreement it agrees to, just like any other licensee.

The rules on commercial software licensing to the US government were different before December 1, 1995. Before that date, it was advisable to affirmatively assert in license agreements that private commercial software was provided with "Restricted Rights." You often see this old form of language in software agreements, but it is no longer accurate for "commercial computer software." In fact, if you license commercial computer software to the federal government, no special language for contracting is required.

Many companies, just to be safe and sure, put language into their various form agreements to declare affirmatively that they are supplying "commercial computer software." It certainly does no harm to do that. Here is some conventional language, which contains references to the appropriate federal acquisition regulations:

> *LICENSE TO THE US GOVERNMENT. The Software programs are commercial computer software programs developed exclusively at private expense. Unless otherwise set forth in a License Agreement, use, duplication, and disclosure by civilian agencies of the U.S. Government shall not exceed those rights set forth in FAR 52.227-19 (c). Use, duplication and disclosure by DOD agencies is subject solely to the terms of a standard software License Agreement as stated in DFARS 227.7202. The manufacturer is [INSERT VENDOR'S COMPANY NAME AND ADDRESS.]*

This sounds very obscure and bureaucratic, but it just means that your software is in commercial distribution, was not developed with any government funds, and then cites the regulations that say that the commercial license agreement applies.

Dealing with the US government is much more complicated for software companies creating software at government expense or providing software development services to the federal government. Those companies must become thoroughly familiar with the applicable procurement regulations. The federal government can get a very broad license to or ownership of software created wholly or in part with the use of government funds. If you are dealing with the federal government in such situations, you should consult legal counsel that is familiar with US Government procurement regulations and procedures.

Special rules also apply to software created for the government under federal Small Business Innovation Research (SBIR) grants. The SBIR program is a US government program under which government agencies give research contracts and grants to small businesses. For information on the SBIR program, see the Web site of the Small Business Administration, www.sba.gov.

State and local governments also have regulations concerning contracting and procurement that may apply to software. A vendor should learn applicable regulations before doing business with state and local government agencies as well.

ACCOUNTING FOR LICENSE REVENUE

One important issue in software licensing generally (not just commercial end-user licensing) is revenue recognition. This is primarily an accounting issue, but companies that get it wrong can get into severe legal trouble. This topic is discussed in Chapter 8, and we suggest you re-read that discussion. If you have any doubt about whether your company's accounting for software revenues is correct, you should consult with your accountant without delay.

SOFTWARE LICENSING AND SALES TAX

Another issue of importance in software licensing generally (again not just for commercial end-user licensing) is sales taxation. Licensing of software is often subject to sales tax (or similar taxes in other countries). When sales tax applies, it is the vendor's obligation to collect it and pay it over to the government.

Sales tax is a very complicated subject because of the many different rules in different jurisdictions. So our main point here is very simple. If you are in the business of licensing software in the United States, you must discuss with your accountant how sales tax requirements affect your company. A high-level overview of general principles is provided below, but this discussion is not a substitute for a review of your business' sales tax situation with your accountant. As you will see here, there is considerable variation in the applicable rules.

Why Sales Tax is Important?

The majority of U.S. states have a sales tax, a flat percentage rate tax applied to retail sales to end users. There are also some city and county sales taxes. There is no US national sales tax. (Many other nations have a value-added-tax or "VAT" which is a form of national sales tax collected at the producer or wholesale level.)

In the US, failure to collect and pay sales taxes can lead to liability for your company, plus interest and penalties and legal expenses. Officers of your company may be personally liable for failure to pay the tax. Moreover, sales taxes paid correctly are deductible expenses that reduce your company's taxable income under state and federal income tax, but penalties and interest on sales taxes are not deductible. It is therefore always best to comply with sales tax law. If you have questions about sales taxation, see your accountant.

The Concept of Nexus

There is an important concept in sales tax law called "nexus" that determines whether your company is obligated to collect sales tax for a particular state.

If your company has nexus to a state, your company must collect sales tax for transactions there. If your company does not have nexus, there is no requirement for your company to collect and pay over sales tax.

"Nexus" is defined as a "sufficient connection" to the state. If you have an office or other location in a state, it is clear that you have nexus with the state. In some cases, a less extensive connection may establish nexus. The rules vary state by state—and there are limitations, imposed by the US Constitution—as to how far the states can go in asserting jurisdiction by expansive definitions of nexus.

Nexus and the Internet is a bit of an unknown area, although most lawyers think that licensing over the Internet will not establish nexus. Virginia reportedly has decided that having an e-commerce site hosted in Virginia by an out-of-state company was not enough to establish "nexus" there. It is not yet clear that other states will see it the same way. Again this is a matter that you should review with your accountant.

Wholesale vs. Retail

Sales to resellers intended for resale are exempt from sales taxes in the United States. The general rule is the burden is on the seller to prove that it qualifies for the exemption. This means that your business needs to get a "tax exemption certificate" from each customer that is buying software licenses for resale. You must follow this practice in every state where you have nexus. If you fail to obtain the certificate, then you may be obligated to pay the sales tax. For this reason, many companies routinely request proof of exemption from sales tax for every customer that claims to be sales tax exempt.

Applicability of Sales Tax to Software Products

Software programs are usually considered taxable goods in most states. In several states, notably in California, software products that are delivered electronically (with no delivery of software media) are exempt from sales tax.

Most states that have a sales tax do not tax most services. In most states, creating and supplying custom-developed software is considered an untaxed service, but several states require that sales tax be paid even on custom software.

Some states have a sales tax on "telecommunication services" and may apply this tax to other digital services such as Web hosting or software-as-a-service.

Products vs. Services

A complicated matter is the sales taxation of services that are provided together with a software product, services such as installation, customization, configuration, and testing. Here are some of the possible rules for this situation:

- In some states, the rule is that if the associated services are separately itemized, even if on the same invoice, the services are untaxed. In those states, sales tax applies only to the software.

- In some states, the rule is that if services and software are charged on the same invoice, sales tax applies to the entire invoice, but that there is no tax on services if they are separately billed.

- In some states, the rule is that if a project for a customer includes both services and software, sales tax applies to the entire project, even if services and software are separately billed.

You will need to contact your accountant to see which rules apply in states where your company does business.

CONCLUSION

With care, your company can create commercial end-user agreements that help you realize the value of software, reinforce relationships, and manage risk—all of which help build value in your software business.

Software as a Service (SaaS)

13

It's a badge labeled 'End of Software'. Each employee at Salesforce.com wears this badge.

—Saleforce.com CEO Marc Benioff,
quoted in September 2006 in saasweek.com

It's not really the end of software, but for some companies it *is* about ending software as a *licensed business asset*. Business software functionality can be supplied remotely through a network. This is known as the Software-as-a-Service (or "SaaS") business model. ("SaaS" is pronounced like the first syllable of "sassy.")

With the SaaS paradigm at its purest, software disappears and all that the customer sees is the service. There is no installation. There are no updates or maintenance charges. There is no upfront license fee. Charges are on a subscription model. SaaS is now a powerful trend that is changing business computing.

IN THIS CHAPTER

We provide information here on:

- The SaaS Business Model

- SaaS and Security

- SaaS and Open Source

- Customer Agreements for SaaS Offerings

SOME SAAS HISTORY

The concept of a SaaS is almost as old as commercial computing. From the mainframe era of the 1960s and into the minicomputer days of the 70s, computers were expensive, and many small- and medium-size enterprises obtained computing resources by means of remote access. This remote computing model, known as "service bureau," never really died, but it retreated into the background with the introduction of PCs, LANs, and client–server computing in the 80s and early 90s.

What has brought back the SaaS model to prominence now are Web browsers and broadband access, as well as robust mobile access. There is now an inexpensive ubiquitous "pipe" to remote computers and there is a universal software client that allows ready access.

During the tech boom of the late 90s, the SaaS model (then commonly referred to as "ASP" for "Application Service Provider") was the subject of a huge buzz. ASP firms raised hundreds of millions from venture capital firms. Pundits theorized that all software would turn into a service and that existing enterprise applications would be rented remotely by the minute as needed—a notion called "apps-on-tap." Many of the highflying ASP companies of the bubble era had a business model that was little more than hosting off-the-shelf applications. There was not enough value-add in this business model. When funding dried up, the majority of the ASP companies of the boom era crashed and burned.

Now the SaaS is back, but it has changed. SaaS technology is more mature; the business models are sounder; and the Internet infrastructure is more robust. There is more value and richer functionality. The current success of SaaS model can be seen as an extension of the outsourcing trend, which moves many "noncore" functions (and even some "core" functions) outside the enterprise.

SAAS BUSINESS VARIETIES

Most SaaS vendors have applications that are constructed or highly customized for SaaS operation. Most SaaS applications are built so that they work efficiently as remote thin-client implements, are customer-configurable over the Web, and are adapted for billing based on the amount of customer use.

Here are some of the principle SaaS categories:

- **Outsourced Business Functions**—Some SaaS vendors provide online applications designed to allow customer to outsource specific business functions.

The best-known SaaS vendor of this type is Salesforce.com, which allows remote access to sales force management tools. There are also SaaS solutions for inventory management, employee benefits management, customer relationship management (or CRM), payroll management, employee recruiting, supply chain management (or SCM), information system help desks, and many others. This type of SaaS model is currently the most important SaaS category.

- **Data Management**—There are SaaS vendors that provide data management and analysis services, such as remote data warehousing, backup, management, or "data mining" services—typically for small- and medium-size businesses. The most sophisticated services upload large amounts of data and provide sophisticated "business intelligence" reports.

- **Collaboration Environments**—Some SaaS vendors provide an online-hosted collaboration environment, sometimes called "teamware." These are online sites for project-based collaboration, providing virtual spaces for storing and sharing documents, scheduling, instant messaging, and project planning among other functions.

- **Vertical Market SaaS Vendors**—There are many SaaS vendors that provide business function solutions that are targeted to vertical market sectors. Examples are companies that manage medical records or reimbursement for hospitals and clinics, those that manage room inventory and block booking for hotels, those that provide donor tracking and campaign management for non-profits, those that provide credit card verification for retailers, and so forth.

- **E-mail and Calendar**—At the "low end" of the SaaS scale are businesses that offer simple server-based services, such as more secure Web mail or online calendaring. In some cases, these functions are integrated with other, more feature-rich categories of SaaS services.

WHAT CUSTOMERS LIKE ABOUT SAAS

These are benefits that customers typically look for when they purchase SaaS services:

- **Short-Term Fee Savings**—The customer avoids a large upfront license fee and pays on a subscription basis. (Many SaaS offerings, however, have a "lock-in" requiring the customer to subscribe for minimum duration, which can be a year or more.)

- **Scale Up**—A SaaS services is a convenient way to start small, with just a few test users and scale up gradually.

- **Simplicity of Management**—The business customer avoids the complexity of internal software maintenance and support.

- **Staff Savings**—The customer saves the cost of internal staff to install, manage, update, and support a licensed software application.

- **Freedom from Corporate IS**—For some large companies, one major benefit of buying SaaS services is a "way around" the bureaucracy that runs corporate information services (known as "IS"). Buying a SaaS service may avoid an IS delay or veto of new functionality.

- **Readily Available Remote Access**—The SaaS vendor, rather than the customer, manages the process of providing remote access to the applications for employees at home or on the road.

- **Expertise**—The SaaS vendor can provide a source of expertise, as for example about employee benefits or medical record keeping. The customer, in some cases, obtains access to specialized functionality not readily available from packaged software.

CUSTOMER CONCERNS WITH THE SAAS MODEL

Along with the benefits of the SaaS model, there come a number of issues and concerns. Several of these topics are discussed further below.

- **Security**—This is probably the largest customer concern. Customers worry about putting their data outside the enterprise and potentially at risk.

- **Risk of Service Outage**—Customers are concerned about critical dependence on a remote vendor for a "mission critical" application. They worry what will happen if the SaaS vendor has a prolonged service outage. Many SaaS vendors offer a supplemental disaster recovery location of software, hardware, and data that can act as a "fail-over" resource.

- **Business Risks**—The customer may be fearful that the SaaS vendor will become bankrupt or insolvent.

- **Customization and Integration Limitations**—SaaS applications (at least to date) lend themselves less to extensive integration and customization than traditional software packages.

- **Regulatory Issues**—The customer may be concerned whether use of the SaaS vendor raises legal compliance issues. Examples would be whether medical files are in compliance with the medical record keeping and security rules of the Health Insurance Portability & Accountability Act of 1996 (more commonly called: "HIPPA"). The Sarbanes-Oxley Act (known as "SOX") requires that public companies verify that they have adequate controls of the accuracy and integrity of material data and systems; this requirement leads them to require SaaS vendors to provide accountants' "Sas 70 reports" as are discussed below.

ADVANTAGES AND ISSUES FOR SAAS VENDORS

From the SaaS vendor's perspective, the SaaS model has both advantages and challenges. Here are some advantages:

- **Steadiness of Cash Flow**—Because customers pay on a subscription model month-after-month and year-after-year, cash flow is much more predictable than with traditional software selling.

- **More Profitable Over Time**—While SaaS customers pay less up front, they end up paying more over time than with traditional software licensing. With a large installed base, the business has the potential to become a "cash cow."

- **Simplification of Support**—Support with the SaaS model is simpler than traditional software. The SaaS vendor usually has to support only one version of its software. The vendor does not have to worry about variations in hardware or software-operating systems. Updates can be made at any convenient time and do not have to be packaged and supplied to customers. Features can be added continually.

Here are some of the challenges:

- **Service Obligations**—On the other hand, the SaaS vendor has to supply services as well as software—and that makes for a more complex offering. The SaaS vendor has to provide not only its software, but also a supporting infrastructure, including hardware, software, and systems for enrolling and managing customers and for billing and/or processing online credit card payments. The SaaS vendor often needs to provide 24/7 data center staffing and always needs to provide firewalls, intrusion detection, secure communication, data backup, and robust Internet connections. (Much of this infrastructure requirements can be outsourced by SaaS providers, but the vendor will remain responsible to the customer for providing it.)

- **Financing Requirements**—Because the SaaS business provides less cash upfront than a traditional "permanent license" model, a startup SaaS business needs more cash to get started. This means that a SaaS business must be well capitalized so that it can survive during an initial "ramp-up" phase.

- **Sales Staff Compensation**—Because SaaS vendors produce less money from customers upfront (but more over the long run), commission compensation to the SaaS vendor's sales staff has to be adjusted accordingly.

- **Competition**—If the customer's cost of switching to a different SaaS vendor is low, the SaaS vendor may find itself in a constant feature and price competition.

- **Partnering Challenges**—Strategies for partnering and distribution are more difficult for SaaS vendors. The compensation structure for "resellers" may have to be adjusted. Also there may be less opportunity for resellers to provide customization services than in a SaaS customer sale.

MIXING TRADITIONAL SOFTWARE LICENSING AND SAAS

There will be many companies where the traditional licensing model and the SaaS model coexist. Because of the increasing popularity of SaaS solutions, traditional software companies may have no choice but to add a SaaS offering. Many vendors believe that SaaS services allow them to penetrate more effectively into the market for small- and medium-size businesses.

There are challenges with managing the two coexisting business models like this:

- **Feature Distinctions**—The SaaS offering may have different features from the existing traditional license software product. If so, that may affect the customer's options to switch between them as discussed below.

- **Marketing**—The SaaS offering may have a different target market and a different marketing and sales strategy.

- **Internal Competition**—The SaaS product might effectively compete against the existing offering.

- **Pricing and Support**—The pricing and support of the different platforms should be coordinated so that one does not drive out the other just do to cheap pricing.

- **Allowing Customers to Switch**—SaaS customers may want an option to switch to traditional software licensing and vice versa. Where the customer has the option to switch, they will likely want the option expressed in their license or service agreement with the vendor. The existing customer that switches to or from the SaaS platform may expect a discount on SaaS pricing.

There are also companies that offer solutions that are not quite true SaaS offerings, but still have elements of remote hosting or administration:

Term Licensed and Hosted. Some companies offer a business software product on a term lease (for example, year-to-year) and in addition provide hosting (as the customer's option) for the product for the duration of the term. In this case, the offering is very similar to a traditional software license, except that the location of the software is elsewhere and there is remote access—usually by secure Internet access.

Managed Services. A managed services provider is a company that offers information system management services remotely. This service is kind of SaaS-in-reverse. The outside provider reaches into the computer infrastructure of the enterprise to manage items such as desktop software security monitoring, routine software patching, backup, network monitoring, and help desk. Charges are typically on a per workstation per month basis.

SAAS AND SECURITY

Customers are, quite understandably, interested in and concerned about the SaaS vendor's ability to provide data and system security. Customers expect (unrealistically) that security will be bulletproof and perfect. In addition, customers often request, in contract negotiations, that the SaaS vendor agree to pay (and indemnify the customer for) for any cost or liability that the customer may incur in case of any security breach. Vendors, of course, do not want that risk—and regularly refuse to take it.

Customers do have good reasons to fear breaches of data security. The SaaS vendor's response is to have reasonable security measures but not to undertake contractual risk from security breaches. In this chapter section, we will discuss first the security risks and then the SaaS vendor's contractual and practical response.

Points of Vulnerability

Companies that hold data have several points of potential data vulnerability. These include:

- External hackers and malicious software
- Employee dishonesty
- Lost or stolen passwords
- Lost or stolen notebook computers, drives, or tapes that contain personal data
- Data handling mistakes

Measures for Data Security

SaaS vendors should put in place a data security plan that provides a reasonable amount of comfort to customers. These measures that you should consider using include (but are not necessarily limited to) the following:

- Use technological security measures, including intrusion detection and data encryption for stored data. Match the highest technological protection to the customer data that carries the highest risk.
- Avoid placing sensitive customer data on laptops and other portable devices.
- Require employees to take security training.
- Have "white hacking" intrusion tests performed to verify that your system can fend off routine hacker attacks.

- Have well-documented procedures for data backup.

- Be careful in providing data copies to customers. Mishandling can easily expose one customer's data to the customer's competitor.

- Make sure that vendors, such as colocation facilities, have data security policies, technologies, and procedures that are complementary to your own.

- Be sure that old equipment and data devices are wiped clean of customer or business data before disposal.

- Remove access privileges of former employees and contractors as soon as they are terminated.

- Review your security planning regularly.

The better your security measures, the more likely you will be able to provide the customer with the comfort it needs to purchase your company's SaaS services.

State Security Breach Notification Statutes

States around the country have data security breach notification statutes. The first state to adopt such a law was California. As of the time that this book is being written, 35 states plus the District of Columbia have such statutes. It is likely that there will be federal legislation on this point at some time—if only for the sake of protecting companies that do business nationwide from the complexities of dealing with 36 different laws on the same topic.

These laws are discussed in more detail in the chapter of this book on privacy (Chapter 18). The gist is as follows:

- **Companies under the Law**—Companies that own or possess personal information (we will call them the "data holder") are subject to these laws.

- **Personal Information**—Personal information generally means a person's name plus a social security number, a credit card number, or a driver's license number. In some states, only unencrypted information is subject to the applicable statute.

- **In Case of a Breach**—When there is a breach, the data holder must notify all data subjects who are citizens of the relevant state (and in some cases state law enforcement personnel) as soon as possible.

- **How Notice Is Given**—Notice must generally be by first class mail, although e-mail can be used if the data subject has given his or her permission.

- **Liability Provisions**—Minnesota amended its data breach notice law, effective August 1, 2007, to add a provision that makes companies that accept credit and debit cards liable to banks for certain costs resulting from a merchant's loss of credit card data. Other states might pass similar laws.

- **Role of SaaS Vendor**—Under these laws, it is the SaaS vendor's customer that would be treated as the data holder, but the SaaS vendor will have an obligation to notify the customer as soon as possible of a breach.

These laws are directed primarily at data breach where the goal of the intrusion is criminal identity theft for illegal commercial gain. However, these laws are not limited to such breaches. They also could apply (depending on the state) to employment, medical, insurance, or many other types of personal data records.

Where there are significant security breaches, the data holder can have significant costs for notifying data subject, investigations, legal fees, and so forth.

Other Potential Harms

If SaaS data security is breached, there are potential harms to the customer. These include:

- The risk of disclosure of the customer's clients, suppliers, and other trade secrets

- The risk of invasion of privacy for sensitive information

- The risk of bad publicity.

Contract Provisions on Security

In spite of these potential risks to customers from data breaches, SaaS vendors, in contract negotiations, reject assuming this potential liability—largely because it is impossible to quantify. SaaS vendors would impair their ability to obtain investors or to sell their business if they had this potentially huge risk profile.

The form contracts that SaaS vendors use have clauses designed to fend of this kind of liability. Typically:

- Vendors disclaim all "consequential" losses. Expenses from data loss would normally be categorized as "consequential." (See discussion of contract damages and disclaimers in Chapter 8.)

- Vendors include caps on liability.

- Vendors avoid representing that customer data will be secure. Rather, they represent that they use or will use specified security measures.

- Vendors disclaim "lost data" liability.

- Vendors reject customer requests to include contract language indemnifying the customer for data breaches.

- Vendors reject customer requests to include contract language indemnifying the customer for vendor "negligence."

Careful contracting can help manage risk from potential data security breach incidents.

Risk from Overstating Your Data Security

Your SaaS company should be very careful to be accurate and factual in all of its representations about its data security and systems. You should avoid hype and broad generalizations. Otherwise, your company could risk being sued for misrepresentation if data loss occurs from your company's systems.

Let's assume that you have protected your SaaS business well by prudent contracting, but your customer has suffered a large financial loss because of data that was stolen from your internal system. Can the customer sue and recover damages against your company on some other *noncontractual* theory of your liability? The answer is that it might—and that your company's biggest risk is likely a claim that it misrepresented its security systems.

We think it unlikely that a customer can recover against your company for *negligence* under the laws in the United States. That's because of the so-called "economic loss rule" which generally disallows negligence claims in a business contract setting where the loss is merely economic and there is no claim of physical damage to property or injury to a person.

On the other hand, the law of *misrepresentation* in the United States can cut through contractual limitations and is not subject to any "economic loss" limitation. The plaintiff in a misrepresentation lawsuit can claim: "Our company only signed the agreement and entrusted the SaaS vendor with sensitive data because the SaaS vendor misrepresented that it had ironclad security," or "We provided our data in reliance on the vendor's false assurance of adequate security measures." This is an "end around" that can evade the best-written contractual limitations and exclusions of damages. Depending on the law in particular states, this claim might include both negligent and intentional misrepresentation. Individuals in your company as well as businesses could be sued for misrepresentation.

How could your SaaS company protect itself against this kind of misrepresentation claim? What you need to avoid is hyping security and making broad categorical statements. Don't say that your business has "ironclad security." Don't say that your company has "state-of-the-art security." Don't claim to be in compliance with any particular security standard unless you are confident that you can prove it.

We prefer that our SaaS client represent in writing what their current security system consists of. For example, they can represent that they have a firewall, that they use intrusion protection software, that they have intrusion vulnerability testing once a year, that they change passwords quarterly and the like. Your SaaS customer agreements can include provisions for updating your list of security measures by reference to a security system document on your company's Web site. As long as the company actually does what it claims to do and is reasonably specific, your risk of liability for misrepresentation will be very low.

SAS 70

Any SaaS vendor will have an advantage in selling services to major public companies if the vendor is certified under what is known as "Sas 70." Sas 70 is the common name for the Statement on Auditing Standards No. 70: Reports on the Processing of Transactions by Service Organizations. ("Sas" is also pronounced like the first syllable in "sassy.")

This is an auditing standard issued by the Auditing Standards Board of the American Institute of Certified Public Accountants (AICPA). This standard is used by certified public accountants to assess the internal controls of service organizations for audited companies, such as SaaS vendors.

The importance of Sas 70 certification comes largely from the Sarbanes Oxley Act, the post-Enron statute that requires public companies to have adequate controls of auditing and financial reporting. Internal controls are about more than counting money. They are also about accuracy, reliability, and security of information generally. When public companies outsource important functions to SaaS vendors, they rely on the SaaS vendor's internal controls. Auditors consider a Sas 70 report to be a means to obtain assurance that the SaaS vendor performs the outsourced function using proper controls.

The Sas 70 review process can vary from company to company, but will typically cover such items as:

- Computer and network operations, including backup and storage
- Physical security, including availability, disaster recovery and troubleshooting
- Information security, including password control and encrypted storage
- Communications, including intrusion detection and encrypted messaging

There are two variants of an accountant's Sas 70 report: Type I, which covers a single point in time and Type II which covers controls over a set period, typically six months. Customers of SaaS vendor normally require Type II reports. Most organizations that have Sas 70 certification get a Type II review once a year.

You can get a Sas 70 report from a certified public accountant. The costs will be professional service fees that are generally charged by the hour. You should discuss the cost with a CPA firm. The Sas 70 report will contain a description of the controls, a description of the examining auditor's testing process and a certification of the adequacy of the controls (or a statement of any deficiencies). You can find the AICPA's "original pronouncement" on Sas 70, which describes how it works, at www.aicpa.com.

MORE MANDATES

In addition to SaaS 70 compliance, customers may insist that SaaS vendors be subject to compliance with industry mandates intended to provide personal data with security and privacy:

These include:

- For the healthcare industry, the Health Insurance Portability and Accountability Act (HIPAA). You can find out about HIPAA compliance from the federal Department of Health and Human Services, www.hhs.gov.
- For financial services, the Gramm-Leach-Bliley Act (GLB). Information about GBL is available from the Federal Trade Commission, www.ftc.gov.

- For credit card transactions, the Payment Card Industry Data Security Standard (PCI-DSS). A good source of information about PCI-DSS is the PCI Security Standards Council, www.pcisecuritystandards.org.

Each of these mandates, if it applies, will require a SaaS vendor to secure the storage, transmission, and processing of data.

FOREIGN DATA PRIVACY LAWS

SaaS vendors may offer services from the United States to companies or individuals in other nations. Such SaaS services may involve processing personal data for customers, including employee data or consumer data. Holding personal data in some cases may require the SaaS vendor to comply with foreign data privacy laws.

Probably the most important step is to comply with the "Safe Harbor" rules that allow US companies to hold data protected by the EU Data Directive. (Complying with this Safe Harbor rule is discussed in Chapter 18 of this book along with other privacy matters.)

Other laws that might be relevant are the Canadian Data Privacy Act, the Japan Data Privacy Act, the German Teleservices Act, the Swiss and Luxembourg banking privacy regulations, and so forth. You should consult legal counsel if you are concerned that any foreign law privacy provisions may apply to your SaaS offerings.

HOT, COLD, AND WARM DISASTER RECOVERY SITES

Some SaaS vendors offer their customers "fail-over" disaster recover sites—which are no different in concept than disaster recover sites used by many enterprises. The idea is quite simple: if the main operational location of the SaaS vendor is lost due to a natural or manmade disaster, there is a stand-by second site from which the SaaS services can be provided. The disaster recover site is normally offered to SaaS customers as an extra price service because implementing and maintaining these sites is expensive.

It is common to divide disaster recover sites into so-called Hot Sites, Cold Sites, and Warm Sites:

Hot Site. Hot sites are a complete operational "mirror" of the SaaS vendor's main operations site—complete with all equipment, the software and all data. Typically, the hot site maintains a complete database in parallel with the main site—updated in real time—so that switchover to the hot site will cause little or no data loss or delay. The hot site is the most expensive disaster recovery option because it requires substantially the same level of investment and cost as the original operation.

Cold Site. This is an essentially empty location that lies ready for the installation of equipment, the software, and data. After the disaster, the vendor would purchase (or lease) the needed computers, router, and other equipment, would install and configure the software, load the data, and start operations. It may take weeks to get operations started. Data recover would typically be from backup storage, which means that transactional data entered after the most recent system backup would have to be re-entered. This is the cheapest option and provides the least protection.

Warm Site. A "warm site" is a disaster recovery solution that is more than a cold site, but not equal to a hot site. Typically, a warm site would include equipment and software ready to turn on, but would require data to be loaded from backup storage. This solution might require a few days to get up and running.

A SaaS vendor may offer any or all of these services. Whatever its disaster recover offerings, the vendor should be careful to spell out clearly what it is providing. Here are some additional points to note about disaster recovery:

- **Alternative ISP**—Many companies that provide disaster recover service use a different Internet service provider for the disaster recovery site.

- **Testing**—Hot site and warm site implementations should include periodic testing to be sure they work as expected.

- **Outage Information**—In some cases, it may be unclear whether a service outage will be prolonged or not. SaaS vendors should inform their customer promptly of the status and likely duration of any service outage.

- **Switchover Planning**—There should be a written plan for switchover to the disaster recover site. The plan should make clear who will be responsible for declaring a disaster, and who will be the contacts for coordinating the switchover. The plan should take account of fact that in some disasters (as we saw with Hurricane Katrina), there may be regionwide communication breakdowns. Vendors and customers should prepare for this risk by having alternative contact persons in a second location in another region.

OPEN SOURCE: THE GENERAL PUBLIC LICENSE AND THE "SAAS LOOPHOLE"

The SaaS business model provides an escape from the restrictions of "copyleft" licenses such as the GNU General Public License (or "GPL"). This means that you can build a SaaS business with open source "copyleft" software and make your service available to the world without granting copyleft licenses to customers or users.

As you recall from our chapter on open source licensing (Chapter 9), the open source licenses that most constrain commercial businesses are the "copyleft" licenses in general and the GPL in particular. Copyleft licenses are characterized with these important restrictions:

- **Required Source Availability**—When you provide the licensed program (or any derivative) to someone else, you are required to make the source code available to each recipient. You are not permitted to grant binary-only licenses.

- **License Inheritance**—A copyleft license provides that any recipient must be given a license to copy, distribute, or modify the program subject to exactly the same copyleft license terms and conditions—with nothing left out and nothing added. Thus as a GPL licensee, you can distribute the program or derivatives to a customer only under the GPL.

SaaS provides a way around these copyleft restrictions because a SaaS vendor need not distribute any binary or source code to customers. The customer merely uses a Web browser (or similar thin client program) to access a service; the customer does not get any SaaS vendor binary or source code. Because SaaS requires network-access rather than copies of software, the Required Source Availability and License Inheritance provisions of the GPL and other copyleft license are never invoked. This SaaS loophole applies both for the 1991 version 2 of the GPL (the most common version of the GPL used, for example, in distribution of Linux) and the newest version of the GPL, version 3, released in 2007.

There are, however, circumstances in which the SaaS Loophole can fail. For example:

- You provide a licensed copy of the copyleft SaaS application to a customer under a copyleft license.

- You place the source code of the copyleft SaaS application into escrow and the code is released from escrow to a customer under the copyleft license.

- You provide the copyleft SaaS application to a distributor or reseller under the copyleft license for use in another implementation.

In short, the SaaS Loophole works only so long as no copies of the copyleft SaaS license are distributed under the required copyleft license.

SAAS AGREEMENTS

The following is a discussion of the distinctive aspects of SaaS agreement and of key provisions. We are not going to discuss, except is passing, the "boilerplate" provisions of these form agreements—which look much like similar clauses in other IT contracts and are covered in Chapter 8, the chapter of this book on digital contracting basics. We have provided a sample SaaS Customer Agreement (Form 13-1) in the Appendix of this book.

Service or License?

In some SaaS agreements, the offering is characterized as a "service" that the customer obtains the right to "access." In other SaaS agreements, the offering is called "software" that the customer "licenses," is "hosted," and the customer "accesses remotely." Is there any difference here? Does it matter whether the customer "accesses" or "licenses"? Does it matter if you call it "software" or a "service"?

The answer is that it might matter—both from a marketing and a sales tax perspective.

> *Marketing Issue.* A SaaS vendor that wants to emphasize how different it is from a traditional software company will more likely term its offering a "service." Companies that want to show continuity with traditional software licensing are more likely to call it "licensing" of "software."

> *Sales Tax Issue.* There are a few states that impose sales tax on "telecommunications services." These states might consider SaaS "services" as such a service and therefore subject to sales tax. There are other states that impose sales tax on leased software products—and these states might consider software that is licensed for a fixed term (even if remotely hosted) to be subject

to sales tax. You should check with your tax accountant (or with state sales tax authorities) to see if SaaS offerings are subject to sales tax in any particular state and whether the way that they are described in a SaaS agreement can affect sale taxability.

No Delivery of Software

Unlike traditional software licensing, with SaaS deals, the vendor normally does not deliver customer with the software that provides the SaaS functionality. Rather than a delivery, there is the moment when access is "turned on" for the customer or "ready for access." In many SaaS agreements, notice to the customer that the software is ready (the "go live date") triggers the beginning of subscription payments.

Customization

Many SaaS vendors provide little customization and some allow for quite a lot. For some SaaS applications, it may be necessary to build interfaces between the customer's own software and the remote SaaS application.

Where there is customization, we lawyers use clauses to manage development and implementation that are similar to those in development deals (as discussed in Chapter 10). There needs to be schedules or collateral documents stating the specifications for the customization work (usually referred to as a work statement).

In the SaaS context, customization work is normally not delivered. The acceptance process will be based on the customer's remote testing of the software on the SaaS vendor's servers. Typical provisions provide for the SaaS vendor to notify the customer that the customization work is done and provide a stated amount of time, often 30 days, for the customer to test and accept or to notify the SaaS of anything that needs to be fixed before acceptance. More complex applications may have a multistage acceptance process.

In addition, the SaaS agreement will normally have:

- A process for change orders

- The option for one or both parties to terminate the SaaS agreement if flaws cannot be cured after a stated number of attempts

- Clauses providing for the ownership of any custom code. Most often (but not always) the provision is that customization will be owed by the SaaS vendors.

Data Ownership

With an ordinary software license, the customer has possession not only of the software, but also all of the data that is stored within its systems. However, with the SaaS model, the customer's data is on the SaaS vendor's servers (which may in fact be at a third party colocation facility). The SaaS vendor may also have a backup copy of the customer's data at another location.

Because the SaaS vendor is handling information from the customer—often very sensitive or valuable information—the agreement between the customer and the SaaS vendor needs to make it clear that the "ownership" of all customer-supplied data remains with the customer. (We put "ownership" in quotes because the legal technicalities of who might own particular data—or even if it is subject to ownership at all—are often subtle. When the parties discuss data "ownership," they often really mean the right to control the data.) The agreement will normally state that the SaaS vendor may hold the data for its intended use only and that the SaaS vendor must return the customer-supplied data upon termination of the agreement or upon demand.

Sometimes, there are provisions for the SaaS vendor to hold the data in archive for 60 or 90 days after the agreement terminates in order to give the customer an opportunity to retrieve it. If the customer does not retrieve the data during that time, the SaaS vendor can erase it.

Security

Simple SaaS agreements may have general provisions that say the vendor will use "reasonable efforts" to maintain the security and safety of data. Customers may expect detailed specifications regarding the technological means that are used to secure its data. SaaS vendors should make sure clauses are written to provide for flexibility in security measures so that security can be modified over time.

Most SaaS agreements disclaim damages due to data security breaches or other data loss.

Other Service Delivery Details

In simple SaaS deals, the technology and systems that the SaaS vendor uses to deliver its services are not specified. But in "high-end" deals there may be specifications of many aspects of the SaaS vendor's information system. These might include:

- **On-Demand Scale Up**—The customer may want a commitment for the SaaS vendor to add additional network, storage, or computing resources to serve the customer as needed to prevent system bottlenecks that would slow the response of the SaaS vendor's services. These clauses can be written to give the SaaS vendor a specified time to increase capacity—and to require customer payment for the increased capacity.

- **Backup**—The customer may want assurance that its data is backed up to a secure location at specified times. Most SaaS agreements have a provision under which the customer may obtain a copy of all customer-supplied data held by the SaaS vendor.

- **Disaster Recovery**—As discussed above, many SaaS agreements (or documents referred to in the agreements) specify hot site, warm site, or cold site disaster recover operations.

Pass Through of Litigation-Related Costs

Because SaaS vendors hold information for customers, they can end up in the midst of their customer's litigation. This can happen if:

- The customer that is either in litigation or believes that litigation is imminent will often request the SaaS vendor to archive data or protect data from erasure in order to secure the evidence. Compliance with this type of request can cost staff time.

- There is a risk that a third party that is in litigation with the customer will subpoena customer data in the SaaS vendor's systems. Compliance with subpoenas also requires expenditure of staff time.

Well-written SaaS agreements often provide that the SaaS vendor can bill its customer for staff time and expenses required for this kind of litigation compliance.

Service Level Agreements

Customers that use SaaS services want them to be "always on" and never interrupted—and want assurance that if, in spite of all precautions, there is bug or other service problem, it will be fixed right away.

SaaS customers often pay substantial sums for important service. Most SaaS agreements include some kind of service guarantees. The provision that provides these assurances is known as a "service level agreement" or, commonly, "SLA." These clauses often are highly negotiated. A vendor that provides a higher level of guaranteed service may want a higher price for it. Here are some of the topics that are commonly covered in an SLA.

Uptime Guarantee

An uptime is a provision providing an assurance that the service will be "up and running" for a specified percentage of the time. Often the provision is stated as a promise that the service will be running 99.9 percent of the time (referred to as "three nines"). Usually, these benchmarks are determined each week or each month.

Also note that SaaS vendors often provide an assurance only that their own system will be running. Most provide no guarantee that the Internet will be available. Many SaaS vendors have systems that test remotely whether their systems can be contacted from other locations. Some vendors include uptime reports as part of their SaaS service.

Be sure you understand the implication of these measurements. For example, 99.99 percent uptime in a month permits 4.3 minutes of downtime. 99.5 percent uptime in a month would allow 3.6 hours of downtime. The time over which compliance is measured is important. The maximum consecutive amount of downtime permitted is more than four times higher if the measurement is per-month than it would be if the measurement were per-week.

A common exception to the uptime guarantee is a provision for reasonable downtime for maintenance of the vendor's system. Some customers may want assurance that uptime will take place only on nonpeak hours in their own time zone and will be scheduled with a defined amount of prior notice.

Uptime guarantees often come with provisions for granting the customer credits if the uptime guarantees are not met. Often there are specified higher levels of downtime that permit the customer to terminate the SaaS vendor agreement. Usually, the agreement provides that these are the "sole and exclusive remedies" for excess downtime.

Service Response Metrics

Another common SLA component is "service response metrics," which are similar to those found in service provisions of end-user agreements. These provisions cover such items as:

- Hours that technicians are available or "on call."

- How soon technicians will respond to different classes of problems, which may graded into categories such as "Critical," "Serious," and "Non-Serious."

- Target times for technicians to fix various types of errors.

The agreement may set standards under which the customer may terminate the Agreement for "Critical" or "Serious" bugs that are not fixed in a specified time.

Response Time Metrics

Another common SaaS metric is "response time," which is the speed with which the system performs a particular function. Some functions require extensive data retrieval and/or calculation, and customers may wish to avoid long delays for such functions.

Response time metrics need to be defined carefully. Often they measure the time between the receipt of an inquiry at the SaaS vendor's system and the time the SaaS vendor's system sends its response to the Internet. That may be different from response time that the user experiences, which may be affected by latency in the Internet or other data network that the user uses to access the SaaS vendor's site.

Bad Customer Data

Under SaaS arrangements, the SaaS vendor will have no control over the particular data that flow in and out of its systems. It keeps, stores and processes whatever the customer and its authorized users put into the system. Some of that data could be illegal or otherwise. It might be defamatory. It might invade someone's privacy. It might be infringing under the copyright law. There is at least some risk that the SaaS vendor will get sued by a third party for supplying "bad" customer data in its system.

For this reason, the SaaS vendor agreement will often provide that the customer is responsible for any problems in the data that the customer's employees and users provide, and that the customer will indemnify the SaaS vendor for any claim that arises from the data.

Source Code Escrow

SaaS agreements often have source code escrow provisions very similar to those found in standard software enterprise licenses.

In the case of SaaS vendors, the value of the source code escrows to customers may be diminished. That's because many "pure SaaS" applications include back-end functionality that is designed for the Software vendor's use only.

Term, Termination, and Transition

Some SaaS agreements permit the customer to sign up for the service for a short period and to terminate at any time for any reason. This "easy-in, easy-out" format fits best the low end of SaaS services.

More often the SaaS vendor negotiates for a longer-term commitment— sometimes for a year or a number of years, and to require that customer that terminates without cause to pay compensation for early termination. Compensation clause may be set as a percentage of the remaining fees for the term. In SaaS agreements that involve large fees, termination clauses and termination payments are often the subject of negotiation.

One common feature of SaaS agreements is provisions that smooth transition to the next vendor in case of termination. The customer will expect to be able to obtain a copy of its data in some agreed format. The customer may also want to arrange for profession services (typical charged for by the hour) to assist in transitioning the customer's data to a new provider.

PRICING IN SAAS AGREEMENTS

There are many ways that vendors price SaaS offerings. The general idea is to find a reasonable metric to quantify the customer's use of the service. Often charges are based on the number of authorized users of the SaaS vendor application. In other cases, the right measure might be the number of transactions processed or the number of employees managed and so forth.

SAAS AGREEMENT FORM

As noted above, to provide assistance with your SaaS contracting, we included a sample SaaS Customer Agreement (Form 13-1) in the Appendix to this book. There is no such thing as a "one-size-fits-all" SaaS form contract. If you need help creating the right agreements for your business, please see qualified legal counsel.

Commercial Distribution—Part I

GENERAL PRINCIPLES, DEAL TYPES, RESELLER DEALS, AND LEGAL RULES

The most important single central fact about a free market is that no exchange takes place unless both parties benefit.

—Milton Friedman, Economist

Software vendors want to reach the maximum number of customers and increase sales of each new product offering. Most software vendors leverage their sales by means of "partnering" or "channel partners"—to benefit from the sales and distribution networks of their "partners." The partners benefit as well by carrying and profiting from the products.

Most distribution relationships are based on a written distribution agreement. Some distribution deals are customized and highly negotiated. Others are unmodified form agreements. Because distribution agreements manage not just a transaction, but a multiyear relationship, it is important to get these agreements right. Having a successful and smooth-running distribution relationship can greatly enhance the profitability and value of your business. Bad deals can waste time and resources.

IN THIS CHAPTER (AND THE NEXT CHAPTER)

Your company may be the vendor of software or the channel distributor of another company's software. Many companies are both. Distribution arrangements for software are a big topic. To cover it fully, we have divided the subject into two chapters.

375

- This chapter deals with some distribution basics and then reviews reseller agreements, which are the most common form of distribution agreement. You can use this chapter as a check list for issues involved in distribution generally. This chapter also explains some legal issues under antitrust law and franchise law that are potential traps in distribution deals. In addition, this chapter provides some comments on "strategic alliances."

- Chapter 15 deals with OEM and bundling deals as well as embedded software and software component deals, retail sales, and sales agent agreements.

There are samples of these agreement types (see Form 14-1 and Forms 15-1 through 15-4) in the Appendix in this book. Chapter 8, our chapter on software basics, is essential background for this discussion.

A NOTE ON TERMINOLOGY—PARTNERS AND RESELLERS

There was a time when the word "partner" was reserved for describing a fellow member of a partnership, a particular form of business entity. (Lawyers, for example, sometimes do business as a partnership.) However, sometime during the late 1980s some clever marketer decided that the word "partner" sounded much nicer and friendlier than "distributor" or "reseller." Now it seems that most software distributors are called "partners." Large volume distributors may be called "premium partners," which sounds even nicer. When you hear a company says "We partner with IBM," it usually means the company buys products or services from IBM to resell.

A distributor of software may also be referred to as a *reseller*, because from a commercial viewpoint, the distributor functions like a reseller that buys and resells tangible products. It is quite common to name a software distribution agreement a "Software Reseller Agreement." This terminology is quite sensible and practical, but legally misleading. From a legal perspective, it is important that transaction documents are worded as *licensing* transactions, not "sales" or "reselling" of software. (Sometimes, software transactions are worded so that the vendor *sells licenses* to the distributor—and the distributor then resells those licenses.)

Form Distribution Agreements for Your Business

If your company is a software vendor that does distribution deals, it needs well crafted and thoughtfully designed forms of agreement. As we discussed in Chapter 8, you can cut negotiation time if you make these forms easy to read and balanced. Your goal should be to create documents that minimize negotiation but still protect your business. Having a "play book" of preapproved attachments and variations that can be cut and pasted into your form agreements can also save time and money.

Getting the right forms for distribution deals is an art rather than a science. The form you use must be tailored to your business and must be updated frequently. Forms from books or on the Web (such as those in this book) can be valuable as starting points and checklists, but they will never be a perfect fit.

If you are the reseller, then it is your job to vet out the vendor's forms very carefully. They may grant rights that are too narrow for your needs or for your customer base. They might impose business and legal risks that you don't want to take. Problematic contracts can often be fixed through negotiation.

SOFTWARE PARTNERING AND CHANNELS

Each vendor needs to consider what channels and partners best fit the features of its software products and their pricing, use, and target users. For some (probably most) software products, the right approach is a combination of distribution channels and strategies.

In the next section of this chapter, you will find a listing and short discussion of the common types of software distribution channels, deals, and relationships. After this introduction, we will "drill down" and discuss these deal types in greater detail. Reseller/VAR agreements are discussed in this chapter. As noted above in Chapter 15, you will find a discussion of other distribution arrangements.

Resellers

The term *reseller* applies primarily to distributors of nonconsumer products (including commercial, governmental, and academic markets) that deal directly with their customers. It is common for resellers to hold themselves out as experts in particular software products or to specialize in solutions for particular vertical markets. A reseller may also refer to itself as a "solutions provider." A reseller will typically arrange for delivery to customers and provide installation and "primary" customer support. (See discussion of support and maintenance below.)

A reseller makes money by charging the customer a mark-up on the wholesale price it pays the software vendor. A reseller also makes money on "value-adds" such as customizing the software, providing integration or configuration services, handling data conversion, supplying training, and so forth. A reseller's "sale" might include installing combinations of software and computer or network hardware.

VARs

VAR stands for *value-added reseller*. The concept behind the term is that the VAR adds something extra to the vendor's software that is of significant value to the customer. The term is most commonly just a synonym for reseller, although some vendors do distinguish between ordinary resellers and VARS, which are perceived of as providing more sophisticated service or solutions.

Distributors and Dealers

In some cases, there are two levels of distribution between the vendor and the customer. In this case, we normally say that the company selling at the wholesale level is a "distributor," and the various companies under the distributor that license to users at retail are "dealers." Having both distributors and dealers adds complexity and costs to distribution.

This two-tier structure is most common in dealing with foreign markets, where the distributor may have responsibility for a large national or multinational territory. The foreign distributor can help arrange for penetration in the foreign market territory by using its existing relationships with regional resellers; it may also arrange for localization of products. (You will find a discussion of issues in international distribution and localization in Chapter 23.)

System Integrators

A system integrator is a company that assembles and integrates a variety of hardware, software, and telecommunication components to create complex computer systems. System integrators work on large contracts for large corporations, government agencies, or the military. System integrators are typically not tied to any one source or vendor, but obtain products from many hardware and software vendors. System integrators may "partner" with software vendors in bidding and performing a particular system development project. The largest system integrators include CMG Logica, Cap Gemini, Ernst & Young, Accenture, and IBM Global Services. (System integrators work for their customers under consulting agreements of the type discussed in Chapter 10.)

Rebranding, OEM, or "White Label" Deals

The term OEM stands for *original equipment manufacturer*, but this is a misnomer. What an OEM arrangement most often means in business is *private labeling*—the customer puts its own branding on the OEM's software or hardware product or markets a system under its own name that includes the software products of others. These are "OEM deals" also called "white label deals." In some cases, the licensee may do nothing to the vendor's software other than change the name. In other cases, the licensee may require the vendor to make substantial additions or alterations to the software. OEM deals can fit both business and consumer products and markets.

In dealings with major personal computer sellers (like Dell and HP), "OEM" can have a different meaning. An "OEM deal" is one in which a vendor provides a software product to be bundled with a PC or other hardware. In this context, the "OEM" is the computer company. The deal, most often, is that the software will come preinstalled on the PC's hard drive, and the software is normally under the vendor's own brand (not under the brand of the PC). An example would be Norton virus-scanning software from Symantec, which is bundled with an HP PC.

Bundling Deals

Bundled software means software that is licensed together with hardware or software as part of a package. If your company licenses software to another company, but permits distribution only in a package together with one of that company's products, that is a "bundling deal." Bundling deals typically trade a price concession for the increased sales volume.

Embedded Software and Software Components

The term "embedded system" or "embedded software" refers to software that is embedded in a hardware device, such as the software in mobile phones, appliances, DVD players, or electronic cameras as well as many other commercial, industrial, and military products. Virtually, all sophisticated devices with electronics include some kind of embedded software.

There are also many products that are "software components" that are designed to be used as components of other products. Examples of components are software for graphic display, communications, encrypting data, converting data from one format to another and managing embedded databases. The software component goes into another product to perform specific functions, and most often the user is not even aware that the end product includes the component.

Retail Distribution

There are some distributors that function as software wholesalers for mass-market retail sales. The largest software distributors in the United States are Ingram Micro Inc. and Merisel Inc. These two companies compete in the distribution of mass-market software and hardware to retailers in the United States. (Both companies handle significant foreign sales as well.) There are other smaller distributors, many of which specialize in niche markets. And there are other retail channels, such as Web sellers, catalog sellers, and retail outlets such as CompUSA. The physical retail channels are gradually being replaced by electronic selling. The "low-end" of retail distribution is shareware. Shareware marketing is typically done though Web sites and Web resellers.

Sales Representatives

The role of a sales representative (or "sales rep") is more limited than a distributor. The sales representative is an independent business or contractor that promotes products and takes orders. The vendor—not the sales representative—accepts the order, ships the product, and provides all required installation and support. Sales representatives normally work on commission. There is almost always a written sales representative agreement between the sales rep and the vendor.

ABOUT STRATEGIC ALLIANCES

Often technology companies will say they have a "strategic alliance" or "strategic partnership" with another company. These are business rather than legal terms. In some cases, the written "strategic alliance agreement" is nothing more than a distribution and marketing agreement of the types discussed in this chapter and in Chapter 15. Sometimes, there is much more to it.

An "alliance" that is truly "strategic" may allow a larger company access to its smaller partner's products, technologies, and intellectual property—and can allow the smaller company access to a large company's financial resources and distribution reach. Large companies enter into this kind of alliance because it is faster and cheaper than developing new technology on its own. Small companies do them in the hopes of accelerating growth and to reach new markets.

A strategic alliance agreement might contain:

- **Development Obligations**—Some agreements require one strategic alliance "partner" to develop products for the other to market. In that case, the agreement would combine distribution provisions with development provisions of the sort that we discussed in Chapter 10. The development provisions of such an alliance agreement would cover all performance and intellectual property ownership issues that we discuss in that chapter.

- **Rebranding and Cobranding**—In some deals, the parties may allow one party to rebrand the other party's products or they may agree to cobranded products. See discussion of rebranding provisions of this type in Chapter 15.

- **Funding**—Some of these agreements can provide development funding for the party that is to supply technology. The funding might be in the form of advances or guaranteed purchases.

- **Equity**—Sometimes, a strategic alliance agreement may provide for a larger "partner" to make an equity investment in a smaller company (that is, to purchase shares of its stock) or for the smaller partner to grant the larger partner warrants, which are options to buy the grantor's stock.

Because these strategic alliance agreements can be combinations of many elements, their contents and provisions vary widely. You will need an attorney's help in structuring strategic alliance agreements. This is especially true when they involve stock or warrants—which raise corporate and securities laws issues in addition to intellectual property, distribution, and licensing issues. (See also our discussion of international strategic alliances and joint ventures in Chapter 23.)

RESELLER AGREEMENTS

We now turn to the topic of vendor–reseller agreements. The following discussion will cover, in some detail, the provisions that make up a reseller agreement and the issues that come up in reseller agreements negotiations.

You will find examples of many of these provisions in the sample reseller agreement included in the form Appendix of this book. Most of the issues and provisions discussed here are also pertinent to the distribution deals outlined in Chapter 15.

Vendor Goals

From the vendor's viewpoint, the goals of a software reseller agreement are:

- **Increase Sales**—The vendor wants to increase distribution without incurring the costs of building or enlarging its direct sales organization. The ultimate goal of the vendor is to sell more of its products without sacrificing too much of the margin on its products to the reseller.

- **Lock in Sales Ability**—The vendor wants a reseller that is effective in making sales, and knows how to deal with customer concerns.

Reseller Goals

Resellers have their own goals:

- **Competitive Products**—Resellers want competitive products with high margins and growth opportunities.

- **Innovative and Reliable Vendors**—Resellers want innovative vendors that will keep their software product lines up-to-date and attractive to customers. Resellers expect vendors to provide reliable support and maintenance for those products.

A reseller's success depends on profitable long-term relationships with strong vendors that continue to innovate high demand, high-margin products. Being saddled with weak products and a stagnant vendor are costly distractions for a reseller and may put its reputation at risk.

The Relationship Between the Vendor and Reseller

Software distribution arrangements can last for years, even decades, but each party in the relationship should understand that the other party's commitment to the relationship is inherently contingent. Both the vendor and the reseller will maintain the relationship only so long as it works. Resellers may find vendor pricing too high. The vendor's products may have too many errors, may be too hard to use, or may be superseded by other technologies. The vendor's support may be inadequate. If the cost of staying with a product is too high, the resellers will drop it. Similarly, if the reseller performs poorly, the vendor will replace it.

When Microsoft was tiny and was dealing with huge IBM as its prime reseller, Microsoft called its strategic engagement with IBM "riding the bear." This aptly describes the relationship that many vendors have with powerful resellers—they can get a strong ride, but they may have little control.

The Risk that the Vendor Will Go Direct

A software reseller's nightmare is that the vendor will go direct—that is, the vendor will replace its reseller's successful operations with an operation run by the vendor's own employees. Because resellers almost always have contracts that can be terminated after a fixed term, they are vulnerable to this type of change in a vendor's distribution strategy.

As a practical matter, software vendors do not commonly eliminate their resellers, in part, because there may be customer loyalty to the reseller and in part because of the costs of going direct. But the risk of such a change remains—and may be increased if software prices fall and vendor margins fall with them. There is also a risk that the vendor will open additional channels of distribution to the same market. For example, the vendor may begin direct marketing through Internet channels or use direct mail and phone solicitations in the area where the reseller operates.

Aside from some rather limited protection afforded by franchising statutes in some states (discussed below), resellers in the United States have little or no legal protection from a vendor's decision to make changes in distribution. In the final analysis, the reseller's protection against change depends on the value that it brings to the vendor, on the reseller's personal relationship with the vendor's officers and staff, and on the expense and risk to the vendor of change. Sometimes, vendors "go direct" by buying out their resellers—which can turn into a good deal for the reseller.

The Negotiation Dynamic for Software Reseller Agreements

A critical factor in establishing the terms of a reseller agreement (as with other business deals) is the relative leverage of the parties. Powerful and prestigious companies may be able to impose their form distribution agreement on the reseller without negotiation, letting the reseller "take it or leave it."

On the other hand, it may be hard for some vendors to get good software resellers. This is particularly true for vendors promoting new software or novel technology. To get a qualified and proven reseller to adopt a new product line, the vendor may have to make important concessions on price and terms.

Products Covered by the Agreement

Every software reseller agreement must specify the scope of the license and the products that the reseller will distribute. The products included in a software reseller agreement may be all the products that the vendor makes or only designated products or lines of products. The scope of products under the agreement included can be the subject of negotiation.

The products that are covered are often listed in a schedule attached to the reseller agreement, although sometime the vendor reserves the right to change the list. Most vendors will reserve the right to discontinue products or product lines.

Resellers normally receive and market products in binary form only (unless the product exists only in an editable form). They rarely receive the source code to the product or the right to alter it.

End Customers Only

In most cases, the reseller will be forbidden to license the software to anyone other than a bona fide commercial end-user customer.

Nonexclusive Reseller Territories

Most commonly, software reseller agreements grant the reseller the right to license in a defined geographic area or "territory." Most vendors will not want to grant a reseller any territory in which the reseller lacks and effective sales reach. The reseller's presence in the territory is particularly important when (as is common) the software product requires direct selling, on-site customization, or on-site support. Some vendors have policies to limit the number of resellers in any given territory to simplify management of their relationships with resellers. The most common territory grants are national or regional. In many reseller agreements, the reseller is prohibited from accepting orders from outside its territory.

A practical problem with reseller territories arises because software sales and installations for many commercial applications can span geographic borders. If a vendor has one reseller in Japan and another reseller in Canada, the vendor must be able to manage distribution if a Canadian bank wants the vendor's application to be installed in a network that requires installations in both Montreal and Tokyo. Any system of territorial resellers needs to have arrangements for reseller cooperation and shared compensation on deals that span the globe; this is part of the burden of administering a reseller network.

In the European Union (EU), it is not legal to prevent resellers from accepting orders from locations within the EU. However, under EU law, a reseller agreement may lawfully restrict a reseller's "active selling" to a defined territory, which may be a single EU nation. The agreement can require that the reseller's promotion and advertising be targeted only to the defined territory, but the reseller must be allowed to do "passive selling," which means filling unsolicited orders, from everywhere in the EU. This distinction between active and passive selling is hard to apply to Web sales and advertising—and therefore these territorial restrictions have become less effective in the EU in the Internet age.

Exclusive Reseller Territories

On occasion, resellers are granted exclusive territories, where they alone have the right to market the licensed software products. The defined geographic territory may be a country, a specified region, a state, part of a state, or any other area the parties designate. Exclusive usually means exclusive of anyone, even the vendor, and when exclusivity is granted, the text usually makes this clear.

Resellers will argue that exclusivity is a necessary incentive for it to commit itself to a new product or to open a new territory. As a practical matter, resellers love exclusives because they provide insulation against competition. Most vendors resist granting exclusive territories. Vendors believe that they can increase sales by having more than one reseller in each territory. Vendors want competition between resellers to increase the level of sales and service. There is a risk that having only one reseller in a territory can lead to complacency.

When vendors do grant exclusives—for example, to induce a powerful reseller in a particular territory to take on its products—it is normally for a short time and the vendor looks to get something in return—such as a guaranteed purchase commitment. Exclusivity clause should be written very carefully because they tie the parties' hands and may become a major obstacle if the relationship between vendor and reseller sours.

Restriction on Competing Products

Some reseller agreements impose a non-competition restriction on the reseller—this is a requirement that the reseller refrains from distributing any product that competes with the vendor's product line. These clauses are quite common, but, of course, resisted by resellers. The resellers fear that they will lose sales to customers that want to use competing solutions.

Usually, the restriction just lasts for the duration of the agreement, but sometimes reseller agreements contain clauses like this:

> *Reseller agrees not to distribute any competing product for the term of the Agreement and for one year thereafter.*

The underlined text is disadvantageous for the reseller because it locks reseller out of the market after the reseller agreement is terminated. Vendors want these clauses for the same reason. In the United States, these posttermination restraints on competition clauses, if reasonable, are generally legal and usually enforceable in court.

Channel and Market Restrictions

Sometimes, vendors put restraints in reseller agreements that confine resellers to certain markets or close off certain classes of customers. For example, a reseller may be appointed with permission to market and license solely to the defense industry. Or a reseller's appointment may be conditioned on its agreement not to market and sell to the financial services industry. Normally, the vendor imposes these restraints to protect existing relationship with other resellers—or to keep control of sales channels in which it makes direct sales.

Provisions of this sort should be worded carefully, because ambiguity over what is open or closed to the reseller could lead to misunderstandings and disputes.

Multiple Marketing Channels

Many vendors use a mixture of direct marketing and resellers. Often vendors will retain the right to market directly to customers and will most often exercise that right with regard to so-called *national accounts* or *major accounts*, the large businesses whose operations span numerous territories or to other categories of customers. Often vendors will, either by contract or by practical effect, close these large accounts to resellers.

Mixed distribution methods can generate tension in reseller networks. Problems may arise, for example, when the vendor's price-cutting or aggressive selling tactics begin to cut into reseller sales. This type of friction between vendors and their resellers is known as "channel conflict." A modest amount of channel conflict is not necessarily bad. Managing a company's various marketing channels so that all of them remain productive is an important part of the marketing process.

Tiers of Partnerships

It is common for established vendors to have form agreements with more than one class or "tiers" of resellers. For example, many vendors have "silver," "gold," and "platinum" reseller "partners."

The classification of reseller levels is often based on two measures: the level of reseller sales of the vendor's products (this is the most important) and the number of reseller employees trained on the vendor's products. Higher-level "partners" may be entitled to a number of revenue-generating perks. Here are a few:

- The vendor might permit only higher-level resellers to provide support to end-users or share in support revenues.

- The vendor might distribute products that require more customization only through higher-level resellers.

- The vendor may provide sales leads preferentially to higher-level partners.

Vendors normally will want the right in the reseller agreement to adjust these categories from time to time.

Pricing

Every software reseller agreement has a provision for the prices that the reseller pays for software products. As a matter of practice, most vendors give the same terms to all resellers of the same type or class. (There may also be legal restraints on discrimination between resellers. See discussion of the federal Robinson-Patman Act below in this chapter.)

There are a variety of ways that pricing can be specified in the agreement. The following are some of the choices and issues.

Specified Prices

One option for pricing is to have the reseller agreement specify the software prices that the reseller will pay for the duration of the agreement. While this is a straightforward way to set prices, it is not very common. Most vendors want the flexibility to adjust these wholesale prices.

The problem with fixed pricing for the duration of the agreement is that it does not allow a response to changed conditions. Flexibility is needed. Prices may turn out to be too high if the competition begins price-cutting, or pricing may turn out to be too low due to customer demand.

Adjustable Pricing or Percentage of List

More commonly, the prices that the reseller pays are set by the vendor from time to time at its discretion. Often, the vendor will have a wholesale price list or grant the reseller an agreed-upon discount off suggest retail list price, which the vendor can change from time to time. With this system, only competition in the marketplace places a lid on wholesale price increases.

Sometimes, the discount from list price increases if the reseller achieves specified levels of product placements. Under some reseller agreements, the vendor grants a discount based on the projected volume of reseller orders, with a provision that removes the discount retroactively (and therefore requires the reseller to pay additional amounts for the software products) if the required volume levels are not met.

Price Rise Protection

When the vendor has the power to raise prices, the reseller agreement may include a promise that price increases during any year will be limited to a specified percentage.

Resellers that hold copies of packaged software in inventory may expect retroactive price adjustments on inventory—which will most often be in the form of credits against future purchases—if the vendor cuts prices. These "price protection" provisions are a "reseller-friendly" means to protect resellers that are willing to invest in inventory of the vendor's products.

Ordering, Delivery, and Payment

The terms of the software reseller agreement specify a process for ordering and delivery. These provisions may include reseller sales forecasts so that the vendor can plan its production.

Replication of the Product

In some cases, the vendor does not actually ship the product to the reseller. Rather, it allows the reseller to duplicate the product and ship copies to customers. Under this system, the vendor provides the reseller with a master file, which contains the object code of the program, and electronic and/or print-ready documentation. It is then the reseller's job to reproduce both disk and documentation. In some cases, the vendor grants permission for the distributor to use electronic distribution to provide the software and documentation to customers. When a reseller agreement permits resellers to copy software, it usually provides that the payment obligation to the vendor is triggered whenever the software is shipped to a customer.

When a vendor allows the reseller to replicate software in foreign countries, it can have an adverse tax effect in countries that have withholding tax requirements. This requirement is explained in Chapter 23, our discussion of "going global."

When Payment Is Due

Normally, when a vendor is shipping packaged software to a reseller, the vendor issues an invoice upon shipment. Payment is then due as specified, normally in 30 days, but a shorter or longer period can be negotiated. Reseller agreements usually have clauses that permit the vendor to restrict or cut off credit, in its discretion— and it will invoke this provision if it thinks the reseller is in financial difficulty.

Less commonly, reseller agreements provide for payment to be based on reseller receipts, that is, the reseller pays the vendor only after the reseller receives the customer's payment for particular licensed software. Vendors don't like these delayed payment provisions and avoid them if they can; vendors are often unwilling to take the risk that the reseller's customers will pay late or not at all.

Under most reseller agreements, the reseller must pay the vendor for the software regardless of whether it collects from its customer. Usually, the reseller bears the risk of customers that delay or default on payment.

Key Locks and License Management

Many vendors use license management software with "software keys." These keys—usually letters and numbers or a binary code—unlock the license management software and enable customer use of the software. In such cases, the vendor may provide a "temporary key" for the customer's use of the software product until the vendor receives payment from the reseller. Upon receipt of payment, the vendor provides the "permanent key" which the vendor can then deliver to the customer.

License management software is also commonly used to limit the number of users to the authorized level.

Records and Audit

Many reseller agreements require that the reseller keep records of its compliance with the financial terms of agreement and provide an audit right for the vendor. These provisions are most common when the reseller has the right to replicate software and is obligated to report its sales. But they are not necessarily limited to financial matters. Some vendors want the right to audit the reseller's compliance with other mandates of the agreement, such as security of confidential information, market restrictions, and so forth.

Term Licenses for Customers

Resellers most often provide end-users permanent licenses to software, but some products are available to customers under leasing arrangements or under licenses for a limited term. The reseller agreement will provide for distribution of products subject to these time-limited arrangements.

License management software and "keys" are often used to enforce these limitations. If the term limit is exceeded and the customer does not arrange for an extension, the software is programmed to simply stop working. Where this kind of "time-out" mechanism is used, the vendor should make sure that the mechanism is mentioned in the end-user's agreement and the end-user therefore assents to the use of this automated license limitation enforcement.

Sales Targets

It is common for a software reseller agreement to have provisions that permit the vendor to terminate the agreement if the reseller fails to achieve specified yearly sales goals. For example:

- The reseller agreement may require the reseller to make a specified minimum level of payments for software products to the vendor every year, a provision sometimes called a "purchase commitment schedule."

- The requirement could be a minimum number of new customers each year.

There can be combinations of such goals. Vendors use these provisions to "weed out" the weaker resellers. In addition to these quotas, some vendors require a specified minimum initial order at the time the reseller agreement is signed.

Customer Information

Vendors often impose a requirement that the reseller report specified information about the reseller's customers that use the vendor's software. Getting customer information has great value for vendor sales and marketing. This information will also be very important to the vendor if the reseller is terminated and the vendor needs to contact the customers.

Here are some ways that vendors get customer information:

- The reseller agreement may require that the reseller periodically supply the vendor with an updated list of licensed users, including their addresses, phone numbers, contact persons, and the products used.

- Many vendors have a reseller-only section of their Web site. (One of our clients calls it the "Partner Zone.") A vendor can have online fill-in-the-blank forms in this portion of their Web site for resellers to enter orders, including required customer-related information.

- Some vendors also use a direct means to get customer information. The vendor requires the customers to register on the vendor's Web site in order to get information about the software, including support information.

- Many reseller agreements provide that the vendor must be given copies of all agreements between the reseller and customers.

Those resellers that jealously guard customer information sometime resist (or fail to comply with) these kinds of provisions because they want to keep control of customer relationships.

Reseller Marketing Obligations

It is quite common for software reseller agreements to require that the reseller undertakes certain marketing obligations. Examples of such reseller obligations are:

- Maintenance of a specified level of inventory (for packaged software)
- Maintenance of a specified level of sales staff and technical staff
- Provision of customization, installation, and/or training for customers
- Maintenance of an office location or locations where the software products will be demonstrated
- Submission of a marketing plan every year or on some other periodic basis

It is also common for reseller agreements to require a reseller to use its "best efforts" or "commercially reasonable efforts" to market, promote, and license the vendor's products.

Marketing, Sale Assistance, and Reseller Training

There are some ways that vendors directly assist resellers. It is not uncommon for vendors to provide sales leads to resellers. Many vendors have "cooperative advertising" programs under which they agree to share the cost of print or online advertising. Under such a program, the vendor will reimburse the reseller part of its out-of-pocket advertising costs. Usually, these programs are handled informally as a matter of vendor policy.

Software reseller agreements sometime impose obligations upon the vendor such as the following:

- **Literature**—Supply of reasonable quantities of sales literature for its software product line.
- **Technical Advice**—Provision of technical advice and support on the use of the software and on coping with technical problems.
- **RFP Support**—Provisions of technical assistance to aid the reseller in responding to requests for proposals received from prospective customers.

It is common for the reseller agreement to require that the reseller send its support staff to vendor-supplied training (which the reseller will pay for). Some vendors have certification programs, which require regular training and testing of the reseller's sales and support staff.

Trademark Issues

A software reseller agreement will usually include a license for the reseller to use the vendor's trademark on signs, on the reseller's Web site, in advertising and promotional literature. The reseller may be required to identify itself as an "authorized reseller" in signage, on stationary or business cards, and the like. Reseller agreements almost always require that reseller's use of the trademarks be in accordance with vendor's written trademark guidelines that are subject to change. Other uses of the trademark normally will not be permitted except with prior written permission of the vendor.

Restrictions

Reseller agreements normally have boilerplate clauses that protect the vendor's products and intellectual property. These may include:

- An agreement of the parties that the software belongs to the vendor
- A provision that any vendor suggestion for features or changes can be used by the vendor without compensation to the reseller
- A requirement that the reseller report any unlawful use of the software by customers or third parties when it comes to the reseller's attention
- Prohibition on the use of the licensed software in Software-as-a-Service, application service provider, or service bureau arrangements
- Prohibition on reverse engineering of the software

Product Warranties and Remedies

The warranties provided to resellers may be different from those given to end-user customers.

In some cases, vendors (those with leverage) will provide no warranty to the reseller at all. The vendor will provide for a limited warranty to the customer—but none at all for resellers.

In other cases, vendors will provide a limited warranty to the reseller that the software "conforms in material respects" to its documentation. However, this warranty normally comes with limitations on remedies. Here is some typical vendor form language used to limit reseller remedies:

> *Reseller's sole and exclusive remedy for Vendor's breach of this warranty is to return the Software to the Vendor. Vendor will use reasonable commercial efforts to supply Reseller with a replacement copy of the Software that substantially conforms to the documentation, provide a replacement for defective media, or refund to Reseller Reseller's license price for the Software, at Vendor's sole option.*

Maintenance and Support

Fixing serious reported bugs in the software promptly is essential to maintaining customer loyalty. The reseller will therefore have an incentive to report serious bugs, errors, and problems quickly, and the vendor will have an incentive to fix serious problems as soon as possible.

Commonly, the reseller agreement divides support and maintenance obligations. The reseller agrees to deal directly with the customer and provide what is often called "primary support." The vendor will normally provide assistance only to the reseller, known as "secondary support."

The primary support to be provided by the reseller typically consists of:

- Providing technical advice to each customer on using the software.

- Providing reasonable installation assistance to the customer for the software and any updates or upgrades.

- Providing customer with training on use of the software.

- When a customer reports a software error, supplying existing cures for the problem, such as software patches. If there are no available cures, the reseller will contact the vendor and report the error. When the vendor provides a fix, the reseller will then provide it to the customer.

The secondary support to be provided by the vendor typically consists of:

- Modifying the software or providing other solutions to fix or circumvent errors that are not the subject of existing patches

- Modifying software documentation to respond to reported errors

- Assisting the reseller in providing primary support, if needed

- Incorporating needed changes into the next release of the software

In some cases, when the reseller does not have the capacity to provide support, the vendor arranges to provide both primary and secondary support directly to the customer.

When the reseller provides primary support, maintenance and support payments are typically shared by the reseller and vendor. A common arrangement is for the customer to pay the reseller for support. The reseller in turn pays the vendor for secondary support provided by the vendor for the benefit of the customer.

Warranty Disclaimers and other Limitation

A software reseller agreement will normally have a section in which the vendor disclaims product warranties and limits damage claims. (The legal background for this type of provision under the Uniform Commercial Code (or UCC) is discussed in Chapter 8.)

To summarize briefly, the need for the vendor to *disclaim* warranties and *limit* liability comes from provisions of the UCC that impose broad product warranty and damage obligations on the vendor that take effect *unless otherwise agreed*.

Here are some of the common disclaimers and limitations (all of these provisions are discussed in more detail in Chapter 8):

- **Disclaimer of Implied Warranties**—Vendors commonly disclaim any implied warranties. Under the UCC, to be effective, the warranty disclaimer is required to be "conspicuous" and it is therefor normally in all capital letters or italics.

- **Replacement or Refund**—It is also common for the reseller's remedy for defects in any copy of the software to be limited to replacing the defective software or, at the vendor's option, refunding the wholesale price of the defective software.

- **Exclusion of Certain Damages**—Usually, vendor will disclaim liability for the consequential, incidental, or exemplary damages.

- **Damage Caps**—Distribution agreements commonly have a limitation or "cap" on the aggregate amount of money damages that a reseller may collect from the vendor in court for breach of the agreement. Damages are commonly limited to the amount that the reseller has paid under the agreement for a specific period, often the one-year period before the claim arose.

- **Carve-Outs**—Sometimes, there are "carve-outs" (exceptions) that allow greater or unlimited liability for breaches of provisions on confidential information or indemnification.

Terms of Licenses to End-Users

The software reseller agreement will often include a schedule with "flow down" license terms required by the vendor. These are terms for the vendor's software that must be included in the reseller's agreements with its end-user customers. Other reseller agreements require that the reseller use only the vendor's specified form of end-user agreement.

These "flow-down" provisions and required end-user agreements always contain damage limitation language and other contractual protections for the vendor. They are usually substantially similar to the "clickwrap" agreements discussed in Chapter 16.

The purpose of these provisions is to ensure that the reseller uses customer agreements that will minimize the legal risks and that help protect the vendor's intellectual property.

Noninfringement Warranties; Indemnification

Reseller agreements also have clauses that deal with the risk of copyright, trademark, or patent infringement suits filed against the reseller based on the vendor's software. Often, the vendor will agree in the reseller agreement to provide indemnification to the reseller for infringement claims based on its source or object code. (This topic of indemnification is also discussed in Chapter 8.)

Vendors normally insist that intellectual property warranty and indemnification clauses be subject to provisions that manage and limit risk. These include:

- **Prompt Notice and Control of Defense**—A provision requiring prompt reporting the infringement claim to the vendor and giving the vendor sole control of the defense and settlement of the claim.

- **Sole Remedy**—A provision that makes indemnification (dealing with third party lawsuits and claims) the reseller's sole remedy for any infringement problem.

- **Termination and Refunds**—A provision that permits the vendor to terminate distribution if it is unable, after reasonable efforts, to resolve the infringement problem with a new design or with a license from the intellectual property owner. In case of such a termination, there may be a provision for limited compensation to the reseller, such as a refund of amounts that the reseller has paid for product that it returns.

Vendors often insist that their resellers provide the vendor with indemnification from any third party lawsuits that arise from misrepresentation of the vendor's products or from combination of the vendor's products with other products.

Term, Termination, and Disengagement

The term of these reseller agreements is commonly one, two or three years. Normally, there are provisions that the agreement will be automatically renewed for another additional one- or two-year terms unless one or the other party gives notice of nonrenewal a specified number of days before the expiration of the agreement. This is known as an "evergreen" clause because the agreement stays in effect forever unless one party or the other stops it. Evergreen clauses prevent accidental termination of the agreement.

Reseller agreements usually provide that they may be terminated for material breaches of the agreement that are not cured after notice. A typical cure period is 30 days, but sometimes the period is shorter in case of nonpayment. Reseller agreements also normally provide that, even if the agreement is terminated, the end-user licenses for the product are unaffected.

Software reseller agreements include provisions imposing certain obligations on the reseller upon termination. Here are a few:

- Payment of all accrued but unpaid license fees

- Cooperation in turning the customers over to the vendor or a new reseller appointed by the vendor

- Return of goods held in inventory—normally for a refund

- Cessation of licensing or use the vendor's product and any use of vendor's trademark

In some cases, the agreement will provide for a limited period of posttermination maintenance. Certain provisions such as those on confidentiality, limitation of remedies, damage caps, audit and indemnification will normally survive termination.

Jurisdiction for Disputes

Jurisdiction seems like a technical point, but it's not. If there is a dispute that turns into litigation, it is worth a lot to have the place for litigation to be your own hometown. Normally, vendor's "standard" forms will provide for exclusive jurisdiction for lawsuits in their home city and state. Resellers may try to get jurisdiction in a neutral city. The parties may also want to consider alternative dispute resolution clauses, such as provisions for arbitration. (See discussion of these topics in Chapter 8.)

Foreign Distributors and Resellers

Dealing with distributors and resellers in other countries involve additional issue. Please refer to Chapter 23 for a discussion of international distribution agreements.

SOME LEGAL ISSUES IN DISTRIBUTION

Distribution arrangements can be subject to the antitrust laws and the laws regulating franchising.

State and Federal Antitrust Laws

Any company that engages in the distribution of products may be subject to state and federal *antitrust* laws. Both vendors and distributors can be at risk for antitrust violations.

The most important federal antitrust statute, the Sherman Act, was passed at the turn of the 20th century to prevent unlawful monopolies and forbid certain anticompetitive contracts. Most states have very similar statutes. Antitrust suits in the United States are serious business, because if a company files a federal antitrust lawsuit and wins, it automatically gets judgment against the loser for triple damages and attorneys' fees.

What is important to most software businesses is the antitrust rule on *how companies may set prices and terms*. (Antitrust also covers monopolization, but unless your company dominates a market, suits alleging monopolization are not an issue for your business.) Here are a few very simple guidelines.

Price Fixing

A company cannot fix prices by agreement with its competitors. Price fixing is a classic antitrust violation that can result in a triple damage suit by the overcharged customers. Price fixing can also lead to *criminal prosecution* by the United States Justice Department or by state governments. A vendor cannot make a price fixing agreement with another vendor. Distributors cannot fix prices with other distributors.

Informal price fixing agreements are as illegal as formal ones. Nothing stops a company from matching a competitor's price. However, if a company sends its competitors its new price list so that the competitors can follow those prices, the practice is illegal and quite dangerous.

License Terms

A company may not fix nonprice terms of licenses with its competitors. Fixing nonprice terms can be as injurious to customers as fixing prices. For example, it would likely be a violation of the law for a company to agree with its competitors on the minimum configuration of software or on credit or warranty terms to be offered.

Restrictions on Pricing to Distributors

There is another federal antitrust statute that may apply to software distribution, called the Robinson-Patman Act. This statute forbids a company from giving one distributor better prices or nonprice terms than those made available to other distributors. The intent of the law is to protect small businesses against the economic power of large distribution operations. Because it is an antitrust law, it bears the same risk of treble damages and attorneys fees for any violation.

It is not wholly clear how the Robinson-Patman Act applies to software distributorships and distribution. The act applies to "sales" of "commodities," and it is not clear how this statutory terminology applies to software licensing. Many lawyers believe that the Act applies to transactions that predominantly have the characteristics of the sales of goods, such as dealings in packaged software, but does not apply to transactions such as software-as-a-service online distribution of services or custom programming.

If the Robinson-Patman Act does apply, the Act has exceptions where price discrimination is permitted, such as meeting competitive prices and genuine cost-based quantity discounts. Some computer hardware and software vendors are careful about the Robinson-Patman Act, and avoid giving special discounts to favored resellers. Instead, they have a standard list of quantity discounts available to all distributors. Certainly, the safest course, from a legal perspective, is to apply pricing and discounts equally to all distributors.

If you are concerned about the possibility of liability under the Robinson-Patman Act, you should contact legal counsel.

Resale Price Maintenance

Resale price maintenance is the practice under which the vendor fixes the minimum price that the reseller can charge the customer for the vendor's software. This rule is designed to keep vendors from discounting prices. In effect, the practice lets the vendor protect its resellers from price competition. In most countries in the world, resale price maintenance is always illegal.

In the United States, from 1911 to 2007, it was also the rule that resale price maintenance was always illegal under US antitrust law. However, due to a 2007 US Supreme Court decision, the rule now is that the practice of resale price maintenance will be illegal only if its anticompetitive effects (higher prices) outweigh any pro-competitive advantages (for example, better service).

In spite of this legal change, resale price maintenance remains a legally uncertain and potentially dangerous practice under US law. It is also possible that it may be illegal under state antitrust law. If you are a vendor and want to sign a deal to fix resale prices, you should consult your legal counsel and make sure you understand how to minimize the risks.

Federal and State Franchise Laws

One important aspect of the law that may affect software distributorships is federal and state franchise law. This body of law is important because a software distributor *might* be deemed to be a *franchisee*, entitled to the protection of federal regulations and state laws. This body of law may impose precontract disclosure rules on companies that recruit distributors. Even more important, this body of law may make it more difficult to terminate a distributor contract in some states.

The Background of Franchise Regulation

Classic examples of franchise operations are fast food operations and operator-owned gas stations, but a great variety of other enterprises including income tax preparers, real estate brokerages, dental offices, optician shops, and many others. In the 1970s, there were many abusive and dishonest franchising schemes that promised riches and delivered heartaches. After these schemes consumed the life savings of some unsuspecting owner-investors, franchising became something of a national shame, and federal and state franchise regulation followed.

Although software resellers may seem far removed from the world of fast food, the courts have on occasion ruled that software resellers are covered by franchise law.

Precontract Disclosure and Registration

The Federal Trade Commission (FTC), an agency of the federal government, reacted to the public outcry against franchise abuses by adopting regulations requiring extensive financial and business disclosure to prospective franchisees. Similar laws requiring disclosure have been enacted by 14 states including California, Illinois, Michigan, and New York. Many of these states require that any offer of a franchise be registered and approved in advance by the state regulatory authorities—after filing a disclosure form with the state that includes specified financial and business information about the franchisor. Failure to comply with the FTC regulations or these state statutes can result in fines, may permit the franchisee to rescind its agreement, and may result in liability to the franchisee. Willful noncompliance may be a criminal violation.

Restrictions on Termination

In addition, 16 states have statutes that regulate a franchisor's ability to *terminate* a franchisee. States with such statutes include California, Connecticut, Illinois, Michigan, and New Jersey. Generally, these statutes mandate that the distributor cannot be terminated except *for cause*—and cause usually means the failure of the franchisee to perform the requirements of its agreement. In these states, when the vendor tries to terminate the franchisee without cause, the franchisee may be able to file a lawsuit and get an injunction forbidding the termination or money damages for improper termination.

Software Distributorship May Be a Franchise

How does one determine whether a software distributor is, as a legal matter, a franchisee? This is not an easy subject. The federal government and the states use slightly differing rules, and this is therefore a matter where counsel's advice is a necessity. As you might expect, the fact that a software distributor agreement *says* that it is not a franchise agreement carries little or no weight. Generally speaking, these are the elements that the court looks at in deciding whether there is a franchise relationship:

- **Licensing of a Trademark**—A franchise arrangement must include permission for a distributor to use the trademark of another company. Most software distributors fit this test because most are granted the right to use the vendor's trademark.

- **Franchise Fee**—Franchise arrangements include a franchise fee, which is money paid by the distributor at the start of the relationship. Under the FTC regulations, a franchise fee may be as little as $500 paid as much as six months before or after the agreement is signed. Any amounts paid to a vendor other than the bona fide retail price of goods may be deemed a franchise fee. A franchise fee can be a payment that is mandatory under a contract or a payment that is required as a practical matter, even if the payment is ostensibly voluntary. Many software distributor agreements have up-front license fees or other payments that might be found to be franchise fees.

- **Some Element of Common Interest, Association, or Control**—The final element of a franchise agreement is phrased differently by the FTC and by various states—but the essential element is *control or influence* over the purported franchisee's business by the vendor. This element might include sales training, operation and marketing manuals or guides, management advice or training sessions, flow-down licensing provisions, marketing plans from the vendor, control of distributor locations, or control of advertising and promotion.

- **Unfair Treatment of Resellers**—There is also a fourth, unwritten factor: the treatment of the distributor. The more it looks like the distributor was unfairly treated, the more likely it is that a court will find that franchise law protection applies.

How Software Vendors Cope with Franchise Laws

Every software vendor with a distributorship network takes the position that its distributors are *not* franchisees. Nonetheless, if they are prudent, vendors take steps to reduce the risk that franchise laws might apply.

- **Advice of Counsel**—In each state where they wish to establish a distributorship, a prudent vendor learns of the applicable franchise laws and other relevant restrictions. Sometimes, if there is any doubt, vendors will require, as a condition of the distributor agreement, that prospective distributors get a written opinion of local counsel that the contract does *not* create a franchise under state or federal law.

- **Terms of the Agreement**—Vendors can draft the software distributor agreement in a way to minimize risks that it will be deemed a franchise agreement. For example, up-front fees that might be deemed franchise fees can be eliminated.

- **Use of Annual Minimums**—Vendors include in the software distributorship agreement a requirement for a minimum yearly level of purchases from the vendor or sales to end-users. Such a provision may allow the vendor to terminate an unproductive distributor *even if* franchise law restrictions apply, because the distributor will have breached the requirements of the agreement.

Franchise law is a complicated subject. Talk to legal counsel if you have questions or concerns about franchise law.

Common Errors

We have dealt with many reseller agreements. Most work well, but some are seriously flawed and break down or result in disputes. Here are some common mistakes.

- **Ambiguity**—Many reseller agreements are written in an informal manner with terms that are not defined or that make sense only to the parties themselves. Good reseller agreements should be sufficiently well defined and clear that they make sense to people that were not involved in the original dealings.

- **Overly One-Sided Agreements**—Some resellers unwisely sign the other side's proposed form agreements that are unfairly one-sided when they could have negotiated a better deal. When disputes arise, they will find they have no remedy and little or no leverage.

- **Lack of Flexibility**—Well written long term reseller agreements include mechanisms to change products, practices, prices, and some business terms over time. Agreements that are too rigid can cause conflict or may be unprofitable.

- **Lack of Disengagement Provisions**—Many reseller agreements lack terms that state what happens when the distribution agreement ends. Reseller agreements should have thoughtful provisions on what happens to inventory, customers, customer information, and support after termination.

- **Exclusives**—Some parties sign exclusive distribution arrangements that leave their product in limbo when their exclusive distributor fails to perform. Most vendors either avoid exclusives or limit them.

- **Omitted Terms**—Some reseller agreements lack liability or other key risk limitation clauses.

- **Unenforceable Agreements to Agree**—Very often parties "paper over" key provisions that they have failed to agree upon with provisions that require them to agree in the future. In most cases, these provisions will be legally unenforceable. There are some provisions where this is relatively harmless. However if the parties leave key provisions such as price or product features "to be agreed," the parties run the risk that they have an unfillable "hole" in their agreement—or perhaps no legally enforceable agreement at all. Well-written agreements do not leave key provisions to be agreed upon some time in the future.

FORM AGREEMENTS IN THIS BOOK

In order to provide you with more guidance, we have provided a sample reseller agreement (Form 14-1) in the Appendix to this book. This agreement is not meant to be a model for either a vendor or reseller. There is no "one-size-fits-all" version.

There is more about distribution agreements in Chapter 15.

Commercial Distribution—Part II

15

EMBEDDED, COMPONENT, AND OTHER DISTRIBUTION DEAL VARIATIONS

New technologies that evolved from the cumulative innovations of the past half-century have now begun to bring about dramatic changes in the way goods and services are produced and in the way they are distributed to final users.

—Alan Greenspan, while Federal Reserve Chairman, at the Boston College Conference on the New Economy, March 2000

IN THIS CHAPTER

This chapter discusses some additional important distribution arrangements in the digital economy:

- Rebranding deals
- Bundling deals
- Embedded/software component deals

These are not exclusive categories; there can be combinations of these deal types, as is discussed below. This chapter also includes a discussion of retail distribution and of sales representative agreements.

Before reading this chapter, you should be familiar with Chapter 8, our basic digital contracting overview, and Chapter 14, which provides a general introduction to the subject matter of distribution deals and a detailed look at reseller agreements. **405**

Forms Agreements

For your review in connection with this chapter, we provide, in the Appendix, the following sample agreements:

- OEM Software Agreement (including Component Software Provisions) (Form 15-1)

- Software Bundling and Distribution Agreement (Form 15-2)

- Retail Software Distribution Agreement (Form 15-3)

- Sales Representative Agreement (Form 15-4)

About "OEMs" and "OEM Deals"

In the discussion that follows you will see the term "OEM." OEM and the related concept of an "OEM deal" have some inconsistent meanings. As mentioned in the last chapter, all agree that the term OEM stands for "original equipment manufacturer." Unfortunately that derivation does not clarify the use and meaning of the term "OEM" in technology-related commerce.

OEM as White Label Supplier
Most often the term OEM is used for rebranding or "white label" deals. An OEM relationship consists of Supplier A making a product and Reseller B buying the product for resale under Reseller B's branding. In that relationship, Supplier A is called "the OEM."

OEM as Mass-Market PC Vendor
To complicate the matter, a different meaning of OEM applies in the personal computer (PC) business; there is an "OEM deal" one in which a vendor provides a software product to be included with mass-market PCs. The software will come preinstalled on the PC's hard drive under the vendor's own brand. For example, some Hewlett-Packard (HP) PCs come with Roxio's branded CD burner software preinstalled. Roxio's deal with HP would be referred to as an "OEM deal," and HP would be referred to as the "OEM."

In this type of arrangement, the software pricing is deeply discounted. That's because the consumer gets less—there is no CD-ROM disk supplied, no pretty box, and no printed manual. Often the consumer gets little or no tech support from the vendor for the OEM version.

Sometimes the vendor supplies an application that "times out" (stops working) after a set number of days. This is "try-and-buy" software; the end user must pay the vendor to get the normal software version that is licensed permanently. With try-and-buy software, the vendor and the PC maker may share the resulting revenue.

Rebranding or White Label Deals

Rebranding (or "white label") deals consist of licensing one company's software or digital product together with permission to rebrand it as the licensee's own product. This category of rebranded distribution arrangements may also be referred to as "private label deals" or "OEM deals." (The vendor is the "OEM" in the first sense we discussed above.) Rebranding agreements often bring together a vendor with valuable software, content, or technology and a "partner" with a powerful brand and strong distribution system.

For example, Sony PDAs feature "Sony Desktop" software that is a rebranded version of the Palm Desktop software from Palm Inc. The Best Buy Digital Music Store is a private-label version of the Rhapsody music service. Many mobile phones contain third-party software that provides calendar or e-mail support, but which is branded with the mobile service provider's brand.

In the following discussion of rebranding deals, we will refer to the company supplying the software as the "vendor" and the company that will resell it as the "Brand Owner." Rebranding can be combined with elements of the bundling deals or embedded component software deals discussed in the following sections.

Here are some considerations to keep in mind when negotiating these rebranding deals:

- **Rebranding Limitations**—The agreement typically limits the branding that can be placed on the vendor's software to the Brand Owner's trademarks only. The agreement will thus forbid the Brand Owner from making or distributing rebranded products with third-party brands. This restriction is designed to prevent the Brand Owner from making its own rebranding deals with the vendor's software.

- **Entry Level Products**—Sometimes the Brand Owner version of product is a lower featured or "entry level" version designed not to compete with more fully featured premium versions offered by the vendor under its own brand.

- **Dollar Minimums**—Vendors in these deals often seek minimum royalty commitments and nonrefundable advances on royalties. The idea here is to get money in the door sooner and ensure that the Brand Owner has "skin in the game."

- **No Vendor Support of End Users**—Vendors normally wish to avoid dealing directly with the Brand Owner's end user customers. End user support and maintenance for "white labeled" products is typically from the Brand Owner (or an outsourcer retained by the Brand Owner). The vendor merely provides secondary support, dealing solely with the Brand Owner's technical staff to address software problems, fix bugs, and provide maintenance updates.

- **Rebranding of Documentation**—In addition to the software itself, the Brand Owner will usually want a license to rebrand software documentation and distribute it with the software.

- **Product Upgrades**—Brand Owners often want assurances that they will receive upgraded and next generation products from the vendor as soon as it is released. Brand Owners will often want to get prerelease copies of new versions of the licensed software for testing and review.

- **Longer Agreement Terms**—Brand Owners will often want to sign long-term agreements (a five-year term is not unusual). This is because Brand Owners and their customers become dependent on the relabeled product. The Brand Owner may also want the right to further extensions of the agreement.

- **Sell-off Periods**—The Brand Owner will typically negotiate for a "selloff" period of six months or more at the time of agreement termination to allow for its continued selling of its work-in-process, inventory, and products in the distribution channel.

- **Replication, Reporting and Audits**—The vendor typically grants the Brand Owner the right to replicate the software. Payment terms are based on the Brand Owner's reporting its shipments of the software. Quarterly payment terms are common. The vendor should always insist on the right to audit reported sales.

- **Volume-Based Royalties**—Brand Owners sometimes seek deals with license fees that decrease when the Brand Owner ships the licensed product in high volumes or prepays the license fees. In some cases the Brand Owner may negotiate a license fee cap (that is, have a maximum for cumulative license fees).

- **Co-branding**—In some cases, a rebranded product will bear the Brand Owner's brand as its principal trademark and display a smaller marking that states "Powered by" followed by the vendor's mark. Vendors often will provide a modest discount in exchange for the benefit of having their own branding included as secondary branding on the Brand Owner's product. Sometimes the brands are actually combined. For example, Skype is a vendor of voice-over-IP (or "VOIP") software that allows users to have PC-to-PC voice communications over the Internet. Skype made a deal with Chinese Internet portal Tom.com to offer Skype software in China branded as "TOM-Skype."

- **Protection against Substitution for Licensed Software**—The vendor may seek to negotiate provisions that forbid the Brand Owner from replacing the vendor's software with a competing product—whether the Brand Owner's own product or a third-party product. The Brand Owner can be expected to resist this request, and the vendor will need to have leverage to be able to get this provision into the agreement with the Brand Owner.

- **Proprietary Notices**—Although its branding is removed from the digital product, the vendor should maintain the right to use its form of proprietary notice in the product (which may cover copyrights and, as applicable, patents). Usually the proprietary notice appears in the "About Box" of a software product and in the documentation.

- **Flow-Down Disclaimers**—The vendor will normally require that the Brand Owner includes specified warranty declaimers and other risk limitation clauses in its EULA (end user license agreement) with end users. Often the Brand Owner is permitted to include these provisions in its own form of EULA.

- **Source Code Escrow Agreement**—Because the Brand Owner will be dependent on the software, it will often request that the vendor put the software's source code in escrow—to be released upon the vendor's failure to support the software and in the case of the vendor's insolvency. This will be the "last resort" protection, because most Brand Owners will just look for another vendor.

- **Rebranding Agreements for Services**—Rebranding agreements may also be used where the vendor is offering services.

Bundling Deals

Sometimes distribution arrangements are conditional on the software being distributed in a "bundle" or as a combined product with another vendors' hardware or software product.

Everyone has seen such bundling deals. Microsoft Works is bundled with many low end PCs; the Linux version of the Opera Web browser is bundled with SuSE Linux; Macromedia's Flash product is bundled with Apple Macintosh PCs; most digital cameras come bundled with photo cataloging software, and so forth. Bundling deals are not limited to consumer products. For example, Sun Microsystems has made a deal to bundle an evaluation copy of BEA Systems' WebLogic Server (a business Web server application) with the Sun Solaris operating system. (All these deals are current as of the time this chapter is being written in 2007.)

In these bundling arrangements, the vendor of the "bundled product" wants to obtain quick and broad distribution by getting "bundled with" an existing valued and widely distributed product (often known as the "core product").

The maker of the core product (we will call it the "core product vendor") wants to make its product more attractive by extending its features and functionality. Often the vendor of the bundled product will require that the bundled product be mentioned in the advertising and press releases for the core product. There are variants on the bundling strategy. In some cases the bundled product is "try and buy" software. When the end user pays for a full version of the bundled software, the parties share the resulting revenue.

There is a difference between: "compulsory bundling" and "optional bundling."

- Compulsory bundling means that the core product vendor is *required* to include the bundled product with each and every core product. Vendors want these deals because they can guarantee large volume distribution.

- Optional bundling means that the core product vendor has the right to include the bundled product with any core product, but is not required to do so.

Because bundled products are usually provided at a below-market license fee, they often come with limited warranties, limited support (unless the end user pays for more), and with constraints on the duration and type of distribution that is permitted.

Embedded Software and Software Components

Many software products are made to be reusable working building blocks of other software. If the software is for hardware devices, it is called "embedded software." Software that is meant to be a building block of a larger computer software program is normally referred to as a "software component." For convenience, I will refer to both kinds of software as "components." It is common for components to be based on standard interfaces and standard protocols; this makes it more readily integrated with other components in the "end product." (See discussion of standards and standard setting in Chapter 19.) Components are important time savers in product development.

Software components are available, for example, for encryption, image manipulation, video and audio compression, network management, Internet messaging, and many other functions. Some components are open source, some are commercial. Some are offered in the form of libraries. One client of our law firm provided database management component software under both open source and commercial licensing.

In this section, I will refer to the party that is supplying commercial components as the vendor and the party that is incorporating components in its hardware or software product as the "end product maker."

Software license agreements for components usually have the following characteristics:

- **Development and Distribution Licenses**—The agreement will usually grant the end product maker a development license and a distribution license. The development license will permit the end product maker to use the software internally (or with its contractors) to develop its end products. The distribution license will allow the end product maker to replicate and distribute the components, but only as part of the end product. In some cases, the development and distribution license are in two separate agreements. The end product maker will begin with the development license. If development is successful and it wants to begin distribution, it will then purchase a distribution license.

- **Normally Nonexclusive**—Most software component agreements are nonexclusive. The end product maker will want to remain free to use components made by other component vendors. Technologies might change, and the end product maker may need to switch to a competing product. In addition, the end product maker will likely want the benefit of price and service competition.

- **Components in Binary Form**—Most components are provided in binary form. They are designed to allow the end product maker to integrate them into its own product by means of "application program interfaces" or "APIs" that permit interoperability.

- **Components in Source Code Form**—In some cases, components are supplied to the end product maker in source code form. In such a case, the vendor will grant the end product maker a license to use the source code only to make binary versions of the component (usually called "binary derivatives") and to integrate the binary derivatives into the end product. The end product maker will be required by the agreement to hold the source code version of the component securely as the confidential information of the vendor, and will usually be required to erase all copies of the source code when the agreement terminates.

- **SDKs**—It is common for component vendors to supply software design tools or sample software products designs for use with their components. The combination of the component and these related items is commonly referred to as a "software development kit" or "SDK." The tools and samples are normally licensed to the end product maker for internal use only and are designated as the confidential information of the vendor.

- **Intellectual Property Grantback**—If the component is provided in source code form and the end product maker has the right to modify it, the vendor's form of agreement may require that the end product maker deliver back to the vendor a copy of any modified versions. Such an agreement will also give the vendor a nonexclusive license (called a "license back") allowing the vendor to make, use, and distribute the customer's modifications (and derivatives of the modifications). If both the vendor and the end product maker are in the same or related technology markets, such a grant-back provision will be controversial and likely the subject of negotiation—especially if the license back to the vendor could include a license under the customer's patent rights.

- **Support**—Component agreements often have a provision for the end product maker to purchase support services consisting of advice on integration of the component into an end product.

- **Maintenance**—Component agreements normally have provisions for bug fixing and maintenance updates in exchange for support fees. These would cover both the component itself and the other contents of the SDK.

- **Limited or No Branding Obligations**—Component agreements typically have no requirement that the end product mention the component or the component vendor in marketing or branding. Component vendors with famous brands or market power are sometimes able to obtain a requirement of secondary branding—such as the famous "Intel Inside" branding on PCs.

- **Proprietary Legends**—In many agreements, the end product maker is required to include the Software component's proprietary legends (such as its copyright and trademark notices) in the end product's "about box" and product documentation. Sometimes there is not even this requirement and the use of the component is invisible to end customers.

- **Publicity and PR**—Vendors like to issue press releases and publicize the fact that major technology companies use their components. They often propose a clause in component agreements that permit this. For their part, many technology companies do not want their vendors known and do not want smaller companies trading off their reputation. So often the end product makers may insist that they have the right to control or prevent press and publicity about the relationship.

- **Volume-Based Pricing**—Pricing of the software component may depend on volume commitments made by the end product maker. In some cases, the end product maker agrees to a fixed minimum volume commitment or pays a substantial part of the license fees in advance to secure lower pricing.

- **Longer Agreement Terms**—As with OEM deals, the end product maker will normally want a long agreement term so that it can avoid the expense of integrating a replacement component into its end products. Multiyear agreements for important components are common. Like OEM deals, it is common to see provisions for a "sell-off" period at the time of termination for completing work-in-process and sales of inventory and products in the distribution channel.

Retail Distribution

There are some distributors that function as software wholesalers of packaged software products to retailers. Large retail outlets also purchase software directly from vendors.

Sales of Packaged Software through Retail Channels

Retail software can generate large sales and high margins, but retailing of packaged software products is a very tough business. There is only so much shelf space in any retail store—and some of the space is better than others. Similarly online retail merchants can prominently feature only a limited number of products. Consumers can be very fickle. Trends and fads come and go. One year's hot product can be the next year's dog. Customers are free to return products that they don't like. Retailers hold inventory, which ties up their capital.

For all these reasons, retailers look for arrangements that place on their vendors much of the risk of inventory of products that won't sell. Large and powerful vendors may be able to resist these pressures and push back. Smaller retail vendors with little leverage are more likely to get stuck with the risk. Following are some typical characteristics of retail distribution agreements:

- **Returnable Goods**—When customers return products, either because they are defective—or just because they don't like them, the returns will flow back to the vendor. The retailer will usually get a credit for the return that it can use for other purchases from the vendor; but in some cases, the retailer may have so much leverage that it can insist upon a cash refund. Retail goods that have been opened may have to be scrapped.

- **Stock Balancing**—"Stock balancing" refers to the right of the retailer to return vendor products that are slow sellers or superceded and obtain the vendor's new and better products. The retail distribution agreement may set a cap on the percentage of the goods sold to the reseller that can be returned under this arrangement.

- **Price Protection**—"Price protection" means the right of the retailer to get the benefit of any reduction in price not only for new purchases but for its inventory as well. It works like this: if the retailer bought products at a twenty-dollar wholesale price and the wholesale price falls to fifteen, then the retailer is entitled to a five-dollar credit for each copy of the product it held in stock on the day when the price changed.

- **Payment Terms**—Retailers like long payment terms so that, in effect, they pay for products after they have sold them to consumers. Vendors will try to shorten credit terms and include provisions for interest on late payments.

- **Payment for Placement**—Vendors may have to pay retailers, in credit or with cash, for favorable shelf placements. For example, the vendor may charge for placement on special displays or at the end of shelf "end cap" locations.

- **Cooperative Advertising**—Vendors may offer credits or cash that retailers can use to defray the cost of advertising that features the vendor's product.

If the vendor has any bargaining leverage, it may be able to negotiate more favorable versions of these provisions. Many of these provisions (such as those regarding returns or credits) may have revenue recognition and other accounting effects. If your company is selling products into retail channels, you should be sure you discuss the accounting issues with your company's accountant.

Retail Download Distribution

An alternative form of retail distribution is download distribution. Download distribution is commonly found in the "low end" of retail products. However, download distribution is so fast and cost-effective (and generates such high margins) that it is found in many other product categories, including high end enterprise software.

Here are some common features of this model in mass market retail sales:

- The online retailer commonly does not make physical delivery of the software at all. Usually it simply puts a copy on a server and allows consumers to download the software.

- In consumer markets, this model lends itself to "try-and-buy products." To remove the limitations of the trial version, the consumer makes an online credit card purchase and receives a software "key" by e-mail. This "key" unlocks the software.

- Products are supplied with click-through end user license agreements of the type discussed in Chapter 16.

In many ways, download distribution is an answer to the retailer's headaches. There is no "shelf space" limitation to the titles that the retailer can carry, so the online retailer can afford to have a very lengthy catalog. There is no inventory. There are no returns. The labor cost is low due to the high level of automation. For this reason, the percentage of the sales revenue that goes to the vendor is higher than in traditional boxed software sales.

Sales Representatives

The role of a sales representative (or "sales rep") is an old one, going back centuries. As noted in the preceding chapter, a sales representative (also known as a "sales agent" or "commission agent") is an order taker for a software vendor. The vendor—not the sales representative—accepts the order, ships the product, and provides all required installation and support. Today many sales representatives use telemarketing and the Internet to extend their reach.

Sales Representative Agreements

If you want to appoint sales representatives (usually a company—but the sales rep can be an individual), you need a form of sales representative agreement. These forms are rather simple agreements, although they do require customization to fit the needs of your particular business. Here are the kinds of provisions that they normally contain:

- Assignment of a territory to the representative

- Product and price lists provided by the vendor and subject to change by the vendor, usually on short notice

- Commissions splitting arrangements when more than one representative is involved or the sale crosses representative territories

- "Easy-in, easy-out" terms allowing either party to terminate the agreement on relatively short notice

Compensation to Sales Representatives

Sales representatives are normally paid for results—compensation to the sales representative is commission-based. The commission structure is usually set out in the Agreement. Because payment in sale agent arrangements goes directly from the customer to the vendor, the sale agent normally receives payment monthly or quarterly together with reports of transactions.

Sometimes commissions are based on the vendor's *revenues* resulting from the actions of the sales representative and sometimes on *receipts*. What is the difference? Revenue is an accounting concept. While there are exceptions, most companies recognize revenue on software licenses when the product is shipped and invoice is mailed to the customer. Receipts mean money actually received. If you need more information on the significance of this distinction, you should discuss it with your accountant or attorney.

Compensation upon Termination of the Sales Representative

Under many sales representative agreements, payments to the sales representative simply end when the agreement terminates. In others, there are provisions for a period of continued commissions that apply for ongoing revenue that arises from the sale rep's customers—unless the sales representative was terminated "for clause." Post-termination commissions are limited in time, often to a year or two—under some agreements they also diminish over time. In the European Union and in a number of other nations, there are mandatory legal provisions requiring payment of post-termination compensation unless the sales representative was terminated for cause.

FORM AGREEMENTS

As noted above, in the form appendix, we have provided a form of OEM software agreement (including component software provisions) (Form 15-1), a software bundling and distribution agreement (Form 15-2), an agreement for retail software distribution (Form 15-3), and a sales representative agreement (Form 15-4). Remember that these are samples—not models. Each reflects the give and take of business negotiations, and there is no assurance that a form will fit your own dealings.

As we noted in the preceding chapter, distribution is often quite complicated, and distribution arrangements may be crucial for the development of your business. You should craft your own "standard forms" that best fit your business and revise them as your business evolves.

Clickwraps and Browsewraps

16

Dilbert to Dogbert: "I didn't read all of the shrinkwrap license on my new software until after I opened it. Apparently I agreed to spend the rest of my life as a towel boy in Bill Gates' new mansion."

Dogbert: "Call your lawyer."

Dilbert: "Too late. He opened software yesterday. Now he's Bill's laundry boy."

—From *Dilbert* by Scott Adams, 1997

This chapter is about form digital product and service agreements primarily in electronic form—the "clickwraps" and "browsewraps." You have seen these form documents hundreds of times, although you may not have bothered to read them. Nonetheless they are a big part of the legal foundations of the modern IT industry. These form documents allow a single company to be a party to tens of millions of contracts. They make mass contracting fast, efficient, and very low cost.

This kind of form-based mass contracting is not limited to software products. Over the past decade, the Internet and the Web have made necessary new breeds of electronic form agreements as, for example: the terms of use on Web sites, the legal terms for multiplayer online games, and the contract terms used when providing software-as-a-service (SaaS). Writing these documents—particularly for new and innovative business models—can be a challenge.

IN THIS CHAPTER

This chapter covers:

- Uses and goals of electronic contracting

- Categories of form agreements in volume electronic contracting

- Enforceability of electronic agreements

- Contents of clickwrap agreements for software products

- Suggestions, options, and cautions about how to use electronic contracting

In Chapter 17, you will find a discussion of a related topic, Web site terms of use; this chapter is essential background to that discussion. This chapter assumes that you read Chapter 8, which discusses digital contract basics.

In the form appendix, you will find two samples of "clickwrap agreements," one for a consumer product (Form 16-1) and one for a business software product (Form 16-2). (Of course, you can find countless additional examples of these forms on the Web.) Any clickwrap agreement for your business will need to be customized to fit its products, services, and business needs. These forms may need to change over time as your business or commercial and legal requirements change.

USES OF ELECTRONIC CONTRACTING

Many companies that distribute software use the form agreements that we call clickwraps or browsewraps. Electronic contracts under US law can serve some important purposes. They can be used to:

- Specify the license grant.

- Obtain permissions from the user.

- Forbid unwanted conduct such as reverse engineering, circumvention of data protections, or unlicensed use.

- In some cases, provide contractual protection for data and information even if it is outside the protection of US copyright law.

- Disclaim warranties and limit money damages.
- Specify the means of resolving disputes (such as arbitration) or select the forum state for any litigation.

There are two cautions, however. One is that their effect—particularly as applied against consumers—can be limited by state and federal law. Second is that their terms may be cut back or disregarded by the courts if deemed oppressive or unfair.

CATEGORIES OF MASS-MARKET FORMS CONTRACTS

When we talk about these mass contracting form documents, we break them down into categories:

Shrinkwrap Agreements

Shrinkwrap is now largely a historic term. Shrinkwrap refers to paper-based rather than electronic contracting. The 1997 reference in the *Dilbert* quoted above to a "shrinkwrap license" is thus a bit dated. In the 1980s and early 1990s, it was common to include an "in the box" form end user license agreement (or "EULA"). When you bought PC software, you opened the box and often found the software diskettes in a sealed white paper envelope. The envelope contained a notice in capital letters across the top that says:

> *BY OPENING THIS SEALED DISK PACKAGE YOU ARE AGREEING TO BE BOUND BY THE TERMS OF THIS AGREEMENT. IF YOU DO NOT AGREE TO THE TERMS OF THIS AGREEMENT, RETURN THIS PRODUCT TO THE PLACE OF PURCHASE PROMPTLY FOR A FULL REFUND.*

Following this notice was a page of legalese, which was the "shrinkwrap" EULA. The EULA stated the terms and conditions of the software license—written, of course, by lawyers like us to protect the licensor.

The term "shrinkwrap" comes from clear plastic wrap used to cover packaged software and other products—a thin polymer film that shrinks to a snug fit when heat is applied. A "shrinkwrap license" therefore meant the EULA included in the software box. The white envelope is now gone—it has been replaced by electronic means of assent for packaged software discussed below. However, it is still a good idea to provide users with EULAs as part of any printed documentation supplied to users, such as printed user manuals. The EULA can also be put in electronic documentation or online documentation.

Printed form agreements are still common with mass-market hardware products such as mobile phones, electronic cameras, or PDAs. Open source licenses commonly come as a text file included with a software download and usually do not display automatically or come with a form of "click" acceptance. (See Chapter 9 in this book for a discussion of open source licensing.)

Clickwrap Agreements

The term "clickwrap" (also commonly known as a "click-through" agreement) refers to agreements that obtain the user's affirmative acceptance electronically. You see clickwrap contracting virtually every time you install PC software. During the install routine, you are presented with check boxes labeled "I accept the terms of the License Agreement" and "I do not accept the terms of the License Agreement." There is typically a scroll box that allows you to view the text of a EULA. The install routine works only if you accept. The EULA begins with language like this:

THE ACCOMPANYING PROGRAM (THE "PRODUCT") IS MADE AVAILABLE TO YOU UNDER THE TERMS OF THIS END-USER SOFTWARE LICENSE AGREEMENT (THE "AGREEMENT"). BY CLICKING THE "ACCEPT" BUTTON, OR BY INSTALLING OR USING THE PRODUCT, YOU ARE CONSENTING TO BE BOUND BY THE AGREEMENT. IF YOU DO NOT AGREE TO THE TERMS AND CONDITIONS OF THIS AGREEMENT, DO NOT CLICK THE "ACCEPT" BUTTON, AND DO NOT INSTALL OR USE THE PRODUCT. RATHER YOU SHOULD PROMPTLY CONTACT SUPPLIER FOR A REFUND.

A similar, but slightly different form of clickwrap for products is sometimes used on Web sites. For example, a Web page that makes available software for downloading may have a notice like this:

BY DOWNLOADING THE SOFTWARE YOU ARE CONSENTING TO BE BOUND BY TO VENDOR'S END-USER LICENSE AGREEMENT. IF YOU DO NOT AGREE TO ALL OF THE TERMS OF THIS LICENSE, DO NOT DOWNLOAD OR USE THE SOFTWARE.

This may be accompanied by a link that states "Click here to see the text of the End-User License Agreement." Or, less commonly, there may be a scroll box on a Web page that has the license text.

Use of clickwraps is not limited to software. This mechanism is commonly used to capture assent to contracts for online services—as discussed in Chapter 13 of this book on Software as a Service (or "SaaS"). In that case, the online text invites the customer to click to accept the terms of a service agreement covering the SaaS offering. Clickwraps are used with terms of use for online games and online mass services such as instant messaging. There are more specialized forms of clickwraps for online mortgage applications, travel reservations, banking accounts, and other online consumer services.

Browsewrap Contracts

The term "browsewrap" refers to an agreement that claims to bind the user of a Web site merely by the user's use of a Web site. By definition, there is no attempt to require any overt act of user acceptance. The browsewrap presumes that the user knows of and accepts the agreement. Most browsewraps are meant to deal with anonymous Web site use.

Browsewraps include "Terms of Use" that are found in many commercial and noncommercial Web sites (discussed in Chapter 17). These documents are normally found by clicking a link (often rather in small type) to the "Terms of Use" at the bottom of each page on the site. The terms of use normally begin with text like this:

THE FOLLOWING NOTICES, TERMS, CONDITIONS AND POLICIES GOVERN THE USE OF THE THIS WEB SITE AND ANY PRODUCTS OR SERVICES AVAILABLE ON THIS WEB SITE. BY ACCESSING OR USING THIS WEB SITE, YOU AGREE TO BE BOUND BY THE TERMS AND CONDITIONS SET FORTH BELOW.

Web site privacy statements are a form of browsewrap too. (See the discussion of privacy statements in Chapter 18.) Some sites have rules of conduct that function as browsewraps. Many Web sites include clickwrap terms as well.

ARE ELECTRONIC FORM CONTRACTS LEGALLY ENFORCEABLE?

Electronic form contracts contain important provisions regarding rights, prohibitions, liabilities, and remedies. Digital product and service companies often want to know if these electronic form contracts actually bind users.

Are Clickwraps Binding?

Generally speaking the courts in the United States have treated clickwrap agreements as enforceable agreements. There was never really much doubt that clickwraps would be binding if the buyer agreed to the contract *before* paying for the product or service offered. However, it was less clear that a company could bind the buyer if the contract was first presented *after* the sale.

A fundamental idea in our contract law, from its medieval roots in England to the present, is the *bargain*—what lawyers sometimes call a meeting of the minds. The terms are bargained out; *then* the sale takes place as agreed. The potential problem with the clickwrap was that the software payment and delivery transaction were over before the customer sees the terms of the agreement. After the sale of a license to the product is already made (for example for a boxed consumer software product), we wondered if was it too late to try to impose agreement terms.

In spite of this history, the clear trend in the court decisions over the last decade is to find clickwraps enforceable even if the contract is first presented after the fact—provided that the customer must be given the right to return the goods for a full refund if not satisfied with the contract terms. The courts have regarded this form of electronic contracting as a practical necessity. Shrinkwrap agreements (in paper form) that users first see after buying packaged software have also been enforced on the same theory.

So the bottom line is the clickwraps that you use with your software will likely be enforceable in the United States, but the court may not enforce provisions that seem unfair or impose unexpected burdens, especially on consumers—and there may be other limitations that apply as well (discussed below).

Software in the Box

When mass-market software is sold in packaged form, we think it is best to have a notice on the outside that mentions that there is a clickwrap license agreement that governs the bargain. This notice is designed to make the use of the clickwrap appear (to the court) to be more fairly presented and fairly accepted. A typical on-the-box notice looks like this.

> *Installation and use of this software product is subject to an end user license agreement within. If you do not accept this agreement, you may return the software and accompanying contents in this package to the place of purchase within 30 days of purchase for a refund.*

As noted above, we also recommend including the EULA in the product documentation (electronic or in paper form) or in the help files in the product or both.

Electronic Signatures, E-SIGN and Clickwraps

Over the last decade, the law has adapted to the reality that many "signatures" on documents are no more than "clicks" of a mouse. Many states have passed laws making the electronic signatures binding to the same extent as the traditional pen-and-ink signature. More importantly, in 2000, the federal government enacted the Electronic Signatures in Global and National Commerce Act, or E-SIGN. Under E-SIGN, contracts that affect interstate and foreign commerce can be signed digitally.

An electronic signature is defined under E-SIGN as:

an electronic sound, symbol, or process, attached to or logically associated with a contract or other record and executed or adopted by a person with the intent to sign the record.

This means that virtually any form of electronic signature can be effective. The law provides that a contract "may not be denied legal effect, validity, or enforceability solely because it is in electronic form." Many foreign nations have similar laws.

These state and federal laws mean that most of any commercial contracts in the United States of the sort that we are discussing in this book can be digitally signed. There are some limits and exceptions, of course. For example, you cannot execute your last will or testament or convey real estate with a click.

Authenticity

There is, however, an issue that is not resolved by E-SIGN or state electronic signature laws—proving the *authenticity* of an electronic signature. Just as is the case with traditional pen-and-ink signatures, digital signatures can be forged. The law leaves it to science and technology to create verifiable electronic signatures and to supply proof in court of authenticity.

E-SIGN also has a provision under which consumers may validly consent to get certain notices that are normally required to be in writing (for example bank account statements) in electronic form. If you want to include this kind of consent provision in electronic contracting with consumers, you should see your lawyer for details.

Who is Authorized to (Digitally) Sign What?

Generally speaking business software vendors like using clickwraps. They provide no opportunity for negotiation and have near zero transaction cost. However, in some cases, it may be better for the vendor to use an old-fashioned signed contract. That's because of a legal issue involving both clickwraps and browsewraps: whether employees have "legal authority" to bind their employers to these electronic contracts.

The legal question of the scope of employees' authority can be complicated. In US law we have doctrines of "actual authority" (the company expressly gave the employee power to sign), "apparent authority" (the company made it look as if the employee had the power to sign) and ratification (the company acted later on as if it was bound by the contract). A company that wants to walk away from a particular clickwrap agreement may well argue that the employee who "clicked" was not authorized to bind the company. Written contracts are much less likely to have this authority problem because the form of contract is normally sent to someone at a customer location that has authority or apparent authority to deal with the particular negotiation, license, or purchase (although it can happen on occasion that signers are unauthorized as well).

There is no magic solution to this issue. We do our best to deal with this authority issue with text such as this:

> As used in this Agreement, the terms "you" or "your" will include the company or other entity with which you are employed or otherwise affiliated, to the extent that you are acting on its behalf. You represent that you are 18 years old or older and are authorized by your company or other entity to enter into this Agreement.

However, there is no guarantee that the person who clicks really has legal authority to bind anyone. The quoted language regarding being "18 years old or older" deals with the legal reality that minors have the legal right to back out of (or "void") any contract that they make. This is true even if the customer claimed falsely to be 18 or older.

Are Browsewraps Enforceable?

The enforceability of browsewraps is a bit more uncertain. Browsewraps by definition are not signed digitally or in any other way. They have nonetheless been enforced in some key legal cases, but it is not clear that they work all the time—or that all of the clauses in them will be enforceable.

Let's begin with an important situation where browsewraps have been effective.

Protecting Web Site Data

This issue of enforcing browsewrap has been addressed in just a few court cases. Two that are worth noting are *Ticketmaster Corp. v. Tickets.com, Inc.* (decided in 2003) and *Register.com, Inc. v. Verio, Inc.* (also in 2003). Both of these cases involved "spidering" to collect data on the Web, and in each case the target Web site relied on a browsewrap for legal protection.

Many Web businesses are based in large part on data and databases. When that data is merely factual or public, it has no copyright protection under US law. (The gap in copyright protection is explained in Chapter 2.) For that reason, there is a temptation for other businesses to use automated "spiders" (also called "bots" or "scrapers") to take that data. So, is systematically downloading a Web site's factual data an illegal rip-off or just good business? It turns out that protecting non-copyrighted data depends on enforcing browsewraps electronic agreements.

Ticketmaster's Web site listed sports and entertainment events for which it was selling tickets. The site included times and prices. Ticket.com used a spider program to extract this data from Ticketmaster's Web site; the data then went on Ticket.com Web site. Ticketmaster site's terms of use stated that of the information on the Web site was for the "personal use" of the user only and not to be used for commercial purposes—a common provision. The court ruled that the terms of use were an enforceable contract that could be enforced to place the data off-limits to Ticket.com.

Register.com provided domain name registration services. It maintained an online "WHOIS" database, which allowed users to identify the holders of Internet domain names. Verio provided Web-hosting services. Verio deployed a spider to download the daily updates to the WHOIS database from the Register.com site. Verio used this information to solicit new domain owners via e-mail, telephone, and direct mail to purchase its hosting services. Register.com had programmed its Web site so that each data record retrieved included a prominent notice that stated that all solicitations using the data, via e-mail, direct mail, or telephone, were prohibited. The court ruled that the notice was enforceable as a contract; and the court ordered Verio to stop its downloading.

These cases appear to mean that companies can offer uncopyrighted factual information to the public and have a remedy in court for commercial use by other companies—at least when those companies are engaging in systematic downloading. In this way, uncopyrighted data can get protection in the online world—using a contract law theory—that it could not have had in the physical world. This is an example of using a well written electronic agreement to achieve some key business protection.

Other Aspects of Browsewrap Enforceability

Here are some other aspects of browsewrap enforcement:

- **Limits Unclear**—The cases stand for the proposition that reasonable provisions in browsewrap will be enforced in some circumstances; however the limits of this protection—and even to what degree other courts will follow these precedents—is not yet clear. This is an area of the law that is still developing.

- **Hard to Find Terms**—Sometimes you see sites where the link to the terms of use is gray and in tiny type—so that it is difficult to see if you are not looking hard. Companies that use such "hard to find" formats run a risk that a court of law will find that the terms are not binding.

- **Occasional Spidering**—The cases reviewed above address situations of repeated and comprehensive spidering of a single site. What about companies, such as search engines, that gather information across the Web from thousands or millions of sites? Is it possible that their spiders are electronically accepting the terms of use of each site that they hit? There is not much case law on search engines, but the cases so far say that search engine spidering is "fair use" under copyright law and apparently cannot be forbidden or affected in this contractual way. (If a party does not want its Web site spidered by the search engines, there are simple *electronic* techniques to block search engine spiders. See, for example, the discussion in "Webmaster Help" on *google.com*.)

PRODUCT CLICKWRAP AGREEMENTS

Let's turn to the provisions and clauses that you may want to put in a clickwrap EULA for the software products that your company may distribute in the United States.

The clickwraps that your company uses should be customized for your products, your markets and your business strategy. There is no such thing as a "one-size-fits-all" form. A good starting point is to look at other clickwrap forms from other companies in your market space and then think about how the forms you find might need to be changed to work for your product.

Acceptance of the EULA

The clickwrap EULA should have language, of the type quoted at the beginning of the clickwrap discussion above, under which the user expressly accepts the agreement by indicating assent—or, if not, can return the software for a full refund.

Limitations on Installation and Use of the Product

The clickwrap EULA needs a provision that states how the software may be installed and used. There are many possible variations; here are a few that you may choose to use:

- Use of the software might be limited to a single PC or workstation or other device. (It could also be a single iPod, PDA or mobile phone.) Or the provision could be made to permit several installations. For example, Apple sells "Family Pack" licenses that permit up to three Macintosh installations.

- There may be limitations as to the number of "instances" (that is copies running concurrently).

- Use may be permitted on a single server.

- Use might be permitted on an intranet only.

- With client–server architecture, there may be provisions allowing for use on the number of servers and workstation licenses purchased—as evidenced by certificates from the vendor and/or controlled by software or hardware "keys."

- With a software programming tool, there may be permission for the user to distribute the products that the user creates using the tool—sometime together with a "runtime" program supplied by the vendor.

Most clickwrap EULA agreements grant licenses that are permanent unless terminated for breach. However, there is no reason why licenses for time-limited terms cannot be granted.

Additional Restrictions

A clickwrap EULA form typically has restrictions. For example:

- If the software is for consumer use, you will likely want to limit the license grant to the user's "personal noncommercial use."

- If the software is for business use, you need to consider limiting the software to "internal business use only."

- You will normally want to include a prohibition of reverse engineering. This is an important provision because it extends protection against reverse engineering beyond the US copyright law defaults. (See the discussion of Copyright law and reverse engineering Chapter 3.)

- You should include a prohibition of use of the product to provide commercial services to third parties (sometimes referred to as "service bureau use").

- There is also commonly a restriction against leasing or lending the software to anyone else.

Specification of Program Ownership

The clickwrap normally says that the licensor and its suppliers or licensors retain ownership of the product including all intellectual property and grant a non-exclusive license only.

Restriction of Copying, Transfer and Use

The clickwrap usually provides that unauthorized copying is forbidden, often with the exception of a single backup copy. (Sometimes a "reasonable number" of back-up copies are allowed). Many EULAs allow the licensee to transfer the program so long as she uninstalls all her own copies. Some EULAs do not allow transfer. There are other alternatives. Windows Vista, for example, comes with a license that allows on the "first user of the software" to make a "one time transfer" after uninstalling the software. The usual goal here is to be reasonable with buyers.

Limited Warranties and Support

Many clickwrap EULAs have express warranties. These warranties generally promise that the software will "substantially conform" to the documentation.

Most clickwrap EULAs have a limited period of warranty. Commonly it is for 60 or 90 days. Typically these warranties give the vendor (not the customer) the choice of remedies—usually repair, replace, or refund.

Clickwrap EULAs generally disclaim implied warranties and consequential damages. However, the federal Magnuson-Moss Act, which is discussed below, puts some limitations on these disclaimers for consumer products and also affects the wording of warranty provisions in consumer EULAs. State consumer laws may also impose limitations.

Despite the limitations of warranties to 60 or 90 days, companies in mass markets often support products for years after they are shipped—fixing bugs and patching securities holes. For example, Microsoft supported Windows 98 for six years before bug fixing and security vulnerability patching was stopped. In some cases, companies sell extended maintenance and support services—often using clickwrap agreements to do so. Clickwrap EULAs sometimes contain clauses expressly reserving the right to discontinue support. The bottom line is that support and maintenance policies often diverge from EULA limitations—and that both need to be adjusted to customer expectations and the practices common to your market sector.

There may be other relief for unhappy customers. Many consumer software vendors will allow returns for full credit "no-questions-asked" within 30 days of purchase. Business products also often come with an express short-term "satisfaction" guarantee. Many software products come with "try-and-buy" EULA provisions under which the software is obtained for free but time-out (stops working) unless the user pays for the software license and obtains a software key to enable permanent operation. This try-and-buy form of marketing is ideal for electronic software distribution, because the cost to deliver each copy is so low.

Disclaimers and Liability Limitation

Your clickwrap EULA should disclaim implied warranties, including implied warranties of merchantability and fitness for a particular purpose. There is a rule that disclaimers of these implied warranties are ineffective unless "conspicuous" which is why you normally see the disclaimer in ALL CAPS. Under the law of many states and under the federal Magnuson-Moss Act discussed below, you may not be able to effectively disclaim these implied warranties for consumer products.

In addition, it is normal to exclude consequential damages and to set a cumulative "cap" for the vendor's money damage exposure; the limit is normally the license fee that the licensee pays. (These basic contract concepts are discussed in Chapter 8.)

No-Warranty EULAs

When vendors charge for software, they normally include a so-called "Limited Warranty" of the type discussed below. Where software is offered for free, vendors usually disclaim *all* warranties.

Why would you distribute software for free? There are many scenarios:

- You may want to drive adoption of other products. For example, makers of video cards and other electronic components often provide free software "drivers" for use of their hardware.

- You may want to introduce free low-featured version of your products in the hope that users will upgrade to a "premium" version. For example, Realnetworks licenses its software media player, RealPlayer, for free and offers a version with richer functionality, RealPlayer Plus, for a one-time license fee.

- You may want to establish a standard that helps drive adoption of for-pay software. A prime example of this strategy is Abode, which gives away millions of copies of Acrobat Reader in order to establish the PDF format and thereby create a market for Adobe Acrobat, which is used to create and edit PDF documents.

- You may want the no-charge software to be the "front-end" of a service, as, for example, the iTunes online music store which is promoted by Apple's giveaway of iTunes software.

Here is some language for use in the United States to all warranties.

DISCLAIMER OF WARRANTIES. TO THE MAXIMUM EXTENT PERMITTED BY APPLICABLE LAW, VENDOR AND ITS SUPPLIERS PROVIDE TO YOU THE SOFTWARE "AS IS" AND "WITH ALL FAULTS"; AND VENDOR AND ITS SUPPLIERS DISCLAIM ALL WARRANTIES, EXPRESS, IMPLIED OR STATUTORY, INCLUDING, BUT NOT LIMITED TO: TITLE, NON-INFRINGEMENT, MERCHANTABILITY, AND FITNESS FOR A PARTICULAR PURPOSE. THE ENTIRE RISK ARISING OUT OF USE OR PERFORMANCE OF THE SOFTWARE REMAINS WITH YOU. THE SOFTWARE COMES WITHOUT SUPPORT.

Note that the "entire risk" and "without support" language is suggested to help meet your company comply with California requirements for warranty disclaimers.

We cannot assure you, however, that you can successfully disclaim all state law implied warranties for consumer products with this language.

When we have "no warranty" software, we also have remedy limitations. Consequential damages are excluded. Some EULAs use a nominal sum, such as $5.00 as the "cap" of vendor liability. This is out of concern that a judge might find no damages at all to be legally insufficient. However, many lawyers use provisions that say the user can recover no damages at all under these contracts. (No one is sure that a nominal damage amount will make a difference.) There is no assurance the state law will enforce these limitations against consumers.

Export Control Clause

It is customary to have a clause in the EULA that requires the licensee to be responsible for compliance with United States and foreign import and export control laws. This clause refers to laws that restrict and control export of military technology and of "dual use" technology (technology that has both civil and military applications). Many products are affected by the export control on encryption technology, which is considered "dual use." There are also restrictions on exports to embargoed countries such as Cuba. Some countries, such as France, have technology import controls as well.

There is no legally required format or formulation of words for a shrinkwrap provision on obeying export controls. In fact there is no legal requirement that you include this kind of clause at all, although it is deemed prudent. We recommend including it in all forms, including those for consumer products. Generally speaking it is sufficient to write in your form agreement:

> *The software is subject to United States export laws and regulations. You agree to comply with all export laws and regulations that apply to the software.*

If your product is mass market software, I don't recommend elaborate export control clauses that have a list of excluded nations or of the applicable US regulations because they can become obsolete and no one seems to update them.

While writing this kind of clause is easy, export compliance itself may not be, depending on what you are selling and where you are selling it. Encryption functionality, including encryption in mass-market products, has special export rules. Compliance with US requirements is straightforward for most mass-market products, but less so for advanced technologies. Violation of these laws can be a criminal offense. The topic of export and import controls is discussed more fully in Chapter 24. Do not hesitate to contact counsel or an export control consultant if you need export control advice.

Licensing to the Federal Government

In the past, there was a need to include special language limiting license grants to the US federal government agencies and departments. Due to changes in federal and military procurement regulations, that special language is no longer required. Now federal government agencies, unless otherwise agreed, get essentially the same limited license rights as other licensees for software that is in commercial distribution and was not created at government expense. However, as a matter of caution, many EULAs include federal government licensing clauses of the type that are discussed in Chapter 12.

Choice of Law, Jurisdiction

Most clickwrap EULAs have a choice of law clause (selecting the law of a particular state) and a choice of jurisdiction (selecting the place for any litigation). Most often the law chosen is that of the licensor's home state, and the jurisdiction chosen is most often in or near of the headquarters location of the licensor. The courts have upheld these clauses in some cases, but there is a risk that the court will refuse to do so if the jurisdiction is inconvenient—particularly when the other party is a consumer.

Arbitration

Arbitration causes do have one important advantage for deep-pocket licensors—they are a potential means to stop class action litigation. (Class actions are a litigation process that joins large numbers of persons with similar claims into one law suit—and therefore multiply legal risk for licensors.) There is no class action process under arbitration rules.

Some EULAs have arbitration clauses—although most do not. These clauses may or may not be enforceable. As I noted above, some judges have refused to let consumers be forced into arbitration far from home. If the arbitration procedure is expensive to invoke (they often have substantial filing fees), the court may rule the requirement unfair and unenforceable.

Some arbitration clauses in consumer product EULAs have provisions designed to make them more acceptable to the courts and therefore more likely to be enforced. For example, some clauses permit the arbitration to be conducted by phone or online. Some clauses provide for lower arbitration fees to the consumer. Here is an example of such language:

> *Your arbitration fees and your share of arbitrator compensation shall be governed by the AAA Rules and, where appropriate, limited by the AAA Consumer Rules. If such costs are determined by the arbitrator to be excessive, Vendor will pay all arbitration fees and expenses. The arbitration may be conducted in person, through the submission of documents, by phone or online.*

"AAA Rules" and "AAA Consumer Rules" in this text refer to the Arbitration Rules and Consumer-Related Dispute procedures of the American Arbitration Association (AAA), a non-profit organization that offers arbitration and mediation services. The AAA Consumer Rules have provisions for lower fees (or in some cases no fees for the consumer) and expedited and simplified arbitration of consumer product and service claims. For more information, see your lawyer or the AAA Web site, www.adr.org.

Termination

Clickwrap EULAs typically permit the licensor to terminate for any licensee breach. In some cases they provide for automatic termination in case of the licensee's breach. Normally they provide that licensee must cease use of the product and destroy all copies upon termination.

Boilerplate Provisions

Clickwrap EULAs typically have boilerplate at the end such as clauses on waivers, amendment, assignment, and an "entire agreement" provision. To keep these agreements short, the boilerplate is often written in a "barebones" abbreviated fashion.

Other Provisions that You Might Consider

The list of provisions is not exhaustive—the possible variations are limited only by human imagination. Here are some other types of provisions that you *might* want to include in clickwraps for particular software and situations.

Distribution

There are many programs that allow licensees to use licensed programs to create software or media and to distribute the resulting product (sometimes with a "runtime" that is needed to make it work). A typical clause looks like this:

> *You may distribute programs that you create by use of the Software and you may include the Runtime in your programs without paying the Vendor royalties. However, you may not distribute any other portion of the Software. In addition, you cannot distribute any software-creation or software-authoring product based on the Software.*

If you do have a clause that permits distribution by the licensee, you should consider having the licensee indemnify you for any legal problems you suffer that are caused by the licensee's distribution activity. Here is a typical provision:

> *You agree to indemnify, hold harmless, and defend Licensor from and against any claims or lawsuits, including attorneys' fees, that arise or result from the use or distribution of your application.*

Keys and Anticircumvention

Some programs come with extra components that are "turned on" only if the user buys software keys for them. If so, the EULA will prohibit circumventing or defeating the key mechanism.

Privacy Related Provisions

If your software product monitors any aspect of the customer's use of your software, the EULA should disclose the monitoring and state that the user expressly consents to it. You will be in a much better position to defend your accessing this data if the EULA mentions it expressly. (This may not be enough to bring you into compliance with privacy laws in the EU, in Canada, and in other nations. See also Chapter 18 of this book which is about digital privacy matters.)

Assent to DRM

Many media (sound and video) programs have "digital rights management" (or "DRM") to prevent unauthorized copying of content. It is good practice to obtain the user's consent to use of DRM measures. That is because some DRM protections may involve monitoring the user anonymously (and therefore raise privacy issues) and because some may impose material restriction on use.

No Benchmarking

Sometimes a company that has high performance product will be concerned that its competitors will use its products for benchmarking. Benchmarking means running a series of tests ostensibly designed to assess relative performance of two or more competing products. Many companies that run benchmarks do them in ways that favor the features of their own products, and use the result in advertising. For that reason, companies want to discourage this use by all licensees. In an attempt to stop such tests, vendors put antibenchmarking provisions in their agreements. For example:

> *The Licensee agrees not to use the software to run benchmark tests or to disclose the results of any benchmark test to any third party.*

Publicity Provisions

Some business software companies have a clause in their clickwrap EULAs like this:

> *You agree to permit Licensor to use Your name and trademarks to identify You as a Licensor customer on Licensor' Web site(s), in Licensor marketing materials and in other sales and marketing activities.*

Even if you use this kind of provision, you may wish to contact your customers before using their name on any marketing materials, because they may not be happy about your unexpected use of their name and trademarks.

User Feedback

Sometimes clickwrap EULAs will have provisions under which their licensee grants back to the licensor a license to the vendor. Most commonly these are rights to "feedback" that the licensee may provide. Here is a typical clause:

> *Feedback. You may provide feedback to Vendor. If you do so, Licensor, without compensation to you, may use, copy, commercialize or exploit your feedback in any manner and for any purpose.*

Clickwraps Are Not Limited to Product EULAs

Clickwrap EULAs for software products are not the only way to use this form of contracting. It also works for Web services. For example:

- Most SaaS vendors use clickwraps to sign up service customers. (See the discussion of SaaS agreements in Chapter 13.)

- When Google sells online advertisements, it uses a clickwrap to obtain assent by the ad buyers.

- When Amazon pays referral fees to other sites that link to Amazon, it uses a shrinkwrap form to manage its legal relationship to the referring Web site owner.

Your attorney can help you craft the right form of services clickwrap agreement for your needs.

The Magnuson-Moss Act and Consumer Product Warranties

The warranty-related language that you will use for consumer product clickwraps in the United States are affected by a federal statute called the Magnuson-Moss Act, which Congress passed in 1975. (We will call it the "MMA.") The MMA was passed to help protect consumers from deceptive warranties. It regulates aspects of the wording of consumer product warranties—including software and other digital products. If your digital business is in a consumer field, you should know about it.

Here is a short overview of how the MMA affects product warranties in EULAs. Compliance with MMA is relatively easy.

- The MMA applies to warranties for "consumer products" costing more than $15 where a supplier uses a written warranty. "Consumer products" means goods normally used for personal, family, or household purposes. The MMA does *not* apply to warranties on services or to business products. Sometimes you may see form contracts for service offerings or business products that use the special "magic words" of the MMA discussed below, but this is not legally required.

- The MMA does not require that you provide any warranty with consumer goods—the MMA lets you supply your digital goods "AS IS." Note that state law may have different requirements.

- If you do provide a written warranty for a consumer product, the MMA says that you must label the warranty as either a "Full Warranty" or "Limited Warranty." A "Full Warranty" is very rare, because it requires a long period of coverage and requires that product service be supplied to anyone who owns a product—not just the original purchaser. So you will be giving a "Limited Warranty" and your shrinkwrap form will say so—using the "Limited Warranty" terminology.

- If you do give a Limited Warranty for your consumer product, then the MMA says that you cannot disclaim the UCC (Uniform Commercial Code) implied warranties of merchantability and fitness for a particular purpose for the duration of the Limited Warranty. (These implied warranties and the UCC are discussed in Chapter 8.)

Due to these requirements, consumer product shrinkwraps have language like this:

Any applicable implied warranties, including warranties of merchantability and fitness for a particular purpose, are limited in duration to the duration of this warranty.

Or sometimes:

We disclaim, to the fullest extent permitted by law, all warranties of any kind, either express or implied, including, but not limited to, warranties of merchantability, fitness for a particular purpose, or non-infringement of rights.

In this text, the words "to the fullest extent permitted by law" are added because the MMA or state law may not permit full waiver of these implied warranties.

Federal Trade Commission (FTC) regulations have further requirements regarding Limited Warranties for consumer products that are mandatory in the United States. In effect the FTC has prescribed "magic words" that you need to use with consumer products:

- You must include the following text:

This warranty gives you specific legal rights, and you may also have other rights which vary from state to state.

- If you limit the duration of implied warranties (which everyone does), you must include the following text:

Some states do not allow limitations on how long an implied warranty lasts, so the above limitation may not apply to you.

- If you exclude incidental or consequential damages (which everyone does), you must include the following text:

Some states do not allow the exclusion or limitation of incidental or consequential damages, so the above limitation or exclusion may not apply to you.

The bottom line is that compliance with MMA requirements is actually pretty simple and formulaic. If you review the consumer shrinkwrap form in the Appendix to the book, you will see forms reflecting these federal requirements.

Foreign Customs, Language, and Law

We live in a global economy. If your company has products, services and Web sites that are directed to non-US markets, it may have to adapt and localize all contracts—including your clickwraps and your business' online terms of use.

Most foreign customers expect to see contract documents in their own language. In some nations, it is illegal to use form consumer agreements that are not in the local language. Local laws, including privacy and consumer protection laws, may require different provisions than are common in the United States. Your lawyer can help you find foreign legal counsel in major foreign markets to help you comply with local law and meet local customer expectations regarding form agreements.

Terms of Use for Web Sites and Online Applications

17

Even if you don't spend the time to read this, you accept you have notice of it and are bound by it.

—from the Terms of Use for Wikipedia

IN THIS CHAPTER

This chapter is about terms of use for your Web site and for online applications. These are the form agreements that you find all over the Web linked to the home page. These electronic documents are designed to set the rules between your company and your online users. Much of their content is for your company's protection.

This is not a long chapter. That is largely because much of the important information about this subject is elsewhere in this book. Before getting into the substance of this chapter, let us list for you the relevant background and where to find it.

- **Enforceability**—The legal foundation for these Web form agreements is covered in Chapter 16.

- **Legal Basics**—Terms of use include basic legal clauses—shorter versions of those discussed in Chapter 8, which is our review of digital contract basics.

- **User-Supplied Content**—User-supplied content is discussed in Chapter 20, our chapter on clearing content.

- **Notice and Take-Down Rules**—Web sites that have any user-supplied content also will need protection from the risk that users may upload infringing content. That means they absolutely should take advantage of the "notice-and-take-down rules" under the Digital Millennium Copyright Act (or DMCA). This important US copyright protection—and how to get it—is explained in Chapter 3.

- **Privacy Statements**—Web sites need accurate and comprehensive privacy statements. These are covered in Chapter 18, the privacy chapter.

So what's left? This answer is the terms of use document itself. In the Appendix to this book, you will find a sample form of Terms of Use for a Web site (Form 17-1). You can use this form as a starting point for terms for your own Web site. There are many tens of thousands of other examples of these terms of use (from very good and to very bad) to be found on the Web. If you are writing terms of use for your site, you may want to start by looking at terms of use for other sites that are like yours—as well as looking at the form included here.

ABOUT WEB TERMS OF USE

Many Web sites are about the "three C's"—content, community, and commerce:

- *Content* means all the materials and information that the user can access through the site. You should be thinking about the particular type of content that your site will offer, what forms of use you want to permit, and what restrictions you should place on content use.

- *Community* means the ways that users can use the site to interact with one another and the world. This includes posted testimonials, blogs, and chat spaces. It also includes sites that feature user-supplied videos or Web pages.

- *Commerce* means the goods or services (free or for a fee) that your site may provide. If you provide commerce opportunities on your site, your site terms of use—or separate clickwrap agreements—will set the terms for licensing or sale.

Terms of use documentation addresses each of these areas in ways discussed below. Terms of use are both business and legal documents. Every business changes over time, but online business changes faster than any other businesses.

For this reason, you should give your terms of use and other Web site legal documentation a legal and business review periodically.

When Should Your Terms Be a Clickwrap, a Browsewrap, or Both?

Terms of use can be a clickwrap (the user expressly gives consent), a browsewrap (user consent is presumed), or a combination of the two.

- Unregistered users of a Web site normally have no way to "accept" the terms of use. For them, the terms of use have to function as a browsewrap.

- Sites that feature user registration usually have a button to click to make registration effective. That button usually sits on the Web page next a link to the terms of use together with a message such as: "*I have read and agree to the terms of use.*" When the user clicks and registers, the terms of use become a digitally signed clickwrap.

- For some sites, the user may have a choice of proving assent or not. Or your site could use a combination—that is, you might require click-acceptance as a condition for use of selected online services.

We recommend that your company uses a clickwrap model (and thus captures express user consent) in the following situations:

- Whenever there is any money involved—as for example with a paid online service or a paid-for download.

- Whenever you obtain and intend to use personally identifying data. This rule is because of privacy concerns.

You may also consider getting click acceptance from Web site users that register anonymously (by giving a username and password but without identifying information). From a lawyer's perspective, it never hurts to get assent.

Acceptance of the Terms of Use and of Changes
As discussed above, Web site terms should begin with a statement that use of the site constitutes acceptance of the terms of use.

Registration Rules
For business-oriented sites, provisions in the terms of use on registration are straightforward. The user should be required to provide accurate information

and select a username and password. There should also be a requirement that address, e-mail and other contact information be kept accurate and up-to-date.

For consumer sites, particularly those that are youth oriented, there may be other issues. For example, there may be a requirement that the username that an end-user selects and uses in a blog on your site not be a famous trademark, a celebrity's name or nickname, or an obscenity.

Checkback Clauses

Most terms of use have what we call "checkback clauses." These provisions say the Web site terms may change, that any change will bind the user, and that the user must check the terms of use from time to time. Here, for example, is language from AOL.com's terms of use:

> We may change these Terms of Use at any time. You can review the most current version of these terms by clicking on the "Terms of Use" hypertext link located at the bottom of our Web pages. You are responsible for checking these terms periodically for changes. If you continue to use AOL.COM after we post changes to these Terms of Use, you are signifying your acceptance of the new terms.

It is a fair assumption that the number of users that will be "checking these terms periodically for changes" is zero. There is an (as yet unanswered) question as to whether these clauses will work and bind users to changes. Obviously, giving actual notice of changes is better. If users have affirmatively agreed to be bound by changes (by clicking a clickwrap), that is also better. Our recommendation is that any company that wants to change its Web terms of use in any significant way should contact its registered users by e-mail (at their registered e-mail address) telling them of the change.

There are limits to what you can change by altering the terms of use. It is very doubtful, for example, that a Web business can make retroactive changes in past transactions. It is also unlikely that you can change terms of use in order to give your site permission to use personal information from your users in ways that are inconsistent with the restrictions in effect when the information was received.

Even if there are doubts about how far "checkback clauses" can take you, you should definitely include them in your Web site's terms of use. That is because they might work some of the time or all of the time and they certainly do no harm.

Termination of User Registration

Terms of use often provide that site owner reserves the right to cancel the registration of any user at any time for any reason. Some sites have a similar provision for any user that violates the terms of use on any Web site policy, such as policies for chat rooms and Weblogs.

Minimum Age

As discussed in Chapter 18 (the chapter on digital privacy), there is a strict federal law, with criminal penalties for violation, that requires verifiable parental permission for a site to obtain and use identifying information from any child under 13 years old. For this reason, many sites' terms of use do not permit registration or use by any persons under 13.

Many sites have terms of use that have provisions that permit registration and use only by persons 18 and older—this is the age that persons are generally able to make binding contracts under state law in the United States.

These provisions do not stop minors from using Web sites. But they can help the Web site owner prove that it did not invite use by minors.

Acceptance of the Privacy Policy

As discussed in some detail in Chapter 18, every Web site that obtains any personal information must have a privacy policy that discloses the site owner's use of personal information. The terms of use should state that the user agrees to and accepts the privacy policy.

Permitted Use

The terms of use always state what is the permitted use of the Web site and what is not allowed. This listing will vary depending on the site's functionality and content:

- The terms of many consumer sites limit use of a site to "personal noncommercial use."

- Business sites may permit use by corporations for "internal noncommercial use."

- Sometimes terms of use have rules that permit printing of the Web pages for personal use. Otherwise copying and distribution of content is normally not permitted.

- On the other hand, if you have a site that is about open source software or public domain content, your site use rules might encourage persons to take and exploit much of what you have on offer.

Where there is downloadable software or Web site plug-ins on the site, your terms of use should say that the EULAs (End User License Agreements) that accompany the downloaded programs will apply.

Acceptance of Behavior Rules

When persons interact on the Internet, there can be problems involving the same behaviors (sexual invitations, aggression, and so forth) that get people in trouble in the real world. For that reason, Web sites that facilitate chat and blogs or other user interaction have rules of conduct.

If your Web site permits user-supplied content, you are likely to worry that users will give you "bad" content that will get you sued. Bad content might include copyrighted or trademarked materials used without permission (and therefore infringing), content that is obscene, or content that is defamatory or indecent. Rules of conduct will prohibit these as well. If your site has such rules, the terms of use should say that the user agrees to comply with them.

Indemnification by the User

In addition to forbidding bad conduct, terms of use will often include user indemnification provisions. Here is typical language:

> *Upon our request, you agree to defend, indemnify, and hold harmless us and our parent and other affiliated companies, and our respective employees, contractors, officers, directors, and agents from all liabilities, claims, and expenses, including attorney's fees that arise from your use or misuse of the Site, violation of these Terms of Use, or the Rules of Conduct on our site. We reserve the right, at our own expense, to assume the exclusive defense and control of any matter otherwise subject to indemnification by you, in which event you will cooperate with us in asserting any available defenses.*

This means that if something that the user does causes the site owner a loss or leads to a law suit, the site owner can sue the user and recover all losses, expenses, and fees.

Of course, it would be rare that a Web site owner would actually sue a user for indemnity. Many users don't have the financial resources to provide indemnification in any case. But you should include it because it might be needed and it certainly cannot hurt.

License to User-Submitted Content

Many Web sites include a terms of use provision that the user grants the site owner a license to user-supplied content. The principles of getting electronic permission from users are discussed in Chapter 20.

Liability Limitation

Key provisions of terms of use are their liability limitation clauses. These include:

- Exclusion of all warranties. Most sites present any content and material on the Web site "AS IS" and disclaim all warranties. Many sites have disclaimers of any warranty that their content is accurate.

- Consequential damages exclusion.

Where the site is directed to consumers, this language should follow the rules on writing these clauses that we discussed in Chapter 16 with regard to "magic words" that the law requires in consumer warranty disclaimers. (For example, use of phrases such as "APPLICABLE LAW MAY NOT ALLOW THE LIMITATION OR EXCLUSION OF LIABILITY FOR INCIDENTAL OR CONSEQUENTIAL DAMAGES, SO THE ABOVE LIMITATION OR EXCLUSION MAY NOT APPLY TO YOU.")

No Spidering or Bots

Many Web sites have content that is vulnerable to third party automated harvesting of their content by "spiders." Many terms of use have no-spidering-permitted provisions. Here is a typical clause, with some common synonyms for spiders:

You agree not to use or attempt to use any "spider," "robot," "bot," "scraper," "data miner," or any other program, device, algorithm, process, or methodology to access, acquire, copy, or monitor this Site or pages, data or content found on this Site.

As noted in Chapter 16, some Web site owners have had some success in using term of use provisions in court to stop other companies from systematically spidering information off their site.

No Framing

Another technology that terms of use on a Web site may forbid is "framing." When this technology is used, one Web site (the "framing site") provides the user a Web page that has a "frame" (like a picture frame) or a banner across the top of the site. In the frame—or under the banner—the Web page displays the content of another site (the "framed site"). Sometimes, the user may be confused as to the source of the content—although most framing sites make it clear that framing is going on. (There is a discussion of copyright aspects of framing in Chapter 3.)

While Google often frames other sites (by use of its cached page service), it does not want anyone else to frame Google. So Google uses this language in its terms of use:

You may not in any way frame or cache the Results produced by Google.

No Deep Linking

"Deep linking" means displaying Web site links that, when clicked, brings the user directly to a specific page within another Web site, as opposed to the home page.

For example, www.copyright.gov/forms/formtxi.pdf is a "deep link" that will take you directly to Form TX on the US Copyright Office Web site (the form that we most often use for copyright registration of software works). The home page of the copyright office is www.copyright.gov.

The site owners of many consumer-oriented e-commerce Web sites do not like deep linking into their site. This is because deep links take away opportunities to deliver promotions and advertisements that are displayed on the home pages that the user would have to view before getting to the deep-linked page.

Say, for example, I want shop at Ticketmaster.com for tickets to see the Dave Matthews Band in Boston. I can start at the Ticketmaster home page (where I see a banner ad for Nissan) and then I need to see two more pages of Ticketmaster content and promotions before I get to page where I can actually start ordering tickets. A deep link from a Dave Matthews fan site might take me directly to the ordering page—and that would prevent Ticketmaster from getting paid for that banner ad display (known as an "ad impression") or showing me the other promotional materials.

There was one well-publicized 1997 case in which Ticketmaster sued Microsoft because Microsoft's Sidewalk Web site deep linked (just as in my example) to pages on Ticketmaster.com to purchase tickets to a particular concert event. The case was settled and reportedly Microsoft stopped its deep link practice. More recently, in 2006, there was a case in India in which a New Delhi court enjoined an Indian search engine from deep linking into a job site.

If you want to discourage deep linking into your Web site, you should include a prohibition on deep linking in your site's terms of use. It is unclear whether the courts will enforce these restrictions, but they do no harm.

You can include automated instructions in Web pages that will stop search engines from indexing particular pages of your Web site or the Web site as a whole. Your supplier of Web development services can help you accomplish this.

No Responsibility for Links and Linked Content

Most site terms of use make it clear that any hyperlinks to third-party Web sites take the user away from the site. Terms of use usually add that the site owner has no responsibility for the contents or functionality of third party sites.

Intellectual Property (IP) Ownership

The terms of use should make it clear that content on the site belongs to the site owner and its content suppliers and should also state that no use of the content or the site is permitted except as expressly permitted in the terms of use.

Electronic Communications

Some terms of use include a provision stating that the user consents to receiving notice by e-mail. This type of provision typically says that notice may be given by an e-mail sent to the e-mail address that the user provides in registering—as updated in the user's account functionality on the site.

Patent and Other IP Grantbacks

While it is not common, some sites have clauses that purport to obtain licenses from users under the user's patents rights. For example, Salesforce.com has a service called "AppExchange" that allows users to build and upload software applications that interact with Saleforce.com's online software-as-a-service platform. In the current (as of late 2007) online terms of use for AppExchange, which apply if you use the AppExchange service for your application, we find this language:

> To the extent you possess now or in the future any copyright, patent or other intellectual property rights that may be infringed by the operation of the AppExchange itself (excluding the content of individual applications), you hereby grant to Salesforce.com a nonexclusive, worldwide, irrevocable, perpetual, transferable (only to a successor of Salesforce.com by way of merger, acquisition or corporate reorganization), fully paid-up, royalty-free license to all such rights with respect to the operation of the AppExchange as it may be modified from time to time.

This means that if you put any application on AppExchange under this agreement, you grant a broad permanent IP license to Salesforce.com. Under this license, if any aspect of the AppExchange service now or in the future uses your IP, you license your relevant IP rights permanently and for free to Salesforce.com for use with the service.

It is a matter of judgment whether to include this type of clause in your terms of use. Many users might consider it overly aggressive. We also do not yet know whether the courts will enforce this kind of provision.

Public Companies

Public company Web sites have information that might affect decisions of investors to purchase or sell shares of stock in their company. For this reason, some include securities law-related disclaimers in their terms of Use. For example:

> *Forward-Looking Statements.* This Web site contains forward-looking statements that relate to future events or the Company's future financial performance. Such forward-looking statements involve risks and uncertainties that could cause actual results to differ materially from those predicted by such forward-looking statements. They also include other risks detailed from time to time in The Company's publicly filed documents, including its most recent Annual Report on Form 10-K and subsequent Reports on Form 10-Q and 8-K, all of which are available on this Web site and at www.sec.gov. The Company undertakes no obligation to publicly update any forward-looking statement, whether as a result of new information, future events, or otherwise.

Other Common Clauses

Terms of use normally also include some clauses that we discussed in Chapter 16 with regard to clickwraps:

- Choice of law and jurisdiction. Some Web sites have arbitration clauses; the majority do not.

- Other "boilerplate" provisions.

To see typical language on these points, please see the sample terms of use in the Appendix to this book.

Regulated Businesses

There are special rules and regulations that apply to many regulated industries and businesses that may profoundly affect what online terms of use will say. For example, there are banking laws that will affect the terms of use on banking sites. Securities law will affect the terms of use for broker's Webs sites. Even law firms are subject to regulations in most states that affect the contents of their Web sites. If your business is in a regulated field, be sure to obtain legal advice about rules affecting the electronic relationship that you have with customers.

Web Site Proprietary Notice

Web sites also often have proprietary notices that include a list of the site owner's trademarks, a copyright notice covering the site contents and, of applicable patents that apply. You are not required by law to include such a notice, but it helps when suing infringers and therefore these proprietary notices are recommended.

Other Applications

The Web is not the only Internet service that needs terms of use. For example:

- Massively Multiplayer Online Games (or "MMOs") are a form of online role-playing game (RPG) in which tens of thousands of players interact in a virtual world. MMORPGs all have terms of use that touch most of the bases of the terms of use forms discussed above, but also add rules that are designed to control behavior and set standards in the online world of the game. (See the discussion of MMOs and MMORPGs in Chapter 22.)

- Internet communication applications such as Apple's iChat and AOL Instant Messenger have terms of use not dissimilar to those for Web communication sites.

- Some electronic services are marketed through the Web, but delivered in other media. These include services for mobile applications that run on smartphones, mobile PDAs, or Blackberry devices.

In each case, drafting the appropriate terms of use requires an understanding of the application, its technology, its use, its users, its potential abuse, and the IP that it uses or delivers. With these in mind, your business (with the help of skilled legal counsel) can craft the right terms of use for any digital service.

More Web Site Forms

We have included in the Appendix a form of Content Guidelines for user-submitted content (Form 17-1) and rules for Weblogs (or "blogs") (Form 17-2). These documents are extensions of the terms of use and provide additional rules. You should read these documents together with the discussion of user-created content in Chapter 20. Privacy policies for Web sites, another important subject, are discussed in Chapter 18.

Privacy and Use of Personal Data

18

Privacy is not something that I'm merely entitled to, it's an absolute prerequisite.

—Marlon Brando

An American has no sense of privacy. He does not know what it means. There is no such thing in the country.

—George Bernard Shaw

Companies around the world hold huge volumes of personal data, meaning data associated with a particular person. Companies collect personal data, process it, analyze it, and transmit it in the course of their every day business. Many IT and Internet businesses are based on creating, operating, and maintaining software applications to process such data.

Data processing technology and the creation of mass databases inevitably erode privacy. In January 1999, then Sun Microsystems CEO Scott McNealy famously told news reporters in Silicon Valley: "You have zero privacy anyway! Get over it!"

In the United States, many aspects of data collection and processing by business are unregulated. However, there are some laws that do importantly affect information technology companies that collect or process personal data. A number of companies have been stung by regulators and slammed in the press for privacy violations. The federal law involving personal data gathered from children from the Internet is quite tough. A number of foreign nations also have comprehensive data laws that cover all of their citizens. As a result digital business needs to be aware of privacy issues and needs well-conceived privacy policies. (There is, of course, a huge concern about broad US government data collection and databases, but that is a topic beyond the scope of this book.)

IN THIS CHAPTER

Here are the topics covered in this chapter:

- What are legal rules on personal data and privacy?

- How can you stay out of the trouble but still exploit the personalization potential of the Internet?

- How can you write an Internet privacy policy that actually works for your business? How can you stay in compliance with your own policy?

- What are the rules that apply if your business suffers a breach of security that compromises personal data? How do data security breach notification laws work?

- What is the Children's Online Privacy Protection Act (COPPA) and why does it impact your online business—even if your site is not oriented to children?

- What are US legal rules on spam?

- How about the rest of the world? What are the privacy rules outside the United States?

This chapter has a business focus and does not cover (except in passing) state and federal criminal laws on intrusion to electronic data systems and data theft. If your company is the victim of a data crime, you may want to consult legal counsel and law enforcement authorities.

Personal Data and IT

There are different kinds of electronic data relating to persons that we will discuss in this chapter:

Individual Information. This data is associated with a particular person, such as a person's name, address, phone, e-mail address, social security number, credit card numbers, race, gender, health, finances, sexual orientation, interests, and so forth. This data is found in:

- **Direct Marketing Databases**—By way of example, InfoUSA, a large public company, has a marketing database that covers 210 million consumers.

Responsys.com, a major e-marketing mailer, reportedly sends out more than 200 million e-mails a month. Your company may buy or use data or data services of this kind.

- **Corporate Databases**—These are the customer information databases held by banks, telecommunication companies, insurance companies, retailers, and so forth. Smaller companies have smaller versions.

- **Web Site Registration Data**—This is the information that Web users give voluntarily, often for a free service or as part of a commercial transaction.

<u>Anonymous Individualized Data</u>. This is a new data type of the Internet Age. When your company collects anonymous individualized data via the Web, your company does not know who the user is or where he or she lives, but your site develops a profile of the user by gathering a profile or following her "clickstream." Although this is a less intrusive form of data collection, as you will see from the examples discussed below, it has attracted legal scrutiny.

USE OF THE INTERNET TO OBTAIN PERSONAL DATA

Most businesses on the Internet that deal with individuals need to obtain user data. Here are some of the ways that Web sites can obtain personal data:

- Require customer registration as a condition of using the site. Users must register, for example, to use the *New York Times* site on the Web.

- Obtain user information in online transactions involving sales of goods or services.

- Give additional benefits for registration. Users don't have to register to use Yahoo!. If they want to use Yahoo! Calendar, however, then they need to register.

- Providing notifications on request. To get e-mail notices of sales at bloomingdales.com, users need to register.

- Offer online sweepstakes to obtain registration information.

What can site owners do with personal data that they gather on the Internet? Here are some examples:

- Use customer profiling to customize content and target advertisements.

- Send users additional electronic communications, such as newsletters and "sale" announcements by e-mail or other messaging.

- Build the company's customer and marketing database for other forms of marketing, such as direct mail or telemarketing.

- Share the data with strategic partners.

Web Profiling and Cookies

A Web technology that facilitates consumer tracking possible is the "cookie." A cookie is a string of text data that a Web server puts on a PCs hard disk to identify the computer and record information about the user. Cookies can be used to track use of Web sites either by known users or by anonymous users.

Many cookies are used to record the user's preferences when using a particular site. However, some cookies are placed by advertising servers that are not tied to any particular Web site. The Web ad delivery company DoubleClick pioneered the use of "cookies" as a means of tracking everyone who sees banner ads on the "DoubleClick network," which is DoubleClick's system of Web servers. DoubleClick reports to advertisers how may times a user sees a particular banner ad for a particular advertiser, regardless of which sites on the DoubleClick network the user saw it. It can track all the sites on the DoubleClick network that a user visits. (At the time this is written, Google has signed an agreement to purchase DoubleClick.

This kind of tracking system can learn a lot about the user of a particular PC, even if the identity of the user is not known. A company with this technology would record, for example, if the user accesses sites on its network involving pop music or mutual funds or cancer. Compiling of data about users' tracking their click behavior is known as "online profiling."

From the advertiser's viewpoint, the effectiveness of cookies has been impaired to some extent in the last few years by consumer use of some anti-spyware programs that delete many cookies.

Other Identifiers

Cookies are not the only forms of identifiers. Many computer programs generate (or obtain over the Web) unique identification numbers (or combinations of numbers and letters) so that remote server computers can identify them uniquely. These identifiers can be used to identify computers for marketing or other purposes.

One well-known example is Microsoft's Windows Genuine Advantage (WGA) program that validates a copy of Windows XP on a PC as authorized by Microsoft. After examination of the PC, WGA installs an anonymous identifier on the PC that indicates that the PC has passed or failed validation. If the PC fails validation, WGA will display warnings to the user and will prevent the PC from receiving any Microsoft update except those that Microsoft labels critical.

OVERVIEW OF US LAW ON PERSONAL DATA

In some countries, including all the states of the European Union (EU) and Canada, there are comprehensive national privacy protection statutes that place important limits on the gathering and use of personal data, but that is not the case in the United States. There is no comprehensive data privacy act here.

As a broad generalization, under current law (which could change), your company will be in compliance with US law regarding privacy and the Internet if:

- You provide users with the fair disclosure regarding Web and Internet collection of personal data as discussed in this chapter.

- You are honest with Internet users, have an adequate privacy policy, and actually do what you promise in your privacy policy.

- You follow the special—and very strict—laws relating to dealing over the Internet and online services with children under 13. This is the Children's Online Privacy Protection Act or COPPA. Note (as is explained later in this chapter) COPPA can apply to you, even if your Web site does not target children.

- You follow, if applicable, special rules regarding some regulated industries, particularly banking and health care.

- You follow applicable state laws that may apply.

Subject to those qualifications, and based on current law, you generally have freedom as to how you can collect, buy, sell, use, and exploit personal data. You should watch for legal developments, however, because additional legislation on the state or federal level is possible.

The FTC Act and Little FTC Acts

The is no general law that controls personal data, but nonetheless authorities such as the Federal Trade Commission (FTC) or state attorneys general bring legal enforcement actions regarding privacy. How do they do so? For the FTC, the answer is a federal law called the Federal Trade Commission Act that outlaws "unfair and deceptive practices" in commerce. Most states have similar laws often called "consumer protection acts" or, more informally, "little FTC Acts." The state attorneys general enforce these state versions and in some states private citizens may sue as well. These acts are important weapon in privacy cases, although other legal theories such as fraud may apply as well.

The Geocities Case
The first federal enforcement action involving Internet data privacy was the FTCs 1998 case against Geocities. (Geocities is now owned and operated by Yahoo!).

Geocities was an "online community" that provided free Web site hosting to nearly two million member users. Geocities, privacy policy promised members of Geocities that personal information would be used only to provide members the specific advertising offers and products or services they requested and that their personal information "would not be released to anyone without the member's permission."

However, according to the FTCs Bureau of Consumer Protection: "Geocities misled its customers, both children and adults, by not telling the truth about how it was using their personal information." The FTC charged that Geocities engaged in "disclosure of personal identifying information of children and adults to third-party marketers."

Geocities denied liability but, under great public pressure, entered into a consent order with the FTC in which it agreed never to engage in such practices.

Other Examples
Here are some further examples of the problem that the legal system and public pressure can create for Internet business:

RealNetworks
In October 1999, RealNetworks, the streaming Web media company, was hit with a class action lawsuit alleging the company was violating the privacy of millions of online pop music fans. RealNetworks had assigned unique identi-fication numbers to users of its RealJukebox music player without informing

its users. The software would have allowed RealNetworks to track its users' listening habits without their knowledge—RealNetworks would know if the user were playing Brittany Spears or Nine Inch Nails—and they could use that information to target content or ads. When the suit was filed, RealNetworks disabled the feature.

It would have been permissible under US law for RealJukebox to use functionality to track user listening, but RealNetworks should have disclosed clearly that its software would do so during installation. It would also have been smart for RealNetworks to allow users the option to opt out. RealNetworks' legal mistake was failing to disclose, and its practical mistake was failing to allow consumer choice.

AOL Smart Downloads

In June 2000, a consumer in New York filed a class action lawsuit alleging that AOL subsidiary Netscape's SmartDownload product sent information about user downloads (including third-party products) back to Netscape. AOL denounced the lawsuit as "without merit," but also announced that Netscape will remove the feature from SmartDownload in future versions.

DoubleClick Data Merger

In February 2000, DoubleClick came under fire for plans to merge its anonymous individualized data about Web surfers' online activities with personal data such as names, postal addresses, and catalog-purchase histories. Merging the data would have allowed DoubleClick to make anonymous individualized data into individualized data—to figure out the name and address of persons seeing banners and clicking on its clients' ads. In response, a watchdog organization, the Electronic Privacy Information Center, filed a complaint with the FTC alleging that DoubleClick was in violation of law for failure to disclose in advance this use of the anonymous data. In the face of a firestorm of criticism, DoubleClick announced that it had abandoned its plan to combine the data.

DoubleClick Tracking System

Doubleclick's tracking system (described above) also generated consumer class actions law suits beginning in 2002. In all, 13 separate suits were filed based on claims of invasion of users' privacy and misrepresentation. The suits were settled in 2002 when DoubleClick agreed to provide consumers with a clear and easy-to-understand privacy policy about its service, technologies, and use of cookies, as well as information on ways to opt out of its system.

Theories of Liability

The theory of the Geocities case and the ones that followed it are that a Web site or service operator violates the law by not telling the whole truth about use of personal information and/or its manipulation of the user's computer. This theory treats the sites' privacy policy as a promise and treats any variation or failure to disclosure the whole truth as an unfair and deceptive practice that victimizes consumers. An extension of the theory is that if Web sites use personal information without any disclosure at all, that is also unfair and deceptive.

From these principles, it follows that, if your company collects and uses personal information—or uses cookies or other identifiers—and you don't want to take a risk of legal action, then:

- Your company needs a privacy policy for Internet sites and applications.

- The privacy policy should be one that is carefully written to provide full disclosure of your relevant practices and procedures.

- Your company should actually do what the privacy policy says.

No Right of Access to Data

Under US law, consumers have no general right to access and/or correct data collected about them. (There are some narrow exceptions discussed below.) This is quite different from the state of the law in the EU, where citizens have a general statutory right of access to data about them.

Opt-In vs. Opt-Out

Often Web sites have options for users—for example the option as to whether or not to receive e-mails from the site owner or whether the user will receive offers for other products. Making a choice is normally indicated by a check box.

The site can make the default that a user's information is used *unless* the user affirmatively says *"no"* by unchecking the box. This manner of biasing the choice is called "opt-out."

Or the Web site can require the user to affirmatively choose by affirmatively checking what he or she wants. This is called "opt-in."

Businesses in the United States have freedom to use "opt-out." This is different from the EU where use of the "opt-in" mechanism is generally required.

YOUR WRITTEN PRIVACY POLICY

Whether you have a consumer- or business-oriented site, as a practical matter, you must have a written privacy policy. As noted above, companies that fail to make disclosure can get into regulatory trouble. In addition, a privacy policy helps build trust. It is a good idea to have a link to the privacy policy, in a readily visible format, on every page of your business Web site, starting with the home page.

Goals of the Process

Privacy policies sound simple, but often are not. Here are some key tasks in creating one:

- Find out what data your company actually collects and what it does with it.
- Keep privacy policies up to date as your company's business changes.
- Decide what promises you actually want to make.
- Be sure that your company actually obeys its own privacy policies.

In addition, you want to take steps to avoid:

- Making promises that you can't keep.
- Making promises that handcuff your business—privacy obligations that sound all right now, but could hurt your company in the future.

Using Privacy Policy Forms

Many companies begin with a privacy policy form that they find on the Web. There are a lot of model forms and good examples around. There is a form that we like in the Appendix in this book (Form 18-1), which you can use as a starting point in drafting your own policy.

Starting with a form is not a bad idea, as long as it is only one step in the process. Just remember that your privacy policy needs to fit *your* business.

A Team Approach

In a company with a sophisticated Web strategy, you need a team approach to creating a privacy policy. You need to think of a "privacy policy" as not just the notice on your Web site, but as the set of practices that governs how you use personal data.

The first step in creating a privacy policy is to figure out what your company is actually doing. This involves finding out what information is actually gathered, how it is stored, how it is processed, how it is used, what third parties use it, what security measures protect it, and so forth.

A team is required because your privacy policy for any sizable company involves information systems, Web developers, marketing, public relations, legal, and sales. For smaller companies, the team will be smaller, but an approach that crosses functional lines is going to be necessary.

What's Covered and What's Not

Generally speaking, the privacy policy is about information gathered at a Web site (or by Internet applications)—not about information that you got in other ways. The practical necessity of having a privacy policy may actually mean that you can do *less* with information from the Web site than with your other data. This may be a good reason to track data in your systems that came from the Web site.

The Substance of Your Privacy Policy

Here's an overview of the topics and considerations that your written privacy policy should cover. You may find it convenient to organize your policy around these general categories—although, of course, there is no particular required format and some categories may not apply to you at all.

Disclosing the Information that You Obtain from Users

Your policy should tell users what kind of personal information you gather via your Web site. This could include:

- **Information that you capture in Web registration**—It might be only user name and password—or it could include name, address, phone, e-mail, and information about interests, even financial or medical information. Some information may be required and some may be optional.

- **Information about other persons requested from a Web site user—**Sometimes users are asked to provide information about other persons. One example is offering the option to "e-mail this page to a friend" and requesting the friend's name and e-mail address.

- **Information that you capture in transactions—**Credit card and mailing information are an example.

- **Information about users obtained from third parties—**An example might be credit checks that you may run.

- **Information that you may collect by tracking—**Many sites capture the user's "click stream" to build a profile of use.

Some information may be collected for special purposes. For example, a site that does not normally capture user's name and address may do so for the purpose of a contest.

Disclosing Cookies and other Forms of Automated Information Collection

This category may include whether your site uses cookies and if so:

- What information is stored in the cookie?

- What functionality the user will lose by disabling cookies?

- Whether your site has tools to disable cookie use?

- Other tools used by your site (such as downloadable software that may install a persistent identifier and collect information).

Disclosing Your Use of Information from Users

This category includes what you will do within your own organization with user's personal information. Uses may include:

- Contacting consumer by e-mailing newsletters, direct mail, telephone, and other forms of follow-up contact

- Personalization of the Web content or advertising messages

Disclosing Information Shared with Other Sites and Users

This category deals with personal data that leaves your company and goes to someone else. For example:

- It may be your practice to pass on information about users to advertisers and direct marketers. (See the discussion below of California's "Shine the Light Law" which relates to this kind of information sharing.)

- Many businesses have relationships with "partner" businesses to share leads and make referrals.

- Some sites subcontract some services and sales of goods to other parties, and in connection with doing so, pass customer information onto third parties.

Access by Children

As is discussed later in this chapter, your privacy policy and site design need to take account of the COPPA which relates to dealing with children under 13 years old. Many sites state that children (persons under 18) and particularly children under 13 cannot use the site or provide personal information to the site.

Third-Party Ad Servers and Framing and Linking

As we mentioned in our discussion of cookies, some online advertising agencies (known as "advertising networks") have the ability to place their own cookies and track users across a number of sites. DoubleClick (mentioned above), and 24/7 Real Media (now owned by advertising and communications giant WPP) are companies in this field. If your site has advertising with its own cookies and data collection, this is a necessary disclosure item.

Opt-In and Opt-Out

The subject here is the kind of user choice you offer. Most sites give users the choice to decide whether they will be on a mailing list, or whether their data will be passed onto other companies (or used to provide offers for other company's goods or services). Whether you use "opt-in" or "opt-out," your privacy policy will explain how the choices are made.

Privacy Management

Your disclosure should inform the user as to how to grant or revoke permission for sharing or use of personal data. Most often, this is controlled by a "user profile" page that the user may access and change on the Web site.

This functionality may also relate to how the user can get access to and update user profile information.

Information Retention Policies

The topic here is how long you keep data. Is it forever or is inactive data discarded after a set amount of time?

Data Security

This category is about how you safeguard information both on your site and as it flows through the Internet (such as the use of secure transaction technology). Most often, the technology employed is described in general terms.

Changes to Site

You will want to explain that your privacy policies may change and that the changes will be posted on the Web site. You may (or may not) want to state that you will send notice of changes to the e-mail address given by the use in registration.

Sale of Your Company

Your privacy policy should explain that personal data may be transferred along with the sale of a company or line of business. Otherwise there is a risk that your company will be unable to transfer its customer list to a buyer of its assets.

Dating the Policy

When you post a privacy policy, you should include its effective date. If you change the privacy policy, you should archive the old policy. This is so that you can reconstruct later what policy applied on what date.

Be Careful about Promises

Your lawyer will want you to make sure the promises of a privacy policy in ways that don't promise perfection. For example, rather than saying "Your data will be absolutely safe," it would be better to say:

> *Our policy is to limit access to your personal data to those of our employees who need access to perform their duties. Any employee who violates our privacy and/or security policies may be subject to disciplinary action.*

Your lawyer can help you scrub your policy so that you don't make promises that you may not be able to keep.

Follow Up

Creating and maintaining a privacy policy is not something that you "set and forget." The deals that you will want to do with data, the partnerships you make, and changes in technology you implement—all of this can require changes in your published privacy policy.

It is therefore sensible to review your policy periodically and make sure that practices and policy are in sync.

Making the Technology Fit the Policy

It is not enough to make up a policy that sounds good. You may have to make your site functionality fit the privacy. You site should have functionality:

- To allow users to edit their registration data
- To allow users to change their "opt-out" choices

Use Seal-of-Approval Programs

One aim of a privacy policy is to make your users "feel good" about your site. That effect, some believe, can be reinforced by having your site "certified" as being a "good citizen" in data privacy.

There are two well-known voluntary organizations that allow your site to display a "seal" of approval. They are BBBOnLine, a service of the Better Business Bureau (www.bbbonline.com) and TRUSTe (www.truste.org). Both are nonprofit organizations that issue a certification seal or "trustmark" to Web sites. (This is what trademark lawyers call a "certification trademark.")

Both organizations work the same way. To get a license to use the trustmarks, a site must submit answers to a self-assessment questionnaire. The site must also agree to certain dispute resolution procedures if there are user complaints, and it must agree to let the certifying organizations investigate complaints in some cases. A site that uses the trustmarks agrees to pay yearly fees that are based on the volume of business that the licensee does on its site.

Neither organization imposes any real limitations on what you can do with personal data. Rather each focuses on *disclosure*. Each organization takes the position that, as long as your privacy policy discloses fairly and fully what you do, your site will be deemed acceptable.

California Online Privacy Protection Act

There is a California statute that mandates that companies have privacy policies for any Web site that collects personally identifiable information about any Californian. It is called the California Online Privacy Protection Act (CalOPPA).

Who Is Subject to CalOPPA?

CalOPPA is about any commercial Web site or other commercial online service that collects personally identifiable information regarding a person who resides in California. The statute applies to any person or entity that "owns" such a site or service. Any site with a national or international focus is likely to include Californians in its users, so the reach of CalOPPA is potentially very broad.

Nature of the CalOPPA Statute

In spite of its impressive name, CalOPPA is a rather mild-mannered statute. Violation of CalOPPA occurs only if the owner's site does not have the required privacy (as discussed below) within 30 days after notice. The law is about disclosure only and does not mandate any particular privacy policy. The disclosures that CalOPPA mandates are no more than most companies would do as matter of good business practice.

Requirement for a Privacy Policy

When CalOPPA applies, the statute says that owner must post a privacy policy. The policy:

- Must state what types of personally identifiable information are collected.

- Must state the process (if any) that permits the user to review and change such personally identifiable information.

- Must list the categories of third parties with which the site owner shares such information.

- Must include a statement of the process by which the user is notified of privacy policy changes.

- Must state the effective date of the privacy policy.

Conspicuous Privacy Policy

Under CalOPPA, each owner must have a privacy policy that is "conspicuous." It is deemed conspicuous if:

- The privacy policy appears on the home page of the Web site. (No one does this.)

- The privacy policy is linked to the home page with an icon that has the word "privacy," and the icon's color is different from the homepage background, or

- The privacy policy is linked to the home page via a hypertext link that contains the word "privacy," which is (1) written in capital letters equal to or greater in size than the surrounding text, (2) written in a type, font, or color that contrasts with the surrounding text of the same size, or (3) otherwise distinguishable from surrounding text on the home page.

Normal practice in US Web sites is to have a hyperlink to "Privacy" at the bottom of the home page. Few pages actually have icons or all capital letters text.

California's "Shine the Light Law" and "Your California Privacy Rights"

When you look at many consumer companies Web sites, you may notice a home page link to "Your California Privacy Rights." This text is there because of another California statute—which is about disclosure of information to third parties for the third parties' "direct marketing purposes."

In 2003, California adopted California Civil Code Section1798.83 or the "Shine the Light Law" (sometimes called S.B. 27 [for Senate Bill 27]). As originally drafted, the bill would have allowed all California residents to get a list of the every third-party direct marketer to whom their personal information was disclosed. However, as passed, the law included a big exception. A company does not have to send the disclosure list if (a) the company has a privacy policy that allows customers to "opt out" of having their information transferred to third parties for marketing, (b) the company provides information on opting out upon request, and (c) the company notifies consumers that they have these rights.

This exception, has, in most cases, become the rule for most companies, and many Web companies simply provide the opt-out option together with instructions (sent to customers by e-mail on request) on how to opt out, in a manner discussed further below. (The same how-to-opt-out information would normally be in the company's online privacy policy.)

Does the Shine the Light Law Apply to Your Web Company?
This law will apply if your company:

- Obtains personal information about California residents.

- Has 20 or more employees.

- Has provided personal information to one or more third parties for their direct marketing use during the past calendar year.

There are certain companies that are exempt from the law—primarily for companies that are under other privacy regulations, such as financial and medical service providers. If you need details on exceptions, you should consult legal counsel.

What Individuals Does the Law Protect?
Any California resident is covered by the law. This means that the law applies to companies outside the state that have Californians as customers.

How Do Web Companies Comply with this Law?
The Shine the Light Law potentially applies to all types of companies, not just those on the Web, so it has various notice provisions that apply to California "brick and mortar" locations. (If you want information on compliance with this law for non-Internet operations, please see your lawyer.) Companies that are on the Web need to do the following to comply:

- **The Link**—Have a link on the Web site home page that uses the words "Your Privacy Rights" or "Your California Privacy Rights." (Most sites use the words "Your California Privacy Rights" to avoid confusion.)

- **Providing an E-mail Address**—Have that link take the user to a Web page, which normally is entitled "Your California Privacy Rights." (Sometimes this disclosure is combined with the site's privacy policy.) On that Web page, the site owner should indicate an information source that the consumer can contact for information required under this law. The source that Web companies normally provide is an e-mail address. (The statute also allows the provider to use a postal address, toll-free phone number, or in-person advice, but each of these options is more expensive than e-mail.)

- **Web Page Statement**—Include on the same Web page a statement explaining the statute generally and providing information on how to opt-out of disclosure of the user's personal information to direct marketers.

470 CHAPTER 18 Privacy and Use of Personal Data

- **E-mail Response**—If the consumer sends an e-mail to the address provided to request information, your site should promptly respond by return e-mail with the same opt-out information.

It may strike you as odd that the law requires that Web site companies provide information by e-mail (or by one of the other permitted means) rather than just requiring that opt-out information be put on the Web site itself. However, this process is what the California legislation requires, so companies must comply using this method.

What If a Company Does Not Provide an Opt-Out?

If your business does *not* provide customers a chance to opt out of information sharing with direct marketers, then it must make the following disclosure to the customer free of charge by e-mail (or by the other permitted means of providing information):

- **Information Disclosed**—A list of the kinds of personal information that the business has disclosed to third parties for direct marketing purposes during the preceding calendar year.

- **List of Marketers**—The names and addresses of all of the third parties that received personal information from the business for direct marketing purposes during the preceding calendar year.

Enforcement

The law allows consumers to sue for violation—but the law also allows a company 90 days to cure a violation when first brought to its attention.

Example of the Web Notice

Here is what a "Your California Privacy Rights" notice looks like. As you can see, it is a pretty simple form:

YOUR CALIFORNIA PRIVACY RIGHTS

Residents of the State of California, under the California Civil Code, have the right to request from companies conducting business in California a list of all third parties to which the company has disclosed personal information during the preceding year for direct marketing purposes and a disclosure of the shared information. Alternatively, the law provides that if the company has a privacy policy that provides you with an "Opt-Out" choice for use of your personal information by third parties for marketing purposes, the company may instead provide you with information on how to exercise your disclosure choice options.

This Site qualifies for the alternative option. Its privacy policy provides you with information on how you may Opt-Out from the use of your personal information by third parties for direct marketing purposes. Therefore, we are not required to maintain or disclose a list of the third parties that received your personal information during the preceding year for marketing purposes.

If you are a California resident and request information about how to exercise your third party disclosure choices, send a request to the following e-mail address: privacy@[URL].

If your Web company does disclose information and does *not* provide an opt-out, then the online notice could be even simpler:

YOUR CALIFORNIA PRIVACY RIGHTS

California residents can ask companies with whom they have an established business relationship to provide certain information about the sharing of personal information with third parties for direct marketing purposes during the past year. If you want a copy of the information disclosure provided by this Site, send your request by e-mail to Privacy Administrator at privacy@[URL].

DATA SECURITY BREACH NOTIFICATION LAWS

Many Americans have experienced identity theft, the organized criminal misuse of personal information such as social security numbers and credit card and debit card information to commit fraud.

There have been some high profile cases of identity theft. For example, in February 2005, data vendor ChoicePoint disclosed that it mistakenly sold personal identification of some 145,000 individuals to a criminal identity theft operation. In a well-publicized case, the federal Veterans Administration lost the identity of 26 million veterans on a stolen laptop. TJX Corporation, the owner of T.J. Maxx stores, disclosed that hackers had installed hidden software in its systems that resulted in the theft of 45 million credit and debit card numbers from its information systems.

Part of the cause of the identity theft problem has been poor security by the many companies that hold personal data. To make things worse, many data holders historically kept secret about data thefts, so that data subjects had no notice that their personal information had been compromised. As a result, many state legislatures have now enacted data security breach notification acts that require data holders to inform data subject if their personal information has been stolen or compromised.

California was the first state to enact a law requiring data holders that suffer data security breaches to notify the potentially affected data subjects. Many other states followed California's lead; they have enacting statutes that are similar to California's but often differ in the details. As of the time this is written, 39 US states and two territories have such statutes.[1] Because of the near national coverage, the practice of companies that hold large amounts of personal data is now to notify all data subjects in all US states and territories of a data security breach.

California Law on Security Breach Notification

Let's take a look first at the California Security Breach Notification Law and then discuss some ways that the laws in other states vary. Here is a summary of the California statute:

Personal Information—The statute applies to "unencrypted computerized data" that includes a name (first name or initial and last name) plus any of the following: Social Security number, driver's license or California ID card number, credit or debit card number (with PIN number if required for access).

Security Breach—The statute covers any unauthorized acquisition of computerized data that compromises the security, confidentiality, or integrity of personal information.

Notice—The data holder must notify all data subjects that reside in California. Notice is to be provided "in the most expedient time possible and without unreasonable delay," but may be delayed if law enforcement officials advise that prompt notice would impede a criminal investigation or to the extent time is needed to learn the scope of the breach and restore reasonable integrity to the system.

---

[1] This jurisdictions (as of late 2007) are Arizona, Arkansas, California, Colorado, Connecticut, Delaware, District of Columbia, Florida, Georgia, Hawaii, Idaho, Illinois, Indiana, Kansas, Louisiana, Maine, Massachusetts, Michigan, Minnesota, Missouri, Montana, Nebraska, Nevada, New Hampshire, New Jersey, New York, North Carolina, North Dakota, Ohio, Oklahoma, Oregon, Pennsylvania, Puerto Rico, Rhode Island, Tennessee, Texas, Utah, Vermont, Washington, Wisconsin, and Wyoming. You can find a listing of the states laws on the Web site of the National Conference of State Legislatures, www.ncsl.org. You can also check with your legal councel as to any states that that may have joined this list.

Data Holders—If the breach occurs to a data holder (such as a hosting facility or outsource data processor), the data holder's obligation is to notify the company for which it holds the data, and that company would then have the obligation to notify data subjects.

Means of Notice—Generally notice will be by mail. There is a provision for e-mail notice if permitted under the federal digital signature act (E-Sign, discussed in Chapter 16 of this book). However, E-Sign allows electronic notice only if the data subject has provided prior consent to notice in electronic form, so it likely will not apply in many cases. There is a provision that "substitute notice" may be used if the cost of notifying data subjects is more than $250,000 or if more than 500,000 people need to be notified, or the organization or if contact information is lacking. Substitute notice means: e-mail when the e-mail address is available, Web site notice, *and* notification in statewide media. There is a somewhat vague provision that allows for notice under the company's own notification procedures under its own data security plan, but only if its procedures are consistent with the timing requirements of the law and if it actually notifies subjects in accordance with its policy.

Remedies—Consumers can sue companies that fail to comply.

The Law in Other States

The security breach notification laws in other states do vary, sometimes in signification ways. Variations include:

Definition of Personal Information—The definition is broadened in some states to include mother's maiden name, digitized or other electronic signature, biometric information, or other identifying information.

The Entities Covered—Some states require the data holder be holding the personal data of a minimum number of data subjects for the law to apply, such as 500, 5,000, or 10,000. Some states have exceptions for entities that are covered by other disclosure statutes or regulations (such as the Gramm-Leach-Bliley Act or HIPPA, both discussed below).

Breach—Most states require disclosure if there is likelihood of access, but some states require a reasonable likelihood of harm to the data subjects. While most states require notice of compromise of "unencrypted" information, some (sensibly) include theft of the encrypted information, if the encryption key has been compromised.

Means of Notice—Some states allow telephone or fax notification.

Notice to Authorities—The New York law requires notice to "the state attorney general, the consumer protection board, and the state office of cyber security and critical infrastructure coordination." New Jersey's law requires notice to the Division of State Police in the Department of Law and Public Safety before notice to data subjects.

Remedies—Some follow the California model that allows data subjects to sue. In others, the state's attorney general enforces the statute.

Merchant Liability in Minnesota—The state of Minnesota amended its data breach notice law, effective August 1, 2007, to add a provision that makes companies that accept credit and debit cards liable to banks for certain costs resulting from a merchant's loss of credit card data, including notifying customers, replacing credit cards, refunding fraudulent consumer charges, closing accounts, and dealing with customer queries. The law also prohibits entities that do business in Minnesota from retaining data credit cards, including security codes and PINs, for more than 48 hours after the transaction. The California legislature passed a very similar law in 2007 but it was vetoed by Governor Arnold Schwarzenegger. It is possible that other states may enact similar laws. These laws would certainly raise the financial risk of data breaches for companies that accept credit card transactions.

For a detailed review of these state laws (as of early-2007), a good reference is a book called *US Data Breach Notification Law: State by State*, edited by John P. Hutchins and published by the American Bar Association. You can order it from the ABA Web site, www.aba.org. This book can give you a good baseline, but you will have to check for changes in these laws after the date of publication.

The costs of complying with these statutes after a data breach incident can be very high. For holders of large amounts of data, the costs include investigation, remediation, cost of notice to data holders, and legal costs. For major breaches for large data holders, it runs into the millions of dollars.

If you have more questions on these laws, you should contact your attorney.

More Potential Liability for Financial Loss

Data breaches can lead to costs that may be borne by other businesses. The clearest case of this is credit card data, where, as noted above, retailer's loss of information imposes credit card fraud losses on banks.

Banks have filed lawsuits to recover these losses against the retailers that have suffered data breaches. The banks have asserted theories under contract law and have also accused merchants of fraudulently misrepresenting the capabilities of their security systems. These cases have not (at this time in late 2007) gone far enough to draw any firm conclusions about whether merchants will be liable to banks, but it does underline the potential risks from holding data insecurely.

Data Security and Planning

Good data security practices will reduce a company's risk of data breaches. Data security plans should address all the many points of data vulnerability that companies have, including hacking and "Trojan horse" programs, employee dishonesty, stolen passwords, lost or stolen notebooks, and data handling and transfer mistakes. Companies should do periodic risk assessments and keep abreast of new threats and new technologies for data protection. The use of encrypted data and careful control of encryption keys can prevent incidents under many of these statutes. Firewalls can protect internal networks and individual applications. If your business holds significant amounts of personal data, it should certainly consult a computer system security expert on a regular basis. Companies should also have in place procedures for response (internal and external) to data breach incidents and for timely notification of data subjects.

The Payment Card Industry (PCI) data security standard issued (and updated from time to time) by a consortium of credit card processing companies is the de facto standard for companies that process credit card information. You can get information about PCI at www.pcisecuritystandards.org.

Possible Congressional Action on Data Breach Notification

Because of the variations in local laws, companies that handle data have asked Congress to pass a uniform national law on data breach notification. Although a number of bills have been filed in the House and Senate, no federal legislation has passed as of the time that this book is being written. Companies that handle personal data should watch for both state law and federal law developments.

Credit Report Security Freeze Laws

A related set of state laws allows consumers to impose a credit freeze on credit reporting by credit reporting agencies. These state laws will not impose any obligation on your business unless you are in the credit reporting business.

These freeze laws apply to any company in the credit reporting business but the main target is the three major US consumer credit reporting agencies: Equifax, Experian, and TransUnion. These laws are designed to enable consumer to prevent use of stolen personal information to open new credit card accounts. By 2008, there will be 34 states with such freeze laws in force. Some states allow a freeze to be imposed only by persons that are previous victims of identity theft. If you are interested in this law, you should contact your legal counsel.

Under the federal Fair Credit Reporting Act, US consumers also have a right to access information about them held by credit reporting companies and to require credit reporting companies to correct false information. (For information on this law, see the FTC site at www.ftc.org and look for information on the Act.)

ANTI-SPYWARE LAWS

There are two states, California and Utah, that have passed anti-spyware laws. The California law makes it illegal to provide software that surreptitiously installs software, modifies settings, disables protection, and collects information. The Utah law has similar provisions. The key to these laws is intentional deception as to functioning of the software. Knowingly providing deceptive software of this kind is also illegal under the FTC Act and the state "little FTC Acts" discussed above.

The member states of the EU have generally similar anti-spyware statutory provisions, which were mandated by the EUs 2002 Directive on Privacy and Electronic Communications.

Children's Online Privacy Protection Act

In 1998, Congress passed Children's Online Privacy Protection Act, or COPPA for short. It became effective on April 21, 2000. *COPPA likely affects the way you should operate your online business even if you don't have "for-kids" content.*

A Serious Law
COPPA is a serious law. The fines under COPPA are up to $11,000 per violation. That means that if you collect personal data from 1000 children in violation of COPPA, you could be fined up to $11 million dollars!

The FTC enforces COPPA. State governments also have the power to enforce it. You can find information about COPPA at the FTCs Web site at www.ftc.gov.

Every Business on the Web that Obtains Personal Data Is Affected by COPPA
Every Internet (or other network) business that deals with consumers and solicits personal information from anyone in the United States is affected to some

extent by COPPA—including sites that have no child-oriented content. Staying out of trouble under this law, if your Web site is not child-oriented, normally requires just a few changes in your privacy policy and site registration functions.

If you do have or want to have a child-oriented site, COPPA profoundly impacts your businesses. You need to be very careful that all operations are 100 percent COPPA-compliant.

We will cover the practice pointers for general audience sites and then focus in on the rules that affect sites with Internet content for children.

Who Is Covered by COPPA?

The law provides that a site is under COPPA if it is a commercial business that is either:

- *Directed* to children under 13 years old or

- *Knowingly* receives personal information from children under 13 years old

Does your online business collect any kind of personal information from preteens? If so, you are under this law. Note also that COPPA applies not only to Web sites, but also to any "online service." The latter term that is probably broad enough to apply to any Internet-based application. (It is unclear if COPPA applies to all wireless applications, but the prudent course is to assume that it applies to wireless networks as well.)

On the other hand, COPPA does not cover data on preteens that is collected by other means. For example, this law does not restrict data obtained by mail. This is thus another instance where it may make sense to segregate data by source.

Foreign Web sites must comply with COPPA if they are directed to children in the US or knowingly collect information from children in the US.

How Can General-Purpose Sites, with No Children's Content, Stay Clear of COPPA?

If you have a general-purpose Web site (not oriented to preteens), how can you prevent the application of COPPA?

The answer is you must make sure that you never knowingly receive personal information from any preteens. In addition, you make sure that you never knowingly have children under 13 in chat rooms or other forums where they could easily disclose personal information.

Provisions in Terms of Use

Most commercial Web sites have provisions in their terms of use that provides the user is 18 (which is the age that in most states they can legally make a binding contract) and in any case under 13 (because of COPPA). Here is a typical provision:

You affirm that you are either more than 18 years of age and are legally competent to enter into the terms, conditions, obligations, affirmations, representations, and warranties set forth in these Terms of Use. In any case, you affirm that you are over the age of 13. This Site is not intended for children under 13. If you are under 13 years of age, then you are not permitted to use this Site.

Banning Preteens

When COPPA became law, a large number of content, chat, games, and entertainment sites changed terms of use and privacy policies and make a rule that children under 13 were not permitted to register, participate in contests, or use chat rooms.

How does this work in practice? If your site is not children-oriented and you want to avoid COPPA exposure, here's what you need to do:

- When you ask users for age information, omit any age category for the 0-12 year range—or just don't ask for any age information at all.

- Put a notice on your Web site in your privacy policy stating that the site is not for children under 13.

Here is a sample notice:

The Services and Information available to registered users on this site are NOT FOR USE BY CHILDREN UNDER 13 YEARS OF AGE. Please note that if it comes to our attention through reliable means that a registered user is a child under 13 years of age, we will cancel that user's account.

Try downloading the instant chat application AOL Instant Messenger (known as AIM) from the AOL Web site. If you enter a birth date that is too recent, you will get this message:

Thank you for your interest in AIM. At this time, children under the age of 13 may not register for AIM. We regret any inconvenience.

No doubt many clever children will do the arithmetic, enter an earlier birth date and succeed in getting AIM. Of course, there is a difference between shutting preteens out of your Web site, which is impossible, and not *knowing* that they are there. Some may say that Web sites have become like the monkey who puts his paws over his eyes to "see no evil." However, AOLs practice seems acceptable under the COPPA law, so long as AOL does not knowingly provide its instant chat service to preteens.

Full COPPA Compliance

If a site comes under COPPA and does have a site directed, wholly or in part, to children under 13 years old, then it must comply with COPPAs requirements.

The basic concepts of COPPA are these:

- **Disclosure**—Sites that are under COPPA must disclose their actual privacy policies. Mom and Dad must be able to find out what is going to be done with the personal information that little Jane might disclose.

- **Parental Consent**—Preteens are not permitted to disclose personal information without parental consent. Little Jane cannot be allowed to type out her first and last name online unless Mom or Dad has given *prior verifiable permission*. There are some narrow exceptions, but this is the general rule.

Sites Directed to Children Under 13 Years Old

What is the definition of a site "*directed to kids under 13 years old*?" It depends primarily on the content and use of the site. If any part of the site is content that young children like to see or do, it will be under COPPA. Unfortunately that is a rather unclear standard.

What's "Personal Information" under COPPA?

From the FTCs perspective, *any* of the following for a preteen would be considered to be "personal information":

- First name or initial and last name

- Home address

- E-mail address or screen name revealing an e-mail address

- Social Security Number

- Telephone number

- Any information about a child's age, gender, hobbies, preferences, etc. when associated with identifying information

What does the FTC consider *not* to be personal information?

- First name only, without other identifying information.

- A screen name or "handle" that is not tied to an e-mail address or other identifying information.

When do the Parental Permission Obligations Apply?

The requirement to get permission applies whenever the child is *requested* or *permitted* to disclose personal information. The site must get parental consent *first*, and then the site may ask the child for personal information:

- The requirement of *prior* parental consent applies if the site requests personal information from a preteen—for example in registration.

- The requirement of *prior* parental consent also applies if the site functionality would *allow* a child to disclose personal information. As noted above, any kind of chat or messaging function requires prior consent.

What Is a Site's Privacy Policy Obligation under COPPA?

Web sites that are covered by COPPA must post a privacy policy that includes a section clearly labeled as a notice of the site's information practices regarding children. The privacy policy must include:

- Types of personal information that the site collects from preteens—for example, name, home address, e-mail address, or hobbies.

- How the site will use the information—for example, to market to the child who supplied the information, to notify contest winners, or to make the information available through a child's participation in a chat room.

- Whether the site forwards personal information to advertisers or other third parties—and if so, what kind of businesses they are in, how they use the information, and whether they have agreed to maintain the confidentiality of the information.

- A contact at the site in charge of privacy matters.

- Whether personal information about the child is disclosed to third parties.

For sites under COPPA, there should be a "clear and prominent" privacy policy link, in the home page, on the child's area of the site, and at each place where personal information can be collected.

Exceptions

There are a few exceptions where prior parent consent does not apply. The site can take personal information without prior parental consent in the following ways:

- It is permitted to get the parent's or child's name and e-mail address for the purpose of seeking parental consent. The site must delete this information within a reasonable time if it does not get a response.

- The site may obtain a child's e-mail address to respond on a *one-time basis* to a child's request—for example, to send an e-mail to the child. However, the site must delete the e-mail address immediately after use.

- The site may obtain a child's e-mail address to send repeated requested e-mailing, such as an e-zine. But the site must promptly e-mail the parents and give them a chance to cancel the subscription.

- The site can get a postal address to send a free gift, a prize, or other postal mailing to the child.

These requirements of deleting information and e-mailing follow-ups mean that the site owner needs to invest in an automated system with good audit tracking to carry all of this out.

Chat Rooms, Message Boards and Kids

As a general rule, any site that has any chat room, message board, or instant messaging always requires prior parental consent. Such functionality is deemed to involve a child's personal information. This is because there is a risk that the child will disclose her real name or other personal information.

Moderated chat and message boards without parental consent are permitted if the site pre-screens messages before they appear online and the moderator screens out any personal information. The moderator should also screen out any content that is inappropriate for the age group. If you have such a moderated chat function, you should note:

- Your site should contain clear notice to parent about the nature of the moderated chat or message service offered and the rules that apply. Here is an example from the privacy policy at kidzworld.com:

Kidzworld has chat rooms, message boards, discussion groups and forums. These are accessible to our registered users. Users should be aware that any posts and conversations in these areas becomes public information. You should NOT disclose any personally identifiable information. Your username is the only identity you should have, and that is how people should know you on the Internet. Kidzworld's chatroom and message boards are monitored at all times by experienced Kidzworld staff. Our chat room is open from noon to 7:00PM Pacific Time (PST). Our chat moderators take extraordinary steps to ensure our users do not divulge personal information. Anyone who tries to reveal, or ask for, personal information will be removed from both the chat and message boards for 24 hours. If problems continue with the same user, their IP address could be permanently blocked and future access denied to the web site from that IP address.

- Your site should include a notice regarding comments and complaints and e-mail address, so that parents can notify your site if the moderators are not doing their job. Needless to say, your company should respond to any reported problem or complaint without delay.

How Do You Get Valid Parental Consent?

If a site owner wants to get or use personal information from a child, and what it wants to do is not in the exception list, it needs valid prior parental content. COPPA is based on the assumption that reliable parent verification cannot come through Internet certification. How do you know it isn't a 10-year old pretending to be Mom or Dad giving consent?

Parental permission must be by Non-Internet Verification, which means:

- Providing the parent a paper form for the parent to sign and mail or fax back; or

- Getting the parent to use a credit card in connection with a transaction (but note that credit card companies probably will not provide verification without a purchase); or

- Maintaining a toll-free telephone number for parents to call in their consent (this is probably the most efficient means)

The Cost of Getting Verification May Be Worth It!

Getting parental permission is not cheap. Child-oriented Web sites that achieve compliance often have operators that do nothing all day but listen to phone calls from parents giving consent for their children to use the site. Getting personal information from children definitely raises the cost of doing business. It also pays to have a legal review of compliance.

However, there is another side of the cost of compliance. COPPA may be a pretty effective *barrier to your competition*. A site that has consent from a half million parents has quite a competitive jump on a competing site that has none.

Additional Requirements

There are a few additional rules:

- Sites need to notify parents and get consent again if they plan to change the kinds of information they collect, change how they use the information, or offer the information to new and different third parties.

- Sites must give parents a way to revoke consent.

- Sites must limit information to that reasonably required for its use.

- Sites must keep personal data secure.

- Sites cannot commercially exploit the personal information they get from patents in the permission process.

Safe Harbor

COPPA has a provision that allows private associations to propose rules and practices that the FTC may approve as "safe harbors"—meaning that if your company complies with the private rules, it will be deemed in compliance with COPPA.

One set of approved safe harbor rules is the guidelines from the Children's Advertising Review Unit (CARU) of the Council of Better Business Bureaus. The CARU programs provide for self-certification based on a questionnaire—very much like the "trustmark" programs of Trust-E and BBOnline.

The FTC approved the CARU's safe harbor program in February 2001. For more information, see the FTCs Web site at www.ftc.gov and learn about CARU at www.bbbonline.com.

ANTI-SPAM PROVISIONS OF US FEDERAL LAW

In 2003, Congress passed the CANSPAM Act. The name stands for "Controlling the Assault of Non-Solicited Pornography and Marketing Act." The law sets rules for commercial e-mails. The Act has (as we all know) failed to stop spammers (because they hide their tracks and are hard to find), but it has been more effective in setting rules for legitimate commercial users of e-mail.

The Commercial Rules

The law applies to commercial e-mails that have the primary purpose of advertising or promoting a commercial product or service.

The law makes an exception for a "transactional or relationship message" which is an e-mail message that is part of an agreed-upon transaction (such as an order confirmation) or updates a customer in an existing business relationship (such as a message about a service to which the consumer is subscriber). Such a message cannot contain false routing information, but otherwise is generally exempt from the CANSPAM Act rules.

Here are CANSPAM rules that apply to commercial e-mail messages:

- **Header Information**—The Act forbids false or misleading header information. E-mail's "From," "To," and routing information—including the originating domain name and e-mail address—must be accurate and identify the person or organization who initiated the e-mail.

- **Subject Lines**—The Act prohibits deceptive subject lines. The subject line cannot mislead the recipient about the contents or subject matter of the message.

- **Opt-Out**—The Act requires that the e-mails give recipients an opt-out method. It can be a return e-mail or a Web-based mechanism. There can be other options presented to the user aside from stopping mail, but there must be a simple way to stop all commercial e-mail messages from the sender. The opt-out opportunity provided must be good for at least 30 days after the e-mail data. When the sender receives an opt-out request, it has a maximum of 10 business days to stop sending e-mail to the requestor's e-mail address.

- **Transfer Restrictions**—Once a person has opted out, the sender cannot have or assist another sender to contact the same e-mail address. It is illegal to transfer or sell e-mail addresses of persons who opt-out (even if they are on a pre-existing mailing list).

- **Identification**—The commercial e-mail must be identified, with a clear and conspicuous notice, as an advertisement, and it must include the sender's valid physical postal address. Your message must tell the recipient that he or she may opt-out of receiving more commercial e-mail.

- **Sanctions**—Each violation can lead to a fine of up to $11,000.

Rules for Hardcore Spammers

The CANSPAM Act also has provisions designed to outlaw activities used by hardcore spammers (We are sure you would never violate any of these provisions):

- **Harvesting E-mail Addresses**—Commercial e-mails may not "harvest" e-mail addresses from Web sites or Web services that have published a notice prohibiting the download or transfer of e-mail addresses for the purpose of sending e-mail.

- **Address Generators**—Commercial mailers cannot generate e-mail addresses using programs that combine names, letters, or numbers into multiple permutations.

- **Automated E-mail Account Registration**—Commercial mailers cannot use scripts or other automated ways to register for multiple e-mail or user accounts to send commercial e-mail. This is a way that spammers have used to find out names of registered users at Hotmail or Yahoo! Mail, because the sites will reject attempts to register existing user account names.

- **Using Zombies**—Commercial mailers cannot relay e-mails through a computer or network without permission—for example, by breaking into and controlling computer without authorization. Spammers commonly hijack unprotected computers, install mail program "malware," and use the hijacked computers (known as "zombies") to blast out spam.

The law has criminal penalties for violations of these rules.

OTHER REGULATION OF PERSONAL DATA REGULATION

While the US does not have a comprehensive data protection scheme, there are industry-based laws and regulations that are important to know about if your business is in financial services or health care.

Financial Services

Federal law imposes personal data controls on the financial services industry. In 1999, Congress enacted the Financial Services Reform Act (better known as "The

Gramm-Leach-Bliley Act" for the names of the legislators that sponsored the law). Various federal agencies have adapted regulations to implement this law. The following is a high-level overview.

The scope of the new regulation of financial privacy is broad:

- It applies to any financial institution that is engaged in a financial activity, including banks, insurance companies, stock brokers, and finance companies.

- It covers disclosures of information by a financial institution to any "nonaffiliated third party."

- The regulation applies to all "nonpublic personal financial information."

The regulation imposes three basic requirements:

- Financial institutions must provide an *initial notice* to consumers about their privacy policies. The notice will explain the conditions under which they may disclose nonpublic personal information to nonaffiliated third parties and affiliates. The institutions must provide this notice *before* disclosing the information to nonaffiliated third parties.

- Financial institutions must provide *annual notices* of their privacy policies to consumers with whom they establish a customer relationship.

- Financial institutions must provide a method for consumers to *"opt-out"* of disclosures to nonaffiliated third parties.

There are two major affects on banks under this new law. They need to maintain the technical infrastructure to deal with the requirements of the statute and regulation. And they are much less free to commercialize personal data.

There is, of course, much more detail to be learned. If your business is involved in the financial sector, you may wish to contact legal counsel to learn more about provisions that affect your business in the Gramm-Leach-Bliley Act and the regulations that implement it.

Health Care

Each time a patient visits a doctor, enters a hospital, buys drugs at the pharmacy, or makes a health plan claim, an electronic record is made of their health information. There is also a federal regulation that sets base standards for health-care data privacy. It's called the "Standards for Privacy of Individually Identifiable Health Information" adopted under the Health Insurance Portability &

Accountability Act of 1996 (more commonly called: "HIPAA"). Here's a brief summary of the regulatory provisions:

- **Covered Entities**—The regulation covers health plans and all care providers (doctors, hospitals, clinics, and so forth). Vendors that process or handle patient information are also covered.

- **Information Protected**—The regulation covers all medical records and all other individually identifiable health information in electronic form and on paper. Even information transmitted orally is covered.

- **Consent Required**—The regulation requires patient consent before information is released, even for routine uses such as insurance approval. It also requires that information released be only that which is needed. With some narrow exceptions, an individual's health information can be used for health purposes only.

- **Patient Access**—Patients must be able to see and get copies of their records, and request amendments. In addition, a history of most disclosures must be made accessible to patients.

- **Written Policies**—Organizations under the regulation must adopt written privacy procedures. These must include who has access to protected information, how it will be used within the entity, and when the information would or would not be disclosed to others. There must be a designated privacy officer.

- **Penalties**—For violation there are civil fines, and for willful violation, criminal penalties up to one year in prison.

There are many state laws that regulate data privacy. If applicable state rules are more restrictive, they apply as well. There are much more to HIPAA privacy compliance than is stated in this overview. If your digital business is the medical sector, you should contact legal counsel to learn more about restrictions under the Gramm-Leach-Bliley Act and the regulations that implement it.

PRIVACY AND THE INTERNATIONAL DATA ECONOMY

This is a global economy. The more your company grows, the more it will come under the law of other nations. There is a simple general rule: when collecting personal data in a foreign state—or transferring personal data out of it, you need to know about the data privacy laws there (if any).

There have been significant data protection enactments in Argentina, Canada, Chile, Israel, Korea, Japan, New Zealand, Switzerland and other nations. However, it is the EU and its 27 member nations that have taken the lead in data protection laws.

EU Directive on Data Protection

In October 1998, the EU adopted the *Directive on Data Protection* (better known as the "Data Directive") which contains strict rules for companies that handle personal data about EU citizens. If your company does business in Europe, or "partners" with companies that collect data there and send it your way, you need to understand the Data Directive (and European national laws that implement it).

The Data Directive is much broader than any US regulation or law. It covers all forms of person data collection, processing, and transmission, including, for example, information about employees, financial information, and health information. The Data Directive is based on the philosophy that data privacy is a human right. Its provisions are based on a few fundamental principles:

- **Notification**—The right of data subjects to notice regarding the information about them that is being collected and how it is being used

- **Choice**—The right to authorize data transfer (or not) in advance, and the right to stop use of data in direct marketing

- **Access**—The right of users to know what data is collected and to correct errors

- **Data Integrity**—The obligation of holders of data to take reasonable steps to ensure that data is reliable, accurate, and current

- **Security**—The right to have data kept in secure storage

- **Enforcement**—The right to have adequate official remedies for violation.

The Directive requires each company to have a data controller to oversee data handling. Each EU country must have a regulatory organization, a privacy commission that controls the data controllers. The Data Directive requires each EU state to permit civil remedies (that is the right to sue) for violation of data privacy. Violation can also lead to fines and other sanctions.

Of course, the Data Directive has exceptions. National governments are not required to disclose information used for national security or law enforcement, for example. There are exceptions for files of journalists.

The bottom line in the EU is that data holders have to build and maintain automated systems to provide these rights. If you have issues that arise under the Data Directive, your need to consult foreign counsel. Your US-based lawyer is likely to have corresponding counsel in the foreign states involved.

Transferring Personal Data from the EU to the United States

Does the Data Directive permit transfer of personal data from the EU to the USA? For a while, we thought that, in spite of the need for data transfers, the answer would be "no." That's because there is a provision of the Data Directive that *prohibits* export of personal data from the EU to countries or regimes that fail to provide an "adequate level of protection" for personal data.

For example, the EU has decided that Switzerland does provide sufficient data protection. However, based on the state of the law in the US, it looked pretty clear in 1998 and 1999 that the US would fall far short of having an "adequate level of protection."

Prohibiting the export of personal data would have had some serious and unfortunate consequences. Personal data transfers are routine in sales, telecommunications, travel, banking, and other fields. They are also needed for international e-commerce.

Nonetheless, when the Data Directive went into effect, the Europeans threatened to cut off the flow of data to the US. The US asked for talks, and two years of hard bargaining followed.

Taking Advantage of the EU–US "Safe Harbor Agreement"

In the end, the EU and the United States made a deal. The EU bureaucrats realized that to cut data flows between the United States and Europe would do more harm to commerce than good to privacy.

The results of the negotiations were the adoption by the United States and the EU of something called "Safe Harbor Privacy Principles" that permit US companies to adopt and adhere voluntarily to a set of measures that are rather like the EU Privacy Directive. The system is administered by the International Trade Administration (ITA) of the Department of Commerce.

To qualify for "safe harbor," a company must provide for its own measures and policies, with contents very much like those that we discussed above: *Notification, Choice, Access, Data Integrity,* and *Security.* The rules impose some burdens and require administration. Here is an overview of the rules:

Notice

Data holders must notify individuals about the purposes for which they collect and use information about them. Data holders must provide information about how individuals can contact the data holder with any inquiries or complaints, the types of third parties to which it discloses the information, and the choices and means the data holder offers for limiting its use and disclosure.

Choice

Data holders must give individuals the opportunity to choose (opt-out) whether their personal information will be disclosed to a third party or used for a purpose incompatible with the purpose for which it was originally collected or subsequently authorized by the individual.

For sensitive information, affirmative or explicit choice (opt-in) must be given if the information is to be disclosed to a third party or used for a purpose other than its original purpose or the purpose authorized subsequently by the individual.

Transfers of Personal Information to Third Parties

To disclose information to a third party, data holders must apply the Notice and Choice principles above.

There is an additional rule that applies if a data holder wishes to transfer information to another company acting as its agent. This would apply, for example, if the agent were a shipper and needed personal data to ship a product or if the agent was a bank and needed personal data for credit card approval. In that case, the agent must also be qualified to hold personal data under EU rules.

This means the agent must itself subscribe to the safe harbor principles or must otherwise be subject to the EU Data Directive. Alternatively, the data holder can enter into a written agreement with the agent obligating the agent to provide the same level of privacy protection as is required by the safe harbor principles.

Access

Individuals must have access to the personal information about them held by the data holder. Individuals must be able to correct, amend, or delete that information where it is inaccurate, except where the burden or expense of providing access would be disproportionate to the risks to the individual's privacy in the case in question, or where the rights of persons other than the individual would be violated.

Security
Data holders must take reasonable precautions to protect personal information from loss, misuse and unauthorized access, disclosure, alteration, and destruction.

Data Integrity
Personal information must be relevant for the purposes for which it is to be used. A data holder should take reasonable steps to ensure that data are reliable for its intended use, accurate, complete, and current.

Enforcement
In order to ensure compliance with the safe harbor principles, there must be:

(a) Readily available and affordable independent recourse mechanisms so that each individual's complaints and disputes can be investigated and resolved and damages awarded

(b) Procedures for verifying that the safe harbor principles have been implemented

(c) Obligations to remedy problems arising out of a failure to comply with the principles

The safe harbor system relies on self-certification—that is, your company certifies, once a year, that it complies. You can obtain a great deal more information on how this "safe harbor" system works at the ITA Web site, www.trade.gov or at www.export.gov/safeharbor/. Self-certification can be carried out online via the ITA Web site and is quite straightforward. The rules state that data holders that fail to provide annual self-certification will be dropped from the safe harbor system. There is a list of certified safe harbor companies online at the ITA site.

This is a pretty "soft" regulatory system. Washington is not planning to police companies to ensure they are complying with their promises. Unlike European countries, we have, at present, no "national privacy commission." However, this does not mean that the safe harbor system is meaningless. The actions that a certifying company promises to carry out go far beyond what is required under US law or normal at most US companies. Your company might face lawsuits or FTC enforcement actions if you promise to observe these rules and do not—and you may find that your European partner companies withhold needed personal data.

CONCLUSION

Personal data is a very important subject for companies that use the Internet and other electronic communications. Many of the rules and practices are now well established, but there are still open issues. It is an area with significant risks and therefore it is important that you make sure your business is in full compliance with the law.

Digital Technology Standards—Opportunities, Risks, and Strategies

In the computer industry, new standards can be the source of enormous wealth, or the death of corporate empires.

—*The Economist* Magazine, 1993

There is growing tension between patents and standards in information technology.

—Brian Kahin, writing for the Computer & Communications Industry Association, 2007

IN THIS CHAPTER

"Standards" are technical specifications that are designed to promote interchange, communication and commonality in products. This chapter discusses participation in standards setting for digital technology, communications, computers, and software—all of which we will call, for simplicity's sake, "digital technology standards."

There are many organizations that set standards. This chapter focuses on the standard organizations known as "consortia" or "alliances" that have a leading role in defining, promoting, and guiding emerging digital technology standards. This chapter also focuses on the interaction between digital technology standards, the standard setting process, and patents. At our law firm, we have advised clients in dealing with many digital technology standards related issues.

WHO IS THIS CHAPTER FOR?

This chapter is for persons in any digital technology enterprise that are deciding its technical direction, including the CTO, the head of engineering, the tech gurus and evangelists, and other senior technologists, as well as its legal counsel. The topic matters for senior executives and managers in any company that has a strong technology focus in emerging technologies. It is also for the managers, engineers, scientists, and programmers that participate and contribute to standards setting organizations around the world.

DIGITAL TECHNOLOGY STANDARDS AND THE MODERN WORLD

Digital technology standards, of course, are everywhere. The Internet is built with TCP/IP, the Domain Name System (DNS), HTML, XML, and many more. Databases are queried with SQL. Documentation is supplied in the form of PDFs. Local area networks run on Ethernet. Cellular communications are based on CDMA, GSM, and EDGE. Short-range communication relies on WiFi (IEEE 802.11b) or BlueTooth. Fiber optic networks run on Sonet. Digital technology standards are so ubiquitous that they have become part of the ordinary speech: for example, a music download is an "MP3"; a movie on an optical disk is a "DVD."

There are standards for integrated circuits, networks data transmission, document formats, processor interfaces, video display, computer ports, PC power management, digital sound processing, geographic positioning, and on and on. The world of IT, communications, computers, software, and "convergence" as we know it today could not exist without digital technology standards.

HOW DO NEW DIGITAL TECHNOLOGY STANDARDS MATTER TO YOUR BUSINESS?

Digital technology standards multiply endlessly and change constantly. To innovate your company also needs to embrace new digital technology standards that define emerging technologies and new markets. There are opportunities for your company to play a role in the standard setting for market advantage. Why should your company (small or big) participate in standard organizations and participate in setting new standards? There are a number of reasons:

- **Catching the Wave**—Your company may get an "early mover" advantage by introducing products and services in new markets just being defined by new standards.

- **Staying in the Leader's Wake**—Your company may be able to build on research and development done by large and powerful companies—or benefit by interacting with their newest products.

- **Steering the Technology**—Your company may be able to influence the contents of a key technology standard with your contributions and suggestions.

- **Getting Ahead of the Curve**—By knowing a standard early, your company may be able to move its own product (or its strategy) *beyond* the standard—in anticipation of the next iteration of the standard.

- **Market Insights**—Your company may get information about where other companies are going in your technology field.

- **Technical Know-How**—Participating in a consortium can provide access to knowledge about techniques used in emerging technologies.

- **Obtaining Licenses**—In some cases, participating in a standards organization brings patent licenses—in some cases for free.

- **Strength in Numbers**—Your company and other companies in a standards organization can help build credibility and critical mass for a new technical standard in a way that your company alone could not do.

- **Stamp of Approval**—Your company may be able to get a certification of standards compliance from a standards setting body.

There is, of course, a potential business risk in committing to cutting edge standards—you might choose wrong—and end up committing money and resources to a standard that fails. In addition, your company will pay fees to participate and will invest time and effort.

SOURCES OF STANDARDS

Many standards come from standards organizations. (A common generic term for such an organization is an "SSO" for Standards Setting Organization.) However, there are other sources of standards as well.

Single Company

Standards can come from a single company. An example is the Microsoft .NET Framework, which has many standards and interfaces formalized and promoted by Microsoft. The PDF standard comes from Adobe. We usually call these "proprietary standards." Some proprietary standards, PDF is an example, include patented technology of their sponsors.

De Facto Standards

A "de facto standard" is one that becomes dominant without anyone proclaiming it a standard. De facto standards may or may not be proprietary. There are many common examples of de facto standards such as:

- Business use of Microsoft Office and its file formats for word processing and other common office information processing

- The "desktop" metaphor used by PC operating systems with "folders," "windows," "files," a "trash can," and a desktop "pointer"

- Web page design elements such as the company logo at the upper left of the page that links to the home page, the "shopping cart," the search box, and so forth

- JavaScript for developing Web application.

Establishment Standard Setting Organizations

There are national and international standard organizations that constitute the establishment of standards setting. There are dozens of these organizations located around the world. This type of organization is sometimes referred to as an "SDO" for Standards Development Organization. The most prominent of these in digital technology standards setting include:

- **ISO**—The International Organization for Standardization. Located in Geneva, Switzerland, ISO is a global standards organization whose members are national standards organizations.

- **ITU**—The International Telecommunication Union. Also in Geneva, Switzerland, ITU is a UN specialized agency that focuses on standards for telecommunications and wireless.

- **IEEE**—The Institute of Electrical and Electronics Engineers. IEEE is a worldwide engineer's standards, publishing, and educational organization.

- **ANSI**—The American National Standards Institute. ANSI is a US national organization but many of its standards are used worldwide.

While these standard organizations vary in process and rules, they share a general approach. They function with specialized committees that include professionals and specialists from industry, government, and academia. Their standards process starts with a proposal followed by a comment period. Standards emerge based on consensus and are subject to formal adoption and publishing processes. They issue only standards that are published and accessible by any member of the public. They typically have patent policies. (I will give a short overview of these below.)

The prestige of these organizations and the value of the standards they promulgate cannot be overestimated. Companies and standards consortia commonly seek adoption by one of these SDOs of new standards in order to establish their technology's acceptability and increase its prestige. (An example is Microsoft's successful efforts to get its Office Open XML format for Web documentation accepted as an ISO standard.) International organizations are especially important for telecommunications because the standards require government approval in many nations.

Other Broadly Based Organizations

There are other standards organizations organized outside the old-line organizations that are more informal in style but still broadly based—with an interest in advancing technology while keeping the technology accessible and "open" in other ways. (I will discuss below the multifaceted meaning of "open" as applied to standards.) The most prominent of these "open" standards organizations are:

- **ISOC**—The Internet Society is an international organization and includes committees responsible for Internet infrastructure standards, including the Internet Engineering Task Force (IETF) and the Internet Architecture Board (IAB).

- **W3C**—The World Wide Web Consortium is an international standards organization for the World Wide Web. It has a technical staff and issues standards known "W3C Recommendations."

CONSORTIA AND ALLIANCES

Now let me turn to the main subject of this chapter—smaller ad hoc organizations that are the predominate form of standard setting body for emerging digital technologies. These standards organizations are known as "consortia," "forums," or "alliances." (We will call them "consortia.") This is an organizational model for setting standards that has become popular around the world over the last 15 years. There are hundreds of these consortium organizations. For growing technology companies, this is where most of the innovation in standards takes place and where you are likely to obtain an advantage by participation.

In digital technology, there are consortia for technologies used in connection with the Web and Internet, wireless, personal computing, semiconductors, vertical sectors (such as defense, industry, or health care), and many more areas.

Here are some examples:

- **OSGi Alliance**—(formerly the Open Services Gateway Initiative) adopts and promotes standards for Java-based software for devices. The Web site is www.osgi.org.

- **Continua Health Alliance**—adopts and promotes standards for interoperable "tele-health" systems and services. The Web site is www.continuaalliance.org/home.

If you are interested in reviewing examples of consortium documents, including incorporation, documents, by-laws, membership agreements, and intellectual property policies (all these document types are discussed below), you can find such documents on the Web sites of many consortia.

These organizations are not hard to form. Major software, electronics, or communications companies may belong to as many as a hundred consortia or more and may join ten or more consortia each year. These companies are also often among the founders of new consortia.

For reasons that we will discuss below, your company should examine carefully from a practical and legal perspective each consortium it may wish to join.

Consortia Characteristics

Here are some characteristics of consortia:

- **Industry-Founded**—Usually, a relatively small group of companies forms the consortium. The founders often include at least one or two leading large companies, but smaller companies may also be founders or early participants. They may end up with hundreds of members.

- **Selected Technologies**—Most consortia have a particular technology or set of technologies, often quite narrowly defined, that they want to define, standardize, and propagate.

- **Emphasis on Interoperability**—Consortia are ways to link suppliers and customers in a value chain. For this reason, their standards often focus on interfaces, components, and inter-device messaging. They often begin with one or a few standards, but their standards may diversify, broaden, and evolve over time.

- **Commercial Mission**—Consortia usually have a commercial objective—to help secure adoption of a technology that the members can commercialize or that will help sell their other technologies and products. These standards are designed to get suppliers and customers in sync on an emerging technology early in the adoption cycle.

- **Availability of Membership**—Most consortia are, as a practical matter, open to anyone that wants to join and pay the requisite fees. But most consortia do reserve the right to reject any proposed applicant.

- **Membership Classifications**—In consortia, there are membership grades with different membership prices and privileges. The most common gradations are: "Founder," "Promoter," and "Adopter." Usually, Founders and Promoters pay the highest yearly fees (unusually in the tens of thousands of dollars annually) and make most of the decisions. The basic idea is the companies that have created the base technologies—and pay most of the expenses—get the most say. In most consortia, the Founders and Promoters have equal privileges, but there are some consortia where the Founders have superior rights. Adopters (commonly paying several thousand dollars a year for membership) usually have no voting rights but may be able to participate in committee discussions.

- **Confidentiality of Discussions**—Most consortia keep standard proposals and deliberations confidential by agreement.

- **Standards and Implementation**—In addition to issuing standards, many provide documentation regarding embodiments (sample implementations) of their standards.

- **Patent Rules**—Most consortia have rules permitting and/or requiring patent disclosure and licensing to other members. These rules are important, and they vary greatly. We discuss patent rules below.

- **Intellectual Property**—With a few exceptions, most consortia do not hold patent themselves. They do, however, often have copyrights (or copyright licenses) on their standards documents and documentation. Most consortia adopt a trademark.

- **Certification Services**—Some consortia have a service to certify a "standards-compliant" device. These consortia often have a certification trademark that members can place on or use to promote the approved product.

- **Structure**—Most consortia are nonprofit corporations or limited liability companies (LLCs) that file for tax-exempt trade association status. Sometimes companies form an unincorporated grouping to promulgate a standard and only get around to forming an entity later on when the standard begins to catch on.

PARTICIPATING IN A CONSORTIUM—BUSINESS ISSUES

How do you decide if your company should be in any particular consortium? There are both business and legal factors. Let's look at the business side first. Here are some factors to consider:

- **The Fit**—How important is the standard for your current markets and customers?

- **The Market**—What is the market size of the products that will use the standard?

- **The Membership**—What is market power and technology skill of the other members of the consortium?

- **The Culture**—What is the business and social culture of the consortium? Is participation by new members encouraged? Is needed information readily available?

- **Your Competitiveness**—Can your business compete and excel in the technology and market area targeted by the consortia?

- **Resources**—What is your company's willingness and ability to commit the time and effort to the area?

- **Consequences**—What will your business lose if it does not participate?

Consortium Documents

If you do want to participate in consortium, you need to review the operative documents of the consortium. These are:

- The Charter (or Articles of Incorporation)

- The By-Laws

- The Membership Agreement

- In some cases, there are patent policy documents (or other policy documents such as work group procedures) that are usually (but not always) binding on the members.

You can often find the relevant documents on the consortium's Web site. You must read *all* of the documents, as each will contain rules applicable to your company if it joins the consortium. It would be foolhardy to join any consortium without fully understanding the rules that apply. We strongly recommend a legal review of the operative documents before your company joins any consortium. (Major corporations do a legal review before joining a consortium as a matter of course.)

Process and Organization

Before joining a consortium (and deciding whether to participate at a "Sponsor" or "Adopter" level), it is important to get a practical understanding of how the consortium operates. Here are some process and procedure issues that you will want to focus on:

- **Overall Organization**—How is the organization managed? How are board members selected?

- **Working Groups**—How are working groups formed? Who can participate in them? Do all members have access to the information exchanged in the working groups? Can your company join any working group that interests it?

- **Proposing Standards**—How are standards proposed? What is the process for refining the standard and getting comments within working groups? Once a standard is proposed by a committee, what is the process for comments on and objections to the proposed standard?

- **Patent Issues**—How (if at all) are patent issues managed?

- **Approvals**—What is the process for final approval of a standard? Who gets to vote at the committee and organization level? To what extent does the board of directors of the consortium control the process? How are standards amended?

In reviewing the standards documents, you will want to be sure that your company obtains the level of participation, influence, and access to information that it needs.

TENSION BETWEEN PATENTS AND STANDARDS

Today's technical standards often involve technologies that are covered by patents. There are a number of reasons for this.

- Patent filings in software and communications have increased enormously—driven in part by an explosion of software patenting. (Software patents are discussed in Chapter 5.)

- The founders promoting standards may control patents or patent applications that are relevant to the standard—but not necessarily all of them. Where multiple parties hold patents, the resulting "patent thicket" can be a barrier to adoption of a technology. Consortium rules are often designed to help clear out—or at least sort out—potential patent barriers.

Digital technology standard setting can interact—and sometimes come into conflict with—the legal power of patent systems around the world.

- Patents that are licensed free or cheaply can help drive digital technology standards adoption—high patent licensing fees can block adoption from happening.

- Your company might be able to get technology licenses to another party's enabling technologies at low rates or even free through standards organizations.

- If you are not careful, some standard organization rules that apply to its members can cause your company to grant free permanent licenses to your valuable patents—without your even being aware of it.

If you are considering participating in any consortium, you should consider whether member companies have relevant patents and if your own company has, or plans to get, patents in the technical area covered by the proposed standard. Then you need to look at patent-related rules and policies that the consortium has adopted.

One caution: Your company may obtain patent licenses from all the members of a consortium, but still not get all the patent licenses that you need to exploit the relevant technology. That is because holders of significant patents may remain outside the consortium organization and free to assert its patents unrestrained by any consortium rules. Often (but not always) consortium members will know of patent licenses needed that are outside of their members' control.

Key Concepts in Standards-Related Patent Licenses

Most (but not all) consortium agreements have provisions for licensing patents that relate to the standards. Under these license clauses, members that have patents that relate to standards license those patents to other members. These agreements use licensing concepts that are complicated and may be unfamiliar to you. As a result, the licensing provisions are often difficult for lay persons to read and understand.

In the hope of making these licensing provisions more understandable, let me introduce some key terminology and concepts that appear time-and-again in key consortium documents. We will need these concepts to explain the patent-related rules that apply under consortium documents. (We sometimes also use these concepts in private company-to-company patent licensing as well.)

"Compliant Portions" of Products
The term "Compliant Portions" is defined in consortium documents to mean those portions of a software application or hardware device that actually implement the specification that constitutes the standard.

Assume, for example, that there is a standard that relates to coding digital audio files to make them more compressed. If you designed a streaming audio Internet broadcasting system that used the standard, only those portions of your application that actually implement the standard specification would be "Compliant Portions."

Some consortium documents use the defined term "Scope" to express a similar concept. The Scope of the license grant is defined by and limited to the specification that constitutes the standard.

"Necessary Claims" of Patents

License grants in consortium documents typically grant members a license to other members' "Necessary Claims" required for Compliant Portions. Necessary Claims is a fundamental concept in standards licensing. (Sometimes, the terms "Essential Claims" is used.)

As you may recall, patents are issued with one or more "claims" that define their legal scope. (For background on patent claims, see the discussion in Chapter 5 of this book.) "Necessary Claims" is defined in consortium documents to refer to those particular claims of a members' patents that other consortium members need to use in Compliant Portions in order to implement the standard.

The use of the words "necessary" or "essential" here is a bit misleading. It is not really that the patent claims are "necessary" in the sense that it is absolutely impossible to design around them. Rather the concept is that there is no *commercially feasible* alternative. Definitions use phrases such as: "no reasonable alternative way to implement." In some cases, people might disagree about whether alternative technologies are commercially feasible, so the concept of Necessary Claims can be imprecise.

Necessary Claims are likely to include all patent claims that a member is free to license without paying royalties—this could include not only patents the member owns, but also licensed patents that the member has the right to sublicense without paying a third party any fee.

Reasonable and Non Discriminatory (RAND) Licensing

Some consortia require that the licenses referred to above be granted free of license fees. However, most consortia have rules requiring that their members license their Necessary Claims to all other members on a "reasonable and nondiscriminatory" or "RAND" terms. Sometimes, the term used is "fair, reasonable and nondiscriminatory" or "FRAND," but this appears to be a distinction without a difference. RAND is also a fundamental concept in consortium licensing.

What RAND really means is unfortunately indistinct. It is unclear what level of royalties might be "reasonable." The term "nondiscriminatory" is also subject to interpretation. For example, some companies have lower royalties for China than for the United States. Is that "discriminatory" or just bowing to economic reality in the Chinese market?

What is clear is that the concept of RAND patent licensing allows a broad range of pricing and is compatible with charging minimums, offering pricing based on quantity and other common patent licensing terms. Refusing to grant any license or treating various licensees differently in an arbitrary way violates RAND. Beyond that, the constraints of RAND licensing are not very clear.

Consortium rules rarely set the royalties for members' patent licensing. That's in large part because there is a risk that fixing royalties would constitute "price fixing" by competitors in violation of the antitrust laws or similar competition laws in other countries. (See the discussion of patent pools later in this chapter.)

Because the price of RAND licenses can powerfully affect the potential license for a new technology, your company should learn all that it can about the pricing of licenses that are needed to practice any technology standard. That means contacting the licensors and finding out what licensing terms are offered.

Patents vs. Patent Applications

The consortium's rules may or may not cover patent applications—as opposed to issued patents. You should check this point in any consortium your company is thinking of joining. Undisclosed patent applications may spring an unpleasant future surprise.

Assume, for example, that Company X is a member of a consortium that has licensing rules that include issued patents but do not include patent applications. Company X notices that the consortium has, unbeknownst to its members, included technology that is covered by Company X's pending patent application. Company X then resigns from the consortium before the patent issues. In that case, when the patent does issue, Company X can bring a patent infringement law suit against any company that uses the standard. Company X would have no obligation to offer a RAND license.

Defensive Termination

Many consortium documents have a "Defensive Termination" provision. This is a provision designed to discourage patent litigation among members. Here is how it works:

Assume consortium member Company A has granted a license to its Necessary Claims that consortium member Company B is using. Assume Company B then sues Company A for patent infringement. A consortium "defensive termination" clause would allow Company A to terminate its Necessary Claims license to Company B. After the license is terminated, Company A is free to sue the now-unlicensed Company B for patent infringement if Company B keeps on using Company A's Necessary Claims.

"Contributions" and Patent Licenses

Many consortia have rules that apply whenever a member makes a "Contribution" (sometimes termed a "Submission") to a standard. The Contribution occurs when the standard is in the process of being formulated. If a member makes a suggestion as to how the standard should be written, that suggestion is a Contribution.

The rules about Contributions are designed to prevent one patent-holding member from "sandbagging" the other members by getting the consortium to adopt a standard that is controlled by the contributor's undisclosed patent (or patent application).

Some consortia require that a member that makes a "Contribution" that ends up in a standard must choose either to:

- Agree to provide a royalty-free license to any Necessary Claims that cover the Contribution to all members; or

- Identify, at the time it makes the Contribution, any Necessary Claims used in the Contribution that it declines to license royalty-free and agree to license all of those excluded Necessary Claims on a RAND basis.

Some consortia simply require that a member automatically licenses royalty-free any Necessary Claims that cover its Contribution that is included in the resulting standard.

Consortium rules vary on what is a "Contribution." Sometimes, Contributions are written proposals or suggestions for what the standard should be. Under some rules, any oral suggestion that is recorded in meeting minutes will also be a Contribution. Before participating in any consortium, your company needs to know the rules and obligations that relate to Contributions.

Proposed and Final Standards

Consortiums usually circulate a "Proposed Specification" for a new or revised standard to members for review for 30 or 60 days. Many consortia require that, when a Proposed Specification is received, each member must either:

- Agree to provide a royalty-free license to any Necessary Claims that cover the Contribution; or

- Identify any Necessary Claims used in the draft specification that it declines to license royalty-free and agree to license all of those Necessary Claims on a RAND basis.

What if the member does not want to license a particular patent at all? Most often the rule is that if the member has relevant Necessary Claims that it wants to *exclude* from all licensing, it must identify each patent and opt-out in writing in the review period. Less commonly, the rule is that the member can avoid licensing Necessary Claims only if it both opts-out of the standard *and* terminates its membership in the Consortium.

Under some consortium rules, the company that is "asleep at the switch" during this period and fails to respond will inadvertently license its Necessary Claims royalty-free.

Rules on patent claims and the standard adoption process vary considerably. It is essential for you to understand the rules before you join any consortium.

Identifying Your Necessary Claims

What if your company has a patent that *might* apply to a proposed standard or to your Contribution to a standard? What if you are just not sure whether or not your patent would apply? Should you designate the patent to the consortium as including a Necessary Claim or not?

Under many consortium rules, failure to identify a Necessary Claim means granting other members a royalty-free license. If you identify a Necessary Claim, on the other hand, you fully preserve your right to obtain RAND royalties and lose nothing. For that reason, it may be prudent to identify all patent claims that appear potentially relevant—even if their applicability is somewhat uncertain.

Based on this logic, companies' identification of their Necessary Claims may be over-inclusive—which is something that you need to take into account when your company is deciding if it needs to be the licensee of these patents.

The rules on licensing make it clear that patent holders that participate in consortiums must read the rules and must pay attention to each technical proposal. Failure to be diligent can result in granting an inadvertent free license to Necessary Claims for use in the proposed standard.

One word of warning: It may be an antitrust violation or an illegal unfair business practice to assert a patent that you *know* does not apply or that you know to be invalid. Seek patent law advice if you are in doubt.

Standards Bodies and Mergers and Acquisitions

When you go to sell your company, you are likely to find that prospective buyers will want to know what standards bodies your company has participated in and what your RAND and/or free patent licensing obligations may be. If your company has given away licensing opportunities, it might decrease the value of your company. This is another reason why you should be careful with consortium-based obligations.

Do You Really Need a License to All So-Called Necessary Claims?

What do you do, if you need a license from a consortium member for its Necessary Claims that cover a standard? The answer is simple. You contact the patent holder and make your best deal.

Before seeking a license to Necessary Claims from a patent holder, it is often a good idea to check with patent counsel to be sure that you need the license. Here are some factors to keep in mind:

- Check to be sure the patent claim actually applies to your application or device.

- Be sure that the patent involved is unexpired and valid. When the patent expires, the need to pay royalties does too.

- Due to prior art, litigation, or other factors, the patent may have become legally or practically unenforceable. Your patent lawyer can help you make this determination.

- Check the geographic reach of the patent. If it is a US patent with no Canadian counterpart and you intend to use it only in Canada, you will often not need a license.

- Check to see if your company already has licensed the same patent in another deal. (It happens.)

Copyright

Consortium documents often have terms governing copyrights as well. Here the goal is just to make sure that the consortium has the right to copy, modify, and distribute its standard documents and other related documentation.

Consortium documents commonly require that members grant the consortium a copyright license to any Contributions that they provide. It is common that the consortium itself will own the copyright to the documents that consist of the standard, the implementation examples, and other official documentation. The consortium then grants members the right to make copies, in some cases only internal copies, of the documents.

Termination

Members can withdraw from consortia or they can be terminated. The most common termination is probably for nonpayment of yearly membership fees.

Most consortium agreements provide that if your company leaves a consortium:

- Any licenses that your company has granted to other members will remain in effect and in some case may even apply to new standards that use the same Necessary Claims.

- Any license that other companies have granted to your company will be lost.

This means that once your company has joined a consortium and adopted its patented technologies, it may be unwise to discontinue membership if the technology is relevant to your business.

PATENT RULES AND SDOs

The establishment standards organizations such as ISO, ITU, and ANSI also have patent policies (which you can find on their Web sites). If your company participates in the standards processes of any SDO, you need to be aware of their policies. These policies could change (and this account of them might become obsolete), so you do need to review them from time to time.

Let's look for example at the ANSI Patent Policy (which is quite similar to the rules at the ISO and ITU). Under the policy, ANSI can issue a query to one or more potential patent holders. (This is known as a "Call for Patents.") Requests of this kind are most commonly issued at the working group level when standards reach the proposal stage. Requests are often sent to all working group participants and can be sent to other members as well.

Under the policy:

- The member that receives such a request is required to either (a) state that it does not have patents relevant to the standard; or (b) identify each relevant patent.

- If there are relevant patents, the member must also state, for each patent: (a) that the patent will be licensed for use with the standard royalty-free; or (b) that the patents(s) will be licensed for use with the standard on a RAND basis. There is no option not to license at all.

There are some perceived weaknesses of this kind of rule:

- The requirement applies only to known patents without the obligation for a participant to search its patent portfolio.

- The process applies to contacted members only.

- The policy does not cover patent applications.

Another paradigm is represented by the W3C's patent rule. The W3C requires that its standards must all be royalty-free. It requires its members to disclose relevant patents and applications. W3C's policy is to withdraw a standard if a patent affecting the standard is later revealed and the patent holder does not agree to royalty-free licensing. The advantage of this policy is that it keeps standards (mostly) free of royalty claims. The disadvantage is that it omits all nonfree patented technology—no matter how valuable to users.

STAYING OUT OF TROUBLE WITH STANDARDS

Standards bodies can be good for your business—but not if your company engages in illegal conduct. There are two bodies of law that can threaten your business in this context—antitrust law and unfair competition law.

Antitrust Concerns

Antitrust is the body of law (both state and federal) that protects competition. Violation of antitrust law can give rise to lawsuits by injured competitors and federal enforcement actions. Price-fixing is a criminal antitrust violation.

In 2004 and 2005, the US government obtained guilty pleas from Samsung and from executives of Hynix Semiconductor of Korea and German chipmaker Infineon for criminal violations of the antitrust laws. The case was based on their fixing the prices of dynamic random access memory (DRAM) chips. The executives served prison sentences.

Standards bodies are places where competitors talk to and cooperate with one another. On the whole, antitrust authorities consider standards to be pro-competitive—because they help create a level playing field for competition on the merits. Most consortia focus on technical rather than the business matters, so the antitrust risk level generally is low. However, standards setting meetings will become very dangerous if competitors use them to do anticompetitive things—like fix prices, exclude competitors, and divide markets.

Here are some general pointers to keep you and your company out of trouble with antitrust law while meeting with competitors over standards:

- Don't talk about license or product pricing.

- Don't talk about markets and market share.

- Don't allocate product or geographic markets and sub-markets among companies.

- Don't discuss the validity of patents. (As noted above, asserting worthless patents to bar or extract money from competitors can be a violation of antitrust law.)

Many consortia or other standards organizations have rules or guidelines similar to these—to help the membership say out of antitrust trouble. If you see other companies violating these rules, seek legal counsel. If any question comes up about antitrust compliance, you should seek advice from your legal counsel immediately.

Unfair Competition and Standards

Another way that a company can get into trouble in standards setting is by concealing patents that ought to be disclosed.

There have been a few cases where companies have "sandbagged" other companies. They participated in standards-setting discussions that they steered successfully to include their own technology—without disclosing that their preferred standard was covered by a patent or pending patent application. After the other member companies became reliant on the standard technology, the patent holder then "held up" the other members for royalties.

This conduct is very sharp and aggressive—but is it illegal? It all depends on the rules of the standard organization at the time.

- If the rules called for patent disclosure, then a patent holder that willfully is silent about its relevant patent filings will very likely violate unfair competition law by knowingly failing to disclose them. The patent holder could be held liable in a lawsuit brought by other members. In addition, the Federal Trade Commission may bring proceedings against some companies that abuse standards setting in this way for unfair business practices.

- On the other hand, if the rules of the standards organization do not require disclosure, then the practice of keeping silent about relevant patents and patent applications is legal under US law—although it certainly will not win friends.

PATENT POOLS

Sometimes, the companies that have patents that are relevant to a standard or set of standards will be for an organization for joint licensing of their patents—a so-called patent pool. Patent pool organizations normally operate separately from standard setting bodies. Patent pool organizations tend to charge a single royalty for a full set of "essential" patents and have provisions for pool members to share resulting royalties. An example of a patent pool is the RFID Consortium, which was formed in 2005 to provide access to patent licenses needed for the ultrahigh-frequency (UHF) RFID technology standards.

Patent pooling has advantages and disadvantages for licensees. The main advantage is that it can allow "one-stop" shopping for patent licenses. The main disadvantage is that it is potentially anticompetitive—which is why patent pool arrangements are normally submitted for review by federal antitrust authorities (and often by their counterparts in other nations).

Because of the antitrust issues, patent pooling agreements need to be drafted with a great deal of care and planning. If you want to form a patent pool or add your patents to an existing patent pool, you need to seek legal advice in advance.

WHAT IS AN "OPEN" STANDARD?

You will often hear companies claim to use or promote "open standards." But what does it mean that a standard is open?

There are two aspects of "open" standards. First, is it the result of a truly open process? Second, can it be used royalty-free? It is the latter, practically speaking, that means the most to users.

Open Adoption Process

The process for adoption of a standard can be "opened up" in a number of ways. For example, each proposed standard can be published on the Web. Comments and objections can be received from the public. There can be broad member voting on proposed standards.

Most of the traditional standards setting organizations have rather open models, whereby proposed standards are published for comments and participation is broad. Most consortia chose a less open model where proposals and deliberations are kept confidential and voting at the working group level is typically limited to a select (and more expensive) class of membership.

Royalty-Free

For most users, the most important meaning of an "open standard" is that anyone can use the standard royalty-free—either because there are no blocking patents or because all the patent holders have made their patents available royalty-free.

Companies do adopt many "open" technologies. And most of the time, the standards-based technologies widely believed to be available royalty-free are indeed royalty-free. However, there is always some risk that there is a relevant patent out there that has not surfaced. It would be difficult and very costly to be certain that relevant patents do not exist. Standards organizations do not render legal advice or do patent searches—they will not give you assurance that there are no relevant patents. Even if you were to pay for a patent lawyer's search, the results may be inconclusive. There is not much you can do about this risk, but you should be aware of it.

The recent *Eolas vs. Microsoft* case provides an example of a patent that turned up unexpectedly and applied to standards-based technology. Eolas Technologies Inc. is a company that holds a US patent, filed for in 1994 and granted in 1998, that covers the automatic activation of certain Web browser plug-in functions.

The patent covered functionality commonly used in HTML and the world believed that this HTML functionality was "open" and royalty-free. Eolas sued Microsoft for patent infringement and won a half-billion-dollar jury verdict against the software giant in 2004. (Further proceedings in the case are still going on as of the time that this chapter is being written.) This example indicates how a patent can surface unexpectedly even for standards universally believed to be royalty-free.

FORMING YOUR OWN CONSORTIUM

If your company perceives the need for a new standard—or if your company wants to establish an alternative standard, you (with other like-minded companies) may want to form a new consortium of your own.

There is no great magic to this. It is simply a matter of careful and systematic planning. There are a number of steps that you need to take to decide the scope and focus of the consortium, its structure, its rules of operation, and some practical aspects of operating it. There are many models of consortia documentation that are publicly available to guide you.

In large part, putting together a consortium requires a checklist of the business and legal issues that we have reviewed in this chapter.

- Be sure that there is (or will be) a market need for the standard.

- Identify likely players that may be cofounders.

- With legal counsel's help, think through the issues of how decision-making should work and working group organization.

- Decide on classes of membership and the fee structure.

- Decide how open or closed the decision-making should be.

- Decide on a patent policy.

- Decide if you want to (or might want to) provide certification of compliance with your standards.

- Select a trademark for the consortium.

- Consider the known patents in the subject matter area and how they might affect the standards to be issued.

- With the assistance of legal counsel, be sure that potential anti-trust issues are considered.

In addition, you will need to consider some pragmatic financial issues—such as funding for initial operations, an initial budget, staffing, and the "home" of the consortium. It is common to start a consortium in the home office of one of its founders.

CONCLUSION

Participation in a standards consortium may put your company on the cutting edge of emerging technologies and set it apart as an innovator in its field. Banding together with other companies in your field, large and small, may give your company insight into the future and affordable access to technologies necessary to grow your business. However, joining a standards consortium is not a casual decision. Your company can have significant rights and obligations as a result. It is most important to read and understand the standards body documentation, know how the rules work, and then comply with them.

Content for Digital Media

20

Content is king.

—Attributed to Sumner Redstone, majority owner of media giant Viacom

The value of the software is proportional to the scale and dynamism of the data it helps to manage.

—Tim O'Reilly in "What Is Web 2.0?" September 30, 2005, published in oreilly.com

IN THIS CHAPTER

This chapter is about how to obtain content with the right to use it. This chapter is for any business that uses digital content. That includes Web sites owners, mobile content providers, multimedia businesses, and digital entertainment companies, including video game companies.

In this chapter, the term "content" is used in a broad sense. It means text, graphic, audible, and video information in digital form. Content includes, for example, videos, music, business news, sports news, stock prices, economic data, blogs, baseball scores, weather data, geographical data, and so forth.

How do we use content in digital media? Here are a few examples:

- **Featured Digital Content**—Media offered as a Web or mobile onscreen display, downloads (including podcasts), and streaming or videos or music. Access to content can be for a fee or can be advertising supported (or both).

517

- **Content to Support Creation of Products**—Content used in the creation of other digital content, for example sound and graphics in video games or other multimedia products.

This chapter offers three different topics on the issue of obtaining and getting rights to use content:

- **Topic One: Traditional Clearance**—The most common way to get rights to content is the tried-and-true road of licensing rights from content owners and their distributors. This is traditional "clearance," the process of identifying the owner and procuring the rights you need to specific content. This is the first major topic of this chapter (and by far its longest part). The section also includes an overview of the provisions typically found in agreements that license content for use in digital works. (In Chapters 21 and 22, you will read about using licensed content in Internet and mobile applications and in video games.)

- **Topic Two: User-Supplied Content**—Another way to get data is to get people to contribute content for free. This is the method of the blogosphere and video sites like YouTube. This has turned out to be a complex legal area.

- **Topic Three: Content Gathering**—Another way to get content is to just take it! You could do that by copying it on a large scale from the Web or from other data sources. This is what the search engines do; in this area, the amount of content gathered is huge but the use is very narrow. Or you could take content from Web sites and combine it to produce something new—which is what "mashups" do. We discuss the rules that apply to these new ways to get content.

We introduce this discussion with a review of some intellectual property principles that apply to this rich and multifaceted subject.

FORMS FOR CONTENT

In the form Appendix to this book, we have included some sample clearance agreement forms (also called "releases"). These are forms for persons or companies to authorize use of content (Form 20-1), locations (Form 20-2), and personal names and images (Form 20-3) in digital media. See also the forms for Content Guidelines for user-submitted content (Form 17-1) and rules for Weblogs

(Form 17-2). Digital content licensing forms are offered in connection with Chapter 21, which is about the Web and mobile value chain.

SOME BACKGROUND: CONTENT AND INTELLECTUAL PROPERTY

Let's look first at how the intellectual property laws relate to content and digital media.

There are three sources of content-related rights that we need to pay attention to: copyrights (covering the content itself), trademarks (branding and logos), and rights of the personality (the images and names of artists and stars). Background for this discussion is Chapter 2 (copyright basics), Chapter 3 (copyright on the Internet), and Chapter 4 (trademarks).

Copyright and Content

Under US law (and in most other nations as well), a copyright holder has the exclusive right to make and sell copies of copyrighted works, to display them, and to create derivative works.

Exploitation of content always requires copying and often involves derivatives and public display, so copyright law is almost always in play in content deals. Copyright law applies to most content that is not in the public domain. (There are certain kinds of factual data that are not copyright protected, but are still licensed as digital content. See the discussion of data and copyrights in Chapter 2.)

Literal Copying and Digital Derivatives

One important copyright concern is exact copying—what copyright lawyers call "literal" copying. Many digital copies are exact copies. There is also the creation of digital derivatives created by processing files, such as compressed files, encrypted files, and so forth. Although technically derivatives, these are akin to literal copies because there is minimal transformation of the content.

Unauthorized literal digital copying or sales or display of literal copies of copyrighted content is infringing—unless a defense to infringement applies. The more important copyright defense for literal copying is "fair use." You may wish to review the discussion in Chapter 2 of the fair use defense. As a broad generalization, literal copying of other owners' content for your own profit in your site, service, or product will usually lie outside the bounds of the fair use. That means it will likely be infringing unless you get a license.

Non-Literal Copying

Copyright concerns with content do not end with literal copying. Because content can have artistic elements, themes, and storylines, your company also has to worry about copying (or making derivatives of) of "non-literal elements." You may be accused of copying the look of objects, the melody of tunes, the appearance of artwork, the form or names of characters, the aesthetic design of Web pages, or the story and plot of a video game. The more the elements of your work that are similar to another copyrighted work and the closer they sound or appear, the more likely that your borrowing may be held an infringement.

It is not uncommon for creative people to seek out the published work of others for "inspiration." There is nothing wrong with looking for ideas. Watch out, however, for the tipping point where inspiration becomes copying and infringement. Close imitation is dangerous.

Infringement analysis in this area is done by closely comparing the visual and sound elements of one copyright work to the other (after disregarding unprotectable generic elements). If your product (or a significant element in it) looks like (or sounds like) a copy to the average person and you do not have a license, there's a significant risk of copyright trouble.

Borrowing from other media is another area in which you have to be careful about nonliteral copying. If your Web site has a superhero animation that looks almost like Spiderman or a well-known rock star or your video game has a song that sounds almost like a hit song, there could be a problem. Other than parody (which we discuss below), most nonliteral copying will not be justified by the fair use doctrine.

The Public Domain

In the discussion above, we mentioned the "public domain." These include works on which the copyright has expired, US government works, or works dedicated by the copyright owner to the public domain.

Subject to some exceptions, the copyright on a published work has expired if:

- The work was created and first published *before January 1, 1923*, or, if published later, then

- *70 years after the death of the author*, or if work-made-for-hire for a company, *95 years from publication.*

There are other technical rules under which works published before 1989 may have lost copyright protection. There are also rules for unpublished works. If you want to rely on the public domain status of a work, you may want to consult your attorney to be sure you are correct.

Whether something is the public domain can have more than one answer. For example, a 19th century tune will be out of copyright, but not its 1975 sound recording. A 19th century novel will be out of copyright, but not a translation of the novel made in 1985.

Trademarks and Clearance

Much of the value of content can be tied up in associated trademarks. This is true, for example of famous rock bands and movies. Most people understand that they cannot use a third party brand without permission to brand their own site, services, or product. For example, "Star Wars" is a famous brand, and a Web site developer could not lawfully make a commercial Star Wars site without consent from the brand owner Lucasfilm.

While there is some use of trademarks that can be fair use, generally speaking, famous brands should not be used without permission. This is especially true when they imply endorsement or approval or when their reputation will likely be tarnished or diluted. Trademark owners are often quite aggressive in asserting their trademark rights. If you want to use famous branding for commercial advantage, you will normally need a trademark license as part of your content deal.

Publicity Right (Right of Personality)

Digital content also involves an intellectual property right that we haven't met before in this book—the "publicity right" also known as the "right of personality." This is the right of famous persons to control the commercial use and exploitation of the name, signature, and image—even the sound of their voice.

If you want a personality from sports, TV, music, movie, or a celebrity in a game or Web site, you need to negotiate a license agreement that permits your intended use. This is a state-law created right—not surprisingly the largest share of the court decisions on these rights have occurred in California and New York. A number of states have laws that extend this right of publicity after death. In California, for example, publicity right protection lasts 70 years after death of the celebrity.

Beware also of names that sound similar to names of celebrities or characters that look like famous people. The courts in New York have held that commercial use of look-alike models and sound-alike singers violates the right of personality.

This publicity right rule does not, however, prevent reporting on or photographs of famous personalities for news and comment.

The Right of Privacy

There is another personal right that should be mentioned, which is the right of privacy. This is right (recognized under US state law) for ordinary persons to be left alone.

This is a right that is most relevant when you make commercial use an image (or a video) of a person that is not famous at all and has not consented to use of their image. Using the image without permission could get you sued. And it would be much worse if the picture is used in a way that causes embarrassment or emotional distress. When you deal with images, remember that you normally need both a license to the photo copyright *and* the permission of the subject. Again, there is an exception for news reports of an individual who is involved in a newsworthy event.

A "Clearance Culture"

In traditional media—radio, TV, movies, and the press—commercial use of content usually requires clearance under some or all of the intellectual property concepts mentioned above. If a traditional media company publishes someone else's content without permission, there is a significant risk that it will be sued—and often have the losing case. That's because under applicable principles of copyright, trademark and right of personality, the media company will be liable without regard to fault. This is what we call "strict liability"—good faith reliance on a supplier who claimed to have the required rights is not a defense.

Because of this risk, in traditional media, there is what we call a "clearance culture." It is the general rule in traditional media companies that content must be cleared. With limited exceptions, every third party photo, song, script, and video clip will need a written license or permission. This can be a laborious process.

This clearance culture carries over to much of the digital world as well. If you are going to sell a copyrighted song online, you need permission. If you are going to display a story and photos from the Associated Press (AP) on a mobile phone, you need permission. And so forth.

Blending of the Old and the New

On the Internet, there are certainly commercial sites that use a different paradigm—far removed from traditional clearance culture. An example is YouTube that obtains user-supplied content that is uploaded and displayed with no clearance process—or Google that spiders the Web-gathering content with no one's permission.

However, those new media companies are also involved in the traditional clearance as well. For example, Google has made deals with the major news services to clear content for *Google News*. YouTube has made deals with record labels to put music videos on its site.

To deal with content in digital media, you need to understand the old rules for content and the new rules as well. Both are covered below.

TOPIC ONE: PRACTICAL GUIDANCE IN CLEARING CONTENT

The following is an overview of many aspects of clearing content. As you will see, there are many issues in content in a digital world.

Getting Started in Clearance

There are several relevant questions regarding clearance of content for your site, product, or project that you need to start with:

- What third party rights do you need to clear?
- Who has the rights you need?
- What are the limitations, restrictions, and risks that come with the content?
- What are the form, scope, and terms of the license agreement that you can negotiate?
- What will the content cost to get?

For a simple project, these may be rather simple questions. For a complex project, getting the license agreement or agreements that you will end up with may also be complex. In the following pages, we present an overview of how to deal with these issues.

What Content Items Need Clearance

Individual items of third party content that your company exploits commercially in a Web site or mobile application will usually require clearance by means of a written license. A single work may need more than one clearance. A photo of a famous baseball player in his uniform would require the copyright clearance for the photo, right of personality clearance from the player, and trademark clearance for the uniform and its markings.

Getting clearance for a major project can involve many licensors and time and money. Say, for example, that you want to make a realistic online game based on major league baseball—with representations of the real ballparks and with the names and faces of players of real teams. You would need to obtain permissions for the players, the teams, the ballpark owners, and the major leagues. You would need to clear all copyrighted music. Any photos or other art in the game would need clearance. If there were famous-make baseball gloves and bats in the game, you would need permission for those as well. You would need permission for the famous brand advertisements on the fence of your virtual ball parks (you may be able to get advertisers to pay for such placement). Even the digital fonts that you use for text in your virtual score card will likely need clearance. In each instance, your task would be to get a suitable signed agreement permitting use of each item of the needed content from some person or entity that has the right to grant the license. To put together, this collection of content licenses requires careful planning, contacts, time, and money. You can see why clearance culture needs to be meticulous.

Copyrights Clearance for Prose and Graphic Works

There are some works for which copyright clearance is relatively straightforward once you find the rights holder.

- **Prose Works**—For prose, the copyright originally goes to the author. The author might hold the rights or she might have transferred them to someone else, such as a publisher or a news service. In some cases there may be more than one copyright owner for a work. For example, if one person wrote a book and a second person translated it, there are two copyrights. The translation would be a derivative work, and under copyright principles, to use the translated work, you would need a license under both copyrights.

- **Graphic Works**—With graphic works, the copyright also starts with the creator. The rights may have been transferred to a publisher or a news service. It is also true that new copyrights are created when a second person manipulates an existing image. To use an altered graphic image may require clearing two or more copyrights. Digital "sampling" of graphic works normally requires permission as well.

Once you have found the rights holder(s), the next step is a negotiating process to see if you can agree upon a license that fits your intended use and distribution for the right price. What the deal will look like for obtaining text and graphics content will depend on what content is involved and its value. The clearance of text for a recipe for a food-related Web site will be very different from clearance of illustrations from a Harry Potter novel for an online advertising campaign.

For "stock" photos and graphics, you can check out the many sources of this material on the Web. Many stock content licenses are available on a "click-and-use" basis on the Web for modest payments. Be sure that when you license such a stock work that you read very carefully the license that comes with it. Be sure the terms fully cover your intended use.

Another tip: when sourcing materials, it is in your interest to deal with reputable sources. Just because a person claims to hold the copyright to a work is not a guarantee that they are the true owner.

A Note about Fonts

A typeface is a form of printed letters (for example, the letters in each word on this printed page). A font is the computer equivalent—a digital file that a computer uses to generate typefaces on a screen. Many font developers license fonts for use in games and other commercial multimedia products on a royalty or flat-fee basis. It is best practice to buy a license for use of the fonts in these commercial products, unless you are sure the font can be used royalty-free.

You may have heard that fonts are not copyrightable—but it's not that simple. It is true that the US Copyright Office takes the view that typefaces are not subject to copyright. However, many countries other than the United States take the position that typefaces are copyrightable. The Copyright Office believes that *scalable* fonts are subject to copyright, but that *bitmapped* (fixed) fonts are not. That's because scalable fonts are really software programs that tell a computer how to generate a typeface on the screen, and software programs are subject to copyright.

In addition, some font downloads come with restrictive clickwrap agreements that make the font royalty-free for personal use only and require that commercial use require royalty payments. Those agreements are likely to be binding.

Therefore a developer that uses a particular font may need a license, and, if so, the developer should be sure that terms of any applicable font license cover the intended use.

Locations

You will need written permission to record images or videos in a particular private location, such as home, a restaurant, or a retail store. There are several reasons for this. Being on site without permission might be trespassing. The location may have a name which is its trademark. There may be a copyright in the building as an architectural work—or there may be images inside the location that are copyrighted. If you are recording in a leased location, it is best to get permission from both the owner and the lessee.

Copyright and Clearing Music

Plato wrote 25 centuries ago that music "gives soul to the universe, wings to the mind, flight to the imagination, and charm and gaiety to life." Musical content is fundamental. It is impossible to imagine digital entertainment without it.

For better for worse, clearing music can be tricky. To begin with, a music recording is subject to two different copyrights:

- **Composition**—One is the composition copyright—covering the words and musical notes. This is the work created by the composer and lyricist. For example, there are hundreds of recordings of White Christmas, but there is only one composition copyright for the song, which Irving Berlin wrote in 1940. (Sometimes, the composition copyright consists of two works, the music, that is, the musical notes, and the lyrics.) The composition copyright is indicated with the traditional ©, 'C in a circle' copyright symbol. The composition copyright must be licensed for any copying and sales of copies, performance, and derivatives of the composition, including sheet music, live performance, and recordings.

- **Master Recording**—The other kind is the copyright in the sound recording. This copyright covers the recorded sound and is known as the "master recording," the "master," or sometimes the "phonogram." An example is Frank Sinatra's 1987 recording of White Christmas on the Capital label. The master recording copyright covers just the recorded sound. This copyright is symbolized by the 'P in a circle' symbol or ℗. The sound recording copyright is normally controlled by the recording company—known as the "label." This copyright in the recording covers copying of the master recording and also "digital performance," as discussed below.

To copy recorded music, you need to obtain rights to both the composition copyright *and* the master recording copyright. Take, for example, Green Day's recording of "My Generation" which is on Green Day's debut album.

- **Composition**—The composer of My Generation is Peter Townshend of the Who. The publisher of the composition is the Devon Music Inc. in New York City. Devon Music licenses the composition copyright.

- **Master Recording**—Green Day's label is Reprise, which is part of Warner Music Group. Warner Music Group controls the master recording.

This means that if you wanted to include the Green Day version of this song in a Web site, multimedia product, or game, you would need permission from both Devon Music and Warner Music. You need to make two different deals for use of these two different aspects of the same recorded music. (Licensing the sound recording for a popular song is often considerably more expensive than the composition rights.) For some uses, such as selling CDs or music downloads, Warner Music may be able to provide you with a license under both copyrights, if (as is likely) it has a prior arrangement with the music publisher for recorded music sales.

Of course you don't have to use Green Days' version of this song. You could license the master recording of the Who's version. (The Who's recording is on the MCA label, which is owned by Universal Music Group.) Or you could license the composition copyright only and hire musicians and a music producer to supply a new recording of the song. (If you do, be sure to secure, by written agreement, the master recording copyright from the artists and producer that you hire to record the song.)

There may be intermediate derivative forms in music. For example, a new arrangement of a song (in the form of the sheet music) would be a derivative of the composition copyright. There is a separate sound recording copyright in each of the tracks that are made in a recording session. Similarly, a remix would be a separate recording copyright as well a derivative of the master recording copyright for the song's tracks.

You would need these same permissions not only for the song, but also for portions of the song. The legal issues to clear an excerpt used as a ringtone are the same as for clearance of the whole song.

Finding Music Copyright Holders

To find music rights holders is usually not difficult. The label that holds the performance copyright can be found in music catalogs—and is listed on music CDs. (Sometimes, rights to recordings are bought and sold or otherwise moved, so the CD is not always the final guide.)

To find the composition copyright publisher, the best source is usually the online catalogs of the performing arts societies in the US. These are:

- BMI (Broadcast Music, Inc.), www.bmi.com

- ASCAP (American Society of Composers, Authors and Publishers), www.ascap.com

- SESAC (originally called the Society of European Stage Authors & Composers), www.sesac.com

These performing arts organizations mission is to collect royalties for public performance for most public performances of compositions. They obtain royalty payments from broadcasters, Webcasters, night clubs, bands, and any other business or entity that performs compositions. They then share the royalty proceeds with the composition copyright holders.

Other Music-Related Clearance for Groups

The music copyrights are not the only clearance that you may need when dealing with recorded music. If you wanted to use a rock band's logo, you will need a trademark license from the owner of the mark—which is likely to be the band itself. If you want to use the likenesses of the band members in the game, you will need to license their personality rights. The band's talent agency is normally the place to go to propose such a licensing deal.

"Promotion Use" of Thumbnails and Clips

It is a rather common practice for services that sell or stream music on the Web to use album cover art in "thumbnail" form together with 30-second clips of the recorded music. This is sometimes done without permission from the labels.

There is a folk myth that "promotional use" of album cover art or music clips is legally permissible even if unlicensed. In fact, album cover art is undoubtedly covered by copyright and is no different from any other copyrighted work. While the labels may well tolerate your unlicensed use of album cover art or sound clips to promote their works, you will be living on their sufferance—there is no guarantee that they will allow you to do so.

Sampling

Audio sampling occurs if you take a portion of one sound recording and reuse it in another sound recording. The sound taken could be a bit of music, speech, or a sound effect. In almost all cases, there is a potential legal issue if you don't have a license or written consent.

Because there has been a lot of sampling of music in recent years, particularly in hip-hop music, there have been some court decisions regarding sampling. However, it is too early to say that the law is fully settled. Based on the decisions to date (as of the time that we are writing this book late in 2007), we can distinguish two situations with two different rules:

- **Sampling from the Sound Recording**—Based on the cases to date, it appears that any amount of copying from a sound recording, no matter how small, will be deemed an infringement. The courts have so far rejected arguments of "fair use" or "*de minimus*" copying. This means that any electronic sampling of third party recorded content without consent is likely to be infringing under current US law. So, negotiating license for each sampled recording is a necessity (at least until your attorney advises you otherwise).

- **Copying Phases from a Composition**—Here the issue is not "sampling" of sound, but rather the inserting of a note pattern or music phrase from another piece of music into your own composition. Here the rule is that there can be *de minimus* copying for a composition—a few notes may not be enough to render you liable. However the more that is taken and the more distinctive the musical phrasing is, the more likely it will be held infringing. This kind of copying without consent is inherently risky because it is never clear how much copying is too much.

The only really safe way to do any sampling or other copying of recorded music is with a written license and that includes licenses from both the music publisher *and* the label of the sampled music.

Public Performance and Webcasting

Let's take a look at a special copyright problem—clearing music for Webcasting. This section applies to you if you are streaming music over the Internet or a mobile network.

Under US law, the composition copyright and the performance copyright are different in one important respect:

- The *composition copyright* includes a legal monopoly on *all public performances.* This "performance right," controlled by the composition copyright, extends to all means of performance, including Webcasting over the Internet.

- The *master recording copyright* includes a legal monopoly on *public performance only by means of digital audio transmission.* The "digital performance right" under the master recording copyright extends to Webcasts in the United States as well as other digital broadcasts such as satellite radio.

This means that:

- If you want to broadcast a song over the radio or play it in a club, you do not need permission from the record label. You only need deal with ASCAP, BMI, or SESAC. The license needed is only under the composition copyright.

- If you want to do a streaming Internet Webcast of the same song, *you need a license to the master recording copyright* (normally held by the label) —*in addition to* a composition performance license from ASCAP, BMI, or SESAC.

Special Rules for Webcasting

So, how do you get a master recording license for Webcasting? There are two paths:

- The first is the old-fashioned way—negotiate a deal with each label whose music you want to use. If you do this, you can make your best deal and get whatever rights you can for the best prices you can negotiate.

- The second (and most common approach) is use of a unique "statutory license" that you can get under a special provision of the Digital Millennium Copyright Act (or DMCA). The good news about the DMCA statutory license is that it covers all performance copyrights automatically for Webcasts to the USA. The bad news is that there are many restrictions, and Webcasters have complained bitterly that the royalty rates are too high. (This statutory license does not apply to music downloads or podcasts; these require traditional clearance by means of permission. It also does not supply the required composition copyright license which, as noted, you still need to get from ASCAP, BMI, or SESAC.)

The (Many) Restrictions for Webcasters

Tight restrictions on the DMCA statutory digital broadcast license are designed to protect the labels. The rules allow Webcasters to provide music, but prevent online listeners from getting the same experience as buying a music CD. Here is a (long) list of the major legal restrictions on Webcasting under the DMCA statutory license:

- In any three-hour period, the Webcaster:
  - May not play more than three songs from a single album.
  - May not play more than two songs consecutively from a single album.
  - May not play more than four songs from a single featured artist or from boxed set.
  - May not play more than three songs consecutively from a single featured artist or from boxed set.

(These four restrictions are called the "sound recording performance complement" in the DMCA.)

- If the service permits users to make requests, the Webcaster must wait at least one hour before playing any requested song. This rule prevents the Webcaster from having an on-demand or "interactive service."

- If a Webcaster archives programs and makes them available on its Web site, then each program must be at least five hours long and it cannot be available on the Webcaster's Web site for more than two weeks.

- Any continuous loop prerecorded Webcast music programs must be at least three hours long.

- Webcaster must identify the sound recording, the album, and the featured artist on screen, if it can display this information. However, the service must not preannounce songs in any way.

- Frequency of re-broadcasting is restricted. A program of less than an hour can be broadcast no more than three times in any two-week period. Longer programs can be broadcast no more than four times in any two-week period.

- The Webcaster must pass on, and not disable, any included copyright information or protections in the recorded music (if any).

- The Webcaster must not encourage users to copy or record Webcast music and must disable recording and copying to the extent that it can do so.

- Webcasts under the statutory license are for US audiences only.

Webcast License Royalty Payments

Complying with these rules is not the end of it. The Webcaster also must pay. To take advantage of this statutory license, the Webcaster has to pay royalties to SoundExchange, Inc., a company set up by the Recording Industry Association of America (RIAA). The RIAA is the labels' industry association.

The rules also require the Webcaster to record a variety of information about the music played in the Webcasts and report this information to SoundExchange. SoundExchange distributes this royalty money and provides usage reports to copyright owner and artists. (Fifty percent of the fees are paid to the performance copyright owner, normally the record label, and 50 percent is paid to the recording artists.) The Webcaster must also file a form with the US Copyright Office, called the "Notice of Use of Sound Recordings under Statutory License." You can find the form on the copyright office Web site.

Different statutory license rates apply for commercial and noncommercial Webcasters. For 2008, the official commercial royalty rate (which is set by a federal government panel) is $.0014 (fourteen hundredths of a cent) per performance, where a "performance" is defined as the streaming of one song to one listener. If you Webcast one song to 1000 listeners, this royalty would be $1.40. Rates go up yearly to $.0019 in 2010. These rates have been hugely controversial. Webcasters believe they are outrageously high and are lobbying Congress for changes in this system. The labels (no surprise) think the rates are fair. Under pressure (as of time that this chapter was written in 2007), the labels had been offering a discounted rate to Webcasters—less than the full amount permitted. This is an area to watch. It is possible that rates will be reset or that Congress will make other changes in the law.

If you want to be a Webcaster:

- You can find information at www.soundexchange.com on how to sign up for the statutory master recording license and how to report and pay royalties. The site also has the reporting forms that you will need.

- There are also blanket composition copyright licenses needed. You can get information about Webcast composition copyrights licenses at the Web sites of ASCAP, BMI, and SESAC.

- There is more information on the DMCA license and the copyright issues of the US Copyright Office Web site at www.copyright.gov.

If you still have questions about this system, the DMCA, or how to comply, you should consult your legal counsel.

Public Performance and Downloading

How the public performance right (both for the composition and for the recording) plays out for music *downloads* is a bit more uncertain. It seems clear that providing a downloadable file or a podcast to a customer, without more, is not a performance.

An issue arises however when there is a download that promptly plays (or plays while downloading), a process sometimes called "pseudostreaming." In this case (although the matter is not free from doubt), it is likely that there *is* a public performance, and the same rules would apply as for streaming; that is, you most likely need to get licenses under the same rules.

If this is an issue that matters for your digital business, you should ask your attorney if there have been recent legal developments or decisions in this area.

Movies and Television Content

Traditional video content (motion pictures and television) is an amalgam of rights—a mixture of images, music, story, sounds, rights of personality, brands, and so forth. It is the job of the movie or TV producer to assemble all the relevant rights.

With popular films and shows, licensing for auxiliary products and services of all sorts—from game or Web promotions to dolls and T-shirts—is common, particularly for films and shows for children and action-adventure films.

Rights for auxiliary products may be licensed by the distributor (for example, Twentieth Century Fox) or the producer (for example, Lucasfilm). Video games rights or right for Web exploitation of the most popular television or movies content is likely to be very expensive and available only to leading game and Web companies. Other older or less popular video or motion picture content may be available for much less.

As with the other content types that we have discussed, the issues involved include the copyrights in the images and sound (including music), the branding, and the rights of personality for the stars. Content included under license may include not only the film itself, but also stars and director interviews, on-set photos, separate sound track, and so forth.

There may be additional obligations that come with this type of content. The producer may be subject to a contractual requirement to require you to make certain payments to motion picture unions such as the Screen Actors Guild (SAG) or TV unions such as the American Federation of Television and Radio Artists (AFTRA).

If you are seeking to license rights from the movies or TV from a television or the movies, you should use an attorney or agent with experience in the field. Most of the practitioners in this legal specialty, not surprisingly, work in Los Angeles and New York.

Creative Commons

Sometimes, developers use music, sound effects, graphics, or graphic effects that are available under the Creative Commons or other "open" content licenses. These are license forms, loosely based on the "open source" concepts from software licensing, that are designed to permit content to be shared and used. There are even Creative Commons "Sampling Licenses" that expressly permit sampling of music and sound. You can find lots of Creative Commons licensed content on the Web.

However, just because content is under Creative Commons license does not mean that it is available for use in any Web site, multimedia product, or game. There are various Creative Commons licenses, and the rights granted in these licenses vary. Some Creative Commons licenses permit commercial use and some do not. Some permit derivative works and some do not. This means that someone in your company must be responsible for reading, tracking, and keeping records of any Creative Commons license (or similar license) relied upon.

Remember also that just because someone makes content available under a Creative Commons license does not necessarily mean he or she actually has the rights needed to permit you to use it. There is always some risk that the copyright really belongs to somebody else.

Parodies and Other Fair Use

When you do a parody, you can use characters, themes, and tunes without the copyright holder's consent. The lead case involved 2 Live Crew's explicit-lyrics song "*Pretty Woman.*" The allegation in that case was that the song infringed the composition copyright for the Roy Orbison ballad "*Oh Pretty Woman.*" 2 Live Crew lost in the lower courts, but won its case in the US Supreme Court. The Court held that their song was a parody and, as such, protected fair use. That gave the Crew an absolute defense to copyright infringement.

A couple of points on parodies:

First: Be very sure that your content really is a parody, which must provide commentary (usually social, ethical, or political) on the original work. Just because your song or other game content is funny or clever and uses third party content does not make it a parody of that work.

Second: Even if you don't need *permission to do a parody, you may still want to get it. For example, "Weird Al" Yankovic is the king of music and video parodies, but always gets permissions from the rights holders in the songs that are the object of his craft. In general, you will be far more likely to get cooperation and maintain good will if you can work out mutually agreeable terms for the use of another company's material.*

Facts and Factual Databases

The application of copyright law to factual information and data is a topic covered in the previous chapters of this book on copyrights. In summary, this is the rule. If the contents of a database are *facts*, US copyright law does *not* protect those facts. In the famous case of *Feist Publications v. Rural Telephone Service* in 1991, the US Supreme Court ruled that no infringement occurs if one phone book company copies all the contents of a rival's phone book—despite the fact that it took millions of dollars and years of effort to create the phone book in the first place. The court ruled that copyright law simply did not apply. There is a lot of data that is in the same uncopyrightable category; for example, stock market data, baseball statistics, lists of homes for sale, and the like.

There is a rule that if a selection or arrangement of data is original, then copyright protection will extend to that selection or arrangement of data, but not to the facts themselves. An example of an original selection and arrangement would a "ten best" list. Where the arrangement is unoriginal—such as alphabetical order—there is no copyright protection.

Under this rule, you might assume that you are free to take any factual data on the Web that is not the subject of an original selection or arrangement without fear of suit. However, the rule is not quite so simple because of two sets of legal rules.

The Impact of Web site "Browsewrap" Agreements

Whether facts are copyright protection or not, data and fact holders may have protection under an entirely different body of law—contract law. This is a topic covered in Chapter 16 in the discussion on clickwrap and browsewrap agreements. A prime example is the case of *Ticketmaster Corp. v. Tickets.com, Inc.* (decided in 2003) discussed in that chapter. Tickets.com used a spider program to extract sports and entertainment event data including price, venue, date, and time information from Ticketmaster's Web site. Tickets.com then put up the data on its own Web site. The "terms of use" on the Ticketmaster site stated that of the information obtained from the Web site was for "personal use" only and not to be used for commercial purposes. The court ruled that these terms of use were an enforceable contract that could be enforced against Tickets.com to bar its taking the data. This case and others like it mean that factual data that would be unprotectable if published in a book or newspaper may be protectable by contract if it appears on a Web site.

As we noted in the chapter on clickwrap and browsewrap agreements, it is not clear how far the courts will carry this contract-based doctrine. My best guess is that this law will end up being a mirror image of "fair use" law. Most likely if you take a lot of data from all across the Web and use it in a "transformative" and noncompetitive way, the law will probably not hold you liable. If you take a lot of data from one site or a few sites and use the copied data to "piggyback" on that site and compete with it, there is more risk under contract law that the court will conclude that you violated the terms of use.

This body of law is not settled. If you are engaging in this kind of data gathering, you should consult legal counsel for guidance.

The Hot News Doctrine

Generally speaking law on copying content in the United States is exclusively under US federal copyright law—which means that it displaces any state law regarding copying. However, there is a narrow exception in the law of some states—notably New York—under the so-called "Hot News Doctrine." This doctrine applies if the copying party takes highly time-sensitive information that the originator has gathered at considerable expense, and the copying party "free rides" on the data in direct competition in a manner that seriously harms the originator.

The originator of this kind of "hot news" can sue the copying party under state law. The remedy can be an injunction that stops the competition or money damages.

There is tension between this doctrine and First Amendment freedom of speech. As a result, the hot news doctrine has not been widely applied. But the case law is still out there and a potential threat. If you have an idea for a business that piggybacks on "hot news" under this principle, you should discuss this issue with your attorney.

What if You Get the Facts Wrong

Sometimes, new media publishers want to know if they risk liability for publishing incorrect information that causes harm. The general answer under US law is "No." The courts have said that inaccurate publications to the public at large, even if negligent, and even if very harmful, are immune from lawsuits. For example, the courts have held that a publisher was not liable for wrong stock market prices in articles that led to economic loss. As long as your misinformation is published generally and not *intentionally* wrong, it is most unlikely that you will be liable.

A Note on Dealing with Employees and Contractors

A lot of digital media companies obtain content from their own employees and contractors. While copyright law generally awards employers ownership of copyrights created by employees, it is certainly best practice to have each employee sign a rights transfer and confidentiality agreement of the type described in this book. See discussion of these agreements in Chapter 7.

With regard to contractors, there is the additional circumstance that the default copyright rule is the reverse. Remember that under US law, your company cannot obtain ownership of a copyright or patent or any other exclusive interest in a copyright from an independent contractor without a *written* agreement—no matter how much you pay the contractor. So written contracts with contractors are a necessity. These agreements and their "work-made-for-hire" clauses are covered in Chapter 10.

Agreements that License Content for Digital Products and Services

Agreements that license content for use in digital products and services can go from the very simple (for inexpensive or "stock" content) to very elaborate—for the most valuable and most attractive content. This section of the chapter presents a high-level overview of the terms that are likely to be included in a deal for highly valued content. Of course, each deal must be adapted to the particular content and your particular licensed use.

Let's assume that you are negotiating for a license for some popular music, movie, comic book or novel that you wish to use in creating a game or other online or wireless property. What are the provisions that you are likely to negotiate over in a deal like that? In this section, we review some of the provisions and clauses we would expect to see.

For the purpose of this discussion, let's call the company that has the rights to provide as the "Content Supplier" and the other party the "licensee."

Note also that this overview is not a substitute for legal help. Unless you have a lot of experience, you will need a lawyer's help with these deals.

The Deliverables

The Agreement should specify what it is that the Content Supplier must deliver to the licensee. For recorded music, this could be the sound recording, the logos, pictures of the artists, and so forth. For movies, other video, or text, there would be a similar list of assets. The agreement may also provide for the Content Supplier to generate and supply additional deliverables, such as additional promotional photographs. The agreement would also state when the assets are to be delivered.

Grant of Rights

The agreement will have to specify the rights that the licensee is permitted to exercise using the delivered content. For example, for a video game deal, the agreement might authorize the making of a game, its distribution, its promotion, and so forth. The agreement for a game might also allow content packs, hint books, or other related merchandise. For a Web site or wireless use of the content, there would be a corresponding list of license grants, specifying how the content can be used or transformed, distributed, downloaded, and promoted. The agreement will state whether the rights granted are nonexclusive or exclusive in any respect. The agreement will state expressly the various licenses, as applicable, granted for each item of content, for brands, for use of personality or character names and images. The more detailed these provisions, the more control the Content Supplier will have.

Restrictions and Limitations

The agreement will usually impose definite limitations on the rights granted. Here are some of those that might apply:

- The grant may be for specified territories or languages.

- The grant may be limited in duration.

- The agreement may control the timing of the introduction of the licensed product or service. For example, there may be a requirement that use of a rock band video be timed to coincide with the "street date" (first sale date) of its new album.

Style and Quality Controls

Content Suppliers usually have large investments in the creation and promotion of their content properties. They don't want their brands to be cheapened or tarnished. So many licenses come with restriction and mandatory guidelines on how content and branding must look or can be used. Commonly, the Content Supplier will want the right to review in advance and approve (or reject) any licensee product or service that uses the delivered content. The Content Supplier may insist on quality standards as well as "decency" standards.

Branding Restrictions

Content suppliers will often want to control the branding and prevent cobranding of its content. For example, if a Content Supplier provided sports video supplier licensed content to *ABC News* online, it would normally specify that it can be used only on ABC News-branded Web sites. It would not want the content showing up under *The New York Times* branding or on a site that was cobranded by *ABC* and *The New York Times*. The reason for these restrictions is to allow the Content Supplier to keep control of the exploitation in its markets and to avoid competing against its own licensees.

Compensation, Reports, and Audit

Compensation deals for content user can be simple or complex. Commonly charges are based on the amount of use (for example, for each download or display) or royalty-based or a combination of the two. There are many possible variations.

The Advance. An agreement for content of high value is likely to include an advance payment that is an advance payment of licensee fees or royalties to the Content Supplier upon closing the deal and/or delivery of the content. The advance payment is designed to make sure the licensee has some "skin in the game." The advance is almost always nonrefundable.

Minimum. These deals also usually featured yearly (or other periodic) minimum royalty or license fee payment commitments. If the licensee's payments fall short, it may have to make up the difference—and the Content Supplier may also be able to terminate the deal. (Termination would usually include a reasonable period for the licensee to sell off any inventory.)

Required Advertising and Promotion

The Agreement may require the licensee to spend a specified budgeted amount on advertising and promotion of the product that features the content. There may be requirements as to the types of advertising required, for example a requirement of specified television or Web promotion.

Ownership

The agreement will have provisions to make it clear that the Content Supplier retains all ownership rights in its content and brands.

Indemnification and Insurance

The licensee will expect the Content Supplier to provide indemnification that backs up the content that it supplies. Most often the Content Supplier agrees, in an indemnification clause, to "defend, indemnify, and hold harmless" the licensee from third party intellectual property claims arising from use of the content as licensed.

For its part, the Content Supplier will often expect that the licensee will indemnify it for all other risks, including, for example product defect claims, false advertising claims, claims of injury from the licensee products, and so forth. The Content Supplier's view is that it is being paid for content, not to take any product-related risks—and that therefore the licensee should provide contractual protection.

We reviewed indemnity clauses in some detail in Chapter 8 (the contract basics chapter). As we discussed there, there are many ways to expand or contract the protection offered by an indemnity clause. Small changes in wording in these clauses can have large effects. You may wish to seek your attorney's advice on whether the indemnity you are offered in a content agreement is good enough and whether you can try to get a better one.

Any party's indemnification is no more valuable than its balance sheet. In some cases, the Content Supplier will insist that the licensee provide insurance (such as general liability, infringement, errors and omissions or e-commerce insurance policies) to reinforce its indemnity obligations.

Confidentiality, Limitation of Liability; Other Boilerplate
Agreements to supply content have much of the other "boilerplate" provisions that we commonly see in digital agreements. For a discussion of these clauses, please review Chapter 8.

TOPIC TWO: USER-SUPPLIED CONTENT

This section of the chapter is about user-supplied content. There is no doubt that this kind of data can be, in the aggregate, of great value. Here are some examples from the commercial world (and there is much more that is noncommercial):

- Core content for Amazon.com's business is comments and ratings from readers. With enough money you could duplicate Amazon's book sales technology, but you would not have its user-supplied content and, without that content, you could not be competitive.

- News, sports, and many other content sites include user comments on stories.

- Social Web sites like Facebook and MySpace are created by aggregation of user-supplied data.

- User-generated content is a key asset of massively multiplayer online games such as Worlds of Warcraft and Second Life.

- Perhaps the most famous example: YouTube was founded in 2005 and was sold in 2006 to Google for $1.65 *billion* in Google stock. Its value was built on content that it acquired from users for free.

Most user-supplied content (except on sites directed to children) is not screened by a human before it goes up on these Web sites. These sites have automated processes for uploading content and posting it on the site. This means content that may be problematic and readily flow into Web sites.

Rights Clearance in User-Supplied Content

How can your business legally use and display this kind of user-supplied content without violating third party intellectual property rights? There are two clearance issues involved, one easy and one not-so-easy.

- It's easy to get permission to use the rights to an end-user's own creations, as for example a video that the user made herself.

- It is not easy to get permission to use all the third party content that the user may have included (usually without permission) in her content upload to your site or service, as for example the movie sound track song that she included in her home-made video.

In addition, as is explained below, user-supplied content may come with other legal problems.

Carefully Crafted Terms of Use

To get a license from the user for rights that she is legally able to grant you, the key is to have the right terms of use on your Web site (or other digital service) terms of use. (To review how Web site terms of use work, you may wish to refer back to Chapter 17.) You want the user to grant your business a clearly stated broad license to user-supplied content.

One place to start is the page on your site that has instructions and functionality for uploading content. (We call it the "Uploading Page.") On the Uploading Page, the text should state prominently that "User Submissions are subject to the Terms of Use," and should have a link to the full text of your site's terms of use.

Your terms of use document should include a license grant stating that the user provides your company a license for all "User Submissions." Here are some examples of license grant clauses that may work for you.

- For user-submitted text content, the terms of use could provide for the user to grant your company:

a permanent worldwide, non-exclusive, royalty-free, sublicenseable and transferable license to create derivatives of and to, copy, store, edit, display, archive, reproduce, reprint, publish in other forms, include in archives, and distribute each User Submission and derivatives in any format or channel.

- For video content, they could provide for the user to grant your company:

a permanent worldwide, non-exclusive, royalty-free, sublicenseable and transferable license to create derivatives of and to display, and perform each User Submission and to, copy, store, edit, display, archive, reproduce, perform, and distribute the User Submission and derivatives in any format or channel.

You should also include an assurance from the user (for what it's worth) that the user has all required rights. The text could look like this:

You represent that you have all necessary licenses, rights, consents, and permissions to provide the User Submission and to grant the foregoing licenses.

For more examples of terms of use provisions on user-supplied content, you only have to search the Web. There are hundreds of examples. Be sure to use only text that you understand clearly and that really fits your business. Get a lawyer's advice if you have any doubts about how to set up your terms of use correctly.

There is much more that belongs in your terms of use than these few clauses. For a review of many additional provisions, please see the discussion in Chapter 17. As your digital business changes and evolves, you may want to revisit and revise your terms of use to make sure it fits your needs.

Content Guidelines

You terms of use should contain a requirement that the user comply with "Content Guidelines" or "Community Standards." This is a separate document of rules regarding content that will offend other users.

Content Guidelines will normally ban content that is pornographic or sexually explicit, about illegal activity, violent, racist or sexist, anti-gay, threatening, and so forth. Content Guidelines include a requirement that content that violates copyright or trademark rights should not be submitted. It is common for such guidelines to limit content that includes advertising or promotion of businesses or commercial Web sites.

You can find many examples of such guidelines on the Web. The guidelines do, of course, need to be adapted to each Web site, its users, and content types.

Having guidelines may not be enough to actually keep harmful content off your Web site. If you have lots of user submitted content, it is a good idea to include functionality that allows users to report offensive content. Some sites (for example, MySpace) have employees whose only job is to hunt for and take down pornography and other offensive content.

Blogging Terms of Use

It is common for many Web sites to have separate terms of use for their Weblogs (usually known as "blogs"). Examples of these supplemental terms of use are also commonly available on the Web. We have included in the form appendix a version of "Blog Terms of Use" that we like. It comes, as with all forms in this book, with the caveat that it may or may not fit your business.

Issues and Opportunities from User-Supplied Video Content

There are many sites on the Internet that based their business on aggregating user-supplied video content. These sites use the traffic to sell advertisements. Current sites of this sort include Metacafe, iFilm, Yahoo Video, MySpace, AOL Uncut, YouTube, and others. There will no doubt be many new variations in the future on this business model.

YouTube, the most popular site of this type to date, has been sued by a number of content owners. They apparently resent YouTube's benefiting from their content that YouTube has not paid for. User-supplied video content presents challenges, along with its opportunities. Here are some of the reasons:

- Much of the content posted on video sites has been simply illegally copied from network and cable television or from other commercial video sources.

- Much of user-supplied video content is partly original. For example, the user takes a movie scene (recorded digitally from a DVD or television image) but substitutes a new sound-track. In that case, the user has (without permission) made a derivative work. Or the user may make an original short video, but may use a popular song (without permission, of course) as background music. A user's video lip-syncing a song would be another instance.

- Taking down *all* commercial content may not be consistent with the content owner's wishes. For example, a movie distributor might have no objection to fan-submitted content that consists of movie clips or previews.

Back in Chapter 3, we provided a discussion in considerable detail about the "Notice-and-Take-Down" rules of the DMCA. These are the so-called "safe harbor" rules, also known as DMCA Section 512(c). These rules can provide a "service provider" with immunity from copyright liability if it follows to the letter the procedures stated in the law.

The importance of these safe harbor rules for user video content contribution on the Internet cannot be overstated. It's fair to say that sites like YouTube could not have been possible without the protection of the safe harbor rules. *If you have a Web site and allow users to contribute content of any sort, you must take advantage of the protection of these rules; they are especially important for video content.* We will not repeat the discussion in Chapter 3 here, so please refer to that overview of the safe harbor rules, follow the procedures, and take advantage of these statutory provisions.

The safe harbor rules are certainly the first line of defense, but they are not a full answer to dealing with user-supplied video content. That's because:

- Under the wording of the law, the DMCA safe harbor rules will not protect your business if you are aware of *"facts or circumstances from which the infringing activity is apparent."* Whether infringing activity is "apparent" will depend on all the facts. It is likely that if your site gets infringing content repeatedly from the same users, for example, the court may decide that your business knew about the infringement and is not entitled to the protection of the DMCA safe harbor.

- The rules do not apply if there is a direct financial benefit tied to the download—such as "pay to view."

- Depending how you run your business, you may be accused of inducing infringement under the theory of the *Grokster* case (discussed in Chapter 2). For example, if your video site accepts 90-minute-long videos, the courts may conclude that you encouraged posting of infringing motion pictures and TV shows.

- Applying the safe harbor rules requires labor and attention. It is an informal "rule of thumb" for Web sites that you should take down challenged content within 24 hours of notice. It is expensive and tedious to be dealing, day after day, with "take down" notices from media companies.

- The safe harbor rules don't apply outside the USA.

- There may be opportunities from making deals with media companies rather than continually fending them off using the DMCA rules.

Here are some of the measures that YouTube uses—or is planning to use—as of the time that we are writing this chapter to pro-actively deal with the risks and enhance the opportunities of this business:

- The YouTube site limits user-submitted videos to 10 minutes in length.

- The YouTube site includes instructions and advice on its site about music in user-submitted videos, including advice on avoiding infringement and on getting royalty-free stock music.

- The site uses a "digital hash" technique (generating a unique short identifier from processing a file) and automated filters to stop repeated posting of infringing content.

- The site is building a "digital signature"-based content registration database that will allow content owners to preregister content and inform YouTube if they want specified content allowed or forbidden on the site—or if they just want notice of its use on the site. A digital signature is a technique for processing digital files into unique identifiers.

- In the UK, YouTube has made a deal for a blanket license from music publishers (the holders of the composition copyrights) to cover popular music in videos viewed in the UK from the YouTube site. (In the US, YouTube has been sued by music publishers.)

- YouTube has also made deals with the major record labels covering label-supplied music videos. These deals are based on sharing advertising revenue.

As you can see, notwithstanding the "safe harbor" of the DMCA, being in the user-supplied content business requires a fair amount of obtaining content by traditional techniques of clearance and deals.

TOPIC THREE: "JUST TAKING" CONTENT

In this section, we deal first with the subject of spidering the Web and then follow that with a short discussion of the legal issues in the Internet applications known as "mashups."

About Spidering

Search on with any search engine, and what you are really searching is its database. The heart of a search service business model is amassing, controlling, and retrieving these terabytes of data. That data comes primarily from "spidering" the Web. Search services get most of their data without paying a dime for it.

Probably not many of our readers are planning to launch a search service to go head-to-head with Yahoo! and Google search. However, there are many other business models that might be based on taking large amounts of data by automated means without paying for it. These include specialized search engines and specialized content sites such as "price grabbers" and specialized news and information aggregators. We will refer to these businesses generally as "search engines."

Copying Without Permission and Fair Use

Let's now look at the legal questions involved in copying and using massive amounts of the Web content without permission and without pay, as search engines do.

The process begins with massive and systematically copying known as "spidering" or "Web crawling." The programs that carry out spidering are known as spiders, Web crawlers, indexers, or bots. The spider program will copy and store millions of Web pages and index them. Search engines, as we all know, use the information to provide matches to search queries and respond with "snippets" of text, images (usually as "thumbnails"), and even entire Web pages in "cached" form. After spidering, search engines carry out ranking, indexing, reproduction, and display of the spidered content, all of which involves various rights under copyright law. We will call this entire process "search engine operations."

As we have discussed, in the United States, it is copyright infringement to copy, make derivatives of, or display content that is subject to copyright without the copyright holder's permission, unless you have a legal defense. Most of the content on the Web is subject to copyright law, and most search engine use of content is done without express permission. There is no DMCA "safe harbor" for these search engine operations. When a copyright owner objects to the use of its content by a search engine, the only defense open to the search engine is "fair use" under copyright law. For that reason, legal justification for search engine operations comes down to the application of copyright doctrine of "fair use." As we discussed back in Chapter 2, the fair use doctrine is situation-dependent, requires judgment to apply, and is often unclear.

Search Engines and Fair Use

The law on search engines and fair use is a work in process. We lawyers have some answers and some guidance to give, but the law on this topic will surely become clearer over time. The law is likely to be affected by changes in technology. So the following is a summary of what appears to be the rules, as best as we can tell now. If you are making important decisions in this area, you should consult your legal counsel.

Complaints Against Search Engines

As you might expect, to date search engines have been sued by content owners that are unhappy when search engines display their copyrighted content without their permission and in spite of their objection or link to sites where infringing copies can be found.

Search engines all include provisions that allow Web site owners to prevent spidering. The site owner can include in its site a "metatag" (which is HTML code that does not display on the page) that tells the spider not to copy the page. So why is there a problem of copying without consent? The answer is that problems occur because the copyright owner is not the same as the Web site owner.

The News Services

One example of a dispute over search engines involves news services. As you know, the *Google News* service indexes and displays stories from Internet news sites. Other providers have similar services. Google provides snippets of text, often with a thumbnail picture. *Google News* provides a link to the news site that text and pictures were copied from. The *Google News* pages are updated frequently every day.

This service drives millions of users to Web news sites, so they don't complain. In fact, *Google News* is a great aid to them and raises their advertising revenues. The problem is that much of the news text and photos originally comes from news services, such as Associated Press (AP) and Agence France-Presse (AFP). The news services own the underlying copyrights, and Google was not driving traffic to *them.* AP has complained about *Google News* (privately and publicly) and in 2005 AFP sued Google. During 2007, Google settled with AFP and announced licensing deals with both *AP* and *AFP*.

Perfect 10

Another example of conflict with content owners is the important lawsuit *Perfect 10 v. Google*. Perfect 10 is in the business or providing "soft porn" nude pictures from a for-pay Web site that, naturally, blocked spidering. The problem was that Perfect 10's customers download images and then often post them on Web sites around the Web. (There is no doubt that the users were thereby infringing Perfect 10's copyright of these images.) Google's spider then copied the images as posted by users and incorporated them into Google Image search. As a result, blocking by Perfect 10 was ineffective. Google kept copying the copyright Perfect 10 pictures from other Web sites, displaying thumbnails, and directing Google Images users to sites on the Web where the Perfect 10 pictures could be seen and downloaded for free. So Perfect 10 sued Google for copyright infringement.

In May 2007, there was federal appeals court decision in the *Perfect 10* case, but it provided only a partial answer. The court held that the indexing Perfect 10 pictures and displaying the thumbnails were fair use. However, the court was clearly troubled by the fact that Google was facilitating the distribution of infringing copies from sites around the Internet. Perfect 10 asserted that this was "contributory infringement." (You may recall, from Chapter 2, that this is type of copyright infringement that arises from encouraging or assisting another to infringe.) The court stated the rule this way:

> *A computer system operator can be held contributorily liable [for copyright infringement] if it has actual knowledge that specific infringing material is available using its system, and can take simple measures to prevent further damage to copyrighted works, yet continues to provide access to infringing works.*

The key words here are "simple measures." The appeal court ordered the lower court to review the fact and determine if there are indeed available "simple measures" that would stop the linking of Google users to the full size infringing copies of Perfect 10's content on the Web. If there are such measures and it is found that Google failed to use them, Google may be liable for infringement. The case is still ongoing, but it is possible that the result could be to force search engines with image search functionality to implement some kind of image-based screening technology to eliminate links to identified infringing content. The *Perfect 10* decision is likely not the last word on this topic. It is possible that other courts might decide differently. So this is an area to watch.

Libraries and Publishers

Google has a project to scan a major proportion of the world's books. As with Web content, Google provides Google Books users access on its site to snippets from scanned works. Google has permission from some major libraries that have possession of the books, but in many cases, not from the publishers who control the copyrights. A number of publishers have sued Google, and, as this is being written, the case is pending. The argument is about whether this copying and exploitation of printed works is fair use. This is another area to watch.

Some Additional Observations

Here are some further observations about search engines and the law.

- **Search Engine Operations Generally**—It appears clear that search engines are generally permitted under US law to spider and carry out their normal operations as a "fair use."

- **How Much to Display**—Is there a limit to how much of copied content a search engine can display? This currently is an open issue. Certainly, it will be more defensible to display short snippets than paragraphs. There is also no decision to date on whether it is or is not permitted to display cached pages.

- **Music Search Engines**—Is it legal to operate search engines for MP3 (or other music file formats) downloadable on the Web? This is most likely illegal if most of the links are primarily to infringing downloads and that fact is obvious to the search engine company, because it would be deemed inducement of infringement. This is the same logic under which the Grokster service was held to be infringing. (See discussion of the *Grokster* litigation in Chapter 2.)

- **The Rest of the World**—While there are search engines everywhere, their legal status is quite unclear. Fair use is a distinctively American legal doctrine. There is a narrower concept of "fair dealing" in England, Canada, Australia, and some other nations that have legal systems that derive from English law, but it is not clear that it would apply to search engine operations. You should not assume that US concepts in this area will apply to other nations.

About Mashups

According to Wikipedia, a mashup is a "Web application that combines data from more than one source." The idea of a mashup is using the data or functions of more than one Web site and "mashing" them together to make something new. The term "mashup" originally comes from hiphop music where it means music created by mixing two or more recorded music tracks together.

During the 2007 to 2008 presidential campaign, there has been a mashup on the Slate.com online magazine site that combines candidate Web site data and Google Maps to list every day each candidate's campaign appearance stops on a Slate.com national map, including each place name and time of day information for each candidate event. You can "zoom in" on Iowa or New Hampshire or any other location in the USA. Every candidate's stops automatically shows up as a small balloon on the map. Pass your mouse cursor over the balloon and the data pop up.

Data and graphics that show up in mashups like this can come from Web sources such as:

- **Application program interfaces (APIs)**—Some sites have Web-based applications interfaces or "APIs" specially built for making applications such as mashups. For example, if you sign up to be an eBay developer, you can use its API to build applications. The eBay API allows a developer to create a Web application that includes functions such as: showing all the items for sale on eBay in a particular category; submitting items to eBay for auctioning; retrieving high bidder information; listing items that a particular eBay seller has to offer; and so forth. Developers that sign up with Google can similarly use the functions of Google Maps APIs to make mapping applications that place geocoded information at specified map locations.

- **RSS Datafeeds**—Really Simple Syndication or RSS is a format for publishing and receiving frequently updated content such as news headlines and stories. Many news services, newspapers, magazines, and other publishers provide free RSS feeds on the Internet. Mashups typically aggregate RSS data.

- **Screen Scraping**—This is a technique to copy text out of Web pages by means of rendering the page and capturing (or "scraping") text electronically from selected positions on the page.

Mashups are hosted on a server on the Internet (the mashup site), but access other locations. The functionality of the mashup can be run on the mashup site, on other servers accessed through the Internet, or on the user's computer or on a combination.

Mashups currently feature use of shopping data feeds, news, photos, online lists, and maps. While many of the first generation of mashups are simple and rather casual, it is inevitable that more sophisticated mashup applications will appear by the thousands for both consumer and business use.

Mashups and Clearance of Content

The first question that developers of mashups must ask is whether they need permission from all the data sources that they use in making mashups. The answer is that permission is most often (but not always) required. Here are some of the issues.

Mashups and Terms of Use of Source Web Sites

Mashup developers need to pay attention to the terms of use on the Web sites from which they obtain data. As we discussed in Chapters 16 and 17, courts have ruled that terms of use on Web sites are enforceable, including restraints on third party "spidering." The same legal principle likely applies to mashups.

Many Web site terms of use have limitations that say their contents are for a user's "personal noncommercial use." Most mashups are probably not "personal" use. In addition, any mashup that makes money (for example, from advertising) cannot be classified as "noncommercial."

Mashup developers should try to observe all applicable restrictions of the Web sites they may tap for data. They should ask for written permission to use data from Web sites in any manner other than as Web site's terms of use permit.

API Terms of Use

In order to use a Web API (as for example the eBay or Google APIs discussed above), the developer must register with the site and agree to rather strict terms of use.

For example, Google's terms of use for its Google Map API requires that each developers display a notice to users that the mashup is based on Google technology. Google requires that the resulting mashup shall not: "(1) tarnish, infringe, or dilute Google's trademarks, (2) violate any applicable law, and (3) infringe any third party rights." eBay has similar rules for its API and also requires that the developer's applications clearly segregate eBay and non-eBay content. In each case, the API provider has the right to shut off API access, and thus shut down its use in the mashup, for the developer's noncompliance.

Mashups under Copyright

In addition to issues under Web site terms of use, there are copyright issues. If a developer takes content from a Web site, copyright law requires consent for its copying unless one of the following applies:

- **Fair Use**—In some cases, the developer may be able to argue that its limited use of the data copied was "fair use."

- **Public Domain**—Some information may be in the public domain (for example, data from the US government or under an expired copyright).

- **Not Copyrighted**—For some items, the developer may be able to show that the information taken was pure data (that is, it has no copyrighted content, and there was no original selection or ordering of the data) and therefore not copyrighted.

(See discussion of fair use and the relationship of copyright and data in Chapter 2. There is a summary of the public domain and copyright above in this chapter.) In many cases, the developer will find that copyright applies and that consent is legally required.

Owning and Running the Mashup

Some developers want to know whether they "own" their mashup. The answer is really quite simple. The mashup, as written by the developer, is a "computer program" under US copyright law. (See discussion of this term in Chapter 2.) That means that developer will own the copyright to the mashup program that he or she creates. Of course, this would not grant the developer any ownership of third party copyrighted content that the mashup imports. In addition, because copyright does not cover concepts and methods, copyright will not stop others from producing very similar mashups with substantially the same functionality.

Mashup developers should take the same steps with their mashup sites that other Web site owners do. They should protect themselves with the DMCA "notice and take-down" rules discussed in Chapter 3. They should have their own Web site terms of use with the normal disclaimers. They should protect and register their own trademarks. There will surely be technical innovations in the field of mashups that are patentable.

CONCLUSION

Content truly is the king in digital media. As you have seen from this chapter, there is traditional clearance and then there are new ways for accessing and amassing content. Whatever combination of these techniques and source you use, be sure you know when you need permissions and when you do not. With some care and planning, you can have content-rich sites and applications and stay always on the right side of the law.

Deals in the Web and Mobile Value Chains

21

We see telephones exchanging information with computers, and computers play-
ing compressed audio data files or live audio data streams that play music over
the Internet like radios. Computers can play movies and tune in to television …
These are just some of the features of a digital world.

—Wikipedia on the "Information Age"

IN THIS CHAPTER

This chapter is about technology, content, and services deals in the Internet and mobile communications markets. The goal of this chapter is to help you make sound agreements in the rich and ever-changing digital communications environment.

The value chain for content production, distribution, and use has changed radically in recent years. Online and wireless entertainment and information have taken mind share and market share away from traditional broadcast, print and cable media around the world. This change is forcing traditional media companies to become providers and purchasers of technology-based services and is creating new content providers.

Most of the action and the money in the US are in Web-based media and services, but mobile-based entertainment and applications are growing in importance. In the third world countries, such as India and China, where there are a huge number of cell phones and fewer PCs, mobile media is very important.

This chapter covers a lot of ground, and you may wish to read all of it or only those portions that concern your business and its issues. The topics presented consist of:

- **Background**—We present an overview of the current Web and wireless business and legal environment.

- **Topic I: Technology Deals**—We discuss deals to license and distribute communications technology components and systems, for example: software components that provide video compression and decompression, play media files, or control communications in devices or systems that store, manage, and process payment for media content.

- **Topic II: Content Deals**—We examine agreements to obtain or supply digital content (or links to digital content) for video, music, text, and graphics. These agreements involve digital content licensing and distribution and digital rights management (or DRM).

- **Topic III: Services**—Next is a short section about supporting services for Web and mobile services, such as hosting, security, and content management. These services may be provided in the same agreement as digital content, or in a separate deal.

At the end of this chapter, we offer some observations about "widgets"—mini software applications that are created or distributed to be placed in others' Web or mobile applications.

Relationship with Other Chapters

To make sound agreements in this digital communications environment, you will draw upon many principles and approaches that are discussed throughout this book.

The discussion in this chapter assumes that you are familiar with the chapters of this book on intellectual property (Chapters 3, 4, 5, and 6), contract basics (Chapter 8), distribution deals (Chapters 14 and 15), privacy (Chapter 18), on standards and standards setting (Chapter 19), and clearing data and content (Chapter 20). You also should be familiar with the discussion of the Digital Millennium Copyright Act (DMCA) "Notice and Take Down" rules discussed in Chapter 3. To avoid repetition, the discussion in this chapter is focused only on what is different and distinctive about deals in the digital communications environment.

Forms

The form Appendix in this book includes three examples of digital content distribution agreements:

- **A Mobile Content License Agreement**—(Form 21-1) covering the supply of digital entertainment content, such as games and ring tones, from the content owner to a wireless communications carrier.

- **A Media Publishing and Services Agreement**—(Form 21-2) under which a content aggregator agrees to manage and publish through the Internet a supplier's video or audio content; the aggregator's customer or any other supplier of video or audio content for such an agreement could be a television or cable network, or a record label.

- **An Affiliate Media Services Agreement**—(Form 21-3), a click-through agreement under which a content aggregator distributes video media content; the customer would be a Web site which, as a member of the aggregator's "affiliate network," provides its end users access to the aggregator-supplied online video or audio content.

The form Appendix in this book also includes a sample distribution license agreement for a technology component (Form 15-1). That form agreement can also be used as a foundation for communications technology deals of the type discussed in this chapter.

There are unlimited possible variations in digital media transactions. So these forms can serve as starting points, checklists, and examples but they are not templates. You will have to adapt and change them to fit your own business deals.

THE WEB AND MOBILE COMMUNICATIONS ENVIRONMENT

Let's start with a look at the Web and mobile communications universe. Here are some of the great variety of functionality deployed in this environment:

- **Entertainment**—Music, games, contests, and video

- **Information**—News, sports, weather, market updates, currency rates, and other news and reports

- **Communications and Community**—Text-based instant messaging, VOIP (Voice over Internet Protocol), video chat, blogging, social networking, instant messaging and SMS messaging

- **Personalization**—Personal Web pages and individualized e-mail designs on the Internet and personal ring tones on mobile devices

- **Productivity**—Calendars, order entry, maps, supply chain applications, and asset management

- **Security and Protection**—Content filtering, firewalls, and spam filters

- **Commerce**—Advertisements, shopping, auctions, and payment systems

- **Location Based Services**—GPS-based mapping, child locator services

It requires intellectual property, content, and technology to create, assemble, distribute, deliver, supply content for, and monetize these communications services. These services are assembled and provided through licensing and services agreements.

The Players

In the digital communications value chain there are many players—all needed for the system to function:

- **Application and Technology Suppliers**—the hardware and foundation software companies including computer makers, handset makers, and manufactures of network and communications hardware and software. This category includes companies like Cisco, Microsoft, Motorola, Nokia, and many other vendors.

- **Access Providers and Carriers**—the telecom companies that provide broadband and mobile network connectivity. This category includes providers like NTT DoCoMo, Verizon, AT&T, and others around the world. This category also includes caching-and-replication service companies, such as Akamai, which assist in efficient network distribution of rich media content such as video and music.

- **Content Owners**—the companies that have or make content, including news organizations, Hollywood, the record labels, and so forth. (Calling these parties "owners" is a bit of an over-simplification, because they are often suppliers of rights they own and rights they license from others.)

- **Content Sites**—the Web sites and mobile portals that provide consumers with access to content. These could be a content site, an entertainment, information and news Web site (such as ESPN or nytimes.com), a portal (such as Yahoo!), a social Web site (such as MySpace), or any other Web site with significant third party content.

- **Content Aggregators**—These companies are content publishers and service providers that sit in the middle of the food chain—getting music and video content from Content Owners (like the game companies, record labels, or television studios) and distributing content for various customers (such as Web or mobile portals or entertainment sites). Examples are video and audio aggregators such as Veoh Networks, Joost, and Brightcove.

- **Advertising Networks**—(also known as "ad networks" or "ad agents"). Examples of Web ad networks are DoubleClick and 24/7 Media (both mentioned in our discussion of privacy in Chapter 18). The advertising network acts as an advertising aggregator, connecting advertising buyers with web sites that display advertising content. The ad network's business model is to charge advertisers for site visitors' "click-through" and to share that revenue with web sites where ads are displayed. Advertising networks allow buyers to plan advertising buys online and track advertising results in near real time.

- **Other Service Providers**—the companies that provide the variety of services that support Internet and mobile operations. These include the companies that host online or mobile applications. They also include supporting services such as authentication, payments, and security.

In order for the digital content network to operate, there needs to be an extended network of contract-based relationships starting at the content creator and ending at the final consumer or user. Each of the players in the content chain adds value in exchange for a price. Each of the parties is tied to those above and below them through a content intellectual property licensing and distribution structure.

Internet and Mobile

As noted, this chapter is about both Internet and mobile communications. There are some important differences in these media environments (these differences are discussed below), but from a dealmaker's perspective they are similar. Platforms, interfaces, and technical standards differ in important ways, but the issues, legal principles, and deal structures are largely the same. To deal successfully in this complex environment, your company needs to have a clear understanding not only of technology, but also of intellectual property strategy and smart digital contracting.

Convergence and Differences

There is a functional overlap between Internet and mobile communications. Most of the communication services listed at the beginning of this chapter exist in both

Internet and mobile versions. Some applications and content can be accessed from either Internet or mobile devices. The "mobile web" is a system that brings Internet functionality onto a mobile platform.

On the other hand, we are still a long way from a seamless Web and mobile communications system. There are still significant differences between Internet and mobile environments that affect technology and business deals. Among the most important are these:

Carrier Control and the "Walled Garden"

Carriers (like Verizon Wireless, Sprint Nextel, or T-Mobile) in the United States have a large measure of control of over use of mobile phones on their own networks as a platform for applications. The carriers sell mobile handsets; they therefore control which handsets are sold for use on their networks. Many mobile devices sold by carriers are designed to limit third party application access—with some carriers implementing more restrictions than others. In the industry, the end-to-end domination of data services by communication carriers is called the "walled garden."

The walled garden data services (that is non-voice services) that the carriers offer come from the carrier itself or often from content-provider "partners" that have revenue sharing deals with the carrier. The approved applications are listed in a menu accessible on the mobile handset—this list is known as "the deck." Carrier-offered applications are therefore called "on deck" applications. Those applications that a customer obtains without going through the carrier are "off deck." (Off-deck applications might be downloaded or accessed as Web sites optimized for mobile access.) So far, it has been inconvenient for customer to obtain and use off-deck applications. Most US mobile customers use primarily "on deck" data services.

Mobile carriers have also imposed technical restrictions that tend to restrict mobile applications and commerce. For example, most US carriers, at present, do not allow their mobile handsets to accept "cookies" that allow tracking of users. This restriction makes the mobile handset less suitable for e-commerce. (For discussion of cookies on the Web, see Chapter 18.)

It is likely that in the next few years mobile phones and other mobile devices will become more "open" and more friendly for off-deck applications. For example, Google has promoted a more open mobile phone platform known as Android. Some carriers have announced plans to make it easier for third party software applications and devices to use their mobile networks. As we write this, the transition to a more open model is underway, but it is uncertain how fast this will happen.

Technology businesses should watch closely to see how opportunities in this space develop.

Spectrum

Wireless spectrum is a relatively scarce and expensive resource compared to broadband Internet access. Acquiring spectrum is expensive for carriers. It costs more to move a megabyte wirelessly than through the Internet. This cost structure affects pricing for wireless data services. The US government is increasing the supply of wireless spectrum for advanced wireless services and carriers are building more capacity, so the relative cost of mobile data services may decrease over time.

Device Limitations

Mobile devices are currently more limited than PCs in computing power, display capability and means of data input. There is also great variation in mobile devices, which means that applications may need to be released in different versions for different mobile devices—which can raise programming costs. However devices are changing and improving. Apple's iPhone appears to have quickened the trend to richer functionality in mobile devices.

Adoption Ratios

Mobile devices are more widely adopted than computers. In developing areas in the world—most importantly in India and China—PC penetration is a fraction of mobile phone use. This is one reason why the most successful markets for non-voice mobile services such as music, video, and news are in the developing world.

Internet Openness and "Net Neutrality"

The providers of broadband Internet connectivity (cable companies and communication carriers) want to exert more control over mass market wired and fiber optic broadband Internet connectivity in the future. Specifically, they have been discussing charging higher fees for new applications and content (like Internet high-definition video) that will require more intensive use of their network's resources. The providers call this "Quality of Service" pricing. Internet content companies oppose the carriers' proposals; they say that the right position is "Net Neutrality"—the principle that all users of the Internet should be able to access the same system resources without pricing or access variations. This is an important technology, regulatory, and political debate to follow if your business is in communications technology or content markets.

TOPIC I: COMMUNICATIONS TECHNOLOGY LICENSE AGREEMENTS

Content is king but technology licensing supports the kingdom. The following discussion is about the deals to supply technology for use in the Web or mobile communications world.

Defining the Basic Deal

A communications technology software license agreement is, at its business and commercial core, no different from a distribution deal for any other information technology component or product. The key provisions of these agreements are covered at some length in Chapters 14 and 15. You should look in particular at the discussion of component software deals in Chapter 15.

Your communications software license agreement must define the component or product to be delivered. There needs to be a license grant stating how the licensee may integrate, use, and distribute these deliverables. The agreement must have provisions on pricing and payment, intellectual property owner-ship, warranties, risk limitation, termination, and so forth. We will not repeat the discussion of all these items. However, we do want to bring to your atten-tion some differences in issues and approach in communications technology software deals.

Duration of the Deal

When a company's software component is designed into a mobile device, such as a mobile PDA or a cell phone, or a communications infrastructure device such as an Internet switch, it is likely to be included in product production for as long as the product (and perhaps successor products) are made. That means that duration of communications technology software license agreements often are written to fit the life cycle of the products that the components support.

Where the licensee wants to insure a long-term supply of a technology, it may press for:

- **Renewal Rights; Price Reductions**—Licensees do not like to deal with unexpected price increases and therefore may press for options to extend the license at preset pricing. They may ask that the price of the software go down over time as the product gradually ceases to be the most advanced or "high end."

- **Wind-Down Periods**—The licensee may ask for a long "wind down" and "sell off" period at the end of the agreement term when the licensee can complete goods in production and sell inventory.

- **Distributed Copies**—The licensee normally wants all end user licenses to be permanent.

- **Licensee Usage Rights that Survive**—The licensee may often want to keep copies of the licensed software after termination of the Agreement. Licensee may want post-termination rights to archive the software and to use software to support existing customers.

Technology Distribution through Multiple Levels

Communications technology often flows through multilayers of distribution. A company's component software product to be integrated into a mobile phone might go through several intermediate software integration companies before it reaches the mobile phone handset maker. The same could be true for components that go into complex Internet applications.

Where this situation applies, technology license agreements must be written to fit multilevel distribution. The agreement must grant the licensee the sublicensing rights needed for those farther down the value chain. These may include:

- **Integration Rights**—Some parties down the distribution chain may need a license to integrate the software into a software or hardware product.

- **Replication Rights**—The licensee may need to give some parties farther down the distribution chain the right to replicate the software component (often as part of the end product).

- **Support Rights**—The licensee may need to give its customers (or its customers' customers) the right to support component software, provide patches, outsource support, and so forth.

It is in the best interests of both licensor and licensee to get these multi-level distribution clauses right—they facilitate rational and efficient distribution and support of components through the manufacturing and distribution chain.

Control of Sub-Distribution

Licensors often wish to impose use limitations on sublicensees in this multi-level distribution chain. The licensor can exert this control by means of required sub-distribution terms (known as "mandatory flow-down terms") that the licensee promises to implement. Here is some sample agreement text:

> *Licensee agrees to offer and provide the Software to its manufacturer and OEM customers only pursuant to Licensor's form of distribution license, a copy of which is found in Schedule X (the "Mandatory Flow-Down Terms").*

(For discussion of the term "OEM," see Chapter 15.)

Source Code Integration and Transformation

Licensors sometimes supply source code that licensees need to use in integrating the licensor's product into its own. This could be the source code for program interfaces only or it could be the source code for the licensor's product as a whole.

Source code usually comes with a limited license that permits only the licensee (and perhaps its contractors) to use the source code. The license grant normally allows the licensee to edit the code and to create and distribute binary derivatives only. There are some deals where the source code can be passed down the distribution chain for this limited use.

The communications technology agreement will normally require that each source code licensee or sublicensee agree in writing to treat the source code as the confidential information of the licensor and abide by other distribution restrictions.

Indemnification for Digital Communications Products

If you are a supplier of digital communications components or products, you need to be quite careful about the intellectual property indemnities that your company provides. Licensors usually try very hard to impose a limit on liability.

The issue and threat in communications technology are patents. There is enhanced risk that comes from the way that US law calculates patent infringement money damages. When one component of a complex product is found to be infringing, a US federal court has considerable latitude in determining contract damages—which are commonly based on determining a "reasonable royalty" for the infringed invention. (Congress has been considering proposals to change the law on calculating patent damages to reduce money damage awards, so this is an issue to watch. See the discussion of possible patent law changes in Chapter 4.)

An example that illustrates the risk is the famous Blackberry patent litigation, involving patents covering the synchronizing mechanism used to update Blackberry devices. (The case name is *NPT, Inc. v. Research in Motion, Ltd.*) After finding that Blackberry manufacturer Research in Motion, Ltd. ("RIM") infringed NPT's patents, the court awarded NPT damages equal to 8.55 percent of the revenue from US sales of Blackberry products and services. RIM ended up settling the case in 2006 by paying NPT $612.5 million.

This money damages risk is added to the fact that patent cases can carry treble damages if infringement is found to be willful and there are huge distributed volumes of some communications products. These factors make it possible for infringement in small device components to end up causing huge damages. Added to this is the multimillion dollar cost of patent litigation. Indemnification obligations to cover this kind of customer loss could wipe out small and medium size technology suppliers.

Normally licensors are expected to "stand behind" the products they supply and to indemnify their customers. But the licensors should always look for a limit to this potentially crushing liability if possible. Common ways to do this are:

- A dollar limit or "cap" on intellectual property indemnification.

- A clause that allows the licensor to withdraw the license in case of an infringement if the licensor cannot design around the problem or obtain a patent license. Licensees commonly resist any clause like this unless it has a "long trigger." If licensee has built a software component into its end product, it does not want the component to be removed on short notice.

Another indemnity point: the agreement the parties make with regard to responsibility for standards-based patents (discussed below) may require some corresponding fine tuning in the indemnification provisions.

Technology On or Over the Copyright Edge

A communications technology application can infringe copyrights in two different ways. One is *direct* infringement—the technology might include infringing software code. The other is *indirect* infringement—an application might contribute to or induce infringement of copyrighted content. There are communications applications that can get your company into trouble for indirect copyright infringement;

these include file sharing applications (like Napster and Grokster) and applications for defeating encryption or other copyright protection technologies. (See the discussion of copyright limits and anti-circumvention law in Chapters 2 and 3.)

If your company makes or distributes (and perhaps if it assists another company in making or distributing) products that contribute to or induce violations of copyright or anti-circumvention law, your company may be liable to copyright holders. In some cases, it may be unclear if products or technologies are over the line or not. If you have any doubt whether a product is compliant with copyright and anti-circumvention law, you should consult legal counsel.

Standards and Patents

Communications technology products and components often must meet specifications that require compliance with communications, software, or hardware standards. Products may be required to pass compliance testing administered by standards organizations. (See discussion of standards setting in Chapter 19.) Patents often dominate standards. Sometimes the necessary patents are held by single parties and sometimes by patent pools.

Technology licensing agreements often assign responsibility for standards-based intellectual property compliance. Patent licenses that you may need for standards-based intellectual property include:

- **Development License**—A developer/technology supplier may need a development license under patents just to create software and deliver a prototype to the next party in the distribution chain. It also may be necessary to obtain a license to gain access to confidential development documentation regarding the standard.

- **Distribution License**—Commercial replication and distribution of the product may require a separate (more expensive) patent license.

If licensor and licensee each assume, without verifying, that the other party is getting required standards-related patent permissions, the result will be an unlicensed and infringing product. Here are sample provisions to allocate responsibility expressly:

"Standards-Based IP" means Intellectual Property Rights including copyrights and patents (and applications for the same) that are reasonably required to develop, make,

sell, otherwise dispose of, support, or use Products compliant with the industry standards that the applicable Specification requires.

The parties agree that [Licensor] [Licensee] will be responsible for procuring all required licenses and permissions for Standards-Based IP.

These clauses can be targeted on specific standards that the parties have identified as a matter of particular concern.

Other Patent Issues

Patent issues do not stop with standards. There may be other blocking third party patents that need to be licensed. Patent awareness is a first step to sound deals and smart communications technology negotiations.

Other Technology Licensing Issues

Here are some other important issues in communications technology licensing that are discussed elsewhere in this book:

- **Open Source Licenses**—Communications components and products often include software under open source licenses—including "Copyleft" and others types. See Chapter 9 for a review of open source rules.

- **Export Compliance**—Communications software often includes encryption, which is regulated by US (and other) export control laws. See Chapter 24 for a discussion of US export controls.

- **Component Branding**—Some communications technologies are a sufficient "value add" that they can support "component branding"—such as the famous "Dolby" or "Intel Inside" trademarks. See Chapter 4 for a discussion of this kind of trademark use.

TOPIC II: DIGITAL CONTENT DEALS

Now let's turn to our next major topic: content deals in the digital communications environment. We are talking about any kind of content, including video, music (including songs and ring tones), graphics, text, financial data, and so forth. While each medium has its own technical issues—and can have different content clearance issues—they are all digital information. The principles and deal structures that apply are much the same.

The Flow of Content

We begin with an overview of the different ways that digital content can get from the Content Owner to the consumer through the value chain. We begin with an example:

Let's start with a music video owned by a record label. (We'll call it the "Label.") That video is represented by a static thumbnail graphic on a Web page of a Content Site such as Yahoo!, AOL, YouTube, or MySpace. Any end user of the Content Site who wants to see and hear that music video on her PC clicks the graphic and the music video plays on-screen.

From a technological point of view, this is a comparatively simple transaction. Somewhere on the Internet, a server is hosting that video. The Content Site embeds in a Web page a small piece of computer code that, when clicked, triggers the video play. (These snippets of code, often written in JavaScript or Flash, are known as "Web widgets." There is more about widgets at the end of this chapter.) When the end user clicks, the Web widget triggers a link, a server then transmits the video to the consumer's PC either by file transfer (the video plays as it transfers) or by streaming.

From a business point of view, there are many possible business arrangements that could be behind this transaction. For example:

- **Direct License**—There could be a direct content supply agreement between the Label and the Content Site. The agreement could provide, for example, that the Label delivers videos to the Content Site, and the Content Site is licensed to host the videos and distribute them to its end users.

- **Direct License and Hosting**—There could be the same content supply agreement between the Label and the Content Site except that one party or the other could provide for a third company to host the video content and broadcast it to Content Site's end users. The end user who clicks on a video does not know (or care) that a third party hosting company is carrying out digital distribution.

- **Content Aggregator**—A Content Aggregator is a company that sits in the middle. It has an agreement with the Label under which it obtains videos together with rights to host and distribute them. The Content Aggregator has another agreement with the Content Site in which it supplies the videos to end users of the Content Site. Under this arrangement, the Content Aggregator manages the content, services, and the technology for the convenience of both the Label and the Content Site.

Here are some additional important services that a Content Aggregator could contract to provide:

- **Syndication**—The Content Aggregator can provide syndication, that is, the sublicensing of content to many outlets. This is a digital equivalent to the role that traditional publishers play—gathering content from many sources and distributing it to many retail outlets.

- **Advertising Sales**—The Content Aggregator can arrange for advertising for "ad-supported" content and pay the resulting ad revenues (net of a commission for the Content Aggregator) to the Content Owner. Or the Content Aggregator can make a deal with third party advertising network to do the same.

- **Content Management Services**—The Content Aggregator can provide content management functions for the Content Owner. For example, the Content Aggregator can agree to:

  - Add or remove content or change the content "mix" on demand or under agreed rules and procedures.

  - Distribute pricing information and other relevant data for pay-to-play or pay-to-download content.

  - "Take down" (quickly remove) content found to be infringing.

  - Provide "geo-filtering" to direct content to designated areas of the world.

  - Manage digital rights management systems and information.

  - Track and report usage of content assets.

These functions for digital distribution are not limited to video. They apply to distribution of text, graphics, games, and music.

Digital Content Agreements

We now turn to designing and negotiating a digital content agreement for video, music or other content types. There are many varieties of these agreements. We have tried, in this section, to put together a topic list that covers most of the issues that will arise in most of the agreements that you might do.

In this discussion, we will refer to a party supplying rights and content as the "licensor" and the party getting rights in the deal as the "licensee." For example, a Content Owner would be a licensor. A Content Site would be a licensee. A Content Aggregator could be either licensee or licensor, depending whether it was obtaining or supplying content in the deal.

The following discussion is not intended to cover every section and topic that is likely to be in a content distribution agreement. The focus is on issues that apply generally to digital content deals. (The chapter on digital contracting basics in this book (Chapter 8) is essential background for this discussion. You may want to review the discussion of copyrights on the Internet in Chapter 3 and the discussion of clearing content in Chapter 20.)

As noted above, there are form agreements in the Appendix in this book that you can also use as examples and checklists for content licensing agreements in the Web and mobile value chain. To create the right agreements for your company, your company may need experienced legal counsel to help you conceptualize deal structures, to draft your form agreements and to assist you in negotiations.

Specifying the Offering

Any digital content distribution agreement needs to define the content to be supplied, including:

- **The Deliverables**—The specification of the content to be provided, including content types, titles and formats. There may also be metadata (text information) about the content, associated promotional material, graphics, brands, and logos.

- **Availability**—When the content must be made available to the licensee. (For example, before the "street date" of a recording or the release date of films.)

- **Updating**—How the content must be added to, updated, or refreshed.

- **Prohibitions and Ratings**—Any excluded content categories, for example racist, offensive or indecent content, or any exclusion of content based on suitability standards or parental advisory ratings.

- **Mechanics**—The process, technology, and format for the licensor's delivery of the content.

The License Grant

The license grant for content—like a license for software or any other digital offering—will need to be customized for the particular commercial setting. Each licensor's goal will be "value licensing"—creating permissions and restrictions so that the permitted use matches closely to the payment provisions. Each licensor should make sure that it only grants rights that it owns or has cleared. Each licensee should be sure it obtains all the rights that it needs.

Here are some factors to consider:

- **Permitted Distribution Method**—Is the licensee's permitted distribution by streaming or download or both? Is distribution permitted in podcast downloads or on optical media form (such as a DVD or Blu-ray disk)?

- **Brand-Based Restrictions**—Is distribution by the licensee limited to Web sites or mobile portals that are branded with the licensee's trademark? What about co-branded pages that include the licensee's trademark and also include third-party branding?

- **Syndication**—Does the license include the right for the licensee to syndicate the content and place it into many different Content Sites? If so, what are the limits and controls on the Content Sites that can display the content?

- **Target Platforms**—Is the licensee's distribution to PCs only? Mobile devices only? Some combination? Pricing structures may be different for different target media.

- **Associated Advertising**—Is the licensee permitted to (or required to) combine the content with advertising—and if so, what kind? Does the licensor select and supply advertising to be displayed or played together with the content?

- **Geographic Limits to Distribution**—Is distribution permitted only in the United States or other specified national or regional markets? Is worldwide distribution allowed? (For some media, such as music and film, rights clearance is done country by country, so the parties may have no choice but to live with geography limitations.)

- **Duration**—For how long may the licensee continue to receive and distribute the content?

If you are the licensee of digital content, be very careful about rights you are getting and which are not in the deal. For example, a license to distribute digital music recordings will usually come without any right to display the lyrics. Anyone that arranges for or redistributes digital content should be sure to understand the rules.

Related matters are the licensee's obligations. For example:

- **May Carry or Must Carry**—Is the licensee *permitted* to make the content available online or *required* to do so?

- **Marketing and Distribution**—How is the licensee required to market, promote, or distribute the content?

Hosting and Data Management

Digital content agreements often include the obligation to provide hosting and data management services, and may include other service obligations as well. (Service delivery is covered in the next section of this chapter.)

Digital Rights Management

Content Owners usually (but not always) require that their content be distributed to distributors or end users only under a digital rights management (DRM) protection scheme. DRM refers to various technical mechanisms that restrict copying, use, and transfer of digital media. DRM is more than "anti-piracy" protection—it is a way of authorizing and metering end user access, copying, and use. DRM systems are also used to "lock" and "unlock" content that is subject to an end user's month-to-month subscription. The goal is to place limits on use of the content (while keeping it easy to use) and, at the same time, deterring (if not fully preventing) unauthorized copying and transmission.

Most DRM schemes for PCs and mobile devices are software-based and use encryption. Examples of DRM are:

- The Window Media Audio (or WMA) system used to protect music files for Windows PCs and WindowsCE devices.

- The FairPlay music-control system used in Apple's iTunes and iPods.

- The Content Scrambling System (or CSS) on DVD videos.

- Adobe DRM that protects "e-books" provided in Adobe PDF format

These systems have become quite sophisticated. Apple's FairPlay system, for example, features software and file structures that (under its current version):

- Allow a music track to be copied on up to five DRM-protected PCs.

- Allow a music track to be copied onto an unlimited number of DRM-protected portable devices (such as the iPod, iPhone, and Apple-authorized third party mobile phones).

- Allow a music track to be played an unlimited amount of times.

- Allow a music track to be "burned" from PCs to non-DRM-protected audio CDs an unlimited number of times.

If you are a Content Aggregator, it is your job to make sure the permissions that you get from Content Owners include all of the permissions that you provide to your customers and end users. For example, Apple can authorize the copying listed above only because it has already negotiated a grant of rights from the record labels and music publishers to allow end users to make these various copies.

DRM-related provisions in content license agreements may include provisions on:

- Which form or forms of DRM are permissible or mandatory.

- Whether it is the licensor or the licensee that is responsible for placing the content in its DRM format.

- Who pays license fees for DRM technologies.

- Whether "unlocking" content is controlled or authorized separately from distribution. (For example having distribution of locked content that can be unlocked at a later time.)

- Whether the agreement includes any licensing or distribution of DRM software.

- What the licensee's reporting obligations are if it learns that the DRM scheme has been "cracked" and what technical measures the licensee can be required to take in case of such an incident.

DRM is a bit of a paradox because it is a "value-add" for Content Owners but consumers often see it as reducing content value. There is a current trend in digital music to provide both DRM-protected and unprotected versions of music files, with the unprotected versions at a premium price.

See the discussion of the anti-circumvention provision of the Digital Millennium Copyright Act (or DMCA) in Chapter 2. The DMCA includes statutory provisions (including criminal penalties) that forbid circumvention of DRM protections and outlaw production or distribution of technical means to circumvent DRM protection. Similar restrictions apply in the countries of the European Union and in a number of other nations.

Licensor's Branding and Attribution

Digital content agreements often include provisions for the licensee to display the licensor's branding with licensor-supplied content. These provisions may be voluntary ("Licensee may display Licensor's branding") or mandatory ("Licensee must display Licensor's branding"). Any licensor that includes this kind of provision must include provisions for "branding guidelines" that specify the look and use of the licensor's online branding. (See discussion of branding guidelines in Chapter 4.) Some agreements have provisions for "co-branding"—allowing both the licensor's and the licensee's branding (or third party branding) to appear on an Internet or mobile display that lists the licensor-supplied content.

Content Owners commonly supply and require that licensees display attribution information for content. Attribution information for music, for example, could include the copyright and trademark notices, publisher's name, recording artist, producer, record label, studio, and so forth, all as specified by the licensor. Attribution data and attribution requirements tend to follow content down through the digital distribution chain.

Restrictions

The use, display, and distribution of data and content may be subject to additional restrictions stated in the content licensing agreement. For example, there might be one or more of the following:

- The licensee agrees not to use or display the content in any manner or context that is negative, indecent, unsavory, or bad for the content supplier's reputation.

- The licensee agrees not to defeat or circumvent any copy protection or reverse engineer any licensor software or system technology.

- The licensee agrees not remove any proprietary legends or attribution information.

- The licensee agrees not to copy or exploit the data and content except as expressly permitted in the agreement.

Exclusivity

The licensee may want to negotiate for the right to exclusivity to the content. The licensor may want the licensee to agree to promote or prominently feature the licensor's content and may wish to exclude competing content. There are many variations on exclusivity provisions of course. Exclusivity may be limited in time, dependent on upfront payments, subject to payment minimums, and so forth.

Links to Content Rather Than the Content Itself

Licensors often will supply links, widgets, or identifiers rather than the content itself. This method is not limited to the Web widgets to enable videos that we discussed above. Here is another example from a different application:

If your PC displays cover art on an Internet-based music store, there's a good chance that the cover art comes from All Media Guide LLC (known as AMG). AMG supplies media-related data and content, including album cover art in the form of image "thumbnails." However, AMG does not transfer its digital album cover art thumbnails to the online music stores. Here is how it works:

- AMG supplies the online music store with thousands of "identifiers" which are alphanumeric codes that uniquely refer to a particular album's cover art. These identifiers are each linked in the music store's system with particular recording albums. For example, the music stores' data on *Led Zepplin II* is linked to a unique identifier for the cover art for that particular album.

- When the online music store Web page loads on an end user's PC, the online store's Web server supplies the required identifier to the end user's PC. Links in the Web page then sends the identifier from the user's PC to AMG's servers on the Internet.

- AMG's servers find the cover art files and send them through the Internet to the end user's PC, which displays the cover art at the appropriate places in the music store Web page.

It all happens seamlessly. End users do not know that the *Led Zeppelin II* album cover art thumbnail image displayed on the Web page of their favorite online music store actually comes from another online source.

There are a number of advantages to using this method of supplying Web widgets, identifiers and links:

- **Restriction on Access**—The content licensee (in our example, the music store) does not obtain possession of the content, so there is less danger of unauthorized access or use of the content.

- **Monitoring**—Usage of the content by end users can be monitored precisely. This allows for highly accurate "per use" license fee schemes.

- **Effective Shutdown**—If the licensee fails to pay license fee—or otherwise breaches the agreement—end user access to the content can be turned off in an instant.

This same system can be used in many digital contexts to insert content from one company's servers into the online content of another.

No Warranty of Accuracy

As we mentioned in Chapter 20, suppliers of data or content normally expressly disclaim any warranty that the facts reflected in any licensed content are accurate. This is the case especially when the content has a business function, such as currency price data or stock market data, or might impact human life or health, such as content about diseases. Suppliers of content will want to disclaim and exclude any warranty or potential liability regarding information supplied through network distribution.

Who Do You Trust to Supply Clearance?

It is important that one of the parties provide intellectual property clearance of the content that is being supplied. Normally (but not always) this is the content supplier's responsibility. In most deals, the licensor will warrant that it has all rights required to supply the specified content and to permit the licensee to use and distribute it in accordance with the agreement.

Each party should be sure that it understands the clearance issues that might arise. For example, as discussed in Chapter 20, clearance of music, movies, or video content can be complicated and can vary from country to country. The agreement should expressly allocate responsibility for all known clearance obligations.

Indemnities

In most deals, the licensor will indemnify the licensee against any claim of infringement arising from the content used and distributed as permitted in the agreement. The licensee will want indemnification to cover copyrights, trademarks, right of personality (for content regarding famous persons), defamation, and privacy. When the licensor is providing services or technology, the licensee will likely seek patent indemnification as well.

Limitations to Indemnity

However, the licensor's obligation to indemnify may not be absolute. In some agreements, the licensor may be able to limit its exposure for potential intellectual property infringement claims to some extent:

- The agreement will often make indemnification the sole remedy for a breach of intellectual property warranties regarding the data; or

- The agreement may limit total indemnification liability to a set figure (or "liability cap").

"Take Down" Provisions

Often a licensor provides content where its rights to particular content might change over time. For example, a publisher might lose rights to distribute a particular book or a recording company may loose the master recording distribution rights for a particular artist. For this reason, licensors may want the right to require the licensee to "take down" and cease offering specified content on very short notice.

Licensee's Indemnification

It is common in content agreements for the licensor to seek, in turn, indemnification from the licensee—covering any claim or liability arising from the use of the content other than as licensed, privacy violations, or any other claim arising from the licensee's acts or operations.

Payment Terms

The payment terms of a content agreement must fit the type of content, its distribution, and the market. Pricing terms are often highly negotiated.

Broadly speaking, there are four models for copyrighted Web site content licensed to a Content Site:

- **Free Content**—Distribution without royalties could apply for content such as advertisements, infomercials, and promotional videos.

- **Content Site Pays**—The Content Site may simply pay for the content and distribute it without obtaining revenue directly connected to the content. This would apply only if the content is low cost.

- **For-Pay Content**—In this model, the end user pays. This could be a subscription payment, pay-per-view or pay-per-download. The money paid, after expenses, will be shared by the parties, that is the Content Site and its supplier, which could be the Content Owner or a Content Aggregator.

- **Advertising Supported**—In this model, one of the parties sells advertising (or arranges for advertising) that is played or displayed in connection with the content display (such as a video ad or embedded banner ad), and the parties share the revenue.

To date (as is noted above) the wireless carriers' "walled garden" controls have limited the content and services that can be readily accessed on mobile devices. This means that Content Owners, Content Aggregators, and providers of mobile services have needed to strike deals with carriers in order to get onto the carriers' mobile phone "deck." This circumstance has limited most on-deck mobile content and services deals to end-user-paid-for models. As we noted above, there appear to be changes coming in the mobile space—and mobile phones and devices may become more open to different revenue and business models in the future.

More about Revenue Sharing Provisions

Content deals often have revenue sharing provisions, often referred to as "Rev Share." These clauses can vary widely and are often negotiated. Crafting Rev Share provisions is not fundamentally different from other royalty or license fee provisions in distribution deals. Here are some issues to watch out for:

- **Roles of the Parties**—The parties must agree on which party will generate revenue that will be shared. For example, a Content Owner could be the party that bills for and receives the advertisers' payments for the content or a Content Site could collect those payments.

- **Frequency of Payment**—Payments on Rev Share deals can be calculated monthly or quarterly (or on some other periodic basis).

- **Revenue vs. Receipts**—Rev Share payments can be based either on "revenue" (based on billings) or "receipts" (moneys actually received). Where the money comes from credit card payments by consumers, there may be little difference between revenues and receipts.

- **Deductions**—Revenue sharing may be based on revenue net of certain costs, such as third party commissions and sales taxes.

- **Minimum Guarantees**—Content Owners that provide content for Rev Share deals may want minimum guaranteed payments.

For a more extensive discussion of royalty issues (in a similar context), you may wish to review royalty provisions in game publishing discussed in Chapter 22.

The DMCA Safe Harbor

In Chapter 3, there is a discussion of the "safe harbor" protection under the "Notice-and-Takedown" provisions of the Digital Millennium Copyright Act or DMCA. This law protects service providers (which would include any companies providing content electronically) against copyright infringement liability for content supplied by any "user."

If your company is handling and distributing content supplied by others (including Content Owners), you should review Chapter 3, follow the applicable procedures, and take full advantage of this safe harbor protection. Be sure to read the Copyright Office resources referenced in that chapter. See your legal counsel if you have any doubts about this important protection.

TOPIC III: HOSTING AND OTHER SERVICES

Services are often an essential part of a digital content agreement. In addition, services can be contracted for separately. In this section, we will refer to the parties to a deal for Internet or mobile services as the "Service Provider" and the "Customer."

One very common digital content service is hosting of digital content. Services may also include all the other service types that we listed at the beginning of this chapter, including personal and public communications, personalization, productivity services, e-commerce, advertising, location-based services, and so forth.

Here are issues to watch for in agreements regarding Web and mobile services:

- **Content Warranty and Indemnity**—If the Service Provider is hosting the Customer's content, the Service Provider will want the Customer to warrant that it has all required rights to the content. It will also want the Customer's indemnification against any third party claim that arises from the content or any issues of privacy.

- **Customer Data Ownership**—Where the supplier of services is handling end user data for its Customer (such as name, address information), the Customer will want contractual provisions to make it clear that the Customer "owns" the end user data and that such information will not be used for the Service Providers benefit.

- **Security Measures**—Customers often want detailed specifications regarding the security that will be provided for any remote service and hosted data. Customers will want very prompt notice if there is a security failure and may want specific remedies, including termination of the agreement, for any material security breach. Customers may ask for (and Service Providers will resist) guarantees that there will never be a security breach.

- **Data Backup**—Customers will want to be sure that any data held or processed for the Customer is securely and reliably backed-up. Often Customers want access to or delivery of back-up copies.

- **Disaster Recovery**—Customers may require that the Service Provider has a disaster recovery "hot site" facility, complete with all required data, that can start-up as soon as the supplier's principal location fails.

- **Scale-Up**—The online demand for the supplier's service may vary greatly and may grow quickly. Customers often want specific assurances (and supporting technical data) to provide assurance that the Service Provider can scale up services quickly.

- **Service Level Agreement or "SLA"**—Many service agreements require that the Service Provider guarantee a high level of system "uptime." If the "uptime guarantee" is not met, the Customer will often be entitled to compensation—in the form of a discount or credit. For serious or repeated failures, many agreements allow the Customer to terminate the agreement. Agreements also often have "problem response" metrics—requirements on how quickly the supplier must respond to a trouble report.

ABOUT WIDGETS

Let's talk a bit about widgets—a topic that we touched upon briefly above. A "widget" is a software component that provides discrete functionality and runs in another application or environment through a graphic user interface. The number, power, and sophistication of these programs are growing. There are several types of widgets:

- **Web Widgets**—These are "chunks" of computer code that can be "plugged into" Web pages to provide bits of user functionality. Because they are written with the same code that Web pages use and can access remote services, Web widgets can provide virtually any Web functionality. They commonly provide access to video, music, images, maps, news, sports, text, or social networking functionality. Google's AdSense service (which allows Google to put targeted advertising in any Web page) is implemented with a Google-supplied widget. Widgets are used to put YouTube videos on any Web page. Like the "mashups" that we discussed in Chapter 20, widgets often interact with application programming interfaces (APIs) on the Internet to provide content to the end user. Some social Web sites and media sites have functionality for users to add Web widgets to their personal Web sites.

- **Desktop Widgets**—These are code applets that are programmed to run in special software environments designed to support multiple widgets. An example of such an environment is Dashboard, the "widget engine" in Macintosh OS X. There is a similar environment in Microsoft Windows Vista to support "gadgets" (a synonym for widgets), and Google Desktop includes an environment that runs "gadgets." These various widgets provide sports, news, weather, clocks, and many other useful functions—with many of them interacting through the Internet with sources of content outside the end user's PC.

- **Mobile Widget**—This is an emerging category of small applications for mobile handsets that will run on mobile widget engines.

Licensing and Widgets

Because widgets are so varied, it is impossible to give a comprehensive guide to widget licensing. We do, however, offer the following overview of issues and concerns that you should keep in mind.

General Observations

First, some basic legal observations about widgets that affect their licensing and use:

- **Intellectual Property**—Intellectual property applies to widgets just like any other software. The code of any widget is protected under copyright law against unauthorized copying and distribution. Your company (or others) may be able to patent aspects of the widget technology. You may have widget trade secrets. Widgets commonly have branding. All of these aspects of the software are relevant to licensing.

- **Clearance**—Widgets have all the clearance issues of any other software, Web, or network application. If you provide a widget, you need to be sure to obtain the licenses and permissions needed for the code and intellectual property that the widget uses and for the content that it accesses and provides to the user.

- **Commercial Widgets**—Many widgets are used to implement a service or system that has a commercial purpose—which may include advertising, promotion, and brand development as well as for-pay services. When two companies conclude a negotiated contract that includes Web or mobile services and involves delivery and use of widgets, the issues are no different from any other deal involving combination of services and software for Internet or mobile use.

- **Noncommercial Widgets**—Some widgets are completely noncommercial. If you create a widget and want to just give it away to the world, you may consider open source licensing. Because widgets go within other commercialized works, a "copyleft" type license may not be the best choice. (See the discussion of open source licenses in Chapter 9.)

Inviting Widget Contributions onto Your Site or Mobile Application

Let us say that you create a Web site or mobile application that is widget-friendly; your site invites developers to upload and contribute widgets to showcase their programming skills. Your site might also offer resources and APIs that developers will use in creating widgets that your site will host and provide to the public. There is such a developer widget-friendly strategy used, for example, by the online video firm Joost.

If your site accepts contributed widget uploads, your site's terms of use will have to manage the legal interaction of the widgets and your Web business. Here are some of the issues that you may want to address in your online terms of use:

- **License Grant**—Under the terms of use, the developer will grant your company a license to install, copy, archive, display and use the widget permanently and royalty-free for your Web business. You may want to include a grant allowing your company to modify the widget in its discretion.

- **Registration**—Any contributor of widgets should register and include in the widget accurate identification of his, her, or its authorship.

- **Testing and Control**—The terms of use should include the contributor's consent to your company's process for review and acceptance of the widget before it goes online on your site.

- **Content Limitations**—You will want to avoid offending or annoying users; so your terms of use will forbid racist content, infringing content, pornography, or other offensive content or any links to such content. You would also forbid spyware and "malware" in contributed widgets.

- **Platform Protection**—There should be a prohibition against any application that degrades or disrupts your site or its functionality.

- **Limits on Commercial Use**—You might wish to exclude widgets with an overt commercial purpose, such as any advertisement display or ad streaming, except in accordance with a separate agreement for which your site would charge fees.

- **Privacy Protection**—Your terms of use will require that widget contributors cannot use the widgets to capture end user personal information or otherwise interfere with user privacy.

- **Branding and Reputation**—You would have rules on branding of the widgets, so that it would be clear that the widget is not supplied or endorsed by your company. You may want to permit (or require) "powered by" branding that indicates your company's technology is used in the widget.

- **Termination** Your company should retain the right to terminate its use or display of any widget at will.

- **IP Warranty**—The terms of use will have the developer represent that all technology and content used in or access by the widget is non-infringing and in compliance with applicable laws.

- **Indemnification**—Your terms of use will provide for the widget developer to indemnify your company from any third party claims arising from the widget or its use.

- **Other Boilerplate**—Your site would have typical warranty disclaimer and limitation of liability provisions to protect your company against claims by the contributor.

Putting Web Widgets Out in the World

Assume that your company creates Web widgets and distributes them to others—perhaps to provide access to content and information from your own Web-based service. In that case, you also need to address the risks of the Internet environment—but in this case, the risks come from the various Web sites around the world into which your Web widget and your service are being placed.

Say that you put your widget in a mass distribution and license thousands of Web sites to use them. You will want each person or business that downloads and embeds your widget in their site to assent to terms of an end user license agreement (EULA) that imposes controls and sets boundaries. Here are some of the issues that you should consider in crafting that EULA:

- **Grant of License**—Your company will grant the licensee a license to download, install and use the widget and/or the licensor's service in the licensee's own Web site. You might (or might not) allow redistribution of your widget code by these licensees.

- **Registration**—You will want each individual and company licensee that is using your widget or your Web service to register with your site or with your company.

- **Excluded Web Sites**—You will not want your widget to be placed, or your service associated with, any content or any site that will cause your company embarrassment or give offense. Therefore your agreement will forbid your widget and service from being used in any licensee Web site that has offensive content.

- **No Modification**—Most likely you will want to forbid the licensee from any changes in your widget's code or the functionality of your service.

- **Branding and Reputation**—Your agreement will forbid the licensee from changing the widget's branding. You will also want to require that any licensee's Web site that uses the widget or your service does not claim that your company is affiliated with or endorses its Web site.

- **Permitted Use**—You may want to preclude any use of your widget or your service other than by placing the widget on the licensee's own Web page for end users' personal use.

- **Limits on Content Aggregation**—You will want to forbid the licensee's aggregating your company's content or data.

- **Privacy Protection**—Your EULA will require that any site that incorporates your widget or service must have a privacy policy and must respect user privacy rights.

- **Termination**—Your company would retain the right to terminate any use of the widget or the supply of your company's service at any time, including the right to close the licensee's access to your service.

- **IP Warranty Disclaimer**—You would likely want to disclaim any warranties for your widget or service or your service, including any warranty that the supplied technology or content is non-infringing.

- **Indemnification**—Your agreement will provide for the licensee to indemnify your company from any third party claims arising from its usage or deployment of the widget in breach of the agreement.

- **Other Boilerplate**—Your site would have other typical terms of use provision to limit your company's liability.

For more information on these topics, please refer to the discussion in this book about clickwraps and browsewraps (Chapter 16), terms of use (Chapter 17), and user-provided content (Chapter 21).

CONCLUSION

There is enormous opportunity in the rapidly changing field of digital and mobile content and technology. Planning, intellectual property awareness, and smart contracting can maximize the benefits for your company and minimize the risks.

Video Games! Developing Games and Doing Deals

22

The only legitimate use of a computer is to play games.

—Arcade game designer Eugene Jarvis

This chapter provides practice guidance about legal issues and publishing deals in the world of video games. There are lots of deals to be done. Video game industry sales in 2007 (hardware and software) reportedly were about $1.25 billion *per month*. Top tier video games gross more money in America than the movies. Video games are a tough business with huge potential rewards. For example, in 2006, our law firm negotiated the sale of a game developer client Harmonix Music Systems (developer of *Guitar Hero*, *Guitar Hero II* and *Rock Band*) to MTV for $175 million in cash. Building value in a game development company requires a skilled development team and great game products, but it also requires valuable intellectual property (IP) and smart deals.

IN THIS CHAPTER

The chapter is divided into three sections:

- **Overview**—A look at some of the characteristics of video games and the video game industry that underlie its legal issues and affect video game deals.

- **Intellectual Property and Games**—A brief review of how intellectual property laws apply to video games.

- **Game Publishing Deals**—This section of the chapter explains key legal issues and negotiation strategies for publishing agreements. If you have   **587** a game in development—or an idea for one—a publishing agreement can get your game to market.

■ **Massively Multiplayer Games**—The final section provides an overview of some legal and practical issues for MMOs.

In the Appendix to this book you will find a form of Game Development and Publishing Agreement (Form 22-1), with a number of annotations and including some alternative and optional provisions. Of course, that form would have to be adapted to your company's own game development and publishing deals.

In preparation for the chapter, you may wish to review the chapter of this book on clearing content (Chapter 20) and contract basics (Chapter 8).

THE GAME INDUSTRY

Here is a high-level overview of the video games business; it is presented as a preface to the discussion of legal issues that follows.

The Players

Here are some of the players in the video game business:

Developers (sometimes called a "development studio") are the companies that produce games in exchange for payment. The staff of a developer can range from hundreds of persons down to a single person. Some developers serve as subcontractors on a "work-made-for-hire" basis.

Publishers are the companies that finance, promote, and distribute games. Publishers can be large or small companies.

Platform Owners are the companies that make and distribute game consoles and game controllers. There are currently three platform owners in mainline video games: Sony, Microsoft, and Nintendo. It takes enormous amounts of capital to break into this business and sustain a presence. Platform owners also develop and publish their own branded video games.

Mobile Operators provide for downloading of games and/or operation of networked games. Mobile games in the United States come primarily from portals operated by the major mobile communications carriers such as Verizon and ATT.

These are not all the players in this universe. There are contractors, content licensors, technology suppliers, distributors, retailers, investors, lawyers, various agents, and so forth.

Industry Segments and Genres

The game business is divided into a number of segments:

Console Games

This is the biggest and most profitable game segment with the highest production values. This segment is defined by game consoles—the hardware and software platform that the games run on. This segment is characterized by periodic "generation" changes in the console platform that allows for ever more stunning graphics and sound. The current generation (as this book is written) is the Sony PlayStation 3 (or "PS3"), the Microsoft Xbox 360 and the Nintendo Wii. There are also handheld variants such as the Sony PlayStation Portable. Each generation of hardware has required richer and more complex game software and this has lead to a big run-up on the price of creating console games.

The platform owners lose money on game consoles sales. However, they control disk replication for all publishers; they charge every publisher several dollars for each disk copy. They also use their consoles as a download game distribution and sales channel and charge users for "premium" subscriptions to online services. In addition, they publish their own games. Their plan is to profit on games in all these ways, which is why hit games are so important. Hit games also drive more console sales—because gamers will buy hardware only if there is exciting game software content available for the platform.

PC Games

These are games that run on PCs, Windows computers and (to a lesser extent) on Apple Macintosh computers. In many cases, these are versions of console games. Improvements in PCs have also increased the complexity of PC games and therefore the cost to make a game.

Mobile Games

These are games that run on mobile phones. Mobile games are a segment of mobile "value added services," which also include news, sport videos, SMS messaging, mobile instant messaging, and other mobile consumer information and communication services.

Mobile games have tended to be simpler and cheaper to make because of the limits of mobile display screens, memory, and processors. There are technical challenges in serving the mobile game market because mobile phones vary widely in the parameters of processing power, memory, and screen size and use different operating environments. Some believe that the improvements in mobile device interfaces (such as in Apple's iPhone) and better mobile game controller devices will lead to richer products for the mobile game market.

Other Platforms

There are other platforms for games that are relatively small markets. For example, there are games that play on PDAs. We will likely see the emergence of other video game platforms over time. It is possible that Apple iPods or other consumer electronic devices will become significant game platforms.

Types and Genres

Video games come in many different types and genres. There are adventure games, racing games, role-playing games, strategy games, arcade games, and so forth. Console games are usually divided into the highest quality video games (known as "AAA" titles), the less expensive second tier products (known as "A" titles), and budget games. There are casual games, online games and, as mentioned above, mobile games. One of the most interesting and fastest growing categories is the massively multiplayer online game (or MMO)—a form of computer game hosted on servers connected to the Internet in which many thousands of players participate and interact in a virtual online world. (There is more about MMOs later in this chapter.)

The cost and difficulty of development can vary greatly by game type. Developers usually specialize in one type or another. Developers may start with the lower end and simpler games and work up to the more complex high-end products. Barriers to entry to new game developers are lowest for the least elaborate and least expensive games, so the competition there is the fiercest.

Features of the Video Game Business

Here are some observations about the video game business as a whole that will be relevant to the discussion to come about clearance and deals:

- **Hit Driven**—The video game business is "hit driven." Game players tend to follow trends and converge on certain games and leave others to languish. Due to the popularity of game sites on the Web, players' opinions about games—positive or negative—spread like wildfire. Hit games can be hugely profitable. Unpopular games can lose millions. This can make successful developers very valuable.

- **Sequels and Ancillary Products**—Hit video games are a gift that keeps on giving. Every hit game is followed with one or more sequels. Video games can also be exploited through "ancillary products" such as content packs, strategy guides, and t-shirts. Games can spawn Web sites, movies, and TV shows. Music written for games may become popular songs. A super-hit can generate a "franchise" that lasts for many years.

- **Rising Costs for Games**—Because this is a hit-focused business, game publishers have increased their investment in prime games in the hopes of creating the next big winner. Each generation of game consoles features more functionality, richer graphics, and better sound effects—new technology which increases the cost of production. As a result, the development of high-end console games and PC games requires ever-increasing multimillion dollar development budgets.

- **Content and Branding Deals**—Because games are consumer entertainment products, they can be based on other mass marketing entertainment products, such as sports, movies, video, and pop music. Selling a game can be easier if it has a brand and content that is already popular with the target audience. This means that there are many game-related deals with other entertainment industries for brands, celebrity names and images, fictional characters, popular songs, and so forth. Many of these deals require significant upfront payments and/or guaranteed payments to secure exclusive rights. All of this requires content licensing deals based on principles that we discussed in Chapter 20.

- **Development Uncertainties**—Specifications for games are necessarily incomplete—many of the details of a game are conceived in the development process. Development time for games is therefore inherently uncertain. The more ambitious and innovative the game is, the more the risk that the game will end up behind schedule. Behind schedule usually also means over budget, because the longer that the game development process continues, the higher the payroll cost for its creation. There is also a risk of "feature creep" when the developer (often at the publisher's request) adds functionality during the course of development. All this means that there are big risks in game development. Video games require creativity and inspiration, but they also require planning, efficient production, and well-managed teams to keep them on track.

- **Marketing Costs**—Marketing expenses for top games can be as high or higher than the production budgets. Marketing expenses include advertising, promotional events, public relations, and market development funds (or "MDF"), which are payments for allocation of prominent shelf space in retail stores or other retail promotions. Game promotion and marketing for many games are focused on game launch, and launch is often targeted to meet the Christmas season.

- **Christmas Concentration**—For many console and PC video game products, as much as half of all sales occur during the Christmas season. So if a developer runs late and misses Christmas, its game product can lose a significant percentage of its sales potential.

- **Limited Space in Retail**—There is limited game display space in retail locations—much less than would be needed to display all titles well. Online retailers can also feature a limited number of titles. As a result space is initially allocated to those who pay for the best placement with MDF. But payment does not buy success. Regardless of the money spent on MDF, retailers usually retain the right to return poorly selling titles for cash or credit.

- **Control of the Platform**—Platform owners exercise control over their platform that gives them leverage over developers that create games for their respective platforms and third party publishers. The platform owner publishes proprietary development software used to create the games. They control encrypted interfaces to the game platform and only allow authorized parties to have the keys. They control the use of their branding on the games. They also control downloading of games and game content packs (additional levels or other added content for games) from their online channel accessed through the game console.

- **Approval of Developers**—The platform owners require all would-be developers to submit an application and can reject any would-be developer they deem insufficiently skilled or financed. They have branding and quality requirements. They require developers (or publishers) to submit games for their approval before release.

- **Platform Fees for Console Games**—The manufacturing cost of a single video game unit is not high (unless the games include an expensive peripheral such as a special game controller). However, each of the platform owners charges a fee for making each DVD copy of a video game—the fees are substantial and must be paid at the time each copy is made. This means that these "platform fees" are incurred whether games sell or not and can run into millions of dollars for the copies required for launch of a new game. Because of the platform owners' technology and branding control, publishers have no choice but to pay these platform fees.

- **Piracy**—Piracy is a fact of life for the game business. In China or India, it is hard to find anyone who has bought a "genuine" PC video game. Game consoles have more powerful anti-copying protections, which makes piracy more challenging, but not so powerful that technically sophisticated hackers are stopped. In Asia in particular, there are many shops that sell and install "mod" (modification) chips in game consoles that allow them to play pirated copies of games. As is discussed below, MMO games are much less exposed to piracy.

- **Marketing Issues in Mobile Games**—Currently, most mobile game titles are sold primarily through mobile phone handsets, and the small screen on the devices limits promotion. This tends to limit the number of mobile game titles, because there is only so much space available for promotion on mobile phone displays.

- **Competition and Imitation**—When a popular game emerges, it draws imitators with similar game projects. The result can be over-competition and poor sales in crowded genres.

All of the foregoing makes contracting in the game industry quite challenging.

What's in a Video Game?

From a legal (and practical) perspective, games development requires combining technologies and content.

Game Engine
At the heart of any game is the "game engine" which is the background software that renders and manipulates graphics and sound, controls object interaction (for example collision detection that decides if object are touching), tracks the state of the game, processes input from the game controller, and provides networking. The game engine would normally exclude graphics, sound, content creation tools, and the game scripting.

A developer may have significant amounts of internally developed game engine code. Game engines are developed in source code and compiled into executable code, which means that the source code of an internally developed game can be a very important trade secret asset. On the other hand, the developer could license all or most of the game engine technology from others.

Code Libraries and Software Tools

Libraries are collections of software components that game developers may include in games to perform particular game functions. They may be incorporated in the game engine. Some may be commercially licensed and others may be open source. Developers may create their own collections of software components, which may be part of the game engine.

In addition, game developers use specialized software tools to create and manipulate graphics and sound, to aid in development and management of source code, and for many other functions. Some tools may be developed in-house, but most are licensed from suppliers. Unlike components, such tools are not included in game code.

Game Scripts

Scripts are the instructions that contain the game logic. They are sets of instructions to the game engine telling it what to do in response to input from the players and the state of the game. Scripts are largely game-specific.

Video and Sound Assets

Games are also full of visual and sound assets. Visual assets consist of data that the game engine renders as a visible (2D or 3D) object. Sound objects are data that the game engine renders as sound. The developer often creates the visual assets, although parts of the process of doing so may be outsourced. Sound—music and sound effects—may also be created by the developer; however it is also very common for the developer to license third party music and sounds for a video game.

Content Rights

Games may have important third party licensed assets, such as pop music, brands, personality rights, video content, other graphics, and so forth. There is an overview of the licensing and clearance of these assets in Chapter 20.

Game Title

Titles for games may include both the name of a particular game and the name of a game series. An example is *Grand Theft Auto: Vice City*, a 2002 game product in the monstrously successful *Grand Theft Auto* franchise published by Rockstar Games. These can be extremely valuable trademarks.

GAMES AND IP

Let's look briefly at how intellectual property laws relate to video games. There are two reasons that this topic is important to game companies. First, there can be hidden IP traps. Second, IP law is background for the discussion of clearance and game publishing that follows. You may wish to review the chapters of this book on copyrights, trademarks, and patents (Chapters 2 through 4) as background for this discussion.

Copyright and Games

Under US law (and in most other nations as well), a copyright holder has the exclusive right to make and sell copies of copyrighted works and to create derivative works. Because video games (and their components) are digital copies and are full of code and content, copyright law applies in one way or another to all of the contents of video games.

Literal Copying and Digital Derivatives

Most developers know that they need written permission to use third party content in their games. (But there is more to avoiding copyright problems than that.)

One important copyright concern is exact copying—what copyright lawyers call "literal" copying (that is, copying of the bits and bytes of content and technology). Developers put hundreds of different objects into their games—library code, sound, images, and so forth. Much of these are exact copies. Some objects are processed or compiled and therefore are digital derivatives that are, in essence, literal translations. With this kind of literal copying (except for the rare item that might be in the public domain), each copy of each object from a third party is covered by copyright law. That means incorporation of any unauthorized code or objects in a game is likely to be an infringement.

It is possible for your company to become an infringer due to mistakes by your employees or contractors. Your employee or contractor may embed a third party's code or content in your video game without your knowledge and without proper authorization. The fact that the company's management did not know of a copyright infringement is not a defense. It is important for the development staff to understand that just because something can be downloaded from the Web does not mean it is cleared for use in a game. An IP-aware workforce is a must.

There is a myth that a little bit of literal copying without permission is OK. In fact, there is substantial risk that very small amounts of copying will render your company liable. In one reported copyright case, the copying of 27 lines of code out of 525,000 lines was found to be infringing, where the copied code had significant functionality.

If you do have infringing content in your video game, you run the risk that you will be sued and that a judge will order your game off the market until and unless the infringing matter is replaced. (Usually it is a disgruntled employee that spills the beans.) And your company can be sued for damages. Of course unauthorized copying of an entire video game (what the industry calls "piracy") is an infringement under this same principle.

Non-Literal Copying

Because games are creative objects, game developers must also avoid "non-literal" copying, which is copying of the creative expression of other works. You may be accused of copying the look of objects, the melody of tunes, the appearance of art-work, the form or names of characters, the appearance of scenes, or the story and plot of another game. The more the elements are similar and the closer they sound or appear, the more likely that the borrowing from another game will be held an infringement.

An example is the case of *Marvel vs. NCSoft*, a law suit filed in 2004. Korea-based NC Software is the publisher of City of Heroes, a massively multiplayer online role playing game with a superhero comic book theme. Marvel, of course, is the famous comic-book publisher that licenses its character, like Wolverine and Spiderman, for use in games and film. Marvel's suit alleged that NCSoft promoted and encouraged the creation of look-alike characters that infringed copyrights and trademarks owned by Marvel. The suit was ultimately settled.

For more information on literal and non-literal copying, please see the chapters of this book on copyright basics (Chapter 2) and on clearance of content (Chapter 20). Your attorney can provide more guidance on copyright matters.

Trademarks and Video Games

Most developers understand that they cannot use a famous third party brand to name their game. Developers also need to be careful about brands slipping into the scenes of a video game. The game's street scenes should not have signs for Coke or McDonalds unless you have consent from those companies. Characters in your game should not drive Chevys unless you have consent from GM.

You should not use famous brands in dialog. The American Red Cross has written game publishers to demand that its famous trademark not be used in violent video games. In 2007, the Church of England has threatened to sue Sony over the inclusion of a virtual Manchester Cathedral in Sony's game Resistance: Fall of Man (although no suit has been brought as this chapter was written). It is also risky to use look-alike or sound-alike branding.

We are not saying that this kind of "embedded" trademark use in a game is always illegal. In some cases, you could cogently argue that that trademark use to make a storyline or scene feel more realistic is a fair use or constitutes protected artistic expression under the First Amendment. The problem here is that the application of these legal doctrines is uncertain. In addition, the law on these topics varies from nation to nation, and video games are normally distributed internationally. It is seldom worth the risk of a lawsuit. So the common practice is to get a written license or do without.

Also relevant is the concept of trade dress, which is the nonfunctional appearance of goods and packaging and appearance that identifies it in much the same way as a brand. If you want a Ferrari in your game, there is both a trademark and a trade dress issue. You should get written permission for both and that will likely require a negotiation and a license.

The good news here is that, in the right kind of game, brand holders will often give consent if they think that your game will help sell their product and may actually pay for brand placement.

Patents and Games

Patents can be infringed without knowledge or fault. As a result, a development company and its staff could respect all known rights, license all third party content and code used in a game and the company could still get sued for patent infringement. (Patents are the subject of Chapter 4 of this book.)

The world of video games is full of patented technology and there are more game-related patents coming all the time. A quick search of the patent database at the US Patent and Trademark Office (USPTO) will show you hundreds of game patents covering hardware and software. Patented technology covers inventions in many areas, including graphics, game play, shadow-generation, Internet play, character movement, controller functionality, antipiracy, and more. Some game-related patents are well known in the industry. Many more are obscure, but might still be the basis of claims. Because of the enormous stakes in high-end gaming, more and more companies that can afford to do so are developing and acquiring patent portfolios in video games.

There have been a number of well-publicized patent lawsuits involving games. For example:

- In 2002, technology inventor Immersion sued Sony and Microsoft for their use of "tactile feedback" in game controllers.

- In 2003, Sega sued Fox Filmed Entertainment, Electronic Arts, and others over the video game "Simpsons Road Rage." Sega claimed the game used its patented technology on software car game controls for its own game "Crazy Taxi."

- In 2003, Peer-to-Peer Systems sued Palm for alleged infringement of a patent on software coordination of multiplayer wireless games.

- Gibson Guitar has a patent on a system for guitar-based video games. In 2008, it asserted alleged patent infringement claims against Activision, the publisher of the popular *Guitar Hero* games and Harmonix Music, the developer that created *Guitar Hero* and *Guitar Hero II*. As of the time this book was written, the Gibson litigation was ongoing.

Game patents that generate lawsuits are the tip of the iceberg. Many more patents are licensed after demand and negotiation. Still more are held in reserve until needed for a competitive threat.

In addition to the game-related patents, there are the pending patent applications, many of which will issue as patents in the years to come. Applications are normally secret for 18 months after filing—so you could be using technology that is subject to a patent application and have no way of knowing.

Video game developers should be patent-aware. They should watch for new stories about patents being asserted against other companies that make similar games. Getting patent legal advice is always a good idea but particularly so when entering into new game fields. Finally, we recommend consistently evaluating the patentability of novel game technology.

Publicity Rights (Right of Personality)

Games (and media generally) that feature celebrities often involve an intellectual property right known as the "publicity right" also known as the "right of personality." This is the right of famous persons to control the commercial use and exploitation of their names, signatures, and images—even the sound of their voices. This is a right that we met in the chapter on clearing content (Chapter 20).

Trade Secrets

Much of the information that game companies possess (particularly makers of novel and innovative products) constitutes a trade secret. That includes programming techniques, code libraries, business plans, and other nonpublic information. Even though game developers often have an informal culture, they must protect trade secrets using the commercially reasonable efforts described in Chapter 6 of this book like any other technology business.

Note on Dealing with Employees and Contractors

A lot of content for games come from your own employees and contractors. A developer should be sure that each employee signs a rights transfer and confidentiality agreement of the type described in this book. (See Chapter 7.)

With regard to contractors, game companies should read and take seriously the discussion of consulting contracts in Chapter 10 and use form agreements like those discussed in that chapter. Be sure that contractors all sign agreements with "work–made-for-hire" clauses. (The copyright principles underlying such clauses are discussed in Chapter 2.) Agreements with contractors should also have provisions under which each contractor agrees to assign all IP the contractor creates while working on your assignment including copyrights (to the extent not covered by the work-for-hire clause), patents, trademarks, and trade secrets. Remember that under US law, you cannot obtain ownership of or any other exclusive right in a copyright or patent from a contractor without a written agreement that conveys the interest—no matter how much you pay the contractor.

Third Party Game Engines/Game Tools/Libraries

Licensing third party game engines, tools and code libraries is important. Here are a few tips to help you get the rights you need:

- Appoint someone in your organization to manage the licensing process. Do not leave it to programmers to decide what software licensing is sufficient.

- Review all licenses carefully. Some license schemes have one form of license for development and another (more expensive) license for distribution. Make sure that the licenses permit the types of distribution that you plan for. (If you have any doubts, get legal assistance.)

- Many licenses will disclaim warranties, including warranties of non-infringement. That means that the suppliers are not responsible if they provide you with code that infringes a third party's patent. There may not be much you can do about this, but you should be aware of the risk.

- Be careful about the use of open source licenses. Some have "Copyleft" provisions that make them inadvisable to use in games. Developers should be sure that use of open source complies with publisher requirements. See the chapter of this book on open source licensing (Chapter 9) for more details.

PUBLISHING AGREEMENTS

This section is about the "publishing agreement"—the contract that manages the relationship between the video game developer and a publisher. As noted above, the Appendix to this book includes a form of publishing agreement (Form 22-22).

We hope that the following discussion will help both developers and publishers to negotiate better deals. In the form appendix to this book, you will find a sample game publishing agreement. This document is based on actual contracts, but it may not fit your needs or your deal. In fact, because of the great variety of arrangements, any deal that you do will surely diverge from this sample in many ways. So the form is offered for information and can be used as a checklist, but it is not necessarily a guide to the contents of your own deal.

The Role of Publishers

The relationship between developers and publishers is one of mutual dependence. Developers know how to make games, but they most often lack the resources to finance, promote, and get them to market. Publishers offer the resources, skills, and abilities to finance game development and to manufacture (or have manufactured), promote, and distribute games.

Some publishers create games in-house and some do not. (From time to time, publishers buy development firms.) Nonetheless, most publishers are always on the look-out for good video game products from developers. That's because hit video games require creativity, innovation, and inspiration, and there is no way to capture the world's supply of those intangible qualities.

Often the core ideas for games come from developers, but that is not always the case. In some cases, the publisher may come up with the concept or make the key deal with a movie studio or book publisher for licensed content that will become the basis of a game.

Shared and Diverging Goals

The developer and the publisher share a common goal—a hot game that sells in huge quantities, but there are many ways in which their interests diverge. Publishing contracts are about the commitment of resources and the allocation of profit and business risk. Each party wants to reduce its commitment of resources and business risk and maximize its profits.

The tension created by these issues is played out on a number of different levels including:

- **Development Funding**—How much will the publisher have to pay to get a finished game?

- **Development Risks**—Will the project be developed on budget and on time?

- **Market Risks**—Will players buy the game? Will there be other valuable revenue streams?

- **Royalties**—What are the on-going payment obligations of the publisher?

- **Ownership**—Who will end up with ownership of which game assets? Who will control the right to make sequels or ports?

- **IP Risks**—Will third parties threaten or bring lawsuits regarding the game contents or technology?

About Leverage

Leverage counts for a lot in game deal negotiations. Often the publisher has the benefit of the oft-cited "golden rule"—the one with the gold dictates the rules. Publishers usually have in-house counsel and will send their preferred pro-publisher "standard forms." Flexibility to change the form will vary by publisher but there is invariably some "gives" that developers can obtain.

Leverage shifts to the developer if it has a record of hit games or if it has unique skills or game technologies. Publishers may compete for the skills of a hot development shop. Even developers that do not have these advantages may be able to obtain significant concessions through good negotiation skills—however they do need to "pick their spots" and be selective about what they need to have in deals.

Term Sheets and LOIs

As with many other deal types, game deals typically start with "term sheets" or "deal outlines" and proceed to more formal documents. These documents are sometimes signed as nonbinding "Letters of Intent" or "LOI." If you sign a document that you expect to be nonbinding, the document must state unambiguously that it is nonbinding.

A nonbinding LOI would typically have the outline of the business terms of a game development deal, including the general nature of the game, its development time frame, advances for development, IP ownership, perhaps clearance obligations if the game has significant third party content, and royalty structure.

Although an LOI is nonbinding, it can have a powerful effect on the following negotiation of the binding agreement. Departing materially from the term sheet may be seen as bad faith. This means that you should get legal advice before you sign even a nonbinding document—so that you can be sure what you are getting yourself into. Legal costs for help on this kind of preliminary document are usually relatively modest—much less than the legal costs for the publishing agreement itself.

Short Forms/Binding MOUs

Sometimes developers and publishers sign a "short form" *binding* agreement—which, the parties agree, will be followed by a longer and more complete "long form" contract thereafter. Commonly the long form is supposed to be negotiated and signed within the following 30 days—although it often takes considerably longer. Such a document is often titled a "Memorandum of Understanding" or "MOU." Unlike an LOI, the short form MOU is a binding legal agreement. (See the discussion of MOUs in Chapter 8.) This means that a party's failure to perform under the short form will be a breach of contract that can result in termination of the agreement, legal liability for money damages, a costly lawsuit or all the above.

The short form agreement would cover main business points such as:

- Main game functionality and platforms
- Development schedule and milestones
- IP ownership
- Advances and recoupment
- Royalty rates and payment

The major advantage of a short form agreement to the developer is that it almost always triggers payment of a development advance. This gets the publisher invested in the game and makes backing out less likely. It also means that the developer can stop spending its own precious cash on development. The short form also gives the developer the ability to document in binding form (at least provisionally) the key business terms.

But these advantages come with risk. If the parties fail to agree on the long form agreement, the short form MOU will control the parties' relationship throughout development and for the life of game—or even longer depending on the deal. The development requirements, license and financial provisions in a short form agreement, are typically written without many details, so important issue may be unaddressed or left open. Short form (particularly in the form proposed by the publisher) may place many legal risks on the developer and omit legal protections.

If you are asked to sign a short form agreement, get legal advice. You may decide to skip the short form and just negotiate the "long form" agreement. This path likely will save legal fees, because you will have one negotiation instead of two. It will also reduce legal risk. Or you may ask your lawyer to help you negotiate a balanced short form document. During negotiations, it is not uncommon for proposed short form agreements to morph into more complicated documents as each party inserts what it considers to be essential qualifications and protections.

Whether a short form binding agreement is a good idea for a developer or publisher depends on the circumstances and the text of the proposed agreement.

Prototype and Game Design Agreements

There can be intermediate contracts between publisher and developer that are short of a full development agreement. Sometimes the publisher will engage the developer to produce a game design, that is, be a document stating the game's intended look and functionality. Or the publisher may engage for the developer to produce a working game prototype as a proof of concept. These are typically short term, lower budget engagements that are designed to lower the risk of the full scale game development project that may follow.

Although these are short term engagements with less money at stake, both sides need the assistance of legal counsel on these agreements as well. The key issue will be ownership of resulting IP. While it may be reasonable for the publisher to own the IP created "on its nickel" (particularly if the idea for the game came from the publisher), the developer will want to be sure that its proprietary game engine code is not inadvertently conveyed to the publisher.

The Development Provisions

Development agreements normally provide for the publisher to finance game development through advances. While it is possible to develop a game first and then find a publisher, it is not often done that way. Developers usually do not have the resources to self-fund.

Most publishing agreements have negotiated development and payment provisions. The developer promises to develop and deliver the finished game (or game versions) to the publisher by a particular date—meeting milestones tied to deliverables along the way. The publisher agrees to fund development with payments tied to deliverables and milestones. There is an acceptance process for each milestone deliverable and, of course, a process for payment to the developer. The first payment is normally an advance due on signing. Developers commonly have the same kind of milestone-driven payment structure in their agreements with their subcontractors.

Goals of the Parties in Development

What the publisher wants is simple: a top quality game delivered on time with all expected functionality and with no unpleasant surprises. What the developer wants is for someone else to pay all of the development costs and still retain the opportunity for financial success without undue risk.

Most publishing agreements have development provisions that are crafted to favor the publisher and make missing a milestone a default that can lead to termination. Therefore the developer must try to sell the publisher on a development plan that it can deliver on time, within budget, and with very low risk of technical failure—even if the game technology plan is ambitious. There are always some delays and if there is no "give" in the project planning, the game development project will have a higher risk of failure.

A Preliminary Note on Game Funding

Development funding by publishers is typically structured as milestone-driven advances against royalties. This means that the publisher recovers its development investment from the developer's royalties on video game revenues. Typically only after the publisher fully recoups its development payments does the developer get its first royalty check.

Because of the expense of modern video game development, it is the fact of life that many games (even those that sell quite well) never get "into royalties." This means that the developer needs to secure development milestone funding that provides for all its costs and a reasonable profit—even if the royalties never come.

Game Description

Every agreement for game development includes a description of the game to be delivered. It is nearly impossible to have a complete detailed description in advance. The game will include artistic content to be created. Game play and features may change in development.

Nonetheless, the publisher needs to have a reasonably clear idea of what it is getting and that idea needs to match up to what the developer thinks it is suppose to create. For this reason, it is best for all if the game description contains some metrics that indicate the limits of the development obligation. For example, the parties should make clear (as applicable) the number of principle characters in the game, the number of venues that will appear in the game, the number of game levels, the number of weapons and "power-ups," the number of songs that will be licensed, and so forth.

Try to avoid game descriptions that have significant game functionality listed as "TBD" (for "to be decided"). The problem with open items like this is that they can lead to deadlock later on when the parties disagree. Under contract law, an agreement that is incomplete may not be an agreement at all—in spite of the fact that both parties thought they were signing a binding agreement. The practical risk is that the development process may grind to a halt if the parties cannot agree on what milestone deliveries should contain. The legal risk is that neither party may be able to enforce the agreement in case of such a breakdown. It is best to keep TBD items to a minimum and close unspecified items as soon as possible.

Ports and Localization

A "port" is a modification of a software game that makes it playable on one or more additional platform or operating systems. For example, one could port a game from PlayStation3 to Xbox 360 or to a PC.

Localization means the translation or modification of a game's software and related materials (such as the user manual) to meet the needs of a particular foreign country or region. Localization may include translation or adaptations in the text, data, music, voices, sounds, graphics, and/or video format for a target market. Additional changes may be required to adapt the product for Asian language characters. The game description in the publishing agreement must make it clear what ports or localization is required.

Members of the Development Team

The publisher will normally insist on provisions in the agreement that gives it some veto control over staffing of the developer's team. This might include the right to review resumes and to interview manager candidates—or the right to require changes in staff. You will often also see provisions that prohibit the transfer of staff to other projects without permission. The developer may be able to negotiate a limitation of these provisions, but may not be able to remove them altogether.

Game Milestones

The milestone charts set forth the deliverables and events that trigger development payments and the amount of each payment. Some typical milestones used as payment triggers might be:

- **Signing of the Agreement**

- **Initial Deliverables**—In some cases, the developer may deliver technology demonstrations (to validate that the functionality will work) and deliver artwork, design documents and the like.

- **Alpha**—This is a varying concept for an early game version. It is usually defined to mean a playable form of a software game with most of the major functionality graphics, sound, video, and text.

- **Beta**—This normally is defined as a feature complete game that is ready for testing. Sometimes there is an "Initial Beta" for internal testing and a "Second Beta" for release to select outside beta testers.

- **Gold Master**—This means the version of the game that is complete, fully tested, and ready for release. For console games, there may be a further requirement that the game has passed the platform owner's acceptance testing.

The larger and more complex the game, the greater the number of milestones. Some games have dozens of deliverables—each with an associated milestone payment. Careful budgeting, achievable milestones, and sufficient payment for each milestone are keys to make development provisions work.

When the publisher is required to make deliveries that will be used in game development—such as music, artwork, and so forth, it is in the developer's interest to include these in the milestone schedule. The developer should negotiate for a provision that the publisher is responsible for any delay caused by its own late performance and that the milestone schedule will be deemed adjusted accordingly.

Change Control

Development contracts often have formal provisions for changes in scope and budget. Developers should try to avoid or remove language in agreements that give the publisher an unqualified right to "require modifications." Modifications usually require more time and more dollars. Developers that just say 'yes' to unfunded change requests will be creating problems down the line.

It is in the developer's interest—and ultimately in both parties' interest—to have rational change control provisions. These usually require that the developer prepares a written description of proposed changes, together with the proposed impact both on the time milestone schedules and on development funding. Under such provisions, changes are binding only when agreed upon by both parties in writing.

Outsourced Tasks

Developers may outsource a variety of tasks—music production, graphics development, localization, porting of the game to a different platform, quality assurance testing, or other tasks. Many publisher form agreements forbid delegation of obligations without prior publisher permission. Any developer that wants to outsource production to subcontractors should be sure that the publishing agreement permits outsourcing and know what limitations, if any, there are on the outsourcing. If the publishing agreement forbids outsourcing, the developer will need to get the publisher's express written permission prior to the use of any third party resources.

Developers also need to be sure that they use third party subcontractors that are trustworthy and can make deliveries on time. In addition, developers need agreements with subcontractors that capture all of the IP rights required to be passed on to the publisher under the publishing agreement. Often the publisher will want the right to review and approve contracts with subcontractors. Developers should be sure to get experienced legal counsel to help with subcontracting.

Source Code

Publishing agreements normally require the developer to provide the full source code for the games to the publisher. Publishers want source code because it may be needed for maintenance and ports, and because it may be useful in sequels or other similar games. Sometimes, developers successfully negotiate limits to what the publisher may do with the code, and the agreement may make certain source code uses subject to royalties. (See discussion of IP and payment provisions below.)

Sometimes publishers want "commented" source code supplied. This is code filled with annotations as to what each portion does. Needless to say, developers (and their staff) usually resist doing this extra work.

Acceptance and Correction

Publishing agreements usually have provisions for acceptance or rejection of deliverables. These acceptance provisions are important, because acceptance of deliverables is the trigger for milestone payments. Sometimes acceptance clauses have no definite time frame for the publisher to accept or reject a deliverable. This favors the publisher by permitting a leisurely review of the deliverables, which in turn, can delay milestone payments. Developers will, and often successfully argue for a fixed amount of time (say, 10 business days) for the publisher to accept or reject a deliverable by stressing that its delivery of the finished game is dependent on the prompt action of the publisher.

If the publisher rejects a deliverable, the acceptance clause normally requires that the publisher specify in writing the failures and defects of the deliverable. The developer then must respond in a fixed time with a corrected version. Failure to fix is normally grounds for the publisher to terminate the agreement.

In some agreements, the publisher will be "deemed to accept" a deliverable if it fails to make a timely rejection. In other agreements, a publisher's acceptance of every milestone must be in writing. Commonly, the Gold Master can be accepted only in writing and is not subject to "deemed acceptance."

Acceptance criteria for games may be quite subjective. You often see requirements that the game be of the "highest quality" and "free of errors" and provisions that base acceptance on whether the publisher finds "in its sole judgment" that the game conforms to this standard. Under many publishing agreements, the publisher can reject a deliverable (and the game) on the grounds that the graphics do not look good enough or that game play is too easy or not compelling enough and can then legitimately take the position that it has terminated the game for "cause."

Developers can push to lighten these provisions, but will need leverage to do so. For example, the developer may want the publisher to be required to accept a Gold Master that is of "commercially acceptable quality" even if not wholly bug free.

Bug-free code is desired but rarely achieved and not necessarily expected. Gold Masters in practice are often accepted with some known minor bugs or defects. Publishers may (but usually are not obligated to) accept them if they are "good enough" for use—if the flaws are minor and do not interfere in any significant way with customer use and enjoyment. Many publishing deals require developers to provide error corrections for no additional fees even after the game is released. We discuss below (in the section on Termination) what happens if the developer or the publisher has uncured defaults in its development obligations.

Marketing Support Tasks

Publisher's form agreements often require developers to provide, without extra charge, additional deliverables for use in marketing, such as: demo versions of a game, screen shots, concept art, art for use in advertising or packaging, and so forth. It is in both parties' interest that these items are produced, because both the developer and the publisher want the product marketing to be as effective as possible. The issue for the developer, however, is the uncompensated extra time and effort it takes to fulfill these requests. This is another area where the developer can try to push back and see if it can obtain additional payments for these extra services.

The Right to Kill Games

In many publishing deals, the publisher reserves the absolute right to stop development of the game and terminate the agreement at any time for no reason—what is known as "termination for convenience." If the developer has sufficient leverage it may be able to negotiate this provision out of the agreement and permit termination only for an uncured breach of the agreement.

The publisher wants this kind of provision because it fears that the market may change and it may want to redeploy its resources to other game markets. Sometimes publishers' decisions to kill products are driven by politics in the publisher's organization—the firing of a manager may lead to the discontinuance of his or her pet game projects. A developer may not successfully negotiate a "kill" provision out of a publishing agreement but here are some ways that a developer may mitigate its negative consequences:

- **Payments through Termination**—Developers will normally get provisions for payment up to the date of termination based on a percentage of completion calculation (that is, completion or partial completion of milestones).

- **Kill Fees**—Some developers successfully negotiate a "kill fee"—a payment of compensation.

- **Reduced Royalties**—In some cases, the developer may be entitled to a royalty (as a reduced rate) if the publisher has the game finished by another developer. The reduced rate royalty can be based on the percentage of completion of the game on the termination date.

- **Acquiring Rights to the Game**—Developers may negotiate for the option to reacquire the rights to the game if the publisher has terminated for convenience. Under such a provision, the developer would normally obtain only the game rights that it has created (as opposed to any content and rights contributed by the publisher or supplied by third party licensors). If the developer does get the rights back, there will often be a provision that allows the publisher to recoup its milestone payments from advances and/or royalties paid to the developer by the successor publisher of the game.

The publisher usually reserves the right not to publish the game even after acceptance—although it is rare that a publisher would fully fund development and then kill a video game product.

Content and Tools

Unless the publishing agreement says otherwise, the developer will be responsible for obtaining and paying for all content, development software, and hardware that are required to complete the game. The developer needs to make sure that adequate time is built into the milestone schedule to obtain the licenses it needs. Obtaining licenses can be expensive; the developer should make sure that the licensing costs are built into the development budget.

If a publisher agrees to be responsible for obtaining and paying for certain content or development tools (which is frequently the case), the publishing agreement should state clearly what is required and when. If the publisher is providing rights from a movie, for example, the agreement should be very clear as to exactly what assets and what rights are provided: is it the name of the movie, film footage, characters, likenesses of the stars, photos, music, or other assets? The agreement should also specify (as much as possible) the form in which the content will be provided.

Sometimes the publishing agreement will require the publisher to supply (or to pay for) particular development software (such as code libraries or development SDKs from the platform owner) or development hardware. It is in both parties' interest that no clearance tasks fall between the cracks.

Game Asset Ownership and Licensing

A hotly negotiated issue in publishing agreements is the ownership of game assets and related IP.

Effect of Third Party and Publisher-Supplied IP

Third party (or publisher supplied) IP in a video game acts as a constraint on the rights that the developer can transfer or license. In the discussion that follows, I refer to the ownership, transfer, or licensing of "the game" or "the game assets" as a shorthand. In reality the discussion is about only that portion of the game as the developer has the legal right to license or sell and that usually means the IP rights created by the developer.

Owners of Game Assets

The publisher's preference is to own all game assets and the related IP rights. This kind of agreement is often referred to as a "work–made-for-hire" deal—although technically "work made for hire" is a copyright term, and publishers' form agreements normally cover other IP rights, such as trademarks, patents, and trade secrets.

At the other end of the spectrum would be an agreement (rather rare if the publisher provided significant funding) under which the publisher owns nothing and merely obtains a license for game distribution. In between, there are many negotiated agreements that divide the game assets and IP between the developer and the publisher.

When assets are divided, the developer can argue that it should keep ownership of game assets that: (a) it created or improved before or apart from the current game or (b) that will be reusable for a variety of games. The publisher will argue that it should own assets that are game-specific or that were created with funding from the publisher. There can be overlap in these categories; some reusable assets (that the developer may want to own) may be created by use of the publisher's funds.

Game Engine

As is noted above, one asset that developers commonly (but not always) retain is a developer-created game engine, including game engine code created as part of game development for the publisher. Developers seek to impose limits on publisher's licensed use of this asset. For example, the license terms can limit use of the game engine to maintenance, ports, and sequels. If and when the publisher does reuse developer code in a game that the developer does not program, the developer will want a royalty for its use. This can be a negotiation item.

The developer will want provisions in the game publishing agreement requiring that the publisher treat the game engine source code as confidential information of the developer. The developer will want to be sure that there are confidentiality obligations in place, as well, if the publisher provides the code to a third party developer to create a sequel or content packs. Similar considerations will apply to the publisher's use of proprietary tools and libraries that the developer may create.

Visual and Sound Assets and Brands

When the publisher funds the game development, it will normally expect to obtain ownership of all visual and sound assets, characters and venues as well as all trademark rights for the game title, game-related logos, and any other branding that developer may develop. (The publisher would also normally have the right to change the name and branding of the game.) The publisher will also want the exclusive right to register these assets for copyright and trademark registration. All of these assets can be keys for sequels and for creating a game "franchise" from a hit game.

Patent Rights

Most developers do not have patented game technologies. However, some do have patents for particular game programming algorithms or methods. The publisher may see developer's patents as a threat, and if so, will seek broad license rights under them. That's because the patents may control the means to implement key game functionality. Unless the publisher has a license, sequels and work-alike games could be infringing. Of course a developer with a patent position will expect the publisher to pay royalties for use of its patents.

If the developer has a pre-existing patent position and wants to avoid conveying the patents to the publisher, it should negotiate a publishing agreement clearly stating that the developer's patents are licensed and not transferred. If the developer wants to own patented technologies that it may develop in the course of its work, it will normally have to bargain hard for that privilege. If the developer does retain patent rights, the publisher will insist on a patent license covering the game and most likely sequels or other games as well.

Marketing Obligation

A fundamental obligation of the publisher is to promote and market the game. Publishers can spend a lot or a little on marketing, public relations, and advertising. Sometimes publisher do a great job in marketing and sometimes they perform poorly. The hard fact is that it is very difficult to get meaningful measures of a publisher's performance into a publishing agreement.

The best that most developers can do is to obtain early and frequent marketing consultation. If the developer has leverage, it can sometimes obtain a committed marketing budget (which might be in the hundreds of thousands or millions of dollars).

The Money Provisions

Money is the fuel for building games. As mentioned above, the basic structure consists of the publisher paying development funding as advances against royalties. The concept is simple; the devil is in the details. Payment provision negotiations are an art. A good deal of the action is trading one element for another and weighting (or guessing) the value of contingent future payments.

Development Payments

It is normal for the publisher to pay about 15 to 25 percent of the development budget upon signing the publishing agreement and to hold back 10 to 15 percent for the finished and complete Gold Master version of game. The other milestones are largely driven by the needs of the specific game development process and by the parties' negotiations. The developer will want to "front load" payment by increasing amounts payable on the earlier milestones, and the publisher may want to "back load" them by paying more for later milestones.

Some publishing agreements include a bonus payment for early delivery of the Gold Master and reductions in payment if delivery is late—although these penalty provisions may be self-defeating for publishers if they cause the developer to run out of money needed to finish the game.

The developer should not forget that federal and state income tax laws apply to development payments—to the extent that income exceeds business expenses. If there are likely to be taxes, and the developer should take them into account in budgeting.

Recoupment of Development Payments

In most publishing agreements, the provisions for recoupment of advances are fairly simple. Royalties are simply calculated at the applicable rate or rates (set as discussed below) and are kept by the publisher until they equal the development payments.

But that is not the only way that it can be done. Sometimes developers with leverage are able to negotiate accelerated recoupment.

For example, let's say the royalty rate is negotiated to be 10 percent. If the game advances were a million dollars, the publisher's net sales would have to equal $10 million before advances would be recouped and royalty payments would begin.

The developer and the publisher could agree on a special rule that the royalty rate will be deemed to be 20 percent until advances are recouped and that the rate will then revert to 10 percent. Under this special rule, the publisher's net sales would only have to equal $5 million before advances would be recouped and royalty payments would begin.

Or the deal could be that the publisher begins paying royalties at a reduced rate beginning from game launch and pays full royalties only after it recoups all its advances.

The costs of games are mostly upfront. Publishers pay a lot to create the game and for advertising and promotion to launch it. The games themselves are high gross margin goods, and hit games are very profitable. Those who study the economics of games tell us that successful games usually generate profits for publishers long before the publisher begins paying royalties.

The lower the royalty rate the longer it will take for recoupment to occur and the better the developer's argument will be for an alternative recoupment method. Developers may find, however, that this kind of concession is tough to get unless they have a very attractive game offering.

Percentage Royalties

Publishing agreements typically set royalties as a percentage (called the "royalty rate") of "Net Sales" which is defined as "Gross Sales" net of specified deductions. (There is more on royalty rates and deductions below.)

Gross Sales

Most often Gross Sales is defined as the publisher's total revenues. However, sometimes it is defined as the publisher's receipts. There is an important difference between the two. Revenue is normally booked when games are shipped to the buyer (which could be a retailer, wholesaler, or consumer). Receipts are booked when the buyer pays, which in the case of retailers or wholesalers can be considerably later. So, receipts-based royalties will be delayed by months. Developers should be sure that Gross Sales include those of the publisher and its subsidiaries and affiliates anywhere in the world.

Deductions

Allowable deductions from Gross Sales are, to some extent, a matter of custom and practice. Needless to say, publishers will try to broaden applicable deductions to include more expense categories, because this effectively reduces the royalty rate. Developers will try to reduce or cap the deductions, to exclude any publisher internal expenses, and limit deductions to actual out-of-pocket costs.

Here are some of the common categories of deductions from Gross Sales used to calculate Net Sales and some of the positions that publishers and developers can take. These are items that are often subject to negotiation and haggling.

Returns/Reserve for Returns

Returns are a fact of life in games. It is favorable to the developer if the deduction is limited to actual returns. More commonly the provision is for a reserve for returns, which is a deduction that is taken as sales are recorded. The publisher's establishing a "reserve" does not mean that any money is set aside—it is just an accounting adjustment. The amount deducted is a percentage of sales (often set at 10, 15, or 20 percent) which should be adjusted for actual returns at the end of every quarter, or sometimes every sixth months. Developers should try to keep the reserve low and shorten the time for it to be adjusted to the actual return rate.

Taxes and Shipping

Deductions for taxes are normally limited to those paid or payable based on sales. They normally should not include any form of income taxes. Developer will want "shipping" to be limited to amounts paid or due to shipping companies and not include publisher's "handling" charges.

Platform Fees and Third Party License

A common deduction is the platform fee charges, mentioned above, that platform owners (such as Sony or Microsoft) charge for authorized game disks.

When there is a substantial per-game fee to a content supplier (as for example in a game based on a movie), the publisher may want to deduct that fee.

Cost of Goods

Cost of goods is the per-unit cost for manufacturing and assembling the game, that is, the cost of the disk, instructions, packaging and any other included item. Developers often resist a deduction for cost of goods, because manufacturing is a core component of publishing—it is considered just a normal cost of the publisher's operation and it is not costly to manufacture a video game. While most games are not expensive to manufacture and package—normally a few dollars—including cost of goods in deductions is effectively a royalty reduction.

A different rule may apply for games that include costs for peripheral hardware. For example some race car games come with a special game controller that looks like a steering wheel. Karaoke games come with a microphone. Music games may come with a guitar-shaped game controller. The cost of goods for this kind of special hardware in the game package (usually paid to Chinese suppliers) may be a more legitimate deduction, because the cost of those products is a large out-of-pocket expenditure to a supplier. Developers will often take the position that all sales of peripheral hardware for a particular game, net of cost goods, should be included in gross sales—even when sold separately from the game.

Credits to Wholesalers or Retailers

There are various promotional credits that the publisher grants to wholesalers or retailers. An example would be a credit associated with a reduction in price for the game. Another common deduction is MDF, the funding paid to retailers for in-store promotion. A similar item is cooperative advertising credits—money paid to retailers for advertising a video game. Developers will argue that these kinds of marketing costs are not proper deductions, because these are costs of distribution and promotion and that is the publisher's job.

Bundling

Most publishing agreements have rules for calculating royalties when the current game is bundled in a package with other games or with computer hardware. Bundling is most common for games that are several years old and have reached "classic" status.

The normal rule is to apportion the Gross Sales for the entire bundle among the various bundled products based on their list or suggested price. Here is an example:

Assume that the stand-alone list wholesale price of Game A is $18 and the list price of Game B is $22. Assume that Game A and Game B are sold at wholesale in a bundled package for $30. Based on the relative list prices, 45 percent of the gross sales of the bundle are attributed to Game A and 55 percent to Game B. That means that Game A is credited with $13.50 of each $30 sale, and Game B is credited with $16.50.

Royalty-Free Copies

In addition to deductions, most publishing agreements permit the publisher to distribute a reasonable number of royalty-free copies for marketing and promotion purposes. These copies go to reviewers, wholesalers, and retailers. Some could be used for focus-group testing. Publishing agreements may also provide for try-before-you-buy "teaser" versions that are royalty-free until the end user pays for the game.

Royalty Rates on Games and Content Packs

The royalty rate for packaged games (those that come on-disc in a box) range from a low of 10 percent to a high of about 25 percent. Similar rates would also apply to "content packs" which are add-ins, usually sold on disk, that consist of extra game levels, extra virtual venues, additional characters, or other added content. Royalty rates may be negotiated so that they step up as volume increases—based on the reality that high volume sellers are more profitable for publishers.

There is a good argument for setting royalties higher for games that the publisher sells directly to end users from its Web site or (if applicable) from its own stores. That is because it can charge retail rather than wholesale, so the margin and amount of cash it gets is higher.

There is also justification for considerably higher royalty rates for games that are downloaded (rather than sold in a box). This market includes downloaded PC games and console-based download services such as Xbox Live Marketplace and the PlayStation Store, which distribute digital content to Microsoft and Sony consoles. Mobile games are also downloaded. Royalties should be higher for downloads because the marginal reproduction and distribution costs for each downloaded game are very low. Similarly higher royalty rates may apply to downloaded add-ins such as additional game levels or other "digital content packs."

Changes in technology will inevitably change the way the money is made from video games and, as it does, conventional ways of calculating royalties may change. For example, online subscription services require royalties based on fees that end users pay to play a game online. There will always be room for imagination in proposing new ways to measure compensation and divide revenue.

Reports and Audits

It is common that royalty reports and payments be made quarterly 30 or 45 days after quarter end. Royalty payment every six months—which publishers some-time propose—are usually considered unreasonable because they allow the publisher rather free use of the developer's funds. For hot games, the developer can certainly seek to get monthly royalties.

Every publishing agreement should have reasonable audit clauses. Developer should try to avoid audit clauses that foreclose audit after relatively short periods or require the developer to hire an expensive "national accounting firm" to do the audit. A fair audit provision has a requirement that the publisher should pay for the audit if an error of more than 5 or 10 percent in its favor is found in the audit. Developers often discover that they are owed money when they audit. Overdue amounts should be payable with reasonable interest.

Ancillary Products

Ancillary products is a general category of game-related products (and services). These could be hint books, strategy guides, apparel, in-game advertising, even TV shows and music CDs. Most publishing agreements require publishers to pay royalties on ancillary products at negotiated rates similar to those on games.

Developers may argue for a definition of ancillary product that includes products that are "ancillary" not only to the original game, but also to sequels or other games that share the branding of the original game. Such secondary ancillary products may generate a lower royalty rate. The argument for such payments would be strongest if the developer brings an original game idea or novel technology to a publisher.

Cross-Collateralization

Cross-collateralization is a recoupment concept. It means that the publisher can recoup its advances on the game from any royalties that the publisher might owe to the developer. These might be royalties from another unrelated game, from a sequel, or from ancillary products.

The effect of cross-collateralization is bad for developers for two reasons:

- First, it delays payment of royalties to developers, because payments that otherwise would have gone into royalties are held by the publisher and applied to other purposes.

- Second, this kind of clause shifts risk of product failure to the developer. That's because royalties from a hit game may be used by the publisher to recoup advances for a game that was a flop.

Developers should always try to get rid of these clauses if they have the leverage to do so. If not, they may limit them in various ways. For example, one could limit cross-collaterization to a capped amount of money from a particular game, to games only (excluding ancillary products), or to game versions that were released at about the same time (as for example the release of Wii, XBox 360 and PS3 version of a game). Sequels can be excluded. And so forth. There are many possible variations.

Alternatives Means of Game Financing

The most common source of financing for developers is publishers but it is not the only one. Some game companies with innovative business plans or technologies have obtained venture capital investment. There are some companies that will finance video games (particularly high-end games) for first access to royalties until they recover their investment and get a hefty return.

If you do have financing independent of publishers, it can be a mixed blessing. You will certainly be able to get higher royalties in a game publishing deal. On the other hand the publisher will have less commitment to the game if it has no financial stake.

Sequels

Control of the right to make sequels follows ownership and control of certain key game assets: the brand, characters, plot and story. In most cases these belong to the publisher (or to a licensor of the publisher such as a movie or book publisher). These sequel rights are likely to belong to the developer only if the game is the developer's original conception *and* the developer has funded the game development without the publisher's help.

If the publisher controls the sequels, then the developer will want the right to be the developer for the sequel or sequels as well and will try to negotiate some royalties from each sequel developed for the publisher by others. If the developer controls the sequel, then the publisher will try to negotiate rights to publish the sequels as well.

Clauses that deal with sequels are quite thorny because what a sequel might be is an unknown. The sequel might be for a new generation game platform or an unrelated platform. It might have different or increased functionality. It might have higher resolution or more sophisticated graphics. It might have a larger or smaller budget and shorter or longer timeline for development. The milestone structure, IP clauses and royalty clauses of the publishing agreement might not fit the sequel. And so forth. There is no such thing as an agreement to agree, so it is hard to craft meaningful sequel clauses that are not subject to further negotiation.

If the publisher controls the sequel rights, and the developer wants a fair chance to be the sequel developer, there are two classic contractual approaches to consider—a right of first negotiation (ROFN) and a right of first refusal (ROFR).

- The ROFN simply says that the parties will negotiate exclusively with one another regarding the terms of a sequel deal for a specified amount of time, often 30 or 60 days. This is a relatively light constraint and is easy to get, because if the negotiation fails, the publisher is free to deal with others.

- The ROFR is the right to match and pre-emptively take over (on the same terms) any sequel publishing deal that the publisher wants to do with a third party developer. The ROFR is a much more powerful right, because it never goes away as long as the publisher is talking to others. The ROFR can chill negotiations with third parties—because other developers may be reluctant to negotiate a complex publishing deal just to have it snatched away by a party with ROFR rights. For this reason, publishers don't like to grant ROFRs.

What royalties should go to a developer if another company develops the sequel? The amount has to be much less than the original game royalties, because there needs to be enough money left over to pay the new developer. The developer has an argument for a comparatively higher royalty rate if its game engine or other licensed assets are used in a sequel game.

Multigame Deals

Sometimes a publisher wants to "tie up" a valuable developer and limit its ability to work for others by offering a multigame contract. In these deals, the developer agrees to develop exclusively for the publisher and to develop a number of games—typically a current project and a specified number of future games. The details of the future games "are to be agreed."

While these deals can work out as intended and be profitable for both parties, from the developer's perspective, they also carry lots of risk. As long as the publisher and the developer do in fact manage to agree on the financial terms for the follow-on games and both parties work relatively harmoniously, these deals can work fine.

Multigame deals have the same basic problem as sequel deals—there is no such thing as an agreement to agree. So these agreements simply break down if the parties fail to agree on the terms of the following games. If one of the parties becomes unhappy with the performance of the other, the relationship can become deadlocked.

For the developer in particular, the result can be a legal nightmare. That's because the fact that it is under an "exclusive" multigame agreement with one publisher will likely scare off all others. In that case, the developer will be left in a very weak position—with a broken relationship to its current publisher and difficulty in establishing a relationship with any one else.

For this reason, the best way for a developer to do a multigame deal is to be sure that it has a clean "escape clause" from the contract (and to terminate follow-on game obligations of the multigame agreement without fault) if the parties ever fail to agree after reasonable efforts on the next game.

Special Issues in International Sales

Almost all publishing agreements provide the publisher worldwide rights of distribution—but not all publishers have the ability to distribute worldwide. What then happens is that these publishers delegate or sublicense distribution rights to foreign distributor "partners."

If the developer is not careful, this kind of sublicensing can lead to very low royalties. Say that developer has agreed to a royalty from the publisher of 10 percent of Net Sales. And say that the publisher sublicenses distribution for Australia for 10 percent of the Australian net revenues. In this case, unless the developer has provided for this situation, its share of Net Sales from Australia will be 10 percent of 10 percent or just 1 percent. We have seen this happen. Once the deal is in place, there is nothing the developer can do about it.

To avoid this bad result, careful developers negotiate for a clause that provides for much higher royalties in the event that game distribution rights are sublicensed by the publisher. It is common for the rate to be 50 percent. Alternatively, the developer can seek to forbid sublicensing and keep the foreign rights for itself, but that provision is usually harder to get.

Geographic and Platform Limitation and Reversions

When publishers obtain ownership of a game or license game assets, they usually obtain worldwide rights, but that is not always the case. There is no legal reason why rights could not be granted only as to North America—or only as to Europe. In that case, the developer would keep rights to the rest of the world. Furthermore, the publisher may obtain rights only as to certain platforms or for specified languages. The developer will probably be most successful in retaining rights that the publisher is unable or unwilling to exploit.

"Reversion" provisions allow the developer to regain rights originally granted to the publisher due to the publisher's failure to exploit those rights. There could be a provision, for example, that if the developer fails to fund porting for and launch the Nintendo Wii version by a specified date, the rights to exploit the game on that platform would go back to the developer. These provisions should be carefully negotiated so that the conditions of reversion are unambiguous and the agreement specifies very clearly the rights that revert.

Termination

Game publishing agreements always have provisions on termination. These provisions are often quite technical, can be somewhat complicated, and are the subject of much negotiation.

Game publishing agreements are normally perpetual until and unless terminated by a party as permitted in the agreement. The devil in these clauses comes in determining when a party can terminate and what will be the economic result if one side or other pulls the termination trigger. The easier to negotiate clauses are the ones for termination without fault—which we will look at first. The tougher ones are termination for uncured breach, also known as termination "for cause."

Without Fault Termination Provisions

Termination provisions that are not fault-based and usually noncontroversial are:

- Termination on the bankruptcy of the other party

- Termination when the licenses granted by the developer are no longer in use

Some publishing agreements allow the developer to re-acquire the game and its assets at a nominal price if the publisher ceases active marketing efforts or removes the game from its catalog of active products. This is beneficial to the developer (and presumably no threat to the publisher) because it allows the developer to explore ways to re-use or re-license the game assets. Any reacquisition of this type would not include third party content.

What's at Stake in Termination for Breach

The publisher will be sure to propose termination provisions that are designed to deal with its worst nightmare—that the developer will fail in development. To deal with that fear, the publisher will seek the ultimate weapon against the developer—the right to terminate the contract, take the game away from the developer and give it to someone else. For its part, the developer will negotiate to soften the blow if that happens.

For its part (depending on its leverage), the developer will want termination provisions that deal with its own worst nightmare—that the publisher will fail to pay advances (which can push the developer to economic collapse) or will fail to pay royalties. In that situation, the developer will want its own ultimate weapon to block the publisher from selling the game and to get it back. Needless to say, no publisher wants any provision with that result. The following is an overview of some common provisions on termination for breach of contract dealing with these issues, risks, and fears.

Breach by the Developer

The publisher is dependent on the developer until an acceptable Gold Master version is delivered. Until then, there is the risk that the developer will run late, go over budget, or fail to produce a quality game. Under the publishers' preferred termination provisions, if the developer fails to perform with regard to any milestone deliverable, and fails to cure, the publisher can terminate the publishing agreement "for cause." Developers complain that many game publishing agreements are written so that the publisher's decision to accept or reject "for cause" is essentially subjective.

Consequences of Development Failure (Part 1)—Loss of Royalties (or Not)

What is the contractual consequence of termination for the developer's breach during development? Often the publisher wants a provision that allows the publisher to keep the delivered game in its incomplete state. The publisher will be free to get another developer to take over the development of the game. Under the pro-publisher termination clause, the developer typically would be allowed to keep the payments for any completed milestones, but the developer loses all right to any more advances or any royalties.

Developers may try to soften this type of provision. The developer might negotiate for terms, similar to those that we discussed above with regard to the publisher's "for convenience" termination, in which the developer will retain a percentage of game royalties based on accepted milestones. Under this scheme, if the developer has completed two-thirds of the milestones at the time of termination, the developer will keep the right to royalties at two-thirds of the royalty rate that would otherwise apply. (The developer would still have to permit the publisher to recoup its advances fully before it starts receiving royalty checks.) Whether Developer can get this kind of termination protection is a matter of negotiation.

Consequences of Development Failure (Part 2)—Paying Back Advances from the First Money (or Not)

In many deals, the publisher has an additional termination clause remedy. This is the option (which it can exercise or not as it chooses) to transfer all the game rights back to the developer—who will then be free to take the game to another publisher.

This sounds good for the developer, but there is a catch. If the publisher chooses this option, the publisher will expect the developer to pay back to the publisher all development advances. The publisher will likely propose that the developer must repay the advances from proceeds of its next publishing deal for the game— obligating the developer to apply each and every dollar it receives from the next publisher to repayment of advances until the original publisher gets 100 percent of its money back.

The developer will resist this provision too. No new publisher will take over the rejected game, its argument goes, because any would-be next publisher will want its own advances to be used to *finish the game*, not to repay the original publisher. For this reason, the developer will propose that the developer should be permitted to repay the original publisher's advances from a share of the *royalties* it might receive from the next publisher—*not* from the next publisher's development advances. This provision can also be the subject of debate and negotiation.

Developer's (Limited) Termination Remedies for the Publisher's Breach

The Publisher invests in games—often millions of dollars. It never wants to lose its rights in the game it funds—even if it breaches the contract. Therefore the publisher often proposes agreements that provide the developer limited remedies in case of the publisher's breach particularly after the game is completed.

A typical pro-publisher provision allows the developer to sue for money damages if royalties are not paid as its sole and exclusive remedy—but never to terminate the publisher's rights to the game and never to get an injunction blocking distribution and sales.

Publishers like to tie down tightly the rights to games they fund. If the game is made on a "work-made-for-hire" basis, the publisher will own the copyright to the game and its code. That means that even if the publisher breaches its obligation to pay, the publisher will have all the game rights and can keep using them. If the game is licensed to the publisher (wholly or in part), the publisher will want to make the license "permanent" and "irrevocable."

Developers resist these provisions because developers want clauses that can be used to force publishers to pay what is due. If the developer has sufficient leverage, there are some provisions to deal with the publisher's breach:

- A clause that allows the developer to terminate during development if the publisher is late in development payments. (A developer with leverage may seek a "three strikes" clause that allows the developer to terminate the agreement during development if the publisher is late by more than 10 days on three different development payments.)

- A provision that the publisher must pay undisputed portion of any disputed payments amounts.

- A provision that the publisher must pay any disputed amount into an escrow fund controlled jointly by the developer and the publisher.

- A provision that missed payment or late payments bear interest at 1.5 percent per month.

- A provision that *intentional* underpayments or missed payments are grounds for the developer to terminate the publisher's license to the game.

Other Important Provisions

Like other sophisticated contracts, publishing agreements have a variety of "legalese" or boilerplate. See the chapters in this book on contract basics (Chapter 8) and on development agreements (Chapter 12). The issues with these clauses are largely the same for other development agreements. The developer should try to obtain conventional warranty exclusions and limitations of liability, it should try to limit its indemnification obligation, and it should seek protection for its confidentiality. Your company's attorney can help you with these matters.

INTERNET FUNCTIONALITY—THE CASE OF *BLIZZARD V. BNETD*

We now turn to a new topic, the fact that more and more games have Internet functionality. Naturally game publishers want to have sole control of Internet communications carried out by their own games. Thus far, under US law, the courts have allowed game companies this kind of control against third parties that want to link up gamers on the Internet.

The lead court decision is a 2005 decision in a case known as *Blizzard v. bnetd*. That case involved an Internet service offered by Blizzard Games called Battle.net. Battle.net allows players of Blizzard PC games, including StarCraft, Diablo and others, to find other players in an Internet virtual meeting room and then link up to play one other through the Internet. When players compete over the Internet, they use a direct peer-to-peer link of their PCs through the Internet.

Some users of Battle.net occasionally experienced technical difficulties with the Battle.net service. To address their frustrations with Battle.net, a group of nonprofit volunteers formed the "bnetd project." The bnetd project was an informal volunteer group who developed a program called the "bnetd.org server." Their software emulated the Battle.net server and permitted users to meet and play online without using Battle.net. They did this programming work for free and released the bnetd program without charge under the GNU Public License.

Blizzard sued the bnetd developers to force them to stop their distribution. Blizzard won the case; the court ruled that the bnetd program was illegal both under the battle.net terms of use and under the DMCA.

The moral here is that game publishers that offer Internet functionality should be sure that:

- Interaction of games through the Internet is encrypted
- The terms of use and EULA forbid reverse engineering.
- The terms of use and EULA forbid emulation of the online services offered for use with the game.

MASSIVELY MULTIPLAYER ONLINE GAMES

Wikipedia defines Massively Multiplayer Online Game (also called "MMOG" or simply "MMO") as a "computer game which is capable of supporting hundreds or thousands of players simultaneously." Most MMOs are PC-games, but some are on console and mobile platforms.

About MMOs

There are many genres of MMOs, such as strategy games, team shooter games, dance and rhythm games, and so forth. The most popular MMO include fantasy role-playing games know as the Massively Multiplayer Online Role-Playing Game or MMORPG.

The best known MMORPG is Blizzard Entertainment's World of Warcraft or "WoW" in which players' virtual selves (called avatars) roam a medieval world of spells and wizards, interact, go on quests, and slay monsters and demons. (Blizzard is owned by Vivendi Games.) There is a similar experience in the popular Tolkien-licensed MMORPG, Lord of the Rings Online or "LOTRO" offered by Turbine Games. Also popular is the social MMO, such as Linden Labs' Second Life, which features a much less structured virtual reality. In these social games, players' avatars socialize, buy and sell assets and services, build objects and develop virtual real estate locations.

MMOs fascinate sociologists because they allow humans to live in a fantasy reality. From a business and law perspective, they are interesting because:

- They feature different financial models from other games.

- MMOs (particularly MMORPGs) allow social and financial interactions between players that can raise real world legal issues and concerns.

How MMOs Work

Technologically, MMOs are client–server game systems that communicate through the Internet or other networks. They consist of:

- **The Client Software**—The player downloads and installs a client application supplied by game operator. The client application renders the game's graphics, text messages and sound, and communicates with the server via the Internet.

- **The Server Software**—The server software, running on hundreds or thousands of servers hosted by the game operator tracks the status of every player in the game in real time and controls interactions of players with each other and with the virtual world of the MMO.

In addition to their distributed client–server architecture, MMOs have the following characteristics:

- They are *continuous*. The games servers are always on and ready to interact. The game play does not have a beginning or end.

- They are *persistent*. This means that characters get attributes, powers, assets, and properties over time. The game never resets. When characters gain or lose assets in a session, their new status persists into following sessions.

- They are *account-based*. Individual users must sign up to be subscribers.

How MMOs Work Financially

The financial advantage of MMOs is that users usually pay a monthly subscription fee—typical pricing is $10 to $20 per month, paid by credit card. This makes MMOs economically different from other games, because MMOs have the potential to provide the owner earnings over a period of years at a regular (and hopefully growing) pace, free from the seasonal selling spikes of conventional games. The marginal cost of supporting each additional user is small; so profit margins for successful games can be very attractive.

Some MMOs have alternative business models such as in-game advertising, free entry level accounts with premium accounts at a fee, or charging for in-game virtual property. There are likely to be more alternative business models in years to come.

In Asia, the current MMO business model is different; most players use the MMO game in cyber café game parlors (shops with network-connected PCs) and pay by the hour.

Creating MMOs

The financial burden of an MMO is its large upfront cost of creation and deployment. Commercial grade MMOs are expensive and complex systems. It can take years to build an MMO. Building these requires expertise in network systems, databases, three-dimensional modeling, emulation of physical interaction of objects, communications, sound, automation, artwork creation, game and story design, and more. Games need to be engineered so that they can be patched and improved without material interruption of game play. Systems must be scalable to hundreds or thousands of servers and need to be redundant because loss of data could destroy the virtual universe. While much of the infrastructure software to create these complex applications is available from third party vendors (and presumably more will be available over time), it is still an enormous task to create an MMO world.

MMOs have substantial fixed costs to operate, which means they lose money until they build their user base up to a critical mass.

Piracy-Resistant Games

Because MMOs are server-based, they are largely immune from the kind of illegal copying that afflicts conventional video games. It does a pirate no good to clone copies of the client software for an MMO, because the software is useless unless one has an account, which normally come with a monthly charge. This is why MMO games are considered particularly suitable for "high piracy" regions of the world, such as Asia.

A possible piracy-like problem for MMO companies is unauthorized emulation of the server software. Although MMO companies typically encrypt communication between client software and online servers, hackers have occasionally succeeded in reverse engineering and creating alternative "free" servers that replicate the functionality of major MMO games. It is likely that this kind of server emulation (which is not easy to do) is illegal under US law because:

- The usual MMO terms of use forbid reverse engineering and also forbid server emulation

- Circumventing encryption for reverse engineering most likely violates the anti-circumvention provisions of the Digital Millennium Copyright Act or DMCA. (See the discussion of anti-circumvention law in Chapter 2.)

MMORPGs and Virtual Money

A number of MMORPGs have "virtual currency." Examples are gold in World of Warcraft or Linden Dollars in Second Life. Some MMORPGs have complex internal economies in which players sell goods and services in exchange for virtual currency. Secondary markets have sprung up on the Web that allows the purchase and sale of virtual money—or other valuable virtual goods, such as powerful weapons—for real world cash. Because games can produce money in the real world, there are some real world legal issues that result.

No Gambling

In most US states gambling is either completely illegal or legal only in licensed locations. In addition, there is a new federal law that outlaws most Internet gambling. The law is called the Unlawful Internet Gambling Enforcement Act of 2006. Under the Act, (with narrow exceptions for certain in-state legal betting), it is unlawful for any service to provide Internet betting. The law also directs US government agencies to issue regulations to block credit card companies from providing credit or payments for Internet betting. As a practical matter, this makes the United States off limits to Internet gambling.

Under this law, it would be illegal for any MMORPGs to offer gambling functionality in the United States if the virtual money or virtual prizes that are granted are convertible into money or anything else of value. If you offer (or plan to offer) an MMO and have any doubt about what activities are allowed or forbidden, you should contact your attorney.

Gold Mining

Some games have dedicated players that regularly make extra money—or even earn their living—from MMORPGs by repeatedly engaging in activity to amass virtual money or virtual assets (such as killing virtual demons that drop gold or other virtual assets when they "die") that they then sell for cash outside the game.

There have been press reports of businesses established in China that function by retaining contractors to play MMORPGs 12 hours or more a day. These businesses profit by selling on the Web the virtual money and other valuable virtual property.

MMORPG consider this kind of "gold mining" to be unfavorable because it causes distortions in the virtual economy of the MMORPG universe and players consider it unfair. Gold mining is not currently illegal under US federal or state law, but most MMORPGs ban it in their terms of use. MMORPGs are capable of monitoring unexpected and unexplained fluctuations in virtual wealth, and can use that data to decide which players might be mining and selling gold in violation of the rules. MMORPGs usually terminate the accounts of violators.

Taxation

Needless to say, anyone that makes real money (or obtains a real world object of value) through an MMORPG is required to report it and pay taxes under applicable state, federal or local income tax law.

Other Real World Issues

The rules of MMO are determined by their operators. Every MMO has a EULA and/or terms of use documents that grants the operator the right to set the rules and change them. Each MMO has rules for game play and online behavior.

Because MMOs allow real world interactions, there is a risk that users will abuse the service and so MMOs ban "bad behavior." Operators need to provide means for users to make complaints and terminate accounts of users that engage in behavior that is offensive or illegal. The operator runs the risk that it will be seen as tolerating (and may become legally liable for) behaviors that it knows about and does not curtail.

The behaviors commonly banned (in addition to gold mining) include:

- **Spam**—Use of in-game chat and mail functionality to send unwanted commercial messages. (Commonly spam consists of offers to sell virtual currency and assets.)

- **Harassment**—Unwanted attention from another player.

- **Intolerance**—Content that is racist, antigay, or otherwise intolerant.

- **Pornographic messages and content**—Games that allow creation or exchange of images involve this risk factor.

- **Infringement**—User-supplied content can infringe copyright, trademark or rights of personality.

- **Criminality**—Content that encourages criminal conduct, such as use of drugs.

- **Bots**—Use of automated techniques to harvest information from the game about players or any aspect of game play.

- **Cheating**—Use of techniques to manipulate the game or evade rules, including technological means or defrauding other players of money or virtual assets.

For more about EULAs and terms of use generally, please see the discussion in Chapters 16 and 17. Infringement issues in user-generated content are discussed in Chapter 20.

CONCLUSION

The world of video games allows for incredible creativity and imagination, but it also a serious business that can be very profitable. Companies in this industry need to be savvy and careful about IP, contracts, markets, finance, distribution, and negotiation. The law is a key business tool and risk manager in this exciting field.

Going Global—Doing Business in World Markets

23

"It has been said that arguing against globalization is like arguing against the laws of gravity."

—Kofi Annan, secretary-general of the United Nations, in 2001.

This chapter presents an overview of the legal and business issues involved in bringing your company and its products and services into the global marketplace.

BACKGROUND: GLOBALIZATION OF INFORMATION TECHNOLOGY

If you have a compelling digital technology product or service offering and your business is limited to just the USA, you are missing a great opportunity. There are vast and growing markets overseas for information technology. In addition, globalization can provide you resources, technology, talent, and partners.

THE OPPORTUNITY

The international opportunity for digital technology products and services is enormous. According to market consultant IDC, as of 2003, just over half of all software sales worldwide are outside the United States. American software is distributed worldwide, but by far the largest foreign market is the 27 countries of the European Union (EU)[1]—particularly England, France, Germany, Spain, and

---

[1] As of the time that this book is written, the EU consists of Austria, Belgium, Bulgaria, Cyprus, Czech Republic, Denmark, Estonia, Finland, France, Germany, Greece, Hungarian, Hungary, Ireland, Italy, Latvia, Lithuania,Luxembourg, Malta, Poland, Portugal, Rumania, Slovakia, Slovenia, Spain, Sweden, The Netherlands, and United Kingdom. Additional countries that have asked to join are Croatia, the Republic of Macedonia and Turkey.

Italy. There are other large and important software and digital technology markets including Australia, Canada, China, India, Japan, Korea, Russia, and the East Asian "tiger" economies of Malaysia, Taiwan, Hong Kong, and Singapore.

Globalization of Digital Technology Innovation

The Internet has made technical information available worldwide and allows development work done halfway around the world to be coordinated on a daily basis from the United States or from anywhere else. Software development has become sophisticated in India, China, and Russia, and most leading US digital technology companies have overseas development centers. Many laptops and other electronic products are designed in Taiwan. There are also important software development centers in Ireland and Israel. Taiwan and China are leaders in semiconductor production. Japan and Korea are leaders in consumer electronics and gaming technologies. The shift of research and development abroad and the growth of homegrown enterprises in Europe, China, India, and other nations will likely erode US companies' leadership over time. All this suggests that your company must participate in the world economy or be left behind.

Software Designed for One Country or for the World?

There are some products that are specially adapted to particular local regulations or fit particular cultures. Software written for monitoring compliance with US securities regulations may not work for companies in the EU. A Korean language word processor may have limited appeal outside Korea. However, most digital technology products are culture-neutral or can be localized for other nations and languages. Many companies build digital technology products from the start so that they are ready to be adopted for foreign distribution. (See discussion of localization below.)

IN THIS CHAPTER

Going global is a big topic that has the United States, foreign, and international legal aspects. Because every nation has its own laws and regulations and there are many ways you can participate in foreign markets, there is no way any one chapter (or even one book) could cover this topic comprehensively. So this chapter is a survey—a kind of extended checklist of issues. It will not give you all the answers, but it will give you conceptual guidance on key points and help you get your business on the global track.

Topics that you will find in this chapter include:

- Licensing products to foreign customers and markets from inside the United States

- Contracting with distributors in other nations

- Establishing foreign subsidiaries to open new markets

- Foreign technology development subsidiaries

- International joint ventures.

- Localization of digital technology products

- Intellectual property protection abroad

- Choice of law and dispute resolution

- Privacy considerations

- Piracy and enforcement

Chapter 24 addresses US export controls.

At our law firm in Boston, we work with many companies on their international transactions. We also help technology companies "go international" in another way: we assist foreign businesses to enter the vast American market. If your company is entering the great American digital technology marketplace, you can also use this chapter (and indeed this book) as a guide to legal issues you will find here in the United States.

In the Appendix to this book, for use with this chapter, you will find:

- a form of technology international distribution agreement (Form 23-1)

- a form of nonbinding term sheet for an international joint venture agreement (Form 23-2)

GETTING INTO GLOBAL MARKETS

There are many different degrees of participation in foreign markets. You can stick your toe in the water—or you can dive in. You can just sell and support products to foreign markets from inside the United States. You can contract with a foreign distributor. You can establish foreign subsidiaries. You can participate in joint ventures with foreign parties. You can have products developed for US or world markets in foreign locations. Each method of participation in foreign markets involves trade-offs of investment, gain, and risk.

To fully exploit foreign markets and opportunities, your company will need a permanent foreign presence. But a permanent presence in a foreign market requires investment of time and resources and exposes your business (or more often your foreign subsidiary) to foreign laws and regulations.

Use of US and Foreign Professionals

In doing international deals, US lawyers often work with foreign legal counsel and accountants. The need to use foreign professionals varies. For some simple direct license or sale transactions from the United States, we might advise our clients that no foreign legal help is required. Distribution agreements (particularly those that recite that they are governed by the law of a particular US state, such as New York or California) may need a relatively inexpensive check by foreign counsel to be sure there are no unforeseen issues. We also may use foreign counsel to review and "localize" our clients' US form contracts.

If you are setting up a business operation and creating a subsidiary in a foreign nation or if you are doing a foreign joint venture, then you will need more extensive foreign legal and accounting assistance (in coordination with your US counsel and accountant) in order to structure, set up, and run your business. Your US counsel can help you make connections with foreign firms in ways that work well with your US business and tax planning.

Direct Licensing or Sale from the United States

Many smaller software and digital technology companies get their first taste of foreign markets by direct licensing (for software) or direct sales (for digital technology services and hardware) from the United States. Often, the first foreign customer finds the US supplier though advertising, trade shows, the Web, or by word of mouth.

Direct licensing or selling is simply the supplying and support of a product or service from the US to a foreign customer. Contractually this is often a simple process—usually based on the vendor's standard US-oriented end user sales or licensing documents. While there is a risk that your company's standard US agreements may not work under foreign law, the contractual risks are generally low for commercial products sent from or for service performed wholly in the United States.

A few notes about direct sales or direct licensing to customers outside the United States:

- **Payment**—Payment in this kind of transaction is often in advance or "front loaded" because the supplier does not want to take a credit risk.

- **Letters of Credit**—It is possible to secure payment from a foreign customer by means of an international letter of credit. An international letter of credit is a document issued by a bank (usually a foreign bank) which provides an irrevocable payment undertaking. The letter of credit will allow your company to obtain payment from your own bank in the United States after shipping the products. All major banks provide letter of credit services. Letters of credit involve fees and have transaction documentation requirements rules that you must comply with exactly if you want to be paid. If you do not understand how letters of credit work, you should contact your lawyer or your banker.

- **Relationship**—It may be more difficult to sustain a long-term relationship with foreign customers if you are present only in the United States.

- **Local Taxes**—This is not normally an issue for the supplier in direct licensing or sales. When the supplier is not present in the customer's jurisdiction, local transaction-based taxation (such as sales tax or VAT) is normally the responsibility of the customer. You will nonetheless want your form contract to make it clear that the customer will take care of taxes (if any) resulting from the transaction.

- **Export Controls**—Any exporter of goods has to comply with applicable US export controls, which are discussed in Chapter 24.

- **Customs**—Goods that are sent in physical form are subject to customs declaration. Fortunately most nations have zero or nominal tariffs on software.

Can Your Business Be Sued in a Foreign Court?

Many persons that sell overseas from the United States—including those that do Internet-based sales and licensing to foreign states—want to know whether or not they can be sued in a foreign country simply because of a remote licensing or sales made from the United States.

The simple (but incomplete) answer is "yes"; your company can certainly be sued. Most licensees and most buyers in most countries will have the right to file a lawsuit in their local court naming your company as the respondent or defendant. There are international treaties that provide for serving litigation papers internationally. The hard question is what will happen next. In particular, the questions are: What will happen if you ignore the suit and allow a judgment to be entered against your company by default? What will happen if you hire a local lawyer and seek to dismiss the case? What will happen if you defend the case and lose?

International juridical jurisdiction and international enforcement of judgments are unfortunately complex subjects that are beyond the scope of this book. As a general matter, if you send goods into a particular jurisdiction, you do expose your business to a risk that a foreign court will validly exercise jurisdiction over your company. There is also a risk that a foreign judgment might be enforceable in the United States. The higher the volume of commerce and the more targeted to the foreign jurisdiction your product and sales are, the higher the risk.

The bottom line is that any legal claim asserted against your company in any jurisdiction must be taken very seriously. You should obtain legal advice without delay as to the best course of action for your company. No claims should be ignored.

Sales Agents

Sometimes digital technology suppliers first extend their reach into foreign countries by contracting with sales agents—these are individuals or, more commonly, companies that provide sales representation. As the name suggests, a sales agent's job is only to obtain customers. Sales agents do not provide delivery, installation, or support of products.

Many digital technology companies find that working with distributors provides more benefits than working with sales agents. There are several reasons for this:

- **Need for Resources and Technical Sophistication**—Sales agents are often small companies with relatively limited resources, and it may be hard for them to penetrate major markets. Some lack the technical knowledge to effectively sell sophisticated high technology goods.

- **Need for Support**—Most digital technology products require some degree of technical sales support, maintenance, and support in use that sales agents do not provide.

- **Statutory Compensation**—Many nations—particularly those in the EU—require that a supplier must pay sales agent compensation upon termination. In the EU countries, the sales agent will be entitled to such compensation even if his agreement with the principal states the contrary. A typical compensation payment would be an additional year's commissions based on recent sales results.

If you do retain a sales agent, be sure you have a suitable written sales agent agreement that clearly defines the respective duties and rights of your company as the "principal" and of the sales agent. Under these agreements, any sale with a customer must be subject to approval by the principal. Most of these deals are nonexclusive. Your lawyer can help you craft a suitable international sales agent agreement. Some assistance from foreign counsel may also be required.

FOREIGN DISTRIBUTION

Many software and digital technology companies distribute internationally through foreign distribution. In the software field, distribution means a licensing arrangement with a grant of rights to the distributor to pass licenses on to customers (and sometimes to dealers). It is important to have a carefully written international distribution agreement to establish this kind of relationship. As noted above, we have included a sample international distribution agreement in the form appendix to this book.

Benefits and Disadvantages of Distribution

Here are some benefits to using foreign distributors:

- Distributors (if well chosen) already have a presence in the market that allows them to build sales more quickly. They know potential customers and understand local customs and practices as well as the local legal and tax issues.

- Distributors may (depending on the deal) take much of the financial risk of distribution, including the upfront investment in sales staff and marketing.

- Companies that use foreign distributors can avoid the costs of establishing a subsidiary, opening an office, hiring staff, and marketing.

There are also potential disadvantages:

- Distributors may want exclusivity.

- Distributors may fail to make the level of commitment to selling your product that you think is required.

- Distributors may fail to provide adequate support to customers.

- Depending on the deal terms, foreign distributors may handle competing products.

- Distributors may take a substantial share of the revenue from sales.

The bottom line is that by using foreign distributors, you minimize investment but you give up control and potential profit margin.

Companies use foreign distributors in many ways:

- Many companies do foreign distribution only through distributors.

- Some companies have wholly owned subsidiaries to deal with larger customers in a foreign market (so-called "national accounts") but deal with their smaller customers in the jurisdiction through local distributors.

- Large US software vendors often establish foreign sales subsidiaries for major foreign markets but may use local distributors in smaller foreign markets.

- Some companies enter each new foreign market through distribution first and then decide whether to establish a local subsidiary on a country-by-country basis.

- Some companies have, over time, solidified their foreign market position by purchasing their foreign distributors and turning them into wholly-owned subsidiaries.

- There may be business or cultural reasons to use distributors. For example, use of distributors by outside companies is particularly common in Japan.

You will have to decide which strategy or combination of strategies works best for your company.

International Distribution Agreements

To engage in international distribution, your first step (after finding the distributor and conducting due diligence under a nondisclosure agreement) is to negotiate and sign an international distribution agreement. You will want to start by putting a good form of international distribution agreement on the table, customized as you deem fit for the particular deal. Then there will likely be a negotiation. This is a process that typically does not take long—normally the process is over in a few weeks. Some distributors will sign your form agreement with no negotiation at all.

There are two chapters in this book on distribution (Chapters 14 and 15) that discuss the various deal types and contract issues in distribution deals generally. Negotiating an international distribution agreement with a foreign distributor is not fundamentally different from doing a deal with a US distributor. We suggest that you reread those chapters before you tackle international distribution agreement negotiations.

Here are some important additional points to keep in mind in doing deals with foreign distributors.

What the Distributor Should Bring to the Table

An international distributor should have sufficient resources to promote, license, and provide primary support for your product in the territory and/or language version that is the subject of the license. Many foreign distributors for business products are VARs and can provide customization, configuration, and installation services in a particular market. Checking out each distributor thoroughly is essential.

Territories

International distribution agreements normally assign national or regional territories. Sometimes they are defined by language.

You should never give a distributor rights to territories where they have no sales presence or where there is no localized version to promote. The distributor should have concrete plans to exploit every nation and region for which it is licensed.

Be specific about what countries or subdivisions are included. Avoid using vague terms such as "Asia" or "Central Europe" to specify a territory unless these are unambiguously defined with a list of included countries.

In most parts of the world, there is no problem in confining a distributor's marketing and sales to a particular country. However, there is a different rule in the EU. Under EU law, each business has a right to sell to customers anywhere in the EU—and that principle overrides any private agreement. You are, however, permitted to impose contractual restrictions that limit the distributor's "active" sales activity to specified countries within the EU or to specific language versions. You may have restrictions, for example, that require that the distributor's advertisements be placed only in publications or other media that are directed to specified EU countries within a designated territory. But you cannot stop EU-wide "passive" sales. Your agreement can restrict EU-based distributors from making sales outside the EU. Your attorney can help you craft clauses that comply with the applicable EU restrictions.

In most international distribution agreements, the distributor's right to carry out Web selling normally is limited to the same allocated territories and sales restrictions as those imposed on sales activity generally. You may want to add a provision requiring your foreign distributor to send Internet sales inquiries from outside its territory back to your company.

Avoiding or Limiting Exclusivity

Granting long-term exclusivity for foreign distributors is very dangerous, because you could get trapped in a bad deal or chained to an underperforming distribtor. If you give an exclusive deal to a distributor that has financial problems or doesn't perform as agreed, it can take years to disentangle yourself from the relationship.

As a practical matter, you might have no choice but to agree to some form of exclusive deal. In some cases, you may need to give a distributor a short-term market exclusive to induce the distributor to take your product—particularly if the product is new and unproven. But keep the time period as short as possible.

If you do grant exclusivity, you should try to protect your business with other provisions:

- Exclusivity should be mutual. You will agree not to use other distributors, but your foreign distributor should also agree not to carry competing products.

- Your distributor should commit to a clearly defined level of purchases and payments, increasing over time, which the distributor must achieve in order to keep exclusivity.

- Your company should bargain for the right to license directly to multinationals, major accounts, or government entities, notwithstanding the grant of exclusivity.

- Your company should reserve the right to make sales (or allow your other distributors to make sales) involving customers that have locations in more than one sales territory.

Deciding about Sub-distribution

During the negotiating foreign distribution agreements, the distributor often asks for the right to appoint dealers—and thus create a two-level foreign distribution system in the territory. You should consider carefully whether you want to permit this. It can dilute profits and lessen control—but increase reach. If you do have such a provision, you may want to negotiate control over which entity becomes or remains a dealer.

International Software as a Service

If your company supplies a software-as-a-service (or SaaS) solution, you need to decide whether or not to permit the foreign distributor to act as the host of the service—or whether to keep control of this key role for yourself. A similar question is whether the foreign distributor either can or must add local content or functionality to the SaaS site—and if so, which party owns or controls that additional content or functionality.

If your foreign SaaS distributor uses your company's data hosting in the United States, your holding of the data may raise privacy issues in the foreign jurisdiction because US privacy law restrictions are weaker than in other countries. (See the discussion below about privacy laws and the discussion of international aspects of privacy law in Chapter 18.) You need to be sure that all end user customers provide legally valid written consent to the holding of their data in the United States.

Maintenance and Support

Support and maintenance are key issues in making foreign distribution work.

In most foreign arrangements, the foreign distributor supplies primary support to customers, and the vendor from the United States or other location supplies secondary support to the distributor. Distribution agreements can contain provisions requiring a foreign distributor to comply with the supplier's support plan. (The vendor should retain the right under the distribution agreement to make reasonable changes in the support plan.) The support plan would cover required support staffing, training, response to customers, and coordination with the vendor. The goal is to provide quality support to local customers in the local language.

Avoiding Resale Price Maintenance

In most countries around the world, it is illegal for you to dictate to distributors the pricing that they may charge to customers. This practice is called "resale price maintenance" and you should avoid it in all international distribution agreements. The international distribution agreements should set what the foreign distributor pays your company—not what the foreign distributor charges to its customers. Broadly speaking, suggested retail pricing is allowed, and mandatory resale pricing is forbidden. If you have questions about applicable competition law in a foreign nation, your attorney can help you find local counsel that can give you the answer.

There are many ways to set the pricing that the distributor pays. Most schemes provide the foreign distributor a discount from the vendor's list price. There can be variations such as discounts based on quantities, discounts for early payment, special pricing for certain products, bundled pricing, and so forth.

Compliance with Local Packaging Rules

If the product that you are supplying is for consumer use or mass distribution, there may be legal requirements regarding what language the product packing and literature must be written in or what product materials may say. Often, but not always, the international distribution agreement allocates to the distributor the burden of compliance with this kind of local law.

Privacy Laws

Many countries have tighter and much more comprehensive laws on privacy protection than the United States.

There is an EU Privacy Directive that requires all EU nations to impose a comprehensive set of privacy protections. (See, in Chapter 18, the discussion of the EU privacy requirements and the EU–US "Safe Harbor Agreement" regarding US companies' compliance with EU privacy and data sharing requirements.) There are also relatively stringent privacy protection laws in Australia, Japan, and Canada.

Generally speaking these countries require express consent for any use of personal data, require secure data storage, and require destruction of personal data when no longer used. They may also restrict export of personal data. Your international distribution agreement should require your distributor to comply with local privacy laws.

Export Controls

In Chapter 24, you will find a discussion of US export controls. It is always a good idea to include, in every international distribution agreement, the distributor's express undertaking to comply with applicable US export controls. It is important that you explain to the distributor that it cannot knowingly supply your products or services to embargoed nations. (There are nations that are under US export and trading restrictions. There is a list, current as of later 2007, in Chapter 24.) Other US export rules may apply as well. Note that some nations have their own export and import control rules.

Protecting Trademarks

Your international distribution agreement should be very clear that the foreign distributor cannot register or gain any interest in your company's trademarks or in any confusingly similar trademark. Permitted trademark use should be stated. (Your trademark guidelines may have to be adapted to the foreign jurisdiction.) As discussed in Chapter 4, your company should always register its own trademarks in every jurisdiction in which it does business or plans to do business.

End User Licensing

Often, it is necessary to change your end user license agreement (EULA) for foreign nations. You will need a local language text that conforms to local law and practice. This is something your distributor might be willing to get done. However, you will be better off (because you have more control) if you take charge of the process and work with a foreign lawyer to get the EULA terms right.

You should *not* assume that your existing US law English language contracts will work in other countries. They may be invalid legally and they may be wrong from a cultural perspective.

Currencies and Payment

The rate of exchange between the US dollar and foreign currencies can fluctuate. International distribution agreements need a clause that provides a mechanism for setting and converting foreign currency payment obligations to US dollars. Most agreements provide for payment by wire transfer.

Foreign Withholding Tax

When you deal with distribution in some countries, you may find that foreign withholding tax has been deducted from your royalties. This is a subject that you should check out and deal with in advance in negotiations.

If you grant your foreign distributor the right to replicate your software, the license fees that the distributor pays you are often treated as "royalties" on your intellectual property under the law of the foreign nation. If withholding applies to these royalties, then:

- When your distributor pays your company, the distributor is required to withhold and pay over to the government a defined percentage of the royalties as the income tax.

- This withholding tax will be a tax on *your* company, not on the distributor. The distributor's withholding is analogous to the taxes that you withhold from your US employees and pay to the IRS.

The bad news is that most countries have this kind of withholding tax in their laws, which can run up to 30 percent. The good news is that the United States has negotiated deals with many countries to reduce or often eliminate withholding taxes on royalties reciprocally. These treaties are usually known as "double taxation treaties"—because they avoid double tax of transactions—or just "tax treaties."

Under double tax treaties with many nations (including the most developed nations), the deal with the United States is that the tax on IP royalties is reduced to zero. However, there are still a number of countries where there is a significant withholding tax on royalties—often 10 or 15 percent. As of the time that we are writing this in 2007, there are income tax withholding on royalty payments from Taiwan, Singapore, Korea, China, and certain other nations. Before you do a deal with any foreign distributor, you must know the tax law that applies. Your tax accountant or your lawyer can help. If you want to dig into this subject matter yourself, you can find the text of all US treaties (known as "Treaties in Force") on the US State Department Web site, www.state.gov.

Being hit with a foreign withholding tax is not the end of the world. The distributor should give your company tax receipts—and these will often allow your company to get a dollar-for-dollar "foreign tax credit" for your company's US federal income taxes. If your company has taxable profits, you can use the credits when payments to the IRS are due. The problem here is that many growth companies have accumulated losses and therefore cannot put the tax credit to use for years, if at all. Even if you can use the tax credit later, it is not as good as having cash now.

In our international distribution deals, we sometimes include a "tax gross-up clause." This is a provision that requires the distributor to increase its payment so that the amount paid, net of withholding taxes, is the agreed license fee. However, you will find that distributors often balk at this provision, which is, from its perspective, a significant price increase. In the final analysis, you may have to compromise over which party takes any loss caused by the withholding tax.

Distributorship vs. Strategic Alliance

Often, technology companies will hold themselves out as having an "international strategic alliance" with a foreign company. The term "strategic alliance" sounds very impressive, but it is a business rather than a legal term—and a rather loose and indistinct business term at that. When parties say they have a strategic reliance, they are almost always talking about having dealings under one or more contracts that regulate their business relationship.

In many cases, the underlying "Strategic Alliance Agreement" is nothing more than a distribution and marketing agreement, but sometimes there is more to it. The strategic alliance "partners" may share customers and leads and agree to recommend one another. (We use the term "partners" in quotes, because this would rarely be a partnership in any legal sense.) There may be provisions for co-marketing or for cobranded products or services. Some agreements require one strategic alliance "partner" to develop products for the other to market. Or the agreement may provide for one "partner" to make an equity investment in the other or grant warrants, which are options to buy the grantor's stock. You should seek your attorney's help in structuring any international strategic alliance.

Establishing Foreign Subsidiaries of Your Company

If you want a more powerful and direct foreign presence, then your next step would be to establish a direct presence in a foreign market. The most common way to do this is through a foreign subsidiary. There are important advantages of doing so:

- **Control**—Your presence in the foreign market will give you much more control over what is done to promote your products and services.

- **Knowledge**—You will obtain knowledge of the customers and their needs.

- **Financial Gain**—Dealing without a distributor intermediary will allow your company to capture more revenue.

There are some disadvantages of establishing a foreign presence. There will be start-up costs. It will take effort, money, and time to build an organization and develop a customer base. In addition, your company's foreign operation will be exposed to all aspects of local law and regulation.

Foreign Subsidiaries vs. Branch Offices

Legally you have a choice of establishing a foreign subsidiary or opening a foreign branch office:

- A foreign subsidiary is a separate legal entity (essentially a corporation although it might have another name, such as a "limited company," depending on what country you are in). All the stock of this entity will be owned by your US company.

- A branch office is just an office of your US company. It is not a separate company.

While it is simpler to open a branch, we usually recommend that you form a foreign subsidiary. There are three main reasons for this:

- **Liability Protection**—Having a foreign entity establishes a legal barrier between your US company and your foreign operations. This makes it less likely that your US company will be subject to foreign governmental regulation or foreign taxation. In addition, a foreign entity will usually, but not always, insulate your US company from the contractual obligations and debts incurred by your foreign operations.

- **A Local Face**—From a business perspective, it is often better to give your foreign operation a "local face." Having a local company with a local headquarters location may help.

- **Potential Tax Advantages**—There may be important US tax advantages in having a separate subsidiary. These can result in tax deferral or lower effective rates. Note, however, that international tax matters are complicated, and these taxation results are not guaranteed. Before forming a foreign subsidiary, you should consult with your tax advisor.

Establishing a Foreign Subsidiary

Forming a foreign subsidiary is similar to forming a US corporation. You will need local legal and accounting help (in coordination with your US lawyer and accountant).

It is important to understand the rules of the game in each nation that you enter. There are important legal and practical differences. Countries vary in their tax and legal systems, employment law, and intellectual property laws. The rule of law prevails more in some nations than others.

Some countries are easier to work in than others. The World Bank does an annual survey of "Ease of Doing Business" in various countries around the world. In 2006, the UK was ranked 3rd and the United States was ranked 6th. Germany was 21st. France was 35th. China ranked 93rd. (Singapore was the easiest place for the world's companies to do business according to the World Bank.)

Here are some (but by no means all) of the tasks that may be involved in getting your subsidiary started in a foreign country:

- In some nations, obtaining government approval to form or operate the business

- Incorporating the foreign subsidiary

- Obtaining in-country trademark registration (if you don't already have it).

- Putting internal systems in place to comply with tax reporting and withholding requirements and other applicable local law

- Creating bank accounts and money transfer arrangements

- Obtaining real estate by lease or purchase

- Hiring staff in compliance with laws and customs regarding wages, conditions of employment, benefits, and so forth

- Providing for stock options or other equity compensation for key employees

- Localizing your products and documentation

- Retooling your customer contracts to comply with local law and business customs

- Jump starting the marketing and sales process

All of the foregoing actions will be influenced by local law and custom—and will be done with the aid of foreign staff and professionals.

Other Issues with Foreign Subsidiaries

There are many other issues associated with the operation of your foreign subsidiary—again this is not meant to be an exhaustive list:

Setting Up Your Operational Structure—Your company will need to establish the right management, budgeting, and control structures. The goal is to allow the subsidiary's local management to have enough flexibility to operate, but subject to management and fiscal guidance—so that operations will be consistent with company policies. Control of the money flow by the parent corporation is recommended.

Human Resources—Recruiting is a key activity for any foreign operation. It is important to understand that laws affecting employment vary widely. In Europe, employees have benefits and protections that exceed those in the United States. In some (but not all) developing countries, there are weaker employee protections.

Tax Planning—In order to minimize tax liability and avoid problems with taxation authorities, it is important to understand and plan effectively under both the US and foreign taxation rules. The goals are normally to minimize total tax and to defer US taxation if possible.

Employee Agreements—It is also important to have employee agreements that are effective under local law to mandate confidentiality and transfer all intellectual property rights to the subsidiary. You also need to decide if you want a noncompetition clause—after determining first if such clauses are permitted under the applicable local law.

Equity Compensation—Many US-based companies provide employee stock options (to purchase stock in the US parent) to their more valued foreign employees. To do this, you need to be sure that your company's US-based option plan is written to permit this. (You can amend it if need be.) Be sure you award options to foreign employees in accordance with local law, including laws on taxation.

Accounting—You will want to be sure you understand how assets and financial performance at the subsidiary will interface with your overall financial accounting.

Privacy Rules—As noted above, some countries have stricter laws on privacy than the United States. You need to be sure that your subsidiary complies with these laws.

Currency Controls—In some countries, notably China and India, there is not a free market in foreign currency. If you earn money in China in Chinese Yuan, you cannot just change it into US dollars. You need to get permission to buy other nation's currencies. Currency exports are also subject to controls—which may affect or delay your ability to distribute the gains from your subsidiary. You should discuss these controls with bankers and local counsel in applicable jurisdictions.

Consumer Protection—In many countries, there are local laws that regulate dealing with consumers. If your company plans to do Internet sales in Europe, for example, your company will have to comply with the distance selling laws in EU nations. These are in force in all EU nations pursuant to the EU's Distance Selling Directive. These distance selling rules provide for information disclosure about the transaction, written confirmation of the sales terms, a seven day right to cancel, and in the case of cancelled contract, the right to a refund within 30 days. The rules also require that sales based on fraudulent credit card use (such as identify theft) must be cancelled. You should check with local counsel for more information.

Doing Your Homework

The major accounting firms publish "doing business in" guides for major countries that are very helpful and are usually available without cost. Additional information is available from governments and international organizations. However, preliminary homework takes you only so far. Your company will need to check out target countries on the ground and talk to legal and accounting professionals in the United States and abroad.

Foreign Technology Development Subsidiary

Foreign subsidiaries are not only for reaching new markets. You can also use them for engineering and product development as we will discuss below.

Global Trends in Development of Digital Technology

Over the past two decades, companies have increasingly discovered the value of having digital technology products created, supported, or enhanced in developing nations. While the price of trained labor is increasing worldwide, it still costs considerably less to hire software engineers in India, China, or Russia. One way to tap the benefits of this talent is to outsource product development—a topic that we discussed earlier in this book in Chapter 10. However, for many businesses, outsourcing development is not good enough; they need to have their own foreign development subsidiaries.

Forming a development company in a low-cost jurisdiction has some key advantages over simply outsourcing your development work. Here are some:

- You can select, hire, and train staff and managers, who will be wholly dedicated to your technologies and products.

- You will have full control of intellectual property disclosure and patenting decisions.

- You can integrate the foreign engineering and product development efforts with those of the rest of your company.

- You will have better control over security and business practices.

The US–Foreign Hybrid Start-Up

Having a foreign development subsidiary is not just for multinational corporations. In many cases, these development entities are formed by venture-funded start-ups or early stage growth companies.

These days, it is common to see young companies with a "hybrid" structure, part in the United States and part in a developing county. The "head" of the operation, its finance, top managers, sales and headquarters, are in the USA, but its "body," the development staff that creates, improves and maintains its products and services are employed by a subsidiary formed in China, India, or other country.

When your company is seeking angel or venture financing, it may be a point in your favor that you have a credible plan to cut the development costs of proprietary technology by use of an overseas subsidiary operation.

Intercorporate Agreement

Setting up and operating a foreign development subsidiary involves all of the legal, financial management, control, human resources, and compensation issues discussed above and a few more.

If your company has a foreign development subsidiary, you will need, from the beginning, to put in place an intercorporate agreement between the US-based parent and the subsidiary. This should be done before operations begin. The intercorporate agreement serves primarily to manage intellectual property and taxation matters.

Here are some typical components of such an intercorporate agreement:

- **Performance of Tasks**—The foreign development subsidiary undertakes to carry out research assignments from the parent corporation.

- **Cost-Plus Compensation**—The parent corporation agrees to pay the development subsidiary on a "cost-plus" basis for its services—normally at cost plus 10 percent.

- **Intellectual Property**—The foreign development subsidiary agrees to transfer all intellectual property rights at the moment of creation to the parent corporation and acknowledges the parent's right to products, improvements, and confidential information.

This intercorporate agreement structure avoids fragmentation of intellectual property ownership. If you allow intellectual property to accumulate in a foreign jurisdiction, you may find that there is a hefty tax to pay when you try to transfer it out—because the transfer may be treated as a taxable dividend.

This structure is intended to emulate an "arms length" product development agreement in order to avoid potential transfer tax issues. The key here is for both the foreign tax authorities and to the IRS to find the agreement to be "reasonable." Any such agreement should be drafted by your US counsel and reviewed by local counsel in the subsidiary's jurisdiction.

Joint Ventures

An alternative to a foreign subsidiary is an international joint venture. A joint venture (commonly abbreviated as "JV") is an arrangement under which two companies form and share ownership of an entity (often a corporation or a limited liability company or their foreign equivalent) to run a business together. The parties contribute capital and other resources, such as intellectual property or licenses, and they share expenses, profits and control. Joint ventures can serve to reach new markets or to produce or enhance products, or both.

There is some confusion about this term. Some companies say they want a "joint venture" when what they really are seeking is a "strategic alliance" — that is, a contractual relationship only. Sometimes you need to ask a few questions to be sure that everyone at the table has the same understanding of the terminology.

As noted above, we have included, in the appendix to this book, a non-binding term sheet for an international joint venture agreement (Form 23-2). This document is in the nature of an outline that you can use to guide your joint venture discussions and planning.

A Note on Nomenclature

In the following discussion, we will discuss the parties to a joint venture as the "domestic partner" and the "transnational partner." The nation where the joint venture will operate is the "host country." The domestic partner is one already present in the host country, and the transnational partner is the company that is entering the host country. (We use these terms for clarity. It is confusing to use the term "foreign" in this context, because each company in the joint venture is foreign from the other's point of view.) Also note that while we speak of "partners," this is in an informal business sense. Joint ventures are not normally partnerships under applicable law, and their participants should not be referred to as partners in legal documents or correspondence.

The Record of International Joint Ventures

International joint ventures can be powerful drivers for penetrating new markets. Ideally, a joint venture is a "win-win" solution, putting each partner in a much better position than they could have achieved working alone. However international joint ventures actually have a mixed record. Studies have found that about a third of them are considered failures by the transnational partner. To maximize the chance of success, joint ventures require very careful planning covering pertinent legal, financial, technological, operational, taxation, and cultural issues.

While combining and leveraging each party's abilities is a key reason for forming an international joint venture, it is not the only one. There are some nations, notably China, where they are favored because they facilitate government approvals under Chinese law and regulations, and they provide a route to establish relations with local government officials.

Goals for an International Joint Venture

International joint ventures in the digital technology field need to be structured to fit the parties' strategic goals. Here are some goals that might apply:

- Gaining access to the host-country markets quickly, by means of the domestic partner's sales staff, contacts, and skills

- Developing and marketing host-country versions of the transnational partner's products or services

- Arranging for lower cost development of technologies and products that both parties can use in their respective markets

- Overcoming barriers imposed by governments or culture

It is important that both parties understand each other's goals and agree on common goals, methods, and measurements of success.

The International Joint Venture Agreement

International joint ventures are usually formed by a negotiated joint venture agreement. When done right, the agreement sets a solid framework for their relationship.

When negotiating a joint venture, sometimes the parties start with a non-binding term sheet or letter of intent. In some cases, they just dive into drafting the joint venture agreement itself. These are not simple deals and you should expect that it may take several months of meetings, drafts and discussions to put them together. Here are the key issues that typically need to be discussed and resolved:

- **The Business of the Joint Venture**—The parties have to agree on which products and services of the transnational partner and the domestic partner are included in the joint venture. The parties need to agree on the markets in which the joint venture can market and sell its products and services.

- **Contributions**—The parties will need to agree upon what they will contribute to the joint venture. There will be contributions of money (which may be required all at once or over time). There will also likely be transfers of (or licenses to) technology or intellectual property. The parties can also bring intangibles such as market savvy and "good relations" with local officials.

- **Ownership Percentages**—The parties will need to agree on the ownership percentages of the joint venture. This determination will be largely dependent on the value of each party's contributions to the joint venture, including the various intangibles mentioned above.

- **Additional Funds**—The joint venture may require additional money or other assets over time. The joint venture agreement will likely include provisions for requiring additional contributions by the parties and procedures for borrowing funds from a party or third parties. If a party may contribute additional money or other assets to the joint venture, provisions in the agreement will govern how those additional capital contributions affect the ownership percentages.

- **Use of Intellectual Property**—There agreement may state whether technology or intellectual property developed in the joint venture can be used by one or both parties outside the joint venture—and if so, on what terms.

- **Profits and Pay-Outs**—The joint venture agreement will include a mechanism for deciding on distribution or reinvestment of profits.

- **Exclusivity**—Each party will normally have to commit to the development, manufacture or sale of specified products or services in the target markets only through the joint venture.

- **Governance**—The agreement will state how operational control over the joint venture should be administered and what decisions require both parties' approval. One party's control will need to be subject to checks and balances that protect the other.

- **Financial Affairs**—The joint venture agreement will include provisions establishing accounting, finance, reporting and auditing procedures as well as the budgeting process and controls on expenditures. There may be issues in coordination of the transnational partner's worldwide policies on corporate governance, privacy, ethics, tax and accounting with the everyday activities of the joint venture. There may be integration with the information systems of the local or transnational partner.

- **Buy-Sell Provision**—Joint venture agreements often have an exit mechanism allowing one party to compel the other party to buy or sell its interest in the joint venture.

- **Dissolution**—The joint venture agreements will contain mechanisms for dissolving the joint venture and satisfying its obligations when its mission is completed or when the parties wish to part ways. There may be provisions regarding which party gets access to the customers and intellectual property of the joint venture in case of dissolution.

- **Indemnification**—In joint venture agreements, each party typically indemnifies the other with respect to the technology and intellectual property that it contributes.

- **Applicable Law**—What country's law applies to the joint venture should be stated. Joint venture agreements may be governed by a US state law, such as New York or California, under the law of the host country, or under the law of some other "neutral" nation.

- **Dispute Resolution**—There is always a possibility of disputes, so joint venture agreements commonly contain a dispute "escalation" procedure that provides that all disputes be referred to senior management and if senior management is unable to resolve any such dispute, it be referred to mediation and/or arbitration in specified city.

You can look at a joint venture agreement as a work-in-process that may need to be amended over time as the joint venture evolves and the parties' relationship changes.

Taxation of Foreign Operations

Foreign taxation is a complex subject. You need a plan for financial and tax matters and re-examine it from time to time. Some foreign governments, for example, have incentives for foreign investments, including tax breaks. In many cases, there are legitimate benefits to be had due to relative differences in US and foreign tax rates and provisions or due to tax treaties.

Here is a short, and by no means exhaustive, check list of foreign tax issues for foreign subsidiaries (there would be a similar list for a joint venture) that you may wish to discuss with your tax lawyer or tax accountant or with a foreign tax advisor:

- The optimal structure and form of entity for your foreign subsidiary

- Available local tax breaks or other subsidies for investment

- Tax treatment in the foreign jurisdiction and/or in the United States of foreign start-up costs and initial losses

- Tax effect of investments in, and transfers of capital to, the foreign subsidiary, including the advantages of financing by use of equity and or by loaning money to the subsidiary

- Tax effect of agreements under which the US parent transfers or licenses intellectual property to the foreign subsidiary

- Taxation on return of capital to the US parent company

- Tax on payment of dividends and profit distributions to the US parent company

- The effect of double tax treaties of the type mentioned above

- Tax aspects of the sale or other disposition of the foreign subsidiary or its assets

LOCALIZATION

When software is distributed in a foreign country, it may need localization—these are adaptations for local language, culture, and technological standards. This process is a key part of international software marketing, particularly for mass-market software.

Localization by Language

For some products, participating in foreign markets requires adapting those products for different technology standards or translating those products into a different language. For many products language localization is fairly straightforward—involving mainly translation of screen text, help files and documentation. Often, software is written so that it is relatively easy to substitute one language for another. Documentation that is kept simple is likely to be less costly to translate.

For major software companies that have broad international distribution, extensive language localization is routine. For example, in one recent contract we worked on for a large software vendor, this was the list of required languages:

> *American English, Arabic (Saudi), Portuguese (Brazilian), Danish, Netherlands Dutch, Finnish, French (France), German, Hebrew, Italian, Japanese, Korean, Norwegian, Polish, Russian, Simplified Chinese, Spanish (Mexican), Swedish, Thai, and Traditional Chinese.*

There are, of course, many other languages that could be used—it all depends on your target markets.

There is a widely used international standard called Unicode that provides for display of a great variety of fonts and characters needed for English, German, Russian, Thai, Hindi, Chinese, Arabic, and many more languages, as well as the symbols needed for punctuations, currency, and other symbols.

Word-for-word translations will not do of course. The user interface should be idiomatic and easy to understand in its foreign version. The documentation often must be rewritten, as must tutorial programs. Examples given in documentation and illustrations, for example, should be natural situations for the user, particularly for mass-market products. Documentation will also have to be reindexed.

The localizing of your contracts (such as end user agreements) should be done by local lawyers, not by a translator.

Other Localization

Localization of text is not just about foreign languages. Localization also includes the conventional manner for writing dates, for showing a decimal point, and marking the thousands place in numbers. Some software programs process weight, pressure, distance, power, or other parameters in English units that must be converted to metric system equivalents. Many major vendors begin by creating an internationalized version of their products—with varieties of text, units and standards built into the product or product architecture—to facilitate international marketing from launch.

Additional, less obvious changes may also be required. For example, a transaction processing system for banks may need to be adapted to local tax and bank secrecy laws, to local accounting practices, or to government reporting requirements. In addition, there may be content in a program or documentation that is deemed odd or offensive in particular cultures.

Localization may involve technology factors as well. For example, video games or other home products with TV displays may need to be adopted to local analog television standards, the main ones being NTSC (used in North America,[2] much of South America, and Japan), PAL (used in most of Europe and much of Asia), and SECAM (used in France, Russia, and some former French colonies). In China, there are "homegrown" standards for 3G telecommunications and for IP-TV in addition to international standards. Hardware and software vendors that want to address foreign markets need to understand local variations in relevant technologies.

Getting Localization Done
Some companies will do localization with their own employees. There are also many vendors that supply localization services. In some cases, you may want to have your foreign distributor provide localization.

Using a Localization Vendor
Choose a localization vendor carefully. Be sure to check references. Localization is best done by someone that understands your technology and markets, has superior language and technical skills, communicates effectively, and can provide reliable time and cost estimates. Clear and concise text in the original version will save time and money.

---

[2] The US government has mandated that all NTSC analog broadcast transmissions end in the United States on February 17, 2009. Unless the date is extended, television will then switch over to digital broadcasting which uses less of the electromagnetic spectrum. However there will be "set-top boxes" to convert the new digital signals for legacy NTSC equipment, so NTSC televisions may be around for some years to come.

You also need to pay attention to the contract with the localization vendor. Many of the legal issues that are discussed in Chapter 10 of this book with regard to custom development apply to localization contracts as well. Here are some pointers for localization agreements:

- It is important that the contract addresses the ownership of the copyright to the localized version. Under copyright law in most countries, if your contract is silent on ownership, the localization vendor will end up owning its contribution to the version—and perhaps own the localized version itself as a "derivative work." Accordingly, it is essential that the contract has provisions to make the work of the localization vendor "work made for hire" for your company and, further has language stating that, to the extent not work made for hire, the copyright to the localized version is assigned to your company.

- The contract with the localization vendor should also require that the localization vendor has "work made for hire" and "copyright assignment" contracts with its own employees and subcontractors such that it can capture the copyrights from them as well. You may want to provide that subcontracting can be done only with your company's permission.

- The pricing clauses and time-for-delivery clauses are important.

- You may want to include provisions for processing corrections and updates over time.

Localization by Your Distributor

In many cases, companies sign an agreement with a foreign distributor for the distributor to provide (and pay the costs of) localization of your software and documentation. Often, the foreign distributors propose clauses under which they will "own" the localized version. We normally counsel our clients to reject these clauses for several reasons:

- It is generally a bad idea to give any foreign distributor an exclusive on its territory—or if you do provide exclusivity, it should be quite short-lived. However, if you allow the foreign distributor to own the localized version, you may, in effect, be granting an exclusive.

- There will eventually come a time when your company's agreement with the foreign distributor expires or is terminated. At that time, your company will need to have ownership and control of the localized version.

There are several ways that you can handle ownership of the localized version in the distribution agreement:

- The best is for your company to be the owner of the localized version—even if this means that your company pays for all or part of the localization cost. If you chose this route, be sure that your distribution contract has provisions for the distributor to convey all resultant copyright interests to your company in writing.

- Even if you are going to permit the distributor to be an "owner" of the localized version in some sense, you can specify and limit exactly what the distributor will own. For example, the distributor could own the localized version of the software as a whole—or it could own only the particular foreign language text files that it supplies. From your perspective, you want the distributor to own as little as possible. In any case, the agreement should make it very clear that: (a) the rights of the distributor in the localized version are subject to your company's rights as the owner of the underlying program copyright and (b) upon termination or expiration of the agreement, the foreign distributor must cease all distribution of the localized version.

- If the foreign distributor owns the localized version or some part of it, you should have a provision in the distribution agreement providing for your company to purchase all rights to the localized version upon demand. Normally the price of purchase will be set at an amount that is just enough to allow the foreign distributor to recover its original out-of-pocket costs of localization.

DISPUTE RESOLUTION PROCEDURES

Whenever US companies deal with foreign entities (including in distribution, in joint ventures, or in other deals), there is the possibility that the relationship will end up in a dispute. Agreements usually manage this risk by providing for a process for dispute resolution.

There are many different ways to handle this. The law chosen could be that of one of the parties or a neutral country. (Many use English or Swiss law.) Disputes could be resolved by litigation or arbitration. The place of the proceedings (such as arbitration or trial) could be in one of the parties' home town or in a neutral location. All of this is for negotiation.

Many international agreements include an arbitration clause. That is because court judgments of one country are often not enforceable in the courts of another. The United States is not a party to any international treaty or convention providing for international recognition and enforcement of judgments. If you get a judgment in a US court, that judgment may have no legal effect in China, for example.

On the other hand, arbitration awards have quite broad international recognition under the Convention on the Recognition and Enforcement of Foreign Arbitral Awards (commonly known as the "New York Convention"). For this reason, it is quite common to have a clause that provides for disputes that cannot be resolved by negotiation to be decided exclusively by arbitration. There are both advantages and disadvantages to arbitration. You should discuss this important issue with your attorney. Arbitration clauses are technical and need to be crafted carefully.

Even if you are agreeable to an arbitration remedy, you still need to choose applicable law and the forum. It would be best to get US law and arbitration in a US city if possible. Sometimes the parties choose neutral applicable law and a neutral location such as English law and arbitration in London, Swiss law and arbitration in Geneva, Hong Kong Law (which is based on English law) and arbitration in Hong Kong—and so forth.

INTERNATIONAL INTELLECTUAL PROPERTY PROTECTION

It is almost inconceivable that you could "go global" without an international intellectual property protection plan. Your company needs to be smart about its intellectual property in each market that it enters. There are discussions about the international aspects of copyright, trademark, and patent law earlier in this book that we will not repeat here. (Please see discussion of these topics in Chapters 3, 4 and 5). We offer here a summary of matters to focus on.

International Patent Strategy

If you have a US patent only, your US patent has no international reach. Every innovative digital technology company should consider patenting its inventions not only in the United States but in other nations as well. Patenting internationally takes careful planning—not least because obtaining patents in other nations is expensive. On the other hand, patents in other nations can extend the reach and power of your patent portfolio. If your company has a "patent committee" that manages patent affairs, it should be charged with international patent matters as well. You should discuss your international patent strategy with your patent counsel.

Don't forget that your own products may come up against different patents owned by others in each market. Just because your product is noninfringing in the United States does not mean that it is noninfringing everywhere. There are foreign patents that have no US counterpart—and therefore will not be found by a search of US patent records. For example, in 2006, a Korean court held that the international version of Microsoft Office infringed a Korean developer's patent covering a technique to switch the typing input mode of a software program between the Korean and English.

How do you decide whether to file for or search for patents in a nation that your company markets in? A lot depends on the stakes involved and the technology. In some cases, it would be a smart to do so—and in others it would simply not be cost justified. This is a matter you should discuss with patent counsel. In any case, you should be aware of the risk. Any international distribution agreement should include the standard clauses that allow your company as licensor to terminate the agreement if there is an infringement problem that you cannot readily cure with a license or a design-around.

Copyright Protection Abroad

Copyrights are the most international of intellectual property. If you have a US copyright (which is created automatically when a software work is made), then you can also have copyright protection in most other countries in the world. In addition, many nations follow the United States in including computer software within the scope of copyright protection, classifying them as literary works. That means that if there is illegal copying of your computer program or digital content, the law of most nations will provide you with a legal claim against the infringer of your copyright. How effectively you can enforce those rights will vary. (See discussion of copyright piracy below.)

Taking Trademarks Global

Your company must have a trademark strategy before it "goes global." In every country that you plan to have distribution (even if you have no office or employees there), you should register your trademarks. See also the discussion in Chapter 4 of the benefits of the EU's Community Trade Mark that can cover all 27 nations in the EU.

Trade Secrets

Most advanced and developing countries have laws protecting trade secrets or confidential technological and business information. Having such protection is a prerequisite for joining the World Trade Organization, to which most nations now belong. The details of such protection and the enforcement mechanisms vary from country to country. In each country, it is, of course, a very good idea to follow the practical measures set forth in Chapter 5 of this book about trade secrets and confidential information. You should check with local counsel in emerging markets to find out how practical and effective legal protection of trade secrets may be in each jurisdiction.

DEALING WITH SOFTWARE PIRACY

Anyone who travels in the developing world sees in every city, town, and village thousands of unauthorized copies of digital products, including music, movies, and mass-market software. The practice of media and software piracy is simply too widespread, too easy, and too lucrative to stamp out. There is no doubt that the losses to right holders are enormous.

There are only two ways to deal with piracy—through technology or through enforcement. Both approaches may be needed in international markets if you have mass-market products.

Technological Measures

One way to stop piracy is with copy protection measures, which include:

- Hardware keys, known as "dongles." These are quite effective but are expensive, somewhat inconvenient, and are commonly used only on applications costing thousands of dollars. There are some companies that use dongles only in emerging countries.

- License management systems that control copies running on a network.

- Software protection measures requiring typed in keys or key files.

- An "activation" process, such as that used in Microsoft products, that verifies that the software's product key, required as part of product installation, has not been used for more PCs than is permitted.

- Systems (used in online games) that combine software and Internet accounts.

Enforcement Measures

The other way of dealing with piracy is legal enforcement. The primary weapons are copyright law and trademark law. Any pirated product is a blatant infringement on both theories.

Broadly speaking, enforcement is improving in many developing countries, in part as a result of US government pressure. In many countries, there are relatively swift processes for seizure of counterfeit products. More difficult is getting criminal prosecution of those responsible. Civil remedies—suits for damages—are often less effective because they may be slow and money damages awarded may be limited.

Enforcement of your intellectual property rights in any foreign jurisdiction means hiring skilled, experienced, and aggressive local attorneys to bring administrative and judicial proceedings to stop piracy. You should consult with local counsel about the most effective legal measures.

FOREIGN CORRUPT PRACTICES ACT (FCPA)

If you are engaged in selling software to foreign governments, particularly in the third world, you need to be aware of the FCPA, a US federal statute.

Under the FCPA, it is illegal to give or promise any money or anything of value to any foreign official, party, or politician to get business. It is also illegal to make such payments indirectly or through intermediaries. Willful blindness to the obvious purpose of a payment is no defense.

The criminal penalties for corporate violations may include a fine of up to $2,000,000. Officers, directors, stockholders, employees, and agents are subject to a fine of up to $100,000 and imprisonment for up to five years. There is an alternative fine of twice the benefit that the defendant sought to obtain by making the corrupt payment. You should also be aware that fines imposed on individuals may not be paid by their employer.

Your company should never participate in a deal that involves prohibited payments—no matter how lucrative the promised contract seems. Your company must be sure its sales staff understands the rules. If any doubt arises about what is permitted, you must contact legal counsel.

INTERNATIONAL ANTI-ISRAEL BOYCOTT

Some countries, primarily Arab states, have tried to impose an international boycott of the state of Israel and have blacklisted companies that deal with Israel or Israeli companies. You may be requested to participate in the boycott or to certify that you will do so as part of contracting with your customer.

It is a violation of US law to participate or assist this international boycott. Your company is forbidden to sign any agreement or any statement certifying that you have not dealt with Israel or promising not to do so in the future. Nor can you furnish information about whether or not your company has dealings with Israel. If you were asked to join in boycott activity, you may be required to report the request to the federal government. Violation of federal anti-boycott law is a serious matter that can result in substantial criminal penalties and income tax problems. If you are approached to participate in any boycott activity, you should seek legal counsel immediately.

CONCLUSION

With planning and care, your company can exploit its technologies around the world. Being smart about contracts, partnering, distribution, local law, and intellectual property will allow you to optimize your strategies for going global.

United States Export Controls

Security is the condition of being protected against danger or loss. In the general sense, security is a concept similar to safety. The nuance between the two is an added emphasis on being protected from dangers that originate from outside.

—Wikipedia on "Security"

IN THIS CHAPTER

The great majority of contracts in the United States involving software or IT services require one or both parties to comply with US export controls. Export controls are designed to help secure the United States. They do that by restricting export of certain technology, knowledge, and goods to certain persons and nations. This chapter provides an overview of what is involved and how your business can comply with the rules.

WHY EXPORT CONTROLS MATTER

If your company exports controlled technology of the kind discussed below, someone at your company will have to dig into and learn the rules. Violation of federal export control laws can lead to criminal prosecution and prison terms if knowing or even if unwitting to large civil penalties.

The discussion in this chapter will give you a general overview of the export control system of the United States, with enough detail that you should be able to dig into this topic further and comply with the law. We do not give you **667** detailed compliance instructions because the export control system is continually changing and because there is no substitute for looking at the language of the rules. We also did not want to bore you with page after page of regulatory distinction and detail.

On the other hand, many people find the export regulations simply impenetrable without some guidance. We wanted to provide enough information about how it works so that you could really understand the rhyme and reason of the system and then drill down into the rules that affect your business. This overview can also help you decide whether you need expert advice on export control matters.

DO YOU NEED TO WORRY ABOUT EXPORT CONTROLS?

Export controls come in two flavors—those that apply on specific products and technologies (we will call them "technology-based") and those that apply across-the-board to specified persons, countries, or organizations (we will call the "target-based").

The IT companies that must pay most serious attention to technology-based export controls are:

- Companies that are in fields that impact our national security such as aerospace, defense, nuclear, or robotics

- Companies that make advanced solutions or provide advanced technologies that may have defense or intelligence applications

- Companies that include any form of encryption in their products or technologies

If your business has plain vanilla business or consumer applications and uses only off-the-shelf technologies with no encryption functionality, chances are good that no technology-based export controls at all apply to your products and technologies. Even so, you will remain subject to export restrictions that are target-based as discussed below.

All major IT companies deal with at least some technology-based export compliance issues. That is because export of encryption is regulated and there is a lot of secure messaging and secure data storage in the Internet age.

Many large technology companies have staff members that are dedicated entirely to export control compliance. Most of these staff members are nonlawyers; although if there are difficult issues of interpretation, and for any legal proceedings, the lawyers get involved.

PURPOSE OF EXPORT CONTROLS

The current US system of technology-based export controls on products and technologies dates back to the start of the Cold War. The system is designed primarily to stop strategic technologies from going to nations and persons that may use them against US interests. During the 1990s, after the breakup of the Soviet Union, the system was liberalized and rationalized to some extent. The events of September 11, 2001 slowed, but did not stop, the process of liberalization.

By its nature, regulation of exported technologies is a balancing act. The challenge is to stop the flow of specified technologies into the wrong hands without creating a red tape tangle that puts US companies at a competitive disadvantage. Compounding the problem is the fact that regulators play a continual game of catch-up because technologies and markets change quickly and the regulatory changes come more slowly.

MULTIPLE REGULATORS

In this discussion, we will focus mainly on the Department of Commerce's Bureau of Industry and Security (or "BIS") and its processes. BIS is the agency that IT companies are most likely to deal with. BIS' mission is to regulate the export of products and technologies that span the civilian and military worlds—so-called "dual-use" products and technologies (although some of the product and technologies categories that it regulates might not be readily adapted to military use). These technologies comprise hundreds of categories.

For many years, this agency was known as the "Bureau of Export Administration" or "BXA." After the September 11, 2001 attacks, the name was changed to the Bureau of Industry and Security to emphasize its role in the security of the nation. BIS operates under a set of export control regulations known as the Export Administration Regulations (or "EAR").

However, BIS is not the only US government agency involved in security and exports. There are other federal agencies that have a role in export control and, depending on what your business does, some of these might impact your company:

- **Trade Sanctions**—The Treasury Department's Office of Foreign Assets Control (OFAC) administers and enforces certain economic and trade sanctions against targeted foreign countries, terrorism-sponsoring organizations, and international narcotics traffickers.

- **Weapons and Military Technology**—If you are exporting weapons or other military goods or technologies, your product may be subject to the export licensing jurisdiction of the Directorate of Defense Trade Controls at the Department of State. The applicable regulations are the International Traffic in Arms Regulations (or "ITAR"). The discussion in this book does not cover controls on military goods. If you export such goods, you should see a specialist in those regulations.

- **Patent Information**—The US Patent and Trademark Office has a process for clearing patent filing data sent abroad.

There are other agencies involved in other areas of export controls. There is a listing at www.bis.doc.gov/About/reslinks.htm. If you believe any of these areas are relevant to your business, you can start by checking out each relevant agency's Web site and reading their requirements. Your attorney can also help.

EMBARGOED NATIONS AND DENIED PERSONS

Before we discuss the BIS, let me digress briefly to discuss the "target-based" export controls—trade sanctions imposed on disfavored nations and on individuals and entities that our government judges to be dangerous.

Trade Sanctions

As noted above, OFAC in the Department of Treasury is in charge of trade sanctions against selected nations. (Where there is a complete or nearly complete ban on trade, we call the subject state an "embargoed nation.")

As of the time that we are writing this book, there are trade sanctions of one sort or another in effect against Cuba, Cote d'Ivoire (Ivory Coast), Iran, Iraq, Libya, North Korea, Sudan, Liberia, Zimbabwe, Sierra Leone, the UNITA faction in Angola, Syria, and Myanmar (formerly Burma). There are details on the OFAC site on the Web at: www.ustreas.gov/offices/enforcement/ofac/. This list and the sanctions in effect are subject to change. This list is largely parallel with a BIS list of six countries to which especially strict technology export restrictions apply: Cuba, Iran, Libya, North Korea, Sudan, and Syria (known as the "T-6" countries, where "T" stands for "terrorist").

Of this list, the countries on this list most likely to be buying IT goods or services from your company would probably be Iran and Syria. You should not be dealing with them or these other nations, their companies or citizens (other than lawful US permanent residents) either directly or indirectly without talking to your legal counsel.

Your company is not permitted to directly or indirectly violate US government trade sanctions. You should not knowingly permit products, services, or technology to be obtained, acquired for, shipped, transferred, or reexported in violation of these restrictions. Even innocent violations can lead to penalties.

Prohibited Persons

There are various individuals, organizations, and companies that the US government has decided should be restricted in their trade dealings with the United States. These targeted lists come from the Commerce Department (focusing on technology and technological products), the Defense Department (focusing on military goods and arms), and the Treasury Department (imposing bans on all trade). The lists are:

1. **Debarred Parties**—Parties denied export privileges under ITAR, as administered by the Office of Defense Trade Control (ODTC) of the Department of Defense.

2. **Denied Persons List**—Parties denied technology export privileges by BIS.

3. **Entity List**—Entities judged by BIS to be involved in proliferation of weapons of mass destruction and subject to special restrictions.

4. **Specially Designated Nationals, Terrorists, Narcotics Traffickers, Blocked Persons, and Vessels**—Parties subject to various economic sanctions programs administered by the Office of Foreign Assets Control (OFAC) of the Department of the Treasury.

5. **Unverified Parties List**—Parties to past export transactions where BIS prelicense checks or postshipment verifications did not check out.

The government's online Export Administration Regulation Database, maintained by the Department of Commerce, features a "Prohibited Parties Database." Exporters can screen would-be customers against these five government lists of prohibited parties with a single keyword search. There is a modest yearly fee for access to the database. There are also commercial services that will perform similar searches for a fee.

Exporters of export-controlled technology products may wish to search the Prohibited Parties Database before accepting an order. There are many companies that do not do so, because of the bother and because positive matches are relatively uncommon. However, because dealing with Prohibited Parties is illegal and violations can be costly, it may be worth companies while to do this kind of search.

THE REGULATION OF TECHNOLOGY EXPORTS BY BIS

The control system that BIS operates is an export licensing system under the EAR. General information about the system is available at www.bis.doc.gov/licensing/exportingbasics.htm. The BIS site at www.bis.gov also has explanations of rules and of the various export forms. We recommend reading that information along with this chapter.

What Is an Export?

Before we discuss the BIS rules, it is import to understand BIS' expanded view of what is an "export." For example:

- Shipment of goods to a customer is, of course, an export. However, so is carrying a product overseas in your laptop. From the BIS' perspective, technology leaving the United States on a temporary basis is still an export.

- Electronic transmission of files to another country is an export. So, so far as BIS is concerned, is posting it for download on your Web site. E-commerce is a tricky subject for technology-based export controls.

- You may be transmitting controlled technology if you discuss it at an international conference or if you describe it in a publication that will be available outside the United States. Even an international phone call divulging a controlled technology may be an export.

For all of these various "exports," the law requires that your company completes the licensing or other applicable procedures *before* the export. All of this means that export controls must be considered early in the life cycle of controlled products and technologies. Your company should educate its staff about the do's and don'ts.

What Is a "Deemed Export"?

There is a somewhat counter-intuitive concept in BIS rules of a "deemed export." A "deemed export" is a disclosure of controlled technology to a foreign national in the United States. The idea is that if you cannot, under the regulations, export a technology to China, you should not be able to tell a Chinese citizen about it anywhere—even if the conversation takes place in the United States.

The good news about deemed export is that it does not apply to US citizens or permanent residents (holders of a so-called "green card")—and rarely is a problem with Canadians. However, it can be a serious problem with foreign employees from other countries that are in the United States on nonpermanent visas.

Many IT companies have employees with H-1B visa's for example. (H-1B is a nonimmigrant visa category under which a foreign citizen employee may work in the United States for up to five years.) Giving any technological information or product to an H-1B employee is an export. For these various "deemed exports" as well, the law requires that your company goes through licensing or other applicable procedures *before* the "export" takes place.

To make this issue worse, the US government has been enforcing the Deemed Export rules more vigorously over the past several years and imposing large penalties. This means that the HR organizations and managers must screen for potential violations.

Overview of Rules

The BIS system under the EAR is based on the perception that (1) different technologies present different risks and (2) different countries present different kinds of threats. For example, the US government may be concerned about terrorists in one country and about the danger of nuclear proliferation in another. Therefore the system is designed to require licensing in transactions where the technology risks and foreign policy concerns match up. It works like this.

Lists of Technologies and ECCNs

BIS maintains a written master list of technology categories called the "Commerce Control List" (or CCL). In the CCL, there are a series of technology product types listed. Each is specified and given an Export Control Classification Number (or ECCN). For example: ECCN 5B002 is for "Information Security—test, inspection, and production equipment." If you have trouble figuring out the right ECCN categorization, there is also a process whereby BIS will determine the applicable classification for you upon written application.

Each ECCN in the CCL listings includes one or more codes indicating the "Reason for Control." For example, "AT" means antiterrorism and "EI" mean encryption item. There are subcategories of the Reasons for Control codes in the form "AT Column 1" or "AT Column 2." The ECCN also lists "Exceptions" that may apply.

EAR99 is a designation for goods that are covered by the EAR but are not specifically listed on the Commerce Control List. EAR99 items can be shipped without a license to most destinations other than T-6 countries (as long as other export restrictions do not apply). The majority of commercial exports from the United States fall into this category.

Commerce Country Chart

BIS also has issued a Commerce Country Chart that lists the various countries of the world and states the "Reasons for Control" that apply to that nation, including the Column 1 and Column 2 subcategories.

If you want to export a product, you first look up its ECCNs and listed Reason for Control categories. Then you look up the destination country in the Commerce Country Chart and find the Reason for Control categories that apply to it. If the Reasons for Control categories in both lists match up, you know that an export license is required on an individual transaction basis for the export, unless there is an applicable Exception.

Licenses Generally

If you need a license for exporting, the next step is to apply for one. Licensing generally is either for a single export to a single customer or for a distribution transaction. Forms for license applications are available on the BIS Web site. There is also a convenient online system for a paperless license application on the BIS site. Instructions on its use are also on the site. License application processing is generally in 30 to 45 days. Where licenses are required, exports must be held in abeyance until the license issues.

Exceptions

As noted above, some ECCN indicate applicable "Exceptions." There are several categories of Exceptions. There is one, for example, for temporary exports. One Exception applies to beta test products. And so forth. You should see the BIS site and regulations for more details on what Exceptions apply and how to qualify for them. Some special rules (discussed below) apply to encryption.

REGULATION OF ENCRYPTION EXPORTS

For most software and IT companies, it is the encryption controls that are most likely to impact your operations.

Encryption regulations are probably the most controversial of the regulations of exports, because sophisticated encryption products are available from many offshore sources. Many question the effectiveness of this scheme. The rules have been softened and simplified over the years—particularly with regard to a group of favored nations that we will discuss below, but they are still complex and often a barrier. Like all US export controls, violating these rules can be a crime or can lead to civil penalties. Any company that has products that contain encryption functionality must learn about these regulations.

BIS regulates export of "encryption items" which are hardware, software, and technology that carry out secure messaging, secure storage, or encryption key management. As with the other aspects of export regulation, these rules change with some frequency and they are, unfortunately, rather complex. So to explain them in detail would be overkill. We will, however, provide an overview of the system, as it currently exists. Detailed information and the most current regulations will be available on the BIS Web site. Making software available on the Internet is treated as an export under the encryption rules.

Please note that it is possible for a product to be subject both to the encryption rules and also other non-encryption export controls under the applicable regulations.

What's Not Regulated Under the Encryption Rules

Before we look at BIS encryption rules (which are part of EAR), let me make clear what is *not* included in the encryption rules. The BIS does not regulate any transfer of encryption items within the United States (other than deemed export). The BIS does not regulate *import* of encryption items. The BIS rules do not affect encrypted data or content—the rules are about the technological means of encryption and decryption.

Some Countries Are Treated Differently

Under the regulations, there is a group of countries informally called the "License-Free Zone" or "LFZ" in which the barriers are lower and most products can be exported, although some red tape may still be involved. The License-Free Zone is, as of the time that we write this, the European Union nations plus Switzerland, Norway, Australia, New Zealand, and Japan.

There is also a group of disfavored nations that are areas to which you should not directly or indirectly export encrypted goods. These currently are the T-6 nations mentioned above.

Also note that there are some categories of encryption items that may be sold to ordinary citizens, but not to foreign governmental users.

Range of Technologies

The encryption rules range from encryption technologies with minimal perceived threat to very powerful encryption products. Different classifications get different treatment. Note that, in most cases, once your product qualifies for export, you can ship it to all customers other than T-6 customers or in some cases to foreign governmental buyers. Individual export licenses are not often required under these rules.

For details, see the BIS website. Here, in summary, is how it works.

No Notice, No Review

Some products require no notification of BIS and no BIS review of an application to classify the product. These products include limited-functionality consumer devices such as cell phones, some short-range radios, smart cards, and the like.

The same no-notice, no-review rule applies to temporary export of standard consumer encryption software in your laptop when you go overseas. A similar rule applies when your company supplies its foreign subsidiaries with technology for research and development use.

Notice, No Review

Next are items where export requires notice to the BIS before foreign distribution, but there is no written application for classification by BIS. Low-key length product is the key here. That's presumably because if the key lengths are short, the encryption can be readily "cracked" by the US security services such as the National Security Agency (NSA).

In this low-scrutiny category are "mass market" encryption products with encryption key lengths up to 64 bits. "Mass market" includes items such as cable modems, laptops, routers, firewall software, e-mail programs, and encrypted instant messaging software. The same "notice, but no review" treatment, is given to nonmass market products with key lengths not exceeding 56 bits for symmetric algorithms and 512 bits for asymmetric key exchange algorithms.

A similar notice-only provision also applies to publicly available source code encryption software products (such as open source software). In case of such open source products, the source code needs to be made available to the government, presumably so that the NSA can take a look if it wants.

You can export items in this classification worldwide (except to T-6 countries) after submitting a form of notice to BIS. The procedure for giving the required notice BIS is on the BIS Web site.

Notice and Review

Next up the ladder comes the class of products that requires notice to BIS before foreign distribution *and* a BIS review of the exporter's written classification application. (BIS generally reviews your company's description of products, not the products themselves.) In this class are "mass market" encryption products with key lengths greater than 64 bits. BIS can reject the applications if it decides that the application is not justified or incorrect. No action by BIS in 30 days constitutes automatic approval. Applications can be made online via an interactive system on the BIS site.

Also in a category are the ENC-Unrestricted items (ENC stand for "encryption"), which are strong encryption items that are not on a list of even more restricted encryption technologies described below. The same written classification application and 30-day review process apply.

After review and approval (or deemed approval) of the classification, the encryption item can be sent worldwide (except to T-6 countries).

Further Restricted

Next, there is a class of items that are ENC-Restricted (a tighter ENC Exception). These also require notice and review of a written classification application. This is a category of specified powerful encryption devices and software such as specified high-speed communications equipment, certain virtual private network (VPN) and "data tunnel" products, quantum encryption products, and encryption cracking software and equipment. Also included are products that have an "open cryptographic interface" meaning that they do not have encryption functionality, but are designed to be ready for encryption functionality to be easily "plugged in."

Again the written application and 30-day review process apply. For most, but not all of these items, export to the License-Free Zone is allowed when a full review application has been docketed—the exporter does not have to wait for the 30-day review to be completed.

Even after you get this approval, there is an important restriction: you cannot export the product directly or indirectly to a non-License-Free Zone "government end users." This is significant because it means your company must screen your customers. In order to provide the encryption item to a proposed government licensee or outside the License-Free Zone, you would need to get a BIS export license for that one customer.

Reporting

In addition to the review procedure set forth above, exporters of some classes of encryption process have to report exports to BIS every six months, including customer names where available. You can find the process and details of this reporting obligation on the BIS site.

Other Countries Laws on Encryption

The United States is not the only country that regulates encryption. France has restraints on encryption imports. Russia has encryption export controls. If your company makes encryption products (or products that include encryption functions), your firm will need to learn the applicable rules in each nation in which it operates.

CONCLUSION

With reasonable care, your company can comply with export controls while going global. There are experts in this field that can advise you company, and your legal counsel can help.

Proactive Management of Your Legal Affairs

Every digital technology company needs an ongoing internal process that keeps the company's legal strategy and legal affairs on track. If your company pays attention to legal matters, it will pay off.

THE NEED FOR CONTROL OF LEGAL AFFAIRS

There are key moments in the life of a digital technology business when your company must be able to prove that it has control of its legal affairs. When the company borrows funds, obtains a venture capital investment, sells stock to the public, or is acquired, it must be ready to undergo due diligence scrutiny of its legal affairs. If your company has done its legal job right, its value will be much greater, and it will sail through due diligence. If the party conducting the due diligence examination finds legal problems, your deal may slow or come to a dead stop or your bargaining position may be undermined, because you will be unable to deliver the full value the other side expects.

It is not enough to implement the concepts discussed in this book on a sporadic basis. Your digital technology business needs to foster a culture in which intellectual property (IP), legal compliance, and smart contracting are valued. No less than once a year, there should also be a legal audit (more on this below) to verify that legal affairs are under control. Your company should periodically review its legal strategies to be sure they support your business plan or to fix them if they are out of sync.

There are legal matters that affect companies that are beyond the scope of this book, such as federal, state, and local taxation, employee health and retirement benefits, corporate and securities law, liability insurance, and real estate issues, **679** among others. These too need attention and the assistance of professional advisors. However, the main focus in this discussion is on those legal matters that uniquely determine the value and core assets of your digital technology businesses—those are the legal issues that we have covered in this book.

Keeping legal affairs in order is not cost-free. In a small company, it requires the owners to assume one more burden. In large companies, it means hiring staff to manage contracts and IP matters. There are administrative costs for security measures and copyright filings; there are legal costs for trademark and patent applications. These are the unavoidable costs of building value; the cost of failing to attend to legal affairs will be much higher.

In the following pages, you will find lists of measures for IP and contract management that are used by many digital technology businesses. This list represents a distillation; it is designed to cover the main topics, and you will have to adapt it to your business. Your legal counsel and other advisors can help you do this.

INTELLECTUAL PROPERTY PROTECTION PROCEDURES

Procedures for IP protection should be a matter of routine. Good practice includes the following:

1. Implement a process to have the copyright on each major version of the company's software products registered with the Copyright Office before release.

2. Make sure that registration, use, and licensing of trademarks and service marks conform to good legal practice.

3. Encourage employees to disclose patentable inventions. Form a patent committee that meets regularly to review inventions and patent matters. Consult counsel on the patentability of inventions.

4. Monitor patent trends and patent litigation in your business segment.

5. Hold periodic meetings to educate officers and employees about the importance of trade secrets, and implement appropriate security measures for the company.

6. Create and maintain a program for security of the premises, including, alarms, after-hours access control, badges, and sign-in logs.

7. Verify use of appropriate copyright, trademark, and patent legends.

8. Give each officer and employee a copy of the company's policy on IP protection.

INFORMATION PROTECTION AND CONTROL

Because digital technology and confidential data are critical assets, your company should use the following measures to protect them:

1. Implement appropriate computer security systems, including password or biometric controls that provide a high degree of assurance that only authorized users have access. Use security software that records each log-in, including the identity of the user and the time and duration of use. Monitor for unusual or inappropriate access. Change passwords periodically. Be sure that names of former employees are promptly removed from access lists.

2. Plan and document network security measures for Internet and mobile systems. Engage consultants to test system vulnerabilities.

3. Implement systems for tracking changes to source code for the company's software products and proprietary software tools, so that the company is in a position to prove what technology it had at various points in time. For the same reason, archive older versions of the software and documentation.

4. Perform regular backups of computer code and business data.

5. Have copies of proprietary source code and master disks in a secure location off-site, so that fire or other disaster will not destroy the software (and the company along with it).

6. Arrange for backup computer facilities off-site to ensure the continuation of key business functions in case of an emergency.

7. Arrange for regular compliance with your escrow agreement updating obligations; verify compliance by your suppliers with any escrow obligations that were set up to protect your company.

8. Maintain lists of each piece of third-party software incorporated in the company's products, including memory management programs, printer

drivers, and so forth. Verify that your company is licensed to use the third-party code and that your company's field of use and geographic distribution is authorized by license.

9. Monitor competing products to see if your company's copyrights, trademarks, or patents are being infringed. Monitor the markets for counterfeit versions of your company's products.

10. Avoid cloning competitors' products in order to avoid copyright infringement concerns. Seek legal advice before any reverse engineering activity.

MANAGING THE DOCUMENTATION OF YOUR BUSINESS

It is important for companies to manage contract documentation. (Storage can be physical storage, in an electronic system based on scanned documents or both.) Your company should take the following steps to securely store the following.

Contract Management

1. Monitor and control the process of licensing third-party components. Be sure the license grants fit your business.

2. Monitor and control the adoption of open source licenses.

3. Maintain files containing every agreement, together with each amendment, schedule, and addendum. Contract files should be maintained for dealings with suppliers, dealers, independent programmers, and others with whom the company has a commercial relationship.

4. Maintain files of all nondisclosure agreements or other written agreements providing for confidential sharing of confidential information.

5. Maintain files of documentation relating to end-user agreements, such as shipping documentation, customer acceptance forms, reports of errors and bugs, records of service calls, release of software patches, upgrades, and new software versions. Be sure that you date document and product versions.

6. Use a database system to record installation dates, renewal and expiration dates, upgrade deliveries, and other key milestones for each end-user agreement.

7. Establish controls on who is authorized to sign or negotiate changes in contracts.

8. Maintain export control documentation including export licenses, and correspondence with Commerce Department and State Department personnel.

Intellectual Property Documentation

1. Copyright registration certificates and copyright applications

2. Trademark registration certificates and applications for trademark registration

3. Invention disclosure forms, patents, and patent applications

4. Legal counsel's patent opinions

5. Correspondence with government agencies involved in IP protection

6. Agreements with other companies in which your company or the other has agreed to keep information confidential

7. Agreements under which the company has acquired digital technology or other IP rights, including licenses, assignments, development agreements, publishing agreements, and so forth

8. Agreements under which the company has granted digital technology or IP rights to others, including assignments, development and publishing agreements, and so forth

9. Agreements relevant to security measures, including guard service contracts, contracts for purchase and service of alarm and entry control systems, contracts for procurement of encryption and password protection digital technology, and any consultant reports on such matters

10. All correspondence relating to IP matters

11. Relevant insurance policies and records

Dispute and Litigation Records

1. All pleadings, correspondence, and other documents relating to any actual or threatened suit, claim, or arbitration concerning licensing or use of IP or infringement of any IP rights

2. All pleadings, correspondence, and other documents relating to any actual or threatened suit, claim, or arbitration concerning alleged defects in the company's products

Content and Permissions Documentation

1. Branding and co-branding agreements
2. Consents and permissions for use of content of any kind
3. Content licenses for advertising, promotions, or otherwise
4. Agreements with content suppliers and licensors

Form Documents

1. Standard forms such as beta test agreements, employee confidentiality and noncompetition agreements, confidential disclosure agreements, exit interview forms, end-user agreements, shrink-wrap licenses, bug reports and logs, and the like
2. Online documentation, including terms of use, privacy statements, browse-wraps, and the like
3. Standard sales, service, and other commercial contracts
4. Samples of all CD-ROM labels and physical and electronic documentation with appropriate copyright, patent, and government contract legends
5. Employee policy statements concerning IP matters

Marketing and Sales Material

Your company should keep records of advertisements (in printed and online media), sales literature, and other documents used to promote the company's products. These should be kept in order to monitor the company's use of its trademarks and its representations concerning its products.

Lists of Consultants and Professionals

1. A list of technical consultants and experts used by the company
2. A list of professionals used by the company: lawyers, accountants, marketing consultants, advertising agencies, and so forth

IP-RELATED EMPLOYEE DOCUMENTATION

Managers in charge of hiring, or in the human resources department of large companies, must require and maintain appropriate employee documentation, including the following:

1. Employee confidentiality and noncompetition agreements

2. Confidentiality and noncompetition agreements signed by consultants

3. Records regarding employee access to laboratory notebooks and other trade secret information

4. Completed exit interview forms for each departing employee

PERIODIC LEGAL AUDITS AND STRATEGIC REVIEWS

In addition to the ongoing process of protecting its IP, a digital technology company should conduct an audit of its IP and contract management at least once a year. An audit is needed in the same way that a person needs a regular physical examination. The process is designed to make sure that systems are functioning properly and to attempt to catch any problems before they become serious.

The audit should cover both the implementation of the existing procedures and their effectiveness. An attorney can aid in the design of the process, in assessing its results and in recommended actions to deal with any deficiencies found.

The audit should address the subjects listed above. Key managers should take responsibility for verifying compliance with company procedures and for reporting exceptions and problems. From time to time, you should have counsel review form agreements and company policies to be sure that they reflect any changes in the law, in technology, or in your company's strategy. Needless to say, problems found in policies or practices should be addressed and cured.

In addition to a legal audit (or combined with it), at least once a year, your company should take a look at how its legal strategies fit with its business and financial strategies. This should include a review of:

1. Patent strategies and risks

2. Branding strategies and trademark protection

3. Trade secrets protection

4. Copyright protection and risks

5. The relationship and fit of your IP strategies, business strategies, and contracting strategies

6. Privacy management and compliance

7. System security

8. Contract forms and contracting tactics

9. Web site legal compliance

10. Open source issues

CONCLUSION

Your company must manage its legal affairs. Control of legal matters will make your company better prepared to compete and better capable of developing strategies that build and protect the value of your company. Managing legal matters will also make your company prepared for investments and its most important transactions.

About These Forms

This Appendix contains 38 contract and web forms for your use and review. These forms are available online for download by purchasers of this book in Microsoft Word format. Instructions on how to download the forms follow this discussion.

As we have emphasized in this book, agreements and web forms usually need to be customized. These forms are not "templates," because they may need modification to fit the particular situations of your business, its technologies or its deals. You should read them carefully and think about them before using them in any way.

The agreement forms are based on actual deals. The web forms were based on text prepared for actual web sites. Of course, we have removed all reference to particular companies and deal terms. In many cases, we have combined agreement text from several sources or edited language. While these forms cover a lot of ground, they are by no means comprehensive, because the potential varieties of transactions and issues are endless.

In these forms you will see some alternatives and optional language. There are some combinations that will not make sense when used together, so you need to be sure you think through how sections interact. Many of the forms require additions, such as blanks to be filled in or schedules to be added. Please add these elements with care. We have provided explanatory annotations where we thought the rationale for variations or options was not self-explanatory.

We cannot claim that these forms represent ideal agreement language. There is no "standard" license grant wording or standard indemnification clause, for example. Indeed these forms vary in the wording they use for similar clauses. Their provisions may differ from sample language included in the chapters. This variation occurs because we took sample language from a variety of agreements. There is no "best" way to write contracts, and the choice of wording for a particular form or particular deal, in the final analysis, is a matter of judgment. We encourage you to compare wording in various forms as well as from examples that you may obtain from other sources.

The forms are related to chapters. For example, Form 10-1, a development agreement, relates to content on development deals that you can find in Chapter 10. The discussion of intellectual property in Chapter 2 through Chapter 6 and the overview of contract basics in Chapter 8 are relevant to most of these forms.

If you edit these forms, combine them, or add additional language, be careful that your resulting draft is consistent in logic and in terminology. Be sure to double-check that all cross-references are correct.

We cannot guarantee the results that you will obtain with these forms. They are provided for your use and education, but you use them at your own discretion and risk. These forms do not constitute legal advice. When you need legal assistance, you should consult your qualified legal counsel.

Please note that the forms are subject to copyright and are provided for your own personal or business use. You may not publish these forms, post them on the web, or distribute them without the publisher's express prior written permission.

We hope that you will benefit from these forms. If you have any suggestions for their improvements, you may contact Gene Landy at gkl@riw.com.

Form Downloading Instructions for the *IT/Digital Legal Companion*

About the Forms in The IT/Digital Legal Companion

There are 38 contract and web forms in the Appendix at the end of this book. The purchaser of this book can download the forms from a special web page at no additional charge. The forms are available in PDF and Microsoft Word format. You can also download a zip file on the web side that includes all of the forms in both formats.

To get the forms, you need to register and then downloading just requires a few clicks.

The site is optimized for Internet Explorer v6+ or Firefox v2.0+.

How to Register

You must register to download the forms.

1. Find the 8-digit passcode listed at the back of this book inside the cover.

2. To access the website, go to this URL: http://booksite.syngress.com/Landy

3. Beneath the "Log In" button, you will see a "Register" link. Click this link to open the registration form.

4. Enter your 8-digit passcode. Choose a username and password. Enter your first and last name as well as a current email address. This information can be used to retrieve your password if you lose it. If you would like to receive additional information on product updates, you may opt-in by checking the Opt-In box.

5. Be sure to write down or save your username and password. It is your key to downloading forms. Once you have obtained a username and password, your 8-digit passcode will be invalid.

Downloading Forms

Once you have registered, you are redirected to the Logon Page. Use your username and password to logon to the site.

You may open the forms through the browser and then save them or you may right-click on the form links and save them directly to your drive.

You may logon to and use the download site as often as you wish.

If You Have a Problem or Lose Your Password

If you have problems in registration or downloading forms or if you lose your password, please contact Technical Support at technical.support@elsevier.com.

Use of Forms

Please note that the forms are subject to copyright and are provided for your own personal or business use. You should not use them for distribution or sale.

DMCA Web Site Copyright Policy

3-1

Introductory Note

This is a web site copyright policy designed to help the site owner secure the benefits of the notice-and-take-down "safe harbor" under the Digital Millennium Copyright Act. Please see Chapter 3 for details on the purpose and use of this form, including information on how to register an agent for notifications with the Copyright Office.

Copyright Policy

Repeat Infringers

We respect the intellectual property rights of others, and we prohibit users from uploading, posting or otherwise transmitting on this web site or by use of any of our services any materials that violate another party's intellectual property rights.

It is our policy, in appropriate circumstances and at our discretion, to disable and/or terminate the accounts of users who may repeatedly infringe or violate the copyrights or other intellectual property rights of any party.

Notification of Alleged Copyright Infringement

If you believe that your work has been copied in a way that constitutes copyright infringement, or that your intellectual property rights have been otherwise violated, please provide our Copyright Agent with the following information:

1. An electronic or physical signature of the person authorized to act on behalf of the owner of the copyright or other intellectual property interest;

2. A description of the copyrighted work or other intellectual property that you claim has been infringed;

3. A description of where the material that you claim is infringing is located on the web site, with enough detail that we may find it on the web site;

4. Your address, telephone number, and email address;

5. Your statement that you have a good faith belief that the disputed use is not authorized by the copyright or intellectual property owner, its agent, or the law;

6. Your statement, made under penalty of perjury, that the above information in your notice is accurate and that you are the copyright or intellectual property owner or authorized to act on the copyright or intellectual property owner's behalf.

This web site's Agent for Notice of claims of copyright or other intellectual property infringement can be reached as follows:

By Mail: *[Supply Mailing Address]*
By phone: *[Supply number]*
By fax: *[Supply number]*
By email: *copyright@[domain name]*

Counter Notification

If you believe your own copyrighted material has been removed from our website and/or service as a result of mistake or misidentification, you may submit a written Counter Notification to our Agent for Notice pursuant to 17 U.S.C. § 512(g)(2) and (3). To be effective, your Counter Notification must include substantially the following:

1. Identification of the material that has been removed or disabled and the location at which the material appeared before it was removed or disabled.

2. A statement that you consent to the jurisdiction of the Federal District Court in which your address is located, or if your address is outside the United States, for any judicial district in which the service provider for the web site may be found.

3. A statement that you will accept service of process from the party that filed the Notification of Alleged Copyright Infringement or from the party's agent.

4. Your name, address, and telephone number.

5. A statement under penalty of perjury that you have a good faith belief that the material in question was removed or disabled as a result of mistake or misidentification of the material to be removed or disabled.

6. Your physical or electronic signature.

You may submit your Counter Notification using our automated form, or send it to our designated Agent for Notice of by fax, mail, or email as set forth below:

Agent for Notice
By Mail: *[Supply Mailing Address]*
By phone: *[Supply number]*
By fax: *[Supply number]*
By email: *copyright@[domain name]*

If you send us a valid, written Counter Notification meeting the requirements described above, we will restore your removed or disabled material after 10 business days but no later than 14 business days from the date we receive your Counter Notification, unless our designated Agent for Notice first receives notice from the party filing the original Notification of Alleged Copyright Infringement informing us that such party has filed a court action to restrain you from engaging in infringing activity related to the material in question.

Please note that if you materially misrepresent that the disabled or removed content was removed by mistake or misidentification, you may be liable for damages, including costs and attorney's fees. Filing a false form may constitute perjury.

Royalty-Free Trademark License Agreement

Introductory Note

This is a form of trademark license agreement for a particular setting: The Licensor has (in a prior agreement) licensed component software to Licensee. That component software is now in the Licensee's software product. The Licensor wants to permit the Licensee to use the Licensor's branding royalty-free in connection with the promotion and marketing of the resulting Licensee product. This form can be adapted to any situation in which a supplier wants to permit another to use its branding in a specified fashion without charge.

This is a variation on the kind of trademark licensing strategy under which Intel allowed PC companies to use its "Intel Inside" branding on products and in advertising. This agreement is written to be permissive (i.e., the Licensee <u>may</u> use the branding), but could be made mandatory (i.e., the Licensee <u>must</u> use the branding).

Any trademark license should be conditioned upon the Licensee's meeting certain product quality and trademark usage standards. This form gives Licensor a right of inspection to monitor use of its branding.

Trademark License Agreement

This Trademark License Agreement ("Agreement") is entered into as of _____ ("Effective Date") by and between _____, with principal offices at _____ ("Licensor") and _____, with principal offices at _____ ("Licensee").

RECITALS:

A. Licensor has developed a line of embedded software ("Licensor Components") for use in certain software products developed, manufactured, and/or sold by Licensee ("Licensee Products").

B. Licensor has adopted certain trademarks and stylized logos and has proprietary rights in such trademarks and logos for use with the Licensor Components (collectively referred to as the "Marks"), which are identified on <u>Schedule A</u> to this Agreement.

C. The parties, for their mutual benefit, desire to promote end user recognition of Licensor Components as used in Licensee Products through Licensee's use of the Marks.

NOW, THEREFORE, the parties agree as follows:

1. **License Grant**

   1.1. *Grant.* Subject to the terms of this Agreement, Licensor hereby grants to Licensee a non-exclusive, non-transferrable, royalty-free license for the Territory (as defined below) to reproduce and use the Marks solely in connection with the promotion, marketing, and sale of those Licensee Products which comply with the requirements stated in <u>Schedule A</u> to this Agreement ("Qualified Products"). This grant includes a license to place the Marks on the Qualified Products. Licensor may amend <u>Schedule A</u> in Licensor's discretion and may specify different requirements for use of different Marks on 30 days' written notice.

   1.2. *Territory.* The "Territory" is [*define geographic reach of license*]. All license grants under this Agreement are limited to the Territory.

2. **Trademark Usage Requirements**

   2.1. *Trademark Use Guidelines.* The license granted in this Agreement is subject to Licensor's trademark use guidelines ("Trademark Use Guidelines") as provided by Licensor from time to time. The current form of Licensor's Trademark Use Guidelines is attached as <u>Schedule B</u>. Licensor may amend the Trademark Use Guidelines, in Licensor's discretion, upon thirty (30) days' written notice. Additionally, Licensee will comply with any additional trademark usage requirements stated in <u>Schedule A</u> for specific Marks and Qualified Products.

2.2. *Use Only for Qualified Products.* The Marks may only be used on or in connection with the promotion, marketing, and sale of Licensee Products that are Qualified Products. In the event that previously Qualified Products cease to be Qualified Products, Licensee will cease use of the Marks for such non-Qualified Products.

2.3. *Multiple Licensee Products.* In the event that Licensee includes multiple Licensee Products in its advertising in any media, some of which are not Qualified Products, Licensee will separately use the Marks in conjunction with its Qualified Products only, so that it is clear to the reader or viewer which are the Qualified Products.

2.4. *Accuracy in Promotion.* Licensee will exercise care in the use of the Marks so as not to indicate to the public that Licensee is a division or affiliate of Licensor or otherwise related to Licensor, or to misrepresent or create the misimpression that the Qualified Product is produced or has been tested, approved, and endorsed by Licensor.

2.5. *Reputation.* Licensee agrees to safeguard and maintain the reputation and prestige of the Marks and to avoid tarnishing the image of or adversely impacting the value or reputation associated with the Marks.

2.6. *No Alterations to Marks.* No Mark will be altered. If the Mark is in the form of a logo, such Mark will be reproduced from the supplied logo sheet as provided by Licensor from time to time as part of the Trademark Use Guidelines.

2.7. *Failure to Comply.* Failure to comply with any requirement of this Agreement regarding the Marks or their use is a material breach of this Agreement.

3. **Goodwill and Protection of Marks**

   [*Comment:* *The term "goodwill" in trademark law refers to the reputation associated with the Marks among customers and in the public at large.*]

3.1. *Sole Owner of Goodwill.* Licensee acknowledges the value of goodwill associated with the Mark(s) and agrees that Licensor is and will be the sole owner of such goodwill.

3.2. *No Registrations.* Licensee agrees that it will not apply for registration or otherwise seek to obtain ownership of any Marks or any confusingly similar trademarks anywhere in the world.

4. Product Quality

4.1. *Quality Control.* Licensee agrees to maintain the quality of Qualified Products at a high level equaling or exceeding the current quality of Qualified Products. For avoidance of doubt, Licensee must use Licensor Components in all Qualified Products for so long as such Qualified Products are being promoted using the Marks.

4.2. *Deficient Quality.* If Licensor determines the Qualified Products, collectively or individually, are no longer maintained at the required level of quality, Licensor will so notify Licensee in writing. Licensor will have the right to terminate this Agreement with respect to the Qualified Product(s) which are the subject of such deficient quality notice, if Licensee does not re-establish the quality of the Qualified Products within 30 days following its receipt of the deficient quality notice.

5. Right to Inspect.

Upon reasonable notice, Licensee agrees to allow Licensor to inspect Qualified Products and peripheral materials, such as packaging, manuals, instruction materials, brochures, web pages, PDFs and email messages, catalogs, point-of-purchase displays, etc., which make use of the Marks, to ensure that usage of the Marks is in compliance with the terms of this Agreement. Licensee will promptly provide samples of the foregoing to Licensor upon request.

6. Term of Agreement and Termination for Default

6.1. *Term of Agreement.* This Agreement will remain in effect until terminated in accordance with the provisions of this Section 6.

6.2. *Termination for Convenience.* Either party may terminate this Agreement on no less than ninety (90) calendar days prior written notice to the other party. Termination pursuant to this Section 6.2 may be for any reason or no reason.

6.3. *Termination for Default.* In addition to the right to terminate this Agreement pursuant to Paragraph 6.2 above, either party will have the right to terminate this Agreement if the other party defaults on any of its material obligations under this Agreement unless within thirty (30) calendar days after written notice of such default, the defaulting party cures the default.

6.4. *Effect of Termination.* Upon termination of this Agreement, the license grants terminate, and Licensee will immediately cease use of the Marks; provided that Licensee may continue to dispose of any existing inventory of Qualified Products and collateral materials which include the Marks, in the event such termination is under Section 6.2, for up to 90 days after termination.

6.5. *Continuing Obligations.* The respective obligations of Licensee and Licensor under the provisions of Paragraphs 6.4, 6.5, and Sections 7, 8, and 9 will remain in force after the termination of this Agreement.

7. **Notices.** Any notice required or permitted to be sent hereunder will be in writing and will be sent in a manner requiring a signed receipt, such as courier delivery, or if mailed, registered or certified mail, return receipt requested. Notice is effective upon receipt. Notice to Licensor will be addressed to [*specify name, title, and address*] or such other person or address as Licensor may designate. Notice to Licensee will be addressed to [*specify name, title, and address*] or such other person or address as Licensee may designate.

8. **Indemnification**

8.1. *Indemnification by Licensor.* Licensor will defend, indemnify, and hold harmless Licensee and its officers, employees, and agents from and against any loss, damages, or liability resulting from or arising out of a claim that Licensee's use of the Marks as permitted in this Agreement infringes the proprietary rights of any third party. As a condition to such defense and indemnification, Licensee will provide Licensor with prompt written notice of the claim, tender the defense and settlement of the claim to Licensor, and cooperate in the defense.

8.2. *Indemnification by Licensee.* Licensee will indemnify, hold harmless, and defend Licensor and its officers, employees, and agents against any and all claims arising out of Licensee's use of any Mark or out of the manufacture, use, sale, license, promotion, or other disposition of Qualified Product(s) that include any Mark, including without limitation, product liability and infringement claims (other than those claims for which Licensor provided indemnification under Section 8.1). As a condition to such defense and indemnification, Licensor will provide Licensee with prompt written notice of the claim, tender the defense and settlement of the claim to Licensee, and cooperate in the defense.

9. **General Provisions**

9.1. *LIMITATIONS OF LIABILITY.* EXCEPT WITH REGARD TO UNAUTHORIZED USE OF THE MARKS OR LICENSEE'S UNAUTHORIZED USE OR REGISTRATION OF THE SAME OR CONFUSINGLY SIMILAR MARKS, NEITHER PARTY WILL BE LIABLE TO THE OTHER FOR SPECIAL, INCIDENTAL, OR CONSEQUENTIAL DAMAGES ARISING OUT OF OR IN CONNECTION WITH THIS AGREEMENT, EVEN IF SUCH PARTY HAS BEEN ADVISED OF THE POSSIBILITY OF SUCH DAMAGES. EXCEPT WITH REGARD TO UNAUTHORIZED USE OF THE MARKS, LICENSEE'S UNAUTHORIZED USE OR REGISTRATION OF THE SAME OR CONFUSINGLY SIMILAR MARKS OR INDEMNIFICATION OBLIGATIONS, NEITHER PARTY WILL BE LIABLE TO THE OTHER UNDER THIS AGREEMENT FOR MORE THAN $_____.

9.2. *Assignment.* This Agreement will be binding upon and inure to the benefit of the successors and permitted assigns of the parties hereto. Neither party may assign any of its rights or delegate any of its obligations under this Agreement to any third party without the express prior written consent of the other party, except in the instance of a merger, company sale, sale of business operations, line of business sale, or acquisition of either party.

9.3. *Choice of Law; Jurisdiction.* The validity, construction, and performance of this Agreement will be governed by the laws of the State of _____ and applicable US federal law. The state and federal courts located in _____ will have exclusive jurisdiction and venue of any dispute arising from this Agreement or its subject matter.

9.4. *Relationship of the Parties.* No agency, partnership, joint venture, or employment is created between Licensor and Licensee as a result of this Agreement. Neither party is authorized to create any obligation, express or implied, on behalf of the other party, nor, except to the extent expressly provided in this Agreement, to exercise any control over the other party's methods of operation.

9.5. *Entire Agreement.* This Agreement, including the Schedules attached hereto as amended from time to time by the parties, constitutes the entire agreement between the parties concerning the subject matter hereof and supersedes all proposals, oral or written, all negotiations, conversations, and/or discussions between the parties relating to this Agreement and all past courses of dealing or industry customs. This Agreement may not be amended except by a written instrument executed by each of the parties hereto.

9.6. *Miscellaneous.* No delay or omission by either party in exercising any right under this Agreement will operate as a waiver of that or any other right. A waiver or consent given by either party on any one occasion will be effective only in that instance and will not be construed as a bar or waiver of any right on any other occasion. This Agreement may be executed in one or more counterparts, each of which will be deemed to be an original (a facsimile will be deemed an original), but all of which taken together will constitute one and the same instrument. If any provision of this Agreement will be found to be invalid by any court or arbitrator having competent jurisdiction, the invalidity of such provision will not affect the validity of the remaining provisions.

IN WITNESS WHEREOF, the parties, by their duly authorized representatives, have executed this Trademark License Agreement.

Licensor: _____   Licensee: _____

By: _____   By: _____
(Name)   (Name)
(Title)   (Title)
(Date)   (Date)

Schedule A

Licensed Marks and Qualified Products

Licensed Mark(s):

[Specify]

Qualified Products Requirements:

[List product specifications and requirements]

Schedule B

Trademark Use Guidelines

[*Attach current guidelines*]

Royalty Bearing Trademark License Agreement

Introductory Note

This is a basic form of trademark licensing agreement. The form is for the situation where the Licensor has a widely known and valuable trademark. The Licensee pays the Licensor for use of the trademark on Licensee's products and for promotion of those products.

The Licensee expects to be able to increase sales and prices by its use of the well-known trademark. Trademark licenses of this type normally feature required minimum royalties.

Bracketed provisions are optional or provide alternatives.

Trademark License Agreement

This Trademark License Agreement ("Agreement") is entered into as of _____ ("Effective Date") by and between _____, with its principal office at _____ ("Licensor") and _____, with its principal office at _____ ("Licensee"). This Agreement is effective as of *[date]* (the "Effective Date").

Purpose of This Agreement

A. Licensor is the owner of certain designations comprising designs, trademarks, and service marks listed on <u>Schedule A</u> ("Marks").

B. Licensee wishes to obtain a license to use the Marks on or in connection with certain Licensed Product(s) in the Territory.

1. **Definitions**

   1.1. "Licensed Product(s)" means the Licensee product(s) listed on <u>Schedule A</u> and bearing one or more of the Mark(s).

   [**Comment:** *The following is a pro-Licensor definition of "Net Sales." A Licensee might want various deductions, depending on the nature of the product and the sales channels.*]

   1.2. "Net Sales" means the total dollar amount of gross sales and proceeds from licensing and sales [and support and maintenance] of Licensed Product(s) by Licensee after deducting any credits for returns actually made or allowed. In computing Net Sales, no direct or indirect expenses or costs incurred in manufacturing, selling, distributing, or advertising the Licensed Product(s) (including cooperative and other advertising and promotion allowances) shall be deducted, nor shall any deduction be made for uncollectible accounts, cash discounts, or similar allowances, provided, however, that any taxes actually paid and any universally offered published discount actually applied may be deducted. Except as expressly provided in this paragraph, no deductions shall be made from gross sales. Net Sales resulting from sales to any party directly or indirectly related to or affiliated with Licensee shall be computed based on regular selling prices to non-affiliated parties.

   1.3. "Term," "Initial Term," and "Renewal Term" have the meaning set forth in Section 11.

   1.4. "Territory" means [*indicate territory*].

2. **License Grant**

   2.1. Licensor hereby grants and Licensee hereby accepts a nonexclusive license to use the Mark(s) solely on Licensed Product(s) distributed in the Territory and for advertising and promotion of such Licensed Products in the Territory.

   2.2. Licensee understands and agrees that this Agreement does not permit export of Licensed Products outside of the Territory or any other use of the mark(s) in or outside of the Territory. [This provision will not be violated by incidental sale or licensing via Internet downloads outside the Territory, provided that Licensee must use and require reasonable means to screen out and minimize such transactions.]

3. **Trademark Use**

   3.1. *Trademark Use.* The license granted in this Agreement is subject to Licensor's trademark use guidelines ("Trademark Use Guidelines") as provided by Licensor from time to time. The current form of Licensor's Trademark Use Guidelines is attached as Schedule B. Licensor may amend the Trademark Use Guidelines, in Licensor's discretion, upon thirty (30) days written notice. Additionally, Licensee will comply with any additional trademark usage requirements stated in Schedule A for specific Marks and Licensed Products.

   3.2. *Accuracy in Promotion.* Licensee will exercise care in the use of the Marks and in its promotional activities and public communications so as not to indicate to the public that Licensee is a division or affiliate of Licensor or otherwise related to Licensor.

   3.3. *Reputation.* Licensee agrees to safeguard and maintain the reputation and prestige of the Marks and to avoid tarnishing the image of or adversely impacting the value or reputation associated with the Marks.

   3.4. *No Alterations to Marks.* No Mark will be altered. If the Mark is in the form of a logo, such Mark will be reproduced from the supplied logo sheet as provided by Licensor from time to time as part of the Trademark Use Guidelines.

   3.5. *Failure to Comply.* Failure to comply with any requirement of this Agreement regarding the Marks or their use is a material breach of this Agreement.

4. **Quality Assurance**

   4.1. *Approval.* Licensee shall submit, at Licensee's expense, samples of proposed Licensed Product(s) including any related packaging, documentation, or materials to Licensor prior to any use, sale, or other distribution to the public. Licensee shall not use, sell, or otherwise distribute proposed Licensed Product(s) until they are approved in writing by Licensor. Licensor will not unreasonably withhold such approval.

   4.2. *Quality Assurance.* Licensee shall ensure that Licensed Product(s) meet or exceed the quality stated in the specifications and shown in the samples approved by Licensor. Licensee shall remove from public sale or distribution any previously approved Licensed Product(s) to which Licensor reasonably rescinds approval.

4.3. *Changes.* Licensee shall submit to Licensor for its written approval any proposed change to a Licensed Product(s) affecting its design, structure, or quality, and Licensee shall not use, sell, or otherwise distribute such proposed changed Licensed Product(s) until receiving approval in writing by Licensor.

4.4. *Inspections.* Licensee agrees that Licensor's representatives may visit and inspect the premises of Licensee, which may include inspecting the manufacturing operations and Licensed Product(s), at any time during normal business hours to ensure conformance to the terms and conditions of this Agreement.

4.5. *[Promotional Use.* All promotional use of the Mark(s) under this Agreement, including any advertising and promotion material, in any media will be subject to Licensor's prior approval, not to be unreasonably withheld.]

*[**Comment:** There are many possible pricing provisions. This is one variation offered as a sample. Your own deal may require different terms.]*

5. **Financial Terms**

5.1. *Royalty.* Licensee shall pay Licensor a royalty ("Royalty") of _____ percent (___%) on Net Sales calculated and paid quarterly as stated below.

5.2. *Advances.* Licensee agrees to pay in advance a minimum advance on earned Royalties for each year of the Term in the amount of $_____ ("Minimum Annual Payment"). The Minimum Annual Payment for the first year of the Term is due within ___ days of the Effective Date of this Agreement. The Minimum Annual Payment for each succeeding year is due on the anniversary of the Effective Date. Each Minimum Annual Payment is creditable against earned Royalties due Licensor for that particular year. Unused credits will expire at the end of the Term.

5.3. *Non-Refundability.* Each Minimum Annual Payment and all Royalty payments are non-refundable, except that, in case of Licensee's termination for Licensor's uncured material breach, Licensor shall refund the amount of the Minimum Annual Payment that is not credited to Royalties.

6. **Reports, Payments, and Audit**

   6.1. *Quarterly Royalty Payment and Report.* Licensee will, for each calendar quarter of each year, provide Licensor with written reports and make Royalty payments to Licensor within thirty (30) days of calendar quarter end. The report shall state the number, description, and aggregate sales and licensing of Licensed Products, any deductions relevant to calculation of Net Sales during such completed calendar quarter, and resulting calculation of Royalty payments due Licensor for such completed calendar quarter. The report will also show the application, as applicable, of the credit for the Minimum Annual Payment paid by Licensee.

   6.2. *Payment.* Together with such report, Licensee shall include payment due Licensor of Royalties for the calendar quarter covered by such report. If there were no Net Sales during any calendar quarter, a statement to that effect shall be provided to Licensor by Licensee.

   6.3. *Accounting and Audit.* Licensee shall keep reasonably detailed records for a period of three (3) years showing the manufacturing, licensing, sales, use, and other disposition of Licensed Products licensed or otherwise disposed of and any other transactions relevant to calculation of Net Sales in sufficient detail to verify the correct Royalties payable hereunder by Licensee to Licensor. Licensee shall permit its books and records to be examined by Licensor or Licensor's designated representative from time to time to the extent necessary to verify reports and Royalties under this Agreement. Such examination is to be made at the expense of Licensor, except in the event that the results of the audit reveal a discrepancy in Licensee's favor of ___ percent (___%) or more, then the audit fees and costs shall be paid by Licensee.

7. **Disclaimer of Warranty**

   7.1. Except as expressly stated, nothing in this Agreement is or shall be construed as: (a) a warranty or representation by Licensor as to the validity or scope of any Mark(s) or (b) a warranty or representation that anything made, used, sold, or otherwise disposed of under any license granted in this Agreement is or will be free from infringement of trademarks, copyrights, and other proprietary rights of third parties. No licenses are granted by implication. All rights not expressly granted are reserved.

7.2. EXCEPT AS EXPRESSLY SET FORTH IN THIS AGREEMENT, LICENSOR MAKES NO REPRESENTATIONS AND EXTENDS NO WARRANTIES OF ANY KIND, EITHER EXPRESS OR IMPLIED. THERE ARE NO EXPRESS OR IMPLIED WARRANTIES OF MERCHANTABILITY OR FITNESS FOR A PARTICULAR PURPOSE, OR THAT THE USE OF THE LICENSED PRODUCT(S) WILL NOT INFRINGE ANY COPYRIGHT, TRADEMARK, OR OTHER PROPRIETARY RIGHTS.

8. **Indemnity**

8.1. *Indemnification by Licensor.* Licensor will defend, indemnify, and hold harmless Licensee and its officers, employees, and agents from and against any loss, damages, or liability resulting from or arising out of a claim that Licensee's use of the Marks as permitted in this Agreement infringes the trademark rights of any third party. As a condition to such defense and indemnification, Licensee will provide Licensor with prompt written notice of the claim, tender the defense and settlement of the claim to Licensor, and cooperate in the defense.

8.2. *Indemnification by Licensee.* Licensee will indemnify, hold harmless, and defend Licensor and its officers, employees, and agents against any and all claims arising out of the manufacture, use, sale, license, or other disposition of Licensed Product(s), including without limitation, product liability and infringement claims (other than to the extent based on the Marks). As a condition to such defense and indemnification, Licensor will provide Licensee with prompt written notice of the claim, tender the defense and settlement of the claim to Licensee, and cooperate in the defense.

9. **Infringement by Third Parties.** Licensee shall promptly inform Licensor of any suspected infringement of any Mark(s) by a third party.

10. **Goodwill and Protection of Marks**

*[**Comment:** The term "goodwill" in trademark licenses refers to the reputation associated with the Marks among customers and in the public at large.]*

10.1. *Sole Owner of Goodwill.* Licensee acknowledges the value of goodwill associated with the Mark(s) and agrees that Licensor is and will be the sole owner of such goodwill.

10.2. *No Registrations.* Licensee agrees that it will not apply for registration or otherwise seek to obtain ownership of any Marks or any confusingly similar trademarks anywhere in the world.

11. **Term and Termination**

11.1. *Term.* The term of this Agreement ("Term"), unless earlier terminated as provided herein, will be as follows: The initial term of this Agreement ("Initial Term") will be for a period of ___ (__) year(s), unless sooner terminated as provided by this Agreement. After the Initial Term, this Agreement will be automatically renewed for successive one (1) year periods (each a "Renewal Term"), unless either Party gives the other written notice of termination at least _____ (__) days prior to the expiration of the then current Initial Term or Renewal Term (as applicable). If such notice is given, the Agreement will terminate at the end of the then current Initial Term or Renewal Term.

11.2. *Termination for Default.* Either party will have the right to terminate this Agreement if the other party defaults on any of its material obligations under this Agreement, unless within thirty (30) calendar days after written notice of such default, the defaulting party cures the default.

11.3. *Effect of Termination.* Upon termination of this Agreement, license grants terminate, and Licensee will immediately cease use of the Marks licensed hereunder, provided that Licensee may continue to make disposal of existing inventory of Licensed Products and collateral materials which include the Marks for the _____ day period following termination in the event such termination is for Licensor's uncured material default. All provisions of this Agreement apply to such post-termination use, including the obligation to pay Royalties.

11.4. *Continuing Obligations.* The provisions of Sections 5 (to the extent applicable), 6, 7, 8, 9, 10, 11.3, 11.4, and 12 will remain in force after the termination of this Agreement as will all accrued and any continuing payment obligations.

12. **General**

12.1. *LIMITATIONS OF LIABILITY.* EXCEPT WITH REGARD TO UNAUTHORIZED USE OF THE MARKS OR LICENSEE'S REGISTRATION OF THE SAME OR CONFUSINGLY SIMILAR

MARKS, NEITHER PARTY WILL BE LIABLE TO THE OTHER FOR SPECIAL, INCIDENTAL, OR CONSEQUENTIAL DAMAGES ARISING OUT OF OR IN CONNECTION WITH THIS AGREEMENT, EVEN IF SUCH PARTY HAS BEEN ADVISED OF THE POSSIBILITY OF SUCH DAMAGES. EXCEPT WITH REGARD TO UNAUTHORIZED USE OF THE MARKS, LICENSEE'S REGISTRATION OF THE SAME OR CONFUSINGLY SIMILAR MARKS OR INDEMNIFICATION OBLIGATIONS, NEITHER PARTY WILL BE LIABLE TO THE OTHER UNDER THIS AGREEMENT FOR MORE THAN AMOUNTS PAID OR REQUIRED TO BE PAID UNDER THE PROVISIONS OF THIS AGREEMENT.

12.2. *Notice.* Any notice required or permitted to be sent hereunder will be in writing and will be sent in a manner requiring a signed receipt, such as courier delivery, or if mailed, registered or certified mail, return receipt requested. Notice is effective upon receipt. Notice to Licensor will be addressed to *[specify name, title, and address]* or such other person or address as Licensor may designate. Notice to Licensee will be addressed to *[specify name, title, and address]* or such other person or address as Licensee may designate.

12.3. *Assignment.* This Agreement will be binding upon and inure to the benefit of the successors and permitted assigns of the parties hereto. Neither party may assign any of its rights or delegate any of its obligations under this Agreement to any third party without the express prior written consent of the other party, except in the instance of a merger, company sale, sale of business operations, line of business sale, or acquisition of either party.

12.4. *Choice of Law; Jurisdiction.* The validity, construction, and performance of this Agreement will be governed by the laws of the State of _____ and applicable US federal law. The state and federal courts located in ___ _____ will have exclusive jurisdiction and venue of any dispute arising from this Agreement or its subject matter.

12.5. *Relationship of the Parties.* No agency, partnership, joint venture, or employment is created between Licensor and Licensee as a result of this Agreement. Neither party is authorized to create any obligation, express or implied, on behalf of the other party, nor, except to the extent expressly provided in this Agreement, to exercise any control over the other party's methods of operation.

12.6. *Entire Agreement.* This Agreement, including its Schedules, constitutes the entire agreement between the parties concerning the subject matter hereof and supersedes all proposals, oral or written, all negotiations, conversations, and/or discussions between the parties relating to this Agreement and all past courses of dealing or industry customs. This Agreement may not be amended except by a written instrument executed by each of the parties hereto.

12.7. *Miscellaneous.* No delay or omission by either party in exercising any right under this Agreement will operate as a waiver of that or any other right. A waiver or consent given by either party on any one occasion will be effective only in that instance and will not be construed as a bar or waiver of any right on any other occasion. This Agreement may be executed in one or more counterparts, each of which will be deemed to be an original (a facsimile will be deemed an original), but all of which taken together will constitute one and the same instrument. If any provision of this Agreement will be found to be invalid by any court or arbitrator having competent jurisdiction, the invalidity of such provision will not affect the validity of the remaining provisions.

IN WITNESS WHEREOF, the parties have executed this Agreement as of the Effective Date.

Licensor: _____   Licensee: _____

By: _____   By: _____
(Name)   (Name)
(Title)   (Title)
(Date)   (Date)

Schedule A

Marks and Licensee Products

Mark(s):

[Specify]

Licensee Products

[List products and any special branding requirements]

Schedule B

Trademark Use Guidelines

[*Attach current guidelines*]

Patent License Agreement

Introductory Note

This is a form of exclusive patent licensing agreement.

Some potential variations in this form are indicated below in bracketed text, but there are many others. Patent license fees can be based on many different royalty arrangements. Sometimes a patent license agreement also includes a license to unpatented know-how or technology. Sometimes the inventor or patent owner agrees to provide consulting services. Some license agreements have grant-backs, under which the Licensor gets a license to the Licensee's improvement patents. The Licensor in most patent licenses will want to carefully define the field of use so that the license extends only to areas where the exclusive Licensee will use the rights.

A non-exclusive patent license agreement would be similar, but would give the Licensor more control of the patent in various ways; for example, a non-exclusive deal would normally give the Licensor, rather than the Licensee, control over patent filings and litigation to enforce the patent. An exclusive patent licensing deal would usually require a substantially higher financial commitment from the Licensee than a non-exclusive one.

Patent licenses are very technical and have many tricks and traps. You may want to consult your attorney with regard to your licensing strategy before you begin negotiations.

Patent License Agreement

This Patent License Agreement ("Agreement") is made as of the _____ day of
_____, 20_____ (the "Effective Date") between _____ ("Licensor"),
a _____ corporation having a business address of _____,

and _____ ("Licensee"), a _____ corporation having its principal place of business at _____. Licensor and Licensee hereby agree as follows:

Purpose of Agreement

A. Licensor is the owner of the Patent Technology, as defined below.

B. Licensor is willing to grant, and Licensee wishes to obtain, a license to the Patent Technology under the terms stated below.

1. **Definitions**

   1.1. "Affiliate" means any entity that controls, is controlled by, or is under the common control of a party to this Agreement.

   1.2. "Field of Use" means the field of *[define the field in which the license may be used]*.

   1.3. "Licensed Product" will mean any product the manufacture, sale, or use of which is covered in whole or in part by a Valid Claim in the country in which the product is made, used, or sold.

   1.4. "Net Sales" will mean the gross amount invoiced for sales of Licensed Products to independent third parties by Licensee or its Affiliates less:

      1.4.1. Transportation charges or allowances actually paid or granted;

      1.4.2. Trade, quantity, cash, or other discounts, if any, allowed or paid by Licensee to independent parties in arms-length transactions;

      1.4.3. Credits or allowances made or given on account of rejects, returns, recalls, or retroactive price reductions for any amount not collected;

      1.4.4. Any tax or governmental charge directly on sale or transportation, use or delivery, or services paid by Licensee and not recovered from the purchaser.

   1.5. "Patent Rights" will mean any United States or foreign patent applications or any patents issued thereon directed to the invention or inventions included in the Patent Technology owned by, or assignable to, Licensor or its Affiliates, together with any divisions, reissues, continuations, continuations in part, extensions, or additions thereof. [In the case of a regional patent, such as a European patent, an application will be deemed to be pending in a country if there is pending a regional patent application for which such country has been designated; and a patent will be deemed to have issued in a country if a regional patent has issued and such patent is registered in such country so as to be enforceable in such country.]

1.6. "Patent Technology" will mean the technology disclosed and claimed in *[indicate patents and/or applications by name, date, and number]* [and any enhancements or improvements made by Licensor thereto during the term of this Agreement].

1.7. ["Sublicense Income" will mean the net amounts actually received by Licensee and its Affiliates from non-affiliated third party sublicensees on their Net Sales under the license herein granted[, after the deduction of all reasonable legal costs actually incurred by Licensee in connection with the negotiation and procurement of the pertinent sublicenses].]

1.8. "Territory" means *[indicate nations or regions or state "worldwide"]*.

1.9. "Valid Claim" will mean any claim set forth in the Patent Rights that, has (i) been maintained, (ii) not expired, and (iii) not been held invalid or unenforceable by a court of competent jurisdiction; or, in the case of a claim set forth in a patent application, has (iv) been diligently prosecuted and (v) not been finally rejected by the patent office of the country in which the application has been filed, such rejection having become unappealable by virtue of a waiver or a failure to file and diligently prosecute an appeal.

2. **Grant**

2.1. *Grant for Licensee Use.* Licensor hereby grants to Licensee during the term of this Agreement, subject to all the terms and conditions of this Agreement, the exclusive right and license under the Patent Rights to make, have made, use, lease, promote, import, market, distribute, and sell the Licensed Products in the Field of Use in the Territory. Licensee may permit its Affiliates in the Territory to exercise the license rights under this Agreement, provided that (a) Licensee guarantees that each Affiliate will comply with this Agreement and (b) Licensee will be responsible for the acts and omissions of its Affiliates as if they were its own.

2.2. [*Sublicense Rights.* Licensee will have the right during the term of this Agreement to sublicense worldwide any of the rights, privileges, and licenses granted hereunder to non-affiliated business entities subject to the terms of this Agreement.]

3. **Royalties Licensed Products**

   [*Comment:* *The following section has a simple percentage royalty. There are many possible alternatives that might be used, for example: per-product royalties, minimum royalties per product, different royalties for different uses or product types, etc.]*

   3.1. *Royalty.* In consideration of the license granted by this Agreement [, subject to Section 4,] Licensee will pay a royalty ("Royalty") of _____ percent (_____%) of Net Sales of Licensed Products by Licensee and its Affiliates.

   [*Comment:* *Royalties payable to the Licensor would normally be considerably higher on revenues that the Licensee obtains from sublicensing the Patent Rights.]*

   3.2. [*Sublicenses to Non-Affiliates.* In the event Licensee grants any sublicenses to non-affiliated third parties during the term of this Agreement, then for each such sublicense, the Royalty payable by Licensee will equal _____ percent (_____%) of the Sublicense Income of Licensee.]

   [*Comment:* *The following optional section deals with a contingency that might affect the value to the Licensee of a licensed patent application.]*

4. **[Royalty Reduction]**

   4.1. *[If No Patent Issues.* If no patent has issued with respect to the Patent Rights by the date when Net Sales by Licensee of Licensed Products exceed _____ dollars ($_____) or *[date]*, whichever first occurs, the applicable Royalty rate will be reduced by _____ percent (_____%) [unless the patent application is involved in a patent interference proceeding in the US Patent and Trademark Office, in which cases the full Royalty rate will apply]. If the Royalty rate is reduced by _____ percent (_____%) as provided by this paragraph and a patent subsequently issues, the full Royalty rate will be payable as of the issue date of the patent. If no patent has issued with respect to the Patent Rights by the _____ anniversary of this Agreement, the applicable Royalty rate will be reduced by one hundred percent (100%) until a patent subsequently issues, at which time the full Royalty rate will be restored.]

5. **[Minimum Royalties**

*[**Comment:** Many patent license agreements—exclusive and non-exclusive—have provisions for minimum royalties.]*

5.1. In each calendar year during the term of this Agreement after *[specify date]*, Licensee will pay minimum Royalties ("Minimum Royalties") of $*[insert amount]* per calendar quarter. Such payment will be made by adding, to Royalties based on Net Sales, an additional payment amount such that total payments of Royalties for the calendar quarter equal such Minimum Royalties amount.

5.2. In addition, if Royalties based on Net Sales for *[number]* consecutive calendar quarters are not at least *[insert amount]*, then Licensee, at its option, may, by written notice, [change the license grant from exclusive to non-exclusive in all respects] [terminate this Agreement in accordance with its terms].]

6. **Records, Reports, and Audit**

6.1. *Records.* Licensee will keep adequate and complete records (including, without limitation, those of its Affiliates) showing all Net Sales of Licensed Products, with respect to which Royalties are due under this Agreement. Such records will include all information necessary to verify the total amount and computation of Royalties [including Minimum Royalties] due hereunder. Licensee is required to retain such records for three (3) years after the close of each calendar quarter.

6.2. *Reports.* Within _____ days after the closing of each calendar quarter during the term of this Agreement, including the quarter in which this Agreement is terminated, Licensee will furnish Licensor with a written report, signed by an authorized representative of Licensee, showing:

6.2.1. The Net Sales of all Licensed Products sold by Licensee and its Affiliates in each country during the preceding calendar quarter;

6.2.2. The total amount of Royalties due on Licensed Products sold by Licensee and its Affiliates during the preceding calendar quarter and the calculation of such amount;

6.2.3. [The total amount of Sublicense Income received by Licensee, its Affiliates, and from non-affiliated sublicensees pursuant to this Agreement during the preceding calendar quarter and the calculation of such amount;]

6.2.4. [Any Minimum Royalty payment due including a statement showing how such amount was computed;] and

6.3. *Audit.* Upon reasonable notice, no more frequently than twice a year, Licensor may, by itself or by its representative or certified public accountant, audit, at its own expense, any and all business records relating to payments made or amounts due to Licensor or to calculations related thereto or regarding other matters of compliance with this Agreement. Licensee will provide reasonable cooperation with such audit. If errors or discrepancies of more than five (5) percent for the audited period are found, Licensee shall reimburse Licensor for the reasonable expense of the audit. Licensee shall promptly pay all unpaid amounts due with applicable interest.

7. **Royalty Payments**

7.1. *Payment.* With each such quarterly report of Royalties, Licensee will remit to Licensor the total amount of Royalties due, subject to any credits which may be taken by Licensee under the provisions of this Agreement. Subject to the provisions of Section 7.3 hereof, payment will be made in lawful money of the United States. Payments not made when due will be paid with interest at the rate of _____ percent per year, compounded daily, or, if less, the maximum permitted legal rate.

[**Comment:** *The following optional sections also deal with the contingency that the Licensee might need other underlying patent licenses in order to exercise the rights under the licensed patent.*]

7.2. [*Third Party Necessary Licenses.* If it is necessary for Licensee to have one or more royalty-bearing licenses from third parties in order to exercise the rights granted by Licensor hereunder, then Licensee will be entitled to credit such royalty payments against the then prevailing Royalty payments it is obligated to pay hereunder, but in no case will the Royalty otherwise due Licensor be reduced by more than _____ percent (_____%) from the Royalty otherwise payable. If such deductions are taken, Licensee will itemize them in each Royalty report, and will provide a written explanation of such deductions, in reasonable detail, upon Licensor's written request.]

7.3. *Currency Conversion.* All payments due hereunder from foreign sales of Licensed Products from time to time will be paid in United States funds to Licensor. For purposes of computing such payments, the Net Sales will first be determined in the foreign currency for which such Licensed Products are sold and then converted into its equivalent in United States funds at the conversion rate published in *The Wall Street Journal* on the last business day of the applicable calendar quarter.

8. **Patent Prosecution**

8.1. *U.S. Patents.* Licensor will use reasonable efforts to file, prosecute, and maintain all U.S. patents and patent applications specified under Patent Rights and Licensee will be licensed under the resulting patents.

[Comment: The sections that follow grant the Licensee some control over foreign patent filings (with several variations on the effect of its exercising that control). These provisions are something that a Licensee might bargain for in an exclusive patent license agreement. The Licensee would normally not have any say in patent filings in a non-exclusive patent agreement.]

8.2. *Foreign Patents.* Licensor will at its expense file and prosecute foreign applications corresponding to United States patent applications [in all such countries as may reasonably be selected by Licensee] [in the following countries and jurisdictions: *[insert list]*. [In any country where Licensor fails to have a patent application filed or to pay expenses associated with filing, prosecuting, or maintaining a patent application or patent and in which Licensee wishes to pursue commercialization of the Licensed Products, Licensee may then file, prosecute, and/or maintain a patent application or patent in its name or the name of Licensor, and Licensee, thereafter, will be fully licensed under such patent or patent application for that country under the terms of this Agreement[, and will not be obliged to pay any Royalty for sales of Licensed Products in such country] [and will have its Royalties for such country reduced by [*number*] percent] [and may credit such foreign patent prosecution and maintenance expenses, to the extent that Licensee makes such payments, against Licensee's Royalty obligations as they become payable to Licensor.]

8.3. [*Licensee Participation.* With respect to any Patent Right, each patent application, office action, response to office action, interference proceeding, request for terminal disclaimer, and request for reissue or reexamination of any patent issuing from such application filed or received by either party, such document will be provided to the other party sufficiently prior to the filing or due date of such application, response, or request to allow for comment by such other party, and in no event later than _____ weeks prior to such date.]

9. **Infringement**

[*Comment:* In this form, the Licensee gets the "first shot" at suing a patent infringer. This mechanism would normally be used only where Licensee has an exclusive patent license. For non-exclusive licensing, it is normal that the Licensor controls any patent enforcement. There are many possible variations on payment for litigation costs and sharing potential money recoveries.]

9.1. *Notice.* If either Licensor or Licensee learns that a Valid Claim in any issued and unexpired patent licensed exclusively under this Agreement is allegedly infringed or contributorily infringed by a third party, the party learning of the alleged infringement or contributory infringement will promptly notify the other party. Within thirty (30) days after learning of such infringement or contributory infringement, Licensee will notify Licensor of its decision whether or not to bring an action against the alleged infringer.

9.2. *Licensee Prosecution of Claim.* In the event that Licensee brings an action for infringement or contributory infringement, it may sue in its own name and/or in the name of Licensor, and Licensee will bear all costs and the expenses relating to the litigation.

9.3. *Credit.* Licensee may credit _____ percent (____%) of its litigation expenses in such an action for infringement or for contributory infringement against its otherwise applicable Royalties payable to Licensor. Unused credits may be carried over to subsequent quarters. Any damages recovered by such suit or action will be first used to reimburse each party hereto for the cost of such suit or action (including attorney's fees) actually paid by each party hereto as the case may be, then to reimburse Licensor for any Royalties waived under this Section and the residue, if any, will be divided equally between the parties hereto.

9.4. *Licensor Prosecution of Claim.* In the event that Licensee elects not to bring an action for infringement or for contributory infringement, then Licensor will have the right, but not the obligation, to bring an action in the name of Licensor and/or the name of Licensee. Licensor will bear all costs and expenses relating to the litigation, and Licensor will be entitled to all damages and other recoveries awarded in such litigation.

9.5. *Cooperation.* In any infringement suit as either party may institute to enforce the Patent Rights pursuant to this Agreement, the other party hereto will, at the request and expense of the party initiating such suit, cooperate in all respects and, to the extent possible, have its employees testify when requested and make available relevant records, papers, information, samples, and the like.

9.6. *Claims Against Licensee.* If Licensee is charged with or sued in any country for infringement of any patent of a third party by doing acts necessary to practice the inventions of the Patent Rights, Licensee will promptly notify Licensor of the circumstances in reasonable detail. Licensor will cooperate and assist Licensee in the disposition and defense of each such case or proceeding at Licensee's expense.

10. **Term and Termination**

10.1. *Term.* Unless earlier terminated as hereinafter provided, this Agreement will remain in full force and effect until the last to expire of any patent included in the Patent Rights or the other termination or cancellation of all such rights.

10.2. *Termination for Default.* Either party will have the right to terminate this Agreement if the other party defaults on any of its material obligations under this Agreement, unless within thirty (30) calendar days after written notice of such default, the defaulting party cures the default.

10.3. *Insolvency.* In the event that either party goes into bankruptcy or insolvency proceedings and such proceedings, if involuntary, are not dismissed in 60 days, or a receiver or trustee is appointed for the property or estate of either party, or either party makes an assignment of substantially all of its assets for the benefit of its creditors, this Agreement and the license and rights herein granted can be terminated at the option of the other party.

10.4. *Rights and Obligations After Termination.* Upon termination of this Agreement for any reason, nothing herein will be construed to release either party from any obligation that matured prior to the effective date of such termination. Licensee and its Affiliates [and any non-affiliated third party sublicensees thereof] may, after the effective date of such termination, sell all Licensed Products which are in inventory at the time of termination, and complete and sell Licensed Products which were in the process of manufacture at the time of such termination, provided that Licensee will pay to Licensor the Royalties thereon as required by this Agreement and will submit the required reports on the sales of Licensed Products.

10.5. The following Sections will also survive termination: 1 (Definitions), 6 (Records, Reports and Audit), 7 (Payments) (as applicable), 9 (Infringement), 10 (Termination), 11 (Indemnification and Insurance), 12.4 (Disclaimers), 14 (Confidentiality), and 16 (Miscellaneous).

11. Indemnification and Insurance

11.1. *Duty to Defend and Indemnify.* Licensee will defend, indemnify, and hold Licensor, its officers, directors, employees, and agents harmless as against any judgments, fees, expenses, or other costs (including reasonable attorney's fees) arising from or incidental to any product liability, infringement, or other lawsuit or claim relating to the Licensed Products or their marketing or sale or arising from the practice of the license granted with regard to the Licensed Products, whether or not Licensor is named as party defendant in any such lawsuit. Licensee will have the right to defend such a lawsuit with counsel of its own choosing and the indemnified parties will cooperate in the defense of such action at Licensee's expense. Practice of any invention encompassed by any of the licenses granted herein by Licensee, an Affiliate, an agent or a sublicensee, or a third party on behalf of or for the account of Licensee or its Affiliate or by a third party who purchases Licensed Products from any of the foregoing will be considered practice of the license by Licensee for purposes of this Section and subject to the obligation of Licensee to defend, indemnify, and hold harmless under this Section.

11.2. *Notice of Claims.* In the event any such action is commenced or claim made or threatened against Licensor or other indemnified parties as to which Licensee is obligated to indemnify it (them) or hold it (them) harmless, Licensor or the other indemnified party will promptly notify Licensee of such event, and Licensee will assume the defense of, and may settle, that part of any such claim or action commenced or made against Licensor (or other indemnified parties) which relates to Licensee's indemnification.

[Comment: In many agreements, the insurance requirements are spelled out in detail, including types of coverage, dollar amounts, required insurer ratings, and so forth.]

11.3. *Insurance.* Licensee warrants that it has and during the term of this Agreement and for _____ year(s) thereafter [will have product liability insurance at a level that is commensurate with the risks to which it is exposed] [will have the following insurance coverage: [*insert statement of coverage required*]. Licensee will provide Licensor certificates of insurance upon request.

12. **Representations and Warranties of Licensor.** Licensor hereby represents and warrants to Licensee that:

12.1. *Power and Authority.* Licensor has the full legal power, authority, and right to grant the license under the Patent Rights and to perform its obligations under this Agreement. This Agreement will constitute a valid and binding agreement of Licensor enforceable against it in accordance with its terms.

12.2. *Title and Validity.* Licensor is the sole owner of all right, title, and interest in and to the Patent Rights. [Except for such Patent Rights, there are no patents issued or, to Licensor's knowledge, other patent applications filed in any country claiming the Patent Technology, except for patents owned or filed by or specifically licensed to Licensor or any of its Affiliates. Licensor has no knowledge of any fact which casts substantial doubt on the validity of any of the Patents Rights as of the Effective Date.]

12.3. *No Conflict.* Licensor hereby represents and warrants that no other person or organization presently has any assignment, option, or license under the Patent Rights with respect to the manufacture, use or sale of Licensed Product that is inconsistent with the license grant in this Agreement. Execution, delivery and consummation of this Agreement will not result in the breach of or give rise to cause for termination of any agreement or contract to which Licensor or its Affiliates may be a party or, to Licensor's knowledge, which otherwise relates to the Patent Rights. Neither Licensor nor any of its Affiliates after the date hereof will enter into any agreement or take or fail to take any action which will restrict its legal right to grant to Licensee the rights and benefits contemplated under this Agreement.

12.4. *DISCLAIMERS.* THE RIGHTS GRANTED HEREIN BY LICENSOR DO NOT INCLUDE AND LICENSOR DISCLAIMS ANY WARRANTY WHATSOEVER WITH RESPECT TO ANY LICENSED PRODUCT INCLUDING ITS SAFETY, EFFECTIVENESS, COMMERCIAL VIABILITY OR MERCHANTABILITY, AND LICENSEE ASSUMES ALL RESPONSIBILITY AND LIABILITY IN THIS REGARD. LICENSOR DOES NOT WARRANT THAT LICENSED PRODUCTS WILL NOT INFRINGE THIRD PARTY PATENTS. LICENSOR MAKES NO REPRESENTATION WITH REGARD TO THE COMMERCIAL RESULTS THAT MAY BE OBTAINED UNDER THIS AGREEMENT.

13. Notices

13.1. All reports, notices and other communications provided hereunder may be made or given by either party by facsimile, by first-class mail, postage prepaid, or by courier to the mailing address or facsimile numbers set out below or such other address or facsimile numbers as such party will have furnished in writing to the other party in writing:

If to Licensor, to: *[supply address, contact person and/or title, and fax number]*

If to Licensee, to: *[supply address, contact person and/or title, and fax number]*

Notice is effective upon receipt.

14. Confidentiality

14.1. "Confidential Information" means non-public information, technical data or know-how of a party and/or its Affiliate, which is furnished directly or indirectly to the other party in written or tangible form in connection with this Agreement. Each oral disclosure of a party will also be deemed Confidential Information if the recipient should reasonably understand it to be non-public information [and its disclosure and confidentiality is confirmed in writing by the disclosing party within 30 days of oral disclosure].

14.2. Licensee and Licensor contemplate that it may be necessary to exchange Confidential Information in connection with the terms of this Agreement. Each party to this Agreement agrees that Confidential Information that is received from the other will be maintained in confidence and that reasonable and prudent practices will be followed to maintain the information in confidence including, where necessary, obtaining written confidentiality agreements from persons not already bound by a written confidentiality agreement having access to information obtained from the other.

14.3. The obligation to maintain the confidentiality of Confidential Information will survive this Agreement for a period of _____ (_____) years. However, a party will not be obligated to maintain information in confidence which it demonstrates was:

14.3.1. publicly known prior to submission by the other; or

14.3.2. known or available to it prior to submission by the other; or

14.3.3. publicly known, without fault on its part, subsequent to submission by the other party; or

14.3.4. received from a third party not under a duty of confidence to the other party; or

14.3.5. required to be disclosed by order of any court or government agency, provided that reasonable advance notice is given to the other to afford an opportunity to protect the information.

15. **Miscellaneous**

15.1. *Relationship of Parties.* For the purpose of this Agreement and all services to be provided hereunder, both parties will be, and will be deemed to be, independent contractors and not agents or employees of the other. Neither party will have authority to make any statements, representations or commitments of any kind, or to take any action, that will be binding on the other party.

15.2. *Severability.* If any one or more of the provisions of this Agreement will be held to be invalid, illegal or unenforceable, the validity, legality or enforceability of the remaining provisions of this Agreement will not in any way be affected or impaired thereby.

15.3. *Successors and Assigns.* This Agreement will be binding upon and inure to the benefit of the successors and permitted assigns of the parties hereto. Neither party may assign any of its rights or delegate any of its obligations under this Agreement to any third party without the express prior written consent of the other party, except in the instance of a merger, company sale, sale of business operations, line of business sale, or acquisition of the assigning party.

15.4. *Amendment and Waiver.* No change, modification, extension, termination or waiver of this Agreement, or any of the provisions herein contained, will be valid unless made in writing and signed by a duly authorized representative of each party.

15.5. *Captions.* The captions are provided for convenience and are not to be used in construing this Agreement.

15.6. *No Presumptions.* The parties agree that they have participated equally in the formation of this Agreement and that the language herein should not be presumptively construed against either of them.

15.7. *Counterparts.* This Agreement may be signed in counterparts, which collectively will constitute a single agreement and may be executed by means of faxed signature pages.

15.8. *Choice of Law; Jurisdiction.* The validity, construction and performance of this Agreement will be governed by the laws of the State of _____ and applicable US federal law. The state and federal courts located in _____ will have exclusive jurisdiction and venue of any dispute arising from this Agreement or its subject matter.

15.9. *Force Majeure.* Neither party will be in breach hereof by reason of its delay in the performance of its obligations hereunder, if that delay is caused by strikes, acts of God or the public enemy, riots, incendiaries, interference by civil or military authorities, compliance with governmental priorities for materials, or any cause beyond its control.

15.10. *Further Assurances.* The parties each, at any time or from time to time, will execute and deliver or cause to be delivered such further assurances, instruments or documents as may be reasonably necessary to fulfill the terms and conditions of this Agreement.

15.11. *Entire Agreement.* This instrument contains the entire Agreement between the parties hereto. No verbal agreement, conversation or representation between any officers, agents, or employees of the parties hereto either before or after the execution of this Agreement will affect or modify any of the terms or obligations herein contained.

IN WITNESS WHEREOF, the parties, by their duly authorized representatives, have executed this Agreement as of the Effective Date.

Licensor: _____   Licensee: _____

By: _____   By: _____
(Name)   (Name)
(Title)   (Title)
(Date)   (Date)

Mutual Non-Disclosure Agreement

Introductory Note

This is a conventional form of mutual non-disclosure agreement.

Bracketed language is optional or provides alternatives.

Provisions that are optional include a clause prohibiting hiring of the other party's personnel and the somewhat controversial "residuals" clause. You should be careful in use of the residuals clause to be sure it fits your needs. (See discussion of this clause in Chapter 6.)

The optional "feedback" clause also carries some risk, because it allows the company that receives feedback to have a free license to information.

Mutual Non-Disclosure Agreement

This Mutual Non-Disclosure Agreement (the "Agreement") is entered into between SoftCo, Inc. ("SoftCo") and _____ ("Company") as of the date that both parties have signed this Agreement ("Effective Date").

Under this Agreement, it is contemplated that each party will disclose and discuss its Confidential Information (as defined below). The parties have entered into this Agreement to define the rights and duties of the parties concerning such disclosure. For the purposes of this Agreement, the term "Disclosing Party" will refer to either party in the case of each such party's disclosure of Confidential Information, and the term "Recipient" will refer to either party, as the case may be, in the case of each such party's receipt of Confidential Information.

1. **Definition of Confidential Information**

    1.1. "Confidential Information" means (subject to Sections 1.2 and 1.3) information that Disclosing Party provides to the Recipient, including, without limitation, information regarding Disclosing Party's technology, software, code, plans, specifications, marketing or promotion, customers, and practices and information received from others that Disclosing Party is obligated to treat as confidential.

    *[**Comment:** Many companies do not want the risk of obtaining Confidential Information of another party that is not documented. Therefore they insist that oral or visual disclosures be confirmed in writing. However, some consider written confirmation to be too burdensome. The text at the end of section 1.2 provides a choice of either approach.]*

    1.2. Information as described in paragraph 1.1 will be deemed Confidential Information only under the following circumstances: (a) if in written or tangible form, is stamped or marked as "proprietary" or "confidential" (or bears a similar legend denoting the Discloser's confidentiality interest therein), or (b) if in oral or visual form, is treated as confidential at the time of disclosure[, and is designated as confidential in a written memorandum to Recipient's primary representative within thirty (30) days of disclosure, summarizing the information disclosed] [, and is the type of information that the Recipient should reasonably have understood to be confidential].

    1.3. Confidential Information does not, however, include any information that: (i) is or subsequently becomes publicly available without Recipient's breach of any obligation owed Disclosing Party; (ii) became known to Recipient prior to Disclosing Party's disclosure of such information to Recipient; (iii) became known to Recipient from a source other than Disclosing Party other than by the breach of an obligation of confidentiality owed to Disclosing Party; or (iv) is independently developed by Recipient.

2. **Non-disclosure and Non-use of Confidential Information**

    2.1. Confidential Information is provided to the Recipient for review and evaluation only. No other use is permitted.

    2.2. Recipient will not disclose Confidential Information to anyone other than its employees [and agents] who legitimately need access to it for permitted use. Recipient will notify its employees [and agents] who are given access to Confidential Information that they have an obligation not to disclose Confidential Information and will take such steps as are reasonably necessary to insure compliance with this obligation.

2.3. Recipient will safeguard Confidential Information with reasonable security means at least equivalent to measures that it uses to safeguard its own confidential information. Recipient will store Confidential Information in a safe and secure location.

2.4. Recipient may make copies of Confidential Information only as is necessary for its evaluation process. Recipient will duplicate on any copy of Confidential Information all copyright, trademark, trade secret, confidentiality, and patent notices found on Confidential Information. Recipient will not reverse engineer any Confidential Information in hardware or software form. Recipient will not use the Confidential Information for any product design or development unless otherwise expressly agreed in writing.

2.5. The obligations regarding Confidential Information in this Agreement will apply [for ___ years after disclosure] [for so long as such information remains Confidential Information as provided in Section 1].

3. **Reservation of Rights.** No rights are granted by implication. In addition to the restrictions of this Agreement, Disclosing Party reserves its rights under any such patents, copyrights, trademarks, or trade secrets except as otherwise expressly provided in this Agreement.

4. [**Residuals.** The terms of confidentiality under this Agreement shall not be construed to limit either the Disclosing Party or the Recipient's right to independently develop or acquire products without use of the other party's Confidential Information. Further, the Recipient shall be free to use for any purpose the residuals resulting from access to or work with the Confidential Information of the Disclosing Party, provided that the Recipient shall not disclose the Confidential Information except as expressly permitted pursuant to the terms of this Agreement. The term "residuals" means information in intangible form, which is retained in memory by persons who have had access to the Confidential Information, including ideas, concepts, know-how or techniques contained therein. The Recipient shall not have any obligation to limit or restrict the assignment of such persons or to pay royalties for any

work resulting from the use of residuals. However, this Section shall not be deemed to grant to the Recipient a license under the Disclosing Party's copyrights or patents.]

5. [**Feedback.** Either party may from time to time provide suggestions, comments or other feedback to the other party with respect to Confidential Information provided originally by the other party (hereinafter "Feedback"). Both parties agree that all Feedback is and shall be entirely voluntary and shall not, absent separate agreement, create any confidentiality obligation for the Recipient, provided that the Recipient will not disclose the source of any feedback without the providing party's consent. Except as otherwise provided herein, each party shall be free to disclose, receive, and use Feedback as it sees fit, entirely without obligation of any kind to the other party. The foregoing shall not, however, affect either party's obligations hereunder with respect to Confidential Information of the other party and this Section shall not be deemed to grant to the Recipient a license under the Disclosing Party's copyrights or patents].

6. **No Warranty.** ALL CONFIDENTIAL INFORMATION IS PROVIDED "AS IS," WITHOUT ANY EXPRESS OR IMPLIED WARRANTY OF ANY KIND.

7. **Return of Confidential Information.** Within ten business days of receipt of Disclosing Party's written request or when negotiations or business relations between Disclosing Party and Recipient cease (whichever is earlier), Recipient will return to Disclosing Party all documents containing Confidential Information. All copies of Confidential Information made by Recipient will be turned over to Disclosing Party or destroyed. For purposes of this Section, the term "documents" includes any medium, including paper, disks, optical media, magnetic memory, and any other means of recording information. The Recipient will, upon request, certify in writing that it has complied with this Section.

8. **Equitable Relief.** Recipient hereby acknowledges that unauthorized disclosure or use of Confidential Information will cause immediate and irreparable harm to Disclosing Party. Accordingly, Disclosing Party will have the right to seek and obtain preliminary and final injunctive relief to enforce this Agreement in case of any actual or threatened breach, in addition to other rights and remedies that may be available to Disclosing Party.

9. [**Hiring Restraint.** From the Effective Date of this Agreement and continuing for one year after business discussions contemplated by this Agreement terminate (which, for the purposes of this Section will be presumed to be the situation if no business discussions under this Agreement have taken place for 30 days), each party agrees not to hire or attempt to hire executive, marketing, sales, or technical employees of the Company whose identity or qualification were disclosed to the other during the negotiations.]

10. **General Provisions**

   10.1. This Agreement constitutes the entire agreement of the parties concerning its subject matter and supersedes all prior or contemporaneous oral or written agreements concerning this subject.

   10.2. This Agreement may not be assigned by either party and neither party's obligations under this Agreement may be delegated without the prior written consent of the other party. Subject to such restriction, this Agreement is binding and inures to the benefit of the permitted successors and assigns.

   10.3. This Agreement may be amended only by a writing signed by both parties.

   10.4. This Agreement will be governed by and construed in accordance with the substantive laws of _____. The state and federal courts located in _____ will have exclusive jurisdiction and venue over any dispute arising from this Agreement or its subject matter.

So Agreed by the parties:

SoftCo, Inc.   Company: _____

By:_____   By:_____
(Name)   (Name)
(Title)   (Title)
(Date)   (Date)

Evaluation Agreement (Pro-Recipient)

6-2

Introductory Note

This simple evaluation agreement is drafted for the benefit of the recipient of software or other material for evaluation use. It is drafted as the form agreement of the fictitious software company SoftCo, Inc.

The company that uses this form promises very little—and that's the whole idea. The form expressly gives the recipient the right to develop products similar to those submitted for evaluation, and it gives no assurances of confidentiality. The person or company that submits information under this form has the protection of the copyright laws and (if applicable) patents, but nothing else.

Evaluation Agreement

IF YOU ACCEPT AND AGREE WITH ALL OF THE PROVISIONS OF THIS AGREEMENT, PLEASE SIGN THIS AGREEMENT AND RETURN IT (BY MAIL, FAX OR AS AN EMAIL PDF) TO SOFTCO, INC. ("SOFTCO") TOGETHER WITH A COPY OF YOUR MATERIAL FOR SUBMISSION. THIS AGREEMENT COVERS BOTH ELECTRONIC AND PHYSICAL SUBMISSION OF YOUR MATERIAL, INCLUDING ANY MATERIAL YOU SUBMIT BEFORE OR AFTER SIGNING AND RETURNING THIS AGREEMENT.

If you do not accept and agree with any provision or paragraph of the Agreement, do not submit your Material to SoftCo.

1. You represent that you are 18 years of age or older. If you are younger than 18, you should include with this Agreement a written consent from your parent or legal guardian for your entering into this Agreement.

2. You hereby authorize SoftCo to use and copy your program, content or other material ("Material") for evaluation. You agree that SoftCo owes you no compensation for submitting the Material to SoftCo. SoftCo may (but is not obligated to) decide to negotiate an agreement with you to exploit the Material for commercial purposes.

3. You represent and warrant (a) that you have all rights to provide the Material, (b) that your submission of the Material to SoftCo and SoftCo's copying and use for its review and evaluation of such Material will not violate or infringe any personal or property right of any person or entity and (c) that your Material does not constitute a defamation of any person or entity. You also represent that you are the sole owner of the Material and all rights therein and that it is your own original work. You agree to indemnify SoftCo and hold SoftCo harmless from any claim asserting actual or alleged infringement or violation of any third party rights that arises from the Material if used by SoftCo as permitted in this Agreement.

4. You represent that the Material you are submitting is not obscene, pornographic, defamatory, or illegal.

5. Your submission of the Material does not create any confidential or fiduciary relationship between you and SoftCo.

6. You represent that you have retained one or more copies of the Material in your possession. SoftCo is not obligated to return the Material. SoftCo will not be liable to you if any Materials are destroyed, damaged or misplaced.

7. SoftCo may, from time to time, receive submissions of material similar to yours, or we may be developing similar materials, content, ideas, or products. SoftCo does not agree to treat as confidential your Material, your ideas or any information which you may choose to disclose to us during the course of our evaluation whether or not marked as confidential or proprietary.

8. SoftCo's acceptance of your material for evaluation does not imply that SoftCo will market your material nor does it prevent us from marketing or developing other products which may be similar in idea or concept so long as we do not infringe your copyright or patent rights.

9. This Agreement will remain in effect indefinitely and covers all Materials that you may provide.

10. This Agreement is subject to the substantive laws of the state of _____. Any disputes or claims that you may have against SoftCo regarding this Agreement or the Material will be resolved exclusively by the state or federal courts located in the state of_____USA in the city of _____ , and you agree and submit to the exclusive jurisdiction of such courts.

11. This is a complete statement of the agreement of the parties and supersedes any other oral or written understanding or agreement.

By signing below, you accept and agree to the foregoing as a binding agreement between SoftCo and you.

_____
[*Signature*]

If you are an individual, print your name and address:

Print Name: _____

Address: _____

_____

Date: _____

If the party entering into this Agreement is a corporation or other business entity, print the name of the entity and its address and the name and title of officer or agent signing this Agreement:

Print Company Name _____

Print Signer's Name and Title: _____

Address: _____

Date: _____

Employee Agreement

Introductory Note

This is a form of Employee Agreement. You should review Chapter 7 before using it, and you may wish to seek advice of your own legal counsel because employment law has significant state-by-state variations.

This form includes both non-competition provisions and restraints on solicitation of other employees or customers.

As noted in Chapter 7, some states require, as condition of enforcing such restraints, that the employer make a payment to the employee in cash (or something else of value) as "consideration" for the restraint, particularly if the agreement is signed after employment begins.

If you are a California employer, you should know that California prohibits most non-competition restraints. California law on non-solicitation clauses is less clear, but it is possible that the non-solicitation restraints in the following form may need to be narrowed or modified to meet California requirements. Another California requirement is to give employees notice of California Labor Code Section 2870. There are analogous notice requirements in some other states. (These laws are discussed in Chapter 7.)

This form contains some optional and alternative provisions in brackets.

Employee Agreement

This Employee Agreement (the "Agreement") is entered into by and between *[name of employer corporation or entity]* ("Employer"), and the individual whose name appears on the signature page below (the "Employee"). This Agreement is effective as of the Effective Date (as defined below).

Purpose of This Agreement. Employer desires to employ Employee, and Employee desires to be employed by Employer subject to the terms and conditions contained in this Agreement. Employee and Employer agree that the following provisions are fair and appropriate for protection of the Employer's interests.

THEREFORE, in consideration of the mutual promises of this Agreement, and other good and valuable consideration, the receipt and sufficiency of which are acknowledged by the parties, Employer and Employee agree as follows:

1. **Definitions.** Capitalized terms used herein and not otherwise defined herein will have the meanings set forth below:

   1.1. "Affiliate" will mean, for a specified business entity, a business entity which directly or indirectly through one or more intermediaries, controls, is controlled by or is under common control with such entity.

   1.2. "Company" will mean Employer and all Affiliates of Employer.

   1.3. "Company Business" will mean the business and technical activities, products and services, and operations of the Company as presently conducted, included plans for expansion of the same, and such other additional activities, products and services, and operations as may be conducted or planned at any time during the Employment Period.

   1.4. "Confidential Information" means any information or data, whether in oral, graphic, written, optical, electronic, machine-readable, hard copy or any other form, possessed by, used by, or under the control of Company that is not generally available to the public. Confidential Information includes but is not limited to inventions, designs, data, source code, object code, programs, other works of authorship, know-how, trade secrets, techniques, ideas, discoveries, technical, marketing and business plans, customers, suppliers, pricing, profit margins, costs, products, and services.

   1.5. "Effective Date" is the earlier of (i) the beginning of Employee's employment with Company, (ii) the date and time at which any Confidential Information was, or is, first disclosed to Employee, or (iii) the date that both parties have signed this Agreement.

   1.6. "Intellectual Property Rights" will mean all copyrights, copyright registrations and copyright applications, trademarks, service marks, trade dress, trade names, trademark registrations and trademark applications, patentable inventions or discoveries, patents and patent applications, trade secret rights, and all other rights and interests existing, created or protectable under any intellectual property law of any nation.

1.7. "Restriction Period" will mean during the period of Employee's employment with the Company and for a period of _____ [months] [years] following the date on which Employee's employment with Company is terminated regardless of cause.

1.8. "Work Product" means any and all inventions, discoveries, original works of authorship, Intellectual Property Rights, developments, improvements, formulas, techniques, concepts, data and ideas (whether or not patentable or registrable under patent copyright, or similar statute) made, conceived, created, discovered, or reduced to practice by Employee, either alone or jointly with others, that (i) result from work performed by Employee for Company or are created in the course of his or her employment, (ii) are made by use of the equipment, supplies, facilities, or Confidential Information of Company or are made, conceived or completed, wholly or in part, during hours in which Employee is employed by Company, or (iii) are related to the Company Business or the actual or demonstrably anticipated business plan, research or development of Company.

2. **Employment**

2.1. Employee acknowledges that he or she is and will be employed by Company "at-will" and that either Company or Employee will have the right to terminate Employee's employment at any time for any reason or for no reason at all. The period of time during which Employee is employed by Company is sometimes referred to herein as the "Employment Period."

2.2. Employee acknowledges that his or her employment with the Company constitutes adequate consideration for this Agreement. [In addition, Employee acknowledges actual receipt of the sum of $_____ in connection with and as consideration for this Agreement.]

3. **Confidential Information**

3.1. Employee acknowledges and agrees that Confidential Information constitutes a valuable asset of Company and is and will be the sole property of Company. Where Employee has any doubt whether information is Confidential Information, Employee will request a determination from his or her supervision.

3.2. Employee agrees to preserve and protect the confidentiality and security of Confidential Information. At all times during and after Employee's employment with Company, Employee will hold in trust, keep confidential and not disclose to any third party or make any use of, the Confidential Information, except as may be authorized by the Company in the course of Employee's employment.

3.3. Employee agrees to abide by policies established by Company for the protection of Confidential Information, and to take reasonable security precautions to safeguard Confidential Information, including without limitation, the protection of documents from theft, unauthorized duplication and discovery of contents, and restrictions on access by other persons.

3.4. Employee acknowledges that unauthorized use or disclosure of Confidential Information will be prejudicial to the interests of Company or the entities with which Company has business relationships and may be an invasion of privacy or a misappropriation or improper disclosure of trade secrets.

3.5. Employee agrees that all documents containing Confidential Information, whether produced by Employee or others, are at all times the property of Company.

4. **Third Party Information**

4.1. Employee acknowledges that Company has received and in the future may receive confidential or proprietary information from third parties, subject to a duty on Company's part to maintain the confidentiality of the information and to use it only for certain limited purposes. Employee agrees to hold all such confidential or proprietary information in the strictest confidence in compliance with the terms of any agreement or other obligation Company may have with such third parties, and not to disclose it to any person, firm or corporation or to use it except as necessary in carrying out Employee's duties for Company, consistent with the terms of any agreement Company may have with such third parties.

5. **Return of Company Property.** Upon termination of employment with Company for any reason, Employee will promptly deliver to Company all Company documents and materials pertaining to (i) Employee's employment, (ii) the Confidential Information of Company or the other entities with which Company has relationships, or (iii) Work Product (as defined above), whether prepared by Employee or otherwise coming into Employee's possession or control. Employee also agrees to return to Company all equipment, files, software programs and other personal property belonging to Company on separation from employment. Employee will not retain any written or other tangible materials (in hard copy or electronic form) that evidence, contain or reflect Confidential Information or Work Product of Company. Employee agrees, on or before the date of termination of employment, to execute and deliver to Employer a Termination Certification in the form set forth as Exhibit A to this Agreement.

6. **Work Product**

    6.1. *Assignment.* All Work Product is and will be the sole property of Company. Employee hereby assigns to Company, without royalty or further consideration to Employee, all right, title, and interest Employee may have, or may acquire, in and to all Work Product including but not limited to all Intellectual Property Rights. Employee agrees that Company or its designee will be the sole owner of all domestic and foreign patents, patent rights, copyrights, and other Intellectual Property Rights included in or pertaining to all Work Product.

    6.2. *Disclosure.* Employee will promptly disclose all Work Product that consists of inventions, discoveries, developments, improvements, formulas, techniques, concepts, data or ideas to Company in writing. Employee agrees to keep adequate and current written records of all such Work Product, in the form of notes, sketches, drawings, electronic records and/or other reports, which records are, and will remain, the property of Company and will be available to Company at all times.

    6.3. *Copyrights.* Employee further agrees that all copyrightable materials that Employee authors, creates, modifies, or prepares, wholly or in part, will be, to the maximum extent permitted by law, work-made-for-hire for the Company under copyright law, and to the extent not work-made-for-hire are hereby assigned to the Company.

6.4. *Execution of Documents.* Whenever requested by Company, Employee will promptly sign and deliver to Company, both during and after employment, any and all applications, assignments and other documents that Company considers necessary or desirable in order to: (a) assign, apply for, obtain, and maintain letters patent or other forms of Intellectual Property protection or registration in the United States and for other countries with regard to Work Product, (b) assign and convey to Company or its designee the sole and exclusive right, title, and interest in and to Work Product, (c) provide evidence regarding Work Product that Company considers necessary or desirable, and (d) confirm or perfect Company's ownership of the Work Product, all without royalty or any other further consideration to Employee.

6.5. *Assistance to Company.* Whenever requested by Company, both during and after employment, Employee will assist Company, at Company's expense, in assigning, obtaining, maintaining, defending, registering and from time to time enforcing, in any and all countries, Company's right to the Work Product including but not limited to Intellectual Property Rights. This assistance may include, without limitation, testifying in a suit or other proceeding and executing all documents deemed by Company to be necessary or convenient for such purposes. If Company requires assistance from Employee after termination of Employee's employment, Employee will be compensated for time actually spent in providing assistance at an hourly rate equivalent to Employee's salary or wages at the time of termination of employment together with Employee's reasonable expenses of providing such assistance.

6.6. *Power of Attorney.* For use in the case that Company cannot obtain Employee's signature on any document that Company considers necessary or desirable in order to assign, apply for, prosecute, obtain, or enforce any patent, copyright or other right or protection relating to any Work Product, whether due to Employee's mental or physical incapacity, non-cooperation, unavailability, or any other reason, Employee hereby irrevocably designates and appoints Company and each of its duly authorized officers and agents as Employee's agent and attorney-in-fact to act for, and on Employee's behalf, to execute and file any such document and to do all other lawfully permitted acts to further the assignment, transfer to Company, application, registration, prosecution, issuance, and enforcement of patents, trademarks, trade secrets, copyrights, or other rights or protections, with the same force and effect as if executed and delivered by Employee.

6.7. *Excluded Work Product*. Employee represents that any inventions, original works of authorship, discoveries, concepts or ideas, if any ("Excluded Work Product") to which Employee presently has any right, title or interest, and which were previously conceived either wholly or in part by Employee, and that Employee desires to exclude from the operation of this Agreement are identified on Exhibit B of this Agreement. Employee represents that the list contained in Exhibit B is complete to the best of Employee's knowledge.

6.8. [*California Labor Code Section 2870.* This Section 6 does not apply to any Work Product to the extent that it is subject to the provisions of Section 2870 of the California Labor Code as described in Exhibit C to this Agreement.]

7. **Non-Competition; Non-Solicitation**

7.1. [*Non-Competition.* During the Restriction Period, Employee will not engage or become interested, directly or indirectly, as an owner, employee, director, partner, consultant, through stock ownership, investment of capital, lending of money or property, rendering of services, or otherwise, either alone or in association with others, in the operation, management or supervision of any type of business or enterprise that at any time during the Restriction Period is in competition with the Company Business, except that this provision will not be breached by Employee's ownership of shares in a publicly-traded corporation or publicly-traded mutual fund or publicly-traded limited partnership in which Employee's ownership interest is five percent (5%) or less. [Employee acknowledges that the scope of the markets in which Company competes is global and therefore agrees that no geographic limitations on this non-competition provision of this Section will apply.] [The geographic scope of the limitations set forth in this Section will extend to every geographic market, state, province or country in which Company or any Affiliate does business during the term of this Agreement or in which the Company or any Affiliate was, during the term of this Agreement, actively planning or preparing to do business.]

7.2. *Non-Solicitation.* During the Restriction Period, Employee will not, directly or indirectly, whether on behalf of himself or anyone else: (i) solicit or accept orders from any present or past customer of the Company for a product or service offered or sold by, or competitive with a product or service offered or sold by, the Company; (ii) induce or attempt to induce any such customer to reduce such customer's purchases from the Company; (iii) use for his or her benefit or disclose the name and/or requirements of any such customer to any third party; or (iv) solicit any of the Company's employees to leave the employ of the Company or hire anyone who is an employee of the Company.

7.3. *Judicial Modifications.* If any restriction set forth in this Section is found by a court of competent jurisdiction to be unenforceable because it extends for too long a period of time or over too great a range of activities or in too broad a geographic area, it will be enforced only over the maximum period of time, range of activities or geographic area for which it may be enforceable.

8. **Remedies of Company**

8.1. *Injunction.* Employee acknowledges that immediate and irreparable damage will result to the Company and its business and properties if Employee breaches the obligations of this Agreement regarding Confidential Information or the provisions set forth in Section 6 or Section 7 of this Agreement and that the remedy at law for any such breach will be inadequate. Accordingly, in addition to any other remedies and damages available, the Company shall be entitled to injunctive relief without the necessity of posting a bond, and Employee may be specifically compelled to comply with such obligations under this Agreement.

8.2. *Expenses.* Company shall be entitled to reimbursement by Employee for all costs and expenses, including reasonable attorneys' fees, which Company may incur in connection with the enforcement of its rights regarding Confidential Information or under Sections 6 and 7 of this Agreement.

9. **Notices and Other Communications.** All notices and other communications will be in writing and will be deemed effectively given upon personal delivery, and in the case where delivery is made by an established courier delivery service, delivery will be deemed to occur on the day after delivery to such

delivery service, upon confirmed completion of transmission in the case where such notice is transmitted by telecopy, or on the fifth (5th) day following mailing by registered or certified mail, return receipt requested, postage prepaid, addressed (a) if to Employee, at his or her address set forth below his or her signature, and (b) if to Company at the following address: *[indicate address for notice]* or addresses as the parties may specify by a written notice to the other from time to time.

10. **Entire Agreement; Amendment; Survival.** This Agreement constitutes the entire agreement between the parties and supersedes all prior agreements and understandings, whether written or oral, relating to the subject matter of this Agreement. This Agreement may be amended or modified only by a written instrument executed by both Company and Employee. The provisions of this Agreement (except for Section 2.1) will survive the termination of Employee's employment and the assignment of this Agreement by Company to any successor-in-interest or other assignee.

11. **Governing Law.** This Agreement will be construed, interpreted and enforced in accordance with the laws of the state of _____, not including its choice of law provisions. Both parties agree to jurisdiction and venue in the state and federal courts located in _____ with regard to this Agreement and its subject matter.

12. **Successors and Assigns.** This Agreement will be binding upon and inure to the benefit of both parties and their respective successors and assigns; provided, however, that the obligations of Employee are personal and will not be assigned by Employee.

13. **Miscellaneous.** No delay or omission by Company in exercising any right under this Agreement will operate as a waiver of that or any other right. A waiver or consent given by Company on any one occasion will be effective only in that instance and will not be construed as a bar or waiver of any right on any other occasion. In case any provision of this Agreement will be invalid, illegal or otherwise unenforceable, the validity, legality and enforceability of the remaining provisions will in no way be affected or impaired.

EMPLOYEE ACKNOWLEDGES AND UNDERSTANDS THAT THIS AGREEMENT AFFECTS HIS OR HER RIGHTS TO INVENTIONS HE OR SHE MAKES DURING HIS OR HER EMPLOYMENT BY THE COMPANY, [CONTAINS NON-COMPETITION AND] NON-SOLICITATION PROVISIONS, AND RESTRICTS

HIS OR HER RIGHTS TO DISCLOSE OR USE THE COMPANY'S CONFIDEN-
TIAL INFORMATION DURING SUCH EMPLOYMENT AND THEREAFTER.

This Agreement is executed as a binding agreement of the parties as of the
Effective Date.

Employee

Name: _____

Address: _____

Signature: _____ Date: _____

[Employer Name] by its authorized agent:

Name: _____

Address: _____

Signature: _____ Date: _____

Exhibit A

Termination Certification

This is to certify that I do not have in my possession, nor have I failed to return, any devices, records, data, notes, reports, proposals, lists, correspondence, specifications, drawings, sketches, materials, equipment, other documents or property or any reproductions of any of these items belonging to Company, its subsidiaries, Affiliates, successors or assigns (collectively "the Company").

I further certify that I have complied with, and will continue to comply with, all the terms of Employee Agreement that I signed with the Company, including, without limitation, those that relate to Work Product, Confidential Information, [Non-Competition], and Non-Solicitation of customers and Company employees.

Upon the termination of my employment with Company, I will be employed by _____ and will be working in connection with the following technologies and business areas: _____.

Employee Name: _____

Date: _____

Signature: _____

Address for Notifications: _____

_____

_____

Exhibit B

Employee Statement Regarding Employee's Prior Work Product

Except as set forth below, I acknowledge that at this time I have not made or reduced to practice (alone or jointly with others) any Work Product relevant to the subject matter of my employment with Company except those (if any) listed below:

[Employee to list any applicable Work Product or write "None".]

Employee certifies that the foregoing is true, accurate and complete.

Employee Name: _____

Date: _____

Signature: _____

[Exhibit C

Notification to Employee of California Labor Code Section 2870

The provisions of this Agreement regarding ownership of Work Product do not apply to Employee's inventions which qualify for protection under California Labor Code ("Section 2870"). As currently in effect, Section 2870 covers Employee's inventions for which no equipment, supplies, facility or trade secret information of Company was used and which were developed entirely in Employee's own time, and (i) which do not relate, at the time of conception or reduction to practice of the invention, to the business of Company, or to Company's actual or demonstrably anticipated research or development, or (ii) which do not result from any work performed by Employee for Company. Employee agrees to disclose to Company during the term of his or her employment in confidence each such invention in order to permit the Company to make a determination as to compliance by Employee with this Agreement. Employee acknowledges that it is his or her burden to prove to Employer that Section 2870 applies.

Employee acknowledges receipt of this notice.

Employee Name: _____

Date: _____

Signature: _____]

Software Development Agreement

10-1

Introductory Note

This is a sample software development agreement. This is a "long form" that is designed for substantial custom software development. It could also be used for major customization of the Developer's pre-existing application. This is a relatively balanced form, but some variations favor one party or the other.

This draft includes many provisions that commonly occur in these agreements, including some common variants and alternatives (but certainly does not have all possible variants). There are further variations discussed in Chapters 9 and 10 of this book. Text in brackets within sections is also optional. There are some combinations and permutations that work together and some that will not make sense when combined, so you need to be sure you think through how sections work with one another.

We left the Schedule letters (or numbers) to be filled in because there are many choices in this text.

Software Development Agreement

This Software Development Agreement ("Agreement") is effective as of *[insert date]* (the "Effective Date") between _____ ("Customer") with an office at _____ and_____ ("Developer") with an office at _____.

Purpose of This Agreement

This is an Agreement for Developer to develop software for Customer in accordance with the terms set forth below.

Wherefore, intending to bound, the parties agree as follows:

1. **Definitions**

   *[**Comment:** Definitions in any agreement need careful attention because they often depart from the "plain meaning" of a word or phrase or resolve ambiguities in ways that favor one side or the other. Additional definitions can appear in the text and in schedules. Depending on choices that you make in the remainder of the Agreement, you may need to add to these definitions or delete some of them.]*

   As used in this Agreement, the following definitions will apply:

   1.1. "Affiliate" means any corporate entity that controls, is controlled by or is under the common control of a party to this Agreement.

   1.2. "Defect" means, with respect to any Deliverable, any material deviation from the Specification[or any defect in quality or operation].

   1.3. "Deliverables" are the items that are specified in the Specification and the Milestone Schedule as items to be delivered to Customer.

   1.4. "Intellectual Property" means all inventions, discoveries, patents, trademarks, domain names, design rights, copyrights, database rights, know-how, trade or business names, and other similar rights (in each case whether or not registered or registerable and including all applications for any registerable rights) throughout the world, for the full duration of such rights.

   1.5. "Milestone" means each stage of development of the Program as set out alongside a Milestone Date in the Milestone Schedule.

   1.6. "Milestone Date" means each of the dates for achieving a Milestone in the Milestone Schedule.

   1.7. "Milestone Payment" means each of the Milestone-based payments set forth in the Milestone Schedule.

   1.8. "Milestone Schedule" means the delivery and payment schedule for the Program [as described in Schedule _____] [as developed under this Agreement], as it may be amended from time to time by written agreement of the parties hereto.

1.9. "Program" will mean the computer program entitled [*name of program*] to be developed by Developer, which will consist of all Deliverables [including the User Manual], as stated in the Specification and the Milestone Schedule.

1.10. "Services" means Developer's services to be provided under this Agreement.

1.11. "Specification" means the specifications for the Program as set forth in Schedule _____, with any modifications that may be agreed upon by the parties in writing. [After the parties' agreement on the Detailed Specification prepared under this Agreement, the term "Specification" will refer to the Detailed Specification.]

1.12. "User Manual" means a manual containing instructions for end users that enables them to operate the Program.

[Optional Provision:]

2. **Preparation of Detailed Specification**

    2.1. Developer will prepare a detailed specification ("Detailed Specification") for the Program on or before [date]. The Detailed Specification will include, at a minimum:

        2.1.1. a detailed statement of the Program's functionality.

        2.1.2. a specification of third party products and technologies to be included in the Program.

        2.1.3. a Milestone Schedule for development.

        2.1.4. the total development cost and expected expenses.

        2.1.5. a detailed schedule of Milestones and Milestone Payments.

    2.2. After submission of the Detailed Specification documents mentioned in the previous Section, the Customer may accept or reject the same in writing. [Failure of Customer to reject the Detailed Specification in _____ days will constitute acceptance.]

    2.3. In the case of rejection of the Detailed Specification, the parties will confer in good faith regarding changes to the Detailed Specification. If there is no written agreement on a Detailed Specification in a further _____ days, either party may terminate this Agreement without fault. In case of such a termination, each party will be discharged of further obligations except as follows:

2.3.1. The parties will remain obligated under provisions regarding Confidential Information (as stated below).

2.3.2. Developer will be paid for the Detailed Specification on the following basis: [*describe compensation; it may be fixed fee or hourly with a cap*].

2.3.3. [Customer will be free to use the versions of the Detailed Specification supplied by Developer for any purpose, provided that Developer makes no warranty as to results that may be obtained from such versions of the Detailed Specification, and Developer will be deemed to supply the Detailed Specification "AS IS."]

3. **Development of Program**

[***Comment:*** *In this section, the Developer undertakes a duty to create the Program in accordance with the Specification.*]

3.1. [On the Effective Date or within [*number*] of days thereafter] [upon acceptance of the Detailed Specification], Developer will begin work [and will use reasonable efforts] to develop the Program.

4. **Change Orders**

[***Comment:*** *Disputes arise from changes to the Specification that are not documented. Often customers will ask for additional features without expecting to pay more. Developers will do extra work as a result and expect extra pay. This draft requires the parties to negotiate changes in specifications, payment, and delivery schedules.*]

4.1. Either Customer or Developer may propose a "Change Order." Change Orders are effective when signed by both parties. The parties agree to include in each Change Order as many of the following as are relevant:

4.1.1. Description of the change.

4.1.2. Description of the additional or changed services to be performed by Developer.

4.1.3. Effects of the change on the Specification.

4.1.4. New or changed Customer obligations.

4.1.5. Effects on the Milestone Schedule, including dates and pricing of services.

4.1.6. Changes in acceptance criteria.

4.2. Customer may not require work or features not set forth in the Specification unless agreed to in writing in a Change Order. Developer will not be compensated, other than as stated in the Agreement, unless such additional payments are agreed to in a Change Order in advance in writing or unless otherwise agreed in writing.

[Optional Provision:]

5. **Resources to Be Provided to Developer**

   [Comment: Sometimes the Developer needs technical or business information from the Customer to do its work. Sometimes the Developer needs access to the Customer's computer system or to a code base in the Customer's possession. The following clause deals with these and other such requirements. Where the Customer's cooperation is substantial or it has to supply software, data, or content for the Developer to use, these requirements could be put in a separate schedule.]

   5.1. Customer will supply to Developer all information and resources that Developer will reasonably require to carry out the work required by this Agreement, including: [*include list or refer to a schedule of Customer tasks*].

   5.2. [Customer grants to the Developer a non-exclusive, non-transferable, and limited license to use the Customer's software and other materials solely as necessary to perform its obligations under this Agreement.]

6. **Responsibility for Employees**

   6.1. Developer is solely responsible for paying the salaries and wages of its employees, for ensuring that all required tax withholdings are made, and for ensuring that each employee has the legal right to work in the United States. Developer further agrees that it is solely responsible for workers' compensation insurance. Developer will defend, indemnify and hold harmless Customer, its affiliates, and their respective officers, directors, employees, servants and agents from any cost, including attorneys' fees, and any liability that arises from Developer's breach of these obligations.

7. Subcontractors

[Option 1. Subcontractors Restricted.]

7.1. [Unless otherwise authorized in writing by Customer, Developer will provide all Services by use of its own employees. Developer will use subcontractors under this Agreement only with Customer's express prior written permission.]

[Option 2. Subcontractors Permitted.]

7.2. Developer may retain qualified subcontractors to work under this Agreement. Developer warrants the performance and full compliance with this Agreement by each subcontractor. Developer will be responsible for all acts and omissions of each subcontractor and each subcontractor's staff, as if they were Developer's own acts and omissions.

8. Assigned Personnel

8.1. "Personnel" means those individuals engaged by the Developer, whether as employees or (if permitted) as subcontractors or the subcontractors' employees.

8.2. [The Personnel assigned to work under this Agreement will be those listed on Schedule _____. The Developer will not reassign such Personnel to any other work without Customer's prior written consent. If any such Personnel are no longer available to Developer, Developer will supply equally qualified replacements, which will be assigned to work under this Agreement only with Customer's prior written consent.]

8.3. Developer will ensure that its employees and permitted subcontractors will, whenever on Customer's premises (or on any Customer's client's premises or other location), obey all applicable work and safety rules.

8.4. Developer has obtained and will at all times obtain and maintain in effect non-disclosure, assignment of rights and other appropriate agreements with its employees and (if use of subcontractors is permitted) subcontractors sufficient to protect Customer's Confidential Information and sufficient to allow it to provide Customer with the assignments and licenses provided for herein. Such agreements must contain terms and conditions no less restrictive than the terms and conditions set forth in this Agreement. [Upon Customer's request, Developer will cause all employees and subcontractor staff members engaged under this Agreement to sign Customer's form of Intellectual Property Transfer and Confidentiality Agreement, as issued by Customer from time to time.]

*[**Comment:** The final text (in brackets) is designed to obtain from each member of the Developer's team an obligation to assign intellectual property. This is prudent if the development work is likely to result in patentable inventions, because a company that wants to patent an invention must get the individual inventor(s) to assign the patent rights.]*

9. **Delivery and Acceptance of Deliverables**

   *[**Comment**: The following provision mandates delivery within dates specified in the Milestone Schedule. Optional language allows the Developer some flexibility in the meeting deadlines. There are many ways to write provisions under which the Customer may accept or reject the Milestones. The version that follows provides a time frame for Customer's acceptance and allows a cure period if the Program is rejected. As an option, this version also allows the Customer to accept a defective Program and to have Defects fixed at the Developer's expense.*

   There is an optional provision stating that Customer's "productive use" of a Program is deemed acceptance. This clause is used by Developers to avoid the Customer using the Program in its business while claiming it is defective and refusing to make the final payments.]

   9.1. Developer will deliver various Deliverables at the times and in the manner specified in the Milestone Schedule. [At its option, Developer may extend the due dates of the Milestone Schedule by giving written notice to the Customer provided that the total of all such extensions will not exceed [*specify number*] days.]

   9.2. Each Deliverable that consists of software [will be delivered in binary form only][will be delivered in binary form together with source code, programming documentation sufficient to permit replication of the binary Deliverables, and any relevant Developer proprietary programming tools].

   9.3. [If Developer fails to make timely delivery of any Deliverable as specified in the Milestone Schedule, Customer may give Developer notice of the failure. After such notice, Developer will have [*specify number*] days to make the specified delivery. Failure to submit the Deliverables within such period will be a material breach that will entitle Customer to terminate this Agreement in accordance with the provisions on termination.]

9.4. Customer may inspect and test each of the Deliverables when received to determine if it [substantially] conforms to the requirements of the Specification. [Testing will be in accordance with the testing procedures specified in *[Name of Testing Procedure Document or Schedule]*]. [Customer will not unreasonably withhold acceptance.]

9.5. [Any Deliverable not rejected in *[specify number]* days will be deemed accepted.] If any Deliverable is rejected, Customer will give Developer reasonably detailed written notice of the rejection and the reasons for rejection. Developer will then have *[specify number]* days to cure deficiencies. After resubmission within such *[specify number]* day period, Customer may again inspect the Deliverable to confirm that it [substantially] conforms to requirements of the Specification. [If the resubmitted Deliverable is not rejected in the *[specify number]* days after resubmission, the Deliverable will be deemed accepted.] [Appropriate adjustments in the dates that Milestones are due will be made for delays caused by Customer's delays in carrying out its obligations.]

9.6. If the resubmitted Deliverable does not [substantially] conform to the requirements of this Agreement, the failure will be a material breach that will entitle Customer to terminate this Agreement in accordance with the provisions of this Agreement regarding termination. If the resubmitted Deliverable is rejected, Customer will give notice to Developer stating the reasons for rejection.

9.7. [Notwithstanding the foregoing, acceptance will be deemed to have occurred if Customer makes Productive Use of the Program for a period of more than *[specify number]* days (not including acceptance test use in accordance with any written acceptance plan agreed to by the parties in writing). "Productive Use" means use in Customer's business.]

[Optional Provision:]

9.8. In case of termination by Customer for Developer's failure to provide Deliverables as required by this Agreement or for Developer's providing Deliverables that are properly and finally rejected by Customer, Customer will pay for completed Milestones only. Developer will deliver to

Customer all work in process, including binary code, source code and any relevant proprietary Developer tools, all of which will be deemed provided "AS IS" and "WITHOUT WARRANTY" but with all rights granted to Customer regarding ownership and/or exploitation otherwise provided for in this Agreement. [Remedies expressly provided in this Agreement for termination under such circumstances will be Customer's sole and exclusive remedies for such breach.]

[Optional Provision:]

9.9. In case of termination by Customer for Developer's failure to provide Deliverables as required by this Agreement or for Developer's providing Deliverables that are properly and finally rejected by Customer, Developer will refund to Customer [all] [*specify percentage or other refund formula*] of amounts paid by Customer under this Agreement as liquidated damages for such breach. [Remedies expressly provided in this Agreement for termination under such circumstances will be Customer's sole and exclusive remedies for such breach.]

[Optional Provision:]

9.10. As an alternative to termination of this Agreement, if Developer has failed to complete development and/or to cure Defects as required in this Agreement, Customer, at its option, may accept the Program as nonconforming. If it does so, it will give prompt notice to Developer stating the known Defects, and may withhold and deduct, from amounts otherwise due and payable to Developer for development of the Program, the amount of reasonable out-of-pocket costs to correct, modify, and/or complete the Program in accordance with the Specification. From time to time, and as soon as is practicable, Customer will provide Developer with notice of all sums withheld and expended and will turn over to Developer all funds withheld that are not so applied when such remedial work is completed. Such remedy [will be Customer's sole and exclusive remedy for failure to deliver the Program in accordance with this Agreement] [will be in addition to any other remedies that may apply].

10. **Payment**

[***Comment:*** *The following text sets a time limit for payments and a remedy if prompt payment is not made.*]

10.1. Customer will pay Developer the amount due upon the execution of this Agreement as specified in the Milestone Schedule. Upon acceptance of each Deliverable, Customer will pay Developer the amounts as specified in the Milestone Schedule. Payment will be due within _____ (_____) days of acceptance of each Deliverable. Payment by mail will be deemed made [when mailed] [when received].

10.2. Payments for any fee or amount other than Milestone Payments under this Agreement will be due _____ (_____) days after invoice or other written request for payment.

10.3. If any payment is not made as required, Developer may give notice of the failure to pay. The failure to pay, if not cured within _____ (_____) days after notice, will entitle Developer, at its option, to suspend work and/or terminate this Agreement in accordance with the provisions upon termination of this Agreement.

10.4. Payments not received within _____ (_____) days of their due date will be subject to late charges of one (1%) per month, or if lower, at the highest legal rate.

[Optional Provision:]

11. **Early and Late Performance**

11.1. *Early Delivery.* If Developer provides Final Deliverables (as defined in the Milestone Schedule) suitable for acceptance on or before [*specify earlier than otherwise scheduled date*], then the final Milestone Payment will be increased by _____.

11.2. *Late Delivery.* In the event that Final Deliverables suitable for acceptance are not provided to Customer until [date] or thereafter, then (in addition to other remedies that may apply) the final Milestone Payment will be decreased by [*specify amount*] for each day's delay, provided that the maximum cumulative decrease in such Milestone Payment cannot be more than [*specify percentage*]. Developer will not incur any reduced payment to the extent that delays are caused by Customer, by a third party vendor, or a Force Majeure event.

12. **Intellectual Property; Grant of License**

[**Comment:** *Option 1 provides that the Customer obtains all Intellectual Property that the Developer creates in the engagement and all interests that the Developer has* *to provide in the Deliverables. The only exception in this version is the Developer retains ownership of Developer Background Technology—which is limited to technology that the Developer has from before or outside of this Agreement. If there is no relevant Developer Background Technology, that exception can be omitted.*

Option 2 provides that the application will be owned by the Developer and licensed to the Customer. This is a provision that a Developer will be most likely to obtain when (a) the Program is largely based on Developer's pre-existing code base or (b) the Customer does not have any business reason to obtain sole control of the Program. If the Developer provides binary code only, it will want to include a "no reverse engineering" and "no service bureau use" provision as provided below.]

[Option 1. Transfer of Ownership, Except for Developer Background Technology]

12.1. "Customer Technology" means software, materials, software development tools, supplies, proprietary information, work product, files, technology, related scripting and any related Intellectual Property owned or provided by Customer.

12.2. "Developer Background Technology" means Developer's software, materials, software development tools, supplies, proprietary information, work product, files, technology, related scripting and programming and any related Intellectual Property that Developer owned on the Effective Date of this Agreement or that Developer creates or acquires independently of Developer's services under this Agreement.

12.3. [Conditioned upon Customer's payment of all amounts due to Developer,] Customer will be the sole owner of all Intellectual Property created by or for Developer under this Agreement. Subject to the paragraph below with regard to Copyrighted Works, Developer will assign, and does hereby assign, to Customer all of Developer's present and future right, title, and interest in all such Intellectual Property.

12.4. With regard to any works subject to copyright ("Copyrighted Works") created under this Agreement or included in any Deliverable (other than Developer Background Technology), [conditioned upon Customer's payment of amounts due to Developer,] Developer agrees that, to the maximum extent permitted by law, Copyrighted Works are and will be "works made for hire" for the benefit of Customer, and to the extent not "works made for hire," Developer hereby assigns such rights exclusively to Customer.

12.5. Customer (and Customer's suppliers, if applicable) owns and will continue to own the Customer Technology (including all Intellectual Property in them), and this Agreement will not transfer any ownership of such Customer Technology to the Developer. Except for Developer Background Technology, Customer will own all the Deliverables (including all Intellectual Property in them).

12.6. The Developer owns and will continue to own the Developer Background Technology (including all of Developer's Intellectual Property in them). Developer will grant and does hereby grant Customer a perpetual paid-up sublicensable license under Developer Background Technology to use, alter, distribute, make, have made, copy or otherwise exploit any Deliverables and Services or any derivatives of the Deliverables.

12.7. [Conditioned upon Customer's payment of amounts due to Developer,] Developer will, upon request of Customer, execute, acknowledge, deliver and file any and all documents necessary or useful to vest in Customer all rights allocated under this Section or to transfer, perfect, obtain, confirm and enforce any such rights and will cause its Personnel to do the same. [Developer hereby irrevocably designates and appoints Customer and its duly authorized officers and agents as its agent and attorney-in-fact, to act for and in its behalf, in the event Customer is unable, after reasonable efforts, to secure its signature on any application for patents, copyright or trademark registration or other documents regarding any legal protection, to execute and file any such application or applications or other documents and to do all other lawfully permitted acts to register, transfer, perfect, obtain, confirm and enforce patents, copyrights or trademarks or any other legal protection with the same legal force and effect as if executed by it.]

12.8. Upon transfer of such rights, Customer may register the copyright to the Program [and any derivative work] in any and all countries and jurisdictions, and take such further steps as it deems fit to provide legal protection to intellectual property relating to the Program.

[Option 2. Developer Grants a License Only]

12.9. Developer and its suppliers will own all rights to the Program. This Agreement grants Customer license rights only. [Conditioned upon Customer's payment of amounts due to Developer,] Developer grants

Customer the worldwide, non-exclusive, perpetual right, solely for its own internal business operations:

12.9.1. To install and use the Programs on one [or more] computer[s] [and on testing and backup computers].

12.9.2. To use the User Manual and any training materials solely for purposes of supporting Customer's use of the Program.

12.9.3. To permit third parties (such as consultants, contractors and system integrators), so long as they are subject to a reasonable written confidentiality agreement, to install, integrate, and implement the Program.

12.9.4. To copy the Program for the purpose of installation and licensed use and to make a reasonable number of backup copies.

12.9.5. To copy the User Manual for internal use.

12.10. [Customer will not: (a) copy the Program except as expressly authorized in this Agreement; (b) create derivative works of or otherwise modify the Program, (c) decompile, disassemble or reverse engineer (except as and to the extent permitted by applicable local law) the Program, or (d) use the Program to provide remote access, software-as-a-service, service bureau or similar services to third parties.]

[Optional Provision:]

13. **Exclusivity**

[Comment: If the Program is licensed only, the Customer may want assurances that, for a period of time, it will not be licensed to others.]

13.1. For a period of _____ years from the Effective Date of this Agreement, Developer will not grant to any competitor of Customer any right to use the Program developed by Developer for Customer hereunder, or any portion or derivative of the Program, without the prior written consent of Customer.

[Comment: Regardless if the Program is transferred to the Customer or only licensed, the Customer may want assurances that the Developer will not supply similar software to competitors.]

13.2. For a period of _____ years from the Effective Date of this Agreement, Developer will not supply or agree to supply to any party other than Customer computer software with functionality similar to the Program or software that will or is likely to be competitive with the Program.

14. **Confidentiality**

14.1. "Confidential Information" means non-public information, technical data or know-how of a party and/or its Affiliates, which is furnished directly or indirectly to the other party in written or tangible form in connection with this Agreement. Oral disclosure will also be deemed Confidential Information if it would reasonably be considered to be of a confidential nature or if it is confirmed at the time of disclosure to be confidential. [Conditioned upon Customer's payments of amounts due to Developer,] Confidential Information created by Developer under this Agreement will be deemed to be the Confidential Information of Customer and may be used only for the purposes of this Agreement.]

14.2. Notwithstanding the foregoing, Confidential Information does not include information which is: (i) already in the possession of the receiving party and not subject to a confidentiality obligation to the providing party; (ii) independently developed by the receiving party; (iii) publicly disclosed through no fault of the receiving party; (iv) rightfully received by the receiving party from a third party that is not under any obligation to keep such information confidential; (v) approved for release by written agreement with the disclosing party; or (vi) disclosed pursuant to the requirements of law, regulation, or court order, provided that the receiving party will promptly inform the providing party of any such requirement and cooperate with any attempt to procure a protective order or similar treatment.

14.3. Neither party will use the other party's Confidential Information except as reasonably required for the performance of this Agreement. Each party will hold in confidence the other party's Confidential Information by means that are no less restrictive than those used for its own confidential materials. Each party agrees not to disclose the other party's Confidential Information to anyone other than its employees or permitted subcontractors who are bound by confidentiality obligations and who need to know the same to perform such party's obligations hereunder. [The confidentiality obligations set forth in this Section will survive [for _____ (_____) years after the termination or expiration of this Agreement.]

14.4. Upon termination or expiration of this Agreement, except as otherwise agreed in writing or otherwise stated in this Agreement, each party will, upon the request of the disclosing party, either: (i) return all of such Confidential Information of the disclosing party and all copies thereof in the receiving party's possession or control to the disclosing party; or (ii) destroy all Confidential Information and all copies thereof in the receiving party's possession or control. The receiving party will then, at the request of the disclosing party, certify in writing that no copies have been retained by the receiving party, its employees or agents.

14.5. In case a party receives legal process that demands or requires disclosure of the disclosing party's Confidential Information, such party will give prompt notice to the disclosing party, if legally permissible, to enable the disclosing party to challenge such demand.

15. **Warranty**

15.1. Subject to Customer's payment of applicable amounts under this Agreement, Developer represents and warrants that the Program will conform in all material respects to the Specification for _____ (___) days after the date of acceptance of the Program ("Warranty Period"). In the event that Customer provides written notice of a material Defect during the Warranty Period, Developer's sole obligation under this warranty is to respond promptly and [to use all reasonable efforts] to promptly remedy such Defect within a reasonable time[; provided that if the Defect cannot be reproduced with reasonable efforts, Developer's warranty will not apply and Developer will have no obligation to remedy the cited Defect].

15.2. This warranty does not apply to corrections or remedies for any issues arising from any Program modification, system change, or improper configuration or use of the Program, any third party software, or other causes external to the Program. If Customer requests Developer assistance with any non-warranty issue or problem, Developer will provide assistance, subject to Developer Personnel's availability, on its then standard time and material terms.

16. **No Harmful Code**

16.1. Developer warrants and represents that the Program will contain no routine, program, "virus" or code which [functions so as to] [has been intentionally designed or created by Developer to]: (a) allow unauthorized access to, or use of, the Program by any agent or employee of Developer or by any third party; or (b) cause the Program or other program or programs to malfunction; or (c) allow unauthorized access to, or use of, Customer's network computing environment, individual client computers or any other computing resource, by any agent or employee of Developer or any third party.

17. **Program Maintenance and Support**

[*Comment: Most software development agreements have a provision for maintenance, that is, ongoing error correction and some kind of technical support. In some cases, there would be a schedule that states the maintenance and support offering. In Option 1, we provide a provision that refers to such a schedule that could be added. (You can find an example of such a maintenance and support schedule in Form 12-2, the Commercial End User License Agreement.) Option 2 is the provision of such services on an as-agreed basis.]*

[Option 1. Maintenance and Support Schedule]

17.1. Developer agrees to provide Customer with ongoing maintenance and support for the Program and other software supplied under this Agreement as set forth in Schedule ___. Developer agrees to provide qualified personnel as necessary to provide such maintenance and support service. Annual minimum support fees are stated in Schedule ___.

17.2. Provided that Customer continuously purchases annual maintenance, Developer agrees to maintain and support the Program distributed by Customer for at least _____ years after acceptance.

[Option 2. Maintenance and Support to Be Agreed]

17.3. Upon request by Customer, Developer agrees to negotiate in good faith with Customer with respect to providing maintenance, support or other ongoing services with respect to the Program after acceptance.

[Optional Provision:]

18. Program Improvements

18.1. Customer may from time to time request additional functionalities to be made to the Program. Upon request by Customer, Developer agrees to make such adaptations, or develop such enhancements, subject to agreement on terms and conditions to be mutually agreed upon in writing, which will provide for additional payments to Developer. The fee for any such adaptations or enhancements [will be at the Developer's then current rates] [will be negotiated].

[Optional Provision:]

19. Technical Assistance and Training

19.1. Developer agrees to provide to Customer training [and training materials] for Customer personnel on use of the Program as further set forth in Schedule ___. Payment for such training shall be as set forth in Schedule ___.

20. Warranty Disclaimer and Limitations of Liability

The language about warranties being "DISCLAIMED" is keyed to statutory provisions of the Uniform Commercial Code (UCC), which are discussed in Chapter 8. Liability limitation "carve-outs" is also a topic that is discussed in Chapter 8.]

20.1. EXCEPT FOR WARRANTIES EXPRESSLY STATED HEREIN, DEVELOPER DISCLAIMS AND EXCLUDES ALL WARRANTIES, EXPRESS AND IMPLIED, INCLUDING WARRANTIES OF MERCHANTABILITY, FITNESS FOR A PARTICULAR PURPOSE, AND OF NON-INFRINGEMENT.

20.2. The procedures for repair and replacement of the Program during the Warranty Period [and purchase of maintenance and support services] are Customer's sole and exclusive remedy for any Defect or other issue or problem in the Program or any Deliverable.

20.3. [Except for breach of the confidentiality provisions of this Agreement] [or under the provisions on indemnification,] Developer shall not be liable for any special, incidental, indirect or consequential damages, even if warned of the possibility of such damages. Developer does not warrant that use of the Program will be uninterrupted or error free.

20.4. [Except for breach of the confidentiality provisions of this Agreement] [or under the provisions on indemnification,] Developer's aggregate liability to the Customer for any and all claims in any way arising from or related to the Program or this Agreement will not exceed [*specified amount*] [the total of the Milestone Payments made to or owed to Developer under this Agreement].

21. **Third Party Software**

21.1. Developer may use and incorporate third party software products or components ("Third Party Software") as indicated in the Specification. Developer will not incorporate into the Deliverables any Third Party Software without the prior written authorization of Customer. [Developer will be solely responsible for obtaining licenses to any such Third Party Software.] [Customer will be solely responsible for obtaining licenses to any such Third Party Software.]

21.2. DEVELOPER MAKES NO WARRANTIES OR REPRESENTATIONS, EXPRESS OR IMPLIED, AS TO THE QUALITY, CAPABILITIES, OPERATIONS, PERFORMANCE OR SUITABILITY OF THIRD PARTY SOFTWARE, INCLUDING THE ABILITY OF NEW RELEASES TO INTEGRATE WITH THE PROGRAM. [Responsibility for the quality, performance, support, and maintenance of such Third Party Software lies solely with the vendor or supplier of such Third Party Software.]

[Optional Provision:]

22. **No Open Source**

22.1. Except as is expressly stated in the Specification, Developer will not include any software or code that is under the GNU General Public license or any open source license.

[Optional Provision:]

23. **Software Escrow**

[*Comment: This provision would only be appropriate if (a) Developer delivers the Program solely in binary form and (b) the Customer is insisting on a software escrow.*

This version requires a "mutually acceptable" escrow agent and escrow form. An alternative is to designate an escrow agent in the Agreement and to include as a Schedule the form of escrow agreement.]

23.1. Within _____ days after acceptance of the Program, Developer will deposit a copy of all materials relating to the Program, including the binary and source code for the Program, and all tools used by Developer to generate such software that are not generally commercially available, such as Developer-authored development tools, etc., such that a reasonably skilled programmer could understand and modify such Program (collectively, the "Source Materials") in escrow with a mutually acceptable escrow agent and the parties will enter into a mutually acceptable source code escrow agreement on customary terms consistent with the provisions of this Section. Developer will deposit all Source Materials with the escrow agent in accordance with the escrow agreement, but in no event shall such deposits be required more frequently than once in each six month period. Customer shall have the right to inspect any deposited Source Materials after delivery to the escrow agent, but only on the premises of the escrow agent and only as is necessary to verify the completeness of such Source Materials. Customer shall pay all fees of the escrow agent.

23.2. In the event that Developer ceases to carry on business for thirty (30) consecutive days or ceases to provide maintenance and support for the Program to which Customer is entitled under this Agreement, which inability continues for thirty (30) days after Customer notifies Developer in writing of the alleged failure in maintenance and support, the deposited Source Materials shall be delivered to Customer by the escrow agent.

23.3. Delivery of the deposited materials will be made to Customer after written request by Customer to the escrow agent, with written notice also to Developer, stating the grounds upon which the request is made. On receipt of the request from Customer, the escrow agent will mail a copy of the request to Developer and will then deliver the deposited Source Materials to Customer forthwith thirty (30) days after the copy of the request is mailed to Developer. If Developer disputes the occurrence of any release event specified in Customer's request, the escrow agent will not deliver the requested Source Materials to either party until directed to do so by Customer and Developer jointly, or until ordered to do so by final order of a court of competent jurisdiction or pursuant to an arbitration proceeding initiated by either of the parties, in accordance with the then-current rules of the American Arbitration Association. The arbitration shall take place in_____. The decision of the arbitrator will be binding and either party will have the right to enter such order in a court of competent jurisdiction.

23.4. On the occurrence of the escrow agent's release of the Source Materials to Customer under the terms of the escrow agreement, Customer may use the Source Materials, either directly or indirectly, through a third party programmer or analyst engaged by Customer only as follows: to complete or continue Developer's work, to maintain [and enhance] and support the Program, and to make a reasonable number of copies of the Source Materials to assist in the performance of such tasks.

23.5. Customer acknowledges that the Source Materials constitute Confidential Information of Developer. Customer may disclose the Source Materials only to those employees of Customer (or Affiliates) required to have knowledge of such information to perform their duties. Customer shall protect the Source Materials with the same degree of care as it protects its own confidential information, and in no event less than a reasonable degree of care and shall ensure that any third party that is permitted to access or use the Source Materials is under equivalent contractual restrictions.

24. **Intellectual Property Warranty**

[*Comment: Many software development agreements contain an intellectual property warranty—a guarantee that the code provided is original and does not infringe the intellectual property rights of third parties. There are potential variants to this provision, as explained in Chapter 8.*

The following text makes warranties only as to rights under United States law. Some developers will resist warranties concerning foreign intellectual property laws, because it is more difficult to determine what foreign intellectual property rights the program might infringe. However when the Customer plans to use the program in one or more foreign states, it way wish to negotiate an indemnification provision that includes the law of some or all foreign countries.]

[Option 1. Warrants No Knowledge of Infringement:]

24.1. Developer represents and warrants that it knows of no fact or circumstance indicating that the Program, used and copied as permitted in this Agreement, will infringe any Intellectual Property rights existing under the laws of the United States or any state thereof of any other person or entity.

[Option 2. Broadly Warrants Non-Infringement:]

24.2. Developer represents and warrants that Developer has full and absolute right to [transfer] [license] the Program as required in this Agreement and that the permitted use and copying of the Program will not infringe any rights existing under the laws of the United States or any state thereof. [Customer's sole and exclusive remedy for breach of this warranty will be indemnification as provided in this Agreement.]

25. **Indemnification**

*[**Comment:** In the following Section, the Developer indemnifies the Customer against infringement claims. Sometimes there is broad indemnification: the Developer must pay all costs and liability for any intellectual property suit against the Customer (even if it turns out that the suit is without merit). Sometimes there is a narrow indemnification: the Developer must pay only if it turns out that there was infringement and the Developer was aware of it. Obviously, the Customer, if it is sophisticated, will seek the broad one. The scope of indemnification is a matter for negotiation. The rather quaint terminology of "holding harmless" the other party is a promise to pay any and all costs arising from a third party infringement claim.]*

[Option 1. Broad Indemnification:]

25.1. Developer agrees to defend, indemnify and hold harmless Customer, its officers, directors, employees, agents and representatives, at its own expense, from and against any and all costs, demands, losses, damages, liabilities, costs and expenses (including reasonable attorney's fees) and any award of damages or costs made against Customer that is based on any claim that the Program or its permitted use infringes any Intellectual Property rights of a third party (collectively, "Claim"). Developer's obligations under this Section do apply to or cover any claim or liability arising from the combination of the Program and any technology or content not provided by Developer.

[Option 2. Indemnifies for Knowing Infringement Only:]

25.2. Developer agrees to defend, indemnify and hold harmless Customer, its officers, directors, employees, agents and representatives, at its own expense, from and against any and all fees, costs and expenses (including reasonable attorney's fees) and any award of damages or costs made against Customer that arises from Developer's intentionally creating and supplying the Program and Deliverables while knowing that such Program or Deliverables infringe the Intellectual Property rights of a third party (collectively, "Claim"). Developer's obligations under this Section do apply to or cover any claim or liability arising from the combination of the Program and any technology or content not provided by Developer.

25.3. If Developer deems that the Program or any Deliverable furnished under this Agreement is subject to a substantial threat of a Claim or is held to constitute an infringement and its use enjoined, Developer [may] [must], at its own expense, use commercially reasonable efforts to: (1) procure for Customer the right to continue using the Program; or (2) replace or modify the Program with a functional, non-infringing equivalent.

25.4. Customer will defend, indemnify, and hold Developer harmless from and against any and all third party claims arising or alleged to arise from (i) any unlicensed use of the Program or (ii) any claim or liability arising from the combination of the Program and any technology or content not provided by Developer, to the extent that the Program alone is non-infringing.

25.5. The party requesting indemnity under this Section shall provide the indemnifying party with prompt and reasonable notice of the Claim, and shall allow the indemnifying party to conduct the defense or settlement in its sole discretion, and provide reasonable cooperation with the indemnifying party in such defense or settlement.

25.6. [The foregoing is the parties' sole and exclusive remedies for infringement or claimed infringement of third party Intellectual Property rights.][Developer's maximum aggregate liability under this Section will not exceed the sum of $_____.]

25.7. [Notwithstanding the foregoing, Developer's obligation under this Section will be effective only if Customer has made all or substantially all of the payments required by this Agreement.]

26. **Term and Termination**

   [*Comment: The term and termination clause of some development contracts grants the Customer an absolute right to cancel at will on no notice, or on short notice. This would allow the Customer to get out of further obligations if it decides that there no longer is any market for the Product that is being developed. Often the Developer will resist the inclusion of such an "escape" clause unless there is a termination fee to compensate the Developer for loss of expected revenues.]*

26.1. The term of this Agreement will commence on the Effective Date, and will continue until this Agreement is terminated in accordance with the provisions set forth in this Agreement.

26.2. Either party may terminate this Agreement:

26.2.1. In accordance with the provisions stated in this Agreement that provide for termination.

26.2.2. In the event that the other party ceases business operations or is in any bankruptcy, state law insolvency or receivership proceeding, or other equivalent proceeding that is not dismissed in _____ (_____) days or assigns its assets for the benefit of creditors, or

26.2.3. In the event of any material breach by the other party which is not cured within _____ (_____) days after notice.

[Optional Provision:]

26.3. Customer may terminate this Agreement for convenience on _____ days written notice. If Customer terminates for convenience, Customer will pay Developer for completed Milestones and on a percentage-of-completion basis for uncompleted Milestones. On receipt of such payment, Developer will deliver to Customer all work in process, including binary code, source code and any relevant proprietary Developer tools, all of which will be deemed provided "AS IS" and "WITHOUT WARRANTY" but with all rights granted to Customer regarding licenses, ownership and/or exploitation otherwise provided for in this Agreement. [In case of Customer's termination for convenience, an additional termination fee of *[state amount or formula for a termination fee]* will also be due and payable to Developer.]

27. **Effect of Termination**

27.1. Upon any termination of this Agreement by any party, the following Sections will survive termination: 12 (Intellectual Property), [13 (Exclusivity)], 14 (Confidentiality), 15 (Warranty) (if applicable), 16 (No Harmful Code), 20 (Warranty Disclaimer and Limitations of Liability), 24 (Intellectual Property Warranty), 25 (Indemnification), 27 (Effect of

Termination), [28 (Non-Solicitation of Staff),] and 29 (General Provisions) together with accrued obligations and any provisions that recite that they survive or by their terms apply after termination.

[Optional Provision:]

28. **Non-Solicitation of Staff**

28.1. Customer agrees not to solicit to hire, hire, or otherwise obtain the services of, or to assist any third party to solicit to hire, hire, or obtain the services of any Developer employee or other person assigned by Developer to work under this agreement while engaged in Services or for one year thereafter.

28.2. The parties agree that it is impossible to fix with certainty the damage to Developer for breach of this Section, and the parties therefore agree that Customer will pay, for each breach of this Section, as liquidated damages, an amount equal to one hundred percent (100%) of the affected employee's average monthly compensation over the most recent six full months multiplied by twelve. Such amount will be due and payable by the Customer within ten (10) days of receipt of an invoice from Developer.

29. **General Provisions**

*[**Comment:** The following are some general (or "boilerplate") provisions. Similar provisions are found in many commercial contracts.]*

29.1. *Relationship of Parties.* Developer will be deemed to have the status of an independent contractor, and nothing in this Agreement will be deemed to place the parties in the relationship of employer-employee, principal-agent, partners or joint venturers. Developer is responsible for all payments to its subcontractors [, and guarantees their observance of their confidentiality requirements referred to herein.]

29.2. *Payment of Taxes.* Developer will be responsible for any withholding taxes, payroll taxes, disability insurance payments, unemployment taxes, and other taxes or charges incurred in the performance of the Agreement for its Personnel.

29.3. *Force Majeure.* Neither party will be deemed in default of this Agreement to the extent that performance of their obligations or attempts to cure any breach [other than with regard to payment] are delayed or prevented by reason of any act of God, fire, natural disaster, accident, act of government, shortages of materials or supplies, or any other cause beyond the control of such party ("Force Majeure") provided that such party gives the other party written notice thereof promptly and, in any event, within fifteen (15) days of discovery thereof and uses its best efforts to cure the delay. In the event of such a Force Majeure, the time for performance or cure will be extended for a period equal to the duration of the Force Majeure but not in excess of sixty (60) days. If a Force Majeure delay exceeds sixty (60) days, the other party may terminate this Agreement without fault.

*[**Comment:** The following provisions relate to assignment of the Agreement by the Developer or the Customer. There are a number of options presented in the following text. If there is an assignment, the Developer may want the Customer to remain responsible for payment if the assignee fails to pay. Owners of businesses may want the freedom to sell or assign all the assets of a business, including all its contracts. Normally the Customer, who contracted for the skills of a particular developer, may resist granting the Developer any right to assign the agreement.]*

29.4. *Assignments.* This Agreement may not be assigned by Customer in whole or in part without consent of Developer [which consent will not be unreasonably withheld]. [Customer may assign this Agreement, without Developer's consent, to any third party which succeeds by operation of law to, purchases, or otherwise acquires substantially all of the assets of Customer and assumes Customer's obligations hereunder.] [Notwithstanding the above, Customer will retain the obligation to pay if the assignee fails to pay as required by the payment obligations of this Agreement.] [Developer may not assign its obligations under this Agreement without Customer's written consent, which Customer may withhold in its complete discretion.]

29.5. *Partial Invalidity.* Should any provision of this Agreement be held to be void, invalid, or inoperative, the remaining provisions of this Agreement will not be affected and will continue in effect as though such provisions were deleted.

29.6. *No Waiver.* The failure of either party to exercise any right or the waiver by either party of any breach will not prevent a subsequent exercise of such right or be deemed a waiver of any subsequent breach of the same or any other term of the Agreement.

29.7. *Notice.* Any notice required or permitted to be sent hereunder will be in writing and will be sent in a manner requiring a signed receipt, such as courier delivery, or if mailed, registered or certified mail, return receipt requested. Notice is effective upon receipt. Notice to Customer will be addressed to [*specify name, title and address*] or such other person or address as Customer may designate. Notice to Developer will be addressed to [*specify name, title and address*] or such other person or address as Developer may designate.

29.8. *Modifications.* No modification of this Agreement will be effective unless in writing and signed by both parties.

29.9. *Injunction.* The parties acknowledge that damages may not be an adequate remedy for breach of the Sections of this Agreement on confidentiality [and exclusivity] [and non-solicitation]. Without limiting other rights or remedies, the parties will have the right in the event of breach or anticipated breach of such provisions to seek injunctive or other equitable relief to remedy or prevent the breach or anticipated breach.

29.10. *Governing Law.* This Agreement will be governed and interpreted in accordance with the substantive law of the State of _____.

29.11. *Venue and Jurisdiction of Legal Actions.* Any legal action brought concerning this Agreement or its subject matter will be brought only in the state and federal courts located in [*indicate and county*], and both parties agree to the exclusive jurisdiction and venue of these courts.

[*Comment: The following "entire agreement clause" (also known as an "integration clause") is designed to eliminate any claim that oral promises not in the Agreement are effective. This clause, a standard feature of many types of agreement, will usually be enforced. If there are promises made or "side agreements" outside the text of the Agreement, it is important to get them into the text before the Agreement is signed.*]

29.12. *Entire Agreement.* This Agreement, including the Schedules thereto, states the entire agreement between the parties on this subject and supersedes all prior negotiations, understandings, and agreements between the parties concerning the subject matter.

29.13. *Counterparts.* This Agreement may be executed in multiple counterparts, each being deemed an original and this being one of the counterparts. Execution by fax is permitted.

IN WITNESS WHEREOF, the parties have executed this Agreement.

Developer: _____   Customer: _____

By: _____   By: _____

Name: _____   Name: _____

Title: _____   Title: _____

Date: _____   Date: _____

Schedule _____

Specifications

[To be added]

Schedule _____

Milestone and Payment Schedule

*[**Comment:** Every development agreement will have its own Milestone and Milestone Payment schedule. The following are some terms that might fit a Milestone Schedule.]*

The following Schedule will govern milestones and payments for the development of the Program.

1. **Definitions.** The following definitions and provisions apply to this Schedule:

   1.1. "Working Model Code" will mean Program code written by Developer that has Critical Features (as defined in the Specification). This version of the Program demonstrates the technical feasibility of the Program.

   1.2. "Alpha Code" will mean Program code written by Developer that includes all operations, functions, capabilities, and performance in the Specification implemented, integrated and fully functional. It is code that is not necessarily "bug free" and may be in need of adjustment and tuning of functions, operations, and graphics.

   1.3. "Beta Code" will mean Program code written by Developer that includes all operations, functions, capabilities, and performance implemented, integrated and functional substantially in accordance with the Specification. This version will have all known serious bugs and errors corrected.

   1.4. "Final Deliverables" will mean the version of the Program written by Developer that has passed through user tests and which [fully] [substantially] complies with the Specification. [This version is the Beta Code version that has been corrected to address the bugs and errors that have been documented during testing.]

[Optional Provision:]

   1.5. "Technical Documentation" will mean commented source code and other documentation sufficient to permit the Program to be modified by a reasonably skilled technician with knowledge of the languages in which the Program is written but no prior knowledge of the Program. Technical Documentation is further defined as follows: *[specify]*.

2. Delivery and Payment Schedule

The delivery and payment schedule will be as follows:

[Specify Dates, Milestones and Payment Amounts]

[Add other Schedules as Required]

Software Consulting Agreement (Favors Consultant)

Introductory Note

This is a software consulting agreement with a variety of clauses that "lean" toward Consultant rather than Customer. These include the provisions on the performance obligations of Consultant, acceptance, correction of defects, warranties, intellectual property ownership, and indemnification.

You can contrast these provisions with those of Form 10-3, which is a pro-Customer version of a consulting agreement.

This form is for use when Consultant is a corporation or other legal entity. It will requirew some modification if Consultant is an individual.

Bracketed language is optional.

Software Consulting Agreement

This Software Consulting Agreement ("Agreement") is entered into this _____ day of 20___, by and between _____ , having its principal place of business at _____("Customer"), and _____, having its principal place of business at _____ ("Consultant").

   In consideration of the mutual covenants and promises set forth below, the parties agree as follows:

1. **Services**

   1.1. *Statement of Work.* All services to be performed by Consultant under this Agreement ("Services") will be set forth in a written statement of work ("Statement of Work") signed by authorized representatives of both parties. Each Statement of Work will set forth the description of the Services to be done and the hourly, daily or other fees for the Services to be performed, and other matters as the parties may agree upon. The initial Statement of Work(s) is (are) attached as <u>Schedule 1</u>.

1.2. *Provisions of Services.* Consultant agrees to use commercially reasonable efforts to provide the Services to Customer in accordance with the terms and conditions of this Agreement and the applicable Statements of Work.

1.3. *Support Not Included.* Unless expressly included in a particular Statement of Work or otherwise agreed in writing, Consultant is not obligated to provide any support or maintenance services for any deliverables provided pursuant to this Agreement.

1.4. *Estimated Times.* The parties agree that, unless otherwise expressly stated in a particular Statement of Work or otherwise agreed in writing, where a time or amount of Services required for a particular task or deliverable is described in a Statement of Work, it is an estimate only. [Consultant will use reasonable efforts to advise Customer as soon as is practicable if the time or amount of Services required is likely to exceed the estimate by more than ____ percent.]

2. **Third Party Products and Services**

   2.1. Unless otherwise stated in a particular Statement of Work, Customer will arrange for third party products and services required for implementation of the Statement of Work, including third party software and tools. CONSULTANT MAKES NO WARRANTY REGARDING THIRD PARTY PRODUCTS AND SERVICES.

3. **Performance of Services; Changes**

   3.1. Consultant will determine the details and means of performing the Services to be performed for Customer under Customer's general guidance and direction. Services will be performed at such times and at such places set out in the Statements of Work or as the parties may otherwise agree in writing.

   3.2. Changes to any Statement of Work can be made only by written change order signed by both parties or by an additional Statement of Work. Any change to a Statement of Work which is agreed to by the parties will specify the changes ordered, any increase or decrease in the estimated charges for performance, timing issues, and any changes to other matters as may be affected.

4. **Payment**

   4.1. Customer will pay Consultant at the fee rates specified in the Statements of Work. If rates are not specified in the relevant Statement of Work, Services performed by Consultant on behalf of Customer will be undertaken on a time and materials basis at Consultant's applicable standard rates.

   4.2. Customer will reimburse Consultant for reasonable out-of-pocket expenses incurred in the provision of Services, including, without limitation, all travel, accommodation, and meal expenses for Services performed at Customer site or Customer's client's site.

   4.3. Consultant will render invoices to Customer on a monthly basis, indicating the Services for which the invoice is rendered, the period of time it covers, the fees due, and any other additions, expenses or taxes (evidenced by receipts), and any other detail reasonably required for Customer to verify the amount invoiced. All invoices submitted under this Agreement and the Statements of Work will refer to this Agreement and the applicable Statement of Work.

   4.4. Customer will pay all invoices within thirty (30) days of receipt. In the event that Customer wishes to dispute an item or items on an invoice, Customer will notify Consultant in writing within fourteen days of receipt of that invoice, setting out its reasons in reasonable detail. If no notice of dispute is received by Consultant fourteen days after receipt of an invoice by Customer, the invoice will be deemed accepted, and Customer will be obliged to pay the invoice in accordance with its terms. In case of a dispute regarding billing, Customer must pay all undisputed charges and items.

   4.5. Customer is responsible for all taxes resulting from the Services, including any sales taxes, but excluding taxes on Consultant's net income. Consultant may bill for such taxes and pay them to the relevant tax authorities.

4.6. If Customer fails to pay any amount payable by it under this Agreement within 30 days of receipt of an invoice, Consultant will be entitled to charge and Customer will pay 1.50% interest per month (or if less the highest legal rate), compounded daily, on the overdue amount.

5. **Personnel**

5.1. Consultant will perform the Services by means of the services of suitably experienced staff and/or may delegate its obligations hereunder by commercially reasonable use of one or more subcontractor individuals or firms, provided that, in any case, Consultant will remain responsible for provision of Services as required by this Agreement. The individuals who provide Services under this Agreement are the "Personnel." [Consultant will use reasonable efforts to provide Customer with a list of the Personnel assigned to Services under each Statement of Work.]

5.2. Consultant will seek to ensure continuity of staffing for Services under each Work Statement. Consultant, from time to time, may replace Personnel with suitably experienced alternative Personnel or subcontractors. [In this event, Consultant will use reasonable efforts to provide to Customer reasonable notice of each replacement.]

5.3. Consultant will determine matters such as Personnel's working hours and holidays taking into account Customer's business requirements. Personnel may take state and local holidays.

6. **Cooperation; Facilities to Be Provided by Client**

6.1. Customer agrees to provide reasonable cooperation to Consultant and access to information that Consultant reasonably requires to perform its obligations under this Agreement.

6.2. Customer will make available to Consultant (including its subcontractors and any third parties contemplated within this Agreement) free of charge any premises, facilities, assistance, information, and services reasonably required to enable them to perform the Services. Such facilities will include, but not be limited to, desks, PCs, office facilities and telephones.

6.3. Where the Services are to be provided at the premises of a client of Customer, it is the responsibility of Customer to ensure that the foregoing are provided at such location.

7. **Independent Contractor**

   7.1. The parties agree that Consultant is acting, in performance of this Agreement, as an independent contractor. The parties agree that the Personnel supplied by Consultant hereunder are not Customer's employees or agents.

   7.2. Consultant will be solely responsible for the payment of compensation and any benefits to the Personnel, and the Personnel will not be entitled to the provision of any Customer employee benefits.

   7.3. This Agreement is mutually non-exclusive. Customer will retain the right to have services of the same or a different kind performed by its own personnel or other consultants, and Consultant will retain the right to provide similar services to others.

8. **Confidentiality**

   8.1. "Confidential Information" means non-public information, data or know-how of a party and/or its affiliates, which is furnished directly or indirectly to the other party in written or tangible form in connection with this Agreement. Each oral disclosure of a party will also be deemed Confidential Information if the recipient should reasonably understand it to be non-public information.

   8.2. Notwithstanding the foregoing, Confidential Information does not include information which is: (i) already in the possession of the receiving party and not subject to a confidentiality obligation to the providing party; (ii) independently developed by the receiving party; (iii) publicly disclosed through no fault of the receiving party; (iv) rightfully received by the receiving party from a third party that is not under any obligation to keep such information confidential; (v) approved for release by written agreement with the disclosing party; or (vi) disclosed pursuant to the requirements of law, regulation, court order or other applicable require-ment, provided that the receiving party shall promptly inform the providing party of any such requirement and cooperate with any attempt to procure a protective order or similar treatment.

   8.3. Neither party will use the other party's Confidential Information except as reasonably required for the performance of this Agreement. The confidentiality obligations set forth in this Section shall survive for five (5) years after the termination or expiration of this Agreement. Each party will hold in confidence the other party's Confidential Information by means that are no less restrictive than those used for its own confidential materials but in any case by commercially reasonable means. Each party agrees not to disclose the other party's Confidential Information to anyone other than its employees or subcontractors who are bound by confidentiality obligations consistent with this Agreement and who need to know the same to perform such party's obligations hereunder.

8.4. Upon termination or expiration of this Agreement, except as otherwise agreed in writing or otherwise stated in this Agreement, each party shall, upon the request of the disclosing party, either: (i) return all of such Confidential Information of the disclosing party and all copies thereof in the receiving party's possession or control to the disclosing party or (ii) destroy all Confidential Information and all copies thereof in the receiving party's possession or control. The receiving party shall then, at the request of the disclosing party, certify in writing that the requirements of this Section have been carried out and that no copies have been retained by the receiving party, its employees or agents.

8.5. In case a party receives legal process that demands or requires disclosure of the disclosing party's Confidential Information, such party shall give prompt notice to the disclosing party, if legally permissible, to enable the disclosing party to challenge such demand.

8.6. The parties acknowledge that damages may not be an adequate remedy for breach of this Section. Therefore, without prejudice to any other rights or remedies, the parties will have the right in the event of such breach or anticipated breach to seek injunctive or other equitable relief to remedy or prevent the breach or anticipated breach.

9. **Ownership of Software**

9.1. From time to time, Consultant has created software tools and code and/or will during the course of the Agreement create, and/or improve, software tools and software code that are reusable or are useful for one or more other products, tasks and projects. Such tools and code provided to Customer under this Agreement are termed "Reusable Software." Software created and delivered under this Agreement other than Reusable Software is "Customer Specific Software."

9.2. Upon payment of amounts due to Consultant with regard to each Statement of Work, Customer Specific Software under such Statement of Work will belong to Customer and will be, to the fullest extent permitted under the US copyright act, a work-made-for-hire for Customer. To the extent that it is not work-made-for-hire, Customer Specific Software (including, as applicable, ownership of the binary code and source code) is hereby assigned to Customer.

9.3. Customer agrees that the Consultant Reusable Software will be the property of and will belong to Consultant. Upon payment of amounts due to Consultant with regard to each Statement of Work, Consultant will be deemed to grant to Customer a non-exclusive, worldwide, perpetual, irrevocable and fully paid up license to use, modify, adapt, sublicense, and otherwise exploit the Consultant Reusable Software solely for use with the deliverables under such Statement of Work and derivatives of such deliverables.

9.4. Each party agrees to provide, at the other party's expense, the documents necessary or useful to vest in each party its respective Intellectual Property under this Agreement.

9.5. Except as expressly stated in this Agreement, each party retains its own rights. No rights are created or transferred by implication.

9.6. Customer hereby grants to Consultant a non-exclusive and non-transferable license to access and use Customer's computer and network systems and proprietary software and to use Customer Specific Software as reasonably required for Consultant to carry out its obligations under this Agreement.

10. **Warranty and Indemnity**

10.1. Each party warrants that it has all required corporate authority to execute and perform this Agreement.

10.2. Consultant warrants that to the best of its actual knowledge that all deliverables provided or to be provided under this Agreement do not and will not infringe or violate any valid third party patent right, copyright or trade secret right in the United States.

10.3. Customer warrants that it has all required ownership, rights and/or permissions for any materials, software or other items that it provides for Consultant's use under this Agreement.

10.4. Consultant agrees to defend, indemnify and hold harmless Customer from any litigation or proceeding arising from Consultant's breach of the warranty in Section 10.2. Customer agrees to defend, indemnify and hold harmless Consultant from any litigation or proceeding arising from Consultant's breach of the warranty in Section 10.3.

10.5. In case of any claim that is subject to indemnification under this Agreement, the Party entitled to indemnification ("Indemnitee") shall provide the indemnifying party ("Indemnitor") prompt notice of the relevant claim. Indemnitor shall defend and/or settle, at its own expense, any demand, action, or suit on any claim subject to indemnification under this Agreement. The Indemnitee shall cooperate in good faith with the Indemnitor to facilitate the defense of any such claim. Claims may be settled without the consent of any Indemnitee unless the settlement includes an admission of wrongdoing, fault or liability on behalf of the Indemnitee.

11. **Limitations of Liability**

11.1. *Warranty Exclusion.* EXCEPT AS EXPRESSLY STATED IN THIS AGREEMENT, CONSULTANT DISCLAIMS ALL EXPRESS AND IMPLIED WARRANTIES, INCLUDING IMPLIED WARRANTIES OF NON-INFRINGEMENT, MERCHANTABILITY AND FITNESS FOR A PARTICULAR PURPOSE.

11.2. *Damage Disclaimer.* Consultant will not be liable to Customer for any special, indirect, consequential, incidental or exemplary damages including without limitation, damages for loss of Customer's business profits, cost of procurement of substitute goods, technology or services, business interruptions or loss of information, even if Consultant has been advised of the possibility of such damages.

11.3. *Limitation of Liability.* In no event will Consultant be liable to Customer for any amounts in excess in the aggregate of the fees paid by Customer to Consultant during the six (6) month period prior to the date the cause of action arose or, if less, the amount paid to Consultant with regard to the Statement of Work that is relevant to the liability.

12. **Non-Solicitation**

   12.1. Customer agrees not to solicit to hire, hire, or otherwise obtain the services of, or to assist any third party to solicit to hire, hire, or obtain the services of any Consultant employee or other person assigned by Consultant to work under any Statement for Work for the duration of Services under such Statement of Work or for one year thereafter.

   12.2. Because it is any Consultant impossible to fix with certainty the damage to Consultant for breach of this Section, the parties agree that Customer will pay, for each breach of this Section, as liquidated damages, an amount equal to one hundred percent (100%) of the affected employee's average monthly compensation over the most recent six full months multiplied by twelve. Such amount will be due and payable by Customer within ten (10) days of receipt of an invoice from Consultant.

13. **Term and Termination**

   13.1. Unless otherwise agreed in writing by the parties, either Customer or Consultant may terminate this Agreement, or any Statement of Work, at any time by giving the other _____ (__) days written notice of termination, whereupon this Agreement or (as appropriate) the Statement of Work will terminate on the effective date specified in such notice. Termination of a Statement of Work will not operate to terminate this Agreement, unless this Agreement is also terminated in accordance with its terms.

   13.2. Either Party may terminate his Agreement for cause in the event of: (a) a material breach or default by the other party of an obligation under this Agreement which is not remedied within thirty (30) days after written notice; (b) the other party's filing for bankruptcy or becoming an involuntary participant in a bankruptcy proceeding, if such involuntary proceedings are not dismissed within sixty (60) days after commencement; or, (c) notice of the inability of the other party to perform due to the existence of a force majeure event for more than thirty (30) days.

   13.3. Where this Agreement is terminated, each Statement of Work will also be terminated and any Services being provided under that Statement of Work will cease. Consultant will issue, and Customer will pay, an invoice for Services provided up to the date of termination. In case of Customer's termination without cause, an additional termination fee of *[amount]* will also be due to Consultant.

13.4. On receipt of payment of all amounts due, Consultant will deliver to Customer all work in progress. Uncompleted work in progress will be provided "AS IS" and "WITHOUT WARRANTY," but otherwise subject to the terms and conditions of this Agreement.

13.5. The Sections of this Agreement regarding Confidentiality, Intellectual Property, Warranties, Limitation of Liability, Term and Termination, Non-Solicitation and General provisions will survive termination, as will accrued rights to payment.

14. Notices

Any notice required to be given by either party hereunder will be in writing and will be hand delivered or sent by courier or pre-paid first class post or by confirmed fax transmission to the party receiving such communication at the address and fax numbers specified below or such other address or fax numbers as either party may in the future specify to the other party. Notice is effective upon receipt.

If to Consultant: *[add address, contact person and/or title, and fax number]*

If to Customer: *[add address, contact person and/or title, and fax number]*

15. General

15.1. *Compliance with Laws.* Each party hereby represents and warrants that it will comply with all applicable, local, state, provincial, and national laws and regulations, including, without limitation, US export control laws.

15.2. *Assignment.* Customer may not assign this Agreement. Consultant reserves the right to transfer this Agreement to any affiliate. Consultant may also, without Customer's consent, transfer this Agreement in connection with the sale or disposition of its business or a line of business relevant to this Agreement, by asset transfer, merger, stock sale or otherwise.

15.3. *No Third Party Beneficiary.* This Agreement is not intended to confer a benefit on, or to be enforceable by, any person who is not a party to this Agreement.

15.4. *Status as Independent Contractor.* Each party is an independent contractor and neither party's employees will be considered employees of the other party for any purpose. This Agreement does not create a joint venture or partnership, and neither party has the authority to bind the other to any third party.

15.5. *Applicable Law and Jurisdiction.* This Agreement will be governed and construed in accordance with the laws of the State of _____ without regard to the conflicts of laws or principles thereof. Exclusive jurisdiction and venue for any disputes, claims or litigation arising from or related in any way to this Agreement or its subject matter will lie exclusively in the state and federal courts located in _____, USA. Each party expressly agrees to submit to the personal jurisdiction of such courts.

15.6. *Waiver.* No waiver of a breach of any of the provisions of this Agreement will be deemed a waiver of any preceding or succeeding breach of the same or any other provisions hereof. No such waiver will be effective unless in writing and then only to the extent expressly set forth in writing.

15.7. *Partial Invalidity.* If any provision of this Agreement is invalid or unenforceable under any statute or rule of law, the provision is to the extent to be deemed omitted, and the remaining provisions will not be affected in any way.

15.8. *Force Majeure.* Neither party will be responsible for any delay or failure in performance resulting from acts beyond such party's control ("Force Majeure"). Force Majeure will include but not be limited to: acts of God, government or war; riots or strikes; epidemics, fires, floods, or disasters.

15.9. *Modifications.* No modification of this Agreement will be effective unless in writing and signed by both parties.

15.10. *Counterparts.* This Agreement may be executed in multiple counterparts, each being deemed an original and this being one of the counterparts. Execution by fax is permitted.

15.11. *Entire Agreement.* This Agreement, including the attached Statement of Work and any supplements, constitutes the entire agreement between Consultant and Customer.

SIGNED: By, or on behalf of the parties on the date which first appears on this Agreement.

Consultant: _____   Customer: _____

By: _____   By: _____

Name: _____   Name: _____

Title: _____   Title: _____

Date: _____   Date: _____

Schedule 1

SCHEDULE OF WORK

This is a Statement of Work referred to in the Software Consulting Agreement dated [_____] ("the Agreement") by and between [_____] ("Consultant") and _____ Inc. ("Customer"). This Statement of Work will be effective immediately after it has been signed by both Customer and Consultant.

[_____] Statement of Work Reference:

<u>Personnel</u>	<u>Role</u>	<u>Start Date</u>	<u>End Date</u>	<u>Fee Rate</u>

Consultant's time and materials fee billing rates are reset annually on no less than thirty (30) days' notice.

Description of Services

Location(s) where Services are to be performed

Normal working hours

Customer Relationship Manager

Consultant Relationship Manager

Agreed upon by the parties:

Consultant: _____   Customer: _____

By: _____   By: _____
Authorized Signatory   Authorized Signatory

Name: _____   Name: _____

Title: _____   Title: _____

Date: _____   Date: _____

Software Consulting Agreement 10-3
(Favors Customer)

Introductory Note

This is a software consulting agreement with a variety of clauses that favor the Customer rather than Consultant. In essence, this form provides protection for the Customer and places most risks on Consultant. You may see forms of this kind used by large corporations for the purposes of procurement of consulting services.

The provisions of note include the performance obligations of Consultant, acceptance, correction of defects, warranties, intellectual property ownership, third party software, and indemnification. All of these points could be the subject of negotiation, and most Consultants would seek to "soften" many of the following provisions if they have the leverage to do so.

You can compare and contrast these provisions with those of Form 10-2, which is a pro-Consultant version of a consulting agreement.

Bracketed language is optional.

Software Consulting Agreement

This Software Consulting Agreement ("Agreement") is entered into this _____ day of 20_____, by and between _____, having its principal place of business at _____ ("Customer"), and _____, having its principal place of business at _____ ("Consultant").

    In consideration of the mutual covenants and promises set forth below, the parties agree as follows:

1. **Legal Status of Consultant**

Consultant represents and warrants that it is a corporation or other legal entity that is capable of contracting. (This form of agreement is not intended for use with a consultant who is an individual person.)

2. **Duties of Consultant**

   2.1. Consultant agrees to provide the professional services ("Services") described on statements of work (each, a "Statement of Work"). Each Statement of Work will describe the Services to be performed, the schedule or term of Services, specifications and requirements ("Specifications"), means of delivery, applicable rates and charges, and other appropriate terms.

   2.2. Each item prepared, provided, delivered or required to be prepared, provided, or delivered under any Statement of Work is a "Deliverable."

   2.3. No Services are authorized and no payment is due except as expressly stated in writing in a Statement of Work signed by the parties.

   2.4. A Statement of Work cannot be varied or amended unless agreed in writing by the parties. Any change to a Statement of Work which is agreed to by the parties will specify the changes required, any increase or decrease in the charges for performance, any change in the times for performance, and other applicable changes.

3. **Standard of Performance. Acceptance of Deliverables**

   3.1. Consultant agrees to provide all Services and Deliverables in conformity with the applicable Specifications, the Statement of Work, this Agreement and applicable industry standards and laws. Consultant agrees to: (a) perform the Services in a professional manner, (b) keep Customer advised of the progress of the Services, (c) permit any representative of Customer to obtain and review from time to time the results of the Services, (d) provide Customer with such Deliverables, including any work in process, upon request, (e) keep records of work performed which such records Customer may review from time to time upon reasonable notice to Consultant, and (f) ensure that Consultant and its employees comply with Customer's safety, security and code of conduct regulations. Consultant will comply with all reasonable instructions given by Customer in connection with the Services. Consultant will supply all tools and equipment necessary to perform the Services unless otherwise agreed to in the applicable Statement of Work.

3.2. Unless otherwise stated in an applicable Statement of Work, Deliverables are subject to acceptance ("Acceptance") under the following procedure: Customer will make reasonable efforts to carry out inspection and accept or reject each Deliverable within thirty (30) days from receipt. Acceptance of each Deliverable will occur only upon written notice of Acceptance by Customer; no other act or failure to act by Customer will constitute Acceptance. [Customer will not unreasonably withhold Acceptance.]

3.3. Unless otherwise expressly stated in the applicable Statement of Work, Deliverables consisting of software will include Consultant's delivery of source code and binary code, together with all relevant technical documentation. Customer reserves the option to require daily or other periodic deliveries of source code and binary code.

3.4. In case Customer discovers one or more deficiencies in a Deliverable, Customer will notify Consultant in writing (which may be by email) within a commercially reasonable time. Upon receiving such a notice, Consultant will promptly correct any such deficiency or make such changes within fifteen (15) days after receiving such notice and resubmit the Deliverable. If Consultant fails to provide a conforming Deliverable, Customer in its discretion may (but is not obligated to) terminate this Agreement and/or the applicable Statement of Work, or, at its option, may, by written notice, require Consultant to continue work and provide conforming deliverables within a further fifteen (15) days under the same procedure.

4. **Fees for Services Performed**

4.1. Consultant will be paid the fees set forth in each Statement of Work for Consultant's performance of Services under this Agreement as follows: Consultant will submit to Customer invoices setting forth the Services rendered in reasonable detail. Any relevant backup documentation regarding the Services that Customer may require will be included. Conditioned on performance satisfactory to Customer of the Services under a Statement of Work, Customer will pay proper invoices within forty-five (45) days of receipt of invoice. Such fees will be Consultant's sole compensation for rendering Services to Customer. In no event will

Customer be obligated to pay Consultant any more than the maximum fee amount stated in the Statement of Work.

4.2. If the Statement of Work provides for reimbursement of expenses, Customer will reimburse the reasonable pre-approved costs or expenses incurred by Consultant in performing the Services. Each invoice will cite the applicable agreement number and purchase order number. Consultant will submit invoices to: [*Insert billing address*].

4.3. [Consultant represents and warrants that pricing and terms for the Services performed hereunder are and at all times will be at least as favorable as that charged to any other customer for the same or similar services.]

5. **Confidentiality**

5.1. Consultant acknowledges that in connection with the Services, Customer may deliver to Consultant non-public information. For purposes of this Agreement, "Confidential Information" is information provided by Customer, or created or discovered by, for or on behalf of Customer (including, without limitation, Deliverables and information created under this Agreement). Confidential Information includes, but is not limited to, information relating to products, processes, techniques, formulas, ideas, know-how, works of authorship, copyrightable works, inventions (whether patentable or not), technical information, trade secrets, computer programs, computer code, designs, technology, compositions, data, drawings, schematics, customers, product development plans, and other business, technical and financial information.

5.2. At all times, both during this Agreement and after its termination, Consultant will protect Confidential Information from unauthorized dissemination and use with the same degree of care that Consultant uses to protect its own confidential information, but with not less than reasonable care and diligence, and will not disclose any Confidential Information without the prior written consent of Customer. Consultant may use such Confidential Information solely for the purpose of performing the Services under this Agreement and for no other purpose.

5.3. Consultant agrees that immediately upon Customer's request and in any event upon completion of the Services, Consultant will deliver to Customer all Confidential Information including all copies, derivatives, and extracts thereof.

5.4. Consultant will not be obligated under this Section with respect to information that Consultant can document: (a) is or has become publicly known through no fault of Consultant or its employees or agents; or (b) is received without restriction from a third party lawfully in possession of such information and lawfully empowered to disclose such information; (c) was rightfully in the possession of Consultant without restriction prior to its disclosure by Customer; or (d) is independently developed by or on behalf of Consultant.

5.5. Consultant will treat the terms and conditions and the existence of this Agreement as Confidential Information of Customer. Consultant will obtain Customer's written consent prior to any publication, presentation, public announcement or press release concerning the existence or terms and conditions of this Agreement.

5.6. Consultant acknowledges that any disclosure or unauthorized use of Confidential Information will constitute a material breach of this Agreement and cause substantial and irreparable harm to Customer for which damages would not be a fully adequate remedy, and, therefore, in the event of any such breach, in addition to other available remedies, Customer will have the right to obtain appropriate injunctive relief.

6. **Intellectual Property Ownership**

6.1. "Intellectual Property" means all rights pertaining to developments, inventions and discoveries, whether or not patentable, copyrights, trademarks, trade secrets, mask works or other proprietary rights, or any applications for the above including, without limitation, those owned, conceived, improved, created, developed, discovered, reduced to practice, or written by Consultant, alone or in collaboration with others, in connection with any Services.

6.2. Customer will be the sole owner of all Intellectual Property that is: (a) created by or for Consultant under this Agreement or (b) included in any Deliverable. Subject to the paragraph below with regard to Copyrighted Works (as defined below), Consultant will assign, and does hereby assign, to Customer all of Consultant's present and future right, title, and interest in all such Intellectual Property.

6.3. With regard to any works or content subject to copyright created under this Agreement or included in any Deliverable ("Copyrighted Works"), Consultant agrees that, to the maximum extent permitted by law, Copyrighted Works are and will be "works made for hire" for the benefit of Customer, and to the extent not "works made for hire," Customer hereby assigns such rights exclusively to Customer. Consultant hereby waives all "moral rights" under the law of any nation and under any treaty with regard to all Deliverables and the results of any Services.

6.4. Consultant will, upon request of Customer, execute, acknowledge, deliver and file any and all documents necessary or useful to vest in Customer all of Consultant's rights, under this Section or to transfer, perfect, obtain, confirm and enforce any such rights. Consultant hereby irrevocably designates and appoints Customer and its duly authorized officers and agents as its agent and attorney-in-fact to act for and in its behalf, in the event Customer is unable, after reasonable efforts, to secure its signature on any documents regarding any legal protection. Customer's rights under this Section include the right to execute and file any such application or applications or other documents and to do all other lawfully permitted acts to register, transfer, perfect, obtain, confirm and enforce patents, copyright or trademarks or any other legal protection with the same legal force and effect as if executed by Consultant.

6.5. Consultant will not incorporate into the Deliverables any software, code or other work product of any third party without the prior written authorization of Customer. Consultant will not disclose to Customer, and will not induce Customer to use any Intellectual Property, confidential information, or trade secrets of any third party.

7. **License Grants**

7.1. Consultant will give, and hereby grants, to Customer a perpetual paid-up sublicensable license under Consultant's patents, trade secrets, trademarks, copyrights, and other proprietary rights which are reasonably required for Customer, its licensees, transferees, successors, and assigns to use, alter, distribute, copy or otherwise exploit any Intellectual Property created or supplied under this Agreement, Deliverables and any derivatives of Deliverables, Services, or any other subject matter or result of this Agreement.

7.2. Consultant is licensed to use any Intellectual Property created under this Agreement solely as is necessary to carry out its obligations under the applicable Statement of Work. Consultant may keep original materials that it creates under this Agreement in its possession as reasonably required for follow-up Services, but must turn over all originals and copies of such materials to Customer upon Customer's request.

8. **Consultant's Personnel**

8.1. Unless otherwise authorized in writing by Customer, Consultant will provide all Services by use of its own employees. Consultant will use subcontractors under this Agreement only with Customer's express prior written permission. Any subcontract made by Consultant with the written consent of Customer will incorporate by reference the terms of this Agreement. Consultant warrants the performance and full compliance with this Agreement by any subcontractor used in performance of the Services.

8.2. Consultant is solely responsible for paying the salaries, wages and benefits of its employees, for ensuring that all required tax withholdings are made, and for ensuring that each employee has the legal right to work in the United States. Consultant is solely responsible for its permitted subcontractors' compensation. Consultant will defend, indemnify and hold harmless Customer, its Affiliates (as defined below), and their respective officers, directors, employees, servants and agents from any cost, including attorneys' fees, and any liability that arises from Consultant's breach of these obligations. "Affiliate" means a person or entity that directly, or indirectly through one or more intermediaries, controls, or is controlled by, or is under common control with a Customer (with "control" meaning ownership of more than 50 percent of the voting stock of the entity or, in the case of a non-corporate entity, an equivalent interest).

8.3. Consultant will ensure that its employees and permitted subcontractors will, whenever on Customer's premises (or on any Customer's client's premises or other location) obey all applicable work and safety rules.

8.4. Consultant has obtained and will at all times obtain and maintain in effect non-disclosure, assignment of Intellectual Property, and other appropriate agreements with its employees and (if permitted) subcontractors sufficient to protect Customer's Confidential Information and sufficient to allow it to provide Customer with the assignments and licenses provided for herein. Consultant will provide Customer with copies of such agreements upon request. Upon Customer's request, Consultant will cause all employees and (if permitted) subcontractors engaged under this Agreement to sign Customer's form of Intellectual Property Transfer and Confidentiality Agreement in its most current form as issued from time to time.

9. **Warranties of Quality.** Consultant represents and warrants the following with respect to Services performed:

9.1. *Compliance with Specifications.* Upon delivery, the Deliverables will comply with the requirements, descriptions and representations as to the Services and Deliverables (including performance capabilities, completeness, Specifications, configurations, and function) that appear or are referred to in the Statement of Work.

9.2. *Compliance with Specifications after Acceptance.* For a period of 180 days after Acceptance under this Agreement, any computer programs, materials, or other Deliverables developed under this Agreement will operate in conformance with the Specifications for such computer programs unless such computer programs are modified by Customer, without Consultant's written permission, within the 180-day time period. Any non-conformity found during that period will be fixed by Consultant promptly without additional charge.

9.3. *Non-Infringement of Third Party Rights.* The Services and the Deliverables will not violate or in any way infringe upon the rights of third parties, including any trademark, copyright, patent or other Intellectual Property rights.

9.4. *No Open Source.* No open source software code or any derivative of any open source software code will be included in any Deliverable, except as may be expressly permitted in the applicable Statement of Work.

10. **Remedies**

10.1. In the event that Consultant breaches any representations or warranties hereunder or fails to comply with any term or requirement of this Agreement, including but not limited to timely delivery of Services and/or Deliverables or if Consultant fails to cure deficiencies in Deliverables as permitted in this Agreement, Customer will be entitled to, in addition to any other remedies, at its sole option and without any liability to Customer:

10.1.1. Terminate or cancel this Agreement in its entirety or as it relates to any specific Services and/or Deliverables;

10.1.2. Reject non-conforming Services and/or Deliverables, in whole or in part;

10.1.3. Withhold any payments relating to non-conforming Services and/or Deliverables;

10.1.4. Recover any and all actual, incidental and consequential damages to Customer, including but not limited to actual or estimated loss of profits or sales and costs to cover, attorney's fees and costs;

10.1.5. Require that Consultant either re-perform the Services, at no additional charge to Customer, or alternatively, refund to Customer the fees paid for such non-conforming Services and/or goods; and/or

10.1.6. Offset any amounts due Consultant by any actual or estimated loss incurred by Customer.

10.2. Remedies of Customer herein will not be exclusive but will be accumulative of any other remedy of Customer under this Agreement or under any statute or law.

11. Exclusivity and Non-Competition

In order to safeguard Customer's Confidential Information and secure to Customer the full value of this Agreement, Consultant will not directly or indirectly work for any other company with respect to technology or Services substantially similar to those under or used in any Statement of Work and/or Deliverable during the term of this Agreement and for one (1) year after the termination or expiration of the relevant Statement of Work or Acceptance of the Deliverable.

12. Limits on Access to Introduced Clients

12.1. For purposes of this Agreement, an "Introduced Client" is a legal entity or individual that has purchased the software or services from Customer where (1) Customer introduced Consultant to such entity or individual and (2) the introduction led to Consultant performing services for the use or benefit of such entity or individual.

12.2. Consultant agrees that Consultant will maintain its primary business and technical dealings with Customer with regard to each Introduced Client and will not deal with the Introduced Client on business or payment matters.

12.3. Consultant further agrees that it will refrain from promoting or soliciting to provide or arrange to provide similar or competing services to any Introduced Client for a period during and for six (6) months after the completion of all Statements of Work ("Restriction Period") that relate to such Introduced Client.

12.4. Should an Introduced Client contact Consultant directly for similar or competing services at any time during any Restriction Period, Consultant agrees to notify Customer and allow Customer to contact the Introduced Client and to cooperate in permitting such services to be contracted and arranged solely through Customer.

13. **Insurance**

13.1. Consultant will, at its own expense, at all times during the term of this Agreement and for one year thereafter, provide and maintain in effect those insurance policies and minimum limits of coverage as designated below. Coverage will be for the benefit of Customer, its Affiliates and their respective officers, directors, employees, servants, and agents. These requirements do not limit liability of Consultant assumed elsewhere in this Agreement:

13.1.1. *Workers' Compensation.* Workers' Compensation insurance will be provided as required by any applicable law or regulation and, in accordance with the provisions of the laws of the nation, state, territory or province having jurisdiction over Consultant's employees.

13.1.2. *General Liability.* Consultant will carry Commercial General Liability insurance covering all operations for bodily injury, property damage, personal injury and advertising injury, as those terms are defined by Commercial General Liability insurance policies, with limits of not less than $_____ for each occurrence and an aggregate of $_____.

13.1.3. *Automobile Liability Insurance.* Consultant will carry Business Automobile Liability insurance, including bodily injury and property damage for all vehicles used in the performance of Consultant's Services under this Agreement. The limits of liability will not be less than $_____ combined single limit for each accident.

13.1.4. *Errors and Omissions.* Consultant will carry insurance for Errors and Omissions/Professional Liability with limits of not less than $_____ per occurrence or per claim and $_____ in the annual aggregate.

13.2. Consultant will supply Certificates of Insurance for the foregoing to Customer before work on any Services or Deliverables are commenced hereunder by Consultant and 30 days prior to policy renewal. The policy(ies) will be endorsed to stipulate that Consultant's insurance will be primary to and non-contributory with any and all other insurance maintained or otherwise afforded to Customer, its Affiliates and their respective officers, directors, employees, servants, and agents. Consultant and its respective insurers waive all rights of recovery or subrogation against Customer, its Affiliates and their respective officers, directors, employees, agents, and insurers except as prohibited by law.

13.3. Consultant will obtain insurance or will reimburse Customer and its Affiliates for loss or damage to any property of Customer or its Affiliates in the care, custody, or control of Consultant, for all losses including, but not limited to theft, loss, misappropriation or destruction caused by Consultant, its employees, agents, or other representative.

13.4. In the event Consultant utilizes the services of subcontractors to perform any Services contemplated hereunder, Consultant will require from or provide for all subcontractors the same minimum insurance requirements detailed above. Customer reserves the right to require and obtain copies of Subcontractor's certificates and/or certified copies of insurance policies from Consultant upon request.

14. Indemnification

14.1. Consultant will defend, hold harmless and indemnify Customer, its Affiliates, and their respective officers, directors, employees, servants and agents (collectively the "Indemnitees") from and against any and all losses, claims, liabilities, damages, costs and expenses (including taxes, fees, fines, penalties, interest, reasonable expenses of investigation and attorneys' fees and disbursements) as each Indemnitee may incur arising out of or relating to:

14.1.1. Acts or omissions of Consultant that breach any term or condition of this Agreement;

14.1.2. Any claim or allegation by any third party of damage to or destruction of property or death or injury of persons, including but not limited to employees or invitees of such party, which damage, destruction, death or injury results from or is alleged to result from any Deliverable or Services or any negligent act or omission of Consultant, its employees, agents or subcontractors; or

14.1.3. Any claim or allegation by any third party that any Deliverable or Services, or use, copying, distribution or exploitation thereof infringes (whether directly, contributorily, by inducement or otherwise), misappropriates or violates such third party's Intellectual Property or proprietary interest.

15. Limitation of Liability

15.1. *Consequential Damages.* Customer will not be liable to Consultant with respect to any subject matter of this Agreement under any contract, negligence, strict liability or other legal or equitable theory for any special, indirect, consequential, incidental or exemplary damages including without limitation, damages for loss of Consultant's business profits, cost of procurement of substitute goods, technology or services, business interruptions or loss of information, even if Customer has been advised of the possibility of such damages.

15.2. *Limitation of Liability.* In no event will Customer be liable to Consultant for any amounts in excess of the aggregate of the fees paid by Customer to Consultant hereunder during the six (6) month period prior to the date the cause of action arose.

16. Term

16.1. This Agreement will commence on the Effective Date and will continue until the later of (i) [DATE], or (ii) so long as a Statement of Work is in effect and has not been completed to the satisfaction of Customer, unless this Agreement is terminated earlier as provided in this Agreement.

16.2. Immediately upon the expiration or termination of this Agreement, Consultant will turn over all Confidential Information (including all copies, extracts, modifications and derivatives thereof) to Customer and will deliver to Customer all Deliverables, Intellectual Property and work product (whether completed or not) developed or created under this Agreement in the performance of the Services.

17. Termination

17.1. Customer may terminate this Agreement or any Statement of Work, in whole or in part:

17.1.1. For convenience upon thirty (30) days' written notice to Consultant; or

17.1.2. If at any time after the commencement of the Services, Customer, determines that such Services are inadequate, unsatisfactory, or substantially non-conforming to the Specifications, descriptions, warranties, or representations contained herein and the problem is not remedied within thirty (30) days of Consultant's receipt of written notice describing the issue or problem.

17.2. Either Party may terminate his Agreement for cause in the event of: (a) a material breach or default by the other party of an obligation under this Agreement which is not remedied within thirty (30) days after written notice; or (b) the other party's filing for bankruptcy or becoming an involuntary participant in a bankruptcy proceeding, if such involuntary proceedings are not dismissed within sixty (60) days after commencement.

17.3. The Sections of this Agreement regarding Confidentiality, Intellectual Property Ownership, Warranties, Remedies, Exclusivity and Non-Competition, Limits on Access to Introduced Clients, Insurance, Indemnification, Limitation of Liability, Termination, and General provisions will survive termination, as will accrued rights to payment.

18. Assignment

Consultant may not assign this Agreement without Customer's express prior written consent. Customer reserves the right to transfer this Agreement to any Affiliate. Customer may also, without Consultant's consent, transfer this Agreement in connection with the sale or disposition of its business or a line of business relevant to this Agreement, by asset transfer, merger, stock sale or otherwise.

19. **General**

    19.1. *Notice.* Any notice to be given hereunder will be in writing and addressed to the party and address stated below, or such other address as the party may designate from time to time by written notice in accordance with this Section. Except as otherwise expressly provided in this Agreement, notices hereunder will be deemed given and effective: (i) if personally delivered, upon delivery, (ii) if sent by overnight rapid-delivery service with tracking capabilities, upon receipt; (iii) if sent by fax or electronic mail, at such time as the party that sent the notice receives confirmation of receipt by the applicable method of transmittal, or (iv) if sent by certified or registered United States mail, upon receipt.

    If to Consultant: *[add address, contact person and/or title, and fax number]*

    If to Customer: *[add address, contact person and/or title, and fax number]*

    19.2. *Compliance with Laws.* Consultant hereby represents and warrants that it will comply with all applicable, local, state, provincial, and national laws and regulations. Consultant will comply, to the extent applicable, with US export control laws.

    19.3. *No Third Party Beneficiary.* This Agreement is not intended to confer a benefit on, or to be enforceable by, any person who is not a party to this Agreement.

    19.4. *Status as Independent Contractor.* Consultant is an independent contractor, and neither party's employees will be considered employees of the other party for any purpose. This Agreement does not create a joint venture or partnership, and neither party has the authority to bind the other to any third party.

    19.5. *Applicable Law and Jurisdiction.* This Agreement will be governed and construed in accordance with the laws of the State of _____ without regard to the conflicts of laws or principles thereof and applicable US federal law. It is further agreed that any and all disputes, claims or litigation arising from or related in any way to this Agreement or any provisions herein will be resolved exclusively in the state and federal courts located in _____. The parties hereby waive any objections against and expressly agree to submit to the personal jurisdiction and venue of such state or federal courts.

19.6. *Waiver.* No waiver by Customer of any breach by Consultant of any of the provisions of this Agreement will be deemed a waiver of any preceding or succeeding breach of the same or any other provisions hereof. No such waiver will be effective unless in writing and then only to the extent expressly set forth in writing.

19.7. *Customer Affiliates.* Customer may cause or permit all rights and permissions granted in this Agreement to be exercised by or through any Affiliate.

19.8. *No Delegation.* Consultant's performance and obligations under this Agreement may not be delegated without the prior written consent of Customer.

19.9. *Severability.* If any provision of this Agreement is invalid or unenforceable under any statute or rule of law, the provision is to the extent to be deemed omitted, and the remaining provisions will not be affected in any way.

19.10. *Force Majeure.* Neither party will be responsible for any delay or failure in performance resulting from acts beyond such party's control ("Force Majeure"). Force Majeure will include but not be limited to: acts of God, government or war; riots or strikes; epidemics, fires, floods, or disasters. At its option, Customer may terminate any Statement of Work that is delayed more than 30 days by Force Majeure event(s).

19.11. *Entire Agreement.* This Agreement, including the attached Statement of Work and any supplements, constitutes the entire agreement between Consultant and Customer with regard to this subject matter.

19.12. *Modifications.* No modification of this Agreement will be effective unless in writing and signed by both parties.

19.13. *Counterparts.* This Agreement may be executed in multiple counterparts, each being deemed an original and this being one of the counterparts. Execution by fax is permitted.

IN WITNESS WHEREOF, the parties hereto have executed this Agreement as of the Effective Date set forth above.

CONSULTANT: _____   CUSTOMER: _____

By: _____   By: _____

Print Name: _____   Print Name: _____

Title: _____   Title: _____

Date: _____   Date: _____

Web Site Development Agreement

10-4

Introductory Note

This is a straightforward web site design and development agreement. It could also be used, with minor changes, for adding functions or content to an existing web site.

Web development ranges from quite simple and low cost to complex and expensive. The more functionality, the more integration with back end data systems, the more complicated the graphics, and the higher the traffic that the web site must handle, then the more prolonged and expensive web development will be. This form is more suited to web site development that is more toward the lower end of the scale. If you want to contract for a more complex web site development, your agreement would look more like Form 10-1, which is a "long form" milestone-driven software development agreement.

Web development can be charged for on an hourly or daily rate basis, on a fixed fee basis, or on a milestone-based billing and payment scheme. This form uses a simple hourly time-and-expense pricing model.

This form is written to be generally favorable to the Developer. It has liability risk limiters that protect the Developer, and it provides the Customer with only a limited intellectual property warranty and indemnity.

Some of the important provisions to pay particular attention to (in addition to the payment provisions) when negotiating web development deals are:

- The task description.
- Acceptance.
- Limitations on liabilities and damages.

- Indemnification.

- Ownership of intellectual property.

This draft includes a few common variants and alternatives. The bracketed text provides optional or alternative language.

The next form in this book (Form 10-5) is for web hosting. Sometimes the provider of web services will offer a combined web development and web hosting agreement, which would be a combination of these forms.

Web Site Development Agreement

This Web Site Development Agreement ("Agreement") is effective as of the ___ day of _____ 20___ ("Effective Date") between *[Insert Developer company name]* (hereinafter "Developer"), with its principal office at _____, and *[Insert Customer company name]* ("Customer") with its principal office at _____ (each a "Party"; together the "Parties").

Purpose of This Agreement

A. Developer is in the business of providing web site design and development services.

B. Customer wishes to have a web site created in accordance with the specifications in this Agreement (the "Site").

In consideration of the mutual agreements set forth herein, Developer and Customer agree as follows:

1. **Design and Development**

   1.1. *Development.* Customer hereby engages the services of Developer to provide web development services. Developer will carry out the development of the Site in substantial compliance with the statement of work (the "Statement of Work") attached as <u>Schedule A</u>. The Parties may, by mutual agreement, execute additional Statements of Work under this Agreement.

   1.2. *Development Timetable.* Developer will use commercially reasonably efforts to complete development of the Site in accordance with the development timetable set forth in the Statement of Work. Developer will promptly notify Customer of any circumstances that may reasonably be anticipated to lead to a material delay.

1.3. *Change Orders.* Customer may request additional services or modifications to the Site by delivering a written change order request to Developer. In the event that Developer receives a change order request, Developer will determine the cost and/or schedule impact, if any, of the requested change, and provide to Customer a proposal for a change order ("Change Order"). Each Change Order will be effective when signed by both Parties. Customer will not be liable for any charges under the Change Order, and Developer will not be obliged to perform the requested changes unless the applicable Change Order has been executed by the Parties.

1.4. *Use of Third-Party Consultants.* Developer may retain qualified third parties to furnish services to it in connection with its work on the Site, provided that Developer will be responsible for the activities of such third parties as they relate to this Agreement.

2. **Customer Materials**

2.1. Customer will supply content and materials, including any graphics, pictures, audio, video, logos and text for the Site ("Customer Materials"). Customer will retain ownership of Customer Materials. Customer grants Developer a license to use Customer Materials solely for the purpose of performance of its obligations under this Agreement. Customer represents and warrants that it has or has or will obtain all necessary ownership, licenses and/or permissions to grant such license and will defend, indemnify and hold Developer harmless with regard to any third party claim or allegation that the Customer Materials or Developer's licensed use of the Customer Materials infringes or violates any third party rights or violates any law.

3. **Acceptance Testing and Access**

[*Comment: With web site development, the Developer will typically give the Customer initial access to a web site on a test server for acceptance testing purposes. The following text is based on a testing of the entire Site that is provided as a single "Deliverable." For a large-scale project, it would be common to break down the work into a series of deliverables and milestones that are subject to a corresponding series of acceptance tests. For examples of such deliverable-driven acceptance language see Form 10-1 and Form 10-3. In some cases, the Customer's initial acceptance of the web site may be subject to final acceptance after the web site "goes live." In that case, review on the test server would be a pre-final milestone, and acceptable performance during an agreed period of live deployment would be the last and final milestone.]*

3.1. *Access to Site for Review.* Developer will make the Site accessible to Customer on a non-public test server ("Test Server") for review and acceptance testing. Developer will notify Customer by mail, email or fax when the Site is available for testing on the Test Server.

3.2. *Acceptance Tests.* Customer will access the Site on the Test Server and perform all tests necessary to determine whether the Site conforms to the specifications set forth in the Statement of Work. Customer will have *[specify number]* days from the date upon which Developer provides notice that the Site is available for such testing (the "Initial Test Period"). In the event that the Site does not conform to the specifications set forth in the Statement of Work, Customer will deliver a written notice specifying each non-conformity in reasonable detail (a "Non-Conformity Notice") to Developer on or before the expiration of the Initial Test Period.

*[**Comment**: There are a number of choices on how to deal with errors and non-conformities on the Site. The most common provision simply requires that the Developer fix any errors. If the web site development tasks are relatively simple, there is a high probability that any errors and bugs can be readily fixed. An alternative approach includes language to allow the Customer to terminate the Agreement if non-conformities are not fixed after one or two opportunities to cure. In such a termination, the Developer might receive only partial payment, or in some deals (where the Customer has substantial leverage), the disappointed Customer is given a refund of some or all development fees. This form takes the first approach and simply requires that errors be fixed.]*

3.3. *Corrective Action.* Developer will correct [at no additional cost to Customer] [on a time and materials basis] the non-conformities stated in the Non-Conformity Notice within a reasonable period of time. After Developer makes such corrections to the Site and makes the Site available to Customer for access on the Test Server, then Customer will have *[specify number]* days to re-test the Site ("Additional Test Period"). If any non-conformities remain, the process stated above will be repeated.

3.4. *Deemed Acceptance.* Customer's failure to deliver a Non-Compliance Notice prior to the expiration of the applicable Initial Test Period or Additional Test Period will be deemed Customer's acceptance of the Site.

3.5. *Delivery.* Upon the completion and acceptance of the Site, Developer will deliver a copy of the Site's computer code to Customer and will also [host the Site pursuant to the separate Web Hosting Agreement between the Parties] [deliver a copy of the Site's computer code to Customer's designated hosting provider].

4. **Compensation**

4.1. *Fees.* Unless otherwise provided by the Statement of Work, all services hereunder will be performed on a time and materials basis billed at the rates set forth on the Statement of Work.

4.2. *Expenses.* Developer will be entitled to reimbursement of its reasonable [pre-approved] expenses incurred in connection with the Statement of Work for travel-related expenses and for such other items as the Parties may agree upon in writing. Expenses will be documented with receipts or other reasonable written evidence.

4.3. *Payment.* Developer will submit a [monthly] [weekly] statement and invoice to Customer for services rendered hereunder and its reimbursable expenses. Such invoices will be due and payable within ____ (___) days of the invoice date.

4.4. *Taxes.* The fees set forth herein are exclusive of taxes. Customer will be responsible for all taxes, levies, and assessments, excepting taxes based on the income of Developer.

4.5. *Records and Audit.* Developer will maintain books and records in connection with its services, billings, and expenses. Customer, by its independent certified public accountant, may audit Developer's records to determine whether Developer's billings, charges, and fees comply with the terms of this Agreement. Any such audits will be conducted during Developer's regular business hours at Developer's facilities subject to a reasonable confidentiality agreement, will not unreasonably interfere with Developer's business activities, and will take place not more than once in every calendar year. In the event of any overpayment or over-billing or underpayment, appropriate adjustments will be made within thirty (30) days of receipt of the audit report. In case that Developer has over-billed in an amount in excess of ten percent (10%) of the aggregate billings, accrued fees, and charges for the audited period (but in any case in excess of $_____), then Developer will pay Customer's reasonable accounting costs for conducting the audit.

5. **Ownership**

   [**Comment**: *The following provisions allow the Developer to retain ownership in "Background Technology" which consists of Developer's existing code and technologies and any derivatives. The Background Technology is licensed to Customer for use in the Site. All other code or content created under this Agreement and included in the Site will be the Customer's property under the "work made for hire" clause. This formulation allows the Developer to keep what it already owns and improve it, but any wholly new code would belong to the Customer. A possible alternative, even more favorable to the Developer, is to give the Developer ownership of all code that is "reusable." For an example of such a formulation, see the "Intellectual Property" section of Form 10.2.]*

   5.1. *Ownership of Work Product.* Except as provided in Section 5.2 with regard to Background Technology (as defined below), upon Customer's payment of fees due for the Site, Developer hereby assigns and agrees to assign to Customer all right, title and interest in and to all source code, object code, data, and works of authorship, including those that constitute the Site (collectively, the "Work Product"). Except as provided in Section 5.2 with regard to Background Technology, upon Customer's payment of fees due for the Site, the Work Product will be deemed a "work-made-for-hire" to the extent provided by law, and to the extent not a work-for-hire, is hereby assigned to Customer. Developer agrees to cooperate with Customer in confirming Customer's ownership rights in the Work Product.

   5.2. *License to Background Technology.* Developer will retain all right, title and interest in all of (i) its pre-existing programs, materials, software development tools, supplies, proprietary information, files, technology, scripting, and programming, including, without limitation, those items which are utilized by Developer in providing the Site or the services under this Agreement, (ii) all improvements and derivatives of the foregoing and

(iii) all intellectual property rights in the foregoing (the "Background Technology"). Upon payment in full of all development fees set forth herein, Developer hereby grants to Customer, a perpetual, non-exclusive, non-transferable (except as specifically provided in Section 11.1), world-wide right and license (the "License") to use, modify, copy or otherwise exploit the Background Technology as used in the Site (but not for resale or for the purpose of creating additional web sites, products, applications or other programs separable from the Site as it may be modified, used, copied or exploited).

6. **Warranty and Disclaimers**

[Comment: When a Site is provided on a time-and-materials basis, it is most common that error correction also is charged for in the same way. Developers do sometimes provide error correction for a period at no extra cost. This form allows a choice of how error correction will be handled.]

6.1. *Limited Warranty.* Developer warrants that for a period of ninety (90) days following the acceptance date, the Site will perform in accordance with the specifications set forth in the Statement of Work. Should the Site, during such warranty period, not perform as warranted herein, Developer will resolve the problem [on a time and materials basis] [free of additional charge] within a commercially reasonable period of time. The foregoing are Customer's sole and exclusive remedies.

6.2. *Exclusions from Warranty.* Developer will not be obligated under Section 6.1 to correct, cure, or otherwise remedy any nonconformity if (1) Customer has made any alteration to the Site without Developer's authorization; (2) the Site has been misused or damaged other than by personnel of Developer; or (3) Developer has not been notified of the existence and nature of such nonconformity or defect within the warranty period.

6.3. *Disclaimer.*   EXCEPT AS EXPRESSLY STATED IN THIS AGREEMENT, DEVELOPER DISCLAIMS ALL WARRANTIES, EXPRESS OR IMPLIED, INCLUDING, WITHOUT LIMITATION, IMPLIED WARRANTIES OF TITLE, NON-INFRINGEMENT, AND MERCHANTABILITY OR FITNESS FOR ANY PARTICULAR PURPOSE.

6.4. *Limitation of Liability.* The cumulative liability of Developer to Customer for all claims whatsoever related to the Site, the services provided hereunder or this Agreement, including any cause of action sounding in contract, tort, or strict liability, will not exceed the total amount of all fees paid to Developer by Customer under this Agreement.

*[**Comment**: The foregoing is a unilateral damage cap clause. Sometimes, a Customer will insist that the damage cap be "bilateral" (i.e., that Customer also has the benefit of a cap on claims made by Developer). If a bilateral clause is used, Developer should consider excluding unlicensed use or copying of any Developer-licensed software or Background Technology from the mutual liability cap and from the consequential damages clause. The Developer should also make sure that its unpaid fees are not limited by the cap. See also the discussion of "Mutual Consequential Damages Exclusions and Carve-Outs" in Chapter 8.]*

6.5. *Consequential Damages.* In no event will Developer be liable for any lost profits, incidental, exemplary, or consequential damages, even if Developer has been advised of the possibility of such damages.

6.6. *Third-Party Materials.* Developer may, pursuant to the terms of the Statement of Work, incorporate third party software, code, content or materials (collectively, "Third Party Materials") in the Site; Developer makes no warranty with regard to Third Party Materials. Customer's sole and exclusive rights and remedies with respect to the Third Party Materials, including remedies in the event the presence of such a Third Party Material gives rise to an intellectual-property infringement claim, will be against the third party vendor of such materials and not against Developer.

6.7. *Authority.* Each Party warrants that it has all required authority to enter into this Agreement.

7. Intellectual Property Warranty and Indemnification

*[**Comment**: It is not unusual for a Customer to argue that the Developer should provide broad non-infringement warranties and indemnification with respect to the software code embodied in the Site. Developer will want to provide non-infringement provisions subject to various "carve outs" and "a knowledge qualifier" like those in the following Section. There is probably not a lot of infringement risk in "plain vanilla" web development, but generally speaking Developers should try to avoid assuming material infringement risk.]*

7.1. *Developer's Intellectual Property Warranty.* To the best of its knowledge (but without an obligation to make any investigation), Developer's

Contribution (as defined below) does not and will not infringe or violate any third party patents, copyrights, trademarks, trade secrets or other intellectual property rights. "Developer's Contribution" means the Site except for Customer Materials and Third Party Materials.

7.2. *Developer's Indemnification of Customer.* Developer will defend, indemnify, and hold harmless Customer with respect to any third party lawsuit or proceeding arising from Developer's breach of the warranty in Section 7.1 (each, a "Claim"). Indemnification under this Section is Customer's sole and exclusive remedy for the Claim and for breach of the warranty in Section 7.1.

8. **Procedure for Indemnification.** For any Claim that is subject to indemnification under this Agreement, the obligation to indemnify is subject to the Party entitled to indemnification (the "Indemnitee") providing the indemnifying Party (the "Indemnitor") reasonably prompt notice of the relevant Claim. Indemnitor shall defend and/or settle, at its own expense, any Claim subject to indemnification under this Agreement. The Indemnitee shall cooperate in good faith with the Indemnitor to facilitate the defense of any such Claim and shall tender the defense and settlement of the Claim to the Indemnitor. Claims may be settled without the consent of the Indemnitee, unless the settlement includes an admission of wrongdoing, fault or liability of the Indemnitee.

9. **Term and Termination**

[Comment: This Agreement is written to terminate when the development tasks and any warranty period is completed. If a web development agreement includes provisions for the Developer to provide hosting or ongoing support services, it would need provisions under which the Agreement continues in effect.]

9.1. *Term.* This Agreement will commence on the date first written above and will continue in effect until such time as all obligations (including services and the warranty period) hereunder are completed, unless terminated earlier in accordance with this Agreement.

9.2. *Material Breach.* Either Party may terminate this Agreement for a material breach which remains uncured for thirty (30) days after the breaching Party receives notice of such breach from the non-breaching Party.

[Comment: Permitting a Customer to terminate for convenience fits a time and materials agreement. For a fixed fee agreement, there is commonly some compensation

to the Developer (sometimes informally called a "kill fee") that will apply if the Customer terminates for convenience before the Site is done.]

9.3. *Termination for Convenience.* Customer may terminate this Agreement for convenience upon ten (10) days' prior written notice to Developer. Upon the receipt of payment in full for all services performed through the effective date of termination, Developer will promptly deliver to Customer all work in-progress within ten (10) days of such payment. If Customer terminates before completion of the Site as described in the Statement of Work, all Deliverables will be deemed provided "AS IS," and the warranty in Section 6.1 will not apply.

9.4. *Survival.* The following Sections will survive the termination of this Agreement as applicable: 4.5 (Audit), 5 (Ownership), 6 (Warranties and Disclaimers), 7 (Intellectual Property Warranty and Indemnification), 8 (Procedure for Indemnification), 9.4 (Survival), 10 (Confidentiality) and 11 (General), together with accrued payment obligations.

10. **Confidentiality**

10.1. *Use of Confidential Information.* The Parties, from time to time, may disclose Confidential Information (as defined below) to one another. Accordingly, each Party agrees as the recipient (the "Receiving Party") to keep strictly confidential all Confidential Information provided by the other Party (the "Disclosing Party"). The Receiving Party further agrees to use the Confidential Information of the Disclosing Party solely for the purpose of exercising its rights and fulfilling its obligations under this Agreement. The Receiving Party may not use for its own benefit or otherwise disclose any of the Confidential Information of the Disclosing Party for any other purpose.

10.2. *Definition of Confidential Information.* "Confidential Information" means, subject to Section 10.3, information in any form, oral, graphic, written, electronic, machine-readable or hard copy consisting of (i) any non-public information provided by the Disclosing Party, including but not limited to, all of its inventions, designs, data, source and object code, programs, program interfaces, know-how, trade secrets, techniques, ideas, discoveries, marketing and business plans, pricing, profit margins, and/or similar information or (ii) any information which the Disclosing Party identifies as confidential information or the Receiving Party should understand from the context of the disclosure, to be confidential information.

10.3. *Exclusions.* The term "Confidential Information" will not include information that (a) is publicly available at the time of disclosure by the Disclosing Party; (b) becomes publicly available by publication or otherwise after disclosure by the Disclosing Party, other than by breach of this Section by the Receiving Party; (c) was lawfully in the Receiving Party's possession, without restriction as to confidentiality or use, at the time of disclosure by the Disclosing Party; (d) is provided to the Receiving Party without restriction as to confidentiality or use by a third party without violation of any obligation to the Disclosing Party, or (e) is independently developed by employees or agents of the Receiving Party who did not access or use the Confidential Information.

10.4. *Protection of Confidential Information.* The Receiving Party will inform those employees and consultants who have access to the Confidential Information of the Disclosing Party that such information is confidential and proprietary information of a third party. The Receiving Party agrees to disclose the Confidential Information of the Disclosing Party solely to its employees and consultants who need to know such information for the purpose of exercising the Receiving Party's rights and fulfilling the Receiving Party's obligations hereunder and who agree in writing to keep such information confidential. The Receiving Party will ensure compliance by its employees and consultants having access to the Confidential Information of the Disclosing Party and will be responsible for any breach by any such parties. The Receiving Party will notify the Disclosing Party without delay if it has reason to believe that any Confidential Information of the Disclosing Party has been used or disclosed in violation of this Section.

10.5. *Return of Confidential Information.* Promptly upon the written request of the Disclosing Party or upon termination of this Agreement, the Receiving Party will return to the Disclosing Party or destroy all copies of the Disclosing Party's Confidential Information.

10.6. *Legal Proceedings.* In the event that the Receiving Party becomes legally compelled to disclose any of the Confidential Information of the Disclosing Party, the Receiving Party will provide the Disclosing Party with prompt notice so that the Disclosing Party may seek a protective order or other appropriate remedy.

10.7. *Remedy.* Each Party acknowledges that the other Party will not have an adequate remedy in the event that it breaches the provisions of this Agreement regarding Confidential Information and that such Party may suffer irreparable damage and injury in such event. The breaching Party agrees that the non-breaching Party, in addition to seeking any other available rights and remedies as may apply, will be entitled to seek an injunction restraining the breaching Party from committing or continuing such violation.

11. General Provisions

[*Comment: The following clause, allowing assignment of the Agreement (and the included license to the Background Technology) under specified conditions is common. Some Customers may want broader rights to transfer the Site, including, for example, making the Site available to related companies or spin-off companies.]*

11.1. *Transfer or Assignment.* A Party will not have the right to transfer or assign this Agreement or rights granted under it except in connection with (a) the sale of all or substantially all of the Party's assets or a line of business sale; (b) the sale of a majority of the capital stock of the Party or (c) the merger of the Party with another entity. In each such instance, the Party may transfer the Agreement to the acquirer or surviving company (in the case of a merger). Any such transfer or assignment will become effective only if and when the transferee or assignee agrees in writing to be bound by the terms of this Agreement.

11.2. *Force Majeure.* Neither Party will be responsible for any delay or failure in performance resulting from acts beyond such Party's control ("Force Majeure"). Force Majeure will include but not be limited to: acts of God, government or war, riots or strikes, epidemics, fires, floods, or disasters. At its option, Customer may terminate any Statement of Work that is delayed more than sixty (60) days by Force Majeure event(s). Force Majeure may not extend any payment obligation by more than fifteen (15) days.

11.3. *Publicity.* All public announcements of the relationship of Developer and Customer under this Agreement shall be subject to the prior written approval of both Parties; provided, however, that Developer may list

Customer as a customer of Developer on its web site and in marketing materials, press releases, and other promotional documents [subject to Customer's approval which is not to be unreasonably withheld].

11.4. *Non-Solicitation.* During the term of this Agreement and for a period of one (1) year thereafter, each Party agrees not to directly or indirectly solicit for employment any employee of the other Party who is or was materially involved in providing services pursuant to this Agreement unless the other Party consents in writing. This provision does not prevent general job solicitations, such as web and newspaper postings.

11.5. *No Agency.* Developer is an independent contractor and neither Party's employees will be considered employees of the other Party for any purpose. This Agreement does not create a joint venture or partnership, and neither Party has the authority to bind the other to any third Party.

11.6. *Notices.* Any notice to be given hereunder will be in writing and addressed to the Party and address stated below or such other address as the Party may designate from time to time by written notice. Except as otherwise expressly provided in this Agreement, notices hereunder will be deemed given and effective: (i) if personally delivered, upon delivery, (ii) if sent by overnight rapid-delivery service with tracking capabilities, upon receipt; (iii) if sent by fax or electronic mail, at such time as the Party that sent the notice receives confirmation of receipt by the applicable method of transmittal, or (iv) if sent by certified or registered United States mail, upon receipt.

For notice to Customer: *[Insert address information and officer to whom notice should be addressed]*

For notice to Developer: *[Insert address information and officer to whom notice should be addressed]*

11.7. *Governing Law.* This Agreement will be governed and construed in accordance with the laws of the State of _____ without regard to the conflicts of laws or principles thereof and applicable US federal law. Any and all disputes, claims or litigation arising from or related in any way to this Agreement or any provisions herein will be resolved exclusively in the state and federal courts located in _____. The Parties hereby waive any objections against and expressly agree to submit to the personal jurisdiction and venue of such state or federal courts.

11.8. *Entire Agreement; Amendment.* This Agreement constitutes the entire agreement between the Parties and supersedes all prior agreements and understandings, whether written or oral, relating to the subject matter of this Agreement. This Agreement may be amended or modified only by a written instrument executed by both Parties.

11.9. *Miscellaneous.* No delay or omission by either Party in exercising any right under this Agreement will operate as a waiver of that or any other right. A waiver or consent given by either Party on any one occasion will be effective only in that instance and will not be construed as a bar or waiver of any right on any other occasion. This Agreement may be executed in one or more counterparts, each of which will be deemed to be an original (a facsimile will be deemed an original), but all of which taken together will constitute one and the same instrument. If any provision of this Agreement is found to be invalid by any court or arbitrator having competent jurisdiction, the invalidity of such provision will not affect the validity of the remaining provisions.

IN WITNESS WHEREOF, the Parties have executed this Web Site Development Agreement on the date first above written.

Developer: _____   Customer: _____

By: _____   By: _____

Name: _____   Name: _____

Title: _____   Title: _____

Date: _____   Date: _____

STATEMENT OF WORK

[Insert provisions of the Statement of Work, which may include:

Description of Project/Specifications.

Schedule of Work.

Milestone Deliverables (if any).

Fees and Payment Schedule /Standard Rates.

Third Party Software.]

Web Hosting Agreement

Introductory Note

This is a form of web hosting agreement for a commercial web site. This form is written to protect and favor the hosting provider, but provides a significant amount of services to the Customer.

Bracketed language indicates options or alternative language. As you will see, some of the optional language adapts the form for use in hosting of online retail e-commerce sites that require credit card clearance. This form includes a sample Service Level Agreement (or "SLA"). There are many variations in the content of SLAs.

The form is intended to be used as a signed agreement. A simpler (but similarly pro-hosting-provider) version would be used for a "clickwrap" hosting agreement.

Web Site Hosting Agreement

This Web Site Hosting Agreement (this "Agreement") is made and entered into as of the ____ day of ___ 20__ (the "Effective Date"), by and between _____, a _____ corporation with offices at _____ ("Provider"), and _____a _____ corporation with offices at _____ ("Customer") (each being referred to individually as a "Party" and collectively, the "Parties").

Purpose of This Agreement

    A. Provider is in the business of providing Internet services for hosting of Internet sites on the World Wide Web (known as the "Web"); and

    B. Customer desires to engage Provider to provide such Web services on the terms and subject to the conditions set forth below.

833

Intending to be bound, the Parties agree as follows:

1. **Services**

   1.1. *Hosting Services.* Provider agrees to provide Customer with services for hosting of a site on the Web (the "Web Site") as described on <u>Schedule A</u> hereto (the "Hosting Services"). The Hosting Services are expected to make the Web Site accessible to third parties via the Internet.

   1.2. *Additional Services.* If Customer wishes to receive from Provider services other than the Hosting Services, for example, setup, configuration, software updating, FTP, or email (collectively, the "Additional Services"), arrangements for such services may be set forth in a separate addendum to this Agreement (the "Additional Services Addendum"). An Additional Services Addendum will be effective when executed by both Parties. Unless otherwise agreed in writing, each Additional Services Addendum will be incorporated into and be subject this Agreement. (The Hosting Services and any Additional Services are referred to as the "Services.")

   1.3. *Liaison.* Each Party will designate a person who will act as the primary liaison for all communications regarding the Hosting Services and any Additional Services.

   *[**Comment:** The term "PCI" in the following section refers to the Payment Card Industry Security Standards Council. This organization, formed by American Express, Discover Financial Services, JCB, MasterCard Worldwide and Visa International, sets security standards for credit card and debit card transactions and data storage. In an optional schedule to this Agreement are provisions relating to Provider's compliance with PCI standards. In essence, they say that Provider will try to comply with PCI security rules but will not be liable to either the Customer or the banks if there is a data breach that results in identity theft or financial loss.]*

   1.4. [*PCI Compliance.* Provider agrees to use commercially reasonable efforts to provide services compliant with the transaction security standards of the Payment Card Industry Security Standards Council ("PCI") as further stated in and subject to <u>Schedule D</u> to this Agreement.]

2. **Supply of Customer Content**

Except to the extent that Provider has been separately engaged to develop and/or update the Web Site for Customer, Customer will provide to Provider all materials comprising the Web Site, including, but not limited to, any software, code, images, photographs, illustrations, graphics, audio, video or text (the "Customer Content"), which will be in Provider's acceptable format (as specified by Provider in consultation with Customer). Unless otherwise agreed in writing, Customer is solely responsible for Customer Content and its functionality.

3. **Availability of the Web Site**

   3.1. Unless otherwise indicated on <u>Schedule A</u> hereto, the Web Site will be accessible to third parties via the Internet twenty-four (24) hours a day, seven (7) days a week after installation and configuration, except for scheduled maintenance and required repairs, and except for any loss or interruption of Hosting Services due to causes beyond the control of Provider.

   3.2. Subject to Section 3.1, Provider agrees to provide the Hosting Services in accordance with the Service Level Agreement set forth in <u>Schedule C</u>. In the event of any loss or interruption of Hosting Services other than as permitted in Section 3.1 of this Agreement, Customer's sole and exclusive remedy and Provider's sole liability will be as stated in the Service Level Agreement.

4. **Domain Name Registration**

As part of the initial Hosting Services, Customer will provide Provider with a registered domain name. Upon Customer's written request, Provider will register a domain name selected by Customer provided that such domain name is available for registration and does not violate any policies of the registrars used by Provider or any law or regulation. Customer agrees to promptly reimburse to Provider the fees paid by Provider for registration and maintenance of such domain name.

5. **[Third Party Services**

In the event that any of the Hosting Services and any Additional Services provided Customer (including, if applicable, credit card services or any third party content or data feeds) are supplied to Provider by third party ("Third Party Services"), such Third Party Services will be listed in <u>Schedule A</u> (as it may be amended from time to time) or an Additional Services Addendum. Payments that apply to Third Party Services, if applicable, are to be set forth in <u>Schedule B</u> (as it may be amended from time to time) or the applicable Additional Services Addendum.]

6. **Additional Hardware and Software**

In the event that the Web Site requires additional hardware and software not included in the Hosting Services, Customer may request in writing that Provider (a) upgrade the level of Hosting Services, or (b) acquire additional hardware or software to be included in the Hosting Services. Provider will promptly review such request and submit to Customer, for its written acceptance, a proposal for additional hardware, software and/or any Additional Services Addendum required to fulfill Customer's request, including applicable pricing. If Customer accepts Provider's proposal in writing, Provider will proceed to use reasonable efforts to implement such proposal, and Customer will pay Provider as provided in such proposal.

7. **Web Site Updating**

    7.1. *Updating by Customer.* As part of the Hosting Services, on reasonable notice, Provider will provide Customer with reasonable access to one or more test servers to allow Customer to supply, transmit and apply revisions, updates, deletions, enhancements or modifications of the Web Site (the "Updates") and to test and review the Web Site as so modified.

    7.2. *Customer Consultants.* Customer may engage a third party ("Customer Consultant") to update and make other modifications to the Web Site, and Provider will cooperate with such Customer Consultant. Provider will provide each Customer Consultant with the same access to make Updates to the Web Site as Provider provides to Customer. Customer will require each Customer Consultant to sign a confidentiality agreement consistent with Customer's confidentiality obligation under this Agreement. Customer will be responsible for the acts and omissions of its Customer Consultant as if they were its own.

    7.3. *Additional Services.* If Customer's Updates require additional services or technology that are not within the scope of the Hosting Services as stated in this Agreement, Customer and Provider may negotiate and enter into an Additional Services Addendum setting forth the terms and conditions for Provider's support of such Updates.

8. **License and Proprietary Rights**

    8.1. *Proprietary Rights of Customer.* As between Customer and Provider, unless otherwise agreed in writing by the Parties, Customer Content will remain the property of Customer, including, without limitation, all copyrights, patents, trademarks, trade secrets and any other proprietary rights.

8.2. *License to Provider.* Customer hereby grants to Provider a non-exclusive, worldwide, royalty-free license for the term of this Agreement to use, copy, install, archive, adapt, test, display, distribute and transmit through the Internet or other networks, modify and otherwise use Customer Content solely as is reasonably necessary to render the Hosting Services or any Additional Services to Customer under this Agreement.

8.3. *Proprietary Rights of Provider.* The materials and technology, including but not limited to software, data, content, or information developed, supplied or provided by Provider or its suppliers, the means used by Provider to provide the Hosting Services and any Additional Services to Customer, and the copyrights, patents, trademarks, trade secrets, and other proprietary rights of Provider or its suppliers (collectively "Provider Technologies") will remain the property of Provider or its suppliers.

9. **Customer Data Ownership and Use**

   9.1. "Customer Data" means (a) Customer's data, (b) data submitted by Web Site end users, and (c) data resulting from or used in transactions on the Web Site, including, without limitation, transaction and sales data from Web Site activity, end user contact information, and all other individually or personally identifiable information.

   9.2. As between Customer and Provider, Customer Data will be Customer's property. Provider will use such Customer Data only in the manner and for the purposes set forth in this Agreement or as otherwise authorized by Customer. Upon termination of this Agreement or Provider's Services for any reason, all such Customer Data will be made available to Customer, and Provider will thereafter make no copies, use or disclosure of Customer Data. Provider reserves the right to erase all copies of Customer Data ___ days after the termination of this Agreement.

   9.3. [Provider agrees to provide the measures for data security for Customer Data as stated in the Hosting Services stated in <u>Schedule A</u>.]

10. **Confidentiality**

    10.1. *Definition of Confidential Information.* Each Party agrees that during the course of this Agreement, information that is confidential may be disclosed to the other Party, including, but not limited to, software, technical processes and formulas, source code, product designs, sales, cost and other unpublished financial information, product and business plans, advertising revenues, usage rates, advertising relationships, projections and marketing data ("Confidential Information").

10.2. *Exclusions from Confidentiality.* Confidential Information, however, will not include information that the receiving Party can demonstrate (a) is, as of the time of its disclosure, or thereafter becomes publicly available without fault of the receiving Party, (b) was known to the receiving Party as of the time of its disclosure, (c) is independently developed by the receiving Party, or (d) is subsequently learned from a third party not under a confidentiality obligation to the providing Party. Except as provided for in this Agreement, each Party will not make any disclosure of the Confidential Information to anyone other than its employees and/or contractors who have a need to know in connection with this Agreement. Each Party will ensure that its employees and/or contractors are under confidentiality obligations with respect to the Confidential Information that are consistent with this Agreement. Each Party is responsible for the acts and omissions of its employees and/or contractors with regard to these obligations. The confidentiality obligations regarding Customer Data (including credit cardholder data) survive expiration or termination of this Agreement indefinitely; all other confidentiality obligations of the Parties and their employees and/or contractors will survive the expiration or termination of this Agreement for a period of two (2) years.

10.3. *Compelled Disclosure.* In the event that the receiving Party becomes legally compelled to disclose any of the Confidential Information of the disclosing Party, the receiving Party will provide the disclosing Party with prompt notice so that the disclosing Party may seek a protective order or other appropriate remedy.

10.4. *Remedy.* Each Party acknowledges that the other Party will not have an adequate remedy in the event that it breaches the provisions of this Agreement regarding Confidential Information and that such Party may suffer irreparable damage and injury in such event. The breaching Party agrees that the non-breaching Party, in addition to seeking any other available rights and remedies as may apply, will be entitled to seek an injunction restraining the breaching Party from committing or continuing such violation.

11. **Customer Content Matters**

11.1. *Responsibility for Customer Content.* Customer assumes sole responsibility for (a) obtaining authorizations and permissions for Customer Content (including without limitations any permissions for links to or interaction with third-party web sites), (b) ensuring the accuracy of Customer Content, (c) ensuring that the Customer Content does not infringe or violate any right of any third party and is not defamatory, and (d) complying with privacy law and other applicable legal requirements.

11.2. *Interactive Functionality.* Subject to Provider's written consent, not to be unreasonably refused, Customer may facilitate user forums, blogs, chat, user content uploads, and other interactive features ("Interactive Functionality") using the Web Site and the Hosting Services. Depending on the nature of such functions and services, Provider reserves the right to require Customer to purchase Additional Services in order for Provider to support such functions and services. If Customer implements Interactive Functionality, it agrees to implement reasonable procedures to process complaints about resulting user-generated content and, if appropriate, remove infringing, illegal or offensive materials. [Customer agrees to include in the terms of use of the Web Site provisions binding on each user of the Web Site or the Hosting Services that the user will indemnify, defend, and hold harmless Provider from any such liability to the extent caused or contributed to by the end user.]

11.3. *Other Harmful Content or Conduct.* Customer will exclude and will not provide or permit Customer Content that is infringing, illegal or harmful to Provider or Provider's computer infrastructure, including, without limitation: copyrighted material used without permission, threatening, disparaging, or hate-related content, pornographic or indecent materials or advertising for adult content, pirated software, or links to any of the above. Use of the Service for transmission of bulk unsolicited email (spam) is forbidden. Provider may suspend the Service or terminate this Agreement for Customer's breach of the provisions of this Section.

11.4. *Excluding Customer Content.* Provider reserves the right, in its sole discretion, to exclude, disable, or remove from the Web Site any Customer

Content on the Web Site that in Provider's good faith judgment materially impairs or degrades the operation of the Provider's systems, poses a risk of violating any law or violating or infringing third-party rights or which otherwise exposes or potentially exposes Provider to civil or criminal liability or public ridicule, provided that such right will not place an obligation on Provider to monitor or exert editorial control over the Web Site. Provider agrees to notify Customer promptly by email of any such removal of Customer Content.

12. **Fees and Taxes**

12.1. *Hosting Services Fees.* Customer will pay Provider all fees for the Hosting Services in accordance with the applicable fee and payment schedule set forth in <u>Schedule A</u> hereto. Provider expressly reserves the right to change its rates charged hereunder for the Hosting Services during any Renewal Term (as defined below). [Provider reserves the right to pass through to Customer any increase in rates charged for any Third Party Services.] Customer will pay to Provider all fees for Additional Services on a time and materials basis as set forth in <u>Schedule B</u> hereto, on an applicable Additional Services Addendum, or as otherwise agreed in writing.

12.2. *Out-of-Pocket Expenses.* Customer will pay, or promptly reimburse Provider for, any reasonable [pre-approved] out-of-pocket expenses, including, without limitation, travel and travel-related expenses, incurred by Provider in connection with the performance of the Hosting Services and any Additional Services.

12.3. *Late Payment.* Unless otherwise agreed in writing, Customer will pay to Provider all fees. expenses and any other amounts due under this Agreement within thirty (30) days of receipt of the applicable Provider invoice. Late charges will apply to late payments at the annual rate of ____ percent, compounded daily, or if less, the maximum rate allowable under applicable law.

12.4. *Default for Non-Payment.* The failure of Customer to pay fees due[, unless disputed in good faith,] within ____ days after receiving written notice from Provider specifying that such fees are overdue is a material breach of this Agreement. For such breach, Provider may, at its option, suspend performance of the Hosting Services and/and any Additional Services or terminate this Agreement. Suspension will not relieve Customer from paying past due fees plus interest. Provider will be entitled to recover attorneys' fees and costs of collection in case of payment delinquency.

12.5. *Taxes.* Customer will pay or reimburse Provider for all sales, use, VAT, and all other taxes and all duties that are levied or imposed by reason of the performance by Provider under this Agreement; excluding, however, income taxes on net income which may be levied against Provider.

13. **Warranties**

13.1. *Provider Warranties.* Provider represents and warrants that Provider has the power and authority to enter into and perform its obligations under this Agreement.

13.2. *Customer Warranties.* Customer represents and warrants that Customer has the power and authority to enter into and perform its obligations under this Agreement.

13.3. *Disclaimer of Warranty.* EXCEPT FOR THE LIMITED WARRANTY SET FORTH IN THIS AGREEMENT, PROVIDER EXPRESSLY DISCLAIMS ALL WARRANTIES, EXPRESS OR IMPLIED, INCLUDING, WITHOUT LIMITATION, WARRANTIES OF MERCHANTABILITY, NON-INFRINGEMENT, AND FITNESS FOR A PARTICULAR PURPOSE.

14. **Indemnification**

14.1. *By Provider.* Provider agrees to defend, indemnify, and hold harmless Customer, its officers, directors, employees and agents from any and all costs, liabilities, damages and reasonable attorneys' fees incurred in or resulting from any third party claim or lawsuit alleging that any of the Provider Technologies infringes or violates any rights of third parties, including without limitation, rights of publicity, rights of privacy, patents, copyrights, trademarks, trade secrets, and/or other proprietary rights.

14.2. *By Customer.* Customer agrees to defend, indemnify, and hold harmless Provider, its officers, directors, employees and agents from any and all costs, liabilities, damages and reasonable attorneys' fees incurred in or resulting from any third party claim or lawsuit arising or alleged to arise from Customer Content, Customer Data, and use of the Web Site by Customer or any user, or any Interactive Functionality, including, without limitation, any end user material or content posted, communicated, published, or distributed by means of the Web Site and any claim that such use or such content or material infringes or violates any rights of third parties, including without limitation, rights of publicity, rights of privacy, patents, copyrights, trademarks, trade secrets, and/or other proprietary rights or constitutes defamation or any illegality or criminal offense.

15. **Procedure for Indemnification**

As a condition of obtaining indemnification and a defense under any applicable provision of this Agreement, the indemnified Party will promptly provide the indemnifying Party with written notice of any claim which the indemnified Party believes falls within the scope of the foregoing paragraphs and will cooperate in the defense of the claim. The indemnifying Party will control such defense and all negotiations for the settlement of any such claim. Any settlement intended to bind the indemnified Party will not be final without the indemnified Party's written consent, which will not be unreasonably withheld, provided that consent is not required if the disposition has no adverse impact on the indemnified Party and provides the indemnified Party with an unconditional release of all asserted claims.

16. **Limitation of Liability**

16.1. Provider shall have no liability for consequential, exemplary, special, incidental or punitive damages even if Provider has been advised of the possibility of such damages.

16.2. Provider shall have no liability for unauthorized access to, or alteration, theft or destruction of, the Web Site, Customer Data, Customer Content, or Customer's data files, programs or information through accident, fraudulent means, loss, devices or any other cause.

16.3. The aggregate liability of Provider to Customer shall be limited to the amount actually paid to Provider by Customer under this Agreement during the _____ months immediately preceding the date on which such claim(s) accrued. This limitation applies to all claims and liabilities in the aggregate, including, without limitation, breach of contract, breach of warranty, negligence, strict liability, or misrepresentations.

17. **Termination and Renewal**

17.1. *Term.* This Agreement will be effective on the Effective Date and thereafter will remain in effect for _____ (__) years from the initial date of public availability of the Web Site, unless earlier terminated as otherwise provided in this Agreement (the "Initial Term"). This Agreement will automatically be renewed beyond the Initial Term for successive one (1) year terms (each, a "Renewal Term") unless a Party provides the other Party with a written notice of termination at least sixty (60) days prior to the expiration of the Initial Term or the then-current Renewal Term.

17.2. *Termination*

17.2.1. Either Party may terminate this Agreement if a bankruptcy or insolvency proceeding is instituted against the other Party which is acquiesced in and not dismissed within sixty (60) days or if the other party ceases business operations.

17.2.2. Either Party may terminate this Agreement if the other Party materially breaches any of its representations, warranties or obligations under this Agreement, and such breach is not cured within thirty (30) days of receipt of notice specifying the breach, [except that the cure period for failures of payment obligations will be ___ (__) days].

17.3. *Termination and Payment.* Upon any termination or expiration of this Agreement, Customer will pay all unpaid and outstanding fees through the effective date of termination or expiration of this Agreement.

17.4. [*Termination of Third Party Services.* Should any Third Party Services no longer be available for any reason outside the control of the Provider, Provider may terminate such Third Party Services by providing Customer with thirty (30) days' notice. Provider will use commercially reasonable efforts to assist Customer in obtaining the same or similar services as those terminated from an alternate third-party provider.]

17.5. *Survival.* The following Sections, together with accrued obligations, will survive termination: 8.1 (Proprietary Rights of Customer), 8.3 (Proprietary Rights of Provider), 9 (Customer Data Ownership), 10 (Confidentiality), 12 (Fees and Taxes), 13.3 (Warranty Disclaimers), 14 (Indemnification), 15 (Procedure for Indemnification), 16 Limitation of Liability, 17.5 (Survival) and 18 (Miscellaneous).

18. **Miscellaneous**

18.1. *Independent Contractors.* Provider and Customer are independent contractors and not employees or agents of one another.

18.2. *Amendments.* No amendment, change, waiver, or discharge hereof will be valid unless in writing and signed by the Party against which such amendment, change, waiver, or discharge is sought to be enforced.

18.3. *Customer List.* Provider may use the name of and identify Customer as a Provider client in advertising, publicity, or similar materials distributed or displayed to prospective clients, subject to Customer's written consent, which is not to be unreasonably refused.

18.4. *Force Majeure.* [Except for the payment of fees by Customer,] If the performance of any part of this Agreement by either Party is prevented, hindered, delayed or otherwise made impracticable by reason of any flood, riot, fire, judicial or governmental action, labor disputes, act of God or any other causes beyond the control of either Party, that Party will be excused from such to the extent that it is prevented, hindered or delayed by such causes.

18.5. *Governing Law.* This Agreement will be governed in all respects by the laws of the State of _____ without regard to its conflict of laws provisions. Customer and Provider agree that the sole venue and jurisdiction for disputes arising from this Agreement or its subject matter will be the appropriate state or federal courts located in the city of _____, and Customer and Provider hereby submit to the exclusive jurisdiction of such courts.

18.6. *Assignment.* This Agreement will be binding upon and inure to the benefit of the successors and permitted assigns of the Parties hereto. Neither Party may assign any of its rights or delegate any of its obligations under this Agreement to any third party without the express prior written consent of the other Party, except in the instance of a merger, company sale, sale of business operations, line of business sale, or acquisition of the assigning Party.

18.7. *Notice.* All notices and other communications provided hereunder may be made or given by either Party by facsimile, by first-class mail, postage prepaid, or by courier to the mailing address or facsimile numbers set out below or such other address or facsimile numbers as such Party will have furnished in writing to the other Party in writing:

If to Customer, to: _____

If to Provider, to: _____

Notice is effective upon receipt.

18.8. *Waiver.* The waiver or failure of either Party to exercise any right in any respect provided for herein will not be deemed a waiver of any further right hereunder or any later exercise of such right.

18.9. *Severability.* If any provision of this Agreement is determined to be invalid under any applicable statute or rule of law, it is to that extent to be deemed omitted, and the balance of the Agreement will remain enforceable.

18.10. *Counterparts.* This Agreement may be executed in several counterparts, all of which taken together will constitute the entire agreement between the Parties hereto.

18.11. *Headings.* The Section headings used herein are for reference and convenience only and will not enter into the interpretation hereof.

18.12. *Entire Agreement.* This Agreement and attached Schedules constitute the entire agreement between Customer and Provider with respect to the subject matter hereof and there are no representations, understandings or agreements which are not fully expressed in this Agreement.

IN WITNESS WHEREOF, the Parties have caused this Agreement to be executed by their duly authorized representatives as of the date first written above.

Customer   **Provider**

By: _____   By: _____
      (Signature)   (Signature)

Name: _____   Name: _____

Title: _____   Title: _____

Date: _____   Date: _____

Schedule A
Hosting Services and Fees

Hosting Services and Fees:

[*This Schedule can itemize application management and support services provided, such as installation and update support, web server and database software management, data and software backup, disaster recovery, security system operations, third party services, and help desk. It may also include a list of hardware and software that Provider will supply.*]

[*This Schedule should also include a list of fees for Hosting Services and any applicable Additional Services. Such fees might include amounts for lease, use or purchase of hardware or software, monthly fees for the Provider's Web Site management and oversight, and extra fees for excess use of data storage or bandwidth.*]

Schedule B

Fees for Additional Services

[*This Schedule would include labor charges, by the hour or the day, for professionals that provide Additional Services.*]

Schedule C
Service Level Agreement

For the purposes of this Service Level Agreement (or "SLA"), "System" means the hardware, software, and other items provided by Provider (as detailed in Schedule A) and Provider's network infrastructure and Internet connectivity.

The remedies provided herein are the sole and exclusive remedies with respect to Provider's performance guarantee as stated in this SLA.

Provider's Uptime Guarantee

Based on the equipment and service configuration selected by the Customer, Provider offers performance guarantee that the System will be operational and available to interact with the Internet ("the Uptime Guarantee") of ____ percent. This guarantee and applicable remedies are subject to the terms and conditions below.

Credits for Customer

Periods of unavailability in excess of those specified in the Uptime Guarantee will entitle Customer to a credit applicable to future monthly charges which Customer is obligated to pay Provider. The amount of the credit will be the greater of (a) 10% of the monthly fees outlined in Schedule A or (b) an amount calculated based upon the number of hours during a particular month (see example below) and the duration of any and all periods of unavailability in excess of Uptime Guarantee during such month. The formula for any such credit or refund is as follows:

$$\text{Credit} = \frac{\text{Hours in Excess of Uptime Guarantee in Month}}{\text{Hours in Month}} \times \text{Monthly Fee (in Schedule A)}$$

For the purposes of this formula, a period of unavailability will be deemed to occur entirely in the month in which such period of unavailability begins.

Procedure

When a period of unavailability is detected by the Customer, the Customer should contact the Provider by email or phone and advise Provider's staff of the problem. If the staff of Provider are able to confirm the Customer's report, the period of unavailability will be recorded. Such period of unavailability will be deemed to have begun at the earlier of the time such unavailability was reported to the Provider by Customer or the time such unavailability was detected by the Provider's monitoring tools.

Customer Termination Option

[In addition to the foregoing credit, Customer may terminate the Agreement at any time by providing Provider with ___ (__) days written notice of termination in the event that (i) the Web Site is unavailable for a total of ___ hours within any ___ day period or (ii) the Uptime Guarantee is not met for ___ or more weeks in a ___ consecutive week period.]

Limitations

Provider will not be responsible for periods of unavailability resulting from failure by Customer to approve reasonable modifications to the System reasonably recommended by Provider to prevent periods of unavailability if Provider has provided Customer with documentation to show the reason for such modification(s) and the manner in which such modification(s) will affect the System.

In addition, Provider will not be responsible for periods of unavailability to the extent Provider is able to prove that such periods of unavailability resulted from the following:

- Failure of networks, hardware or software which are not part of the System.

- Customer modifications to the System which are not approved by Provider, resulting from Customer's use of customizable software provided by a third party (i.e., a software provider other than Provider).

- Any modifications made to operating systems without the consent of Provider.

- Modifications to the System implemented by Provider, at the request of Customer, but not recommended or approved by Provider.

- Unavailability occurring during periods of System testing, development, or problem diagnosis which are scheduled in advance with Customer's approval (and in such case, only during the period of scheduled downtime).

- Planned facility and equipment maintenance upgrades and migration, which are scheduled in advance.

- Normal maintenance periods which are scheduled every Wednesday between 4:00 am and 6:00 am [(*Indicate applicable time zone*)].

- Content or applications, developed by third parties and installed or run on the System by the Customer or others authorized by Customer to have access to the System without Provider's approval or recommendation.

- Incidents of force majeure.

- Interruption of Hosting Services due to a denial of service or other hostile attack on the System or due to unexpected and unusually peak demands for access to the Web Site.

- Co-located hardware not managed by Provider.

[System Monitoring

Provider will actively monitor the System for unavailability and proper operation 24 hours per day, 7 days per week, every day of the year. Provider does not guarantee that remote monitoring will be able to detect all problems or interruptions at the time they occur.]

[Schedule D

Terms and Conditions Regarding PCI Compliance

1. **Data Protection Compliance**

   1.1. *Compliance.* Provider will use commercially reasonable efforts to remain in compliance with the Payment Card Industry ("PCI") Data Security Standards for a Level 1 Service Provider.

   1.2. *Additional Services.* If due to changes in PCI-related requirements, additional hardware, software, or procedures are required, Provider may require Customer to purchase mutually agreed Additional Services as a condition of providing further PCI compliance.

   1.3. *Compliance Audit.* Customer may audit the compliance with such standards at Provider's site. These audits may take place no more than once per calendar year. PCI representatives or third party PCI-approved representatives may audit Provider on Customer's behalf, at Customer's sole cost. Customer agrees to provide to Provider reasonable notice of such audit.

2. **Nature of Obligations; Remedies**

   2.1. Compliance by Provider with the requirements of PCI is an agreement between Provider and Customer and there are no third party beneficiaries of such obligation. For the avoidance of doubt, no third party customer, bank, card issuer, network member, association or any other third party will have any right to assert any claim or cause of action against Provider. Provider disclaims any liability to any third party arising out of or relating to such standards.]

Beta Test Agreement – Consumer Application

Introductory Note

The following form is an agreement for a beta test for a downloadable consumer application. It is advisable to require that the user assent to the agreement when downloading or installing the Beta Software.

With minimal editing, the form could be adapted for a broadly distributed business (rather than consumer) application, provided that the application is one that the user will self-install and use without support (other than information on the Vendor's web site).

Bracketed text is optional or provides choices. You will note that some of the optional language relates to combining downloaded software with online services (such as data or content services).

Beta Test Agreement

BY DOWNLOADING, INSTALLING, OR USING THE BETA SOFTWARE, USER AGREES UNCONDITIONALLY TO THE TERMS OF THIS BETA TEST AGREEMENT ("Agreement"). IF YOU DO NOT AGREE WITH THESE TERMS, DO NOT DOWNLOAD, INSTALL, OR USE THIS BETA SOFTWARE.

This Agreement is between you (entity or person, hereinafter referred to as "you" or "your") and *[Vendor Name]* ("Vendor") for the Vendor software product(s) [provided herewith] [available from the Vendor Beta Test web site], which includes computer software and documentation [together with related online services] (collectively, the "Beta Software").

1. Age and Capacity; No Conflict of Interest

You represent and warrant that you are an individual user that is eighteen (18) years of age or older. IF YOU ARE UNDER 18 YEARS OF AGE, YOU MAY NOT PARTICIPATE IN THE BETA TEST PROGRAM OR DOWNLOAD OR USE THE BETA SOFTWARE.

[You certify that (a) you are not an employee or affiliated with an organization offering a competing product, (b) you are not involved in the testing, marketing, development or production of any competing product and (c) you are not affiliated with or acting for the benefit of anyone who is involved in such activities. IF YOU HAVE A CONFLICT OF INTEREST, YOU MAY NOT PARTICIPATE IN THE BETA TEST PROGRAM OR DOWNLOAD OR USE THE BETA SOFTWARE.]

2. Beta Test License

Subject to the terms of this Agreement, Vendor grants you, during the Test Period (as defined below), a non-exclusive, limited license to use one copy of the Beta Software in binary form only as authorized in this Agreement. You may install such single copy on a computer under your control for your own personal use. Vendor authorizes you to use and evaluate the Beta Software under the terms and conditions of this Agreement solely for the purposes of providing information and feedback to Vendor.

3. Test Period

You are licensed to use the Beta Software only during the Test Period. The "Test Period" will begin upon the installation of the Beta Software, and may be terminated at any time by either you or by Vendor, by providing email or written notification of such intent. In any case, the duration of the Test Period ends on the date when the Beta Software is announced by Vendor as being commercially generally available, _____ (___) months from the date that you download or otherwise obtain the Beta Software, or upon termination of this Agreement, whichever comes first. Vendor may include license management functionality in the Beta Software that disables it after the Test Period is completed.

4. [Registration and Personal Information

You may be required to provide to Vendor, as a condition to testing the Beta Software, certain personally identifiable information ("Personal Information"). Vendor's retention and use of all Personal Information shall be subject to Vendor's privacy policy posted on *[provide Web URL]*, as that policy may be updated by Vendor in its discretion from time to time.]

5. [Automated Reporting

The Beta Software may be configured to periodically check your computer system for, and report back to Vendor without additional notice to you, anonymous information relating to your use of the Beta Software, such as the frequency of your use of the Beta Software and/or certain of its features, your Beta Software configuration settings and information on computer errors occurring during your use of the Beta Software. Such configuration may include functionality that allows for the transmission of data about your computer to Vendor (for instance the version of operating system you are using, or details of other programs you may be running) to enable Vendor to better understand why bugs may occur and to enable Vendor to improve the Beta Software. Some Beta Software may contain a specific identification number for the purpose of tracking the number of unique instances of such Beta Software being used by you.] [This functionality may continue to function post-termination, but can be disabled by uninstalling the software; you consent to any such continuing operation.]]

6. [Updating

The Beta Software may contain an "Automatic Update" feature that may gather information from your computer in connection with its updating functionality, and, if so, you consent to its use.] [This functionality may continue to function post-termination, but can be disabled by uninstalling the Software; you consent to any such continuing operation.]]

7. Ownership

You acknowledge and agree that the Beta Software is a proprietary product of Vendor protected under United States copyright laws, other applicable intellectual property laws, and international treaty provisions. The Beta Software is owned by Vendor and/or its third party contributors. Vendor retains all rights not expressly granted to you.

8. Feedback

You agree to evaluate the Beta Software. For this purpose, you agree to provide Vendor with reports, data, and suggestions ("Feedback") concerning the Beta Software as Vendor may reasonably request.

856 FORM 11-1 Beta Test Agreement – Consumer Application

You agree that all right, title and interest to any Feedback (and all relevant intellectual property rights) will become the exclusive property of Vendor, and Vendor may disclose or use Feedback for any purposes whatsoever, entirely without obligation of any kind to you.

9. **Confidential Information**

Definition of Confidential Information. All non-public information disclosed by Vendor will be referred to collectively in this Agreement as "Confidential Information." Such information will include, but not be limited to, the Beta Software (including its documentation), marketing information, product test results and Feedback.

Ownership of Confidential Information: All Confidential Information and any derivative thereof will be the property of Vendor, and no license, intellectual property rights or other rights to Confidential Information will belong to you. You are licensed to use Confidential Information as reasonably required for your use of the Beta Software as permitted by this Agreement.

Non-Disclosure of Confidential Information. You will not disclose, publish or disseminate the Confidential Information to any third parties.

10. **Restrictions**

You agree not to:

- Disclose the results of any benchmark tests of the Beta Software to any third party without Vendor's prior written approval;

- Work around or circumvent any technical limitations or any copying or use restriction mechanisms in the Beta Software;

- Reverse engineer, decompile or disassemble the Beta Software, except and only to the extent that applicable law expressly permits, despite this limitation;

- Publish the Beta Software for others to copy;

- Rent, lease or lend the Beta Software; or

- Transfer the Beta Software or this Agreement to any third party.

11. **Disclaimers**

You acknowledge that the Beta Software has not been completely tested and may contain material defects or deficiencies. You agree to determine for yourself the suitability of the use of the Beta Software for your purposes. The Beta Software is provided without maintenance or support.

You acknowledge that Vendor has no express or implied obligation to announce or introduce the Beta Software or any similar or compatible product. You acknowledge that all testing that you perform pursuant to this Agreement is done entirely at your own risk. VENDOR MAKES NO REPRESENTATIONS OR WARRANTIES, EXPRESS OR IMPLIED, REGARDING THE USE OR PERFORMANCE OF THE BETA SOFTWARE, INCLUDING WITHOUT LIMITATION ANY IMPLIED WARRANTIES OF MERCHANTABILITY, FITNESS FOR A PARTICULAR PURPOSE AND NON-INFRINGEMENT.

YOU ACCEPT THE BETA SOFTWARE "AS IS," AND VENDOR SHALL NOT BE LIABLE FOR ANY DIRECT, INDIRECT, INCIDENTAL, SPECIAL, CONSEQUENTIAL OR PUNITIVE DAMAGES, SOURCE, EVEN IF VENDOR HAS BEEN ADVISED OF THE POSSIBILITY OF SUCH DAMAGES. Vendor shall not be liable for money damages under this Agreement.

12. **General**

You may not assign or transfer this Agreement, the Beta Software, or the license contained herein without the express written consent of Vendor.

Any notices or other communication will be addressed to any email address that you may provide and will be deemed communicated when so emailed.

This Agreement will be governed by the laws of the State of _____, USA, without regard to conflicts of law rules. You agree to comply with US export control laws, as applicable. You consent to the exclusive jurisdiction and venue of the state and federal courts located in _____ with regard to any dispute relating to this Agreement or its subject matter.

Your breach of this Agreement will result automatically in immediate termination of this Agreement and may be cause for exclusion in all other Vendor-sponsored beta programs, in addition to other remedies available to Vendor under applicable law. This Agreement may be terminated by either party upon ten days' notice. This Agreement will terminate upon the general release of the commercial version (Version 1.0 or later) of the Beta Software.

The following provisions of Sections shall continue in full force and effect even after termination of this Agreement: 4 (Registration and Personal Information), 7 (Ownership), 9 (Confidentiality), 10 (Restrictions), 11 (Disclaimers) and 12 (General) together with all provisions of this Agreement that recite that they survive termination.

You hereby acknowledge that unauthorized disclosure or use of the Beta Software or Confidential Information could cause Vendor irreparable harm and significant injury that may be difficult to ascertain and for which Vendor would not have an adequate remedy of monetary damages, and that accordingly, Vendor will be entitled to seek injunctive relief to curtail such disclosure or use.

This Agreement is the entire agreement of the parties and supersedes any other agreement governing your use of this Beta Software.

Beta Test Agreement – Business Application

Introductory Note

The following form is for a beta test for use where (1) the software requires installation, training, and support from the Vendor and (2) the parties have agreed upon a Beta Test Plan specifying how the Vendor and Tester will cooperate during the test. This form is written on the assumption that the Tester is a business rather than an individual.

The provision of a Beta Test Plan will vary with the application and the market it is for. The Vendor should consider including the following:

- *Required hardware and software. The number and specification of computers, networks and the hardware and software platforms to be used.*

- *Test sites. The business locations where the software will be installed and used.*

- *Installation details. The timing and sequencing of installation, and the services needed from both sides to prepare for and carry out installation.*

- *Training and technical support. Provision for how and when training and technical support for users will be supplied, often including a hotline for quick troubleshooting. The Vendor may require remote access to the installed software.*

- *Contact persons. The personnel of the Tester that will be in charge of coordinating the beta test and the contact persons for the publisher.*

- *Bug and error reports. The method and format of reporting problems and bugs.*

- *Meetings. The scheduling of regular meetings with the Tester's staff to assess problems and progress.*

- *Final or periodic evaluation of the software. Evaluation procedures in which the software is compared to projected results and user satisfaction is rated.*

859

This agreement assumes the use of installed software. The form of agreement would need modifications for a hosted or software-as-a-service application beta test.

Beta Test Agreement

1. Introduction

The undersigned company ("Tester") and [*Name of Vendor*] ("Vendor") agree that Tester will participate in the [*Name of Software Product*] beta test (the "Beta Test") under the terms of this Beta Test Agreement ("Agreement"). As used in this Agreement, the term "Beta Software" refers to the [*Name of Software Product*] software program and its user manual and other documentation.

2. Agreement of Vendor and Tester to Carry Out Planned Beta Test

Vendor and Tester agree to use the reasonable efforts to carry out their respective tasks and procedures set forth in the Beta Test Plan attached hereto as <u>Schedule A</u>. The schedule or tasks may be changed only by mutual agreement in writing.

3. Testing License

Tester is granted a limited license to use the Beta Software solely for the purpose of this Beta Test and solely at the location specified in the Beta Test Plan attached as <u>Schedule A</u> hereto. Tester may not copy the Beta Software except as provided in the Beta Test Plan, and may not provide any copy to any other person.

Each authorized user at the Tester's business location may install the Beta Software on such hardware specified in the Beta Test Plan. Except as the parties may otherwise agree in writing, Tester agrees to remove all copies of the Beta Software at the end of the Beta Test, upon termination of this Agreement, or upon Vendor's written request, whichever is earlier.

4. [Discounted Copies of Commercial Version

Vendor intends to release the Beta Software as a commercial product. When Vendor does so, Tester shall have option, which it may exercise within ____ (__) months of the date of commercial release or within ____ (__) months of the conclusion of the Beta Test (whichever is later) to purchase one or more licenses of the [*Name of Software Product*] released for commercial sale in the version and configuration specified in <u>Schedule B</u> ("Commercial Version") at [*specify percentage*] discount from the then current list price (provided that Tester shall pay shipping and any applicable taxes). The Commercial Version delivered under the option shall be subject to the Vendor's applicable standard User Agreement[, a copy of which is attached as <u>Schedule C</u>] [, which will be available on Vendor's web site].

5. **Confidential Information**

Tester agrees that the characteristics, performance, potential shipment date, and all other information about the Beta Software (including errors), the Beta Software itself (including all software and any documentation) and this Agreement are all confidential information and constitute trade secrets of Vendor. (Such information is referred to, collectively, as "Confidential Information.") Tester acknowledges that under the Agreement, Vendor will make Confidential Information available to Tester.

Tester agrees to take all reasonable steps to prevent disclosure of Confidential Information and to ensure that its employees, officers, and agents prevent disclosure of Confidential Information. Tester further agrees that information will be available to its employees, officers and agents strictly on a need-to-know basis.

6. **Restrictions**

Tester agrees not to:

- Disclose the results of any study, review or benchmark tests of the Beta Software to any third party without Vendor's prior written approval;

- Work around or circumvent any technical limitations or any copying or usage restriction mechanisms in the Beta Software;

- Reverse engineer, decompile or disassemble the Beta Software, except and only to the extent that applicable law expressly permits despite this limitation;

- Publish the Beta Software for others to copy;

- Rent, lease or lend the Beta Software; or

- Transfer the Beta Software or this Agreement to any third party.

7. **Ownership of the Beta Software**

Tester acknowledges that the Beta Software, its copyright, its trademark, and any other intellectual property rights in the Beta Software are owned by Vendor and its suppliers.

Tester acquires no ownership of the Beta Software from this Agreement and no license to use the Beta Software beyond the term of this Agreement. Tester acquires no license to copy or use the Beta Software (except as expressly permitted by this Agreement), prepare derivative works, or participate in development, manufacturing, marketing, and maintenance of the Beta Software.

8. **Disclaimers**

Tester acknowledges that the Beta Software has not been completely tested and may contain material defects or deficiencies. Tester agrees to determine for itself the suitability of the use of the Beta Software for Tester's purposes. The Beta Software is provided without maintenance or support, except as expressly stated in the Beta Test Plan.

While Vendor intends to introduce a commercial version of the Beta Software, Tester acknowledges that Vendor has no express or implied contractual obligation to announce or introduce the Beta Software or any similar product.

Tester acknowledges that all testing that Tester performs pursuant to this Agreement is done entirely at Tester's own risk. THE BETA SOFTWARE IS PROVIDED "AS IS," AND VENDOR EXCLUDES ALL REPRESENTATIONS OR WARRANTIES, EXPRESS OR IMPLIED, INCLUDING WITHOUT LIMITATION ANY IMPLIED WARRANTIES OF MERCHANTABILITY, FITNESS FOR A PARTICULAR PURPOSE AND NON-INFRINGEMENT.

VENDOR SHALL NOT BE LIABLE FOR ANY DIRECT, INDIRECT, INCIDENTAL, SPECIAL, CONSEQUENTIAL OR PUNITIVE DAMAGES, EVEN IF VENDOR HAS BEEN ADVISED OF THE POSSIBILITY OF SUCH DAMAGES. Vendor shall not be liable for cumulative money damages under this Agreement in excess of US$500.00.

Tester agrees not to allow any third party to use or access the Beta Software and agrees to defend, indemnify, and hold Vendor harmless from any damages or claims arising from use by any third party. Tester agrees to back up data and take other appropriate measures to secure and protect its programs and data.

9. **Feedback**

Tester agrees that the contents of all oral and written reports to Vendor and any other materials, information, ideas, concepts, and know-how provided by Tester (including corrections to problems in the Beta Software and documentation) (collectively "Feedback") become the property of Vendor. Vendor may use or exploit Feedback without any accounting or payment to Tester. Under no circumstances will Vendor become liable for any payment to Tester for any information that Tester provides, whether concerning the Beta Software or otherwise.

Tester agrees not to disclose to Vendor, as Feedback or otherwise, any information that is confidential or proprietary to Tester or any third party.

10. **[Publicity**

Tester grants Vendor permission, to be exercised in Vendor's sole discretion, to use the facts, contents and outcome of the Beta Test, Tester's comments, quotations from Tester's employees and officers, and Tester's trade name and trademark in Vendor's promotions, press releases, public relations, advertisements, and other sales and marketing activities. Such use will be subject to Tester's written permission for each use, not to be unreasonably refused. No compensation shall be required for Vendor's exercise of such right.]

11. **[Automated Reporting**

The Beta Software may be configured to periodically check Tester computers or system for, and report back to Vendor without additional notice, non-personal technical information relating to Tester's use of the Beta Software, such as the frequency of the use of the Beta Software and/or certain of its features, Beta Software configuration settings and information on computer errors occurring during use of the Beta Software. Such configuration may include functionality that allows for the transmission of data about the computers or systems to Vendor (for instance the version of operating system in use or details of other programs that Tester may be running) to enable Vendor to better understand why bugs may occur and to enable Vendor to improve the Beta Software. Some Beta Software may contain a specific identification number for the purpose of tracking the number of unique instances of such Beta Software being used by Tester.] [This functionality may continue to function post-termination, but can be disabled by uninstalling the Beta Software; Tester consents to any such continuing operation.]

12. **[Updating**

The Beta Software may contain an "Automatic Update" feature that may gather information from your computer in connection with its updating functionality, and, if so, you consent to its use.] [This functionality may continue to function post-termination, but can be disabled by uninstalling the Beta Software; Tester consents to any such continuing operation.]

13. **Termination**

Vendor may terminate this Agreement for Tester's material breach by written notice. This Agreement may be terminated by either party upon ten days' notice. This Agreement will terminate 30 days after the general release of the commercial version (Version 1.0 or later) of the Beta Software.

The following provisions of Sections shall continue in full force and effect even after termination of this Agreement as applicable: 4, 5, 6 through 11, 13 and 14, together with any provisions of this Agreement that recite that they survive termination.

14. **General Provisions**

Notice may be given at the addresses stated in this Agreement or to such other addresses as to which a party has given written notice.

Neither Tester nor Vendor has any obligation to purchase anything under this Agreement. No agency, partnership, joint venture, or other joint relationship is created by this Agreement. Vendor may enter into the same, similar or different agreements with others.

This Agreement will be governed by the laws of the State of _____, USA, without regard to conflicts of law rules. Tester agrees to comply with US export control laws, as applicable. Tester agrees to the exclusive jurisdiction and venue of the state and federal courts located in _____ with regarding to any dispute relating to this Agreement or its subject matter.

U.S. Government Users. The Beta Software is a "Commercial Item," as that term is defined at 48 CFR §2.101, consisting of "Commercial Computer Software" and "Commercial Computer Software Documentation," as such terms are used in 48 CFR §12.212 or 48 CFR §227.7202, as applicable. Consistent with 48 CFR §,12.212 and 48 CFR §§227.7202-1 through 227.7202-4, as applicable, the Beta Software is being provided to U.S. Government end users (1) only as a Commercial Item, and (2) with only those rights as are granted to all other end users pursuant to the terms and conditions of this Agreement.

Tester is responsible for compliance with US export control laws as applicable.

The Beta Software is not designed, manufactured or intended for use in connection with hazardous or "high risk" activities nor with applications that require fail-safe performance (together, "High Risk Activities"). High Risk Activities include but are not limited to activities or applications relating to the operation of nuclear facilities, air traffic control, aerospace operations, or direct life support machines, and any other activities or applications in which the failure of the software could lead directly to death, personal injury, or severe physical or environmental damage. Vendor disclaims any and all express or implied warranties of fitness for High Risk Activities, and Tester agrees that Vendor will have no liability or responsibility relating to use or operation of the software in connection with High Risk Activities.

This document is a complete statement of the contract between the parties, and any change or addition to this Agreement must be in writing and signed by Tester and Vendor.

SO AGREED on the date set forth below between [*Name of Vendor*] and Tester:

To Tester: Please sign and fill in blanks as indicated:

Type or Print Name of Tester Company: _____

Tester Signature: _____

Type or Print Name and Title of Person Signing this Beta Test Agreement on behalf of Tester_____

Street Address: _____

_____

Contact Person and email: _____

Date: _____

[*Vendor Name*]

Signature: _____

Print Name and Title of Person: _____

Signing on Behalf of [*Vendor*]

Street Address: _____

_____

Contact Person and email: _____

Date: _____

Evaluation License Agreement 12-1

Introductory Note

This is a form agreement to license software to a user (a potential customer) for evaluation use only. This license agreement is designed to "time out" after a relatively short period of trial use.

This form is written for SoftCo, a fictitious software company. Bracketed language is optional.

The form could require customization, for example, for:

- *Use might be limited to one personal computer or a single server.*

- *The license might be for business or personal use.*

- *There may be interaction with the SoftCo's online services (such as data services) that need to be covered in the agreement.*

- *The license may need to manage open source or third party components.*

Evaluation license agreements of this kind can be combined with a permanent license (or a license for a fixed term or subscription license) to form a "try-and-buy" license agreement.

Evaluation License Agreement

PLEASE READ THIS EVALUATION END-USER LICENSE AGREEMENT ("EULA") CAREFULLY. BY INSTALLING OR USING THE SOFTWARE THAT ACCOMPANIES THIS EULA (THE "SOFTWARE"), YOU AGREE TO THE TERMS OF THIS EULA. IF YOU DO NOT AGREE, DO NOT USE THE SOFTWARE AND, IF APPLICABLE, RETURN IT TO THE PLACE OF PURCHASE.

THE SOFTWARE CONTAINS FUNCTIONALITY TO DISABLE THE SOFT-
WARE AFTER A DEFINED PERIOD (THE "TRIAL PERIOD"). IF YOU WANT
TO USE THE SOFTWARE AFTER THAT TIME, YOU ARE REQUIRED TO
PURCHASE A LICENSE.

You must read and agree to be bound by the terms and conditions of this EULA
before you use or activate the Software. If you are an individual, then you must be
at least 18 years old and have attained the age of majority in the state, territory or
jurisdiction where you live to enter into this EULA. If you are using the Software
on behalf of an entity, then you must be properly authorized to represent that
entity and to accept this EULA on its behalf. <u>If you do not agree to be bound
by the terms and conditions of this EULA, do not install or use the Software</u>.

1. COVERAGE OF THIS EULA. This EULA governs the Software, which
   includes computer software (including online and electronic documentation)
   and any release, plug-in or add-on [and any associated online services] that
   SoftCo may supply.

2. TRIAL USE LICENSE. SoftCo grants you the right to use the Software on one
   server computer (the "Server Hardware") during the Trial Period. [You are
   permitted to use the Software to access SoftCo's associated online services
   only during the Trial Period.] The Trial Period is the stated or authorized trial
   period as specified on your order confirmation or in the accompanying documentation, or if not specified, is 30 days. At the end of your Trial Period, this
   EULA expires automatically. You may purchase a paid license to the Software
   [through SoftCo's web site] [by contacting an authorized SoftCo reseller].

3. TIME OUT MECHANISM. You agree not to disable or circumvent the functionality of the Software that causes it to "time out" and cease operation at
   the end of the Trial Period.

4. UPDATES. SoftCo may, but is not required, to provide you with software
   updates ("Updates"). Upon download, Updates become "Software" for the
   purposes of this EULA. Updates may, at SoftCo's option, require additional
   or different license terms that must be accepted before download. [To receive
   Updates, you must register with SoftCo. Registration requires an email
   address for notices.]

5. NO SUPPORT. SoftCo is not obligated to provide maintenance, technical or
   other support to you for the Software. At its option, SoftCo may provide
   information about the Software and its use on its web site.

6. [INFORMATION COLLECTION. SoftCo may also upload information periodically from installed Software about product usage. SoftCo will not capture or retain any personal or private information about you [other than information that you may provide in product registration]. You agree that SoftCo may (i) use uploaded data from installed Software to improve products and services and (ii) use and disclose uploaded data for analysis or reporting purposes only if any such use or disclosure does not identify you or include any information that can be used to identify any individual person. SoftCo reserves the title, ownership and all rights and interest to any intellectual property or work product resulting from its use and analysis of such information.]

7. USE RESTRICTIONS. The Software is licensed, not sold. SoftCo and its suppliers reserve all intellectual property rights in the Software and all rights not expressly granted to you in this EULA. You agree that you will not rent, loan, lease or sublicense the Software or use the Software to provide services to others. You also agree not to attempt to reverse engineer, decompile, modify, translate, disassemble, discover the source code of, or create derivative works from, any part of the Software.

8. WARRANTY DISCLAIMER. TO THE FULLEST EXTENT PERMITTED BY APPLICABLE LAW, SOFTCO SOFTWARE, SERVICES AND RELATED DOCUMENTATION ARE PROVIDED "AS IS" WITHOUT WARRANTIES OF ANY KIND. THIS EULA EXCLUDES, TO THE MAXIMUM EXTENT PERMITTED, ALL EXPRESS OR IMPLIED WARRANTIES, INCLUDING BUT NOT LIMITED TO IMPLIED WARRANTIES OF MERCHANTABILITY, FITNESS FOR A PARTICULAR PURPOSE AND NONINFRINGEMENT. ANY IMPLIED WARRANTIES RELATING TO THE SOFTWARE WHICH CANNOT BE DISCLAIMED SHALL BE LIMITED TO 30 DAYS (OR THE MINIMUM LEGAL REQUIREMENT) FROM THE DATE YOU ACQUIRE THE SOFTWARE. SoftCo does not warrant that the Software will meet your requirements or that your use of the Software will be uninterrupted or error-free.

9. LIMITED LIABILITY. TO THE EXTENT PERMITTED BY APPLICABLE LAW, SOFTCO OR ITS SUPPLIERS WILL NOT BE LIABLE FOR ANY CONSEQUENTIAL, SPECIAL, INCIDENTAL OR INDIRECT DAMAGES OF ANY KIND OR FOR LOST OR CORRUPTED DATA OR MEMORY, SYSTEM CRASH, DISK/SYSTEM DAMAGE, LOST PROFITS OR SAVINGS, OR LOSS OF BUSINESS, ARISING OUT OF OR RELATED TO THIS EULA

OR THE SOFTWARE EVEN IF SOFTCO HAS BEEN ADVISED OF THE POSSIBILITY OF SUCH DAMAGES. IN NO EVENT WILL THE AGGREGATE LIABILITY OF SOFTCO OR ITS SUPPLIERS FOR ANY CLAIM, WHETHER FOR BREACH OF CONTRACT, NEGLIGENCE, STRICT PRODUCT LIABILITY OR ANY OTHER CAUSE OF ACTION OR THEORY OF LIABILITY, EXCEED THE SOFTWARE LICENSE FEES PAID OR OWED BY YOU OR IF NO FEES WERE PAID, THE SUM OF US$10.00.

10. CONSUMER PROTECTION. SOME STATES DO NOT ALLOW CERTAIN EXCLUSIONS OR LIMITATIONS OF LIABILITY, SO THE ABOVE EXCLUSION OR LIMITATION OF LIABILITIES AND DISCLAIMERS OF WARRANTIES (SECTIONS 8 AND 9) MAY NOT FULLY APPLY TO YOU. YOU MAY HAVE ADDITIONAL RIGHTS AND REMEDIES. SUCH POSSIBLE RIGHTS OR REMEDIES, IF ANY, SHALL NOT BE AFFECTED BY THIS EULA.

11. CONSENT TO ELECTRONIC COMMUNICATIONS. SoftCo may need to send you legal notices and other communications about the Software, SoftCo's services or our use of the information you provide us ("Communications"). SoftCo will send Communications via email to your registered email address or will post Communications on its web site. By accepting this EULA and registering with SoftCo, you consent to receive all Communications through such electronic means.

12. TERMINATION. SoftCo may terminate your rights under this EULA immediately and without notice if you fail to comply with any term or condition of this EULA or no longer consent to electronic Communications. Upon such termination, you agree to destroy all copies of the Software. You may terminate this EULA at any point by destroying all copies of the Software. Sections 7, 8, 9, 10, 11, and 15 survive any termination or expiration of this EULA.

13. EXPORT CONTROL. The Software is subject to export controls under US law. By accepting this EULA, you confirm that you are not a resident or citizen of any country currently embargoed by the U.S. and that you are not otherwise prohibited from receiving the Software.

14. UNITED STATES GOVERNMENT RIGHTS. If you are an agency, department or entity of the United States Government ("Government"), then use, reproduction, release, modification or disclosure of the Software, or any part thereof, including technical data, is restricted in accordance with Federal

Acquisition Regulation ("FAR") 12.212 for civilian agencies and Defense Federal Acquisition Regulation Supplement ("DFARS") 227.7202 for military agencies. The Software is a commercial product that was developed at private expense. The use of the Software by any Government agency, department or other agency of the Government is further restricted as set forth in this EULA.

15. GENERAL. This EULA constitutes the entire agreement between you and SoftCo. This EULA supersedes any prior agreement or understanding, whether written or oral, relating to the subject matter of this EULA. In the event that any provision of this EULA is found invalid, the validity of the remaining parts of this EULA will be unaffected. You may not assign or transfer this EULA. This EULA is governed by the laws of the State of _____, USA. You and SoftCo agree to the exclusive jurisdiction and venue of the state and federal courts located in _____ for the purpose of any action or proceeding brought by either of them in connection with this EULA or its subject matter.

Commercial End User License Agreement

Introductory Note

This form is typical of agreements for licensing of enterprise or industrial applications to business or industry. The form is designed to protect the Vendor but offer reasonable assurance and support to the Customer.

As noted in Chapter 12, there is a variety of possible license and revenue models for commercial end user licensing. This form features "named user" pricing, but other variations are possible, such as server-based or concurrent user.

Language in brackets is optional or presents choices.

Software License Agreement

This Software License Agreement ("Agreement") is entered into as of the ____ day of _____, 20__ (the "Effective Date") between _____ ("Vendor") with principal offices at _____ and _____ ("Customer") with principal offices at _____.

In consideration of the mutual promises and upon the terms and conditions set forth below, the parties agree as follows:

1. **Definitions**

    1.1. "Documentation" means any help files, instruction manuals, operating instructions, user manuals, and specifications provided by Vendor which describe the use of the Software and which either accompany the Software or are provided to Customer at any time.

1.2. ["Equipment" means the computer system, including peripheral equipment and operating system software, specified in the Documentation.]

1.3. "Named User" is defined as an individual authorized by Customer to use the Software regardless of whether the individual is actively using the Software at any given time. Each Named User will be assigned a unique user name and password.

1.4. "Releases" shall mean released versions, if any, to the Software. "Major Releases" involve additions of substantial functionality while "Minor Releases" do not. Major Releases are designated by a change in the number to the left of the decimal point of the number appearing after the product name while Minor Releases are designated by a change in such number to the right of the decimal point. Vendor is the sole determiner of the availability and designation of an update as a Major Release or Minor Release. Major Releases exclude software releases which are reasonably designated by Vendor as new products. Where used herein "Releases" shall mean Major Releases or Minor Releases or both as the context requires.

1.5. ["Site" means each physical location specified in Schedule A.]

1.6. "Software" means the computer programs in binary form as described in Schedule A or otherwise agreed in writing.

1.7. "Subsidiary" means all current and future business entities as to which a party owns, directly or indirectly, more than fifty percent (50%) of the equity ownership and voting rights that provide the power to select the management of the entities, for so long as such ownership and control exists.

1.8. ["Third Party Component" will mean any component of the Software, as listed in Vendor's Documentation, provided by a third party vendor to Vendor and utilized as a component of the Software.]

2. **Delivery and License**

2.1. *Delivery.* Delivery of the Software ("Delivery") will be deemed to have taken place when (a) Vendor ships the Software on disk or (b) makes the Software available for download and the Vendor has notified the Customer that the Software is available. Vendor will provide Documentation in paper, on disk, or online form, at Vendor's discretion.

2.2. [*Installation*. Vendor will install the Software on the Equipment at the Site(s) based on a mutually agreed upon schedule, subject to Customer's obligation to pay Vendor's fees for installation as described in Schedule A herein. Customer agrees that if Customer delays the agreed-upon installation schedule through no fault of Vendor (e.g., the Equipment is not available, or is not configured as required in the applicable Documentation) and Vendor is on Customer's Site, ready to install the Software, and the delay extends for one day or more, that in addition to the fee for installation, Customer will pay Vendor's consulting fee for each day required as a direct result of Customer's delay, in excess of those days originally scheduled for the installation, at Vendor's then current rates. Customer agrees to reimburse Vendor for reasonable travel, accommodation, and meal expenses incurred for installation.]

3. **License**

3.1. *Grant of License.* Subject to the terms and conditions of this Agreement, upon Delivery, Vendor grants Customer and Customer accepts a perpetual (unless terminated as expressly provided for below), non-exclusive, non-transferable (except as expressly provided for below) license to install and use the Software solely for Customer's own internal business use. Customer's license to use the Software is limited to the number of Named Users stated on Schedule A (or such greater number as Customer may have purchased from Vendor at Vendor's applicable pricing).

3.2. *Copies.* Customer will be entitled to make a reasonable number of binary copies of the Software for backup or archival purposes only. Customer may make a reasonable number of copies of the Documentation for internal use. Customer may not copy the Software, except as permitted by this Agreement. Whenever Customer is permitted to copy or reproduce all or any part of the Software, all titles, trademark symbols, copyright symbols and legends, and other proprietary markings must be reproduced.

3.3. [*License Management Software*. Vendor reserves the right to use license management software to limit Customer's use of the Software to the limits stated in this Agreement. Customer will not circumvent or attempt to circumvent such license management software.]

3.4. [*Additional Software*. By written agreement, the parties may add additional Vendor software programs to this Agreement. Upon such written agreement (together with Customer's appropriate purchase order), the additional programs will thereafter be included in "Software" under this Agreement. No terms stated in Customer's purchase order or other form document will modify this Agreement. Vendor reserves the right to require different or additional terms and conditions for the licensing of any additional software.]

3.5. [*Third Party Components.* Any Third Party Component used in or with such additional Vendor software may be licensed to Customer subject to its different or additional terms and conditions.]

4. **License Restrictions.** Customer agrees not to: (a) sell, lease, license or sub-license the Software or the Documentation; (b) decompile, disassemble, or reverse engineer the Software, in whole or in part; (c) write or develop any derivative software or any other software program based upon the Software or any Confidential Information; (d) use the Software to provide services on any ASP, software-as-a-service or service bureau basis; or (e) use, copy, exploit, or permit use of the Software except as expressly authorized in this Agreement.

5. **Ownership.** This Agreement grants a license only and transfers to Customer no ownership interest. Vendor and its suppliers reserve all rights not expressly granted.

6. **Payment**

6.1. **License Fee; Other Amounts.** Customer agrees to pay Vendor the License Fee [and other amounts] specified in <u>Schedule A</u>. Payment is due and payable in [upon the Effective Date] [upon Delivery] [within ____ days of Delivery]. Other amounts due under this Agreement, except as otherwise specifically stated, are due 30 days from invoice date.

6.2. **Taxes.** Customer agrees to pay or reimburse Vendor for all federal, state, or local sales, use, personal property, excise or other taxes, fees, or duties arising out of this Agreement or the transactions contemplated by this Agreement (other than taxes on the net income of Vendor).

7. **Support Services.** Customer's fees for maintenance and support ("Support Fees") shall be as stated in <u>Schedule A</u>. For so long as Customer is current in the payment of all Support Fees, Customer will be entitled to maintenance and support services ("Support Services") for the Software as stated in Schedule B. Initial Support Fees are due in advance together with applicable License Fees and are due annually in advance thereafter.

8. **Limited Warranty**

   8.1. Vendor warrants that for a period of ninety (90) days from the Effective Date (the "Warranty Period") (a) the Software will perform in substantial accordance with the Documentation and (b) the media on which the Software is distributed will be free from defects in materials and workmanship under normal use. If during the Warranty Period the Software or the media on which it is distributed do not perform as warranted (a "Non-Conformity"), Vendor shall undertake to correct such Non-Conformity, or if correction is not reasonably possible, replace such Software or the media free of charge. If neither of the foregoing is commercially practicable, Vendor shall terminate this Agreement and refund to Customer the License Fee. The foregoing are Customer's sole and exclusive remedies for breach of this limited warranty. The warranty set forth above is made to and for the benefit of Customer only. The warranty will apply only if:

      8.1.1. The Software has been properly installed and used at all times and in accordance with the instructions for use; and

      8.1.2. No modification, alteration or addition has been made to the Software by persons other than Vendor or Vendor's authorized representative, except as authorized in writing by Vendor.

9. **Exclusion and Limitations**

   9.1. *Warranty Exclusion.* EXCEPT AS EXPRESSLY SET FORTH IN THIS AGREEMENT, VENDOR MAKES NO WARRANTIES, EXPRESS OR IMPLIED, UNDER THIS AGREEMENT. VENDOR SPECIFICALLY DISCLAIMS ALL IMPLIED WARRANTIES OF MERCHANTABILITY, FITNESS FOR A PARTICULAR PURPOSE AND NON-INFRINGEMENT.

   9.2. *Limitation of Liability.* In no event will Vendor be liable for any loss of profits, loss of use, business interruption, loss of data, cost of cover or indirect, special, incidental or consequential damages even if Vendor has been advised of the possibility of such damages. Vendor will not be liable for any damages caused by delay in delivery or furnishing the Software or services. Vendor's liability under this Agreement for damages of any kind will not, in any event, exceed the License Fees paid by Customer to Vendor under this Agreement.

   9.3. *Claims.* No action arising out of any breach or claimed breach of this Agreement or transactions contemplated by this Agreement may be brought by either party more than one (1) year after the cause of action has accrued. For purposes of this Agreement, a cause of action will be deemed to have accrued when a party knew or reasonably should have known of the breach or claimed breach.

10. **Intellectual Property Warranty and Indemnification**

10.1. *IP Warranty.* Vendor warrants to Customer that it and its suppliers have sufficient rights to the Software to provide the license grants and fulfill its other obligations under the terms of this Agreement. The Customer's sole and exclusive remedy for breach of this warranty is indemnification as provided for in this Agreement.

10.2. *Infringement Indemnity.* Vendor agrees to defend, indemnify, and hold Customer harmless from and against any and all costs, judgments, damages and awards in lawsuits, proceedings or actions brought by any third party, and costs in connection with the defense thereof (including, without limitation, court fees and reasonable attorney's fees), resulting from any claim or allegation that the Software infringes any patent, copyright, trade secret or other proprietary right of any third party ("Claims").

10.3. *Limitation of Indemnification.* The obligations set forth in Section 10.2 will not apply to, and Vendor assumes no liability for, any Claims to the extent arising from (i) use of a modified version of the Software, (ii) the combination, operation or use of the Software with non-Vendor programs, data, methods or technology if such infringement would have been avoided without the combination, operation or use of the Software with other programs, data, methods or technology, or (iii) unlicensed use of the Software.

10.4. *Procedure for Indemnification.* Vendor's obligations under Section 10.1 and 10.2 applies only if Customer gives Vendor: (i) prompt written notice of the Claim; (ii) sole control of the defense and settlement of such Claims; and (iii) assistance reasonably requested by Vendor at Vendor's expense.

10.5. *Actions by Vendor.* In the event any such infringement, Claim, action or allegation is brought or threatened or if Vendor deems that there is a material risk of a Claim, Vendor may, at its sole option and expense:

10.5.1. procure for Customer the right to continue its use of the Software; or

10.5.2. modify or amend the Software or infringing part thereof, or replace the Software or infringing part thereof with other software having substantially the same or better capabilities; or, if neither of the foregoing is commercially practicable,

10.5.3. terminate this Agreement and repay to Customer a portion, if any, of the License Fee equal to such fee less one-sixtieth (1/60) thereof for each month or portion thereof that this Agreement has been in effect.

10.6. *Exclusive Remedy*. This Section 10 states the entire liability of Vendor and Customer's exclusive remedy with respect to actual or alleged infringement of any patent, copyright, trade secret or other proprietary right.

11. **Confidentiality**

11.1. "Confidential Information" means non-public information, technical data or know-how of a party and/or its Subsidiaries, which is furnished to the other party in written or tangible form in connection with this Agreement. Oral disclosure will also be deemed Confidential Information if it would reasonably be considered to be of a confidential nature or if it is confirmed at the time of disclosure to be confidential. [The parties agree that Vendor's Confidential Information includes this Agreement and its terms, the Documentation, binary copies of the Software, source code relating to the Software, and any other proprietary information supplied to Customer by Vendor, or by Customer to Vendor and marked as "confidential information" or the like.]

11.2. Notwithstanding the foregoing, Confidential Information does not include information which is: (i) already in the possession of the receiving party and not subject to a confidentiality obligation to the providing party; (ii) independently developed by the receiving party; (iii) publicly disclosed through no fault of the receiving party; (iv) rightfully received by the receiving party from a third party that is not under any obligation to keep such information confidential; (v) approved for release by written agreement with the disclosing party; or (vi) disclosed pursuant to the requirements of law, regulation, or court order.

11.3. Neither party will use the other party's Confidential Information during the term of this Agreement except as reasonably required for the performance of this Agreement. In addition, the confidentiality obligations set forth in this Section 11 will survive for five (5) years after the termination or expiration of this Agreement. Each party will hold in confidence the other party's Confidential Information by means that are no less restrictive than those used for its own confidential materials. Each party agrees not to disclose the other party's Confidential Information to anyone other than its employees or subcontractors who are bound by confidentiality obligations and who need to know the same to perform such party's obligations hereunder. In case a party receives legal process that demands or requires disclosure of the disclosing party's Confidential Information, such party will give prompt notice to the disclosing party, if legally permissible, to enable the disclosing party to challenge such demand.

11.4. *Injunctive Relief.* In the event of actual or threatened breach of the provisions of Section 11, the non-breaching party will have no adequate remedy at law and will be entitled to seek immediate injunctive and other equitable relief, without bond and without the necessity of showing actual money damages.

*[**Comment:** This form provides for the parties to agree on a form of source code escrow agreement. A common alternative is for the parties to attach the form of software escrow agreement as an exhibit.]*

12. **[Escrow of Source Code.** A mutually agreed code escrow agreement with respect to the Software (excluding the Third Party Software) shall be established within 30 days of the Effective Date. Customer shall pay all costs of the source code escrow.]

13. **Verification of Proper Use; Audit**

13.1. Vendor by its employees or agents may audit, with thirty (30) days' prior written notice, Customer's available records related to the use of the Software, to verify that Customer's use of the Software is in accordance to the constraints of this Agreement. Vendor will bear the expense of an audit with the exception of instances where the Customer is found, through such an audit, to be materially in violation of this Agreement, in which case, Customer will reimburse Vendor for the time, travel and material costs and fees reasonably associated with the audit. Audits will be conducted during regular business hours at Customer's facilities and will not unreasonably interfere with Customer's business. Audits will be conducted no more than [once] [twice] in any twelve-month period. Customer will promptly pay any adjustments to License Fees or other amounts due revealed by such audit. Payment will be due together with interest at 1.0 percent per month, compounded daily, or if less, at the highest legally permitted rate. The audit and its results will be subject to the restrictions of this Agreement regarding Confidential Information.

14. **Term and Termination**

14.1. *Term.* This Agreement will take effect on the Effective Date and will remain in force until terminated in accordance with this Agreement.

14.2. *Termination.* This Agreement is terminated as elsewhere provided in the Agreement or as follows:

14.2.1. *Termination without Cause.* Customer may terminate this Agreement upon thirty (30) days' prior written notice to Vendor, with or without cause.

14.2.2. *Termination with Cause.* Either party may terminate this Agreement and its license grants by written notice upon the occurrence of any of the following events: (i) in the event the other party materially fails to comply with any of the terms and conditions of this Agreement and such default has not been cured within thirty (30) days after receiving written notice of the breach; or (ii) in the event the other party (A) terminates or suspends its business, (B) becomes subject to any bankruptcy or insolvency proceeding under Federal or state law, (C) becomes insolvent or subject to control by a trustee, receiver or similar authority, or (D) has wound up or liquidated, voluntarily or otherwise.

14.3. **Effect of Termination.** All licenses terminate upon termination of this Agreement. Termination does not entitle Customer to any refund or return of payment except as expressly stated in this Agreement. Within fourteen (14) days after the date of termination or discontinuance of this

Agreement, Customer shall erase or destroy all copies of the Software and the Documentation and all Confidential Information in its possession. Upon request, Customer shall furnish Vendor with a certificate signed by an executive officer of Customer verifying that the same has been done. The following provisions will survive termination: 5 (Ownership), 9 (Exclusions and Limitations), 10 (Intellectual Property and Indemnification), 11 (Confidentiality), 13 (Verification Audit), 14.3 (Effect of Termination) and 17 (Miscellaneous), along with accrued financial obligations.

15. **Viruses and Disabling Devices.** Neither the Software nor any enhancements, modifications, upgrades, updates, revisions or releases thereof shall contain (i) any mechanism such as a "trap door," "time bomb," or "logic bomb," software protection routine or other similar device, that would enable Vendor to disable the Software or make the Software inaccessible to Customer after the Software is installed; or (ii) to the best of Vendor's knowledge, any computer "virus," "worm" or similar programming routine.

16. **Assignment**

   16.1. Either party may assign this Agreement together with the Software license to a Subsidiary or in connection with a sale of all or substantially all of its assets or stock, provided each assignee or successor party agrees in writing delivered to the non-assigning party to be bound by all terms and conditions of this Agreement[, except that Customer may not assign this Agreement or the license to a competitor of Vendor].

   16.2. [In the case of the transfer of all or substantially all of Customer's assets or stock (a "Transaction") to an entity that prior to the Effective Date of this Agreement held no controlling interest in Customer, the license under this Agreement shall be restricted to Customer and its Subsidiaries as constituted prior to the acquisition. In such a case, Vendor will have no obligation to extend price discounts or any other non-standard terms and conditions to operations of the acquiring or new controlling entity's businesses outside the scope of the businesses or operations of Customer as they existed before the Transaction.]

   16.3. The terms and provisions of this Agreement will be binding upon and inure to the benefit of the parties to this Agreement and to their respective heirs, successors, and assigns.

17. **Miscellaneous**

17.1. *Notice.* Any notice required or permitted under the terms of this Agreement or required by law must be in writing and must be (a) delivered in person, (b) sent by first class registered mail, or air mail, as appropriate, (c) sent by overnight air courier, or (d) transmitted by facsimile, in each case properly posted to the appropriate address set forth below. Either party may change its address for notice by notice to the other party given in accordance with this Section. Notices are effective on receipt.

[Insert parties' addresses for notice]

17.2. *Force Majeure.* Neither party will incur any liability to the other party on account of any loss or damage resulting from any delay or failure to perform all or any part of this Agreement if such delay or failure is caused, in whole or in part, by events, occurrences, or causes beyond the control and without negligence of the parties. Such events, occurrences, or causes will include, without limitation, acts of God, strikes, lockouts, riots, acts of war, earthquakes, fire and explosions, but the inability to meet financial obligations is expressly excluded.

17.3. *Waiver.* Any waiver of the provisions of this Agreement or of a party's rights or remedies under this Agreement must be in writing to be effective. Failure, neglect, or delay by a party to enforce the provisions of this Agreement or its rights or remedies at any time will not be construed and will not be deemed to be a waiver of such party's rights under this Agreement and will not in any way affect the validity of the whole or any part of this Agreement or prejudice such party's right to take subsequent action. Except as expressly stated in this Agreement, no exercise or enforcement by either party of any right or remedy under this Agreement will preclude the enforcement by such party of any other right or remedy under this Agreement or that such party is entitled by law to enforce.

17.4. *Severability.* If any term, condition, or provision in this Agreement is found to be invalid, unlawful or unenforceable to any extent, the parties shall endeavor in good faith to agree to such amendments that will preserve, as far as possible, the intentions expressed in this Agreement. If the parties fail to agree on such an amendment, such invalid term, condition or provision will be severed from the remaining terms, conditions and provisions, which will continue to be valid and enforceable to the fullest extent permitted by law.

17.5. *Standard Terms of Customer.* No terms, provisions or conditions of any purchase order, acknowledgment or other business form that Customer may use in connection with the acquisition or licensing of the Software will have any effect on the rights, duties or obligations of the parties under, or otherwise modify, this Agreement, regardless of any failure of Vendor to object to such terms, provisions or conditions.

17.6. *Amendments to This Agreement.* This Agreement may not be amended, except by a writing signed by both parties.

17.7. *Vendor's Prior Consent.* Unless expressly provided otherwise in this Agreement, any prior consent of Vendor that is required before Customer may take an action may be granted or withheld in Vendor's sole and absolute discretion.

17.8. *Export of Software.* Customer may not export or re-export this Software without the prior written consent of Vendor and without compliance with applicable US export control laws.

17.9. *Governing Law and Jurisdiction.* This Agreement will be governed by the laws of _____. Each party hereby agrees that the exclusive jurisdiction and venue for any action arising out of or related to this Agreement or its subject matter will lie exclusively in the state and federal courts located in _____. This Agreement is not subject to the United Nations Convention of Contracts for the International Sale of Goods.

17.10. *Public Announcements.* Customer acknowledges that Vendor may desire to use its name and logo in its web site, press releases, product brochures and financial reports indicating that Customer is a customer of Vendor, and Customer agrees that Vendor may use its name and logo in such a manner. Customer reserves the right to review any use of its name or logo and to grant or withhold permission, provided that permission will not reasonably be withheld.

17.11. *Counterparts.* This Agreement may be executed in counterparts, each of which will be deemed an original and all of which together will constitute one instrument. Execution by fax is permitted.

17.12. *Entire Agreement.* This Agreement (including the Schedules and any addenda hereto signed by both parties) contains the entire agreement of the parties with respect to the subject matter of this Agreement and supersedes all previous communications, representations, understandings and agreements, either oral or written, between the parties with respect to said subject matter.

IN WITNESS WHEREOF, the parties have executed this Agreement.

Vendor: _____   Customer: _____

By: _____   By: _____

Name: _____   Name: _____

Title: _____   Title: _____

Date: _____   Date:_____

Schedule A Software and License Fees

Software

[Add Description]

License Fee

[Add License Fee Schedule]

Annual Support Fee

[Add Annual Support Fee Schedule]

[This schedule may also include place and date of installation, any required site preparation, required hardware and software platform, etc.]

Schedule B

Support Services

1. **Definitions**

    1.1. "Class 1 Error" means a reported problem in the Software which renders the Software unusable with no obvious work-around.

    1.2. "Class 2 Error" means a reported problem in the Software, not considered as a Level I Error which causes material disruption but permits operation.

    1.3. "Class 3 Error" means a reported problem in the Software which is not affecting the Software's ability to perform substantially in accordance with the applicable Documentation.

    1.4. "Service Response Time" means the elapsed time between the receipt of a service call and the time when Vendor begins the Support Services, including a verbal or written confirmation to the Customer thereof.

2. **Hours of Operation.** *[State hours of operation, including time zone information]*

3. **Contact Information.** *[Provide email and phone contact information]*

4. **Support Services.** Support Services will be provided only with respect to versions of the Software that are being supported by Vendor. The Vendor's policy is to support the current Major Release version and the next preceding Major Release version. Customer is obligated to install the most recent Minor Releases for such versions as a condition of support.

5. **Error Response.** Vendor agrees to use commercially reasonable efforts to meet the following Service Response Times: *[Indicate target response times for Class 1, 2 and 3 Errors.]*

6. **Other Services.** Support Services includes, during Vendor's standard hours of service: (i) [Major Releases and] Minor Releases with related Documentation, and (ii) email and telephone assistance for the Software, including (a) clarification of functions and features of the Software; (b) clarification of the Documentation; (c) guidance in the operation of the Software; and (d) error verification, analysis and correction to the extent possible by telephone.

7. **On-Site Assistance.** At Vendor's discretion, Vendor may provide Support Services at the Customer site of installation. In such event Customer will reimburse Vendor for all related traveling expenses and costs for board and lodging.

8. **Causes not Attributable to Vendor.** Support Services will not include services requested as a result of, or with respect to, causes which are not attributable to Vendor.

9. **Responsibilities of Customer.** As a condition of Support Services, Customer shall properly train its personnel in the use and application of the Software and deal with Vendor through such trained personnel.

10. **Assignment of Duties.** Vendor may assign its duties of Support Services to a third party, provided that Vendor will remain responsible for the actions of such third party. [Any such assignment is subject to Customer's consent, which consent shall not be unreasonably withheld.]

Source Code Escrow Agreement

Introductory Note

This is a sample Source Code Escrow Agreement. The basic concept of an escrow is that a neutral third party (here called the "Escrow Agent") holds a software product's source code – and will release it to the licensee only in situations where there is a compelling need for it, such as the Depositor ceasing business operations.

It is conventional to call the vendor the "Depositor" because it is the party that "deposits" the source code with the Escrow Agent. In this form, the licensee is referred to as the "Beneficiary" because it obtains the benefit of the escrow arrangement.

Usually the Escrow Agent for a source code escrow is a specialized company known as an escrow house. These companies are chosen to hold source code in escrow because they can provide reasonably secure, climate-controlled storage and because they have the expertise to conduct verification of the escrow contents if needed. It is possible to have other types of Escrow Agents, such as banks, attorneys, or other third parties. Any Escrow Agent will charge fees for its services.

The following is a form designed for a rather simple escrow agreement, in which there is a single Beneficiary and a single software product. Escrow houses each have their own preferred forms of escrow agreements. Some are simple forms like this one. Other standard forms allow for multiple beneficiaries—so that a single source code "deposit" can service many software Beneficiaries—or cover multiple products.

If you are a software Depositor, you will find that "off the shelf" escrow house forms are too pro-Beneficiary and almost always require modification. (You will also find that the escrow house will permit modifications that do not adversely impact its own interests or increase its risk.) The key issues that Depositors often modify are:

- *Escrow Contents. Depositors may wish to clarify what materials other than the Depositor-created source code (such as the types and quantity of documentation) are required in the escrow.*

- *Updating. It is a considerable amount of work to assemble and adequately document source materials. Some Depositors want to avoid too frequent an obligation to update the deposited source code. Depositors also resist updating when Beneficiaries are not purchasing support services that entitle them to new binary versions of the relevant product.*

- *Release Conditions—the provisions which trigger release (also called a "release event"). Because source code is a trade secret, Depositors want the conditions of release to be narrow.*

- *Permitted Use. The issue is what the Beneficiary can do with the source code after release. Depositors want the permitted scope of use to be narrow.*

- *Conditions of Use. Most Depositors want provisions that require source code to be kept confidential after release. Depositors will also resist provisions that waive or can be read to waive applicable license fees after an escrow release.*

Most escrow agreement forms (including the one below) provides that if the Beneficiary and the Depositor disagree on whether a release condition exists, the Escrow Agent will continue to hold the source code pending arbitration of whether the source code should be released. Sometimes escrow agreements provide the opposite: that the code will be released immediately and may be used by the Beneficiary until the arbitration requires that it go back into escrow.

The parties do not need to use arbitration; it is possible to provide that a dispute over releasing code from escrow will be settled by a court of law; however most parties prefer arbitration because it is a private process.

The following agreement is written so that new versions of the source code placed into escrow are substituted for old ones; only source code for the most recent version of the software product remains in escrow. It is also possible to provide that each new version of the source code is added to the previously deposited material.

This form provides for payment of escrow fees by the Beneficiary. Some forms require the Depositor to pay such fees. This is a negotiated term.

For technical reasons relating to bankruptcy law, the escrow agreement should recite that it is "supplementary" to the related license agreement "pursuant to 11 United States

Code (Bankruptcy Code), Section 365(n)." This language is designed to help keep the agreement from being blocked by a bankruptcy proceeding.

A further legal note: Section 15 of this form allows the Escrow Agent the option to file an "interpleader" lawsuit if it is at a loss as to its proper action in a dispute over possession of the source code. Interpleader is a legal way of placing an object or money before a court of law and asking the court to decide who is entitled to get it.

Bracketed language is optional or indicates choices in wording.

Source Code Escrow Agreement

This Source Code Escrow Agreement ("Agreement") is effective as of the date all Parties have signed, among *[Name of Escrow Agent]* ("Escrow Agent"), *[Name of Software Company]* ("Depositor"), and *[Name of Beneficiary]* ("Beneficiary") (collectively the "Parties"; each a "Party").

1. **Purpose of This Agreement**

    1.1. Depositor and Beneficiary have entered or will enter into a license agreement regarding Product (as defined below) of Depositor (the "License Agreement").

    1.2. Under this Agreement, Depositor will deposit Source Materials (as defined below) for the Product to be held in escrow by Escrow Agent. The Source Materials will be released to Beneficiary only upon the occurrence of certain conditions specified herein.

2. **Certain Definitions.** As used in this Agreement:

    2.1. "Product" shall mean the current generally released version of the software product identified in <u>Schedule A</u>, as it may be modified from time to time and provided to Beneficiary in binary form during the Support Term. Product excludes versions to which Beneficiary is not entitled under the License Agreement. ["Product" also includes any additional code, functions or programs developed or supplied by Depositor for the Beneficiary from time to time under the License Agreement during the Support Term.]

    2.2. "Source Code" shall mean the human readable version of software used to edit, write and/or compile the binary code version of the Product[, excluding third party commercially or publicly available code, utilities, libraries, compilers and proprietary tools used in creating the Product.] Required third party materials will be listed in the Source Materials.

2.3. "Source Materials" shall mean the Source Code for the current general release of the Product together with [the available] [all reasonably required] documentation for use of the Source Code. This definition of Source Materials may be supplemented in Schedule A.

2.4. "Support Term" means the period for which Beneficiary purchases maintenance and support services from Depositor for the Product.

3. **Deposit in Escrow**

3.1. Within ten (10) days after execution of this Agreement, Depositor shall deliver to Escrow Agent the current version of the Source Materials.

3.2. Each delivery to the Escrow Agent (a "Deposit") shall be made together with a written description of the contents of the Deposit and with Depositor's certification of the completeness and accuracy of description of each deposit in the form set forth as Schedule B. Within five (5) days after receipt of the Source Materials, Escrow Agent shall notify Depositor and Beneficiary of receipt.

3.3. Depositor shall provide a new version of the Source Materials [every ____ months (provided that a Deposit is required only if a more recent release has been issued)] [within thirty (30) days of each new release of the Product]. These updating obligations apply only to versions issued during the Support Term.

3.4. Escrow Agent shall inspect each Deposit visually to confirm that the description matches the contents (so far as can be determined visually) and shall promptly notify Depositor and Beneficiary in writing of any discrepancies.

3.5. Each new Deposit shall replace the earlier Deposit which earlier version Escrow Agent shall then destroy by a reasonably secure means of doing so, provided that if there are discrepancies identified as stated above, the earlier version will be held until the discrepancies are resolved.

3.6. Escrow Agent shall hold the Source Materials in a reasonably secure climate-controlled facility under reasonable conditions of confidentiality and shall release the Source Materials only upon the terms and conditions provided in this Agreement.

3.7. Escrow Agent is licensed to make copies of the Source Materials as reasonably necessary to perform this Agreement. Escrow Agent shall copy all copyright, non-disclosure, and other proprietary notices contained on the Deposit Materials onto any copies made by Escrow Agent.

3.8. Escrow Agent will keep an accurate record of its actions hereunder which will be available for inspection by Depositor or Beneficiary upon request.

4. **Definition of Release Condition**

4.1. As used in this Agreement, "Release Condition" shall mean [any of the following] [any of the following that occurs during the Support Term]:

4.1.1. Depositor's failure to continue to do business in the ordinary course.

4.1.2. Depositor's bankruptcy proceeding or the appointment of a receiver that is not dismissed within sixty (60) days or Depositor's assignment of its assets for the benefit of creditors. [However if Depositor is operating in Chapter 11 of the US Bankruptcy Code and is continuing to provide commercially reasonable maintenance support, there shall not be deemed to be a Release Condition.]

4.1.3. [Depositor's discontinuing maintenance and support for the most current version of the Product.]

4.1.4. [Depositor's material breach, uncured after 30 days' written notice to Depositor, of its maintenance and support obligations under the License Agreement.]

5. **Release from Escrow.** The Source Materials shall be released and delivered to Beneficiary only in the event that:

5.1. Depositor directs Escrow Agent in writing to make delivery to Beneficiary at a specific address; or

5.2. Escrow Agent has received from Beneficiary (to be sent with a copy to Depositor):

5.2.1. Written notification that a Release Condition exists;

5.2.2. Evidence satisfactory to Escrow Agent that Beneficiary has previously notified Depositor of such Release Condition in writing (including notice to the Depositor of the nature of the Release Condition);

5.2.3. Beneficiary's written demand that the Source Materials be released and delivered to Beneficiary;

5.2.4. A written undertaking from Beneficiary that the copy of the Source Materials being released to Beneficiary will be used only as permitted under the terms of the License Agreement and this Agreement; and

5.2.5. Specific instructions from Beneficiary on where and how to make delivery.

5.3. In the event that the provisions of paragraph 5.2 are met, Escrow Agent shall, within five (5) days of receipt of all of the items specified, send Depositor notice that Beneficiary has demanded release of the Source Materials and shall include a photocopy of the items specified in paragraph 5.2. Depositor shall have thirty (30) days from the date such items are mailed or sent by Escrow Agent to provide to Escrow Agent written notice of any objection to the release of the Source Materials. Depositor shall send a copy of any such objection to Beneficiary.

5.4. If, within thirty (30) days after mailing or sending the items specified in paragraph 5.2 to Depositor, Escrow Agent has not received written notice of objection to the release of the Source Materials, then Escrow Agent shall release the Source Materials to Beneficiary in accordance with the delivery instructions referred to in paragraph 5.2. Escrow Agent is entitled to require payment of any fees due Escrow Agent before making the release.

6. Arbitration

In the event that Depositor sends such notice of objection to Escrow Agent within the thirty (30) day period, the matter may be submitted to binding arbitration by either Depositor or Beneficiary. Three (3) arbitrators shall be chosen by the American Arbitration Association office located in *[specify city and state]* in accordance with the rules of the American Arbitration Association ("AAA"). The Parties shall request that, if feasible, the AAA appoint one arbitrator to the panel of three arbitrators who shall possess knowledge of the computer software industry; however the arbitration shall proceed even if such a person is unavailable. The decision of the arbitrators shall be binding and conclusive on all Parties involved. Judgment on the arbitrator's decision may be entered in any forum, federal or state, having jurisdiction. All costs of the arbitration, including reasonable attorneys' fees and costs incurred by the prevailing Party and Escrow Agent, shall be paid by the non-prevailing Party.

7. **Delivery by Escrow Agent to Depositor.** Escrow Agent shall return and deliver the Source Materials to Depositor upon the occurrence of mutual termination or non-payment to Escrow Agent as follows:

   7.1. If mutual termination occurs upon the presentation to Escrow Agent of a written notice of termination:

      7.1.1. Executed by authorized representatives of Depositor and Beneficiary, stating that this Agreement has been terminated by the written agreement of Depositor and Beneficiary, and

      7.1.2. Directing Escrow Agent to release and deliver the Source Materials to Depositor by a specified method of delivery to a specified address within ten (10) days of receipt by the Escrow Agent.

   7.2. In case of non-payment to Escrow Agent, Escrow Agent shall give notice to both Beneficiary and Depositor of the non-payment of any fees due and payable hereunder. Both Beneficiary and Depositor shall have the right to pay the unpaid fee within thirty (30) days from the date of mailing or sending the notice from Escrow Agent. Upon timely payment of the unpaid fee by either Beneficiary or Depositor, this Agreement shall continue in force and effect; otherwise termination shall take place under this Section.

8. **Ownership of Source Materials**

Ownership of the Source Materials shall remain with Depositor and its suppliers. No rights of ownership are granted by this Agreement.

9. **License Upon Release to Beneficiary**

   9.1. *License Grant.* Upon Escrow Agent's release of the Source Materials to Beneficiary in accordance with this Agreement, the Beneficiary shall have the right to use the Source Materials solely for purposes of maintaining [and modifying] the Product for its own internal use in accordance with the License Agreement. Beneficiary shall not distribute, license or release any copy of the Source Materials. Except as is reasonably required for licensed use, Beneficiary may not copy the Source Materials (except for [one backup copy] [a reasonable number of backup copies]). The Source Materials may not be used for any other function or purpose. [Nothing in this Agreement discharges either of the Parties to the License Agreement of their obligations under it, including any applicable payment obligations.] Rights not expressly granted are reserved to the Parties respectively.

9.2. *Continuing Confidentiality Obligation.* In case of release to the Beneficiary, the Parties agree that the Source Materials will be confidential information of Beneficiary under the terms of the License Agreement and the Beneficiary shall treat them accordingly. After release, Beneficiary shall be under a continuing obligation to keep the Source Materials secure and confidential. Failure to do so will be a material breach that will entitle Depositor to terminate the license grant.

10. Subpoenas

10.1. If Escrow Agent receives a subpoena or any compulsory demand pertaining to the disclosure or release of the Source Materials, Escrow Agent will immediately notify the Depositor and Beneficiary unless prohibited by law. It shall be the right of Depositor and/or Beneficiary to challenge any such subpoena or any compulsory demand. Escrow Agent may obey any legally valid order or any law without violating this Agreement.

11. Bankruptcy

If Depositor or its trustee in bankruptcy rejects the License Agreement or this Agreement under the provisions of the Bankruptcy Code, Beneficiary may elect to retain its rights under the License Agreement and this Agreement as provided in Section 365(n) of the United States Bankruptcy Code. Depositor or such trustee in bankruptcy shall not interfere with the license and contractual rights of Beneficiary as provided in the License Agreement and this Agreement, including the right to obtain the Source Materials from Escrow Agent.

12. Warranties of Depositor. Depositor warrants to Beneficiary and Escrow Agent:

12.1. Depositor has sufficient rights and permissions to provide the deposited Source Materials and grant the licenses and permissions stated in this Agreement; and

12.2. The Source Materials are as described in their applicable description and, if encrypted, the decryption tools and decryption keys have also been deposited.

13. **Liability Limitation of Escrow Agent**

Except for actual fraud, gross negligence, or intentional misconduct, Escrow Agent shall not be liable to Depositor, Beneficiary or to any other party for any act or failure to act. Any liability of Escrow Agent under this Agreement, regardless of cause, shall be limited to the actual cost of new magnetic or optical media of the same type and quality of any lost or destroyed Source Code copy. Escrow Agent will not be liable for special, indirect, incidental, or consequential damages.

14. **Indemnity**

Depositor and Beneficiary shall defend, indemnify and hold harmless Escrow Agent and each of its directors, officers, employees, agents, and stockholders from any and all claims, damages, suits, liabilities, obligations, costs, fees, and any other expenses whatsoever, including legal fees, that may be incurred by Escrow Agent or any of its directors, officers, employees, agents, or stockholders relating to the duties or performance of Escrow Agent under this Agreement, except for the results of their actual fraud, gross negligence, or intentional misconduct.

15. **Certain Disputes**

15.1. In the event of any dispute between Depositor and Beneficiary or any other party claiming rights under this Agreement, Escrow Agent may submit the matter to any court of competent jurisdiction in an interpleader or similar action. However, Escrow Agent shall not be obligated to bring such a proceeding. Depositor and Beneficiary shall defend, indemnify and hold harmless Escrow Agent from all costs and fees incurred in such a proceeding, including legal fees.

15.2. If Escrow Agent shall be uncertain as to its duties or rights hereunder, Escrow Agent may, without incurring any liability, refrain from taking any action until it receives direction in writing in the form of the order, decree, or judgment of a court of competent jurisdiction; but Escrow Agent shall be under no duty to institute or defend any such proceeding.

16. **Verification**

16.1. Upon receipt of a written request from Beneficiary and payment by the Beneficiary of the applicable fee as set by Escrow Agent from time to time, Escrow Agent shall compile and inspect the Source Materials to verify its contents, completeness, accuracy, and functionality, and shall send its written report ("Technical Verification Report") to Beneficiary. Escrow Agent will send Depositor a copy of its written Technical Verification Report.

16.2. Depositor shall cooperate with Escrow Agent by making available promptly facilities, computer systems, object code, technical and support personnel, and all other materials and assistance as Escrow Agent may reasonably request for the purpose of verification. Upon request by Beneficiary, Depositor shall permit one employee of Beneficiary to be present at Depositor's facility during verification of Source Materials.

16.3. Except as otherwise expressly provided in this Agreement, Escrow Agent shall have no responsibility with respect to the accuracy or completeness of the Source Materials or any revisions thereto.

17. **Fees and Term**

17.1. Escrow Agent shall be entitled to the fees for its services under this Agreement. Fee amounts will be as described in Escrow Agent's applicable fee schedule as it is in effect from time to time. The current fee schedule is attached as <u>Schedule C</u>. Such fees will paid by Beneficiary. [The fees set forth on <u>Schedule C</u> may be increased, by Escrow Agent in its sole discretion, by a maximum of ___ (__) percent per year after the initial ____ years of the term of this Agreement.]

17.2. Escrow Agent shall issue an invoice for its initial fee to Beneficiary which shall be due at the time of the execution of this Agreement, and shall issue additional invoices to Beneficiary from time to time as additional fees become due under <u>Schedule C</u>. Payment is due within thirty (30) days of invoice date.

17.3. Subject to Section 7.2, if invoiced fees are not paid, Escrow Agent may terminate this Agreement.

17.4. The initial term of this Agreement shall be one (1) year commencing the date all Parties have signed. The term of this Agreement shall be automatically renewed for successive one (1) year terms unless otherwise terminated by the written agreement of Beneficiary and Depositor or as permitted in this Agreement.

17.5. This Agreement shall terminate upon the delivery of the Source Materials to any Party, provided however that all fees due to Escrow Agent shall remain due and owing notwithstanding the termination of this Agreement. No fee shall become refundable or be discharged on account of such termination.

17.6. The following Sections of this Agreement shall survive termination: 8 (Ownership), 9 (License upon Release to Beneficiary), 12 (Warranties of Depositor), 13 (Liability Limitation of Escrow Agent), 14 (Indemnity), 15 (Certain Disputes), and 18 (Miscellaneous) together with any accrued payment obligations.

18. **Miscellaneous**

18.1. *Notices.* All notices required or permitted by this Agreement shall be in writing and sent by registered or certified mail, return receipt requested, or by any form of express delivery that generates a receipt. The following addresses shall be used for notice:

> If to Depositor: *[Insert notice information.]*
>
> If to Beneficiary: *[Insert notice information.]*
>
> If to Escrow Agent: *[Insert notice information.]*

It shall be the responsibility of the Parties to notify each other as provided in this Section in the event of a change of addresses.

18.2. *Invalidity.* The invalidity of any provision of this Agreement shall not affect the validity of the Agreement or its other provisions.

18.3. *Successors and Assigns.* This Agreement shall be binding upon and shall inure to the benefit of the successors and assigns of the Parties.

18.4. *Waiver.* Delay or failure to exercise any right or remedy shall not be deemed the waiver of that right or remedy.

18.5. *Entire Agreement.* This Agreement, which includes the Schedules described herein, embodies the entire agreement of the Parties with respect to its subject matter and supersedes all previous communications, representations or understandings, either oral or written. Escrow Agent's obligation to Depositor or Beneficiary is limited to this Agreement, and Escrow Agent is not responsible with regard to the License Agreement.

18.6. *Legal Compliance.* Depositor and Beneficiary are responsible for and warrant compliance with all applicable laws that may relate to this Agreement.

18.7. *No Third Party Rights.* This Agreement is made solely for the benefit of the Parties to this Agreement. There are no third party beneficiaries.

18.8. *Authority to Sign.* Each of the Parties herein represents and warrants that it has sufficient authority to execute and perform this Agreement.

18.9. *Counterparts.* This Agreement may be executed in any number of counterparts, each of which shall be an original, but all of which together shall constitute one instrument, and it may be executed by fax copies.

So agreed among the Parties to this binding Agreement:

[Name of Escrow Agent]

By: _____

Print Name and Title: _____

Title: _____

Date: _____

[Name of Depositor]

By: _____

Print Name and Title: _____

Title: _____

Date: _____

[Name of Beneficiary]

By: _____

Print Name and Title: _____

Title: _____

Date: _____

Schedule A

Description of Source Materials

[Insert Description]

Schedule B

Form for Deposit Source Materials

Depositor Name: _____

Beneficiary Name: _____

Product Name: _____

Version No.: _____

Date of Deposit: _____

Additional Description of Materials Deposited:

_____

_____

_____

Depositor hereby certifies to the accuracy and completeness of the foregoing description.

[Name of Depositor]

By: _____

Print Name and Title: _____

Title: _____

Date: _____

Schedule C

Escrow Fees

[To be added]

SaaS Customer Agreement

Introductory Note

This is a form for a software-as-a-service (or SaaS) offering to a customer. This form is written to be a signed agreement but can be adapted to be an online clickwrap agreement.

The form is written to favor and protect the Vendor, but does include reasonable promises of service and support to the Customer, including a service level agreement that promises a specified remedy if "uptime" falls below a specified level.

Bracketed language is optional or provides alternatives.

Service Agreement

This Service Agreement ("Agreement") is made between [*Vendor Name*] ("Vendor") with its principal address at _____ and the Customer (as defined below). This Agreement, including the attached Schedule(s), is effective on the date that both parties have signed this Agreement (the "Effective Date").

1. **Definitions.** The following definitions (and additional definitions provided below) will apply:

   1.1. "Activation Date" is defined in Section 23.

   1.2. "Customer" means the legal entity or individual that enters into this Agreement as described on the Signature Page.

   1.3. "Customer Data" means data, information or material provided or submitted by Customer or any User to Vendor in the course of utilizing the Service.

1.4. "Customer Representative" means the Users designated by Customer as authorized to create User accounts, administer Customer's use of the Service and otherwise represent Customer for the purpose of this Agreement.

1.5. "Pricing Schedule" means <u>Schedule A</u> to this Agreement.

1.6. "Service" means Vendor's online service as described in <u>Schedule B</u> and applicable documentation on Vendor's web site.

1.7. "Term" means the term of this Agreement as specified in Section 23.

*[**Comment:** Some SaaS agreements have restrictions on who can be a "User." For example, Users might be limited to employees. In this form, the Customer can allow anyone to be a User.]*

1.8. "User" means one of Customer's employees, representatives, consultants, contractors or agents and other persons expressly permitted by Customer in connection with Customer's business affairs who are authorized to use the Service and have been supplied User identifications and passwords by Customer (or by Vendor at Customer's request).

1.9. "Vendor Content" means Vendor-supplied text, audio, video, graphics and other information and data available by means of the Service or on Vendor's web site.

2. **Customer Use of the Service**

   2.1. Vendor grants Customer a license to access and use the Service during the Term via the Internet under and subject to the terms of this Agreement. Vendor will host the Service. Vendor reserves the right to make changes and updates to the functionality and/or documentation of the Service from time to time.

   2.2. Customer is licensed during the Term to store, print, and display the Vendor Content and to permit Users to access it only in connection with use of the Service. No other use of Vendor Content is permitted. [Customer will maintain and will require its Users to maintain Vendor Content as Confidential Information (as defined below) of Vendor.]

3. **Number of Authorized Users**

   Customer is initially authorized to permit use by the number of Users listed in the Pricing Schedule. Customer, by its Customer Representative, may add to the number of Users by contacting Vendor customer support by email or phone or by utilizing applicable management features of the Service. Customer will be bound by the instructions and authorizations provided by its Customer Representative.

4. **Fees Generally**

   Customer agrees to pay fees as set forth in the Pricing Schedule or as Vendor and Customer otherwise agree in writing.

5. **User-Based Fees; Payment**

   5.1. Subject to the fee structure and calculations stated in the Pricing Schedule, license fees are due for the Service based on the number of billable Users in the immediately preceding month. A User is considered billable if his or her account (with a username and password) is available for login and use [at any time during a month] [for at least ___ days during any month]. Customer agrees that charges will apply for all billable User accounts including those that have been inactive during a particular month. A User account may not be shared or used by more than one User.

   5.2. Vendor will invoice monthly for use of the Service at the beginning of the month. All invoices for any charges under this Agreement are due and payable within 15 days of invoice date. [For customers paying via credit card, customer's credit card is charged simultaneously with the creation of the customer's invoice.] Customer's account will be considered delinquent (in arrears) if payment in full is not received by the due date specified on the invoice. Amounts due are exclusive of all applicable taxes, levies, or duties, and Customer will be responsible for payment of all such amounts. All amounts are payable in U.S. dollars. If Customer believes that any specific charge under this Agreement is incorrect, in order to obtain a credit, Customer must contact Vendor in writing within 30 days of invoice date setting forth the nature and amount of the requested correction; otherwise invoices are final.

*[**Comment:** In this form, the Vendor charges the Customer for storage used in excess of a specified amount. Where SaaS applications involve heavy bandwidth usage (for example services involving video or audio), there could also be bandwidth charges for data transmission in excess of a specified volume.]*

6. **Excess Data Storage Fees**

The maximum disk storage space for Customer Data provided to Customer at no additional charge is specified on the Pricing Schedule. If the amount of disk storage required for Customer's use exceeds this limit, Customer will be charged per-megabyte (MB) at the applicable rate stated in the Pricing Schedule, based on the maximum storage used [at the end of] [during] the month.

7. **Non-Payment**

7.1. In addition to other applicable remedies, Vendor reserves the right to suspend and/or terminate Customer's access to the Service and/or terminate this Agreement, upon five days' email notice, if Customer's account becomes delinquent (falls into arrears).

7.2. Delinquent invoices are subject to interest of 1.5% per month on any outstanding balance, or the maximum permitted by law, whichever is less, plus all expenses of collection, including reasonable attorneys' fees and court costs. Customer will be charged all applicable fees, including fees for all Users then authorized, during any period of suspension.

8. **Account Information Submitted to Vendor**

Customer agrees to provide Vendor in writing with billing and contact information as Vendor may reasonably require, including Customer's legal company name, street address, email address, and name and telephone number of an authorized billing contact, as well as the name, User name and password of the Customer Representative. Customer agrees to update this information promptly by means of email to accounting@[*vendorURL*].com, and in any case within 15 days, if there is any change.

9. **Appropriate Use of the Service**

9.1. While Users may be any persons that Customer authorizes to use the Service for its business, including, but not limited to, Customer's employees and contractors, Customer may not sublicense, resell or supply the Service for use in or for the benefit of any other organization, entity, business, or enterprise without Vendor's prior written consent.

9.2. Customer agrees not to submit to the Service any material that is illegal, misleading, defamatory, indecent or obscene, in poor taste, threatening, infringing of any third party proprietary rights, invasive of personal privacy, or otherwise objectionable (collectively "Objectionable Matter"). Customer will be responsible to ensure that its Users do not submit any Objectionable Matter. In addition, Vendor may, at its option, adopt rules for permitted and appropriate use and may update them from time to time on the Vendor web site; Customer and Customer's Users will be bound by any such rules. Vendor reserves the right to remove any Customer Data that constitutes Objectionable Matter or violates any Vendor rules regarding appropriate use, but is not obligated to do so. Customer and Customer's Users will comply with all applicable laws regarding Customer Data, use of the Service and the Vendor Content, including laws involving private data and any applicable export controls. Vendor reserves the right to terminate this Agreement for cause in case the Customer materially breaches the provisions of this Section 9.

9.3. Vendor reserves the right to suspend or terminate immediately any Customer or User account or activity that is disrupting or causing harm to Vendor's computers, systems or infrastructure or to other parties, or is in violation of state or federal laws regarding "spam," including, without limitation, the CAN-SPAM Act of 2003. Any such spamming activity by Customer will be a material breach of this Agreement.

10. **Passwords and Access**

Customer is responsible for all activities that occur under Customer's User accounts. Customer is responsible for maintaining the security and confidentiality of all User usernames and passwords. Customer agrees to notify Vendor immediately of any unauthorized use of any Service username or password or account or any other known or suspected breach of security.

11. **Customer Data**

11.1. All Customer Data submitted by Customer to Vendor, whether posted by Customer or by Users, will remain the sole property of Customer or such Users to the full extent provided by law.

11.2. Customer will have sole responsibility for the accuracy, quality, integrity, legality, reliability, appropriateness of and copyright permissions for all Customer Data. Vendor will not use the Customer Data for any purpose other than to provide the Service to Customer and for statistical reporting purposes. Vendor may aggregate anonymous statistical data regarding use and functioning of its system by its various Users. Such aggregated statistical data will be the sole property of Vendor.

11.3. On a [weekly] [monthly] basis during the Term, Vendor will (at Customer's request, in writing or by email, to Vendor customer support) make one backup of the then current Customer Data available to the Customer via FTP server in Vendor's standard format. Additional backup services are available at additional cost; Customer may contact Vendor customer support for details.

11.4. Vendor will use commercially reasonable security measures to protect Customer Data against unauthorized disclosure or use. Vendor's security policies in effect from time to time can be accessed on Vendor's web site.

12. Limited License to Customer Data

Subject to the terms and conditions of this Agreement, Customer grants to Vendor a non-exclusive license to use, copy, store, transmit and display Customer Data to the extent reasonably necessary to provide and maintain the Service.

13. Vendor's Ownership

Vendor and its suppliers retain all rights in the Service and Vendor Content. This Agreement grants no ownership rights to Customer. No license is granted to Customer except as to use of the Service as expressly stated herein. The Vendor name, the Vendor logo, and the product names associated with the Service are trademarks of Vendor or third parties, and they may not be used without Vendor's prior written consent.

14. Restrictions on Use of the Service

Customer may not alter, resell or sublicense the Service or provide it as a service bureau. Customer agrees not to reverse engineer the Service or its software or other technology. Customer will not use or access the Service to: (i) build a competitive product or service, (ii) make or have made a product using similar ideas, features, functions or graphics of the Service, (iii) make derivative works based upon the Service or the Vendor Content or (iv) copy any features, functions or graphics of the Service or the Vendor Content.

Customer will not "frame" or "mirror" the Service. Use, resale or exploitation of the Service and/or the Vendor Content except as expressly permitted in this Agreement is prohibited.

15. **Privacy**

Vendor agrees to implement its privacy policies in effect from time to time. Vendor's privacy policies can be accessed on Vendor's web site. Vendor reserves the right to modify its privacy and security policies from time to time in its business judgment and as it deems required for compliance with applicable law.

16. **Warranty Regarding the Service**

Vendor warrants that the Service will perform in all material respects to the functionality as described in applicable online user documentation available via Vendor's web site.

*[**Comment:** In this form, the Vendor makes an "uptime warranty" and provides the Customer with compensation if the uptime goals are not met. In some agreements, the Vendor agrees to use automated means to monitor uptime and to report its failure to meet targets to the Customer. In some agreements, on the other hand, it is up to the Customer to notice a Service outage and ask for a credit. The following section in this form is written in the latter fashion.]*

17. **Service Level Warranty**

Vendor warrants during the Term of this Agreement that the Service will meet the applicable service level stated in <u>Schedule C</u>. If Vendor does not achieve such service level, Vendor will provide Customer upon request with a credit as described in <u>Schedule C</u> as Customer's sole and exclusive remedy. To claim a remedy under this Section, Customer is required to notify Vendor within 15 days of the occurrence of the failure to provide the applicable service level.

18. **Additional Warranties**

Each party represents and warrants that it has the legal power and authority to enter into this Agreement. Customer represents and warrants that it has not falsely identified itself or provided any false information to gain access to the Service and that Customer's billing information is correct.

*[**Comment:** The following section allows for customization of the Customer's SaaS implementation.]*

19. **Professional Services**

19.1. Customer may retain Vendor to perform professional services ("Professional Services") as the parties may agree upon in writing in the form of a work order or other writing ("Work Order"). Vendor will use reasonable efforts to carry out the Professional Services stated in the Work Order and to provide any resulting functionality in the Service made available online to Customer and Customer's Users. Except as the parties otherwise agree in a Work Order, Professional Services and the results thereof are made available "AS IS."

19.2. Unless otherwise agreed in writing in the Work Order, Professional Services are provided by Vendor on a time and materials basis at Vendor's then applicable rates and subject to such deposit or advance payment as Vendor may require. Maintenance and support of code or functionality created by means of Professional Services will likewise be on a Work Order basis under this Section unless otherwise agreed in writing. The code and functionality made or provided under this Section and all interests therein, including copyrights, will be Vendor's property. Access to the results of Professional Services will be available as part of the Service during the Term unless otherwise agreed in writing. The initial Work Order (if any) is attached as <u>Schedule D</u>. Unless otherwise agreed in a Work Order, Vendor may bill for Professional Services on a weekly or monthly basis, at its discretion.

20. **Indemnification**

20.1. Vendor will defend, indemnify, and hold Customer (and its officers, directors, employees and agents) harmless from and against all costs, liabilities, losses, and expenses (including reasonable attorneys' fees) (collectively, "Losses") arising from any third party claim, suit, action, or proceeding arising from the actual or alleged infringement of any United States copyright, patent, trademark, or misappropriation of a trade secret by the Service or Vendor Content (other than that due to Customer Data). In case of such a claim, Vendor may, in its discretion, procure a license that will protect Customer against such claim without cost to Customer, replace the Service with a non-infringing Service, or if it deems such remedies not practicable, Vendor may terminate the Service and this Agreement without fault, provided that in case of such a termination, Customer will receive a pro-rata refund of the license fees prepaid for use of the Service not yet furnished as of the termination date. THIS SECTION STATES CUSTOMER'S SOLE AND EXCLUSIVE REMEDIES FOR INFRINGEMENT OR CLAIMS ALLEGING INFRINGEMENT.

20.2. Customer will defend, indemnify, and hold Vendor (and its officers, directors, employees and agents) harmless from and against all Losses arising out of or in connection with a claim, suit, action, or proceeding by a third party (i) alleging that the Customer Data or other data or information supplied by Customer infringes the intellectual property rights or other rights of a third party or has caused harm to a third party or (ii) arising out of breach of Sections 9 (Appropriate Use of the Service) or 10 (Passwords and Access) above.

20.3. Customer will defend, indemnify, and hold Vendor (and its officers, directors, employees and agents) harmless from any expense or cost arising from any third party subpoena or compulsory legal order or process that seeks Customer Data and/or other Customer-related information or data, including, without limitation, prompt payment to Vendor of all costs (including attorneys' fees) incurred by Vendor as a result. In case of such subpoena or compulsory legal order or process, Customer also agrees to pay Vendor for its staff time in responding to such third party subpoena or compulsory legal order or process at Vendor's then applicable hourly rates.

20.4. In case of any claim that is subject to indemnification under this Agreement, the party that is indemnified ("Indemnitee") will provide the indemnifying party ("Indemnitor") reasonably prompt notice of the relevant claim. Indemnitor will defend and/or settle, at its own expense, any demand, action, or suit on any claim subject to indemnification under this Agreement. Each party will cooperate in good faith with the other to facilitate the defense of any such claim and will tender the defense and settlement of any action or proceeding covered by this Section to the Indemnitor upon request. Claims may be settled without the consent of the Indemnitee, unless the settlement includes an admission of wrongdoing, fault or liability.

21. **Disclaimers and Limitations**

21.1. THE WARRANTIES EXPRESSLY STATED IN THIS AGREEMENT ARE THE SOLE AND EXCLUSIVE WARRANTIES OFFERED BY VENDOR. THERE ARE NO OTHER WARRANTIES OR REPRESENTATIONS, EXPRESS OR IMPLIED, INCLUDING WITHOUT LIMITATION, THOSE OF MERCHANTABILITY OR FITNESS FOR A PARTICULAR PURPOSE. EXCEPT AS STATED IN SECTIONS 16, 17 AND 18 ABOVE, THE SERVICE AND VENDOR CONTENT ARE PROVIDED TO CUSTOMER ON AN "AS IS" AND "AS AVAILABLE" BASIS. CUSTOMER ASSUMES ALL RESPONSIBILITY FOR DETERMINING WHETHER THE SERVICE OR THE INFORMATION GENERATED THEREBY IS ACCURATE OR SUFFICIENT FOR CUSTOMER'S PURPOSES. VENDOR DOES NOT WARRANT THAT USE OF THE SYSTEM WILL BE ERROR-FREE OR UNINTERRUPTED. VENDOR IS NOT RESPONSIBLE FOR SOFTWARE INSTALLED OR USED BY CUSTOMER OR USERS OR FOR THE OPERATION OR PERFORMANCE OF THE INTERNET.

21.2. Except with regard to Customer's payment obligations and with regard to either party's indemnification obligations, in no event will either party's aggregate liability exceed the license fees due for the 12 month period measured by the monthly payment obligation at the time of the event or circumstance giving rise to such claim. Except in regard to Customer breach of Sections 9 or 10, in no event will either party be liable for any indirect, special, incidental, consequential damages of any type or kind (including, without limitation, loss of data, revenue, profits, use or other economic advantage).

21.3. The Service may include gateways, links or other functionality that allows Customer and/or Users to access third party services ("Third Party Services") and/or third party content and materials ("Third Party Materials"). Vendor does not supply and is not responsible for any Third Party Services or Third Party Materials, which may be subject to their own licenses, end-user agreements, privacy and security policies, and/ or terms of use. VENDOR MAKES NO WARRANTY AS TO THIRD PARTY SERVICES OR THIRD PARTY MATERIALS.

22. **Confidentiality**

22.1. "Confidential Information" means non-public information, technical data or know-how of a party and/or its affiliates, which is furnished to the other party in written or tangible form in connection with this Agreement. Oral disclosure will also be deemed Confidential Information if it would reasonably be considered to be of a confidential nature or if it is confirmed at the time of disclosure to be confidential.

22.2. Notwithstanding the foregoing, Confidential Information does not include information which is: (i) already in the possession of the receiving party and not subject to a confidentiality obligation to the providing party; (ii) independently developed by the receiving party; (iii) publicly disclosed through no fault of the receiving party; (iv) rightfully received by the receiving party from a third party that is not under any obligation to keep such information confidential; (v) approved for release by written agreement with the disclosing party; or (vi) disclosed pursuant to the requirements of law, regulation, or court order, provided that the receiving party will promptly inform the providing party of any such requirement and cooperate with any attempt to procure a protective order or similar treatment.

22.3. Neither party will use the other party's Confidential Information except as reasonably required for the performance of this Agreement. Each party will hold in confidence the other party's Confidential Information by means that are no less restrictive than those used for its own confidential materials. Each party agrees not to disclose the other party's Confidential Information to anyone other than its employees or subcontractors who are bound by confidentiality obligations and who need to know the same to perform such party's obligations hereunder. [The confidentiality obligations set forth in this Section will survive for _____ (_) years after the termination or expiration of this Agreement.

22.4. Upon termination or expiration of this Agreement, except as otherwise agreed in writing or otherwise stated in this Agreement, each party will, upon the request of the disclosing party, either: (i) return all of such Confidential Information of the disclosing party and all copies thereof in the receiving party's possession or control to the disclosing party; or

(ii) destroy all Confidential Information and all copies thereof in the receiving party's possession or control. The receiving party will then, at the request of the disclosing party, certify in writing that no copies have been retained by the receiving party, its employees or agents.

22.5. In case a party receives legal process that demands or requires disclosure of the disclosing party's Confidential Information, such party will give prompt notice to the disclosing party, if legally permissible, to enable the disclosing party to challenge such demand.

*[**Comment:** The following section allows time for customization of the Customers' SaaS implementation before monthly billing begins. The billing for the first year of service is also adjusted to allow for this process. If there is no customization required, the following clauses can be simplified to allow monthly billing to begin on or a specified number of days after the Effective Date.]*

23. **Term and Termination**

23.1. The Term commences on the "Effective Date." Vendor will use commercially reasonable efforts to make the Service available to Customer on the "Target Activation Date" stated on Schedule A. The "Activation Date" will be the date that Vendor first makes the Service available to Customer and provides email or written notice of such availability to Customer. In most cases, the Target Activation Date and the Activation Date will be the same; Vendor will inform Customer of any likely delay. Billing of monthly license fees will start as of the Activation Date and thereafter on or after the first of each month.

23.2. The initial term of this Agreement ("Initial Term") will begin on the Effective Date and will end one year from the Activation Date. This Agreement will automatically renew for successive one-year periods (each a "Renewal Term") beginning at the end of the Initial Term, unless Customer provides notice of termination not less than 60 days before the end of the Initial Term or current Renewal Term, as applicable. Applicable pricing, including monthly minimum fees, will continue unchanged from the previous term unless Vendor notifies Customer of changes in pricing at least 30 days prior to the expiration of the Initial Term or current Renewal Term, as applicable. Vendor reserves the right to terminate this Agreement for convenience not less than one year's notice.

23.3. Vendor, in its sole discretion, may suspend or terminate Customer's username and password, account, or use of the Service and/or terminate this Agreement if Customer materially breaches this Agreement and such breach has not been cured within 10 business days of notice of such breach.

23.4. In the event that this Agreement is terminated (for any reason), Vendor will, within 5 days of a Customer's request, make available one backup of the Customer Data in Vendor's standard format. Customer agrees and acknowledges that Vendor has no obligation to retain and may delete Customer Data that remains in Vendor's possession or control more than 60 days after termination.

*[**Comment:** This form contains a provision that commits the Customer to a defined amount of services and requires that the Customer pay the Vendor compensation in case of any early termination. Sometimes SaaS services are offered on an "easy-in-easy-out" basis under which Customer can terminate on short notice, in which case the following clause would not be used.]*

23.5. Any termination by Customer prior to the end of the Initial Term or any Renewal Term will subject Customer to an early termination (acceleration) fee. The early termination fee is calculated as the remaining months of the then contract term (that is the Initial Term or the current Renewal Term) multiplied by the applicable minimum monthly User fees under the Pricing Schedule plus any other outstanding fees or amounts due.

23.6. The following provisions will survive termination: all definitions, Customer's accrued financial obligations, the license to Customer Data to the extent reasonable for Vendor's discharge of its post-termination obligations, and the following Sections and paragraphs: 1 (Definitions), 7.2 (Overdue Payments), 11.1 (Customer Data), 13 (Vendor's Ownership), 14 (Restrictions on Use of the Service), 20 (Indemnification), 21 (Disclaimers and Limitations), 22 (Confidentiality), 22.4 (Return of Customer Data), 23.6 (Survival of Provisions), 24 (Notice), [26 (Arbitration),] [27 (Non- Solicitation),] and 28 (Miscellaneous).

24. **Notice**

Vendor may give notice by means of electronic mail to Customer's email address on record in Customer's account or by written communication sent by first class mail or by courier service to Customer's address on record in Customer's account. Such notice will be deemed to have been given upon the expiration of 36 hours after mailing (if sent by first class mail) or sending by courier or 12 hours after sending (if sent by email), or, if earlier, when received. Customer may give notice to Vendor by [*specify method and address*]. A party may, by giving notice, change its applicable address, email, or other contact information.

25. **Assignment**

This Agreement may not be assigned by Customer without the prior written approval of Vendor but may be assigned by Vendor to (i) a parent or subsidiary, (ii) an acquirer of all or substantially all of Vendor's assets involved in the operations relevant to this Agreement, or (iii) a successor by merger or other combination. Any purported assignment in violation of this Section will be void. This agreement may be enforced by and is binding on permitted successors and assigns.

26. **[Arbitration**

Any dispute arising under this Agreement or the termination of this Agreement will be subject to arbitration in the city of _____, under the commercial rules of the American Arbitration Association before a single arbitrator. The parties will share the arbitration fees equally. Any award will be enforceable in any court of competent jurisdiction and will not be inconsistent with the terms of this agreement. Nothing herein will prevent a party's application to a court of law for injunctive relief to prevent irreparable harm.]

27. **[Non-Solicitation**

During the Term of this Agreement and for a period of one year thereafter, Customer will not, and will ensure that its affiliates will not, directly or indirectly: (i) solicit for employment or for performance of any services any person employed by Vendor or (ii) hire or engage for any services any person employed by Vendor.]

28. **Miscellaneous**

28.1. *Choice of Law; Jurisdiction.* This Agreement will be interpreted fairly in accordance with its terms, without any strict construction in favor of or against either party and in accordance with the laws of the State of _____ and applicable US federal law. [Except as provided in the arbitration clause, the] [The] state and federal courts located in the city of _____ will have exclusive jurisdiction and venue over any dispute or controversy arising from or relating to this Agreement or its subject matter.

28.2. *Severability*. If any provision of this Agreement is held by a court of competent jurisdiction to be invalid or unenforceable, then such provision(s) will be construed, as nearly as possible, to reflect the intentions of the invalid or unenforceable provision(s), with all other provisions remaining in full force and effect.

28.3. *No Agency*. No joint venture, partnership, employment, or agency relationship exists between Customer and Vendor as a result of this Agreement or use of the Service.

28.4. *No Waiver*. The failure of Vendor to enforce any right or provision in this Agreement will not constitute a waiver of such right or provision unless acknowledged and agreed to by Vendor in writing.

28.5. *Force Majeure*. Except for the payment by Customer, if the performance of this Agreement by either party is prevented, hindered, delayed or otherwise made impracticable by reason of any flood, riot, fire, judicial or governmental action, labor disputes, act of God or any other causes beyond the control of such party, that party will be excused from such to the extent that it is prevented, hindered or delayed by such causes.

28.6. *Entire Agreement*. This Agreement, together with any applicable Schedule(s), comprises the entire agreement between Customer and Vendor and supersedes all prior or contemporaneous negotiations, discussions or agreements, whether written or oral, between the parties regarding the subject matter contained herein. No amendment to or modification of this Agreement will be binding unless in writing and signed by an authorized representative of each party.

Signed as a binding Agreement by the parties as of the Effective Date:

Vendor: _____

By (Authorized Signatory): _____ Date: _____

Print Name: _____ Title: _____

Customer

Company Name: _____

By (Authorized Signatory): _____ Date: _____

Print Name: _____ Title: _____

Street Address: _____

City, State: _____

Postal Code, Country: _____

Email Address for Contact: _____

Schedule A

Pricing Schedule

[To be added]

Schedule B

Service Description

[To be added]

Schedule C

Service Level Agreement

1. Service Level Warranty: Vendor's warranty is no less than 99.5% *[or other percentage]* Uptime (as defined below).

2. Remedy: If the warranted level of uptime is not provided, the Customer will be entitled to a credit to Customer (subject to the applicable procedures in this Agreement) in accordance with the following schedule, as follows:

Uptime Level	Available Credit
99.5%–99.0%	Credit equal to ___% of monthly user fees
99.0%–98.5%	Credit equal to ___% of monthly user fees
98.5%–98.0%	Credit equal to ___% of monthly user fees
98.0%–97.5%	Credit equal to ___% of monthly user fees
Below 97%	Credit equal to ___% of monthly user fees

3. "Uptime" means the service is operational and is available to communicate with the Internet in Vendor's server location (which may be at a co-location facility).

4. This credit does not apply to the extent that the failure to achieve the Uptime is due to (a) circumstances that are subject to the Force Majeure clause of this Agreement, (b) scheduled maintenance and system upgrades, or (c) Customer's misuse of the Services.

Schedule D

Work Order for Professional Services
[To be added or state "None"]

Reseller Agreement

Introductory Note

This is a form of Reseller Agreement. Agreements of this type are used for enterprise and industrial software applications which the Reseller will (with help from the Vendor) market, install, customize and support. Sometimes they are called "partnering agreements."

This form does not permit the Reseller to replicate copies. One can write these agreements to license Resellers to make copies, in which case, it would be necessary to include addition provisions for reporting and audit of Reseller's replication, licensing and distribution activity.

Terms in these agreements that are often subject to negotiation include pricing, products covered, territories, indemnification, access to Customer contact information, and duration of the agreement.

Provisions in brackets are optional language or provide alternatives.

Software Reseller Agreement

This Software Reseller Agreement (the "Agreement") is entered into this ___ day of _____, 20__ (the "Effective Date"), by and between *[Name of Vendor]* with a place of business at _____ ("Vendor") and *[Name of Reseller]* with a place of business at _____ ("Reseller") (each a "Party").

Purpose of This Agreement

    A. Vendor markets certain computer applications more particularly described in <u>Schedule A</u>.

B. Reseller, as a value-added software reseller, is engaged in the business of marketing and distributing software applications in connection with its own provision of services and wishes to market and distribute the Products.

C. Vendor desires to grant Reseller a license to market and distribute the Products on the terms hereof.

In consideration of the mutual promises set forth in this Agreement, the Parties agree as follows:

1. **Definitions.** The following definitions (and additional definitions in the text) will apply to this Agreement:

   1.1. "Customer" means an end-user customer of Reseller.

   1.2. "Customer License Agreement" means Vendor's applicable form of license and support agreement for Customers as it may be in effect from time to time. Vendor may modify the terms of its Customer License Agreement any time on thirty (30) days' written notice to Reseller. The current form of Customer License Agreement is attached as <u>Schedule C</u>. Vendor may adopt differing Customer License Agreement forms for different Products.

   1.3. "Products" mean the software products listed on <u>Schedule A</u>, which Vendor may amend as provided in Section 2.3. Where Vendor has provided any upgrade, maintenance, release or other replacement software, such software is included in "Products." "Products" also includes accompanying written, electronic and online user manuals and documentation ("Documentation").

   1.4. "Support Services" means maintenance and support services for the Products under Section 7 of the Agreement.

   1.5. "Vendor Marks" means the trademarks, service marks, trade names, slogans, and brand names, domain names and any other source identifier of the Vendor as specified by Vendor from time to time.

   1.6. "Term" means the term of the Agreement specified in Section 13.

   1.7. "Territory" means those territories and countries listed on <u>Schedule B</u> or as may be chosen by the written agreement of the Parties.

2. **License.** Upon the terms and subject to the conditions of this Agreement:

   2.1. *Distribution License.* Vendor hereby grants to Reseller, during the Term, a non-exclusive, revocable (as stated in this Agreement) and non-transferable license to market and distribute the Products and to sell Vendor licenses for the Products only to Customers in the Territory.

   2.2. *Usage License.* Vendor hereby grants to Reseller, during the Term, a non-exclusive, revocable (as stated in this Agreement) non-transferable license to use the Products for the purpose of demonstrating the Products to Customers. Vendor will supply a reasonable number of "not-for-resale" copies of the Products for such use.

   2.3. *Products Changes.* Vendor retains the right, in its sole discretion, to upgrade or modify the Products from time to time. In addition, upon thirty (30) days' prior written notice to Reseller, Vendor may add or delete Product(s) from <u>Schedule A</u>. Upon receipt of any notice of an upgrade or modification of a Product or upon the expiration of such 30-day notice period for deletion of a Product from <u>Schedule A</u>, Reseller will cease to market and distribute superseded or discontinued versions of the Product.

   2.4. *No Duplication.* Reseller may distribute and deliver Vendor's Products in their original form and packaging. No rights of replication or duplication are granted unless otherwise expressly agreed in writing. The Products will be distributed in executable binary code form only. Reseller will have no license to the source code of Products.

   2.5. *License Management.* Vendor may use such temporary and permanent hardware and software license management software, devices or "keys" as it deems appropriate with regard to Products under such procedures as Vendor may issue from time to time. Reseller may not circumvent or defeat any such means of license management.

   2.6. *Use of Customer License Agreement.* Reseller may grant a Customer a Vendor license to a Product only by means of Vendor's form of Customer License Agreement as it may be in effect from time to time. [Reseller is required to send Vendor a duly signed Customer License Agreement to Vendor before shipment of each order.]

3. **The Territory**

   3.1. *Restriction to the Territory.* Reseller agrees to sell licenses for and promote the Products only in the Territory unless otherwise agreed in writing. Sale of licenses, advertising, or solicitation of orders for the Products by Reseller outside the Territory will be considered a material breach of this Agreement and, at Vendor's option, cause for termination. Reseller will take such reasonable steps as Vendor may direct to avoid conflict resulting from Internet or Web promotion or marketing. With Vendor's prior written permission, Reseller may initiate licensing transactions for the Products that are both inside and outside the Territory. In such cases, Vendor will have the right to allocate to itself or other distributors such transactions to the extent that deliveries or intended use is outside the Territory. With regard to such transactions, Vendor may resolve any competing interests, conflicts or disagreements. Decisions of the Vendor in such matters will be final.

   3.2. [*Sub-distribution Channels.* Reseller may propose to Vendor the use of subdistributors or other channel arrangements for the Territory. Vendor in its discretion may consent to or decline to accept such a proposal. No such permission will be effective unless approved in writing by Vendor.]

4. **Orders and Shipment**

   4.1. *Purchase Orders.* Reseller will submit all orders for Products via a purchase order specifying: the Products ordered, quantity, requested shipping date, and shipping address. All purchase orders submitted by Reseller will be subject to acceptance by Vendor. Reseller reserves the right to require electronic ordering and to confirm order through a designated web site or by other electronic communication.

   4.2. *Packaging.* Each Product may, at Vendor's option, be shipped in boxes or other packaging. Vendor may, at its option, provide for electronic delivery of Products from Vendor to Customer. The Parties may, by mutual agreement, arrange for other means of delivery.

   4.3. *Additional or Contrary Terms.* The terms of this Agreement will govern all sales or licenses and deliveries of Products hereunder notwithstanding any additional or contrary terms contained in any purchase order, quotation, acknowledgment, invoice, or other document issued by Vendor or Reseller.

4.4. *Shipments.* Shipment will be made F.O.B. from the place of business of Vendor, its subsidiary, or a designated agent ("Shipment Location"). Risk of loss, and title, for Products ordered hereunder will pass to Reseller upon delivery to a carrier for shipment, and Reseller will then be responsible for and will bear the entire risk of loss or damage to such Products. Vendor will invoice Reseller for shipping and insurance charges if paid by Vendor.

4.5. *Returns.* Reseller will inspect all Products promptly upon receipt thereof and may reject any visibly damaged or defective Product, provided that Reseller will (i) within ten (10) days after receipt of such alleged defective Product, notify Vendor of its rejection and request a Return Material Authorization ("RMA") number, and (ii) within ten (10) days of receipt of the RMA number from Vendor return such rejected Product freight prepaid and properly insured to Vendor at the Shipment Location or such other location as Vendor will designate in writing. Reseller will only return Products to Vendor after issuance of an RMA.

5. **License to Trademarks.** Vendor hereby grants to Reseller during the Term a non-exclusive, revocable (as stated in this Agreement), and non-transferable license to the Vendor Marks only as follows:

5.1. The Vendor Marks will be used for the purpose of identifying the Products to the Customers within the Territory for normal advertising and promotion of the Products. Reseller may hold itself out in the Territory as Vendor's authorized reseller.

5.2. Reseller will not remove the Vendor Marks from any portion of the Products or the Documentation.

5.3. Reseller may use its own marks in connection with integration services provided with the Products, but may not create the commercial impression that the Vendor Marks pertain to the Reseller.

5.4. Any and all trademarks and trade names licensed hereunder are and remain the exclusive property of Vendor. Reseller may not adopt or register any trademark in any jurisdiction that is the same as or confusingly to the Vendor Marks. Reseller agrees to adhere to all applicable trademark usage guidelines, as may be prescribed by Vendor from time to time. Nothing contained in this Agreement will be deemed to give Reseller any right, title or interest in any Vendor Mark, and all goodwill associated with each Vendor Mark will belong to Vendor.

6. **Price and Payment**

6.1. *Price.* Reseller will pay to Vendor the wholesale license price ("Price") as may be specified and due in accordance with <u>Schedule D</u> or as otherwise provided in this Agreement. Vendor may set Prices both for Products and for Support Services. Vendor may increase or decrease the Price upon thirty (30) days' written notice to Reseller. Payment by Reseller is due in full thirty (30) days from invoice date. Vendor may change its credit terms if it deems that payment is uncertain. If Reseller fails to make payment when due and fails to cure such failure within ten (10) days of notice regarding the default, Vendor may suspend or terminate this Agreement at its option. All amounts are stated in United States Dollars.

6.2. *Late Payment; Credit Policies.* A late payment charge of the lesser of one percent (1.0%) per month or the highest interest rate allowed by applicable law will be charged upon all unpaid amounts that are due hereunder for more than thirty (30) days. Acceptance of late payment in any given instance will not obligate Vendor to accept late payment on other occasions.

6.3. *Taxes.* In addition to the Price and other fees payable hereunder, Reseller will pay any federal, state, local or other duties and excise taxes, including sales tax, value added tax or similar tax.

6.4. *Records; Inspection.* Reseller will maintain detailed records of receipts, revenues, and costs relating to the sale of Product licenses and any associated services, including Support Services (as defined below). Vendor may, upon reasonable notice, inspect the records of Reseller during Reseller's normal business hours to monitor and verify compliance with this Agreement. Vendor may conduct such inspection of such records by its certified public accountant, employee, or agent, provided such person may be required to sign, at Reseller's request, a reasonable non-disclosure agreement.

7. **Support Services; Training; Additional Services**

7.1. *Support Services.* Reseller agrees to promote and sell Support Services to Customers to which Reseller has sold licenses. Vendor's Support Services offering, which is subject to change, is described on <u>Schedule E</u>. Support Services may be provided to Customers subject to the following:

7.1.1. Vendor will have the right to require purchase by Customers of a certain amount of Support Services at the time of the Customer's purchase of a license to a Product. The current requirement, which Vendor may change, is that one year of pre-purchased Support Services is required.

7.1.2. Unless otherwise permitted by Vendor in writing, Reseller may sell Support Services only to Customers that it has licensed in the Territory and who are current in Support Service payments ("Supported Customers"). To provide such Support Services to Customers, Reseller is required first to pay fees to Vendor for Secondary Support for such Customer, as stated in <u>Schedule D</u>.

7.1.3. To each Supported Customer, Reseller will provide the primary support services ("Primary Support") as Vendor may reasonably specify from time to time. The current version of the requirements of Primary Support is stated in <u>Schedule E</u>. Vendor will, unless otherwise agreed, provide secondary support services ("Secondary Support") for support of such Supported Customer as described in such Schedule.

7.1.4. Where Vendor has sold a license to one or more Products to a Customer inside the Territory other than through Reseller, Vendor may request that Reseller provide Primary Support to such Customer. The provision of such Primary Support by Reseller will be subject to the Parties' agreement on the fees and other terms for provision of such Primary Support.

7.2. *Training.* At all times, Reseller will maintain a minimum of one (1) dedicated sales person for the Products and two (2) technical people trained in the then-current Products. Reseller's current pricing and terms for training services are set forth on <u>Schedule G</u> to this Agreement. Training materials will be billed at Vendor's prices for such materials in effect from time to time. Reseller may not replicate Vendor's training materials or authorize others to do so.

7.3. *Customer Services and Vendor Consulting.* Reseller may provide consulting services to Customers. Subject to availability, Vendor will provide services of the type listed on <u>Schedule G</u> to Reseller, which Reseller may, in turn, provide to its Customers. Vendor's current pricing and terms for such consulting services is set forth on <u>Schedule G</u>. Vendor's standard work order form will apply.

8. **Confidentiality and Proprietary Rights**

8.1. *Confidentiality.* Each Party acknowledges that in the course of dealings between the Parties, each may acquire information about the other, its business activities and operations, its technical information and trade secrets (the "Confidential Information"). Confidential Information does not include: (i) information generally available to or known by the public, (ii) information independently developed outside the scope of this Agreement without reference to that made available under this Agreement, or (iii) information which was known to the recipient prior to receipt from the other Party. For the Term, and for a period of five (5) years thereafter, each Party will use commercially reasonable efforts to (i) hold all such Confidential Information in strict confidence and will not reveal the same except pursuant to a court order or upon written permission from the disclosing Party and (ii) use such Confidential Information only as expressly permitted hereunder. Each Party will safeguard the Confidential Information with at least as great a degree of care as the Party uses to safeguard its own most confidential materials or data relating to its own business, but in no event less than a reasonable degree of care. Each Party will immediately return to the other Party or destroy all Confidential Information of the other Party upon termination or written request and upon written request will certify that it has done so.

8.2. *Proprietary Rights; Restrictions.* Reseller acknowledges and agrees that the Products and all copies thereof are the intellectual property of Vendor and its suppliers. Reseller will not reverse engineer or decompile the Products. Reseller may not, and may not permit Customers or third parties, to use, reproduce, sublicense, distribute, dispose of or exploit the Products except as expressly permitted under this Agreement.

8.3. *Notice of Violations.* Reseller agrees to promptly notify Vendor of any actual or suspected infringement of some or all of the rights licensed or any unauthorized use or copying of any Product by any third party.

9. [**Non-Competition.** Reseller agrees, during the Term, not to market any products that compete with the Products and not to promote goods or services that tend to diminish licensing or distribution of the Products.]

10. **Limited Warranty and Disclaimer**

   10.1. *Limited Warranty.* For thirty (30) days after delivery of a Product to Reseller, Vendor warrants that media upon which the Products is delivered will be of good quality and workmanship. Upon written notice from Reseller of defective media for a Product, Vendor will provide replacement media. Any warranties in any Customer License Agreement are solely for the benefit of the Customer.

   10.2. *Disclaimer of Warranties.* EXCEPT AS EXPRESSLY STATED HEREIN, VENDOR SPECIFICALLY DISCLAIMS ALL WARRANTIES EXPRESSED OR IMPLIED, INCLUDING BUT NOT LIMITED TO, IMPLIED WARRANTIES OF MERCHANTABILITY, FITNESS FOR A PARTICULAR PURPOSE AND NON-INFRINGEMENT.

   10.3. *Vendor's Options.* Vendor may, at its option, repair or replace defective Products, provide patches, maintenance releases, or work–arounds or other solutions, or, at Vendor's sole option, may accept returns for refunds.

11. **Damage Exclusions; Limitation of Liability**

   11.1. Except with regard to unlicensed use or exploitation of the Products or a Party's intellectual property or breach of a Party's obligations regarding Confidential Information:

      11.1.1. Neither Party will have any liability for consequential, or other indirect damages, or exemplary, special, incidental or punitive damages even if it has been advised of the possibility of such damages; and

      11.1.2. The cumulative liability of each Party will be limited to the amount paid or payable under this Agreement by Reseller to Vendor.

12. **Reseller Obligations**

   12.1. *Marketing Efforts.* Reseller agrees to use commercially reasonable efforts to promote the sale of the Products. Reseller agrees to permit Vendor to review all of Reseller's promotion and advertising material for the Products prior to use. Reseller will withdraw any promotion or advertising that Vendor finds unsuitable.

12.2. *Web Linking.* During the Term, Reseller may link its web site to Vendor's web site, subject to Vendor's assent, which will not be unreasonably denied or withdrawn. During the Term Vendor may link its web site to Reseller's web site, subject to Reseller's assent, which will not be unreasonably denied or withdrawn.

12.3. *Customer Information.* Reseller will provide Vendor with up-to-date information on Customer name, address and contact information as Vendor may reasonably request. Vendor may require Customers to register with Vendor at Vendor's web site or by other means.

12.4. *Forecasting.* Each Party will use commercially reasonable efforts to carry out its obligations under the Joint Marketing Plan, attached as Schedule F. During the Term, Reseller will, at the beginning of each calendar quarter, provide to Vendor its non-binding sales forecasts for the next following four quarters, according to a reasonable format that Vendor will provide. Both Parties may use the forecast to plan and predict licensing revenue.

12.5. *Prohibited Conduct.* Reseller may not make any contracts or commitments on behalf of Vendor nor make any warranties or other representations regarding the Products other than those authorized herein or by Vendor in a separate writing. Reseller will not engage in any conduct that in Vendor's reasonable determination would diminish public perception of Vendor or the Products.

13. **Term and Termination**

13.1. *Term.* Unless otherwise terminated as permitted in this Agreement, the term of this Agreement ("Term") will have an initial term of two (2) years from the Effective Date (the "Initial Term") and will thereafter be renewed for successive one (1) year periods (each a "Renewal Term") unless either Party provides notice of termination no less than ninety (90) days before the end of the Initial Term or any Renewal Term.

13.2. *Termination.* This Agreement may be terminated immediately by written notice under any of the following conditions:

13.2.1. by a Party, if the other Party is declared insolvent or bankrupt;

13.2.2. by a Party, if a petition is filed in any court to declare the other Party bankrupt or for a reorganization under the US Bankruptcy Code or any similar statute and such petition is not dismissed in sixty (60) days or if a Trustee in Bankruptcy or a receiver or similar entity is appointed for the other Party;

13.2.3. by Vendor, if Reseller breaches its payment obligations and fails to cure within ten (10) days after written notice of such breach; or

13.2.4. by a Party, if the other Party otherwise materially breaches the terms of this Agreement, and such breach is not cured within thirty (30) days after written notice of such breach is given by the non-breaching Party.

13.3. *Duties upon Termination.* Upon termination, Reseller will cease use and distribution of the Products and all of Reseller's rights and licenses granted hereunder will immediately cease.

13.4. *Transition.* Customer License Agreements executed before termination will survive termination in accordance with their terms. Reseller will cooperate before and after termination in transition of Support Services to Vendor or its designee, at such time and manner as Vendor may direct.

13.5. *Survival.* Sections 8 (Confidentiality), 10.2 (Disclaimer), 11 (Damage Exclusions; Limitation of Liability), 13.4 (Transition), 13.5 (Survival), 14 (Indemnification) and 15 (General) will survive the termination of this Agreement and continue for such time as they may remain applicable. Accrued payment obligations will survive.

14. **Indemnification**

14.1. *Vendor Indemnification.* Vendor will, at its expense, defend or settle any claim, action or allegation brought against Reseller that the Products infringe any patent, copyright or other proprietary right of any third party that is enforceable in the Territory and will pay any final judgments awarded or settlements entered into, provided that, as conditions of indemnification, each of the following is met: (i) Vendor is given written notice of the claim within ten (10) business days of its receipt; (ii) Vendor is given immediate and complete control over the defense and/or settlement of the claim, and Reseller fully cooperates with Vendor in such defense and/or settlement; (iii) the alleged infringement is not based upon the use of the Products or provision of services in a manner not authorized under this Agreement; and (iv) the exclusions in Section 14.2

do not apply. Any indemnity payments to Reseller will be net of any tax benefits to it. In case Vendor perceives an infringement risk, it may suspend Reseller's distribution of any Product involved until the matter is resolved to Vendor's satisfaction.

14.2. *Altered Version; Combination.* Vendor will have no liability under this Section for any claim of infringement based on the use of a superseded or altered version of the Products if infringement would have been avoided by the use of a current or unaltered version of the Products which Vendor made available to Reseller. Vendor will have no liability under this Section for any claim of infringement based on the combination of a Product with any hardware, products, software or data not supplied or approved in writing by Vendor to the extent that the use of the Products alone would have been non-infringing.

14.3. *Reseller's Indemnification.* Reseller will indemnify, defend and hold Vendor harmless from any claims, demands, liabilities or expenses, including reasonable attorneys' fees, incurred by Vendor as a result of any claim or proceeding against Vendor arising out of or based upon (i) the combination, operation or use of the Products with any hardware, products, software or data not supplied or approved in writing by Vendor, if such infringement would have been avoided but for such combination, operation or use or (ii) the modification of the Products by Reseller or Customers, or (iii) any claims that arise from unauthorized representations by Reseller.

14.4. *Exclusive Remedy.* To the extent that the foregoing concerns claims regarding actual or alleged intellectual property infringement or violation of any proprietary right, the foregoing states the Parties' sole and exclusive remedy with regard to actual or alleged claims.

15. **General**

15.1. *Authority.* Each of the Parties represents and warrants that (i) its entry into this Agreement is duly authorized, and binding upon it and (ii) in entering into and performing this Agreement, it does not violate third party agreement.

15.2. *Non-Solicitation.* During the Term and for one (1) year thereafter, each of the Parties agrees not to solicit services from or solicit to employ any employee of the other Party or any consultant of the other Party with whom such Party had contact during the Term. This provision does not prohibit general solicitation by the web, newspapers or other media.

15.3. *Reservation of Rights.* All licenses granted to Reseller are non-exclusive. Without limiting the foregoing, Vendor will have the right, at its discretion, to license, sell, distribute and provide Products or Support Services to any entity or person inside or outside the Territory.

15.4. *Remedies.* If Reseller uses or copies the Products other than as licensed, breaches the obligations of this Agreement regarding Confidential Information or has violated Vendor's intellectual property rights, Vendor will have, in addition to all other remedies, the right to seek injunctive relief. The Parties agree that such relief is required to prevent immediate and irreparable harm to Vendor.

15.5. *Headings.* The headings and captions used in this Agreement are for convenience only and are not intended to be used as an aid to interpretation.

15.6. *Severability.* The provisions of this Agreement are severable, and if any part of this Agreement is held to be illegal or unenforceable, the validity or enforceability of the remainder of this Agreement will not be affected.

15.7. *Binding.* This Agreement will be binding upon and inure to the benefit of the Parties, their respective successors and assigns. Reseller may not assign its rights or obligations under this Agreement without the prior written consent of Vendor.

15.8. *No Waiver.* Failure by either Party to exercise any right or remedy under this Agreement does not signify acceptance of the event giving rise to such right or remedy. No waiver in any particular circumstance should be construed as a bar to a Party's refusal to waive other or subsequent defaults.

15.9. *Force Majeure.* Neither Party will be deemed in default of this Agreement to the extent that performance of their obligations or attempts to cure any breach are delayed or prevented by reason of any act of God, fire, natural disaster, accident, act of government, shortages of materials or supplies, or any other cause beyond the control of such Party ("Force Majeure"), provided that such Party gives the other Party written notice thereof promptly and, in any event, within fifteen (15) days of discovery thereof and uses its commercially reasonable effort to cure the delay. In the event of such Force Majeure, the time for performance or cure will be extended for a period equal to the duration of the Force Majeure but not in excess of three (3) months. Force Majeure, however, will not apply to or delay any obligation to make payments of money required by this Agreement for more than twenty (20) days.

15.10. *Applicable Law and Jurisdiction.* This Agreement will be governed by and construed in accordance with the laws of the State of _____, without regard to the choice of law provisions thereof. The United Nations Convention on Contracts for the International Sale of Goods will not apply. The Parties hereby irrevocably consent to the exclusive jurisdiction and venue of the state and federal courts located in _____ for the purpose of any action or proceeding brought by either of them in connection with this Agreement or the relationship of the Parties.

15.11. *Notice.* Unless otherwise agreed to by the Parties, any notice required or permitted to be given or delivered under this Agreement will be given in writing and delivered to the address set forth in this Agreement, and addressed to the attention of:

> if to Vendor: *[Insert contact information]*
>
> if to Reseller: *[Insert contact information]*

Notice will be deemed to have been received by any Party, and will be effective, (i) on the day given, if personally delivered or if sent by confirmed facsimile transmission, receipt verified or (ii) on the third day after which such notice is deposited, if mailed by certified, first class, postage prepaid, return receipt requested mail.

15.12. *Assignment.* This Agreement may not be assigned by Reseller, whether by operation of law or otherwise, without the consent of Vendor. Vendor may assign this Agreement upon a merger, consolidation, sale of all or substantially all of its assets or of the line of business involved in this Agreement, or similar transaction without regard to the form thereof.

15.13. *Counterparts.* This Agreement may be executed in counterparts, by facsimile transmission, with original signatures following by courier or mail, each of which will constitute an original and all of which taken together will constitute one and the same instrument.

15.14. *Independent Contractors.* Vendor and Reseller are acting hereunder as independent contractors, and under no circumstances will any of the employees of one Party be deemed the employees of the other for any purpose. This Agreement will not be construed as authority for either Party to act for the other Party in any agency or other capacity, or to make commitments of any kind for the account of or on behalf of the other except to the extent and for the purposes provided for herein.

15.15. *Entire Agreement.* This Agreement, including the Schedules, constitutes the entire agreement between the Parties with respect to the subject matter hereof and supersedes all previous proposals, both oral and written, negotiations, representations, commitments, writings and all other communications between the Parties. This Agreement may not be modified except by a writing signed by a duly authorized representative of each of the Parties.

IN WITNESS WHEREOF, the Parties have executed this Agreement under seal by a duly authorized representative as of the date set forth above.

Vendor: _____   Reseller: _____

By: _____   By: _____

Name: _____   Name: _____

Title: _____   Title: _____

Date: _____   Date: _____

Reseller Agreement
Schedule A
Products

1. <u>Products</u>

[List software products.]

Reseller Agreement
Schedule B
Territory

[Specify licensed territory.]

Reseller Agreement
Schedule C
Customer License Agreement

[Attach current form of Customer License Agreement.]

Reseller Agreement
Schedule D
Price and Payment

1. **Suggested List Prices**

Vendor provides the following suggested list prices ("List Price") with respect to the Products and annual fees for Support Services:

a) License Fees: *[To be supplied.]*

b) Annual Support Fee. *[To be supplied.]*

List Pricing is subject to change on thirty (30) days' notice. Reseller may establish its own pricing as to the Customers for the Products.

2. **Vendor Pricing**

The Prices that Reseller must pay Vendor for Products and Support Services, stated as a percentage of List Prices, are as follows:

a) Products.

[Formula to be supplied.]

b) Support Services.

[Formula to be supplied.]

Reseller Agreement
Schedule E
Support Services

"Primary Support" will mean the following maintenance and support services to be provided by Reseller to Customers:

1. Providing the Customer with a reasonable level of assistance in installing the Products(s);

2. Providing the Customer with a reasonable level of training;

3. Providing technical advice to the Customer on using the Products(s) by means of telephone support;

4. When a Customer reports a software error, accessing Vendor's error tracking system to determine whether the error matches an error previously reported and whether a software patch, a change to the current version of the Products or other recommendation, has been identified as a response to the error;

5. Providing the Customer a reasonable level of assistance in installing any available software patch or version of the Products or in implementing any recommendation or solution to deal with software errors;

6. With regard to software errors not matching those in Vendor's error tracking system, acquiring and using tools required to acquire diagnostic reports, memory dumps, and other materials, and providing and employing such diagnostic services as may be required by the circumstances or requested by Vendor to aid in resolution of software errors;

7. Providing such other assistance to Customers in dealing with Product errors as Vendor may request;

8. Providing Updates [and Upgrades] to Customers as released by Vendor;

9. Providing Customer assistance in implementing fixes or recommendations as implemented by Secondary Support.

"Secondary Support" will mean the following services to be provided by Vendor to Reseller:

1. Using reasonable efforts to modify the Products to correct, fix, or circumvent errors, and modifying Documentation, as Vendor will deem appropriate, to respond to reported errors.

2. Using reasonable efforts to assist Reseller in providing Primary Support.

3. Delivering Updates [and Upgrades] to Reseller for supply to those Customers that are entitled to the same;

4. Vendor is required to support only the most recent version and the next preceding version of each Product.

Reseller Agreement
Schedule F
Joint Marketing Plan

[To be supplied.]

Reseller Agreement
Schedule G
Charges for Consulting Services

In the event that Reseller requires that Vendor perform services on Reseller's behalf or for Reseller's customers, Vendor may invoice for, and Reseller will pay at the rates then in effect.

Rates for Services (as of the date of the Agreement)

Consulting:

[Specify Rates.]

Training:

[Specify Rates.]

Prices are subject to change on 30 days' written notice. Vendor may charge for travel time as reasonably required for its Support Services. Vendor will invoice for and Reseller will reimburse Vendor for its out-of-pocket expenses incurred in providing services, including, without limitation, travel-related expenses incurred by Vendor.

OEM Software Agreement

Introductory Note

This is a form of OEM agreement. This form is designed for the Vendor's software that is licensed for use and distribution solely as an embedded component of the Licensee's Software product offering. The combination of the Vendor Software and the Licensee Software is called an "Integrated Product" in this form.

As noted in Chapter 15, the term "OEM" usually refers to a supplier of product to be sold under the licensee's brand, but the usage of the term in the trade is not consistent.

This form contains optional language on branding, including:

- *A provision requiring that the license is limited to Integrated Products that are marketed solely under the Licensee's brand. This clause may be important if the Vendor Software is licensed to the Licensee at a deep discount.*

- *A provision requiring that the Licensee use "powered by the [Vendor brand]" on the Integrated Product itself and on related promotional literature and documentation. This can help promote the Vendor's brand.*

This form also features optional language that can be used if the Vendor Software includes open source components.

This document is based on a contract used for a "high end" business software product that is to be inserted into a licensee's software. The form can be adapted for other software and hardware markets, such as components of consumer software or software components for consumer electronics hardware products (such as music players or mobile phones).

This form leaves the payment and royalty structure to be added. It would depend largely on the means by which Licensee charges for the Integrated Product. For example, if the

Licensee charges its customers on a per-server basis, it would be normal for the Vendor to charge the Licensee on the same basis.

<h2 style="text-align:center">OEM Agreement</h2>

This OEM Agreement ("Agreement") is effective as of the ___ day of _____ 20___ ("Effective Date") between *[Insert vendor company name]* (hereinafter "Vendor"), with its principal office at _____ and *[Insert Licensee company name]* ("Licensee") with its principal office at _____ (each a "Party"; together the "Parties").

Purpose of This Agreement

A. Vendor has developed Vendor Software that is suitable for integration, as a component, in various third party software products. (Capitalized terms are as defined below).

B. Vendor has developed a Software Development Kit ("SDK") to assist in integrating the functionality of the Vendor Software into various software products.

C. Vendor is willing to license the Vendor Software and the SDK to Licensee on the terms and conditions set forth herein that provide for the integration of the Vendor Software with the Licensee Software (resulting in the Integrated Products) so that Licensee may market such Integrated Products to Customers in the Territory.

THEREFORE, in consideration of the promises made in the Agreement, the Parties agree as follows:

1. **Definitions.** For the purposes of this Agreement, the definitions set forth in this Section will apply:

    1.1. "Affiliate" means any entity that directly or indirectly controls, or is controlled by, or is under common control with, a Party. "Control" means: (a) for corporate entities, direct or indirect ownership of 50% or more of the stock or shares entitled to vote for the election of the board of directors or other governing body of the entity, and (b) for non-corporate entities, direct or indirect ownership of 50% or greater of the equity interest.

    1.2. "Customer" will mean a third party entity or individual that is granted a Sublicense.

1.3. "Documentation" means instructions, manuals, and diagrams pertaining to the Vendor Software in electronic or printed form. Documentation includes instructions for Licensee's use of the SDK and also may include User Documentation.

1.4. "Error" means a defect in a Vendor Software that prevents it from functioning in substantial conformity with the applicable Documentation.

1.5. "Integrated Product" means a product, as further described in Schedule B, resulting from integration of the Vendor Software with Licensee Software in accordance with this Agreement.

1.6. "Licensee Software" means Licensee software products that Licensee creates for marketing and distribution [under its own brands].

1.7. "Primary Support" means the following services to be provided by Licensee to Customers:

   1.7.1. Providing Customers with a reasonable level of assistance in use of Integrated Product by means of documentation, online aids, email and/or telephone support.

   1.7.2. When a Customer reports an Error in the Vendor Software, contacting Vendor and reporting the Error under such procedure as Vendor will reasonably specify.

   1.7.3. Providing Customers with a reasonable level of assistance in obtaining or installing any available Vendor Software patch or maintenance version or in implementing any recommendation or solution to deal with an Error.

1.8. "Secondary Support" means the support and maintenance services to be provided by Vendor to Licensee as further specified in Schedule D.

1.9. "Software Development Kit" or "SDK" means the Vendor Software together with Documentation to assist Licensee in integration of the Vendor Software in an Integrated Product.

1.10. "Sublicense" means a non-exclusive license granted by Licensee to an entity, individual or end user to use the Vendor Software in binary form as embedded in an Integrated Product for his, her or its own business or personal use.

1.11. "Sublicense Agreement" means the form or forms of license agreement that Licensee uses to provide the Vendor Software (as included in the Integrated Products) to a Customer. Licensee must require the Customer's assent to the Sublicense Agreement by electronic acceptance (such as "click to accept") or by means of a signed written contract as a condition of Customer's installation and use of the Integrated Product.

1.12. "Term" is as defined in Section 21.

1.13. "Territory" is *[specify applicable territory]*.

1.14. "Update" will mean a subsequent release of the Vendor Software denoted by a change in Vendor Software release number to the right side of such release number decimal point. (For example, the change from version 3.0 to 3.1.) Updates may include, but not be limited to, Error corrections (provided as stated in Schedule D) and minor changes to existing functionality. Updates do not include significant new functionality, features or options. An Update may include changes to the SDK, if applicable.

1.15. ["Upgrade" will mean a subsequent release of the Vendor Software denoted by a change in the Vendor Software release number to the left of the release number decimal point. (For example, the change from version 3.0 to 4.0.) Upgrades may include, but not be limited to, Error corrections (provided as stated in Schedule D) and major changes to existing functionality. An Upgrade may include changes to the SDK, if applicable.]

1.16. "User Documentation" means the Documentation that Vendor designates for use by Customers.

1.17. "Vendor Software" means the Vendor's software in binary form as further described in Schedule A, including Updates [and Upgrades] provided by Vendor to Licensee under this Agreement.

1.18. "Vendor Branding Guidelines" means Vendor's guidelines for use of the Vendor Marks and proprietary legends that Vendor may issue from time to time.

1.19. "Vendor Marks" means Vendor's trade names, trademarks and logos associated with the Vendor Software.

2. **License to the Vendor Software**

    2.1. *License to Integrate and Distribute.* During the Term, subject to the payment of the applicable fees, Vendor grants to Licensee a non-exclusive, non-transferable (except as provided below) license to the Vendor Software and the SDK for the Territory as follows:

        2.1.1. To install and use the SDK internally for the purpose of integrating the Vendor Software with one or more Licensee Software products thereby creating Integrated Products.

        2.1.2. To use subcontractors ("Subcontractors") for the purpose of such integration of the Vendor Software into Integrated Products, provided that (a) Licensee will be responsible for the acts and omissions of each Subcontractor and (b) Licensee will require each Subcontractor to sign a written agreement no less protective of Vendor and its suppliers with regard to confidentiality than the provisions of this Agreement.

        2.1.3. To replicate, demonstrate, and distribute the Vendor Software for the purpose of sublicensing the Vendor Software to Customers solely as a component of the Integrated Products;

        2.1.4. To provide training and support to Customers regarding the Vendor Software solely as a component of the Integrated Products; and

        2.1.5. To make a reasonable number of the copies of the Vendor Software for archival purposes.

3. **License to Documentation**

    3.1. Licensee is licensed to use and copy the Documentation internally (and provide Documentation in confidence to Subcontractors) as reasonably required for the purpose of integrating the Vendor Software with the Licensee Software and for the maintenance of Integrated Products.

    3.2. Licensee may modify the User Documentation and may integrate the User Documentation into the Licensee's own user documentation for any Integrated Product, provided that Licensee shall be solely responsible for any modified version. Licensee may distribute User Documentation (including such modifications) in connection with the Integrated Product.

4. **Conditions of Distribution.** Licensee agrees to carry out the following obligations with regard to distribution of the Vendor Software (as included in Integrated Products) and Licensee's license to distribute the Vendor Software shall be conditioned upon Licensee's carrying out such obligations:

4.1. [The Vendor Software will be included only in Integrated Products that are marketed under Licensee's own brand.]

4.2. Licensee will not: (a) distribute, transfer, sell, license or otherwise make available the Vendor Software as a single product or on a stand-alone basis; (b) customize, modify, enhance or otherwise exploit the Vendor Software or Documentation other than as expressly permitted by this Agreement; (c) distribute or sublicense the Vendor Software or Documentation other than as expressly permitted by this Agreement; or (d) use the functionality of the Vendor Software for its own internal business operations unless it enters into a separate license agreement with Vendor.

4.3. Licensee will distribute the Integrated Product solely with a Sublicense Agreement (which may be integrated into Licensee's own license agreement for the Integrated Product) that includes, at a minimum, contractual provisions as follows:

4.3.1. A requirement that the Vendor Software be used only for the Customer's own personal or business use;

4.3.2. A prohibition of assignment or transfer of the Vendor Software (except in Customer's sale of business transaction) and of any timesharing, service bureau, software-as-service or rental use of the Vendor Software;

4.3.3. A prohibition of the reverse engineering, disassembly or decompilation of the Vendor Software;

4.3.4. A general prohibition on use or copying of the Vendor Software for any purpose other than as licensed or for any use separately from the Integrated Product;

4.3.5. A clause on intellectual property ownership, disclaimer of warranties, and limitation of liability no less protective of Vendor than this Agreement;

4.3.6. Standard disclaimers of implied warranties, exclusions of consequential and incidental damages, and limits of liability that protect Licensee and its suppliers (including Vendor);

4.3.7. A requirement that the Customer cease use of and destroy all copies of the Vendor Software upon any Sublicense Agreement termination; and

4.3.8. A provision permitting Vendor and its suppliers to enforce the Sublicense Agreement insofar as it relates to the Vendor Software.

4.4. Licensee agrees to report to Vendor material breaches of the Sublicense Agreement that involve breach of the provisions regarding the Vendor Software. Licensee and Vendor agree to cooperate in enforcement of the Sublicense Agreement with regard to the Vendor Software.

5. **License Restrictions.** The license granted to Licensee is subject to the following:

5.1. Licensee may not engage in timesharing, service bureau, software-as-service or rental of the Vendor Software.

5.2. Licensee will not carry out or authorize the reverse engineering, disassembly or decompilation of the Vendor Software.

5.3. Licensee will not use the Vendor Software to create any product or service that replicates the functionality or serves as a substitute for the Vendor Software.

5.4. Licensee agrees not to copy, distribute, use or exploit the Vendor Software except as licensed in this Agreement.

6. **Branding; Proprietary Notices**

6.1. [Each Integrated Product will be branded as follows: Licensee agrees to include the Vendor "Powered by *[Vendor Brand]*" logo in any place that Licensee's own brand or logo appears when the Vendor Software operates and on all Licensee User Documentation and promotional literature concerning the Integrated Products. Licensee will not remove such logo from any portions of the Vendor Software. Use, appearance, and sizing of Vendor Marks will be consistent with the Vendor Branding Guidelines.]

6.2. Vendor's proprietary notices (as set forth in the Vendor Branding Guidelines) will not be removed from any Vendor Software and will be placed on the documentation, the Integrated Product sign-on screen, in the Integrated Product's "About Box, and on the labeling of digital media.

6.3. Vendor Marks and any associated goodwill belong to Vendor; Licensee may use Vendor Marks only as expressly set forth herein. Licensee's use of Vendor Marks will be consistent with the Vendor Branding Guidelines. Licensee agrees not to use the Vendor Marks or any other trademark or trade name likely to cause confusion with the Vendor Marks.

7. **Marketing Obligations of Licensee.** Licensee will use commercially reasonable efforts to create and introduce to the market one or more Integrated Products as soon as is reasonably feasible [and in any case no later than *[date]*]. Licensee will use commercially reasonable efforts to promote and market such Integrated Products.

8. **Ownership.** Vendor and its licensors retain all rights in the Vendor Software. Licensee will have solely the license rights expressly granted in this Agreement. Each Party reserves all rights not expressly granted.

9. **Support Services**

9.1. During the Term, Vendor will provide to Licensee Secondary Support for the Vendor Software as provided in Schedule B. Secondary Support does not cover any Customer or Licensee modifications or additions to the Vendor Software. Support for any custom additions or modifications will be as may mutually be agreed upon in writing by the Parties.

9.2. Licensee will be responsible to provide Primary Support to Customers and (if applicable) installation and training. Vendor is not responsible for supporting Customers.

9.3. Vendor will provide to Licensee consulting and training agreed to by the Parties. Such consulting and training will be subject to the terms of this Agreement. Except as otherwise agreed by the Parties, Licensee will pay Vendor for all consulting services and training services on a time, materials and expenses basis at Vendor's standard consulting rates. For any on-site services provided to Licensee, Licensee will reimburse Vendor for actual, reasonable travel and out-of-pocket expenses incurred.

10. **Integration Support.** During the Term, Vendor will assist Licensee with the technical assistance for the integration of the Vendor Software and the Licensee Software at mutually convenient times. Such assistance will be at Vendor's standard consulting rates and be subject to a mutually agreed statement of work.

11. **Payment**

11.1. [Licensee agrees to pay to Vendor in addition to other amounts due under this agreement, the Initial License Fee as set forth in Schedule C. Such fee is due and payable __ days from the Effective Date.]

11.2. Licensee agrees to pay Vendor the Royalties as set forth in Schedule C (and defined in such schedule). Such Royalties are due any payable quarterly, within thirty (30) days of the end of each calendar quarter, together with the relevant Payment Report (as defined below). The Royalty obligation accrues when each Integrated Product is shipped or transferred by Licensee.

11.3. For promotional purposes only, Distributor may make and distribute a reasonable number (not to exceed *[number]* copies) of "not-for-resale" review and promotion copies of Integrated Product and such copies shall not be subject to the Royalties.

11.4. Licensee agrees to pay Vendor annual fees for secondary support ("Secondary Support Fees") as set forth in Schedule C. Secondary Support Fees are due in advance. Licensee shall owe and pay to Vendor a Secondary Support calculated as provided for in Schedule C for each Customer to whom Licensee provides or agrees or arranges to provide Primary Support. Licensee will not provide Primary Support with regard to the Vendor Software to any Customer unless Licensee has paid to Vendor a Secondary Support Fee for such Customer. Licensee may provide Customers support for Integrated Products only in the form of support packages that include Primary Support for the Vendor Software.

11.5. Within thirty (30) days of the last day of each calendar quarter, Licensee will send to Vendor a report detailing for that quarter the quantity of Licensee Software shipped or licensed during that month, total Royalties and Secondary Support Fees due to Vendor. Calculations shall be consistent with the fees and charges shown in Schedule C and shown in sufficient detail that the calculation can be replicated ("Payment Report"). Licensee will make payment of the amounts due to Vendor together with such Payment Report. Licensee will pay any other amounts due to Vendor under this Agreement within thirty (30) days from Vendor's invoice.

11.6. Any amounts payable by Licensee under this Agreement which remain unpaid after the due date will be subject to a late charge equal to one percent (1%) per month (or if lower, the highest legal rate) from the due date until such amount is paid. Amounts due under this Agreement are net of taxes. Licensee will pay all sales, use, property, value-added or other taxes or custom duties, but not including taxes on Vendor's net income. All payments will be in United States dollars.

11.7. Licensee is free to determine unilaterally its own license and support fees to its Customers. Licensee will not be relieved of its obligation to pay fees owed to Vendor by the non-payment of amounts billed or due to Licensee.

12. **Audit.** Licensee will maintain books and records in connection with its Vendor Software use and sublicensing activity during the Term and for two (2) years thereafter. Vendor, by its accountant, employee or agent, may audit Licensee's records to determine whether Licensee has complied with the terms of this Agreement. Any such audit will be conducted during Licensee's regular business hours at Licensee's facilities, will not unreasonably interfere with Licensee's business activities, and will take place not more than twice in every calendar year. If an audit reveals that Licensee has underpaid fees to Vendor, Licensee will be invoiced for such underpaid fees. If the underpaid fees are in excess of five percent (5%), then Licensee will pay Vendor's reasonable costs of conducting the audit. If discrepancies in Licensee's favor of more than fifteen percent (15%) for the audited period are found, Vendor may, at its option, terminate this Agreement.

13. **Confidentiality**

13.1. Each Party may have access to non-public information provided by the other Party ("Confidential Information"). Confidential Information includes, without limitation, the SDK, the Documentation (other than User Documentation), the Vendor Software functions and interfaces, and all information identified as confidential. The terms and conditions set forth in this Agreement will be Confidential Information, provided, however, that either party may reveal the contents of this Agreement in confidence to auditors or other professionals, as well as advisors, investors, and parties conducting due diligence in connection with such party's efforts to obtain financing, comply with legal or regulatory requirements or negotiate a merger, acquisition, or sale of substantially all the assets of such party's business or line of business.

13.2. A Party's Confidential Information will not include information that: (a) is or becomes publicly known through no act or omission of the other Party; (b) was in the other Party's lawful possession prior to the disclosure; (c) is lawfully disclosed to the other Party by a third party without restriction on disclosure; or (d) is independently developed by the other Party.

13.3. The Parties agree to hold each other's Confidential Information in confidence during the Term and for a period of ___ (__) years after termination of this Agreement. The Parties agree, unless required by law, not to make each other's Confidential Information available in any form to any third party (except to each such Party's permitted Subcontractors) or use Confidential Information for any purpose other than as reasonably required for this Agreement. Each Party agrees to take all reasonable steps to ensure that Confidential Information is not disclosed or distributed by its employees or permitted Subcontractors in violation of the terms of this Agreement.

14. **[Publicity**

14.1. Licensee and Vendor agree to promptly issue a joint press release mutually agreed upon by the Parties announcing the Parties' cooperation.

14.2. Upon successful integration of the Vendor Software with the Licensee Software, Licensee will cooperate with Vendor to be the subject of a Vendor "success story" for publication on Vendor's web site, in print, or in other media.

14.3. Licensee agrees that Vendor may use the Licensee's company name and logo on Vendor's web site and on collateral and related marketing materials to show that Licensee is a partner of Vendor.]

15. **[Open Source Programs**

15.1. Vendor represents and warrants to Licensee that (i) the software obtained under Open Source or freeware licenses ("Open Source Programs") identified on <u>Schedule E</u> represent all of the Open Source Programs integrated into or bundled with the Vendor Software, and (ii) the source code for all such Open Source Programs and the text of all relevant open source license agreements have been delivered to Licensee for review before the Effective Date.

15.2. Vendor represents and warrants that, as of the Effective Date, and during the Term of this Agreement, [to the best of its knowledge,] Vendor has and will have the rights to grant to Licensee the rights and license to copy, market, sublicense, distribute, and use the Open Source Programs.

15.3. Licensee acknowledges that the terms and conditions applicable to the Open Source Programs are contained in the various applicable open source licenses rather than by this Agreement.]

16. **Warranty, Exclusions and Limitations**

16.1. *Warranty.* For Vendor Software licensed to Licensee, Vendor warrants to Licensee that for a period of _____ (__) days after the initial delivery of the Vendor Software, the Vendor Software will operate substantially in accordance with the functional description provided the applicable Documentation when used as licensed. For breach of such warranty, Licensee's exclusive remedy, and Vendor's entire liability, will be as follows: Vendor will correct the Vendor Software Errors that cause the breach of warranty or Vendor will replace the Vendor Software with conforming software.

16.2. *Warranty Disclaimer.* EXCEPT FOR THE WARRANTIES EXPRESSLY STATED IN THIS AGREEMENT, VENDOR DISCLAIMS ALL WARRANTIES, EXPRESS OR IMPLIED, INCLUDING THE IMPLIED WARRANTIES OF MERCHANTABILITY AND FITNESS FOR A PARTICULAR PURPOSE. Vendor does not warrant that the Vendor Software will operate without interruption or be error-free. Any beta or other preliminary or non-public releases of programs to Licensee will be provided "AS IS" and "WITHOUT WARRANTY."

16.3. *Damages Exclusion and Limitation.* Except with regard to unlicensed use or exploitation of the Vendor Software or for breach of the confidentiality provisions of this Agreement, in no event shall either Party be liable for any indirect, incidental, special or consequential damages, or damages for loss of profits, revenue, data or use, incurred by either Party or any third party, whether in an action in contract or tort, even if the other Party has been advised of the possibility of such damages. Except with regard to unlicensed use or exploitation of the Vendor Software or for breach of the confidentiality provisions of this Agreement, in no event shall either Party's cumulative liability for damages hereunder exceed the total amount of payments made by and/or due from Licensee under this Agreement.

16.4. *Risk Allocation*. The provisions of this Agreement allocate the risks between Vendor and Licensee. Vendor's pricing reflects this allocation of risk and the limitation of liability specified herein.

17. **Vendor's Intellectual Property Indemnity**

17.1. Vendor will defend, indemnify and hold harmless Licensee (and its officers, directors, employees, servants and agents) against any third party claim that the Vendor Software infringes any U.S. copyright, patent or other intellectual property right, provided that Vendor will have no liability for any claim of infringement based on (a) use of a superseded or altered release of Vendor Software by Licensee if the infringement would have been avoided by the use of a current unaltered release of the Vendor Software which Vendor provides to Licensee or (b) the combination or use of the Vendor Software with software, hardware or other materials not furnished by Vendor to the extent that infringement would not have occurred but for the software, hardware or other materials not furnished by Vendor.

17.2. If the Vendor Software is held to be infringing or if Vendor believes that there is a material infringement risk, Vendor will have the option, at its expense, to (a) modify the Vendor Software to be non-infringing or (b) obtain for Licensee a license to continue using the Vendor Software. If Vendor determines, in its sole discretion, that it is not commercially reasonable to perform either of the above options, then Vendor may terminate the license for the relevant Vendor Software on no less than ninety (90) days' notice.

17.3. This Section states Vendor's entire liability and Licensee's exclusive remedy for actual or alleged infringement.

18. **Indemnity by Licensee**

18.1. Licensee hereby agrees to defend, indemnify and hold harmless Vendor (and its officers, directors, employees, servants and agents) from and against any and all claims, actions, or demands alleging that the Licensee Software or Integrated Product (except to the extent such claim is based on the Vendor Software only) infringes any patent, trademark, copyright, or other intellectual property right of any third party. Vendor shall permit Licensee to replace or modify any affected Licensee Software so to avoid infringement, or to procure the right for Customers to continue use and remarketing of such items. This Section states Licensee's entire liability and Vendor's exclusive remedy for actual or alleged infringement.

18.2. Licensee hereby agrees to defend, indemnify and hold harmless Vendor (and its officers, directors, employees, servants and agents) from and against any and all claims, actions, or demands arising from or alleged to arise from or due to Licensee's marketing or distribution of the Vendor Software or any Integrated Product (other than due to Errors in the Vendor Software).

19. **Procedure for Indemnification**

19.1. In case of any claim that is subject to indemnification under this Agreement, the Party entitled to indemnification ("Indemnitee") shall provide the Party providing indemnification ("Indemnitor") prompt notice of the relevant claim.

19.2. Indemnitor shall defend and/or settle, at its own expense, any demand, action, or suit on any claim subject to indemnification under this Agreement.

19.3. The Indemnitee shall cooperate in good faith with the Indemnitor to facilitate the defense of any such claim and shall tender the defense and settlement of any action or proceeding under the indemnification provisions of this Agreement to the Indemnitor upon request. Claims may be settled without the consent of any Indemnitee unless the settlement includes an admission of wrongdoing, fault or liability on behalf of the Indemnitee.

20. **Term and Termination**

20.1. *Term.* The "Term" of this Agreement will begin on the Effective Date of this Agreement and will continue for ____ (__) years unless terminated earlier as provided in this Agreement. The Term may be extended by mutual agreement in writing.

20.2. *Termination for Breach.* Either Party may terminate this Agreement upon written notice if the other Party materially breaches this Agreement and fails to cure the breach within thirty (30) days following receipt of written notice specifying the breach.

21. **Effect of Termination**

21.1. Upon expiration or termination of this Agreement, all of Licensee's rights to market, distribute, and use the Vendor Software will cease except as provided below; provided, however, that a Sublicense granted by Licensee will continue in full force and effect until and unless the Customer breaches or has breached its Sublicense Agreement in which case Licensee or Vendor may terminate the Sublicense Agreement within thirty (30) days if such breach remain uncured after notice to the Customer.

21.2. Licensee may continue to use the Vendor Software for twelve (12) months after termination for the sole purpose of providing Primary Support to Customers. At Vendor's direction, Licensee agrees to cooperate with Vendor in transition of Customer Primary Support to Vendor or its designee.

21.3. The Parties' rights and obligations under Sections 8 (Ownership), 12 (Audit), 13 (Confidentiality), 16 (Warranty, Exclusions and Limitations), 17 (IP Indemnity), 18 (Indemnity by Licensee), 19 (Procedure for Indemnification), 21 (Effect of Termination), 22 (Non-Solicitation) and 23 (General), together with accrued obligations survive termination of this Agreement.

22. **Non-Solicitation.** Each Party agrees that during the Term and for a period of one year thereafter, it will not solicit or contact for the purposes of hiring employees of the other Party with whom the Party had material contact under this Agreement. This provision will not apply to employment resulting from general solicitation for employment or contractors on the Internet, the press, or through other mass media.

23. **General**

23.1. *Affiliates.* Licensee may permit its license rights to be exercised by one or more Affiliates, provided that Licensee will be responsible for the acts and omissions of each Affiliate as if they were its own, and Vendor shall have no obligation to deal with any Affiliate of Licensee.

23.2. *Force Majeure.* Neither Party will be liable to the other for failure or delay in the performance of a required obligation if such failure or delay is caused by strike, riot, fire, flood, natural disaster, or other similar cause beyond such Party's control ("Force Majeure") provided that such Party gives prompt written notice of such condition and resumes its performance as soon as possible, and provided further that the other Party may terminate this Agreement if such condition continues for a period of sixty (60) days. Force Majeure may not extend payment obligations more than thirty (30) days.

23.3. *Relationship between Parties.* In all matters relating to this Agreement, the Parties are independent contractors. The relationship between Vendor and Licensee is that of licensor/licensee. Neither Party will represent that it has any authority to assume or create any obligation, express or implied, on behalf of the other Party, nor to represent the other Party as agent, employee, or in any other capacity. Nothing in this Agreement will be construed to limit either Party's right to independently develop or distribute software that is functionally similar to the other Party's product, so long as done so in compliance with this Agreement.

23.4. *Governing Law; Jurisdiction.* This Agreement, and all matters arising out of or relating to this Agreement, will be governed by the laws of the state of _____. This Agreement is not governed by the U.N. Convention on Contracts for the International Sale of Goods. The parties agree to the exclusive jurisdiction and venue of the courts located in _____ with regard to any dispute relating to this Agreement or its subject matter.

23.5. *Injunctive Relief.* The Parties agree that in case of a breach of the provisions of this Agreement relating to Confidential Information or intellectual property rights or in case of the unlicensed use or exploitation of the Bundled Software, a remedy at law will not be adequate for the non-breaching Party's protection, and accordingly the non-breaching Party will have the right to seek, in addition to any other relief and remedies available to it, preliminary and final injunctive relief to enforce the provisions of this Agreement.

23.6. *Notice.* Any notice to be given hereunder will be in writing and addressed to the Party and address stated below, or such other address as the Party may designate from time to time by written notice in accordance with this Section. Except as otherwise expressly provided in this Agreement, notices hereunder will be deemed given and effective: (i) if personally delivered, upon delivery, (ii) if sent by overnight rapid-delivery service with tracking capabilities, upon receipt; (iii) if sent by fax or electronic mail, at such time as the Party that sent the notice receives confirmation of receipt by the applicable method of transmittal, or (iv) if sent by certified or registered United States mail, upon receipt.

> Address for Notice for Vendor: *[to be added]*
>
> Address for Notice for Licensee: *[to be added]*

23.7. *Assignment.* Neither Party may assign this Agreement, or any part thereof, to a legal entity separate from such Party, without the prior written consent of the other Party hereto, such consent not to be unreasonably withheld. Notwithstanding the foregoing, either Party may assign this Agreement to the surviving entity in a merger or reorganization or the purchaser of the line of business involved in this Agreement, [provided however that in the event that the acquiring entity is a direct competitor of the other Party, the prior written consent of the other Party hereto will be required].

23.8. *Severability.* If any provision of this Agreement is held to be invalid or unenforceable, the remaining provisions of this Agreement will remain in full force.

23.9. *Waiver.* The waiver by either Party of any default or breach of this Agreement will not constitute a waiver of any other or subsequent default or breach.

23.10. *Exports.* Each Party agrees to comply fully with all relevant export laws and regulations of the United States as applicable.

23.11. *Entire Agreement.* This is the entire agreement of the Parties and supersedes all prior or contemporaneous agreements or representations, written or oral, concerning the subject matter of this Agreement. This Agreement may not be modified or amended except in a writing signed by a duly authorized representative of each Party. It is expressly agreed that the terms of this Agreement will supersede the terms in any Licensee purchase order or other ordering document and such terms will have no force or effect.

So agreed by the Parties as of the Effective Date.

[Vendor Name]   *[Licensee Name]*

By: _____   By: _____

Print Name: _____   Print Name: _____

Title: _____   Title: _____

Date: _____   Date: _____

Schedule A

Vendor Software

[Insert Description]

Schedule B

Integrated Products

[Insert Description]

Schedule C

Royalties and Fees

[Insert Initial Licensee Fee (if applicable), and rules for calculation of Royalties and Secondary Support Fees.]

Schedule D

Secondary Support

Secondary Support is provided for Errors that are demonstrable in the applicable release of Vendor Software running unaltered on an appropriate hardware and operating system configuration.

Secondary Support services are provided over annual support periods ("Support Periods"). Initial-year annual Secondary Support services for each unit of Vendor Software in Integrated Products commence on the date of delivery to Licensee's Customer or if no delivery is required, commence on the effective date of the order for such product. Thereafter, Secondary Support services may be renewed for successive annual periods of one year. Licensee's purchase of at least one year of Secondary Support for each Product is delivered to each Customer is mandatory.

Secondary Support Fees are due and payable annually in advance of commencement of the applicable Support Period. Licensee's failure to pay Secondary Support Fees with regard to any Customer will result in suspension of Secondary Support Services to Licensee for the benefit of such Customer.

Secondary Support includes:

- Telephone support assistance to Licensee, available on the following business hours *[specify times, days of the week, exceptions (such as holidays and weekends) and time zone].*

- Web-based access to Secondary Support patches and support-related information.

- Updates when issued generally.

- [Upgrades when issued generally.]

- Documentation for Updates [and Upgrades].

Maintenance Procedures

For the Secondary Support Services level specified above, Vendor's Support Engineers (SEs) field incoming calls, email and fax messages. SEs provide the following:

- Verifying any reported Error, including by obtaining additional information from Licensee. (Licensee is responsible for obtaining information from Customers.)

- Communicating to the Licensee a resolution, or work-around, or supplying a bug fix or other remedy, as appropriate

- Coordinating the resolution of the Error with the Licensee.

Error Classification

Vendor categorizes reported Errors as provided in the table below and responds to reported Errors according to the schedule indicated. "Acknowledgment" means confirming receipt of an Error, verifying details, attempting to duplicate the Error and confirming status to Licensee. "Response" means providing Licensee with an answer, a patch or a resolution action plan.

Classification	Acknowledgment	Response
Priority 1	1 Business Day	2 Business Days
Priority 2	2 Business Days	4 Business Days
Priority 3	3 Business Days	8 Business Days
Priority 4	3 Business Days	15 Business Days

Priority Categories are as follows:

Priority 1 Critical: Production stops due to the Error or data are corrupted by the Error. Also includes major security "hole" or vulnerability.

Priority 2 Serious: Major impact. Major feature/product failure; inconvenient work-around or no work-around exists.

Priority 3 Minor: Minor impact. Minor feature/product failure, convenient work-around exists.

Priority 4 Informational: Functionality works but does not match documented specifications in some way.

A non-conformity is not considered an Error if (a) the Vendor product is combined or merged with any hardware or software not supported by Vendor; or (b) the Error is caused by Licensee's or Customer's misuse or improper use of the Vendor product.

Technical Contacts

For the purpose of Secondary Support services, the Licensee must designate one primary and one backup employee ("Technical Contacts") to serve as liaisons with Vendor. The designated Technical Contacts are the sole liaison between Licensee and Vendor for all software product support and will be based at the Licensee's premises. To avoid interruptions in support services, Licensee must notify Vendor whenever the Technical Contact responsibilities are transferred to another individual. The Licensee will ensure that each Technical Contact is trained on Vendor's products.

Prior Versions

Vendor provides support for a specific release or version of a Vendor product for a minimum of six (6) months after Vendor makes a subsequent release or version of such product available, as an Update or otherwise. At its sole discretion and control, Vendor may replace specific components of the Vendor Software with other components and Vendor will only provide Secondary Support for the new components.

Custom Software

Custom-made applications, alterations or additional software, created by the Licensee, by Vendor's professional services or other means, are not covered by this maintenance offering.

Applicability of Agreement

All services, including Updates [and Upgrades], are provided subject to the terms of this Agreement between Licensee and Vendor.

Reinstatement Fees

In the event that Secondary Support services lapse, are not renewed for particular Vendor Software for a particular Customer, a Reinstatement Fee will be assessed upon re-commencement of Secondary Support services equal to the amount of Secondary Support fees which would have been applicable during the period of lapse, calculated based on the current Secondary Support Fee in effect at the time the renewed Secondary Support is ordered.

[Schedule E

Open Source Programs included in the Vendor Software

[Insert List]]

Software Bundling and Distribution Agreement

Introductory Note

This is a form designed for distribution of a stand-alone software product (referred to as "Bundled Product") with the limitation that the Distributor can sublicense it only bundled together with its own product, that is, as a "Software Package." These agreements are typically quite explicit as to which of the Distributor's products can be included in the Software Package with the Bundled Product.

This form is designed for use with business products but could be adapted to consumer products.

You will notice that this form has provisions requiring that the Software Package include the Vendor's branding. You may wish to have more detailed provisions regarding required branding and how it will appear to the customer.

This form is designed generally to favor the Vendor, but to have enough balance to reduce the amount of negotiation.

Provisions in brackets are optional or provide alternatives.

Software Bundling and Distribution Agreement

This Software Bundling and Distribution Agreement ("Agreement") is made between [*Vendor Name*] ("Vendor"), with its principal address at _____ and [*Distributor Name*] ("Distributor") with its principal address at _____ (each a "Party"; together the "Parties"). This Agreement, including the attached Schedule(s), is effective on the date that both Parties have signed this Agreement (the "Effective Date").

1. **Definitions**

   1.1. "Bundled Product(s)" means the Vendor's software programs, identified on <u>Schedule A</u>, including all updates and versions, which Vendor may choose to supply to Distributor. The Parties may amend this Agreement to add additional Bundled Products and provide for additional licensing and other fees for such additional Bundled Products by attaching one or more additional schedules ("Supplemental Schedules"). Each such Supplemental Schedule will be effective on the date signed by both Parties, unless otherwise agreed.

   1.2. "Customer" means each sublicensee of the Bundled Product who will obtain such sublicenses from Distributor to the Bundled Product(s) together with the Distributor Product(s) in the form of a Software Package for its own business use pursuant to distribution under this Agreement.

   1.3. "Customer License Agreement" means a written agreement of Distributor that licenses the Customer to use Bundled Product(s); such agreement is to be provided together with the Software Package.

   1.4. "Distributor Product" means the Distributor's software products as listed on <u>Schedule B</u> to this Agreement that are distributed under Distributor's own branding. The Parties may amend this Agreement to add additional Distributor Products by attaching one or more Supplemental Schedules to this Agreement.

   1.5. "Error" means a defect in a Bundled Product that prevents it from functioning in substantial conformity with the applicable User Documentation.

   1.6. "Primary Support" means the following services to be provided by Distributor to Customers that arrange for maintenance and support of the Software Package:

      1.6.1. Providing the Customer with a reasonable level of assistance in installing the Bundled Product and a reasonable level of training in its use, by means of documentation, online aids, or telephone support, if needed.

      1.6.2. Providing technical advice to the Customer on using the Bundled Product by means of documentation, online aids, or telephone support, if needed.

1.6.3. When a Customer reports an Error in a Bundled Product, contacting Vendor and reporting the Error under such procedure as Vendor will reasonably specify.

1.6.4. Providing the Customer a reasonable level of assistance in obtaining or installing any available Bundled Product patch or version of the Bundled Product or in implementing any recommendation or solution to deal with Bundled Product Errors.

1.7. "Secondary Support" means the following services to be provided by Vendor to Distributor for the benefit of Customers that arrange for maintenance and support of the Software Package:

1.7.1. Using reasonable efforts to modify the Bundled Product to correct, fix, or circumvent Errors and modify User Documentation, as Vendor may reasonably deem appropriate, to respond to reported Errors, and advising Distributor in providing Primary Support.

1.7.2. Providing maintenance releases and updates for Bundled Products to Distributor during the Term as they are released.

1.8. "Software Package" means a form of sales unit for commercial distribution that includes both a Bundled Product and a Distributor Product incorporated on the same CD-ROM or other optical disk, downloadable file, or other distribution medium, with a single price for the combination.

1.9. "Term" is as defined in Section 21.

1.10. "Territory" means the geographic area described on <u>Schedule C</u> subject to the conditions and limitations set forth in such Schedule.

1.11. "User Documentation" means user guides for the Bundled Product provided by Vendor in written or electronic form.

1.12. "Vendor Branding Guidelines" means Vendor's guidelines for use of the Vendor Marks and proprietary legends that Vendor may issue from time to time.

1.13. "Vendor Marks" means Vendor's trade names, trademarks and logos associated with the Bundled Product.

2. Appointment and Grant of License

2.1. Subject to this Agreement, Vendor grants to Distributor a non-exclusive and non-transferable (except as provided below) license to market, demonstrate, sublicense, and support the Bundled Products within the Territory, provided that Vendor is permitted to exercise these rights with regard to each Bundled Product *only* when distributed together with a Distributor Product in the form of a Software Package.

2.2. Vendor also grants Distributor a non-exclusive and non-transferable (except as provided below in Section 23.9) license to replicate the Bundled Products for distribution solely together with a Distributor Product in the form of and as part of a Software Package for the purpose of such commercial distribution of such Software Packages.

3. Customer License Agreements

3.1. Unless otherwise directed by Vendor, each Customer License Agreement granted by Distributor or in permitted subdistribution pursuant to this Agreement will contain provisions no less protective of and advantageous to Vendor and Vendor's suppliers than Vendor's standard customer license agreement as it may be in effect from time to time. Vendor's current version of its standard customer license agreement is attached to this Agreement as <u>Schedule D</u>. Vendor may change its standard customer license agreement on thirty (30) days' written notice.

3.2. Each Customer License Agreement granted by Distributor or in permitted subdistribution pursuant to this Agreement will recite that Vendor has the right to enforce the Customer License Agreement on its own behalf.

3.3. Distributor will submit to Vendor, for Vendor's prior approval (not to be unreasonably withheld) the Customer License Agreement forms used for the Bundled Products by Distributor or in permitted subdistribution pursuant to this Agreement.

3.4. Each Customer License Agreement granted by Distributor or in permitted subdistribution pursuant to this Agreement will conspicuously describe Vendor as the supplier of the Bundled Product, using and displaying the Vendor Marks in accordance with the Vendor Branding Guidelines.

4. **Ownership of Intellectual Property**

   4.1. Distributor acknowledges that each Bundled Product is owned by Vendor and its suppliers. No ownership right is granted to Distributor for any intellectual property relating to any Bundled Product.

   4.2. Distributor will not copy, use, distribute, rent, lease, lend, supply, or market any Bundled Product except as expressly provided for in this Agreement. Distributor may not decompile, disassemble, or reverse engineer any Bundled Product.

5. **Distributor's Marketing Obligation**

   5.1. Distributor agrees to:

      5.1.1. Introduce Bundled Products into distribution promptly and in any case no later than _____ (__) days from the Effective Date;

      5.1.2. Train its salesperson(s) and customer support personnel in the characteristics, support, and use of the Bundled Product;

      5.1.3. Use its commercially reasonable efforts to promote, market, distribute and sublicense and provide support for the Bundled Product during the Term.

   5.2. The Vendor Marks will be conspicuously displayed on Software Package media, documentation, packaging, and any splash screen in conformity with the Vendor Branding Guidelines. If the Bundled Product is accessed from within the Distributor Product, Vendor will receive "About Box" credit in Distributor Product including its proprietary legends. Such Software Package media, documentation, packaging, splash screen and proprietary legend display will be subject to Vendor's prior approval, not to be unreasonably withheld.

   5.3. Distributor will include prominent references to Vendor and the Bundled Product, including Vendor Marks, in all of its presentations and sales materials relating to Software Packages that are used or created during the Term, including such copyright and trademark or other proprietary notices as Vendor may specify. Use of Vendor Marks will conform to the Vendor Branding Guidelines.

5.4. Distributor will make no representations concerning the functionality or performance characteristics of the Bundled Product except as set forth in the User Documentation furnished by Vendor.

6. **Additional Obligations of Distributor**

6.1. Distributor will perform its duties in compliance with all applicable laws. To the extent applicable, Distributor will comply with all United States export laws and procedures.

6.2. Distributor will use its commercially reasonable efforts to assist Vendor in the protection of its legal rights and to enforce the Customer License Agreements. Any recovery on account of third party violation of such rights by Vendor will be solely for the benefit of Vendor.

6.3. Distributor may suggest features or improvements for the Bundled Product or ideas for additional products. Such information and suggestions and any product, modification or improvement that results from such information or suggestions will be the sole property of Vendor and may be used by Vendor without obligation to Distributor.

7. **[Information Concerning Sales and Support**

7.1. Vendor will use its commercially reasonable effort to obtain the names of and compile a list of registered users of Software Packages. No later than thirty (30) days after the end of each quarter, Distributor will deliver to Vendor, in such printed or software format as Vendor will reasonably require, a report of the following information, to the extent available to Distributor:

7.1.1. A description of the amount and type of Bundled Products newly licensed to each Customer during the quarter and the revenues derived from each such licensing transaction;

7.1.2. Disclosure of the name, address, phone, fax, and email address and the name of contact persons for each Customer.

7.2. Vendor may use such information for marketing products, including versions of the Bundled Products.]

8. **Use of Trademarks**

8.1. This Agreement authorizes sublicensing of Bundled Products only under the Vendor Marks. Unless otherwise agreed by the Parties in writing,

Distributor will use the Vendor Marks only for purposes of advertisement, promotion, and sale of the Bundled Products and Software Packages and for no other purposes. Distributor will use the Vendor Marks in accordance with the Vendor Branding Guidelines issued by Vendor from time to time. Vendor will have all ownership of the Vendor Marks and associated goodwill.

8.2. Neither Party obtains rights in the other Party's trademarks except for licenses expressly granted in this Agreement. Neither Party will use or authorize use of any of the other Party's trademarks, service marks, logos, or slogans in any manner likely to confuse, mislead, or deceive the public, or in any way that is injurious to the other Party's reputation.

9. **Shipment and Payments**

9.1. [In connection with the execution of this Agreement, within _____ (_) days of the Effective Date, Distributor will pay Vendor an initial fee ("Initial License Fee") in the amount stated in <u>Schedule E</u>. Such Initial License Fee will be in addition to other amounts due hereunder.]

9.2. For each Bundled Product in each Software Package that Distributor ships, delivers or provides to any Customer, reseller, distributor or other person (each a "Shipment"), Distributor agrees to pay Vendor a fee ("Vendor License Fee") calculated as set forth in <u>Schedule E</u> to this Agreement. Payment of the Vendor License Fee to Vendor is due unconditionally, regardless of whether Distributor is paid by any Customer, subdistributor or other person.

9.3. Distributor agrees to pay Vendor an annual fee for secondary support ("Secondary Support Fees") as set forth in <u>Schedule E</u>. Secondary Support Fees are due in advance. Distributor shall owe and pay to Vendor a Secondary Support Fee calculated in accordance with the metrics stated in <u>Schedule E</u> for each Customer to whom Distributor provides or agrees or arranges to provide Primary Support for a Bundled Product. Distributor may provide Customers support and maintenance for a Software Package (or a Distributor Product in a Software Package) only in the form of a support package that includes Primary Support for the Bundled Product. Distributor will not provide Primary Support with regard to the Bundled Product to any Customer unless Distributor has paid to Vendor the required Secondary Support Fee for such Customer.

9.4. Distributor will at all times maintain records, systems and procedures to accurately count Bundled Product Shipments and sales of Primary Support for Software Packages.

9.5. Within thirty (30) days of the end of each month, Distributor will report to Vendor, in writing or in such electronic format as Vendor may specify, the total number of Bundled Product Shipments during the previous month ("Payment Report"). Included in such report will be a Distributor's calculation, in reasonable detail, of the total amount of Vendor Licensee Fees due for such month. The Payment Report will also show the Secondary Support Fees due to Vendor and the calculation thereof. Distributor will make payment of the amounts due to Vendor together with such Payment Report. Distributor will pay all other amounts due to Vendor under this Agreement within thirty (30) days from Vendor's invoice.

9.6. [For promotional purposes only, Distributor may make and distribute a reasonable number (not to exceed *[number]* copies) of "not-for-resale" review and promotion copies of each Bundled Product as included in a Software Package; such copies shall not be subject to the Vendor License Fee.]

9.7. Distributor is free to determine unilaterally its own license fees and support fees to its Customers.

10. **[License Fee Quotas**

10.1. The Parties stipulate that this Agreement has sufficient value to Vendor only if Distributor meets certain sales minimums. Accordingly Distributor's sales performance will be measured by minimum Vendor License Fee quotas under the methodology set forth in Schedule F ("Quotas"). If Distributor fails to achieve sufficient sales to cause Vendor to be paid such Quota amount for a particular period in accordance with the measurement criteria set forth in such Schedule, Vendor may, within thirty (30) days of the end of such period, give Distributor notice that Vendor may terminate this Agreement unless Quotas are met. After such notice, if Distributor fails during the next succeeding period to achieve sufficient sales to cause Vendor to be paid in accordance with the applicable Quota, Vendor may terminate this Agreement on thirty (30) days' written notice.]

11. **Payment and Currency**

   11.1. Unless otherwise agreed in writing, all payments to Vendor will be by wire transfer. Distributor will pay all costs and fees of wire transfer. Payments from Distributor to Vendor will be in United States dollars.

   11.2. Payments to Vendor not made when due will bear interest, compounded monthly, at a rate of one percent (1%) per month or the highest rate then lawful, whichever is lower, from the date the payment was due until it is received by Vendor. Arrearage that is not paid within ten (10) days of demand will be grounds for termination of this Agreement at the option of Vendor. Distributor will suspend Shipments and licensing of Bundled Product upon Vendor's request, if any payment is not made when due.

   11.3. All amounts payable by Distributor to Vendor under this Agreement are exclusive of any tax (including, but not limited to, income tax and value-added tax), duty, levy or similar governmental charge that may be assessed by any jurisdiction, except for income taxes assessed on Vendor.

12. **Audit**

   12.1. Distributor will maintain books and records in connection with its Vendor Software use and sublicensing activity during the Term and for two (2) years thereafter. Vendor, by its accountant or agent, may audit Distributor's records to determine whether Distributor has complied with the terms of this Agreement. Any such audit will be conducted during Distributor's regular business hours at Distributor's facilities and will not unreasonably interfere with Distributor's business activities and not more than twice in every calendar year. If an audit reveals that Distributor has underpaid fees to Vendor, Distributor will be invoiced for such underpaid fees. If the underpaid fees are in excess of five percent (5%), then Distributor will pay Vendor's reasonable costs of conducting the audit. If discrepancies in Distributor's favor of more than fifteen percent (15%) for the audited period are found, Vendor may, at its option, terminate this Agreement.

13. **Vendor's Technical Support**

   13.1. Vendor agrees to disclose to Distributor such interface and other technical information as Distributor may reasonably require to integrate the

Bundled Product into a Software Package. Such information will be Confidential Information (as defined below) of Vendor under this Agreement.

14. **Warranties**

14.1. Distributor may offer and may authorize its subdistributors to offer Customers a warranty of up to _____ (___) days from delivery on Bundled Products ("Warranty") that the Bundled Product will substantially conform to its specification. Such Warranty is subject to Vendor's approval of the Warranty text as included in the Customer License Agreement, which Vendor agrees will not unreasonably be withheld. Distributor will be responsible for dealing with Customers with regard to all maintenance support and warranty matters, and Vendor's sole obligation with regard to the warranty will be to provide Distributor with Secondary Support as stated in this Agreement with regard to any reported and confirmed Error or other non-conformity.

15. **Disclaimer of Warranty and Limitation of Liability**

15.1. *Warranty Disclaimer.* EXCEPT FOR THE WARRANTIES EXPRESSLY STATED IN THIS AGREEMENT, VENDOR DISCLAIMS ALL WARRANTIES, EXPRESS OR IMPLIED, INCLUDING THE IMPLIED WARRANTIES OF MERCHANTABILITY, NON-INFRINGEMENT AND FITNESS FOR A PARTICULAR PURPOSE. Vendor does not warrant that the Bundled Product will operate without interruption or be error-free. Any beta or other preliminary or non-public releases of programs to Distributor will be provided "AS IS" and "WITHOUT WARRANTY" for internal review and testing only.

15.2. *Damages Exclusion.* Except with regard to unlicensed use of any Bundled Product or for breach of the confidentiality provisions of this Agreement, in no event shall either Party be liable for any indirect, incidental, special or consequential damages, or damages, even if the other Party has been advised of the possibility of such damages.

15.3. *Damages Limitation.* Except with regard to unlicensed use of any Bundled Product or for breach of the confidentiality provisions of this Agreement, in no event shall either Party's cumulative liability for damages hereunder exceed the total amount of payments made by and/or due from Distributor under this Agreement.

15.4. *Risk Allocation.* The provisions of this Agreement allocate the risks between Vendor and Distributor. Vendor's pricing reflects this allocation of risk and the limitation of liability specified herein.

16. **Vendor's Intellectual Property Indemnity**

16.1. Vendor will defend, indemnify and hold harmless Distributor (and its officers, directors, employees, servants and agents) against a claim that the Bundled Product infringes any U.S. copyright or patent, provided that Vendor will have no liability for any claim of infringement based on (a) use of a superseded or altered release of Bundled Product by Distributor if the infringement would have been avoided by the use of a current unaltered release of the Bundled Product which Vendor provides to Distributor or (b) the combination or use of the Bundled Product with software, hardware or other materials not furnished by Vendor to the extent that infringement would not have occurred but for the software, hardware or other materials not furnished by Vendor.

16.2. If the Bundled Product is held to be infringing or if Vendor believes that there is a material infringement risk, Vendor will have the option, at its expense, to (a) modify the Bundled Product to be non-infringing or (b) obtain for Distributor a license to continue using the Bundled Product. If Vendor determines, in its sole discretion, that it is not commercially reasonable to perform either of the above options, then Vendor may terminate all licenses to Distributor with regard to such Bundled Product on no less than ninety (90) days' notice.

16.3. This Section states Vendor's entire liability to Distributor and Distributor's exclusive remedy for actual or alleged infringement.

17. **Indemnity by Distributor**

17.1. Distributor hereby agrees to defend, indemnify and hold harmless Vendor (and its officers, directors, employees, servants and agents) from and against any and all claims, actions, or demands alleging that the Distributor Product or the Software Package including the Bundled Product and Distributor Product (except to the extent such claim is based on infringement by the Bundled Product only) infringes any patent, trademark, copyright, or other intellectual property right of any third party. Vendor shall permit Distributor to replace or modify the affected Distributor Product so to avoid infringement, or to procure the right for Customer to continue use and remarketing of such items. This Section states Distributor's entire liability to Vendor and Vendor's exclusive remedy for actual or alleged infringement.

17.2. Distributor hereby agrees to defend, indemnify and hold harmless Vendor (and its officers, directors, employees, servants and agents) from and against any and all claims, actions, or demands arising from or due to Distributor's marketing or distribution of the Bundled Product or the Software Package including the Bundled Product and Distributor Product (other than due to Errors in the Bundled Product).

18. **Procedure for Indemnification**

18.1. In case of any claim that is subject to indemnification under this Agreement, the Party entitled to indemnification ("Indemnitee") shall provide the Party providing indemnification ("Indemnitor") prompt notice of the relevant claim.

18.2. Indemnitor shall defend and/or settle, at its own expense, any demand, action, or suit on any claim subject to indemnification under this Agreement.

18.3. Each Party shall cooperate in good faith with the other to facilitate the defense of any such claim and shall tender the defense and settlement of any action or proceeding by the indemnification provisions of this Agreement to the Indemnitor upon request. Claims may be settled without the consent of any Indemnitee unless the settlement includes an admission of wrongdoing, fault or liability on behalf of the Indemnitee.

19. **[Non-Competition**

19.1. During the Term, Distributor will not promote, represent, distribute, install, maintain, support or otherwise market or service computer products that compete with or perform functions similar to the Bundled Products.]

20. **Confidentiality**

20.1. Each Party may have access to non-public information provided by the other Party ("Confidential Information"). Confidential Information includes, without limitation, technical and business information, the Bundled Product interfaces the terms and pricing under this Agreement, and all information identified as confidential.

20.2. A Party's Confidential Information will not include information that: (a) is or becomes publicly known through no act or omission of the other Party; (b) was in the other Party's lawful possession prior to the disclosure; (c) is lawfully disclosed to the other Party by a third party without restriction on disclosure; or (d) is independently developed by the other Party.

20.3. The Parties agree to hold each other's Confidential Information in confidence during the Term and for a period of _____ (__) years after termination of this Agreement. The Parties agree, unless required by law, not to make each other's Confidential Information available in any form to any third party or use Confidential Information for any purpose other than as reasonably required for this Agreement. Each Party agrees to take all reasonable steps to ensure that Confidential Information is not disclosed or distributed by its employees in violation of the terms of this Agreement. Each Party may, however, disclose information about this Agreement, its terms, and relevant financial matters to its lawyers, accountants, advisors, directors, investors, owners and to parties that may be conducting due diligence with regard to the Party, subject to reasonable confidentiality measures.

20.4. Either Party may use subcontractors for the purposes of this Agreement and provide Confidential Information of the other Party to such subcontractors as reasonably necessary for the contractors' performance, provided that each subcontractor must be subject to contractual confidentiality obligations consistent with this Agreement.

21. **Term and Termination**

21.1. *Term*. The term of this Agreement ("Term"), unless earlier terminated as provided herein, will be as follows: The initial term of this Agreement ("Initial Term") will be for a period of _____ (__) year(s), unless sooner terminated as provided by this Agreement. After the Initial Term, this Agreement will be automatically renewed for successive one (1) year period (each a "Renewal Term"), unless either Party gives the other written notice of termination at least _____ (__) days prior to the expiration of the then current Initial Term or Renewal Term (as applicable). If such notice is given, the Agreement will terminate at the end of the then current Initial Term or Renewal Term.

21.2. In the event that Distributor fails to maintain a satisfactory credit rating or financial condition or if Vendor reasonably concludes that, for any reason, Distributor is or will become unable to discharge its obligations hereunder, Vendor may, at its option, terminate this Agreement upon thirty (30) days' notice. Alternatively, and without waiving its termination rights hereunder, if Vendor deems that Distributor has failed to maintain a satisfactory credit rating or financial condition, Vendor may require that payment be secured by letter of credit or other form of security acceptable to Vendor in its absolute discretion.

21.3. In the event of a filing by or against either Party of a petition for relief under the United States Bankruptcy Code or any similar petition under the insolvency laws of any jurisdiction or nation that is not dismissed in thirty (30) days, or in the event that either Party will make an assignment for the benefit of creditors, permit or suffer any attachment on a substantial portion of its assets to remain undissolved for a period of thirty (30) days, or discontinue the business operations relevant to this Agreement, then the other Party may immediately terminate this Agreement upon written notice.

21.4. In case of any material breach of this Agreement by a Party that is not cured within thirty (30) days of written notice, the other Party may terminate this Agreement upon written notice.

22. **Effect of Termination.** Upon termination of this Agreement, and except as otherwise provided in this Agreement:

22.1. The license and all rights to license, bundle, distribute, exploit, sublicense or resell the Bundled Product granted to Distributor by this Agreement will be terminated immediately. Distributor will make no further use of all or any part of the Bundled Product or any Confidential Information received from Vendor.

22.2. Distributor will cease any public statement or representation that it is an authorized Distributor, and will immediately cease use of the Vendor Marks, except as may otherwise be authorized in writing by Vendor.

22.3. Distributor will cooperate fully with Vendor and perform all acts appropriate to carry out the provisions of this Agreement relating to termination.

22.4. Licenses granted to Customers during the Term will survive termination.

22.5. The following provisions of this Agreement will survive termination: Sections 4 (Ownership of Intellectual Property), 12 (Audit), 15 (Disclaimer of Warranty and Limitation of Liability), 16 (Vendor's Intellectual Property Indemnity), 17 (Indemnity by Distributor), 18 (Procedure for Indemnification), 20 (Confidentiality), 22 (Effect of Termination), and 23 (General Provisions) together with accrued liabilities and any provisions that state that they are effective after termination.

22.6. Termination of this Agreement will not affect the license of a Customer, duly licensed under this Agreement to utilize the Bundled Product in accordance with the terms of a Customer License Agreement.

23. General Provisions

23.1. *Relationship of Parties*. Distributor will be deemed to have the status of an independent contractor, and nothing in this Agreement will be deemed to place the Parties in the relationship of employer-employee, principal-agent, partners, or joint venturers.

23.2. *Product Changes or Discontinuance*. Vendor reserves the right to discontinue sale, distribution or support of any Bundled Product at any time or may introduce new versions thereof.

23.3. *No Waiver*. The failure of either Party to exercise any right or the waiver by either Party of any breach will not prevent a subsequent exercise of such right or be deemed a waiver of any subsequent breach of the same or any other term of the Agreement.

23.4. *Notice*. Any notice required or permitted to be sent hereunder will be in writing and will be sent in a manner requiring a signed receipt, such as Federal Express, courier delivery, or if mailed, registered or certified mail, return receipt requested. Notice is effective upon receipt. Notice to Vendor will be addressed to the address set forth above or such other person or address as Vendor may designate. Notice to Distributor will be addressed to the address and contact person set forth above or such other person or address as Distributor may designate in writing.

23.5. *Partial Invalidity*. Should any provision of this Agreement be held to be void, invalid, or inoperative, the remaining provisions of this Agreement will not be affected and will continue in effect as though such provisions were deleted.

23.6. *Force Majeure*. Neither Party will be deemed in default of this Agreement to the extent that performance of their obligations or attempts to cure any breach are delayed or prevented by reason of any act of God, fire, natural disaster, accident, act of government, shortages of materials or supplies, or any other cause beyond the control of such Party ("Force Majeure"), provided that such Party gives the other Party written notice thereof promptly and, in any event, within fifteen (15) days of discovery thereof and uses its commercially reasonable effort to cure the delay. In the event of such Force Majeure, the time for performance or cure will be extended for a period equal to the duration of the Force Majeure but not in excess of three (3) months. Force Majeure, however, will not apply to or delay any obligation to make payments of money required by this Agreement for more than twenty (20) days.

23.7. *Licensing to Government.* The Bundled Product and Documentation are "Commercial Items," as that term is defined at 48 CFR §2.101, consisting of "Commercial Computer Software" and "Commercial Computer Software Documentation," as such terms are used in 48 CFR §12.212 or 48 CFR §227.7202, as applicable. Consistent with 48 CFR §12.212 or 48 CFR §§227.7202-1 through 227.7202-4, as applicable, the Commercial Computer Software and Commercial Computer Software Documentation are being licensed to U.S. Government end users (a) only as Commercial Items and (b) with only those rights as are granted to all other end users pursuant to the terms and conditions herein.

23.8. *Non-Solicitation.* Each Party agrees that during the Term and for a period of one (1) year thereafter, it will not solicit or contact for the purposes of hiring employees of the other Party with whom the Party had material contact under this Agreement. This provision will not apply to employment resulting from general solicitation for employment or contractors on the Internet, the press, or through other mass media.

23.9. *Assignment.* Either Party may assign and transfer this Agreement in connection with the sale or disposition of the line of business that is involved in this Agreement[, provided, however, that upon assignment of this Agreement to a competitor of Vendor or such competitor's obtaining control of the Agreement or of Distributor, Vendor may terminate this Agreement upon written notice]. Subject to the foregoing, this Agreement will be binding upon and inure to the benefit of the Parties to this Agreement and their respective heirs, legal representatives, successors, and permitted assigns.

23.10. *Injunctive Relief.* The Parties agree that in case of a breach of the provisions of this Agreement relating to Confidential Information or intellectual property rights or in case of the unlicensed use or exploitation of the Bundled Product, a remedy at law will not be adequate for the non-breaching Party's protection, and accordingly the non-breaching party will have the right to seek, in addition to any other relief and remedies available to it, preliminary and final injunctive relief to enforce the provisions of this Agreement in any court of competent jurisdiction.

23.11. [*Enforcement Expenses.* In case of any default or breach by Distributor under any provision of this Agreement or any violation of Vendor intellectual property rights, Distributor agrees to pay, in addition to such other amounts as may be due, all costs of enforcement or collection incurred by Vendor, including reasonable attorney's fees.]

23.12. [*Arbitration.* Any dispute relating to the terms, interpretation or performance of this Agreement or the dealing of the Parties with regard to Bundled Products (other than claims for preliminary injunctive relief or other pre-judgment remedies) will be resolved at the request of either Party through binding arbitration. Arbitration will be conducted in _____ under the rules and procedures of the American Arbitration Association ("AAA"). The Parties will request that the AAA appoint a panel of three arbitrators and, if feasible, include one arbitrator of the three who will possess knowledge of computer Bundled Product and its distribution; however the arbitration will proceed even if such a person is unavailable. The award may be enforced in any court of competent jurisdiction.]

23.13. *Entire Governing Law.* This Agreement will be governed and interpreted in accordance with the substantive law of the State of _____ applicable to contracts made and performed there. The United Nations Convention on Contracts for the International Sale of Goods will not apply.

23.14. *Agreement.* This Agreement, including the Schedules attached to this Agreement, states the entire agreement between the Parties on this subject and supersedes all prior negotiations, understandings and agreements between the Parties concerning the subject matter. No amendment or modification of this Agreement will be made except by a writing signed by both Parties.

IN WITNESS WHEREOF, the Parties have executed this Agreement as of the Effective Date set forth above.

[Vendor Name]   *[Distributor Name]*

By: _____   By: _____

Print Name and Title:_____   Print Name and Title: _____

Date: _____   Date: _____

Schedule A
Bundled Products

[To be specified]

Schedule B
Distributor Products

[To be specified]

Schedule C
Territory

Distributor may license and authorize sublicensing of Bundled Products only in the *[define Territory]*.

Schedule D
Vendor Standard End User License Agreement

[To Be Supplied]

Schedule E
Payments Due to Vendor

[To Be Supplied]

Schedule F
Quotas

[To Be Supplied]

Retail Software Distribution Agreement

Introductory Note

This is an agreement in which a Vendor provides its software to a Distributor that is specialized in distributing the software to Retailers in a defined Territory. This form is for non-exclusive distribution of packaged software. Distributor does not have a license under this form to replicate the software.

This kind of agreement is normally written to favor the Distributor rather that the Vendor, and you will see that the following is not an exception. Commercial terms, such as details of the pricing and payment, are frequently negotiable.

As written, this agreement does not permit the Distributor or its Retailers to carry out electronic delivery of software over the Internet, but does not prevent the Retailers from selling licenses to Products over the Internet so long as there is physical delivery of the packaged software Products in the Territory.

This form can be adapted for licensing directly to a Retailer.

Bracketed language is optional or provides alternatives.

Software Distribution Agreement

This Software Distribution Agreement ("Agreement") is effective as of the ___ day of _____, 20___ ("Effective Date") between *[Insert Vendor company name]* (hereinafter "Vendor"), with its principal office at _____, and *[Insert Distributor company name]*. ("Distributor") with its principal office at _____ (each a "Party"; together the "Parties").

Purpose of This Agreement

A. Vendor is engaged in the business of development and distribution of the Products.

B. Distributor is engaged in the business of distribution of various software products to Retailers in the Territory.

C. Vendor wishes to retain Distributor and Distributor wishes to serve as a distributor of Vendor's Products to Retailers within the Territory on the terms and conditions set forth in this Agreement.

Intending to be bound, the Parties have agreed as follows:

1. **Definitions**

   1.1. "End User" means an individual or entity that purchases a license to a Product at retail for his, her or its own use and not for resale.

   1.2. "Product(s)" means certain packaged computer software products manufactured, distributed, or marketed by Vendor during the Term as set forth in Schedule A [and such other computer software products as may be added by agreement of the parties or as otherwise provided by the terms of this Agreement].

   1.3. "Retailer(s)" means any third party entity to which Distributor markets any Products for remarketing to End Users in the Territory.

   1.4. "Term" means the term of this Agreement as specified below in Section 15.

   1.5. "Territory" means [specify territory or state worldwide].

2. **Grant of Marketing and Distribution License**

   2.1. Vendor grants to Distributor and Distributor accepts from Vendor a non-exclusive license during the Term to market and distribute Products to Retailers located in the Territory solely for distribution in the Territory.

3. **Certain Vendor Obligations**

   3.1. *Product Availability.* Vendor agrees to use commercially reasonable efforts to maintain sufficient Product inventory to fill Distributor's orders. If a shortage of any Product exists, Vendor agrees to allocate its available inventory of such Product to Distributor fairly and in any case to not less than in proportion to Distributor's percentage of all of Vendor's customer orders for such Product during the previous sixty (60) days. Vendor reserves the right to discontinue any Product on thirty (30) days' written notice.

3.2. *Product Marking.* Vendor will clearly mark each unit of Product with the Product name and computer compatibility. Such packaging will also bear a machine-readable bar code identifier in standard Uniform Product Code (UPC) format. The bar code must identify the Product as specified by the Uniform Code Council (UCC).

3.3. [*New Products.* Vendor will endeavor to notify Distributor at least ninety (90) days before the date any new Product ("New Product") is introduced in the Territory and provide Distributor information regarding New Product features, marketing and suggested retail pricing. Vendor will make such Product available for distribution by Distributor no later than the date it is first offered for sale in the Territory. Unless otherwise agreed in writing, each New Product, when so introduced, will be deemed an additional Product for purposes of this Agreement.]

4. **Orders and Shipment and Delivery of Products to Distributor**

4.1. *Orders and Shipment.* Vendor will ship Products pursuant to Distributor purchase order(s) ("Order"). Distributor will issue each Order in writing (which will include faxes and email PDFs sent to a designated email address). Product will be shipped F.O.B. Distributor's designated warehouse with risk of loss or damage to pass to Distributor upon delivery to the warehouse specified in Distributor's Order. Vendor will make commercially reasonable efforts to ship all Products ordered by Distributor within times reasonably specified in Orders. Distributor's pricing, as shown in Schedule B or otherwise agreed upon in writing, includes freight to Distributor's facility. A packing list showing Distributor's Order number, quantity ordered, quantity shipped and an identification of the Products must accompany all shipments. Pre-printed or standard terms of purchase orders, confirmations, and other transactional documents of the Parties will not supplement or vary the terms of this Agreement.

4.2. *Order Cancellation.* Distributor may cancel all or part of any Order prior to the date of shipment with written notice seven (7) working days before Distributor's requested delivery date.

4.3. *Certain Charge Backs.* Distributor may charge back to Vendor costs incurred by Distributor or its Retailers (if chargeable by Retailers to Distributor) for missing, defective or inaccurate UPC codes[, provided that such charges will not exceed ___ percent (__%) of the suggested retail price of the Products].

4.4. *Invoices.* For each Product shipment to Distributor, Vendor will issue to Distributor an invoice showing Distributor's Order number, the Product part number, description, price and any applicable discounts. Upon written request on reasonable notice, Vendor will provide Distributor with a current statement of account, listing all invoices outstanding and any payments made and credits given since the date of the previous statement.

5. **Purchase Price**

5.1. *Pricing Generally.* The current suggested retail list price and the price payable by Distributor for each Product is shown on Schedule A and Schedule B respectively. The suggested retail price and the price payable by the Distributor for any Product may only be increased on thirty (30) days' advance written notice given by Vendor to Distributor. Vendor will notify Distributor in writing of the availability of new versions of existing Products. Distributor agrees to pay Vendor license fees and other amounts due calculated under the terms and conditions stated in Schedule B.

5.2. *Price Protection.* Any price decrease by Vendor will apply to Distributor Orders shipped on or after the date the price decrease was announced or published. In addition, Vendor will credit to Distributor's account an amount equal to the difference between the pre-existing price to Distributor for a Product and the new price, times the total number of units of the Product held in Distributor's inventory. Vendor will also provide Distributor with a credit, calculated in the same manner, for all affected Product held by Distributor's Retailers at the time of a price decrease. Vendor will cooperate with Distributor to implement the credit for Retailers' stocks of Product affected by a price decrease. Distributor agrees to track and inform Vendor of Distributor's inventory of Products held by Distributor's Retailers affected by such a price change so that Vendor can provide such credit.

5.3. [*Most Favored Pricing.* Vendor represents and warrants that the price, discounts, payment terms and return and other provisions set forth with respect to any Product will never be less favorable to Distributor than those made available by Vendor to any similar distributors of such Product. Vendor agrees that if a more favorable sales offer to a third party occurs, Vendor will offer to Distributor all the same terms and conditions.]

6. **Payment**

   6.1. On or after the date of shipment, Vendor will invoice Distributor for the purchase of Product. All amounts specified in any net invoice will be paid by Distributor within _____ (___) days from the date of receipt of the Products. Distributor will be granted a ____ (__%) percent discount on pre-paid purchases. Distributor will have the option to deduct from invoices due Vendor any credits due Distributor. [Payments not made when due will accrue interest at the rate of ____ percent per month or the highest legal rate, if lower from the date due.] In case there is a balance due Distributor, Vendor will issue a check for the required amount to Distributor within sixty (60) working days for the credit balance.

7. **Stock Balancing, Returns, Product Recalls and Credits**

   7.1. Distributor may return for credit to Vendor any unit of a Product which, in the opinion of Distributor or Distributor's Retailer is defective in material or workmanship, is overstocked or has been outdated by the release of a new version. Distributor may return for credit any product that has been returned by an End User. Upon receipt of such Product, Vendor will credit Distributor's account with the amount originally paid for the Product net of any applicable credits or discounts. All transportation charges incurred with respect to defective Products or recalled Product will be paid by Vendor. Distributor will pay transportation charges for other Product returns.

   7.2. Credits for returns, any applicable advertising allowances, or other credits relating to Products will be handled by the issuance of charge backs by Distributor and the issuance of a credit memo by Vendor.

8. **Audit**

   8.1. Each Party (the "Auditing Party"), at its own expense, will be entitled to retain an independent certified public accounting firm reasonably acceptable to the other Party (the "Audited Party") solely for the purpose of auditing, at mutually agreed upon times during normal business hours, those records of the Audited Party that relate to the financial terms of this Agreement. Prior to an audit, the Auditing Party will require the certified public accounting firm (the "Auditor") to sign a confidentiality agreement reasonably acceptable to the Audited Party. If an audit reveals an underpayment or overpayment, the benefited Party will promptly make a curative payment to the other Party [together with interest at the rate of ___ percent (__%) per year, compounded daily from the date of such underpayment or overpayment]. If an audit reveals a miscalculation of more than ____ percent (__%) in favor of the Audited Party, then the Audited Party will pay the reasonable cost of the audit.

9. **Warranties and Disclaimer**

   9.1. *End User Warranties.* Vendor shall provide a commercially reasonable warranty for each Product for the End User's benefit. This warranty shall commence upon Product delivery to an End User.

   9.2. *Content of Products.* Vendor warrants that each Product offered for distribution does not contain any obscene, indecent, defamatory or libelous matter or violate any right of publicity or privacy.

   9.3. *Disclaimer.* OTHER THAN AS EXPRESSLY SET FORTH HEREIN, VENDOR DISCLAIMS ALL EXPRESS AND IMPLIED WARRANTIES, INCLUDING WARRANTIES OR CONDITIONS OF MERCHANTABILITY, FITNESS FOR A PARTICULAR PURPOSE, AND NON-INFRINGEMENT OF THIRD PARTY RIGHTS.

10. **Liability Limitation**

    10.1. Neither Party will be liable to the other Party for consequential, incidental, indirect or special damages, even if such Party has been apprised of the likelihood of such damages occurring.

    10.2. Except with regard to indemnification, each Party's aggregate liability to the other Party under this Agreement will be limited to the aggregate sum that Distributor has paid to or owes to Vendor.

11. **Indemnification**

    11.1. Vendor agrees to defend, indemnify and hold Distributor (and its officers, directors, employees, servants and agents) harmless from and against any claim, loss, damage, expense or liability (including legal fees and costs) that may result from:

11.1.1. Any infringement, or any claim of infringement of any patent, trademark, copyright, trade secret or other proprietary right with respect to the Products.

11.1.2. Any warranty or product liability claim with respect to the Products.

11.2. In case of any claim that is subject to indemnification under this Agreement, the party entitled to indemnification ("Indemnitee") shall provide Vendor prompt notice of the relevant claim. Vendor shall defend and/or settle, at its own expense, any demand, action, or suit on any claim subject to indemnification under this Agreement. The Indemnitee shall cooperate in good faith with the Vendor to facilitate the defense of any such claim and shall tender the defense and settlement of any action or proceeding under the indemnification provisions of this Agreement to the Vendor upon request. Claims may not be settled without the consent of any Indemnitee unless the settlement includes an admission of wrongdoing, fault or liability on behalf of the Indemnitee.

12. **Insurance**

Vendor will carry product liability insurance coverage for the Products during the Term and for ___ years thereafter as follows: *[indicate insurance coverage required]*.

13. **Advertising**

13.1. Distributor will have the right to utilize in the Territory Vendor's trade name and any trademarks and service marks associated with the Products to identify the origin of the Products in advertising and promotional materials. With respect to Products made or supplied wholly or in part by a third party, Vendor will ensure that Distributor has the right to use in Distributor's advertising and promotional materials the third party's trademarks and service marks associated with the Products. Distributor will follow the written trademark guidelines of Vendor or such third party regarding such use as have been supplied to Distributor.

13.2. Vendor may from time to time make available to Distributor and/or Distributor's Retailers advertising, market development, and promotional support. Distributor will be provided an opportunity to participate in such programs and to provide such programs to its Retailers under conditions no less favorable than those available to other distributors for the Territory.

14. Confidentiality

14.1. Each Party may have access to non-public information provided by the other Party ("Confidential Information"). Confidential Information includes, without limitation, information regarding product plans and promotional plans, the terms and pricing under this Agreement, and all information identified in writing as confidential.

14.2. A Party's Confidential Information will not include information that: (a) is or becomes publicly known through no act or omission of the other Party; (b) was in the other Party's lawful possession prior to the disclosure; (c) is lawfully disclosed to the other Party by a third party without restriction on disclosure; or (d) is independently developed by the other Party.

14.3. The Parties agree to hold each other's Confidential Information in confidence during the Term and for a period of ___ (__) years after termination of this Agreement. The Parties agree, unless required by law, not to make each other's Confidential Information available in any form to any third party or use Confidential Information for any purpose other than as reasonably required for this Agreement. Each Party agrees to take all reasonable steps to ensure that Confidential Information is not disclosed or in violation of the terms of this Agreement. Each Party may, however, disclose information about this Agreement, its terms, and relevant financial matters to its lawyers, accountants, advisors, directors, investors, owners and to parties that may be conducting due diligence with regard to the Party, subject to reasonable confidentiality measures.

15. Term and Termination

15.1. The Term, unless earlier terminated as provided herein, will be as follows:

15.1.1. The initial term of this Agreement ("Initial Term") will be for a period of ___ (__) year(s), unless sooner terminated as provided by this Agreement.

15.1.2. After the initial term, this Agreement will be automatically renewed for successive one (1) year periods (each a "Renewal Term"), unless either Party gives the other written notice of termination at least ninety (90) days prior to the expiration of the then current Initial Term or Renewal Term (as applicable). If such notice is given, the Agreement will terminate at the end of the then current Initial Term or Renewal Term.

15.2. In the event of a material breach of this Agreement, the Party not in breach may terminate the Agreement after the failure of the other Party to cure such breach within thirty (30) days of written notification to cure.

15.3. Upon expiration or termination of this Agreement, Distributor will have the right, for 120 days after the termination, to return to Vendor all or a portion of the Products in Distributor's inventory. Vendor agrees to repurchase any such returned Products at the prices paid for them by Distributor less any applied credits and discounts.

16. Survival

The following provision will survive termination: Sections 8 (Audit), 9 (Warranties and Disclaimer), 10 (Liability Limitation), 11 (Indemnification). 12 (Insurance), 14 (Confidentiality), 15 (Term and Termination), 16 (Survival) and 17 (Miscellaneous) together with accrued obligations.

17. Miscellaneous

17.1. *Relationship of Parties*. Distributor will be deemed to have the status of an independent contractor, and nothing in this Agreement will be deemed to place the Parties in the relationship of employer-employee, principal-agent, partners, or joint venturers.

17.2. *No Waiver*. The failure of either Party to exercise any right or the waiver by either Party of any breach will not prevent a subsequent exercise of such right or be deemed a waiver of any subsequent breach of the same or any other term of the Agreement.

17.3. *Notice*. Any notice required or permitted to be sent hereunder will be in writing and will be sent in a manner requiring a signed receipt, such as Federal Express, courier delivery, or if mailed, registered or certified mail, return receipt requested. Notice is effective upon receipt. Notice to

Vendor will be addressed to the address set forth above or such other person or address as Vendor may designate. Notice to Distributor will be addressed to the address set forth above or such other address as Distributor may designate in writing.

17.4. *Partial Invalidity.* Should any provision of this Agreement be held to be void, invalid, or inoperative, the remaining provisions of this Agreement will not be affected and will continue in effect as though such provisions were deleted.

17.5. *Force Majeure.* Neither Party will be deemed in default of this Agreement to the extent that performance of their obligations or attempts to cure any breach are delayed or prevented by reason of any act of God, fire, natural disaster, accident, act of government, shortages of materials or supplies, or any other cause beyond the control of such Party ("Force Majeure"), provided that such Party gives the other Party written notice thereof promptly and, in any event, within fifteen (15) days of discovery thereof and uses its commercially reasonable effort to cure the delay. In the event of such Force Majeure, the time for performance or cure will be extended for a period equal to the duration of the Force Majeure but not in excess of three (3) months. Force Majeure, however, will not apply to or delay any obligation to make payments of money required by this Agreement for more than twenty (20) days.

17.6. *Assignment.* Either Party may assign and transfer this Agreement in connection with the sale or disposition of the business unit that is involved in this Agreement. Subject to the foregoing, this Agreement will be binding upon and inure to the benefit of the Parties to this Agreement and their respective permitted legal representatives, successors, and assigns.

17.7. *Governing Law; Jurisdiction.* This Agreement will be governed and interpreted in accordance with the substantive law of the State of _____ applicable to contracts made and performed there. The United Nations Convention on Contracts for the International Sale of Goods will not apply. The Parties agree that the state and federal courts located in _____ will have exclusive jurisdiction and venue over any action or claim arising from this Agreement or its subject matter.

17.8. *Export Law Compliance*. With regard to any Products to be exported by Vendor to a location outside the United States for distribution, Vendor will arrange for compliance with all applicable export laws and regulations.

17.9. *Entire Agreement*. This Agreement, including the Schedules attached to this Agreement, states the entire agreement between the Parties on this subject and supersedes all prior negotiations, understandings and agreements between the Parties concerning the subject matter. No amendment or modification of this Agreement will be made except by a writing signed by both Parties.

17.10. *Counterparts*. This Agreement may be executed in counterparts, each of which will be deemed an original and all of which together will constitute one instrument.

IN WITNESS WHEREOF, the Parties have executed this Agreement as of the Effective Date set forth above.

Vendor: _____   Distributor: _____

By: _____   By: _____

Printed Name: _____   Printed Name: _____

Title: _____   Title: _____

Date: _____   Date: _____

Schedule A

List of Products and Suggested Retail Prices

[Insert List]

Schedule B

Product Pricing

[To be added. Pricing would commonly be stated as a discount from list price. Distributor would often be able to qualify for various credits, such as credits for money spent on cooperative advertising and other market development activities and costs, price tagging on goods and in-store inventory management.]

Sales Representative Agreement

Introductory Note

This is a form of sales representative agreement. This form would normally be used for business software products. As you will recall, a sales representative obtains orders but does not provide, install or support the product. In this form, the vendor reserves the right to sell directly to customers that it selects, called "House Accounts."

There are special legal characteristics of the relationship of a sales agent with a vendor that are discussed in Chapter 15. You should review that discussion before using this form.

Brackets indicate options or alternative provisions.

Sales Representation Agreement

This Sales Representation Agreement ("Agreement") is effective as of the ___ day of _____, 20___ ("Effective Date") between *[Insert Vendor company name]* (hereinafter "Vendor"), with its principal office at _____, and *[Insert Representative company name]*. ("Representative") with its principal office at _____ (each a "Party"; together the "Parties").

1. **Definitions.** The following definitions shall apply:

    1.1. "Territory" shall mean the geographic area identified in <u>Schedule A</u> to this Agreement.

    1.2. "Customers" shall mean all customers that license Products with purchasing locations within the Territory, except distributors and House Accounts (as hereinafter defined).

1.3. "House Account" shall mean any Customer, including corporate, individual or any agency of local, state or national government (including those who are Customers prior to such designation) which Vendor at any one or more times during the term of this Agreement advises Representative in writing is to be so designated.

1.4. "Products" means the Vendor's software products that are available for licensing as listed in Schedule A.

2. **Appointment of Representative.** Vendor appoints Representative as a non-exclusive sales representative of Vendor for the Products for the Territory. Vendor reserves the right to appoint other distributors and representatives in the Territory.

3. **Duties of Representative**

3.1. *Assigned Task.* Representative's assigned task under this Agreement is supplementing Vendor's licensing efforts for Products by providing adequate sales coverage in the Territory for Customers and prospects, not including House Accounts.

3.2. *Sales Promotion.* Representative will use its best efforts to promote the licensing of the Products to Customers and prospects in the Territory. All advertisements by Representative must receive Vendor's prior approval.

3.3. *Orders and Inquiries.* Representative will send promptly to Vendor any proposed order or inquiry from prospective Customers. Representative will follow such order processing rules and procedures as Vendor may specify, including procedures relating to written and electronic (online) licensing and order processing.

3.4. *Assistance and Advice.* Upon request, Representative will assist Customers in the Territory concerning selection of Products and render advice as needed for that function. Representative represents that it is and will at all times remain qualified to give such assistance and advice.

3.5. *Reports and Visits.* Representative will give written and oral reports to Vendor as to its promotion activities in such form and in such frequency as Vendor may reasonably require.

3.6. *Limits of Responsibility.* For clarification, Representative will have no obligations or function under this Agreement other than selling; delivery, installation, any customization, maintenance and support of Products will be subject to Vendor's sole control.

4. **House Accounts**

    4.1. In the event that Vendor decides to provide direct sales coverage to any Customer, it will so advise Representative by giving not less than thirty (30) days' prior written notice designating such Customer as a House Account. Representative's consent will not be required for any such designation.

    4.2. Representative shall not be entitled to any compensation for sales made to House Accounts subsequent to the effective date specified in each such notice. Representative shall not call on or solicit any House Account with regard to the Products without Vendor's express prior written permission.

5. **Confidentiality and Intellectual Property Matters**

    5.1. *Confidential Information.* Representative acknowledges that during the course of this Agreement, it may learn non-public information regarding Vendor's products, customer, pricing, technology, and other non-public information of Vendor ("Confidential Information").

    5.2. *Confidentiality Obligation.* Except with Vendor's prior written authorization, Representative shall not disclose Confidential Information and shall not use Confidential Information other than for the purpose of this Agreement. Representative shall take all necessary steps to assure that its employees comply with this obligation regarding confidentiality.

    5.3. *Works and Inventions.* All copyrightable works ("Works") relating to or arising from Representative's services under this Agreement shall belong to Vendor, shall be considered "work for hire" that becomes Vendor's property upon creation, and to the extent not deemed "work for hire" are hereby assigned to Vendor. Representative also hereby assigns to Vendor all patents, inventions, improvements, trade secrets, or developments ("Inventions") conceived by Representative, solely or jointly, relating to the Products of Vendor or to Vendor's business, from their moment of creation. Upon Vendor's direction, Representative will execute all papers that Vendor may deem appropriate to assign, register, protect or confirm Vendor's rights in Works and Inventions, including, without limitation, as required for copyright, patent or other legal assignment or registration.

5.4. *Trademarks.* Representative shall recognize at all times Vendor's exclusive ownership of Vendor's trademarks, service marks, logos, domain names and trade names ("Marks"). Unless otherwise agreed by the Parties in writing, Representative shall use the Marks only for purposes of advertisement, promotion, and sale of the Products and for no other purposes. Representative shall use Marks solely in accordance with the written guidelines established by Vendor from time to time. Representative may identify itself on stationery, advertisements, and promotional literature as a "*[Vendor name]* Authorized Sales Representative." Representative shall not hold itself out as or create the impression or suggestion that it is the author, creator, manufacturer or source of the Products. All good will arising from use of the Marks will belong to Vendor. Representative shall not register the Marks or any confusingly similar marks.

6. **Non-Competition**

6.1. Commencing on the date hereof, Representative agrees not to represent, sell or otherwise solicit sales in the Territory for any product in competition with (or which Vendor, after consultation with Representative, considers to be in competition with) the Products ("Non-Competition Restraint"). Such Non-Competition Restraint shall continue for the term of this Agreement and, in addition, for one year after the expiration of this Agreement.

6.2. If Representative violates the Non-Competition Restraint, Representative agrees that the period of such Non-Competition Restraint shall not run during the period of the violation. Representative understands that the purpose of this paragraph is to give Vendor the protection of the restraint for the full agreed-upon duration.

6.3. If the period of time or the geographic scope of the Non-Competition Restraint is judged by a court of law to be unreasonable, Representative agrees that the time and/or geographic scope for such Non-Competition Restraint will be reduced so that this restraint can be enforced in such area and for such time as the court decides is reasonable.

7. **Promotional Aids**

7.1. Vendor will supply Representative with such sales literature and Product samples it believes will reasonably assist Representative in promoting the Products.

8. **Product Changes**

   8.1. Vendor shall have right to change and discontinue any at the Products at any time.

9. **Prices**

   9.1. Representative shall quote only from Vendor's current price list as it may be in place from time to time. Representative shall have no right to vary pricing or sales terms and conditions. Vendor may make changes or adjustments to its price list at any time. Special quotations, including but not limited to "off list" pricing for large volumes or customized products, may be granted by Vendor from time to time in Vendor's discretion.

10. **Acceptance of Orders**

    10.1. In its discretion, Vendor may accept or reject orders from prospective Customers in Territory. No order shall be binding until accepted by Vendor in writing. Representative does not have authority to accept orders or otherwise bind Vendor.

    10.2. Unless Vendor otherwise elects, all sales will be made subject to Vendor's standard licensing terms and conditions, a copy of which is attached hereto as Schedule B. Vendor reserves the right to change its standard terms and conditions at any time or to have different terms apply to different Products.

    10.3. Representative shall follow such sales and ordering procedures as Vendor may specify.

11. **Representative's Compensation**

    11.1. *Commission Schedule.* Vendor shall pay to Representative the commissions stated in Schedule A attached hereto based upon the Net Value (as defined below) of the orders accepted by Vendor for delivery during the term of this Agreement in the Territory to Customers (other than House Accounts) located there. Vendor's obligation to pay a commission shall apply only when the Representative, in Vendor's judgment, is the effective cause of the sale. [Commissions are conditioned upon Customer's payment of the invoiced license fee for the Product(s).]

11.2. *Net Value Definition.* "Net Value" shall mean the gross invoice price *minus*:

11.2.1. Development, installation, customization and professional service charges billed to Customers;

11.2.2. Delivery charges, taxes and handling billed to Customers;

11.2.3. Customer credits for returns or rejections;

11.2.4. Credits, discounts or adjustments made for the Customer's benefit.

11.3. [*Adjustment for Pre-Existing Contacts.* Where the Vendor has material contact with a Customer prior to Representative, the Vendor, at its discretion, may reduce the applicable commission rate for such Customer by up to ___ percent (__%) of the rate that would otherwise apply. Rates may also be adjusted for particular Customers by written mutual Agreement of the Vendor and Representative. Such adjustments will continue for the term of this Agreement unless otherwise agreed in writing. Customers subject to such an adjustment shall be known as "Adjusted Commission Accounts." Adjusted Commission Accounts agreed to by the Parties as of the date of the Agreement, and the applicable commission rates for such Adjusted Commission Accounts are set forth in Schedule A.]

11.4. *Time of Payment.* [Commissions are due and payable to Representative on or before the thirtieth (30th) day of the month following the month in which Vendor invoices the Customer.] [Commissions are due and payable to Representative on or before the thirtieth (30th) day of the month following the month in which Vendor receives payment of its invoice to the Customer.]

11.5. *Methods of Correction.* In case that, due to adjustment, return, delinquent payment, default, mistake or otherwise, Vendor has paid Representative more than the commission that was due, Vendor, in its discretion, may recover such amount by deductions from Representative's current or future commissions, or by requiring Representative to repay such amount ten (10) days from demand.

11.6. *Dividing Commissions.* Where Vendor deems more than one sales representative or distributor is responsible for a licensing transaction with a Customer or in case of transactions that are both inside and outside the

Territory, Vendor may divide commissions among Representative, other representatives, and other distributors. Only Vendor will decide if Representative is entitled to a portion of a commission and the amount of such portion. If Representative disagrees with Vendor, Representative will send, within ten (10) days after Vendor's decision, written reasons for its disagreement to the *[insert name of Vender officer]* of Vendor (or other person designated by Vendor, holding a comparable or higher management position). Such representative of Vendor shall review such reasons and notify Representative of his or her conclusion, which shall be final and binding on the Parties.

12. **Injunctive Relief**

   12.1. Representative agrees that in case of Representative's breach of provisions regarding the Non-Competition Restraint, Confidential Information, Works, Inventions or Marks, Vendor will suffer immediate and irreparable injury. In such a case, Representative agrees that, in addition to any other remedies that may apply, the Court shall require Representative's strict compliance with this Agreement, and Vendor shall be entitled to preliminary and final injunctive relief to enforce this Agreement.

13. **Term and Termination**

   13.1. This Agreement shall have a term of one (1) year and shall terminate upon the first anniversary of its date unless extended by written mutual agreement of the Parties; provided, however, that either Party may elect to terminate this Agreement during its term and with or without cause by giving the other Party not less than thirty (30) days' prior written notice of its election to so terminate this Agreement.

   13.2. To the maximum extent permitted by law, Representative waives any statutory rights it may have arising out of such termination, such as any right to compensation or to require a showing of "just cause."

   13.3. If either Party is in material default, the other Party may, upon not less than fifteen (15) days' prior notice, terminate this Agreement; provided that the Party in default has not cured the default during such notice period.

14. **Effect of Termination.** The following terms and conditions shall apply upon termination of this Agreement:

14.1. Termination shall not affect any debt, claim or cause of action that has accrued to the benefit of either Party against the other before termination.

14.2. Representative shall earn commissions earned on orders booked before termination if within ten (10) days after termination Representative sends to Vendor a list of Customers and sales for which commissions are sought, provided that such orders are subsequently shipped and paid for.

14.3. Within fifteen (15) days of termination, all written technical and business material furnished to Representative by Vendor shall be returned, and all property of the Vendor shall be turned over to it.

14.4. Representative will no longer use Vendor's Marks and Representative will not adopt or use any trademark, service mark, trade name or brand that reasonably could be confusingly similar to names used by Vendor.

14.5. Sections 5, 6, 12, 14, and 15 shall survive the termination of this Agreement.

15. Miscellaneous Provisions

15.1. *Terminology.* While this Agreement uses terms such as "sales" and the like, the Parties agree that Vendor licenses its Products to Customers and does not sell them.

15.2. *Reputation of Vendor.* Representative will at all times act professionally and in a manner that enhances the reputation of Vendor and the Products.

15.3. *Force Majeure.* Neither Party shall be liable for loss or damage, failures or delays because of causes beyond its reasonable control, such as but not limited to strikes, lockouts, or labor disputes, fires, acts of God or public enemy, riots, incendiaries, interference by civil or military authorities, compliance with the law, orders or policies of any governmental authority, delays in transportation or communications or failures of sources of raw materials or production facilities.

15.4. *Entire Agreement.* This is the entire agreement of the Parties and supersedes any earlier representation, discussion, promise or agreement regarding this subject matter.

15.5. *Relationship of the Parties.* Representative is an independent contractor and not an agent, partner or employee of Vendor. Representative may not commit Vendor to any obligation.

15.6. *Damage Limitation*. Other than Vendor's claims for Representative's breach of provisions regarding the Non-Competition Restraint, Confidential Information, Works, Inventions and Marks, neither Party shall be liable to the other for any indirect, incidental or consequential damages, including but not limited to, loss of profits, loss of business opportunities or loss of business investment.

15.7. *Insurance*. Representative warrants that it has, and agrees to provide Vendor with, certificates of insurance evidencing that Representative has purchased the following insurance: Comprehensive General Liability insurance, including automobile liability insurance, with limits not less than $1,000,000 per occurrence for bodily injury or property damage. At Vendor's option, on thirty (30) days' notice, higher limits and additional coverage may be specified.

15.8. *Legal Compliance*

15.8.1. Representative will comply with all laws, rules and regulations issued by any governmental entity having jurisdiction over it.

15.8.2. Representative shall take no steps and have no understanding, written or verbal, to encourage, arrange, pay or receive any payment or consideration: (a) which involves any illegal purpose, or (b) which, whether legal or illegal, involves government officials or employees, political candidates or parties or (c) which consists of kickbacks or bribes.

15.8.3. Documentation of all business transactions shall properly describe the pertinent events and such records must not be false, distorted or misleading. No undisclosed or unrecorded fund or asset shall be established for any purpose.

15.9. *Assignment*. Representative shall not assign this Agreement without prior written consent of Vendor, granted or withheld in the Vendor's discretion, and any unapproved assignment shall be void. Representative will not appoint subrepresentatives or otherwise delegate its duties.

15.10. *Notice*. Notices to either Party shall be in writing and will be deemed made when deposited in the United States Mail, First Class, postage paid, to the addresses set forth in <u>Schedule A</u> hereto, or when received by electronic mail or facsimile, or when delivered by hand. Either Party may change its addresses by giving notice to the other Party.

15.11. *Changes in Writing.* Any change to this Agreement shall not be binding unless approved in writing by persons authorized by the Parties.

15.12. *No Waiver.* Failing to perform a term or a condition, or waiving breach thereof, shall not prevent a subsequent enforcement of such term or condition nor be a waiver of any subsequent breach.

15.13. *Applicable Law.* This Agreement will be governed and interpreted in accordance with the substantive law of the State of _____ applicable to contracts made and performed there. The United Nations Convention on Contracts for the International Sale of Goods will not apply. The parties agree that the state and federal courts located in _____ will have exclusive jurisdiction and venue over any action or claim arising from this Agreement or its subject matter[, except that, in case of Representative's breach, Vendor, in its discretion, may enforce the Agreement against the Representative in any court with jurisdiction over Representative].

So agreed by the Parties:

[Vendor Name]	*[Representative's Name]*
By: _____	By: _____
Printed Name: _____	Printed Name: _____
Title: _____	Title: _____
Date: _____	Date: _____

Schedule A

Products and Commission Rates

1. Products and Commission Rates are as follows:

    <u>Products</u>   <u>Commission Rate</u>

2. Territory shall mean _____

3. The addresses to which notices shall be sent are:

If to Vendor: If to Representative:

Schedule B

Vendor Current Standard Licensing Terms and Conditions

[Add Standard License Agreement. The form of agreement should have a prominent notice indicating that the Representative cannot bind the Vendor, and that all Agreements are subject to Vendor's written approval.]

EULA – Consumer Product 16-1

Introductory Note

This is a form of EULA for a mass market consumer application.

You should not consider a consumer application EULA to be an unvarying "template," because consumer product offerings have become quite complex and varied; this form illustrates some of this complexity. You will need to adapt the form to fit your business and your applications.

The following is a EULA for a fictitious "Media Player" offered by a fictitious company named "SoftCo, Inc." It could, of course, be adapted for any other consumer application. This EULA covers the Media Player's entry-level "Free Version" and a more richly featured for-pay "Premium Version." The EULA also covers (a) related online services (which could be data or content provided through the Internet), (b) software "add-ins" from SoftCo and third parties, and (c) hyperlinks from the application to third party web sites. The form also refers to related documents such as SoftCo's online terms of use and privacy policy.

This EULA is designed to function as a "clickwrap" form that would be on the SoftCo web site and would also be in the Media Player's installation routine.

End User License Agreement

This End User License Agreement (EULA) applies to the Media Player (as defined below) provided by SoftCo, Inc. ("SoftCo"). BY CLICKING THE ACCEPTANCE BUTTON OR BY DOWNLOADING, INSTALLING OR USING THE MEDIA PLAYER, YOU ASSENT TO AND ARE BOUND BY THIS EULA. YOU ALSO ACCEPT AND ASSENT TO THE SOFTCO PRIVACY POLICY LOCATED AT *[insert SoftCo URL]* AND YOU AGREE TO RECEIVE NOTICES FROM SOFTCO ELECTRONICALLY.

1. **Definitions**

   a. "Free Version" means the executable code version of the SoftCo Media Player, including only those features listed for the Free Version listed at the following URL: *[insert applicable SoftCo URL]*.

   b. "Documentation" means the user documentation for the Media Player available on SoftCo's Web Site.

   c. "SoftCo Plug-in" means a plug-in (software that adds functionality to the Media Player) offered by SoftCo together with the Media Player download and/or from *[insert applicable SoftCo URL]* for use with the Media Player.

   d. "Premium Version" means the executable code version of the Media Player, including both the Free Version features and all features of the "Premium" application as listed at the following URL: *[insert applicable SoftCo URL]*.

   e. "Media Player" means the Free Version and/or the Premium Version, as applicable to Licensee, associated software, Upgrades, Updates, plug-ins, Documentation, and any associated online services provided by SoftCo or its suppliers.

   f. "SoftCo Web Site" means the web site accessed at: *[insert applicable SoftCo URL]*.

   g. "Update" means a revision to the Media Player designated by a change in the version number to the right of the decimal place.

   h. "Upgrade" means a revision to the Media Player designated by a change in the version number to the left of the decimal place.

2. **License Grant**

   a. *Free Version.* Subject to the terms and conditions of this EULA, SoftCo grants Licensee a free-of-charge, non-exclusive, and non-transferable license to install and use the Free Version solely for Licensee's own personal use.

   b. *Premium Version.* When Licensee has paid the applicable license fee, SoftCo agrees to supply an alphanumeric key ("Key") that will unlock the additional features of the Premium Version. Licensee may access and use such features only by use of the Key. Subject to the terms and conditions of this

EULA and provided Licensee has paid the applicable license fee for an upgrade to the Premium Version, SoftCo grants Licensee a non-exclusive and non-transferable license to use the Premium Version (as enabled by use of the Key) solely for Licensee's own personal use.

3. **Upgrades and Updates.** In its discretion, SoftCo may make Updates or Upgrades available for the Free Version and/or the Premium Version. SoftCo may, in its discretion, provide any Updates or Upgrades subject to its then current forms of end user license agreement, which may contain additional or different terms. This license does not entitle Licensee to Updates or Upgrades.

4. **Restrictions on Use.** Licensee may not: (i) modify or create any derivative works of the Media Player; (ii) decompile, disassemble, or reverse engineer the Media Player, or (b) defeat, bypass, or otherwise circumvent any software protection mechanisms in the Media Player (except to the extent applicable laws specifically prohibit such restriction); (iii) attempt to access or use the additional features of the Premium Version if Licensee has not paid the applicable license fee or other than by using the Key; (iv) redistribute, encumber, sell, rent, lease, sublicense, or otherwise transfer the Media Player; (v) use the Media Player in a timesharing or service bureau arrangement; or (vi) remove or alter any trademark, logo, copyright or other proprietary notices, legends, symbols or labels in the Media Player. SoftCo Plug-ins that may be provided with or for the Media Player may only be used with the Media Player and may not be used with any other product. The Media Player may not be used for any revenue generating or broadcast activities or for creation of any physical or electronic media or content for distribution or sale.

5. **Responsibility for Copyright Content.** Licensee alone is responsible for ensuring that any audio or video content that is played or displayed on the Media Player is properly obtained, licensed and used under copyright and all other applicable law. Licensee agrees not to use the Media Player to reproduce, display, perform, or distribute audio and/or video content in any manner that violates any U.S. or foreign laws or any third party rights.

6. **Online Support.** Support for the Media Player consists of online FAQ, blogs, and other online materials that SoftCo may make available at: *[insert applicable SoftCo URL]*. Online materials are subject to SoftCo's applicable online Terms of Use and this EULA.

7. **Payment.** There is no license fee for the Free Version. A fee is required for the Premium Version in connection with obtaining the Key. Pricing is stated at: *[insert applicable SoftCo URL].*

8. **Online Services.** SoftCo and/or its suppliers may provide online services for use with the Media Player. You may be required to register with SoftCo for such services. Online services are subject to applicable legal terms and conditions stated on SoftCo's Web Site and this EULA. SoftCo may change or discontinue online services at any time.

9. **Consent to Electronic Notice.** If for any purpose under this EULA, you provide SoftCo with your email address, you agree to receive all notices and communications ("Notices") from SoftCo in electronic form at such email address. Delivery of any Notice from SoftCo is effective when sent by SoftCo, regardless of whether you actually receive or read the Notice. If you have provided your email address and do not wish to consent to electronic notice, you must uninstall and discontinue all use of the Media Player. You can update your email address by using the features on the SoftCo Web Site for managing your user account.

10. **Ownership.** The Media Player is protected by copyright and other intellectual property laws and by international treaties. No ownership rights are granted by this EULA. SoftCo may use in any manner and without limitation all comments, suggestions, complaints and other feedback that Licensee provides relating to the Media Player. All rights not expressly granted to Licensee are reserved to SoftCo and its suppliers.

11. **[Included Open Source Code.** Portions of the Media Player use open source software components and programs. The licenses and availability of source code for such components are specified in the copyright and license notice text file delivered with the Media Player.]

12. **Indemnification.** Licensee agrees to indemnify, hold harmless, and at SoftCo's request, to defend SoftCo and its suppliers from any and all costs, damages and reasonable attorneys' fees resulting from any breach of this EULA or any allegation or claim that Licensee's use of the Media Player has violated any right of any third party or violated any law.

13. **Termination.** Should Licensee breach this EULA, Licensee's right to use the Media Player will terminate automatically without notice. The respective rights and obligations of SoftCo and Licensee under the following provisions will

survive termination: 4 (Restrictions on Use), 5 (Responsibility for Copyright Content), 9 (Consent to Electronic Notice), 10 (Ownership), 12 (Indemnification), 13 (Termination), 14 (Disclaimer of Warranty), 15 (Limitation of Liability), 19 (Third Party Services or Products) and 20 (Miscellaneous). Upon termination, Licensee will erase all copies of the Media Player.

14. **Disclaimer of Warranty.** THE MUSIC PLAYER IS PROVIDED "AS IS." SOFTCO AND ITS SUPPLIERS DISCLAIM ALL WARRANTIES, WHETHER EXPRESS OR IMPLIED, INCLUDING IMPLIED WARRANTIES OF MERCHANTABILITY, FITNESS FOR A PARTICULAR PURPOSE, AND NON-INFRINGEMENT. THE ENTIRE RISK ARISING OUT OF USE OR PERFORMANCE OF THE SOFTWARE REMAINS WITH YOU. SoftCo and its suppliers do not make any representations regarding the results of the use of the Music Player.

15. **Limitation of Liability.** TO THE MAXIMUM EXTENT PERMITTED BY APPLICABLE LAW, IN NO EVENT WILL SOFTCO OR ITS DIRECTORS, EMPLOYEES, DISTRIBUTORS, SUPPLIERS, AGENTS OR RESELLERS OR SUPPLIERS ("SOFTCO PARTIES") BE LIABLE FOR ANY INDIRECT, SPECIAL, INCIDENTAL, CONSEQUENTIAL, OR EXEMPLARY DAMAGES, EVEN IF SUCH PARTY HAS BEEN ADVISED OF THE POSSIBILITY THEREOF. THE SOFTCO PARTIES' ENTIRE LIABILITY WILL NOT EXCEED IN THE AGGREGATE THE SUM OF THE FEES LICENSEE PAID FOR THIS LICENSE, REPLACEMENT OF DEFECTIVE MEDIA OR PROVISION OF A REASONABLY SIMILAR SOFTWARE PRODUCT, AT SOFTCO'S DISCRETION.
Some jurisdictions do not allow the exclusion or limitation of incidental, consequential or special damages, so this exclusion and limitation may not be applicable to you. The SoftCo Parties will not be liable for any claims or damages arising out of: (i) content provided by Licensee or a third party that is accessed through or used with the Music Player and/or any material linked to or through such content; or (ii) the use of third party plug-ins (even if made available on SoftCo's Web Site).

16. **Export Controls.** Licensee agrees to comply with all export and import laws and restrictions and regulations of the United States or any foreign nation, and not to export, re-export or import the Media Player in violation of any such restrictions, laws or regulations.

17. **Injunctive Relief.** Licensee acknowledges and agrees that, notwithstanding any other provisions of this EULA, any breach or threatened breach of this

EULA by Licensee will cause SoftCo irreparable damage for which recovery of money damages would be inadequate and that SoftCo therefore may obtain timely injunctive relief to protect its rights under this EULA in addition to any and all other remedies available at law or in equity.

18. **U.S. Government Users.** The Media Player is a "commercial item," as that term is defined in 48 CFR 2.101, consisting of "commercial computer software" and "commercial computer software documentation," as such terms are used in 48 CFR 12.212 and 48 CFR 227.7202. Consistent with applicable laws and regulations, all U.S. Government users acquire the Media Player with only those rights as set forth herein.

19. **Third Party Services or Products**

    a. The Media Player may contain links to other web sites, resources and advertisers. SoftCo is not responsible for such external sites.

    b. Third parties may offer from time to time applications or services to access, "plug-in" to or interact with the Media Player. Licensee's use of such third party applications will be at Licensee's own risk and subject to the terms and conditions of those third parties. SOFTCO MAKES NO REPRESENTATION OR WARRANTIES REGARDING THIRD PARTY PRODUCTS EVEN IF DOWNLOADED FROM SOFTCO'S WEB SITE OR BY MEANS OF A LINK ON SUCH SITE.

20. **Miscellaneous**

    a. Licensee represents and warrants that Licensee has all required legal capacity to enter into this EULA as a binding agreement.

    b. This EULA is subject to the law of the state of _____. This EULA will not be governed by the United Nations Convention on Contracts for the International Sale of Goods. Licensee agrees that the exclusive jurisdiction and venue for any claim or dispute relating to or arising out of this EULA or its subject matter will be in the federal and state courts located in _____, and Licensee consents to the personal jurisdiction in such courts.

    c. If any provision in this EULA should be held illegal or unenforceable, the other provisions of this EULA will remain in full force and effect.

    d. A waiver by either party of any term or condition of this EULA or any breach thereof, in any one instance, will not waive such term or condition or any subsequent breach thereof.

e. Licensee may not assign or otherwise transfer by operation of law or otherwise this EULA or any rights or obligations herein. SoftCo may assign this EULA to any entity at its sole discretion. This EULA will be binding upon and will inure to the benefit of the parties, their successors and permitted assigns.

f. Neither party will be in default or be liable for any delay, failure in performance (excepting the obligation to pay) or interruption of service resulting directly or indirectly from any cause beyond its reasonable control.

g. This EULA constitutes the entire agreement between the parties concerning the subject matter hereof, which may only be modified by a written amendment signed by an authorized executive of SoftCo.

Clickwrap EULA—Commercial Product 16-2

Introductory Note

This is a form of "clickwrap" agreement that can be used for a commercial software product.

The form presents text for licensing of software in binary form for installation and use by the customer. We have also included some alternative grant language that can be used to grant the customer a development license and/or a run-time distribution license.

This form is provided for installation on either one or a specified number of work stations. It could be edited to provide for installation on one or a specified number of server computers.

Optional or alternative text is in brackets.

End-User License Agreement

[VENDOR NAME] ("VENDOR") IS WILLING TO LICENSE THE SOFTWARE IDENTIFIED BELOW TO YOU IF YOU ACCEPT THE TERMS IN THIS AGREEMENT. PLEASE READ THE AGREEMENT CAREFULLY. BY DOWNLOADING, INSTALLING OR USING THIS SOFTWARE, YOU ACCEPT THE TERMS OF THE AGREEMENT. INDICATE ACCEPTANCE BY SELECTING THE "ACCEPT" BUTTON AT THE BOTTOM OF THE AGREEMENT. IF YOU ARE NOT WILLING TO BE BOUND BY ALL THE TERMS, SELECT THE "DECLINE" BUTTON AT THE BOTTOM OF THE AGREEMENT AND THE DOWNLOAD OR INSTALL PROCESS WILL NOT CONTINUE. IF YOU ARE ACCEPTING THESE TERMS ON BEHALF OF ANOTHER PERSON OR A COMPANY OR OTHER LEGAL ENTITY, YOU

REPRESENT AND WARRANT THAT YOU HAVE FULL AUTHORITY TO ACT FOR AND TO BIND THAT PERSON, COMPANY, OR LEGAL ENTITY TO THESE TERMS.

1. **Definitions.** "Software" means the software that you obtain from Vendor in binary form and all other machine readable materials that are included with such software or are provided for use with it, including (a) any updates or error corrections provided by Vendor and (b) any user manuals and other documentation provided by Vendor. "Agreement" refers to this End-User License Agreement.

[**Optional Provision.** *Money-Back Guarantee*]

2. [**Sixty-Day Money Back Guarantee.** If you are the original licensee of this copy of the Software and are dissatisfied with it for any reason, you may return the complete product, together with your receipt, to Vendor or an authorized dealer, postage prepaid, for a full refund at any time during the sixty (60) day period following your receipt of the Software.]

   [*Comment: The following text presents two ways to specify the number of permitted copies. One is to simply state a limit in the EULA—often but not always limited to use of a single copy and one backup copy. The other is for the Vendor to issue the customer separately a "License Certificate" that states how many copies can be made.*]

3. **Use.** Under this Agreement, Vendor grants you a non-exclusive license to do the following:

   - [Install and use one copy of the Software on a single computer.] [If Vendor has provided you with a Vendor-issued license certificate ("License Certificate")] that authorizes a different number of copies, then you may make the number of copies of the Software licensed to you by Vendor as provided in your License Certificate;]

   - Make [one copy] [a reasonable number of copies] of the Software for backup and archival purposes only;

   - [Use the Software on a network, provided that you have a licensed copy of the Software for each computer that can access the Software over that network;]

- After written notice to Vendor, transfer the Software on a permanent basis to another person or entity, provided that you retain no copies of the Software and the transferee agrees to the terms of this license; and

- [Use the Software in accordance with any additional permitted uses set forth below.]

[Optional Provision. *Development Use. This provision would apply to software that was a development tool.*]

4. **[Development License Grant.** Subject to the terms and conditions of this Agreement, Vendor grants you a non-exclusive, non-transferable, royalty-free license to use the Software internally for the purpose of designing, developing, and testing your own original software programs. This Agreement does not license you to distribute the Software [except as expressly stated herein].]

[Optional Provision. *Distribution License. This provision is for application development software that includes a distributable "run time" component.*]

5. **[Distribution License Grant.**

- "Run Time Module" means the binary components of the Software designated as the Run Time Module in the Software user documentation that are required for programs created by use of the Software to operate.

- Subject to the terms and conditions of this Agreement, Vendor grants you a non-exclusive, non-transferable, royalty-free license to reproduce and distribute the Run Time Module, provided that (i) you distribute the Run Time Module complete and unmodified and only bundled as part of, and for the sole purpose of running your original software programs, (ii) your original software programs add significant functionality and value, (iii) you do not modify the Run Time Module, (iv) you do not remove or alter any proprietary legends or notices contained in the Run Time Module, (v) you do not distribute the Run Time Module as part of a software or application development program, and (vi) you only distribute the Run Time Module subject to a license agreement that protects Vendor with terms and conditions consistent with the terms contained in this Agreement.

- If you distribute the Run Time Module, you agree to defend, indemnify and hold harmless Vendor, its officers, employees and agents and its licensors from and against any damages, costs, liabilities, settlement amounts and/or expenses (including attorneys' fees) incurred in connection with any claim, lawsuit or action by any third party that arises or results or is alleged to arise or result from the use or distribution of your original software programs and/or the Run Time Module.]

6. **Restrictions.** You may not:

■ Copy the printed documentation that accompanies the Software;

■ Use the Software as part of a facility management, timesharing, service provider, software-as-a-service or service bureau arrangement;

■ Sublicense [(except as expressly permitted with regard to the Run Time Module)], rent, or lease any portion of the Software; reverse engineer, decompile, disassemble, modify, translate, make any attempt to create derivative works from the Software;

■ Use a previous version or copy of the Software after you have received a replacement disk or an upgraded version; or

■ Use the Software in any manner not authorized by this Agreement.

[**Optional Provision.** *Activation*]

7. [**Product Installation and Activation.** The Software contains license management technology that requires activation as stated in the documentation. The Software will only operate for a limited period of time, as stated in the documentation, prior to your activation of the Software. During activation, you will provide Vendor with your unique Vendor-supplied product key accompanying the Software and computer configuration over the Internet to verify the authenticity of the Software. If you do not complete the activation within the specified period of time set forth in the documentation, or as prompted by the Software, the Software will cease to function until activation is complete, which will restore Software functionality. In the event that you are not able to activate the Software over the Internet, or through any other method specified during the activation process, you may contact Vendor customer support using the contact information provided by Vendor.]

[**Optional Provision.** *Copy Management Technology*]

8. [**Copy Management Technology.** This Software may contain license management technology that limits the ability to install and uninstall the Software on a computer to not more than a specified number of times for a specified number of computers. You agree not to disable or circumvent such technology.]

[**Optional Provision.** *Data Gathering for Installation and Updating*]

9. [**Installation and Auto-Update.** The Software's installation and auto-update processes transmit a limited amount of data to Vendor (or its service provider) about those specific processes from your computer to help Vendor understand and optimize them. Vendor does not associate the data with personally identifiable information.]

[**Optional Provision.** *Third Party Software*]

10. [**Third Party Software.** Additional copyright notices and license terms applicable to portions of the Software from third parties may apply. Any such terms can be found [on vendor's web site] [in the user documentation] [in an on-disk text file named "*[filename]*"]. By accepting this Agreement, you also accept the third party terms.]

11. **License Only.** The Software is the property of Vendor or its licensors and is protected by copyright law. You are granted non-exclusive license rights only, which take effect after your acceptance of this license. No right, title or interest is granted except as expressly stated in this Agreement.

12. **Limited Warranty.** [Vendor warrants to you that for a period of ninety (90) days from the date of purchase, as evidenced by a copy of the receipt, the media on which Software is furnished (if any) will be free of defects in materials and workmanship under normal use.] [Vendor warrants to you that: (a) for a period of ninety (90) days from the date of purchase, as evidenced by a copy of the receipt, the Software will function substantially in accord with its applicable documentation and (b) the media on which Software is furnished (if any) will be free of defects in materials and workmanship under normal use.] Except for the foregoing, the Software is provided "AS IS". Your exclusive remedy and Vendor's entire liability under this limited warranty will be at Vendor's option to replace the Software or refund the fee paid for Software. Any implied warranties on the Software are limited to 90 days. Some states do not allow limitations on duration of an implied warranty, so the above may not apply to you. This limited warranty gives you specific legal rights. You may have others, which may vary from state to state.

13. **Disclaimer of Warranty.** EXCEPT AS EXPRESSLY SPECIFIED IN THIS AGREEMENT, ALL EXPRESS OR IMPLIED CONDITIONS, REPRESENTA-TIONS AND WARRANTIES, INCLUDING ANY IMPLIED WARRANTY OF MERCHANTABILITY, FITNESS FOR A PARTICULAR PURPOSE OR NON-INFRINGEMENT, ARE DISCLAIMED, EXCEPT TO THE EXTENT THAT THESE DISCLAIMERS ARE HELD TO BE LEGALLY INVALID.

14. **Limitation of Liability.** TO THE EXTENT NOT PROHIBITED BY LAW, IN NO EVENT WILL VENDOR OR ITS LICENSORS BE LIABLE FOR ANY LOST REVENUE, PROFIT OR DATA, OR FOR SPECIAL, INDIRECT, CONSEQUENTIAL, INCIDENTAL OR PUNITIVE DAMAGES, HOWEVER CAUSED REGARDLESS OF THE THEORY OF LIABILITY, ARISING OUT OF OR RELATED TO THE USE OF OR INABILITY TO USE SOFTWARE, EVEN IF VENDOR HAS BEEN ADVISED OF THE POSSIBILITY OF SUCH DAMAGES. In no event will Vendor's liability to you, whether in contract, tort (including negligence), or otherwise, exceed the amount paid by you for Software under this Agreement. The foregoing limitations will apply even if the above stated warranty fails of its essential purpose. Some states do not allow the exclusion of incidental or consequential damages, so some of the terms above may not be applicable to you.

15. **Termination.** This Agreement is effective until terminated. You may terminate this Agreement at any time by destroying all copies of Software. This Agreement will terminate immediately without notice from Vendor if you fail to comply with any provision of this Agreement. Either party may terminate this Agreement immediately should any Software become, or in either party's opinion be likely to become, the subject of a claim of infringement of any intellectual property right. Upon termination, all license grants end and you must destroy all copies of Software and cease all use.

16. **Export Regulations.** All Software and technical data delivered under this Agreement are subject to U.S. export control laws and may be subject to export or import regulations in other countries. You agree to comply with all such laws and regulations.

17. **U.S. Government Restricted Rights.** If Software is being acquired by or on behalf of the U.S. Government or by a U.S. Government prime contractor or subcontractor (at any tier), then the Government's rights in Software and accompanying documentation will be only as set forth in this Agreement; this is in accordance with 48 CFR 227.7201 through 227.7202-4 (for Department

of Defense (DOD) acquisitions) and with 48 CFR 2.101 and 12.212 (for non-DOD acquisitions).

*[**Comment:** You may want to select arbitration to resolve any disputes. Here is some suggested text on that subject.]*

18. **[Binding Arbitration.** You agree that any disputes or claims that arise from this Agreement or its subject matter will be (except as stated below) finally and exclusively resolved by binding arbitration. Any election to arbitrate by one party shall bind the other. The arbitration shall be conducted under the Commercial Arbitration Rules of the American Arbitration Association ("AAA") (available on the AAA web site www.adr.org) before a single arbitrator conducted in *[specific location]*. The decision will be final and binding. YOU UNDERSTAND THAT ABSENT THIS PROVISION, YOU WOULD HAVE THE RIGHT TO SUE IN COURT AND HAVE THE RIGHT TO A JURY TRIAL. Each party reserves the right to seek temporary, preliminary and final injunctive relief in court in cases for which such relief applies under applicable law.]

19. **Governing Law.** Any action related to this Agreement will be governed by the law of the State of _____ and controlling U.S. federal law. No choice of law rules of any jurisdiction will apply. Exclusive jurisdiction and venue for any claim regarding this Agreement or its subject matter will lie in the state and federal courts located in _____, USA [except that any arbitration decision may be enforced in any court of law with jurisdiction over the party against which enforcement is sought]. The provisions of the United Nations Convention on the International Sale of Goods do not apply.

20. **Severability.** If any provision of this Agreement is held to be unenforceable, this Agreement will remain in effect with the provision omitted, unless omission would frustrate the intent of the parties, in which case this Agreement will immediately terminate.

21. **Usage Limitations.** You acknowledge that Software is not designed or intended for use in the design, construction, operation or maintenance of any nuclear facility or any other use that may affect individual health and safety. Vendor disclaims any express or implied warranty of fitness for such uses.

22. **Entire Agreement.** This Agreement is the entire agreement between you and Vendor relating to its subject matter. It supersedes all prior or contemporaneous oral or written communications, proposals, representations and warranties

and prevails over any conflicting or additional terms of any quote, order, acknowledgment, or other communication between the parties relating to its subject matter during the term of this Agreement. No modification of this Agreement will be binding, unless in writing and signed by an authorized representative of each party.

Web Site Terms of Use

Introductory Note

This is a sample of web site terms of use. It is written for the fictitious company WebCo, Inc.

Terms of use are not generic; they need to be customized to each web site; so this form may need to be modified for your own web site. Terms of use need to take into account:

- *The technology and functionality of the site.*

- *The content that is available on or through the site.*

- *The interaction of users with the site or its other users.*

- *Other user-oriented documents on the site, such as the copyright policy (see Form 3-1), content guidelines (see Form 17-1), weblog rules (see Form 17-3) and privacy policy (see Form 18-1).*

- *Applicable state and federal law.*

Optional language is bracketed. Underlined terms in the text should be hyperlinked to the content that they refer to.

WebCo Terms of Use

Welcome to the WebCo Site (the "Site"). These Terms of Use govern your use of the Site and its contents. The terms "WebCo," "we," "us" and "our" refer to WebCo, Inc.

BY USING THE SITE, YOU AGREE TO THESE TERMS OF USE, THE WEBCO <u>PRIVACY STATEMENT</u>, AND THE WEBCO <u>COMMUNITY GUIDELINES</u> AND YOU AGREE TO RECEIVE REQUIRED NOTICES AND TO TRANSACT WITH US ELECTRONICALLY. IF YOU DO NOT AGREE, PLEASE DO NOT USE THE SITE.

1. **Registration**

You must register on this Site in order to use certain of the Site functions, such as our blogs. If you just want to browse this Site, registration is optional.

During registration, you will be required to provide contact information, consisting of an email address, username and password. You can select any username as you like, except that your username cannot be an impersonation of another person, a term that is the same or confusingly similar to a famous trademark, or a term that is offensive in any way. You may, but are not obligated to, use your own name. If you do use your own name, you consent to it being passed to others by use of certain of the functions of WebCo and the Site such as our blogs. WebCo reserves the right to reject or remove any username.

For certain of our functions, such as the purchase of products and services, you are required to provide your name, address and billing and credit card information. You are required to provide accurate and complete information.

> [**Comment:** *The following provisions on age of users serve two functions. By banning users under 13 the Site seeks to comply with the Children's Online Privacy Protection Act or COPPA discussed in Chapter 18. Its provisions regarding children 13 to 18 deal with the fact that, under US state law, persons under 18 cannot make binding contracts. This form assumes that there is no content that is unsuitable for children 13 to 18 on the Site.*]

2. **Age of Users**

Children under the age of 13 may not use this Service and parents or legal guardians may not agree to these Terms of Use on their behalf. If we become aware that a child under 13 has provided or attempted to provide us with personal information, we will use our best efforts to remove the information permanently from our files.

If you are under the age of 18 but at least 13 years of age, you may use this Site only under the supervision of a parent or legal guardian who agrees to be bound by these Terms of Use. If you are a parent or legal guardian agreeing to these Terms of Use for the benefit of a child between the ages of 13 and 18, be advised that you are fully responsible for his or her use of this Site, including all financial charges and legal liability that he or she may incur.

3. **Non-Commercial Use**

This Site and its contents are for your own personal non-commercial use only.

4. Additional Terms and Conditions for Software; EULAs

When you [download and/or install and use WebCo's downloadable software] [register for or purchase the Site's services], you will be required to agree to one or more End-User License Agreements (or "EULAs") which may include additional terms. You will be bound by any EULA that you agree to.

5. WebCo Privacy Statement

Your use of this Site signifies your continuing consent to the WebCo <u>Privacy Statement</u>, which you can examine any time by clicking on the "Privacy" link on the Site.

Personal information that you supply to WebCo, and any information about your use of WebCo that we obtain will be subject to the WebCo <u>Privacy Statement</u> on this Site.

6. Changes to WebCo

We may discontinue or change any WebCo content, service, function or feature at any time with or without notice.

7. Proper Use of This Site

When you use our blogs or other social and communications functions, you agree at all times to comply with the WebCo <u>Community Guidelines</u>, which you may access with the <u>Community Guidelines</u> link on the Site. You may use WebCo for lawful purposes only and may use the Site only in ways consistent with the law.

You may not use any program, spider or "bot" to gather or "harvest" information from this Site.

8. Proprietary Rights

WebCo and its suppliers reserve all rights under intellectual property law in WebCo and in any content that is on the Site.

Except as WebCo may expressly state in writing, you may not reproduce, reprint, publish, or otherwise exploit content or technology from WebCo or its suppliers on the Site without our express prior written consent.

9. Changes to the Terms of Use

We may change the Terms of Use at any time. You can review the most current version of the Terms of Use by clicking on the Site's "Terms of Use" link. If you continue to use this Site after we make changes to the Terms of Use, you are signifying your acceptance of the new terms. You are responsible for checking these terms periodically for any changes.

10. **Electronic Delivery Statement and Your Consent**

You agree that we may provide to you notices and other information concerning WebCo or this Site electronically, including notice to any email address that you may provide.

11. **Content That You Supply**

WebCo may allow you to supply content for the Site or its functions that can be accessed and viewed by others. You agree not to post any content that violates these terms, any applicable EULA or the Community Guidelines. Content that violates applicable rules may be removed.

If you post any content on any blog or other public area of the Site, you grant us and our affiliate companies the perpetual sublicensable right and license to use, copy, display, perform, distribute, modify, adapt, abridge, exploit, and promote this content in any way and in any commercial or non-commercial medium or form without charge.

12. **No Duty to Monitor**

You agree that we are not liable for content that is provided by others. We have no duty to screen content that you may supply or post, but we have the right to refuse to post or to edit submitted content. We reserve the right to remove any content for any reason at any time.

13. **Third Party Sites and Advertisers**

WebCo may include on its Site links to third party web sites. You agree that we are not responsible or liable for any content or other materials on third party sites. You also agree that we are not responsible for content or claims supplied by our advertisers. We are also not responsible for any transactions or dealings between you and any third party or any advertiser. You agree that WebCo is not responsible for any claim or loss due to a third party site or any advertiser.

14. **Disclaimer of Warranties**

We provide this Site and its contents "AS IS." We and our suppliers make no express warranties or guarantees about this Site. TO THE EXTENT PERMITTED BY LAW, WE AND OUR SUPPLIERS DISCLAIM IMPLIED WARRANTIES

INCLUDING ANY WARRANTY THAT THE SITE IS OR WILL BE MERCHANT-ABLE, OF SATISFACTORY QUALITY, ACCURATE, TIMELY, FIT FOR A PARTICULAR PURPOSE OR NEED, OR NON-INFRINGING. WE DO NOT GUARANTEE THAT THIS SITE OR ITS CONTENT WILL MEET YOUR REQUIREMENTS, IS ERROR-FREE, RELIABLE, OR WILL OPERATE WITHOUT INTERRUPTION. Because some states do not permit disclaimer of implied warranties, you may have additional consumer rights under your local laws.

15. Limitation of Liability

You may not assert claims for money damages arising from this Site or its contents. We and our suppliers shall not be liable for any indirect, special, incidental, consequential or exemplary damages, even if we knew or should have known of the possibility of such damages. Because some states or jurisdictions do not allow the exclusion or the limitation of liability for consequential or incidental damages, in such states or jurisdictions, our liability, and the liability of our company and suppliers, shall be limited to the extent permitted by law.

16. Indemnification

You agree to defend, indemnify, and hold harmless us and our parent and other affiliated companies, and our respective employees, contractors, officers, directors, and agents from all liabilities, claims, and expenses, including attorney's fees, that arise from your use or misuse of this Site. We reserve the right, at our own expense, to assume the exclusive defense and control of any matter otherwise subject to indemnification by you, in which event you will cooperate with us in asserting any available defenses.

17. International Use

We make no representation that content on this Site is appropriate or available for use in locations outside the United States. If you choose to access this Site from a location outside the US, you do so on your own initiative and you are responsible for compliance with local laws.

18. Choice of Law and Location for Resolving Disputes

You agree that the laws of the state of _____ USA and US federal law govern these terms of use, its subject matter, your use of the Site, and any claim or dispute that you may have against us, without regard to its conflict of laws rules, and that the United Nations Convention on Contracts for the International Sale of Goods shall have no applicability.

[You further agree that any disputes or claims that you may have against us will be resolved by a court located in the state of _____USA in the city of _____, and you agree and submit to the exercise of personal jurisdiction of such courts for the purpose of litigating any such claim or action. BY AGREEING TO THESE TERMS OF USE, YOU ARE: (1) WAIVING CLAIMS THAT YOU MIGHT OTHERWISE HAVE AGAINST US BASED ON THE LAWS OF OTHER JURISDICTIONS, INCLUDING YOUR OWN; (2) IRREVOCABLY CONSENTING TO THE EXCLUSIVE JURISDICTION OF, AND VENUE IN, THE STATE OR FEDERAL COURTS IN THE STATE OF _____ OVER ANY DISPUTES OR CLAIMS YOU HAVE WITH US; AND (3) SUBMITTING YOURSELF TO THE PERSONAL JURISDICTION OF SUCH COURTS FOR THE PURPOSE OF RESOLVING ANY SUCH DISPUTES OR CLAIMS.]

> [**Comment:** *You may want to select arbitration to resolve any disputes with users. Be aware that (as discussed in Chapter 16), the courts have sometimes declined to enforce these arbitration clauses because arbitration fees are too high or because the location is inconvenient. The following text seeks to provide means to manage both issues—by providing the arbitrator the right to allocate the fees to WebCo and permitting the arbitration to be done by phone or online.]*

19. [Binding Arbitration

You agree that any disputes or claims that you may have against us will be (except as stated below) finally and exclusively resolved by binding arbitration. Any election to arbitrate by one party shall be final and binding on the other. The arbitration shall be commenced and conducted under the Commercial Arbitration Rules of the American Arbitration Association ("AAA") and, where appropriate, the AAA's Supplementary Procedures for Consumer Related Disputes ("AAA Consumer Rules"), both of which are available that the AAA web site www.adr.org. The determination of whether a dispute is subject to arbitration shall be governed by the Federal Arbitration Act and determined by a court rather than an arbitrator. Your arbitration fees and your share of arbitrator compensation shall be governed by the AAA Rules and, where appropriate, limited by the AAA Consumer Rules. If such costs are determined by the arbitrator to be excessive, WebCo will pay all arbitration fees and expenses. The arbitration may be conducted in person, through the submission of documents, by phone or online. The arbitrator will make a decision in writing, and will provide a statement of reasons if requested by a party. Except as otherwise provided in this Agreement, you and WebCo may litigate in court to compel arbitration, stay proceeding pending arbitration, or to confirm, modify, vacate or enter judgment on the award entered by the arbitrator. YOU UNDERSTAND THAT ABSENT THIS PROVISION, YOU WOULD HAVE THE RIGHT TO SUE IN COURT AND HAVE THE RIGHT TO A JURY TRIAL.]

20. Severability and Integration

This contract and any supplemental terms, policies, rules and guidelines posted on this Site constitute the entire agreement between you and us and supersede all previous written or oral agreements. If any part of the Terms of Use is held invalid or unenforceable, that portion shall be construed in a manner consistent with applicable law to reflect, as nearly as possible, the original intentions of the parties, and the remaining portions shall remain in full force and effect.

21. Termination

We reserve the right to terminate your use of this Site if you violate the Terms of Use or any rules or guidelines posted on the Site or for any other reason in our discretion.

> [**Comment:** *The following Section refers to the "Notice-and-Take-Down" copyright infringement "safe harbor" under the Digital Millennium Copyright Act. See Chapter 3 for details. This underlined text should have a link to the site's form of notification under those rules. (See Form 3-1).]*

22. Claims of Copyright Infringement

If you believe that your work has been copied and is accessible on this Site in a way that constitutes copyright infringement, please follow the <u>instructions</u> on how to contact us to report possible copyright infringement. See the <u>Copyright</u> link on our home page.

Revision Date: _____

Copyright © *[year]* WebCo, Inc. All Rights Reserved.

Content Guidelines

Introductory Note

This is a simple form for use on a web site that allows users to chat, blog or otherwise communicate with each other or the world. As written it is for WebCo, a fictitious Internet company. It is customary to include in any such site a set of guidelines for online good behavior. The terms of use for the web site should refer to and contain a link to these guidelines, so that their observance becomes part of the contractual agreement under which the user accesses and uses the web site and its functionality. You may want a link to these guidelines from each web page.

This form can be modified for particular web sites to address the user behaviors and issues that are of most concern.

Online Community Guidelines

About WebCo's Online Community

The WebCo online community consists of all those people that use the online resources of the WebCo web site (the "Site") to exchange information, content and ideas. The community will thrive based on mutual respect and consideration. Your use of Site and its resources is subject to these Guidelines. We can change these Guidelines at any time by posting the changed version on the Site.

Here are rules that apply to the Site and its resources for the purpose of making our community better:

No Objectionable Content. You should not supply or post any content or message that is abusive, belligerent, slanderous, racist, vulgar or sexually explicit or otherwise offensive. Never use the Site or its resources to insult or attack other persons. Don't write in all capital letters; it is considered shouting and it is also harder to read. You should not promote or encourage illegal conduct.

No Commercial Activities. You may not use the Site or its functions to promote your own or any other business or commercial activity. Do not make offers to buy or sell using the Site or its resources. You may not attempt to drive traffic to any other site for commercial gain. You may not promote or run any contest, chain letter, investment opportunity, or any other form of solicitation or pyramid scheme by means of the Site or its resources.

Truthful Dealings. Any information that you supply should be true to the best of your knowledge. You should not use any false identity and should not claim false credentials.

Respecting Privacy of Others. You should not disclose the name, address or other personal information about third parties without their express permission. You should not encourage or request others to disclose personally identifying information.

Age Restriction. Children under the age of 13 are not permitted to register on this Site or use any functionality for which registration is required. You should not permit or encourage any violation of this rule.

Titles for Posting. Please give your posts a meaningful title so that members and visitors do not spend time reading posts about things they have no interest in. Make your title descriptive, reflecting the topic you are addressing, rather than a generic title such as "Question" or "I Need Help."

Legal Compliance; No Illegal Filesharing. You may use the Site and its resources only in full accordance with applicable law. In particular, you should never post or exchange content, data, or files that infringe any third party copyright, trademark or other proprietary rights. Unauthorized sharing of copyrighted content is not permitted.

No Hacking or Spamming. You may not circumvent any Site protections and safeguards, and you may not redirect messages and communication to other sites. You should never use the Site's functionality for unauthorized mail or messages or any form of "spamming."

Password Security. Keep your password private. You should not share your account with others.

Violations and Reports

Feel free to report violations or abuse. Contact WebCo at the following email address: *[insert email address for reporting]*.

WebCo does not monitor content that is exchanged or posted by means of WebCo. However, we reserve the right to remove any content that we determine, in our sole discretion, to be inappropriate. We also may remove any content or activity in violation of these rules or the Site Terms or Use. We may terminate any user account or any user's access to the Site and its functionality if we believe that there has been any violation.

Weblog Rules

Introductory Note

This is a web site form to set user rules for a weblog or "blog" for the fictitious company WebCo, Inc. This form is for use in addition to the web site's terms of use and privacy policy. Your company's web site should have a link from the page in which users read blogs or access blog functionality to these weblog rules. Weblog rules may need to be customized to take account of the content and subject matter of the web log.

Underlined terms in the text should be hyperlinks to other legal materials on the Web site, specifically to the site terms of use and the DMCA notice and take-down disclosure.

WebCo Weblog Terms of Use

Your Agreement to These Terms of Use

The WebCo Site provides weblogs or "blogs" ("Weblogs") for exchange of information and opinions. The following are the terms of use of the Weblogs ("Weblog Terms").

By accessing or viewing a Weblog, contributing any content, or participating in a Weblog in any way, you agree to these Weblog Terms. These Weblog Terms are subject to the <u>Terms of Use</u> that apply for the WebCo Site generally. Please read these Weblog Terms and the Terms of Use carefully. If you do not want to be subject to any of these terms and conditions, do not read, use, or contribute to the Weblogs.

WebCo Contributions

WebCo may contribute content (each a "WebCo Contribution"). WebCo Contributions belong to WebCo and are subject to WebCo's copyright ownership. **1043**

You are permitted to access WebCo Contributions through the Internet. You can save, display, and print a copy of WebCo Contributions for your own personal use only. You may not otherwise copy, transmit, publish, distribute, display or in any way exploit any WebCo Contributions.

If any WebCo Contribution is provided by a named employee or agent of WebCo, then, unless otherwise expressly stated, the statements and opinions expressed in such WebCo Contribution are those of the *author only* and are not the statements or opinions of WebCo or its management.

User Registration Required for Contributors

WebCo requires users who wish to contribute to a Weblog (each a "Contributor") to register. You may register to be a Contributor by choosing a username and password. You are not required to provide your true name or any identifying information. However you may not choose a username that is misleading or that misidentifies you as another person. Your username may not be indecent or offensive. Registration is not required to access and read the content of the Weblogs.

WebCo reserves the right to remove the user registration for any person for any reason.

User Contributions

By posting content to any Weblog (each a "User Contribution"), you grant WebCo a non-exclusive, royalty-free, perpetual, and worldwide license to such User Contribution. This license includes the perpetual right for WebCo to post the User Contribution in any Weblog and to copy, archive, distribute, abridge, transmit, display, edit, translate and reformat any User Contribution, and/or to incorporate it into a collective work, database or archive.

You agree not to provide any User Contribution that is illegal, misleading, defamatory, indecent or obscene, in poor taste, threatening, infringing of any third party proprietary rights, invasive of personal privacy, or otherwise objectionable. By posting any User Contribution, you represent that you have all required rights and permissions to do so.

You are not required to include any information in any User Contribution that identifies you. If you choose to provide personal identifying information, you do so at your own risk.

WebCo reserves the right not to post or to remove any User Contribution from any Weblog for any reason. WebCo may, but is not required to, screen content before posting or use. WebCo may limit the length of User Contributions.

Non-Commercial Use

The Weblogs are for non-commercial use only. You agree not to provide any Contribution that includes a request for money or contains any promotion, advertising, or any solicitation involving goods or services. You agree not to solicit other users of Weblogs to join any organization. You will not solicit or collect personal data about Contributors or other users. You may not claim that WebCo endorses you, your activities, your business, or your User Contributions.

Third-Party Sites and Links

Links to third party Internet sites will be in WebCo Contributions and in many User Contributions. WebCo does not approve or endorse the contents of any third party site or data that may be reached by means of any link. WebCo has no control over such third party sites, and WebCo is not responsible for any content on such sites.

No Guarantee Regarding WebCo Contributions or User Contributions

WebCo assumes no responsibility for the accuracy, completeness, or usefulness of information in any material in any Weblog, including any WebCo Contributions and any User Contributions. WebCo does not approve or endorse any statements, opinions or recommendations in any WebCo Contributions and any User Contributions.

WebCo grants no license to any user of any Weblog under any patent, trademark, trade secret, copyright or any other intellectual property right, except for the permissions to view and print WebCo Contributions as expressly stated above.

No Robots and Spiders

Use of Weblogs is for participants and readers only. You agree not to use any automated means, including, without limitation, agents, robots, scripts, or spiders, to access, monitor or copy any part of any Weblog. This provision does not prevent you from using RSS feeds provided in the WebCo Site. Weblogs may be indexed by search engines that survey the Web and are available to the public generally.

Indemnification

You agree to indemnify, defend and hold harmless WebCo, its subsidiaries, and their officers, directors, owners, employees, and agents from and against any and all liability, losses, costs and expenses (including attorneys' fees) incurred by any of them in connection with any claim arising out of any User Contribution that you provide, your violation of these Weblog Terms, or your violation of the Terms of Use that apply for the WebCo Site generally.

Disclaimers and Exclusions of Warranties

THE WEBLOGS AND THEIR CONTENTS ARE PROVIDED "AS IS." WEBCO MAKES NO WARRANTIES OF ANY KIND. INACCURACIES OR MISTAKES ARE POSSIBLE. WEBCO DOES NOT WARRANT THAT THE WEBLOGS AND THEIR CONTENT WILL MEET YOUR REQUIREMENTS OR WILL BE UNINTERRUPTED OR ERROR FREE. WEBCO EXPRESSLY EXCLUDES AND DISCLAIMS ALL EXPRESS AND IMPLIED WARRANTIES OF MERCHANTABILITY, FITNESS FOR A PARTICULAR PURPOSE AND NON-INFRINGEMENT OF ANY THIRD PARTY INTELLECTUAL PROPERTY RIGHTS. WEBCO SHALL NOT BE RESPONSIBLE FOR ANY DAMAGE OR LOSS OF ANY KIND ARISING OUT OF OR RELATED TO YOUR USE OF THE WEBLOGS OR THEIR CONTENT.

Limitation of Liability

IN NO EVENT SHALL WEBCO OR ITS SUPPLIERS BE LIABLE FOR ANY SPECIAL, INCIDENTAL, PUNITIVE, MULTIPLE, INDIRECT OR CONSEQUENTIAL DAMAGES OF ANY KIND, EVEN IF WEBCO HAS BEEN ADVISED OF THE POSSIBILITY OF SUCH DAMAGES, AND REGARDLESS OF THE FORM OF ACTION.

Compliance with Law

You agree that your use of any Weblog will comply with all applicable laws, rules and regulations.

Changes to Terms of Use

WebCo reserves the right to make changes to these Weblog Terms at any time. Your continued access to, viewing, contribution to, or other use of any Weblog will constitute your acceptance of any new terms and conditions.

Privacy Policy

To see WebCo's privacy policies, click <u>here</u>.

Copyright Complaints

If you believe that your work has appeared on any Weblog in a manner that infringes a copyright, please follow our <u>procedures</u> for reporting copyright infringements.

Revision Date: _____

Copyright © 20__ by WebCo, Inc.

Privacy Policy

Introductory Note

This is a sample privacy policy. The form is for WebCo, a fictitious web enterprise which we have provided with a hypothetical set of technologies and policies that are reflected in the following text. Those technologies and policies may be different from those that apply to your own company; so this form can be used as a checklist and starting point, but each privacy policy needs to be customized.

For more information, please review the discussion of privacy issues in Chapter 18.

WebCo Privacy Policy

Effective on: [DATE]

WebCo, Inc. ("WebCo") knows that you care how information about you is used and shared. This notice describes WebCo's privacy policy for our web site (the "Site") including all online services and functions.

Registration

You must register on this Site in order to use certain of the Site's online services and functions, such as our blogs. If you just want to browse the Site, registration is optional.

During registration, you will be required to provide contact information, consisting of an email address, username and password.

You can select any username you want, except that your username cannot be an impersonation, the same or confusingly similar to a famous trademark, or be a term that is offensive in any way. You may, but are not obligated to, use your own name. If you do use your own name, you consent to it being passed to others by use of the functions of the Site. WebCo reserves the right to reject or remove any username that does not meet applicable standards.

Cookies

A cookie is a small text file that is stored on a user's computer for record-keeping purposes. WebCo use cookies on the Site.

WebCo uses both "session ID cookies" and "persistent cookies." WebCo uses session cookies to make it easier for you to navigate the Site. A session ID cookie expires when you close your browser. If you check "remember me on this computer" when logging in to the Site, WebCo also sets a persistent cookie to store your username passwords, so you do not have to enter it more than once. The persistent cookie also enables WebCo to track and target the interests of users to enhance the experience on the Site. The persistent cookie is removed when you uncheck the "remember my email address" check box.

Your web browser allows you to control and limit cookies on your computer. If you reject cookies, you may still use the Site, but your ability to use some areas or functions of the Site may be limited.

Some of WebCo's business partners (such as advertisers) use cookies on the Site. WebCo has no access to or control over these cookies. This privacy policy covers the use of cookies by WebCo only and does not cover the use of cookies by any advertisers.

Email from WebCo for Newsletters and Announcements

WebCo may use your username and email address to provide you with email newsletters and announcements. If you do not wish to receive these kinds of communications, you can opt out by unchecking the email newsletters and announcements boxes during registration. WebCo also offers you the option to unsubscribe from newsletters and announcements by return email or by changing your profile on the Customer Profile page on the Site.

Product Information and Offers

The email address information that you provide on the Site may be used to contact you about other product and service offers from WebCo. WebCo may also use that information to let you know of additional products and services from other companies that you might be interested in. If you do not wish to receive these kinds of communications, you can opt out by unchecking the appropriate email offer announcements boxes during registration. In addition, you can choose not to receive such information by opting-out on the Customer Profile page on the Site.

Significant Announcements by Email

WebCo may also use your registered name and email address to provide you with significant announcements about Site functions or services that you are registered to use, about this Site, about any user account you may create, about fulfillment of a specific transaction you have requested, or about other significant developments that may affect your use of the Site. You cannot opt-out of this kind of email.

Additional Information for Specific Purposes

This Site may request additional information from you on product order forms or other online transaction forms. Such forms may require you to provide contact information (such as name and mailing or shipping address) and payment information (such as credit card number and credit card expiration date). Information that you provide in this way may be used for billing and accounting purposes, for recording products and services that you have licensed, bought or downloaded, and to fill your orders. WebCo may use this contact information to communicate about orders, products, services, or fees or charges.

WebCo may use an outside shipping company to ship orders and uses a credit card processing company to process payments for goods and services. These companies have access to user information in order to perform their functions.

WebCo may partner with other third parties to provide specific goods or services. When you sign up for such goods or services, WebCo will share names or other contact information that is necessary for the third party to provide these goods or services. WebCo does not authorize third party providers to use personally identifiable information except for the purpose related to these goods or services.

Communications with Others

The Site may allow you to contribute to one or more blogs or communicate by means of online functions.

Nothing requires you to disclose your identity to others. If you choose to disclose your identity to third parties using any Site function or service, you do so at your own risk. WebCo is not responsible for the privacy or security of any information, personal or otherwise that you may choose to communicate or exchange using the functionality of the Site.

Each item of information or any materials you contribute for such purposes is your "Public Content." Public Content must be content and information that you have a right to disclose and transfer and must not violate any other person's privacy or intellectual property rights.

Feedback to WebCo

WebCo has feedback functionality on the Site that allows you to submit comments, suggestions, or bugs found. WebCo may collect your name or username and email address in order to follow up with you or thank you for a suggestion.

Anonymous Data

WebCo may track the Site to analyze trends, administer the Site, track your actions and use of the Site, record transactions, and gather demographic information for aggregate use. Such analysis is not linked to personally identifiable information.

WebCo may share aggregated demographic and usage information with its partners and advertisers. This aggregated information is not linked to any personal information that can identify any individual person.

Links

This Site may contain links to other sites. WebCo is not responsible for the privacy practices of such other sites. WebCo encourages users to be aware when they leave the Site and to read the privacy statements of sites that collect personally identifiable information. This privacy policy applies only to information collected on this Site.

Security Technology

When a Site's registration/order form asks users to enter financial information (such as credit card number), that information is encrypted and is protected during transmission through the Internet using Secure Socket Layer (SSL) software. You should see the lock icon on the bottom of web browsers such as Microsoft Internet Explorer becomes locked, as opposed to unlocked or open when you are just surfing. If you have any questions about the security, you can send an email to *[add email address for queries.]*.

Correction/Updating of Personal Information

If you provide personally identifiable information changes (such as an email address or zip code), WebCo will endeavor to provide a way to correct, update or remove your personal data. This can usually be done at the Customer Profile page.

Protection of Minors

Children under the age of 13 are not permitted to register on this Site or use any functionality for which registration is required.

Business or Asset Transfer or Sale

WebCo may be sold, might sell or buy businesses or assets of businesses, or WebCo might merge with another business. In such transactions, customer information generally is one of the transferred business assets. Also, in the event that WebCo, a line of business of WebCo, or substantially all the assets of WebCo are transferred, customer information may well be one of the transferred assets. WebCo will make reasonable effort to provide notice on the Site and to notify you via email to the most recent email address that you have provided to WebCo of any such change in ownership or control of your personal information.

Release of Information for Legal Reasons

WebCo may release information concerning your use of WebCo (including, but not limited to, posted Public Content, registration information, and network records) when it believes in good faith that such release is appropriate to comply with the law (for example, pursuant to a statutory demand, subpoena, warrant or court order), to protect against fraudulent, abusive or unlawful use of the WebCo, to protect WebCo's rights or property, enforce any contract between you and WebCo, or if WebCo reasonably believes that a situation involving danger of death or injury to any person requires disclosure.

Limited Use

WebCo does not intend to sell, share, or rent information obtained on this Site other than as discussed in this privacy policy.

Changes in This Privacy Policy

If WebCo decides to change its privacy policy, WebCo will post those changes on WebCo's Site so WebCo's users can remain aware of what information WebCo collects, how WebCo uses it, and under what circumstances, if any, WebCo discloses it.

Your California Privacy Rights

Residents of the State of California, under the California Civil Code, have the right to request from companies conducting business in California a list of all third parties to which the Company has disclosed personal information during the preceding year for direct marketing purposes and a disclosure of the shared information. Alternatively, the law provides that if the company has a privacy policy that provides you with an "opt-out" choice for use of your personal information by third parties for marketing purposes, the Company may instead provide you with information on how to exercise your disclosure choice options.

This Site qualifies for the alternative option. Its privacy policy provides you with information on how you may opt-out from the use of your personal information by third parties for direct marketing purposes. Therefore, we are not required to maintain or disclose a list of the third parties that received your personal information during the preceding year for marketing purposes.

If you are a California resident and request information about how to exercise your third party disclosure choices, send a request to the following email address: *[provide email address for queries]*

Release for Video, Images and Music

Introductory Note

This is a simple form for clearance for content such as video, images, music and other items supplied to a company for non-exclusive use. The form is written to be used as a signed agreement, but could easily be adapted as a "clickwrap" on a web site for uploaded content. This form is for content provided without consideration, but could be adapted to add a license fee.

An agreement for clearance of this type is traditionally called a "release."

Content Release

This agreement ("Agreement") is a binding contract between *[name of entity]* ("Company") and me (the undersigned) as follows:

1. **Materials.** This Agreement applies to all video, images, photographs, mixed media or multimedia works, music, text, and other forms of content, information, data or copyrighted materials that I may supply, provide, upload or submit or provide to Company (collectively "Materials") [including those listed on Schedule A].

2. **License.** I hereby grant Company an irrevocable, unconditional, worldwide, royalty-free, sublicensable, transferable, non-exclusive license to use, reproduce, distribute, publish, prepare derivative works of, display, perform and otherwise exploit the Materials or any part thereof in perpetuity in any and all media (existing or later created or made available) and in any manner as the Company may determine or authorize in its discretion.

3. **Name and Likeness.** In connection with the Material, I grant the Company irrevocable, unconditional, worldwide, royalty-free license to use my name,

1055

likeness, image, voice, and biographical information in connection with the Material (including, if applicable, my voice or image in the Material), including without limitation, the distribution and promotion of any works made with or including the Materials as permitted in this Agreement.

4. **Restriction.** I agree that I will not submit any material that is copyrighted by third parties, protected by trade secret or otherwise subject to third party proprietary rights, including privacy and publicity rights, unless I am the owner of such rights or have express written permission from the rightful owner of such rights to supply such material and to grant Company all of the license rights granted herein. I will provide the Company with copies of such written permissions upon request.

5. **Warranty.** I represent and warrant that I own or have the necessary licenses, rights, consents, and permissions to use and authorize Company to use all copyright, patent, trademark, trade secret, or other proprietary rights in and to any and all Materials required for all the licenses that I grant in this Agreement. I hereby waive all so-called "moral rights" or other similar rights in such Materials to the maximum extent permitted by law. I represent and warrant that use of such Materials is not subject to any payment obligation to any third party, including, without limitation, for any actors, musicians, artists, or performers union or guild.

6. **Consideration.** I understand and agree that this Agreement is made in consideration of the resources and efforts that the Company expends to store and evaluate the Material for its potential use and other good and valuable consideration, the receipt and adequacy of which is hereby acknowledged.

7. **No Obligation to Use.** I acknowledge that Company is under no obligation to use the Materials.

8. **Indemnity.** I hereby agree to indemnify and hold harmless the Company, its officers, directors, employees, and agents from any or other rights and licenses granted by this Agreement actual or alleged claims that arise from licensed use of the Materials, including, without limitation, any claim of infringement, defamation, or any breach of my representations and warranties.

9. **Jurisdiction; No Injunction.** This Agreement is governed by the laws of the state of _____ and applicable US federal law. Exclusive jurisdiction and venue for any claim arising from this Agreement or its subject matters will lie in the state and federal courts located in _____. I acknowledge that, in the event of a

breach of this Agreement by Company or any third party, the damage or harm, if any, caused to me will not entitle me to seek injunctive or other equitable relief, and I will not have the right to enjoin the production, exhibition, distribution or other exploitation of the Materials under any circumstances.

10. **General.** This Agreement is the entire agreement of the parties. This Agreement inures to the benefit of and binds the parties' heirs, successors, representatives, and assigns.

I have read this Agreement and I understand and agree to its terms and conditions:

Signed: _____

Print or Type Name: _____

Address: _____

_____

Date: _____

Age: _____

Email: _____

Parent or Guardian's Consent. (If the party providing this Agreement is a minor)

I represent that I am either the parent (with sole or shared custody, as applicable) or the legal guardian of the minor child (the "Minor") whose name appears above and that I have the legal capacity to enter into the irrevocable, binding agreements on behalf of the Minor. The Minor and I, both individually, and additionally, I, on behalf of the Minor and as the Minor's parent or legal guardian, agree to be bound by all the provisions of this Agreement and I guarantee all the Minor's obligations and duties under the Agreement.

Signed: _____

Print or Type Name: _____

Address: _____

_____

Date: _____

Email: _____

Agreed to by *[Company Name]*

By its authorized representative

Signed: _____

Print or Type Name: _____

Address: _____

_____

Date: _____

[**Schedule A**

List of Materials

[To be supplied]]

Right of Personality Release and Permission

Introductory Note

This is a simple form that is used to secure permission from an individual whose image, voice or name is to be used in a digital multimedia or audiovisual work. An agreement for clearance of this type is traditionally called a "release."

This is a form that you would use for persons that appear without pay (or for nominal pay) in an informal video, such as a street scene. This form is not intended for situations in which payment is based on sales of products or services; you should see your legal counsel if you need to contract for personality rights or endorsements from celebrities for pay.

This form is written to include permissions under rights of privacy and personality. It also includes copyright clearance, because there is a possibility that the subject may have contributed to the creation of the work such as making changes to a script, directing or in some other manner.

The grant of rights, which is quite broad in this form, may be narrowed, if appropriate. For example the use could be limited in time or reuse rights could be restricted. Bracketed language is optional.

Right of Personality Release Agreement

For one dollar and other valuable consideration, the sufficiency and receipt of which is hereby acknowledged, I, the undersigned, hereby stipulate and agree with *[name of entity]* ("Company") as follows:

1. **Attributes of Personality.** I hereby irrevocably agree and consent to the use and distribution of my name, voice, image, likeness, and any and all attributes of my personality:

1.1. In, on, for promotion of, and/or in connection with any digital or analog work, copyrighted work, recording, text work, graphic work, video, audio tape, multimedia work, audiovisual work, photograph, illustration, animation, web site, webcast, and/or broadcast or any derivative of the above, to be made, published, or distributed in or by means of any media or any technology now existing or hereinafter developed, that are made by or for the Company or at its request [in connection with [*Name or Project or Work*]] (collectively the "Works"); and

1.2. In any advertising and promotion, including all promotional material in any media, in connection with or for the Works (collectively the "Promotional Materials").

2. **Copyright.** I irrevocably assign to Company any and all claims of copyright I may have in and to the Works and the Promotional Materials. My contribution (if any) to each of the foregoing shall be "work made for hire" to the maximum extent permitted by law, and to the extent not "work made for hire" is hereby irrevocably assigned to Company.

3. **Discharge of Claims.** I hereby waive to the fullest extent that I may lawfully do so, any causes of action in law or equity I may have or may hereafter acquire against the Company, its officers, directors, employees and agents for libel, slander, invasion of privacy, copyright or trademark violation, right of publicity or personality, or false light arising out of the Works or the Promotional Materials or the use of the license that I grant in this Agreement.

4. **Acknowledgments.** I hereby acknowledge and confirm that I have no right of approval with regard to any use of the rights granted herein or any Works and the Promotional Materials. I acknowledge that the Company is not obligated to use the rights granted in this Agreement.

5. **Age and Capacity.** Unless otherwise stated below, I represent and warrant that I am over the age of eighteen (18) years, and that the authorizations and rights granted hereunder do not conflict with or violate the rights of any third party. (If I am under 18, my parent or guardian has signed as stated below.)

6. **Miscellaneous.** This Agreement is the entire agreement of the parties. This Agreement inures to the benefit of and binds the parties' heirs, successors, representatives, and assigns. This Agreement is governed by the laws of the

state of _____ and applicable US federal law. Exclusive jurisdiction and venue for any claim arising from this Agreement or its subject matters will lie in the state and federal courts located in _____.

I have read this Agreement and I understand and agree to its terms and conditions:

Signed: _____

Print or Type Name: _____

Address: _____

_____

Date: _____

Age: _____

Email: _____

Parent or Guardian's Consent. (If the party providing this agreement is a minor)

I represent that I am either the parent (with sole or shared custody, as applicable) or the legal guardian of the minor child (the "Minor") whose name appears above and that I have the legal capacity to enter into the irrevocable binding agreements on behalf of the Minor. The Minor and I, both individually, and additionally, I, on behalf of the Minor and as the Minor's parent or legal guardian, agree to be bound by all the provisions of this Agreement and I guarantee all the Minor's obligations and duties under the Agreement.

Signed: _____

Print or Type Name: _____

Address: _____

_____

Date: _____

Email: _____

Agreed to by *[Company Name]*

By its authorized representative:

Signed: _____

Print or Type Name and Title: _____

_____

Address: _____

_____

Date: _____

Email: _____

Location Release

20-3

Introductory Note

This is a simple form that is used to secure permission for video and audio recording in a location such as a building, garden, or other private enclosed space.

This form is for the location only; it is not written to obtain clearance of use of the likenesses, voices, or names of persons who may be at such location or for third party branding or logos or third party copyrighted works (such as signs or works of art) that may be visible in the location.

This form should be signed by a person that has the legal right to provide access to and use of the location and otherwise enter into the obligations of this Agreement. This might be the owner or a lessee. If you are in doubt that you have the right person, you should consult your legal counsel.

Location Release Agreement

I, the Authorized Property Representative listed below, agree that this agreement "Agreement") is a binding contract between [name of entity] ("Company") and me as follows:

1. **Location; Time.** This Agreement relates to the property located at *[Address]* (the "Location").

2. **Warranty.** I hereby represent and warrant that I have the right (as owner, lessee, as a representative of the owner or lessee) to grant all permissions stated in this Agreement.

3. **Grant of Permission.** In my capacity as warranted in Section 2, I hereby grant permission for Company to video, photograph, sound record or otherwise **1065**

record or transmit images, sounds, performances, and/or scenes at the Location. This grant of permission covers entry into the Location during the following period of time: *[Indicate start and end dates]*.

4. **Equipment and Personnel.** This Agreement includes permission for the Company or its agents or contractors to bring equipment and personnel onto the Location and to remove them after completion of work.

5. **Right of Exploitation.** The Company shall have the unlimited permanent irrevocable right to copyright, copy, exploit, use, modify, make derivatives of, exhibit, display, print, distribute and reproduce, for any lawful purpose, in whole or in part, through any means now existing or hereafter created, any content or works created, transmitted, recorded or produced as permitted in this Agreement without inspection by the undersigned or further consent or approval. Without limiting the foregoing, the permission granted to the Company covers all promotion in any media for the foregoing content and works.

6. **Location Names and Trademarks.** All permissions herein granted shall include a permanent irrevocable non-exclusive license (but not the obligation) to make recordings, publications, and transmissions of the names and identifying trademarks associated with the premises and to use such names and trademarks in connection with the recorded images, video and/or sounds, any works that include such recorded images, video and/or sounds, and/or any derivatives thereof or in the promotion of the above.

7. **Indemnity.** I agree to defend, indemnify and hold harmless the Company, its officers, directors, employees, and agents from any claim arising from or based on my breach or alleged breach of my representation and warranty that I have the right to grant the permissions in this Agreement as stated in Section 2.

8. **Discharge.** I hereby release and discharge Company, its officers, directors, employees, servants and agents from any liability or claim arising from the exercise of the rights granted by this Agreement, except those caused by their grossly negligent acts or deliberate misconduct.

9. **Miscellaneous.** This Agreement is the entire agreement of the parties. This Agreement inures to the benefit of and binds the parties' heirs, successors, representatives, and assigns. This Agreement is governed by the laws of the state of _____ and applicable US federal law. Exclusive jurisdiction and

venue for any claim arising from this Agreement or its subject matters will lie in the state and federal courts located in _____.

I have read this Agreement and I understand and agree to its terms and conditions:

Authorized Property Representative

Signed: _____

Print or Type Name and Company Name (if applicable):

_____

Print or Type Title: _____

Address: _____

_____

Date: _____

Email: _____

Agreed to by *[Company Name]*

By its authorized representative

Signed: _____

Print or Type Name and Title: _____

_____

Address: _____

_____

Date: _____

Mobile Content License Agreement

Introductory Note

This is a form of agreement under which a content supplier (referred to as the "Supplier") provides mobile content (such as news, music, games, videos, etc.) to a mobile aggregator (referred to as the "Licensee"). The Licensee intends to sublicense that content through Carriers (that is, mobile telecommunications companies) and other channels in a particular territory for use on mobile handset devices, such as mobile phones or "smart phones." Payment to Supplier in this form is based on a "revenue share" pricing model.

As written, this form is relatively balanced between Supplier and Licensee interests.

The bracketed text below is optional or provides alternatives.

Mobile Content License Agreement

This Mobile Content License Agreement ("Agreement") is entered into as of [*date*] (the "Effective Date") by and between _____ of [*address*] ("Supplier") and _____ of [*address*] (Licensee").

Purpose of This Agreement

  A. Supplier is the owner or provider of certain digital content in formats suitable for certain mobile devices;

  B. Licensee aggregates content and supplies such content to the mobile carrier industry and other channels in the Territory for further distribution to consumers;

  C. Licensee seeks a license from Supplier to distribute such content in a specified territory.

Therefore, intending to be bound, Supplier and Licensee agree as follows:

1. **Definitions**

   1.1. "Affiliate" means any corporate entity that controls, is controlled by or is under the common control of a party to this Agreement.

   1.2. "Carrier" means a provider of consumer mobile telecommunications services.

   1.3. ["Initial Fee" means US$_____.]

   1.4. "Intellectual Property Rights" means property rights under the patent, copyright, trade secret, trademark or other intellectual property or moral rights law of any jurisdiction and all registrations and applications for registration of the same.

   1.5. "Licensed Content" means the Supplier content identified in Schedule A.

   1.6. "Mobile Devices" means the handheld mobile devices listed on Schedule B hereto. Such list may be updated from time to time by the written agreement of the parties.

   1.7. "Mobile Distribution" means distribution for delivery to mobile end user customers of the Mobile Devices, including distribution through Carriers and other channels. Mobile Distribution may include, without limitation, wireless and Internet download distribution, Carriers' online or mobile stores, retail locations where Mobile Devices are generally sold, and other channels that provide mobile content or services in the Territory.

   1.8. "Net Revenue" means the monies actually collected by Licensee from revenue attributable to the Mobile Distribution of the Licensed Content in the Territory ("Gross Revenue") less (a) third party out-of-pocket distribution fees due and payable to a Carrier and/or other distributors; (b) sales, value added, use tariffs, and similar taxes (excluding income tax); (c) any credit card transaction charges or similar fees charged for the relevant transactions; and (d) credits, discounts, promotions, rebates or similar charges.

   1.9. "Product Launch Date" means the date on which the Licensed Content is first made available by Licensee to consumers via Mobile Distribution in the Territory.

   1.10. "Territory" means: _____.

2. **License Grant**

   Subject to the terms of this Agreement, Supplier grants to Licensee a non-transferable license [on an exclusive basis] [on a non-exclusive basis] in the Territory for the Term to distribute, display and perform (or have distributed, displayed or performed) the Licensed Content for Mobile Distribution in the Territory. [Licensee will use all reasonable efforts to confine all distribution to the Territory and avoid sales and distribution in other areas.]

3. **Responsibilities of the Parties**

   3.1. *Supply of Licensed Content to Licensee.* Supplier will deliver the Licensed Content to Licensee in accordance with the schedule set forth on <u>Schedule C</u> hereto.

   3.2. *Clearance and Permissions.* Supplier will be solely responsible for obtaining all rights, clearances and permissions required for the use and distribution of the Licensed Content as permitted herein and for paying the cost of any and all fees, royalties, commissions and all other payments and charges for the same for the Territory. Such required clearances and permission include, without limitation, rights of copyrights, rights of personality, trademarks, music, video, patents and all obligations, if any, to any actors, musicians, artists, professional, or performer or any union or guild.

   3.3. *Distribution and Hosting.* Licensee will be responsible for arranging for distribution of the Licensed Content for Mobile Distribution. Licensee will be responsible for all costs of its delivery and distribution of the Licensed Content. Licensee will host or arrange for the hosting to supply the Licensed Content in the Territory under this Agreement.

   3.4. *Mobile Devices.* Supplier will provide the Licensed Content in formats suitable for the various Mobile Devices listed on <u>Schedule B</u> which may be updated from time to time by mutual agreement.

   3.5. *Carrier Relations.* Licensee will be responsible for dealing with Carriers serving the Territory and meeting all Carrier requirements for delivery of the Licensed Content.

   3.6. [*DRM.* Licensee will cooperate in the protection of the Licensed Content by means of Supplier's methods of encryption, watermarking, copy protection and other digital rights management (collectively "DRM").

Licensee will report to Supplier any "cracking" or circumvention of any DRM measure and cooperate with Supplier in responding to the same. Licensee will not defeat or circumvent any DRM measure.]

3.7. [*Branding.* Distribution is authorized for Licensed Content with Supplier's included trademarks and logos ("Branding") only. Supplier will not alter or obscure or permit its distributors, including, without limitation, Carriers, to alter or obscure any Supplier Branding on or for any Licensed Content without Supplier's express written consent.]

3.8. [*End User EULA.* Licensee will sublicense and arrange for distribution of Licensed Content only together with and subject to an end user license agreement ("EULA") that is no less restrictive or protective of Supplier than Supplier's form of EULA issued to Licensee from time to time.]

3.9. [*Content Advisories.* If Supplier designates an appropriate parental advisory warning or rating with regard to particular licensed content, Licensee shall display and will arrange with all distributors, including, without limitation, distribution Carriers, to conspicuously display such parental advisory warning or rating whenever marketing or sales information about such Licensed Content is displayed.]

3.10. [*Proprietary Legends.* Supplier may include a copyright notice or other proprietary legend in or with any item of Licensed Content. Supplier will not alter or obscure or permit its distributors, including, without limitation, Carriers, to alter or obscure any such notice or proprietary legend.]

3.11. [*Reputation.* Licensee shall cause and permit Licensed Content to be distributed only by means that will enhance the reputation and image of Supplier and the Licensed Content.]

4. [Subcontracting

Subject to the terms of this Agreement, Licensee may subcontract with and permit third party suppliers to host the Licensed Content in the Territory provided that Licensee will be responsible for all acts and omissions of subcontractors. In advance of any such subcontracting, Supplier will provide Licensee with reasonably detailed written plans for such subcontracting for Supplier's approval, not to be unreasonably withheld.]

5. **Ownership**

Supplier and its licensors reserve all rights of ownership to the Licensed Content and all applicable intellectual property rights. This Agreement grants licenses only. All rights not expressly granted are reserved. Licensee agrees not to use, copy, distribute, and exploit the Licensed Content except as provided in this Agreement.

6. **Pricing in Distribution**

The Supplier may issue suggested retail pricing, but will not determine the retail prices for end users.

7. **Payment and Reports**

7.1. [*Initial Fee*. Licensee will pay Supplier the non-refundable Initial Fee within _____ (__) days of the Effective Date.]

7.2. *Tracking and Payment*. Licensee agrees to track and pay Supplier the Revenue Share from the Net Revenue arising from all Mobile Distribution of the Licensed Content that occurs during the Term under or as a result of this Agreement.

7.3. *Revenue Share*. "Revenue Share" means _____ percent (__%) of Net Revenue. [Licensee shall arrange to create secure records, by automated and auditable means, of each download or other delivery of each item of Licensed Content.] All payments will be made via wire transfer to a bank account designated by Supplier. [Notwithstanding the actual pricing for Licensed Content by Licensee, for each download or other delivery of Licensed Content under this Agreement, Licensee will owe to Supplier a minimum Revenue Share of *[state amount]* each.]

7.4. [*Bundling*. If Licensee licenses or supplies the Licensed Content in a package with other content at a single price, the Gross Revenues from such package or group will be prorated according to the published list prices established for the separate content item contained in the package [provided however that, for the purpose of this allocation, the list price assigned to each item of Licensed Content will be no less than *[state amount]*.]

7.5. *Payment and Reports*. Revenue Share payments will be due and payable within thirty (30) days after the end of each calendar quarter in which

Licensee actually receives any Net Revenue. Licensee will provide to Supplier, together with payment, a written statement for the applicable calendar quarter of: (i) the total number of downloads or other transfers of items of Licensed Content under this Agreement from each form and channel of distribution, (ii) Gross Revenues for the quarter and deductions therefrom used to calculate Net Revenue, (iii) the Net Revenue, and (iv) a reasonably detailed explanation of the calculation of the Revenue Share due to Supplier. Licensee will, to the extent required to provide such information to Supplier, require its distributors (including Carriers) to report the number of downloads and transfer of items of Licensed Content. Overdue amounts will bear interest at the rate of ____ percent per year compounded daily (or if less, the highest legal rate) until paid.

7.6. *Currency.* Payments will be in US dollars. The exchange rate used for conversion from non-US currency will be the exchange rate quoted in the *Wall Street Journal* on the last business day of the quarter for which payment is due.

8. **Records and Audit**

8.1. Licensee will make and maintain reasonably detailed business records for a period of no less than three (3) years that are relevant to and support the calculation of Gross Revenues and Net Revenue.

8.2. Supplier will have the right to have an independent certified accountant or other agent audit the relevant financial records of Licensee to verify amounts payable, paid or due. Audits will be conducted under reasonable conditions of confidentiality with reasonable notice during regular business hours no more often than once per year. Licensee will cooperate in each such audit. If an audit reveals an error of more than ____ (__%) in the favor of the Licensee, the Licensee will reimburse the Supplier for the reasonable cost of the audit. Payment of the amounts found due to Supplier will be made promptly.

9. **Marketing/Promotion**

9.1. *Marketing by Licensee.* During the Term, Licensee will use its commercially reasonable efforts to advertise and promote the Licensed Content at Licensee's expense. [Licensee's efforts will be in accordance with the Marketing Plan attached as Schedule D.]

9.2. *Use of Brands.* Licensee agrees to include Supplier's branding, in accordance with Supplier's guidelines for Suppliers Branding issued from time to time ("Branding Guidelines") on all marketing and promotional materials, including online promotion. All such materials are subject to Supplier's prior review and written prior approval, which will not be unreasonably withheld. Except as expressly permitted, Licensee will not use Supplier's trademarks or brand names without Supplier's express prior written approval. Licensee shall not brand Licensed Content with its own brands or create the commercial impression that it is the supplier of the Licensed Content. Licensee will not register Supplier's trademarks or any confusingly similar trademark. All goodwill associated with Supplier's trademarks belongs to Supplier.

10. **Confidentiality**

10.1. "Confidential Information" means non-public information, technical data or know-how of a party, which is furnished to the other in written or tangible form in connection with this Agreement and marked as "Confidential." Oral disclosure will also be deemed Confidential Information if such disclosures are such that a reasonable person would understand them to be confidential. The terms and conditions set forth in this Agreement will be Confidential Information, provided, however, that either party may reveal the contents of this Agreement in confidence to auditors or other professionals, as well as advisors, investors, and parties conducting due diligence in connection with such party's efforts to obtain financing, comply with legal or regulatory requirements or negotiate a merger, acquisition, or sale of substantially all the assets of such party's business or line of business.

10.2. Notwithstanding the foregoing, Confidential Information does not include information which is: (a) already in the possession of the receiving party or its subsidiaries and not subject to a confidentiality obligation to the providing party; (b) independently developed by the receiving party; (c) publicly disclosed or in the public domain through no fault of the receiving party; (d) rightfully received by the receiving party or its subsidiaries from a third party that is not under any obligation to keep such information confidential; (e) approved for release by written agreement with the disclosing party; or (f) disclosed pursuant to the requirements of law, regulation or court order.

10.3. Neither party will use the other's Confidential Information during the term of this Agreement or for _____ (_) years thereafter. Each party will use commercially reasonable efforts to hold in confidence the other party's Confidential Information by means that are no less restrictive than that used for its own confidential materials.

10.4. Upon expiration or termination of this Agreement, each party will either: (a) return all of the other party's Confidential Information and all copies thereof in the party's possession or control to the other party or (b) at the other party's instruction, destroy all Confidential Information and all copies thereof in the party's possession or control. This obligation of the parties also extends to Confidential Information in the possession of any of its subcontractors. The party will then certify that no copies have been retained by it, its employees, or agents or Contractors.

10.5. In case a party receives legal process that demands or requires disclosure of the disclosing party's Confidential Information, such party will give prompt notice to the disclosing party, if legally permissible, to enable the disclosing party to challenge such demand.

11. **Supplier's Warranties, Representations, and Indemnities**

11.1. Supplier represents and warrants that the Licensed Content is and will be of commercially acceptable quality.

11.2. Supplier represents and warrants that (i) it has the full power and authority to enter into this Agreement and to perform the acts required of it hereunder; (ii) Supplier and/or its licensors have all necessary rights, title and interest in all Licensed Content and all required permissions to grant Licensee the rights granted in this Agreement; (iii) none of the Licensed Content or any of Supplier's obligations or actions hereunder infringe or violate or will infringe or violate any intellectual property rights in the Territory of any third party or are illegal under any law; (iv) the rights granted herein are free and clear of any claims, demands, licenses or encumbrances, and there are no current disputes or claims relating thereto; (v) none of the Licensed Content is or will be defamatory, indecent, libelous, pornographic or obscene, invade any person's privacy, or constitute unlicensed use of rights of personality or publicity; and (vi) none of the Licensed Content contains or will contain any viruses, bugs, spyware, time-outs, or any programming routines that detrimentally interfere with or corrupt mobile distribution equipment, software, networks or data.

12. **Supplier's Indemnification and Certain Remedies**

12.1. At its own expense, Supplier shall defend, indemnify and hold harmless Licensee (and its officers, directors, employees, servants and agents) (each a "Licensee Indemnitee") against any third party any lawsuit, proceeding or demand against any Licensee Indemnitee (a) alleging that the Licensed Content, used as permitted in this Agreement, infringes a copyright, patent, trademark, trade secret or other proprietary right held by another or violates any right of privacy, publicity or personality, or otherwise violates applicable law or (b) that arises or is alleged to arise from any alleged fact or circumstances that, if true, would breach Supplier's warranties under Section 11.2 (collectively, a "Claim"), including, without limitation, against any liabilities, judgments, settlement amounts, fees, costs and attorneys' fees arising from any such Claim. As a condition of Supplier's obligation under this Section 12.1, the Licensee Indemnitee will notify Supplier of the Claim in a timely manner, tender the defense and settlement of such claim to Supplier, and cooperate (at Supplier's expense) in the defense.

12.2. In case that any such Licensed Content is held to infringe or the use of such Licensed Content is otherwise permanently or temporarily enjoined or if Supplier considers that there is a material risk that Licensed Content may be infringing, then Supplier may, at its option either: (i) produce for Licensee a license to continue to use the Licensed Content as contemplated under this Agreement; (ii) terminate its license grant for such Licensed Content; or (iii) modify the Licensed Content.

12.3. Supplier reserves the right to require Licensee, by written notice, to remove from marketing and distribution in the Territory [within 24 hours] [within __ day(s)] any Licensed Content for which there is an infringement risk or risk of any other claim or liability or which Supplier otherwise deems unsuitable for distribution. Licensee is likewise not obligated to distribute or promote any License Content that it reasonably deems subject to an infringement risk or risk of any other claim or liability or which it otherwise deems unsuitable for distribution.

12.4. With regard to actual or alleged intellectual property infringement of any third party right arising or alleged to arise from Licensed Content, the remedies in this Section are Licensee's sole and exclusive infringement indemnification remedies against Supplier.

13. Licensee's Indemnification

13.1. At its own expense, Licensee shall defend, indemnify and hold harmless Supplier (and its officers, directors, employees, servants and agents) (each a "Supplier Indemnitee") against any third party lawsuit, proceeding or demand against any Licensee Indemnitee arising or alleged to arise from the distribution, copying, promotion, marketing, supply or delivery of the Licensed Content pursuant to this Agreement (other than to the extent arising from a Claim for which Supplier provides indemnification under Section 12) (collectively, a "Distribution Claim"), including, without limitation, against any liabilities, judgments, settlement amounts, fees, costs and attorneys' fees arising from any such Distribution Claim. As a condition of Licensee's obligation under this Section 13.1, the Supplier Indemnitee will notify Supplier of the Distribution Claim in a timely manner, tender the defense and settlement of such claim to Licensee, and cooperate in the defense.

13.2. With regard to actual or alleged intellectual property infringement of any third party right arising or alleged to arise in a Distribution Claim, the remedies in this Section are Supplier's sole and exclusive infringement indemnification remedies against Licensee.

14. Warranty Disclaimers

EXCEPT AS SPECIFICALLY SET FORTH IN THIS AGREEMENT, SUPPLIER DISCLAIMS ALL WARRANTIES OF ANY KIND, EITHER EXPRESS OR IMPLIED, INCLUDING BUT NOT LIMITED TO WARRANTIES OF TITLE, NONINFRINGEMENT, MERCHANTABILITY OR FITNESS FOR A PARTICULAR PURPOSE. In addition, Supplier makes no warranty that the services, products, materials and/or other items provided hereunder will be uninterrupted, secure, or error free.

15. Limitation of Liability

15.1. Except with respect to obligations regarding confidentiality or unlicensed use or exploitation of the Licensed Content, neither of the parties shall be liable for any indirect, incidental, special, reliance, punitive or consequential damages.

15.2. Except with respect to obligations regarding confidentiality, unlicensed use or exploitation of the Licensed Content, or indemnification, neither party's aggregate liability will exceed amounts paid or payable under this Agreement.

15.3. Any claim or action arising from this Agreement by one party against the other must be brought no later than _____ year(s) from the date that it accrues.

16. **Notice**

All notices to be given under this Agreement will be in writing and will be sent by certified mail, return receipt requested, or by a recognized courier service, return receipt requested, to the address of the other party set out at the commencement of this Agreement (or to such other address as either party may notify to the other under the provisions of this sub-Section). Notices will be deemed delivered upon receipt.

17. **Term and Termination**

17.1. Unless earlier terminated as permitted herein, the Agreement will remain in effect for _____ year(s) (the "Initial Term") and thereafter will automatically renew for additional _____-year terms in succession (each a "Renewal Term") unless either party serves notice of non-renewal at least ___ days prior to the expiration of the Initial Term or any Renewal Term.

17.2. Notwithstanding the foregoing, if [on or before [*date*]][during any one year period][during any ___ consecutive calendar quarters], the Revenue Share due and paid to Supplier under this Agreement is less than [*amount*], Supplier in its discretion, may terminate this Agreement on ___ days' written notice.

17.3. Either Party may terminate this Agreement for cause in the event of: (a) a material breach or default by the other party of an obligation under this Agreement which is not remedied within ___ days after written notice; or (b) the other party's filing for bankruptcy or becoming an involuntary participant in a bankruptcy proceeding, if such involuntary proceedings are not dismissed within ___ days after commencement.

17.4. Upon termination or expiration of this Agreement, Licensee will discontinue use of the Licensed Content [except as follows]. [In the event of termination of this Agreement before the end of the Initial Term or a Renewal Term, if Licensee has contractually committed to a Carrier to allow Mobile Distribution of Licensed Content, Licensee will use reasonable efforts to request that such Carrier discontinue distribution, but, failing to do so, such Mobile Distribution may continue, subject to all other terms and conditions of this Agreement (including Supplier's payment rights), until the end of the current Initial Term or a Renewal Term as applicable or the end of such contractual commitment, whichever is earlier.

17.5. The following Sections survive termination: 1 (Definitions), as applicable, 5 (Ownership), 8 (Records and Audit), 10 (Confidentiality), 12 (Supplier's Indemnification), 13 (Licensee's Indemnification), 14 (Warranty Disclaimers), 15 (Limitation of Liability), 16 (Notice), 17.4 and 17.5 (Survival) and 18 (Miscellaneous), as well as accrued obligations.

18. Miscellaneous

18.1. *Export Controls.* Each party shall be responsible for its own compliance with US or any other nation's export control laws as they may apply.

18.2. *Waiver.* A waiver of any provision of this Agreement will not waive that provision for the future or waive any subsequent breach of it.

18.3. *No Agency.* The relationship of the parties is that of independent contractors and nothing in this Agreement will render either party an agent of the other.

18.4. *Force Majeure.* Neither party will be liable for any delay or failure to perform its obligations hereunder if such delay or failure is caused by an unforeseeable event beyond the reasonable control of a party ("Force Majeure Event"). If any Force Majeure Event affecting a party's material performance lasts more than ____ (___) days, the other party may terminate this Agreement by written notice. A Force Majeure Event may not delay a payment obligation of Licensee for more than ___ days.

18.5. *Applicable Law and Jurisdiction.* This Agreement will be construed in accordance with the substantive laws of the State of _____ applicable to agreements entered into and performed there and the federal laws of the United States. The courts located in _____ will have exclusive jurisdiction and venue over this Agreement and its subject matter. The provisions of the United Nations Convention on the International Sale of Goods do not apply to this Agreement or any transactions hereunder.

18.6. *Assignment.* This Agreement shall be binding upon and inure to the benefit of the successors and permitted assigns of the parties hereto. Neither party may assign any of its rights or obligations under this Agreement to any third party without the express prior written consent of the other party[, except that consent is not required in the case of a merger or acquisition of the assigning party's business or line of the business involved in this Agreement].

18.7. *Counterparts.* This Agreement may be executed in counterparts, each of which shall be deemed an original and all of which together shall constitute one and the same document. Execution by exchange of signed fax or PDF copies is permitted.

18.8. *Remedies.* To the extent permitted by applicable law, the rights and remedies of the parties provided under this Agreement are cumulative and in addition to any other rights and remedies of the Parties at law or equity. Supplier reserves the right to seek injunctive relief for any unlicensed or unauthorized use of Licensed Content, which the parties agree is likely to cause immediate and irreparable harm.

18.9. *No Third-Party Beneficiaries.* This Agreement is for the sole benefit of the Parties hereto and their authorized successors and permitted assigns. There are no third party beneficiaries.

18.10. *Entire Agreement.* This Agreement contains the entire understanding of the parties and cannot be changed, amended or terminated except by an instrument signed by an officer of each party.

IN WITNESS WHEREOF, the parties have executed this Agreement as of the day and year first written above.

Supplier: _____   Licensee: _____

By:_____   By:_____

(Name): _____   (Name): _____

(Title): _____   (Title): _____

(Date): _____   (Date): _____

Schedule A

Licensed Content

[Insert list]

Schedule B

Mobile Devices

[Insert list]

Schedule C

Delivery Schedule for Licensed Content

[To be added]

[Schedule D

Marketing Plan]

[To be added]

Media Publishing and Services Agreement

Introductory Note

This is a form agreement offered by a service provider that offers an online content distribution service (here called the "Media Publisher"). Under this agreement, owners of content (e.g., videos and music) (here called the "Customer") can upload, publish, manage and distribute its content; the service allows Customer to distribute through various online channels, including the Customer's own web sites, third party web sites, and through the Media Publisher's distribution network.

Under this agreement, the Customer pays the Media Publisher for its distribution services. This form allows for electronic payment to the Customer via "ACH," the Automated Clearing House Network, which is the payment network used in the US for direct deposit and other electronic payments.

To make money from this distribution, the Customer could separately arrange to include third party advertising with the distributed content, have an agency sell advertising placements on its behalf, or retain the Media Publisher to sell advertising placements under a separate agreement.

Media Publishing and Services Agreement

Customer: _____   Contact: _____

Address: _____   Title: _____

                                        Phone: _____

                                        Fax: _____

                                        E-Mail: _____

Effective Date: _____, 20_____

This Media Publishing and Services Agreement, including all amendments hereto (collectively, the "Agreement") is by and between *[Name of Media Publishing Company]* ("Media Publisher") and *[Name of Content Owner or Supplier]* ("Customer", "You" or "Your"). For good and valuable consideration, the receipt and sufficiency of which are hereby acknowledged by each party, the parties hereby agree as follows:

Terms

1. **Payment Information.** All invoices from Media Publisher shall be sent to the Customer at the following address. The Customer represents that the information provided below sets forth all the information necessary for Customer to timely process invoices issued by Media Publisher to Customer in accordance with the terms of this Agreement.

   [TO BE PROVIDED BY CUSTOMER]

   [Accounts Payable Email Address]

   [Contact Name]

   [Purchase Order # or other required payment processing information]

   All payments made by Customer to Media Publisher pursuant to this Agreement shall be denominated in US dollars and made by check, wire or ACH. Payments made by check shall be sent via regular mail to Media Publisher Inc., Attention: Accounts Receivable.

   Payments made via wire or ACH shall be sent to _____ Bank, for the account of Media Publisher Inc., account number _____.

2. **The Media Publisher Service.** The "<u>Media Publisher Service</u>" is an Internet-based service that enables rights holders ("<u>Content Owners</u>") to upload, publish, manage and distribute their Content (defined below) directly to end users through various distribution channels selected by them, including (a) their own, proprietary web site(s), (b) through selected web site(s) of Media Publisher Affiliates (defined below), and/or (c) through the Media Publisher web site(s) ([insert URL] or other website wholly-owned and/or operated by Media Publisher) (the "<u>Media Publisher Web site</u>"). "<u>Media Publisher Affiliates</u>" are those individuals and/or companies that have entered into agreements with Media Publisher which, subject to authorization from a Content Owner, permits Media Publisher to distribute such Content Owner's Content on or through Media Publisher Affiliate owned and/or operated

web site(s). For purposes of this Agreement, "Content" shall mean and include all content that is provided by Customer to Media Publisher and/or provisioned by Customer into the Media Publisher Service including, without limitation, video, music, photograph, text, any digital file, any live event, advertising creative or other advertising material or metadata. Using the Media Publisher Service, You may also distribute Your Content without Media Publisher's mediation or control to web sites not owned by You or a Media Publisher Affiliate ("Unregistered Affiliates"). By using the on-line, user interface provided through the Media Publisher Service, You may make the selections described above, as well as other choices about the presentation, management, distribution of, and end user access to, the Content. You may change such selections from time to time to the extent permitted by the Media Publisher Service. In all cases, however, Your last submissions reflected in Media Publisher's database shall be conclusive in the event of any dispute.

3. **Access to the Service.** You may establish one or multiple user accounts through the Media Publisher Service. Access to these accounts shall be limited by use of user identification/s and password/s. You are responsible for all activity occurring under Your user accounts and shall abide by all applicable local, state, national and foreign laws, treaties and regulations in connection with Your use of the Media Publisher Service, including those related to data privacy, international communications and the transmission of technical or personal data. You are solely responsible for the confidentiality and use of Your user identification/s and password/s, as well as for any use, misuse or communications using Your user identification/s and/or password/s. Each party agrees to notify the other immediately if it becomes aware of any loss, theft or unauthorized use of Your user identification/s or password/s. Except where Media Publisher has actual notice of loss, theft or unauthorized use of Your user identification or password, Media Publisher shall have the right to rely, without further inquiry, on provision of the user identification/s and password/s as sufficient to authenticate use of the Media Publisher Service by You or on Your behalf.

4. **Your Obligations**

   a. *Provisioning Content.* You may only provide or provision such Content into the Media Publisher Service for which You have sufficient rights and licenses to do so. You agree that you will not provision Content into the Media Publisher Service that contains or constitutes: (a) illegal or unlawful content; (b) pornography or obscenity, or content which would generally be considered to be primarily of an "adult" nature (i.e., content that, if displayed in a movie theater, would be expected to receive an "X" rating); or (c) promotions of hate or incitement to violence.

b. *Restrictions on Use.* You may not use the Media Publisher Service (i) to enable distribution of Content beyond the scope of the rights and/or licenses you possess with regard to such Content, (ii) to offer, for sale or otherwise, or to sell, any illegal or unlawful items or service which would be illegal or unlawful to sell in the jurisdiction in which it is sold (iii) to offer, for sale or otherwise, or to sell any items or service where doing so through the Media Publisher Service would cause Media Publisher to violate any law or regulation (iv) to perform any of the following prohibited acts: (A) Any act which, directly or indirectly, causes to be transmitted to, uploaded by or downloaded by, any end user any "junk mail," "spam," "chain letters," "pyramid schemes," or any other like form of solicitation; (B) Any act which, directly or indirectly, causes to be transmitted to, uploaded by or downloaded by, the Media Publisher Service or any end user any software viruses, worms, trojan horses, time bombs, trap doors or any other computer code, files or programs or repetitive requests for information designed to interrupt, destroy or limit the functionality of any computer software or hardware or telecommunications equipment or to diminish the quality of, interfere with the performance of, or impair the functionality of the Media Publisher Service; or (C) Any act which interferes with or disrupts the Media Publisher Service or servers or networks connected to the Media Publisher Service.

c. *Obligation to Pay.* You shall pay Media Publisher the fees set forth on Exhibit A in accordance with the payment terms set forth in this Agreement.

d. *Observance of Agreement.* At all times, in using the Media Publisher Service, You must observe and abide by the terms and provisions of this Agreement.

5. **Media Publisher's Obligations.** Media Publisher's obligations hereunder, including any Exhibits hereto, shall be to: (a) operate the Media Publisher Service *[in accordance with the Service Level Agreement attached as Exhibit C hereto – omitted in this form document]*; (b) unless Customer has elected to purchase Media Publisher's silver or gold support level package, provide basic support (as described on Exhibit B hereto), with the ability to log support cases

twenty-four (24) hours per day, seven (7) days per week (excluding downtime for routine maintenance), and (c) to perform any other obligations expressly identified in this Agreement.

6. **Payment.** Customer shall pay Media Publisher the fees set forth on Exhibit A for the Media Publisher Service within thirty (30) days of the date of each applicable invoice. Customer shall be responsible for and shall pay any applicable sales, use or other taxes or duties, tariffs or the like applicable to the provision of the Media Publisher Service (except for taxes on Media Publisher's income). All payments hereunder shall be made without deduction for withholding taxes. Late payments by Customer will be subject to late fees at the rate of one and one-half percent (1.5%) per month or, if lower, the maximum rate allowed by law. If Customer fails to pay fees invoiced by Media Publisher within fifteen (15) days following the payment due date, then in addition to any other rights Media Publisher may have, Media Publisher shall have the right to suspend delivery of all or a portion of the Media Publisher Service, provided that Media Publisher has supplied prior notice to Customer and five (5) days' opportunity to cure. In Media Publisher's sole discretion, access to the Media Publisher Service shall not be reinstated until Customer pays all such overdue amounts. At no time may Customer withhold payment of any portion of any fees that are not subject to a good faith dispute between the parties, provided, however, that all such disputes relating to invoices must be raised and presented to Media Publisher in accordance with Section 7 below.

7. **Disputes.** Customer shall use its best efforts to promptly notify Media Publisher of any dispute or claim relating to invoices provided by Media Publisher to Customer, which notice must be brought to the attention of Media Publisher by email at *[insert URL]* or such email other address as Media Publisher may identify on the Media Publisher Website from time to time, accompanied by the details forming the basis for such dispute or claim. In addition, in the event that Customer disputes any fees, Customer shall cooperate with Media Publisher, in good faith, to promptly resolve such dispute.

8. **Term.** The term ("Term") of this Agreement shall commence as of the Effective Date and, unless earlier terminated in accordance with this Agreement, shall remain in effect for two (2) years from the Effective Date.

9. **Termination.** Either party may terminate this Agreement: (a) if the other party is adjudicated bankrupt; (b) if a voluntary or involuntary petition in

bankruptcy is filed against the other party and such petition is not dismissed within ninety (90) days of the filing date; (c) if the other party becomes insolvent or makes an assignment for the benefit of its creditors pursuant to any bankruptcy law; (d) if a receiver is appointed for the other party or its business; (e) upon the occurrence of a material breach of a material provision of this Agreement by the other party if such breach is not cured within thirty (30) days after written notice is received by the breaching party identifying the matter constituting the material breach; or (f) by mutual written consent. In the event of a termination or expiration of this Agreement, (i) all licenses and all sublicenses granted under this Agreement shall terminate automatically and (ii) You expressly acknowledge and agree that Media Publisher may preserve and/or disclose certain Content if required to do so by law or in the good faith belief that such preservation or disclosure is reasonably necessary to: (A) comply with legal process; (B) enforce this Agreement; (C) respond to claims that any Content violates the rights of any third-party; or (D) protect the rights, property, or personal safety of Media Publisher, its users and the public. During the Term, Media Publisher will not review or screen Content on a regular basis for compliance with this Agreement or applicable laws, and Media Publisher shall have no obligation to do so, provided, however, that Media Publisher reserves the right to suspend the Media Publisher Service to the extent that Media Publisher determines, in good faith, that such suspension is necessary to comply with applicable law or to prevent significant harm to any end user or the Media Publisher Service; provided, however, that in such event, to the extent practicable, Media Publisher shall only suspend that portion of the Media Publisher Service causing such violation and/or harm.

10. **Title.** The Media Publisher Service is proprietary to Media Publisher and it is protected by the intellectual property laws of the United States and foreign governments under applicable treaties. Media Publisher owns and continues to own all right, title and interest in and to the Media Publisher Service including associated intellectual property rights under copyright, trade secret, patent, trademark and/or other applicable domestic and international laws. Unless otherwise specified in this Agreement, any and all right, title, and interest in any custom work that Media Publisher performs or creates under this Agreement shall belong solely to Media Publisher, and any work product associated therewith shall be and is the sole property of Media Publisher, and each is made available to You solely pursuant to a license as part of the Media

Publisher Service, and all rights to such custom work granted to You shall terminate upon the termination or expiration of the Term. This Agreement does not convey any ownership interest in or to the Media Publisher Service to You, but only a limited license that is immediately revocable if you fail to comply with the terms of this Agreement. Any and all Marks (as defined below) that Media Publisher uses in connection with the Media Publisher Service or with the services included as part of the Media Publisher Service are marks owned by Media Publisher and any goodwill associated with the use of such Marks shall inure to the benefit of Media Publisher. This Agreement does not grant You any right, license or interest in such marks and you shall not assert any right, license or interest in such marks or any words or designs that are confusingly similar to such marks. Title, ownership rights and intellectual property rights in and to the Content shall be retained by the applicable content owner and You agree to abide by all applicable copyright or other law in such use.

11. **Licenses**

    a. *License to Use the Media Publisher Service.* Subject to the terms and conditions of this Agreement, and limited solely to the extent necessary to use the services identified in this Agreement, Media Publisher hereby grants You a limited, revocable, non-transferable, non-exclusive, worldwide right to use the Media Publisher Service. All rights not expressly granted to You are reserved by Media Publisher and its licensors. Except as expressly permitted by Media Publisher or to the extent expressly authorized by the Media Publisher Service, You shall not: (a) license, sublicense, sell, resell, transfer, assign, distribute or otherwise commercially exploit or make available to any third party the Media Publisher Service in any way; (b) modify or make derivative works based upon the Media Publisher Service; (c) reverse engineer, decompile, modify, translate, disassemble (except to the extent that this restriction is expressly prohibited by law) or create derivative works based upon Your access to or usage of the Media Publisher Service; (d) rent, lease or otherwise transfer rights to any aspect of the Media Publisher Service; or (e) take any act to remove, obscure, interfere with or modify the presentation or functionality of any aspect of the Media Publisher Service.

    b. *License to Marks.* Subject to the terms and conditions of this Agreement, Media Publisher grants You, and You grant Media Publisher, the non-transferable (except as provided herein), non-exclusive, royalty-free, worldwide right to reproduce and display the other's logos, trademarks, trade names and other similar identifying material (the "Marks") solely for the purposes described herein and in accordance with the owner's established usage policies and procedures, as may be modified from time to time in the owner's sole discretion and as supplied to the other party, and to grant sublicenses thereto on the same terms and conditions to end users, Media Publisher Affiliates and Your Unregistered Affiliates, if you have selected such distribution channels for your Content. In connection with such licenses, each party shall have the unilateral right to establish such quality standards and additional terms and conditions as such party deems reasonably necessary to protect its Marks. Any and all use of a party's Marks hereunder shall inure exclusively to the benefit of the owner of the Marks.

c. *License to Content.* To the extent necessary for Media Publisher to provide the Media Publisher Service, and subject to Your selections made through the Media Publisher Console or otherwise, You hereby grant Media Publisher a non-transferable (except as provided herein), non-exclusive, royalty-free, worldwide license: (i) to deliver the Content to end users of website/s selected by You (or otherwise permitted by You); (ii) to transmit, exhibit, broadcast, publicly display, publicly perform, distribute, copy, store, provision into and/or reproduce the Content on or through the Media Publisher Service, either in its original form, copy or in the form of an encoded work; (iii) to secure, encode, reproduce, host, cache, route, reformat, analyze and create algorithms based on the Content; (iv) to distribute, transmit, and/or display the Content and encoded works via such technologies as are supported by Media Publisher from time to time; and (v) to perform such other acts with respect to the Content as are necessary from time to time to provide the Media Publisher Service as specified by You through the Media Publisher Console or otherwise permitted by You through the Media Publisher Service. This license also includes the right, but not the obligation, for Media Publisher to offer or provide access to the Content on or through the Media Publisher Website, subject to Your selections made through the Media Publisher Console or otherwise. FOR THE AVOIDANCE OF ANY DOUBT, THE PARTIES EXPRESSLY AGREE AND ACKNOWLEDGE THAT THE VENDOR SERVICE DOES NOT INCLUDE TAKING TITLE TO ANY CONTENT SUPPLIED BY YOU.

12. **Representations, Warranties and Covenants**

   a. *Corporate.* Each party represents and warrants at all times that: (i) it is duly organized and validly existing and in good standing under the laws of the state of its incorporation; (ii) it has full power and authority to enter into this Agreement and to carry out the provisions hereof; (iii) it is duly authorized to execute and deliver this Agreement and duly authorized to perform its obligations and exercise its rights hereunder; (iv) this Agreement is a legal and valid obligation, binding and enforceable in accordance with its terms; and (v) the execution, delivery and performance of this Agreement does not conflict with any agreement, instrument or understanding, oral or written, to which it is a party or by which it may be bound, nor violate any law or regulation of any court, governmental body or administrative or other agency having jurisdiction over it.

   b. *Rights, Approvals, Licenses, etc.* Media Publisher represents and warrants that it either owns fully and outright or otherwise possesses and has obtained all rights, approvals, licenses, consents and permissions as are necessary to perform its obligations hereunder, exercise its rights hereunder and to grant the licenses granted by it under this Agreement.

   c. *Customer Warranty.* Customer represents and warrants that (i) it either owns fully and outright or otherwise possesses and has obtained all rights, approvals, licenses, consents and permissions as are necessary to perform its obligations hereunder, exercise its rights hereunder and to grant the licenses granted by it under this Agreement; (ii) the Content and the distribution and/or publication of the Content through the Media Publisher Service or through and/or by any Media Publisher Affiliate and/or Unregistered Affiliate, to the extent enabled by You, directly or indirectly, does not, and shall not, infringe or misappropriate any third party's rights, nor shall doing so violate any right of any person; (iii) it has obtained and paid for all consents, licenses, permissions, and authorizations necessary in the territory, and shall be solely responsible for paying any fees attributable to any and all: (w) required consents and licenses from artists, actors, directors, performers, writers, producers, or any other individuals who appear in the Content or the results and proceeds of whose services are utilized in the Content; (x) required synchronization, and master use licenses from the owners of the musical compositions and sound recordings embodied in the Content (or their designated representatives); (y) consents from and payments to any labor unions and guilds, to the extent required under applicable collective bargaining agreements or otherwise (e.g., residuals, re-use, rerun and other similar fees or payments required by any applicable union or guild agreement); (z) public performance licenses from applicable public performance rights collection organizations (e.g., ASCAP, BMI or SESAC); and (iv) You have paid all other license fees and/or other fees required to be paid to third parties for performance of Your obligations or exercise of Your rights hereunder, for the grant of the licenses hereunder, and for any other act by You under this Agreement (collectively, subsections (iii) and (iv) herein are "Third Party License Fees") and you covenant to timely pay any Third Party License Fees required to be paid in the future for such actions. You further covenant to timely pay any Third Party License Fees required for the licenses granted by You in Section 12 of this Agreement. For clarity and avoidance of doubt, You expressly agree that, as between You, on the one hand, and Media Publisher, on the other hand, any obligation to pay Third Party License Fees as a result of distribution of the Content pursuant to this Agreement shall be Your obligation and not the obligation of Media Publisher.

13. **Indemnification**

    a. *By You.* You agree to indemnify and hold harmless Media Publisher and Media Publisher's officers, directors, shareholders, employees, accountants, attorneys, agents, affiliates, subsidiaries, successors and assigns (collectively, the "Media Publisher Indemnitees") from and against any and all third party claims, damages, liabilities, costs and expenses (including reasonable attorney's fees and litigation expenses) (each a "Claim"), arising out of or related to any breach or alleged breach of any representation, warranty, covenant and/or agreement made by Customer in this Agreement. For the avoidance of doubt, You agree that regardless of whether any representation, warranty, covenant or agreement is qualified by Customer's knowledge, Customer shall provide indemnification for said representation, warranty, covenant or agreement as if there was no such qualification.

    b. *By Media Publisher.* Media Publisher agrees to indemnify and hold harmless Customer and Customer's officers, directors, shareholders, employees, accountants, attorneys, agents, affiliates, subsidiaries, successors and assigns (the "Customer Indemnitees") from and against any and all third party Claims, arising out of or related to any breach or alleged breach of any representation, warranty, covenant and/or agreement made by Media Publisher in this Agreement. For the avoidance of doubt, Media Publisher agrees that regardless of whether any representation, warranty, covenant or agreement is qualified by Media Publisher's knowledge, Media Publisher shall provide indemnification for said representation, warranty, covenant or agreement as if there was no such qualification.

c. *Conditions and Procedure.* The foregoing indemnities are conditioned upon: (a) written notice by the indemnified party to the indemnifying party of any claim, action or demand for which indemnification is claimed; (b) the opportunity to have reasonable control of the defense by the indemnifying party, with counsel reasonably acceptable to the indemnified party, and settlement thereof by the indemnifying party; and (c) such reasonable cooperation by the indemnified party in the defense as the indemnifying party may request, all provided, however, that failure to provide reasonable notice, control and/or cooperation shall not relieve the indemnification obligations hereof unless the party seeking to avoid such obligations can demonstrate material prejudice to the defense of such Claim caused thereby. The indemnifying party shall not, without the prior written consent of the indemnified party, settle, compromise or consent to the entry of any judgment with respect to any pending or threatened claim unless the settlement, compromise or consent provides for and includes an express, unconditional release of all claims, damages, liabilities, costs and expenses, including reasonable legal fees and expenses, against the indemnified party.

14. **DISCLAIMERS.** EXCEPT AS EXPRESSLY PROVIDED IN THIS AGREEMENT OR IN ANY APPLICABLE ATTACHMENT OR EXHIBIT HERETO, VENDOR MAKES NO REPRESENTATION OR WARRANTY OF ANY KIND TO YOU, EITHER EXPRESS OR IMPLIED, AS TO ANY MATTER IN CONNECTION WITH THIS AGREEMENT INCLUDING, WITHOUT LIMITATION, IMPLIED WARRANTIES OF FITNESS FOR A PARTICULAR PURPOSE, MERCHANTABILITY, NON-INFRINGEMENT, TITLE, SUITABILITY OR OTHERWISE. EXCEPT AS EXPRESSLY SET FORTH HEREIN, THE VENDOR SERVICE IS PROVIDED ON AN "AS IS" BASIS ONLY, AND VENDOR MAKES NO REPRESENTATION, WARRANTY OR ASSURANCE TO YOU THAT IT WILL BE ERROR-FREE OR PERFORM IN ACCORDANCE WITH ANY PARTICULAR STANDARD, LEVEL OR METRIC. YOU ALSO EXPRESSLY ACKNOWLEDGE AND AGREE THAT THE VENDOR SERVICE

RELIES UPON THIRD-PARTY SOFTWARE FOR CERTAIN FUNCTIONS, AND EXCEPT AS EXPRESSLY SET FORTH HEREIN, VENDOR MAKES NO REPRESENTATION, WARRANTY, PROMISE OR GUARANTEE TO YOU THAT SUCH SOFTWARE WILL BE ERROR FREE, ACCOMPLISH THE SPECIFIED INTENT OR PERFORM IN ACCORDANCE WITH ANY PARTICULAR STANDARD, LEVEL OR METRIC AND VENDOR WILL NOT BE LIABLE FOR ANY FAILURE THEREOF TO YOU. YOU ALSO ACKNOWLEDGE AND AGREE THAT TECHNOLOGY MAY EXIST OR BE DEVELOPED TO COPY, DOWNLOAD OR OTHERWISE ACQUIRE CONTENT WITHOUT YOUR AND/OR VENDOR'S AUTHORIZATION AND/OR KNOWLEDGE, AND THAT ANY SECURITY AND PROTECTIONS AS ARE OFFERED BY VENDOR MAY NOT BE SUFFICIENT TO PREVENT SUCH UNAUTHORIZED ACTS.

15. **LIMITATIONS AND EXCLUSIONS OF LIABILITY.** UNDER NO CIRCUMSTANCES SHALL EITHER PARTY BE LIABLE TO THE OTHER FOR INDIRECT, INCIDENTAL, CONSEQUENTIAL, SPECIAL OR EXEMPLARY DAMAGES (EVEN IF THAT PARTY HAS BEEN ADVISED OF THE POSSIBILITY OF SUCH DAMAGES) FOR ANY REASON, INCLUDING, WITHOUT LIMITATION, THOSE ARISING FROM THE PERFORMANCE UNDER OR FAILURE OF PERFORMANCE OF ANY PROVISION OF THIS AGREEMENT (INCLUDING SUCH DAMAGES INCURRED BY THIRD PARTIES), SUCH AS, WITHOUT LIMITATION, LOSS OF REVENUE OR ANTICIPATED PROFITS OR LOST BUSINESS. UNDER NO CIRCUMSTANCES WILL EITHER PARTY BE LIABLE TO THE OTHER FOR DAMAGES IN EXCESS OF $100,000 OR AMOUNTS DULY INVOICED, PAYABLE AND OUTSTANDING, WHICHEVER IS GREATER. NOTWITHSTANDING ANY OF THE FOREGOING IN THIS ENTIRE SECTION, TO THE EXTENT PERMITTED BY APPLICABLE LAW, THE LIMITATIONS SET FORTH IN THIS SECTION SHALL NOT APPLY IN THE CASE OF (A) DAMAGES RESULTING FROM INTENTIONAL TORTS OR BREACHES OF SECTIONS 4(a) AND/OR 4(b) ABOVE, (B) AMOUNTS PAYABLE PURSUANT TO SECTION 13 ("INDEMNIFICATION") OR (C) BREACHES OF SECTION 16 ("CONFIDENTIALITY").

16. **Confidentiality.** Each party agrees not to disclose the other party's Confidential Information without their prior written consent. "Confidential Information" includes, without limitation: (a) all intellectual property, including, without limitation, all software, technology, programming, technical specifications,

materials, guidelines and documentation relating to each party's service; (b) any click-through rates, financial information (including pricing), business information, including, without limitation, operations, planning, marketing interests, products and any other reporting information (including revenue, if any, paid to You by Media Publisher); and (c) any other information designated in writing as "Confidential" or an equivalent designation or that would otherwise be reasonably considered confidential or proprietary given its nature or the circumstances under which it was disclosed. Confidential Information does not include information that has become publicly known through no breach by You or Media Publisher of these confidentiality obligations or information that has been: (x) independently developed without access to Confidential Information, as evidenced in writing; (y) rightfully received from a third party without a breach of confidentiality by such third party; or (z) required to be disclosed by law or by a governmental authority.

17. **Co-Marketing; Promotion.** Subject to each party's prior approval, which approval shall not be unreasonably withheld or delayed, each party agrees to participate in co-marketing activities with the other identifying Customer's use of the Media Publisher Service, including the following: (a) issuance of a press release announcing entry into the Agreement immediately following the first publicly available launch of Customer's Content using the Media Publisher Service; and (b) permission to use each other's Marks in marketing materials and on such party's website, subject to established usage restrictions and policies. Notwithstanding the foregoing, Media Publisher shall have the right to identify Customer as a customer, and Customer shall have the right to identify Media Publisher as the provider of the Media Publisher Service, without obtaining the other party's prior approval.

18. **General**

    a. *Force Majeure.* In the event that either party is prevented from performing or is unable to perform any of its obligations under this Agreement due to any cause beyond its reasonable control, then that party's performance shall be excused and the time for performance shall be extended for the period of delay or inability to perform due to such occurrence;

    b. *Independent Contractors.* Media Publisher and You are independent contractors under this Agreement and nothing herein shall be construed to create a partnership, joint venture or agency relationship between Media Publisher and You, and neither party has authority to enter into agreements of any kind on behalf of the other;

c. *Assignment.* Neither party may assign performance of this Agreement or any of its rights or delegate any of its duties under this Agreement without the prior written consent of the other;

d. *Merger or Acquisition.* Notwithstanding the provisions of Section (c) above, each party may assign its performance of this Agreement or any of its rights or delegate any of its duties under this Agreement without the other party's prior written consent in the case of a merger, acquisition or other change of control (as that phrase is interpreted under Delaware law), and in such event this Agreement shall be binding upon and inure to the benefit of the parties hereto and their respective heirs, successors and assigns;

e. *Governing Law.* This Agreement, its interpretation, performance or any breach thereof, shall be construed in accordance with, governed by and all questions with respect thereto shall be determined by, the laws of the _____ applicable to contracts entered into and wholly to be performed within said state;

f. *Forum and Jurisdiction.* You hereby consent to the personal jurisdiction of the state of _____, acknowledge that venue is proper in any Federal or state court in _____, agree that any action arising out of or related to this Agreement must be brought exclusively in a Federal or state court in _____ and waive any objection You have or may have in the future with respect to any of the foregoing;

g. *Good Faith.* Each party agrees to act in good faith with respect to each provision of this Agreement and any dispute that may arise related hereto;

h. *Effect of Waivers.* The waiver by either party of a breach or a default of any provision shall not be construed as a waiver of any succeeding breach of the same or any other provision;

i. *Severability.* Each provision of this Agreement shall be severable from every other provision of this Agreement for the purpose of determining the legal enforceability of any specific provision;

j. *Survival.* All terms of this Agreement which by their nature extend beyond their termination, remain in effect until fulfilled and apply to respective successors and assigns;

    k. *No Modification Unless in Writing.* Except as specifically and expressly addressed in a writing executed by both parties, the terms and conditions of this Agreement in effect between the parties shall govern; and

    l. *Headings.* The section headings and subheadings contained in this Agreement are included for convenience only, and shall not limit or otherwise affect the terms of this Agreement.

19. *Notices.* All notice required to be given under this Agreement must be given in writing and delivered either by hand, by email, by certified mail (return receipt requested, postage pre-paid) or by Federal Express or other recognized overnight delivery service (all delivery charges pre-paid) and addressed, if to Customer, to the contact identified in the lead-in of this Agreement and, if to Media Publisher, to *[name of company]*, _____, attn: _____.

20. *Entire Agreement; Precedence.* This Agreement constitutes the entire understanding of the parties hereto with respect to the matters and transactions contemplated hereby, supersede all previous agreements between Media Publisher and You concerning the subject matter hereof and cannot be amended except by a writing signed by authorized representatives of both parties. No party hereto has relied on any statement, representation or promise of any party or representative thereof in executing this Agreement.

Intending to be bound the parties hereby accept and agree to this Agreement.

[Name of Media Publishing Company]   **[Customer]**

By: _____   By: _____

Name: _____   Name: _____

Title: _____   Title: _____

Date: _____, 20____   Date: _____, 20____

Exhibit A

Fees

[Insert Fee Schedule]

[May include per download and storage fees.]

All fees are non-refundable.

Exhibit B

Support

[Insert Support Offerings. Include service hours, response times, etc.]

Exhibit C
Service Level Agreement

[To be added. See sample included in Form 10-5 as Schedule C]

Affiliate Media Services Agreement

Introductory Note

This is a form agreement offered by a content aggregator/service provider (here called the "Provider") that offers an online service that distributes streamed digital content. This form is the contractual link between such a Provider and a web site owner (referred to as a "Provider Affiliate") that wishes to arrange to feature on its web site streamed video or audio content (such as news, sports clips, user-contributed content, recorded music, music videos, etc.) that the Provider will make available.

As you can see, this is a web-ready, user-friendly form that allows the Provider to offer the Provider Affiliate online "click-and-go" selection of content. This form is most suited to smaller customers. (Major web properties that consume high volumes of content would likely have a negotiated agreement with the Provider rather than this kind of clickwrap form).

This form is written to cover both free and for-fee distribution of digital content.

Affiliate Media Services Agreement

Here is a short summary of how You can use the Provider Service as a Provider Affiliate (full legal terms and details follow this summary):

Step 1. *Register, Accept this Agreement.* Read this Agreement and then click "Accept" in order to become a Provider Affiliate.

Step 2. *Access the provider's online interface (the "Provider Console").* Once You have registered, You will have access to the Provider Console. There, You will be able to search for and select content and players from Publishers for Your web site.

Step 3. *Paste the Player to Your Web Site.* The Provider Console will provide You with a small piece of code that you can simply paste into Your web site where you choose to display the player which will run the content You select to offer to Your End Users. When they want to watch the content, Provider delivers it to them!

That's it. The legal details follow below.

Terms and Conditions

PLEASE READ THIS AGREEMENT VERY CAREFULLY. IT IS A LEGAL DOCUMENT. IT CONTAINS BINDING RIGHTS AND OBLIGATIONS. BY CLICKING "I ACCEPT" AT THE END OF THIS DOCUMENT, YOU ARE AGREEING TO BE BOUND BY THESE TERMS.

IF YOU ARE ACCEPTING ON BEHALF OF YOUR EMPLOYER OR ANOTHER ENTITY, YOU REPRESENT AND WARRANT THAT YOU HAVE FULL LEGAL AUTHORITY TO BIND YOUR EMPLOYER OR SUCH ENTITY TO THESE TERMS AND CONDITIONS. IF YOU DO NOT HAVE THE LEGAL AUTHORITY TO BIND, YOU MAY NOT ACCEPT THIS AGREEMENT. BY ACCEPTING THIS AGREEMENT, YOU ARE REQUESTING TO UTILIZE THE PROVIDER SERVICE AS AN AFFILIATE. "YOU" MEANS YOU OR, IF YOU ARE ACCEPTING ON BEHALF OF YOUR EMPLOYER OR ANOTHER ENTITY, THEN "YOU" MEANS THAT EMPLOYER OR ENTITY.

1. **Account Creation**

    a. *Registration.* In order to use the Provider Service as a Provider Affiliate, You must first complete and submit all required fields of the Provider Service registration pages and accept this Agreement. Provider reserves the right, exercised at any time in its sole discretion, to reject any registration submission.

    b. *Password.* During the registration process for this Site, you will be asked to create a unique sign-in name ("Sign-In Name"), which will be Your email address. Provider will then supply You with a password ("Password") associated with that Sign-In Name. Each Sign-In Name and corresponding Password can only be used by one User. You are solely responsible for the confidentiality and use of your Sign-In Name and Password, as well as for any use, misuse or communications using your Sign-In Name and Password. You agree to notify us immediately if you become aware of any loss, theft or unauthorized use of your Sign-In

Name or Password and we reserve the right to delete or change one or both of them at any time and for any reason. Provider shall have the right to rely, without further inquiry, on provision of the Sign-In Name and Password as sufficient to authenticate use of the Provider Service by You or on your behalf.

2. **Obtaining Content for Your Web Site**

    a. *Content Available for Affiliation.* The Provider Console will identify what Content is available to Provider Affiliates for distribution from time to time. Availability is subject to the sole discretion of Publishers who choose to publish their Content through the Provider Service, and who addition-ally choose to make such Content available for distribution by Provider Affiliates. Provider makes no promise or representation that any particular Content or any amount of Content will be available for Affiliate distribu-tion at any time. "Publisher Packaged Content" is Content and a Player or Players, and related Titles and/or Lineups all selected by a Publisher for distribution by Publisher-approved Provider Affiliates. In order to obtain a Publisher's approval to distribute Publisher-Packaged Content, You must identify and submit, as prompted by the Provider Console, the URLs of the web sites where You want to make such Content available to end users (the "URLs"). You may only identify the URLs of web sites You own or otherwise have the legal right to operate. Your iden-tification and submission of URLs shall serve as a representation and war-ranty that You are the owner of such URLs and/or otherwise have sufficient legal rights to offer the Provider Service on and through such URLs. Your submission of a URL of a web site not owned by You, or for which You do not possess sufficient rights to offer the Provider Service on and through such web sites, shall constitute a material breach of this Agreement. Approval of Your request to distribute Publisher-Packaged Content is in the sole discretion of each Publisher, as applicable, and may be revoked by such Publisher at any time, for any reason, and in all cases is limited to the specific URLs identified for approval by the Publisher. If Your submission is approved by the Publisher through the Provider Service, then Provider will make available to You HTML code (the "Provider Player Code") to enable You to embed this Player on these URLs only (the "Approved URLs"). This will enable end users of the Approved URLs to access the Content made available to You by the Publisher. The availability of, and the look, feel, and composition of, any particular Content and/or Players is solely at the discretion of the Publisher. From time to time, through the Provider Console, Publishers and/or the Pro-vider Service may make Content available to Affiliates according to different procedures or offer additional features to Affiliates.

b. *Terms of Use of Provider Affiliate Services.* In addition to the terms of the various licenses granted in this Agreement, You expressly agree to the following Terms of Use:

i. You agree to take the Content and Players supplied through the Provider Service on an "AS IS" and "AS AVAILABLE" basis. Provider makes no promises or representations about the Content or the Players or their suitability for any particular purpose or audience, their perfor-mance, the accuracy of any description thereof, that either will be error free or complete, or that either will remain available for any particular period of time.

ii. You agree not to take any action or permit any action that obscures or interferes with, in part or in whole, the presentation of either the Content within the Player, the Player itself, or any branding or advertising presented within or on the Player.

iii. You agree not to copy, capture, edit, cache, reverse engineer, stream grab, crack, or otherwise misappropriate any Content, Players, adver-tising, branding, code, or anything else supplied by or through the Provider Service, and you agree not to take any action or knowingly permit any action, directly or indirectly, that enables, allows, facilitates or assists any end user or other party to do so.

iv. You agree that You may only make the Content and the Players avail-able to end users on and through the Approved URLs (i.e., the URLs for which You applied and received Publisher approval through the Provider Console).

v. You agree that Provider's General Terms and Conditions of Use for End Users, available at *[insert URL]*, shall apply with respect to access by end users to the Content and the Players on the Approved URLs (collectively, the "Terms of Use").

3. Distribution of Content to End Users of the Approved URLs

Unless otherwise indicated by the Provider Console, each Publisher sets the usage terms under which end users may access the Publisher's Content (e.g., free to view online, free to download for a fixed period, pay to own, pay to rent, etc.). Provider and/or the Publisher shall be responsible for encoding the Content to conform to such usage rules. Provider will deliver the Content to end users of the Approved URLs at such times as requested through the Players. Absent the permission of the Publisher and/or Provider, You agree not to take any act, directly or indirectly, to vary the terms of the usage rules set by the Publisher. Provider reserves the right to sell and serve advertising within the Player and/or Content itself.

4. **Payments**

   There is no fee for registering as a Provider Affiliate. To the extent any fees or payments are required to be paid to Provider by You in order to enable the distribution of Content to end users of the URLs, such fees or payments will be identified by Provider in conjunction with Your selection of Content through the Provider Console. Unless otherwise indicated in the Provider Console, Provider shall not have any obligation to pay any amount to You, or share any revenue with You.

5. **Licenses**

   a. *License to Content.* To the limited extent required in order to be able to participate in the Provider Affiliate Services program as available from time to time, Provider hereby grants You a non-transferable (except as provided herein), royalty-free (except as provided herein), non-exclusive, worldwide sublicense to make the Content available to end users of the Approved URLs through the Provider Service. This license and all sublicenses thereto shall terminate automatically upon the effective date of termination or expiration of this Agreement, subject to the usage rights granted to end users through the Provider Service (i.e., termination of this Agreement shall not serve to divest any end user of usage rights acquired through the Provider Service which by their nature extend beyond the effective date of termination).

   b. *License to Marks.* Subject to the terms and conditions of this Agreement, Provider grants You, and You grant Provider, the non-transferable (except as provided herein), non-exclusive, royalty-free right to reproduce and display the other's logos, trademarks, trade names, and other similar identifying material (the "Marks") solely for the purposes described herein and in accordance with the owner's established trademark usage policies and procedures as changed from time to time in the owner's sole discretion and as supplied by link. In connection with such licenses, each party shall have the unilateral right to establish such quality standards and additional terms and conditions as such party deems necessary to reasonably protect its trademarks. This license and all sublicenses thereto shall terminate automatically upon the effective date of termination or expiration of this Agreement, subject to the usage rights granted to end users through the Provider Service (i.e., termination of this Agreement shall not serve to divest any end user of usage rights acquired through the Provider Service which by their nature extend beyond the effective date of termination).

c. *License to Provider Player Code.* Subject to the terms and conditions of this Agreement, Provider grants You a non-transferable (except as provided herein), non-exclusive, royalty-free (except as provided herein), worldwide license to use the Provider Player Code in order to display the Provider Service at Your owned and/or operated Approved URLs. Provider shall have the unilateral right to change or modify the Provider Player Code and to establish such quality standards and additional terms and conditions with respect to use of the Provider Player Code as Provider deems necessary to reasonably protect its rights to the Provider Player Code and/ or the Provider Service with or without any notice to You. You may not modify the Provider Player Code or otherwise perform any act to obscure or interfere with the display or functionality of any feature of any Provider-supplied Player, including, without limitation, the Provider Mark or logo, or any hypertext link built into any Provider Player. Your violation of any of the prohibitions in the preceding sentence shall constitute a violation of the terms of this License grant resulting in automatic termination thereof. This license shall terminate automatically upon the effective date of termination or expiration of this Agreement. Unless specifically and expressly permitted by Provider, You agree that You will not (i) permit any other entity to use the Provider Player Code; (ii) modify, translate, reverse engineer, decompile, disassemble (except to the extent that this restriction is expressly prohibited by law) or create derivative works based upon any of the software/code licensed to You hereby or based upon any access or usage of the Provider Player Code; (iii) copy the software/code licensed hereby (except as expressly permitted or for backup or archival purposes); (iv) rent, lease, transfer, or otherwise transfer rights to any aspect of the Provider Player Code; or (v) remove any proprietary notices or labels, branding or designations on the Provider Player Code. You further agree that upon termination or expiration of this license, You shall no longer have the right to use the Provider Player Code, display the Provider Player, or stream or make available for download any Content from the Provider Service.

d. *License to Offer Provider Service.* Subject to the terms and conditions of this Agreement, Provider grants You a non-transferable (except as provided herein), non-exclusive, royalty-free (except as provided herein), world-wide license to display and offer the Provider Service to End Users at the Approved URLs owned, licensed, and/or operated by You. Provider shall have the unilateral right to change or modify the Provider Service and to establish such quality standards and additional terms and conditions with respect to use of the Provider Service as Provider deems necessary to reasonably protect its rights to the Provider Service with or without any notice to You. This license shall terminate automatically upon the effective date of termination or expiration of this Agreement. Unless specifically and expressly permitted by Provider, You agree that You will not (i) permit any other entity to use the Provider Service except under the terms of this Agreement; (ii) modify, translate, reverse engineer, decompile, disassemble (except to the extent that this restriction is expressly prohibited by law) or create derivative works based upon any of the software/code licensed to You hereby or based upon any access or usage of the Provider Service; (iii) copy the software/code licensed hereby (except as expressly permitted or for backup or archival purposes); (iv) rent, lease, transfer, or otherwise transfer rights to any aspect of the Provider Service; or (v) remove any proprietary notices or labels, branding or designations on the Provider Service. You further agree that upon termination or expiration of this license, You shall no longer have the right to offer the Provider Service.

e. *Ownership/Reservation of Rights*

   i. *For You.* You retain all right, title and interest in and to Your web sites, Your Marks, and all components thereof. This Agreement shall not be construed in any manner as transferring any rights of ownership to or license of Your web sites, Your Marks, or any component thereof, and/or to the features, or information therein, except as expressly licensed by this Agreement. All rights not expressly granted by You are reserved by You. Under no circumstances will the license grants set forth in this

Agreement be construed as granting, by implication, estoppel or otherwise, a license to any of Your intellectual or other property or components thereof other than as specifically granted in this Agreement.

ii. *For Provider*. Provider retains any and all right, title and interest in all of Provider's intellectual property and other rights, including but not limited to the Provider Service, the Provider Player Code, and the Provider Marks and all components thereof. This Agreement shall not be construed in any manner as transferring any rights of ownership of or license to the Provider Service, the Provider Player Code, and the Provider Marks, or any component thereof, and/or to the features, or information therein, except as expressly licensed by this Agreement. All rights not expressly granted by Provider are reserved by Provider. Under no circumstances will the license grants set forth in this Agreement be construed as granting, by implication, estoppel or otherwise, a license to any Provider intellectual or other property or components thereof other than as specifically granted in this Agreement.

6. Representations and Warranties

a. *Corporate Power*. If You are a corporation, You represent and warrant that You are duly organized and validly existing under the laws of the state of Your incorporation and have full corporate power and authority to enter into this Agreement and to carry out the provisions hereof.

b. *Due Authorization*. You represent and warrant that You are duly authorized to execute and deliver this Agreement and that You are duly authorized to perform Your obligations hereunder.

c. *Binding Agreement*. You represent and warrant that (i) this Agreement is a legal and valid obligation binding upon You and enforceable with its terms, and (ii) the execution, delivery and performance of this Agreement does not conflict with any agreement, instrument, or understanding, oral or written, to which You are a party or by which You may be bound, nor violate any law or regulation of any court, governmental body or administrative or other agency having jurisdiction over You.

d. *No Infringement*. You represent and warrant that You either own fully and outright or otherwise possesses and have obtained all rights, approvals, licenses, consents and permissions as are necessary to perform the obligations hereunder and to grant the licenses granted under this Agreement for the duration of the Term.

e. *DISCLAIMERS*

    i. PROVIDER MAKES NO REPRESENTATIONS OR WARRANTIES OF ANY KIND, EITHER EXPRESS OR IMPLIED, AS TO ANY MATTER IN CONNECTION WITH THIS AGREEMENT INCLUDING, BUT NOT LIMITED TO, IMPLIED WARRANTIES OF FITNESS FOR A PARTICULAR PURPOSE, MERCHANTABILITY, NON-INFRINGEMENT, TITLE OR OTHERWISE. YOU EXPRESSLY ACKNOWLEDGE AND AGREE THAT, IN ADDITION TO THE FOREGOING DISCLAIMER, THE CONTENT, THE PROVIDER SERVICE, AND THE PROVIDER PLAY-ER CODE ARE PROVIDED ON AN 'AS IS' BASIS ONLY, AND PRO-VIDER MAKES NO REPRESENTATION, WARRANTY, OR ASSURANCE THAT THEY WILL BE ERROR-FREE OR PERFORM IN ACCORDANCE WITH ANY PARTICULAR STANDARD, LEVEL, OR METRIC, OR THAT THEY ARE SUITABLE FOR ANY PARTICULAR PURPOSE OR AUDIENCE.

    ii. YOU ALSO EXPRESSLY ACKNOWLEDGE AND AGREE THAT THE PROVIDER SERVICE UTILIZES AND RELIES UPON THIRD-PARTY SOFTWARE FOR CERTAIN FUNCTIONS, INCLUDING BUT NOT LIMITED TO THE ENCODING AND APPLICATION OF SECURITY AND DRM FUNCTIONALITY AND PROTECTIONS, AND PROVIDER MAKES NO REPRESENTATION, WARRANTY, PROMISE OR GUARANTEE THAT SUCH SOFTWARE WILL BE ERROR FREE, ACCOMPLISH THE SPECIFIED INTENT OR PERFORM IN ACCORDANCE WITH ANY PARTICULAR STANDARD, LEVEL, OR METRIC AND PROVIDER TAKES NO RESPONSIBILITY AND WILL NOT BE LIABLE FOR ANY FAILURE THEREOF. YOU ALSO ACKNOWLEDGE AND AGREE THAT TECHNOLOGY MAY EXIST OR BE DEVELOPED TO COPY, DOWNLOAD, OR OTHERWISE ACQUIRE THE CONTENT WITHOUT YOUR AND/OR PROVIDER'S AUTHORIZATION AND/OR KNOWLEDGE, INCLUDING WITHOUT LIMITATION CONTENT DELIVERED THROUGH STREAMING TECHNOLOGY, AND THAT SUCH SECURITY AND DRM FUNCTIONALITY AND PROTECTIONS AS ARE OFFERED BY PROVIDER

MAY NOT BE SUFFICIENT TO PREVENT SUCH UNAUTHORIZED ACTS. THE ENTIRE RISK ARISING OUT OF USE OF THE PROVIDER SERVICE AND THE PROVIDER PLAYER CODE REMAINS WITH YOU.

iii. IN ADDITION TO THE FOREGOING DISCLAIMERS, PROVIDER SPECIFICALLY DISCLAIMS MAKING ANY EXPRESS OR IMPLIED REPRESENTATION OR WARRANTY OF NON-INFRINGEMENT, OWNERSHIP, OR TITLE WITH RESPECT TO THE "PUBLISHER'S" CONTENT. SPECIFICALLY, PROVIDER REPRESENTS AND WARRANTS ONLY THAT IT HAS RECEIVED FROM EACH PARTY IDENTIFIED IN THE PROVIDER SERVICE AS THE "PUBLISHER" OF A GIVEN UNIT OF CONTENT A REPRESENTATION THAT IT IS EITHER THE OWNER OF THAT CONTENT OR OTHERWISE POSSESSES SUFFICIENT RIGHTS TO GRANT PROVIDER THE RIGHT TO DISTRIBUTE THAT CONTENT TO END USERS OF, INTER ALIA, THE APPROVED URLs, AND THAT PROVIDER HAS FURTHER RECEIVED FROM EACH SUCH ENTITY IDENTIFIED AS THE "PUBLISHER" OF SUCH CONTENT A LICENSE FOR THE DISTRIBUTION OF SUCH CONTENT TO END USERS OF THE APPROVED URLs. PLEASE BE ADVISED THAT PROVIDER HAS NOT INDEPENDENTLY CONFIRMED THE ACCURACY OR TRUTHFULNESS OF SUCH ENTITY'S REPRESENTATION.

7. Indemnification

a. You agree to indemnify and hold harmless Provider and Provider's officers, directors, shareholders, employees, accountants, attorneys, agents, affiliates, subsidiaries, successors, and assigns (the "Indemnitees") from and against any and all third party ("third party" includes, without limitation, End Users, Provider Affiliates, Provider Syndication Partners, advertisers, guilds, associations, licensing organizations, and other third parties) claims, damages, liabilities, costs and expenses (each a "Claim"), arising out of or related to any breach of any warranty or representation made by You in this Agreement. In addition, You shall indemnify and hold harmless Provider and the Provider Indemnitees for any Claims arising out of or relating to any breach by You or by end users of web sites on which You permit access to the Provider Service of any term or condition of use set forth in this Agreement, the Terms of Use, or in Provider's General Terms and Conditions of Use for End Users. The foregoing indemnities are conditioned upon (i) written notice by Provider or the indemnified party to the indemnifying party of any claim, action or demand for which indemnification is claimed, (ii) the opportunity to have reasonable control of the defense with counsel reasonably acceptable to the indemnified party and settlement thereof by the indemnifying party, and (iii) such reasonable cooperation by the indemnified party in the defense as the indemnifying party may request, all provided, however, that failure to provide reasonable notice, control and/or cooperation shall not relieve the indemnification obligations hereof unless the party seeking to avoid such obligations can demonstrate material prejudice to the defense of such Claim caused thereby. You shall not, without the prior written consent of Provider, settle, compromise, or consent to the entry of any judgment with respect to any pending or threatened claim unless the settlement, compromise or consent provides for and includes an express, unconditional release of all claims, damages, liabilities, costs, and expenses, including reasonable legal fees and expenses, against the indemnified party.

8. Confidentiality

You agree not to disclose Provider Confidential Information without Provider's prior written consent. "Provider Confidential Information" includes without limitation: (i) all Provider intellectual property, including without limitation all Provider software, technology, programming, technical specifications, materials, guidelines and documentation relating to the Provider Service; (ii) any usage or click-through rates, financial information (including pricing), business information, including operations, planning, marketing interests, products, and any other reporting information (including revenues, if any, paid to You by Provider) provided by Provider; and (iii) any other information designated in writing by Provider as "Confidential" or an equivalent designation or that would otherwise be reasonably considered confidential or proprietary under the circumstances. It does not include information that has become publicly known through no breach by You or Provider, or information that has been (a) independently developed without access to Provider Confidential Information, as evidenced in writing; (b) rightfully received by You from a third party without a breach of confidentiality by such third party; or (c) required to be disclosed by law or by a governmental authority.

9. Term

The term ("Term") of this Agreement shall commence on the Effective Date and shall continue for three years unless terminated earlier pursuant to the terms of this Agreement. Upon the end of the Term and the end of each subsequent renewal term ("Renewal Term"), this Agreement shall automatically renew for a Renewal Term, unless either party sends Notice to the other at least sixty days in advance of the commencement of such Renewal Term. Each Renewal Term shall continue for one year from the commencement date of such Renewal Term.

10. Termination

Either party may terminate this Agreement if (a) the other party is adjudicated bankrupt; (b) a voluntary or involuntary petition in bankruptcy is filed against the other party and such petition is not dismissed within ninety days of the filing date; (c) the other party becomes insolvent or makes an assignment for the benefit of its creditors pursuant to any bankruptcy law; (d) a receiver is appointed for the other party or its business; (e) upon the occurrence of a material breach of a material provision by the other party if such breach is not cured within thirty (30) days after written Notice is received by the breaching party identifying the matter constituting the material breach; or (f) by mutual written consent. In addition, Provider may terminate the Agreement on thirty days' written Notice for any reason or for no reason. In addition, Provider may suspend its performance or any aspect thereof at any time, without giving prior Notice, for any act which Provider, in its sole discretion, determines to be harmful to it, the Provider Service, or any End User, or which in Provider's sole discretion violates or fails to comply with any applicable law or regulation.

11. General

a. Provider and You are independent contractors under this Agreement and nothing herein shall be construed to create a partnership, joint venture or agency relationship between Provider and You. Neither party has authority to enter into agreements of any kind on behalf of the other;

b. You may not assign performance of this Agreement or any of its rights or delegate any of its duties under this Agreement without the prior written consent of Provider. Notwithstanding the provisions of the preceding sentence, however, in the case of a merger, acquisition, or other change of control (as that phrase is interpreted under Delaware Law), this Agreement shall be binding upon and inure to the benefit of the parties hereto and their respective heirs, successors, and assigns;

c. This Agreement, its interpretation, performance or any breach thereof, shall be construed in accordance with, governed by, and all questions with respect thereto shall be determined by, the laws of _____ applicable to contracts entered into and wholly to be performed within said state. You hereby consent to the personal jurisdiction of _____, acknowledge that venue is proper in any Federal or state court in _____, agree that any action arising out of or related to this Agreement must be brought exclusively in a Federal or state court in _____, and waive any objection You have or may have in the future with respect to any of the foregoing;

d. You agree to act in good faith with respect to each provision of this Agreement and any dispute that may arise related hereto;

e. If You click on the "I Accept" button below, this will constitute Your acceptance of this Agreement, including all of its terms and conditions;

f. The waiver by Provider of a breach or a default of any provision shall not be construed as a waiver of any succeeding breach of the same or any other provision, nor shall any delay or omission on the part of Provider to exercise or avail itself of any right, power or privilege that it has, or may have hereunder, operate as a waiver of any right, power or privilege of Provider.

12. Notices

All notice required to be given under this Agreement must be given in writing and delivered either in hand, by email, by certified mail, return receipt requested, postage pre-paid, or by Federal Express or other recognized overnight delivery service, all delivery charges pre-paid, and addressed:

If to Provider:

Provider, Inc.

Attn: General Counsel

If to You:

Email sent to the address You supplied at the time of Registration shall constitute sufficient Notice under this Agreement.

13. Entire Agreement

This Agreement constitutes the entire understanding of the parties hereto with respect to the matters and transactions contemplated hereby, supersede all previous agreements between Provider and You concerning the subject matter, and cannot be amended except by a writing signed by authorized representatives of both parties. No party hereto has relied on any statement, representation, or promise of any party or representative thereof in executing this Agreement except as expressly stated therein.

14. Limitation of Liability

UNDER NO CIRCUMSTANCES SHALL EITHER PARTY BE LIABLE TO THE OTHER FOR INDIRECT, INCIDENTAL, CONSEQUENTIAL, SPECIAL OR EXEMPLARY DAMAGES (EVEN IF THAT PARTY HAS BEEN ADVISED OF THE POSSIBILITY OF SUCH DAMAGES) FOR ANY REASON INCLUDING, WITHOUT LIMITATION, THOSE ARISING FROM THE PERFORMANCE UNDER OR FAILURE OF PERFORMANCE OF ANY PROVISION OF THIS AGREEMENT (INCLUDING SUCH DAMAGES INCURRED BY THIRD PARTIES), SUCH AS, BUT NOT LIMITED TO, LOSS OF REVENUE, OR ANTICIPATED PROFITS OR LOST BUSINESS. UNDER NO CIRCUMSTANCES WILL PROVIDER BE LIABLE FOR DAMAGES IN EXCESS OF UNPAID AMOUNTS OWED TO YOU, IF ANY, OR WILL YOU BE LIABLE TO PROVIDER FOR DAMAGES IN EXCESS OF UNPAID AMOUNTS OWED TO PROVIDER, IF ANY. NOTWITHSTANDING ANY OF THE FOREGOING IN THIS ENTIRE SECTION, TO THE EXTENT PERMITTED BY APPLICABLE LAW, THE LIMITATIONS SET FORTH IN THIS SECTION SHALL NOT APPLY IN THE CASE OF (A) INTENTIONAL TORTS OR DAMAGES RESULTING FROM BREA-CHES OF ANY APPLICABLE TERMS AND CONDITIONS OF USE, INCLUDING WITHOUT LIMITATION, THE TERMS OF USE SET FORTH IN SECTION 2, (B) AMOUNTS PAYABLE PURSUANT TO SECTION 7 ("INDEMNIFICATION"), OR (C) BREACHES OF SECTION 8 ("CONFIDENTIALITY").

15. Survival

All terms of this Agreement which, by their nature extend beyond its termination, remain in effect until fulfilled and apply to respective successors and assigns.

Updated: *[Insert date of last Agreement update]*

Video Game Publishing Agreement

Introductory Note

This is a video game publishing agreement with annotations to aid you in negotiation of game deals. This is drawn from a variety of actual agreements.

This form includes many provisions that commonly occur in these agreements, including some common variants and alternatives. Optional and alternative clauses are indicated. Text in brackets within sections is also optional. There are some combinations and permutations that work together and some that will not make sense. So be careful to think through your choices.

This form covers a lot of ground, but is not comprehensive. Because the variety of deals and game types is limitless, your own negotiated agreement will almost certainly require different terms or choices or may raise concerns not addressed here.

In negotiating these agreements, you should read the text of each clause carefully and think through the way that each clause will affect your business. Your own perception of the technical, financial, and business risks will determine which clauses are most important to your business.

The following form is for the case where the game software is to be created and supplied to the Publisher under the agreement. If the software were already in existence, the form would be simplified to require a single delivery and acceptance.

In the following form, the schedules are skeletal; the details would vary with the particular deal.

Video Game Publishing Agreement

This Video Game Publishing Agreement ("Agreement") is effective as of *[insert date]* (the "Effective Date"), between _____ ("Publisher") with its principal office at _____ and _____ ("Developer") with its principal office at _____.

Purpose of This Agreement

Publisher desires to retain Developer, and Developer desires to be retained by Publisher, to develop and supply a video game software program and related materials in accordance with the terms and conditions set forth in this Agreement,

Intending to be bound, Publisher and Developer hereby agree as follows:

1. **Certain Definitions.** As used in this Agreement the following definitions will apply:

   [**Comment:** *The definitions section should define key terms of the agreement to avoid ambiguity and to simplify drafting by providing shorthand names for persons and things. Additional definitions can appear in Schedules and in the text. Depending on choices made in the remainder of the agreement, you may need to add to these definitions or delete some of them.*]

   1.1. "Affiliate" means any corporate entity that controls, is controlled by or is under the common control of a party to this Agreement.

   1.2. "Alpha" means a playable version of the Game containing substantially all features listed in the Specification with all software modules integrated and working together in a usable and testable fashion. The Alpha is expected to undergo further tests and revisions for design tuning and elimination of Defects. Some functions or content may be placeholders for purposes of this version, and this version may not include title and legal screens. Alpha will also include a draft of the User Manual text.

   1.3. "Ancillary Product" means any form, now known or hereafter devised, in which the Game or its plot, branding, characters, storyline concept, scenes, and setting may be recast, transformed, exploited or adapted, including, but not limited to, books, merchandising, radio and television programs, motion pictures, video, web sites, animation and musical recordings.

   1.4. "Beta" means the complete software Game containing all features of the Game as specified in the Specifications with corrections of Defects and any improvements or changes that Developer may have made. The Beta version includes the final User Manual text.

1.5. "Branding Elements" means any branding or trademark that Developer has created that is specific to the Game. Branding Elements do not include trademarks that Developer applies to its products generally.

1.6. "Defect" means, with respect to any deliverable, any material deviation from the applicable Specifications or any defect in quality or operation.

1.7. "Development Materials" means, with regard to each Milestone, the necessary materials of Developer, including but not limited to Source Code and data, that would allow Publisher to independently build such deliverables (but excluding Publisher or third party software code or libraries).

1.8. "Developer's Tools" means any of Developer's software tools used for Game content creation or game design (but excluding Publisher or third party software tools).

1.9. "Documentation" means documentation for the Developer's Tools and programming, compilation and assembly instructions for the Game.

1.10. "End User" means anyone who is the user of any Game as distributed.

1.11. "Executable Code" means the fully compiled version of the Game that can be executed by a computer.

1.12. "Final Acceptance" means (a) Publisher has provided its written acceptance of the complete Game in Gold Master form following successful completion of all testing and approvals and (b) the Game has received all third party verifications that the Game is ready for manufacturing and replication.

*[**Comment:** The reference in this definition and in the Gold Master definition below to "third party" approval refers to game platform owners or other third parties that must approve games before they can be released.]*

1.13. "Game" means the consumer video game entertainment product described in <u>Schedule A</u>.

1.14. "Game Assets" means the Source Code, Developer's proprietary libraries, sound files, video files, graphic files, and other digital assets used in the compilation of the Game (other than those supplied by Publisher or third parties) together with the Documentation.

1.15. "Game Engine" means the core operating functionality of the Game supplied by Developer in binary code form that interacts with the computer or game console environment and executes the game programming or game play. The Game Engine includes, without limitation, software that provides object rendering, object positioning and movement, object-user interaction, and sound control.

1.16. "Gold Master" means the final gold master of the Game for use on all required platforms that: (a) is suitable for release to manufacturing for commercial release and shipment in all required languages and platforms and (b) has been accepted for manufacturing and distribution by any applicable third party whose approval is required prior to manufacturing and distribution.

1.17. "Intellectual Property Rights" means all present and future rights regarding copyrights, patents, trademarks, trade secrets, and trade names, or rights analogous to above in any jurisdiction, in each case registered or unregistered, including, without limitation, all rights in any jurisdiction required to copy, adapt, translate, broadcast, transmit, publish, perform, reproduce in any medium and otherwise exploit the Game.

1.18. "Milestone" means each stage of development of the Game set out alongside a Milestone Date in the Milestone Schedule.

1.19. "Milestone Date" means each of the dates for achieving a Milestone in the Milestone Schedule.

1.20. "Milestone Payment" means each of the development advance payments set forth in the Milestone Schedule.

1.21. "Milestone Schedule" means the delivery and payment schedule for the Game described in <u>Schedule B</u>, as may be amended from time to time by written agreement of the parties.

1.22. "Publisher's Property" will means assets and Intellectual Property Rights arranged for or supplied by Publisher for the purpose of this Agreement or for the Game.

1.23. "Quarter" or "Quarterly" means a calendar quarter or, as applicable, a portion thereof.

1.24. "Royalties" means payments to Developer that are to be paid as stated in Section 9 and 10 and in <u>Schedule D.</u>

1.25. "Sequel" means one of a series of games that End Users perceive as related in a sequence with the Game that feature both branding and content that plainly indicates such a relationship.

1.26. "Source Code" means all source code, build scripts and batch files in human readable form needed to generate the Game in binary form (but excluding Publisher or third party software code or libraries).

1.27. "Specifications" means the specifications for the Game as set forth in <u>Schedule E</u>, with any modifications that may be agreed upon by the parties in writing.

1.28. "Territory" means *[state geographic areas of distribution].*

1.29. "User Manual" means a manual containing instructions for End Users written in a style suitable for the intended age of targeted End Users.

2. **Development of the Game**

   2.1. *Development Undertaking*

      2.1.1. Subject to the terms of this Agreement, Developer agrees to develop the Game. [The Game as developed will be of "AAA" quality as that term is understood in the interactive video game software industry.]

      2.1.2. Except as otherwise provided in this Agreement, Developer agrees to perform all services and provide at Developer's sole cost and expense all necessary programming and other materials in order to develop the Game in accordance with the Specifications and the Milestone Schedule.

   *[**Comment:** A source of many disputes is changes to specifications. Often publishers may ask for additional or different features without expecting to pay more. Conflicts and misunderstandings can be avoided by documenting requests for extra work and extra compensation. Similar problems can arise when delivery is late and arguments arise over whether this was agreed to. This form requires the parties to negotiate changes in specifications and delivery schedules.]*

2.2. *Changes in Specifications and Milestone Schedule*

2.2.1. Either Publisher or Developer may propose changes in the Specifications or to the Milestone Schedule. No such change will be effective unless Publisher and Developer agree, in writing, to the change.

2.2.2. Publisher may not require work, levels, characters or features not set forth in the Specifications unless agreed to in writing. Developer will not be compensated, other than as stated in the Milestone Schedule, unless such additional payments are agreed to in advance in writing by Publisher.

2.3. *Publisher Contributions*

Publisher will provide to Developer, at Publisher's own expense, the development tools, licenses, permissions, and sound and video assets and other assets for the Game listed on <u>Schedule F.</u>

*[**Comment:** The Publisher's contribution might be third party programming tools or licensed content, such as brands, or rights to video, graphics, music, etc.]*

2.4. *Developer Personnel*

2.4.1. Developer will assign qualified personnel to carry out the development tasks stated in this Agreement.

2.4.2. [**Optional Provision:**] Developer will appoint a project manager to coordinate development of the Game and to serve as Publisher's primary contact for all issues related to the services provided hereunder. The Developer's project manager and any replacement thereof will be subject to Publisher's prior review and approval, not to be unreasonably withheld.

2.4.3. [**Optional Provision:**] Developer will utilize the efforts of the personnel of Developer listed on <u>Schedule C</u> for the development of the Game from the Effective Date until Final Acceptance. Developer will not, without Publisher's prior written consent, reassign any of the personnel listed on <u>Schedule C</u> to another Developer account or project or utilize personnel who are not employees of Developer in the development of the Game. Developer agrees that Publisher will be entitled, at any time, to review Developer's technical capabilities and related development resources.

2.5. *Subcontractors*

*[**Comment:** The following language permits the Developer to use subcontractors. It is possible, of course, to include language that forbids use of outside firms.]*

2.5.1. [Developer may retain third parties to work on the Game. All such third parties [and each of their employees who work on the Game] shall execute, before providing such services, an agreement, in a form reasonably satisfactory to Publisher, which shall include a promise to maintain confidentiality as required by this Agreement and which includes an assignment to Developer of all rights in such work so that such rights may be licensed or transferred to Publisher as required by this Agreement.] [Developer may not retain or permit third parties to work on the Game.]

2.6. *Payment of Compensation*

2.6.1. Developer's personnel involved in development of the Game will at all times be employees or (as otherwise permitted) subcontractors of Developer. Developer will be solely responsible for payment of all compensation for such personnel and all related taxes and benefits.

2.7. *Developer Reports*

2.7.1. Developer will, as Publisher may reasonably request from time to time, furnish Publisher with periodic progress reports regarding the development of the Game.

2.7.2. [**Optional Provision:**] Publisher will have the right, on prior notice to Developer, to have one or more representatives present at the offices of Developer or any place at which the development of the Game is taking place. Such representatives will have the right to monitor performance of Developer's services under this Agreement and consult with Developer's personnel with respect to any aspect of the development of the Game. Publisher's right of monitoring and consultation will be exercised so as not to unreasonably interfere with Developer's business.

2.7.3. [**Optional Provision:**] Developer authorizes Publisher to obtain such credit reports and other information regarding Developer from reporting agencies and others as Publisher may deem necessary from time to time and to investigate and verify any such reports and information. In addition, as a condition precedent to any of Publisher's obligations under the terms of this Agreement and at any other time Publisher may deem necessary, Developer will provide to Publisher for Publisher's approval evidence of Developer's financial solvency. Developer will provide to Publisher proof of financial solvency in the form of financial records, which will include balance sheets, income statements, and cash flow projections. Publisher will have the right, in its sole discretion, to determine whether to proceed with this Agreement based on whether Developer is financially capable of fulfilling its obligations under the terms of this Agreement. It is understood and agreed that all financial information provided to Publisher pursuant to this Section is Confidential Information of Developer.

2.8. *Delivery*

2.8.1. Developer will develop and deliver to Publisher the various deliverables in accordance with the dates set f rth in the Milestone Schedule.

*[**Comment:** The Schedules would make clear whether Developer's delivery is only binary code or includes Source Code and tools. The latter is more common.]*

2.9. *Acceptance*

2.9.1. Upon receipt of any of Developer's deliverables, delivered in accordance with the Milestone Schedule, Publisher will have a period of fifteen (15) business days within which to test such items (the "Acceptance Period") and to notify Developer in writing of its test results with respect thereto. Failure to notify Developer with regard to any Defects during the Acceptance Period will constitute acceptance of the Milestone unless otherwise agreed in writing.

2.9.2. Publisher will perform testing to verify that Developer's deliverables conform to the Specifications and other applicable requirements for completion of the applicable development Milestone.

2.9.3. **[Optional Provision:]** Publisher will have the sole right, in its discretion, to determine, approve and disapprove the quality and content of the Game and any development Milestone, including, but not limited to, text, graphics, characters, music, banners, screens, etc.

*[**Comment:** This type of pro-Publisher language makes acceptance of the Game and each Milestone essentially discretionary on the part of the Publisher.]*

2.9.4. If Publisher notifies Developer of any Defect, Developer will, within fifteen (15) business days after receipt of notice (the "Cure Period"), make all necessary and appropriate corrections to eliminate such Defect and redeliver the revised or corrected version of such deliverable to Publisher. The applicable Acceptance Period will thereupon be renewed for an additional fifteen (15) business days from Publisher's receipt of the corrected version of the deliverable. At the end of such extended Acceptance Period, if there are any remaining or additional Defects in any affected deliverable, Publisher may in Publisher's sole discretion (a) exercise the remedies set forth below or (b) repeat the testing and cure process set forth above.

*[**Comment:** These provisions can be written to allow the Developer two or even three attempts to fix code before the Developer can be held to have failed to make the required deliverable.]*

2.10. *Failure to Cure*

2.10.1. If Publisher notifies Developer of a Defect and Developer fails to revise or correct the deliverable to Publisher's satisfaction within the Cure Period, Publisher may, at its option, elect to terminate this Agreement as provided for below, in which case the termination will be deemed to be for Developer's uncured default [, and/or by itself or through third parties make revisions or corrections to the deliverables]. [Developer will pay to Publisher the costs of any such revision or correction incurred by Publisher (including any advances and royalties paid by Publisher to third parties), and Publisher may deduct such costs from any amounts otherwise owed by Publisher to Developer.]

2.10.2. [Notwithstanding, delivery of the Game will not be considered complete until Publisher has given Final Acceptance in writing for the Gold Master.]

3. **[Optional Provision:] Modification by Publisher**

   3.1. Publisher may also modify, change or alter the Game in any respect at any time, whether during development or before, at or after Publisher's first commercial shipment of the Game; *provided, however,* that any such modification, change or alteration will relieve Developer of its warranty and maintenance obligations with regard to any issue, problem or defect caused by such Publisher modification, change or alteration.

   *[**Comment:** This pro-Publisher provision provides the Publisher with the option to take over aspects of development.]*

4. **[Optional Provision:] Demonstration Versions and Materials**

   4.1. Developer will develop and deliver to Publisher the following quantity of interactive demonstration versions of the Game (which will be suitable for introduction at industry trade shows or for incorporation into sampler discs and other promotional compilations): *[insert list of demonstration versions required].* Developer will also provide Publisher with certain materials (e.g., high resolution character art, high resolution "screen shots," concept artwork, etc.), as Publisher may request from time to time, to use in connection with the marketing and promotion of the Game. To the extent such materials are not already in existence and they require more than one hundred (100) hours of Developer's personnel time in the aggregate to create, Developer will be entitled to additional compensation for its time in excess of one hundred (100) hours in accordance with the payment terms and conditions of <u>Schedule D</u>.

5. **Ownership**

   *[**Comment:** These are many ways in which ownership of the copyrights (and any other relevant Intellectual Property Rights) in the Game can be allocated. Here are a few.]*

[Option 1. Work Made for Hire for Publisher]

   5.1. *Work for Hire; Publisher's Rights*

      5.1.1. Developer acknowledges and agrees that the Intellectual Property Rights in the Game created under this Agreement will be the sole and exclusive property of Publisher except that the Developer makes no representations with respect to the assets provided by Publisher and commercially available third party development tools and libraries. The parties agree that the Game created pursuant to this Agreement was specifically commissioned by Publisher as work made for hire, as such term is used in the US Copyright Act.

5.1.2. If the Game or any portion thereof is determined not to be a work made for hire, Developer hereby irrevocably assigns to Publisher in perpetuity throughout the universe, all right, title and interest of Developer in and to the Game, including without limitation, all Intellectual Property Rights embodied in or pertaining to the Game created under this Agreement, and the complete right to exploit or otherwise use the Game (including the right to sublicense the Intellectual Property Rights through multiple tiers of sublicensees, in any form of medium, expression or technology now known or hereafter devised.)

[Option 2. Ownership by Developer]

5.2. *Developer's Ownership Rights.* Publisher acknowledges and agrees that the Intellectual Property Rights in the Game will be the sole and exclusive property of Developer. Publisher's sole rights to the Game will be those licenses granted elsewhere in this Agreement.

[Option 2. Divided Ownership]

5.3. *The Parties' Respective Ownership Rights*

5.3.1. Publisher will own Game elements that are perceptible by sight or sound to the End User, such as the name of the Game, storyline, character design, artwork, text and sound files as well as the User Manual ("Publisher Property"). To the extent that Publisher Property is copyrightable, it will be deemed work made for hire for Publisher.

5.3.2. Developer will own all rights to the Game other than Publisher Property. For clarity, and without limiting the foregoing, Developer will own all rights to the Game's Source Code, object code, script and animation data, technology, the Game Engine, and the Developer's Tools. (The foregoing is, collectively, the "Developer Property,") No Developer trade secrets or patent rights are transferred under this Agreement.

6. Other Intellectual Property Rights Matters

6.1. Each party agrees to provide the other party with reasonable cooperation in the documentation, registration, and confirmation of the allocation of Intellectual Property Rights as stated in this Agreement.

6.2. **[Optional Provision:]** Developer will deliver to Publisher, within thirty (30) days after the Effective Date, and at any time upon Publisher's request, (a) assignments to Developer from each person retained by Developer in connection with the development of Publisher's Property (as defined in this Agreement) of all of that person's right, title and interest in and to Publisher's Property, as well as all Intellectual Property Rights embodied in any of the foregoing, free and clear of any and all rights, liens, claims and encumbrances by that person, the Developer, or any third party, and (b) waivers from each such person of any right to assert any moral rights or artist's rights against Developer, Publisher, or any licensee or assignee with respect to such person's rights in and to Publisher's Property and the Intellectual Property Rights embodied in this Agreement. Such assignments and waivers will be in writing and in form and substance satisfactory to Publisher. Developer will bear all costs and expenses associated with obtaining such assignments and waivers.

6.3. **[Optional Provision:]** Developer acknowledges that Publisher may select a trademark for the Game, and Developer shall gain no rights in the trademark.

6.4. All rights owned by the parties that are not licensed or transferred by the Agreement are reserved to parties respectively; no rights or licenses are granted by implication.

7. Grant of License to Publisher

*[**Comment:** The following section is not necessary if the Agreement provides that the Publisher owns the work under Option 1 above. The following form of license grant is exclusive for the Territory, which is normal in publishing agreements.]*

7.1. Developer hereby grants to Publisher, and Publisher hereby accepts, the exclusive right to manufacture, distribute, sell and market the Game in the Territory through any and all normal channels of distribution during the term of this Agreement.

[*Comment: If the Developer retains ownership of the Game, the Publisher will need this kind of license.*]

7.2. [**Optional Provision:**] The license shall be subject to the following restrictions: [list restrictions by field of use, market, platform, language, customer type, etc.]

[*Comment: If the Developer retains ownership of the Game, the parties may agree on limitations to the license grant.*]

7.3. [**Optional Provision:**] Developer hereby grants and will grant to Publisher a non-exclusive, irrevocable, worldwide, royalty-free, fully-paid right and license, with full right to sublicense, in perpetuity to use, reproduce, create derivatives, exploit, modify, alter, integrate with other works and enhance Game Assets solely in connection with the development, marketing and distribution of ports, versions, Sequels and Ancillary Products for the Game.

[*Comment: This additional text allows the Publisher to create additional products, including ports, Sequels, etc. Whenever the Publisher obtains the right to make these additional products, it will normally have corresponding Royalty payment obligations.*]

7.4. To the extent of the license grant stated above, the license to Publisher shall include Developer's copyrights, patents, patentable inventions, trade secrets, and all other proprietary rights in the Game under the terms and conditions stated in this Agreement.

8. **Sublicensing of Distribution**

[*Comment: Sometimes Publishers will want to sublicense marketing and distribution in other nations to other companies—this would apply if the Publisher does not have its own distribution organization in some geographical markets. In some cases, the publishing agreement is written to prevent this kind of sublicensing—allowing the Developer to find the foreign distributor.*]

8.1. [**Option 1. No Sublicensing**] *No Sublicensing*

8.1.1. Publisher may not sublicense or delegate its rights or obligations with regard to the Game, including its obligations to market, replicate, promote and distribute the Game.

8.2. [**Option 2. Sublicensing Permitted**] *Sublicensing of Distribution*

8.2.1. Publisher may sublicense or delegate its license to market, replicate, promote and distribute the Game only for the following territories: [insert list] [and only subject to Developer's prior written consent, not to be unreasonably withheld.]

9. **Advance Payments**

9.1. Publisher will pay Developer the advance payments (each an "Advance Payment") specified in the Milestone Schedule, within ten (10) business days of acceptance of each Milestone deliverable. Payment by mail will be deemed made [when mailed] [upon receipt].

9.2. Each Advance Payment will be treated as an advance on Royalties (as defined below) subject to recoupment by deductions from Royalties as provided below, provided however that each Advance Payment will otherwise be a non-refundable payment to Developer [except that should the Agreement be terminated due to Developer's failure to deliver acceptable Milestone deliverables as required by this Agreement that are properly and finally rejected by Publisher, Developer will return [all] [_____ percent (__%)] of the Advance Payments to Publisher] [WHICH SHALL BE PUBLISHER'S SOLE REMEDY FOR ANY DAMAGES OR CLAIMS FOR SUCH FAILURE OR BREACH].

9.3. If any Advance Payment to Developer is not made on time and as required, Developer may give notice of the failure to make payment. Upon such notice, failure to make required payments will automatically extend all remaining Milestone Dates by the number of days from the date of notice until the required Advance Payment to Developer is made. If any such failure to pay is not cured within ten (10) days after receipt of notice, Developer will have the option to terminate this Agreement, effective upon Publisher's receipt of notice of termination from Developer, including all license grants to Publisher. Notwithstanding such termination, in addition to any other remedy that Developer may have, Developer will forthwith be paid all amounts due for Milestones completed under the Milestone Schedule that remain unpaid, plus the reasonable value of any additional work rendered in good faith and in accordance with the Agreement prior to termination. [Publisher will pay Developer interest on late payments at the rate of [_____ percent (__%)] per year, compounded daily, or if less, the highest legal rate.] [If payment is reasonably in dispute by Publisher, Publisher is obligated to pay only the undisputed amounts pending resolution of the dispute.]

*[**Comment:** This text allows the Developer to have a claim for full payment and to terminate license grants to Publisher in case of a material default in payment of advances. However this text would not recapture Game ownership for the Developer if the Publisher has ownership of the Game under a work-made-for-hire clause under Option 1 above. It would be possible to add language to the Agreement requiring the Publisher to convey the Game back to the Developer in case of unjustified non-payment. See also termination provisions below.]*

10. **Royalties**

10.1. *Payment of Royalties*

10.1.1. Royalty payments will be calculated for each Quarter as described on <u>Schedule D</u> and in this Section.

10.1.2. Royalty payments to Developer will be due thirty (30) days after the end of each Quarter [provided that if accumulated and unpaid Royalties do not exceed $1000.00, payments will be held until a Quarter when the balance exceeds $1000.00 at which time the full balance will be paid]. [Any payments over 30 days overdue will bear interest at the rate of [_____ percent (__%)] per year, compounded daily, or if less, the highest legal rate.] [If payment is reasonably in dispute by Publisher, Publisher is obligated to pay only the undisputed amounts pending resolution of the dispute.]

10.2. *Reserve*

10.2.1. Publisher may create a reasonable Reserve for refunds, credits, and allowances for returns, stock balancing, and price protection[in an aggregate amount not to exceed _____ percent (___%) of Gross Revenues (as defined in <u>Schedule D</u>) for the Quarter]. [Such Reserve will be reconciled with actual refunds, credits, and allowances for returns, stock balancing, and price protection in the following Quarter and such reconciliation will be reflected in each Quarterly Royalty Report (as defined and provided for below).]

10.3. *Bundling*

    10.3.1. If Publisher licenses or supplies the Game in a package or bundle with other products at a single price, the Net Revenues (as defined in <u>Schedule D</u>) from such package or bundle will be prorated according to the published list prices established by Publisher for the separate works contained in the package [provided however that, for the purpose of this allocation, the list price assigned to any Game unit will be no less than $*[number]*].

10.4. **[Optional Provision.]** *Minimum Per-Unit Royalties*

    10.4.1. Notwithstanding the above, Publisher will pay Developer, for each Quarter, a minimum Royalty of no less than $*[number]* for each copy of the Game shipped or licensed to a third party (promotional copies not included) during the Quarter.

10.5. **[Optional Provision:]** *Percentage Royalties from Exercise of Foreign Sublicensing Right*

*[**Comment:** If the Publisher sublicenses a foreign distributor to publish the Game outside the United States as a sublicensee (see Section 8 above), the Developer should get a substantially larger share of the Publisher's resulting revenue. This is because in the foreign market, the foreign distributor, not the Publisher, will be taking the risks and paying all the costs of publication.]*

    10.5.1. Publisher will pay Developer a Royalty on Gross Revenues from a party to which Publisher has delegated publishing or distribution as permitted herein based on the formula set forth in the section of <u>Schedule D</u> entitled "Sublicensing Revenues."

10.6. *Recoupment of Advance Payments*

*[**Comment:** This Agreement is written so that the Publisher may recoup the Advance Payments paid to the Developer by deducting them from Royalties. This is a common provision. The parties could negotiate a deal in which the Advance Payments are not deducted from Royalties or only partially reduce Royalties.]*

    10.6.1. Publisher will recoup the Advance Payments made to Developer by deductions from Royalties [provided however that in any Quarter, the amount of Royalties credited to or payable to

Developer may not be reduced by such deduction in the aggregate by more than *[number]* percent].

10.7. **[Optional Provision:]**   *Developer's Right to Terminate Based on Performance Criteria*

*[**Comment:** Under the following section, the Developer may terminate the Agreement if Net Revenues or Royalties are below a specified level.]*

10.7.1. After the [second] *[specify other]* anniversary of the Effective Date, Developer may at its option terminate this Agreement at any time by notice during the *[number]* day period after receipt of the Royalty Report for the most recent Quarter, if the aggregate [Net Revenues] [Royalties credited to recoup advances or paid to Developer] on account of the Game during such Quarter plus the preceding three Quarters were less than $*[amount]*.

10.8. *Royalty-Free Copies*

10.8.1. Notwithstanding the foregoing, no Royalties will be due for [up to *[number]*] copies of the Game created and shipped by Publisher solely for demonstration purposes and clearly labeled: "Demonstration Copy; Not for Resale or Relicense." Publisher will keep records of the number of such copies created and will make such records available to Developer upon request.

10.8.2. Notwithstanding the foregoing, no Royalties will be due for End User copies of the Game created and shipped by Publisher for marketing and promotion purposes which have sufficient functions disabled or removed or are limited in the number of times they may be used, so as to render them substantially unusable for the functions for which the Game is normally intended.

10.8.3. No Royalties will be due for the first *[number]* copies of the Game used by Publisher for its own internal purposes. Thereafter, Developer will be paid the Royalties for copies that Publisher uses internally at the rate that would have applied if the Games were sold at *[number]* percent of retail list price. Publisher will keep records of the number of copies put to use internally and will make such records available to Developer upon request.

11. **Accounting**

[*Comment: The purpose of the accounting provision is to require the Publisher to keep adequate financial records and to allow the Developer to audit the Publisher's records to verify that Royalties are being calculated and paid properly.*]

11.1. Publisher will maintain detailed records of receipts, revenues, and costs relating to the computation of the Royalty payments required by this Agreement and will maintain the same, with regard to each Quarter's Royalty Report, for no less than three years after rendering such Royalty Report.

11.2. Publisher will deliver to Developer a report ("Royalty Report") within thirty (30) days after the close of each Quarter which will provide all information reasonably required for computation of the Royalty payments required by this Agreement.

11.3. Developer will have the right to appoint at its own expense an independent auditor reasonably acceptable to Publisher to examine the relevant books and records of Publisher for the purpose of verifying the accuracy of the Royalty Reports and payments provided to Developer. Developer may, upon reasonable notice, cause such independent auditor to inspect the records of Publisher on which the Royalty Reports and payments are based during Publisher's normal business hours. Such audits will be conducted under reasonable conditions of confidentiality with reasonable notice during regular business hours and no more frequently than one time in any twelve (12) month period. Developer will provide Publisher with the results of the audit in the event of any underpayment or overpayment, appropriate adjusting payments or refunds will be made within ten (10) days from the last day of audit. [Such payment will be due with interest at the rate of 10 percent per annum, compounded daily from the due date.] If Publisher has underpaid and/or underreported amounts due for the audited period by ___ percent (___%) or more (but in any case in excess of $_____), then Publisher will pay Developer's reasonable accounting costs for conducting the audit.

11.4. Without limiting the foregoing, if Publisher makes an overpayment to Developer hereunder for any reason, Developer will return to Publisher such overpayment upon the earlier of (a) receipt of Publisher's written demand, together with documentation supporting such demand, or (b) Developer's otherwise becoming aware of such overpayment. Notwithstanding the foregoing, Publisher will have the election to deduct an amount equal to such overpayment from any sums that may become due or payable to Developer by Publisher, in lieu of Developer's reimbursement to Publisher for such overpayment. In the event of any underpayment, appropriate adjusting payments or refunds will be made within ten (10) days from the last day of audit.

12. **Marketing of the Game**

*[**Comment:** Depending on the bargaining power of the parties, the Agreement may impose specific marketing obligations. Some agreements give the Publisher absolute discretion in marketing, including the option (rarely taken) not to market at all. A common (but not very specific) provision is an agreement of the Publisher to use "best efforts."]*

[Option 1: Specified Marketing Requirement]

12.1. Publisher will provide marketing, distribution and promotion of the Game throughout the Territory at Publisher's sole expense in accordance with a written marketing plan (the "Marketing Plan") to be drafted by Publisher and approved by Developer. Publisher will provide to Developer the Marketing Plan for Developer's reasonable approval, such Marketing Plan to be delivered to Developer on or before [date] and to be updated on a Quarterly basis for Developer's reasonable approval.

12.2. The Marketing Plan will include, without limitation, the promotional activities for the Game and the applicable budget. [The budget for expenditures for the launch of the Game will be no less than $_____, and Publisher agrees that it will expend an amount no less than the budgeted amount in connection with the Game launch.] [Publisher will provide a summary of its marketing expenditures Quarterly in reasonable detail.] [Such Marketing Plan will include a sales forecast for each country in the Territory.]

[Option 2: No Marketing Requirement]

12.3. Publisher will not be required to promote the Game except as it deems appropriate; the level of effort and spending in promotion will be in

Publisher's sole discretion. Marketing of the Game will be solely within the control of Publisher, including all decisions as to promotional means, and all matters of terms, conditions and prices.

[Option 3: Best Efforts Marketing Requirement]

12.4. Publisher will use its best efforts to promote the Game. Marketing of the Game will be solely within the control of Publisher, including all decisions as to promotional means.

12.5. Publisher will use its best efforts to commence distribution by no later than: [date] [[number] days after acceptance of the final Gold Master deliverables].

13. **Additional Marketing Provisions**

13.1. Publisher will price the Game as it sees fit consistent with its good faith effort to maximize Game Gross Revenues.

13.2. Publisher will have the option to suspend or cease marketing of the Game if in the judgment of Publisher results of marketing are insufficient to justify keeping the Game on the market. Publisher will promptly notify Developer of any decision to suspend or cease marketing of the Game.

14. **Manufacturing**

14.1. Publisher will be responsible for the manufacturing. [Without limiting the foregoing, Publisher will be responsible for fees and payments required by the platform owners ([Sony, Microsoft and Nintendo games systems] *[or indicate other applicable platforms]*) in connection with manufacturing or distribution of the Game for their respective video game console systems.]

14.2. Publisher will use reasonable effort to produce units sufficient to meet market demand. Publisher will advise Developer upon request of its manufacturing and inventory planning.

15. **Complimentary Copies**

15.1. Publisher will provide Developer with [number] complimentary copies of the Game on first publication, and Developer will be entitled to buy a reasonable number of additional copies of the Game at Publisher's wholesale price at the time such copies are purchased; *provided, however,* that such units are not for resale.

16. **Credits**

16.1. The text credit "Developed by *[Developer brand]*" will be displayed in the Game and in the User Manual for the Game in type no smaller than the most common size text for the User Manual. In addition, Developer's logo will be prominently displayed on the back packaging of the Game, in the User Manual and in the title sequence of credits in the Game.

16.2. Upon receipt of written notice from Developer specifying in reasonable detail any failure by Publisher to accord the credit required hereunder, Publisher will use commercially reasonable efforts prospectively to cure such failure in future pressings of the Game and/or packaging.

16.3. Developer may include the names and titles of personnel involved in or responsible for the Game in the "Credits" section of the in-game documentation of the Game.

17. **Publicity**

17.1. Publisher will be entitled to use and publish and permit others to use and publish the names of Developer and/or its personnel (including any professional or business identity adopted by Developer), photographs, biographical material, or any reproduction or simulation thereof in connection with the promotion, marketing and/or distribution of the Game. Developer will have the right to reasonably approve any photograph or biographical materials concerning Developer or its personnel that are not furnished to Publisher by Developer. Developer will have ten (10) business days to approve or disapprove a particular photograph or biographical material not supplied by Developer. Developer will be deemed to have approved the photograph or biographical material if Developer fails to approve the same within such period.

17.2. Once Developer has approved any particular photograph or biographical material, Developer will be deemed to have approved such photograph or material for all subsequent uses. In addition, Developer agrees to make its employees available for any press interviews as Publisher may reasonably request from time to time.

18. **Non-Competition**

[Comment: It is often part of development deals that Developers not create competing products for other Publishers.]

18.1. *Non-Competition Period.* The "Non-Competition Period" will mean the period from the signing of this Agreement until *[date]*. The Non-Competition Period may be extended by the parties by written agreement.

18.2. *Restriction on Negotiations.* During the Non-Competition Period, Developer will not engage in negotiations of any kind with any third party for the creation or publication of any software product which is directly competitive, or substantially similar to the Game.

18.3. *Restrictions on Publication.* During the Non-Competition Period and for *[number]* months thereafter, Developer will not publish, release, distribute or market, directly or indirectly through a third party, any product which is directly competitive with or substantially similar to the Game [in the Territory] [whether in the Territory or in any other area or place].

18.4. **[Optional Provision:]** Nothing in this Agreement will be deemed in any way to prevent or restrict Publisher from the development and/or marketing of any product of any kind.

19. **[Optional Provision:] Developer's Right of First Negotiation**

[Comment: This following section is written on the assumption that the Publisher controls Sequels. (This would be the case if the Publisher has obtained the copyright to the Game or if it obtained an exclusive license to these rights. See Section 5, Option 1 and Section 6.2, above.) In the text that follows, the Developer gets a right of first negotiation to create these future products. Sometimes these provisions are written the other way around—so that the Developer retains the rights to Sequels and the Publisher get a right of first negotiation to distribute them. Note also that in this form, the Developer gets a Royalty on follow-on products whether it creates them or not.]

19.1. In the event that Publisher desires to publish any conversions, extensions, add-on content packs and/or Sequels (collectively, "Future Versions") of the Game and provided that Developer is capable of developing such computer software programs or content then Publisher will furnish Developer with written notice of its intention regarding such Future Versions and will negotiate exclusively with Developer for a period of thirty (30) days following Developer's receipt of such written notice (the "Negotiation Period").

19.2. If, after good faith negotiations, Publisher and Developer are unable to reach an agreement for Future Versions, then Publisher will be free to contract with a third party for the Future Version referenced in the written notice, provided, however, that if the Agreement is terminated by Publisher for cause, then Developer will have no further right of first negotiation to Future Versions.

19.3. In the event that Publisher creates and exploits a Future Version in which Publisher utilizes Development Materials without Developer's development services, then Publisher will pay to Developer a Royalty of five percent (5%) of the Future Version Net Revenues (as defined below). In the event that Publisher creates and exploits a Future Version without utilizing any of Development Materials and development services, then Publisher will pay to Developer a Royalty of two and one-half percent (2.5%) of the Future Version Net Revenues. "Future Version Net Revenues" are the same as Net Revenues under this Agreement except that they apply solely to Future Versions.

20. **Support**

20.1. *Support Services.* Developer agrees to provide to Publisher, at Publisher's request, the following reasonable Game support services during the development of the Game and ending one (1) year after Publisher's first commercial shipment of the Game:

20.1.1. Developer will use any and all reasonable efforts, without limitation, to correct any Defects in the Game of which Publisher notifies Developer in writing;

20.1.2. [**Optional Provision:**] Developer will respond to Publisher in connection with any reasonable inquiries that Publisher may receive from End Users of the Game; and

20.1.3. [**Optional Provision:**] Developer will provide reasonable enhancements or modifications to the Game requested by Publisher from time to time.

20.2. [**Optional Provision:**] *Compensation for Support.* Developer will provide such Game support services at times reasonably requested by Publisher for no additional compensation other than the Royalties to be paid to Developer, *provided, however,* that if Developer's total time spent providing the services described in this Section, other than correction of Defects, exceeds one hundred (100) hours, then Developer will have no further obligations to provide the services described in this Section other than Defect correction without mutually agreed additional compensation.

21. **Representations and Warranties**

[**Comment:** *Publishing agreements can have a variety of "Rep and Warranty" provisions. These are typical.*]

21.1. *Developer's Representations and Warranties.* Developer represents, warrants and agrees that:

21.1.1. It is a corporation, validly existing and in good standing under the laws of the state in which it was incorporated.

21.1.2. It has all necessary rights and authority to execute and deliver this Agreement.

21.1.3. The Game will be the original work of Developer or licensed from third parties under written license agreements.

21.1.4. Nothing contained in this Agreement or in the performance of this Agreement will place Developer in breach of any other contract or contractual obligation.

21.1.5. Developer has [to the best of its knowledge] all necessary rights and authority to grant to Publisher the rights and licenses purported to be granted in this Agreement. [To the best of Developer's knowledge] the Game will not misappropriate, violate or infringe upon any Intellectual Property Right of any third party.

[**Comment:** *The Developer will likely not have done any patent infringement review. That is why Developers might want to try to include a "knowledge qualification" here.*]

This warranty does not extend to materials, content and technology supplied by Publisher. [Developer makes no representation or warranty with regard to any Branding Elements used in or on the Game (other than its own company branding)].

21.1.6. With regard to all legal rights other than Intellectual property the Game will not violate or infringe upon any other common law or statutory rights of any person or entity including, without limitation, rights related to defamation, contractual rights and rights of privacy and publicity.

21.1.7. **[Optional Provision:]** No "Open Source" software code (as defined by the Open Source Initiative), "Free" software code (as defined by the Free Software Foundation), or any derivative of any Open Source or Free software code will be included in the Game or any deliverable, unless expressly agreed to in writing by Publisher.

21.1.8. Developer has not sold, assigned, leased, licensed, allowed any lien to be placed on, or in any other way disposed of, or encumbered the rights granted to Publisher hereunder.

21.1.9. The Game will contain no computer code designed to (a) disrupt, disable, harm or otherwise impede in any manner the operation of a computer program or computer system or (b) damage or destroy any data files residing on a computer system without the End User's consent and will not adversely affect the hardware, Publisher's development or test equipment, or other software of the End User thereof in any way.

21.2. *Publisher's Representations and Warranties*

21.2.1. Publisher represents and warrants that it has all necessary rights and authority to execute and deliver this Agreement and perform its obligations hereunder and that nothing contained in this Agreement or in the performance of this Agreement will place Publisher in breach of any other contract or obligation.

21.2.2. Publisher warrants that it has [to the best of its knowledge] all necessary rights and authority to grant to Developer the rights and licenses rights granted to Developer under this Agreement.

21.3. **[Optional Provision:]** *Exclusive Remedy.* To the extent that any of the foregoing warranties are breached on account of alleged or actual infringement of any patent [other than willful infringement], the sole and exclusive remedy for each party will be indemnification under the provisions of this Agreement regarding indemnification.

[*Comment: This remedy limitation is generally favorable to the Developer. Its rationale is explained in Chapter 8.*]

22. **Warranty Exclusions and Remedy Limitations**

22.1. *Warranty Exclusion.* EACH PARTY DISCLAIMS ALL WARRANTIES, EXPRESS OR IMPLIED, EXCEPT THOSE EXPRESSLY STATED HEREIN, INCLUDING, BUT NOT LIMITED TO, IMPLIED WARRANTIES OF MERCHANTABILITY, FITNESS FOR A PARTICULAR PURPOSE, TITLE AND NON-INFRINGEMENT.

[*Comment: Developer may want to seek to place a second [usually higher] cap on its potential exposure for indemnification of intellectual property infringement—particularly if the Agreement does not have a "knowledge qualifier" for patent infringement.*]

22.2. *Limitation on Damages.* Except as to indemnification, breach of obligations regarding Confidential Information, or use of the other party's Intellectual Property Rights in breach of this Agreement, each party's right to recover damages against the other for any reason whatsoever relating to or arising out of this Agreement or any breach thereof will not exceed the sum of $*[amount]*[, provided that such limit will not apply to amounts payable as Advance Payments or Royalties under this Agreement]. [With regard to its obligations of indemnification, as a separate liability "cap," each party's aggregate liabilities may not exceed $*[amount]*.

22.3. *Exclusion of Consequential Damages.* Notwithstanding anything contained in this Agreement in no event, except as expressly provided in this Agreement, and except as to indemnification, breach of obligations regarding Confidential Information, or use of the other party's Intellectual Property Rights in breach of this Agreement, will either party be liable to the other for any indirect, special, or consequential damages or lost profits arising out of or related to this Agreement or the performance or breach thereof.

23. **Intellectual Property Indemnification**

[*Comment: Indemnification provisions vary greatly. Here are two sample provisions. The first, pro-Publisher, puts Game-related intellectual property risks on the Developer. The second is a more even-handed provision.*]

[Option 1: Developer Indemnifies—Favors Publisher]

23.1. Developer will indemnify, defend and hold harmless Publisher and its officers, directors, employees and agents against any and all losses, liabilities, claims, obligations, costs and expenses (including, without limitation, reasonable attorneys' fees) which arise in connection with any third party lawsuit or legal proceeding based on allegations that, if true, would constitute a breach or alleged breach by Developer of any of its warranties regarding Intellectual Property Rights as stated above.

[Option 2: Mutual Indemnification—Written to Be More Favorable to Developer]

23.2. Each party agrees, with regard to its contributions to the Game, to defend and indemnify the other party and hold the other party harmless against judgments, awards, fines, damages, costs, and fees (including reasonable expert and attorney's fees) arising from or resulting from third party claims or suits brought against the indemnified party by reason of infringement, actual or alleged, under the intellectual property laws, where the allegations, if true, would violate the indemnifying party's warranties regarding Intellectual Property Rights as stated above. [Each parties' obligations under this Section do not include or extend to actual or alleged infringement of (a) US patents not known to such party as of Effective Date or (b) to infringement of non-US patents.]

24. **Procedure for Indemnification Claims**

24.1. Each party agrees to notify the indemnifying party promptly of a claim subject to indemnification and to cooperate, at the indemnifying party's expense, with the defense of the claim. No indemnifying party shall, without the prior written consent of the indemnified party, effect any settlement of any pending or threatened proceeding in respect of which any indemnified party is a party and indemnity could have been sought hereunder by such indemnified party, unless such settlement includes an unconditional release of such indemnified party from all such liability on claims that are the subject matter of the proceedings.

25. **[Optional Provision:] Insurance**

*[**Comment:** Publishers may require Developers to have insurance, including errors and omissions and intellectual property infringement.]*

25.1. Developer will obtain and maintain, at its own expense, insurance coverage as follows from a nationally recognized and qualified insurance company(ies):

25.1.1. *[List required insurance coverage.]*

25.2. Such insurance will be in effect during the development of the Game and for *[number]* years after development is completed.

26. Third-Party Infringement

26.1. Publisher will have control of litigation against third party infringers of any Intellectual Property Rights in or to the Game for so long as it has the rights in the Game granted in this Agreement.

26.2. Any amounts recovered by judgment or settlement against third party infringers of such rights will, after recoupment of the expenses of litigation, be treated as Net Revenue subject to the Royalties.

27. Confidentiality

27.1. "Confidential Information" means non-public information, technical data or know-how of a party, which is furnished to the other in written or tangible form in connection with this Agreement and marked as "Confidential." Oral disclosure will also be deemed Confidential Information if such disclosures are reduced to a writing that is transmitted by the disclosing party to the other within thirty (30) days of the original disclosure and marked as provided above. The terms and conditions set forth in this Agreement will be Confidential Information, provided, however, that either party may reveal the contents of this Agreement to auditors or other professionals, as well as advisors, investors, and parties conducting due diligence with a need to know in connection with such party's efforts to obtain financing, comply with legal or regulatory requirements or negotiate a merger, acquisition, or sale of substantially all the assets of such party's business or line of business. Any disclosure of the contents of this Agreement to auditors or other professionals pursuant to the immediately preceding proviso will only be made pursuant to an appropriate confidentiality agreement unless such professionals are bound to confidentiality by virtue of an attorney-client relationship with a party.

27.2. Notwithstanding the foregoing, Confidential Information does not include information which is: (a) already in the possession of the receiving party or its subsidiaries and not subject to a confidentiality obligation to the providing party; (b) independently developed by the receiving party; (c) publicly disclosed or in the public domain through no fault of the receiving party; (d) rightfully received by the receiving party or its subsidiaries from a third party that is not under any obligation to keep such information confidential; (e) approved for release by written agreement with the disclosing party; or (f) disclosed pursuant to the requirements of law, regulation or court order.

27.3. Neither party will use the other's Confidential Information for five (5) years after the earlier of termination of this Agreement or the Final Acceptance of the Gold Master, except as reasonably required for the performance of this Agreement. Each party will use commercially reasonable efforts to hold in confidence the other party's Confidential Information by means that are no less restrictive than that used for its own confidential materials.

27.4. Upon expiration or termination of this Agreement, each party will either: (a) return all of the other party's Confidential Information and all copies thereof in the party's possession or control to the other party, or (b) at the other party's instruction, destroy all Confidential Information and all copies thereof in the party's possession or control. This obligation of the parties also extends to Confidential Information in the possession of any of its subcontractors. The party will then certify that no copies have been retained by it, its employees, or agents or subcontractors.

27.5. In case a party receives legal process that demands or requires disclosure of the disclosing party's Confidential Information, such party will give prompt notice to the disclosing party, if legally permissible, to enable the disclosing party to challenge such demand.

27.6. Each party acknowledges that unauthorized disclosure or use of the Confidential Information may cause irreparable harm to the other party for which recovery of money damages would be inadequate, and the other party will therefore be entitled to obtain timely injunctive relief to protect its rights under this Agreement, in addition to any and all remedies available under applicable law.

28. **Term and Termination**

28.1. The term of this Agreement will be perpetual except in the case of termination permitted under the terms of this Agreement.

28.2. [**Optional Provision:**] Publisher may terminate this Agreement for convenience at any time [before delivery of a copy of the Gold Master that meets applicable acceptance criteria] upon 10 days' written notice.

28.3. Either party will be entitled, without prejudice to its other rights, to terminate the Agreement with immediate effect by giving written notice to the other party if the other party is in breach of any of its material obligations under this Agreement, and, if the breach is capable of remedy, it has continued unremedied for a period of thirty (30) calendar days after the other party has been given written notice specifying the breach and the steps required to remedy it.

28.4. Either party shall be entitled, without prejudice to its other rights, to terminate the Agreement by giving written notice to the other party if the other party shall have a receiver or an administrative receiver or an administrator or liquidator appointed over it or shall pass a resolution for winding up or shall enter into any voluntary agreement with its creditors or shall become bankrupt or file for voluntary bankruptcy or anything analogous to any of the above under the law of any jurisdiction occurs in relation to such party.

29. **Effect of Termination**

[**Comment:** *As is discussed in Chapter 22, there are many variations in clauses that state the effect of agreement termination. Following are two examples. The first example comes from a Publisher's form. The second is much more favorable to the Developer.*]

[Option 1: Provisions Generally Favor Publisher]

29.1. If Publisher terminates this Agreement for Developer's uncured material breach, Publisher will be discharged of any obligation to pay for unaccepted Milestones[, and Developer will pay back to Publisher [all] [___ percent of] the Milestone Payments that have been paid to Developer within ____ days of Publisher's written request].

29.2. In the event Publisher terminates this Agreement for convenience or the Developer terminates this Agreement for cause, then Publisher will pay

Developer amounts due for all completed Milestones and for any uncompleted Milestones on a percentage of completion basis within _____ days of the date of termination.

29.3. Upon any termination of this Agreement regardless of cause, unless otherwise agreed in writing, Publisher will retain all rights regarding the Game and other assets granted in this Agreement, Developer will have no further development obligation except to deliver to Publisher the latest copy of all of the Source Code, Executable Code, Developer's Tools (in Source Code and Executable Code forms), Documentation and any other material created under this Agreement [*Indicate any additional or different final deliveries or tasks*].

29.4. [The foregoing will be each party's sole remedy and sole compensation for termination and for the failure, non-performance, claim, breach, action, omission or events, if any, that gave rise or allegedly gave rise to or preceded termination.] [The foregoing will be in addition to any remedies that the Publisher may have for Developer's breach.]

[Option 2: Provisions Generally Favor Developer]

29.5. In the event Publisher terminates this Agreement for convenience or the Developer terminates this Agreement for cause, Publisher will pay Developer for all completed Milestones and for any uncompleted Milestones on a percentage of completion basis within _____ days of the date of termination.

29.6. In addition, in the event Publisher terminates this Agreement for convenience or the Developer terminates this Agreement for cause, then within thirty (30) days of the date of termination, Developer will have the option ("Rights Recapture Option") to obtain rights to the Game as follows:

29.6.1. Developer may, during such thirty (30) day period, give notice of its exercise of the Rights Recapture Option.

29.6.2. Publisher will, upon such notice, promptly assign its rights in the Game (including, without limitation, rights with regard to Game ports, versions, Sequels and Ancillary Products) to Developer (but not including any third party rights or rights in Publisher's content or branding) and confirm in writing the termination of all licenses granted to Publisher. Developer may thereafter arrange for alternative publication.

29.6.3. If Developer, having recovered such rights, arranges for alternative publication, then Developer will then be obligated to pay to Publisher a [number] percent Royalty to be paid out of any and all revenue [not including revenue for development advances or expense reimbursement by the subsequent publisher] which Developer receives with respect to the Game until the advances that Publisher has made under this Agreement are fully reimbursed to Publisher.

29.7. In the event of termination (regardless of cause) before the Publisher's Final Acceptance of the Gold Master, if Developer fails to exercise the Rights Recapture Option as permitted above, then:

29.7.1. Developer will provide Publisher with the latest copy of all of the Source Code, Executable Code, Developer's Tools (in Source Code and Executable Code forms), Documentation and any other necessary materials to allow Publisher, at its option, to rebuild or complete the Game, if unfinished, and to support and maintain the Game, and Publisher will pay Developer within fifteen (15) business days for any prior approved Milestone submissions plus the next following additional Milestone.

29.7.2. All licenses to Developer Property granted to Publisher will remain in place, and Publisher will be free to complete the Game itself or by use of subcontractors, so long as it provides reasonable confidentiality measures to protect Developer Property.

29.7.3. Notwithstanding such termination of this Agreement, Developer will maintain, post-termination, its Royalty rights with regard to the Game and Ancillary Products, and Publisher's obligations to report, pay and permit audit with regard to such Royalty will survive termination; provided, however, that in the case of termination for Developer's material uncured default, Royalties will be reduced by a percentage based on the number of completed Milestones prior to termination divided by the total number of Milestones. For example if Developer had completed 40 percent of the Milestones, the Royalty will be 40 percent of the amount otherwise due and payable.

29.8. [The foregoing will be the parties' sole remedy and sole compensation for termination and for the failure, non-performance, claim, breach, action, omission or events, if any, that gave rise or allegedly gave rise to or preceded termination.] Termination discharges all development, performance and support obligations of either party. [The foregoing will be in addition to any other remedies that may apply.]

29.9. The following provisions will survive any termination or expiration of this Agreement: Sections 5 (Ownership), 11 (Accounting), 18 (Non-Competition), 21 (Representations and Warranties), 22 (Warranty Exclusions and Remedy Limitations), 23 (Indemnification), 24 (Procedure for Indemnification), 27 (Confidentiality), 28 (Term and Termination), 29 (Effect of Termination), and 30 (General), together with accrued rights and obligations and provisions that recite that they survive.

30. **General Provisions**

30.1. *Notices.* All notices, approvals and other communications to be given under this Agreement will be in writing and will be sent by certified mail, return receipt requested, or by a recognized courier service, return receipt requested, to the address of the other party set out at the commencement of this Agreement (or to such other address as either party may notify to the other under the provisions of this sub-Section). Notices will be deemed delivered upon receipt.

30.2. *Variations.* No addition to or modification of any provision of this Agreement will be binding upon the parties unless made by a written instrument signed by a duly authorized representative of each of the parties.

30.3. [**Optional Provision:**] *Subcontracting.* Developer may not subcontract any of its development or support obligations under this Agreement without the prior written consent of Publisher [, which is not to be unreasonably withheld]. This Agreement will inure to the benefit of and be binding upon the parties, their permitted assigns and successors in interest.

30.4. *Waiver.* No failure on the part of either party to exercise or to enforce any right given under this Agreement or at law or any custom or practice of the parties at variance with the terms of this Agreement will constitute a waiver of either of the parties' respective rights under this Agreement or operate so as to prevent the exercise or enforcement of any such right at any time.

30.5. *Force Majeure.* Notwithstanding anything contained in this Agreement, neither party will be in default in performance of this Agreement if such failure arises from causes not reasonably foreseeable by such party, including acts of God or war, governmental acts in either a sovereign or contractual capacity, fire, flood, and/or freight embargoes, provided that no such delay will apply to an obligation to pay money for more than forty-five (45) days.

30.6. *Certain Taxes.* All sums due under this Agreement are exclusive of any applicable Value Added Tax or other tax, except for taxes on Developer's net income.

30.7. *Law and Jurisdiction.* This Agreement will be governed by and construed in accordance with the substantive laws of _____. The state and federal courts located in _____ will have exclusive jurisdiction and venue over any dispute arising from this Agreement or its subject matter.

30.8. *Announcements.* The parties agree to issue a joint press release regarding their respective roles in development of the Game. Subject to Publisher's consent and approval of content, which will not be unreasonably withheld, Developer can show still pictures and video clips of the Game on its web site. Otherwise, except as otherwise expressly stated in this Agreement, Developer may not make any public announcement concerning the Game or this Agreement without the prior written consent of Publisher.

30.9. *Partial Invalidity.* If any provision of this Agreement is held by a court of competent jurisdiction to be invalid, void, or unenforceable, the remaining provisions will nevertheless continue in full force and effect without being impaired or invalidated in any way.

30.10. *No Partnership or Joint Venture.* Publisher and Developer are independent contractors and neither party is the legal representative, agent, joint venturer, partner, or employee of the other party for any purpose whatsoever. Neither party has any right or authority to assume or create any obligations of any kind or to make any representation or warranty on behalf of the other party, whether express or implied, or to bind the other party in any respect whatsoever.

30.11. *Assignment.* Neither party shall assign any right or obligation under this Agreement (excepting solely the right to moneys due or to become due) or delegate any obligation under this Agreement without the prior written consent of the other party; provided, however, that a party may assign this Agreement in full in connection with the sale or disposition of all or substantially all of its assets or business relating to the subject matter hereof without the consent of the other party, provided that the purchaser unconditionally accepts in writing the obligations of this Agreement.

30.12. *Headings.* The Section headings used in this Agreement are for reference and will not determine the construction or interpretation of this Agreement or any portion hereof.

30.13. *Use of Names and Trademarks.* Subject to Publisher's approval, which will not be unreasonably withheld, and only after Publisher issues a press release announcing the Game to the public, Developer may issue press releases with regard to this Agreement and the Game, may mention the Game in promotional material and may mention the Game on its web site. Except as expressly set forth above, Developer may not use any name, logo, trademark or service mark of Publisher without Publisher's prior, written consent for each use, which consent may be given or withheld in Publisher's sole discretion.

30.14. *Non-Solicitation.* During [state period of time], neither party will solicit for employment any employees of the other party that are or have been engaged in development under this Agreement.

30.15. *Counterparts.* This Agreement may be executed in two (2) or more counterparts, each of which will be deemed an original, and all of which together will constitute one and the same instrument.

Entire Agreement. This Agreement (including the Schedules and any documents attached or exhibited) sets out the entire agreement and understanding between the parties and supersedes all prior agreements, understandings or arrangements (whether oral or written) regarding the subject matter of this Agreement. Both parties acknowledge that they have entered into this Agreement in reliance only on the representations, warranties and promises expressly set out in this Agreement, and neither party will be liable in respect of any other representation, warranty or promise made prior to the date of this Agreement.

IN WITNESS WHEREOF, the parties have executed this Agreement as of the day and year first written above.

Publisher: _____   Developer: _____

By: _____   By: _____

(Name): _____   (Name): _____

(Title): _____   (Title): _____

(Date): _____   (Date): _____

[Neither an offer nor an agreement until executed by both parties.]

Schedule A

Description of Game

Game Title: _____

Genre: _____

Platforms: _____

Schedule B
Milestone Schedule

		Delivery Date	Advance Payment
1	Execution of Development Agreement		
2	Detailed Design Document		
3	Alpha Version		
4	Beta Version		
5	Release Candidate		
6	Gold Master		

Total Advances:

Schedule C
Developer's Personnel

POSITION	NAME	START DATE

[To Be Added]

Schedule D
Game Royalties and Other Payments

1. **Definitions used for Royalties**

    1.1. "Net Revenues" means Publisher's Gross Revenues less deductions for: (a) the amount of any credits or cash refunds for returns [and any platform fees actually paid by Publisher to third parties such as Nintendo, Sony and Microsoft] [*or indicate other applicable third party license fees*]), and (b) the amount of any discounts, price protection, rebates, and promotional allowances [provided that all such deductions may not exceed [number] percent of Gross Revenues for any Quarter].

    1.2. "Gross Revenues" means any and all revenues recognized by Publisher (exclusive of sales, use, excise and other taxes and exclusive of all insurance and shipping costs) from all sales, licenses, or other exploitation.]

2. **Royalties Calculation**

    2.1. Upon first commercial release of the Game, Publisher will pay to Developer the following Royalties on Net Revenues arising from sales, licenses, or other exploitation of the Game:

    [*Define amount due.*]

    [**Comment:** *There can be many variants on pricing provisions. Royalties are normally set as a percentage of Net Revenues. The percentage may increase with volume. Higher percentages may apply when the cost of making sales is lower. For example, download sales (where the Publisher does not have the cost of manufacture) may have a significantly higher Royalty percentage. Additional rules may apply for Royalties on sequels or derivatives that use Game assets.*]

3. **Sublicensing Revenues**

    3.1. In case Publisher sublicenses or delegates its license to market, replicate, promote and distribute the Game in specified territories as permitted in this Agreement, Royalties on resulting Gross Revenues shall be as follows:

    [*Define amount due as a percentage of revenues.*]

4. Ancillary Product Royalties

4.1. In the event that Publisher desires to exploit the Game via any Ancillary Products, Publisher will pay to Developer the following Royalties on resulting Gross Revenues:

4.1.1. *[Define amount due as a percentage of revenues.]*

4.1.2. [Royalties on all Ancillary Products will be less any and all out-of-pocket direct costs arising out of or related to the exploitation of such Ancillary Products including, but not limited to: (a) agent or licensing manager fees; (b) development costs; (c) collection and audit costs which may be incurred by Publisher with regard to its agent(s) or licensee(s); (d) all copyright and trademark search and registration fees incurred by Publisher; (e) any legal fees associated with protecting the Ancillary Products; (f) costs of goods and costs related to the advertising, marketing and distribution of the Ancillary Products; and (g) any local, state, federal and/or foreign withholding, sales, excise or value added taxes, duties, freight and tariffs.]

5. Payments for Services

*[**Comment:** Insert provisions for professional services. These are normally prices by the hour or by the day plus expenses.]*

[TO BE ADDED]

Schedule E
Specifications

[TO BE ADDED]

Schedule F
Publisher's Contributions

[TO BE ADDED]

International Distribution Agreement

Introductory Note

This is a form of international reseller agreement. The form allows a Vendor to benefit from the sales and marketing resources of the Distributor for a country or region of the world where the Distributor has a distribution network. It can be used for business or consumer products.

The form will likely need to be customized to fit the products involved, the mode of distribution in the Territory, the nature of the distribution network there, the pricing for products and services, and the type of support that Customers receive.

This text provides alternatives for handling the localization of the Software Products to the Local Language. In the first alternative, this is done by the Vendor. In the second, it is provided by the Distributor.

Language in brackets is for optional or alternative provisions.

International Distribution Agreement

This International Distribution Agreement ("Agreement") is effective as of the ___ day of _____, 20___ ("Effective Date") between *[Insert Vendor company name]* (hereinafter "Vendor"), with its principal office at _____, and *[Insert Distributor company name]*. ("Distributor") with its principal office at _____ (each a "Party"; together the "Parties").

Purpose of This Agreement

A. Vendor supplies and markets certain Software Products.

B. Distributor licenses computer products to Customers and to its authorized Resellers and offers post-sales support services in the Territory.

C. The Parties intend, under the terms of this Agreement, to arrange for Localized Versions of the Software Products.

D. Distributor desires to license the Software Products from Vendor in order to sublicense the Software Products (solely in the form of the Localized Versions) in the Territory to Resellers for the purpose of providing such Software Products for distribution to Customers, and Vendor desires to make such Software Products available to Distributor for these purposes.

In consideration of the mutual promises stated herein, the Parties agree as follows:

1. **Definitions**

   1.1. "Customer" means the person or entity in the Territory who obtains a Software Product under the Customer License Agreement pursuant to distribution authorized by this Agreement.

   1.2. "Customer License Agreement" means the written agreement under which the Customer is licensed to install and use the Software Products in the Territory.

   1.3. "Error" means any reproducible failure of the Software Products to perform its intended functions as stated in the applicable User Documentation or any significant inaccuracies in the User Documentation.

   1.4. ["Initial License Fee" has the meaning set forth in Section 8.1.]

   1.5. "License Fee(s)" has the meaning set forth in Section 8.2.

   1.6. "Local Currency" means the currency in use in the Territory.

   1.7. "Local Language" means the following language: [specify].

   1.8. "Localized Version" has the meaning set forth in Section 2.

   1.9. "Marketing Materials" means product literature, product data sheets, and similar materials that Vendor may supply to Distributor.

   1.10. "Primary Support" means the following services to be provided by Distributor to Customers:

      1.10.1. Providing the Customer with a reasonable level of assistance in installing the Software Product and a reasonable level of training in its use by means of documentation, online aids, or telephone support, if needed.

1.10.2. Providing technical advice to the Customer on using the Software Product by means of documentation, online aids, or telephone support, if needed.

1.10.3. When a Customer reports an Error in a Software Product, contacting Vendor and reporting the Error under such procedure as Vendor will reasonably specify.

1.10.4. Providing the Customer a reasonable level of assistance in obtaining or installing any available Software Product patch or version of the Software Product or in implementing any recommendation or solution to deal with Errors.

1.11. "Reseller" means a business entity or individual in business in the Territory that obtains Software Products from Distributor and distributes the Software Products to Customers in the Territory.

1.12. "Secondary Support" means the following services to be provided by Vendor to Distributor:

1.12.1. Using reasonable efforts to modify the Software Product to correct, fix, or circumvent Errors, and modifying User Documentation, as Vendor may reasonably deem appropriate, to respond to reported Errors, and advising Distributor in providing Primary Support.

1.12.2. Providing maintenance releases and updates for Software Products to Distributor during the Term as they are released.

1.13. "Software Product" means all current and future versions of each of the Vendor software products listed in Schedule A. Vendor reserves the right to discontinue any Software Product.

1.14. "Term" means the term of the Agreement as set forth in Section 17.1.

1.15. "Territory" is [specify national or regional territory].

1.16. "User Documentation" means documentation in written or electronic form for use of the Software Products.

1.17. "Vendor Branding Guidelines" means Vendor's guidelines for use of the Vendor Marks and proprietary legends that Vendor may issue from time to time.

1.18. "Vendor Marks" means Vendor's trade names, trademarks and logos associated with the Software Products.

2. **Localization**

[**Option 1. Localization by Vendor**]

2.1. Distributor agrees to provide reasonable assistance to Vendor, at Vendor's expense, with localization, translation, and other work by Vendor or arranged for by Vendor required to create the Local Language versions of the Software Products and Marketing Materials. The resulting version in Local Language of each Software Product (including packaging and documentation) is the "Localized Version." Vendor will own the copyrights to the resulting Localized Version. The agreed non-binding target date for completion of the localization of the Software Products is *[date]*.

[**Option 2. Localization by Distributor** (This option includes paragraphs through 2.8)]

2.2. *License Grant.* Vendor hereby grants Distributor an exclusive, non-transferable, and non-assignable license to: (a) translate and localize each Software Product into a Local Language version (the "Localized Version") of each Software Product, solely as set forth in this Agreement and (b) to incorporate the Vendor Marks and any artwork used in each Software Product English language version in the Localized Version of each Software Product in accordance with this Section.

2.3. *Cooperation.* Vendor will provide such cooperation and information as Distributor may reasonably require for localization. Information provided by Vendor is Confidential Information of Vendor (as defined below) under this Agreement.

2.4. *Localization Services.* Distributor will create the Localized Version of each Software Product. Upon receipt of all translatable elements of each Software Product, Distributor will translate all translatable files included in such elements, including without limitation, menus and dialog boxes, animations, graphics, audio tracks, online help system, textual content, installation program, and packaging. The agreed non-binding target date for completion of the localization of the Software Products is *[date]*.

2.5. *Review and Approval.* Distributor will deliver to Vendor a preliminary review copy of the Localized Version of each Software Product, including packaging and jewel case liners, together with a translated copy of each translatable file. Distributor will make any changes reasonably requested by Vendor and incorporate such changes in the Localized Version. Distributor will provide Vendor with a proposed final review copy for approval. If further corrections are, in Vendor's opinion, reasonably required, Distributor will make them. The approval process will be repeated until Vendor grants its written final approval for each Software Product. Vendor agrees that final approval will not be unreasonably withheld.

2.6. [*Credit Against License Fees.* In consideration of such localization, Vendor agrees to grant Distributor a credit against amounts otherwise payable to Vendor as License Fees under this Agreement in the amount of $_____. Such credit may be used for no other purpose and expires upon the termination of this Agreement.]

2.7. *Updates and Upgrades.* When Vendor releases any maintenance release, updates or upgrades after the date of this Agreement, the Parties will review any localization requirements and negotiate, in good faith, the terms under which Distributor will localize the same.

2.8. *Copyright.* Vendor will own the copyright of each Localized Version, including, without limitation, documentation and all packaging and other associated materials. Distributor will ensure that each individual that provides services with regard to localization assigns and conveys all copyright interests to Distributor so that it can convey the same to Vendor. The Localized Version (and all other work product created by or for Distributor with regard to the translation or localization for any Software Product) will be work-made-for-hire for Vendor to the maximum extent permitted by law. To the extent not work-made-for-hire, Distributor hereby grants and assigns to Vendor all right, title and interest whatsoever, throughout the world, in and to the copyright of the Localized Version and all other material relating to each Software Product adapted or created by or for Distributor in accordance with this Agreement. Distributor will not assert (or permit any other Party to assert on its own behalf) any right, title or interest (including, without limitation, copyright) in or to any Software Product or any Localized Version. Distributor will, upon request, confirm in writing Vendor's ownership rights as provided for in this Section.

3. **Appointment**

3.1. Vendor appoints Distributor as [the exclusive (subject to the terms and condition of this Agreement)] [a non-exclusive] distributor of the Software Products to Resellers in the Territory for the sole purpose of distribution of Software Products to Resellers and Customers, and Distributor accepts this appointment.

3.2. To enable Distributor to perform its obligations, Vendor grants to Distributor the non-transferable (except as stated below), fee-bearing right to reproduce the Software Products, market and distribute them to Resellers in the Territory, subject to the terms of the Customer License Agreement that will accompany each Software Product.

3.3. [The exclusive license granted by Vendor to Distributor may be changed to a non-exclusive license by Vendor (without obligation, penalty or other change in the terms and conditions of this Agreement) upon 60 days' prior written notice by Vendor at any time during the Term (or any renewal term) subsequent to Distributor's failure to meet or exceed the required levels of performance ("Performance Targets") set forth in Schedule D.]

4. [All replication, manufacture, and distribution rights granted under this Agreement, unless the Parties otherwise agree in writing, pertain and extend solely to the Localized Version of the Software Products. No rights or licenses are granted under this Agreement for Distributor to distribute or sublicense the Software Products other than in the Local Language. Each reference in this Agreement to the Software Product will be deemed subject to this limitation.]

5. **License for Manufacture and Distribution**

5.1. *Manufacture.* Distributor is licensed to and agrees to manufacture or arrange for manufacture of sufficient quantities of packaged Software Products and maintain a sufficient inventory of the Software Products to satisfy anticipated demand. Distributor may not sublicense manufacturing, except to a contractor acting under its direction. Distributor will be responsible for the acts and omissions of any such contractor.

5.2. *Distributor's Distribution License*

5.2.1. Distributor will distribute the Software Products to Customers in the Territory and to Resellers located in the Territory solely for distribution to Customers in the Territory. Such distribution will be at Distributor's own risk and expense.

5.2.2. Distributor may set its own pricing and terms of sale, provided that license grants to Customers must be under the Customer License Agreement.

5.2.3. The distribution of Software Products by Distributor to Resellers will be governed by an agreement with each Reseller ("Reseller Agreement") in form and substance acceptable to Vendor. A Reseller Agreement will not grant to any Reseller any license exceeding the rights granted to Distributor under this Agreement and will be no less favorable to and protective of Vendor than this Agreement. No Reseller may be granted any license to replicate or copy any Software Product or for any electronic distribution. Prior to use of a proposed Reseller Agreement, Distributor will submit the same to Vendor for approval. If the Reseller Agreement is written in the Local Language, Reseller will supply the proposed Reseller Agreement to Vendor in the original Local Language form together with a summary in English of its business and legal terms. Distributor will make such changes in the Reseller Agreement as Vendor may reasonably require. Vendor will not unreasonably withhold or delay its consent to the form of a Reseller Agreement proposed by Distributor.

5.3. *Online Distribution.* Distributor is licensed to sell, supply or distribute the Software Products via the Internet to Customers solely in the Territory. Such online sales and marketing will be solely in the Local Language, and Distributor will use all commercially reasonable means (such as geocoding) to limit online distribution to access within the Territory and will obtain Vendor's approval of such means (not to be unreasonably withheld) before commencing any online distribution. In the Territory only, Distributor is licensed to distribute updates or upgrades of the Software Products via the Internet to Customers that are entitled to them. If Distributor attempts or carries out commercially significant licensing or distribution beyond the Territory by online distribution or otherwise, Vendor may, in its discretion, terminate or limit Distributor's license for online distribution or may terminate this Agreement by written notice.

5.4. *Use of Customer License Agreement.* The Customer License Agreement in the Local Language will be included with each Software Product. The contents of the Customer License Agreement will substantially conform to Vendor's form set forth in <u>Schedule C</u>. Distributor will be responsible for insuring that the contents of the Customer License Agreement conform to applicable local law. Distributor will provide each proposed Customer License Agreement form, in the Local Language and with an English translation, for Vendor's pre-approval before any use by Distributor. Such approval will not be unreasonably withheld.

5.5. *Other Legal Compliance.* Distributor will be responsible for ensuring that packaging and other included materials of Software Products for the Territory are in compliance with local law.

6. **Marketing**

6.1. *General.* Distributor will use commercially reasonable efforts to market the Software Products to Customers and Resellers in the Territory to the best of its ability, and to that end will:

6.1.1. Provide a sufficient number of competent sales and support representatives trained and knowledgeable about the Software Products to demonstrate the Software Products to Resellers and provide Resellers with technical assistance, service and support for the Software Products;

6.1.2. Conduct marketing activities to Resellers and Customers; and

6.1.3. Conduct its business in a manner that reflects favorably upon the Software Products and Vendor.

6.2. *Advertising; Use of Trademarks.* Solely within the Territory, Distributor will advertise and promote the Software Products in a commercially reasonable manner and, subject to the provisions of Section 6.3, may use the Vendor Marks in connection therewith, provided that all such promotions and advertising will be consistent with Vendor's Branding Guidelines and the provisions of this Agreement.

6.3. *Trademarks Rights.* Vendor owns any and all trademarks, trade names, and service marks for the Software Products and all associated goodwill. Vendor does not grant Distributor any license to any Vendor Mark, trade name, or service mark in or outside of the Territory except as expressly stated herein. Distributor will not attempt to register any Vendor Mark, or any trade name or service mark which is similar to any Vendor Mark in or outside of the Territory during or after the Term.

6.4. *Vendor Marketing Support*. Vendor may make available Marketing Materials to Distributor from time to time. Translations of such Marketing Materials into the Local Language will be subject to Vendor's prior written approval, not to be unreasonably withheld.

6.5. *Sales and Technical Training*. Vendor will provide Distributor with reasonable sales and technical training on existing and new Software Products [at Vendor's standard prices for training].

6.6. *Quarterly Progress Meetings*. Representatives of each Party will meet on a quarterly basis to discuss the progress of product development, localization and marketing.

6.7. [*No Competing Software Products*. During the Term, Distributor agrees not to promote or market to Customers or Resellers any products that directly or indirectly compete with the Software Products, and will not engage in any competitive activities or make any investments in or with any competitor offering competing products without the prior written consent of Vendor. Distributor may not use or exploit the Software Products to distribute, market, promote, license or sell any third party product or service without the prior written consent of Vendor.]

6.8. *No Modification*. Except with the express prior written approval of Vendor, Distributor agrees not to alter the copyright or other proprietary notices contained in or on the Software Products or any materials supplied under this Agreement. Distributor will not apply its own or any other trademarks, logos or notices to the Software Products.

7. **Maintenance and Support**

7.1. During the Term, Vendor will provide to Distributor Secondary Support for the Software Products. Secondary Support will be provided in English at Vendor's normal business hours.

7.2. Distributor will be responsible to provide Primary Support to Customers. Vendor is not responsible for supporting Customers.

8. **Fees, Reports, Payments, Taxes**

8.1. [*Initial License Fee.* In connection with the execution of this Agreement, within ___ (__) days of the Effective Date, Distributor will pay Vendor an initial fee ("Initial License Fee") in the amount stated in <u>Schedule B</u>. Such Initial License Fee will be in addition to other amounts due hereunder.]

8.2. *Vendor License Fees.* For each Software Product that Distributor ships, delivers or provides to any Customer or Reseller (each a "Shipment"), Distributor agrees to pay Vendor a fee ("License Fee") calculated as set forth in <u>Schedule B</u> to this Agreement. For these purposes, a Shipment will be deemed to occur when Vendor delivers the goods to a common carrier at its place of business or otherwise transfers possession. Payment of the Vendor License Fee to Vendor is due unconditionally, regardless of whether Distributor is paid by any Customer, Reseller or other person.

8.3. *Secondary Support Fees.* Distributor agrees to pay Vendor annual fees for Secondary Support ("Secondary Support Fees") as set forth in <u>Schedule B</u>. Secondary Support Fees are due in advance. Distributor will owe and pay to Vendor such a Secondary Support Fee, calculated as stated in <u>Schedule B,</u> with respect to each Customer to whom Distributor provides or agrees or arranges to provide Primary Support for a Software Product. Distributor will not provide Primary Support with regard to the Software Product to any Customer unless Distributor has paid to Vendor the required Secondary Support Fee for such Customer.

8.4. *Records and Reports.* Distributor will at all times maintain records, systems and procedures to accurately count Software Product Shipments and Secondary Support Fees. Within thirty (30) days of the end of each [month][calendar quarter], Distributor will report to Vendor, in writing or in such electronic format as Vendor may specify, the total number of Software Product Shipments during the previous [month][calendar quarter] ("Payment Report"). Included in such report will be the Distributor's calculation, in reasonable detail, of the total amount of License Fees due for such [month][calendar quarter]. The Payment Report will also show the Secondary Support Fees due to Vendor and the calculation thereof for the [month][calendar quarter]. Distributor will make payment of the amounts due to Vendor together with such Payment Report. Distributor will pay any other amounts due to Vendor under this Agreement within thirty (30) days from Vendor's invoice.

8.5. *Forecasts*. Distributor will also provide a non-binding, two-quarter fore-cast report in a format acceptable to Vendor within five (5) business days after each quarter end during the Term. All such reports will be sent via email to Vendor.

8.6. *Promotional Copies*. For promotional purposes only, Distributor may make and distribute a reasonable number of copies (but not to exceed *[specify number]* copies) of each Software Product. Such copies will not be subject to License Fees. Distributor may not charge for such copies, and each such copy shall be marked "not-for-resale."

8.7. *Unpaid Amounts*. Any amounts payable by Distributor under this Agreement which remain unpaid after the due date will be subject to a late charge equal to 1.5% per month (or if lower, the highest legal rate) from the due date until such amount is paid.

8.8. *Currency*. Payments will be in US dollars. The exchange rate used for conversion from Local Currency will be the exchange rate quoted in *The Wall Street Journal* on the last business day of the [month] [quarter] for which Licensee Fees are due. All payments will be made via wire transfer to a bank account designated by Vendor.

8.9. *Taxes*. All amounts payable under this Agreement are exclusive of any tax, withholding tax, levy, or similar governmental charge that may be assessed by any jurisdiction in the Territory or in the United States. Withholding for income taxes, if any, required by the government of the Territory on the amounts payable pursuant to this Agreement will be withheld and paid by the Distributor to the appropriate tax authorities, and the amounts payable will be subject to deductions of amounts equivalent to such withholding taxes. The Distributor will cooperate with the Vendor and provide any documentation necessary to reduce the withholding tax rate to the lowest legal rate. Promptly after each such tax payment, the Distributor will forward to the Vendor the official tax receipts or other evidence issued by the tax authorities concerned. The Distributor will assist the Vendor in preserving and exercising whatever right the Vendor may have to contest by appropriate proceedings the validity or amount of any tax thus withheld.

9. **Records and Audit.** Distributor will maintain books and records in connection with the Software Products during the Term and for two (2) years thereafter. Vendor, by its accountant or agent, may audit Distributor's records to

determine whether Distributor has complied with the terms of this Agreement. Any such audit will be conducted during Distributor's regular business hours at Distributor's facilities not more than twice in every calendar year and will not unreasonably interfere with Distributor's business activities. If an audit reveals that Distributor has underpaid fees to Vendor, Distributor will be invoiced for such underpaid fees. If the underpaid fees are in excess of five percent (5%) of the amount due , then Distributor will pay Vendor's reasonable costs of conducting the audit. If discrepancies in Distributor's favor of more than fifteen percent (15%) for the audited period are found, Vendor may, at its option, terminate this Agreement.

10. **Warranties**

   10.1. *Limited Warranty.* Vendor warrants that for a period of sixty (60) days from the date of delivery to Distributor that (i) any media on which the Software Product is furnished will be free from defects in materials and workmanship under normal use; and (ii) the Software Products will contain in all material respects the functionality described in the applicable User Documentation. Distributor's exclusive remedy and Vendor's entire liability under this limited warranty will be, at Vendor's option, repair or replacement of the Software Product.

   10.2. *No Other Warranties.* OTHER THAN AS EXPRESSLY SET FORTH HEREIN, VENDOR DISCLAIMS ALL EXPRESS AND IMPLIED WARRANTIES, INCLUDING WARRANTIES OR CONDITIONS OF MERCHANTABILITY, FITNESS FOR A PARTICULAR PURPOSE, AND NON-INFRINGEMENT OF THIRD PARTY RIGHTS.

11. **Limitation of Liability.** Except for Distributor's unlicensed use, copying or exploitation of the Software Products, Vendor's intellectual property or either Party's breach of its obligations with regard to Confidential Information, neither Party's liability will include consequential, incidental, special or other indirect damages, such as lost profits, even if the Party has knowledge of the likelihood of such damages. Vendor's aggregate liability to Distributor under this Agreement will be limited to the aggregate sum that Distributor has paid to Vendor as License Fees.

12. **Intellectual Property Indemnification**

   12.1. Vendor will defend, indemnify and hold harmless Distributor (and its officers, directors, employees, servants and agents) against a claim that the Software Product infringes any copyright or patent in the Territory, provided that Vendor will have no liability for any claim of infringement based on (a) use of a superseded or altered release of Software Product if the infringement would have been avoided by the use of a current unaltered release of the Software Product which Vendor has provided to Distributor or (b) the combination or use of the Software Product with software, hardware or other materials not furnished by Vendor to the extent that infringement would not have occurred but for the software, hardware or other materials not furnished by Vendor.

12.2. If the Software Product is held to be infringing or if Vendor believes that there is a material infringement risk, Vendor will have the option, at its expense, to (a) modify the Software Product to be non-infringing or (b) obtain for Distributor a license to continue using the Software Product. If Vendor determines, in its sole discretion, that it is not commercially reasonable to perform either of the above options, then Vendor may terminate the license for the infringing Software Product on no less than ninety (90) days' notice.

12.3. This Section states Vendor's entire liability and Distributor's exclusive remedy for actual or alleged infringement.

13. **Indemnity by Distributor**

13.1. Distributor hereby agrees to defend, indemnify and hold harmless Vendor (and its officers, directors, employees, servants and agents) from and against any and all claims, actions, or demands arising from or due to Distributor's marketing or distribution of the Software Product (other than due to Errors in the Software Product).

14. **Procedure for Indemnification**

14.1. In case of any claim that is subject to indemnification under this Agreement, the Party entitled to indemnification ("Indemnitee") shall provide the indemnifying Party ("Indemnitor") prompt notice of the relevant claim. Indemnitor shall defend and/or settle, at its own expense, any demand, action, or suit on any claim subject to indemnification under this Agreement. The Indemnitee shall cooperate in good faith with the Indemnitor to facilitate the defense of any such claim. Claims may be settled without the consent of any Indemnitee unless the settlement includes an admission of wrongdoing, fault or liability on behalf of the Indemnitee.

15. **Confidentiality**

   15.1. Each Party may have access to non-public information provided by the other Party ("Confidential Information"). Confidential Information includes, without limitation, technical and business information, the Software Product interfaces (other than the user interface disclosed in the User Documentation), the terms and pricing under this Agreement, and all information identified in writing as confidential.

   15.2. A Party's Confidential Information will not include information that: (a) is or becomes publicly known through no act or omission of the other Party; (b) was in the other Party's lawful possession prior to the disclosure; (c) is lawfully disclosed to the other Party by a third party without restriction on disclosure; or (d) is independently developed by the other Party.

   15.3. The Parties agree to hold each other's Confidential Information in confidence during the Term and for a period of ___ (__) years after termination of this Agreement. The Parties agree, unless required by law, not to make each other's Confidential Information available in any form to any third party (except to each such Party's permitted contractors under a confidentiality agreement that is consistent with this Agreement) or use Confidential Information for any purpose other than as reasonably required for this Agreement. Each Party agrees to take all reasonable steps to ensure that Confidential Information is not disclosed or distributed by its employees or permitted contractors in violation of the terms of this Agreement. Each Party may, however, disclose information about this Agreement, its terms, and relevant financial matters to its lawyers, accountants, advisors, directors, investors, owners and to parties that may be conducting due diligence with regard to the Party, subject to reasonable confidentiality measures.

16. **Ownership.** Vendor and its licensors retain ownership of all intellectual property rights in the Software Products and Localized Versions. Distributor will not remove, alter or obscure any copyright or other proprietary rights notices contained on the Software Products. Distributor will not apply any other trademarks, logos or notices to the Software Products.

17. **Term and Termination**

   17.1. *Term.* The term of this Agreement ("Term") unless earlier terminated as provided for herein will be as follows: The initial term of this Agreement is _____ (_) years from the Effective Date. This Agreement will automatically renew for up to one additional ___ (__) year term, if Distributor has (i) used its best efforts to promote the sale of Software Products to Resellers in the Territory and (ii) has met or exceeded the Performance Targets set forth on Schedule D.

17.2. *Termination for Breach.* Unless otherwise specified, if either Party fails to comply with any of the terms and conditions of this Agreement, the other Party may terminate this Agreement upon thirty (30) days written notice to the breaching Party specifying any such breach, unless the breach specified therein has been remedied within such thirty (30) day period.

17.3. *Termination by Vendor.* Vendor may terminate this Agreement upon ten (10) days' written notice for the following breaches by Distributor unless such breaches are cured within such ten (10) day period: (i) Distributor fails to pay amounts due as provided in this Agreement; [(ii) Distributor markets or promotes any competing products in breach of this Agreement without Vendor's prior written consent;] or (iii) Distributor breaches its obligations under this Agreement with regard to Vendor Marks.

17.4. *Termination for Change in Business.* Vendor may terminate this Agreement immediately if (i) there is any material change in the ownership or management of Distributor, or Distributor's business or assets where ownership or control is transferred to a competitor of Vendor; (ii) a receiver is appointed for Distributor or its property; (iii) Distributor becomes insolvent or unable to pay its debts as they mature; (iv) Distributor makes an assignment for the benefit of creditors; or (v) Distributor becomes the subject of any proceeding under any bankruptcy, insolvency, company reorganization, or debtor's relief law. Distributor will notify Vendor in writing not less than thirty (30) days in advance of any planned change in the control of Distributor.

17.5. *Effect of Termination.* Upon termination, all outstanding License Fees and all other outstanding payment obligations will be immediately due and payable. Distributor will have no further license to distribute the Software Products or any related materials and will cease any copying, use or distribution of the Software Products.

17.6. *No Liability, Damages.* Neither Party will be liable for damages or costs of any nature arising from the expiration or termination of this Agreement in accordance with its terms.

17.7. *Survival Beyond Termination.* Those rights and obligations that by their nature extend beyond the Term will survive any termination or expiration of this Agreement together with accrued rights and obligations, including payment obligation.

18. **General**

18.1. *Relationship of Parties.* Distributor will be deemed to have the status of an independent contractor, and nothing in this Agreement will be deemed to place the Parties in the relationship of employer-employee, principal-agent, partners, or joint venturers.

18.2. *Reports of Violations.* Distributor agrees to report promptly to Vendor all known violations of the Customer License Agreement.

18.3. *Government Approvals.* Distributor will, at its own expense, obtain and arrange for the maintenance in full force and effect of all government approvals, consents, licenses, authorizations, declarations, filings, and registrations as may be necessary for the performance of the terms and conditions of this Agreement, including without limitation under all laws, regulations, and other legal requirements within the Territory that apply to this Agreement or its performance.

18.4. *Export.* Distributor acknowledges that the laws and regulations of the United States or other nations may restrict the export and re-export of certain commodities and technical data. Distributor agrees that it will not export or re-export the Software Product other than in compliance with applicable US and local law.

18.5. *No Waiver.* The failure of either Party to exercise any right or the waiver by either Party of any breach will not prevent a subsequent exercise of such right or be deemed a waiver of any subsequent breach or the same of any other term of the Agreement.

18.6. *Notice.* Any notice required or permitted to be sent hereunder will be in writing and will be sent in a manner requiring a signed receipt, such as Federal Express, courier delivery, or if mailed, registered or certified mail, return receipt requested. Notice is effective upon receipt. Notice to Vendor will be addressed to the address set forth above or such other person or address as Vendor may designate in writing. Notice to Distributor will be addressed to the address set forth above or such other address as Distributor may designate in writing.

18.7. *Partial Invalidity.* Should any provision of this Agreement be held to be void, invalid, or inoperative, the remaining provisions of this Agreement will not be affected and will continue in effect as though such provisions were deleted.

18.8. *Force Majeure.* Neither Party will be deemed in default of this Agreement to the extent that performance of their obligations or attempts to cure any breach are delayed or prevented by reason of any act of God, fire, natural disaster, accident, act of government, shortages of materials or supplies, or any other cause beyond the control of such Party ("Force Majeure"), provided that such Party gives the other Party written notice thereof promptly and, in any event, within fifteen (15) days of discovery thereof and uses its commercially reasonable efforts to cure the delay. In the event of such Force Majeure, the time for performance or cure will be extended for a period equal to the duration of the Force Majeure but not in excess of three (3) months. Force Majeure, however, will not apply to or delay any obligation to make payments of money required by this Agreement for more than twenty (20) days.

18.9. *Non-Solicitation.* Each Party agrees that during the Term and for a period of one year thereafter, it will not solicit or contact for the purposes of hiring employees of the other Party with whom the Party had material contact under this Agreement. This provision will not apply to employment resulting from general solicitation for employment or contractors on the Internet, the press, or through other mass media.

18.10. *Assignment.* Either Party may assign and transfer this Agreement in connection with the sale or disposition of the business unit that is involved in this Agreement [, provided, however, that upon assignment of this Agreement to a competitor of Vendor or such competitor's obtaining control of the Agreement or of Distributor, Vendor may terminate this Agreement upon written notice and obtain return of all Confidential Information]. Subject to the foregoing, this Agreement will be binding upon and inure to the benefit of the Parties to this Agreement and their respective permitted legal representatives, successors, and assigns.

18.11. *Injunctive Relief.* The Parties agree that in case of a breach of the provisions of this Agreement relating to Confidential Information or intellectual property rights or in case of the unlicensed use or exploitation of the Software Product, a remedy at law will not be adequate for the non-breaching Party's protection, and accordingly the non-breaching

Party will have the right to seek, in addition to any other relief and remedies available to it, preliminary and final injunctive relief to enforce the provisions of this Agreement in any court of competent jurisdiction.

18.12. [*Enforcement Expenses.* In case of any default or breach by Distributor under any provision of this Agreement or any violation of Vendor intellectual property rights, Distributor agrees to pay, in addition to such other amounts as may be due, all costs of enforcement or collection incurred by Vendor, including reasonable attorney's fees.]

18.13. [*Arbitration.* Any dispute relating to the terms, interpretation or performance of this Agreement or the dealing of the Parties with regard to Software Products (other than claims for preliminary injunctive relief or other pre-judgment remedies) will be resolved at the request of either Party through binding arbitration. Arbitration will be conducted in the city of _____ under the rules and procedures of the American Arbitration Association ("AAA"). The Parties will request that the AAA appoint a panel of three arbitrators and, if feasible, include one arbitrator of the three who will possess knowledge of computer Software products and their distribution; however the arbitration will proceed even if such a person is unavailable. The award may be enforced in any court of competent jurisdiction.]

18.14. *Governing Law.* This Agreement will be governed and interpreted in accordance with the substantive laws of the State of _____ applicable to contracts made and performed there. The United Nations Convention on Contracts for the International Sale of Goods will not apply. [Except as provided with regard to claims subject to arbitration] Any legal action brought concerning this Agreement or its subject matter will be brought exclusively in the courts of the State of _____ [in the county of _____] or in the federal courts located in such state [and county], and both parties agree to submit to the jurisdiction of these courts.

18.15. *Entire Agreement.* This Agreement, including the Schedules attached to this Agreement, states the entire agreement between the Parties on this subject and supersedes all prior negotiations, understandings and agreements between the Parties concerning the subject matter.

No amendment or modification of this Agreement will be made except by a writing signed by both Parties.

18.16. *Counterparts.* This Agreement may be executed in two or more counterparts, each of which will be deemed an original and all of which together will constitute one instrument.

So agreed by the Parties:

[Vendor Name]   *[Distributor Name]*

By: _____   By: _____

Printed Name: _____   Printed Name: _____

Title: _____   Title: _____

Date: _____   Date: _____

Schedule A

Software Products

[List of Products to be Distributed]

Schedule B

Amounts Payable by Distributor to Vendor

[State details of the Initial License Fee (if applicable), License Fees, Secondary Support Fees and any other charges]

Schedule C

Form of Customer License Agreement

[Insert form to be localized per the Agreement]

Schedule D

Performance Targets

[State applicable performance targets]

FORM 23-1 Rec. Bottom Distribution Agreement 21 S.

Term Sheet (Non-Binding) for an International Joint Venture

Introductory Note

This is a sample of a non-binding term sheet for an international joint venture. As we discussed in Chapter 23, there are many possible variations on the purpose and terms of joint ventures for digital technology companies.

This form shows the way that a term sheet outlines the essentials of a proposed joint venture deal such as the business purpose, structure, finance and management of the proposed venture. The term sheet is a conceptual document that does not bind the parties to form or fund the entity.

The following term sheet outlines a fictitious deal between a US-based software supplier called SecureSoft, Inc. and a Korean company named KoreaSoft Corp. The two companies are contemplating forming a joint venture to localize SecureSoft's security software line of products and market these products in the Korean market. This is a deal that might be structured as a straight distribution agreement (as in Form 23-1); the difference is that the joint venture structure allows the companies to share ownership, management, costs and profits.

This term sheet would be followed by a much more formal and detailed set of joint venture documents. The term sheet acts as a guide to the negotiation of the binding documents.

We have also included a letter of intent "wrapper," a simple document (binding in part) that provides a framework for the Parties to negotiate the joint venture documents that will follow.

Letter of Intent and Non-Binding Term Sheet

This letter of intent ("LOI") is between SecureSoft, Inc., a Delaware corporation ("SecureSoft") and KoreaSoft Corp., a Korean corporation ("KoreaSoft"). SecureSoft and KoreaSoft may be collectively referred to as the "Parties and each individually as a "Party."

1. **Term Sheet.** The Parties intend to form a joint venture. The overall structure and purpose of the proposed joint venture is set forth in the attached Term Sheet. The Parties intend to (but are not legally bound to) negotiate definitive agreements regarding the proposed joint venture.

2. **Definitive Agreements.** The Parties intend to use reasonable efforts to conclude and sign the definitive agreements during the sixty (60) days following the date that both Parties have signed this LOI. Either Party may terminate negotiations at any time for any reason.

3. **Confidentiality of Negotiations.** The Parties will use best efforts to maintain at all times as confidential information the fact that both have executed this LOI, the terms of this LOI and the existence and content of any negotiations between them except that both Parties may (a) inform advisors, counsel, and employees with a need to know as each Party reasonably deems necessary, (b) make appropriate disclosures if required by applicable securities laws, and (c) issue press releases regarding substance of the negotiations if they have been pre-approved in writing by both Parties.

4. **Governing Law.** This LOI will be governed by the substantive laws of the State of _____ in the United States of America.

5. **Entire Agreement.** This LOI constitutes the entire understanding and agreement between the Parties hereto and their affiliates with respect to its subject matter and supersedes all prior or contemporaneous agreements, representations, warranties and understandings of such Parties (whether oral or written). No promise, inducement, representation or agreement, other than as expressly set forth herein, has been made to or by the Parties. This LOI may be amended only by written agreement, signed by the Parties to be bound by the amendment.

6. **Binding in Part.** This LOI is binding as to paragraphs 3, 4 and 5 and is otherwise non-binding; the terms of the attached Term Sheet are non-binding.

So Agreed by the Parties:

SecureSoft, Inc.   **KoreaSoft Corp.**

By: _____   By: _____

Name: _____   Name: _____

Title: _____   Title: _____

Date: _____   Date:_____

Joint Venture Term Sheet

Names of Parties:

SecureSoft, Inc. ("SecureSoft"), a Delaware corporation.

KoreaSoft, Corp. ("KoreaSoft"), a Korean corporation.

In this Term Sheet, SecureSoft and KoreaSoft are each a "Shareholder" and together the "Shareholders."

Name of Joint Venture: SecureSoft-Korea Corp. ("Company").

Type of Entity: Korean Joint Stock Company. All costs to form the entity will be borne equally by the Parties.

Purpose of Joint Venture: The Company will pursue the following business purposes: (a) the localization importation, marketing, distribution, licensing and sale of the Products (as defined below) in the Territory (as defined below) through all legitimate channels, including direct, through sub-distributors and OEMS; (b) the provision of technical support services for the Products and contract services relating to the Products; and (c) other related business activities which the Board of Directors of the Company may from time to time determine.

Products: The family of software products known as "DataSecure Suite" and any other security software products developed by SecureSoft during the term of the Distribution Agreement (as defined below) as localized by the Company for the Territory.

Territory: The Republic of Korea (South Korea)

Exclusive Distribution Agreement: SecureSoft will enter into an exclusive royalty-bearing license and distribution agreement (the "Distribution Agreement") with Company for the localization, marketing, distribution and sale of licenses for the Products in the Territory. The Distribution Agreement will have an initial term of five (5) years with the opportunity for the Company to renew for additional terms. The Distribution will contain other provisions to be mutually agreed upon by the Parties.

Management of Company: Company will be managed by the Board of Directors (the "Board") consisting of three (3) Directors. Each Shareholder will be entitled to designate a Director. The third Director will be chosen by the mutual agreement of the Shareholders.

Adoption and Implementation: All operating procedures, including, without limitation, pricing policies with respect to the licensing of the Products in the Territory, staffing and hiring, compensation of employees, supervision of work, and marketing of the Products, will be determined under guidelines (including but not limited to an annual budget) established by the Board.

Board Voting Requirements: Decisions of the Board will be determined by an affirmative vote of a majority of the Directors; provided, however, that the following matters will be adopted by the Board only with the affirmative votes of each of the Directors designated by the Shareholders: (i) selling Company, (ii) acquiring another entity, (iii) spending more than US$_____ in any single transaction not contemplated in the Company budget, (iv) incurring over US$_____ of indebtedness in any single transaction or over US$_____ in indebtedness, in the aggregate, in any fiscal year, (v) granting a security interest, mortgage, pledge or lien on any assets of Company, (vi) issuing shares in Company, (vii) declaring a capital call or accepting additional capital contributions from a Shareholder, (viii) conducting any business other than the localization, replication, marketing, distribution, or licensing of Products in the Territory, and (ix) the liquidation of Company.

Initial Capital Contributions and Ownership Percentages

SecureSoft: US$_____: _____ shares (___% ownership).

KoreaSoft: US$_____: _____ shares (___% ownership).

Additional Capital: The Board may require additional capital contributions by the Shareholders.

Voting: Each Shareholder will be entitled to one vote per share.

Dividends: The Board will have the power to declare and distribute dividends. Any such distributions will be pro rata based on ownership.

Transfer Restrictions: No Shareholder will be permitted to transfer its shares in Company without the prior consent of Company. For the purposes hereof, a transfer will include a transfer by operation of law through a merger, stock sale or otherwise.

Non-Competition: Neither Shareholder will import, market, distribute, license or sell a product competitive with the Products in the Territory.

Financial Statements: Company will provide the following financial statements to the Shareholders: (i) within 90 days after the end of each fiscal year of Company, audited financial statements prepared in accordance with United States generally accepted accounting principles ("GAAP") consistently applied and will contain a balance sheet as of the end of the fiscal year and statements of income and cash flows for such fiscal year and (ii) within 45 days after the end of each fiscal quarter of Company, unaudited financial statements of Company for such fiscal quarter also prepared in accordance with US GAAP (except for financial footnote presentation and year-end adjustments).

Index